R. W. Lynch

R.W. Level

R.W. food.

American Casebook Series
Hornbook Series and Basic Legal Texts
Nutshell Series

of

WEST PUBLISHING COMPANY
P.O. Box 64526
St. Paul, Minnesota 55164–0526

ACCOUNTING

Faris' Accounting and Law in a Nutshell, 377 pages, 1984 (Text)

Fiflis, Kripke and Foster's Teaching Materials on Accounting for Business Lawyers, 3rd Ed., 838 pages, 1984 (Casebook)

Siegel and Siegel's Accounting and Financial Disclosure: A Guide to Basic Concepts, 259 pages, 1983 (Text)

ADMINISTRATIVE LAW

Davis' Cases, Text and Problems on Administrative Law, 6th Ed., 683 pages, 1977 (Casebook)

Gellhorn and Boyer's Administrative Law and Process in a Nutshell, 2nd Ed., 445 pages, 1981 (Text)

Mashaw and Merrill's Cases and Materials on Administrative Law–The American Public Law System, 2nd Ed., 976 pages, 1985 (Casebook)

Robinson, Gellhorn and Bruff's The Administrative Process, 3rd Ed., 978 pages, 1986 (Casebook)

ADMIRALTY

Healy and Sharpe's Cases and Materials on Admiralty, 2nd Ed., 876 pages, 1986 (Casebook)

Maraist's Admiralty in a Nutshell, 2nd Ed., 379 pages, 1988 (Text)

Schoenbaum's Hornbook on Admiralty and Maritime Law, Student Ed., 692 pages, 1987 (Text)

Sohn and Gustafson's Law of the Sea in a Nutshell, 264 pages, 1984 (Text)

AGENCY—PARTNERSHIP

Fessler's Alternatives to Incorporation for Persons in Quest of Profit, 2nd Ed., 326 pages, 1986 (Casebook)

AGENCY—PARTNERSHIP—Cont'd

Henn's Cases and Materials on Agency, Partnership and Other Unincorporated Business Enterprises, 2nd Ed., 733 pages, 1985 (Casebook)

Reuschlein and Gregory's Hornbook on the Law of Agency and Partnership, 625 pages, 1979, with 1981 pocket part (Text)

Selected Corporation and Partnership Statutes, Rules and Forms, 621 pages, 1987

Steffen and Kerr's Cases and Materials on Agency-Partnership, 4th Ed., 859 pages, 1980 (Casebook)

Steffen's Agency-Partnership in a Nutshell, 364 pages, 1977 (Text)

AGRICULTURAL LAW

Meyer, Pedersen, Thorson and Davidson's Agricultural Law: Cases and Materials, 931 pages, 1985 (Casebook)

ALTERNATIVE DISPUTE RESOLUTION

Kanowitz' Cases and Materials on Alternative Dispute Resolution, 1024 pages, 1986 (Casebook)

Riskin and Westbrook's Dispute Resolution and Lawyers, 223 pages, 1987 (Coursebook)

Riskin and Westbrook's Dispute Resolution and Lawyers, Abridged Ed., 223 pages, 1987 (Coursebook)

Teple and Moberly's Arbitration and Conflict Resolution, (The Labor Law Group), 614 pages, 1979 (Casebook)

AMERICAN INDIAN LAW

Canby's American Indian Law in a Nutshell, 2nd Ed., about 319 pages, 1988 (Text)

Getches and Wilkinson's Cases on Federal Indian Law, 2nd Ed., 880 pages, 1986 (Casebook)

List current as of July, 1988

LAW SCHOOL PUBLICATIONS—Continued

ANTITRUST LAW

Gellhorn's Antitrust Law and Economics in a Nutshell, 3rd Ed., 472 pages, 1986 (Text)

Gifford and Raskind's Cases and Materials on Antitrust, 694 pages, 1983 with 1985 Supplement (Casebook)

Hovenkamp's Hornbook on Economics and Federal Antitrust Law, Student Ed., 414 pages, 1985 (Text)

Oppenheim, Weston and McCarthy's Cases and Comments on Federal Antitrust Laws, 4th Ed., 1168 pages, 1981 with 1985 Supplement (Casebook)

Posner and Easterbrook's Cases and Economic Notes on Antitrust, 2nd Ed., 1077 pages, 1981, with 1984–85 Supplement (Casebook)

Sullivan's Hornbook of the Law of Antitrust, 886 pages, 1977 (Text)

See also Regulated Industries, Trade Regulation

ART LAW

DuBoff's Art Law in a Nutshell, 335 pages, 1984 (Text)

BANKING LAW

Lovett's Banking and Financial Institutions in a Nutshell, 2nd Ed., about 455 pages, 1988 (Text)

Symons and White's Teaching Materials on Banking Law, 2nd Ed., 993 pages, 1984, with 1987 Supplement (Casebook)

BUSINESS PLANNING

Painter's Problems and Materials in Business Planning, 2nd Ed., 1008 pages, 1984 with 1987 Supplement (Casebook)

Selected Securities and Business Planning Statutes, Rules and Forms, about 475 pages, 1987

CIVIL PROCEDURE

American Bar Association Section of Litigation—Reading on Adversarial Justice: The American Approach to Adjudication, edited by Landsman, 217 pages, 1988 (Coursebook)

Casad's Res Judicata in a Nutshell, 310 pages, 1976 (text)

Cound, Friedenthal, Miller and Sexton's Cases and Materials on Civil Procedure, 4th Ed., 1202 pages, 1985 with 1987 Supplement (Casebook)

Ehrenzweig, Louisell and Hazard's Jurisdiction in a Nutshell, 4th Ed., 232 pages, 1980 (Text)

Federal Rules of Civil-Appellate Procedure—West Law School Edition, about 600 pages, 1988

Friedenthal, Kane and Miller's Hornbook on Civil Procedure, 876 pages, 1985 (Text)

Kane's Civil Procedure in a Nutshell, 2nd Ed., 306 pages, 1986 (Text)

CIVIL PROCEDURE—Cont'd

Koffler and Reppy's Hornbook on Common Law Pleading, 663 pages, 1969 (Text)

Marcus and Sherman's Complex Litigation–Cases and Materials on Advanced Civil Procedure, 846 pages, 1985 (Casebook)

Park's Computer-Aided Exercises on Civil Procedure, 2nd Ed., 167 pages, 1983 (Coursebook)

Siegel's Hornbook on New York Practice, 1011 pages, 1978 with 1987 Pocket Part (Text)

See also Federal Jurisdiction and Procedure

CIVIL RIGHTS

Abernathy's Cases and Materials on Civil Rights, 660 pages, 1980 (Casebook)

Cohen's Cases on the Law of Deprivation of Liberty: A Study in Social Control, 755 pages, 1980 (Casebook)

Lockhart, Kamisar, Choper and Shiffrin's Cases on Constitutional Rights and Liberties, 6th Ed., 1266 pages, 1986 with 1988 Supplement (Casebook)—reprint from Lockhart, et al. Cases on Constitutional Law, 6th Ed., 1986

Vieira's Civil Rights in a Nutshell, 279 pages, 1978 (Text)

COMMERCIAL LAW

Bailey and Hagedorn's Secured Transactions in a Nutshell, 3rd Ed. about 390 pages, 1988 (Text)

Epstein, Martin, Henning and Nickles' Basic Uniform Commercial Code Teaching Materials, 3rd Ed., 704 pages, 1988 (Casebook)

Henson's Hornbook on Secured Transactions Under the U.C.C., 2nd Ed., 504 pages, 1979 with 1979 P.P. (Text)

Murray's Commercial Law, Problems and Materials, 366 pages, 1975 (Coursebook)

Nickles, Matheson and Dolan's Materials for Understanding Credit and Payment Systems, 923 pages, 1987 (Casebook)

Nordstrom, Murray and Clovis' Problems and Materials on Sales, 515 pages, 1982 (Casebook)

Nordstrom, Murray and Clovis' Problems and Materials on Secured Transactions, 594 pages, 1987 (Casebook)

Selected Commercial Statutes, about 1525 pages, 1988

Speidel, Summers and White's Teaching Materials on Commercial Law, 4th Ed., 1448 pages, 1987 (Casebook)

Speidel, Summers and White's Commercial Paper: Teaching Materials, 4th Ed., 578 pages, 1987 (Casebook)—reprint from Speidel, et al. Commercial Law, 4th Ed.

Speidel, Summers and White's Sales: Teaching Materials, 4th Ed., 804 pages, 1987 (Casebook)—reprint from Speidel, et al. Commercial Law, 4th Ed.

COMMERCIAL LAW—Cont'd

Speidel, Summers and White's Secured Transactions—Teaching Materials, 4th Ed., 485 pages, 1987 (Casebook)—reprint from Speidel, et al. Commercial Law, 4th Ed.

Stockton's Sales in a Nutshell, 2nd Ed., 370 pages, 1981 (Text)

Stone's Uniform Commercial Code in a Nutshell, 2nd Ed., 516 pages, 1984 (Text)

Uniform Commercial Code, Official Text with Comments, 1155 pages, 1987

Weber and Speidel's Commercial Paper in a Nutshell, 3rd Ed., 404 pages, 1982 (Text)

White and Summers' Hornbook on the Uniform Commercial Code, 3rd Ed., Student Ed., about 1200 pages, 1988 (Text)

COMMUNITY PROPERTY

Mennell and Boykoff's Community Property in a Nutshell, 2nd Ed., 432 pages, 1988 (Text)

Verrall and Bird's Cases and Materials on California Community Property, 5th Ed., about 587 pages, 1988 (Casebook)

COMPARATIVE LAW

Barton, Gibbs, Li and Merryman's Law in Radically Different Cultures, 960 pages, 1983 (Casebook)

Glendon, Gordon and Osakive's Comparative Legal Traditions: Text, Materials and Cases on the Civil Law, Common Law, and Socialist Law Traditions, 1091 pages, 1985 (Casebook)

Glendon, Gordon, and Osakwe's Comparative Legal Traditions in a Nutshell, 402 pages, 1982 (Text)

Langbein's Comparative Criminal Procedure: Germany, 172 pages, 1977 (Casebook)

COMPUTERS AND LAW

Maggs and Sprowl's Computer Applications in the Law, 316 pages, 1987 (Coursebook)

Mason's Using Computers in the Law: An Introduction and Practical Guide, 2nd Ed., 288 pages, 1988 (Text)

CONFLICT OF LAWS

Cramton, Currie and Kay's Cases-Comments-Questions on Conflict of Laws, 4th Ed., 876 pages, 1987 (Casebook)

Scoles and Hay's Hornbook on Conflict of Laws, Student Ed., 1085 pages, 1982 with 1986 P.P. (Text)

Scoles and Weintraub's Cases and Materials on Conflict of Laws, 2nd Ed., 966 pages, 1972, with 1978 Supplement (Casebook)

Siegel's Conflicts in a Nutshell, 469 pages, 1982 (Text)

CONSTITUTIONAL LAW

Barron and Dienes' Constitutional Law in a Nutshell, 389 pages, 1986 (Text)

Engdahl's Constitutional Federalism in a Nutshell, 2nd Ed., 411 pages, 1987 (Text)

Lockhart, Kamisar, Choper and Shiffrin's Cases-Comments-Questions on Constitutional Law, 6th Ed., 1601 pages, 1986 with 1988 Supplement (Casebook)

Lockhart, Kamisar, Choper and Shiffrin's Cases-Comments-Questions on the American Constitution, 6th Ed., 1260 pages, 1986 with 1988 Supplement (Casebook)—abridgment of Lockhart, et al. Cases on Constitutional Law, 6th Ed., 1986

Manning's The Law of Church-State Relations in a Nutshell, 305 pages, 1981 (Text)

Marks and Cooper's State Constitutional Law in a Nutshell, about 300 pages, 1988 (Text)

Miller's Presidential Power in a Nutshell, 328 pages, 1977 (Text)

Nowak, Rotunda and Young's Hornbook on Constitutional Law, 3rd Ed., Student Ed., 1191 pages, 1986 with 1988 Pocket Part (Text)

Rotunda's Modern Constitutional Law: Cases and Notes, 2nd Ed., 1004 pages, 1985 with 1988 Supplement (Casebook)

Williams' Constitutional Analysis in a Nutshell, 388 pages, 1979 (Text)

See also Civil Rights, Foreign Relations and National Security Law

CONSUMER LAW

Epstein and Nickles' Consumer Law in a Nutshell, 2nd Ed., 418 pages, 1981 (Text)

Selected Commercial Statutes, about 1525 pages, 1988

Spanogle and Rohner's Cases and Materials on Consumer Law, 693 pages, 1979, with 1982 Supplement (Casebook)

See also Commercial Law

CONTRACTS

Calamari & Perillo's Cases and Problems on Contracts, 1061 pages, 1978 (Casebook)

Calamari and Perillo's Hornbook on Contracts, 3rd Ed., 904 pages, 1987 (Text)

Corbin's Text on Contracts, One Volume Student Edition, 1224 pages, 1952 (Text)

Fessler and Loiseaux's Cases and Materials on Contracts, 837 pages, 1982 (Casebook)

Friedman's Contract Remedies in a Nutshell, 323 pages, 1981 (Text)

Fuller and Eisenberg's Cases on Basic Contract Law, 4th Ed., 1203 pages, 1981 (Casebook)

Hamilton, Rau and Weintraub's Cases and Materials on Contracts, 830 pages, 1984 (Casebook)

LAW SCHOOL PUBLICATIONS—Continued

CONTRACTS—Cont'd

Jackson and Bollinger's Cases on Contract Law in Modern Society, 2nd Ed., 1329 pages, 1980 (Casebook)

Keyes' Government Contracts in a Nutshell, 423 pages, 1979 (Text)

Schaber and Rohwer's Contracts in a Nutshell, 2nd Ed., 425 pages, 1984 (Text)

Summers and Hillman's Contract and Related Obligation: Theory, Doctrine and Practice, 1074 pages, 1987 (Casebook)

COPYRIGHT

See Patent and Copyright Law

CORPORATE FINANCE

Hamilton's Cases and Materials on Corporate Finance, 895 pages, 1984 with 1986 Supplement (Casebook)

CORPORATIONS

Hamilton's Cases on Corporations—Including Partnerships and Limited Partnerships, 3rd Ed., 1213 pages, 1986 with 1986 Statutory Supplement (Casebook)

Hamilton's Law of Corporations in a Nutshell, 2nd Ed., 515 pages, 1987 (Text)

Henn's Teaching Materials on Corporations, 2nd Ed., 1204 pages, 1986 (Casebook)

Henn and Alexander's Hornbook on Corporations, 3rd Ed., Student Ed., 1371 pages, 1983 with 1986 P.P. (Text)

Jennings and Buxbaum's Cases and Materials on Corporations, 5th Ed., 1180 pages, 1979 (Casebook)

Selected Corporation and Partnership Statutes, Rules and Forms, 621 pages, 1987

Solomon, Schwartz' and Bauman's Materials and Problems on Corporations: Law and Policy, 2nd Ed., 1391 pages, 1988 (Casebook)

CORRECTIONS

Krantz's Cases and Materials on the Law of Corrections and Prisoners' Rights, 3rd Ed., 855 pages, 1986 with 1988 Supplement (Casebook)

Krantz's Law of Corrections and Prisoners' Rights in a Nutshell, 2nd Ed., 386 pages, 1983 (Text)

Popper's Post-Conviction Remedies in a Nutshell, 360 pages, 1978 (Text)

Robbins' Cases and Materials on Post Conviction Remedies, 506 pages, 1982 (Casebook)

CREDITOR'S RIGHTS

Bankruptcy Code, Rules and Forms, Law School Ed., 792 pages, 1988

Epstein's Debtor-Creditor Law in a Nutshell, 3rd Ed., 383 pages, 1986 (Text)

Epstein, Landers and Nickles' Debtors and Creditors: Cases and Materials, 3rd Ed., 1059 pages, 1987 (Casebook)

CREDITOR'S RIGHTS—Cont'd

LoPucki's Player's Manual for the Debtor-Creditor Game, 123 pages, 1985 (Coursebook)

Riesenfeld's Cases and Materials on Creditors' Remedies and Debtors' Protection, 4th Ed., 914 pages, 1987 (Casebook)

White's Bankruptcy and Creditor's Rights: Cases and Materials, 812 pages, 1985, with 1987 Supplement (Casebook)

CRIMINAL LAW AND CRIMINAL PROCEDURE

Abrams', Federal Criminal Law and its Enforcement, 882 pages, 1986 (Casebook)

Carlson's Adjudication of Criminal Justice, Problems and References, 130 pages, 1986 (Casebook)

Dix and Sharlot's Cases and Materials on Criminal Law, 3rd Ed., 846 pages, 1987 (Casebook)

Federal Rules of Criminal Procedure—West Law School Edition, about 500 pages, 1988

Grano's Problems in Criminal Procedure, 2nd Ed., 176 pages, 1981 (Problem book)

Israel and LaFave's Criminal Procedure in a Nutshell, 4th Ed., 461 pages, 1988 (Text)

Johnson's Cases, Materials and Text on Criminal Law, 3rd Ed., 783 pages, 1985 (Casebook)

Johnson's Cases on Criminal Procedure, 859 pages, 1987 with 1988 Supplement (Casebook)

Kamisar, LaFave and Israel's Cases, Comments and Questions on Modern Criminal Procedure, 6th Ed., 1558 pages, 1986 with 1988 Supplement (Casebook)

Kamisar, LaFave and Israel's Cases, Comments and Questions on Basic Criminal Procedure, 6th Ed., 860 pages, 1986 with 1988 Supplement (Casebook)—reprint from Kamisar, et al. Modern Criminal Procedure, 6th ed., 1986

LaFave's Modern Criminal Law: Cases, Comments and Questions, 2nd Ed., 903 pages, 1988 (Casebook)

LaFave and Israel's Hornbook on Criminal Procedure, Student Ed., 1142 pages, 1985 with 1987 P.P. (Text)

LaFave and Scott's Hornbook on Criminal Law, 2nd Ed., Student Ed., 918 pages, 1986 (Text)

Langbein's Comparative Criminal Procedure: Germany, 172 pages, 1977 (Casebook)

Loewy's Criminal Law in a Nutshell, 2nd Ed., 321 pages, 1987 (Text)

Saltzburg's American Criminal Procedure, Cases and Commentary, 3rd Ed., 1302 pages, 1988 with 1988 Supplement (Casebook)

LAW SCHOOL PUBLICATIONS—Continued

CRIMINAL LAW AND CRIMINAL PROCEDURE—Cont'd

Uviller's The Processes of Criminal Justice: Investigation and Adjudication, 2nd Ed., 1384 pages, 1979 with 1979 Statutory Supplement and 1986 Update (Casebook)

Uviller's The Processes of Criminal Justice: Adjudication, 2nd Ed., 730 pages, 1979. Soft-cover reprint from Uviller's The Processes of Criminal Justice: Investigation and Adjudication, 2nd Ed. (Casebook)

Uviller's The Processes of Criminal Justice: Investigation, 2nd Ed., 655 pages, 1979. Soft-cover reprint from Uviller's The Processes of Criminal Justice: Investigation and Adjudication, 2nd Ed. (Casebook)

Vorenberg's Cases on Criminal Law and Procedure, 2nd Ed., 1088 pages, 1981 with 1987 Supplement (Casebook)

See also Corrections, Juvenile Justice

DECEDENTS ESTATES

See Trusts and Estates

DOMESTIC RELATIONS

Clark's Cases and Problems on Domestic Relations, 3rd Ed., 1153 pages, 1980 (Casebook)

Clark's Hornbook on Domestic Relations, 2nd Ed., Student Ed., 1050 pages, 1988 (Text)

Krause's Cases and Materials on Family Law, 2nd Ed., 1221 pages, 1983 with 1986 Supplement (Casebook)

Krause's Family Law in a Nutshell, 2nd Ed., 444 pages, 1986 (Text)

Krauskopf's Cases on Property Division at Marriage Dissolution, 250 pages, 1984 (Casebook)

ECONOMICS, LAW AND

Goetz' Cases and Materials on Law and Economics, 547 pages, 1984 (Casebook)

See also Antitrust, Regulated Industries

EDUCATION LAW

Alexander and Alexander's The Law of Schools, Students and Teachers in a Nutshell, 409 pages, 1984 (Text)

Morris' The Constitution and American Education, 2nd Ed., 992 pages, 1980 (Casebook)

EMPLOYMENT DISCRIMINATION

Jones, Murphy and Belton's Cases on Discrimination in Employment, 1116 pages, 1987 (Casebook)

Player's Cases and Materials on Employment Discrimination Law, 2nd Ed., 782 pages, 1984 (Casebook)

EMPLOYMENT DISCRIMINATION—Cont'd

Player's Federal Law of Employment Discrimination in a Nutshell, 2nd Ed., 402 pages, 1981 (Text)

Player's Hornbook on the Law of Employment Discrimination, Student Ed., 708 pages, 1988 (Text)

See also Women and the Law

ENERGY AND NATURAL RESOURCES LAW

Laitos' Cases and Materials on Natural Resources Law, 938 pages, 1985 (Casebook)

Rodgers' Cases and Materials on Energy and Natural Resources Law, 2nd Ed., 877 pages, 1983 (Casebook)

Selected Environmental Law Statutes, about 650 pages, 1988

Tomain's Energy Law in a Nutshell, 338 pages, 1981 (Text)

See also Environmental Law, Oil and Gas, Water Law

ENVIRONMENTAL LAW

Bonine and McGarity's Cases and Materials on the Law of Environment and Pollution, 1076 pages, 1984 (Casebook)

Findley and Farber's Cases and Materials on Environmental Law, 2nd Ed., 813 pages, 1985 with 1988 Supplement (Casebook)

Findley and Farber's Environmental Law in a Nutshell, 2nd Ed., about 348 pages, 1988 (Text)

Rodgers' Hornbook on Environmental Law, 956 pages, 1977 with 1984 pocket part (Text)

Selected Environmental Law Statutes, about 650 pages, 1988

See also Energy Law, Natural Resources Law, Water Law

EQUITY

See Remedies

ESTATES

See Trusts and Estates

ESTATE PLANNING

Lynn's Introduction to Estate Planning, in a Nutshell, 3rd Ed., 370 pages, 1983 (Text)

See also Taxation, Trusts and Estates

EVIDENCE

Broun, Meisenholder, Strong and Mosteller's Problems in Evidence, 3rd Ed., about 420 pages, 1988 (Problem book)

Cleary, Strong, Broun and Mosteller's Cases and Materials on Evidence, 4th Ed., about 1050 pages, 1988 (Casebook)

Federal Rules of Evidence for United States Courts and Magistrates, 370 pages, 1987

LAW SCHOOL PUBLICATIONS—Continued

EVIDENCE—Cont'd

Graham's Federal Rules of Evidence in a Nutshell, 2nd Ed., 473 pages, 1987 (Text)

Kimball's Programmed Materials on Problems in Evidence, 380 pages, 1978 (Problem book)

Lempert and Saltzburg's A Modern Approach to Evidence: Text, Problems, Transcripts and Cases, 2nd Ed., 1232 pages, 1983 (Casebook)

Lilly's Introduction to the Law of Evidence, 2nd Ed., 585 pages, 1987 (Text)

McCormick, Sutton and Wellborn's Cases and Materials on Evidence, 6th Ed., 1067 pages, 1987 (Casebook)

McCormick's Hornbook on Evidence, 3rd Ed., Student Ed., 1156 pages, 1984 with 1987 P.P. (Text)

Rothstein's Evidence, State and Federal Rules in a Nutshell, 2nd Ed., 514 pages, 1981 (Text)

Saltzburg's Evidence Supplement: Rules, Statutes, Commentary, 245 pages, 1980 (Casebook Supplement)

FEDERAL JURISDICTION AND PROCEDURE

Currie's Cases and Materials on Federal Courts, 3rd Ed., 1042 pages, 1982 with 1985 Supplement (Casebook)

Currie's Federal Jurisdiction in a Nutshell, 2nd Ed., 258 pages, 1981 (Text)

Federal Rules of Civil-Appellate Procedure—West Law School Edition, about 600 pages, 1988

Forrester and Moye's Cases and Materials on Federal Jurisdiction and Procedure, 3rd Ed., 917 pages, 1977 with 1985 Supplement (Casebook)

Redish's Cases, Comments and Questions on Federal Courts, 878 pages, 1983 with 1988 Supplement (Casebook)

Vetri and Merrill's Federal Courts, Problems and Materials, 2nd Ed., 232 pages, 1984 (Problem Book)

Wright's Hornbook on Federal Courts, 4th Ed., Student Ed., 870 pages, 1983 (Text)

FOREIGN RELATIONS AND NATIONAL SECURITY LAW

Franck and Glennon's United States Foreign Relations Law: Cases, Materials and Simulations, 941 pages, 1987 (Casebook)

FUTURE INTERESTS

See Trusts and Estates

HEALTH LAW

See Medicine, Law and

IMMIGRATION LAW

Aleinikoff and Martin's Immigration Process and Policy, 1042 pages, 1985 with 1987 Supplement (Casebook)

IMMIGRATION LAW—Cont'd

Weissbrodt's Immigration Law and Procedure in a Nutshell, 345 pages, 1984 (Text)

INDIAN LAW

See American Indian Law

INSURANCE

Dobbyn's Insurance Law in a Nutshell, 281 pages, 1981 (Text)

Keeton's Cases on Basic Insurance Law, 2nd Ed., 1086 pages, 1977

Keeton and Wydiss' Insurance Law, Student Ed., about 1024 pages, 1988 (Text)

Wydiss and Keeton's Course Supplement to Keeton and Wydiss's Insurance Law, 425 pages, 1988 (Casebook)

York and Whelan's Cases, Materials and Problems on General Practice Insurance Law, 2nd Ed., about 811 pages, 1988 (Casebook)

INTERNATIONAL LAW

Buergenthal International Human Rights in a Nutshell, about 275 pages, 1988 (Text)

Buergenthal and Maier's Public International Law in a Nutshell, 262 pages, 1985 (Text)

Folsom, Gordon and Spanogle's International Business Transactions – a Problem-Oriented Coursebook, 1160 pages, 1986, with Documents Supplement (Casebook)

Folsom, Gordon and Spanogle's International Business Transactions in a Nutshell, 3rd Ed., about 484 pages, 1988 (Text)

Henkin, Pugh, Schachter and Smit's Cases and Materials on International Law, 2nd Ed., 1517 pages, 1987 with Documents Supplement (Casebook)

Jackson and Davey's Legal Problems of International Economic Relations, 2nd Ed., 1269 pages, 1986, with Documents Supplement (Casebook)

Kirgis' International Organizations in Their Legal Setting, 1016 pages, 1977, with 1981 Supplement (Casebook)

Weston, Falk and D'Amato's International Law and World Order—A Problem Oriented Coursebook, 1195 pages, 1980, with Documents Supplement (Casebook)

INTERVIEWING AND COUNSELING

Binder and Price's Interviewing and Counseling, 232 pages, 1977 (Text)

Shaffer and Elkins' Interviewing and Counseling in a Nutshell, 2nd Ed., 487 pages, 1987 (Text)

INTRODUCTION TO LAW STUDY

Dobbyn's So You Want to go to Law School, Revised First Edition, 206 pages, 1976 (Text)

LAW SCHOOL PUBLICATIONS—Continued

INTRODUCTION TO LAW STUDY—Cont'd

Hegland's Introduction to the Study and Practice of Law in a Nutshell, 418 pages, 1983 (Text)

Kinyon's Introduction to Law Study and Law Examinations in a Nutshell, 389 pages, 1971 (Text)

See also Legal Method and Legal System

JURISPRUDENCE

Christie's Text and Readings on Jurisprudence—The Philosophy of Law, 1056 pages, 1973 (Casebook)

JUVENILE JUSTICE

Fox's Cases and Materials on Modern Juvenile Justice, 2nd Ed., 960 pages, 1981 (Casebook)

Fox's Juvenile Courts in a Nutshell, 3rd Ed., 291 pages, 1984 (Text)

LABOR LAW

Gorman's Basic Text on Labor Law—Unionization and Collective Bargaining, 914 pages, 1976 (Text)

Grodin, Wollett and Alleyne's Collective Bargaining in Public Employment, 3rd Ed., (The Labor Law Group), 430 pages, 1979 (Casebook)

Leslie's Labor Law in a Nutshell, 2nd Ed., 397 pages, 1986 (Text)

Nolan's Labor Arbitration Law and Practice in a Nutshell, 358 pages, 1979 (Text)

Oberer, Hanslowe, Andersen and Heinsz' Cases and Materials on Labor Law—Collective Bargaining in a Free Society, 3rd Ed., 1163 pages, 1986 with Statutory Supplement (Casebook)

Rabin, Silverstein and Schatzki's Labor and Employment Law: Cases, Materials and Problems in the Law of Work, (The Labor Law Group), about 1000 pages, 1988 with Statutory Supplement (Casebook)

See also Employment Discrimination, Social Legislation

LAND FINANCE

See Real Estate Transactions

LAND USE

Callies and Freilich's Cases and Materials on Land Use, 1233 pages, 1986 (Casebook)

Hagman's Cases on Public Planning and Control of Urban and Land Development, 2nd Ed., 1301 pages, 1980 (Casebook)

Hagman and Juergensmeyer's Hornbook on Urban Planning and Land Development Control Law, 2nd Ed., Student Ed., 680 pages, 1986 (Text)

Wright and Gitelman's Cases and Materials on Land Use, 3rd Ed., 1300 pages, 1982, with 1987 Supplement (Casebook)

LAND USE—Cont'd

Wright and Wright's Land Use in a Nutshell, 2nd Ed., 356 pages, 1985 (Text)

LEGAL HISTORY

Presser and Zainaldin's Cases on Law and American History, 855 pages, 1980 (Casebook)

See also Legal Method and Legal System

LEGAL METHOD AND LEGAL SYSTEM

Aldisert's Readings, Materials and Cases in the Judicial Process, 948 pages, 1976 (Casebook)

Berch and Berch's Introduction to Legal Method and Process, 550 pages, 1985 (Casebook)

Bodenheimer, Oakley and Love's Readings and Cases on an Introduction to the Anglo-American Legal System, 2nd Ed., 166 pages, 1988 (Casebook)

Davies and Lawry's Institutions and Methods of the Law—Introductory Teaching Materials, 547 pages, 1982 (Casebook)

Dvorkin, Himmelstein and Lesnick's Becoming a Lawyer: A Humanistic Perspective on Legal Education and Professionalism, 211 pages, 1981 (Text)

Greenberg's Judicial Process and Social Change, 666 pages, 1977 (Casebook)

Kelso and Kelso's Studying Law: An Introduction, 587 pages, 1984 (Coursebook)

Kempin's Historical Introduction to Anglo-American Law in a Nutshell, 2nd Ed., 280 pages, 1973 (Text)

Murphy's Cases and Materials on Introduction to Law—Legal Process and Procedure, 772 pages, 1977 (Casebook)

Reynolds' Judicial Process in a Nutshell, 292 pages, 1980 (Text)

See also Legal Research and Writing

LEGAL PROFESSION

Aronson, Devine and Fisch's Problems, Cases and Materials on Professional Responsibility, 745 pages, 1985 (Casebook)

Aronson and Weckstein's Professional Responsibility in a Nutshell, 399 pages, 1980 (Text)

Mellinkoff's The Conscience of a Lawyer, 304 pages, 1973 (Text)

Pirsig and Kirwin's Cases and Materials on Professional Responsibility, 4th Ed., 603 pages, 1984 (Casebook)

Schwartz and Wydick's Problems in Legal Ethics, 2nd Ed., 341 pages, 1988 (Casebook)

Selected Statutes, Rules and Standards on the Legal Profession, 449 pages, 1987

Smith's Preventing Legal Malpractice, 142 pages, 1981 (Text)

Wolfram's Hornbook on Modern Legal Ethics, Student Edition, 1120 pages, 1986 (Text)

LAW SCHOOL PUBLICATIONS—Continued

LEGAL RESEARCH AND WRITING

Child's Materials and Problems on Drafting Legal Documents, 286 pages, 1988 (Text)

Cohen's Legal Research in a Nutshell, 4th Ed., 450 pages, 1985 (Text)

Cohen and Berring's How to Find the Law, 8th Ed., 790 pages, 1983. Problem book by Foster, Johnson and Kelly available (Casebook)

Cohen and Berring's Finding the Law, 8th Ed., Abridged Ed., 556 pages, 1984 (Casebook)

Dickerson's Materials on Legal Drafting, 425 pages, 1981 (Casebook)

Felsenfeld and Siegel's Writing Contracts in Plain English, 290 pages, 1981 (Text)

Gopen's Writing From a Legal Perspective, 225 pages, 1981 (Text)

Mellinkoff's Legal Writing—Sense and Nonsense, 242 pages, 1982 (Text)

Ray and Ramsfield's Legal Writing: Getting It Right and Getting It Written, 250 pages, 1987 (Text)

Rombauer's Legal Problem Solving—Analysis, Research and Writing, 4th Ed., 424 pages, 1983 (Coursebook)

Squires and Rombauer's Legal Writing in a Nutshell, 294 pages, 1982 (Text)

Statsky's Legal Research and Writing, 3rd Ed., 257 pages, 1986 (Coursebook)

Statsky and Wernet's Case Analysis and Fundamentals of Legal Writing, 3rd Ed., about 450 pages, 1988 (Text)

Teply's Programmed Materials on Legal Research and Citation, 2nd Ed., 358 pages, 1986. Student Library Exercises available (Coursebook)

Weihofen's Legal Writing Style, 2nd Ed., 332 pages, 1980 (Text)

LEGISLATION

Davies' Legislative Law and Process in a Nutshell, 2nd Ed., 346 pages, 1986 (Text)

Eskridge and Frickey's Cases on Legislation, 937 pages, 1987 (Casebook)

Nutting and Dickerson's Cases and Materials on Legislation, 5th Ed., 744 pages, 1978 (Casebook)

Statsky's Legislative Analysis and Drafting, 2nd Ed., 217 pages, 1984 (Text)

LOCAL GOVERNMENT

Frug's Cases and Materials on Local Government Law, about 1000 pages, 1988 (Casebook)

McCarthy's Local Government Law in a Nutshell, 2nd Ed., 404 pages, 1983 (Text)

Reynolds' Hornbook on Local Government Law, 860 pages, 1982, with 1987 pocket part (Text)

Valente's Cases and Materials on Local Government Law, 3rd Ed., 1010 pages, 1987 (Casebook)

MASS COMMUNICATION LAW

Gillmor and Barron's Cases and Comment on Mass Communication Law, 4th Ed., 1076 pages, 1984 (Casebook)

Ginsburg's Regulation of Broadcasting: Law and Policy Towards Radio, Television and Cable Communications, 741 pages, 1979 with 1983 Supplement (Casebook)

Zuckman, Gaynes, Carter and Dee's Mass Communications Law in a Nutshell, 3rd Ed., 538 pages, 1988 (Text)

MEDICINE, LAW AND

Furrow, Johnson, Jost and Schwartz' Health Law: Cases, Materials and Problems, 1005 pages, 1987 (Casebook)

King's The Law of Medical Malpractice in a Nutshell, 2nd Ed., 342 pages, 1986 (Text)

Shapiro and Spece's Problems, Cases and Materials on Bioethics and Law, 892 pages, 1981 (Casebook)

Sharpe, Fiscina and Head's Cases on Law and Medicine, 882 pages, 1978 (Casebook)

MILITARY LAW

Shanor and Terrell's Military Law in a Nutshell, 378 pages, 1980 (Text)

MORTGAGES

See Real Estate Transactions

NATURAL RESOURCES LAW

See Energy and Natural Resources Law

NEGOTIATION

Edwards and White's Problems, Readings and Materials on the Lawyer as a Negotiator, 484 pages, 1977 (Casebook)

Peck's Cases and Materials on Negotiation, 2nd Ed., (The Labor Law Group), 280 pages, 1980 (Casebook)

Williams' Legal Negotiation and Settlement, 207 pages, 1983 (Coursebook)

OFFICE PRACTICE

Hegland's Trial and Practice Skills in a Nutshell, 346 pages, 1978 (Text)

Strong and Clark's Law Office Management, 424 pages, 1974 (Casebook)

See also Computers and Law, Interviewing and Counseling, Negotiation

OIL AND GAS

Hemingway's Hornbook on Oil and Gas, 2nd Ed., Student Ed., 543 pages, 1983 with 1986 P.P. (Text)

Kuntz, Lowe, Anderson and Smith's Cases and Materials on Oil and Gas Law, 857 pages, 1986, with Forms Manual (Casebook)

Lowe's Oil and Gas Law in a Nutshell, 2nd Ed., about 402 pages, 1988 (Text)

See also Energy and Natural Resources Law

LAW SCHOOL PUBLICATIONS—Continued

PARTNERSHIP

See Agency—Partnership

PATENT AND COPYRIGHT LAW

Choate, Francis and Collins' Cases and Materials on Patent Law, 3rd Ed., 1009 pages, 1987 (Casebook)

Miller and Davis' Intellectual Property—Patents, Trademarks and Copyright in a Nutshell, 428 pages, 1983 (Text)

Nimmer's Cases on Copyright and Other Aspects of Entertainment Litigation, 3rd Ed., 1025 pages, 1985 (Casebook)

PRODUCTS LIABILITY

Fischer and Powers' Cases and Materials on Products Liability, 685 pages, 1988 (Casebook)

Noel and Phillips' Cases on Products Liability, 2nd Ed., 821 pages, 1982 (Casebook)

Phillips' Products Liability in a Nutshell, 3rd Ed., 307 pages, 1988 (Text)

PROPERTY

Bernhardt's Real Property in a Nutshell, 2nd Ed., 448 pages, 1981 (Text)

Boyer's Survey of the Law of Property, 766 pages, 1981 (Text)

Browder, Cunningham and Smith's Cases on Basic Property Law, 4th Ed., 1431 pages, 1984 (Casebook)

Bruce, Ely and Bostick's Cases and Materials on Modern Property Law, 1004 pages, 1984 (Casebook)

Burke's Personal Property in a Nutshell, 322 pages, 1983 (Text)

Cunningham, Stoebuck and Whitman's Hornbook on the Law of Property, Student Ed., 916 pages, 1984 with 1987 P.P. (Text)

Donahue, Kauper and Martin's Cases on Property, 2nd Ed., 1362 pages, 1983 (Casebook)

Hill's Landlord and Tenant Law in a Nutshell, 2nd Ed., 311 pages, 1986 (Text)

Kurtz and Hovenkamp's Cases and Materials on American Property Law, 1296 pages, 1987 with 1988 Supplement (Casebook)

Moynihan's Introduction to Real Property, 2nd Ed., 239 pages, 1988 (Text)

Uniform Land Transactions Act, Uniform Simplification of Land Transfers Act, Uniform Condominium Act, 1977 Official Text with Comments, 462 pages, 1978

See also Real Estate Transactions, Land Use

PSYCHIATRY, LAW AND

Reisner's Law and the Mental Health System, Civil and Criminal Aspects, 696 pages, 1985 with 1987 Supplement (Casebooks)

REAL ESTATE TRANSACTIONS

Bruce's Real Estate Finance in a Nutshell, 2nd Ed., 262 pages, 1985 (Text)

Maxwell, Riesenfeld, Hetland and Warren's Cases on California Security Transactions in Land, 3rd Ed., 728 pages, 1984 (Casebook)

Nelson and Whitman's Cases on Real Estate Transfer, Finance and Development, 3rd Ed., 1184 pages, 1987 (Casebook)

Nelson and Whitman's Hornbook on Real Estate Finance Law, 2nd Ed., Student Ed., 941 pages, 1985 (Text)

Osborne's Cases and Materials on Secured Transactions, 559 pages, 1967 (Casebook)

REGULATED INDUSTRIES

Gellhorn and Pierce's Regulated Industries in a Nutshell, 2nd Ed., 389 pages, 1987 (Text)

Morgan, Harrison and Verkuil's Cases and Materials on Economic Regulation of Business, 2nd Ed., 666 pages, 1985 (Casebook)

See also Mass Communication Law, Banking Law

REMEDIES

Dobbs' Hornbook on Remedies, 1067 pages, 1973 (Text)

Dobbs' Problems in Remedies, 137 pages, 1974 (Problem book)

Dobbyn's Injunctions in a Nutshell, 264 pages, 1974 (Text)

Friedman's Contract Remedies in a Nutshell, 323 pages, 1981 (Text)

Leavell, Love and Nelson's Cases and Materials on Equitable Remedies and Restitution, 4th Ed., 1111 pages, 1986 (Casebook)

McCormick's Hornbook on Damages, 811 pages, 1935 (Text)

O'Connell's Remedies in a Nutshell, 2nd Ed., 320 pages, 1985 (Text)

York, Bauman and Rendleman's Cases and Materials on Remedies, 4th Ed., 1029 pages, 1985 (Casebook)

REVIEW MATERIALS

Ballantine's Problems

Black Letter Series

SECURITIES REGULATION

Hazen's Hornbook on The Law of Securities Regulation, Student Ed., 739 pages, 1985, with 1988 P.P. (Text)

Ratner's Securities Regulation: Materials for a Basic Course, 3rd Ed., 1000 pages, 1986 (Casebook)

Ratner's Securities Regulation in a Nutshell, 3rd Ed., 316 pages, 1988 (Text)

LAW SCHOOL PUBLICATIONS—Continued

SECURITIES REGULATION—Cont'd

Selected Securities and Business Planning Statutes, Rules and Forms, 493 pages, 1987

SOCIAL LEGISLATION

Hood and Hardy's Workers' Compensation and Employee Protection Laws in a Nutshell, 274 pages, 1984 (Text)

LaFrance's Welfare Law: Structure and Entitlement in a Nutshell, 455 pages, 1979 (Text)

Malone, Plant and Little's Cases on Workers' Compensation and Employment Rights, 2nd Ed., 951 pages, 1980 (Casebook)

SPORTS LAW

Schubert, Smith and Trentadue's Sports Law, 395 pages, 1986 (Text)

TAXATION

Dodge's Cases and Materials on Federal Income Taxation, 820 pages, 1985 (Casebook)

Garbis, Struntz and Rubin's Cases and Materials on Tax Procedure and Tax Fraud, 2nd Ed., 687 pages, 1987 (Casebook)

Gelfand and Salsich's State and Local Taxation and Finance in a Nutshell, 309 pages, 1986 (Text)

Gunn and Ward's Cases and Materials on Federal Income Taxation, about 815 pages, 1988 (Casebook)

Hellerstein and Hellerstein's Cases on State and Local Taxation, 5th Ed., about 1060 pages, 1988 (Casebook)

Kahn and Gann's Corporate Taxation and Taxation of Partnerships and Partners, 2nd Ed., 1204 pages, 1985 (Casebook)

Kaplan's Federal Taxation of International Transactions: Principles, Planning and Policy, 635 pages, 1988 (Casebook)

Kragen and McNulty's Cases and Materials on Federal Income Taxation: Individuals, Corporations, Partnerships, 4th Ed., 1287 pages, 1985 (Casebook)

McNulty's Federal Estate and Gift Taxation in a Nutshell, 3rd Ed., 509 pages, 1983 (Text)

McNulty's Federal Income Taxation of Individuals in a Nutshell, 4th Ed., about 500 pages, 1988 (Text)

Pennell's Cases and Materials on Income Taxation of Trusts, Estates, Grantors and Beneficiaries, 460 pages, 1987 (Casebook)

Posin's Hornbook on Federal Income Taxation of Individuals, Student Ed., 491 pages, 1983 with 1987 pocket part (Text)

Rose and Chommie's Hornbook on Federal Income Taxation, 3rd Ed., 923 pages, 1988 (Text)

TAXATION—Cont'd

Selected Federal Taxation Statutes and Regulations, about 1400 pages, 1989

Solomon and Hesch's Cases on Federal Income Taxation of Individuals, 1068 pages, 1987 (Casebook)

TORTS

Christie's Cases and Materials on the Law of Torts, 1264 pages, 1983 (Casebook)

Dobbs' Torts and Compensation—Personal Accountability and Social Responsibility for Injury, 955 pages, 1985 (Casebook)

Keeton, Keeton, Sargentich and Steiner's Cases and Materials on Tort and Accident Law, 1360 pages, 1983 (Casebook)

Kionka's Torts in a Nutshell: Injuries to Persons and Property, 434 pages, 1977 (Text)

Malone's Torts in a Nutshell: Injuries to Family, Social and Trade Relations, 358 pages, 1979 (Text)

Prosser and Keeton's Hornbook on Torts, 5th Ed., Student Ed., 1286 pages, 1984, with 1988 pocket part (Text)

See also Products Liability

TRADE REGULATION

McManis' Unfair Trade Practices in a Nutshell, 2nd Ed., about 430 pages, 1988 (Text)

Oppenheim, Weston, Maggs and Schechter's Cases and Materials on Unfair Trade Practices and Consumer Protection, 4th Ed., 1038 pages, 1983 with 1986 Supplement (Casebook)

See also Antitrust, Regulated Industries

TRIAL AND APPELLATE ADVOCACY

Appellate Advocacy, Handbook of, 2nd Ed., 182 pages, 1986 (Text)

Bergman's Trial Advocacy in a Nutshell, 402 pages, 1979 (Text)

Binder and Bergman's Fact Investigation: From Hypothesis to Proof, 354 pages, 1984 (Coursebook)

Goldberg's The First Trial (Where Do I Sit?, What Do I Say?) in a Nutshell, 396 pages, 1982 (Text)

Haydock, Herr and Stempel's, Fundamentals of Pre-Trial Litigation, 768 pages, 1985 (Casebook)

Hegland's Trial and Practice Skills in a Nutshell, 346 pages, 1978 (Text)

Hornstein's Appellate Advocacy in a Nutshell, 325 pages, 1984 (Text)

Jeans' Handbook on Trial Advocacy, Student Ed., 473 pages, 1975 (Text)

Martineau's Cases and Materials on Appellate Practice and Procedure, 565 pages, 1987 (Casebook)

McElhaney's Effective Litigation, 457 pages, 1974 (Casebook)

Nolan's Cases and Materials on Trial Practice, 518 pages, 1981 (Casebook)

LAW SCHOOL PUBLICATIONS—Continued

TRIAL AND APPELLATE ADVOCACY—Cont'd

Sonsteng, Haydock and Boyd's The Trialbook: A Total System for Preparation and Presentation of a Case, Student Ed., 404 pages, 1984 (Coursebook)

See also Civil Procedure

TRUSTS AND ESTATES

Atkinson's Hornbook on Wills, 2nd Ed., 975 pages, 1953 (Text)

Averill's Uniform Probate Code in a Nutshell, 2nd Ed., 454 pages, 1987 (Text)

Bogert's Hornbook on Trusts, 6th Ed., Student Ed., 794 pages, 1987 (Text)

Clark, Lusky and Murphy's Cases and Materials on Gratuitous Transfers, 3rd Ed., 970 pages, 1985 (Casebook)

Dodge's Wills, Trusts and Estate Planning, Law and Taxation, Cases and Materials, 665 pages, 1988 (Casebook)

Kurtz' Cases, Materials and Problems on Family Estate Planning, 853 pages, 1983 (Casebook)

McGovern's Cases and Materials on Wills, Trusts and Future Interests: An Introduction to Estate Planning, 750 pages, 1983 (Casebook)

McGovern, Rein and Kurtz' Hornbook on Wills, Trusts and Estates including Taxation and Future Interests, about 924 pages, 1988 (Text)

Mennell's Wills and Trusts in a Nutshell, 392 pages, 1979 (Text)

Simes' Hornbook on Future Interests, 2nd Ed., 355 pages, 1966 (Text)

TRUSTS AND ESTATES—Cont'd

Turano and Radigan's Hornbook on New York Estate Administration, 676 pages, 1986 (Text)

Uniform Probate Code, Official Text With Comments, 578 pages, 1987

Waggoner's Future Interests in a Nutshell, 361 pages, 1981 (Text)

Waterbury's Materials on Trusts and Estates, 1039 pages, 1986 (Casebook)

WATER LAW

Getches' Water Law in a Nutshell, 439 pages, 1984 (Text)

Sax and Abram's Cases and Materials on Legal Control of Water Resources, 941 pages, 1986 (Casebook)

Trelease and Gould's Cases and Materials on Water Law, 4th Ed., 816 pages, 1986 (Casebook)

See also Energy and Natural Resources Law, Environmental Law

WILLS

See Trusts and Estates

WOMEN AND THE LAW

Kay's Text, Cases and Materials on Sex-Based Discrimination, 3rd Ed., about 979 pages, 1988 (Casebook)

Thomas' Sex Discrimination in a Nutshell, 399 pages, 1982 (Text)

See also Employment Discrimination

WORKERS' COMPENSATION

See Social Legislation

BASIC TEXT

ON

LABOR LAW

UNIONIZATION

AND

COLLECTIVE BARGAINING

ROBERT A. GORMAN

Professor of Law
University of Pennsylvania

ST. PAUL, MINN.

WEST PUBLISHING CO.

1976

Gorman-Labor Law
4th Reprint—1989

To My Parents

*

PREFACE

The objective of this book is to explain in a straightforward manner the principles of what has come to be known as Labor Law. These are the principles that have been developed by the National Labor Relations Board and the courts under a fairly elaborate piece of federal legislation enacted in three major stages: the Wagner Act or National Labor Relations Act of 1935, the Taft-Hartley Act or Labor-Management Relations Act of 1947, and the Landrum-Griffin Act or Labor-Management Reporting and Disclosure Act of 1959. For convenience, this legislation will usually be referred to herein as the Labor Act; its text, and that of other pertinent federal legislation, is set forth in an Appendix to this book. The subjects covered relate to the formation of labor unions, the use of economic weapons such as strikes, picketing, boycotts and lockouts, the establishment of collective bargaining and the enforcement of the collective bargaining agreement. Obviously, the title Labor Law is rather overbroad, for neither this book nor the conventional law course so titled deals with other legal rules which govern the employment relationship, such as wage and hour laws, laws barring discrimination in employment on the basis of race or sex, health and safety laws, laws governing compensation for industrial accidents, pension laws, unemployment compensation and social security. These omitted subjects are regulated by legislation, judicial decisions and administrative rulings, at both the federal and state levels, in increasing volume and importance.

The title of this book has therefore been "colon-ized" to denote its scope with greater accuracy: Unionization and Collective Bargaining. This narrower aspect of the employment relationship merits discrete examination. The Labor Act constitutes a single coherent (some would question the adjective) body of legislation. It has created an administrative agency responsible for shaping and applying most of its directives; that agency, its decisions, and its relationship to the judiciary justify special attention for lawyers and for students of governmental regulation. Unlike laws which regulate working conditions directly, the Labor Act—by fostering employee freedom in the choice of collective bargaining representatives and good faith bargaining if a representative is selected—attempts merely to regulate the process by which the parties themselves shape their substantive working conditions. The study of Labor Law is the study of group action, of the relationship between organized capital and organized labor, of the relationship between the individual and the

PREFACE

labor organization. These common threads justify an attempt to order the pertinent legal principles and to understand their evolution and their foundation in policy.

The intended audience for this book is principally the law student and the practicing lawyer. For the law student, the book will hopefully provide an orientation, will answer many questions and will raise others. I have purposely refrained from venturing a great number of personal appraisals of the soundness of Board and court rules and decisions. Although, in order clearly to communicate principles—the objective of this book—the author must inevitably show his predilections merely by organizing and analyzing materials, I have assumed that the reader would prefer, in a work necessarily limited by economies of time and print, that the author's personalized appraisals be kept to a minimum. While that might for some be a short-coming, I have tried instead to give to the reader enough information and perspective to reach his or her own conclusions about the soundness of the legal doctrines developed in the cases. The student should treat this not as a terminal point for thinking about Labor Law but rather as a starting point. Hopefully, the book can serve this purpose not only for the student in law schools but also for the student in divisions of arts and sciences or business who are studying such subjects as labor history, labor economics or industrial relations.

The book should also be of use to the practicing lawyer. The general practitioner who occasionally confronts a problem in labor-management relations should find orientation and direction in these pages. The more sophisticated specialist in Labor Law will already have that orientation, and will be more adept at handling the arcane reference tools in the field; but this book can serve many as a "refresher" and others as a source of new insights or of new legal references.

These objectives help to explain the somewhat unusual format of this book. Since it is not designed to compile references, it has no "string citations" of cases from many circuits on each principle. While this book can facilitate legal research, the only way to do thorough and up-to-the-minute research is through the usual library methods, particularly in the reference services. No book between two covers can adequately deal with the great volume of cases on the great number of issues in Labor Law or can catch the decision handed down just yesterday. Rather than attempt to substitute for what can only be found in a research library, this book is designed principally to be read in one's own study or office. Therefore, only a single case is generally cited in support of an announced principle. That case has been chosen because it either first announced the principle in question, or has otherwise "given its name" to that principle, or (whenever possible) has the most thorough and illuminating analy-

PREFACE

sis of that principle, or has a useful catalogue of the pertinent cases. In short, the cited case is one which I regard as particularly helpful to the reader who might be moved to go beyond what is in these printed pages. (No attempt has been made to incorporate cases reported after January 1, 1976, the approximate date on which the manuscript of this book was delivered to the publisher.)

The somewhat implausible omission of footnotes is explainable for additional reasons. The constant—for many of us, seemingly instinctive—flitting of the eye from text to page-bottom is rather a nuisance; it consumes time and destroys continuity. Moreover, Labor Law is a field in which it is often quite important to know such information as when a case was decided or principle announced; whether it was announced by the NLRB or by a court of appeals or by the Supreme Court; if by a court of appeals, which circuit; if by the Board, whether its decision was reviewed and whether it was denied enforcement; in which industry and with which union did this case arise. Case citations, ordinarily rather dull and annoying, can be most illuminating on matters of import in the field of Labor Law, and they have been accordingly elevated (quite literally) to a location in text where they can be quickly seen by those interested in doing so and quickly leaped over by those not. (The frequent use of post-citation synopses of holdings and reasoning, placed within parentheses, is another reason for locating them in text.)

In order to limit the citations-in-text to this substantive role, the citations have been stripped of their volume and page numbers and of such non-substantive history as the denial of certiorari; these matters can be ascertained simply by reference to the alphabetical table of cases at the back of this volume. The citations-in-text convey only the name of the case, the year of decision, and the decisionmaker; the identity of the court is shown by customary designations before the date, while decisions of the Board will show the date only (and will obviously be Board decisions because bearing the name of only a single party, the respondent, without the usual adversary caption). As is customary, the year date of two decisions in the same proceeding within the same calendar year will be reflected only once in the citation.

* * *

There are a number of persons who, wittingly or not, have contributed substantially to the preparation of this book. My colleagues at the University of Pennsylvania Law School, Howard Lesnick and Clyde W. Summers, have for many years—both through their writings and in personal discourse—demonstrated for me an incomparable acuity concerning matters of law and labor relations. A number of able and good friends have looked at portions of the manuscript and

PREFACE

have given me the benefit of their suggestions: Robert A. Goldstein of the New York Bar, Patrick Hardin of the University of Tennessee College of Law (and formerly Associate General Counsel of the NLRB), Dr. Bernard Samoff of the Wharton School of the University of Pennsylvania (and formerly Regional Director of the Philadelphia Office of the NLRB), and George Schatzki of the University of Texas School of Law. Along with the many students I have had the pleasure to teach and learn from at the University of Pennsylvania Law School, and who have contributed to my thinking about many of the legal issues addressed herein, there were a number of law students who rendered substantial assistance in the research for and revision of this text; perhaps the most sustained assistance was contributed by Marquerite J. Ayres, Barbara Fick, Thomas W. Meiklejohn, Barry J. Rubenstein, and Howard Zucker, of the University of Pennsylvania Law School. To Winifred Cole must go the author's most profound gratitude for wrestling with a cumbersome manuscript and converting it to order and legibility, always with inner calm, good humor and flawless accuracy, often under the most trying pressures. I owe to my wife Caryl an unbounded debt of thanks not only for her assistance on many technical matters in the processing of the manuscript but particularly for that special kind of incentive (at once persistent and tolerant) that ideal spouses are meant to provide.

It is with sadness that I extend my final word of thanks to the late Bernard Dunau, a stimulating teacher and scholar and a consummate attorney, whose passion for both analytical rigor and industrial justice has left its mark on the law of labor relations and upon those who were fortunate enough to know and work with him. He helped constructively to shape many of the principles discussed in this volume.

ROBERT A. GORMAN

Philadelphia, Pa.
August, 1976

SUMMARY OF CONTENTS

SUMMARY OF CONTENTS

THE DUTY TO BARGAIN IN GOOD FAITH WITH THE MAJORITY REPRESENTATIVE

ENFORCEMENT OF THE COLLECTIVE BARGAINING AGREEMENT

THE UNION AND THE INDIVIDUAL EMPLOYEE

REGULATORY CONFLICT AND ACCOMMODATION

APPENDICES

TABLE OF CONTENTS

TABLE OF CONTENTS

CHAPTER IV. REPRESENTATION CASES: PROCEDURES
—Continued

CHAPTER V. REPRESENTATION CASES: THE APPROPRIATE BARGAINING UNIT — 66

CHAPTER VI. SECURING BARGAINING RIGHTS THROUGH UNFAIR LABOR PRACTICE PROCEEDINGS — 93

TABLE OF CONTENTS

RESTRAINT AND COERCION OF EMPLOYEE RIGHTS TO ORGANIZE

TABLE OF CONTENTS

TABLE OF CONTENTS

TABLE OF CONTENTS

TABLE OF CONTENTS

THE DUTY TO BARGAIN IN GOOD FAITH WITH THE MAJORITY REPRESENTATIVE

TABLE OF CONTENTS

TABLE OF CONTENTS

TABLE OF CONTENTS

THE UNION AND THE INDIVIDUAL EMPLOYEE

TABLE OF CONTENTS

†

LABOR LAW:
UNIONIZATION AND
COLLECTIVE BARGAINING

INTRODUCTION: LABOR LAW, THE FEDERAL LABOR ACT AND THE NLRB

CHAPTER I

A SKETCH OF THE HISTORY OF AMERICAN LABOR LAW

The National Labor Relations Act is the primary body of federal law controlling labor-management relations in private industry. The Act was shaped in three major cycles: the Wagner Act in 1935, the Taft-Hartley Act in 1947 and the Landrum-Griffin Act in 1959. The basic principle of the NLRA is to be found in its section 7, granting to employees the right to form labor organizations, to deal collectively through such organizations regarding terms and conditions of employment and to engage in concerted activities in support of these other rights. The statute can best be understood as an effort by the Congress to create the conditions of industrial peace in interstate commerce by removing obstacles to—indeed, encouraging—the formation of labor unions as an effective voice for the individual worker.

No more than a sketch can be given of the development of labor relations law in the United States prior to the enactment of the NLRA. Concerted employee activities in support of demands for higher wages and better working conditions were met, in the early decades of the nineteenth century, with criminal prosecution. They were treated as common law conspiracies which were rendered criminal because of the illegality of the means employed or the ends sought. In the latter part of the century, and in the early years of the twentieth century, the civil injunction played a much more pervasive role in combatting unionization. Concerted activities in support of such unionization—strikes, picketing and boycotts (of the employer or its product)—were treated as conspiracies which restrained trade and which inflicted irreparable damage upon the affected employer. The injunction was a far more effective weapon against labor activities than was the criminal proceeding. A temporary restraining order could be promptly secured on the basis of stylized affidavits, the truth of which often could not be challenged because they were presented to the judge ex parte, without notice to the employees. The restraining order might continue in effect for as long as several weeks, at which time the employer would seek a preliminary injunction pending an even later formal trial on the merits of the case. Usually there was no need for the employer to take the case even that far, the earlier orders having successfully halted the collective activities. At each stage the case was tried not to a jury but to a judge, generally hand-picked by the moving party and in any event because of education and upbringing unlikely to be sympathetic to the cause of unionization. The injunctive decrees were worded so broadly as frequently to inhibit conduct, such as peaceful persuasive speech, which was clearly lawful and to reach the actions of individuals who were either remotely connected to the labor strife or who had never had an opportunity to participate in the legal proceedings in protection of their rights; and the sanction for violation of the injunction was a contempt citation and possible imprisonment, the relevant issues frequently being tried before the judge who had granted the injunction initially.

Perhaps the worst abuse of the civil courts was their tendency to outlaw as tortious concerted employee activities which relied upon methods, such as strikes and picketing which were thought inherently intimidating and foreboding of violence, or which set economic goals, such as an improved wage scale or a closed shop, which were thought to be anti-social or unfairly restrictive of the freedom of others. Means or objectives which, when pursued by a single person—or by employer combinations—were deemed perfectly lawful, were enjoined as civil conspiracies when pursued by a group of employees. The standards were vague, inconsistent and preeminently dependent upon the predilections of the presiding judges. Over time, even though many state courts came to treat peaceful strikes, picketing and boycotts as economic duress which was excused or justified by "legitimate" employee self-interest, they still purported to judge "legitimacy" by no lights other than their own, such that there was a difference of opinion from one state to another about the validity of economic pressure designed to secure the assignment of work currently being done by a different group of employees (a jurisdictional or work-assignment dispute), or to induce a customer or supplier of the "primary" employer to cease doing business with him (a secondary boycott), or to secure bargaining rights for a particular union or to induce the employer to compel all of his employees to join that union (the closed shop).

Simultaneously, in the early years of the twentieth century, the federal courts were also active in enjoining concerted labor activities, in part through the diversity-of-citizenship jurisdiction (under which it was thought appropriate to formulate rules of federal common law independent of those obtaining in the courts of the state) and in part through the jurisdiction accorded by the federal antitrust laws. The Sherman Act of 1890 declared illegal "every contract, combination . . . or conspiracy, in restraint of trade or commerce among the several States," and provided in such cases for government injunction, criminal prosecution and private treble-damage actions; the Clayton Act of 1914 added the private injunctive action to the arsenal of sanctions for the antitrust violation. Although obviously designed to counter the abuse of power by manufacturers in combining to set price and supply in the product market, the Sherman Act was applied yet more frequently by the lower federal courts to labor unions. And, in 1908, the Supreme Court in Loewe v. Lawlor (U.S.1908), a case involving a boycott by the hatters' union of retail stores which continued to do business with the struck hat manufacturer, held such a secondary boycott to be outlawed by the Sherman Act and sustained a private judgment for treble damages against the individual employee defendants.

Like the common law of the separate states, the vague provisions of the Sherman Act offered little guidance to the federal courts in applying it to labor unions. The courts, realizing that *any* strike which shut down a plant might be treated as a "combination" or "conspiracy" interfering with interstate trade, tended to narrow the statute's proscription to embrace only those employee activities which either were motivated by a specific intention to inhibit competition in the product market or appeared objectionable for reasons extrinsic to antitrust policy. In the first category was the organizational strike, the object of which was frequently to increase wages and thus product prices in order to eliminate competitive pressure upon companies already organized by the union instigating the strike. *E.g.,* UMW v. Coronado Coal Co. (U.S.1922). In the second category were the secondary boycott, the strike designed to stay the introduction of labor-saving devices, and mass picketing.

In the face of this general current of anti-labor judicial decisions there developed a gradual sensitivity on the part of some courts to the need for fair procedures in the issuance and enforcement of injunctions and, more important, a legislative sensitivity toward the interests of the laborer. The economic recession in the last years of the nineteenth century, and the problems of a wartime economy at the outset of the twentieth, invited some federal regulation of labor-management relations. The National War Labor Board announced the principle of employee freedom to organize in and bargain collectively through trade unions, free from employer interference. Earlier, in 1898, the Erdman Act had brought to the railroad industry the principles of peaceful resolution of disputes by third-party mediation and conciliation, and of protection of employees against discharge for union membership (including the outlawing of the so-called yellow dog contract, by which the contract of hire would provide that the employee would not join a union during his term of employment).

While the latter legislative protection was held unconstitutional by the Supreme Court in Adair v. United States (U.S.1908), comparable provisions were re-introduced in the Railway Labor Act of 1926 and were sustained in Texas & N.O.R.R. v. Brotherhood of Ry. Clerks (U.S.1930), because of a change in Supreme Court attitude on the relative weights to be accorded Congressional interest in avoiding disruption of interstate commerce and the private interest of employers and employees freely to set conditions of employment.

The Clayton Act of 1914 was designed to withdraw the power of federal courts to regulate labor activities through the antitrust laws. Section 20 of the Act listed the conventional concerted activities such as strikes, picketing and boycotts, and declared these to be nonenjoinable and not violative of the Sherman Act. But that section was very narrowly construed by the Supreme Court in Duplex Printing Press Co. v. Deering (U.S.1921), and held not to shelter the secondary boycott because of the lack of a direct employment relationship between the defendant employees and the company which was the ultimate object of the boycott. The legislative response was the enactment by Congress in 1932 of the Norris-LaGuardia Act. That statute declared it to be the public policy of the United States that employees be permitted to organize and bargain collectively free of employer coercion and sought to achieve that goal by regulating and in most cases barring altogether the issuance of injunctions in a "labor dispute." That term was broadly defined so as to engross all persons in the same trade as that in which the dispute occurred or persons having an indirect interest therein, regardless of any proximate employment relationship. Peaceful strikes, picketing and boycotts were sheltered against the injunction and, in the extraordinary cases in which an injunction could lawfully issue, the Act imposed limitations upon the duration of restraining orders and provided for full and fair hearings for preliminary injunctions, specificity of allegations and court findings, and trial by jury and recusal of the judge in contempt proceedings.

In Apex Hosiery Co. v. Leader (U.S.1940), the Supreme Court drastically limited the reach of the Sherman Act as applied to labor unions, acknowledging that even anticompetitive impact in the product market is an allowable byproduct of a union's lawful attempt to eliminate competition from nonunion goods as a means of protecting organizational gains elsewhere. And the next year, in United States v. Hutcheson (U.S.1941), the Court held the broad protections of the Norris-LaGuardia Act not only to bar injunctions against labor activities but also to immunize them against antitrust actions for treble damages and criminal relief.

Until the mid-1930's, then, Congress sought to protect labor by declaring that the federal government should leave essentially unregulated the combat between labor and management, with each side mustering its economic resources—the union by striking and picketing, and the employer by discharge—to bring pressure to bear upon the other. With the Wagner Act, or National Labor Relations Act of 1935, Congress announced a more affirmative policy. Drawing upon antecedents in the Erdman Act and the Railway Labor Act and under the War Labor Board, Congress in section 7 of the NLRA declared to be federally protected "the right to self-organization, to form, join, or assist labor organizations, to bargain collectively through representatives of their own choosing, and to engage in concerted activities for the purpose of collective bargaining or other mutual aid or protection." Section 8 went on to declare illegal certain employer acts, such as restraint, interference or coercion of employees in the exercise of their section 7 rights; domination of unions; discrimination in terms of employment so as to discourage union membership; and refusal to bargain in good faith with the majority employee representative. These "unfair labor practices" were to be monitored through judicial-type proceedings before a newly created administrative agency, the National Labor Relations Board. The Board was also empowered, under section 9, to conduct secret elections by which employees could freely select a labor organization to represent them in dealing with their employer. The Board was authorized to order the employer to remedy its unfair labor practices, and such Board orders were made enforceable or reviewable in the United States courts of appeals. The National Labor Relations Act was sustained by the Supreme Court against constitutional attack in NLRB v. Jones & Laughlin Steel Corp. (U.S.1937).

The years after 1935 witnessed a dramatic increase in union membership, greater use of the strike, and a post-war proliferation of work-assignment disputes between unions, secondary boycotts, mass picketing, and some corruption and undemocratic practices in internal union affairs. This was accompanied by what many viewed as a tendency by the NLRB toward overzealous regulation of employer conduct through its unfair labor practice jurisdiction (accompanied by undue judicial deference). Congressional reaction became manifest in a number of post-war labor bills and finally in the enactment of the Taft-Hartley Act in 1947, reaffirmed over a veto by President Truman. Under the amended law, the prosecutorial and adjudicative functions of the Board were separated and reposed in different branches of the agency, the former in the General Counsel and the latter in the five-member Board (expanded from three); supervisors and independent contractors were removed from the coverage of the Act, and limitations were placed upon the Board in handling election cases; and the courts of appeals were given greater authority to review and set aside findings of the Board in unfair labor practice cases. Congress expressly declared that unfair labor practices were not to be based on any expression of opinion or argument which contained no threat of reprisal (the "employer free speech" section), or on any refusal in bargaining to make a concession or reach an agreement. Reports regarding union finances and internal procedures were to be filed by unions. Section 7 was amended to accord to employees the right to refrain from joining a union or engaging in collective bargaining or concerted activities; and the closed-shop agreement was declared illegal while other union-security agreements were declared subject to outlawry by state "right to work" laws. Most significantly, Congress enumerated several unfair labor practices by labor organizations: restraining or coercing employees in the exercise of their section 7 rights; causing an employer to discriminate illegally against employees; refusing to bargain in good faith; striking or inducing a strike in support of a secondary boycott, of a demand for recognition when another union is certified as employee representative, or of a demand to assign work which is the subject of a jurisdictional dispute; and causing an employer to pay for services not performed ("featherbedding"). The Taft-Hartley Act also reintroduced the labor injunction, but limited it to use only against an unfair labor practice and only at the behest of an official of the National Labor Relations Board; and provided for federal-court jurisdiction over suits to enforce labor contracts, while making unions suable entities in federal actions.

Twelve years later, in 1959, the basic federal Labor Act was amended further. The Landrum-Griffin Act, also known as the Labor-Management Reporting and Disclosure Act, was addressed primarily to the problems of corruption within union leadership, which was to be cured by elaborate reporting requirements, and of undemocratic conduct of internal union affairs, which was to be cured by a "bill of rights" for union members in such matters as union meetings and elections, eligibility for office, and union disciplinary procedures. The Landrum-Griffin Act also imposed further regulation of union activities by amendments to the unfair labor practice provisions enacted in the Taft-Hartley Act. Certain "loopholes" in the secondary-boycott provisions were closed; for example, certain forms of appeals to consumers (rather than employees) of "neutral" employers were outlawed, as were "hot cargo" provisions in collective bargaining agreements. And more substantial restrictions were placed upon picketing to organize employees or to secure bargaining rights.

It is the unfair labor practice and representation-election provisions of these three Congressional acts—which will frequently be referred to generically as the Labor Act—which are the subject of this book.

CHAPTER II

THE STRUCTURE AND OPERATIONS OF THE NATIONAL LABOR RELATIONS BOARD

§ 1. Introduction

Congress in 1935 created an administrative agency, the National Labor Relations Board, to implement both the unfair labor practice provisions (section 8) and the election or representation provisions (section 9) of the Labor Act. The Board was to have three members, appointed by the President and confirmed by the Senate, and had the all-embracing tasks of supervising the election process from the filing of a petition to the certification of the election results, as well as processing unfair labor practice charges through investigation, prosecution and adjudication. Important changes were made in the Taft-Hartley Act of 1947. The Board was expanded to five members to be appointed by the President and to serve for staggered five-year terms. In unfair labor practice cases, the five Board members retained the power to adjudicate, but the functions of investigation and prosecution were (and are today) assigned to the General Counsel (to be appointed not by the Board but by the President with the approval of the Senate). In representation cases, the Board members still have the authoritative voice on such matters as the size of the election unit (known as the "appropriate bargaining unit") and the validity of the election. On a day-to-day basis, however, the tasks of investigating and prosecuting unfair labor practice cases and of investigating and supervising election cases are delegated by the General Counsel and the Board, respectively, to the regional offices in major cities throughout the United States. Each of the 31 regional offices of the NLRB is headed by a regional director and is staffed by a regional attorney and a number of trial attorneys, field examiners and clerical employees. It is in the regional offices that the vast bulk of Board business is done and disputes resolved without any formal participation by the five Board members in Washington.

§ 2. Unfair Labor Practice Cases

An unfair labor practice case is initiated by the filing of a charge in the regional office where the alleged wrongdoing has occurred; the charge must, by statute, relate to conduct occurring within the prior six months. The Board and its agents, such as the regional director, are not empowered as public officials to institute charges. Board regulations provide that the charge may be filed by "any person" and it is usually filed by the aggrieved employee or his union when an employer is the charged party or by the aggrieved employee or employer when a union is the charged party. The charge is then investigated by a field representative of the regional office, who interviews witnesses and prepares a report, and a decision is made by the regional director whether a complaint is to be issued against the charged party. (While a charge may be withdrawn, the regional director must first give his consent, and only after determining that the public interest will be served.) A determination by the regional director not to issue a complaint may be appealed to the General Counsel, whose decision whether or not to issue an unfair labor practice complaint is, significantly, in all cases unreviewable either by the Board members or by a court. Vaca v. Sipes (U.S.1967).

After the regional director issues an unfair labor practice complaint, and the respondent is afforded an opportunity to file an answer, the case is tried—in a court-like proceeding—before an administrative law judge, known until recently as a trial examiner. The examiner or judge has been qualified for placement on a Civil Service roster through competitive examinations and has quite often seen prior service with the Board, some in fact as members but more commonly in regional offices; most are based in Washington and some in San Francisco, and are assigned to cases on a rotating basis. (Because they are subject to civil service regulations regarding appointment and tenure, administrative law judges resemble federal judges in that they serve in effect for life; they may be removed only if cause is shown in a hearing before the Civil Service Commission.) The unfair labor practice case is typically heard in the locality where the alleged illegal conduct occurred and while the "prosecuting" party is technically the General Counsel the case against the respondent is conducted by attorneys from the appropriate regional office.

It is at this stage that the function of the General Counsel and regional offices ceases being investigatory and becomes prosecutory. The charging party need not enter an appearance at all, but it may do so and is entitled to call, examine and cross-examine witnesses as well as to introduce documentary evidence. The administrative law judge presides at the hearings, makes rulings on motions and questions of evidence; section 10(b) of the Labor Act provides that "such proceeding shall, so far as practicable, be conducted in accordance with the rules of evidence applicable" in the federal district courts. The judge then prepares a decision or "intermediate report" in the case, with findings of fact, conclusions of law and a recommended disposition or order. If no party files exceptions to the intermediate report, the Board will endorse it as a matter of course.

If, however, exceptions are filed, the case will be formally reviewed by the Board, usually acting through a three-member panel but by all five members in cases which are thought to be of special importance. The Board—which in 1975 rendered decisions in roughly 1300 unfair labor practice cases—is assisted in research and drafting by a staff of legal assistants, each Board member employing some twenty-five attorneys for this purpose. The Labor Act, in section 10(c), imposes few restrictions upon the Board's decisions. While it empowers the Board to take further testimony or hear argument in passing upon exceptions to the decisions of the administrative law judges, the Board disposes of almost all cases on the written record and briefs, with only significant cases set down for oral argument. It is free to disagree completely with the inferences drawn and the decision rendered by the administrative law judge, but will commonly adopt the judge's findings, particularly on matters turning upon the credibility of the witnesses. The Board will often issue a "short-form order," adopting the report of the administrative law judge in full. The Board is required by section 10(c) to issue an order dismissing the complaint unless it finds "upon a preponderance of the testimony taken" that an unfair labor practice has been committed; in short, the burden of proof or of persuasion is on the General Counsel. If the Board finds an unfair labor practice has been committed, it is required to issue a "cease and desist" order, UAW v. NLRB (Omni Spectra, Inc.) (7th Cir. 1970), and is empowered to issue an order requiring appropriate affirmative relief such as reinstatement and backpay. Compliance with Board orders is usually supervised locally by the staff of the appropriate regional office. Again, compliance or enforcement is technically the responsibility of the General Counsel, who can also press for compliance on behalf of the Board before the federal courts of appeals—which have statutory authority to review Board orders—and the United States Supreme Court.

Some statistics for the Board's 1975 fiscal year illustrate the volume of Board unfair labor practice cases, and the extent to which these cases are resolved short of formal Board action. In 1975, more than 31,000 unfair labor practice charges were filed with the Board, roughly double that of a decade earlier. Of these, 20,300 were filed against employers and some 10,800 against unions; roughly two-thirds in each instance charged illegal coercion or discrimination. Some 94% of cases closed in 1975 were closed by the regional office; roughly ⅓ by dismissal of the charge, ⅓ by withdrawal of the charge, and ¼ by settlement or adjustment under the auspices of the regional office either before the issuance of a complaint or after complaint but prior to a decision by the administrative law judge. Complaints actually issued totalled more than 3000, or only 10% of the charges filed; roughly 80% of the complaints were against employers and 20% against unions. In those cases, the median number of days from the filing of the charge to the issuance of the complaint was 54. Of the almost 30,000 cases closed in 1975, less than 4% went to the five-member Board for decision as contested cases, and thus some 1300 unfair labor practice decisions were issued by the Board. Regional offices distributed a total of $11.3 million in backpay to more than 7,400 employees; of some 3800 employees offered reinstatement pursuant to Board order, more than 2600 (or 68%) accepted. In fiscal 1975, courts of appeals handed down some 260 decisions on review of Board unfair labor practice decisions, and affirmed in whole or in part in 85 percent.

§ 3. Representation Cases

In addition to the work that the regional office does in the unfair labor practice cases, it also plays a most important day-to-day role in processing representation cases. Election petitions are filed there; the regional staff investigates the petition; if a representation hearing is to be held it is conducted by a hearing officer from the regional office; and, most importantly, it is the regional director who makes decisions on such matters as the Board's jurisdiction, the appropriate bargaining unit, voter eligibility and objections to the validity of the election. His decisions on such matters, both those which are made prior to the election and those which are made after the election, are subject to appeal in a limited set of circumstances to the National Labor Relations Board (and not, as in complaint cases, to the General Counsel). Although all of these election issues were determined in the first instance by the Board itself until 1961, in that year section 3(b) of the Labor Act was amended to authorize their delegation to the regional directors. Election procedures will be discussed in greater detail below.

The Board's authority in representation cases touches far more employees than its unfair labor practice authority. In fiscal 1975, almost 502,000 employees voted in Board elections. In that year, the Board closed roughly 13,900 cases in the representation area, the vast preponderance, some 12,175, being petitions for certification of union representatives. Some 8,700 of these cases went to an election, with unions winning 50% of them. In roughly 80% of the elections held, the parties agreed voluntarily to the election particulars, such as appropriate unit, date, and place of election. Formal hearings to decide these matters were necessary in only 20% (or 1700) of the elections. In comparison to some 1300 Board decisions in unfair labor practice cases, the Agency (Board and regional directors) in 1975 issued some 3,600 decisions in election cases. Twenty-three days was the median elapsed time between the filing of an election petition and the close of the representation hearing in the regional office, with twenty-two more days until the issuance of the regional director's decision or order—in all, some six weeks. Elections are usually held one month from the date of the election order.

§ 4. Judicial Review: Background, Standards

A decision or order issued by the National Labor Relations Board is not self-executing. If the Board would enforce an order against a recalcitrant party, it must convert its own order to a court order, and this is done by petitioning a federal court of appeals of appropriate venue under section 10(e) of the Labor Act. Judicial review may also be sought by "any person aggrieved by a final order of the Board," as provided in section 10(f), and this will usually be the charged party or respondent which is the object of a Board order; not infrequently, the charging party, which has been denied some requested relief before the Board, will seek review in order to have the court modify and expand the Board's order. This is the only manner in which the statute explicitly contemplates judicial review of a Board order—through an action to enforce or set aside a "final order" of the Board in an unfair labor practice case.

Board decisions in representation cases—such as the determination of an appropriate bargaining unit or the determination that an election should be set aside because of coercive or inflammatory speeches—cannot be directly reviewed by a court (except in extraordinary circumstances, discussed in detail elsewhere in this work). These representation decisions may be reviewed only after they have been "engrossed" as part of the record in an unfair labor practice case; section 9(d) of the Labor Act explicitly provides that when the unfair labor practice case is reviewed by the court of appeals, the record of the pertinent representation case becomes part of the record before the court. The object of this circuitous machinery is to deter dilatory challenges in the midst of representation cases which will delay the conduct of an election and the prompt recording of employee preferences on collective bargaining; moreover, the outcome of the election will in many instances render moot the challenges to the Board representation findings.

The Labor Act speaks almost not at all to the question of the vigor with which the courts are to review Board decisions and orders. Indeed, all that is said of direct pertinence is in section 10(e): "The findings of the Board with respect to questions of fact if supported by substantial evidence on the record considered as a whole shall be conclusive." The Supreme Court, in the famous case of Universal Camera Corp. v. NLRB (U.S.1951), announced a number of guidelines concerning review of the Board's findings of fact. The case raised the question whether the court of appeals should affirm the Board's conclusion that an employee was discharged not for insubordination but for testifying against the employer's interests in a Board proceeding; this in turn was found to depend upon what was said in a particular conversation between two supervisors, an issue on which the record was in conflict. The trial examiner had concluded that the company's reason for discharge was the employee's insubordination but the Board reversed.

The Supreme Court held that judicial review was to be "on the record considered as a whole," including evidence that undermined the Board's fact finding as well as evidence that supported it; it was not proper to look only to the latter. The Court then noted that a court of appeals reviewing a Board fact finding should give special deference when that finding relates to a matter in which the Board's industrial experience and expertise gives it special competence, but that deference is due even on other matters where the Board's finding is a reasonable one. It held that "the whole record" requirement was not

> intended to negative the function of the Labor Board as one of those agencies presumably equipped or informed by experience to deal with a specialized field of knowledge, whose findings within that field carry the authority of an expertness which courts do not possess and therefore must respect. Nor does it mean that even as to matters not requiring expertise a court may displace the Board's choice between two fairly conflicting views, even though the court would justifiably have made a different choice had the matter been before it *de novo*. Congress has merely made it clear that a reviewing court is not barred from setting aside a Board decision when it cannot conscientiously find that the evidence supporting that decision is substantial, when viewed in the light that the record in its entirety furnishes, including the body of evidence opposed to the Board's view.

The Court proceeded to determine the weight, in making its findings of fact, that the Board must give to the conclusions of its trial examiner. It rejected the arguments that, at one extreme, the Board was free to give these no weight whatever, and that, at the other extreme, the Board was bound by them unless clearly erroneous. The Board was to give the report of the trial examiner some weight, "such probative force as it intrinsically commands," particularly when the credibility of witnesses is at stake, for the examiner has the "opportunity to observe the witnesses he hears and sees and the Board does not."

> The "substantial evidence" standard is not modified in any way when the Board and its examiner disagree. We intend only to recognize that evidence supporting a conclusion may be less substantial when an impartial, experienced examiner who has observed the witnesses and lived with the case has drawn conclusions different from the Board's than when he has reached the same conclusion. .   .   .   The significance of his report, of course, depends largely on the importance of credibility in the particular case.

The Supreme Court has emphasized more recently that the courts of appeals are to give the same measure of deference to Board fact findings regardless whether the remedy in question is reinstatement or the milder cease and desist order. One court of appeals, noting that backpay orders have an impact on the employer much like penalties, imposed in such cases a more exacting standard upon the trial examiner and the Board: before one could disbelieve employer assertions that a discharge was based not on antiunion animus but on work-related reasons, the evidence introduced for the General Counsel had to be a substantial contradiction or a direct impeachment. NLRB v. Tex-O-Kan Flour Mills Co. (5th Cir. 1941). The Supreme Court, in NLRB v. Walton Mfg. Co. (U.S.1962), rejected both this stringent test and the distinction between backpay cases and cease-and-desist cases. The Court noted that the rule of *Universal Camera* was not in its terms limited to any special kind of case, that the decision there in fact involved reinstatement, and that on issues of credibility the court of appeals is in a far worse position than is the trial examiner to draw factual inferences.

The statutory directive in section 10(e) and the Court's reading of it in *Universal Camera* relate only to Board findings of fact. The Board also decides "mixed questions of fact and law" such as whether a particular group of jobs constitutes an "appropriate bargaining unit" or whether particular conduct of union or employer constitutes "coercion" or a refusal to "confer in good faith." The Board also decides "pure" questions of statutory construction, such as whether its jurisdiction over "employees" is to be governed by common law principles of respondeat superior and master-servant or rather by some more expansive economic standard applied in light of the mischief which the Labor Act was designed to remedy. The Board also decides questions of constitutional law, such as those relating to picketing or to speeches made or leaflets disseminated during a union organizing campaign. The Labor Act does not explicitly direct the courts to exercise any particular measure of review over Board decisions on these matters which are not "purely" factual. All that can be said with confidence is that courts tend to believe that their own competence matches that of the Board, and finally surpasses it, as the finding moves from "pure" fact, to mixed questions, to issues of "pure" statutory construction and then finally to issues of constitutional dimension. See generally NLRB v. Marcus Trucking Co. (2d Cir. 1961) (full discussion of distinction between "law" and "fact" and of scope of judicial review). (The courts will also feel especially equipped to deal with issues that raise problems at the intersection of the Labor Act and some other body of federal legislation, such as the antitrust or bankruptcy laws.) Indeed, since the boundaries between these categories are not at all sharp, the courts will sometimes "characterize" the issue as falling within one category or another, arguably rather after the fact, in order to justify the greater or lesser vigor with which they review determinations made by the Board. These matters are discussed at various points in this work, as they relate to particular substantive issues.

In addition to giving special deference to the Board on findings of fact, courts generally accord deference to the remedies selected by the Board to redress statutory violations. The Supreme Court stated, in Phelps Dodge Corp. v. NLRB (U.S.1941):

> [I]n the nature of things Congress could not catalogue all the devices and stratagems for circumventing the policies of the Act. Nor could it define the whole gamut of remedies to effectuate these policies in an infinite variety of specific situations. Congress met these difficulties by leaving the

adaptation of means to end to the empiric process of administration. The exercise of the process was committed to the
Board, subject to limited judicial review.

The Court has also stated that a Board remedial order may not be
overturned (assuming the respondent's conduct is indeed an unfair labor practice) "unless it can be shown that the order is a patent attempt to achieve ends other than those which can fairly be said to effectuate the policies of the Act." Virginia Elec. & Power Co. v. NLRB
(U.S. 1943).

§ 5. Judicial Review: Venue, Parties

As noted above, judicial review may be initiated by the Board
through a petition for enforcement, and section 10(e) provides that
that petition may be filed with the court of appeals in the circuit in
which the unfair labor practice occurred or in which the respondent
resides or transacts business. When the Board does seek enforcement, its practice is to petition in the circuit in which the unfair labor practice was committed. A petition for review, filed by "any
person aggrieved by a final order" pursuant to section 10(f), may be
filed in any circuit in which the unfair labor practice occurred or in
which that person resides or transacts business or in the United
States Court of Appeals for the District of Columbia. It should be
noted that under this section, it is the residence or the business location not necessarily of the respondent which determines the venue of
the appeal but of the "person aggrieved," who may in fact be the
charging party should the Board order the dismissal of the unfair labor practice complaint. Clearly, a charging party may seek review
of a Board order dismissing a complaint, and a charged party (or respondent) may seek review of a Board order sustaining a complaint
in whole or in part. In cases in which the Board sustains the complaint only in part, either the charging party or the charged party
will be a "person aggrieved" and may petition for review in a court
of appeals.

The Act makes no specific provision for participation in an appeal by a party which is wholly successful before the Board—that is,
a charging party when a complaint is sustained in full or a charged
party when the complaint is dismissed. But if a court of appeals is
presented with a petition for review, a completely successful party
may wish to intervene in order better to protect its interests. The
Supreme Court has held that such intervention must be permitted if
sought. This principle was announced in two consolidated cases,
UAW Local 283 v. Scofield and UAW Local 133 v. Fafnir Bearing Co.
(U.S.1965).

In *Scofield,* the Board dismissed a complaint against a union, and
the four employees who had filed the charge petitioned for review, as
aggrieved parties; the union sought to intervene in the court of appeals, and the Supreme Court held that it was error to deny interven-

tion. The Court was moved primarily by a desire to have the case resolved justly and expeditiously. If intervention were denied, and the court of appeals upheld the position of the charging employees and remanded to the Board, the charged union would then become the object of an adverse decision on remand, would be able to take its own appeal (possibly to a different court of appeals from that which considered the first appeal), and its position might be prejudiced by the ruling of the first court, made in its absence; at the least, duplicative proceedings would be inevitable. Permitting the successful charged party to intervene on appeal would avoid this time-consuming and possibly prejudicial procedure. The Court also thought it anomalous that the charged union could protect its interests before a court if it lost before the Board but not if it won, for the very same factual and legal issues would be under judicial consideration in either case.

In *Fafnir,* the Board had sustained a complaint against an employer for a refusal to bargain, and the union—the successful charging party—sought to intervene in the proceeding in which the employer petitioned to set aside the Board's order and the Board cross-petitioned to enforce it. The Court held that the successful charging party is entitled to intervene in a proceeding instituted either by the Board or by the unsuccessful respondent. The Court once again noted the anomaly of granting review to the charging party only if unsuccessful below, and also noted that the "private" interests of the charging party are not altogether absorbed by the Board in its stance as protector of the public interest and that these private and public interests are complementary.

In any event, it is well established that after a court of appeals has in any measure enforced a remedial order of the Board, the decision whether to institute contempt proceedings for violation of that order lies exclusively with the General Counsel of the Board (who requests authority to proceed from the Board itself) and not with a private party however aggrieved. Amalgamated Utility Workers v. Consolidated Edison Co. (U.S.1940).

§ 6. Rulemaking and Adjudication

The National Labor Relations Board makes its decisions in representation and unfair labor practice cases in an adjudicatory or court-like setting. The unfair labor practice case pits the General Counsel, often aided by counsel for the charging party, against the charged party, and testimony and documents are introduced before the administrative law judge who makes rulings on evidence and prepares an opinion and order much like any trial judge. The NLRB itself reviews this "intermediate report" much like an appellate court. Representation proceedings, with decisions typically rendered by the regional director subject to review by the Board, purport to be less "adversary" and more "investigatory" but they nonetheless, like unfair labor practice cases, involve rulings made and principles announced in the context of a particular transaction between two and sometimes three parties.

Section 6 of the Labor Act empowers the Board in addition to exercise authority in a quite different manner: "The Board shall have authority from time to time to make, amend, and rescind, in the manner prescribed by the Administrative Procedure Act, such rules and regulations as may be necessary to carry out the provisions of this Act." This "rulemaking" power casts the Board in a quasi-legislative rather than a quasi-judicial role. The Administrative Procedure Act defines a "rule" as an "agency statement of general or particular applicability and future effect," 5 U.S.C.A. § 551(4), in contrast to an "order"—the product of an "adjudication"—which is "the whole or a part of a final disposition, whether affirmative, negative, injunctive, or declaratory in form, of an agency in a matter other than rule making .   . .," 5 U.S.C.A. § 551(6). The Administrative Procedure Act also provides that a rule may be validly promulgated only after compliance with certain procedures designed to assure wide general publicity and agency access to information from all potentially affected parties. There must be publication in the Federal Register of notice of proposed rulemaking and of hearing, an opportunity to be heard, a statement in the rule of its basis and purposes, and publication in the Federal Register of the rule as adopted. 5 U.S.C.A. § 553.

A principle which the Board announces can in theory be formulated either as a product of generalized rulemaking or in the context of a particular two-party litigation. The major difference is that the "rule" is formulated after a legislative-type hearing open to the public without the strictures of the laws of evidence and judicial procedure, while the "order" is fashioned upon evidence introduced in a particular case against a context of the Board's experience in many similar cases. In either mode, the principle announced by the Board will serve to direct the future conduct of particular employers, employees, unions and government officials, and the validity of the principle will be subject to challenge in particular proceedings before the Board and ultimately in the courts. Because of the ambiguity of the definitions of "rule" and "order," there appears to be no situation in which the Board's articulation of a principle *must* be done through one mode to the exclusion of the other. As the Supreme Court said in SEC v. Chenery Corp. (U.S.1947), referring to federal administrative agencies generally, "[T]he choice made between proceeding by general rule or by individual, *ad hoc* litigation is one that lies primarily in the informed discretion of the administrative agency."

The Court was forced to test the distinction between rulemaking and adjudication in NLRB v. Wyman-Gordon Co. (U.S.1969). There, the Board ordered an election at the Wyman-Gordon Company and ordered the company to give the regional director a list of employee names and addresses, a requirement first announced by the Board in Excelsior Underwear Inc. (1966). When the company refused to produce the list, the Board issued a subpoena which, upon the company's refusal to comply, was enforced by the federal trial court and ultimately by the Supreme Court. The company argued that the requirement to produce the employee list was invalid, since it was announced in the *Excelsior* case and not applied to the respondent Excelsior but only to elections directed thirty days after the decision in *Excelsior*; it was thus, allegedly, a "rule" which the Board invalidly promulgated in the context of an adjudicatory election proceeding.

The case produced a strange splintering among the Supreme Court Justices. The disposition of the case was to require (7–2) compliance by Wyman-Gordon with the subpoena of the employee lists. But only three Justices upheld as valid the requirement to produce the list as that requirement was announced in the *Excelsior* case. Those Justices concluded that the requirement could properly be announced either through rulemaking or through adjudication, that the *Excelsior* proceeding was a valid adjudication, and that the validity of the principle or requirement announced there is not undermined by the Board's decision to apply it prospectively only in view of the company's justified reliance on the law as it then existed. The remaining six Justices reprimanded the Board for circumventing rulemaking procedures and announcing in the *Excelsior* adjudication what was in substance a rule, that is, a general requirement of future effect only, not applicable to the parties in the specific case before it. Two of those six (the two dissenting Justices) would have found the requirement thus defective even when later applied against the Wyman-Gordon Company, but a plurality of four found any defect cured when the *Excelsior* requirement was applied directly to Wyman-Gordon in the context of a valid adjudication in its representation proceeding. In short, in spite of the fact that a majority of the Supreme Court believed the Board to have improperly avoided the procedural safeguards of rulemaking in announcing the *Excelsior* requirement, a different majority found that requirement validly imposed (and enforced by subpoena) on all subsequent respondents.

The Board, which had never before utilized rulemaking procedures to announce substantive-law principles, did so not long after the *Wyman-Gordon* decision for the limited purpose of announcing its minimum jurisdictional requirements in cases involving private colleges and universities, 29 C.F.R. § 103.1 (1975), and symphony orchestras, 29 C.F.R. § 103.2 (1975). Other than that, the Board continues to announce new principles of law, and repudiate old ones, through the process of adjudication.

This power was tested once again, and once again upheld by the Supreme Court in NLRB v. Bell Aerospace Co. (U.S.1974). There, the Board announced what was arguably a new principle: certain buyers for the company, although "managerial employees," were protected by the Labor Act and given rights to organize and bargain, because although managerial, their unionization would not generate a conflict of interest on matters of labor relations. The court of appeals held that this shift of Board policy (from a perceived policy excluding from the Act's coverage all managerial employees) could be validly announced only through rulemaking and not in the context of representation and unfair labor practice proceedings. The Supreme Court disagreed with the Board's reading of the Labor Act and held that Congress intended all "managerial employees" to be excluded, but went on to state that the Board would be free on remand, by adjudication and not rulemaking if it chose, to hold that these buyers were not within the category of managerial employees. The Court reiterated

> that the Board is not precluded from announcing new principles in an adjudicative proceeding and that the choice between rulemaking and adjudication lies in the first instance within the Board's discretion. Although there may be situations where the Board's reliance on adjudication would amount to an abuse of discretion or a violation of the Act, nothing in the present case would justify such a conclusion.

It also noted that even if the industry relied on earlier Board decisions from which the Board might on remand choose to depart, this could validly be done in adjudication. The adverse consequences of such reliance were not viewed as very substantial, no fines or damages were being imposed and "this is not a case in which some new liability is sought to be imposed on individuals for past actions which were taken in good-faith reliance on Board pronouncements."

§ 7. Retroactive and Prospective Board Orders

There have, however, been cases in which a retroactive application of a principle announced in unfair labor practice proceedings has indeed resulted in the imposition of significant liability for conduct which was "lawful when engaged in." Some courts on review have held that the Board exceeds its powers in imposing such liability, the suggestion being (either explicit or implied) that the Board should have invoked rulemaking which would then have resulted in a general mandate prospective only. For example, in NLRB v. E & B Brewing Co. (6th Cir. 1960), the union and the employer had entered into an agreement requiring that all hiring be done through a union-operated hiring hall, an agreement which was lawful when executed. The Board subsequently tightened its requirements for hiring-hall legality, declared this particular agreement not to meet those requirements and found both company and union to have violated the law and thus responsible for reinstatement and backpay. The court of appeals set aside the Board's order, finding it "arbitrary, capricious, and an abuse of discretion," and concluding that "The Board's doctrine would retroactively invalidate every union contract which contains an exclusive hiring hall provision. If the Board's order stands, it is doubtful if even the Board can say how many hundreds or thousands of employers and unions are, as of now, guilty of similar unfair labor practices." The court held this impact to be unjustified by any public interest in retroactive application. In a similar case, NLRB v. Local 176, Carpenters (Dimeo Constr. Co.) (1st Cir. 1960), a "retroactive" order requiring the union to disgorge all dues collected from employees under its hiring-hall arrangement was overturned by the court as "an *ex post facto* penalty."

The problem of the propriety of such retroactive orders has become more significant since the Supreme Court decision in NLRB v. Wyman-Gordon Co. (U.S.1969), because that decision rather clearly discourages the Board from applying only prospectively new principles announced in adjudicatory proceedings. Now, in spite of arguable unfair surprise, the Board may choose to apply new doctrine retroactively to avoid the appearance of rulemaking. A conspicuous example of such arguably unfair retroactive application is found in Laidlaw Corp. v. NLRB (7th Cir. 1969), in which the Board reversed its traditional position and held that a striker, lawfully replaced, was entitled to have his job back after applying for reinstatement if, even though there were no jobs available on the date of his application, an equivalent position opened up subsequently. Although the company's denial of reinstatement when a job came open was on advice of counsel and in accordance with the law at the time of the company's action, the Board not only applied the new principle to the company and found a violation of section 8(a)(3) but also required reinstatement and backpay. Rejecting the company's argument that the imposition of backpay running back to the denial of reinstatement was unduly harsh, the court of appeals balanced the hardship to the employer against the need to vindicate the rights of the employees and concluded:

> Unless the disadvantaged strikers are compensated, they will have been penalized for exercising statutorily protected rights and the effects of discouraging future such exercises will not be completely dissipated. In these circumstances, it was not arbitrary or capricious for the Board to conclude that complete vindication of employee rights should take precedence over the employer's reliance on prior Board law.

The question then arose whether other respondents, who also relied on the pre-*Laidlaw* privilege not to reinstate after the date of application, should be subjected to a backpay order. The Board has imposed such liability, and has met with a somewhat mixed but generally supportive reaction in the courts of appeals. Two major decisions conclude that the Board imposition of backpay was in the context of a valid adjudication and thus that it was not necessary to utilize the rulemaking procedure, and also that the Board in its adjudication could within its discretion find the hardship to the company outweighed by the interests of the employees in restitution for a statutory violation. American Mach. Corp. v. NLRB (5th Cir. 1970); H. & F. Binch Co. v. NLRB (2d Cir. 1972). Both courts noted that the change in the law represented by *Laidlaw* was not entirely unforeseeable at the time the company acted, in view of an earlier decision of the Supreme Court in a somewhat similar setting, in NLRB v. Fleetwood Trailer Co. (U.S.1967). Another court of appeals, however, although agreeing that the Board had the discretion to impose backpay for a period subsequent to *Fleetwood,* held—in light of the lack of any evidence of anti-union animus on the part of the company—that the Board's award of backpay running any earlier must be overturned. In finding such an award to be inequitable, the court considered the following factors:

> (1) whether the particular case is one of first impression, (2) whether the new rule represents an abrupt departure from well established practice or merely attempts to fill a void in an unsettled area of the law, (3) the extent to which the party against whom the new rule is applied relied on the former rule, (4) the degree of the burden which a retroactive order imposes on a party, and (5) the statutory interest in applying a new rule despite the reliance of a party on the old standard.

Retail Union v. NLRB (Coca-Cola Bottling Works, Inc.) (D.C.Cir. 1972). The court explicitly noted that the Board should not be deterred by the *Wyman-Gordon* decision from announcing its principles prospectively only, in adjudicatory proceedings, if that is necessary to avoid unfair surprise and hardship.

> [*Wyman-Gordon*] does not prevent an agency in adjudication from declining in subsequent cases to apply a new rule retroactively if equitable or statutory considerations militate against it, any more than Article III prevents a federal court from limiting the retroactive scope of new legal principles articulated in judicial decisions. Nor does *Wyman-Gordon* prevent reviewing courts from refusing to enforce such retroactive orders when the circumstances so dictate.

CHAPTER III

THE COVERAGE OF THE LABOR ACT AND THE JURISDICTION OF THE BOARD

§ 1. Constitutional and Statutory Jurisdiction: Interstate Commerce

Both the Norris-LaGuardia Act of 1932 and the Wagner Act of 1935 were designed to remedy the commercial disruption attendant upon labor disputes relating to representation and bargaining for employees in private industry. The earlier Act, in great measure because of Congressional concern that its power to regulate interstate commerce would not embrace most such disputes, was drafted as a set of limitations upon the equity jurisdiction of the federal courts, more clearly subject to Congressional control under Article III of the Constitution. The Wagner Act or National Labor Relations Act announced substantive rules of labor law, established an administrative agency, and gave to that agency the power to determine any "question of representation affecting commerce" (section 9(c)(1)) and the power "to prevent any person from engaging in any unfair labor practice . . . affecting commerce" (section 10(a)). Section 2(7) of the Labor Act defines the term "affecting commerce" to mean "in commerce, or burdening or obstructing commerce or the free flow of commerce . . . ."

In NLRB v. Jones & Laughlin Steel Corp. (U.S.1937), the Wagner Act withstood a two-pronged constitutional attack when the Supreme Court marked a new direction in adjudication of New Deal legislation. The Court held, first, that the employer unfair labor practice provisions did not constitute a denial without due process of law of employer liberty to contract and, second, that Congress's power under Article I to regulate commerce among the states extended to the business of the respondent, a manufacturer of steel. Although the Court had in earlier decisions held it beyond the power of Congress to regulate a "local" business, such as production, which had only an "indirect" effect on commerce, it vastly broadened in *Jones & Laughlin* the reach of the Commerce Clause of the Constitution and then proceeded to construe the NLRA to give the Board jurisdiction to the fullest extent permitted by that Clause:

> It is the effect on commerce, not the source of the injury, which is the criterion. . . . Although activities may be intrastate in character when separately considered, if they have such a close and substantial relation to interstate commerce that their control is essential or appropriate to protect that commerce from burdens and obstructions, Congress cannot be denied the power to exercise that control.

In later decisions involving the enforcement of Board unfair labor practice orders, the Supreme Court has given yet wider scope to the reach of the Labor Act under the Constitution. In NLRB v. Fainblatt (U.S.1939), the Court held significant not the relative amount or volume of commerce but rather the fact of transportation (no matter how minor) of raw materials or finished products across state lines. In NLRB v. Reliance Fuel Oil Corp. (U.S.1963), the Court extended the Act's coverage to a fuel oil distributor purchasing oil within the state which had originally come from outside the state; a labor dispute at the respondent company could obstruct or limit the free flow of oil in interstate commerce. The Board is thus free to exercise jurisdiction to hear representation and unfair labor practice cases involving parties having a "substantial" impact on the flow of goods or services across state lines, regardless of an isolated examination of the quantity of commerce in the case before the Board, the nature of the business (i. e., services or production as opposed to transportation), the size of the operations or the location of the business.

§ 2. Discretionary Jurisdiction

The Board, however, has chosen not to exert its power to the fullest constitutional and statutory limit. Its volume of cases would otherwise be unmanageable and its attention would be diverted from the more significant interstate cases by many of truly local significance. Congress in 1947 authorized the Board, as a means of relieving some of the burden of its caseload, to agree to cede jurisdiction of Board cases to an agency within a state or territory having legislation consistent with the federal Labor Act; the Board has to date not done so. But it has exercised its discretion to decline jurisdiction over controversies "essentially local in character." Prior to 1950, the Board had neglected to announce minimum jurisdictional guidelines of general applicability but rather, on a case-by-case basis, determined whether the assertion of jurisdiction would further the purposes of the Act. In that year, the Board announced a change of policy in Hollow Tree Lumber Co. (1950):

> The Board has long been of the opinion that it would better effectuate the purposes of the Act and promote the prompt handling of major cases, not to exercise its jurisdiction to the fullest extent possible under the authority delegated to it by Congress, but to limit that exercise to enterprises whose operations have, or at which labor disputes would have, a pronounced impact upon the flow of interstate commerce.
> . . . The time has come, we believe, when experience warrants the establishment and announcement of certain standards which will better clarify and define where the difficult line can best be drawn.

The Board thus commenced the practice of announcing in general terms minimum standards for the assertion of jurisdiction based on annual dollar amounts of inflow and outflow of interstate products or

services. The minimum standards which for the most part obtain today were announced in 1958 in Siemons Mailing Serv. (1958).
(Characteristically reluctant to fashion such jurisdictional standards
by use of the rulemaking procedure—with advance promulgation and
legislative-type hearings—the Board announced these standards in individual cases and by press release.) In the Landrum-Griffin Act of
1959, Congress enacted section 14(c)(1) of the Labor Act which gave
explicit approval to the Board's discretionary declination of jurisdiction, but which also forebade the Board to make its jurisdictional
standards any more stringent: "[T]he Board shall not decline to assert jurisdiction over any labor dispute over which it would assert
jurisdiction under the standards prevailing upon August 1, 1959."

The Board's present jurisdictional minima announce specific dollar amounts of business for different kinds of enterprises. In computing such amounts, the Board cumulates "direct inflow" of goods
and services (furnished directly to the employer from outside the
state in which it is located) and "indirect inflow" of goods and services (those which originated outside the employer's state but which it
acquired from a seller within the state); and it cumulates "direct
outflow" (goods shipped or services rendered by the employer outside
the state) and "indirect outflow." The Board thus considers the effect on interstate commerce to be the same regardless of whether the
movement of goods or services is to or from the employer's operations. Rather than itemize all of the Board's standards, only three
will be set forth by way of illustration. The Board will assert jurisdiction over a nonretail enterprise if there is a gross annual outflow
or inflow of revenue of at least $50,000; over a retail establishment if
there is a gross business volume of at least $500,000 and substantial
purchases from or sales to other states on a direct or indirect basis;
and over a multiemployer association if any member meets any jurisdictional standard or if the combined operations of all members of
the association meet any such standard. The Board also has such
standards for office buildings and shopping centers; instrumentalities, links and channels of interstate commerce; public utilities;
transit systems; newspapers and communications systems; national
defense enterprises; businesses in the territories or the District of
Columbia (in the District, the Board's jurisdiction is plenary); hotels
and motels; restaurants and country clubs.

In applying all of these dollar standards, the Board will consider
the employer as a "totality"; that is, it will consider all of the employer's operations as a unit whether its business is located in one
state or more. Conversely, it will assert jurisdiction if the employer
is a separate component but integral part of an enterprise which does
not fall within the Board's jurisdiction. And, in secondary boycott
cases, the Board will cumulate the business done at the primary employer and all of the business that the secondary employer does at the
site of the illegal union activity (not just the amount of business

there between the secondary and the primary employers). Teamsters Local 608 (McAllister Transfer, Inc.) (1954).

In recent years, the Board has been more willing than in the past to assert jurisdiction over charitable, educational and other nonprofit enterprises. For some time, the Board had, while acknowledging that private universities and proprietary hospitals fell within its constitutional and statutory jurisdiction, chose not to assert that jurisdiction, except where the activities in question were commercial in nature and essentially unconnected with the institution's charitable or educational purposes. *E. g.,* Henry Ford Trade School (1944) (students and faculty engaged in making and repairing tools for Ford, in order to meet school's expenses). Although the Taft-Hartley amendments of 1947 excluded from the definition of an "employer" only the nonprofit hospital, the legislative history rather clearly appeared to support the Board's continuing declination of jurisdiction over all charitable or educational institutions, and the Board's policy was reaffirmed as to colleges and universities in Trustees of Columbia University (1951), and proprietary hospitals in Flatbush General Hospital (1960).

By the late 1960's, however, the Board saw that these institutions were growing in size and number, were hiring larger staffs, were securing goods and funding from across state lines and were increasingly reliant upon federal financial support and subject to federal legislation; in addition, the anticipated development of applicable state laws regulating their labor relations had not materialized and, to the extent it had, these laws provided no uniformity. Accordingly, the Board announced in 1967 that it would assert jurisdiction over private proprietary hospitals and nursing homes, respectively, in Butte Medical Properties (1967) (if receiving at least $250,000 in annual gross revenues; *Flatbush* case overruled), and University Nursing Home, Inc. (1967) (if receiving at least $100,000 in annual gross revenues). In *Butte,* the Board stated:

> All of the foregoing unquestionably evinces a substantial national interest in, and a vital concern for, public health and welfare which, if affected by unregulated labor disputes in proprietary hospitals, would exert or tend to exert a wholly undesirable impact not only on the suppliers of these institutions, but also on the public, and, inevitably, on interstate commerce. We believe that these numerous private and public health-care efforts have a very substantial effect on interstate commerce and that the public interest would be served by making available the orderly and peaceful procedures of this Act in the hospital industry.

In Cornell Univ. (1970), the Board brought within its jurisdiction nonprofit private colleges and universities, overruling the *Columbia University* case. The Board later announced that it would assert jurisdiction only if such an institution has available for its operating expenses a minimum of $1 million in gross annual revenues, and this is the same yardstick that is applied to private symphony orchestras, also recently brought by the Board within its reach. 29 C.F.R. §§ 103.1, 103.2 (1975). (Apparently in deference to the call of the Supreme Court for greater utilization of its rulemaking powers, see NLRB v. Wyman-Gordon Co (U.S.1969), the Board determined these jurisdictional standards for educational institutions and orchestras through rulemaking rather than as in the past by adjudication). The Board extended the principle of the higher-education cases to justify jurisdiction over nonprofit art museums having educational programs and most recently to an art museum which received its income almost exclusively from a charitable trust, charged no admission, had no formal educational program and offered a very limited number of free concerts and lectures. Helen Clay Frick Foundation (1975) (Board relied largely on gross revenues of $1 million from the trust and expenditures for out-of-state paintings and other goods). The jurisdictional circle was closed yet further when Congress in 1974 amended the Labor Act to eliminate from section 2(2) the statutory exclusion for nonprofit medical institutions; thus all private medical institutions are now covered by the Act. The Board has also moved forward on the profit-making front, and for the first time asserted jurisdiction in 1969 over organized baseball. American League of Professional Baseball Clubs (1969) (the antitrust exemption for baseball does not preclude federal jurisdiction over labor relations, and this will provide a uniform law for this nationwide business).

It should be noted that all of the above dollar standards are adopted and applied as a matter of the Board's discretion—with the exception of course that the Board is forbidden by statute to restrict further its general standards in force when section 14(c)(1) was added by the Landrum-Griffin Act of 1959. Thus, the Board has asserted jurisdiction regardless of whether its dollar standards have been satisfied where "public policy requires the Board to exercise jurisdiction to the fullest extent." Iron Workers Local 577 (Tri-State Erectors) (1972) (allegations charged interference with statutory right of individual to resort to Board processes). Conversely, even when an employer would otherwise fall within the Board's standards, jurisdiction is declined when the operations are closely related to a foreign government or when foreign-policy questions may be implicated. E. g., McCulloch v. Sociedad Nacional de Marineros de Honduras (U.S. 1963) (Board held to lack even discretionary jurisdiction over alien employees represented by foreign union on foreign flagship in American port). And, apart from dollar amounts, the Board will occasionally decline to exercise jurisdiction over an entire category of business if the Board considers that it is "essentially local" and has only a "remote relationship" to interstate commerce. E. g., Seattle Real Estate Bd. (1961). The Supreme Court had initially held that the declination of jurisdiction over an entire category of employer not specifically excluded in the Labor Act was an abuse of the Board's power. Office Employees Local 11 v. NLRB (U.S.1957) (labor union specifically included under definition of employer in section 2(2)); Hotel Employees Local 255 v. Leedom (U.S.1958) (hotel industry). But Congress expressly provided, in section 14(c)(1) enacted in 1959, that the Board

> in its discretion, may, by rule of decision or by published rules adopted pursuant to the Administrative Procedure Act, decline to assert jurisdiction over any labor dispute involving any class or category of employers, where, in the opinion of the Board, the effect of such labor dispute on commerce is not sufficiently substantial to warrant the exercise of its jurisdiction.

There is thus a range of employment enterprises which the Board could constitutionally regulate but—whether by dollar amount or by business category—has in fact refrained from doing so. In Guss v. Utah Labor Relations Bd. (U.S.1957), the Supreme Court considered the question whether state courts and agencies were free to regulate labor relations in these enterprises left unregulated by the National Labor Relations Board. The Supreme Court concluded that the states were barred from doing so, unless they were expressly ceded such regulatory jurisdiction by the NLRB in accordance with section 10(a) of the Labor Act which the Court held to represent a Congressional declaration of the exclusive means for countenancing such state regulation. There being no such Board cession of jurisdiction to this day, the *Guss* decision would have created a "no-man's land" wherein the NLRB declined to regulate and the states were barred from regulating. In 1959, Congress remedied this regulatory vacuum by enacting section 14(c)(2), giving to state or territorial courts or agencies the power to assert jurisdiction over labor disputes where such jurisdiction was declined by the NLRB. In cases brought before state tribunals, where it is uncertain whether the NLRB would assume jurisdiction, the parties or the state tribunal may apply to the Board for an advisory opinion, 29 C.F.R. § 102.98–104 (1975); the opinion addresses only the question of jurisdiction and not the merits. The federal Act does not specify whether state tribunals acting pursuant to section 14(c)(2) are to apply federal or state law, but states have generally applied their own law, a practice which appears consistent with the federal legislative history. *E. g.,* Kempf v. Carpenters Local 1273 (Ore.1961).

§ 3. Statutory Exclusions; Employers and Employees Generally

Even if a dispute might affect interstate commerce sufficiently that the NLRB could constitutionally assert jurisdiction, the specific definitions in the Labor Act may confine the Board's power. Section

7 rights to form and join labor organizations and to engage in collective bargaining and concerted activities are given to "employees." Certain conduct is defined as an unfair labor practice when engaged in by either an "employer" or a "labor organization." Thus, the Board cannot order an election among supervisors or independent contractors, because these are excluded from the statutory definition of "employee." Nor can the Board find an airline company or a municipality responsible for an unfair labor practice, for these are excluded from the statutory definition of "employer." Nor can a union comprised exclusively of agricultural workers be held to have committed an unfair labor practice under the national Act because such workers are excluded from the definition of "employee," and a "labor organization" must have "employees" who participate. The key statutory definitions are thus that of "employer" in section 2(2) and "employee" in section 2(3).

Section 2(2) provides:

The term "employer" includes any person acting as an agent of an employer, directly or indirectly, but shall not include the United States or any wholly owned Government corporation, or any Federal Reserve Bank, or any State or political subdivision thereof, or any person subject to the Railway Labor Act, as amended from time to time, or any labor organization (other than when acting as an employer), or anyone acting in the capacity of officer or agent of such labor organization.

Although the term "employer" is thus defined, rather unhelpfully, with reference to itself, the statute assumes that the common law concepts of the employer-employee relationship will prevail (a matter discussed in greater detail below). Even then, however, certain employers commonly understood as such are excluded from the rights and duties of the Labor Act. Labor relations among employees of the Federal Government are regulated not by the National Labor Relations Act but by federal executive order, the first to bring collective bargaining having been promulgated by President Kennedy in 1962. When postal workers became employed not by the federal government but by a public corporation, special legislation swept these workers within the coverage of the national Labor Act, with the exception that the strike is forbidden and compulsory arbitration of new contract terms substituted. Labor relations between public employers—states, counties, municipalities, towns, school boards and the like—are governed by state law, until recently largely judge-made and rather pervasively now in the form of statutes and administrative regulations. The exclusion has been extended to institutions which have private roots but have substantial state support, such as some libraries, Nassau Library Sys. (1972), and universities, Temple Univ. (1972).

Railway and airline employees are governed by the Railway Labor Act, which has created government agencies to mediate bargaining disputes, resolve contract-grievance disputes and conduct representation elections, but not to adjudicate unfair labor practice cases. Section 2(2) makes clear that the labor relations between a union and its own employees are governed by the national Labor Act, regardless of whether the *members* of the union are themselves "employees" within the coverage of the Act. Brotherhood of Locomotive Firemen (1964). Interestingly, while the secondary boycott provisions of the Act (section 8(b)(4)(B)) had originally been written in 1947 to shelter "employers" against secondary pressures—thus permitting boycotts of neutral airlines, railroads and government employers, to induce them to cease doing business with the primary employer—a 1959 amendment expanded the protection to "persons" specifically in order to remedy this perceived inequity. (Of course, the unfair labor practice can be committed only by a "labor organization," which must have statutorily covered "employees" among its members.)

§ 4. Independent Contractors

Section 2(3) defines "employee" to "include any employee" (again, a definition which on its face is of little utility), but not to include "any individual having the status of an independent contractor." This exclusion was not added until 1947. The Wagner Act of 1935 had only the all-embracing definition, but the NLRB did within its discretion usually hold that independent contractors were not entitled to the benefits of employee status (*e. g.,* representation elections and protection from discrimination for union activities). Field Packing Co. (1943). The Board, in determining whether a person asserting the protection of the Act was an independent contractor would frequently invoke the common law "right of control" test utilized to determine whether the doctrine of respondeat superior applied to impute liability to the master for the torts of the servant. *E. g.,* Klement Timber Co. (1944). A person completing a job by his own methods and without being subject to the control of the employer as to the means of doing the work was an independent contractor; a person performing work subject to the employer's control or right of control as to both the end result and the manner of achieving it was an "employee" within section 2(3).

In NLRB v. Hearst Publications, Inc. (U.S.1944), however, the Board announced a more expansive test, finding an "employment" relationship between newspaper publishers and street-corner newsdealers where there was sufficient economic dependence of the so-called newsboys upon the publishers as to fall within the underlying policies of the Act supporting unionization and collective bargaining. A reversal in the court of appeals was in turn reversed by the Supreme Court, which like the Board rejected the common law test as inapt for the application of a labor relations statute and endorsed instead an examination of the purposes of the Act and a determination whether inclusion of the newsboys within the Act would effectuate those policies. "The broad language of the Act's definitions .   . . leaves no doubt that its applicability is to be determined broadly, in doubtful situations, by underlying economic facts rather than technically and exclusively by previously established legal classifications." The Court held that case-by-case decisions whether particular persons fell within the Act's coverage were to be made primarily by the Board on the basis of its expertise, and that courts were obliged to affirm the Board's decision if reasonable and supported by factual evidence in the record.

Congress promptly reacted, in the Taft-Hartley amendments of 1947, to what it believed was a disregard by the Board of the clear statutory language and an abdication by the Court of its functions in reviewing Board decisions. It expressly stipulated in section 2(3) that the "independent contractor" was to be excluded from the definition of "employee," and thereby imported the common law "right of control" test as a standard of statutory coverage. The House Report accompanying the legislation outlined the distinction between employees and independent contractors:

> ["E]mployees" work for wages or salaries under direct supervision. "Independent contractors" undertake to do a job for a price, decide how the work will be done, usually hire others to do the work, and depend for their income not upon wages but upon the difference between what they pay for goods, materials, and labor and what they receive for the end result, that is, upon profits.

The legislative history also compels the conclusion that Congress accorded no special weight to the Board's expertise in determining whether, on a particular set of facts, a person was an employee or an independent contractor; that was to be a question of "law" for the court definitively to resolve.

The Board has since proceeded to utilize the common law analysis, and does place special weight on the "right of control," frequently indeed deciding that newspaper dealers were independent contractors. E. g., Pulitzer Pub. Co. (1964). It has thus considered the degree of supervision exercised by the alleged "employer," National Freight, Inc. (1964) (because of high degree of supervision, owner-drivers of leased trucks were employees and not independent contractors); and has also utilized the "profit" test suggested in the House Report, Kansas City Star Co. (1948). In applying the common law "right of control" test, however, the Board has blended its concern for control over the manner of performing the job with a concern for the entrepreneurial or risk-taking features of the relationship. Thus, in El Mundo, Inc. (1967), the Board stated:

> The result to be accomplished is, of course, the circulation and sale of the Employer's newspapers. In accomplishing this result, the dealers herein bear slight resemblance to the independent businessman whose earnings are controlled by self-determined policies and personal investment . . . .
>
> Moreover, the dealers' risk of loss and capacity to draw upon personal initiative to increase their earnings are minimized to a significant extent by the Employer's practices and policies . . .
>
> Further, the dealers have no proprietary interest in their routes.

An analysis by a court of appeals of existing Board decisions has led that court to conclude that the Board emphasizes three factors in distinguishing the employee from the independent contractor: (1) the entrepreneurial aspects of the dealer's [*i. e.*, the alleged employee's] business, including the "right to control," (2) the risk of loss and opportunity for profit, and (3) the dealer's proprietary interest in his dealership. Brown v. NLRB (9th Cir. 1972) (utilization of Board criteria requires reversal of Board finding that dealers were employees). The Board has itself stated that it will apply the right of control test only "in light of the economic realities of the particular situation," A. Paladini, Inc. (1967)—and thus has evoked some criticism that it is returning to its pre-Taft-Hartley position of the *Hearst* case. But the Board's examination of such factors as control over the price charged third persons by the alleged employee, the quantity of goods supplied by the alleged employer, the ownership of materials by the alleged employee and the privilege of the alleged employee to handle goods supplied by other persons—while these may not directly relate to actual control over the manner in which the alleged employee performs the job—do fall within the range of the common law test for independent contractors and even within the standards set down in the critical House Report of 1947.

In any event, congressional exclusion of the independent contractor from the coverage of the Labor Act was intended to increase the measure of judicial review of Board decisions—both in formulating the common law test and in applying that test to the facts of particular cases. The courts of appeals have in the past reviewed Board "independent contractor" findings to determine not whether the Board's characterization was reasonable but whether it was correct (*i. e.*, is a decision the court would have made in the first instance). *E. g.*, National Van Lines, Inc. v. NLRB (7th Cir. 1960). But the Supreme Court has mandated greater deference to the Board's judgment. In NLRB v. United Ins. Co. of America (U.S.1968), at issue was the status of debit agents, whose primary functions were to collect insurance premiums, prevent lapses of policies and sell such new insurance as time allowed. The Board's determination that these persons were employees rather than independent contractors was reversed by the court of appeals, which was in turn reversed by the Supreme Court. The Court, while recognizing that the Board exhibits no special expertise on this issue, which is purely of agency law, nonetheless held:

> [T]he Board's determination was a judgment made after a hearing with witnesses and oral arguments had been held and on the basis of written briefs. Such a determination should not be set aside just because a court would, as an original matter, decide the case the other way. . . .
>
> Here the least that can be said for the Board's decision is that it made a choice between two fairly conflicting views, and under the circumstances the Court of Appeals should have enforced the Board's order.

The courts of appeals have since appeared to abide by the Court's mandate and have sustained the Board when its conclusion is reasonable and supported by the record, although there is still apparent an inclination to review the Board's decision at very great length, *e. g.*, Joint Council of Teamsters, No. 42 v. NLRB (D.C.Cir. 1971) (2–1 decision; owner-operators are employees in view of degree of supervision); and even on occasion to reverse, *e. g.*, Brown v. NLRB (9th Cir. 1972) (newspaper dealers are independent contractors in view of, among other things, lack of control by company over manner and means of distribution of newspapers by dealers and profit opportunities for dealers). One court has held that it would be constrained to reverse the Board's finding of an employment relationship if, in a tort case, it would conclude that the trial court had erred in sending the case to a jury on the issue of vicarious liability; in such a case, outside the area of Board expertise, the inferences could not be deemed "fairly conflicting." Lorenz Schneider Co. v. NLRB (2d Cir. 1975) (after exhaustive examination of the record, court finds that distributors are independent contractors, in spite of finding to the contrary by regional director and unanimous Board panel).

§ 5. Agricultural Laborers

The National Labor Relations Act excludes from its coverage "any individual employed as an agricultural laborer." This exclusion, found in section 2(3) of the Wagner Act of 1935, is not successfully explained in the legislative history, and it has been inferred that it represented a concession to agriculture forces in Congress who would have resisted the enactment not only of the Wagner Act but also of the Social Security Act and the Fair Labor Standards Act had the three statutes not included an agricultural exclusion. It may also be attributable to some concern that employment relations on most farms are too local to fall within federal cognizance, or that the perishability of crops is such that strikes would give agricultural employees too strong a bargaining weapon and unionization would make farm operations unduly costly, or that (somewhat inconsistently) farm workers do not need unionization since their relationship with the employer is a friendly and intimate one (akin to the excluded domestic servant or close relative of the employer).

The 1935 Labor Act, even in its present form, has no definition of "agricultural laborer." In the early years of administering the Act, the NLRB tended—in cases in which there was a close question whether a particular group of workers were "employees" within the Act or were excluded "agricultural laborers"—to construe the exclusion narrowly and thus to extend the coverage of the Act. *E. g.,* Indiana Mushroom Corp. (1945) (mushroom growers held to be employees); Knaust Bros. (1941) (greenhouse employees held not agricultural laborers). Perhaps the most numerous and troublesome cases involved persons engaged in the sorting and packing of agricultural products. Some cases analogized these activities to production work rather than field work, resulting in the coverage of the workers, while other cases deemed controlling whether the sorting and packing was done on produce grown by one's own employer (resulting in exclusion) or by others (resulting in coverage).

Since 1946, Congress has given the Board greater guidance in construing the term "agricultural laborer." It has directed, by an annual rider to the NLRB's appropriation, that the Board be guided by the Department of Labor's interpretations of section 3(f) of the Fair Labor Standards Act, which provides (29 U.S.C.A. § 203(f)):

> "Agriculture" includes farming in all its branches and among other things includes the cultivation and tillage of the soil, dairying, the production, cultivation, growing, and harvesting of any agricultural or horticultural commodities . . ., the raising of livestock, bees, fur-bearing animals, or poultry, and any practices (including any forestry or lumbering operations) performed by a farmer or on a farm as an incident to or in conjunction with such farming operations, including preparation for market, delivery to storage or to market or to carriers for transportation to market.

The Board promptly adopted a test designed to incorporate the FLSA definition, and in Di Giorgio Fruit Corp. (1948), it held that it would determine whether the worker's services (usually of packing and sorting) are performed primarily in connection with an agricultural operation or with a commercial one:

> If the practice involved is an integral part of *ordinary* production or farming operations, and is an essential step before the products can be marketed in normal outlets, it retains its agricultural characteristics. However, if the practice . . . is adopted in order to add greater value to the farm products [for example, by converting fruit to

fruit juice], it acquires the attributes of a commercial venture.

This test has been generally applied since that time, and has caused the Board to overrule its decisions on some classes of workers previously held to be "employees" rather than "agricultural laborers." *E. g.*, Hershey Estates (1955) (greenhouse employees exempt as agricultural laborers); Michigan Mushroom Co. (1950) (mushroom growers exempt). See also J. G. Boswell Co. (1953) (ranch-shop employees who repair and maintain ranch equipment are exempt since their duties are incidental to farming operations). For the most part, however, the Board has continued to construe the agricultural exclusion narrowly. *E. g.*, NLRB v. Tepper d/b/a Shoenberg Farms (10th Cir. 1961) (dairy workers are "employees" because products handled by them were produced elsewhere than on employer's farm).

Special problems are posed with respect to workers who spend part of their time in agricultural work and part in non-agricultural work. The Board has concluded that the part-time performance of agricultural work ought not necessarily deprive such workers of the benefits of the national Labor Act in connection with their other work, and workers who so divide their time are covered by the Act if they regularly perform non-agricultural work, irrespective of the amount of time spent in the performance of each type of work. Olaa Sugar Co. (1957).

Because of the exclusion of agricultural laborers from the national Labor Act, farm workers do not have access to the Board's representation election machinery or to the protective employer unfair labor practice provisions of section 8(a) of the Act; nor are such workers constrained by such prohibitions on union activity as the secondary boycott provisions of section 8(b)(4). Agricultural unions are thus free of federal restraints upon their use of the strike or boycott to organize farmers, but they are instead subject to state law of property and torts (which is frequently inhospitable to the secondary boycott anyway). In 1974, the state of California enacted legislation, apparently the first of its kind, giving to agricultural workers within the state the right to vote in representation elections and announcing both employer and union unfair labor practices comparable to those under the National Labor Relations Act, all to be administered by a specially created labor relations agency.

§ 6. Supervisors

Section 2(3) of the Wagner Act of 1935 defined the "employee" within the protection of the Act to include "any employee" and contained no exclusion for supervisory employees. The Board in 1942 certified unions to represent foremen in bargaining with the employer, but the following year reversed position and concluded that no unit comprised of supervisors could be appropriate (except in industries in which supervisors had been organized in 1935). In 1945, the Board returned to its initial position, and in Packard Motor Car Co. v. NLRB (U.S.1947), the Supreme Court approved the Board's extension of the NLRA to supervisory employees. In that case, the Court affirmed a Board order to bargain with the Foremen's Association of America (unaffiliated with any rank-and-file union) on behalf of four ranks of foremen (totalling 1100 supervisors). In response to the employer's assertion that management was entitled to the complete loyalty of supervisors acting in its behalf, the Court concluded that even supervisors have an interest in improving their wages and working conditions, and that any exclusion of supervisors is a matter of policy for Congress to implement by specific statutory language.

Congress promptly accepted this invitation and rejected the position of the NLRB and the Supreme Court by inserting in 1947 an express exclusion from the definition of "employee" for "any individual employed as a supervisor." The legislative reports make it clear that Congress wished in part to assure that rank-and-file employees could unionize and select their leaders free from undue influence by supervisors in the union, but more important to assure that supervisors—whether organized within a rank-and-file union or organized independently—would not fall into league with or become accountable to employees whom they were charged to supervise and thereby renounce the undivided loyalty due the employer. The exclusion in section 2(3) was accompanied by the congressional declaration in a new section 14(a) that:

> Nothing herein shall prohibit any individual employed as a supervisor from becoming or remaining a member of a labor organization, but no employer subject to this Act shall be compelled to deem individuals defined herein as supervisors as employees for the purpose of any law, either national or local, relating to collective bargaining.

These 1947 provisions have the following significance:

(1) Since the representation of supervisors is a matter beyond the jurisdiction of the National Labor Relations Board, the Board may not establish bargaining units composed entirely of supervisory personnel or declare that supervisors are to be included within an appropriate bargaining unit with nonsupervisory employees for purposes of a Board representation election.

(2) Supervisors normally may not invoke the employer unfair labor practice provisions of section 8(a), since they are not "employees" whose joining of unions or engaging in concerted activities is protected by section 7. Thus, an employer is free to discharge a supervisor because he has joined or engaged in activities on behalf of a union which represents either supervisors or rank-and-file employees. NLRB v. Inter-City Advertising Co. (4th Cir. 1951). In certain cases, however, the Board may find that the discharge of a

supervisor will interfere not only with the supervisor's union activities, which are not protected, but also with an "employee's" union activities, which are. A clear example is where the employer discharges a supervisor for failure to spy upon rank-and-file union supporters or for failure otherwise to carry out the employer's instructions to impede unionization. See NLRB v. Talladega Cotton Factory, Inc. (5th Cir. 1954), in which the Board had held:

> [W]here, as here, the discharges followed immediately on the heels of the Union's victory in the Board-conducted election, the discharges plainly demonstrated to rank and file employees that this action was part of its plan to thwart their self-organizational activities and evidenced a fixed determination not to be frustrated in its efforts by any halfhearted or perfunctory obedience from its supervisors. In our opinion, the net effect of this conduct was to cause nonsupervisory employees reasonably to fear that the Respondent would take similar action against them if they continued to support the Union.

In such cases, the Board may order the employer to reinstate the supervisor with backpay. *Ibid.*

(3) Supervisors are not prohibited by the NLRA from organizing, and the employer is free on a permissive basis to recognize a union as bargaining representative for organized supervisory employees, either independently or within a union of rank-and-file employees.

Since supervisors are excluded from the jurisdiction of the NLRB, some state courts have held that the regulation of their economic weapons and bargaining rights are left to state control. *E. g.,* Safeway Stores, Inc. v. Retail Clerks Ass'n (Cal.1953) (injunction issued against strike by clerks union to compel bargaining on behalf of store managers). More recently, however, the Supreme Court has justified state regulation on a narrower theory and held that statecourt injunctions against labor activities by supervisors are proper (that is, are not preempted by federal labor law) only because they are consistent with "[C]ongress' propelling intention [in the 1947 Taft-Hartley amendments] . . . to relieve employers from any compulsion under the Act and under state law to countenance or bargain with any union of supervisory employees." Hanna Mining Co. v. District 2, Marine Eng'rs (U.S.1965). (There, the Board had already clearly held that the persons seeking representation rights were supervisors; but when that issue is unclear, and the persons might arguably be covered "employees," the state court must defer to the NLRB and may not enjoin the concerted activity. Marine Eng'rs Benef. Ass'n v. Interlake S.S. Co. (U.S.1962).) Accordingly, when the applicable state law would frustrate the Congressional policy outlined in *Hanna,* it is preempted even though supervisors are involved. The Supreme Court has thus held that a state may not, by applying its right-to-work law, award damages against an employer for the discharge of a supervisor because of union activities. Beasley v. Food Fair, Inc. (U.S.1974).

With the rights of persons to organize and bargain, and the powers of state and federal tribunals, turning upon the status of those persons as "supervisors" or "employees," it becomes crucial to develop criteria to distinguish the two classes of workers. The status of supervisor under the NLRA is determined by an individual's actual duties, not by his title or job classification. Section 2(11), enacted in 1947, provides:

> The term "supervisor" means any individual having authority, in the interest of the employer, to hire, transfer, suspend, lay off, recall, promote, discharge, assign, reward, or discipline other employees, or responsibly to direct them, or to adjust their grievances, or effectively to recommend such action, if in connection with the foregoing the exercise of such authority is not of a merely routine or clerical nature, but requires the use of independent judgment.

The Board will usually find that one who possesses the *authority* to make these judgmental personnel decisions is a supervisor, even though that authority is rarely *exercised*. Yamada Transfer (1956) (authority to fire members of 12-man crew, although never exercised, along with slightly higher wages, held sufficient to classify as supervisor). Thus, even a person who spends most of his time in normal production or maintenance duties may be a supervisor if he exercises or is merely authorized to exercise any of the functions mentioned in the statutory definition. American Cable & Radio Corp. (1958) (employees spend 40–70% of time at rank-and-file work, but in addition have duties to file reports, schedule overtime, effect transfers, and effectively recommend discharge; held to be supervisors). To be classed as a supervisor, a person need have only one or more of the types of authority mentioned, not all. NLRB v. Budd Mfg. Co. (6th Cir. 1948). Probably the most important single criterion is the authority to hire and fire, or to make effective recommendations therefor.

In addition to the factors mentioned in section 2(11), the Board will also consider the ratio of supervisory to supervised employees in the particular department or plant, the manner and rate of pay of the alleged supervisor, and any special procedures for those employees concerning their discipline or other working conditions which set them apart from other workers in the department or plant. As mandated in section 2(11), the Board will look behind the appearances of authority on hiring, firing and directing other employees in order to determine whether the alleged supervisor is exercising controlling discretion on such matters or is merely making routine or broadly reviewable appraisals. Phalo Plastics Corp. (1960) (group leaders and floor ladies are "employees," though they distribute job assignment cards, select tools, set up equipment and act as liaisons between department heads and employees, in view of limited authority on personnel matters and lack of capacity for independent judgment).

Employees who possess some supervisory authority or who occasionally substitute for an absent supervisor may be included in a bargaining unit as an "employee" if the exercise of their supervisory functions is only sporadic or occasional. NLRB v. Stewart (5th Cir. 1953). (Similarly, supervisors who are demoted to rank-and-file status become "employees." National Dairy Prods. Corp. (1958).) But employees who substitute regularly and periodically for their superior during his absence, or who while part-time supervisors act as such during a substantial portion of their working time, are classified as "supervisors" to be excluded from the bargaining unit. Walgreen Louisiana Co. (1970). So too, persons who are training to become supervisors or who are probationary supervisors are treated as supervisors unless their chances of becoming full supervisors are too remote. Diana Shop, Inc. (1957) (learners in department store, being trained for three to six months for managerial positions, held "supervisors"); Shelburne Shirt Co. (1949) (probationary supervisors with authority responsibly to direct work of others, held "supervisors").

§ 7. Managerial and Confidential Employees

A class of employees closely related to supervisors is what has become known as the "managerial employee." If one reads the Labor Act literally, a company executive who formulates company policy would be an "employee" with rights to organize and bargain, since he would certainly be an employee of the company and yet would not in most cases be deemed an excluded "supervisor" who spends the bulk of his time in directing the work of rank-and-file employees. Prior to 1947, the Board had excluded "managerial employees" from rank-and-file bargaining units, but had not clearly held that they were altogether outside the provisions of the Act as "non-employees." In Ford Motor Co. (1946), the Board stated:

> We have customarily excluded from bargaining units of rank and file workers executive employees who are in a position to formulate, determine and effectuate management policies. These employees we have considered and still deem to be "managerial" in that they express and make operative the decisions of management.

In the Taft-Hartley Act of 1947, Congress excluded supervisors from the definition of "employee" but was silent on the question of the exclusion of managerial employees as a class; statements in the legislative reports, however, could reasonably be read to indicate that Congress thought it unnecessary to spell out this exclusion explicitly. The Board for twenty-three years continued to exclude managerial employees from rank-and-file units, and also held that they were not "employees" at all who could organize and require the employer to bargain; these persons were treated as management itself. American Locomotive Co. (1950).

In 1970, the Board altered its position, and held that it would read the statute to exclude only those managerial employees whose position was such, for example an executive in charge of labor relations or personnel, that to permit bargaining would create too severe a conflict between the employer and that person in his official capacity. That year, a union petitioned for an election among buyers for the company who had authority to commit its credit, select vendors and negotiate purchase prices; although they "formulated and implemented management policies" these policies did not deal with labor relations, and the Board held that these "managerial employees" could organize under Board procedures without placing the employer in an awkward position in relation to its other workers. On appeal to the Supreme Court, this position of the Board was rejected in a 5–4 decision. NLRB v. Bell Aerospace Co. (U.S.1974). The two Court factions read the legislative and Board history differently, with the majority concluding that it was the intention of Congress to exclude *all* persons properly defined as "managerial employees" from the ambit of the Labor Act regardless of whether their policy-formulating activities touch upon the company's labor relations. The Court remanded to the Board for a determination whether the buyers seeking to organize were indeed "managerial employees," with emphasis to be placed not on job titles but on the employee's "actual job responsibilities, authority, and relationship to management." On remand, the Board concluded that the workers in question were employees with whom the company was obligated to bargain collectively, and that they did not fall within the definition of "managerial employee" which it articulated as follows:

> [T]hose who formulate and effectuate management policies by expressing and making operative the decisions of their employer, and those who have discretion in the performance of their jobs independent of their employer's established policy . . . . [M]anagerial status is not conferred upon rank-and-file workers, or upon those who perform routinely, but rather it is reserved for those in executive-type positions, those who are closely aligned with management as true representatives of management.

The Supreme Court, in *Bell Aerospace,* also made it clear that it was the intention of Congress to exclude from the coverage of the Act—although not reflected in express statutory language—the "confidential employee." Confidential employees are those who "assist and act in a confidential capacity to persons who exercise 'managerial' functions in the field of labor relations." Ford Motor Co. (1946).

A classic example is the secretary to the vice-president in charge of labor relations. The secretary is clearly an "employee" of the company, is not a "managerial employee" and is not a "supervisor." Nonetheless, the Board and courts believe that the access of that person to confidential information relating to the company's labor relations or bargaining policy would place him or her in a position of potential conflict of interest. Westinghouse Elec. Corp. v. NLRB (6th Cir. 1968). The employer should not have to be concerned about persons with divided loyalties possibly passing pertinent information to a labor organization with which they are allied.

The Board, however, is cognizant of the prevailing statutory philosophy of freedom for employees to organize and bargain, and has tended to read the exclusion for confidential employees rather narrowly. If the employee has access to confidential information which does not relate to labor relations, there will be no exclusion. Swift & Co. (1961). Nor will the secretary be excluded if the person he or she works for deals with labor relations but not on a plantwide basis, Ethyl Corp. (1957); or even if that person might well engage in the future in formulating labor relations policy but does not do so presently, ITT Grinnell Corp. (1974). In short, in determining whether an employee is to be excluded from the coverage of the Labor Act as "confidential," the Board and courts will inquire into both the labor-relations authority of the managerial employee and the specific functions performed by the employee alleged to be a confidential employee.

SECURING REPRESENTATIVE STATUS

CHAPTER IV

REPRESENTATION CASES: PROCEDURES

§ 1. Introduction

In order that collective bargaining may proceed, determinations must be made as to the group of employees for whom the representative will speak and upon whom its decisions will be binding, and as to the identity of that representative. In most instances, the employer may voluntarily acknowledge the existence of such a coherent group of employees or "bargaining unit" and voluntarily "recognize" a union as representative for employees in that unit. As will be explored elsewhere, however, the privilege of voluntary recognition is subject to such challenges (under sections 8(a)(1) and (2)) as that the union is being dominated or managed by the employer, that the union in truth is the choice of less than a majority of the employees in the unit or that a "question of representation" exists in a battle between two unions which must be resolved by the National Labor Relations Board alone.

In many instances, the union seeking representation rights is not accorded recognition by the employer voluntarily, and a statutory procedure has been established for administrative determination of the fundamental questions of appropriate bargaining unit and authorized employee representative. This procedure is set forth in section 9 of the Wagner Act, as amended. Indeed, even a union which can secure voluntary recognition may choose instead to petition for a Board-conducted election pursuant to section 9, for such an election culminates in formal Board certification of the results, and the Act in several instances gives favored treatment to unions which have been certified rather than merely informally recognized (such as protection for certain forms of concerted activity under section 8(b)(7) and protection against the concerted activity of other unions under section 8(b)(4)). Board procedures are available not only to certify a union but also to decertify an incumbent union, to withdraw employee authorization for the union to enter into certain kinds of union security agreements and to clarify or modify the contours of the bargaining unit in the wake of business changes.

The procedures to be employed by the Board in representation cases are outlined in only the most skeletal form in the National Labor Relations Act. Section 9(c)(1) provides for the filing of a petition for a representation election, either by employees or by a union acting in their behalf after an employer's refusal to recognize, or by an employer to whom a claim of representation has been presented.

This is to be followed by the Board's investigation of that petition and the holding of a hearing in the event there is "reasonable cause to believe that a question of representation affecting commerce exists." If this hearing demonstrates that such a question of representation does exist, then the Board is to order a secret-ballot election and to certify the results. Prior to 1961, these investigations and hearings were conducted in the regional offices, with the transcript transmitted directly to the Board, which made the initial decision as to such questions as the employer's amenability to the Act's jurisdiction and the appropriate bargaining unit. Since 1961, pursuant to the express authorization given in 1959 by section 3(b) of the Labor Act, the Board has delegated the powers of initial decisionmaking, as well as of directing elections, ruling on objections to the fairness of the election and certifying the election results, to the regional directors. The Board will, however, grant a request for review of these decisions of the regional director, but only for certain enumerated "compelling reasons":

(1) That a substantial question of law or policy is raised because of (i) the absence of, or (ii) a departure from, officially reported Board precedent.

(2) That the regional director's decision on a substantial factual issue is clearly erroneous on the record and such error prejudicially affects the rights of a party.

(3) That the conduct of the hearing or any ruling made in connection with the proceeding has resulted in prejudicial error.

(4) That there are compelling reasons for reconsideration of an important Board rule or policy. (29 C.F.R. § 102.67(c) (1975).)

§ 2. Petition, Investigation and Hearing

If the election petition is filed by a union (or employees), the Board requires that it also submit proof of a "showing of interest," *i. e.,* demonstrated support by a substantial number of employees such that a "question of representation" may be said to exist and the invocation of the Board's election machinery rendered administratively worthwhile. Such a showing of interest must come from thirty percent of the employees in the unit requested by the petitioner, and is normally demonstrated by signed cards (known as authorization or designation cards) designating the petitioner the desired bargaining representative. 29 C.F.R. § 101.18a (1975). It will not be sufficient that the cards merely request that an election be held. Levi Strauss & Co. (1968), *enf'd* (D.C.Cir. 1970).

In the early years of the Wagner Act, the Board at first denied to employers the privilege of petitioning for an election, and later extended that privilege only in cases in which two unions were making conflicting representation claims. As amended in 1947, however, the

Act explicitly empowers an employer to file an election petition provided there has been some demand for recognition. When the demanding union is the incumbent representative, the employer must also demonstrate that "objective evidence" affords a "reasonable basis" to believe that the union no longer has majority status in the unit. United States Gypsum Co. (1966); Kingsport Press, Inc. (1965) (election ordered, employer doubt of majority based on lengthy strike and replacement of strikers). Whether the election petition is filed by employer or union, any other contending union may intervene as a party in the representation proceedings by a showing of interest from ten percent of the unit, or may secure a place on the ballot by merely showing support from one unit employee. If the intervenor, however, seeks a substantially different unit, it must satisfy the usual thirty percent requirement in the unit it seeks. Boeing Aircraft Co. (1949) (intervenor seeking severance of a craft unit).

A field examiner or attorney from the regional office will then investigate the petition to determine whether the Board has jurisdiction over the case, whether there is a true question of representation in an appropriate bargaining unit, and whether the filing of the petition has been timely. It is not in order at this early stage to consider whether the petitioning union is incompetent or disqualified to serve as bargaining representative and thus to petition for an election. The regional office will attempt to encourage the parties to enter a "consent election" agreement, pursuant to which the details of the election—such as date, place and voter list—can be agreed upon and disputed issues resolved expeditiously (preferably by the regional director without a formal hearing and without appeal to the Board). Failing that, the regional office (through a staff hearing officer who is an attorney or field examiner) will conduct a formal hearing the object of which is to develop—in a "non-adversary" manner, not subject to the conventional rules of evidence—a full record on such issues as jurisdiction, appropriate unit, question of representation and timeliness. Evidence bearing on the validity of the petitioner's showing of interest may not be offered at the hearing; that issue is for the Board's convenience and within its discretion, and the employer should certainly not be permitted to uncloak on demand the secrecy of the list of employee names.

The hearing officer forwards to the regional director a report summarizing the evidence and analyzing the issues, but making no recommended decision, and the regional director makes a decision on the disputed matters and either orders an election (and determines which employees are within the unit and eligible to vote) or dismisses the petition. As noted above, his determinations are subject to review by the Board on very narrow grounds; if he orders an election, this order is not suspended pending review by the Board unless the Board orders otherwise. Any agency determinations at this pre-election stage are almost completely impregnable to immediate review by the courts. To challenge these determinations, a party must first commit an unfair labor practice, assert as a defense thereto the alleged error of the Board in the representation proceeding—an "error" which the Board will commonly adhere to in the unfair labor practice case—and only then seek appellate review in the federal courts. Even if the Board does not itself open for consideration the determination of the regional director, either in the representation proceeding or later in the dependent unfair labor practice proceeding, an unfair labor practice order is to be enforced by the court if supported by substantial evidence; the party challenging the regional director has no "right" to full Board scrutiny. Magnesium Casting Co. v. NLRB (U.S.1971).

§ 3.   Voter Eligibility

The substantive law relating to these pre-election issues—the scope of the Board's jurisdiction, the timeliness of the election petition, and the appropriate unit—is rather complex and is discussed elsewhere. The issue of voter eligibility is somewhat less complex. Typically, an employee is eligible to vote in the election if that employee holds a full-time position which is within the bargaining unit and if he is on the company payroll both at the end of the payroll period preceding the ordering of the election and on the date on which the election is held. In addition, but without exploring the details of the Board's voter-eligibility rules, it may also be generally said that the following employees may vote provided there is a "reasonable expectation of reemployment or continued employment" and a "substantial interest in common with persons currently employed on a full-time basis": employees on temporary layoff, leave of absence, or sick leave, Whiting Corp. (1952); probationary employees, National Torch Tip Co. (1954) (although usually only twenty percent of such probationary employees working for the company eventually achieve permanent status); part-time workers employed on a regular basis, H & K Mfg. Co. (1969) (employee worked 20 hours per week for several years); and seasonal employees, Toledo Overseas Terminals, Inc. (1960).

One special problem of voter eligibility that has vexed Congress is the status of the employee who, at the time of the election, is engaged in an economic strike and whose job has been assigned by the employer to a permanent replacement. Under the Wagner Act, these strikers were permitted to vote, but under the Taft-Hartley Act this vote was taken away. Section 9(c)(3) of the present Act, added in the Landrum Griffin Act of 1959, provides:

> Employees engaged in an economic strike who are not entitled to reinstatement shall be eligible to vote under such regulations as the Board shall find are consistent with the purposes and provisions of this Act in any election conducted within twelve months after the commencement of the strike.

Pursuant to this compromise, the Board has extended the vote to persons who, on the date of the election, are engaged in an economic strike (not in excess of twelve months) and have been permanently replaced, unless the employer has for legitimate business reasons discharged the employee or phased out his job or unless the employer can show that the striker has obtained employment elsewhere under circumstances which tend affirmatively to demonstrate that he has permanently abandoned his struck job. Pacific Tile & Porcelain Co. (1962) (presumption that economic striker has not abandoned interest in his job). Whether or not the replaced economic striker may vote under these rules, his permanent replacement may vote, provided he satisfies the usual eligibility requirements (*i. e.,* he is employed on the date of the election and, if the strike predates the election order, also on the customary payroll date). Macy's Missouri-Kansas Div. (1969) (strike replacement may vote though strike commenced after election was ordered and terminated before election was held).

In instances in which economic strikers have not been replaced, they are entitled to vote within the twelve-month period even though the impact of the strike and of economic conditions generally is such as to make it unlikely that the employer's post-strike business will expand sufficiently to warrant the recall of the strikers; voting status is retained until the striker abandons interest in his job or his work is permanently abolished. Globe Molded Plastics Co. (1972). Subject to these same limitations, economic strikers not yet replaced are eligible to vote even after the one-year period from the beginning of the strike. Gulf States Paper Corp. (1975). Since employees striking not to extract economic concessions but to protest an employer unfair labor practice may not lawfully be permanently replaced, they are entitled to vote regardless of the duration of the strike, and their replacements are not. Rivoli Mills, Inc. (1953), *enf'd per curiam* (6th Cir. 1954).

§ 4.   The "*Excelsior* List" of Eligible Voters

The Board has held that an employer must, shortly after an election date is determined by the parties or the regional director, supply a list of the names and addresses of all of the employees who will be eligible to vote in the bargaining unit in the impending election. The Board announced this requirement in Excelsior Underwear, Inc. (1966):

> [W]ithin 7 days after the Regional Director has approved a consent-election agreement entered into by the parties . . . or after the Regional Director or the Board has directed an election . . . the employer must file with the Regional Director an election eligibility list, containing the names and addresses of all the eligible voters. The Regional Director, in turn, shall make this information available to all parties in the case. Failure to comply with this requirement

shall be grounds for setting aside the election whenever proper objections are filed.

Production of the *"Excelsior* list" is required not only in representation elections, but also in decertification elections and in elections to rescind the authority of an incumbent union to enter into a union security agreement; the only exception is when a representation election is expedited because of contemporaneous recognition picketing under section 8(b)(7), for then the time between the direction and the conduct of the election is too short to permit the employer to compile the list and the union to make meaningful use of it. The Board in *Excelsior* offered two reasons for the disclosure requirement. First, it gives some assurance that all employees in the unit may be informed more fully of the election issues by all participating parties (particularly by the union, which is typically at a communicational disadvantage). Second, by affording the parties an opportunity well in advance of the election to study the names on the eligibility list, disputes about eligibility may be resolved informally without time-consuming last-minute processing of election challenges, thus furthering the public interest in the speedy resolution of representation issues. Not only does the Board enforce its disclosure requirements by setting aside an election won by the recalcitrant employer, but it has also served court-enforceable subpoenas upon the employer to compel production of the *Excelsior* list. The Supreme Court has upheld both the substantive validity of the *Excelsior* requirement and the power of the Board to enforce it by subpoena. NLRB v. Wyman-Gordon Co. (U.S.1969).

If the employer fails substantially to comply with the *Excelsior* requirement, even if the failure is inadvertent, the election will be set aside. Pacific Gamble Robinson Co. (1970) (employer misunderstanding as to use of payroll lists led to omission of three names; total omission of four in unit of thirty-six is not substantial compliance). But see Kentfield Medical Hosp. (1975) (error factor of seven percent is condoned, in absence of bad faith). All that the employer must do, however, is to provide the best list it has or can compile from the available information. Valley Die Cast Corp. (1966). To promote administrative convenience and to avoid difficult factual inquiries into the probable effects on the election, a failure of substantial compliance with the *Excelsior* requirement will be deemed fatal and a new election ordered without determining the impact of noncompliance on the election results. Thus, in Fuchs Baking Co. (1969), an election was set aside for failure to produce the *Excelsior* list, although a union won the election with 110 votes (to 90 for no-agent) and the second, objecting, union had secured only 8 votes. And in Sonfarrel, Inc. (1971), where the employer omitted the names of five eligible employees from a total of 52, a new election was ordered in spite of an offer of written statements from four of those five employees that they had received union literature and had discussed the election with other employees. The Board also appears to be less lenient than in the past in tolerating time delays in supplying the list of names and addresses. Compare Rockwell Mfg. Co. (1973) (election set aside when list was filed 11 days late although 23 days before the election), with United States Consumer Prods. (1967) (election sustained, with late list received fourteen days before election). The Board has held that strict compliance with the *Excelsior* requirement will be necessary "in the absence of extenuating circumstances of substance," Chemical Technology, Inc. (1974) (absence from list of at least 10 of 120 employees is "substantial" omission, with list six days late; defect not cured by tender of complete list only six days before election); it has also on occasion, somewhat inconsistently, sustained an election in which minor omissions were found not attributable to the employer's gross negligence or bad faith, Dr. David M. Brotman Mem. Hosp. (1975).

The employer may not defend its refusal to supply the names-and-addresses list by asserting the interests of employees in privacy or by speculating that disclosure will cause competitive injury. NLRB v. Beechnut Life-Savers (S.D.N.Y.1967), *aff'd* (2d Cir. 1968). See NLRB v. J. P. Stevens & Co. (4th Cir. 1969) (employees intervened to assert personal privacy). There is some question, however, whether the employer can exact a binding waiver or modification of the *Excelsior* requirement from the union. See NLRB v. Frederick Cowan & Co. (E.D.N.Y.1974) (Board may secure by subpoena the names of all employees but only the addresses of employees who consent to that disclosure, pursuant to agreement between employer and union). Since the *Excelsior* requirement not only aids a particular union but in the public interest expedites the election process, and since there is considerable doubt of the union's capacity in the election context to waive the right of employees to information, see NLRB v. Magnavox Co. (U.S.1974) (contractual no-solicitation rule held invalid), perhaps the better view is that substantial noncompliance ought not be excused by union stipulation.

§ 5. The Election: Conduct and Review

The regional director, in his order of election, will normally set the election date twenty-five to thirty days thereafter. This both permits the union, armed with the *Excelsior* list of employee names and addresses, to communicate fully with the voters; and permits the Board to review, upon the request of any party, any pre-election decisions made by the regional director. The regional director may, however, choose to delay the election somewhat longer if, in a seasonal or a rapidly expanding industry, such a delay will permit the election to be held when the size of the work force is, respectively, at a peak or representative number. General Elec. Co. (1953) (election ordered among 1200 employees, a "substantial and representative group" of the 3500 intended to be hired within a year). The election itself is conducted under the supervision of agents from the regional office, typically on company property but, when circumstances warrant, either elsewhere or by mail. Each voter is given a ballot on which he may designate, by marking in secret in a voting booth, his choice of the union (or one of the competing unions) or no-representative. Each party may, subject to certain limitations, designate observers, who are entitled to challenge voters and generally to assist the Board representative. If a voter is to be challenged as ineligible —for example, as a supervisor or as a replacement for an unfair labor practice striker—this must be done, whether by the Board representative or by an authorized election observer, only in advance of that voter receiving a ballot; if unchallenged at that time and the ballot is cast, it is mingled with all other ballots and cannot be the subject of an unsettling and time-consuming attack after the ballots have been tallied. NLRB v. Tower Co. (U.S.1946). If a voter's eligibility is challenged, his ballot is placed in an envelope on which the voter, the challenger and the reason for challenge are noted; the envelope is placed in the ballot box and is later segregated when the Board agents tally the vote. If these challenged ballots are not needed to determine the election outcome they will be destroyed, but if they may affect the outcome the validity of the challenge is determined after investigation by the regional director.

A party may also attack the election results in a manner far broader than challenging particular ballots. It may, within five days after being supplied with the election tally, file with the regional director objections to the conduct of the election itself (e. g., violation of Board election rules, or breach of secrecy) or objections to campaign activity which arguably destroyed the "laboratory conditions" conducive to an uncoerced, accurately informed and dispassionate electorate, General Shoe Corp. (1948). The challenged activity may have been that of either party or even of third persons (such as local politicians, newspapers or townspeople), and need not constitute an unfair labor practice, but must have been engaged in subsequent to the filing of the election petition; in effect, the filing of the petition is deemed a "waiver" of any challenge to earlier conduct as a basis for setting aside an election. See Goodyear Tire & Rubber Co (1962). (It will also be too late, after the election, to complain for the first time of such matters as the appropriateness of the unit, which should have been raised at the initial hearing on the petition, and the eligibility of the voters, if not raised prior to the casting of ballots.)

In a recent development of importance, the Board has held that the employer may, promptly after an election—by procedures comparable to election objections—challenge the propriety of certifying a union, on the ground that it discriminates in membership upon the basis of race, religion or national origin. In Bekins Moving & Storage Co. (1974), the Board was unanimous in holding that no such attack should be permitted prior to the holding of the election, in view of the desirability of a speedy tally and the possible mootness of the attack were the union to lose the election. But three Board members concluded that such a challenge was properly heard after the election and prior to certification, since a Board certification of a union so discriminating was seen to be subject to attack under the federal Constitution as governmental action in contravention of due process. (A different coalition of three Board members concluded, however, that an attack on the status of a union for membership discrimination on the basis of sex could properly be made only after the union was certified.) This willingness by the Board to disqualify a majority union for certification because of wrongdoing is an exception to its general principle that union misfeasance does not justify denying its certification as bargaining representative, provided it is a "labor organization" within the definition of the Labor Act and has been fairly selected by a majority of employees in an appropriate unit. Alto Plastics Mfg. Corp. (1962) (irrelevant that union is ineffectual representative, that its officers have criminal records, that funds are stolen or misused, or that its officers violate the Labor Management Reporting and Disclosure Act of 1959).

Any timely objections to the election or challenges to ballots, when supported by evidence, will be made the subject of a preliminary investigation in the regional office. If the regional director concludes that the objections or challenges raise substantial and material factual issues, he has the authority to order a formal hearing, which follows substantially the same procedures as a hearing on the election petition. Some courts, relying on the constitutional guarantee of due process, *require* the holding of such a formal post-election hearing when the exceptions do raise such substantial and material factual issues. NLRB v. Singleton Packing Corp. (5th Cir. 1969) (burden is on objecting party, in order to secure hearing, to present specific facts making prima facie case for setting aside election; on the record, no evidentiary hearing necessary for employer claims regarding union coercion, voter eligibility or location of election).

Just as with the determination of pre-election issues, the regional director confronted with challenged ballots or election objections renders a decision which is subject to limited Board review for (1) departure from established Board decisions implicating a substantial question of law or policy, (2) clear and prejudicial error on a substantial factual issue, (3) prejudicial error in the conduct of the proceedings, or (4) compelling reasons to reconsider a Board rule or policy. 29 C.F.R. §§ 102.67(c), 102.69(c) (1975). If it is determined that the election challenges are without merit, the results of the election will be certified, and the union which secures a majority of the votes cast will be certified as the bargaining representative; a tie will be insufficient, since section 9(a) requires that the representative be selected by a majority. If, in a three-way race, no selection (including no-union) receives a majority of the votes cast, the regional director will order a "runoff" election between the two highest vote-getters (including, possibly, no-union); to vote in such a runoff election, the employee must have been eligible to vote in the original election and remain eligible until the time of the runoff. 29 C.F.R. § 102.70 (1975). To be distinguished from the runoff election is the "rerun" election, which the regional director or Board may order to cure the defects in an original election which is set aside on challenge because of coercion or interference or destruction of the "laboratory conditions." The rerun election will be set on a date far enough in the future to assure that any untoward effects have been dissipated.

As already noted—and as will be discussed at greater length below—Board decisions in representation cases, both before and after the holding of the election, are (absent unusual circumstances) not directly reviewable by the courts. AFL v. NLRB (U.S.1940). This includes determination of the Board's jurisdiction, the appropriate bargaining unit, the eligibility of voters, the validity of the election and the certification of the results. These can be judicially reviewed only as an incident to the review of a "final order" of the Board in an unfair labor practice proceeding. Thus, an employer wishing to secure judicial review of a Board determination on any or all of these matters will refuse to bargain with the certified union and will seek to have the Board's unfair labor practice order (under section 8(a)(5)) set aside because of error in the representation proceeding.

§ 6.   Decertification, Deauthorization, and Unit Clarification

The Board is also authorized to act through the representation machinery established by section 9 of the NLRA in three other situations. Section 9(c)(1)(A)(ii) provides for the application of the election machinery described above—filing of petition, showing of interest, Board investigation and hearing, election and certification—in the event employees seek decertification of a union "which has been certified or is being currently recognized" as bargaining representative. In the interest of stability in industrial relations, a petition for decertification will be treated as premature—and subject to Board dismissal—if the certification-bar or contract-bar periods applicable to ordinary election petitions have not yet expired when the petition is filed. (These periods will be considered in detail immediately below.) Similarly, the party filing the petition must tender a showing that thirty percent of the employees in the unit seek decertification. It should be noted that the incumbent union which is the object of the petition need not have been certified in the first instance but may have secured representational rights through informal employer recognition. The unit in which the election is held must be the same as the established bargaining unit; a smaller election unit may not be split off for purposes of decertification.

The Board has also assumed the power to take action resembling decertification, but without any expression of employee preferences in an election. The Board has, upon motion of the employer, in extreme cases revoked the certification of an incumbent certified union. This has been done when a union, in the course of negotiations, repeatedly inflicted or threatened severe physical injury to company negotiators, supervisors, employees and property. Union Nacional de Trabajadores (Carborundum Co.) (1975) (even if revocation of certification leaves union with majority support, the Board will not order the employer to bargain unless the union proves fresh majority support in a secret-ballot election in an uncoerced atmosphere). The Board will also revoke a union's certification if, after a hearing, it can be demonstrated that the union has discriminated on the basis of race, religion, national origin or sex in representing employees in contract negotiation or grievance processing, thereby violating its duty of fair representation. Metal Workers Local 1 (Hughes Tool Co.) (1964). Indeed, even apart from such a fair-representation violation, a divided Board has held that certification may be revoked if it can be shown that the union has discriminated in its *membership requirements* on the basis of race, religion, national origin or sex. (But an attack on certification in the first instance, promptly after an election, will be heard by the Board only if there is membership discrimination on the basis of race, religion, or national origin, as opposed to sex.) Bekins Moving & Storage Co. (1974).

An election procedure similar to the decertification election, known as the deauthorization election, is set forth in section 9(e)(1). Section 8(a)(3) permits an employer and the majority bargaining representative to enter into a so-called union shop agreement, requiring all employees in the unit to join the union (at least to the extent of paying the union an amount equivalent to periodic membership dues) within thirty days of becoming employed. The Taft-Hartley Act had provided that no such provision could be incorporated in an agreement until the employees in the unit had by formal election authorized the parties to do so. In view of the uniform union success in securing such electoral authorization, Congress in 1951 in effect automatically authorized the union to bargain for and to incorporate the union shop in the labor contract and provided instead that the election process would be available after the fact to withdraw that authorization. Congress expressly required that the filing of the deauthorization petition be "by 30 per centum or more of the employees in a bargaining unit," and that deauthorization can be effected only when so voted by "a majority of the employees eligible to vote" (rather than a majority of those actually voting, as in the usual representation election).

Apart from elections for certification, decertification and deauthorization, the Board will also receive petitions, and conduct investigations and hearings pursuant to the procedure discussed above, to clarify or to amend a bargaining-unit determination. Although the Board held in 1957 that these proceedings were available only to clarify a bargaining unit which had been initially determined by the Board through its formal certification procedures, Bell Tel. Co. (1957), this limitation was soon discarded in Brotherhood of Locomotive Firemen (1964), in which it was held that the Board could clarify or amend units which had been initially established by the informal agreement of the employer and union. The petition may be filed either by the employer or by the incumbent union and is called a petition for amendment of certification if the union has been certified or a petition for unit clarification if it has not. The procedure is addressed to the situation in which some ambiguity or dispute about inclusion of employees in an existing bargaining unit has been generated by some change in job structure. Typically, a new job will have been created or the tasks of an existing job modified; or the employer will acquire a new plant or some other group of employees. There may be a dispute between the employer and the union concerning the placement of these new jobs or employees within the unit or outside of collective bargaining altogether; or there may be a dispute between two unions about their placement in one unit or the other. In determining such clarification issues, the Board uses the criteria which ordinarily obtain in making unit determinations in the first instance, such as "community of interest," interchange of employees, similarity of job duties—all of which will be discussed in greater detail below.

As just noted, the Board normally utilizes the unit-clarification procedures only when there has been a recent modification in employment pattern. In Libbey-Owens-Ford Glass Co. (1968), however, the Board took two innovative steps: it held that these procedures could be used when, without any change in job duties or any "accretion" of newly acquired employees, a union currently representing all company employees in three units (two single-plant units and one unit comprised of eight plants) petitioned to "clarify" the unit to be one single multiplant unit; and it held that the preferences of the company's employees on the issue of unit size could properly be determined by an election, in spite of the fact that the Labor Act made no express provision for such an election (the issue being unit size and not bargaining representative). The company's attack on the proceeding failed in court, first because of the court's refusal to invoke the rarely applicable power to enjoin a Board election, McCulloch v. Libbey-Owens-Ford Glass Co. (D.C.Cir. 1968), and later because of the court's conclusion that the Board does indeed have the power to conduct an election in the absence of a technical "question of representation" under the Labor Act, United Glass Workers v. NLRB (3d Cir. 1972). In any event, a change in composition of the Board has resulted in a departure from the Board's holding in the original *Libbey* case, and a majority of a divided Board is now disinclined to utilize unit-clarification procedures to determine the question whether contract negotiations will be companywide rather than the question whether an existing union representative speaks for a newly developed or newly acquired job classification. See Libbey-Owens-Ford Co. (1971, 1973), *enf'd* (3d Cir. 1974).

§ 7. Timing of the Election: Introduction

As noted earlier, the Board will order a certification election only, among other conditions, if there is some manifestation that there is a substantial number of employees seeking to bargain through a representative. An employer petition must allege a union claim for recognition, and a union petition must be accompanied by a "showing of interest" of at least 30 percent of the employees in the requested bargaining unit. The purpose of these requirements— which are set forth in section 9(c)(1) of the Act—is to limit the drain on administrative resources and the disruption within the plant attendant upon an election campaign. Even in cases where there might be such substantial support for collective bargaining, or for a change in collective bargaining representative, the Board will not order an election if the petition is filed within what the Board regards as too short a period of time after a previous valid election has been held or after the execution of a collective bargaining agreement. The so-called election-bar rule, certification-bar rule and contract-bar rule rest in part on the premise that the "too frequent" reassessment by employees of their attitude toward collective bargaining or toward a particular representative is similarly wasteful of administrative resources and disruptive within the plant. Those rules—which "freeze" the collective bargaining situation for a fixed time—also encourage sober and deliberate thought by employees in initially voting for or against a particular union and permit of the maturing of a collective bargaining relationship for a period free of interference from too readily disenchanted employees or insurgent unions. In short, the Board has fashioned rules for timeliness of election petitions which attempt to strike a balance between freedom of employees in choosing or turning out their collective bargaining representative (a "right" arguably embodied in section 7) and some measure of repose and responsibility in the structure of collective bargaining.

§ 8. Election, Certification and Recognition Bars

Congress itself announced the election-bar rule in section 9(c)(3) of the Labor Act: "No election shall be directed in any bargaining unit or any subdivision within which, in the preceding twelve-month period, a valid election shall have been held." Under the Wagner Act of 1935, the Board had held an election petition untimely because filed within twelve months of an election only in the event the first election resulted in the certification of a union; section 9(c)(3) now extends the bar as well to elections in which the union is defeated. Obviously, an election must be a valid one before it may serve as a statutory bar. Thus, a rerun election may be promptly held if an initial election is set aside because tainted by coercion, misrepresentation or inflammatory racial appeals.   Moreover, a runoff election may be promptly held if the top vote-getter has secured merely a plurality of the votes cast.   The election-bar rule applies to all elections, whether to select a representative or to decertify one.   (A "deauthorization election" under section 9(e) is barred only if there has been an election *of that kind* within the preceding year.   Southern Press (1958).)   The Act makes it clear that an election in a particular bargaining unit bars a later election within a year within that same unit or in a smaller unit incorporated therein; it does not bar an election within a more all-embracing bargaining unit.   It has therefore been held that an election in a broad overall unit which includes a group of craft employees bars for the one-year period a subsequent election limited to the craft employees.   Vickers, Inc. (1959).   But if, on the other hand, an election is initially held in a unit limited to craft employees, it will not bar an election in a larger bargaining unit that includes the craft employees, even though the one-year period has not elapsed.   Thiokol Chem. Co. (1959).

The Board has gone beyond section 9(c)(3) and has announced a rule which declares an election petition untimely if filed within twelve months of the *certification* of a union.   This extends somewhat the opportunity for a victorious union to consolidate its collective bargaining position in those instances in which there is a period of time (consumed in proceedings before the regional director and the Board) between the date of election and the date of certification. The United States Supreme Court approved the Board's certification-bar rule in Brooks v. NLRB (U.S.1954), in which an employer refused to bargain with a union certified only days before and attempted to defend the refusal by proving that the employees in the unit had promptly communicated to him their disavowal of the election results and of the union.   The rejection of this defense by the Board and the Court created in effect an irrebuttable presumption that a certified union retains its majority throughout the certification year.   The Court was convinced that such a rule was necessary in order to encourage sober reflection by the employees voting in the initial election; to assure that the procedure for ousting the union was to be no less solemn and subject to no fewer safeguards than the procedure for initially selecting that union; to assure that the employer would not be encouraged to delay serious bargaining in the hopes that employees would soon become disenchanted and turn out their representative; and to insulate the union against pressures for "hothouse" results and undue bargaining militancy generated by some other union watching from the wings, prepared to precipitate a new election at an early and advantageous date.   With many of these same justifications in mind, the Board has extended the certification-bar period when, after the union's certification, the employer engages in a refusal to bargain and thus reduces the period of the union's opportunity for "sheltered" bargaining; the twelve-month bar period will commence with the beginning or resumption of bargaining pursuant to Board order or settlement agreement. Mar-Jac Poultry Co. (1962).

The Board has also developed a rule which bars an election for a "reasonable period" after a union has been informally recognized by the employer rather than certified after a Board election. Keller Plastics Eastern, Inc. (1969). This will give the employer and the lawfully recognized union an opportunity to negotiate a labor contract free of pressures stemming from apprehension of an election petition filed by a rival union. This period will be determined on a case-by-case basis and may well be substantially shorter than a one-year period dating from recognition by the employer. Ruffalo's Trucking Serv., Inc. (1955) (election ordered; two months of bargaining was sufficient, where employer had bargained for that period in good faith, union did not and impasse was reached).

§ 9.   The Contract-Bar Rule

An even more extended period of insulation from an election is afforded by the so-called contract-bar rule. The Board will dismiss as untimely an election petition which is filed during the term of a collective bargaining agreement (having a definite termination date) which has a duration less than three years, or which is filed during the first three years of an agreement of longer fixed duration. Although the Board as early as 1936 rejected the claim that an existing labor contract should bar an election petition, it soon reversed its position in National Sugar Ref. Co. (1939), in which a one-year contract was held to bar "an investigation of representatives until such time as the contract is about to expire and a question exists as to the proper representative." As contracts of longer fixed duration became common in particular industries and as the Board perceived more substantial virtues in a stabilized regime of industrial relations, the contract-bar period was extended for a "reasonable period" beyond a year when such longer contract term was the "custom of a substantial part of the industry." See Reed Roller Bit Co. (1947).

This more flexible bar period proved a source of uncertainty (to parties and to the Board) and of litigation, and the Board once again revised its "contract-bar rule" in one of a number of important decisions on the subject rendered in 1958. Pacific Coast Ass'n of Pulp & Paper Mfrs. (1958). Two years was established as a uniform and reasonable time for all industries, and if a contract had a longer fixed duration, it was to be given bar effect only in its first two years. The present bar period of up to three years was announced by the Board in General Cable Corp. (1962). (It should be noted that the Board has formulated and announced these artificial—and in some sense arbitrary—time periods, based in part on the Board's perception of industrial practices, not through its rulemaking procedure under section 6 of the Act, but rather through decisions in particular representation cases.)   Contracts longer than three years in duration will bar throughout their duration, even beyond three years, election petitions filed by the signatory employer or union (if certified).   Absorbent Cotton Co. (1962) (employer petition dismissed, incumbent union uncertified); General Box Co. (1949) (petition of uncertified union held timely).

Exceptions to the Rule.   The Board has been careful to adjust its contract-bar rule so as not to bar reassessment of employee wishes in those situations in which the prevailing collective bargaining setting does not give promise of continued stability.   It is for this reason that a collective bargaining agreement will not bar the filing of an election petition when that contract has no fixed duration, since such a contract is subject to unilateral dissolution and fails to afford the kind of stability given by a mutually binding commitment for a certain and predictable period of time.   Pacific Coast Ass'n of Pulp & Paper Mfrs. (1958).   Similarly, a contract which is so skeletal as to deal only with one or two aspects of the collective bargaining relationship —such as a promise by the employer simply to recognize the union as bargaining representative or simply to pay a specified wage scale—will not bar the filing of a petition at any time.   The contract must not only contain substantive terms and conditions of employment, but it must also be in writing and executed by both parties. Appalachian Shale Prods. Co. (1958).   The same case held that a contract which has not yet been ratified by union membership will not bar a petition if the terms of the contract expressly require ratification as a condition precedent to its validity; otherwise the contract bar will operate.   So too, an election petition filed at a plant covered by a master multi-plant agreement will be timely if the master agreement by its terms provides it will not be effective at the local plant until a supplementary local agreement has been executed, and no such agreement has been executed at the time the petition is filed. United States Rubber Co. (1950).

The Board will also scrutinize the substantive provisions of the contract asserted as a bar in order to determine whether its terms are such as to coerce employees in the exercise of their rights freely to choose a bargaining representative.   Thus, a contract will not bar an election if it contains a union-security provision (requiring that all unit employees join or pay dues to the union) which is clearly unlawful on its face or which has been adjudicated unlawful in an unfair labor practice proceeding.   Paragon Prods. Corp. (1961).   In order to dissolve the contract bar, the term must unequivocally go beyond the "limited form of union security permitted by Section 8(a)(3) of the Act," such as a provision that non-union employees in the unit must pay to the union an amount in excess of normal union dues and fees or that non-union employees will not be hired at all or will be accorded privileges inferior to those of union employees of comparable seniority. Pine Transp., Inc. (1972) (discrimination in seniority).

If a contract provision violates the Labor Act but does not (in contrast to the provisions just discussed) coerce the employee in his union membership, the Board will tend to apply the normal contract-bar rules. Thus, a labor contract is not removed as a bar simply because it contains a "hot cargo" clause in violation of the secondary boycott provisions in section 8(e) of the Act. Food Haulers, Inc. (1962). But in an exceptional case, the Board may hold a contract not to bar an election if it contains a provision which although not technically coercive as an unfair labor practice violates some law which the Board finds to be of unique significance and urgency in industrial relations. Just such a result was reached in Pioneer Bus Co. (1962), where the contract asserted as a bar contained a provision grouping employees in a racially discriminatory manner.

Just as the Board will process an election petition during the first years of a collective bargaining agreement when the terms of that agreement give little promise of assuring bargaining stability, the same reason justifies an exception to the contract-bar rule when there has been a dramatic change in the scope, size or nature of the employing enterprise. In such a case, the contract is sufficiently likely to prove inapt to the needs and the collective-bargaining preferences of the employees that it is thought appropriate to tolerate a fresh assessment of those preferences in a new election. The Board's 1958 decision in General Extrusion Co. (1958), set forth exceptions to the contract-bar rule which apply today. (1) An agreement will not bar an election if the composition of the unit has changed in either one of two ways—fewer than thirty percent of the workers employed at the time of the current representation hearing were employed at the time the contract was executed, *or* fewer than fifty percent of the job classifications in existence at the time of the current representation hearing were in existence at the time the contract was executed. (2) A contract will not bar an election if subsequent to its execution there has been either "a merger of two or more operations resulting in creation of an entirely new operation with major personnel changes" or "resumption of operations at either the same or a new location, after an indefinite period of closing, with new employees." (A "mere relocation" of a considerable portion of the same employees, doing the same kinds of jobs, to another plant will not remove the bar of an existing contract. Pepsi-Cola Gen. Bottlers, Inc. (1968).) Another exception to the contract-bar rules has been written by Congress into the express provisions of the Labor Act; section 8(f), which validates so-called prehire agreements (executed before the hiring of any employees) in the construction industry, declares that such agreements will not bar an election among unit employees at any later time.

When a merger or consolidation, or purchase of a company's business or assets, results in there being a "successor" employer to one which is party to a collective bargaining agreement, that contract will bar an election among the successor's employees only if the successor and the union agree in writing to abide by the predecessor's contract. American Concrete Pipe, Inc. (1960). But when a larger enterprise purchases and "absorbs" a smaller one, or opens a new additional operation, so as to effect what the Board calls an "accretion" to the bargaining unit, a labor contract at the larger enterprise can be extended to the smaller so as to serve as a bar to an election there. Simmons Co. (1960).

Dramatic changes in the status of the union may also warrant departures from the contract-bar principle. In Hershey Chocolate Corp. (1958), the Board held that a contract will not bar an election petition if the signatory union has become "defunct." If there is evidence that the union is unable or unwilling, for more than a brief period, to represent the employees—as evidenced by a failure to hold meetings, elect officers, process grievances and the like—an election petition will be regarded as timely. In determining this issue, the Board will consider the status only of the union which is signatory to the contract; if, for example, it is only the local union which is party to the contract and that local has become defunct, it is irrelevant that the nonsignatory international union has evidenced a willingness and ability to assume responsibility for the representation functions of the local.

The Board in *Hershey Chocolate* also articulated the "schism" exception to the contract-bar rule, again on the assumption that industrial stability will in these cases be better served by a new election than by the compelled continuation of the status quo. A "schism" exists when there is a basic intra-union conflict over fundamental policy which has reached the highest level of the international union and has become so acute as to result in the disruption of intra-union relationships and the "fracturing" of the bargaining representative in such a manner as to create confusion and instability. Typically, the schism has been precipitated by charges of corruption or Communist domination in union leadership and is made manifest by formal disaffiliation action taken by members of the local union. St. Louis Bakery Employers (1958) (election ordered during term of contract with Bakery & Confectionery Workers after AFL–CIO expulsion of BCW International and local's affiliation with newly chartered American Bakery & Confectionery Workers).

These exceptions to the contract bar—duration longer than three years, extensive employer expansion, schism and defunctness, and the like—make it possible for a timely election to be held and won by an insurgent union at a time when a valid and enforceable contract continues in existence. The certification of the insurgent union does not of its own force dissolve the contract with the incumbent union. But the Board has held that a different union which is newly certified is not to be bound involuntarily to honor the terms of the contract negotiated by the ousted union and is free to negotiate a new one. To bind the new union to the existing contract would run counter to the very purposes of dropping the contract bar and permitting a new expression of employee preference. American Seating Co. (1953). The Supreme Court appears to endorse this principle. NLRB v. Burns Int'l Security Services, Inc. (U.S.1972). It is less clear whether, in the rare instance when the newly-elected union wishes to assume the rights and obligations of the contract negotiated by the ousted union, it has an unqualified power to do so. In one case, involving a schism and a transfer of allegiance by the local from one international union to another, the Board held that the newly affiliated and freshly certified union could not assert rights under the "predecessor's" union-security provision; but this was reversed on appeal, on the theory that the new entity was in substance no different from the signatory union. NLRB v. Hershey Chocolate Corp. (3d Cir. 1961).

Open and Insulated Periods. The Board has fashioned additional rules for timely filing in those instances in which a contract bar exists but is drawing to a close. If, for example, the contract is for a fixed term of two years, an election petition filed after the termination date and before a new contract is executed will of course be timely. The Board has also held that a petition will be timely if it is filed during what is known as an "open period" lasting ninety to sixty days *prior* to the expiration date of such a two-year contract. If filed before the open period the petition will be dismissed, but if filed within that period it will be processed and the employer will normally be obliged to refrain from bargaining with the incumbent union for a new contract or a contract extension. Indeed, in order to preserve for the insurgent union (and the employees) this privilege to petition for an election in the open period, any contract renewal, extension or amendment executed by the employer and incumbent union *prior* to ninety days before the termination date of the existing contract (or prior to ninety days before the running of the three-year bar period, if the contract is longer) will be treated as a "premature extension" which, although lawful and mutually enforceable, will not constitute a new bar to the filing of an otherwise timely election petition.

If no petition is filed within the open period, the next sixty days are treated by the Board as an "insulated period." An election petition filed during that period will be dismissed as untimely and the next date on which a petition may be filed is *after* the contract bar has ended—the termination date if the contract is for three years or less, and three years from the date of execution if the contract is for a longer period. Obviously, it is to the advantage of an insurgent union, or of employees seeking decertification, to compute time carefully and to file a petition in the open period; failing that, the employer and the incumbent union are free to negotiate during the sixty-day insulated period which follows and to execute a new agreement which will start the contract-bar "clock" running again.

All of these elaborate principles were announced by the Board in Deluxe Metal Furniture Co. (1958) (with the current "open period" of sixty to ninety days prior to the running of the bar adopted in 1962 in Leonard Wholesale Meats, Inc. (1962)). Their purpose is nonetheless clear: to furnish for the Board and for all parties fixed and unambiguous time periods by which to guide their conduct; to minimize and concentrate the disruption attendant upon the filing and processing of election petitions and the conduct of pre-election campaigns; and to afford to the employer and incumbent union a period of sixty days at the very end of the contract-bar period when serious negotiations for a new contract may be conducted free of the pressures generated by an election campaign between the incumbent and insurgent unions. (Because of the slightly earlier bargaining schedule which the Act contemplates in health care institutions, where formal notification of termination or modification must be given to the other party and to government mediation agencies thirty days sooner than in other industries, the Board has advanced the "open" period in such institutions. In Trinity Lutheran Hosp. (1975), the Board held that "all petitions filed more than 90 days but not over 120 days before the terminal date of any contract involving a health care institution will hereafter be found timely.")

§ 10.   Judicial Review: The Statutory Route

The National Labor Relations Act makes no express provision for direct judicial review of Board decisions in the course of representation proceedings. The Act provides only for review of "a final order of the Board" in unfair labor practice cases, and such review is activated by petition in a designated federal court of appeals either by the Board (section 10(e)) or by "any person aggrieved" by that final order (section 10(f)). Board decisions in election cases—relating to the determination of the bargaining unit, the eligibility of voters, the conduct of the election, and the propriety of certification—were early held by the Supreme Court not to be "final orders" directly reviewable in the courts of appeals. AFL v. NLRB (U.S.1940). The Court there held that the appropriate statutory route for such review was instead through the section 10 unfair labor practice procedures, in which the Board's challenged decision in the representation proceeding under section 9 is made a part of the record. This is required by section 9(d):

> Whenever an order of the Board made pursuant to section 10(c) is based in whole or in part upon facts certified following an investigation pursuant to [section 9(c)] . . . and there is a petition for the enforcement or review of such order, such certification and the record of such investigation shall be included in the transcript of the entire

record required to be filed under section 10(e) or 10(f), and thereupon the decree of the court . . . shall be made and entered upon the pleadings, testimony and proceedings set forth in such transcript.

The legislative history of both the Wagner and Taft-Hartley Acts makes it plain that Congress intended by this provision to bar resort to the courts for immediate review of Board representation decisions, especially prior to the conduct of an election, since this would provide an opportunity for dilatory litigation and the frustration of the collective bargaining preferences of employees in the unit. In effect, Congress declared that the person aggrieved by a Board representation decision is obliged to precipitate an unfair labor practice proceeding as a means of securing review in the appellate courts.

The most common illustration of this procedure is the employer refusal to bargain with a union which has been certified after a Board-supervised election. If, for example, the employer believes that the Board was in error in finding that persons rendering services for the employer are "employees" within the coverage of the Labor Act rather than excluded "independent contractors," judicial review of the Board's construction of the Act is to be secured not in advance of the election but by a refusal to bargain with the union after certification. In defense to the union's charge under section 8(a)(5), the employer contends that the Board erred in finding that the workers fell within the statutory definition. See NLRB v. Hearst Publications, Inc. (U.S.1944). In such cases, the Board in considering the unfair labor practice complaint will commonly endorse pro forma the representation decision made by the Board or its regional director in the earlier representation case, and that issue will thus be ripe for judicial review upon petition of the employer under section 10(f). (The Supreme Court has held that, in such cases, the person aggrieved by a representation decision, such as a unit determination, made by a regional director has no right in the unfair labor practice proceeding to plenary Board re-examination of that decision. Magnesium Casting Co. v. NLRB (U.S.1971).)

In the great majority of cases, the decision of representation issues will invite the exercise of considerable discretion in the application of vague (or nonexistent) statutory mandates to highly particularized facts. Examples are the appropriate bargaining unit, the inclusion of persons as "employees" within the Act or their exclusion as "independent contractors" or "supervisors," the upsetting of "laboratory conditions" which are a prerequisite to a valid election, the propriety of conduct at election locations, and the like. In such cases, the courts will tend to extend great deference to the conclusions of the Board, and to set them aside only when arbitrary or when grossly belied by the record evidence. The standard of review has been well articulated in a refusal-to-bargain case in which the employer contended that the Board's decision as to the appropriate bargaining unit was illegally controlled by the "extent of organization" on the part of the union, in violation of the express mandate of section 9(c)(5). The court in Local 1325, Retail Clerks v. NLRB (Adams Drug) (D. C.Cir.1969) stated:

> A court obviously should not examine a unit determination of the Board with a disposition to substitute its own judgment for that of the Board if it finds that it might have preferred the selection of an alternative unit. Instead, a court must view the Board's decision to see, first, whether the Board has articulated the factors which underlie its choice of a unit; and second, to see whether those factors, when viewed against the backdrop of other Board decisions and a statute which has given the agency broad discretion in the performance of a difficult task are sufficiently substantial to dispel an impression of unreasoned arbitrariness and to negate an inference that "extent of organization" was the primary basis for the Board's action.

§ 11. District Court Injunctions

There are, however, three narrowly defined classes of cases in which the courts have expressed willingness to depart from the statutorily prescribed mode of review of Board representation decisions and have countenanced actions in the federal district courts against the Board or its regional directors seeking to restrain the holding of an election or the certification of election results.

The most notable and frequently invoked exception was recognized by the Supreme Court in Leedom v. Kyne (U.S.1958). The Board in a representation proceeding had found appropriate a single bargaining unit containing 233 professional employees and 9 nonprofessional employees without first permitting the professional employees to vote for or against inclusion as apparently required by section 9(b)(1) of the Labor Act. An election was held and a union certified as the bargaining representative, but the union brought a district court action against the members of the Board seeking to have the election and certification set aside. The Board conceded that it had violated section 9(b)(1) in not polling the professional employees but claimed that no injunction would lie, in view of the exclusive statutory machinery for judicial review. A divided Supreme Court held to the contrary, and sustained the jurisdiction and order of the district court (which had set aside the Board's unit determination, election and certification). The Court articulated two reasons. First, it held the suit to be one not for review of a decision made by the Board within its jurisdiction but rather "to strike down an order of the Board made in excess of its delegated powers and contrary to a specific prohibition in the Act"; this was a deprivation of a right of the professional employees by the exercise of a power specifically withheld from the Board. Second, in the absence of equity jurisdiction in the districts courts, the workers' statutory right would be obliterated, "for there is no other means, within their control . . . to protect and enforce that right." A vigorous dissenting opinion pointed out that the statute left such rights to the Board to protect, that injunctive relief would ignore the Congressional mandate clearly set forth in the review provisions of the Labor Act, and that even an occasional resulting absence altogether of judicial review was contemplated by Congress as preferable to the potential for dilatory lawsuits while representation proceedings were in progress.

A second exception was articulated in McCulloch v. Sociedad Nacional de Marineros de Honduras (U.S.1963), in which the Board had asserted jurisdiction over the crew (composed of foreign nationals) of a foreign flagship owned by a foreign subsidiary of an American corporation. Both the employer and the foreign labor organization already representing the crew sought to enjoin the Board from conducting a representation election, and the Supreme Court held that an injunction would lie even though, unlike in Leedom v. Kyne, no express statutory prohibition was being violated.

> [T]he overriding consideration is that the Board's assertion of power to determine the representation of foreign seamen aboard vessels under foreign flags has aroused vigorous protests from foreign governments and created international problems for our Government. . . . [T]he presence of public questions particularly high in the scale of our national interest because of their international complexion is a uniquely compelling justification for prompt judicial resolution of the controversy over the Board's power.

The Court took pains to limit the reach of its decision. "No question of remotely comparable urgency was involved in *Kyne,* which was a purely domestic adversary situation. The exception recognized today is therefore not to be taken as an enlargement of the exception in Kyne."

The third exception—like that articulated in *Sociedad Nacional,* available but infrequently invoked—is for Board decisions which deprive a party of a constitutional right. In Fay v. Douds (2d Cir. 1949), the plaintiff union asserted a "property" right in the maintenance of its position as exclusive bargaining agent and claimed that it was being unconstitutionally deprived of that right by the Board's refusal to hold a formal hearing in the course of its investigation of a petition seeking the union's decertification. The court, although denying the union's claim on the merits, held that if the assertion of the constitutional right is not transparently frivolous, the district courts have jurisdiction of the injunction action. This constitutional-right claim is typically joined with a claim of violation of statutory right (commonly more easily proved) falling within Leedom v. Kyne.

E. g., AFSCME Council 19 v. NLRB (N.D.Ill.1968) (due process denied and statute violated by Board's declination of jurisdiction over nonprofit nursing homes while asserting jurisdiction over proprietary homes). The constitutional basis for injunctive relief is rarely sustained, and is most narrowly confined. Parsons v. Levine (N.D.Ohio 1974) (denial of injunction against holding of expedited representation election without hearing).

The reach of the district court's injunctive jurisdiction under Leedom v. Kyne is not at all clear. The Supreme Court has since reaffirmed the narrow range of its applicability in Boire v. Greyhound Corp. (U.S.1964), where it held the district court to have no power to enjoin an election at the behest of a company which claimed that the unit employees were in fact not employees of the plaintiff company (Greyhound) but rather of another company hired as an independent contractor. The Court stated:

> [W]hether Greyhound possessed sufficient indicia of control to be an "employer" is essentially a factual issue, unlike the question in *Kyne,* which depended solely upon construction of the statute. The *Kyne* exception is a narrow one, not to be extended to permit plenary district court review of Board orders in certification proceedings whenever it can be said that an erroneous assessment of the particular facts before the Board has led it to a conclusion which does not comport with the law. Judicial review in such a situation has been limited by Congress to the courts of appeals and then only under the conditions explicitly laid down in § 9(d) of the Act.

The courts have come to endorse the principle that injunctive review is to be invoked only in those highly exceptional circumstances when the statutory provision allegedly violated is clear, specific and mandatory, and only when the Board has acted so clearly in defiance of the Act as to warrant immediate judicial intervention. McCulloch v. Libbey-Owens-Ford Glass Co. (D.C.Cir. 1968).

But courts have disagreed on the application of this standard. Some courts have thought it satisfied when the Board has refused to certify an election in which there was some procedural irregularity but not such as would render the election results invalid. Miami Newspaper Printing Pressmen's Local 46 v. McCulloch (D.C.Cir. 1963) (Board cannot invalidate election results merely because appeal from representation decision of regional director was to single member of Board rather than three as required by statute); Bullard Co. v. NLRB (D.D.C.1966) (Board enjoined from conducting second election where Board agent in first election was seen, among other things, fraternizing with employer). *Contra,* NLRB v. Athbro Precision Eng'r Corp. (1st Cir. 1970) (dictum) (Board has discretion to set aside election for appearance as well as actuality of impropriety by Board agent). Some courts may also be inclined to assert jurisdiction—even in cases in which the substantive right asserted is less than clear on the face of the statute—when the plaintiffs are individual employees who, unlike an employer or union, cannot commit an unfair labor practice for purposes of triggering judicial review. See Templeton v. Dixie Color Printing Co. (5th Cir. 1971) (Board is ordered to proceed with hearings looking toward decertification election, after its three-year failure to process the petition because of "blocking" unfair labor practice charges filed by the incumbent union against the employer). But even in such instances, the district court will be loath to interfere when the Board's action is not a plain abuse of discretion. See Bishop v. NLRB (5th Cir. 1974) (injunction denied on facts similar to *Templeton*, which is read narrowly and distinguished).

On the whole, then, courts have been extremely reluctant to assert jurisdiction to enjoin Board action in representation cases. In some cases, the availability of unfair labor practice proceedings has convinced the court that those should be utilized by the plaintiff rather than direct injunctive relief. Thus, employers as a class have been held by some courts to be ineligible to invoke injunctive jurisdiction under Leedom v. Kyne. Leedom v. IBEW Local 108 (D.C.Cir. 1960). But other courts have disagreed, pointing in part to the Supreme Court's failure to dismiss on that basis employer actions in the *Sociedad Nacional* and *Greyhound* cases; and in part to the fact that employers should be treated no less favorably than unions, which also are in a position to challenge representation determinations by committing unfair labor practices. (The winning union can refuse to bargain for employees arguably improperly included in a bargaining unit, and the losing union can picket after an election which is arguably invalid and test the election under section 8(b)(4)(C) or 8(b)(7)(B).) Bullard Co. v. NLRB (D.D.C.1966).

Most commonly, courts have refused to assert injunctive jurisdiction because the asserted statutory right is not quite so clear; even seemingly unqualified legislative mandates are found to invite the exercise of Board discretion, not properly to be corrected by direct injunctive review. Despite statutory language suggesting that the Board "shall" hold a hearing when an election petition is filed, "shall" certify the results of a valid election, "shall not" rule against a craft unit because of earlier Board unit determinations, and "shall not" give controlling weight to "extent of organization," courts have held these directives subject to Board discretion and have dismissed actions for injunctions. *E. g.*, NMU v. NLRB (United Fruit Co.) (S. D.N.Y.1967). It is correct procedure in these cases for the court simply to hold that the statutory mandate is not unequivocal and compelling; any colorable support for the Board's ruling should be treated as a jurisdictional defect dictating dismissal. See Boire v. Miami Herald Pub. Co. (5th Cir. 1965) (section 9(c)(3) does not clearly require Board to issue regulations concerning voting eligibility of economic strikers). Some courts appear instead to probe the merits of the plaintiff's claim to a determination that the Board has acted properly, and only then dismiss for lack of jurisdiction. See Machinery Employees Local 714 v. Madden (7th Cir. 1965). Courts should guard against this review of Board decisions on the merits conducted in the guise of determining jurisdiction.

CHAPTER V

REPRESENTATION CASES:

THE APPROPRIATE BARGAINING UNIT

§ 1. Appropriate Bargaining Unit: Significance

Section 9(a) of the Labor Act provides that a representative chosen by "the majority of the employees in a unit appropriate for such purposes" is to be the "exclusive" representative of all employees in that unit. As an incident to conducting a representation election, the Board must determine which group of jobs shall serve as the election constituency. That group of jobs is denoted the appropriate bargaining unit, and the persons employed in those jobs at the time of the election are entitled to vote whether they wish to continue to settle terms and conditions of employment on an individual basis—as some would characterize it, by "unilateral" act of the employer—or whether they wish to have one or another employee representative. Any such majority representative, the "exclusive" spokesman in dealing with the employer on these matters, is empowered and obliged to bargain not only for the employees who voted for it or who are its members, but for all employees in the bargaining unit. The model of majority rule within discretely bounded election units is obviously borrowed from the American political tradition.

Several important and sometimes misunderstood features of this statutory design should be noted. First, the unit is comprised of jobs or job classifications and not of the particular persons working at those jobs at any given time. The bargaining unit does not change simply because Machinist Jones retires and is replaced by Machinist Williams. Second, what is commonly known as the "appropriate bargaining unit" might more accurately be denoted the appropriate *election* unit since employees represented in different election units may choose to "re-group" as a single larger entity for purposes of conducting actual negotiations. The composition of the *negotiating* unit will thus frequently depend less upon the Board's unit determination than upon the structure of the employer and the union and upon alliances among employers or unions. Third, a determination of the appropriate bargaining unit by the National Labor Relations Board is not a prerequisite to bargaining; an employer and a union are in most instances free to agree informally upon an appropriate unit and upon the commencement of bargaining for the employees in that unit. Fourth, it is the task of the Board to delineate only "an" appropriate bargaining unit; it is not obliged to select only one which is the *most* appropriate or the optimal unit.

While the Labor Act empowers the Board to make unit determinations, it gives the Board only the most modest guidance in doing so. Section 9(b) begins:

The Board shall decide in each case whether, in order to assure to employees the fullest freedom in exercising the rights guaranteed by this Act, the unit appropriate for the purposes of collective bargaining shall be the employer unit, craft unit, plant unit, or subdivision thereof

and proceeds to add explicit limitations upon the Board's powers in three rather narrowly circumscribed situations (to be discussed more fully later). These latter limitations, and several other pertinent restrictions upon the Board's authority in election cases (such as the election-bar rule), were added in the Taft-Hartley Act of 1947 in the context of a Congressional call for greater legislative and judicial limitation of agency discretion. In spite of that, Board decisions on unit-determination matters typically invite a judgmental assessment of a number of relevant criteria and are typically shielded rather well against extensive judicial review. Judicial review is limited both because of the presumed agency expertise, stemming from a familiarity with the industrial context and, as noted above, the possible appropriateness of a number of different bargaining units in the same case. Moreover, as a matter of procedure, a unit determination can, except in the most extraordinary circumstances, be challenged only by the rather circuitous method of committing an unfair labor practice; this method is sufficiently exhausting and frequently technically obscure so as to serve as an additional obstacle to effective judicial supervision.

Although the jurisdiction of the Board to adjudicate unfair labor practice cases is perhaps the more dramatic, its jurisdiction to make unit determinations is at the heart of our system of collective bargaining and has a most pervasive impact upon industrial relations.

(1) A large unit, commonly favored by the employer, will typically be much more difficult for the union to organize than a small one. The size of the unit may thus determine whether there will be an election at all (since the union must first make a "showing of interest") and if so, whether collective bargaining will be instituted.

(2) A large unit may engross within it employees of differing skills, attitudes and interests. The more diversified the constituency, the more likely there will be conflicts of interest and strains upon the union's ability to represent all unit employees fairly in negotiating and administering the collective bargaining agreement.

(3) The size and composition of the unit will directly affect the structure and composition of the union representative, which not only must represent all in the unit but must also court all unit employees as a source of financial and bargaining power.

(4) The smaller and the more homogeneous the unit, the more likely it is that the individual worker will be effectively represented

and will have his voice heard in a democratic manner within union councils; the larger the unit, the more diluted the impact of any single employee on the shaping of union policy.

(5) The size of the unit will also shape the kinds of issues that will be addressed in collective bargaining and dealt with in the labor agreement.

(6) Fragmented units tend to bring economic headaches to the employer. Not only are they typically easier to organize, but they also involve the greater cost and disruption that come with frequent bargaining cycles and meetings; moreover, they expose the employer to "whipsaw" strikes by employees in one unit which inure, cumulatively, to the benefit of employees in other units.

(7) Fragmented units, represented by different unions, often bring with them disputes between those unions about the right to represent employees of uncertain representational status (*e. g.,* in newly created job titles) or the right of members of one union to oust from their jobs members of another (a work-assignment dispute).

(8) Larger units bring the danger of a more massive work-stoppage in the event of a bargaining dispute; smaller units may permit the employer to transfer work from one unit, shut down by a strike, to some other unit which is still in operation and subject to an existing labor contract.

As can be noted, different unions and different employers may have differing preferences regarding the size of the bargaining unit, depending upon the nature of the industry and the structure and composition of the workforce. On the whole, however, it is likely that unions will favor the smaller unit, since it can be more readily organized. Since 1960, the Board has tended to echo this preference, since the smaller unit assures greater homogeneity of employee interest and maximizes employee self-determination.

§ 2. Criteria for Unit Determinations

The statute tells the Board very little about the criteria or standards which should be employed in making unit determinations. Section 9(b) enjoins the Board "to assure to employees the fullest freedom in exercising the rights guaranteed by this Act." Those rights, enumerated in section 7, are the right to form and join a union, to bargain collectively and to engage in concerted activities to those ends—and the right to refrain from doing so. If the Board holds "appropriate" a very large unit covering, for example, many geographically dispersed plants staffed by employees of differing skills and working conditions, the exercise of section 7 rights may be frustrated: effective communication by the union in organizing and in formulating and administering contract terms may be hampered, intensive interest in collective bargaining within one group of employees may be "cancelled out" by the votes of those elsewhere who oppose it, and negotiation and administration of the labor contract may be impeded by the conflicting interests of employees within the unit. Conversely, a unit which is "too small," and which excludes some employees with common skills, working conditions and economic interests, may curtail the bargaining power of the union representing only the unit employees, may generate (perhaps with the aid of the employer) divisions and in-fighting among employees in the plant or conversely may generate pressures to settle terms of employment for the non-unit employees along the lines negotiated for the unit employees (in spite of the possible desire of the non-unit employees to "refrain from" unionization and collective bargaining). For these reasons, the Board in making its unit determinations seeks an employee group which is united by *community of interest*, and which neither embraces employees having a substantial conflict of economic interest nor omits employees sharing a unity of economic interest with other employees in the election or bargaining constituency.

The Board draws upon this criterion of community of interest in order to determine whether, for example, employees with special craft skills and training should be separated out for purposes of voting and bargaining or whether they should be grouped along with semi-skilled and unskilled employees in an "industrial" unit; whether "production and maintenance" employees should be grouped in a single unit with "white-collar employees" doing technical or clerical work; whether the unit should comprise only employees working in a single plant, store or office of the employer or whether there should be a grouping of employees in several—or indeed all—of the employer's plants, stores or offices; and whether it is sound to go even beyond the employees of a single employer and to group those employees with persons employed by other employers in the same industry in the same competitive market. In making judgments about "community of interest" in these different settings, the Board will look to such factors as: (1) similarity in the scale and manner of determining earnings; (2) similarity in employment benefits, hours of work and other terms and conditions of employment; (3) similarity in the kind of work performed; (4) similarity in the qualifications, skills and training of the employees; (5) frequency of contact or interchange among the employees; (6) geographic proximity; (7) continuity or integration of production processes; (8) common supervision and determination of labor-relations policy; (9) relationship to the administrative organization of the employer; (10) history of collective bargaining; (11) desires of the affected employees; (12) extent of union organization.

It can easily be seen that community of interest is a vague standard which does not readily lend itself to mechanical application. It is a multi-factor criterion, and it is rare in any given case that all of the factors point conveniently in the direction of the same size unit. As already noted, it is indeed possible that on the basis of community of interest, the Board may conclude that there are several units any one of which may be, in the language of the statute, "a unit appropriate" for collective bargaining. Black & Decker Mfg. Co. (1964). The Board considers these factors in all of the several different procedural settings in which a unit-determination issue presents itself: (a) *initial organization,* when there is no history of collective bargaining; (b) *severance,* when there is an existing unit —either by informal recognition or certification—and a group of employees wish to split off from the larger group and to bargain separately; (c) *accretion,* the opposite of severance, when there is an existing unit and through merger or other acquisition a group of employees (whether organized or not) is absorbed into the existing business enterprise; and (d) *unit clarification,* when the creation of a new job or the change in description of an existing job (and accretion as well) creates uncertainty as to the inclusion of those jobs in or their exclusion from an existing unit.

While most of the above-listed factors engrossed within "community of interest" are self-explanatory, certain of them require more extended comment.

Centralized Employer Policymaking. If the employer's administrative or management structure is highly centralized, such that supervision of employees and the determination of labor relations policy are directed in the "home office" rather than "in the field," the employer will commonly prefer to group the uniformly affected employees in a single bargaining unit. Such centralization and uniformity of personnel policy, from department to department within a plant and from plant to plant within a company, can be present in two different situations. In one, the processes of production, or of production and distribution, are functionally integrated and continuous. In these cases, the combination of administrative centralization and integrated employee tasks creates a community of interest and ordinarily invites grouping all of the affected employees in the larger unit. Public-utility industries such as electric, telephone and communications offer a common example. Red Hook Telephone Co. (1967). (The employer in such cases reaps the incidental benefit of avoiding fragmented and frequent bargaining, where a strike in one unit can effectively cripple the entire operation.) Even in such cases, however, functional integration standing alone may not be sufficient to outweigh the interest of a smaller and more homogeneous group of employees with special training, skills and interests; the craft-severance cases, to be discussed more fully below, are instructive on this issue. In a second class of case involving centralized formulation and implementation of labor policy, the employees in the different plants or stores or departments may be engaged in work which is not functionally integrated but is simply performed in the same manner under similar working conditions. Examples are the employees working in different stores in a department-store chain or in different restaurants in a quick-service food-store chain. In this class of case, the

Board's policy has vacillated and although it at one time held the single-store or single-plant unit to be inappropriate it currently treats that unit as presumptively appropriate. This too will be discussed more fully below.

In both the integrated-production and chain-store cases, the impetus toward the larger bargaining unit is less weighty when different aspects of personnel policy are determined by different levels of management, and less significant yet when a large degree of supervisory control over employees is vested in local management. Fragmentation of the unit has also been permitted in companies in which, in spite of industrial relations policy being effectively set at the national or multistate regional level, this administrative unit is too large for any union effectively to organize. The Board in the early 1960's held this to be the case in the insurance industry, reversing a long-standing policy favoring comprehensive bargaining units. Quaker City Life Ins. Co. (1961), *unit determination sustained in* (4th Cir. 1963).

Bargaining History. When there is some history of successful bargaining in a unit sought by one of the parties to the representation proceeding—whether the original bargaining relationship was initiated by certification or by informal recognition—the Board will be anxious to retain that unit in existence, as a means of stabilizing industrial relations. The bargaining history will normally demonstrate that collective bargaining on that basis is viable. The expectations of the parties concerning their future bargaining duties may have derived in great measure from both the peaceful and stressful experiences in prior negotiations. Prior bargaining patterns may have themselves established a community of interest among employees even though such a community might have been initially tenuous; for example, a common seniority system or pension plan, or a uniform or correlated scale of wages or of other benefits, may create a sense of common interest and needs. St. Louis Indep. Packing Co. (1952) (washers and spotters may not be severed from production and maintenance unit, in view of common hours, wages and fringe benefits). Although it is the bargaining history between the same employer and employees that is of primary concern, the Board may also look to practices of the same industry in the same locality as indicators of what has produced stability under similar conditions. Toffenetti Restaurant Co. (1961) (area pattern of separate bargaining by restaurant kitchen employees).

Again, however, if the bargaining history runs counter to other elements of Board policy, it may well be deemed of subordinate importance. In a rare departure from its legislative silence on unit-determination issues, Congress declared in section 9(b)(2) that "the Board shall not .   .   . decide that any craft unit is inappropriate .   .   . on the ground that a different unit has been established by a prior Board determination." The negligible impact of this restriction will be noted more fully below in a discussion of the craft unit.

Employee Preferences. The Board will sometimes find that on the record in a particular case either of two units may be an appropriate bargaining unit; this will commonly be so when the larger unit is plantwide or storewide and when the smaller unit is a craft or departmental group. In such cases, the Board may permit the employees to determine by a two-stage balloting procedure both the union they seek as their spokesman and the unit in which bargaining will be conducted. What is today known as a "Globe election" takes its name from Globe Mach. & Stamping Co. (1937), in which the Board permitted a group of craft employees to express a preference for representation in an independent bargaining unit. The device is usually used when two unions are vying for the same group of employees, but one union seeks to represent them in a small unit while the competing union seeks to include them with other employees in a more comprehensive unit. The device is also used when there is only one union seeking representation rights but the Board concludes that either of two units would be appropriate. See NLRB v. Underwood Mach. Co. (1st Cir. 1949) (separate votes among production employees and among maintenance employees, with employer challenging union's request for combined unit; held, Board had not improperly delegated to employees its authority to determine appropriate units).

In its most simplified form, the *Globe* election is conducted by the Board as follows. In a two-union election, the employees in the prospective smaller unit can choose between the union seeking that unit (*e. g.,* a "craft" union) and the union seeking the more comprehensive unit (*e. g.,* an "industrial" union); these employees generally are not given the option to vote "no-agent." The other employees in the prospective larger unit can choose between the industrial union and no-agent. If the craft union secures a majority in the smaller unit, that union will represent those employees in that separate unit; the votes of the remaining employees will be tallied as a separate group to determine whether the industrial union has been selected by a majority of that separate unit or whether those employees will go unrepresented. If, on the other hand, the employees in the smaller unit do not give the craft union a majority vote, then the votes of all employees in both the large and small units will be pooled. The industrial union will be certified if selected by a majority of employees in the pooled group. Parke Davis & Co. (1968).

Extent of Organization. In the early years of the administration of the Wagner Act, the Board sometimes fragmented out from a larger cohesive but unorganized employee group a smaller included group which the union had succeeded in organizing. In declaring these to be appropriate bargaining units—commonly subdivisions within a single plant, or an entire plant in a multiplant company—the

Board emphasized the directive in section 9(b) of the Wagner Act "to insure to employees the full benefit of their right to self organization." *E. g.,* Botany Worsted Mills (1940) ("[E]ven if, under other circumstances, the wool sorters or trappers would not constitute the most effective bargaining unit, nevertheless, in the existing circumstances, unless they are recognized as a separate unit, there will be no collective bargaining agent whatsoever for these workers."). The Board soon came under criticism for certifying units which were thought to lack a true community of interest and to be distinguished only by virtue of the union having organized the employees (frequently after failure to organize the employees in the larger and more apparently suitable unit).

In 1947, Congress made two changes in the Labor Act which directly bore upon the Board's use of the "extent of organization" criterion. First, it modified section 9(b) to require that the Board, in making its unit determinations, seek "to assure to employees the fullest freedom in exercising the rights guaranteed by this Act"; this included not merely the "right to self organization," as mandated by what was section 9(b) of the Wagner Act, but also the right to "refrain" therefrom as accorded by the 1947 amendment of section 7. More pertinently, Congress in that year enacted section 9(c)(5) of the Act which provides: "In determining whether a unit is appropriate for the purposes specified in subsection (b) the extent to which the employees have organized shall not be controlling." Logically, it would appear that this section renders extent of organization wholly irrelevant to unit determination: if a unit which has been organized is not appropriate on the basis of criteria *other* than extent of organization, then the statute forbids use of that factor to find the unit appropriate, and if that unit *is* appropriate when tested against criteria other than extent of organization, then the latter factor is merely cumulative and thus superfluous.

Nonetheless, the Board purports to accord extent of organization some weight, to be considered along with other community-of-interest factors in determining the unit, and the Supreme Court has approved this practice. Metropolitan Life Ins. Co. v. NLRB (U.S.1965). While the Court's opinion and decisions of other courts and of the Board have left the law on the subject rather murky, two propositions can be asserted with some assurance. First, the statute forbids only the *Board* to make extent of organization "controlling" in unit determinations; it does not forbid the Board to find a unit appropriate in cases in which the petitioning *union* seeks an election in that unit because it was unsuccessful in organizing on a wider basis. (The latter will of course be the case in many representation proceedings.) Second, the Board cannot rely on extent of organization as the *sole* justification for finding a unit appropriate; there must be other more conventional criteria which support the unit determination. Indeed, some courts have gone further and have concluded that extent of organization must be in effect ignored and a unit determination bottomed exclusively on criteria *other* than that. NLRB v. Western & S. Life Ins. Co. (3d Cir. 1967).

A well-reasoned decision of the Court of Appeals for the District of Columbia Circuit has concluded that it is the task of the reviewing court to assure itself that the factors articulated by the Board in its unit determination "negate an inference that 'extent of organization' was the *primary* basis for the Board's action" (emphasis added). Local 1325, Retail Clerks v. NLRB (Adams Drug Co.) (D.C.Cir. 1969). In that case, the Board had drawn a unit line around twenty-five drugstores within the geographical limits of the State of Rhode Island, twenty-four of which were in the Providence metropolitan area; it excluded a Massachusetts drugstore in that metropolitan area but included a Rhode Island store at some distance from Providence. In view of the lack of substance in the Board's reasons for severing the unit at the state lines, and in view of the inconsistency in the Board's application of the criterion of geographical proximity, the court surmised that the Board's unit determination rested in truth on no more than the extent of union organization. Similar inconsistencies in the grouping of insurance company district offices—sometimes single-office, sometimes several offices on a strict city-limit basis, sometimes several offices across city or state lines in a metropolitan area, and sometimes several offices within strict state lines—have precipitated careful judicial scrutiny and occasional reversal of Board unit determinations. See Metropolitan Life Ins. Co. v. NLRB (U.S.1965).

§ 3. Statutory Limitations

In addition to the statutory proscription against making "extent of organization" a "controlling" factor in unit determinations, Congress in 1947 imposed three further limitations upon the discretion of the Board. Section 9(b)(2) forbids the Board to "decide that any craft unit is inappropriate . . . on the ground that a different unit has been established by a prior Board determination, unless a majority of the employees in the proposed craft unit vote against separate representation." Congress sought to curb somewhat the Board's impetus toward certification on an "industrial" rather than a "craft" basis, and the section has been understood to bar the Board's holding a craft unit inappropriate if the *only* reason for doing so is a bargaining history derived from an earlier Board certification of a more comprehensive unit. See Mallinckrodt Chem. Works (1966). In an endorsement of the *Globe*-election principle, Congress expressly provided that the wishes of the craft employees could be honored if they approved incorporation in the larger unit.

That principle was also incorporated in section 9(b)(1), which forbids the Board to include in a single unit "both professional employees and employees who are not professional employees unless a majority of such professional employees vote for inclusion in such unit." In essence, Congress was writing the community-of-interest principle into the Act, for it feared that such a hybrid unit would submerge the distinct interests of the professionals (defined in section 2(12) of the Act as employees engaged in work which is predominantly intellectual and which requires discretion and judgment as well as knowledge of an advanced type acquired through prolonged intellectual instruction). Only by a vote of the professionals can the Board include them in a unit with nonprofessionals, and this is true regardless of whether the professionals would comprise a small minority or a great majority of the unit. Leedom v. Kyne (U.S.1958). Even in a case in which there was a well-established history of bargaining in a broader unit, the Board has permitted the severance of a group of professional employees. S.S. White Dental Mfg. Co. (1954). As that case demonstrates, the self-determination election under section 9(b)(1) will offer to the professionals the opportunity to vote on two questions: whether they desire separation from or inclusion in the more comprehensive unit and which of the competing unions they desire to represent them. If a majority vote for separate representation, the ballots on the second issue are tabulated separately; if a majority vote for inclusion, their votes on the second issue are combined and tabulated with those of the nonprofessional employees. The statutory proscription of the hybrid unit speaks only to the Board, and does not bar the informal agreement of employer and union to combine professionals and nonprofessionals in a single unit.

Section 9(b)(3) imposes a far greater restriction upon persons employed as "guards" who "enforce against employees and other persons rules to protect property of the employer or to protect the safety of persons on the employer's premises." Like the section dealing with professionals, this section forbids the Board (but not the parties by informal agreement) to group together guards and other classes of employees in a single unit. But Congress desired not simply to shelter guards against the dissipation of their special group interests in a more comprehensive unit. Congress was more concerned with the conflict of loyalties generated among the guards if they were expected to enforce their employer's security rules, in periods of economic confrontation, against fellow unit-members. Accordingly, section 9(b)(3) makes no provision for sampling the preferences of guards for inclusion in a larger unit through a *Globe*-type election. The same Congressional concern explains the further proscription in section 9(b)(3) against the Board's certifying as the representative of guards—even in a distinct bargaining unit for guards alone—any employee organization which "admits to membership, or is affiliated directly or indirectly with an organization which admits to membership, employees other than guards."

§ 4. Single-Location Versus Multi-Location Units

In the vast preponderance of unit determinations made by regional directors and by the Board, no issue is seriously taken with the announced criteria set forth above or with their application to the facts of the particular case. There has, however, been considerable controversy over the Board's unit determinations in two classes of cases: (1) cases raising the question whether the appropriate unit is all of, or a group of, an employer's plants, stores, or offices, or only one plant, store or office; and (2) cases raising the question whether the appropriate unit is all production and maintenance employees in a plant (an "industrial" unit) or a smaller group of employees allegedly set apart by special training, skills or duties (a "craft" unit). These two situations will be discussed in turn.

The employer may be comprised of several plants, or may be a chain-store operation (typified by supermarkets, drugstores, or "fast-food" restaurants), or an insurance company with many district offices within and across state lines. Obviously, the union will find it easier to organize one or two of these plants, stores or offices than to organize many or all; election petitions will invite the Board to decide that the smaller unit is appropriate. The employer in these cases will typically argue for the larger unit, for it will be more difficult for the union to organize, will minimize the number of negotiations and will frequently correspond to the administrative structure of the employer (that is, the group of employees whose working conditions have traditionally been set by a single responsible company official in charge of labor relations).

Section 9(b) of the Labor Act provides that "The Board shall decide in each case whether, in order to assure to employees the fullest freedom in exercising the rights guaranteed by this Act, the unit appropriate for the purposes of collective bargaining shall be the employer unit, craft unit, plant unit, or subdivision thereof." The Board now holds that, in order to maximize the freedom of employee choice with regard to collective bargaining and not to impose unrealistic barriers to self-organization, there will be a presumption of appropriateness to the single-plant, single-store or single-office bargaining unit. This policy was announced in a number of Board decisions in 1961 and 1962, coincidental with a change in Board membership.

In Dixie Belle Mills, Inc. (1962), the Board announced what was in substance a presumption that one plant of a multiplant industrial operation is an appropriate unit. In that case, in which the union petitioned for an election at a single textile plant, the Board found the employees at that plant an appropriate bargaining unit, in spite of the fact that the same employer operated other mills and warehouses twenty miles away, and in spite of the finding of the regional director that the company's operations at the different locations were integrated. The Board emphasized the low degree of employee interchange and the autonomy of supervision at the individual-plant level on day-to-day business and labor-relations decisions.   The Board announced the following guidelines:

> A single plant unit, being one of the unit types listed in the statute as appropriate for bargaining purposes, is presumptively appropriate.   Therefore, unless such plant unit has been so effectively merged into a more comprehensive unit by bargaining history, or is so integrated with another as to negate its identity, it is an appropriate unit even though another unit, if requested, might also be appropriate. Moreover, even assuming that the unit urged by the Employer and found by the Regional Director here may be the most appropriate unit, this does not establish it as the only appropriate one.   .   .   .   [T]he crucial question in each case is whether the unit requested is appropriate.   The facts here do not reveal such a degree of integration or merger of operations as would require rejection of a request for a single-plant unit.

The Board, apparently from a sense of symmetry—but also from what it contends are the developing economic and labor-relations realities—proceeded to announce that the single retail store and the single insurance company district office are, by analogy to the single plant, also presumptively appropriate units.

Retail Chain Stores.   In the 1950's, the Board had generally disapproved single-store units in a retail chain-store business.   In 1951, it held that "absent unusual circumstances, the appropriate collective bargaining unit in the retail grocery trade should embrace all employees within the categories sought who perform their work within the Employer's administrative division or [geographical] area." Safeway Stores, Inc. (1951).   When labor policy was formulated and implemented on an administrative basis more extensive than a single store, the latter was held an inappropriate unit.   *E. g.,* Quality Food Markets, Inc. (1960) (two stores of five, held inappropriate; not an administrative division, not located far from other stores, justified only by extent of organization).

In Sav-On Drugs, Inc. (1962), however, the Board announced a reversal in policy.   Speaking of its earlier policy on unit determinations in retail-chain cases, it stated:

> [W]e believe that too frequently it has operated to impede the exercise by employees in retail chain operations of their rights to self-organization guaranteed in Section 7 of the Act.   In our opinion that policy has overemphasized the administrative grouping of merchandising outlets at the expense of factors such as geographic separation of the several outlets and the local managerial autonomy of the separate outlets; and it has ignored completely as a factor the extent to which the claiming labor organization had sought to or-

ganize the employees of the retail chain. We have decided
to modify this policy and to apply to retail chain operations
the same unit policy which we apply to multiplant enterprises in general. Therefore, whether a proposed unit which is
confined to one of two or more retail establishments making
up an employer's retail chain is appropriate will be determined in the light of all the circumstances of the case.

In that case, the Board was confronted with substantial centralized
administration of business and labor-relations policy among nine
drugstores in New York and New Jersey, but nonetheless held an
election appropriate for nonsupervisory and nonprofessional employees in a single New Jersey drugstore. The Board noted geographic separation, substantial authority of the store manager, minimal interchange of employees, absence of bargaining history on a
broader basis and lack of any union seeking representation on a
broader basis. Employing the same reasons, the Board has also
grouped in a single unit a few or several of the employer's stores but
less than all and less than the number alleged by the employer to
comprise a single administrative unit. *E. g.,* U–Tote–Em Grocery Co.
(1970) (3 of 11 stores held an appropriate unit).

The Board soon went beyond its rule in *Sav-On Drugs,* and held
that a single store in a chain-store operation is "presumptively appropriate," Frisch's Big Boy Ill-Mar, Inc. (1964), *bargaining order reversed and case remanded* (7th Cir. 1966). In significant part, this
rule was based on a desire by the Board for even-handedness in affording a free choice for collective bargaining in comparable cases,
and was also designed to assure that unit determinations are made
authoritatively by the Board rather than by the employer. See Haag
Drug Co. (1968):

> [T]o draw a distinction between the single chain store and
> the single plant in a multiplant enterprise or the insurance
> district office would artificially disadvantage the organiza-
> tional interests of chain store employees, simply because
> their employer operates a chain rather than a single store
> enterprise and would vest the chain operator with absolute
> power alone to control the scope of the appropriate unit.

Perhaps the three most significant factors in the Board's unit determinations in retail chain-store cases are the degree of local managerial independence (measured by the distribution of authority between local store managers and area or district managers), the geographic proximity of the stores within the proposed unit (in contrast
to those which would be excluded), and the degree of employee interchange among the included and excluded stores. However, there is no
sure way to determine how the Board will apply these criteria. In any
given case, the Board's analysis is likely to be conclusory, with quantitative labels such as "substantial" or "mere" appended without elab-

oration; and in different cases, there is quite often inconsistency in the Board's use of any one of the three fundamental criteria. Compare Gray Drug Stores, Inc. (1972), with Walgreen Co. (1972) (local managerial authority); and Frisch's Big Boy Ill-Mar, Inc. (1964), *bargaining order reversed and case remanded* (7th Cir. 1966) (single-restaurant unit held appropriate, with ten restaurants within a few blocks of one another), with Mott's Shop-Rite, Inc. (1969) (single-store unit held inappropriate, with "proximity" of stores 7 to 34 miles away).

Given the Board's changing attitude over the years toward unit breadth, and its elusive application of criteria from case to case, one might imagine that courts would frequently set aside Board unit determinations on judicial review. (Such determinations are most commonly reviewed after the Board has issued an unfair labor practice order against an employer for refusing to bargain with the union elected within the challenged unit.) In fact, this is not the case. There has been rather pervasive judicial deference to Board decisions in the retail chain-store cases, because of an assumed expertise by the administrative agency, the general utility of presumptions, and the Board's tendency to back its single-store presumptions with other factual support on a case-by-case basis. A court of appeals has recently stated:

> The Board is vested with wide discretion in determining bargaining units and it is not the province of the courts to displace the Board's choice of a unit from among two or more appropriate units, even though the court might have made a different choice were the case here de novo. .   .   .   Furthermore, in cases involving chain stores, as here, there is a presumption that a single store is an appropriate bargaining unit.   .   .   .

> This single store presumption may be overcome by evidence establishing that the requested unit lacks "meaningful identity as a self-contained economic unit"; or that the "day-to-day" supervision of unit employees is "done solely by central office officials"; or that such unit is contrary to an established practice of bargaining in a different grouping; or the stores are geographically proximate or the extent of the union organization was the controlling factor in violation of § 9(c)(5) of the Act. The Board's unit determination as to each of these factors was supported by substantial evidence.

NLRB v. Lerner Stores Corp. (9th Cir. 1974).

Other courts of appeals, however, especially when confronted with what appear to be conclusory and inconsistent Board decisions, can be conspicuously dubious concerning the Board's expertise. At least two courts of appeals have reversed and remanded Board unit decisions, and have then proceeded to reverse again when the Board on remand reaffirmed the result reached initially. NLRB v. Purity Food Stores, Inc. (1st Cir. 1965), (1st Cir. 1967); NLRB v. Davis Cafeteria, Inc. (5th Cir. 1966), (5th Cir. 1968). Some reviewing courts have been particularly critical of the weight accorded by the Board to an assumed community of interest arising from what the court regards as spurious geographic considerations, *e. g.,* NLRB v. Adams Drug Co. (D.C.Cir. 1969) (Rhode Island law regulating pharmacists held irrelevant in grouping non-professional employees in state drugstores; Board improperly controlled by extent of union organization), or spurious decision-making powers of local store managers, *e. g.,* NLRB v. Frisch's Big Boy Ill-Mar, Inc. (7th Cir. 1966) ("the decisions left to the managers do not involve any significant element of judgment as to employment relations"). The Board in Haag Drug Co. (1968), acknowledged the court decisions in *Purity Food Stores* and *Frisch's Big Boy,* but nonetheless—after undertaking a review of the cases in the area—affirmed the single-store presumption, downplayed centralized employer administration and emphasized "substantial autonomy" in the local store manager.

On occasion, the Board will be asked to declare appropriate a unit which is smaller than storewide. The Board is indeed prepared to find that a group of employees *within* a single store have sufficient community of interest setting them apart from other store employees, and thus to declare such a group an appropriate bargaining unit. For many years, the Board had held that a storewide unit, rather than a smaller one, was basically or optimally appropriate. May Department Stores Co. (1952). It did, however, declare smaller groups of employees to be appropriate units if homogeneous and possessing distinctive skills. *E. g., ibid.* (hair stylists and beauticians); F. W. Woolworth Co. (1963) (kitchen staff). And, if there was a history of bargaining or an agreement among the parties, separate units of selling employees and nonselling employees (*e. g.,* stock clerks, packers, elevator operators, boiler operators) were held appropriate. *E. g.,* Root Dry Goods Co. (1960). In 1965, the Board reconsidered its reluctance to authorize units smaller than storewide, and found that bargaining patterns and community of interest justified finding separate appropriate units within a single retail department store for selling employees, for nonselling employees, for restaurant workers and for clerical employees. Allied Stores, Inc., d/b/a Stern's Paramus (1965). This willingness to fragment a storewide unit has been judicially approved. Retail Store Union v. NLRB (Saks & Co.) (D.C.Cir. 1967).

Insurance District Offices. The course of unit determinations in the insurance industry parallels that in the retail-store cases. In 1944, the Board held that, in the absence of unusual circumstances, units for insurance agents smaller than statewide in scope should be avoided. Metropolitan Life Ins. Co. (Toledo and Akron) (1944). The Board's expectation was that collective bargaining could be achieved in this industry—where the administrative structure was commonly statewide or multistate/regional—through statewide units. When this expectation failed to bear fruit, the Board saw this long-standing unit presumption as imposing undue obstacles to self-organization, and in 1961 it held presumptively appropriate a unit of insurance agents limited to a single district office. Quaker City Life Ins. Co., *enf'd* (4th Cir. 1963). While some critics have argued that this avowed justification for the endorsement of the single-office unit shows the Board to be relying on extent of union organization in violation of section 9(c)(5), it can probably just as readily be argued that it was the 1944 *Metropolitan Life* decision which relied on extent of organization (then not yet outlawed by the Taft-Hartley Act) and that it was the 1961 *Quaker City* decision which abandoned that as the controlling factor and reinstated once more the conventional and unobjectionable tests for community of interest, such as homogeneous and distinct employee interests, common supervision, geographic proximity, employee interchange and bargaining history. In any event, the Board has since reaffirmed that

> the district office is the insurance industry's analogue of the single manufacturing plant, or the single store of a retail chain. Accordingly, if petitioned for, we will ordinarily find a single district office to be an appropriate unit for insurance agents, and will direct an election in that unit, just as we normally do for a manufacturing plant or a retail store.

Metropolitan Life Ins. Co. (Woonsocket) (1966).

It is arguable that the insurance industry should not be analogized to the retail chain store in view of the characteristically more centralized decisions in an insurance company establishing company-wide uniformity as to such matters as commission rates, quotas, employment benefits, and sales practices and procedures. Nonetheless, while the Board's finding of the appropriateness of the single-office unit has been challenged before the Supreme Court, which reversed and remanded for further articulation of reasons (in order to overcome an inference of controlling weight given to "extent of organization"), Metropolitan Life Ins. Co. v. NLRB (U.S.1965), the single-office presumption appears to have secured judicial support, NLRB v. Western & S. Life Ins. Co. (3d Cir. 1967) (virtually no employee interchange, no overlap of job territories with other offices, no communications with other offices).

What has been far more controversial is the Board's grouping of several district offices into a single unit on the basis of "coherent geographic or administrative considerations." The Board has come under criticism for grouping all offices within a single city or state to the exclusion of one or more offices very close by (but outside the legal boundaries of the city or state) in a metropolitan area, commonly when the metropolitan offices are closer than many of the offices within the unit. Metropolitan Life Ins. Co. (Chicago) (1963). The criticism is intensified when in seemingly indistinguishable situations in other cases, the metropolitan-area offices are grouped in a single unit to the exclusion of other offices within the legal boundaries of the city or state. Metropolitan Life Ins. Co. (Cleveland) (1962). The criticism is intensified yet further when in many cases the Board sustains the unit request made by the petitioning union—often after the union's failure to organize a more comprehensive unit—thus suggesting that the union is seeking a gerrymandered unit and that the Board has made extent of organization surreptitiously controlling. The Board has attempted to justify these groupings and to dispel the apparent inconsistencies. Metropolitan Life Ins. Co. (Woonsocket) (1966). It is difficult indeed to discern any consistent thread in the Board's decisions—other than its conclusions that each of several units may be appropriate and that a petition seeking an election in any one of those units will be granted provided there is no union which is seeking a more comprehensive one.

§ 5. Craft Versus Industrial Units

Section 9(b), as noted already, authorizes the Board to select as an appropriate bargaining unit "the employer unit, craft unit, plant unit, or subdivision thereof." At approximately the same time as the Board announced that a single-plant (or single-office or single-store) unit is presumptively appropriate, as against arguments that it should not be fragmented from a larger multi-plant employee group, it was announcing somewhat the reverse position on craft units. Broadly stated, there is an assumption that the fragmentation, from a larger plantwide grouping, of craft (or departmental) employees is a source of industrial instability and is justified only when those employees have very distinct economic interests which cannot fairly be represented on a larger industrial basis.

Over its history, the Board has taken a number of different positions concerning the respective merits of craft-unit bargaining and industrial-unit bargaining. While this issue is of some significance today, it was of far greater significance in the latter years of the 1930's, when the more established unions affiliated with the American Federation of Labor—organized since the 1880's on a craft basis, rooted in special training and skills (such as electricians, plumbers, patternmakers)—were confronted with claims for plantwide or companywide bargaining for all employees, skilled and unskilled, asserted by the industrial unions affiliated with the newly created Congress of Industrial Organizations. The Board had to resolve these conflicting unit claims in two kinds of representation cases: initial-organization cases, with no existing bargaining or representation pattern; and "craft severance" cases, with bargaining presently conducted on an industrial basis but with a craft union seeking severance and separate bargaining rights.

The Board at first evidenced some preference for the larger industrial unit, although in 1937 it announced its *Globe* doctrine, in Globe Mach. & Stamping Co. (1937), permitting self-determination elections among craft employees in initial-organization cases.   In 1939, the Board announced what became known as the doctrine of American Can Co. to the effect that a craft unit would not be severed if there existed a stable history of bargaining on an industrial basis. In that case, the larger unit had been established one year earlier by formal Board certification, and the union showed that it had provided adequate representation for the craft employees in the unit.   Within five years, the Board announced a "craft identity" exception to *American Can,* in which craft severance would be granted even in the face of a bargaining history on a broader basis provided the craft group was a "true craft" which had maintained its identity as such and had protested inclusion in the larger unit.   General Elec. Co. (1944).   In spite of this exception, the movement toward the Taft-Hartley amendments saw the AFL challenging what it regarded as a too hospitable Board position toward industrial units at the expense of free choice by craftsmen on issues of collective bargaining.

In 1947, Congress enacted section 9(b)(2), forbidding the Board to "decide that any craft unit is inappropriate . . . on the ground that a different unit has been established by a prior Board determination, unless a majority of the employees in the proposed craft unit vote against separate representation."   Although this appeared to constitute a legislative overruling of the *American Can* doctrine, the Board—as soon after as 1948—dismissed a petition for severance of bricklayers from an existing production and maintenance union; it held that section 9(b)(2) prohibited using a prior unit determination as the *sole* basis for disallowing craft severance but that it was still proper to give considerable weight, in addition, to a *history* of successful and stable collective bargaining.   That history, when combined with the high degree of integration of plant processes in the basic steel industry, outweighed the severance claims of the bricklayers. National Tube Co. (1948).   Over the next three years, denials of severance for the same reasons, in the wet milling, lumber and aluminum industries, gave to these industries the name of the *National Tube* industries.   Craft severance was there seen as inimical to the statutory policy of industrial stability, in light of bargaining history and functional integration.

The Board changed its position in 1954 in American Potash & Chem. Corp. (1954), in which it announced: (1) A craft group should not be denied separate representation merely because the industry is characterized by highly integrated production processes and the prevailing pattern of bargaining is industrial in character.   (2) Nonetheless, in the interest of preserving the bargaining patterns now firmly established in the *National Tube* industries, craft severance would continue to be denied in those industries. (3) In other industries, craft employees could opt for severance provided the petitioning union could show that the craft (or departmental) group is "functionally distinct and separate" and that the petitioner is a union "which has traditionally devoted itself to serving the special interest of the employees in question." As such decisions go, *American Potash*—and its strong receptivity toward organization and bargaining along craft lines—exhibited considerable longevity. The doctrine was sustained on judicial review, with the notable exception of NLRB v. Pittsburgh Plate Glass Co. (4th Cir. 1959), which condemned the doctrine as disregardful of the interests of the industrial union, as an abdication to the craft employees of the Board's responsibility to make unit determinations, and as arbitrary in its retention of the *National Tube* doctrine in four industries but in no others (even though equally functionally integrated) and thus also plainly in violation of section 9(b)(2).

The Mallinckrodt Decision. The current disposition of the Board is reflected in its decision in 1966 in Mallinckrodt Chem. Works (1966). In that case—and two others decided the same day, involving both initial organization on a craft basis and craft severance from an existing industrial unit—the Board repudiated the craft-favoring criteria of *American Potash* (as well as that case's automatic negation of craft claims in the four *National Tube* industries). In *Mallinckrodt,* twelve instrument mechanics sought severance from an existing bargaining unit of 280 production and maintenance employees of a company manufacturing uranium metal. The Board found these instrument mechanics to be a "true craft group"—*i. e.,* distinct and homogeneous journeymen, working with apprentices and helpers, and possessing skills acquired after a substantial period of apprenticeship —but nonetheless dismissed the petition for severance. The Board could have justified the dismissal by its finding that the petitioning union did not traditionally represent this craft, the second requirement of *American Potash,* but it chose instead to repudiate *American Potash* for its failure to consider "all relevant factors" and its failure to:

> balance the interest of the employer and the total employee
> complement in maintaining the industrial stability and re
> sulting benefits of an historical plantwide bargaining unit as
> against the interest of a portion of such complement in hav
> ing an opportunity to break away from the historical unit
> by a vote for separate representation.

Among the factors which the Board announced as pertinent to the issue of craft versus industrial bargaining—in cases involving either initial organization or severance—were these: (1) whether the proposed unit consists of a "distinct and homogeneous group of skilled

journeymen craftsmen" or comprise a "functionally distinct department" working at a trade for which there is a tradition of separate
representation;   (2) whether there is a stable history of collective
bargaining in the plant, and at other plants of the employer, and
whether unit fragmentation would unduly disrupt such stability;   (3)
whether, if there has been a broader pattern of bargaining, the craft
or departmental employees have maintained a separate identity, as
well as whether they have participated in maintaining the established
bargaining pattern and have had prior opportunities for separate representation;   (4) the history and pattern of collective bargaining in
the industry involved;   (5) the degree of integration of the employer's production processes and the degree of dependence of normal operations upon the performance of work by the employees seeking separate representation;   (6) the qualifications of the petitioning union,
including its experience in representing employees like those sought
in the proceeding.   Thus, at the same time as the Board was trying
to simplify the task of adjudication by creating a presumption that a
single-store or single-office unit is appropriate, it moved in the opposite direction in *Mallinckrodt* by announcing a multi-factor test in
craft-unit cases, which was to be applied in all industries.   The Board
rested its decision against severance in *Mallinckrodt* on the operational interdependence of instrument mechanics and other production employees, the twenty-five year history of bargaining on a companywide
basis, the adequacy of representation accorded by the incumbent union to the craftsmen, and the importance of labor relations stability
in this national-defense industry.

The Board has, since *Mallinckrodt*, appeared to give greatest
weight to the existence or nonexistence of a history of bargaining on
a basis broader than the craft group.   In two companion cases to
Mallinckrodt—Holmberg, Inc. (1966); E. I. Dupont de Nemours &
Co. (1966)—the employer's production processes were functionally
integrated.   The former case involved craft severance, and the Board
denied the petition, giving primary emphasis (as in *Mallinckrodt* itself) to the integration *and* the long history of bargaining.   The latter case involved a request for bargaining on a craft basis where
there had been no bargaining before, and the Board held that the separate unit would be appropriate, concluding that functional integration alone would not preclude such a unit "unless it results in such a
fusion of functions, skills, and working conditions between those in
the asserted craft group and others outside it as to obliterate any
meaningful lines of separate craft identity."

There are critics of the Board—indeed, critics within the Board,
witness the separate opinions of Member Fanning in all three of the
1966 decisions—who assert that it has made bargaining history conclusive at the expense of legitimate craft interests, and that it has
thus returned to the Board's earliest policies of *American Can* and
National Tube, in effect ignoring section 9(b)(2).   The Board is also

not free from criticism of other features of its craft-severance decisions. For example, it sometimes points to a bargaining history in
which the craft employees have independently and vigorously asserted their own distinct interests within a more comprehensive unit as
evidence in support of craft severance while, in other cases, it finds
such evidence to demonstrate that the incumbent industrial union has
not been unconcerned with the interests of the craftsmen and thus
that severance is unwarranted. Compare Buddy L Corp. (1967),
with Trico Prods. Corp. (1968). On occasion, the Board is also inclined to include in support of a denial of severance observations of
dubious relevance, such as the sharing between craftsmen and industrial employees of such facilities as lockerroom, lunchroom, wash-
room, parking lot and time clock.

In any event, it is not likely that the Board will encounter serious difficulties in sustaining these unit determinations on those rare
occasions when they are brought for judicial review to a federal court
of appeals. The several factors listed in *Mallinckrodt* are clearly consistent with the statutory purpose and with Board unit criteria generally; and the Board's emphasis in particular cases upon bargaining
history—at least when reinforced by other factors pointing toward
the larger unit—does not appear arbitrary or unreasonable, given the
need to balance employee self-determination with the needs of industrial stability. Such stability can be undermined by unit fragmentation, with its attendant frequency of bargaining, escalating demands from one unit to another, and the risk of recurrent disruptions
of production by small employee groups, particularly in functionally
integrated industries. But this stability ought not be regarded by the
Board as worth the price if the concededly special interests of craftsmen are materially ignored by the union which is charged to represent them as part of a more comprehensive unit. *E. g.,* Buddy L
Corp. (1967) (severance of toolmakers permitted, where production
union did not represent them, did not extend last wage increase to
them, did not process grievances for them).

§ 6. Multiemployer Bargaining Units

Much collective bargaining in the United States is conducted on a
multiemployer basis. A number of employers within a single area or
industry may band together to bargain as a group with a single union
which represents employees at all of the companies. This is a common if not dominant bargaining pattern in such industries as clothing, construction, longshore and maritime, trucking and warehousing,
coal mining, wholesale and retail trades and newspaper printing. The
multiemployer pattern may reflect the desire of several small employers who seek greater leverage in dealing with a single common union
(*e. g.,* clothing, trucking, retail stores), or of unions representing employees whose work for any given employer is likely to be short-lived
(*e. g.,* construction and maritime). Such bargaining brings less ex-

pensive, less frequent and more informed negotiations than would obtain on an individual-employer basis, and gives to union and employers the bargaining benefits (or detriments) attendant upon full knowledge and uniformity of the wage rates and working conditions obtaining among all employers in the area or industry. It also has some anticompetitive implications, and creates the risk of a more massive work stoppage in the wake of a bargaining deadlock than would otherwise attend individual-employer bargaining.

Although a very substantial proportion of organized employees in the private sector are covered by multiemployer agreements, the Labor Act says nothing about the multiemployer unit. Indeed, section 9(b) states that "The Board shall decide in each case whether . . . the unit appropriate for the purposes of collective bargaining shall be the employer unit, craft unit, plant unit, or subdivision thereof . . . ." Although multiemployer bargaining antedated the Wagner Act, and that Act explicitly acknowledged no more all-embracing unit than employerwide, the Board early certified multiemployer units as appropriate. Section 2(2) of the Act as then written defined "employer" to include "any person acting in the interest of an employer," and section 2(1) defined "person" to include "associations"; a multiemployer association, acting on behalf of individual employers for collective bargaining, was thus within the definition of "employer" and its employees constituted an appropriate unit. Shipowners' Ass'n (1938). (The Taft-Hartley redefinition of "employer" to include "any person acting as an agent of an employer" works no pertinent change.) Attempts during the formulation of the Taft-Hartley Act of 1947 sharply to limit multiemployer bargaining failed, and this was read by the Supreme Court to represent congressional satisfaction with the Board's prior practice of certifying multiemployer units. NLRB v. Truck Drivers Local 449 (Buffalo Linen) (U.S.1957) (lockout by nonstruck members of multiemployer association).

Formation. The Board does, however, make a concession to the failure of Congress explicitly to authorize it to certify a multiemployer unit. It holds that the employerwide unit is presumptively appropriate, that any larger unit can be justified only if all parties consent or agree to bargain on a multiemployer basis, and that such consent or agreement will normally be demonstrated by a substantial history of collective bargaining on that basis. The Board's rules regarding the formation of multiemployer units have been succinctly summarized in its Twenty-Third Annual Report 36 (1958):

> . . . no controlling weight [is] given to multiemployer bargaining which was preceded by a long history of single-employer bargaining, was of brief duration, did not result in a written contract of substantial duration, and was not based on any Board unit finding.

The existence of a controlling multiemployer bargaining history may also depend on whether the employer group has in fact bargained jointly or on an individual basis. Generally, the Board will find that joint bargaining is established where the employers involved have for a substantial period directly participated in joint bargaining or delegated the power to bind them in collective bargaining to a joint agent, have executed the resulting contract, and have not negotiated on an individual basis. Execution of the contract by each employer separately does not preclude a finding of a multiemployer bargaining history where the employers are clearly shown to have participated in a pattern of joint bargaining.

A multiemployer unit may include only employers who have participated in and are bound by joint negotiations. The mere adoption of a group contract by an employer who has not participated in joint bargaining directly or through an agent, or has indicated his intention not to be bound by future group negotiations, is insufficient to permit his inclusion in a proposed multiemployer unit.

A petition for a single-employer unit, in the face of a multiemployer bargaining history, will be granted if it appears that the employer involved has effectively withdrawn from the multiemployer group and has abandoned group bargaining.

The Board at first held that if any group of a company's employees was certified within a multiemployer unit, that larger unit would be the only appropriate one for all other employee groups within the company. This position was in substance abandoned in Joseph E. Seagram & Sons (1952), in which the Board acknowledged (in the context of multiplant units of a single employer) that this policy imposed unreasonable impediments to organization on a companywide (or smaller) basis. See NLRB v. E–Z Davies Chevrolet (9th Cir. 1968) (single-employer unit appropriate for salesmen in spite of 14-year history of multiemployer bargaining for mechanics). Whether the employer seeks to bargain on a multiemployer basis for all of its employees, or only for some groups within the company, the employer is not free unilaterally to sweep those employees within the multiemployer association but must honor the usual principles of majority employee choice. Thus, in NLRB v. Local 210, Teamsters (Dancker & Sellew, Inc.) (2d Cir. 1964), the employer, which had signed a multiemployer agreement with a union representing its warehouse employees, proceeded to extend a multiemployer agreement with the same union to the employer's sales and office workers, although the union had no support whatever among those latter workers; indeed, they had signed and delivered to the employer a petition stating their opposition to the union. The multiemployer agreement required all the sales and office employees to join the union. The employer was held to violate section 8(a)(1) by coercing employees, 8(a)(2) by favoring a minority union, and 8(a)(3) by executing the union-shop agreement, and the union was held to violate sections 8(b)(1) and (2). (Of course, once a multiemployer unit exists, certain employees doing work closely related to that done by unit employees may be swept into the unit by application of the Board's normal rules of bargaining-unit "accretions." Steamship Trade Ass'n of Baltimore (1965).)

If all of the usual manifestations of consent to multiemployer bargaining are given by a single employer, the appropriateness of that unit will not be undermined by the fact that that employer continues to deal on a limited range of local matters with its own employees who are covered by the multiemployer arrangement. Kroger Co. (1969). Indeed, it has been held that the duty to bargain under section 8(a)(5) may *require* an employer member of a multiemployer unit to engage in local bargaining on uniquely local matters, such as plant rules. NLRB v. Miller Brewing Co. (9th Cir. 1969).

Withdrawal. With the passage of time, a union or a particular company engaged in multiemployer bargaining may find that arrangement uncongenial and may wish to withdraw. Seeking to minimize the uncertainties and disruptions that would be introduced into ongoing bargaining were withdrawals freely permitted, the Board in 1958 abandoned its position that any withdrawal would be upheld if in "good faith" (rather than as a temporary bargaining stratagem) and it announced certain specific guidelines regarding the manner and timing of withdrawal from the multiemployer unit. The leading case is Retail Associates, Inc. (1958), in which the Board held that the announcement of intention to withdraw must be unequivocal and must precede the commencement of negotiations:

> The decision to withdraw must contemplate a sincere abandonment, with relative permanency, of the multiemployer unit and the embracement of a different course of bargaining on an individual-employer basis. .   .   .

> [The Board] would . . . refuse to permit the withdrawal of an employer or a union from a duly established multiemployer bargaining unit, except upon adequate written notice given prior to the date set by the contract for modification, or to the agreed-upon date to begin the multiemployer negotiations. Where actual bargaining negotiations based on the existing multiemployer unit have begun, we would not permit, except on mutual consent, an abandonment of the unit upon which each side has committed itself to the other, absent unusual circumstances.

In effect, the Board created a per se rule, which converted an untimely withdrawal into a refusal to bargain, regardless of the good faith of the party seeking to withdraw from the multiemployer unit. This principle was approved in NLRB v. Sheridan Creations, Inc. (2d Cir. 1966), where the court noted:

> In a case such as this, good faith withdrawal of a small unit might in practice have minimal or no effect. However, the potential for disruption is sufficient to justify the Board in adopting a uniform rule for all cases that withdrawal is not timely once bargaining has begun. We cannot say that no such potential exists, or that its incidence would be so infrequent that the Board's judgment that the uniform rule is needed is without a reasonable foundation or arbitrary in nature.

That case also stands for the proposition that while a timely pre-negotiation withdrawal will be sustained regardless of an employer's reasons (or lack thereof), it is no defense to an untimely withdrawal that the union has no majority among the employees of the particular employer; it is sufficient, in order to raise a continued duty to bargain on a multiemployer basis once negotiations have begun, that the union retains majority support within the overall multiemployer unit.

Even after the Board had held that employers could withdraw from multiemployer bargaining simply by giving timely and unequivocal notice to the union, employer representatives argued that no comparable privilege should be given the union. Two reasons were given to justify greater limitations upon union withdrawal: while employer withdrawal permitted the continuation of multiemployer bargaining among the remaining employers, union withdrawal had the much more disruptive effect of destroying the unit altogether; and union withdrawal typically favored a strong union against the now fragmented weaker employers, while employer withdrawal brought upon the weak employer the hazards of confronting the strong union. The Board, however, rejected such arguments. It concluded that since multiemployer bargaining is rooted in consent, such a unit may be terminated by the union's withdrawal of consent; that Congress did not authorize the Board to consider the relative bargaining strength of the parties in administering the Act, more particularly in determining bargaining units; and that denial of the union's right to withdraw might in fact discourage multiemployer bargaining, since unions might fear becoming locked into what becomes an uncongenial bargaining relationship. Evening News Ass'n (1965), *enf'd* (6th Cir. 1967). This "equal right of withdrawal" doctrine was soon judicially approved. Publishers' Ass'n of New York City v. NLRB (2d Cir. 1966).

The Board has relied on these decisions in order to hold that a union may engage in a "partial withdrawal" from a multiemployer unit, that is, "a union may withdraw from a multiemployer unit with respect to one or more employers while continuing multiemployer bargaining with those employers remaining in the multiple unit." Pacific Coast Ass'n of Pulp & Paper Mfrs. (1967). The Board reasoned that this would ameliorate the union's fear of being "locked into" the unit, would permit withdrawal without destroying the entire unit, and would hold open the prospect of the employees of the now separated employer working out their local problems and returning to the unit. Moreover, the employers remaining in the unit which the union has "partially" left cannot complain, since they too are free to withdraw after the union's withdrawal. The Board did, however, limit the right of partial withdrawal by holding that neither the union nor any employer could withdraw selectively with respect to some of the employer's plants (or employees) but not others; to try to take some but not all of a company's employees out of an established multiemployer unit is thought to interfere unduly with the Board's authority to make unit determinations.

The Board will permit withdrawal from a multiemployer unit even after negotiations have begun, if the other party consents. Although a failure to protest the withdrawal is not normally sufficient, it is a nice factual issue as to what further conduct will be deemed by Board or court to manifest consent. See Fairmont Foods Co., *enf't denied* (8th Cir. 1972). Untimely withdrawal may also be excused if there are "unusual circumstances." The Board has recently sharply limited the latter exception to "cases in which the withdrawing employer has been faced with *dire* economic circumstances, *i. e.,* circumstances in which the very existence of an employer as a viable business entity has ceased or is about to cease." Hi-Way Billboards, Inc. (1973), *enf't denied* (5th Cir. 1974). In that case, the Board cited earlier decisions in which one of the following circumstances was held to justify an otherwise untimely withdrawal: the employer was undergoing an arrangement under the bankruptcy laws; the employer was confronted with the imminent prospect of a plant closing; the employer was likely to go out of business for lack of qualified employees and lack of union cooperation in securing replacements. It had earlier been held not sufficient to justify withdrawal after the beginning of negotiations that the employer was suffering a sharp decline in business, or was being subjected to a strike, or had been suspended from the multiemployer association for failure to pay dues, or no longer had employees who supported the union, or could foresee that the terms of the multiemployer contract would be unusually onerous. On the important question whether a bargaining impasse is in itself sufficient to warrant withdrawal in the midst of negotiations, the Board and the courts have parted company. At least two courts of appeals have concluded that an employer should have the privilege to withdraw on impasse, in part in order to facilitate the breaking of the impasse. Fairmont Foods Co. v. NLRB (8th Cir. 1972) (court holds that impasse justifies employer withdrawal, and concludes that record fails to support Board conclusion that impasse had not been reached); NLRB v. Hi-Way Billboards, Inc. (5th Cir. 1974). In the last cited case, the Board had concluded that an impasse is a common and expectable occurrence in collective bargaining, and that it would destroy multiemployer bargaining if employers, dissatisfied with the contract that is taking shape, were free to withdraw from the multiemployer unit and commence bargaining on an individual basis.

CHAPTER VI

SECURING BARGAINING RIGHTS THROUGH UNFAIR LABOR PRACTICE PROCEEDINGS

§ 1. Introduction

In the vast majority of instances, unions demonstrate majority support and are recognized as bargaining representative either informally with the employer's consent or through NLRB election and certification. In some instances, however, the union may use the unfair labor practice machinery of the Board in order to prove that it has majority backing and to secure an order against the employer requiring it to bargain. This might be attempted in three different cases: (1) When employer unfair labor practices render it unlikely that an uncoerced election can be held and bargaining rights are secured instead by a Board bargaining order designed to remedy the employer violations; (2) When the union clearly demonstrates its majority support by some means other than an election, and the employer repudiates this clear demonstration and refuses to bargain; (3) When the union has already been representing the employees but changing circumstances give rise to a good-faith doubt by the employer that the union continues to represent a majority of employees in an appropriate bargaining unit. These cases will be discussed in sequence.

§ 2. The Bargaining Order as a Remedy for Employer Coercion: the *Gissel* Decision

Cases frequently arise in which a union gathers, from a majority of employees in the bargaining unit, authorization or designation cards naming that union as exclusive bargaining representative. Although these cards are commonly used to make a "showing of interest" to the NLRB in support of a petition for a representation election, they may also be shown to the employer directly in order to demonstrate majority support and thus to induce the employer to bargain. In many instances, the employer will reject the union's request for recognition and will take steps—often in violation of law—to undermine the union's support. In a leading decision that set the guidelines for roughly fifteen years, the Board with court approval held that the employer could lawfully reject a "card showing" (or other clear evidence of majority support, such as union membership rolls) only if it doubted in good faith that the union did in fact possess uncoerced majority support within an appropriate bargaining unit. If, however, the employer's refusal to recognize was in order to buy time to undermine the union's majority, this was a violation of the duty to bargain under section 8(a)(5), which the Board could remedy by issuing an order to bargain. Joy Silk Mills, Inc. v. NLRB (D.C.Cir. 1950). Under the *Joy Silk Mills* rule, employer violations committed after the refusal to recognize—typically coercive surveillance, discharges, interrogation or threats—were held to demonstrate bad faith; the bargaining order was viewed as a remedy not for the violations of sections 8(a)(1) and (3) but rather for the bargaining violation under section 8(a)(5). In the mid-1960's, the Board moved away somewhat from *Joy Silk Mills,* suggesting both that an employer's distrust of the inherent validity of authorization cards might furnish a legitimate basis for refusing to recognize the union, and that a bargaining order would issue only when employer acts of coercion were rather serious.

A major reformulation of the law was made by the Supreme Court in NLRB v. Gissel Packing Co. (U.S.1969). There, the Court consolidated four cases having in common a union showing of majority support based on authorization cards, a refusal by the employer to recognize the union, and a number of subsequent acts of employer coercion; in one of the cases the union never petitioned for an election, in another the union petitioned but the election was stayed because of the employer violations, and in two others an election was held which the union lost and sought to set aside. The Court explicitly reserved the question whether the employer has an automatic duty to recognize the union on the basis of a card majority and limited its consideration to cases in which the refusal to recognize is followed by "independent unfair labor practices which tend to preclude the holding of a fair election." The Court held, first, that the duty to bargain can arise not only when the union wins a Board-certified election but in some instances when the union has other "convincing evidence of majority support" (giving as examples a union-called strike or strike vote or possession of authorization cards from a majority of employees in the bargaining unit). The Court relied on section 9(a) of the Labor Act which gives exclusive representation status to the union "designated or selected" by a majority, unaccompanied by a limitation on the manner of designation or selection, and by legislative history to the Taft-Hartley Act of 1947 which showed that Congress rejected a proposal that the duty to bargain under section 8(a)(5) be limited to unions which won a Board-certified election.

The Court then addressed the question whether authorization cards are indeed sufficiently reliable indicators of majority support for the union. It held that in spite of the "acknowledged superiority of the election process," cards may become a yet more reliable indicator of employee preferences when employer unfair labor practices so disrupt the election process as to make a future fair election impossible or a recent past election invalid. "[W]here an employer engages in conduct disruptive of the election process, cards may be the most effective—perhaps the only—way of assuring employee choice." Of course, the relative reliability of cards and an election will be affected if the employer can show that the cards were gathered by the union under threats of harm to the signing employees or were gathered by misrepresentations as to the purpose of the cards. For example, an authorization card may on its face authorize only a request for an election, the signer obviously reserving the right to vote by secret ballot either for or against the union; this is not tantamount to a designation of the union as exclusive bargaining representative. When, however, the card on its face explicitly and solely so designates the union, an employee signature on that card will count toward a valid union majority, and will not be undermined by statements made by the card solicitor that the card will no doubt be used if the union wishes to secure an election; only if the solicitor clearly states that the *sole* purpose of the card is to precipitate an election will this representation overcome the designation of the union on the face of the card. The Court thus endorsed the position of the Board in Cumberland Shoe Corp. (1963), *enf'd* (6th Cir. 1965), which forbade the counting of designation cards toward a union majority in an unfair labor practice case "where union organizers solicit cards on the explicit or indirectly expressed representation that they will use such cards *only* for an election .   .   . ." The Court in *Gissel* upheld the findings of the Board that the representations made there by union organizers fell just barely within the protection of the *Cumberland Shoe* doctrine.

After thus finding that the authorization cards were validly gathered and that they could therefore serve as the basis of a duty to bargain if employer unfair labor practices were so serious as to render a free election improbable, the Court turned to the propriety of a bargaining order as a remedy in the cases at hand. The Court held that a cease and desist order would frequently be inadequate to remedy employer coercion and that a bargaining order might be necessary "to re-establish the conditions as they existed before the employer's unlawful campaign," those conditions including a majority designation of the union as reflected in authorization cards. The Court outlined three kinds of cases in which the Board could consider the issuance of a bargaining order as a remedy. Such an order could surely issue in the "exceptional" case of "outrageous" and "pervasive" unfair labor practices; the Court appeared to suggest that it would not be necessary in such cases to inquire into majority status of the union on the basis of cards. The Board could also use the bargaining order

> in less extraordinary cases marked by less pervasive practices which nonetheless still have the tendency to undermine majority strength and impede the election processes. The Board's authority to issue such an order on a lesser showing of employer misconduct is appropriate, we should reemphasize, where there is also a showing that at one point the union had a majority; in such a case, of course, effectuating ascertainable employee free choice becomes as important a goal as deterring employer misbehaviour. .   .   .   If the Board finds that the possibility of erasing the effects of past

practices and of ensuring a fair election (or a fair rerun) by the use of traditional remedies, though present, is slight and that employee sentiment once expressed through cards would, on balance, be better protected by a bargaining order, then such an order should issue.

The third category of cases, that of minor or less extensive unfair labor practices, involves only slight impact on the election machinery and will not warrant a bargaining order.

In cases, then, in which the employer commits unfair labor practices which interfere with or restrain the exercise of protected employee rights, the Board has the power to order the employer to bargain with a union as a remedy for those unfair labor practices. This is surely true if the union offers clear evidence that it had majority support prior to the employer's wrongdoing, and is arguably true even if it did not, provided the unfair labor practices are sufficiently severe and lasting. Since the bargaining order serves to remedy employer coercion under sections 8(a)(1) and (3), it is not necessary that the employer have been found independently to violate section 8(a)(5) by rejecting a formal union demand for recognition; it is not even necessary that the complaint against the company contain an allegation that section 8(a)(5) was violated. Walgreen Co. v. NLRB (7th Cir. 1975). Thus, no longer do the employer's unfair labor practices serve the incidental purpose of reflecting on its state of mind in establishing a refusal to bargain "in good faith" under section 8(a)(5). The Court in *Gissel* viewed its decision as reinforcing the Board's developing policy of avoiding any inquiry into the employer's state of mind at the time of its refusal to recognize and as making the central issue the Board's judgment as to the relative reliability of the secret-ballot election and the union-gathered authorization cards.

The Supreme Court in *Gissel* made it clear that it was the task primarily of the Board, and not of the courts, to determine which of the three categories of severity embraced the employer's coercive and discriminatory conduct and whether a bargaining order would better protect the interests of employees than would an election:

> It is for the Board and not the courts . . . to make that determination, based on its expert estimate as to the effects on the election process of unfair labor practices of varying intensity. In fashioning its remedies . . . the Board draws on a fund of knowledge and expertise all its own, and its choice of remedy must therefore be given special respect by reviewing courts.

While the Board's case-by-case categorizations have generally been endorsed by the courts of appeals, a number of appellate decisions (to be discussed more fully below) have taken the Board to task for failure responsibly to exercise its discretion under the principles announced in *Gissel*.

§ 3. Implementation of the *Gissel* Decision

It has rarely mattered whether the Board characterizes a case as within "category one," the outrageous or pervasive violation, or "category two," the less serious violation which is nonetheless sufficiently coercive of employee freedom as to warrant doubt of the validity of an election. In either case, the Board is empowered to remedy the violation by issuing a bargaining order. One major difference between the two categories, however, lies in the suggestion of the Court in *Gissel* that the Board may issue a bargaining order in the "category one" cases even in the absence of any demonstration that the union at one time had majority support which was dissipated by the employer's coercion. Interestingly, the Board appears unwilling to concede that it can issue a bargaining order in the absence of proof of an earlier majority, even when the employer's violations have been outrageous and pervasive, Loray Corp. (1970), while at least one court has stated that the Board does have this power. In J. P. Stevens & Co., Gulistan Div. v. NLRB (5th Cir. 1971), in which both Board and court characterized the employer's violations—threats of discharge and plant closing, surveillance and interrogation, promises and grants of benefits, promulgation of an unlawful no-solicitation rule, discriminatory discharges and refusals to hire—as "extraordinary," "egregious," "pervasive" and "outrageous," the court in an alternative holding stated that the Board could issue a bargaining order even if there had been no proof of union majority before the employer's unlawful campaign; the court proceeded, however, to sustain the Board's finding that the union did in fact have such a majority. In another case, in which the Board found that the union had majority support and that the employer had committed "outrageous and pervasive" unfair labor practices, it issued a bargaining order even in the face of record evidence demonstrating that a valid election was possible; but the Board was reversed on appeal. In view of the finding of the administrative law judge that a fair election could be held after the issuance of an order to cease and desist and to post notices, the court concluded that the "pattern does not meet the definition of a first category case" and that a bargaining order thus "becomes punitive, rather than remedial." NLRB v. Gibson Prods. Co. (5th Cir. 1974).

At the other end of the spectrum of employer coercion, the Board has found a number of cases to fall within "category three" in *Gissel* and not to justify the imposition of a bargaining order. Such an order would without warrant interfere with the wishes of a majority of employees in the bargaining unit whose uncoerced preferences can be validly tested in a secret-ballot election held after the issuance of conventional Board remedies. Examples of cases in which bargaining orders have been denied are NLRB v. Gruber's Super Market, Inc. (7th Cir. 1974), where the evidence showed only one borderline unfair labor practice, a unilateral wage increase, and no evidence of antiunion bias; and Poughkeepsie Newspapers, Inc. (1969), where the employer's unfair labor practices were directed at only a few employees in a large unit and were not pervasive enough to interfere with the holding of a fair rerun election. The Board has also taken into account voluntary restorative action by the employer to help dissipate any coercive impact of earlier action. Central Soya of Canton, Inc., *enf'd per curiam* (5th Cir. 1970) (employer voluntarily rescinded its unlawful rule prohibiting the wearing of union badges and reinstated with backpay employees suspended for violating the rule). But the Board has even placed in "category three" a number of cases in which the employer violations were arguably rather severe—and at least as severe as in other cases which the Board assigned to "category two" and in which bargaining orders were issued. Thus, in Stoutco, Inc. (1969), no bargaining order was issued although the employer threatened to eliminate existing benefits, to impose harsher working conditions and to close the plant, made promises of benefits, engaged in unlawful interrogations and "suggested" that a union activist quit. In Schrementi Bros. (1969), the employer made threats to and induced physical assaults upon union organizers in the presence of employees, threatened loss of existing benefits, and threatened surveillance. And in Hennessy Serv. Corp. (1973), the employer engaged in coercive interrogation, forbade talk about the union, promised benefits, created the impression of surveillance and warned that the selection of the union would be futile.

In most of the cases decided by the Board prior to *Gissel* and subsequently remanded, as well as cases decided after *Gissel*, the Board has contented itself with a recounting of the employer violations and a rather sketchy or conclusory finding on the question whether they were severe enough so as likely to preclude a fair election. Although most court decisions have endorsed the Board's conclusions as supported by the record, many decisions—rendered by a broad cross-section of courts of appeals—have criticized the Board for allegedly perfunctory performance of its responsibilities in these *Gissel*-type cases. One court has invited the Board to articulate its position on bargaining orders through one of three methods (in descending order of desirability). First, the Board could use its rulemaking power to hold hearings and to formulate general principles as to the kinds of employer coercion that would most commonly lead to bargaining orders and those that would normally be curable through milder remedies. Second, the entire membership of the Board could attempt to announce such general principles in the context of a particular unfair labor practice case. Third, the Board could explain fully in each case "just what it considers to have precluded a fair election and why, and in what respects the case differs from others where it has reached an opposite conclusion." NLRB v. General Stencils, Inc. (2d Cir. 1971).

On remand, in General Stencils, Inc. (1972), the Board eschewed any general rules, particularly rules which would declare that a specified employer violation would in all cases lead (or not) to a bargaining order; it found instead that a threat of plant closing and job loss in the context of the case would clearly interfere with employee freedom, would surely be spread among the plant employees, and would not be curable by conventional Board remedies. One Board member attempted in dissent to formulate working guidelines. He suggested that two forms of conduct should be treated as sufficient per se to justify imposition of a bargaining order: the grant of significant benefits during an organizing campaign (since the usual Board order does not require rescission of the grant), and a pattern of violations of section 8(a)(3) through discriminatory discharge, demotion or reassignment of union adherents (since reinstatement and backpay come long after the event, and the effects of the discrimination are unlikely ever to be undone). These per se cases involve employer action, rather than mere words, and thus demonstrate clear employer intention to punish union adherents unlawfully. The dissenting member went on to suggest that the impact on employees is more speculative when what is unlawful is the employer's words rather than its actions. When the wrongful conduct is employer threats (or interrogation or promises of benefit or "isolated" section 8(a)(3) conduct rather than a pattern), he suggested that one must consider: (a) the actions threatened (with plant closing being a threat of gravest consequence, much more so than threatened strict adherence to work rules); (b) whether the threats would be seriously regarded (with attention given to the position of the person uttering the threats, the deliberate or casual nature with which they were uttered, and their specificity); and (c) how widely the threats were disseminated (with the burden cast upon the General Counsel to prove dissemination rather than upon the company to prove absence of dissemination). On review, the court of appeals (2d Cir. 1972) lauded this attempt to provide guidelines for bargaining-order cases and refused to enforce the Board's bargaining order for lack of record support on such issues as dissemination and employee fear; a dissenting judge took the court to task for substituting its own judgment for the knowledge and expertise of the Board, contrary to the mandate of the Supreme Court in *Gissel.*

The Board continues to insist that the issuance of bargaining orders for violations of sections 8(a)(1) and (3) does not lend itself to per se rules or even to rather generalized guidelines. Indeed, the Board has explicitly rejected the distinction between employer action and employer speech as an indicator of the need for a bargaining order, particularly when the "speech" is a threat to close the plant. Lawrence Rigging, Inc. (1973). The Board found support in a court of appeals opinion which appeared to discredit any investigation, in determining whether to issue a bargaining order, into whether threats were made by low-level rather than high-level supervisory employees. NLRB v. Kaiser Agric. Chems. (5th Cir. 1973).

Most courts of appeals have faulted the Board not so much for its failure to articulate universal guidelines but for its failure, even on a case-by-case basis, to give detailed reasons why the employer conduct could not be cured by conventional remedies and a secret-ballot election conducted. The Board has also frequently been taken to task for failing to distinguish other decisions which would appear to dictate a result contrary to that actually reached. Some courts have indeed been quite open in chastising the Board; that is particularly true when a court had heard the same case months and sometimes years earlier and had remanded to the Board expressly in order to have the benefit of Board findings and reasons. In NLRB v. American Cable Systems, Inc. (5th Cir. 1970), the court expressed dissatisfaction with the Board's action on remand:

> The response which we received was a litany, reciting conclusions by rote without factual explication. We believe that the questions involved in this area of labor law are far too important for such formalistic and perfunctory treatment. Since *Gissel* teaches us that authorization cards are not as trustworthy as ballots all concerned must be particularly careful lest the principles of majoritarianism in union representation be unnecessarily frustrated by the cavalier use of bargaining orders.

(This very concern for the possible subordination of majority preferences when a bargaining order issues has moved some courts which have enforced such an order to include within it an explicit reminder to employees that they are entitled to petition for an election to decertify their bargaining representative within a reasonable time. NLRB v. Drives, Inc. (7th Cir. 1971).)

Some courts have manifested their impatience with sparely reasoned Board decisions not simply by reversing and remanding, but— in the face of the Supreme Court's declaration that it is principally for the Board to determine whether to issue a bargaining order —by overturning the Board's decision and making an independent determination of the impact of the employer's coercion and the likelihood of a free election. The courts, in screening the records for themselves, have noted the inefficiency and the administrative and judicial burden of remand. Most of these courts have reached a conclusion different from that of the Board and have refused to enforce the bargaining order. *E. g.,* Peerless of America, Inc. v. NLRB (7th Cir. 1973). Other courts, after an independent analysis, have enforced the Board's bargaining order. Walgreen Co. v. NLRB (7th Cir. 1975) (court agreed with Board's assessment that employer coercion was "pervasive"). The courts which have refused to remand usually note that years have gone by since the employer had violated the law, and that a very substantial risk thus exists that an unwanted union will be the beneficiary of the bargaining order, long after the coercive impact of the employer violations has been dissipated and the composition of the labor force changed.

Similar concerns have moved some courts of appeals to hold that should the Board be confronted on remand with determining whether to issue a bargaining order for violations of sections 8(a)(1) and (3), the Board must consider the dynamics of the plant as of the time of the remand and not as of the time of the original order recommended by the administrative law judge or issued by the Board. In NLRB v. American Cable Systems, Inc. (5th Cir. 1970), the Board in the course of a remand in late 1969 endorsed its bargaining order issued earlier to remedy the company's 1965 violations, and excluded evidence both of a complete turnover of employees since that time and of the departure of the only management official involved in the unfair labor practices. The court reprimanded the Board for not following the declaration of the Supreme Court in *Gissel* that a judgment as to the likely fairness of an election must be made as of the time the Board issues its order:

> [O]n remand the Board refused to look at the contemporary necessity for such an order, satisfying itself with a jejune regurgitation of the Company's 1965 waywardness. We deem such findings insufficient under the teachings of *Gissel* to justify a 1970 bargaining order. *Gissel* does not apply a nunc pro tunc principle, giving the then sins of the Company a now application.

Other decisions have equivocated, suggesting that the Board should open the record to investigate employee turnover and the departure of culpable personnel in cases where the finding that no fair election could be held was "marginal," NLRB v. General Stencils, Inc. (2d Cir. 1972); or in cases where these factual issues can be disposed of expeditiously, General Steel Prods., Inc. v. NLRB (4th Cir. 1971) (concurring opinion).

In any event, the Board rejects the position that it must reopen on remand the question whether a fair election could be held at that time rather than as of the time the Board originally issued its bargaining order. Gibson Prods. Co (1972), *enf't denied* (5th Cir. 1974) (Board holds that it will look to the time when employer violations occur, in determining whether to issue bargaining order). Most of the courts of appeals appear to agree with the Board. Perhaps the leading authority is NLRB v. L. B. Foster Co. (9th Cir. 1969), in which the employer argued that the passing of three years and the turnover of personnel since a 3–2 union election defeat warranted the court's refusal to enforce a bargaining order, but the court held that the determination of the likelihood of a fair election is to be made as of the time the Board issues its order and not the time at which the court enforces it:

> [T]o deny enforcement, with or without remand for reconsideration on the basis of facts occurring after the Board's decision, is to put a premium upon continued litigation by the employer; it can hope that the resulting delay will produce a new set of facts, as to which the Board must then readjudicate.
>
> .   .   .
>
> Emphasis is given to the rapid turnover in the employer's personnel as a reason for not enforcing the order. But we think that this is a reason to enforce. Otherwise there will be an added inducement to the employer to indulge in unfair practices in order to defeat the union in an election. He will have as an ally, in addition to the attrition of union support inevitably springing from delay in accomplishing results, the fact that turnover itself will help him, so that the longer he can hold out the better his chances of victory will be.

See generally General Steel Prods., Inc. v. NLRB (4th Cir. 1971) (one judge holding that validity of order is to be tested at time of remand, one judge stating that ordinarily validity is tested at time of Board order, one judge stating that validity is tested as of time of employer unfair labor practices).

When the Board does make an initial determination as to whether employer coercion has so influenced employees that an election will be an invalid test of employee preferences, it is free to look to events that transpire after the employer's coercive conduct has occurred. Thus, in Arbie Mineral Feed Co. v. NLRB (8th Cir. 1971), the employer engaged in interrogation and threats and discriminatorily discharged an employee; thereafter, the union secured the bulk of its authorization cards to demonstrate its majority within the bargaining unit. The court endorsed the Board's findings of section 8(a)(1) and (3) violations, but refused to enforce its bargaining order, since the record demonstrated that the coercive actions did not undermine the union's majority and that a fair election was thus possible.

Another difficulty concerning the timeliness of the bargaining order has caused the Board to reassess its position as to the need to find a section 8(a)(5) violation in order to warrant issuing such an order. Although the Supreme Court in *Gissel* had sustained the Board's findings of section 8(a)(5) violations, it appears clear that the Court's justification for sustaining the remedy of a bargaining order was rooted not so much in the employer's technical refusal to bargain but rather in employer coercion and discrimination, which rendered the authorization cards a more reliable indicator of employee desires than an election would be. For this reason, a divided Board held, in Steel-Fab, Inc. (1974), that the Board could issue a bargaining order as a remedy in cases of section 8(a)(1) and (3) violations, even if no violation of section 8(a)(5) was alleged or proved. The Board majority assumed this to mean that such a bargaining order was to take effect only from the date of the Board's decision, as a cure for employer wrongdoing of (typically) many months before. Two dissenting Board members argued that section 8(a)(5) is also violated in the *Gissel*-type case, for the employer's coercion and discrimination ousts the union of the representative status to which it was entitled at the time of the employer's wrongdoing. For the dissenters, the function of the bargaining order is not merely to shape the conduct of the employer *in futuro* but also to restore the union to its rightful position as employee representative as of some date in the past.

This distinction was more than abstract philosophizing, for the application of one theory or the other would determine whether—in the event the employer took "unilateral action" after engaging in coercion or discrimination such as by withholding a bonus or granting a pay increase—such unilateral action was itself an attack on the union's rightful status and thus independently subject to remedy (for example, by repaying employees for benefits improperly withheld without first bargaining with the union). The position of the Board majority in *Steel-Fab* would have permitted the employer, after engaging in wrongdoing, to be free thereafter not to deal with the union, until the Board entered a bargaining order. Because the Board soon perceived that this would not restore the employees' representation rights to what they would have been had the employer acted lawfully and permitted a fair election to be conducted, the Board abandoned its position in *Steel-Fab,* and announced a new principle soon after in Trading Port, Inc. (1975):

> We find that an employer's obligation under a bargaining order remedy should commence as of the time the employer has embarked on a clear course of unlawful conduct or has engaged in sufficient unfair labor practices to undermine the union's majority status. . . . An employer . . . has a right to an election so long as he does not fatally impede the election process. Once he has so impeded the process, he has forfeited his right to a Board election, and must bargain with the union on the basis of other clear indications of employees' desires. It is at that point, we believe, the employer's unlawful refusal to bargain has taken place.

The Board found that refusing to bargain while at the same time acting to undermine the union's majority was a violation of section 8(a)(5), sufficient to warrant giving its bargaining order retroactive effect. The Board also concluded that certain employer acts in derogation of the union's representative status (*e. g.,* eliminating jobs without bargaining with the union), committed after its acts of coercion and prior to the Board proceeding, violated section 8(a)(5).

It is not clear whether the Board's rationale in *Trading Port* requires—in order to make out a section 8(a)(5) violation—that the union (as in that case) actually have made a demand for recognition, or whether it is enough to show a past majority that was undermined by employer coercion. In any event, it appears as though the employer's violation of section 8(a)(1) or 8(a)(3) is still at the heart of the Board's "retroactive" remedial order, and that the label of a section 8(a)(5) violation is less a matter of substance than of analytical symmetry.

Two other noteworthy issues have been generated by the Board's authority to issue bargaining orders to remedy employer coercion. In Donovan v. NLRB (2d Cir. 1975), the court held that the Board was authorized to issue such a bargaining order, even though the union which would benefit from the order was responsible for serious misconduct during a strike and picketing that had been generated by the employer's actions. There, the employer rejected a union request for recognition (which was backed by a card majority) and threatened and effected discharges of union supporters, interrogated employees, solicited grievances and withheld an anticipated wage increase. During a strike sponsored by the union, employees engaged in mass picketing, threats, assault and property damage. When the strike ended, the employer continued to engage in unlawful activity. The court held that the employer's conduct had indeed destroyed the possibility of a fair election, and that the Board had the discretion to remedy such wrongdoing by issuing a bargaining order, in spite of some picket-line violence. It was for the Board to weigh the gravity of the union's misconduct against the effect of the employer violations. The same court of appeals has also upheld the power of a district court to issue a temporary bargaining order, pending the Board's conclusion of an unfair labor practice hearing involving serious employer coercion. In Seeler v. Trading Port, Inc. (2d Cir. 1975), a union which lost an election after the employer had engaged in conduct allegedly in violation of sections 8(a)(1) and (3) filed unfair labor practice charges, and during the hearing before the administrative law judge, the regional director petitioned for temporary relief pursuant to section 10(j). The court of appeals—finding cause to believe that the employer had indeed violated the Act—affirmed the temporary cease-and-desist order issued by the district court against coercive activity; it also held, reversing the district court, that in appropriate circumstances (as these were) an order to the employer to bargain with the union during the Board proceedings would be "just and proper" relief under the Act, in order to preserve the viability of the union and its rights as they would have been had the employer not acted illegally.

§ 4.   Duty to Bargain Upon Showing of Majority Support

Under the principles announced by the Board and affirmed by the court in Joy Silk Mills, Inc. v. NLRB (D.C.Cir. 1950), the employer could justify refusing to bargain with a union which demonstrated its majority status by valid authorization cards only if it had a "good faith doubt" that the union had majority support. The burden would be upon the employer in the section 8(a)(5) proceeding to demonstrate that it had such a doubt, and this might be done, for example, by showing that contemporaneous with the collection of cards, the employees had unanimously presented the employer with a petition repudiating the union or had refused to participate in a union-called strike. It was typically not a defense that the employer had a generalized distrust of the validity of authorization cards and certainly not a defense that the employer, although conceding the union's majority, wished to have some time in which to communicate to the employees without coercion the arguments against unionization. Thus, even though section 8(a)(5) findings and bargaining orders were usually accompanied by findings of violation of sections 8(a)(1) and (3)—with the latter violations demonstrating the employer's bad faith—there were a number of cases in which a bargaining order issued as a remedy when the only violation was of section 8(a)(5). The employer could not lawfully refuse to honor a card majority simply because it wanted the union to demonstrate its majority through the "preferred" method of a Board-conducted election. After some fifteen years of operating under this *Joy Silk Mills* doctrine, the Board staged a gradual retreat, placing greater emphasis upon proof of majority through elections rather than through unfair labor practice proceedings under section 8(a)(5) and less emphasis upon the employer's subjective appraisal of the union's status at the time of the card showing.

In 1972, the Board announced a position which in effect permitted the employer whenever confronted with a card majority and a demand for recognition to refuse that demand and to force the union, as a condition to securing bargaining rights, to demonstrate majority support in a secret-ballot election. This would not violate section 8(a)(5) and—assuming the employer engaged in no coercive conduct in violation of section 8(a)(1) or (3)—the union would thus not be able to use unfair labor practice proceedings to demonstrate that when it demanded recognition it did indeed have majority support within the bargaining unit. Should the employer refuse recognition, the union's recourse would be to invoke the Board's election procedures to demonstrate its majority in unequivocal fashion in the immediate future, rather than to file a section 8(a)(5) charge, litigate on the basis of authorization cards (or other equivocal evidence) its status as of some date in the past, and possibly delay a final disposition until many months after the event. This new Board position was endorsed by the Supreme Court in Linden Lumber Div., Summer

& Co. v. NLRB (U.S.1974). The Court held that since employers as a general matter may properly be suspicious of union-gathered authorization cards, and even more so of apparent majority employee support for a strike (which may be generated principally by fear of or sympathy for the strikers and not by support for the union), the Board was entitled to fashion a rule of law which would relieve it of the need to examine employer state of mind. The Court agreed with the Board that industrial peace would be fostered through the expeditious settling of representation claims through elections rather than through unfair labor practice proceedings under section 8(a)(5). The Court also agreed that the employer, after refusing to recognize the union, was not obliged to petition for an election in order to shelter its refusal; it could properly place the onus on the union. The Court majority paid scant attention to the arguments of the four dissenting Justices that section 9(a) gives bargaining rights to unions when "designated or selected" (and not necessarily elected formally) by a majority of employees, that Congress in 1947 refused to limit the employer's duty to bargain under section 8(a)(5) to certified unions, and that precedents of long standing support the principle that the employer is obligated to bargain whenever the union presents "convincing evidence of majority support."

The Board has countenanced at least one exception to its rule that the employer may reject a card majority, and that is when the employer has actually agreed to abide by a union demonstration of majority status—typically by authorization cards—other than by an election. If, for example, the employer agrees that it will recognize the union if it is shown to have majority support through an independent employer poll, or in a poll conducted by a mutually selected third person, and the employer then repudiates that agreement before it is implemented, or rejects a union victory reflected in such a poll, the Board will find a violation of section 8(a)(5). This doctrine, announced in Snow & Sons (1961), *enf'd* (9th Cir. 1962), was explicitly left unconsidered by the Supreme Court in *Linden Lumber,* and the Board has reaffirmed it since, in Harding Glass Indus. (1975) (employer agreed to have a priest verify the signatures on the authorization cards, but rejected the results; employer "had no basis for reasonably doubting the union's majority status and accordingly was obligated to recognize the union."). Presumably, employers will be discouraged by this doctrine from taking their own polls of union sentiment among the employees or from expressly conceding that the union does indeed have majority support. It is not altogether clear why this vestige of the "good faith doubt" requirement survives, and its breadth and longevity are themselves subject to some doubt.

In the absence of employer coercion and discrimination which itself justifies the issuance of a bargaining order, it appears as though very few bargaining orders will issue for an independent violation of section 8(a)(5). The Court has emphasized its preference for a secret-ballot election rather than authorization cards or strike support to show employee preferences on collective bargaining. If a union's card showing is rejected by the employer under circumstances which the union believes might give rise to a meritorious charge under section 8(a)(5), it may thus be reluctant to process its majority claim in that forum only and may seek simultaneously to petition the Board to conduct a representation election. The Board has changed its position a number of times on the question whether the union's petition is tantamount to an election of remedies, or waiver, which disables it in the event it loses the election from seeking bargaining rights in a section 8(a)(5) proceeding. The Board's present position, announced in Bernel Foam Prods. Co. (1964) (expressly overruling Aiello Dairy Farms Co. (1954)), is that the union may without inconsistency pursue its claim to recognition through both election proceedings and section 8(a)(5) proceedings. In *Bernel Foam,* the Board overturned the union's election loss because the employer had made illegal promises of benefit and illegally induced employees to repudiate the union; it found the employer's refusal to bargain to violate section 8(a)(5) and ordered the employer to bargain. The Supreme Court in NLRB v. Gissel Packing Co. (U.S.1969), sustained the Board's power to issue a bargaining order (for violations of sections 8(a)(1) and (3)) even after the union had gone to an election and lost. The Court made reference to the *Bernal Foam* doctrine, but without expressly either endorsing or criticizing it.

It is not likely that the *Bernel Foam* doctrine—permitting a union to secure a bargaining order under section 8(a)(5) after losing an election—will be of great significance in the future. If the employer has engaged in coercive conduct, *Gissel* permits such a post-election bargaining order regardless of whether the employer has also violated section 8(a)(5). And, even though the employer has committed a violation of section 8(a)(5) alone (for example, by refusing to abide by the results of its own poll showing a union majority), the Board has held that if the union goes to an election and its election loss is not set aside after the filing of objections, no bargaining order will issue as a remedy in the section 8(a)(5) case. Irving Air Chute Co. (1964), *enf'd* (2d Cir. 1965). In most cases then, the employer who does nothing to disturb the election "laboratory conditions" after refusing the union's claim for recognition can be confident that, if the union proceeds with an election, the results will be binding on the union, regardless of any technical violation of section 8(a)(5). The Board has, however, noted that if a union election victory is set aside on the initiative of the employer—for example, because the bargaining unit is inappropriate or ineligible employees were allowed to vote —a bargaining order may issue in a companion case under section 8(a)(5). Photobell Co. (1966). It is doubtful that this would be true if the union's misconduct were the reason for setting aside the election.

§ 5. Incumbent Union's Loss of Majority

A union which has had bargaining rights in the immediate past, either after Board certification or after informal recognition and bargaining, may find itself confronted with an employer claim that it has lost its majority. Rather than counter that claim by petitioning for a representation election, the union may choose to file a charge under section 8(a)(5) and to seek a bargaining order. The Board has, with judicial approval, announced a number of principles to guide the parties when the employer claims that the union's preexisting majority no longer continues.

For a period of one year after it has been certified, the union has the benefit of what is usually referred to as an "irrebuttable" presumption that its majority support continues. Even if it could be demonstrated by the employer that within days after the election and certification, the employees unequivocally repudiated the union, this will not be a defense to a charged violation of section 8(a)(5). The Supreme Court approved this principle in Brooks v. NLRB (U.S. 1954), holding that the Board could, in view of its expertise and in the interest of industrial stability, establish such a conclusive presumption during the "certification year." The Court concluded that thus to bind the employees would promote responsibility in the election process, would afford the union ample time to achieve results in bargaining without being "under exigent pressure to produce hothouse results or be turned out," would minimize inter-union raiding, and would encourage serious bargaining by the employer without attempts to undermine the union's majority status. The Court also approved the few extraordinary exceptions to this rule that the Board had announced:

> (1) the certified union dissolved or became defunct; (2) as a result of a schism, substantially all the members and officers of the certified union transferred their affiliation to a new local or international; (3) the size of the bargaining unit fluctuated radically within a short time.

In each of these three instances, the representative status of the union is so subject to question that it is thought appropriate to free the employer of the duty to bargain and to permit a fresh assessment of employee preferences. (These are also the three exceptions to the Board's "contract bar rule," which governs the timeliness of election petitions, and are discussed in greater detail elsewhere in this work.)

A similar principle has been applied to the union which secures its initial bargaining rights not through Board election and certification but through informal recognition by the employer. Such an uncertified union is entitled to a conclusive presumption of continued majority support "for a reasonable time." Like the certified union, the uncertified union is believed entitled to an "insulated" period when it can consolidate its strength and its bargaining position;

moreover, it is believed necessary to give comparable protection in order to induce unions to content themselves with informal recognition rather than always to invoke the Board's election machinery. As the court said in NLRB v. San Clemente Pub. Corp. (9th Cir. 1969):

> To hold that only a Board-conducted election is binding for a reasonable time would place a premium on the Board-conducted election and would hinder the use of less formal procedures that, in certain situations, may be more practical and convenient and more conducive to amicable industrial relations.

The Board appears not to have announced any firm period which will in all cases be deemed a "reasonable time." Presumably, the uncertified union will not secure the irrebuttable presumption for more than one year, the period which obtains for the certified union; but it will surely be entitled to that presumption when the bargaining period has been as short as three days, NLRB v. Montgomery Ward & Co. (7th Cir. 1968), or ten weeks, NLRB v. Universal Gear Serv. Corp. (6th Cir. 1968). When employer and union have negotiated a contract lawful on its face, the employer is bound by a conclusive presumption that the union had majority support at the contract's inception and that this continues throughout the life of the agreement. Bartenders Ass'n (1974).

During this period of conclusively presumed majority, an employer refusal to recognize is per se an unfair labor practice under section 8(a)(5), and the union can secure a bargaining order as a remedy, without having to prove its actual majority status in an election. After that period passes, it continues to be presumed that the union has majority status, but that presumption becomes rebuttable. That is true regardless of whether the once-conclusive presumption had been based on certification, informal recognition, or a collective bargaining agreement. The burden of rebuttal lies of course upon the employer, and the governing rules have recently been reiterated, *ibid:*

> It is well settled that a certified union, upon expiration of the first year following its certification, enjoys a rebuttable presumption that its majority representative status continues. This presumption is designed to promote stability in collective-bargaining relationships, without impairing the free choice of employees. Accordingly, once the presumption is shown to be operative, a *prima facie* case is established that an employer is obligated to bargain and that its refusal to do so would be unlawful. The *prima facie* case may be rebutted if the employer affirmatively establishes either (1) that at the time of the refusal the union in fact no longer enjoyed majority representative status; or (2) that

the employer's refusal was predicated on a good-faith and reasonably grounded doubt of the union's continued majority status.

Since it will typically be quite difficult for the employer specifically to demonstrate that the union in fact no longer represented a majority of unit employees at the time the employer withdrew recognition, most cases find the employer producing objective evidence which it claims gave rise to a good-faith doubt about the union's majority status. These cases require that the employer's doubt rest on reasonable grounds, not on unfounded speculation or a subjective state of mind only. NLRB v. Gulfmont Hotel Co. (5th Cir.1966). (It should be noted that the employer is not free to avoid proving grounds for its good faith doubt simply by filing an election petition with the NLRB and claiming that the union insists on continued recognition. The presumption of continuing majority has been held by the Board to apply in election proceedings as well as unfair labor practice proceedings, and the Board will require as a condition to ordering an election that the employer "demonstrate by objective considerations that it has some reasonable grounds for believing that the union has lost its majority status since its certification." United States Gypsum Co. (1966).)

The presumption of continuing majority has been successfully rebutted in a number of common situations. The union's majority claim will be most obviously impaired when its own responsible and knowledgeable officials admit that it has lost majority support; if the employer hears this admission, that alone may provide reasonable cause for doubt. Lodge 1746, IAM v. NLRB (United Aircraft Corp.) (D.C. Cir. 1969). Although "plant rumors" and subjective impressions of management that the employees are disaffected will not found a reasonable doubt, Sambo's Restaurants, Inc. (1974), written statements (and even specific oral statements) of repudiation of the union by employees will. NLRB v. Gallaro (2d Cir. 1969). And, although the filing of a decertification petition may not alone serve as the basis for a reasonable doubt of continuing majority support for the union, since the "showing of interest" which supports the petition need only comprise thirty percent of the unit, Rogers Mfg. Co. v. NLRB (6th Cir. 1973), such a doubt is warranted when the petition is supported by a majority of the unit employees, Automated Bus. Systems v. NLRB (6th Cir. 1974). (Indeed, the Board has long held that if a rival union files a petition for an election the employer is obligated to refrain from bargaining with an incumbent union about the terms of a new agreement. Shea Chem. Corp. (1958). Of more recent vintage is the Board doctrine that the employer is similarly obligated when a petition for decertification is filed by individual employees with a proper showing of interest. Telautograph Corp. (1972). This decision will no doubt require that the Board reexamine the statement in many cases that the mere filing of a decertification petition, which requires only a thirty percent showing of employee support, does not in itself justify a doubt of continuing majority.) The employer's case for rebuttal of the presumed majority is stronger when a number of persuasive facts occur in combination, such as a decline in dues checkoff authorizations, the union's failure to process grievances or to recommend employees for promotions or to make safety inspections, and statements by employees that they are no longer union supporters. Ingress-Plastene, Inc. v. NLRB (7th Cir. 1970).

In other fact situations which commonly arise, it has been held that the employer has not produced adequate objective evidence on which to base a good-faith doubt of continuing union majority. The mere passing of a substantial time since initial recognition will not found a reasonable doubt. Bethlehem Steel Co. (1950). Indeed, even when the initial recognition was based on a card check and thirty years had passed, the presumption of continuing majority was not dispelled. NLRB v. Denham (9th Cir. 1972), *vacated on other grounds* (U.S.1973) (successor employer held obligated to bargain). Heavy turnover of personnel since initial recognition will not undermine the presumption of continued majority, NLRB v. Little Rock Downtowner, Inc. (8th Cir. 1969), even in combination with the passing of several years since certification and a union election loss in a nearby branch plant. J. H. Rutter-Rex Mfg. Co. (1974). In effect, the new employees coming into the plant through normal attrition and turnover are assumed to have the same union preferences as those employees they displace. Harpeth Steel, Inc. (1974). Nor will the Board find that the employer is entitled to doubt the union's continuing majority merely because fewer than half of the employees in the unit are union members or have authorized the employer to check off union dues from their periodic paychecks. Bartenders Ass'n (1974). The Board reasons that many employees may be prepared to have the union bargain for them while desiring not to bear some of the concomitant burdens such as paying dues or even joining the union; not agreeing to the checkoff is a particularly weak indicator of non-support of the union, since the employee can be personally paying dues directly to the union. While the courts tend to agree with the Board's conclusions when any of these indicators appears in isolation, they seem to be somewhat more willing than the Board to find that the presumption of continuing majority support has been rebutted when a number appear in combination. *E. g.,* National Cash Register Co. v. NLRB (8th Cir. 1974) (two decertification petitions each supported by at least 30 percent of unit employees, employee turnover, resignations from union, decrease in checkoff authorizations; "[W]hether or not any one of the above factors would itself support an objective good faith doubt, it is not true that all reasons collectively would be insufficient.").

Until recently, there has been some uncertainty in the cases as to whether the employer may, upon the termination of the period of an irrebuttably presumed majority, take a lawful poll of the employees in order to determine whether they support continued recognition of the union. See NLRB v. H. P. Wasson & Co. (7th Cir. 1970) (valid employer poll showing substantial majority opposed to the union apparently held to justify good faith doubt). The Board has now declared that if the employer lacks some independent reason for believing that the union has lost its majority, it may not validly poll the employees to determine their union sympathies; such a poll will be held to violate both sections 8(a)(1) and 8(a)(5) for lack of justification, and the poll results, even though showing less than majority support for the union, will not serve as a defense in the refusal-to-bargain case. Montgomery Ward & Co. (1974). In effect, the Board holds that since the employer is required to demonstrate reasonable grounds to doubt the union's majority before it can secure a Board election, no less a showing should justify the employer's own "election" poll and a re-testing of the union's status.

When the employer's refusal to bargain with the incumbent union occurs during a strike coincident with negotiations for a new contract, other evidence will commonly bear upon the employer's good faith doubt. The Supreme Court has recently held, in Linden Lumber Div., Summer & Co. v. NLRB (U.S.1974), that employee support of a strike call may not be convincing evidence of union majority, since many may support this particular cause only or may be reluctant for other reasons to breach the picket line. Conversely, it has been held that no basis for doubting the union's majority is afforded when many employees report for work during a strike. Crossing the picket line does not constitute repudiation of the union but may merely demonstrate lack of support for this particular strike or, more simply, a need for money. Industrial Workers Local 289 v. NLRB (D.C.Cir. 1973) (filing of decertification petition also inadequate to found good faith doubt). But see Celanese Corp. of America (1951) (good faith doubt created when majority of employees returned to work during strike which union desired to continue). Although employee turnover resulting from normal attrition and new hiring will not justify a good faith doubt of continuing union majority, the result may be different when the "turnover" results from the replacement of strikers. As already noted, the fact that present employees refuse to participate in a strike, or return to work after initially participating, does not mean that these employees can no longer be counted as union supporters; but if a new hire agrees to serve as a replacement for a striker (in union parlance, as a strikebreaker, or worse), it is generally assumed that he does not support the union and that he ought not be counted toward a union majority. When such strikebreakers or permanent replacements constitute a majority of the unit, the presumption of union majority is undermined. Titan Metal

Mfg. Co. (1962).   But in computing the total workforce within which the majority is to be determined, the replaced economic strikers must be counted, at least during the first twelve months of the strike.   C. H. Guenther & Son v. NLRB (5th Cir. 1970).

The governing principles regarding the claim of an incumbent union to continued recognition are thus rather well settled.   Recently, however, two major issues have come to be more hotly debated.   The first question is whether the employer automatically wins its case by demonstrating objective reasons for a good faith doubt of the union's majority.   There is no question that the employer will prevail if it can demonstrate that the union did in fact lose its majority before the employer withdrew recognition;   indeed, continued bargaining with such a minority union as exclusive representative would have violated the Labor Act.   ILGWU v. NLRB (Bernhard-Altmann Corp.) (U.S.1961) (employer gives illegal support to the union and interferes with employee rights).   But it is arguable that if all the employer shows is that it had a good faith doubt, it still can be found to have violated section 8(a)(5) if the General Counsel can then come forward with objective evidence to show that the union in fact did have majority support at the time the employer withdrew recognition. This might be done, for example, through union membership rolls which might not have been brought to the employer's attention at that time.

The view which is currently adopted by a majority of the members of the NLRB is that the employer, in order to defend against a section 8(a)(5) charge, need demonstrate only that it reasonably believed that the union had lost majority support.   Even if the General Counsel can demonstrate a majority in fact, this will apparently not require an unfair labor practice finding and bargaining order.   Faye Nursing Home, Inc. (1974).   Some courts endorse this principle. NLRB v. Dayton Motels, Inc. (6th Cir. 1973) ("A good-faith doubt exculpates the employer even if the Union in fact represented a majority of the employees.").   Most courts which have spoken to the issue (typically in dictum), however, do not.   These decisions place great emphasis under section 8(a)(5) upon the existence in fact of a union majority rather than upon the employer's subjective state of mind.   While this position seems to disadvantage the employer, it appears that the proponents believe it will in fact favor the employer, since it is generally coupled with a substantial willingness to permit the employer to dispel the presumption of continuing majority, at which point the burden will shift to the General Counsel to prove by a preponderance of the evidence that the union possessed majority support in fact.   Thus, the court in Automated Bus. Systems v. NLRB (6th Cir. 1974), quoted and endorsed the language of the

Board in an earlier case (a case which the Board has itself consistently tried to distinguish):

> After the lapse of the certification year, the certifica-
> tion creates only a presumption of continued majority. This
> presumption is rebuttable. Proof of majority is peculiarly
> within the special competence of the union. It may be
> proved by signed authorization cards, dues checkoff cards,
> membership lists, or any other evidentiary means. An em-
> ployer can hardly prove that a union no longer represents a
> majority since he does not have access to the union's mem-
> bership lists and direct interrogation of employees would
> probably be unlawful as well as of dubious validity. Accord-
> ingly, to overcome the presumption of majority the employ-
> er need only produce sufficient evidence to cast serious
> doubt on the union's continued majority status. The pre-
> sumption then loses its force and the General Counsel must
> come forward with evidence that on the refusal-to-bargain
> date the union in fact did represent a majority of employees
> in the appropriate unit.

In most cases, it has not mattered whether the facts are analyzed in
terms of the employer's good faith doubt or the union's majority in
fact. Even under the former theory, it is necessary that the employer come forward with objective evidence to support its doubt, and a
Board finding that the doubt is supportable is generally tantamount
to a finding that the union did not in fact have majority support.

A second issue emerging in the more recent cases is whether section 8(a)(5) is an appropriate vehicle—in contrast to a new election
—in which to test the dispute concerning the union's continuing majority. In cases in which the union seeks to use unfair labor practice
proceedings in order to establish an initial bargaining relationship,
the Supreme Court in Linden Lumber Div., Summer & Co. v. NLRB
(U.S.1974), has both rejected the use of employer state of mind as a
touchstone of recognition and held that the objective datum of union
majority is far better determined in an expeditious secret-ballot election supervised by the NLRB than in unfair labor practice proceedings under section 8(a)(5). Were the initial-bargaining and preexisting-bargaining situations precisely comparable, *Linden Lumber*
would appear to permit the employer always to refuse continued recognition and to force the union periodically to demonstrate its majority by petitioning for an election. (It must be remembered, however,
that if the employer petitions for an election, the Board requires it to
prove objective grounds for a good faith doubt of the union's continuing majority. United States Gypsum Co. (1966). Such proof would
not, of course, be necessary if the union were to petition.) Indeed, at
least one court of appeals has (in a decision considerably predating
Linden) permitted an employer to challenge the union's majority as

a contract was about to expire, primarily because the record showed that the employer had been on amicable terms with the union in the past, was prepared to restore their bargaining relationship if the union prevailed in an election, and had given no indication of antiunion animus or bad faith. NLRB v. Laystrom Mfg. Co. (7th Cir. 1966). One member of the NLRB has recently suggested that a union's refusal to demonstrate its continuing majority through an expeditious election and its insistence on relying on the presumptions which obtain in a much more protracted unfair labor practice case generate suspicion that it is not confident of its majority support. Bartenders Ass'n (1974) (Member Kennedy, dissenting).

The prevailing view, however, appears still to be that the union may use a section 8(a)(5) proceeding to preserve preexisting bargaining rights, thereby in effect shifting to the employer the burden of producing objective evidence which supports either the inference that the union has lost its majority or the employer's good-faith belief that it has (the inference and the belief normally being indistinguishable). A court of appeals has affirmed this principle, in the face of the argument that it was undermined by the Supreme Court decision in NLRB v. Gissel Packing Co. (U.S.1969), in which the Court endorsed the Board's abandonment of a good-faith test in initial-recognition cases. In NLRB v. Frick Co. (3d Cir. 1970), the court distinguished "cases involving a withdrawal of recognition from a validly recognized union":

> In the *Gissel* type of situation, the emphasis is on fulfilling the national labor policy of assuring employees a free choice of representatives by the most reliable method. In the case of withdrawal of recognition, however, competing considerations of assuring the stability of an established bargaining relationship are involved. On this basis, the Board has in the past distinguished between refusals to recognize and withdrawals of recognition. . . . We find no reason in *Gissel* for not continuing to do so. Accordingly, we conclude that the Board's finding in terms of the Company's lack of good faith doubt are proper . . . .

The impact of *Gissel* will, however, be felt in cases in which the employer ceases to recognize a union with which it has been bargaining and contemporaneously commits coercive unfair labor practices. It is precisely in these cases of employer wrongdoing that the Board and courts have traditionally disallowed employer claims that the union had lost its majority by the time of withdrawal of recognition. Celanese Corp. of America (1951). Not only, under a good-faith-doubt test, would the employer's commission of unfair labor practices undermine the claim of good faith, but the employer violations would make it almost impossible in the section 8(a)(5) case, long after the fact, to determine whether any loss of majority reflected the employees' true wishes or reflected only their response to employer coercion. NLRB v. C & C Plywood Corp. (9th Cir. 1969). In any event, the Supreme Court held in *Gissel* that the bargaining order should be used, in the initial-recognition situation, only when employer coercion and discrimination have made it improbable that a fair election can be held to test the union's claim of majority. Some courts of appeals have employed the same analysis in the preexisting-bargaining situation. One court has held that the issuance of a bargaining order is proper—regardless of the union's preexisting majority and the attendant presumptions—only if no fair election can be held, since to do otherwise would risk imposing an unwanted union on a majority of employees. Daisy's Originals, Inc. v. NLRB (5th Cir. 1972). See also Automated Bus. Systems v. NLRB (6th Cir. 1974) (Board based its bargaining order exclusively on section 8(a)(1) and (3) violations in preexisting-majority situation; court held that proof of antecedent union majority was necessary to issue such an order, that the General Counsel may rely on the presumption of continuing majority, but that once sufficient evidence casts doubt, the burden shifts to the General Counsel to prove majority support in fact prior to employer wrongdoing).

In future cases, the Board may have to articulate the difference under section 8(a)(5) between initial-recognition cases and preexisting-majority cases, to justify in the latter cases its resort to unfair labor practice proceedings rather than elections to prove union status. If, in cases in which withdrawal of recognition is accompanied by coercion and discrimination, the Board treats the section 8(a)(5) violation as merely "derivative" of the section 8(a)(1) and (3) violations, this will likely invite judicial use of the *Gissel* standards to test the validity of the Board's bargaining order.

§ 6. The Duty of the "Successor" Employer to Bargain

When one company purchases the stock or the property of another company that is unionized, or acquires control of that unionized company by merger or consolidation, the question arises whether the "successor" company under new management must still bargain with the union that had represented the "predecessor's" employees. Had there been no change in the ownership of the unionized company, the duty to bargain with the union would have continued for at least a year if the union was certified, for a "reasonable time" if the union was granted informal recognition without a Board election, and for longer yet if a labor contract is in existence. When the business operations are transferred, the acquiring company often wishes to be free of the union (which may in fact be a reason why the predecessor wishes to rid itself of the business) while the union along with the predecessor's employees wish the transaction to have no untoward impact on job security or on union security. While the union is often successful in securing the consent of the acquiring company to its continued representation of the employees under new management, it is sometimes necessary for the union to assert its claim to continued recognition against a recalcitrant successor employer by filing a charge under section 8(a)(5) with the National Labor Relations Board. The Board has held, with the endorsement of the Supreme Court, that under certain circumstances—most significantly, when a majority of employees working for the successor company had been formerly employed by the predecessor company—the duty to bargain with the predecessor's union will continue in spite of the change in ownership. The Court has also held, however, that this duty does not require the successor company to honor the terms of any collective bargaining agreement between the union and the predecessor company.

Early in the administration of the Wagner Act, the Board had held that a change in ownership of a business did not eliminate the obligation of the surviving company to remedy existing unfair labor practices, whether the change was the sham creation of an alter ego company under the control of the predecessor, Hopwood Retinning Co., *enf'd as mdf'd* (2d Cir. 1938), or was the result of the death of a partner in the predecessor company, Colten d/b/a Kiddie Kover Mfg. Co. (1938), *enf'd* (6th Cir. 1939). In South Carolina Granite Co. *enf'd* (4th Cir. 1945), the Board went yet further and held that the new employer could be held to the substantive duty to bargain with the predecessor's union even if the transfer was a bona fide arm's length transaction—provided there was continuity of the "employing industry" (regardless of ownership or management) and there was no good faith doubt by the successor of the union's continuing majority. The Board more fully articulated its position on the carryover of the duty to bargain in Stonewall Cotton Mills (1948), where the assets of the Stonewall Cotton Mills were purchased by one Erwin, who continued to produce the same goods in the same plant on the same equipment and with the same employees, changing only the name of the operation from Stonewall to Erwin. Rebuffing Erwin's defense to the refusal-to-bargain charge—that the union had not been certified to represent the Erwin employees—the Board held:

> Where, as here, no essential attribute of the employment relationship has been changed as a result of the transfer, the certification continues with undiminished vitality to represent the will of the employees with respect to their choice of bargaining representatives, and the consequent obligation to bargain subsists notwithstanding the change in the legal ownership of the business enterprise.

Soon after, in a case in which the business acquisition took the form of a lease rather than a purchase, the Board held that the acquiring company—which retained a majority of the former workforce, who continued under the same supervisors to serve the same customers with the same products—was bound to honor the recent certification of the predecessor's union, since the presence of a new employer does not in itself give reason to believe that the employees will renounce their chosen bargaining representative. Krantz Wire & Mfg. Co. enf'd (7th Cir. 1952). The Board did, however, note in dictum that if the new operation is so altered as to change the nature of the employees' jobs and working conditions, this could justify a "good faith doubt" that the employees wish to retain their former union in preference to some other.

Over a number of years, the Board and the courts concluded that the duty to bargain would carry through a change in business ownership if there was "substantial continuity of identity in the business enterprise." Most frequently, this would be said to rest in turn upon a finding of continuity in such factors as: the composition of the workforce; the product and the method of production (or the service and the method of its rendition); job classifications and working conditions; and the supervisory structure and personnel. E. g., J–P Mfg., Inc. (1972). Cited less frequently as indicia of "substantial continuity of identity in the business enterprise," and often seemingly only as makeweights, are the acquisition by the purchaser of the seller's accounts receivable, goodwill, trade name, inventory, obligations, customers, suppliers of raw materials and work-in-progress. E. g., Union Texas Petroleum, Inc. (1965) (servicing same customers); Piasecki Aircraft Corp. (1959) (purchase of goodwill); Investment Building Cafeteria (1959) (same trade name). These latter factors, rather than having independent significance, are usually some evidence of continuity in the more significant factors such as working conditions and processes of production.

Indeed, in Board and court decisions prior to 1972 (when the Supreme Court addressed the issue) the single most significant issue in determining carryover of the duty to bargain was whether a majority of employees in the successor bargaining unit had formerly worked for the predecessor. If such a "successor majority" was present, that was normally sufficient to warrant requiring the successor to continue to bargain with the predecessor's union; minor changes in business operations would not undermine the presumption of continued majority support for the union. Moreover, "successor majority" was normally a *necessary* condition to bargaining carryover; that the preponderance of the successor's employees, who were newly hired by or brought with the successor rather than hired from the predecessor, did the same kind of work under the same working conditions as the predecessor's employees was insufficient to justify imposing the predecessor union on them. Since in substance—although rarely if ever so articulated—the issue was whether the predecessor's union would be regarded by the successor's employees as a congenial and effective representative, such could be assumed when a majority of those employees had formerly worked for the predecessor and been represented by that union (regardless of whether that majority group might only have been a small component of the predecessor's work-force).

Significantly, the Board generally treated as irrelevant the question whether the transfer of the employees and the business took place technically by merger, consolidation, purchase of stock, purchase of assets, lease of assets, or some other form—matters which were usually governed by corporate or tax considerations rather than labor considerations. Indeed, the Board held in a number of cases, with judicial approval, that the duty to bargain could bind a successor even if there were no contractual dealings whatever between the successor and predecessor—even, in fact, if they were business competitors bidding against one another for the right to continue the business. The Board gave its reasons for so holding, in Maintenance, Inc. (1964). There, the new employer, Maintenance, replaced White Castle as the low bidder for a custodial service contract at a NASA facility, and executed the contract with the federal General Services Administration within a year of certification of the union with which White Castle had dealt. Maintenance retained ninety percent of the employees formerly working for White Castle, and of course rendered the same service for the same customer, but it bought no equipment or other assets from White Castle and had no direct corporate or contractual dealings. Nonetheless, the Board held Maintenance to violate section 8(a)(5) when it refused to bargain.

> The duty of an employer who has taken over an "employing industry" to honor the employees' choice of a bargaining agent is not one that derives from a private contract, nor is it one that necessarily turns upon the acquisition of assets or assumption of other obligations usually incident to a sale, lease, or other arrangement between employers. It is a public obligation of the Act. The critical question is not whether Respondent succeeded to White Castle's corporate identity or physical assets, but whether Respondent continued essentially the same operation, with substantially the same employee unit whose duly certified bargaining representative was entitled to statutory recognition at the time Respondent took over.

See also NLRB v. Wayne Convalescent Center, Inc. (6th Cir. 1972) (successor took through mortgage foreclosure). Since the duty to bargain is imposed upon the successor by the mandates of the Labor Act and not by virtue of any private agreement with the predecessor, that duty may be imposed in spite of the fact that the successor has explicitly disclaimed in the contract of purchase (or otherwise) the obligation to recognize the predecessor's union. Colony Materials, Inc. (1961).

In several decisions, the Board went further than merely to hold that the successor was obligated to recognize the predecessor's union.

In Chemrock Corp. (1965), it appeared to hold that a successor which continued to operate an acquired unionized business in the same manner as before was obliged at least initially to retain the employees of the predecessor on its own payroll, to refrain from bargaining individually with these employees about their starting wages and to bargain with the predecessor's union prior to terminating their employment. In Overnite Transp. Co. (1966), *enf'd* (4th Cir. 1967), the Board held that the predecessor's labor contract, although not binding directly on the successor, set the status quo for working conditions at the time of the formal takeover such that those terms could not be altered by the successor without first bargaining with the union. And, further to constrain the successor, the Board in 1970 held in a dramatic reversal of policy that the successor could be obliged under section 8(a)(5) not merely to bargain with the predecessor's union but also to honor the substantive terms of an existing collective bargaining agreement between that union and the predecessor employer for the balance of the contract term. On review of this decision, the Supreme Court sweepingly overturned these three principles, while endorsing the Board's more fundamental and longstanding principle that a bona fide business successor may be obligated under section 8(a)(5) to bargain with the union that had represented the employees of the predecessor company.

The Burns Decision. That significant Supreme Court decision was NLRB v. Burns Int'l Security Services, Inc. (U.S.1972). There, Wackenhut provided plant protection services for Lockheed at a California airport, under a contract to terminate on June 30, 1967. On March 8, the United Plant Guard Workers (UPG) was certified as bargaining representative for Wachenhut employees and a three-year labor contract was executed on April 29. Lockheed invited bids for a new protection-services contract, informing all bidders of the UPG certification and contract with Wackenhut, and although Wackenhut submitted a bid, Lockheed awarded the contract to Burns, effective July 1. Burns retained 27 of the Wackenhut guards, and brought in 15 of its own guards from other locations, but refused to bargain with the UPG or honor its labor contract; indeed, it recognized a rival union, American Federation of Guards (AFG), which represented Burns employees elsewhere. The Board found the Lockheed plant to be an appropriate bargaining unit, and held Burns to be a successor under section 8(a)(5) both to Wackenhut's duty to bargain with the UPG (within four months of its certification) and to its labor contract with UPG. The Supreme Court, by a vote of 5 to 4 sustained the Board's order to bargain with the UPG, but unanimously refused to enforce the Board's order to honor the labor contract. It established a number of significant principles on the question of the duty of a successor to bargain with the predecessor's union.

(1) When a company hires as a majority of its workforce (in an appropriate bargaining unit) employees who had worked for a union-

ized company, and these employees continue to perform the same work in the same setting, the successor company is obligated to recognize and bargain with the predecessor's union during the same period of time as the predecessor would be obligated to do. Indeed, it is possible to read *Burns* to hold that such a "successor majority" (regardless of work similarity) is sufficient in itself to found a duty to bargain. The Supreme Court did note that Burns had not merely retained former Wackenhut employees as a majority of its own workforce at the Lockheed plant, but had also used them to perform the same tasks under supervision organized as before (although the particular supervisors were not those used by Wackenhut). But these latter factors were, if not altogether ignored, clearly treated as less significant than the successor majority comprised of former Wackenhut employees. Indeed, the Court expressly held:

> Burns' obligation to bargain with the union over terms and conditions of employment stemmed from its hiring of Wackenhut's employees and from the recent election and Board certification. It has been consistently held that a mere change of employers or of ownership in the employing industry is not such an "unusual circumstance" as to affect the force of the Board's certification within the normal operative period if a majority of employees after the change of ownership or management were employed by the preceding employer.

(While the Court appeared not to hold that the Board *must* find a continued duty to bargain in such cases, it did hold that the Board was "not unreasonable" in concluding that Burns could not fairly doubt the union's continuing majority and that the Board acted within its discretion in imposing a bargaining order.)

The Court majority was thus not deterred by the observation of the four dissenting Justices that this might well require the successor to bargain with a union which in fact was at no time the freely selected representative of a majority of its employees, since for example of the fifty-one percent of the successor's workforce who had worked for the predecessor only a bare majority in turn might have voted for the union; indeed, a random selection of the predecessor's employees might bring to the successor only a very small proportion of those who had supported the predecessor's union. The Court's rationale would in fact appear to support earlier Board decisions in which the successor was required to bargain after starting its operations on a substantially diminished scale, such that the employees retained from the predecessor's unit, while constituting a majority of the new workforce, had constituted only a small proportion of the predecessor's workforce. *E. g., Johnson Ready Mix Co.* (1963) (workforce reduced from 83 to 56, 36 of whom had worked in predecessor bargaining unit).

The Supreme Court decision in *Burns* made it clear that the duty to bargain would not carry over to a company acquiring a unionized business in any of three (at least) situations: (a) when recruitment by the successor employer results in, for example, "an almost complete turnover of employees," provided of course that the successor does not purposely avoid hiring predecessor employees because they are union members, for such would violate section 8(a)(3) of the Labor Act; or (b) when—even if all of the predecessor's employees are retained—because the successor's "operational structure and practices" differ from those of the predecessor, the former bargaining unit is no longer appropriate (*e. g.,* if the former Wackenhut employees had been dispersed among Burns employees at other locations and the Lockheed location had thus become an "accretion" to a larger Burns-AFG bargaining unit); or (c) when, for other reasons, the successor nurtures in good faith a reasonable doubt that the union continues to represent a majority within the unit, for this defense would have been available even to the predecessor employer had there been no transfer of ownership (but even then such a doubt would presumably be conclusively inapt within the year following the certification of the union). Compare NLRB v. Bachrodt Chevrolet Co. (7th Cir. 1972), *vacated on other grounds and remanded* (U.S. 1973) (doubt of majority not justified by fact that there had been almost complete turnover of employees since union was first recognized), with Davenport Insulation, Inc. (1970) (when the predecessor had recognized a minority union under a construction industry prehire contract, made valid only because of section 8(f), no presumption of continuing majority attached and the successor had no duty to bargain absent the union's demonstration of majority support).

At the heart of the Court's opinion in *Burns* is its willingness to free the successor of any obligation actually to hire the predecessor's employees, provided it recruits its new workforce without discrimination against union members; any contrary suggestions in earlier Board decisions are thus overruled. Also at the heart of the Court's opinion, at least impliedly, is its indifference to the question whether the business was acquired by merger or by sale of assets or by any other consensual arrangement between the two employers, or was indeed acquired—as in *Burns* itself—by direct competitive bidding and without any contract between predecessor and successor. (This indifference contrasted sharply with the position of four dissenting Justices, who would have required as a condition of a continued duty to bargain that there be some assets transferred to the successor by the predecessor, and not merely "a naked transfer of employees.")

(2) The second essential principle established by the Court in *Burns* is that the duty to bargain ordinarily does not commence *until* the successor has hired as a majority of its workforce the former employees of the predecessor, such that the status quo from which bargaining is to begin is that which obtains between the successor and

its own workforce at that time (rather than the earlier status quo between the predecessor and *its* workforce). The Court thus repudiated the Board's earlier position that the predecessor's collective bargaining agreement—even if expired or for other reasons deemed not independently binding on the successor—set the successor's starting wages and working conditions which could be altered only after bargaining with the predecessor's union to an impasse. The Court in *Burns* held that the successor was ordinarily empowered to establish its own starting wages and working conditions, to offer them directly to all job applicants including those then working for the predecessor, and to implement them after the takeover, with the duty to bargain arising only as to future changes and only after the hiring of a majority of the unit from the predecessor's workforce:

> The terms on which Burns hired employees for service after July 1 may have differed from the terms extended by Wackenhut and required by the collective-bargaining contract, but it does not follow that Burns changed *its* terms and conditions of employment when it specified the initial basis on which employees were hired on July 1.

The Court did, however, proceed in dictum to outline a situation where the substantive terms of the predecessor's labor contract will serve as the status quo which binds the successor until it bargains to impasse with the union:

> Although a successor employer is ordinarily free to set initial terms on which it will hire the employees of a predecessor, there will be instances in which it is perfectly clear that the new employer plans to retain all of the employees in the unit and in which it will be appropriate to have him initially consult with the employees' bargaining representative before he fixes terms. In other situations, however, it may not be clear until the successor employer has hired his full complement of employees that he has a duty to bargain with a union, since it will not be evident until then that the bargaining representative represents a majority of the employees in the unit as required by § 9(a) of the Act.

(3) The short-lived Board doctrine that section 8(a)(5) requires the successor employer not only to recognize and bargain with the predecessor's union but also to honor its labor contract was flatly rejected by a unanimous Court. The Court found in the Labor Act a strong policy favoring the voluntary establishment of contract terms by bargaining between the parties, free of government dictation of those terms. An obligation to abide by the predecessor's contract must be found in some express or implied assumption of such an obligation by the successor, and cannot rest merely on the retention of a majority of former employees without consensual dealings between the parties. The Court distinguished its earlier decision in John Wil-

ey & Sons v. Livingston (U.S.1964)—in which a successor was ordered in an action under section 301 of the Labor Act to arbitrate under its predecessor's labor contract—as a case involving the strong federal policy favoring arbitration, a merger which under state law would thrust the predecessor's liabilities upon the surviving company, and an arm's-length negotiation between the two companies. In its analysis, however, the Court did downplay one of the central premises of *Wiley*, the strength of the federal policy in protecting employees against the disruption and loss stemming from business acquisitions in which they are unrepresented. The *Burns* Court instead placed preeminent emphasis upon the need of employers freely to transfer and rearrange physical and human resources in an effort to resuscitate ailing businesses:

> A potential employer may be willing to take over a moribund business only if he can make changes in corporate structure, composition of the labor force, work location, task assignment, and nature of supervision. Saddling such an employer with the terms and conditions of employment contained in the old collective-bargaining contract may make these changes impossible and may discourage and inhibit the transfer of capital. On the other hand, a union may have made concessions to a small or failing employer that it would be unwilling to make to a large or economically successful firm.

Both successor and union should be free to renegotiate working conditions, with economic power rather than the old contract (including many implied terms unknown to the successor) determining the content of the bargain.

The Court thus held it error for the Board to order Burns to reimburse its employees for their contract losses resulting from Burns' refusal to honor the terms of the Wackenhut labor agreement. In the process it gave apparent endorsement to what had been the Board's pre-*Burns* policy on the power of a successor to challenge the representation status of the predecessor's union prior to the termination date of the predecessor's labor contract: The successor is free to assert a good faith doubt of the union's continuing majority support —either by petitioning for an election or as a defense to a refusal-to-bargain charge—even during the term of the predecessor's labor contract unless the successor assumes that contract specifically and in writing (or, of course, signs a new labor contract of its own with that union). Compare Glenn Goulding (1967).

Thus stands the law of bargaining successorship today. A company acquiring a unionized company may, without anti-union discrimination, recruit a new workforce, but if it retains employees of the predecessor in numbers sufficient to comprise a majority of its own workforce, it will ordinarily be obligated to bargain with the predecessor's union—provided the bargaining unit is appropriate and there are no other reasons to doubt the union's continuing majority support. But the successor will not be required against its will to assume the predecessor's labor contract; nor will the predecessor union. And, unless it is perfectly clear from the outset that the "successor majority" test will be satisfied, the successor is free to establish unilaterally the beginning wages and working conditions of its employees, with the duty to bargain arising only thereafter upon the actual retention of the requisite proportion of the predecessor's employees. When the duty does arise, the union's majority is conclusively presumed to continue for a year following certification and the presumption continues thereafter subject to rebuttal, just as in the case of a single employer, by the successor employer's demonstration of a reasonably based good faith doubt that majority support continues. Whether the unwilling successor may be required to arbitrate under the predecessor's contract the union's claim that that contract gives employees substantive rights against the successor is an issue dealt with elsewhere. The successor employer may, of course, assume obligations greater than those required by law and may, for example, expressly agree to abide by the predecessor's contract if the union is willing.

Workforce Majority and the Appropriate Unit. One major issue left unresolved by the Supreme Court decision in the *Burns* case is whether the successor's retention of predecessor employees as a majority of its own workforce will be a necessary element in establishing the successor's duty to bargain. Before the Supreme Court decision in *Burns*, the Board had held in a handful of its many successorship cases that a successor company which continued the organization and production processes of its predecessor's business could be ordered to bargain with the predecessor's union even though less than half of the successor's workforce had worked for the predecessor. While the *Burns* decision does not hold that "successor majority" must be present in order to justify a continuing duty to bargain, the Board appears since *Burns* to have invoked this requirement. But the Board in a recent case was divided on the issue. Two Board members would require that the predecessor's employees comprise a majority of the successor's workforce, regardless of whether they constituted a majority of the predecessor's workforce. One member would require not only successor majority but also retention of a majority of the predecessor's workforce. Two members would be prepared to order continued bargaining even when a successor majority is absent, provided the predecessor's employees constitute a "legally significant portion of the successor's employment force." In Spruce Up Corp. (1974), the takeover of a number of barbershops on a military base was accompanied by a strike, which caused a fluctuation in the proportion of the successor's workforce drawn from the predecessor shops. While two Board members found the successor's duty to bargain to mature only from the date when it continued to employ predecessor employees as a majority of its own workforce, two other members would have imposed the duty throughout the entire period, since the predecessor employees had at all times constituted a "stable nucleus" and a "legally significant portion" of the successor's workforce. Since this latter view creates a risk of imposing an unwanted union on a majority of the employees, and since the predecessor's union can in any event test its strength in a representation election, it is unlikely that the Board and courts will order the successor to bargain when less than a majority of its employees had formerly worked for the predecessor.

Another major issue after *Burns* is the extent to which the Board will treat a successor majority comprised of predecessor employees as in itself sufficient to require the successor company to continue bargaining. It is rather clear that the Board treats "successor majority"—or "continuity in the workforce"—as not itself conclusive but rather as one factor which is relevant to the "continuity of the employing industry" and to the employees' desires with regard to continued representation. Less clear are the indicators of "discontinuity" which when present will outweigh successor majority and free the successor company of the duty to bargain. In one case, Lincoln Private Police, Inc. (1971), although a company which was organized to provide guard services hired sixty-one of its sixty-six employees from the ranks of a unionized company which terminated its service contracts, it was not required to bargain because it took only one-third of the customers of the unionized business (by independent solicitation), secured many new customers of its own, retained none of the same supervisors, moved to a new location, and obtained its own capital, vehicles, equipment and uniforms; the Board also found that the bulk of the predecessor's customers had been taken over by yet other guard-service companies, such that the predecessor should be treated as having been "fragmented" upon its termination. In another case, Radiant Fashions, Inc. (1973), in which the successor retained all of the predecessor's employees, the Board found no substantial continuity in the enterprise and no successor bargaining duty when there was a three-month interruption in production, changes in equipment and customers, a covenant by the successor not to duplicate the predecessor's products and thus a resulting need to retrain retained employees (even though they worked at the same location after the change in ownership). But even a several-month interruption in operations will not free the successor of its duty to bargain if the workforce, location, organization and production processes of the predecessor are continued. NLRB v. Daneker Clock Co. (4th Cir. 1975) (eight-month shutdown does not prevent successorship). Presumably, in the preponderance of cases in which a majority of the successor's workforce had formerly worked for the predecessor, most other indicators of employer continuity will be present.

It has been argued, however, that even if successor majority is present, there is no employer continuity and no continuing duty to bargain when the retained employees had not constituted a majority of the predecessor's workforce. (This could happen when the successor acquires a unionized business and commences its own operations on a substantially diminished scale.) This argument has been squarely rejected by the Board (one member dissenting) and by the courts of appeals. In United Maintenance & Mfg. Co. (1974), where the predecessor workforce numbered thirty-eight and the successor (because of a strike) was able soon after taking over to recruit only fifteen employees (nine of whom had worked for the predecessor), the Board held the successor was obligated to bargain, since the management, operations and customers remained unchanged:

> [U]nder circumstances where operations under the new employer have not been changed in any substantial way, the standard for determining the new employer's obligations to bargain with the union representing the employees of the predecessor is not, as Respondent contends, the percentage of the predecessor's total complement that the new employer retains, but the percentage of the new employer's work force which had previously worked for the predecessor in the bargaining unit.

And, in Zim's Foodliner, Inc. v. NLRB (7th Cir. 1974), a divided court found that the purchaser of one supermarket, formerly owned by a large supermarket chain owning fifty-seven stores in the state, was obligated to bargain with the seller's union which had represented in a single bargaining unit all clerks employed in eleven of the seller's supermarkets. The court noted that the purchaser had retained all of the employees at the acquired store, and rejected its contention "that, in order to be held a successor, an employer cannot have hired less than a majority of the employees in the predecessor unit." It referred to several Board decisions involving sharply contracted successor bargaining units and stated that "mere diminution in the employee complement of the bargaining unit does not relieve the successor of his duty to bargain." The reduction in numbers of the successor employees "warrants no implication that they no longer desired the union to represent them . . . [T]he Board may treat a much-reduced bargaining unit as a miniature of the former unit."

While the cases thus support a continued duty to bargain when there is a successor majority in a sharply reduced workforce in the *same bargaining unit* as before, greater divergence of opinion exists when the successor's employees constitute a bargaining unit which differs in scope from that of the predecessor. Thus, in the *Zim's Foodliner* case just discussed, the successor argued that its continued employment of all of the predecessor's workers in the one supermarket should not subject it to a duty to bargain, since the predecessor's union had been the representative of an eleven-store unit and since employer-employee relations were significantly different in chain-store and single-store operations.   As to the latter point, the court agreed that "Substantial changes in the employing industry may be expected to alter employee expectations and needs, thereby changing employee sentiment with respect to representation," but it upheld as reasonable the findings of the administrative law judge that the employees continued to work under the same general conditions and that "the changes accompanying this business transfer were not such as to significantly affect employee attitudes."   And, while the court noted that inclusion in the former larger unit might in some circumstances justify doubt that the store employees as a separate unit would support the predecessor union, the record showed specifically that the predecessor union had indeed in the past demonstrated majority support in the single store.   (The dissenting judge, however, found the union's representative status "lost in ancient history" and rejected any "continuing presumption of majority status after such a material fragmentation of the bargaining units.")   In this kind of case—as in successorship cases generally—the finding of employer continuity gives rise merely to a presumption of continuing union majority, which the employer is normally free to rebut (after the passing of the "certification year") with objective evidence of employee disaffection.

In some instances, however, a drastic reduction in unit size in the course of a business takeover has been found to justify a fresh assessment by the employees of their bargaining preferences and freedom of the successor employer from any continuing duty to bargain. In IAM v. NLRB (Atlantic Tech. Serv. Corp.) (D.C.Cir. 1974), the respondent was successful in bidding away from Trans-World Airlines certain mail and distribution services at Kennedy Space Center, and retained twenty-seven TWA employees within the new workforce of forty-one; TWA had bargained with a union for all its employees nationwide and had absorbed this small group of mailroom employees into a unit of some 1100 workers at the Space Center.   In spite of the "successor majority" of former TWA employees, the court affirmed the Board's refusal to presume continuing majority support for the union.   It emphasized that the union had become the spokesman for the retained employees only by the "accretion" of the forty-one-worker unit into the much larger TWA unit some seven years before the change in ownership, and that there had never been an election or certification within the smaller unit.

The Board has recently presumed a union's representation status to continue in the reverse fact situation, when the successor's bargaining unit was substantially *larger* than that of the predecessor. In Spruce Up Corp. (1974), the successor was the successful bidder for the contract to operate all twenty-seven barbershops on a military base; formerly, one unionized employer operated nineteen of the shops, and two other employers the remaining eight. The Board held that once a majority of employees from the nineteen shops were re-hired, the successor was obligated to bargain with the union representing the employees there—and the union would be presumed to have a majority not only in those nineteen shops but in the overall twenty-seven-shop unit. The Board held this to follow from the fact that had the predecessor owner of the nineteen shops acquired the other eight, "these like facilities and similarly classified employees" would have been treated as an "accretion" to the nineteen-store unit and the union's bargaining rights extended accordingly. In spite of the risk of imposing an unwanted union on the new hires in the nineteen stores and on the employees in the other eight stores, the "accretion" doctrine was applied to the successor employer who could escape the duty to bargain only by pointing to other facts and circumstances "which under our usual tests would provide the Employer with objective evidence casting doubt on the continuance of the majority status."

In sum, the Board and the courts will likely require that a majority of the successor's workforce have previously worked for the predecessor before imposing a duty to bargain on the successor. It will not also be necessary that the retained workers have comprised a majority of the predecessor's workforce. Even when such a "successor majority" is present, however, other circumstances may show that there has been sufficient "discontinuity in the employing enterprise" to warrant freeing the successor of any duty to bargain in the absence of a new representation election. The Board and courts will determine whether such circumstances, such as a substantial change in the scope of the bargaining unit, indicate that most of the successor's employees are likely to find the predecessor's union an uncongenial spokesman.

When the Duty to Bargain Matures. Another major issue considered in post-*Burns* decisions relates to the precise time at which the successor's duty to bargain matures and the employer becomes obliged to deal with the predecessor's union before modifying the terms of employment. In *Burns,* the Supreme Court held that the successor—even when a majority of its workforce ultimately comes from that of the predecessor—is normally free unilaterally to set the initial wages, hours and working conditions within its bargaining unit unless "it is perfectly clear that the new employer plans to retain all of the employees in the unit." Thus, if an invitation is extended to all or substantially all of the predecessor's employees and they agree to continue on as the successor's workforce, and nothing is said about any departure from the terms governing the predecessor's employees (usually embodied in a labor contract), the successor employer will not be free thereafter unilaterally to declare new initial terms of employment for the retained workers. For example, any attempted change in working conditions three weeks after operating as before with all of the predecessor's employees will be illegal unless first negotiated with the union.   Zim's Foodliner, Inc. v. NLRB (7th Cir. 1974).   Indeed, the successor violates section 8(a)(5) when, after offering employment to the predecessor's employees on a Friday, it unilaterally announces its intention to terminate paid vacations, require Saturday work and introduce a new method of computing mechanics' wages when the employees report for work for the successor the following Monday.   NLRB v. Bachrodt Chevrolet Co. (7th Cir. 1972), *vacated on other grounds and remanded* (U.S.1973).   But see NLRB v. Wayne Convalescent Center, Inc. (6th Cir. 1972) (relying on the *Burns* policy of freeing successors to set initial terms in order to save moribund businesses, court validates employer's setting "initial" terms one month after taking over the business).

The Board has, however, divided on the question whether the successor remains free to set initial terms different from those of the predecessor when, at a time when the predecessor is still operating the business, the successor offers employment to all or substantially all of the predecessor's employees but it is stated or understood that the offer contemplates less favorable working conditions than those currently obtaining.   Two Board members would hold that the duty to bargain with the union attaches immediately upon the successor's manifesting an intention to look primarily to the predecessor's employees to fill its workforce, and that regardless of any statements concerning changed employment terms the employer is bound not to start its business with different terms unilaterally established.   The majority of the Board, however, has rejected this position, and has stated in Spruce Up Corp. (1974):

> When an employer who has not yet commenced operations announces new terms prior to or simultaneously with his invitation to the previous work force to accept employment under those terms, we do not think it can fairly be said that the new employer "plans to retain all of the employees in the unit," as that phrase was intended by the Supreme Court.   The possibility that the old employees may not enter into an employment relationship with the new employer is a real one .   .   . .   We believe the caveat in *Burns,* therefore, should be restricted to circumstances in which the new employer has either actively or, by tacit inference, misled employees into believing they would all be retained without change in their wages, hours, or conditions of employment, or at least to circumstances where the new employer, unlike the Respondent here, has failed to clearly announce its intent to establish a new set of conditions prior to inviting former employees to accept employment.

Since the Board believes the Supreme Court did not intend to bind the successor to bargain prior to takeover unless it actually hires its majority from the predecessor, the Board requires "that there be some substantial likelihood that those offered employment will accept it on the terms offered by the new employer." So stated the Board in United Maintenance & Mfg. Co. (1974), where it was held that the successor was not obligated to bargain with the union about initial terms of employment even though the offer to employ the predecessor's employees did not import any worsening of the terms under which they were presently employed; the employees were on strike against the predecessor in protest of those terms, such that it could not be said that "without question, a sufficient number of those offered employment would have accepted it." The view of the Board majority goes even further than does the *Burns* holding in freeing the successor employer to take over a business unburdened by the working conditions that were set in the labor contract between the predecessor company and its union.

RESTRAINT AND COERCION OF EMPLOYEE RIGHTS TO ORGANIZE

CHAPTER VII

INTERFERENCE WITH EMPLOYEE FREE CHOICE

§ 1. Section 8(a)(1): Coercion, Motive and Business Justification

When Congress passed the Wagner Act in 1935, it utilized very broad language in section 8(1) to declare it illegal for an employer "to interfere with, restrain, or coerce employees in the exercise of the rights guaranteed in section 7" to organize and bargain collectively and to engage in peaceful concerted activities. It also set forth with greater specificity four classes of employer actions which were thought particularly objectionable and which were all considered as sub-classes of the broader 8(1) violation: employer domination of a union (section 8(2)), employer discrimination in hiring, firing or working conditions to encourage or discourage union membership (section 8(3)), employer discrimination for filing charges or giving testimony before the NLRB (section 8(4)), and employer refusal to bargain with a majority union (section 8(5)). Conduct which violated any of the more specific prohibitions of section 8 would also coerce or restrain employees in their section 7 rights and would thus violate section 8(1) derivatively. These more specific prohibitions were not, however, to measure the complete range of section 8(1), for thus to circumscribe the broader provision would render it useless. It has never been seriously debated that section 8(1)—since 1947, section 8(a)(1)—can be violated by conduct other than that proscribed more specifically in the subsections which follow it. Examples are threats of employer reprisal for voting for a union, employer surveillance of employees in their union activities, employer questioning of employees concerning their union membership, employer rules barring union solicitation on company property, and employer discipline of employees for engaging in concerted activities unrelated to a union (and thus not within section 8(a)(3)).

It is also generally agreed that, to establish a violation of section 8(a)(1), it is not necessary to demonstrate—by direct testimony of employees or otherwise—that particular employees were actually coerced; it is sufficient if the General Counsel can show that the employer's actions would tend to coerce a reasonable employee. This objective standard obviously facilitates the development of a record and the trial of an unfair labor practice case, and also avoids the need to place employees in the discomforting position of testifying against their employer. The test for a section 8(a)(1) violation is objective in a second respect. It is sufficient to demonstrate that the employer action has the *effect* of restraint or coercion. It is not necessary to demonstrate that the employer *intended* to produce that effect. In an early and leading case on the meaning of section 8(1), the Supreme Court held unlawful a company rule which forbade solicitation of any kind on company property and which was enforced against employees soliciting for the union on nonworking time; it was not a defense that the no-solicitation rule had been adopted well before the advent of the union, had not been motivated by antiunion bias and had been applied nondiscriminatorily against all forms of in-plant solicitation. Republic Aviation Corp. v. NLRB (U.S.1945).

The Court also, however, announced in that case an important qualification to the seemingly unqualified language of section 8(1). Even conduct which interferes with, restrains or coerces employees in the exercise of their section 7 rights may be held lawful if it advances a substantial and legitimate company interest in plant safety, efficiency or discipline. Thus, no-solicitation rules were held presumptively valid to the extent they barred union activity during working time, when employees were expected to be on the working floor at their machines, and presumptively invalid only concerning nonworking time, such as lunchtime, work breaks and immediately before and after work. Similarly, although the Board believes that employer questioning of employees concerning their union affiliation is bound to have a coercive impact, such questioning is held not to violate section 8(a)(1) when it is done according to certain procedures which minimize the impact and when it is in response to a union claim of majority support. Struksnes Constr. Co. (1967). So, too, employer grants of benefits immediately prior to an election are believed to be tantamount to a threat of employer reprisal, NLRB v. Exchange Parts Co. (U.S.1964), but are permitted if in accordance with plant custom or business necessity, J. P. Stevens Co. v. NLRB (4th Cir. 1972).

In effect, section 8(a)(1) could be rewritten as follows: It shall be an unfair labor practice for an employer to take action which, regardless of the absence of antiunion bias, tends to interfere with, restrain, or coerce a reasonable employee in the exercise of the rights guaranteed in section 7, provided the action lacks a legitimate and substantial justification such as plant safety, efficiency or discipline. Thus construed, section 8(a)(1) requires that the Board strike a balance between the interests of the employer—which are not specifically accorded weight in the statute but which Congress surely intended be considered in administering a statute designed to further industrial peace and efficiency—and the interests of the employees in a free decision concerning their collective bargaining activities. In spite of occasional declarations to the contrary, the courts have tended to hold that the striking of this balance is committed primarily to the judgment, discretion and expertise of the National Labor Relations

Board, subject to only limited judicial review. *E. g.,* NLRB v. Fleetwood Trailer Co. (U.S. 1967).

§ 2. Employer Responsibility for the Conduct of Others

Since coercion of employees in their protected concerted activities will violate section 8(a)(1) only if done by an "employer," and since most employers (and of course any corporate employer) manifest their conduct through individuals other than themselves—most commonly, supervisors—it often becomes necessary to determine whether misconduct of individuals may properly be attributed to the employer. This is true for all subsections of section 8(a) of the Labor Act. The Wagner Act of 1935 included within the definition of "employer" in section 2(2) "any person acting in the interest of an employer, directly or indirectly." This broad imputation of responsibility contrasted with the narrow imputation to unions set forth in section 6 of the Norris-LaGuardia Act of 1932, requiring clear proof that the conduct of officials or members of the union was actually authorized or ratified by the union. In 1947, Congress declared in substance that usual principles of vicarious liability under the law of agency are to be applied to both union and employer. To achieve this, section 2(2) was modified to include within the term "employer" any person "acting as an agent" of an employer; and section 2(13) was added, providing:

> In determining whether any person is acting as an "agent" of another person so as to make such other person responsible for his acts, the question of whether the specific acts performed were actually authorized or subsequently ratified shall not be controlling.

These provisions permit the imputation to the employer not only of actions expressly authorized but also of actions which are impliedly authorized, and, more important, actions which are within the "apparent authority" of the actor. It has long been held that the issue of agency authority is to be gauged from the point of view of the employees. As the Board observed in J. S. Abercrombie Co. (1949), *enf'd* (5th Cir. 1950):

> The test applied by the Board, with the approval of the courts, in determining whether an employer is responsible for coercive statements by a supervisor is not whether the statements were, in fact, within the scope of the supervisor's employment, but whether the employees have just cause to believe that the supervisor is acting for and on behalf of management in the situation under dispute.

Supervisors and foremen are therefore generally presumed to be acting and speaking for the employer. This apparent authority survives even specific instructions to the supervisors to refrain from interfering with organizing activities, and can be dispelled only when these instructions are communicated to the rank-and-file employees. Otis L. Broyhill Furniture Co. (1951) (supervisors' coercive interrogation of an employee imputed to employer). The employer may, however, on occasion escape the imputation of wrongful conduct when it has given general assurances to employees that it will not interfere with their rights and when the specific misconduct of the supervisors is sporadic and isolated. NLRB v. Cleveland Trust Co. (6th Cir. 1954) (reversal of Board finding of employer unfair labor practice based on statements of two supervisors of 200; employer had in several letters informed employees of their rights). In such instances, employees can infer that the coercive acts are unauthorized; this is reinforced when the employer promptly repudiates the incidents and reprimands the supervisors.

It has generally been held that employees who are not supervisors are not presumed to be acting on behalf of the employer unless they are acting within the general scope of their employment or management has instigated such conduct or has ratified it after the fact (either expressly or by silence). Thus, in National Paper Co. (1953), *enf't denied on other grounds* (5th Cir. 1954), the company was charged with the threats made by a security guard, who the Board considered was acting within the scope of his authority. Violent actions by rank-and-file employees may be deemed to have been ratified if the employer fails to avail itself of an opportunity to reprimand the employees, NLRB v. American Thread Co. (5th Cir. 1953) (failure to reprimand employees after learning of their threats and intimidation of union organizers); and more clearly yet if the employer rewards them for their actions, *ibid.* (employee helped beat union man and his wife unconscious and, upon reporting for work the next day with his hand in a cast, was paid without working).

When the coercive conduct sought to be attributed to the employer is not that of supervisory or rank-and-file employees but rather of persons outside the company—such as local businessmen, civic leaders, community groups or newspapers—the burden of demonstrating employer responsibility will be somewhat greater, although the same substantive principle is said to apply in all instances: there must be some showing of an agency relationship, such as employer instigation, implied or apparent authority, or express or implied ratification. The bulk of the cases involve statements (or threats) by these "outsiders" that unionization will bring unfortunate economic consequences—to the employee, the company, and the community. Where there is no connection between the employer and the "outside" third party, the latter's acts will not normally be imputed to the employer even if it benefits from them. NLRB v. Lake Butler Apparel Co. (5th Cir. 1968) (editorial of local newspaper not imputed to employer under section 8(a)(1); court also emphasizes First Amendment considerations). At least one court has held that, in view of the presumption of neutrality of public officials, police surveillance of union organizers will not be attributed to the employer in the absence of clear and convincing evidence. NLRB v. Bibb Mfg. Co. (5th Cir. 1951).

If the employer takes affirmative action to adopt or approve of such third-party action, it will be liable. This was the outcome in NLRB v. Bibb Mfg. Co. (5th Cir. 1951), where the employer supplied a newspaper publisher with names and addresses of employees and ordered it to mail them copies of a threatening publication. Less explicit instigation may still render the employer liable for coercive conduct of nonemployees. In Mid-South Mfg. Co. (1958), the employer invited local businessmen to do whatever they wanted to keep the union out of the plant. Indeed, an employer's silence may in some circumstances be sufficient to charge it with ratification of coercive actions of outsiders. This will normally be the case when the employer is aware of the coercive statements or conduct of the outsiders but fails to utilize an obvious opportunity to repudiate them. Dean Indus., Inc. (1967). For example, when local businessmen or politicians relate to employees the employer's intention to close down the plant if the union is elected, and management is present when these statements are made (or learns of them soon after) but fails to disavow them, it will be deemed to have become a party to the coercion. This is true whether the outsiders were invited to speak by management, Southland Mfg. Co. (1951), or by the employees, L. & H. Shirt Co. (1949). The same is true when the outsiders engage in coercive interrogation or make promises of a wage increase. Waynline, Inc. (1949). It is not necessary that the employer consciously intend to endorse the conduct of the outsider but only that it create such an impression in the minds of the employees. S. D. Cohoon & Son (1952) (employer turned over office to woman who interrogated employees about their union membership, and employer directed employees to see her). Although it is rare, the Board has found (with judicial approval) that a local politician has so allied the interests of the town with those of the company, that the politician himself may be held liable as an agent of the employer for violation of section 8(a)(1) and may therefore be directly subjected to a Board remedial order. Henry I. Siegel Co. v. NLRB (6th Cir. 1969) (court sustains, 2–1, Board order requiring mayor to cease and desist, but refuses enforcement of affirmative order requiring him, now retired, to sign certain company notices).

The need to invoke the law of agency in the above cases stems from the need, in unfair labor practice cases, to find coercive conduct on the part of the "employer." Such a finding is not, however, necessary when the union's claim is that an election should be set aside because of an atmosphere of fear and hostility so pervasive that no reasoned and fair election could have been held, regardless whether the employer is responsible. There are many cases in which, for example, threats of plant closure in the event of unionization are made by local newspapers or businessmen, and such threats cannot be traced to the employer in order to make out an unfair labor practice. If, however, the "laboratory conditions" for a fair election are destroyed, the Board has the power to set the election aside and order a new one. Universal Mfg. Corp. (1966) (regardless whether advertisements and handbills, expressing racist sentiments and threats of blacklisting and economic disaster, were produced by agents of the employer, election should be set aside). Here too, prompt and unequivocal disclaimer by the employer may be sufficient to induce the Board to certify the election results. Claymore Mfg. Co. (1964).

The issue of employer involvement in the conduct of others is of special significance under section 8(a)(2), which bars employer interference in or support of a labor organization. A classic example of a violation of section 8(a)(2) is the involvement of supervisors in the creation and administration of a labor organization which purports freely to represent the wishes of the employees. This kind of violation is discussed in detail elsewhere in this work. The employer will also violate section 8(a)(2), in spite of its communicating to a few employees its neutrality between two competing unions, when the plant manager and other supervisors actively encourage employees to join one of the unions. NLRB v. Fotochrome, Inc. (2d Cir. 1965) (employer also terminated bargaining with incumbent union and failed to repudiate supervisors' support for insurgent).

§ 3. Section 8(a)(3) and Discriminatory Discharge; Proof and Remedies

The most recurrent employer violation of the Labor Act is the imposition of discharge or lesser discipline for an employee's membership in or support for the union. Commonly, the employer claims that the discharge was for work-related reasons, such as incompetence or insubordination; the employee or the union, however, contends that the discharge was a product of antiunion animus. If it can be demonstrated in an unfair labor practice proceeding, by the General Counsel—upon whom section 10(c) of the Act places the burden of proof by "the preponderance of the testimony"—that the actuating motive was reprisal for the employee's union membership or activities, the employer will be held to violate section 8(a)(3) and derivatively section 8(a)(1). Section 8(a)(3) requires that the employer have acted "to encourage or discourage membership in any labor organization" and that this effect be brought about by "discrimination." The requirements for a violation of section 8(a)(1)—interference with, restraint or coercion in the exercise of the section 7 right to organize or support a union—are less exacting and, as already noted, focus more upon the effects of the employer's conduct than upon its motivation. Nonetheless, with the rarest of exceptions, see NLRB v. Burnup & Sims (U.S.1964) (discharge of two employees engaged in organizing for the union, in mistaken belief that they had uttered threats of property damage to the company in order to achieve recognition), the discharge or discipline will not be deemed to violate the Act absent proof of antiunion animus. Presumably, the Board and courts are reluctant to screen employer conduct, short of such discrimination, to test whether the discipline was fitting or the employer's need substantial (although this is often done in cases arising under section 8(a)(1)).

In any event, it is not necessary that the General Counsel demonstrate that union activities were the sole actuating cause for the discharge or lesser discipline. The record in many cases will justify the inference that the discipline was precipitated in part by union activity and in part by a poor work record. In such cases a violation may be found, although there is no consensus as to what should be the required quantum of antiunion animus in order to make out a violation. Some would have it that the improper motive must be "dominant," NLRB v. Fibers Int'l. Corp. (1st Cir. 1971), others that "the employee would not have been fired *but for* the anti-union animus of the employer," NLRB v. Whitfield Pickle Co. (5th Cir. 1967) (improper motive need not be largest "in size" and may constitute violation when "small" if it is the "straw which breaks the camel's back"), and yet others, somewhat more lenient toward the General Counsel, only that the improper motive have contributed in some part, S. A. Healy Co. v. NLRB (10th Cir. 1970). Although the best evidence that discipline was imposed because of union activities is of course statements to that effect by the employer, it will be rare that such statements are available in an unfair labor practice proceeding. Other employer statements which show its hostility to the union, even open speeches to employees, cannot be introduced as evidence to show antiunion animus, unless such statements contain, in the words of section 8(c) of the Labor Act, a "threat of reprisal or force or promise of benefit." This issue is considered in detail below.

Once concluding that the employer has violated the Act by a discriminatory discharge, the Board will ordinarily issue a cease and desist order, will require that the employee be reinstated with backpay, and will require that the employer post a notice in a conspicuous place in the plant for sixty days, such notice informing employees of the violation and the remedy. Section 10(c) of the Act gives the Board express authority to issue a cease and desist order and to require reinstatement and backpay and other "affirmative action . . . as will effectuate the policies of this Act," and also authorizes the Board to require the respondent to file reports from time to time showing compliance with the order.

The calculation of backpay is fairly straightforward, and utilizes the traditional concept of mitigation of damages. Although at one time the Board calculated the difference, over the entire period between discharge and reinstatement, between the amount the employee would have earned had he not been discriminatorily discharged and the amount actually earned elsewhere, the Board now computes back-pay on a quarterly basis. F. W. Woolworth (1950). This prevents excess earnings in one quarter from reducing backpay liability ac-crued in a previous quarter, and is designed to destroy any incentive the employer might have to delay the proceedings and the reinstate-ment order. See NLRB v. Seven-Up Bottling Co. (U.S.1953) (Court approves this formula but suggests that it might be modified in sea-sonal industries). The Board also regularly adds six percent interest to the backpay due the discriminatee. Isis Plumbing and Heating Co. (1962). The backpay order contemplates the payment not only of periodic salary or wages but also of all other income otherwise pay-able for the period in question, including lost overtime, paid holidays and vacations, insurance benefits, board and lodging and bonuses. NLRB v. Exchange Parts Co. (5th Cir. 1965) (Christmas bonus). Moreover, if the rate of pay of the discriminatee would have in-creased had he not been discharged—for example, in the event he would have been promoted in due course—that increase will be taken into account in awarding backpay. NLRB v. Mooney Aircraft, Inc. (5th Cir. 1967).

Section 10(c) expressly provides: "No order of the Board shall require the reinstatement of any individual as an employee who has been suspended or discharged, or the payment to him of any back pay, if such individual was suspended or discharged for cause." The concept of "cause" is not defined in the Act but it is understood to re-fer to work-related justifications for discipline which would ordinari-ly be accepted as such under general industrial usages. See Ohio Ferro-Alloys Corp. (1974) (Board defers to arbitration award and dismisses section 8(a)(3) complaint, when arbitrator found that dis-charge had been for union activities and had ordered reinstatement but not backpay, in view of employee's false statements on his job ap-plication). Generally, this issue does not arise, since if the discharge or discipline was "for cause" there will usually be no violation of the Act and therefore no issue of remedy.

An issue on which there was controversy and confusion for many years is the authority of the Board to impose a reinstatement and backpay order not on the employer responsible for the discriminatory discharge but rather upon a "successor" employer which has pur-chased the business of the culpable employer, or absorbed it by merg-er, or otherwise taken over the assets or workforce of the wrongdoer. Early in the administration of the Wagner Act, the NLRB held that an employer committing an unfair labor practice could not avoid a remedial order simply by changing its corporate form; the order would be issued directly to the "alter ego" of the wrongdoer as well as to the wrongdoer itself. Hopwood Retinning Co. *enf'd as mdf'd* (2d Cir. 1938). The Board had greater difficulty resolving the ques-tion whether an unfair labor practice remedy could be issued against a person whose succession to the business of the wrongdoer was not a sham but was rather a bona fide business transaction. After holding initially in 1944 that only the person committing the unfair labor practice could be ordered to remedy it, the Board in 1947 reversed its position; but after a number of courts of appeals refused enforcement against the successor, the Board reverted in 1954 to its initial refusal to find "remedial successorship," only to reverse course again in 1967 in Perma Vinyl Corp. (1967), *enf'd* United States Pipe & Foundry Co. v. NLRB (5th Cir. 1968), this time with appellate approval. The Board found that the successor, United States Pipe & Foundry, was aware at the time it contracted to purchase the business of Perma Vinyl that charges of discriminatory discharge had been filed with the NLRB against the latter. It also found that Perma Vinyl's former employees were carried over to do the same jobs in the same manner in the same plant, that the jobs of the discriminatees still existed in the United States Pipe operation, and that no reinstatement remedy could be secured against Perma Vinyl which had become defunct by virtue of the transfer of the business. The Board issued a backpay order against the predecessor Perma Vinyl (although not against the successor, in view of the principle of non-liability then obtaining) but ordered United States Pipe to reinstate the discriminatees.

The Supreme Court, in Golden State Bottling Co. v. NLRB (U.S. 1973), upheld the Board in imposing an order of both backpay and reinstatement upon a bona fide successor which had knowledge at the time of the purchase of the business of a similar order against the predecessor-seller. There, All American Beverages bought the soft drink bottling and distribution business of Golden State Bottling Company which, to the knowledge of All American, had been found to have discriminatorily discharged a driver salesman. All American continued the operation of the business without interruption and without substantial change in workforce or method of operation. All American argued that the Board was limited by section 10(c) of the Labor Act to issue a remedial order only against "such person" as was held to have committed an unfair labor practice, and that judicial enforcement of an order against an innocent successor was inconsistent with applicable procedural rules requiring notice and hearing for the successor in the NLRB proceeding. The Supreme Court held that the Board's remedial authority is not thus limited by the Labor Act; that it has discretion to issue an order against persons related in interest to the wrongdoer; that the Board reasonably weighed the interests of the bona fide successor All American, the public and the discharged employee; and that fair procedure is accorded the successor when it is permitted, in a backpay specification proceeding, to present evidence on the issues whether there was sufficient continuity in the employing enterprise and whether the successor knew at the time of the acquisition that the predecessor had been charged with (or found to have committed) unfair labor practices. The Court concluded that the Board could find—in a case where a new employer "has acquired substantial assets of its predecessor and continued, without interruption or substantial change, the predecessor's business operations"—that the retained employees would view the permitted ouster of the discriminatee from the successor's workforce as an expression of continued employer hostility. Reinstatement with back-pay will typically cost the successor little since with advance notice of the Board proceedings against its predecessor, it can adjust its purchase price or secure an indemnity provision in the sales contract with a view toward its own potential liability. Moreover, the remedy permits the Board (in the language of section 10(c)) to "effectuate the policies of this Act," such as avoidance of labor strife, protection of employee rights to unionize, and restoration for the victimized employee.

In short, the successor may be ordered to remedy the predecessor's unfair labor practice when: (a) there is continuity in the employing enterprise; (b) the successor has notice of the predecessor's unfair labor practices at the time of the acquisition; (c) the remedy will effectuate the purposes of the Labor Act; and (d) the successor has an opportunity to try these issues to the Board, typically in a backpay proceeding.

The Court did not consider in detail those factors which warrant a finding of "continuity," but merely held that the Board's conclusion was warranted in the particular case, where operations and workforce continued substantially unchanged. If less than a majority of the successor's workforce had formerly worked for the predecessor, this will ordinarily relieve the successor of a duty to bargain with the predecessor's union, NLRB v. Burns Int'l Security Services, Inc. (U. S.1972); but it will not necessarily relieve the successor of a duty to arbitrate under the predecessor's labor contract, John Wiley & Sons v. Livingston (U.S.1964). There seems little reason why it should relieve the successor of the duty to reinstate with backpay an employee discriminatorily discharged by the predecessor, at least if a comparable job is available in the successor company; surely the equities of the victimized employee seem no less merely because his former co-workers comprise only a minority of the successor's workforce. But in such a case, just as the Board will not find that the successor has an independent obligation to continue to bargain with the predecessor's union, because of the interference with the bargaining preferences of the majority, the Board will not likely go beyond ordering reinstatement and backpay and require the successor to remedy an unlawful refusal to bargain by the predecessor employer. Compare Ramada Inns (1968) (predecessor Ramada's unlawful refusal to recognize the union deprived the union of presumption of majority usually attendant upon certification or recognition, such that successor Maalouf was not obligated to bargain; nor is Maalouf ordered to remedy Ramada's violation of section 8(a)(5)).

If the predecessor company remains in existence after the change in ownership—either elsewhere or in some form at the location of the transferred business—the Board may of course impose a backpay order on the predecessor and may order reinstatement of the discharged employee if that is feasible. The Board has in fact gone so far as to order the predecessor employer to pay the dischargee backpay beyond the date of the termination of its business, if it can be demonstrated that the employee in all likelihood would have continued in the employ of the successor had he not been unlawfully discharged. Hoke Janitorial Serv. (1974).

§ 4. Discrimination for Filing Charges or Giving Testimony to the NLRB

Section 8(a)(4) of the Labor Act declares it an unfair labor practice for an employer to "discharge or otherwise discriminate against an employee because he has filed charges or given testimony under this Act." In NLRB v. Scrivener (U.S.1972), the Supreme Court endorsed a liberal construction of this provision and held that it protected against discharge an employee who, although not filing an unfair labor practice charge or testifying at a hearing, had merely given a written sworn statement to a field examiner of the NLRB who was investigating a charge filed by another. The Court eschewed a literal interpretation of section 8(a)(4) in order that channels of information to the NLRB be kept open to facilitate its investigations. Thus, the Court would protect not only employees who are called to testify by subpoena but also those who come forward with information voluntarily. Presumably, the protection of section 8(a)(4) will be available whether the employee's testimony is oral or written, sworn or unsworn.

Scrivener did not deal with the case of discipline for threatening to file—but not actually filing—an unfair labor practice charge. A court of appeals had earlier held that section 8(a)(4) did not outlaw discipline in such a case, in Hoover Design Corp. v. NLRB (6th Cir. 1968). But the Board has since relied on *Scrivener* (which referred, without apparent enthusiasm, to the *Hoover* decision) to take issue with the lower court and to protect the employee who had merely threatened to file a charge. First Nat'l Bank & Trust Co. (1974).

In determining whether discharge or discipline was motivated by an employee's recourse to the Board, rather than by legitimate work-related reasons, the Board will find facts and draw inferences just as it commonly does in cases of discrimination arising under section 8(a)(3), and the courts will apply the usual review standard in section 10(e) of "substantial evidence on the record considered as a whole." NLRB v. King Louie Bowling Corp. (8th Cir. 1973) (discharge found to be for giving Board a written statement, even though employee's abusive language to her supervisor and fighting with other employees would have been sufficient grounds for discharge); Sinclair Glass v. NLRB (7th Cir. 1972) (discharge of employee who gave statement to Board investigator would be legal only if based solely on legitimate reasons).

If the employer disciplines a supervisor for filing charges or giving testimony to the Board, this will not violate section 8(a)(4), since that section forbids only discrimination against an "employee," and that term is explicitly defined in section 2(3) of the Labor Act to exclude supervisors. Yet such discipline has been held to be an unfair labor practice, under section 8(a)(1), because it may deter or otherwise restrain "employees" in the exercise of *their* rights freely to unionize under section 7, NLRB v. Dal-Tex Optical Co. (5th Cir. 1962) (cited with approval by the Supreme Court in *Scrivener*); and because allowing such discipline would impair the functioning of Board machinery that has been established to vindicate employee rights, NLRB v. Carter Lumber, Inc. (6th Cir. 1974). It is also likely that the discharge of an "employee" under section 8(a)(4) will derivatively violate section 8(a)(1) as well; but the Supreme Court expressly left this question undecided in *Scrivener* and no substantive or remedial rights appear to turn upon it.

§ 5.   Discrimination on the Basis of Race or Sex

In United Packinghouse Workers v. NLRB (D.C.Cir. 1969) the court on its own initiative held that employer discrimination in working conditions among white, black and Latin employees was without more a violation of section 8(a)(1) of the Labor Act. The court found that "invidious discrimination on account of race or national origin" deters the exercise of section 7 employee rights.

> This effect is twofold: (1) racial discrimination sets up an unjustified clash of interests between groups of workers which tends to reduce the likelihood and the effectiveness of their working in concert to achieve their legitimate goals under the Act; and (2) racial discrimination creates in its victims an apathy or docility which inhibits them from asserting their rights against the perpetrator of the discrimination.

The court found these effects to be evidenced in the record and to have been recognized by "union leaders, businessmen, government officials and psychologists," and remanded to the Board to consider the full record in light of the court's theory. The Board found insufficient evidence of racial discrimination and dismissed the claim under section 8(a)(1), without addressing whether it agreed with the court's analysis of that section.

Shortly after, however, the Board did address the issue and held (one member dissenting and one member finding no discrimination in fact and thus avoiding the legal issue) that "discrimination on the basis of race, color, religion, sex, or national origin is not *per se* a violation of the Act." Jubilee Mfg. Co. (1973), *enf'd* (D.C.Cir. 1974) (alleged discrimination in pay rates based on sex). Such discrimination standing alone was held not to be "inherently destructive" of employee section 7 rights and therefore not violative of section 8(a)(1) or (3). "There must be actual evidence, as opposed to speculation, of a nexus between the alleged discriminatory conduct and the interference with, or restraint of, employees in the exercise of those rights protected by the Act." The Board distinguished its decisions holding that the employer's race discrimination might warrant setting aside an election, or finding a refusal to bargain, or finding interference with employees taking concerted action on hiring policies; in all those instances, unlike race or sex discrimination pure and simple, there was "the necessary direct relationship between the alleged discrimination and our traditional and primary functions of fostering collective bargaining, protecting employees' rights to act concertedly" and conducting free and sober elections. The Board has in effect relegated such job-discrimination claims to the court-enforcement machinery of Title VII of the Civil Rights Act of 1964 and the Equal Employment Opportunity Commission, rejecting the conclusion of the court of appeals in *United Packinghouse* that the powers of the Board and the EEOC were intended by Congress to be concurrent.

§ 6. Plant Shutdown and Relocation: The "Runaway Shop"

A number of cases have dealt with the legality, under sections 8(a)(1) and (3), of an employer decision to close or move or subcontract its operations when motivated in some part by a union's organizing drive or its selection as bargaining representative. Prior to 1965, the law on this issue was fairly clear, although the Board's version of the law tended to be different from—and more restrictive of employer action than—the law as developed in the courts of appeals. The Board rather consistently held that the employer committed an unfair labor practice if it closed, moved or subcontracted its operations in any degree because of antiunion animus. Such an illegal motive would be found not only when the action was designed to escape the union or to punish the employees for unionization but also when the employer assumed (prior to bargaining) that the union would force the adoption of demands concerning wages or other working conditions which would render continued operation uneconomical. It was not a defense that the employer had, before the advent of unionization, independently decided to terminate the operation, if unionization accelerated the closing. At its strictest, the Board appeared to suggest that the union's coming would justify termination only when negotiation had made its economic demands a near-reality and were such as to render continued operation of the business actually unprofitable (as opposed to merely less profitable than elsewhere). *E. g.,* Morrison Cafeterias Consol., Inc. (1964).

The courts, on the other hand, were generally far more hospitable to employer decisions to shut down, move or subcontract—even when triggered by unionization—when there was economic justification for the action. Several courts of appeals concluded that a prerequisite to a finding of illegality was an employer purpose to exact reprisals or to avoid a duty to bargain; such illicit animus had to be the "true motive" or the "predominant purpose"—not just a contributing factor in some part—in order to make the employer's action illegal. The motive was not at all objectionable if the employer honestly believed that the union would bring with it sufficient increase in costs or decrease in operational flexibility as to make shutdown, relocation or subcontracting more desirable. Moreover, the courts tended to hold that an acceleration because of unionization of a decision already made to terminate the operation was not illegal. As the court stated in NLRB v. Lassing (6th Cir. 1960):

> The advent of the Union was a new economic factor which necessarily had to be evaluated by the respondent as a part of the overall picture pertaining to costs of operation. It is completely unrealistic in the field of business to say that management is acting arbitrarily or unreasonably in changing its method of operations based on reasonably anticipated increased costs, instead of waiting until such increased costs actually materialize.
>
> . . . Fundamentally, the change was made because of reasonably anticipated increased costs, regardless of whether this increased costs [sic] was caused by the advent of the Union or by some other factor entering into the picture.

See also NLRB v. Houston Chronicle Pub. Co. (5th Cir. 1954) (change in method of distribution and discharge of fifty-nine employees legal, although accelerated to avoid union interference, when initial decision made for economic reasons); NLRB v. Adkins Transfer Co. (6th Cir. 1955) (higher wage rate, under prevailing union scale, was predominant and lawful reason for subcontracting, while union status of employees was merely secondary motive). The court decisions exhibit a reluctance to find unlawful—and to compel the employer to remedy or actually undo—the shift of resources from less profitable to more profitable uses, whether or not profitability is union-related. They also demonstrate reluctance to parse multiple motives or to "second guess" the employer as to the wisdom of its decision, particularly when the termination of operations was in itself sufficiently costly as likely to deter precipitate antiunion retaliation.

In 1965, the Supreme Court decided Textile Workers Union v. Darlington Mfg. Co. (U.S.1965), and construed sections 8(a)(1) and (3) so as to give the employer even freer reign than most of the lower courts had done. In that case, Roger Milliken and members of his family owned controlling shares of Deering Milliken, a textile distributor, which in turn controlled seventeen textile manufacturers operating twenty-seven mills. Milliken also controlled indirectly one of those manufacturers, the Darlington Manufacturing Company, which operated one mill. After threats that the advent of a union at Darlington would result in its closing, and after a union victory in an election, the Darlington board of directors voted to close down, sell the physical assets and go out of business. The NLRB concluded that the entire Deering Milliken operation was a single business enterprise and that the shutdown violated the Act, even conceding that the employer had some economic reasons independent of the advent of the union for going out of business and that the advent of the union was considered by the company in economic terms. The court of appeals reversed, holding that even antiunion motivation would not render illegal a complete or a partial (that is, one of several plants) shutdown. The Supreme Court remanded the case to the Board, holding the legal results to turn upon whether the shutdown was to be viewed as a complete or a partial shutdown:

> We hold . . . that when an employer closes his entire business, even if the liquidation is motivated by vindictiveness toward the union, such action is not an unfair labor practice.
>
> . . . [A] partial closing is an unfair labor practice under § 8(a)(3) if motivated by a purpose to chill unionism in any of the remaining plants of the single employer and if the employer may reasonably have foreseen that such closing would likely have that effect.

The Court began by holding that in shutdown cases, section 8(a)(1)—which can brand as illegal employer action taken without a discriminatory motive—has no independent role to play. If the Act is violated at all, it must be through section 8(a)(3) and thus through proof of antiunion animus, for "some employer decisions are so peculiarly matters of management prerogative that they would never constitute violations of § 8(a)(1) . . . unless they also violated § 8(a)(3)." It then proceeded to state that it would be too startling an innovation to hold that Congress intended to forbid a businessman to go out of business, that a principal purpose of the Act was to bar discrimination designed to reap benefits by discouraging collective activities of employees in the future, and that no effective remedy existed for a complete shutdown motivated by union animus. (The Court's reasoning is suspect, since remedies can be fashioned, such as payment of employees until they secure equivalent employment elsewhere, and since it is surely arguable that the purpose of section 8(a)(3) is primarily to shelter union supporters against job retaliation directed at them personally rather than to shelter the non-victims or to deprive the employer of future benefits.) From these premises followed the conclusions that the complete shutdown, even in retaliation for a union victory, is not illegal; and that a partial shutdown is not illegal unless the General Counsel proves that

> the persons exercising control over a plant that is being closed for antiunion reasons (1) have an interest in another business, whether or not affiliated with or engaged in the same line of commercial activity as the closed plant, of sufficient substantiality to give promise of their reaping a benefit from the discouragement of unionization in that business; (2) act to close their plant with the purpose of producing such a result; and (3) occupy a relationship to the other business which makes it realistically foreseeable that its employees will fear that such business will also be closed down if they persist in organizational activities . . . .

Underlining the very rigorous burden of proof in the partial-shutdown case, the Court held that it was not satisfied by proof that the employees at the Darlington mill were discouraged by the shutdown from future concerted activities and that the shutdown would necessarily have such an impact on other Deering Milliken employees; appearing to ignore its declarations in earlier cases that motivation could be inferred from foreseeable result, the Court held there must be a specific showing that the shutdown was purposely designed to chill unionism at the other plants. On remand, the Board concluded that the closing of the Darlington mill was a partial shutdown and that its object was at least in part to chill unionism in the other mills controlled by the Milliken family. A divided court of appeals sitting en banc enforced the Board's order. Darlington Mfg. Co. v. NLRB (4th Cir. 1968).

The Board's prompt application of the *Darlington* principles represented a sharp reversal of its earlier decisions. In A.C. Rochat Co. (1967), it held that the company's shutdown of its sheet metal department for antiunion reasons was not illegal when the record failed to demonstrate that it was the employer's motive to chill unionism among the two employees in the sales department. And in Motor Repair, Inc. (1968), the Board held that an antiunion shutdown of one of six garage and motor repair facilities did not violate the Act even if it might be concluded that the shutdown discouraged unionization among company employees elsewhere, for failure of proof that this was the employer's object. See also Morrison Cafeterias Consol., Inc. (1969), *enf'd in part* (8th Cir. 1970) (antiunion shutdown of one of several cafeterias was lawful, there being no contemporaneous organizational activity in any of the other distant cafeterias, even though employer told employees of the shutdown later to frustrate organization in other cafeterias).

A recent Board decision may mark a slight movement away from such a strict application of *Darlington*. In George Lithograph Co. (1973), the Board found a violation of section 8(a)(3) when an employer, engaged in the printing and mailing service business, closed down its mailroom (a profitable operation) after repeated statements of opposition and open hostility to the organizing drive there by the Mailers Union. The Board acknowledged that it was impracticable or impossible in most cases to prove actual intent to "chill" and actual subjective "chilling" of specific employees, but went on nonetheless—because of the physical proximity and common supervision of the mailroom and other departments, and the employer's frequent and vehement expression of opposition to the union—to infer both that the chilling of union activities among other company employees was reasonably foreseeable and also therefore that it was intended.

While *Darlington* has thus found greatest application in cases of partial shutdowns, it appears not to have been applied to cases of subcontracting (where the work of the "shut-down" department is contracted out to be done elsewhere) or to cases of plant relocation. It might be argued that in these cases, *Darlington* requires that the employer, to violate section 8(a)(3), must act with the purpose of chilling unionism among its remaining employees in the subcontracting case and its new employees in the relocation case. It appears, however, that these kinds of cases will continue to be decided under section 8(a)(3) according to the pre-*Darlington* criteria; that is, a violation is made out when the subcontracting or plant relocation (the "runaway") is motivated by a desire to retaliate for unionization or to evade the duty to bargain, regardless of the "chilling" impact elsewhere. See Local 57, ILGWU v. NLRB (Garwin Corp.) (D. C.Cir. 1967) ("runaway" from New York illegal, since motivated by opposition to unionization in New York; court sets aside order to bargain in Florida, in part because "there is nothing in the record suggesting that the Florida workers were aware of what had occurred in New York"). Indeed, the Board has stated that in cases of subcontracting to avoid a union, the "chill elsewhere" test of *Darlington* is inappropriate and will not be utilized. Harper Truck Serv., Inc. (1972). Perhaps, as the Court in *Darlington* suggests, the antiunion runaway (or subcontracting) inherently gives the employer future benefits relative to the union, since unionized employees are terminated and nonunion (presumably) employees substituted. In any event, it would appear that plant relocation and subcontracting—like the partial or complete shutdown—will be regarded as "so peculiarly matters of management prerogative" that they will be tested exclusively under section 8(a)(3), with some union animus required for illegality, and not under section 8(a)(1) with its invitation to "interest balancing."

§ 7.   Coercive Speech: The First Amendment, Section 8(c) and Election Proceedings

It was the early position of the Board that any antiunion speeches or literature from the employer constituted "interference, restraint or coercion" in violation of section 8(1) of the Wagner Act. The very employment relationship, characterized by complete economic dependence of the employee upon the goodwill of the employer, made such antiunion statements inherently intrusive upon the employee's free choice. Moreover, the employer was thought to be disinterested in the choice as to collective bargaining made by its employees. This requirement of employer neutrality was sustained by some courts of appeals. See NLRB v. Federbush Co. (2d Cir. 1941) (L. Hand, J.): "What to an outsider will be no more than the vigorous presentation of a conviction, to an employee may be the manifestation of a determination which it is not safe to thwart." Other courts rejected it. E. g., Midland Steel Prods. Co. v. NLRB (6th Cir. 1940).

In 1941, the United States Supreme Court, in NLRB v. Virginia Elec. & Power Co. (U.S.1941), refused to enforce a Board order based upon what appeared to be a finding that two speeches and a bulletin of the company were in themselves illegally coercive. The Court concluded that the Wagner Act could not consistently with the First Amendment prevent an employer from speaking its mind on the merits of unionization provided its communications were free of coercion. The case was remanded in order that the Board might determine whether the employer communications, although noncoercive on their face, became so as a part of a total course of conduct in which the employer had engaged. Although the Board in the years immediately following eased somewhat its restrictions upon employer campaign communications, it held in 1946 that the employer committed an unfair labor practice when it assembled its employees on working time for the specific purpose of delivering an antiunion (but noncoercive) speech. This was the so-called "captive audience" doctrine, announced in Clark Bros. enf'd on other grounds (2d Cir. 1947).

Congress, reacting to the restrictive Board decisions in its first decade of operation, enacted as part of the Taft-Hartley amendments of 1947 section 8(c) of the Labor Act. It provides:

> The expressing of any views, argument, or opinion, or the dissemination thereof, whether in written, printed, graphic, or visual form, shall not constitute or be evidence of an unfair labor practice under any of the provisions of this Act, if such expression contains no threat of reprisal or force or promise of benefit.

The draft of section 8(c) in the House bill would have sheltered all such expression unless threatening force or economic reprisal "by its own terms"; the Senate version would have permitted the Board to condemn such a statement if it "contains under all the circumstances" a threat "express or implied, of reprisal or force." There is some dispute whether section 8(c) as actually written was intended to embody the House or the Senate philosophy. It will rarely matter, however, since it is by now quite clear that a finding of coercion may be sustained even without an explicit and unambiguous threat by the speaker when related intimidating or discriminatory acts give coercive import to an otherwise ambiguous speech. See NLRB v. Kropp Forge Co. (7th Cir. 1949). There is also some dispute whether section 8(c) was intended as merely a statutory restatement of the requirements of the First Amendment, or whether it goes even further in sheltering communications which might (by a broad reading of the surrounding circumstances) be found to be coercive.

What is clear is that Congress intended by the enactment of section 8(c) to restrain the Board in some measure in its earlier tendency to use employer speeches or leaflets in order to attribute motivation for other employer conduct and its tendency to construe employer speeches or leaflets as coercive in themselves. Thus, the legislative history demonstrates that section 8(c) was in large part directed at the case in which the employer makes an antiunion but noncoercive speech and then soon after discharges an employee for reasons which could plausibly relate either to his work record or to his union activities. The statute forbids the Board to treat the speech "as evidence of an unfair labor practice" by inferring from it that the discharge was for antiunion reasons. But see Smith's Transfer Corp. (1966) (section 8(c) does not bar use of antiunion leaflets to show background of discharge and to corroborate other evidence of hostility to union).

Section 8(c) also declared that the noncoercive speech or leaflet was not to "constitute" an unfair labor practice, and the legislative history showed that the draftsmen intended to overrule the *Clark Bros.* decision. The Board thereafter did indeed discard the *Clark Bros.* "captive audience" doctrine, but promptly developed what has become known as the *General Shoe* doctrine. In General Shoe Corp. (1948), the Board held that employer speeches directed against the union and delivered to groups of employees in the president's office, and visits by supervisors to employee homes after working hours—although not necessarily containing the kind of threat of reprisal or force which would justify holding the employer responsible for an unfair labor practice—could warrant setting aside an election which was held thereafter and which was lost by the union. The employer's campaign was held to go "so far beyond the presently accepted custom of campaigns directed at employees' reasoning faculties that we are not justified in assuming that the election results represented the employees' own true wishes." The Board stated further that the standard for setting aside an election would be different from and broader than the restrictions upon campaign techniques imposed in the unfair labor practice provisions of the Act:

> In election proceedings, it is the Board's function to provide a laboratory in which an experiment may be conducted, under conditions as nearly ideal as possible, to determine the uninhibited desires of the employees. . . . When, in the

rare extreme case, the standard drops too low, because of our fault or that of others, the requisite laboratory conditions are not present and the experiment must be conducted over again.

The Board squared its holding with section 8(c) by noting that that section by its own terms forbade the use of nonthreatening communications only in unfair labor practice proceedings and made no mention of representation cases.   While it has been argued that the Board's "sanction" of setting aside an election because of noncoercive communications is barred by the First Amendment (just as much as the sanction of an unfair labor practice order), this claim has been judicially rejected.   Bausch & Lomb, Inc. v. NLRB (2d Cir. 1971) (minimal "chilling" of employer and union speeches by setting aside election for misrepresentations is outbalanced by interest of employees and public in free, fair and informed representation elections).

§ 8.   Implied Threats: Criteria for Decision

The most vexing cases under section 8(c) relate to its mandate that communications "shall not constitute . . . an unfair labor practice" unless they "contain" a threat of reprisal.   Thus, an employer speech or leaflet can itself be found to constitute "interference, restraint or coercion" if it explicitly threatens loss of employment, loss of pay, loss of promotion, or violence if the listener votes for the union or if the union wins the election.   Similarly, as noted above, it is fairly clear that language which on its face can be read either as coercive or not can be held to constitute an unfair labor practice when the language is read in light of other conduct on the part of the speaker, such as discriminatory discharges, surveillance of employees and threatening interrogation, at least when that other conduct is rather directly related in time and space to the speech which is under consideration by the Board.

It is, however, often difficult to determine how to characterize, as either coercive or lawful, statements—orally or in writing, by employer or by union—which *by themselves* may fairly be read in either of two ways: as threats of reprisal or force or as information concerning the possible adverse consequences of unionization which an enlightened employee ought to know.   As was noted by Learned Hand early in the history of the Labor Act, the task for the decisionmaker is essentially to determine which of two elements predominates in an employer's communication: "On the one hand, it is an expression of his own beliefs and an attempt to persuade his employees to accept them; on the other, it is an indication of his feelings which his hearers may believe will take a form inimical to those of them whom he does not succeed in convincing."   NLRB v. American Tube Bending Co. (2d Cir. 1943).   Each case requires a fine assessment of the record, with no case serving as much of a precedent for others because of different combinations of facts such as the commission or non-commission of independent unfair labor practices, the identity of the speaker, the subject matter of the communication, the exact language employed, the nature of the campaign waged in opposition, and the employer's history of past encounters with collective bargaining. Moreover, the Board members will screen these particularized facts through their own differing perceptions of the purposes of the Labor Act and of governmental regulation.

Thus, in the period from 1953 to 1962, when a majority of the Board was appointed by President Eisenhower, the Board tended to sustain employer communications as "predictions," "opinions" or "statements of legal position" in many cases when they might just as plausibly have held them to constitute intrusive threats. The so-called Eisenhower Board also tended more readily to abstract oral and written communications from their factual setting (which might have been thought to give them a coercive overtone) and to downplay the use of the *General Shoe* doctrine in election cases. These tendencies were reversed in 1962 when, coincident with a change in membership, the Board overruled a number of earlier decisions which had refused to set aside elections in the face of charges of coercive speech. In Dal-Tex Optical Co. (1962), the Board announced a higher standard for election speech, and held that:

> Conduct violative of Section 8(a)(1) is, *a fortiori,* conduct which interferes with the exercise of a free and untrammeled choice in an election. This is so because the test of conduct which may interfere with the "laboratory conditions" for an election is considerably more restrictive than the test of conduct which amounts to interference, restraint or coercion . . . .

More recently, the United States Supreme Court spoke to the issue of pre-election speeches in NLRB v. Gissel Packing Co. (U.S. 1969). In an attempt to harmonize the employer (and employee) interest in free and full disclosure of information and the employee interest in an uncoerced decision on collective bargaining, the Supreme Court placed heavy emphasis upon two factors: the extent to which the untoward consequences of unionization are within the power of the employer to implement or are beyond its control, and the extent to which the employer's assertions are based upon demonstrable probabilities:

> Thus, an employer is free to communicate to his employees any of his general views about unionism or any of his specific views about a particular union, so long as the communications do not contain a "threat of reprisal or force or promise of benefit." He may even make a prediction as to the precise effects he believes unionization will have on his company. In such a case, however, the prediction must be careful-

ly phrased on the basis of objective fact to convey an employer's belief as to demonstrably probable consequences beyond his control .   .   .   . If there is any implication that an employer may or may not take action solely on his own initiative for reasons unrelated to economic necessities and known only to him, the statement is no longer a reasonable prediction based on available facts but a threat of retaliation based on misrepresentation and coercion, and as such without the protection of the First Amendment. We therefore agree with the court below that "[c]onveyance of the employer's belief, even though sincere, that unionization will or may result in the closing of the plant is not a statement of fact unless, which is most improbable, the eventuality of closing is capable of proof."

In thus setting a rather high standard for employer campaign communications, the Supreme Court has assisted the speaker in more objectively assessing in advance (and the Board, after the fact) the validity of employer "predictions," "opinions" and "statements of legal position." The Board has applied this high standard and set aside an election because of employer statements that a union victory would induce the company's major customer to deal elsewhere. Blaser Tool & Mold Co. (1972). Over a dissenting opinion which argued that *Gissel* requires a re-run election only when the employer's statement relates to action which is not likely to occur *and* which is within the employer's control, a majority of the Board held that it was sufficient that the employer had failed to demonstrate the likelihood of the customer's desertion.

§ 9. Implied Threats: Recurrent Fact Situations

Perhaps the best way to understand the manner in which the Board and courts have decided cases of arguably coercive election communications is to note several factual patterns which recur in the reports.

(a) Employers often state that the advent of the union will result in increased prices and the consequent desertion of customers and ultimately the removal or shutdown of the business. Depending on the phraseology and the "circumstances," the Board may treat these statements either as thinly veiled threats of reprisal against unionization, see Carpenters & Joiners (1973), particularly when the employer fails to demonstrate that such consequences are likely to occur, Blaser Tool & Mold Co (1972); or as "predictions" of the possible impact of the union's wage demands, see Chicopee Mfg. Corp. (1953). The courts of appeals sitting in review of Board decisions in such cases have been divided. See, *e. g.,* NLRB v. Golub Corp. (2d Cir. 1967).

(b) Employers often state that the union if elected will support its bargaining demands by calling the employees out on strike, thus rendering them subject to permanent replacement. The employer frequently adds that employees out of work because of a strike are not entitled to receive unemployment compensation. In some cases, the Board has found such statements coercive. *E. g.,* Dal-Tex Optical Co. (1962). In others the statements have been upheld as informing employees of the risks they must bear in the event the union makes unreasonable bargaining demands. *E. g.,* Texas Boot Mfg. Co. (1963); Coors Porcelain Co. (1966). (In the latter kind of case, the employer has been held not to forfeit its privilege merely by failing to inform the employees of the reinstatement rights of replaced economic strikers and unfair labor practice strikers. Mississippi Extended Care Center, Inc. (1973).)

(c) Employers often state that upon the initiation of a collective bargaining relationship the employer will be entitled by law to "bargain from scratch" or to "bargain hard" without the obligation to make concessions to the union, thereby indicating that employees may actually lose economic benefits as a result of unionization. In Dal-Tex Optical Co. (1962), the Board treated this as coercive, while a contrary result was reached in Trent Tube Co. (1964).

(d) In *Dal-Tex, supra,* the Board found coercive certain statements by the employer, *inter alia,* that it would litigate the validity of the forthcoming election (since in the opinion of the employer an earlier election which the union lost was invalidly set aside) and that the fruits of collective bargaining might thus be long delayed. The Board noted that the "Employer's statements went far beyond a bare announcement that it intended to test in the courts the legality of the Board's action in setting aside the prior election." In W. T. Grant Co. (1964), just such an announcement by the employer was held not to warrant setting aside an election; *Dal-Tex* was distinguished as involving an employer statement which was tantamount to a claim that it would "in no event" bargain collectively.

(e) In a series of cases before the Board, the employer posted or circulated a notice which warned the employees, among other things, that the advent of the union would work to their "serious harm." In view of the coercive implications which might reasonably be drawn from such an admonition, the Board has tended to find such communications illegal when the employer has committed other independent acts of coercion and discrimination which would tend to dispel any ambiguity; but even when there are no other such acts, the employer appears to have the burden expressly to explain to its employees that the "serious harm" will flow not from the company but from the union itself (*e. g.,* union dues, bargaining strikes). See Greensboro Hosiery Mills, Inc. (1967), *enf't denied on this issue* (4th Cir. 1968). The courts have tended to be much more tolerant of these statements, finding that they are clearly protected by section 8(c) when viewed in isolation and that a rather more substantial showing of an atmosphere of antiunion animus (than that which convinces the Board) will be necessary to convert the protected speech into coercive speech. NLRB v. Aerovox Corp. (4th Cir. 1970).

(f) Employers have frequently exhibited a motion picture entitled "And Women Must Weep," distributed by the National Right-To-Work Committee. The motion picture purports to be factual and portrays a strike in a "middle American" community; the strike is shown to have been precipitated by the arrogance of a clique of union leaders, to lead to hostility and violence on the picket line and within the community, and ultimately to the shooting of the baby of a worker unsympathetic to the union's cause. The Machinists Union has produced and made available for distribution by way of rebuttal a motion picture entitled "Anatomy of a Lie." In 1962, the Board concluded that the showing of "And Women Must Weep" very shortly before an election was in itself sufficient to warrant overturning an employer election victory, the rationale being a combination of the inflaming of employee emotions, the implied employer threat and the serious factual misrepresentations contained in the film. Plochman & Harrison—Cherry Lane Foods, Inc. (1962). The Board subsequently held that the showing of the film in the context of other employer unfair labor practices constituted an implied threat of reprisal (*i. e.,* employer provocation of strikes with attendant risk of grave injury and strife) should the union prevail in the election. Spartus Corp. (1972), *mdf'd on other grounds* (5th Cir. 1973). The courts of appeals, however, almost uniformly reversed these Board unfair labor practice findings and concluded, even in the context of other employer violations, that the showing of "And Women Must Weep" can be discounted by the employees as propaganda and can be understood as no more than a prediction of possible union-induced violence but not threats of employer reprisal. Luxuray, Div. of Beaunit Corp. v. NLRB (2d Cir. 1971) (union had exhibited "Anatomy of a Lie"); Kellwood Co., Ottenheimer Div. v. NLRB (1970). The Board itself has now adopted that position, overruling its earlier decisions to the contrary. Although two Board members are still prepared to hold the exhibition of "And Women Must Weep" to be coercive in the circumstances of a particular case, a Board majority has declared that its exhibition, even in the setting of other employer unfair labor practices, will justify neither an unfair labor practice finding nor the setting aside of an employer victory in a representation election. Litho Press (1974).

As noted above, decisions in these cases tend to be based upon the "totality of the company's activities," as suggested in the Supreme Court decision in NLRB v. Virginia Elec. & Power Co. (U.S. 1941), and there is no litmus-paper test to predict the likely holding of the Board or courts. It is, however, possible to generalize to the extent of saying that campaign communications will more likely be held unlawfully coercive and a basis for upsetting an election when: (1) the speaker has committed independent unfair labor practices, or

(2) when the communications are made very shortly before the election, or (3) when they are not incidental to or otherwise "buried" in a mass of more "objective" communications, or (4) when they have not been provoked by or subsequently addressed by a communication of like kind from the adversary, or (5) when the untoward consequences (such as strikes and permanent replacement) are portrayed as inevitable rather than as merely possible or likely, and, as was held by the Supreme Court in *Gissel,* (6) when the untoward consequences are not demonstrably probable (if they are asserted to be so), and (7) when those consequences are within the volition and control of the speaker rather than of third persons over whom the speaker has no control.

In light of the usual "closeness" of many of these cases, with the record capable of being read to demonstrate either that the communications are coercive or are merely legitimately informative, one would imagine that considerable deference would be given by the courts on review of Board decisions, pursuant to the test of "substantial evidence on the record considered as a whole." However, it is fair to say that many courts have in close cases tended to give little deference to the Board's conclusions, that they have tended to examine the issue of coercion rather independently and that they have far more frequently substituted their own findings of noncoercion for Board findings of coercion rather than the reverse. Although courts rarely advert to or justify this inclination, it is in large part explainable by the fact that federal regulation of the flow of information in labor-election campaigns may trench upon First Amendment protections, see Thomas v. Collins (U.S.1945), a setting naturally characterized by an "uninhibited, robust and wide-open" exchange between labor and management, Linn v. United Plant Guard Workers (U.S. 1966). See NLRB v. Golub Corp. (2d Cir. 1967). It perhaps also is based—at least in those cases in which the unfair labor practice rests on a speech or leaflet itself, isolated from surrounding occurrences—on the court's belief that it is in as good a position as is the Board to assess the impact on the listener or reader.

§ 10. Misrepresentations

Statements made by the contestants in an election campaign may, either by design or by inadvertence, contain factual inaccuracies. Employees may mistakenly rely upon erroneous representations on such matters as employee compensation in comparable industries, the likely fruits of collective bargaining (*e. g.,* mandatory payment of union dues in a stipulated amount), or the extent to which employee benefits in other plants or in this particular plant in the past were products of collective bargaining or of the employer's voluntary action. While such mistaken reliance will not in itself warrant a finding of "interference, restraint or coercion" in violation of the unfair labor practice provisions of the Act, the deviation from the truth may so mislead and confuse the employees as to warrant a conclusion that the election result has been tainted and should be set aside. Considering the volume of oral and written communications by employer and union, and the natural tendency to engage in (and, where discernible, for the employees to discount) exaggeration, ambiguity and half-truth when such is to the speaker's advantage, the Board has stated that it will not void all elections in which such abuses have occurred. It does, however, consider these abuses more properly subject to governmental supervision in the labor election than in the conventional political election.

The Board's present approach to the problem of factual misrepresentation in election cases was announced in Hollywood Ceramics Co. (1962):

> [T]he Board has refused to certify election results where a party has misrepresented some material fact, within its special knowledge, so shortly before the election that the other party or parties do not have time to correct it, and the employees are not in a position to know the truth of the fact asserted.

Moreover, the misrepresentation must be a "substantial departure from the truth." Consistent with its belief that the object is to assure that the employees' vote will not rest on materially erroneous assumptions, the Board does not require that the speaker have an intention to deceive; the Board in *Hollywood Ceramics* announced that it would act whenever the "misrepresentation, whether deliberate or not, may reasonably be expected to have a significant impact on the election." Of course, if it can be demonstrated that the speaker made the misrepresentation with knowledge of its falsity and intent to mislead, this can be properly treated as an admission that in its judgment the representation did indeed relate to a material issue likely to have a significant impact on the outcome of the election. NLRB v. Trancoa Chem. Corp. (1st Cir. 1962). While the Board stated that the election will not be set aside unless the speaker misrepresents some material fact "within its special knowledge," another formulation would focus more upon the employees' *perception* regarding the speaker's special knowledge:

> In judging the effect of a misrepresentation the test cannot be whether the speaker in fact had special knowledge, but must be whether the listeners would believe that he had. A misrepresentation by one having prime access to pertinent facts would be of no consequence if, for some reason, his listeners did not think him believable. On the other hand, a misrepresentation by one in fact having no knowledge at all would be effective if he was thought to be credible.

NLRB v. A.G. Pollard Co. (1st Cir. 1968).

The *Hollywood Ceramics* principle also expresses certain limitations upon the Board's setting aside of elections for campaign misrepresentations. The election will be sustained when the misrepresentation relates to an immaterial issue (that is, one not likely to have affected the results of the election) or, even though on a material issue, when the employees would have been unreasonable to rely on it because of its obvious falseness or because they possess independent knowledge with which to evaluate the statements. Thus, if the employees have—or, more accurately, are in a position to secure in a timely way—access to the information which is the source of the misrepresentation (such as wage levels in stipulated local plants), the Board will not likely set aside the election. NLRB v. Bata Shoe Co. (4th Cir. 1967) (employees can evaluate union representations that employer cheats on computation of their piecework and overtime pay); Convalescent Hosp. Mgt. Corp. (1968) (one union represents wages in nursing homes organized by other union to be below statutory minimum wage).

The Board also rather consistently refuses to set aside an election, even in the face of a serious misrepresentation on a material campaign issue, when the statement has been made long enough in advance of the election that the opponent has ample opportunity to rebut—even though that opportunity might not actually be seized. Lipman Motors, Inc. v. NLRB (2d Cir. 1971). Critics of the Board's position have pointed out that the purpose of the Labor Act is not simply to give the employer and the union a fair opportunity to rebut each other's statements but rather to secure through an election the uninhibited desires of an accurately informed voter; the employee is deceived when, in spite of an opportunity to rebut a material misrepresentation, that opportunity is not seized. NLRB v. Cactus Drilling Corp. (5th Cir. 1972). The Board, however, takes the position that its rule of upholding the election—even when the opportunity to rebut is not utilized and the employees may remain deceived—is justified over the broad range of election cases by the policies of encouraging the rebuttal and thus rectifying the misunderstanding privately and not through Board proceedings and of encouraging prompt settlement of representation questions. *Ibid.* For similar reasons, a misleading statement made even imminently before the election will not likely warrant overturning the election if it is in substance the same as statements made earlier in the campaign, to which rebuttal was or could have been attempted. Lipman Motors, Inc. v. NLRB (2d Cir. 1971).

The extent to which the law does—and ought to—regulate for truth the statements made in vigorous labor election campaigns is quite uncertain. First, the criteria applied by the Board to determine whether an election should be set aside for factual misrepresentations are elusive, and lead to no discernible predictability or consistency in

Board and court decisions. As the Board stated recently, it must make a refined and multi-factored judgment,

> with the aid of such expertise in the field as we may collectively have developed, as to whether the nature of such last-minute departures is such as to constitute a "substantial" departure from the truth, as to whether the issue involved is itself "substantial," as to whether it is likely to have "had a real impact on the election," as well as the collateral, but not unrelated issues of whether there was time for an effective reply, whether employees might reasonably have relied on the misrepresentation, and so on.

Modine Mfg. Co. (1973). The Board must also address the fundamental question whether the speaker can properly be charged with having misrepresented facts at all, when the statements might more charitably be characterized as "allowable" puffing, ambiguity or half-truth with which the Board states it will normally not interfere. Compare Russell-Newman Mfg. Co. (1966), with Cross Baking Co. v. NLRB (1st Cir. 1971) (both cases dealing with union statements regarding bargained wage increase which failed to disclose that increase was not immediate but progressive over three-year contract term); Celanese Corp. (1958), *enf't denied* (7th Cir. 1960) (union statements that fringe benefits at other company plants had been secured by collective bargaining when in fact some had been granted unilaterally by employer). The Board has held in Modine Mfg. Co. (1973), that in weighing all of these factors

> [t]here are many intangibles going into such a judgment. We may, for example, take into account the current degree of sophistication of the voters at a particular time or in a particular area of the country. We may also call into play the expertise we develop in observing through our own eyes and through the eyes of regional personnel directly involved in the conduct of some 9,000 elections a year. For we are faced in each case with a judgment both as to how material alleged misrepresentations in a given subject area may be in a particular place and in a background of the tenor of the particular time. We may also appropriately bear in mind the character of the particular work force involved and what we observe to be the reputation and the relative strength of the employer or the labor organization alleged to have made a material misrepresentation. All of these factors, whether they be labeled "common sense" or "expertise," help mold our conclusions in such cases as this.

Second, there is disagreement within the Board, and between the Board majority and the courts, as to whether certain facts are properly relevant to a decision whether to set aside an election because of misrepresentations. Thus, despite court warnings that "the closeness of the election is obviously relevant," NLRB v. Gooch Packing Co. (5th Cir. 1972), the Board appears no more inclined to order a new election when the margin of victory is slim than when it is substantial. Modine Mfg. Co. (1973). Indeed, while the majority of the Board believe that a "heavily lopsided" election indicates that a misrepresentation has been substantial, *ibid.*, others consider it cause to treat a misrepresentation as unlikely to have affected the election outcome, Allis Chalmers Mfg. Co. (1972) (Chairman Miller, concurring).

Third, there is disagreement among the courts of appeals as to the appropriate standard of judicial review of Board decisions to set aside elections for factual misrepresentations. The courts appear to agree that any findings of fact made by the Board in such election cases are to be set aside if unsupported by substantial evidence on the record considered as a whole; but on the question whether once having found those facts the Board properly exercised its judgment to set aside the election, some courts would hold the Board to a similar "substantial evidence" requirement, see NLRB v. Trancoa Chem. Corp. (1st Cir. 1962), while others will set aside the Board order only if it is arbitrary or an "abuse of discretion," Lipman Motors, Inc. v. NLRB (2d Cir. 1971). (The distinction between these two standards may evaporate in application, but it suggests a differing judicial attitude on the measure of deference due Board election decisions.)

Fourth, there has been some discernible tendency for the courts to be even more critical of campaign representations than is the Board. The Board has recently articulated its growing concern about the expenditure of time and resources in screening elections for minor misrepresentations; even so, it purports to look not for an "actual impact" that misrepresentations have on voters' choice "but rather a tendency materially to mislead." Modine Mfg. Co. (1973). But at least one court has gone further and held that the Board is to set aside an election when the representations are such as to make it "sufficiently likely that it cannot be told whether [the employees] were or were not" misled. NLRB v. Trancoa Chem. Corp. (1st Cir. 1962). Some courts, in announcing that the Board has not been sufficiently rigorous in screening for campaign misrepresentations, have in fact suggested that the Board has improperly displayed a greater tolerance of union statements than of comparable employer statements. *E. g.,* Cross Baking Co. v. NLRB (1st Cir. 1971).

The Board's supervision of the accuracy of election communications has evoked criticism from scholars, from within the Board itself and also from certain members of Congress. One member of the Board, dissenting in Medical Ancillary Services (1974), has urged the abandonment of the *Hollywood Ceramics* guidelines, claiming that they are unduly restrictive of campaign speech, they impose heavier caseloads on the Board, they lead to substantial delays in the processing of representation cases, and they treat "employees not like mature individuals capable of facing the realities of industrial life and making their own choices but as retarded children who need to be protected at all costs"; he would have the Board set elections aside "only upon a showing of intentional deception rising to the level of fraud." Criticisms of this kind have induced the Board to consider departing from the *Hollywood Ceramics* guidelines, but the Board announced in Modine Mfg. Co. (1973), that it was not yet prepared to do so:

> Despite the fact that the voters in most of our elections have benefited, along with the bulk of our citizenry, by improvements in our educational processes, and despite the fact that our elections have now become almost commonplace in the industrial world so that the degree of employee sophistication in these matters has doubtless risen substantially during the years of this Act's existence, we are not yet ready to say that we will leave all our voters in all of our elections and in all circumstances to sort out, with no protection from us, from among a barrage of flagrant deceptive misrepresentations.

Although the validity of the *Hollywood Ceramics* rule has been challenged as in excess of the Board's statutory and constitutional powers, these challenges have been rejected by the courts. Section 8(c) merely forbids the use of misrepresentations (when uncoercive) to support an unfair labor practice finding and does not prevent the Board from setting aside elections which fail to meet the "laboratory conditions" test. Sonoco Prods. Co. v. NLRB (9th Cir. 1968). And, while the courts have recognized that the setting aside of elections may have a "chilling effect" on employer and union speech, it does not violate constitutional safeguards for free speech since "the incidental effects of regulation on the rights of employer and union must be weighed against the interests of employees and the public at large in free, fair and informed representation elections." Bausch & Lomb, Inc. v. NLRB (2d Cir. 1971) (labor elections more properly regulable than political elections).

§ 11.   Racial Appeals

In the early years of the administration of the Labor Act, employer antiunion speeches were sometimes addressed to the racial policies of the union, commonly by way of forecast that job security or working conditions of employees (in most cases white employees) would be threatened upon the advent of the union. In keeping with its early policy of outlawing all antiunion employer speech, the Board found such racial references to be coercive. The Board shifted direction in the 1940's, when the Supreme Court noted the First Amendment implications of banning antiunion speech and when Congress enacted as part of the Taft-Hartley amendments section 8(c) which shelters "the expressing of any views, argument, or opinion   .   .   .

if such expression contains no threat of reprisal or force or promise of benefit." For some fifteen years thereafter, the Board tended to sustain election-campaign appeals—by both employer and union—to racial animosities of the employees, except when those appeals contained threats of reprisal or promises of benefit. *E. g.,* Babcock & Wilcox Co. (1960) (employer threat to lay off black employees in the event of unionization); Empire Mfg. Corp. *enf'd* (4th Cir. 1958) (employer threat to white employees, in event of unionization, to hire black employees to work alongside them).

In 1962, the Board sketched out a more aggressive role for itself in the regulation of campaign communications by holding that under certain circumstances the insistent appeal, by inflammatory propaganda, to the racial animosities of employees would justify setting aside an election. In Sewell Mfg. Co. (1962), the Board—although not finding any employer unfair labor practice (presumably because the inflammatory propaganda contained no threat of reprisal or promise of benefit)—set aside an employer election victory after a campaign in two small Georgia towns in which the employer had periodically distributed copies of newspaper stories and pictures emphasizing the pro-black and pro-Communist activities of labor unions and the "race mixing" implications of unionization. The Board acknowledged that statements about the racial position of the union or employer may be clearly germane to the employees' decision upon the merits of unionization, but expressed concern that appeals to prejudice can ignite the emotions and overpower the reasoning faculty such that extraneous issues of race may prove determinative in the election. Accordingly, the Board stated that propaganda on the racial issue was to be tolerated only if "temperate in tone, germane, and correct factually."

> So long, therefore, as a party limits itself to *truthfully* setting forth another party's position on matters of racial interest and does not deliberately seek to overstress and exacerbate racial feelings by irrelevant, inflammatory appeals, we shall not set aside an election on this ground. However, the burden will be on the party making use of a racial message to establish that it was truthful and germane, and where there is doubt as to whether the total conduct of such party is within the described bounds, the doubt will be resolved against him.

The "laboratory conditions" standard of General Shoe Corp. (1948), was not satisfied in *Sewell* because the employer "calculatedly embarked on a campaign so to inflame racial prejudice of its employees that they would reject the Petitioner [union] out of hand on racial grounds alone."

The Board, in contrast, on the same day sustained an employer election victory, where the employer had informed the employees of the Union's position on segregation and its monetary contributions to integrationist organizations; the information was held to have been temperately presented, factually accurate and germane to a legitimate election issue. Allen-Morrison Sign Co. (1962). The Board believes that it is obliged to tolerate such presentations even though they have racist overtones or cater to the racial or religious prejudices of the employees.

It is not altogether clear that the line drawn by the Board is a happy one. The race issue is in many areas throughout the country inherently volatile and can hardly be "temperately" addressed; some psychological evidence supports the claim that it is the "temperate" appeal to racial hostility which is likely to be more effective and longer-lasting than is the emotionally inflammatory appeal; and much of the thrust of the *Sewell* decision can be circumvented by artful draftsmanship. In any event, the Board continues to apply the *Sewell* decision, and it has received the endorsement of the courts. NLRB v. Schapiro & Whitehouse, Inc. (4th Cir. 1966) (union leaflet referring to contemporaneous racial disturbances in Cambridge, Maryland distributed to black employees in Baltimore).

The Board has, however, treated as distinguishable and unobjectionable certain appeals with racial overtones made to black employees by union organizers and civil rights groups the predominant theme of which is the analogy between organizing for economic gains and organizing for the achievement of full civil rights and personal dignity. In NLRB v. Baltimore Luggage Co. (4th Cir. 1967), a divided court endorsed the distinction, finding a letter and speeches to black employees by representatives of the NAACP to constitute not an appeal to race hatred but rather a response to the peculiar economic plight of black workers and to their traditional hostility and skepticism for organized labor.

Of course, racial appeals by an employer which directly threaten a worsening of economic conditions in response to a union victory, Kay Corp. (1974) (employer suggested that union victory would result in ouster of some white employees or their having to work beside black employees, "a condition which certain employees might consider unpleasant"), or racial appeals by either employer or union which threaten violence, Bush Hog, Inc. (1966), enf'd (5th Cir. 1968), will be treated as coercive and as unfair labor practices. The Board will, however, likely continue to overlook the casual or isolated racist epithet. NLRB v. Bancroft Mfg. Co. (5th Cir. 1975) (union remarks to black employees were "asides," not part of a "racially-oriented campaign").

§ 12. Promise or Grant of Benefits by the Employer

Section 8(c) shelters the expression of views and opinions in campaign oratory and literature only to the extent these lack a "threat of reprisal or force or promise of benefit." The statute thus bars an employer attempt to trade upon its superior economic position not only in the form of a threatened loss of benefits if the union is voted in but also in the form of a promised grant of benefits if the union is rejected. NLRB v. Flomatic Corp. (2d Cir. 1965). The United States Supreme Court has stated that the actual grant of benefits during an election campaign, given with the intention of inducing employees to reject the union, is unlawful since the employees will read this as a demonstration of employer economic power held in reserve ("a fist inside a velvet glove") which can just as readily be used for reprisals. NLRB v. Exchange Parts Co. (U.S.1964). This rationale may be applied in cases where the benefit is promised, conditional on the union's defeat, rather than actually granted, since such a promise is tantamount to a threat, should the listener vote against the employer, to withhold a reward otherwise forthcoming. The employer's assurance that it will deny the "reward" is just as much an intrusive reprisal, likely to coerce and restrain the employee, as is its assurance to deprive the employee of a benefit already in existence. Even when the employer's promise of benefits during an election campaign is not expressly conditioned on a vote against the union, the Board will commonly—subject to exceptions discussed below—infer that the employees will be improperly coerced so to vote. In most of the "promise of benefit" cases, this inference is reinforced by independent employer unfair labor practices, such as direct threats of reprisal, illegal interrogation, or surveillance.

Although the promise by an employer to grant some special benefit in the event the union is defeated thus has coercive implications, it is not at all clear that the same is true when the employer actually grants benefits during the course of an election campaign, without any conditions and without any suggestion that those benefits will be withdrawn if the union prevails. It might be argued that such benefits do not impinge upon the freedom of choice of the employees but rather constitute a permanent improvement in working conditions which inures to the benefit of the employees (even though concededly at the expense of the union). Yet these arguments were rejected by the United States Supreme Court in NLRB v. Exchange Parts Co. (U.S.1964). There, the Court held that the employer violated section 8(a)(1) by announcing certain overtime and vacation benefits shortly before an election "with the intention of inducing the employees to vote against the union." The Court found the grant of benefits so motivated to be an exercise of economic leverage not merely unfair but actually coercive:

> The danger inherent in well-timed increases in benefits is the suggestion of the fist inside the velvet glove. Employees are not likely to miss the inference that the source of benefits now conferred is also the source from which future benefits must flow and which may dry up if it is not obliged. The danger may be diminished if, as in this case, the benefits

are conferred permanently and unconditionally. But the absence of conditions or threats pertaining to the particular benefits conferred would be of controlling significance only if it could be presumed that no question of additional benefits or renegotiation of existing benefits would arise in the future; and, of course, no such presumption is tenable.

Ironically, then, the employer's seeming benevolence is objectionable not because it woos the employees but rather because it intimidates them. To the employer's claim that outlawing the grant of benefits would discourage employers from improving the lot of the employees, the Court responded:

> The beneficence of an employer is likely to be ephemeral if prompted by a threat of unionization which is subsequently removed. Insulating the right of collective organization from calculated good will of this sort deprives employees of little that has lasting value.

The Court's emphasis upon the employer's motive is significant, in two respects. First, the requirement that the employer's grant of benefits be motivated by a desire to oust the union permits the employer to grant benefits during the representation election campaigns for other, more "legitimate," reasons. Second, this requirement is out of keeping with the usual principle that violations of section 8(a)(1) may be found, even without illicit motivation, when the harm to employee rights outweighs even plausible business reasons the employer may have for its conduct. Prior to the Supreme Court decision in *Exchange Parts,* the Board had indeed held that it would test a claimed violation of section 8(a)(1) for an employer grant of benefits by this weighing process, and that specific proof of bad motive was unnecessary; but the Board subsequently reversed its position in reliance on *Exchange Parts.* Tonkawa Ref. Co. (1969), *enf'd* (10th Cir. 1970). The decided cases do indeed tend to invoke the *Exchange Parts* test of "intention of inducing the employees to vote against the union." But there are several cases where the finding of such an intention is dubious at best and where what is articulated as antiunion animus is in truth a finding that the employer has failed completely to explain to the Board why the benefits were granted or a finding that the asserted employer justification is insubstantial. See NLRB v. Styletek (1st Cir. 1975) (prima facie violation is established by showing that benefits were granted while election is pending, and burden shifts to employer to explain; "It is obvious that the closer a wage benefit comes to the day of the election, the harder it will be for the union to answer, and the greater the danger that the benefit will be manipulated to sway the election."). In substance, then, the Board—generally with court approval—does appear to be balancing the discouragement of a vote for the union, stemming from the grant of benefits, against the employer's business reasons for the grant (with the hoped-for defeat of the union not being a substantial business reason). The analysis in the cases is the same regardless whether the employer unconditionally promises that a benefit will be granted or unconditionally grants such a benefit.

Indeed, the Board has found the employer to violate section 8(a)(1), even in the absence of an express promise of unconditional future benefits, when such a promise is implied in employer conduct. The most common example is the unprecedented solicitation by the employer, in the midst of an election campaign, of employee grievances. Without being overly preoccupied with employer motive, the Board holds that such solicitation—even without explicit promises to correct the articulated grievances—is presumed to contain an implied promise to correct them and an implied assurance that the employees need not turn to the union to improve plant conditions. Hadbar, Div. of Pur O Sil, Inc. (1974). Such employer solicitation of grievances has even been read as an implied promise to improve the lot of employees which is conditioned on the defeat of the union. NLRB v. Tom Wood Pontiac, Inc. (7th Cir. 1971). (The presumption of an implied promise to correct may be rebutted if the employer explicitly states that it is not promising or cannot promise corrective action. Uarco, Inc. (1975).)

It is also doubtful that union animus is essential when the employer actually implements an improvement in benefits in the course of an election campaign. Thus, in J.C. Penney Co. v. NLRB (10th Cir. 1967), the employer had a practice of granting a wage increase every 12 to 15 months, and granted such an increase 14 months after the previous one but soon after an election petition had been filed by a union. Although the inference that the increase was motivated by a desire to defeat the union—rather than by a desire to perpetuate the past practice—was by no means compelling, the Board and court drew such an inference, and held that the employer could have waited another month until the election had been held before granting the increase while remaining within the practice. The Board has in fact found illegal the announcement of a benefit during an election campaign even though the company decision was made before the advent of the union. Hineline's Meat Plant, Inc. (1971). Indeed, it has been held that benefits granted by the employer immediately *after* it prevailed in a representation election may violate section 8(a)(1). Even though the employer's motive could not have been to induce the employees to vote against the union in that election, the likely imminence of the Board's overturning that election and ordering a new one was deemed sufficient to warrant a finding of illegal conduct. See Luxuray of N.Y. v. NLRB (2d Cir. 1971) (although the union had not yet filed objections to the election, the employer had failed before the election to supply a list of employee names and addresses, so that objections and an invalidation of the election were certainties; the post-election grant of benefits was of unprecedented generosity and was coupled by the employer with a speech emphasizing the employer election victory). But see NLRB v. Ambox, Inc. (5th Cir. 1966) (post-election benefits lawful, although union objections were pending, when benefits were retroactive to before the election and not conditioned on the ultimate disposition of the election proceeding).

The inference of illicit employer motive that may normally be drawn from a grant of benefits shortly before an election may be dispelled if the employer demonstrates that the grant was compelled by business necessity or by a consistent past practice. Thus, an employer may grant a wage increase when the bulk of its employees have held a meeting and demanded it, and some have already quit to work elsewhere, NLRB v. Gotham Indus., Inc. (1st Cir. 1969) (also proper when there is a tight local labor market and increase is necessary to hold or attract workers); or when all other business competitors have granted an increase, J.P. Stevens & Co. v. NLRB (4th Cir. 1972). See also Doubleday Bros. (1967) (past practice). It matters not that an election is in the offing. In such cases the employees presumably do not regard the grant of benefits as a tactical maneuver or a seeming beneficence beneath which the employer's economic "fist" is clearly perceptible.

But the propriety of the benefits granted depends on their conformity to the business necessity or the past practice; extraordinary generosity will be suspect. If there is an industrywide pay increase and a resulting pay increase in 84 of the employer's plants, this will justify the announcement of a similar increase in the plant in which an election is two days away, for all employees would expect this; but the additional grant of one extra holiday at that plant only will violate section 8(a)(1). J.P. Stevens & Co. v. NLRB (4th Cir. 1972) ("absent a showing by the Company of a proper business purpose or necessity the timing of the announcement of the grant of an additional holiday so close to the election is itself evidence of unlawful motive"). And, if the past practice would dictate a pay increase either before the election or after it, at the employer's option, the employer must wait until the election is over. J.C. Penney Co. v. NLRB (10th Cir. 1967) (with past practice of increase every 12 to 15 months, and 14 months have passed with election pending, employer should wait until election has been held).

There is at least one instance in which a grant of benefits with the object of avoiding unionization will not be unlawful, and that is when there is no specific union which is gathering support in the plant but the employer is merely "seeking to stay one step ahead of unionization." NLRB v. Gotham Indus., Inc. (1st Cir. 1969):

> [T]he situation must have sufficiently crystallized so that some specific orientation exists. It would be a sorry consequence if the Labor Relations Act were to be construed as causing every nonunionized employer to think twice before

initiating a wage increase lest some union should appear and claim that it had been frustrated. . . . At a minimum it must be that to establish improper motivation requires a showing that an employer knows or has knowledge of facts reasonably indicating that a union is actively seeking to organize, or else that an election is, to use the Board's word, impending.

§ 13. Employer Withholding of Expected Benefits

If an employer were to reduce employees' pay during an election campaign, or deny vacations or holidays, without any other announced justification than the advent of the union, the Board would be justified in inferring that this would coerce employees in the exercise of their right freely to choose a union, in violation of section 8(a)(1). It has already been noted that the economic status quo in a plant is viewed dynamically, so that if the employer grants a benefit consistent with a past practice, it simply maintains the status quo and does not violate the Act; but the Act is violated if the employer is extraordinarily generous. A combination of these principles dictates a finding of unlawful coercion when the employer departs from a consistent past practice of granting benefits and denies comparable anticipated benefits, tieing such denial to the presence of the union and the imminence of the election. Gates Rubber Co. (1970). The Supreme Court decision in NLRB v. Exchange Parts Co. (U.S.1964), involving the grant of benefits, by implication invites courts to look for illicit motive as well in the withholding of benefits traditionally granted. E. g., NLRB v. Dothan Eagle, Inc. (5th Cir. 1970) (employer denied a pay increase automatically given every six months in the past; this was an "established scheme of compensation and could not be deviated from for purposes of influencing the vote during the union election [campaign]"). And the mere fact of withheld benefits when an election is pending will normally justify an inference of illicit motive and shift to the employer the burden to demonstrate a legitimate business justification, usually rather difficult to do.

In short, it is the position of the Board and the courts that the company must decide the question of granting or withholding benefits as if there were no union present and no election pending. See McCormick Longmeadow Stone Co. (1966):

> An employer's legal duty in deciding whether to grant benefits while a representation case is pending is to determine that question precisely as he would if a union were not in the picture. If the employer would have granted the benefits because of economic circumstances unrelated to union organization, the grant of those benefits will not violate the Act. On the other hand, if the employer's course is altered

by virtue of the union's presence, then the employer has violated the Act, and this is true whether he confers benefits because of the union or withholds them because of the union.

This simple principle can create a serious dilemma for the employer, for should it attempt to comply with the requirement of the *Exchange Parts* case that there be no grant of benefits to influence employees' votes it may find that its withholding of benefits can also be viewed as an illicit form of influence which coerces employees. The dilemma is not serious when there is wholly absent a past practice of granting benefits which would give rise to employee expectations and thus to employee intimidation when expectations are frustrated; withholding the benefits will not likely violate section 8(a)(1), particularly if the employer refrains from announcing the withholding and tying it to the union's presence. Compare Cotton Producers Ass'n (1971) (employer announcement), with Great Atl. & Pac. Tea Co. (1971) (no employer announcement, no fixed expected date for the benefit).

But the dilemma is serious when there is arguably such a past practice of granting benefits, particularly when the existence or dimensions of that practice are vague. In such cases, the employer will sometimes deal with the risk that the Board will find its denial of anticipated benefits to be illicit, by coupling its denial with a statement to employees (usually at the suggestion of counsel) which explains that the pendency of the election likely renders the grant of benefits illegal. The Board in a number of decisions has held that the employer unlawfully discredits the union (and interferes with unionization) when it thus links its denial of benefits to the union's presence, but in more recent decisions the Board has appeared more willing to approve the action of the employer in assuaging the employees' concern. Uarco, Inc. (1968) (distinguishing other cases, where violations were found, merely as "inapposite"). When upholding the suspension of anticipated benefits, the Board notes that the employer has so explained its conduct as not to lead the reasonable employee to believe that the union is somehow at fault for the deprivation. At least one court of appeals, in reversing a Board finding of coercion, held that "illegal motivation" is a necessary element in proving a violation and that this is absent when the employer withholds benefits in a "good faith effort to conform to the requirements of the law." J.J. Newberry Co. v. NLRB (2d Cir. 1971) (although the wage review, abandoned by the employer during an election campaign, had been granted in the past at regular intervals, the wage increases that had resulted therefrom were subjective and discretionary). The more firm the past practice of granting benefits, the more obviously the employer must adhere to it during an election campaign.

§ 14. Threats and Promises by the Union

A union's intrusive threats during an election campaign are outlawed just as much as are the employer's, including threats that a union loss or a vote against the union will result in physical violence to the person or property of the "victim" or his family, e. g., Mid-States Metal Prods., Inc. (1966), enf'd (5th Cir. 1968) (section 8(b)(1)(A) violation), Sonoco Prods. Co. v. NLRB (9th Cir. 1971) (election set aside); or will result in job loss or denial of other employment-related benefits or status, Red Ball Motor Freight, Inc. (1966), enf'd (D. C.Cir. 1967).

But promises by the union are not of the same quality as employer promises and are thus as a general matter not regarded as coercive or restraining of employee free choice in violation of section 8(b)(1). The union's promise to improve working conditions, which takes the form of specific goals for wages, fringe benefits, grievance processing and the like, is inherent in every election campaign and is not regarded as unlawful. Unlike the employer's promise of benefits conditioned on a rejection of the union, the union's economic promises are not tantamount to a threat which it will be in a position of power to implement in the event a majority of the employees support "no agent." Moreover, the union's campaign promises are normally understood by the employees as "puffing" or at least as requiring some measure of employer cooperation or acquiescence prior to implementation in the event the union prevails. Smith Co. (1971). To that extent they may fairly be discounted, although they are obviously nonetheless relevant to the employee in reaching an informed choice on the merits of unionization.

There are, however, situations in which the union does have control over some economic benefit promised employees in the event they cast a favorable vote. In those cases such a union promise might be treated as coercive, or as a basis for setting aside a union victory in an election. The Board and the courts have in fact concluded that union payments to employees prior to an election, even though not conditioned upon the employee's voting for the union, constitute such a powerful inducement or constraint to vote for the union that a union election victory may properly be set aside by the Board. This was done when the union paid an employee seven dollars to be an observer at an election, Collins & Aikman Corp. v. NLRB (4th Cir. 1967); or made a five dollar gift to employees shortly before an election, General Cable Corp. (1968); or provided for insurance coverage ($500 life insurance, $1000 accidental death, $100 funeral expenses) for employees who joined the union prior to the election, Wagner Elec. Corp. (1967) (constraint to vote for union comparable to constraint when employer grants a wage increase just prior to an election).

More uncertain, until recently, was the status of union assurances that employees who joined the union immediately could do so without paying the customary initiation fee, while the fee would have to be paid by those who waited until after the election. Although the Board first held such union waivers to be cause for setting aside a union election victory, Lobue Bros. (1954), it later reversed its position in DIT–MCO, Inc. (1967), *enf'd* (8th Cir. 1970), in which it held that the union had a legitimate interest in using the waiver to woo new members and that in any event an employee promptly signing a union membership card was still free to vote against the union in a secret-ballot election. The reception of the courts of appeals to the revised Board position was mixed, and led to Supreme Court review in NLRB v. Savair Mfg. Co. (U.S.1973). A divided Court concluded that the union's narrow election victory (22–20) should have been set aside because of the union's waiver of initiation fees conditioned on joining immediately and not after the election. The Court analogized the waiver—which was phrased by union agents as a "fine" for delay in signing recognition slips—to the grant of gifts or benefits by union or employer while an election is pending. It concluded that the pre-election waiver "allows the Union to buy endorsements and paint a false portrait of employee support during its election campaign," and that some employees signing a membership or authorization card may "feel obligated to carry through on their stated intention to support the Union" when they cast their ballot. The Court found this to conflict with the principles of free choice underlying the election provisions of the Labor Act. Although it purposely refrained from deciding whether the waiver of dues was sufficiently intrusive as to constitute an unfair labor practice, in violation of section 8(b)(1), it did note the analogy of employer benefits which do violate section 8(a)(1) and concluded its decision by stating: "The failure to sign a recognition slip may well seem ominous to nonunionists who fear that if they do not sign they will face a wrathful union regime, should the union win."

The Board has since applied *Savair* on several occasions to set aside union election victories for pre-election waivers, but appears not to have ruled on the unfair labor practice issue. It has also departed from the prevailing doctrine that employer or union conduct which takes place prior to the filing of an election petition will not serve as cause to set aside the election; since union waivers of initiation fees will typically be an incident to gathering authorization cards which are in turn used to secure a "showing of interest" necessary to secure an election, the Board can only give full effect to the *Savair* principle by applying it to pre-petition union conduct. Gibson's Discount Center (1974). The Board does, however, distinguish from *Savair*—as the Supreme Court in that case invited in dictum—the case of the union which waives (or reduces) initiation fees for all employees who join the union either before the election or after the election and before a contract is negotiated. This does not put comparable pressure on employees to join the union immediately and is an unconditional and nondiscriminatory offer which does not warrant setting aside a union election victory. B.F. Goodrich Tire Co. (1974). This position has been given judicial approval. NLRB v. Wabash Transformer Corp. (8th Cir. 1975).

§ 15.   Surveillance of Union Activity

Employer surveillance of union activity is a violation of section 8(a)(1), whether the incident is isolated, NLRB v. Clark Bros. Co. (2d Cir. 1947), or part of a continuing program of employer coercion, Consolidated Edison Co. v. NLRB (U.S.1938). The court of appeals in *Clark Bros.* succinctly stated the rationale: "A ruling that an employer was privileged to engage in intentional eavesdropping would be likely to deter free discussion by employees of self-organizational matters." For the same reason, attempted surveillance is unlawful even though the attempt is unsuccessful, Minnesota Mining & Mfg. Co. (1949), *enf'd* (8th Cir. 1950). So too if the employer takes steps designed to lead its employees to believe they are under surveillance even though no surveillance is actually effected. Hendrix Mfg. Co. v. NLRB (5th Cir. 1963).

Although it might be argued that, contrary to open and known surveillance, there is no "interference, restraint or coercion" in violation of section 8(a)(1) when the surveillance is secret and unknown to the employees, the cases uniformly reject this argument. In an early case, the Board announced that allowing secret surveillance would mean allowing only the most effective surveillance, since "to be effective, it must be secret." The long-range goal of espionage always being to interfere with and restrain organizing activity, this first step must be declared unlawful. Virginia Elec. & Power Co. *enf'd* (4th Cir. 1942), *aff'd on other issues* (U.S.1943). The Board more recently reaffirmed this rationale in Cannon Elec. Co. (1965):

> Even if we were to accept the Trial Examiner's finding of lack of employee knowledge of the instructions to supervisors [to engage in surveillance], we would still find that these instructions were unlawful. An employer cannot discriminate against union adherents without first determining who they are. The Board is continually confronted with cases involving unlawful discrimination against employees where the prelude to the discrimination was the employer's attempt systematically to investigate the sympathies of his employees. The frequency of a pattern of employer conduct associating discrimination against union adherents with the employer's efforts to learn the names of union activists supports the conclusion that there is a "danger inherent" in such conduct: a tendency toward interference with the exercise by employees of their organizational rights.

The Board concluded that the tendency of even unknown surveillance to be used for later coercion was sufficient to warrant outlawry in it-

self, in order to thwart the commission of other unfair labor practices.

On occasion, seeming surveillance will be deemed justified—or at
least not outlawed. It is, for example, justifiable for supervisors to
watch over employees at their work stations during worktime, and
this business interest will not be overridden by contemporaneous union activity in the plant. NLRB v. Threads, Inc. (4th Cir. 1962).
But see Florida Steel Corp. (1974) (supervisors from outside the
plant watched three union organizers at work for two days, shortly
after their union activities became known). And rarely the Board
will find that surveillance had no coercive impact in fact. For example, in NLRB v. National Motor Bearing Co. (9th Cir. 1939), the individual engaging in surveillance in an isolated incident had been ordered by the company president not to do so and had been reprimanded afterward. And in Singer Co. (1966), the visits of foremen
to local bars to look for union adherents were found not to coerce,
since the meetings were regarded by both the foremen and the employees as casual and good natured. These cases can certainly not be
relied upon to establish any general exception to the prevailing rule
that surveillance concerning union activities, whether known or unknown to employees, violates the Labor Act.

§ 16.   Interrogation or Polling of Employees

Just as the Board had initially held that antiunion statements by
the employer were inherently coercive and unfair labor practices per
se, the Board also treated as a violation of the Act any systematic interrogation of employees as to their attitudes toward or membership
in a union. Such interrogation was held to intrude into an assumed
right under section 7 to keep such matters (thought by the Board to
be of no concern to the employer) private, and was also held to put
employees sympathetic to unionization in fear that a refusal to answer or an honest answer would be a prelude to job reprisals by the
employer. Standard-Coosa-Thatcher (1949). Section 8(c) was
thought to be no obstacle to such an interpretation, since the Board
refused to characterize interrogation as an expression of "views, arguments, or opinion." This per se approach met with disfavor in the
courts, and the Board in 1954 repudiated it in Blue Flash Express,
Inc. (1954), which held that interrogation regarding union activities
and membership would be deemed coercive only when found to be so
in light of the specific circumstances, such as the "time, place, personnel involved, information sought, and the employer's known preference." This rejection of the easily applied per se approach gave little
guidance to employers who believed they had a legitimate reason to
interrogate (most commonly, upon being presented with a bargaining
demand by a union purporting to have majority support) and also resulted in the prolongation of Board hearings and decisions in unfair
labor practice cases. For a decade, the Board vacillated between an

"all the circumstances" test, which at least one court of appeals rejected as too elusive a standard, Operating Eng'rs Local 49 v. NLRB (Struksnes Constr. Co.) (D.C. Cir. 1965), and a more objective catalogue of conditions which the interrogation would have to satisfy before being sustained, which other courts rejected as too artificial, NLRB v. Lorben Corp. (2d Cir. 1965) (finding of coercion based on a failure to explain reasons for interrogation and to assure against reprisals, set aside as unsupported by substantial evidence).

In Struksnes Constr. Co. (1967), the Board "revised" the rule of the *Blue Flash* case, giving as reasons the "considerable uncertainty" of past decisions, the failure of *Blue Flash* to deter employee intimidation and the availability to the employer of other noncoercive methods for testing a union's majority claim. Henceforth, the Board would apply the following standard:

> Absent unusual circumstances, the polling of employees by an employer will be violative of Section 8(a)(1) of the Act unless the following safeguards are observed: (1) the purpose of the poll is to determine the truth of a union's claim of majority, (2) this purpose is communicated to the employees, (3) assurances against reprisal are given, (4) the employees are polled by secret ballot, and (5) the employer has not engaged in unfair labor practices or otherwise created a coercive atmosphere.

The Board has softened the seeming rigor of these preconditions when, for example, the questioning is casual, isolated or otherwise de minimis. B.F. Goodrich Footwear Co. (1973). In such cases, the Board will continue to determine whether such questioning is intimidating under all of the particular circumstances. But in cases of systematic polling concerning union preferences, the Board does adhere to the *Struksnes* requirements.

The reaction of the courts of appeals has been diverse. Indeed, different decisions within the same circuit have appeared to take contradictory positions on the validity of the *Struksnes* rule. Thus, the Court of Appeals for the Eighth Circuit, after sustaining the *Struksnes* conditions as a reasonable exercise of the Board's expertise, in NLRB v. Harry F. Berggren & Sons (8th Cir. 1969), proceeded not long after to hold—quite contrary to *Struksnes*—that interrogation would not be held to violate the Act absent proof that the employer was motivated by antiunion animus, General Mercantile & Hardware Co. v. NLRB (8th Cir. 1972). It appears to be the prevailing view of the courts of appeals that regardless of the *Struksnes* guidelines, Board findings of coercion must still be supported by substantial evidence and that the failure of the employer to satisfy one of the conditions will not necessarily justify a finding of coercion. *E. g.,* NLRB v. Dorn's Transp. Co. (2d Cir. 1969) (Board finding of coercion reversed, in spite of lack of employer justification and lack of assurances against reprisals). Indeed, the Board has also been reversed in the converse situation where, applying the *Struksnes* rules, the Board found that coercion was dispelled when the employer gave assurances against reprisals, but the court held the Board was nonetheless required, in looking for coercion, to make a "more searching inquiry into the nature of the questioning and the circumstances in which it was conducted." Teamsters Local 633 v. NLRB (Bulk Haulers, Inc.) (D.C. Cir. 1974). No court of appeals appears to have considered itself bound by what might be characterized as a favorable reference to the *Struksnes* case in the Supreme Court's decision in NLRB v. Gissel Packing Co. (U.S.1969).

It follows from the *Struksnes* rules that, as in most cases arising under section 8(a)(1), employer interrogation may be found illegal even in the absence of proof or of any inference that the employer was actually motivated in its questioning by a desire to coerce or intimidate the employees. W.A. Shaeffer Pen Co. v. NLRB (8th Cir. 1973). But see General Mercantile & Hardware Co. v. NLRB (8th Cir. 1972). It is sufficient to make out a violation that the employer has no "legitimate interest" in interrogating the employees. Such an interest—limited by the Board in *Struksnes* to the verification of a union's claim of majority—will be found lacking when, for example, the employer prior to such a union claim is simply "curious" about the extent of union support, or when an election petition has been filed by the union and a representation proceeding is already pending. In the latter case, the Board believes the forthcoming election to be a better test of employee sympathies than the poll which thus lacks justification and which does generally tend to cause a fear of reprisal. Compare Central Merchandise Co. (1972) (post-election interrogation to determine the vote of employees whose ballots had been challenged; held, coercive and without legitimate purpose). For similar reasons, the Board has found coercive and without "legitimate purpose" employer interrogation directed at determining whether the union does indeed have the thirty percent "showing of interest" which the Board considers necessary to precipitate election proceedings. The Board's position concerning employer purpose has been rejected on appeal, however, since the "question, we should suppose in every case is whether the purpose (legitimate or not in the eyes of the Board) would appear to the employees to constitute reasonable grounds for an interrogation" rather than a prelude to employer reprisal; the mere absence of a union request for recognition does not per se convert otherwise nonintimidating questioning into a violation of the Act. S.H. Kress & Co. v. NLRB (9th Cir. 1963). The Board's position is explainable, however, by its assumption that employer questioning regarding union sympathies will always tend in some measure, even if slight, to interfere with an unfettered choice regarding the union; and that such questioning should thus be presumed improper unless clearly justified and unless pursued subject to the rigorous conditions set down in the *Struksnes* case. Compare NLRB v. Great Dane Trailers, Inc. (U.S.1967).

In contrast to the many decisions outlawing systematic interrogation by employers, it is clear that there is no such rule barring comparable interrogation by unions and that unions are free to poll employees to gauge the extent of their support. NLRB v. Springfield Discount, Inc. (7th Cir. 1972). The courts and the Board have found "no merit in the Company's argument that, because such a poll might have been coercive if conducted by the Company, it is likewise coercive when conducted by the Union. The employer occupies a far different position with regard to the coercive impact of its actions upon employees than does a Union." Louis-Allis Co. v. NLRB (7th Cir. 1972). Of course, if the employees reasonably fear that union interrogation is a prelude to reprisal for antiunion sentiments, such interrogation may properly be held to violate section 8(b)(1).

While the *Struksnes* rules are applied by the Board to systematic employer polling of several employees, many interrogation cases involve isolated questioning of particular individuals. In these situations, the Board will continue to apply the "all of the circumstances" rule of the *Blue Flash* case. Blue Flash Express, Inc. (1954). This approach by the Board has secured judicial approval. NLRB v. Harry F. Berggren & Sons (8th Cir. 1969). The Board will thus consider the identity of the questioner, the timing and location of the questioning, the truthfulness of the reply given by the employee, whether the question was a natural product of a conversation about unionization precipitated by the employee or a sharply focused inquiry precipitated by the employer and, perhaps most important, whether the employer has committed other unfair labor practices which give color of intimidation to its interrogation. Questioning which is casual, isolated, the product of friendly discussion and far in advance of an election will normally not be the basis of an unfair labor practice order or an order to set aside an election. B.F. Goodrich Footwear Co. (1973).

The Board has taken a less lenient approach when the single person questioned about his union affiliation is a job applicant. This question is sometimes put by the employer at a job interview or on an application form. Prior to its decision in Struksnes Constr. Co. (1967), discussed above, the Board was prepared to find such questioning coercive in context, when the employer had committed other unfair labor practices; this was so even in the absence of proof that the employer actually used the application-form answers as a basis for discrimination in hiring or retention. Springfield Garment Mfg. Co. (1965). More recently, the Board has declared any questions on application forms which require the applicant to disclose past union membership or union preference to be inherently coercive and unlawful. Rochester Cadet Cleaners, Inc. (1973) (applicant answered truthfully, was not threatened, was hired). It will no doubt be difficult for the employer to demonstrate that such questioning is justified by legitimate business need.   Nonetheless, it is likely that courts of appeals—particularly those unsympathetic to the absolute requirements of the *Struksnes* test—will search for more specific proof of coercion, or of actual use by the employer of application-form answers in personnel decisions, before finding the questions to violate section 8(a)(1).   See NLRB v. D'Armigene, Inc. (2d Cir. 1965). Even the Board appears to look somewhat more kindly on job-application questions which seek to unearth not the applicant's union membership but rather his willingness to report to work through a picket line in the event of a strike.   The Board has stated that it may be prepared to sustain such a question when a strike is actually underway or is imminent; short of imminence, however, the Board will find such questioning of applicants to be unlawful.   W.A. Shaeffer Pen Co. (1972), *enf'd* (8th Cir. 1973).

§ 17.   Interrogation Regarding Pending NLRB Proceedings

The Board has held the employer to have a legitimate purpose in interrogating employees when the information sought relates to an unfair labor practice proceeding pending against the employer and for which it ought properly be permitted to prepare.   As in Struksnes Constr. Co. (1967), the Board has established a number of safeguards which are designed both to facilitate the discovery by the employer of relevant information in advance of the hearing and to curb what the Board considers the inherently coercive impact of employer interrogation.   The Board's formulation was articulated in Johnnie's Poultry Co. (1964), *enf't denied on other grounds* (8th Cir. 1965):

> Thus, the employer must communicate to the employee the purpose of the questioning, assure him that no reprisal will take place, and obtain his participation on a voluntary basis; the questioning must occur in a context free from employer hostility to union organization and must not be itself coercive in nature; and the questions must not exceed the necessities of the legitimate purpose by prying into other union matters, eliciting information concerning an employee's subjective state of mind, or otherwise interfering with the statutory rights of employees.   When an employer transgresses the boundaries of these safeguards, he loses the benefits of the privilege.

The courts as well have acknowledged that while interrogation concerning union activities "is, of itself, coercive, . . .   fairness to the employer requires that a limited amount of such questioning be permitted despite the possible restraint which may result."   (This may reflect the unavailablity of any pretrial discovery comparable to that in the federal district courts.)   The questioning must be "for the purpose of discovering facts within the limits of the issues raised by a complaint" before the NLRB, and must not be used "to pry into matters of union membership, to discuss the nature or extent of union activities, to dissuade employees from joining or remaining members of a union, or otherwise to interfere with the statutory right to self organization." Joy Silk Mills, Inc. v. NLRB (D.C. Cir. 1950).

Subject to these limitations, the employer may take a statement from the employee prior to the unfair labor practice hearing; may ask the employee whether he has given a statement to the Board; and may in fact later secure a copy of any such statement in full in the event the employee testifies at the Board hearing. NLRB v. Winn-Dixie Stores, Inc. (6th Cir. 1965). There is, however, some question whether the employer may lawfully ask the employee to produce in advance of the hearing any statement given by him to the NLRB or its agents. The Board appears to hold any such employer request inherently unlawful. Bayliner Marine Corp. (1974) (employer's counsel sought copy of statement in advance of hearing; dissenting member would allow if assurances are found to dispel coercion). Some courts of appeals endorse the Board's position, see Retail Clerks Int'l Ass'n v. NLRB (Montgomery Ward & Co.) (D.C. Cir. 1967), while other courts would find such a request unlawful only if it is coercive in context, W.T. Grant Co. v. NLRB (7th Cir. 1964) (employer channeled inquiry through company counsel so that employee would remain anonymous, and gave assurances against reprisal).

In these "investigation" cases, as in the "polling" cases, the Board and the courts generally do not require, as part of the burden of proving that interrogation is coercive, that the employer's questioning be motivated by an antiunion or discriminatory object. The central issue is not whether the employer intended to coerce the employees but whether the identity of the questioner along with other circumstances reasonably lead to a perception on the part of the questioned employee that a pro-union response may result in reprisals by the employer; it matters not that in truth the employer may have been motivated secretly by a willingness to expedite the union's entry into the plant rather than by a desire to nip that entry in the bud. Of course, questioning which is in form legitimate "may not be asked where there is purposeful intimidation of employees," that is, where it can be demonstrated that the employer's object is to intimidate. Joy Silk Mills v. NLRB (D.C. Cir. 1950).

CHAPTER VIII

INTERFERENCE WITH UNION ACCESS TO COMPANY PROPERTY

§ 1. Employee Solicitation for the Union on Company Property: Generally

As noted above, the principles relating to coercive speech attempt to accommodate the employees' interest in being free from intrusive pressures upon their freedom of choice with the employer's interest in freely communicating the drawbacks of collective bargaining. Similarly, the Board and courts have found it necessary to accommodate the employees' interest in maximum access to union communications with the employer's interest in the security of his property and the efficiency of his operations. Although section 8(a)(1) outlaws employer "interference" with employee concerted activities, it is obvious that such a proscription should not be read altogether to bar the employer from imposing limits upon the time and manner in which his employees solicit for and are solicited by the union. Frequently an employer will promulgate—either prior to or in the midst of a union-solicitation campaign—a company rule declaring improper (upon pain of job-related discipline) employee solicitation or dissemination of literature on company property. In Republic Aviation Corp. v. NLRB (U.S.1945), such a no-solicitation rule had been adopted by the employer long before the advent of the union and was not applied discriminatorily so as to bar union solicitation while permitting solicitation for social or charitable groups. Nonetheless, the United States Supreme Court sustained the Board's conclusion that the promulgation and enforcement of such a rule constituted illegal "restraint, interference or coercion" to the extent it barred employee solicitation on behalf of the union during nonworking time such as, in the *Republic Aviation* case itself, the employees' lunchtime. The Board's finding of interference with section 7 rights was sustained even though the record contained no specific findings that the inability to solicit on company property and time genuinely "interfered" with the capacity of the union to communicate effectively with the employees and no finding that the employer's purpose in adopting the rule was to frustrate unionization.

The Court in *Republic Aviation,* relying on the Board's special knowledge and experience in such matters, sustained the pair of presumptions announced by the Board in Peyton Packing Co. (1943), *enf'd* (5th Cir. 1944):

> The Act, of course, does not prevent an employer from making and enforcing reasonable rules covering the conduct of employees on company time. Working time is for work. It is therefore within the province of an employer to

promulgate and enforce a rule prohibiting union solicitation during working hours. Such a rule must be presumed to be valid in the absence of evidence that it was adopted for a discriminatory purpose. It is no less true that time outside working hours, whether before or after work, or during luncheon or rest periods, is an employee's time to use as he wishes without unreasonable restraint, although the employee is on company property. It is therefore not within the province of an employer to promulgate and enforce a rule prohibiting union solicitation by an employee outside of working hours, although on company property. Such a rule must be presumed to be an unreasonable impediment to self-organization and therefore discriminatory in the absence of evidence that special circumstances make the rule necessary in order to maintain production or discipline.

In effect, then, the Court agreed that no-solicitation rules, even though applied to all kinds of solicitations and not merely union appeals, intrinsically restrain or interefere with the protected employee rights of "assisting" labor organizations, although the union itself may well have alternative channels of communication. These rules will be sustained, however, if they are reasonably necessary to assure safety and efficiency. That need will be presumed when the ban relates to time when the employees (the solicitor or his listener) are supposed to be at work. That need will be presumed to be absent during nonworking time.

The Board has recently refined its presumptions so as to distinguish no-solicitation rules which in terms relate to "working hours" and those which relate to "working time." The Board holds that "working hours" are normally understood to connote the period of time from the beginning to the end of a workshift, from the time employees "clock in" until they "clock out"; that period would thus embrace lunch and break periods. An employer rule barring solicitation during "working hours" is thus presumed illegal. "Working time," however, is a phrase which connotes time spent in the performance of actual job duties and would thus exclude lunch and break periods. A ban on solicitation during "working time" is thus presumed lawful. The Board articulated and elaborated upon this distinction in Essex Int'l, Inc. (1974):

A rule prohibiting solicitation during "work time" or "working time" is, in our opinion, sufficiently clear to employees to justify requiring the party attempting to invalidate the rule to show, by extrinsic evidence, that, in the context of a particular case, the rule was communicated or applied in such a way as to convey an intent to restrict or prohibit solicitation during breaktime or other periods when employees are not actively at work. On the other hand, in our opinion, a rule prohibiting solicitation during "working hours" is prima facie susceptible of the interpretation that solicitation is prohibited during all business hours and, thus, invalid.   We would therefore require the employer to show by extrinsic evidence that, in the context of a particular case, the "working hours" rule was communicated or applied in such a way as to convey an intent clearly to permit solicitation during breaktime or other period when employees are not actively at work.

(Two dissenting Board members would have applied the principle that ambiguities in the no-solicitation rule should be read against the employer, in order better to protect employee interests under the Act, such that a rule applicable even to "work time" would be treated by them as presumptively unlawful.)

§ 2.   Employer No-Solicitation Rules

The presumption of invalidity that attaches to rules barring solicitation or distribution during other than working time (*e. g.,* lunch or break periods) may be overcome by specific proof by the employer that the rule is indeed necessary for efficiency, safety or discipline. McDonnell Douglas Corp. v. NLRB (8th Cir. 1973) (national security justifies restrictions, by company engaged in production of military and classified aircraft and spacecraft, of access by off-duty employees to parking lots and other nonworking areas).   Perhaps the most common illustration is the retail department store, concerning which the Board has sustained company rules barring solicitation, even during nonworking time, which takes place on the selling floor or on elevators or stairways used by customers.   Such rules are assumed reasonably to safeguard against disruption of customer traffic and transactions.   May Dep't Stores (1944), *enf'd as mdf'd* (8th Cir. 1946).

The Board has also sustained company rules which bar distribution of literature (as opposed to oral solicitation) in working areas even though during nonworking time.   In Stoddard-Quirk Mfg. Co. (1962), the Board sustained such a no-distribution rule since the distribution of union leaflets in working areas of the plant, even during lunch and break periods, could reasonably be thought to create a littering hazard, and since the locus of distribution was not as important as in the case of oral solicitation in view of the employees' ability to carry the leaflet with them for more leisurely study.   A no-distribution ban will, however, be presumed illegal if it applies to nonworking time and to areas, such as company parking lots, other than those in which work is carried on.   The Board has treated the solicitation of signatures on authorization cards as governed by the more hospitable presumptions regarding oral solicitation rather than those governing the distribution of written literature.   *Ibid.*   While the *Stoddard-Quirk* rule will usually give the employer a rather firm idea as to the valid reach of its no-distribution rules, there will be cases in which the distinction between working and nonworking areas will not be easy to draw. Patio Foods v. NLRB (5th Cir. 1969) (truck loading area held a work area in spite of fact that employees traversed it in going to and from plant; Board finding to contrary held unsupported by substantial evidence).

The presumption of validity which ordinarily attaches to no-solicitation rules regarding working time can also be overcome. Most typically, this occurs when specific proof is adduced to demonstrate that the company rule was adopted for discriminatory reasons and with a specific desire to inhibit communication on behalf of the union. Thus, a rule may either on its face or (despite comprehensiveness in its terms) as actually applied bar only union solicitation but permit other kinds of solicitation. If the employer, for example, permits working-time solicitation for charitable organizations, athletic events or funds for injured co-workers—and particularly if it permits solicitation of an antiunion nature—this will be deemed to evidence a discriminatory motive and to undermine any presumed business reason for barring pro-union solicitation. NLRB v. Electro Plastic Fabrics, Inc. (4th Cir. 1967). The standard to be applied in determining whether there has been discriminatory enforcement of a rule is whether the forms of solicitation which the employer allows are "substantial" or "widespread and variegated." Compare Serv-Air, Inc. v. NLRB (10th Cir. 1968) (section 8(a)(1) finding reversed when other solicitation was for flowers for widows of deceased employees), with William L. Bonnell Co. v. NLRB (5th Cir. 1969) (section 8(a)(1) finding sustained when employer permitted raffles for prizes and food, chances in baseball pools, solicitation for flower funds and civic appeals).

A case of discrimination is not established simply by proof that the employer first promulgated a no-solicitation rule (or actively began to enforce a hitherto dormant rule) when the union solicitation campaign got under way. Permian Corp. (1971), *enf'd mem.* (5th Cir. 1972). While the Board will not normally find such a "coincidence" to warrant overturning the presumption of validity, it will find that the General Counsel has made a prima facie case of unlawful discrimination when such coincidence is reinforced by other employer unfair labor practices or by permission to others to engage in solicitation. In such a case, the working-time no-solicitation rule will be struck down unless the employer can demonstrate that it is indeed necessary for production or discipline. State Chem. Co. (1967).

Although a working-time no-solicitation rule will be presumed lawful, it is not altogether clear whether the presumption can be overcome in all instances in which the General Counsel can prove that working-time solicitation will actually not be disruptive of safety or efficiency. An example would be solicitation by an off-duty truckdriver while in the cab along with a working driver. The most common instance in which working-time "solicitation" will be sustained against a company rule is the wearing of union pins or buttons while on the job. The wearing and display of such items are treated as protected activities, Republic Aviation Corp. v. NLRB (U.S.1945), and even though the company ban on their wearing relates to working time, there will be no presumption of validity and the company will have to demonstrate that "special circumstances" warrant an interference with those activities. Such will be the case when it can demonstrate that the button will provoke other employees to serious anger, Caterpillar Tractor Co. v. NLRB (7th Cir. 1956) ("scab" buttons); will affront the company's clientele, NLRB v. Harrah's Club (9th Cir. 1964); or will distract employees at tasks requiring great concentration, Fabri-Tek, Inc. v. NLRB (8th Cir. 1965) (oversized "vari-vue" buttons in electronics assembly plant). Of course, even after the employer attempts to justify its rule banning union pins, the Board is free to disbelieve that it was so motivated when further proof demonstrates that the ban has been applied only to union pins but not to other similar items. Ohio Masonic Home (1973) (employer banned union buttons while tolerating "Smile" and "Jesus Saves" buttons; two dissenting members would have sustained credibility finding of administrative law judge that employer believed only union buttons would unsettle residents of home for aged).

When stated in isolation, the Board's presumptions relating to solicitation and distribution may appear complex and artificial. While they allow of exceptions, whatever rigidity they possess is affirmatively useful. First, they give guidance in advance to employers as to the kinds of limitations which may be validly imposed upon union solicitation and distribution. Second, they give guidance to Board authorities in determining whether or not to issue complaints and how to decide most of these cases without inordinately lengthy hearings and opinions relating to such matters as company need and alternative channels of union communication. Third, they reflect a substantive judgment that inhibitions on employee activities on behalf of the union inherently do "interfere" with and "restrain" the exercise of their section 7 rights and that the burden to justify that inhibition should properly lie with the employer when its needs are not immediately obvious. The courts have for the most part supported the Board in the application of these rules and presumptions, although on at least the issue of no-solicitation rules regarding nonworking time and areas, some courts of appeals have required the General Counsel to go beyond the presumption of invalidity and actually to adduce proof that the rule significantly inhibits the union in communicating its message to the employees, a matter which is speculative and which is likely to prolong proceedings and to proliferate the incidence of litigation. Compare NLRB v. Rockwell Mfg. Co. (3d Cir. 1959) (requiring proof of lack of alternative means of communication), with NLRB v. United Aircraft Corp. (2d Cir. 1963). One may fairly infer, however, from a recent decision of the United States

Supreme Court, that the General Counsel will make out a sufficient case of a section 8(a)(1) violation by showing that the no-solicitation rule reaches nonworking time and nonworking areas; the employer will fail if it comes forward with no proof that production or discipline makes the rule necessary. NLRB v. Magnavox Co. (U.S.1974).

§ 3. Labor-Contract Provisions Limiting Solicitation

Despite the ordinary presumptions which protect employees in the solicitation of union support, an employer and a union with which it is already engaged in collective bargaining may find it to their mutual advantage to impose by agreement limitations upon such employee activities during the term of the labor contract. The Board initially sustained such contract provisions, and any ensuing employee discipline for violation thereof, as a product of free collective bargaining, not unlike bargained-for waivers of other section 7 rights such as the right to strike. May Dep't Stores Co. (1944), enf'd as mdf'd (8th Cir. 1946). The Board in 1963 reversed its position, and denied employers the power to enforce such contractual no-solicitation and no-distribution rules to the extent they apply to nonworking time (and as to distribution, also in nonworking areas) when the communications were on behalf of a union other than the incumbent or were against unionization altogether. Gale Prods. (1963). A conflict developed on the issue in the courts of appeals, and the Supreme Court ultimately endorsed the position taken by the Board. NLRB v. Magnavox Co. (U.S.1974). The Court distinguished allowable union waiver of the section 7 right to strike, which relates to the securing of economic goals, from an attempted waiver of the organizational rights of employees, which are at the very heart of the representation and bargaining provisions of the Labor Act. The Court was not prepared to permit an incumbent union to become entrenched by waiving the right to communicate, on nonworking time in nonworking areas, of employees who would campaign for some other union or against unionization altogether; that the union preserved in its labor contract the right to post notices on the company bulletin board was thus an inadequate substitute. While three Justices would have disabled the union from waiving the solicitation rights only of employees whose interests were adverse, the Court majority went further to hold that the union could not validly waive even the rights of its own supporters. In effect, the Court concluded that the same presumptions of validity—and the employer burden to demonstrate that the nonworking-time rule is necessary for discipline or production—apply when the no-solicitation rule is based on the labor contract as when it is unilaterally promulgated by the employer.

The principle of the *Magnavox* case has since been extended so as to bar labor-contract provisions which would forbid the distribution, in nonwork areas on nonwork time, of literature concerning candidates for an intraunion election of officers. General Motors Corp.

v. NLRB (6th Cir. 1975). The Court reasoned that criticism of incumbent union officials is a protected activity under section 7, and that such literature bears directly on the issue of the selection or retention of a union representative.

§ 4.   Union Solicitation By Nonemployees

The principles just discussed apply to solicitation and distribution by employees of the respondent company. When the union's spokesmen are not employees—and are on the union's payroll as organizers —different rules apply and they are somewhat less hospitable to union solicitation and distribution. Nonemployees will be unfamiliar to the company and its supervisory personnel, and may create problems of identification, discipline, injury and security substantially more serious than those attendant upon solicitation by employees who are known and who themselves know the rules and layout of the plant. Moreover, no-solicitation rules are subject to attack only to the extent they contravene section 8(a)(1), and the Supreme Court has held that the application of these rules to nonemployees (who by virtue of their status are thought to have no claim to the protection of section 7) will be unobjectionable except to the extent that the ban upon communication will actually effect some "restraint, interference, or coercion" upon the rights of employees.

In NLRB v. Babcock & Wilcox Co. (U.S.1956), the Court concluded:

> It is our judgment . . . that an employer may validly post his property against nonemployee distribution of union literature if reasonable efforts by the union through other available channels of communication will enable it to reach the employees with its message and if the employer's notice or order does not discriminate against the union by allowing other distribution.

Since the Board in *Babcock & Wilcox* had erred in treating distribution by employees and nonemployees alike and had not considered the issue of alternative means of communication, the Court took that task upon itself, and found that "the plants are close to small well-settled communities where a large percentage of the employees live. The usual methods of imparting information are available." It therefore sustained a company rule barring nonemployee distribution of union literature on company-owned parking lots. It has thus been held that in those situations where the location of the employees is such as to make solicitation off the company premises impracticable, the employer must open those premises to nonemployee union organizers under reasonable conditions. Classic illustrations are the remote logging camp, see NLRB v. Lake Superior Lumber Corp. (6th Cir. 1948); the mining camp on a distant island, Alaska Barite Co. (1972), *enf'd mem.* (9th Cir. 1973); sailors onboard tankers, Sabine

Towing & Transp. Co. (1973); and mountain-resort employees who spend both working and leisure time on the employer's premises, NLRB v. S. & H. Grossinger's Inc. (2d Cir. 1967).

The determination whether the union will have effective access to employees off company premises by home visits, telephone calls, mailings, and newspaper, radio and television advertisements is typically an elusive one. While the courts ought thus properly defer to the Board in making such assessments, judicial review tends to be rather energetic on this issue. In the major Supreme Court case, for example, the Court announced that "alternative means" had to be considered and itself concluded that the record demonstrated that the union's other methods of communication with employees were adequate, without first having the Board consider the matter under the new legal principle. NLRB v. Babcock & Wilcox Co. (U.S.1956). In two cases involving solicitation of employees at mountain resorts, courts of appeals reversed Board findings that union contacts off company property were inadequate to bring home the union's message, in spite of the fact that the living, dining, recreational and postal facilities were on company property, there were no personal telephones, and the workforce was transitory and had a six or seven day workweek, NLRB v. Tamiment, Inc. (3d Cir. 1971); or in spite of unsuccessful union attempts to communicate with employees at distant union offices, through a local newspaper advertisement, at a local bar or at the main gate to the resort, NLRB v. Kutsher's Hotel & Country Club, Inc. (2d Cir. 1970). These cases suggest that even though employer resistance, or difficulties of geography or work scheduling, render extremely unlikely the success of requesting address lists or bulletin board space or meetings off company property or the accosting of employees at public roadways, the union must pursue such avenues of communication—at least as a prerequisite to securing an order permitting access to company property and perhaps even as a complete alternative thereto.

The Board has itself recently declined opportunities to permit more ready access by nonemployee organizers to company property. Monogram Models, Inc. (1971) (location in large metropolitan area does not make conventional methods of communication inadequate; no "large city" rule announced); Falk Corp. (1971) (exhaustive analysis of alternative means; union can copy car license numbers and thereby obtain list of employee names and addresses from the state). One can thus infer from the Board decisions, and the more stringent readings by the courts of appeals, that section 7 will be read to admit outside organizers to company property only when employees actually live there, and even then only if the union goes through extensive efforts at communication that are likely to be futile.

Of course, if the employer posts its property only against union solicitors, but permits nonemployees upon the property to solicit or communicate for other purposes, the presumed validity of the exclusionary rule is overcome. Stowe Spinning Co. (1949) (sole meeting hall in "company town"); Priced-Less Discount Foods, Inc. (1967) (solicitation permitted in company parking lot for school children, church organizations and community fund drives).

§ 5. The Off-Duty Employee

Because the solicitation rights of nonemployees are so much more restricted than those of employees, unions have attempted, in cases involving solicitation by a company employee who finishes working on his shift and later returns to the plant to solicit among employees on a different shift, to argue that the employee's privileges are to be determined not by the *Babcock & Wilcox* line of cases but rather by the more hospitable *Republic Aviation* line. This would permit the employee to invoke the presumption of invalidity against a no-solicitation rule relating to that employee's nonworking time and would thus require the employer to come forward with a specific business justification for the rule; the union need not come forward with proof that it has no adequate means of communicating with the employees on the shift in question. This attempt has been rebuffed, in court, Diamond Shamrock Co. v. NLRB (3d Cir. 1971), and by the Board, GTE Lenkurt, Inc. (1973). Three members of the Board, rather perfunctorily, chose to characterize the off-duty employee as a nonemployee or stranger who may be excluded without reason from company property; a minority of the Board warned that this would unduly restrict communication by employees of one shift with employees of another, and could even inhibit nonworking-time solicitation on company property by an employee with fellow workers on his own shift should their conversations take place "too long" before their shift begins or after it ends.

§ 6. Constitutional Protection for Union Solicitation on Company Property

Unions have responded to the sharp limitations upon nonemployee solicitation with yet another argument: that many forms of solicitation on company property are protected not primarily by section 7 of the Labor Act but by the free-speech provisions of the federal Constitution. At the same time as population centers have been growing and industrial and retail establishments have been moving to the suburbs, thus making extremely difficult personalized contacts with employees at home, the growth of privately owned industrial parks and shopping centers has created a "buffer" of private property between employees and union organizers, thus rendering impracticable in many instances solicitation or distribution of literature on public ways adjoining the working place. In the face of these communicational difficulties both at home and at work, unions have pointed to the "public" attributes of technically private property surrounding many plants and retail stores.

In Amalgamated Food Employees Union Local 590 v. Logan Valley Plaza, Inc. (U.S.1968), the Supreme Court held that labor picketing within a privately owned shopping center adjoining a supermarket there could not be enjoined as a trespass to private property, since the public had unrestricted access to the mall property and the stores within the mall were functionally equivalent to a shopping district on a public street (where constitutional protections normally applicable to peaceful picketing would clearly obtain). Soon after, a union engaged in solicitation of employees outside a hardware store housed in a large building surrounded by a parking lot owned by the store owner and used by its customers and employees; it sought to invoke *Logan Valley* as a means of securing constitutional protection for its parking-lot solicitation. The Supreme Court distinguished *Logan Valley*, and held that while the solicitation might be protected by section 7 (an issue to be addressed on remand) and the company's no-solicitation rule might thus violate section 8(a)(1), the enforcement of the company's rule did not violate the federal Constitution. Central Hardware Co. v. NLRB (U.S.1972). The Court held that an employer could not be subjected to the limitations of the first and fourteenth amendments (*i. e.*, there could be no "state action") unless its property had assumed "to some significant degree the functional attributes of public property devoted to public use," and that Central Hardware's property had not taken on such attributes by virtue of the fact that its parking lot was open to the public. "Such an argument could be made with respect to almost every retail and service establishment in the country, regardless of size or location" and would drastically impair long-settled property rights which are themselves constitutionally protected.

This emphasis on the control by employers of their private property has ultimately induced the Supreme Court to overrule *Logan Valley*. In Hudgens v. NLRB (U.S.1976), employees working in a warehouse of a shoe company went on strike and picketed the company's retail stores, one of which was inside an enclosed shopping mall. When the owner of the shopping center threatened arrest for trespassing, the union filed a charge under section 8(a)(1). The decisions of the Board and court of appeals, sustaining the charge, appeared to be based in part on a conclusion that the picketing at the shopping center was constitutionally protected under *Logan Valley*. The Supreme Court reversed and remanded, holding that the shopping center could not be assimilated to a governmental entity for purposes of the constitutional protection for freedom of speech, that the picketers thus had no constitutional right to be immune from threats of prosecution for trespass, and that they would have to rest any comparable claims upon sections 7 and 8(a)(1) of the Labor Act. The Court concluded that constitutional protection was available against private landowners only when their property assumed all of the attributes of a municipality (post office, streets, sewers, and other "semiofficial municipal functions") and not merely its business block. It suggested that the Board on remand should consider the applicable precedents under section 8(a)(1) regarding solicitation on private property—such as *Republic Aviation* and *Babcock & Wilcox*—as well as the distinguishing elements in the case at bar (most notably, that the workers were engaged in picketing their own employer, albeit on shopping-center property owned by another, rather than soliciting union membership).

In short, it thus appears—with perhaps the exception of the "company town"—that the right of employees and nonemployees to solicit on company property can no longer plausibly be based on the federal Constitution but must instead be based upon an analysis of the Labor Act and an accommodation between the section 7 rights of workers and the property rights of employers. Obviously, such an analysis cannot be used to protect employees who fall outside the coverage of the Act, such as agricultural workers. In a number of recent cases, reliance was placed upon such constitutional precedents as *Logan Valley* in order to secure access for union organizers (or community organizations) to farmworkers living in privately owned migrant labor camps. In most of these cases, such arguments were successful and access granted. Compare Petersen v. Talisman Sugar Corp. (5th Cir. 1973) (access permitted; exhaustive discussion of precedents), with Asociacion de Trabajadores Agricolas v. Green Giant Co. (3d Cir. 1975) (inadequate proof, on motion for summary judgment, that plaintiffs had no alternative means of communication with employees). While many of these migrant labor camps are more akin to the "company town" than to the suburban shopping center, so that the results of these cases may remain intact in spite of the overruling of *Logan Valley,* future cases will have to take that overruling into account as some expression of Supreme Court concern for the too-ready interference, under constitutional guise, with rights of private ownership.

§ 7. The Union's Right to "Equal Access"; The "Captive Audience"

An employer with a valid no-solicitation or no-distribution rule may frequently wish to "violate" that rule, for example, by assembling its employees on company property during working hours for purposes of delivering an antiunion address. The rule may be concededly valid and the address concededly noncoercive (and thus within the shelter of section 8(c)). Yet the union may believe that it is put at a substantial disadvantage in the absence of a similar opportunity to address a "captive audience" for the purpose of communicating the union message. In Bonwit Teller, Inc. (1951), *remanded on other grounds* (2d Cir. 1952), the Board held the employer's denial of such a request to constitute an unfair labor practice. The employer was held to have interfered with the section 7 right of the employees "to hear both sides of the story under circumstances which reasonably approximate equality." Section 8(c) was thought no obstacle to such a conclusion since the employer's speech was not treated as unlawful but rather its conduct in denying the union equal time.

Two years later, in Livingston Shirt Corp. (1953), the Board, with newly appointed members, departed from the *Bonwit Teller* rationale and concluded that section 8(c) forbade the conditioning of the exercise of the employer's right to speak noncoercively upon its willingness to afford the union comparable time and setting. It stated that as a general matter there was a rough equality between the employer's use of its property to address its employees and the union's use of its property (the union hall) and of other solicitation methods (*e. g.,* by employees on nonworking time and by home visits). The Board held:

> We rule therefore that, in the absence of either an unlawful broad no-solicitation rule (prohibiting union access to company premises on other than working time) or a privileged no-solicitation rule (broad, but not unlawful because of the character of the business), an employer does not commit an unfair labor practice if he makes a preelection speech on company time and premises to his employees and denies the union's request for an opportunity to reply.

In effect, the Board declared that it would require the employer to grant a union's request for equal time in, most typically, the retail and department-store trade (where employers could validly adopt a "broad but not unlawful" rule barring solicitation even during nonworking time on the selling floor); but that there would be no such requirement for manufacturing and wholesale enterprises where valid no-solicitation rules obtained.

The United States Supreme Court was presented in NLRB v. United Steelworkers (Nutone and Avondale) (U.S.1958), with employer denials of union requests to depart from concededly valid no-solicitation rules subsequent to the employers' antiunion solicitation. The Court held that an employer's denial of such a request does not in itself constitute an unfair labor practice, stating that:

> [T]he Taft-Hartley Act does not command that labor organizations as a matter of abstract law, under all circumstances, be protected in the use of every possible means of reaching the minds of individual workers, nor that they are entitled to use a medium of communication simply because the employer is using it.

The Court went on to state in dictum, however, that the result could be different if the no-solicitation rules "truly diminished the ability of the labor organizations involved to carry their message to the employees."

> If, by virtue of the location of the plant and of the facilities and resources available to the union, the opportunities for

effectively reaching the employees with a pro-union message, in spite of a no-solicitation rule, are at least as great as the employer's ability to promote the legally authorized expression of his anti-union views, there is no basis for invalidating these "otherwise valid" rules.

The denial of "equal time" will thus ordinarily be presumed lawful (even, as in the *Avondale* case before the Court, when the employer's solicitation is in itself coercive and unlawful), and the burden will be upon the General Counsel to demonstrate that the union is seriously incapacitated from communicating with the employees by other means. (It is unclear, however, whether this burden is discharged simply upon a showing of "inequality" between the employer's "captive audience" speech and the union's alternative means, or by the more rigorous showing that objectively considered the union has no practicable means of communicating effectively with the employees.) The lack of alternative means will thus become an issue in these "equal time" cases, just as they are in cases of employer denials to nonemployees of access to its property for purposes of solicitation, but as they are not in cases of solicitation restrictions upon employees. The Court ignored the argument, although implicitly rejecting it, that apart from "alternative means" the employer's conduct should be held unlawful because, by "discriminatorily" applying the no-solicitation rule to the union but not to itself, the employer was conclusively demonstrating that the rule was designed to hamper the union rather than to effectuate any legitimate employer interest in plant safety, efficiency or discipline. See James Hotel Co. (1963) (employer's disregarding its own no-solicitation rule does not invalidate it, citing *Nutone*).

In a 1962 decision involving a department store employer with a lawful broad no-solicitation rule relating to nonworking time, the Board found a violation of section 8(a)(1) in the employer's denial of a union request to address employees in a group on company time and property after the employer itself had delivered such an address. May Dep't Stores Co. (1962), *enf't denied* (6th Cir. 1963). Purporting to comply with the *Nutone-Avondale* decision of the Supreme Court, the Board found the broad no-solicitation rule to create a "glaring imbalance in opportunities for organizational communication" when compared with the employer speech, since that rule "relegated the Union and its employee supporters to relatively catch-as-catch-can methods of rebuttal, such as home visits, advertised meetings on the employees' own time, telephone calls, letters, and the various mass media of communication." The dissenting Board member charged the majority with automatically applying an "equal opportunity" doctrine rejected by the Board in *Livingston Shirt* and by the Supreme Court in *Nutone-Avondale* and with failing to make specific findings on the question whether the union "has an adequate opportunity for effectively reaching the employees outside the employer's premises through reasonable efforts." The Court of Appeals for the Sixth Circuit agreed with the dissenting member and refused to enforce the Board's order. To demonstrate the unpredictability of decision in this area, the same court of appeals subsequently enforced a Board order under section 8(a)(1) which found unlawful an employer denial of "equal time" in the face of a no-solicitation rule, even without proof that alternative means of communication were unavailing; the *May* case was thought distinguishable simply because the employer rule in the case at bar (applicable to nonworking time and nonworking areas) was itself illegal. Montgomery Ward & Co. v. NLRB (6th Cir. 1965).

Although no general trend is discernible, these cases show that the Board will sometimes presume "imbalance" or ineffective union alternatives—an assumption which lay at the heart of the now-repudiated *Bonwit Teller* "equal opportunity" doctrine—and thus will require an employer to allow the union to speak to employees "in violation" of a no-solicitation rule when the employer has "violated" the rule. Even if some reviewing courts are unconvinced that such a presumed imbalance justifies an employer unfair labor practice finding, there may be somewhat more receptivity to the Board's invoking against the employer the milder sanction of setting aside an employer victory in a subsequent representation election. NLRB v. Shirlington Supermarket, Inc. (4th Cir. 1955). The theory would be that the employer's refusal of "equal time" and the resulting communicational imbalance destroys the "laboratory conditions" which the Board has held, in General Shoe Corp. (1948), must obtain in a Board election. In any event, it appears as though the same requirement of communicational imbalance will apply in these "equal time" cases regardless whether the context is an unfair labor practice proceeding or a proceeding to set aside an election. See General Indus. Electronics Co. (1967), *mdf'd on other grounds* (8th Cir. 1968).

In recent years the Board has, in cases involving aggravated employer unfair labor practices under sections 8(a)(1) and (3), ordered that the charging union be given access by the employer to company property, either to solicit employees during nonworking time, Decaturville Sportswear Co. v. NLRB (6th Cir. 1969), or to deliver a "captive audience" speech, NLRB v. Crown Laundry & Dry Cleaners, Inc. (5th Cir. 1971). While some courts consider the union's communicational alternatives as relevant to the issuance of such an order, NLRB v. H.W. Elson Bottling Co. (6th Cir. 1967), the better view is that such alternatives bear only on the question whether the employer commits an unfair labor practice when it bars the union from its property and not on the question of remedies after the Board has already found serious employer violations of sections 8(a)(1) and (3), Decaturville Sportswear Co. v. NLRB (6th Cir. 1969).

The Board has announced a firm rule outlawing "captive audience" speeches on company time within the twenty-four-hour period prior to an election. Peerless Plywood Co. (1953). The rule proscribes such addresses whether by company or union, in view of their "unwholesome and unsettling effect" so shortly before the election, and their tendency to "interfere with that sober and thoughtful choice which a free election is designed to reflect." To redress both the "mass psychology" created by the address and the unfair advantage it gives to the last speaker, violation of the *Peerless Plywood* rule will result in the setting aside of an election victory by the speaker and the ordering of a new election. By its terms, the decision does not impede noncoercive employer (or union) speeches before the twenty-four-hour period, the dissemination of other forms of propaganda even during the twenty-four-hour period, and the delivery during that period of campaign speeches on or off company property if employee attendance is voluntary and on the employee's own time.

§ 8.   Employee Names and Addresses

The Board has frequently been invited by unions to return to the equal-opportunity principle of Bonwit Teller, Inc. (1951), *remanded on other grounds* (2d Cir. 1952), should the employer make a "captive audience" speech, and in fact to go further and permit union access to company property for solicitation purposes regardless of any such employer speech. But in General Elec. Co. (1966), the Board explicitly deferred consideration of any such steps pending a determination of the impact of its decision in Excelsior Underwear, Inc. (1966). In *Excelsior,* the Board acknowledged the central importance of having all employees in the election unit hear both sides of the collective-bargaining issues in order to make a rational and informed choice for or against unionization. The Board announced what has become known as the "Excelsior Rule" that within a week of the agreement upon or the ordering of an election, the employer is obliged to furnish the Board for transmittal to the union the names and addresses of all employees eligible to vote. Failure to do so will subject the employer, in the event the union loses the election, to an order setting aside the election and ordering a new one. The obligation is not conditioned upon any prior use of the mailing lists by the employer for election campaigning or upon any proof of a communicational imbalance or inadequate union channels of communication. The Board enforces this rule either after the fact by setting aside the election or in advance of the election, upon an employer's refusal to produce the list, by issuing a subpoena enforceable in a federal district court pursuant to section 11 of the Labor Act. While the Supreme Court criticized the Board for announcing the *Excelsior* requirement (but giving it only prospective effect) in the context of a specific adjudicatory proceeding rather than by formal rulemaking, it sustained both the substantive validity of the requirement and its enforcement by Board subpoena. NLRB v. Wyman-Gordon Co. (U.S. 1969).

The Board has not yet held that failure to disgorge the list of employee names and addresses will constitute an employer unfair labor practice. It has, however, in cases in which the employer has been found to commit serious independent unfair labor practices under sections 8(a)(1) and (3), ordered the employer to furnish the charging union with such a list. The Board will usually note that union contacts off company property have been necessitated by the atmosphere of coercion and employer hostility which pervades the plant itself. J. P. Stevens & Co. v. NLRB (4th Cir. 1968).

CHAPTER IX

EMPLOYER DOMINATION AND SUPPORT
OF UNIONS

§ 1. Background

In the late 1920's and early 1930's, employers confronted with the challenge of unionization frequently took the initiative in organizing employee committees or associations to represent the company's employees in adjusting grievances concerning wages and working conditions. The employer often dominated such "employee representatives" by instigating their creation, shaping the rules of organization and operation, influencing policy by having company representatives in official positions, inducing or requiring employees to join the organization, controlling its pursestrings and giving it special privileges within the plant (such as facilities and time for solicitation and meetings). Such employer domination and support was thought by Congress to interfere with the freedom of employees in selecting their collective bargaining representatives and to substitute for the voice of the employees at the bargaining table the voice of the employer (engaged in a dialogue with itself). In 1935, Congress enacted what is now section 8(a)(2) of the National Labor Relations Act:

> It shall be an unfair labor practice for an employer to dominate or interfere with the formation or administration of any labor organization or contribute financial or other support to it:
>
> *Provided,* That subject to rules and regulations made and published by the Board pursuant to section 6, an employer shall not be prohibited from permitting employees to confer with him during working hours without loss of time or pay.

The proviso makes it clear that adjustment of grievances by an employee group while drawing pay does not constitute illegal "financial support" of that group by the employer. Nor does the Act proscribe per se the "company union" whose membership is limited to the employees of a single company; what is illegal is the employer's domination or support of that union to such an extent that the employee rights given by section 7 are frustrated. Hertzka & Knowles v. NLRB (9th Cir. 1974). It is not, however, a defense to a charge of violation of section 8(a)(2) that the employer is acting with the best of intentions and without antiunion animus. This is true whether the violation takes the form of dominating a labor organization, NLRB v. Clappers Mfg., Inc. (3d Cir. 1972) (domination of employee committee for grievances and suggestions, "although his intentions may have been exemplary"); or of recognition of a union believed to have majority support within the bargaining unit when in truth it does not, ILGWU v. NLRB (Bernhard-Altmann Texas Corp.) (U.S. 1961).

Section 8(a)(2) had its "heyday" in the late 1930's and in the 1940's, when the company-dominated union was much more in vogue than it is today. Litigation involving this section has today slowed to a trickle, the major issues being not employer domination but rather: (1) the fine line between illegal "support" and legal, indeed desirable, "cooperation" by company with union; and (2) the inhibitions upon employer dealing with one union when a second union is engaged in organizing.

§ 2. "Labor Organization"

The employer is forbidden by section 8(a)(2) to dominate or support not any employee association, such as one devoted exclusively to athletic or social pursuits, but an employee group falling within the statutory definition in section 2(5) of a "labor organization":

> [A]ny organization of any kind, or any agency or employee representation committee or plan, in which employees participate and which exists for the purpose, in whole or in part, of dealing with employers concerning grievances, labor disputes, wages, rates of pay, hours of employment, or conditions of work.

It follows that domination is forbidden even if the employee representative is concerned merely with individual grievances rather than pervasive issues such as wages and hours for whole classes of employees. Moreover, because the definition requires only that the representative exist to "deal with" employers, it is not necessary that the representative seek actually to bargain with the employer but need only operate by making recommendations. The Supreme Court so held in NLRB v. Cabot Carbon Co. (1959). Indeed, even if the organization does no more than transmit employee "views" to the employer without making recommendations for their disposition, it falls within the statutory definition. NLRB v. Thompson Ramo Wooldridge, Inc. (7th Cir. 1962). The Board has, however, recently refrained from employing such a broad definition, apparently in an effort to adapt the principles of the Labor Act to the somewhat unusual organs of faculty governance in institutions of higher education. Northeastern Univ. (1975) (university senate comprised of faculty members is not a "labor organization" under the facts, since it "makes recommendations (which are totally different from bargaining demands that a union would make upon an employer during contract negotiations) to the president"; university tried to bar a representation election by arguing senate was labor organization and faculty manual was a collective bargaining agreement).

§ 3. "Domination" and Lesser Assistance: The Distinction and the Remedies

In proscribing employer interference with labor organizations, Congress banned not only domination but also such lesser forms of intrusion as "interference" and "support" (financial and otherwise). Domination, the most egregious form of employer control, is found typically when the employer through its supervisors of other managerial employees directly instigates and encourages, or directly participates in, the organization of the employee representative, and extends financial or other direct support. Many were the cases in the first decade of the administration of the Wagner Act in which the employer urged the formation of a company union, prepared its constitution and bylaws, supplied it with legal advice and financial assistance, and through supervisory employees, shaped its policy decisions. In the eyes of the employees, the employer in such cases had actual control of the union, and their participation was induced largely by fear of reprisal for nonsupport of the company union. NLRB v. Wemyss (9th Cir. 1954). Indeed, membership in the company union was commonly a condition of continued employment, with the employer paying all of the union's operating expenses. See NLRB v. Chardon Tel. Co. (6th Cir. 1963) (company president designated five persons to choose employees' committee, committee met in president's office on company time, president presided over first two meetings and kept minutes).

When the employer's intrusion in the formation and administration of the labor organization is not so extensive as to constitute actual domination and control, it may be determined that under all of the circumstances it still exerts undue influence through other and more subtle forms of interference and support. The need to draw the line between "domination" and "interference" (or "support") is related to the fashioning of an appropriate remedy. When the Board determines that an employer has dominated a labor organization, it will not only issue a conventional cease and desist order but will also order the disestablishment of the union as bargaining representative; the only assurance that employees will freely choose a representative in the future is to bar the employer from ever again recognizing or bargaining with the dominated organization or its successor. When, however, the employer's intrusions are limited to interference or support, the employer is ordered merely to withhold recognition until a fair and free election can be held pursuant to the usual election procedures of section 9 of the Act. In such an election, the previously favored organization may—upon proof that interference or support has ceased and its effects dissipated—be placed on the ballot and certified as bargaining representative.

These remedial principles were announced by the Board in Carpenter Steel Co. (1948), and represented a sharp departure from prior Board practice. Before 1947, the Board's orders in these cases depended upon whether the union in question was affiliated with a national or international federation or was instead an unaffiliated or true company union. In the former case, regardless of the extent of employer domination or interference, the Board would merely order the employer to refrain from recognition until the union was later certified; in the latter case, disestablishment of the unaffiliated union would uniformly be ordered. As the Board stated in *Carpenter Steel:*

> This difference in treatment   .   .   was based upon the Board's belief that a labor organization affiliated with a national or international federation that was outside the ambit of the employer's control could not be permanently and completely subjugated to the will of the employer. It was thought that complete disestablishment was therefore not required to remedy the effects of employer interference or to restore the employees' freedom of self-organization.

This disparity of remedial treatment between the affiliated and unaffiliated union in cases under sections 8(a)(1) and (2) was declared improper by Congress in 1947, when it amended section 10(c) to provide:

> That in determining whether a complaint shall issue   .   .   and in deciding such cases, the same regulations and rules of decision shall apply irrespective of whether or not the labor organization affected is affiliated with a labor organization national or international in scope.

The Board the next year responded to this mandate in *Carpenter Steel* by asserting that it would issue the more severe disestablishment order in cases of employer domination, and the lesser sanction in cases of interference and support—regardless of whether the union is affiliated. (Although it is rare, a court will sometimes endorse the Board's finding of a violation of section 8(a)(2) but classify it as interference rather than domination, and "downgrade" an order of disestablishment. NLRB v. Wemyss (9th Cir. 1954).)

A question will sometimes arise as to whether a newly formed organization is in truth a successor to a "tainted" organization which has been the subject of a disestablishment order. The coercive impact of the original domination may be removed and the successor made eligible for lawful recognition if the employer, prior to the formation of the successor, has established a clear "line of fracture" between the two organizations by publicly and unequivocally disestablishing the old organization and by giving assurances to employees of their freedom from further interference with their choice of bargaining representative. Duro Test Corp. (1949).

§ 4. Employer "Interference"

There appears to be no clear and administrable distinction between domination and "interference" with a labor organization. Indeed, in many cases, what might otherwise have been treated as interference has been elevated to domination by serious independent employer unfair labor practices, such as threatening or implementing discharge of employees unsympathetic to the favored union. The Board and the courts have eschewed any per se rules in construing section 8(a)(2) and have examined the conduct of the employer in light of all the circumstances. As noted above, the major practical significance of the distinction between domination and interference is the issuance, respectively, of either a disestablishment order or merely an order to withdraw recognition pending an election and certification.

Interference will be found when the employer does not, in the eyes of the employees, control the employee representative, but when it exercises some lesser form of influence in the determination of union policy. Perhaps the most common illustration is the participation of supervisory employees in the conduct of union affairs. In many trades, most notably printing, publishing and construction, supervisory employees may wish to retain union membership, both for financial benefits and for job security (especially in the construction industry, where a supervisor on one job may be employed as a journeyman on the next). In itself, retention of union membership by supervisors is not illegal. But it is illegal for supervisors to serve as union officials or on a union bargaining team, for as the Board held in Nassau & Suffolk Contractors' Ass'n (1957):

> *Employees have the right to be represented in collective-bargaining negotiations by individuals who have a single-minded loyalty to their interests.* Conversely, an employer is under a duty to refrain from any action which will interfere with that employee right and place him even in slight degree on both sides of the bargaining table. (Emphasis in original.)

The same Board decision declared it illegal for supervisors even to vote in elections for union officers, since the supervisors might have the balance of power in a close election and could therefore select union officials who will later deal with them in their capacity as employer representatives.

Limitations upon the union activities of supervisors go yet further. The Board has held that it is unlawful for a supervisor to vote in an election of a delegate to be sent by the local union to the annual convention of the international, since that delegate may at the international meeting shape a policy which will affect the local in its dealings with the employer. Employing Bricklayers' Ass'n (1961). It has even been suggested that the supervisor/union-member may not speak out on contentious issues at union meetings, since this will stifle the expression of opposing views by rank-and-file employees who may fear for their job security at the hands of the supervisor. Plumbers Local 636 v. NLRB (D.C.Cir. 1961).

In all of these cases, it will be no defense to a finding of "interference" that the activities of the supervisors were carried on without the express authorization or ratification of the employer, or that the supervisors were acting in what they believed in good faith to be the best interests of the union. *Ibid.*

§ 5. "Financial or Other Support"

Even when the employer does not give the appearance of control over the formation or administration of a labor organization, Congress has forbidden more subtle forms of assistance which may nonetheless sway the independent judgment of the employee representative and improperly influence the employees in their selection of bargaining agent. These forms of assistance are held remediable not by disestablishment but by a cease and desist order and where appropriate by an order to refrain from recognition pending Board certification. It is frequently a fine act of judgment to distinguish between domination and "financial or other support" and, at the other extreme, between such support and legal forms of cooperation by employer with union.

It is not unlawful assistance for an employer simply to state its preference that employees join a particular union, whether or not limited in scope to the company and whether or not presently in competition with another union. NLRB v. Virginia Elec. & Power Co. (U.S.1941); Coppus Eng'r Corp. v. NLRB (1st Cir. 1957). Such expressions are protected by section 8(c) of the Labor Act, provided they contain no "threat of reprisal or force or promise of benefit," such as a threat to discipline employees who are unsympathetic to the favored union or a promise to reward employees who join that union. The employer's *conduct,* however, is not thus sheltered, and the following forms of assistance have (commonly in some combination) been held to violate section 8(a)(2): monetary contributions to the union, NLRB v. Sharples Chems., Inc. (6th Cir. 1954) (monthly contribution of $160 and $140 from vending machine, payment of employee representatives for attendance at committee meetings whether during or after work); payment of union expenses or assumption of union obligations; provision of legal or secretarial services; furnishing of a list of employees as a means of fostering organization by a favored union, Perry Coal Co. v. NLRB (7th Cir. 1960); payment of wages to employees for time spent in formation and organization of the union, NLRB v. Summers Fertilizer Co. (1st Cir. 1958) (test is whether employer benefits represent allowable cooperation with freely chosen employee representative or whether benefits are an inducement to employees to choose an organization which would not likely have been chosen otherwise); allowance of union solicitation or meetings on company time or property; permitting the union to operate a concession on company property and to retain the proceeds thereof, Double A Prods. Co. (1961) (employer forgoes for itself the

profits from the vending machine while profits accrue to union);
permitting the use of other company property, such as stationery or
printing facilities.

Almost all of the pertinent cases take pains to note that any giv-
en employer conduct would not in itself have been a violation of the
Act but rather becomes so in context and in combination with other
acts which either coerce employees or, quite commonly, evidence discrimination against a disfavored union. *E. g.,* Sunnen Prods., Inc.
(1971) (union election on company premises and time, monthly union meetings on company premises and regular pay for members during meetings, held, noncoercive and lawful assistance aiding union
to perform functions effectively; "The result might well be different were other coercive factors present."). It has been held that the
question for decision on judicial review is not whether employer acts
considered separately constitute a violation but rather whether the
facts taken together justify the Board's conclusion. NLRB v. Thompson Ramo Wooldridge, Inc. (7th Cir. 1962).

§ 6.   Cooperation Distinguished from Support

As the Board and courts have become less preoccupied with the
company union, there has been greater willingness to acknowledge
that the zealous prohibition of all forms of employer "support" to a
union can discourage as well much desirable cooperation. A company which is engaged in an arm's-length relationship with an insurgent or incumbent union will often, in full consonance with the purposes of the labor law, be prepared to permit the union to communicate with employees on company time and property, to utilize other
facilities such as company bulletin boards and to facilitate dues
collection. While it is likely that the employer would wish some
form of favorable union consideration in return, any actual intrusion
upon the full representative capacity of the union (and the freedom
of action of the employees) may well be so slight as not to outweigh
the benefits of a cooperative bargaining relationship which may result. The courts have tended to draw the line between cooperation
and illegal assistance rather more favorably to the employer than has
the Board.

In Chicago Rawhide Mfg. Co. v. NLRB (7th Cir. 1955), the court
distinguished support which, even though innocent, constitutes some
degree of control or influence over the union, from cooperation which
only assists the employees or their representative to carry out their
independent intention. "Neither mere cooperation, preference nor
possibility of control constitute [sic] unfair labor practices." Permission to conduct union elections and union business on company
premises or company time was held

> no more than evidence of the presence of potential means
> for interference and support, a possibility that is always

present to some degree in an employer-employee relationship. But, without evidence of the realization of that potential, they do not furnish a substantial factual basis for an unfair labor practice finding.

Even when the employee representative with whom the employer "cooperates" is a committee which has neither provisions for membership of employees generally nor any source of revenue (the employer paying for time spent in union activities and providing facilities and equipment), this has been held to constitute merely "potential means for interference and support" but not illegal support itself. Coppus Eng'r Corp. v. NLRB (1st Cir. 1957). Employer permission to the union to operate certain concessions within the plant and to retain the profits thereof was held not illegal where the profits amounted to roughly $700 per year and were typically devoted to supplying food or flowers for various union social activities; the court found no employer intention to interfere with employees in the free exercise of their right to choose or change their bargaining representative. NLRB v. Post Pub. Co. (7th Cir. 1962).

Although the courts profess to give deference to the Board's expertise in these "close" cases of employer interference and support, these three appellate reversals (and other similar decisions) demonstrate that the courts will examine the record carefully for themselves in order to determine whether the employer's "favors" have been accompanied either by demands for concessions or by the denial of comparable favors to some other and less desired union. More recently, the Board itself took a more flexible position and announced that it would not find a violation in these cases where the employer's assistance is minimal and does not endanger the independence of the union. Coamo Knitting Mills, Inc. (1964).

Perhaps the most significant departure from the traditional approach to domination and interference is represented by the decision of the court of appeals in Hertzka & Knowles v. NLRB (9th Cir. 1974). In that case, after unsuccessful attempts at bargaining on behalf of professional employees in an architectural firm, the union was decertified and promptly thereafter five committees were established to consider such issues as compensation, minimum standards and physical environment. The committee arrangement, initiated by several employees, was enthusiastically embraced by management, and each committee was comprised of five employees and one representative of management (who on some committees was entitled to vote). The Board found the committees to be employer dominated and ordered their disestablishment but the court of appeals reversed. The court noted that the primary purpose of the Labor Act was to facilitate free choice among employees in matters of representation and that such free choice would be frustrated by a too-literal ban on employer "interference," since interference can arguably be found whenever there is salutary employer cooperation with employee representatives. The court suggested that section 8(a)(2) would be violated if the employer was motivated by antiunion animus, that is, a desire to suppress employee rights of self-organization, but that in the absence of such animus, there must be "a showing that the employees' free choice, either in type of organization or in the assertion of demands, is stifled by the degree of employer involvement at issue." While management partners on the committees might mean bargaining is "weaker" than if there were an independent union representative, this mode of cooperation in the adjustment of employee claims was chosen by and satisfactory to the employees. Proof was lacking of any "actual interference with the assertion of employee demands."

> For us to condemn this organization would mark approval of a purely adversarial model of labor relations. Where a cooperative arrangement reflects a choice freely arrived at and where the organization is capable of being a meaningful avenue for the expression of employee wishes, we find it unobjectionable under the Act.

§ 7. Recognition of a Minority Union

A labor organization may be recognized as bargaining representative for all employees only when it has been, in the terms of section 9(a) of the Labor Act, "designated or selected for the purposes of collective bargaining by the majority of the employees in a unit appropriate for such purposes." When the employer deals with the union as exclusive representative in spite of the fact that it represents only a minority of unit employees, the employees' right freely to choose or to reject collective bargaining or a particular union is sacrificed, both by the employer and the minority union; and the union's favored status constitutes employer "support" which improperly induces employees to join. The Supreme Court has thus held, in ILG WU v. NLRB (Bernhard-Altmann Texas Corp.) (U.S.1961), that the recognition of a minority union constitutes a violation of sections 8(a)(1) and 8(a)(2) by the employer and of section 8(b)(1) by the union. Moreover, the inclusion and enforcement of a union-security provision in a contract with a minority union, requiring that all employees join that union as a condition of continued employment, constitute violations of sections 8(a)(3) and 8(b)(2) as well, for this is union-induced discrimination which is explicitly excluded from the shelter of the proviso to section 8(a)(3). That proviso protects such union-security provisions only if made with a labor organization which is "not established, maintained, or assisted by any action defined in section 8(a) of this Act as an unfair labor practice."

In *Bernhard-Altmann,* the employer recognized in a "memorandum of understanding" a union which both employer and union believed to have majority support at that time but which in fact did not; such support was, however, gained by the time the parties entered into a formal collective bargaining agreement. The Court held the after-acquired majority not to remove the taint of the earlier illegal agreement, since that agreement may have afforded the union "a deceptive cloak of authority with which to persuasively elicit additional employee support." The harm done by the agreement with the minority union was that it forced the union upon the nonconsenting majority and gave to it a marked advantage over any other union in securing the adherence of the employees. This harm resulted in spite of the fact that both company and union believed in good faith that the union represented a majority; the Court noted that the Act nowhere prescribes scienter as an element of the unfair labor practice and that to hold otherwise "would place in permissibly careless employer and union hands the power to completely frustrate employee realization of the premise of the Act," freedom of choice and majority rule.

The Board has pushed the holding in *Bernhard-Altmann* yet further and held that the employer violates section 8(a)(2) when it begins to negotiate for a contract with a minority union even though the execution of the agreement is expressly made conditional upon the union's first securing majority status. Majestic Weaving Co. (1964) (employer ordered to reimburse protesting employees for union dues and initiation fees), *enf't denied* (2d Cir. 1966) (sudden reversal of Board policy and unanticipated imposition of reimbursement order warrant utilization of Board rulemaking procedure rather than adjudication). The Board has also held that good faith does not excuse recognition of a minority union when the employer asserts its fear of a strike by the union demanding recognition, Ellery Prods. Mfg. Co. (1964), or its fear that a refusal to recognize will result in the filing of a charge under section 8(a)(5), Kenrich Petrochemicals, Inc. (1964). The effect of all of these decisions is, obviously, to encourage the employer carefully to authenticate the union's majority claim prior to entering upon negotiations.

It should be noted that there are two situations in which dealing with a minority union will not be held to violate sections 8(a)(1) and (2). In light of the short duration of many jobs in the building and construction industry, section 8(f) of the Labor Act, enacted in 1959, authorizes only in that industry the execution of an agreement with a minority union (not otherwise illegally dominated or assisted) which requires membership in the union within seven days (instead of the usual 30 days under the proviso to section 8(a)(3)) as a condition of continued employment; such a "pre-hire agreement" will not, however, serve as a contract bar to a representation election or decertification election under section 9. Even outside the construction industry, moreover, the Act interposes no bar to a contract between employer and minority union when the union acts as spokesman not for all employees in the unit but only for those employees who are members of that union or otherwise authorize it to bargain on their behalf. Such "members only" agreements have been sustained, Retail Clerks Local 128 v. Lion Dry Goods, Inc. (U.S.1962), although their legality becomes somewhat more speculative when the employer either denies comparable members-only bargaining to another organization or extends to one union in a members-only contract such favorable terms that it appears to be affording that union a position of privilege within the plant and an improper inducement for other employees to join.

In a case involving premature recognition of a minority union, the Supreme Court has held that the unfair labor practice occurs at the time of the illegal recognition, such that the passing of more than six months from that date will bar an unfair labor practice charge. The fact that the agreement continues in force until the date of the filing of the charge, by which time the union secures majority support, does not make the violation a "continuing" one embraced within the six-month period of limitations of section 10(b). Local 1424, Machinists v. NLRB (U.S.1960).

When the employer has contracted with a minority union, and the agreement requires employees to join the union and/or pay union dues and initiation fees, the Board order will typically include a provision holding both the employer and the union jointly and severally liable to reimburse such moneys to employees who by their protest assert that they would not otherwise have joined the union and paid such dues and fees. NLRB v. Downtown Bakery Corp. (6th Cir. 1964).

§ 8. Employer Neutrality and the *Midwest Piping* Doctrine

The Board holds that employer preference for one of two rival unions—when manifested not by protected speech but by discriminatory conduct—violates sections 8(a)(1) and (2). Perhaps the ultimate form of preference is recognition of and bargaining with the favored union at a time when another union (or unions) is asserting a claim of substantial employee support. In 1945, the Board held, in Midwest Piping & Supply Co. (1945), that an employer violates the Act when it recognizes and enters into a contract with one union, after another union has made known its claim of majority support and has filed with the Board a petition for a representation election. While the major rationale asserted by the Board is that such recognition arrogates to the employer the task given by statute to the Board of resolving "questions involving representation," it was also held that by its recognition and contracting the employer indicated its approval of the signatory union, accorded it unwarranted prestige, encouraged membership therein (the contract contained a union-shop provision), and rendered it unlawful assistance, all of which interfered with section 7 rights of employees in violation of section 8(a)(1). (One might analogize the employer's conduct to its bestowing economic benefits on employees while an election proceeding is pending; in most cases this is held to be an illegal inducement to reject an insurgent union.) The Board held in *Midwest Piping* that it is no defense that the employer bargained with the union only after the union had tendered signed membership cards as proof of its claim of majority support:

> [I]t is well known that membership cards obtained during the heat of rival organizing campaigns like those of the respondent's plants, do not necessarily reflect the ultimate choice of a bargaining representative; indeed, the extent of dual membership among the employees during periods of intense organizing activity is an important unknown factor affecting a determination of majority status, which can best be resolved by a secret ballot among the employees.

The Board has since held that the recognition of one of two competing unions violates not only section 8(a)(1) but also section 8(a)(2); that it is unlawful to execute an agreement in such a situation even if the agreement contains no union-security provision requiring employees to pay dues to or to join the favored union; and that the employer must withhold recognition even when the rival union raises a "question concerning representation" by means other than formally filing an election petition (for example, by tendering authorization cards). Novak Logging Co. (1958). The Board has also held that a question of representation is raised, under the *Midwest Piping* doctrine, whenever the claim of the rival union is not "clearly unsupportable and lacking in substance," and indeed that such a union need not even have made a formal request for recognition. Playskool, Inc. (1972), *enf't denied* (7th Cir. 1973).

At first the Board chose, in the interests of industrial stability, not to apply *Midwest Piping* when the union recognized in the face of a rival election petition was an incumbent union with which the employer negotiated a successor agreement. William D. Gibson Co. (1954). But the Board soon reversed its position, and now holds that, when an insurgent union raises a "real question concerning representation," the employer is barred from bargaining with an incumbent union at the termination of a labor contract. The incumbent may, however, continue to process grievances under the prevailing agreement pending definitive disposition by the Board of the rival's representation claim. Shea Chem. Corp. (1958). The disability to bargain commences with the filing of an insurgent's election petition accompanied by a thirty percent "showing of interest"; it is not necessary that the Board have held a representation hearing or ordered an election. Peter Paul, Inc. (1970), *enf't denied* (9th Cir. 1972). In these cases, the Board is prepared to tolerate an hiatus in the bargaining relationship for fear that continued dealing with the incumbent will exert pressure on the employees to support the incumbent rather than the insurgent organization. It may be doubted whether the pressure so generated adds much to that which already exists by virtue of the incumbent's past status as such, particularly if prior contracts contain a union-security provision; in any event, any pressure generated by employer favoritism toward an incumbent union will likely be far less than that generated by contracting with one of two rival unions where collective bargaining is new to the plant.

The courts of appeals have not been quite as inclined to make the Board's election processes the exclusive measure of resolving representation disputes, and have not applied the *Midwest Piping* doctrine so as to require quite the broad measure of employer neutrality endorsed by the Board. While adopting the Board's formulation that contracting with one union will violate the Act when a "real question involving representation" exists, the courts have tended to sustain such recognition and contracting when by authorization cards or other evidence the majority claims of the favored union (commonly, the incumbent) are shown to be substantial and those of the insurgent to be spurious. In one case, where the employer continued to bargain with the incumbent union, to which approximately ninety-five percent of the unit employees were still submitting dues by a contract checkoff provision, the court held that no question of representation was raised merely by the insurgent union filing a representation petition with the Board. NLRB v. Swift & Co. (3d Cir. 1961). Another court held that while the filing of an election petition is inadequate to show that a question of representation exists, a Board order of election is; but went on to conclude that nonetheless the employer may defend its bargaining with the incumbent by clearly proving with substantial evidence that the incumbent in truth continues to have majority support. St. Louis Indep. Packing Co. v. NLRB (7th Cir. 1961) (checkoff of dues by approximately ninety-seven percent of unit employees under prior contract with incumbent held insufficient evidence of continued majority support). In effect, the courts have defined "question of representation" in unfair labor practice proceedings under *Midwest Piping* so as to exclude many cases which the Board would include when defining that term for purposes of determining whether it is proper to hold a representation election (where a thirty percent "showing of interest" is all that is necessary).

What appears to be the prevailing judicial approach has been capsulized as follows:

> To recognize one of two competing unions while the employees' choice between them is demonstrably in doubt, is an unfair labor practice under what the courts have accepted as the normal and proper application of the Midwest Piping doctrine. . . . And in principle the same result follows when majority support for the recognized union exists, but has been achieved by coercion or some other unfair labor practice. . . . But where a clear majority of the employees, without subjection to coercion or other unlawful in-

fluence, have made manifest their desire to be represented by a particular union, there is no factual basis for a contention that the employer's action thereafter in recognizing the union or contracting with it is an interference with their freedom of choice.

NLRB v. Air Master Corp. (3d Cir. 1964). See also Playskool, Inc. v. NLRB (7th Cir. 1973).

CHAPTER X

CONSTITUTIONAL PROTECTION FOR PEACEFUL CONCERTED ACTIVITY, AND THE OUTLAWRY OF UNION VIOLENCE

§ 1. The Right to Discharge for Union Membership or Activity

The first major application of the Federal Constitution to the labor-management relationship found the United States Supreme Court declaring it to be a denial of due process for the federal government, Adair v. United States (U.S.1908), or a state government, Coppage v. Kansas (U.S.1915), to outlaw a provision in an employment contract whereby the employee agreed that he would not join a union during the period of his employment. These so-called yellow dog contracts, which were used to render tortious any attempt by laborers to induce employees to organize, were held to be the product of a mutual liberty to contract by employer and employee with which government could not interfere in the cause of securing labor peace. Employers were thus thought to have a constitutionally protected right to discharge employees solely because of their union membership or activities.

This right was short-lived. In 1926, Congress enacted the Railway Labor Act, which gave to both railroad employers and employees the right to designate bargaining representatives "without interference, influence, or coercion" by either against the other. In Texas & N.O.R.R. v. Brotherhood of Ry. Clerks (U.S.1930), even before the enactment of New Deal legislation and the abrupt change in judicial attitudes toward congressional power in the field of commerce, the Supreme Court held that the Railway Labor Act should be construed to empower the courts to issue injunctions against discharges of employees for their union activities (and to order reinstatement) and that such interference with employer action was not unconstitutional. The *Adair* and *Coppage* cases were tersely dismissed as "inapplicable."

> The Railway Labor Act of 1926 does not interfere with the normal exercise of the right of the carrier to select its employees or to discharge them. The statute is not aimed at this right of the employers but at the interference with the right of employees to have representatives of their own choosing. As the carriers subject to the Act have no constitutional right to interfere with the freedom of the employees

in making their selections, they cannot complain of the statute on constitutional grounds.

It was a rather simple matter for the Supreme Court thereafter, relying on the *Texas Railway* case, to sustain the constitutionality of the provisions of the 1935 Wagner Act which declared it illegal to coerce or to discriminate against employees concerning their union membership or activities. This was done in NLRB v. Jones & Laughlin Steel Corp. (U.S.1937).

§ 2.   The Right to Strike

The cases just discussed demonstrate that society can, through its legislature, constitutionally impose limits upon resort by employers to self-help in the face of employee concerted activities. These cases do not, however, mean that such concerted activities are themselves constitutionally immune from legislative regulation, or constitutionally protected against employer self-help. It is perfectly consistent to hold that the peaceful economic weapons of both labor and management are subject to restraints—governmental or private—in the public interest. The employer might wish to respond to a peaceful work stoppage by discharge or other discipline, to rid itself of the employees, or by judicial proceedings designed to secure the return of the employees to work. Moreover, the state might choose to impose governmental sanctions, such as imprisonment or fine, for engaging in a strike. Whether the employee has a constitutional right to be free of such private or governmental sanctions has not often been mooted in litigation in the private sector, although the rapid growth of unionization and concerted activities among employees in the public sector has made the "right to strike" a highly contentious issue there.

The right of a single individual employee to withhold his services as a means of pressuring an employer to come to terms cannot likely be denied by government in light of the Thirteenth Amendment to the Constitution barring involuntary servitude; no injunction could require a return to work, and surely no criminal penalties could be imposed. But no comparable constitutional protection has been accorded the right of employees to strike in concert. In 1926, the Supreme Court upheld a state statute imposing imprisonment and a fine for inducing a work stoppage in the coal mines of the state, holding that "Neither the common law, nor the Fourteenth Amendment, confers the absolute right to strike." Dorchy v. Kansas (U.S.1926) (Brandeis, J.). There, the strike was designed to extort the payment of money to a former employee and was held not to be incident to a trade dispute. The *Dorchy* decision thus does not squarely address the issue—hardly significant today in the private sector in light of the protection for peaceful strikes accorded by the Wagner Act and the Norris-LaGuardia Act—whether a strike incident to a labor dispute can constitutionally be enjoined or otherwise penalized. In the public sector, an absolute prohibition on striking, whether fashioned by the legislature or by the courts, has consistently been sustained against constitutional attack.   United Fed'n of Postal Clerks v. Blount (D.D.C.) (three-judge court), *aff'd mem.* (U.S.1971).   But such an absolute prohibition for private sector employees might well be subject to constitutional attack as a deprivation of liberty without due process of law, at least when the industry in question cannot fairly be treated as essential to the public interest and when no governmental substitute for the strike (such as compulsory arbitration) is afforded as a means of assuring equity in the settling of labor disputes.

§ 3.   The Right to Picket

Unlike the right of private-sector employees to strike, their right to engage in picketing in support of organizational or bargaining demands has been the subject of considerable constitutional litigation, the course of which has been rather serpentine.   At common law, courts readily issued injunctions against labor picketing, at first because such concerted activity was regarded as intrinsically coercive and tortiously disruptive to the employer's business, and later because the picketing was deemed to serve ends, such as the closed shop or the secondary boycott, which the courts disapproved.   In such a legal milieu, the labor injunction could hardly have been viewed as depriving employees of liberty without due process of law or as impinging upon any constitutional right of free speech.   Indeed, the United States Supreme Court held that a state statute making *lawful* all peaceful strikes, picketing and boycotts (in the absence of independent torts) and thus blocking the issuance of an injunction against group picketing amounted to a denial of due process and equal protection of the laws to the complaining employer.   Truax v. Corrigan (U.S.1921).

In Thornhill v. Alabama (U.S.1940), however, the United States Supreme Court drastically revised its position and struck down as unconstitutional on its face a state statute declaring it a crime to picket a place of business for the purpose of interfering with that business. The attempt through peaceful persuasion on the part of a picket to convince a co-employee to honor the strike was assimilated by the Court to an exercise of free speech with the object of communicating the facts concerning the labor dispute, a matter of public interest, and was thus protected by the due process clause of the Fourteenth Amendment against unqualified governmental intrusion.   The Court noted that the statute barring picketing was absolute on its face and had made no exceptions depending upon the number of pickets, the manner in which they conducted themselves, or the cause of the labor dispute.   *Thornhill* was later applied in an injunction case, the Court striking down as unconstitutional an injunction against organizational picketing based on a state policy barring such appeals by "strangers" in the absence of an immediate dispute between an employer and its own employees. AFL v. Swing (U.S.1941).

It was not long, however, before the Court's decisions marked a retreat from this treatment of labor picketing as akin to "pure" political discourse. The Court came to acknowledge that "picketing by an organized group is more than free speech, since it involves patrol of a particular locality and since the very presence of a picket line may induce action of one kind or another, quite irrespective of the nature of the ideas which are being disseminated." Bakery Drivers Local 802 v. Wohl (U.S.1942) (Douglas, J., concurring). This characterization of labor picketing as "speech plus" was not in itself sufficient to alter drastically the constitutional implications, for even "pure speech" can properly be outlawed by government when employed in pursuit of an illicit objective (e. g., criminal conspiracy) and even conduct may be constitutionally protected against governmental interference which is based on no substantial public interest. The Court's increasing willingness to sustain state restrictions upon peaceful picketing was thus attributable to its holding that states could legitimately assert certain specific local policies and thus render their interference with picketing immune to constitutional attack.

In "balancing" the interest of the picketers in dramatically appealing to employees and customers and the countervailing state interests, the Court sustained state-court injunctions against picketing in the nature of secondary boycotts (which violated the state antitrust laws). Carpenters Local 213 v. Ritter's Cafe (U.S.1942); Giboney v. Empire Storage & Ice Co. (U.S.1949). It also upheld against constitutional attack a state-court injunction against picketing designed to induce the employer to hire its employees in proportion to the race of its customers (and which thus violated the state policy against involuntary hiring on the basis of race), Hughes v. Superior Court (U.S.1950); and state-court injunctions against organizational or recognition picketing which was designed to induce the employer to compel its employees to join the union which was sponsoring the picketing (and which thus violated the state policy barring employer coercion of employees in the selection of their bargaining representative), Building Serv. Employees Local 262 v. Gazzam (U.S.1950). See Teamsters Local 695 v. Vogt, Inc. (U.S.1957) (thorough treatment of earlier Court decisions). This disinclination to use the First and Fourteenth Amendments to strike down state control of picketing continues today, even in situations where it might be argued that the communicational interests of the employees and of the public are no less weighty (and the interference with the business of the employer no more severe) than in *Thornhill*. See American Radio Ass'n v. Mobile S.S. Ass'n (U.S.1974) (state court enjoined dockside picketing of foreign ship in American port; Supreme Court found valid state interest in preventing both interference with business of stevedores seeking to unload the ship as well as the potential tie-up of the port and loss to farmers seeking to ship agricultural goods).

Contemporaneously with this constitutional evolution away from comprehensive protection for concerted activities, Congress was utilizing its own statutory authority to forbid and otherwise regulate such union activities as secondary boycotts, work-assignment strikes, strikes and picketing linked to so-called featherbedding, and certain types of recognition picketing. These limits were effected through the enactment of union unfair labor practice provisions in section 8(b) of the Taft-Hartley amendments of 1947. While the Supreme Court's constitutional decisions thus rendered such federal regulation (as much as state regulation) immune from attack, comparable state regulation was soon held to be ousted by the preemptive effect of specific provisions of the federal Labor Act which make picketing either protected under section 7 or prohibited under section 8.

§ 4.   Protection for Concerted Activity on Private Property

In almost all instances leading to reported decisions, the picketing which has been the object of state or federal regulation has been carried on outside the privately-owned property of the employer and on public sidewalks or streets. Should the picketing be conducted on private property, the employer will commonly seek relief in the state courts for trespass. A special constitutional problem has been created by the "quasi-public" uses to which private employers put property which is technically privately owned, such as the so-called company town and the modern suburban industrial park or shopping center with open access to pedestrians and automobile drivers. In a leading case a state court issued an injunction on a trespass theory against organizational picketing in such a shopping center, but the Supreme Court struck down the injunction as unconstitutional in Amalgamated Food Employees Local 590 v. Logan Valley Plaza, Inc. (U.S.1968). It held that the public areas adjacent to the picketed supermarket were "functional equivalents" of a municipal business district and thus could not be foreclosed to those who would peacefully communicate information there to the supermarket patrons regarding its personnel practices.

Although the Court's opinion lent itself to the broad reading that any typical shopping center or commercial enterprise opening its private property to the public could properly be assimilated to public property on which labor picketing could more freely take place, the Logan Valley holding was sharply confined soon thereafter by the majority of a reconstituted Court in Central Hardware Co. v. NLRB (U.S.1972). There, the NLRB had held it to be an unfair labor practice and beyond the constitutional power of the employer—a hardware company owning a large building surrounded by a privately owned parking lot for use by employees and customers—to expel from its parking lot union organizers engaged in communicating with company employees. The Supreme Court rejected the Board's constitutional thesis and held that "state action" (and thus constitutional limitations upon the expulsion of the union solicitors) would be found only when the private landowner was, as in the company-town situation, effectively serving as the equivalent of the municipality, and that this condition was not satisfied merely because the store and its surroundings were open to the general public.

This narrowing of the constitutional rationale soon led to the outright overruling of *Logan Valley,* in a case which like *Logan Valley* involved picketing rather than solicitation of membership. In Hudgens v. NLRB (U.S.1976), employees on strike against a shoe company, and who worked at the company's warehouse, began to picket at the company's retail stores, one of which was within a privately owned enclosed shopping mall. When the owner of the shopping mall threatened arrest for trespass, the union filed a charge under section 8(a) (1). In sustaining that charge, both the Board and the court of appeals appeared to rely in part on an assumed constitutional protection for such picketing on private property, as derived from *Logan Valley.* The Supreme Court, however, held that *Logan Valley* could no longer be considered authoritative, and that it had erroneously analogized a shopping center, which could be said to be much like a business block in a town, to an entire company town, which is in all respects the functional equivalent of a municipality (with homes, businesses, streets, sewers, and an overall assumption of "semi-official municipal functions as a delegate of the State"). One Justice would have merely distinguished *Logan Valley* rather than overrule it; and two Justices, in dissent, urged that *Logan Valley* be kept viable and indeed be deemed controlling in the case at bar (with the emphasis being placed not on the exercise of municipal functions such as a sewer system, but rather upon whether the private landowner has "a virtual monopoly of places suitable for effective communication").

The Court in *Hudgens,* after thus eliminating from the case any possible claim of constitutional protection for the shopping-center picketing, remanded for consideration of the rights of the picketing employees under sections 7 and 8(a)(1) of the Labor Act. The Court observed that this would involve an "accommodation" of the rights of employees to picket in support of their contract demands and of employers to control their private property. It observed that "the primary responsibility for making this accommodation must rest with the Board in the first instance," and noted that, in spite of certain differences, the Board should be alert to analogies between the case at bar and other Board and Court decisions under section 8(a)(1) regarding the rights of employees and unions to solicit membership on company-owned property. The two dissenting Justices were the only ones to assay an analysis under the Labor Act; they concluded that— like the cases of solicitation for union membership—the picketers should be permitted on private property unless there is "ready availability of reasonably effective alternative means of communication with the intended audience." They would have concluded that picketing on public rights-of-way adjacent to the shopping center, and advertisements through the mass media, were not comparable to on-location picketing in reaching patrons of the struck shoe company, and that therefore picketing could proceed within the mall free from employer threats and coercion. Presumably, something akin to this search for reasonable alternative communication will henceforth be made to determine protection for picketing on private property under section 7; indeed, the court of appeals in *Hudgens* had rather clearly made such an analysis, and sustained a finding of a section 8(a)(1) violation for that reason. In any event, if it is held that picketing employees are indeed entitled to access to company property, not only will employer threats of ouster violate section 8(a)(1), but state court actions based on a theory of unlawful trespass should be preempted under the Supremacy Clause of the federal Constitution.

§ 5. Union Violence and Threats

Any constitutional protection normally accorded concerted activity is lost when the actors engage in violence. As the Supreme Court stated in Milk Wagon Drivers Local 753 v. Meadowmoor Dairies, Inc. (U.S.1941), in which union members had engaged in window-smashing, bombings, burnings, the wrecking of trucks, shootings and beating:

> It must never be forgotten . . . that the Bill of Rights was the child of the Enlightenment. Back of the guarantee of speech lay faith in the power of an appeal to reason by all the peaceful means for gaining access to the mind. It was in order to avert force and explosions due to restrictions upon rational modes of communication that the guarantee of free speech was given a generous scope. But utterance in a context of violence can lose its significance as an appeal to reason and become part of an instrument of force. Such utterance was not meant to be sheltered by the Constitution.

The Court cautioned, however, that constitutional rights in labor disputes might be too readily sacrificed were a court to draw "from a trivial rough incident or a moment of animal exuberance the conclusion that otherwise peaceful picketing has the taint of force." Therefore, it is constitutionally appropriate for the Supreme Court to screen a finding of violence for supporting evidence, but such a finding may be set aside "only if we can say that it is so without warrant as to be a palpable evasion of the constitutional guarantee here invoked." Because of the serious violence there committed, the Court held that even wholly peaceful picketing in the future could reasonably generate a "momentum of fear," so that both violent and peaceful picketing in the future could be enjoined.

Violence during a strike or picketing may subject the union and employees to several sanctions. First, as already suggested, state courts may enjoin or issue a judgment of damages (compensatory and punitive) against a union or individuals found to have engaged in such violence; criminal prosecution may also be in order. Although, as will be noted momentarily, the National Labor Relations Board has jurisdiction in many instances to redress such violence, the deeply felt need for local authorities to do the same has justified coordinate state jurisdiction, in spite of the usual preemptive thrust of the federal Labor Act. (This principle is discussed in greater detail elsewhere in this work.) Second, if the individuals engaging in violence are employed by the company which is their ultimate object, they may be discharged or otherwise disciplined for their misconduct which, although concerted, is not within the shelter of section 7 or 8(a)(1) of the Labor Act. (This principle is also elaborated elsewhere in this work.) Third, if the misconduct can be charged to a union, it may be found to violate section 8(b)(1) of the Act; this will subject the union to an unfair labor practice proceeding before the NLRB and ultimately to a cease and desist order.

Just as with employer violence that violates section 8(a)(1), a union violates section 8(b)(1) when its agents shoot, beat or assault an employee in order to force or intimidate him into engaging in concerted activity. Perry Norvell Co. (1948). So too when strikers impose less severe physical discomforts on those who are attempting to cross a picket line, such as pinching or tripping, Central Mass. Joint Board, Textile Workers Union (Chas. Weinstein Co.) (1959), kicking and spitting, United Furniture Workers (Jamestown Sterling Corp.) (1962), or physically barring their automobile from entering the plant, Local 115, Teamsters (Continental-Wirt Electronics) (1970). It is not necessary to a finding of restraint or coercion that the employees intimidated are the direct object of the union's violence. In one case, for example, in which strikers assaulted the employer, coercion of employees was inferred, even though no employees were present, since one could reasonably conclude that they would in fact be coerced upon hearing of the incident. UMW Dist. 31 (Blue Ridge Coal Corp.) (1960), enf'd as mdf'd (D.C.Cir. 1962) (Board order held too broad). Similarly, intentional destruction of company property can violate section 8(b)(1) if such conduct creates a general atmosphere of fear and violence among employees seeking to report for work. North Elec. Mfg. Co. (1949). (Accidental property damage, however, will not violate section 8(b)(1). Amalgamated Meat Cutters (Western Inc.) (1951).)

It is not necessary, to make out a violation of section 8(b)(1), that the agents of the union have actually made a physical impact on person or property. A threat to nonstrikers to do so is sufficient, Perry Norvell Co. (1948), as is an order not to cross a picket line coupled with a threatening gesture, District 20, UMW (Harbert Construction Corp.) (1971). For similar reasons, so-called belly-to-back picketing, or mass picketing, is unlawful. The individual pickets are so numerous and stationed so close together that, if access to the plant is thereby blocked, the conduct is treated akin to a seizure of the plant, giving promise of violence when the nonstrikers seek to force through the line. W.T. Rawleigh Co. v. NLRB (7th Cir. 1951). (When the picketing does not block access to the plant, no unfair labor practice is likely to be found for the mass picketing. Steelworkers Local 2772 (Vulcan-Cincinnati, Inc.) (1962).) Threats may also be found implicit in following nonstrikers from the place of work to their homes, Longshoremen's Local 6 (Sunset Line & Twine Co.) (1948), or picketing the homes of nonstrikers, UMW Dist. 31 (Blue Ridge Coal Corp.) (1960).

In cases in which the union is held to violate section 8(b)(1)(A) by causing or threatening physical violence, the Board will issue a cease-and-desist order but will not require the union to reimburse the employee victims either for loss of pay (caused by the union's blocking access to the plant) or for physical or mental injury. Although this refusal to grant monetary damages against the union is controversial and has divided the Board—especially in cases of particularly flagrant and aggravated violence—the Board has adhered to this policy for some twenty-five years. The reasons were recently reiterated in Union de Tronquistas Local 901 (Lock Joint Pipe & Co.) (1973). The Board noted that, while it deplores violence in the course of a strike or picketing, the award of substantial monetary damages against the union will unduly interfere with the policy of the Labor Act to protect concerted activities. Emotions run high in times of industrial combat; the violent conduct of isolated individuals might all too readily be attributed to the union; the large number of employees refraining from work will both create serious problems of proof as to the reasons therefor and generate the risk of enormous backpay liability for the union. The Board also asserted that remedies against the union for violation of section 8(b)(1)(A) for strike violence were sufficient deterrents: the Board may ultimately issue a cease-and-desist order, court-enforceable through the contempt sanction; while the case is pending before the Board, an injunction may be sought under section 10(j) in aggravated cases; and the union seeking to enforce its bargaining rights through violent action may be denied a bargaining order and forced to demonstrate its majority support in a secret-ballot election. Moreover, the employee suffering physical or mental injury may secure redress against the union in a state-court tort action.

A recent case raised the question whether the kind of union intimidation of employees that would violate section 8(b)(1) would also subject the responsible union officials to federal criminal sanctions. In United States v. DeLaurentis (2d Cir. 1974), the United States Attorney instituted a criminal prosecution of three union officials for alleged acts of violence and duress addressed to employees who did not wish to join in the union's sit-in at the employer's facilities. After a jury trial, a judgment of conviction was entered for violation of 18 U.S.C.A. § 241, a statute enacted after the Civil War which provided for a fine up to $10,000 and imprisonment up to ten years for conspiring

> to injure, oppress, threaten, or intimidate any citizen in the free exercise or enjoyment of any right or privilege secured to him by the Constitution or laws of the United States, or because of his having so exercised the same . . . .

The Government's theory was that the defendants' acts and threats of violence deprived employees of the federal statutory right to refrain from engaging in concerted activities. The court of appeals reversed the conviction and ordered the indictment dismissed. It found no warrant to assume that Congress had intended such coercion of employees to be remedied by the very severe penalties of this federal criminal statute. The court concluded that Congress in 1948 had rejected the use of criminal sanctions under the Taft-Hartley Act, and it held that it is for the National Labor Relations Board rather than a criminal jury to determine whether rights under the Labor Act have been violated and how any such violation is to be remedied. The court did note, however, that it would be appropriate for state criminal law to outlaw "conduct that is violent or endangers life."

§ 6. Union Responsibility

There can be no violation of section 8(b)(1)—or of any other subsection of section 8(b) of the Labor Act—unless the wrongful conduct can be charged to "a labor organization or its agents." Section 8(b)(1) is violated when coercive conduct directed against employees is attributable to the union. Section 2(13) of the Labor Act provides: "In determining whether any person is acting as an 'agent' of another person so as to make such other person responsible for his acts, the question of whether the specific acts performed were actually authorized or subsequently ratified shall not be controlling." This section was added in the Taft-Hartley amendments of 1947 in order to clarify and facilitate the imputation of wrongful conduct to a union, which was given special protection in injunction proceedings under the Norris-LaGuardia Act against liability "except upon clear proof of actual participation in, or actual authorization of . . . or of ratification of" acts of officers or members. In short, the usual principles of agency law apply in determining union liability for unfair labor practices—as well as employer liability under section 8(a) —and such liability can be based not only upon proof of actual authority but also of implied authority or apparent authority.

Of course, union responsibility is clearest when union officials have ordered or directed the unlawful activity. United Furniture

Workers (Colonial Hardwood Flooring Co.) (1949) (union agent told strikers to "go out and get" nonstrikers). Similarly, where union agents have followed a course of conduct advocating coercive acts, the union will be held responsible for particular acts of strikers even though no union agent was present to advocate the particular conduct charged. Woodworkers Local 3–3 (Western Wirebound Box Co.) (1963). When a union agent is present on the picket line and is directing its activities, he may be charged with notice of the misconduct of others on the line. Central Mass. Joint Bd., Textile Workers (Chas. Weinstein Co.) (1959). The union may even be held responsible for the unauthorized and unratified acts of a union agent, even if expressly forbidden, if such acts were within the scope of the agent's authority. Longshoremen's Local 6 (Sunset Line & Twine Co.) (1948) (since union business agent was acting in furtherance of the strike, and he had authority to direct the strike and picketing, union is responsible for his assault and threats against nonstrikers). In such instances of implied or apparent authority to engage on behalf of the union in intimidating conduct, a union will ordinarily relieve itself of liability if it repudiates the misconduct. Such a repudiation must come as soon as possible—on the spot, if there is a union agent present—lest the implication of agency authority be confirmed. UMW Local 7244 (Grundy Mining Co.) (1964).

When an international union gives permission to one of its locals for a strike, the international will not normally be charged with an unfair labor practice for acts of violence occurring in the course of the strike, at least absent knowledge of the misconduct. Amalgamated Ass'n of Street Employees (Plymouth & Brockton St. Ry. Co.) (1963). However, the international may be held responsible for strike misconduct in a local strike if its agent takes an active part in organizing the strike, unless the agents of the international disavow the actions. UMW Dist. 2 (Solar Fuel Co.) (1968), enf'd per curiam (3d Cir. 1969).

CHAPTER XI

RECOGNITION PICKETING

§ 1. Background and History

A union, in order to apply economic pressure upon employees who are indifferent or reluctant to join and upon employers who refuse to recognize and bargain, will sometimes engage in picketing. At an incipient stage of organization, where there is as yet little support for the union among company employees, a strike alone will likely be ineffective, while picketing—even by nonemployees—can result in an interruption of deliveries to and pickups from the employer and of other forms of patronage by customers. Such an interruption, with attendant economic losses, may have the effect of inducing the inside employees to join the union and the employer to bargain with it. Over time, this "organizational" or "recognition" picketing has been subject to varying forms of legal regulation.

At common law, many states treated such picketing as tortious and subject to injunction. *E. g.,* Plant v. Woods (Mass.1900). Even when such picketing was peaceful, the state court would frequently conclude that the organization of employees was an object too remote from the more central union object to increase wages and improve working conditions. It was also frequently held that nonemployee picketers were "strangers" to the company who had no direct economic interest in employment conditions there. Also supporting judicial regulation was the belief that the inside employees, resistant to unionization, should not be subjected to economic pressure (either by a drop in business or the insistence of an embattled employer) to relinquish their freedom of association or of nonassociation. "Stranger" or minority picketing to organize nonunion companies, competition from which was making it difficult to maintain union gains elsewhere, was also held to violate the federal antitrust laws. *E. g.,* Alco-Zander Co. v. Amalgamated Clothing Workers (E.D.Pa.1929).

In the 1930's and 1940's, however, the tide turned somewhat, and courts became more protective of picketing having an organizational or recognitional objective. Courts came to realize that even unions which lacked members among the employees of the picketed company nonetheless were not "strangers" having no economic interest in organization there, since

> [t]o render this combination at all effective, employees must make their combination extend beyond one shop. It is helpful to have as many as may be in the same trade in the same community united, because in the competition between employers they are bound to be affected by the standard of wages of their trade in the neighborhood. Therefore they

may use all lawful propaganda to enlarge their membership and especially among those whose labor at lower wages will injure their whole guild.

American Steel Foundries v. Tri-City Council (U.S.1921). Courts which were prepared to sustain peaceful picketing provided the defendants had a legitimate economic interest (rather than mere malice) found such an interest when the recognition picketing was designed to shelter the union's "area standards." E. g., C. S. Smith Metrop. Mkt. Co. v. Lyons (Cal.1940). The passage of the Wagner Act in 1935, and of a number of state laws patterned thereon, nourished the claims of unionists that organization and recognition for collective bargaining were intended to be fostered by government, and that picketing therefor was thus a protected activity. Some courts upheld picketing allegedly designed to "organize" employees, although employers argued that it was in truth designed to force recognition of —and coercion of employees to join—a minority union in contravention of the statutory policy of freedom of employee choice. E. g., Wood v. O'Grady (N.Y.1954). For a decade, such picketing was indeed thought to be assimilated to constitutionally protected "free speech." A state-court injunction against peaceful picketing, based on a common law policy outlawing picketing when there was no immediate dispute between an employer and its own employees, was held unconstitutional in AFL v. Swing (U.S.1941). But that theory was promptly whittled away, for picketing was soon held to contain elements of coercion beyond "pure speech" and to be subject to state regulation designed to shelter inside employees from coercion in the choice of bargaining representative. Building Serv. Employees Local 262 v. Gazzam (U.S.1950) (recognition picketing); Teamsters Local 695 v. Vogt, Inc. (U.S.1957) (organizational picketing assimilated to recognition picketing).

At the same time as the Due Process Clause was serving less to constrain judicial regulation of recognition picketing, the doctrine of NLRA preemption emerged in its stead. Early under the Wagner Act, a federal court refused to enjoin minority picketing since this would have interfered with the exclusive jurisdiction of the National Labor Relations Board to resolve disputes concerning representation. Fur Workers Local 72 v. Fur Workers Union, No. 21238 (D.C.Cir.), aff'd mem. (U.S.1939). With the passage of the Taft-Hartley Act and its union unfair labor practice provisions which raised close issues as to whether union concerted activities were protected by section 7 or prohibited by section 8, the Supreme Court soon held cases involving peaceful recognition picketing to be beyond the jurisdiction of the common law courts. Garner v. Teamsters Local 776 (U.S.1953); San Diego Bldg. Trades Council v. Garmon (U.S.1959). With this ebbing of judicial restraints upon minority picketing, the National Labor Relations Board attempted to step into the breach, and it held that peaceful picketing by a minority union in order to induce an employer to enter into a labor contract for all its employees constituted restraint and coercion of employee rights in violation of section 8(b)(1) of the Labor Act. The Supreme Court, however, overturned the Board's holding in NLRB v. Drivers Local 639 (Curtis Bros.) (U.S.1960), emphasizing Congress's intention in section 8(b)(1) to address primarily union violence, and the legislative policy embodied in section 13 to limit peaceful strikes and picketing only when the statutory proscription is clear and explicit.

§ 2.   Sections 8(b)(4)(C) and 8(b)(7): Generally

Such explicitness could be found in section 8(b)(4)(C) of the 1947 Taft-Hartley Act and section 8(b)(7) of the 1959 Landrum-Griffin Act, which specifically condemn certain classes of organizational or recognition picketing by labor organizations. Such picketing was regarded as most outrageous when practiced by a minority union while the employer is fulfilling its statutory duty to bargain with a union which was formally elected by a majority of employees and formally certified as exclusive bargaining representative. The law could not, obviously, permit the minority union to exert economic duress as a means of forcing the employer to oust the certified union and to pressure its employees to transfer their allegiance to the picketing union; to do so would be to permit the picketers to force the employer to violate sections 8(a)(1) and (2) of the Labor Act. Accordingly, Congress in 1947 declared, in section 8(b)(4)(C), that a labor organization commits an unfair labor practice if it engages in or induces employees (typically through picketing) to engage in a work stoppage with an object of "forcing or requiring any employer to recognize or bargain with a particular labor organization as the representative of his employees if another labor organization has been certified as the representative of such employees under the provisions of section 9."

By its terms, however, this section did not proscribe "organizational" picketing directed at employees as distinguished from "recognition" picketing directed at the employer; nor, more important, did it bar even recognition picketing in situations which were arguably just as vexing for the employer and the inside employees. It was to these additional situations that section 8(b)(7) was addressed in 1959. Section 8(b)(7) outlaws picketing for organization *or* recognition in three limited circumstances:

> (A) where the employer has lawfully recognized in accordance with this Act any other labor organization and a question concerning representation may not appropriately be raised under section 9(c) of this Act.

> (B) where within the preceding twelve months a valid election under section 9(c) of this Act has been conducted, or

(C) where such picketing has been conducted without a petition under section 9(c) being filed within a reasonable period of time not to exceed thirty days from the commencement of such picketing . . . .

Subsection C contains two somewhat complex provisos which will be discussed below.

Some comparisons with section 8(b)(4)(C) may be useful. First, section 8(b)(7) for the first time in the history of the NLRA explicitly bars conduct labelled "picketing." While section 8(b)(4) addresses more generally the acts of inducing others to engage in a work stoppage, and of threats, coercion and restraint, the later section addresses no form of concerted activity other than picketing, creating thereby some definitional problems. Second, section 8(b)(7) conclusively abandons the distinction between organizational picketing and recognition picketing, for it proscribes not only the kind of picketing addressed in section 8(b)(4)—"forcing or requiring an employer to recognize or bargain with . . . ."—but also picketing an object of which is "forcing or requiring the employees of an employer to accept or select such labor organization as their collective bargaining representative." Congress thus acknowledged the almost universal congruence of goals and tactics in the two kinds of picketing, and henceforth the Board and the courts (and this author) will use the terms recognition picketing and organization picketing interchangeably. For much the same reasons as implied in section 8(b)(4)(C), section 8(b)(7) announces an express exclusion from its coverage of any labor organization which "is currently certified as the representative of such employees." Finally, the remedies for violations of the two sections are very much the same, and will be considered later in greater detail. Suffice it to say that each is remediable through the normal unfair labor practice procedures of the Board, leading to a cease-and-desist order, or through the injunction procedures of section 10(l) in a federal district court. (The private action for damages under section 303 of the Taft-Hartley Act by a person injured by a violation of section 8(b)(4) has not, however, been extended to a person injured by a violation of section 8(b)(7). The draftsmen appear to have feared that damages for recognition picketing would be too severe a sanction, since almost all picketing can be said to have recognition as at least a remote objective.)

§ 3.   The Forbidden Conduct: Picketing

The conduct proscribed by section 8(b)(7) is "to picket or cause to be picketed, or threaten to picket or cause to be picketed." Nowhere, however, is "picket" defined. Commonly, the cases deal with picketing in the long-understood sense of a "patrol" of persons in motion, at or near employee or customer entrances, carrying placards with a terse legend communicating the gist of the union's claims. In a few cases, the union has argued that the conduct of its representatives falls short of picketing for the lack of an ambulatory patrol or of placards. In one instance, union representatives planted signs in a snowbank abutting the entrance to the employer's premises, and located themselves in automobiles parked along an adjacent highway, emerging only to speak to approaching deliverymen. The court held that the stationary location of the signs and the separation of men from signs did not make the appeal any the less picketing. NLRB v. Teamsters Local 182 (2d Cir. 1963). In another case involving union representatives affixing large signs to poles outside the plant, and then retiring to their automobiles, the court announced what appears to be a sensible and administrable principle: conduct can be "picketing" even when there is no parading with placards, provided there is some "confrontation" (even if at a distance) sufficient to have the employees, customers or deliverymen see the union representatives and identify them as such. NLRB v. United Furniture Workers (2d Cir. 1964). By their presence, the union representatives can report on those who ignore their plea and can seek to dispel such ignorance by conversation and entreaty. The question is whether the presence of the representatives "was intended to and did have substantially the same significance for persons entering the employer's premises as if they had remained with the signs."

A similar standard has been recently invoked by the NLRB in determining whether the distribution of handbills at the entrances to an employer's parking lot can be treated as picketing and rendered illegal by its continuation in that case for more than four months. In spite of the fact that the handbillers had themselves spoken of their conduct as "picketing" in conversations with company officials, the Board held the handbilling to fall outside the ban of section 8(b)(7) since, unlike picketing, it did not convey a "signal" that provokes a response without inquiry into the ideas being disseminated. Teamsters Local 688 (Levitz Furniture Co.) (1973) (handbillers also conversed with company employees, and one truckdriver turned away and refused to make delivery). The result is consistent with the legislative history to the 1959 amendments to section 8(b)(4) (more particularly, the publicity proviso to the secondary boycott section), contemporaneous with the enactment of section 8(b)(7); this draws a clear distinction between picketing and (the less objectionable) dissemination of information through the distribution of handbills. The Board has, nonetheless, condemned handbilling under the picketing proscription of section 8(b)(7) when it was a continuation of a prior union demonstration carried out by conventional picketing. Lumber Workers Local 2797 (1965).

§ 4. The Forbidden Purpose: The Legality of Reinstatement Picketing and Standards Picketing

Even if a determination is made that the labor organization has engaged in picketing or a threat of picketing, there will be no violation of section 8(b)(7) unless it is further demonstrated that "an object thereof" is to cause the employer "to recognize or bargain with" or the employees "to accept or select" that union as bargaining representative. If a union were to sponsor picketing of a company for the reason that it engages in trade with Communist countries and with the object of forcing cessation of such trade, this would clearly fall outside the proscription of section 8(b)(7) for lack of a recognitional or organizational object; the picketing will cease when the employer terminates its trade with those countries, regardless of recognition or nonrecognition of the union. Similarly, if the employer discharges an employee for signing a union authorization card, and the union pickets for the purpose (as demonstrated by its communications with the employer and the legends on its placards) of protesting the illegal discharge and securing the reinstatement of the discharged employee, the picketing will not be found to have a recognitional or organizational object.

The Board's position on this matter of "unfair labor practice picketing" (*i. e.,* protesting an employer unfair labor practice) was initially to the contrary. For when the union pickets for the purpose of securing reinstatement it seeks to compel the employer to make a concession in or modification of its personnel decisions; if the employer does so, in response to union demands and pressure, this looks very much like it is bargaining with the union, particularly if it is obliged to confer about the precise terms of reinstatement. The Board thus initially held that picketing seeking the reinstatement of an employee, even when the discharge constituted illegal discrimination, had recognition or bargaining as an objective and thus fell within the reach of sections 8(b)(4)(C) and 8(b)(7). Meat Drivers Local 626 (Lewis Food Co.) (1956). A change in the composition of the Board resulting from appointments by President Kennedy brought with it a reversal of position in Local 259, UAW (Fanelli Ford Sales, Inc.) (1961). In substance, the Board now holds that the immediate objective of the union in these cases—that which would lead to a cessation of the picketing—is not recognition but rather reinstatement of the discharged employee, action which the employer can take without recognizing the union or even meeting with it. The same is true when the union's request for reinstatement stems not from a claim of employer unfair labor practice but from a claim simply that the discharge or layoff works an unjust economic hardship on the individual employee. Teamsters Local 676 (Shell Chem. Co.) (1972), *enf'd on this issue* (5th Cir. 1974).

Also now excluded from the proscription of sections 8(b)(4)(C) and 8(b)(7) is picketing to induce the employer to improve its "substandard" economic benefits in order that union standards embodied in labor contracts with competing companies in the area will not be jeopardized by low-price products manufactured by the nonunion company. Here too, the Board had held that such "standards picketing" was economic pressure in support of a demand concerning wages and working conditions, typically made at the bargaining table. IAM (Indus. Chrome Plating Co.) (1958). Again, a newly constituted Board in 1961 reversed its position in a case arising under section 8(b)(4)(C), Hod Carriers Local 41 (Calumet Contractors Ass'n) (1961); and this new position was reaffirmed under section 8(b)(7) in Houston Bldg. & Constr. Trades Council (Claude Everett Constr. Co.) (1962): "A union may legitimately be concerned that a particular employer is undermining area standards of employment by maintaining lower standards. It may be willing to forgo recognition and bargaining provided subnormal working conditions are eliminated from area considerations."

This distinction between recognition picketing and standards picketing has come in for considerable criticism. First, it makes legality turn upon very fine questions of motive, which in turn requires a frequently burdensome screening of a lengthy record and the drawing of conclusions which often seem arbitrary. Second, it enables an outside or minority union to make economic demands backed by picketing pressures of theoretically indefinite duration—conduct which would frequently be subject to employer reprisal (both direct economic reprisal and the invocation of NLRB sanctions such as charges of bad-faith bargaining) if engaged in by a duly selected majority representative. Third, it places the employer bargaining with or under contract to an incumbent union in almost as untenable a position as do demands for complete recognition; capitulation to the economic demands of the picketing union may involve a departure from the terms of its labor contract, terms which in fact may have been the incentive for the employees' selecting the incumbent union and rejecting the picketing union.

In any event, if the Board finds that the union's object in picketing is *both* to secure area standards (or the reinstatement of an employee) *and* to secure recognition, the picketing will fall within the reach of section 8(b)(7) (or of section 8(b)(4)(C)), which requires no more than that recognition be "an object" of the union. Thus, in Hod Carriers Local 840 (Blinne Constr. Co.) (1962), the union's objects in picketing were found to be: (1) undoing the discriminatory transfer of a union member; (2) payment of the prevailing wage scale under the Davis-Bacon Act; and (3) recognition. The Board held that picketing with only the first two objects would have been outside the ban of section 8(b)(7) and thus could have continued indefinitely. But the further object of immediate recognition as bargaining representative fell within the reach of the section (even though the union, although uncertified, allegedly possessed majority support) and was thus subject to the time restrictions of section 8(b)(7)(C).

§ 5.   Problems of Proof in Determining Union Purpose

The Board must thus determine whether the union's purpose in picketing is solely innocent or is instead (or in addition) to bargain or organize.   It is clear that the burden of proving a proscribed object rests upon the General Counsel.   In discharging that burden, he may point to union activities (such as gathering of authorization cards or earlier picketing with recognitional or organizational legends on the placards) or to conversations between union officials and the company or its employees which took place not only concurrently with the picketing but preceding it.   Retail Clerks Local 345 (Gem of Syracuse, Inc.) (1964) (picketing to protest alleged unfair labor practices also held recognitional, as evidenced by leaflets and picket-line conversation urging unionization).   Evidence which points to a proscribed object will include, of course, prior or contemporaneous demands upon the employer for recognition, appeals (orally, by handbills, or on the placards) to the employees to join the union, or the union's filing of a refusal-to-bargain charge against the picketed employer.   The Board has held, however, that picketing which was clearly recognitional in the past—for example, prior to an election—but which is subsequently altered so as arguably to fall within the protection for area-standards picketing, will not simply because of its earlier recognitional character be presumed to persist as such; the General Counsel must demonstrate the proscribed object by independent evidence.   Retail Clerks Local 344 (Alton Meyers Bros.) (1962).   The union will, of course, frequently introduce evidence of correspondence or communications in which it has expressly denied to the employer any interest in organizing its employees or securing recognition or bargaining rights.   While such disavowals will not be mechanically discounted merely because they are self-serving, they will not be mechanically credited simply because they are uttered.   ILGWU (Coed Collar Co.) (1962).

In cases in which the union asserts that its object was to protest the commission of an unfair labor practice or to secure the reinstatement of an employee, the Board will look closely at the time relationship between the alleged wrongdoing of the employer and the commencement of picketing.   It will also consider whether the union filed an unfair labor practice charge.   It has been held, however, that picketing which began as a protest against an employer's coercion and discrimination will lose its protected status as unfair labor practice picketing if the General Counsel and the employer settle the case against the latter and the case is closed by the Board.   Waiters Local 500 (Mission Valley Inn) (1963) (although such picketing will not be treated as in protest of employer unfair labor practice, that alone does not prove recognitional object).   For substantially the same reason, it has been held that picketing will not be deemed in protest of an employer unfair labor practice when the six-month period of limitations on the alleged misconduct has run and any charges would thus be time-barred. NLRB v. UMW (Blue Diamond Coal Co.) (6th Cir. 1969). These conclusions, however, are not at all compelling, since the issue under sections 8(b)(4)(C) and 8(b)(7) is the union's object, and a Board settlement with the employer (which may satisfy the General Counsel but not the union) is perfectly consistent with a continuing union objection to the manner in which an employee was initially treated or to the terms of any settlement. In any event, even if Board settlement or a time-bar might plausibly undercut the union claim of innocent motive, it alone will certainly not make an affirmative case for recognitional purpose which is always the responsibility of the General Counsel.

In cases in which the union asserts that its object was to protest the substandard pay of the picketed employer, the Board will consider whether union officials actually were aware of the employer's pay scale when the picketing began, whether the union communicated to the employer its concern about any deviation from area standards and whether there was in truth a significant departure by the picketed employer from standards secured by the union among competing enterprises. Carpenters Local 1260 (Selzer Constr. Co.) (1974) (union failed actually to verify employer compliance with area standards, made no mention of same when asked how pickets could be removed); Sales Delivery Drivers Local 296 (1973) (union's inadequate investigation of employer labor costs and union failure to respond to employer offer to meet area standards should cost-analysis show disparity).

Even when all of these conditions are satisfied, however, there have been cases in which the "standards" which the picketing union would have the employer implement are both so comprehensive and specific that discussion or capitulation by the employer will clearly involve mutual dealings which are in substance no different from conventional bargaining; so too, capitulation would far outrun any legitimate interest which the union might have in undoing the nonunion company's competitive advantage over the unionized companies in the area. Thus, it has been held that picketing is not simply to preserve area standards but is in truth to secure recognition when the union demands that the employer match all of the specific money items, both in wages and fringe benefits, embodied in union contracts tendered to the employer, Retail Clerks Local 899 (State-Mart, Inc.) (1967), enf'd (9th Cir. 1968); and when the union demands that the employer execute an agreement binding it to pay wages and fringe benefits comparable to those being paid from time to time to unionized employees and to permit monthly audits of such payments by union accountants, Centralia Bldg. & Constr. Trades Council v. NLRB (D.C.Cir. 1966). The result was otherwise, however, and the picketing held to fall outside the ban of section 8(b)(7), when the union informed the employer that it was not seeking to have the employer adopt for its nonunion employees the terms of the union contract in the area and that it was not seeking to have the employer match specifically the schedule of wages and fringe benefits elsewhere, but that it wanted the employer to pay its employees a total amount equal to the wages and fringes paid by unionized employers. Sachs v. Plumbers Local 5 (D.D.C.1969) (action under section 10(l) for injunction). Surely, a union which goes beyond demanding conformity to the money package secured in area labor contracts and seeks as well to have the picketed employer honor such contract provisions as union security, grievance procedure and seniority, forfeits any credibility for its assertion that its object is nonrecognitional.

§ 6. Picketing for Bargaining Concessions

One other union objective which appears to fall within the ban of section 8(b)(7) merits consideration. Assume that an employer has lawfully and informally recognized a union and has executed a collective bargaining agreement. Midway through the contract term, there is a dispute about whether the employer has lived up to its contract obligations, and the union strikes and pickets. Even though conformity to the contract might require some bargaining between the union and the picketed employer, the union will not be found to have the proscribed object of "forcing or requiring an employer to recognize or bargain with a labor organization." The Board has held this provision to be directed at picketing seeking an employer's *initial* acceptance of the union as bargaining representative. Building & Constr. Trades Council of Santa Barbara County (Sullivan Elec. Co.) (1964). The same is true when the contract has expired, and the recognized incumbent union is picketing in support of economic demands for a new one. Teamsters Local 612 (1964).

In such cases, the employer may exercise its right permanently to replace the employees who are striking and picketing for economic demands and might then refuse to bargain with the union for the reason that it doubts the union's majority status. The Board has held on several occasions that the replacement of employees and the challenge to the union's status are not in themselves sufficient to convert what began as economic picketing into proscribed recognition picketing. *E. g.,* Warehouse Employees Local 570 (Whitaker Paper Co.) (1964). Compare Pennello v. Warehouse Employees Local 570 (D. Md.1964) (such picketing first held nonrecognitional; subsequently held recognitional but no injunction issued under section 10(l)). The issue in these cases of replacement and employer refusal to bargain is a close one, for the employer's doubt of a continuing majority does generate a representational issue which appears to be subject to the congressional preference for resolution through elections rather than picketing. The logic of these decisions would appear, moreover, to require that section 8(b)(7)(B) also be inapplicable in the event our hypothetical union, during the strike and after the replacements, were to compete and lose in a valid Board-conducted election but were to continue picketing thereafter. But the Board has held such post-election picketing in support of bargaining demands to be proscribed under section 8(b)(7)(B) as recognitional in object, with the decertified union being placed in the same position as a union seeking initial recognition. To hold otherwise would be to undermine the post-election stability sought by the draftsmen of section 8(b)(7)(B) and to permit without reason the decertified union to pressure the employees who had just rejected it in a secret-ballot election. Lawrence Typog. Union No. 570 (1966), *enf't denied on other grounds* (10th Cir. 1967).

§ 7. The Subsections of Section 8(b)(7): Generally

Even if it is determined that the union is picketing with a proscribed recognitional or organizational object, such picketing is not banned by the Labor Act unless it also falls within the terms of subsections (A), (B), or (C) of section 8(b)(7). (Of course, recognition picketing by one union when another is *certified* is banned independently by section 8(b)(4).) In effect, these three subsections ban recognition picketing which (A) seeks to disturb a valid and viable bargaining relationship with a union which the employer has informally recognized, or (B) seeks to re-open the issue of union representation when the employees have recently rejected such representation in a valid labor election, or (C) interrupts the employer's business for a protracted period of time without an attempt being made to resolve the union's bargaining claims in a Board-conducted election. The purpose of the section is thus to encourage resort to NLRB election processes rather than to economic warfare as a means of resolving representation issues and also to extend a period of stability and repose to employer and employees after those employees have recently opted for or against unionization.

§ 8. Section 8(b)(7)(A)

Section 8(b)(7)(A) bars recognition picketing "where the employer has lawfully recognized in accordance with this Act any other labor organization and a question concerning representation may not appropriately be raised under section 9(c) of this Act." Section 8(b)(4)(C), enacted in 1947, had responded to the dilemma of the employer which is dealing with a certified union and which under pressure of recognition picketing can choose either to capitulate to the demands of the picketing union and thereby violate the law (the duty under section 8(a)(5) to recognize the incumbent union) or to discharge its legal duties and thereby risk economic destruction. The purpose of section 8(b)(7)(A) is principally to extend that protection to employers and their employees when the incumbent is recognized not after an election but validly and informally by other means, such as the collection and tender of authorization cards from a majority of the unit employees.

Congress wished, however, to assure that the protected bargaining relationship was not to be the product of illegal conduct and was not to be unduly "stale." Thus, subsection (A) requires that the incumbent be "lawfully recognized." If, for example, the contract with the incumbent is a "sweetheart agreement" with a dominated union or is executed with a minority union, the employer has committed an unfair labor practice and the union has not been "lawfully recognized." While these issues can be raised against the employer directly through unfair labor practice proceedings under section 8(a)(2), section 8(b)(7)(A) has been held to permit them to be raised "collaterally" as well by way of defense to a charge of recognition picketing in violation of the Act. Similarly, section 10(l) expressly provides that no injunction against the picketing will be sought by the Board under that section if there is pending against the employer a charge under section 8(a)(2) upon which a complaint is about to issue. But since there is a six-month statute of limitations on the filing of charges under section 8(a)(2), the Board has held that the picketing union may not defensively challenge collaterally a bargaining relationship which is said to have illegally persisted for a period longer than six months. Thus, the incumbent union becomes "lawfully recognized" when its status is immune from challenge under sections 8 and 9 of the Act (unfair labor practice and representation provisions, respectively), and the continuation thereafter of recognition picketing by another union is illegal. Hod Carriers Local 1298 (Roman Stone Constr. Co.) (1965).

Even if the incumbent is lawfully recognized, however, recognition picketing will not violate subsection (A)—although it may violate subsection (C)—of section 8(b)(7) if a "question concerning representation" may "appropriately be raised." If, for example, the contract between the employer and the incumbent is in the second year of its four-year term, the Board would dismiss a petition for an election because of the three-year "contract bar"; the petition would not timely raise a question of representation. So too, recognition picketing in the first three years of the four-year contract would be illegal. This is true even though the incumbent union has lost its majority and the picketing union has gained a majority. *Ibid.* But in the fourth year, when an election petition would be timely, Congress has concluded that—in any event, for the period of time denoted in section 8(b)(7)(C)—it is proper for an outside union to appeal to the inside employees and to the public through recognition picketing.

Read literally, section 8(b)(7)(A) would appear to bar even such picketing, *i. e.,* outside the contract bar, by a union which cannot demonstrate a thirty percent "showing of interest," a requirement which the Board normally imposes as a condition to an election. But it is clear that Congress was contemplating only the time-bar features of the Board's election rules and that even the union with scant support among the employees is allowed to appeal to them to augment that support for a limited period of time.

§ 9.   Section 8(b)(7)(B)

While sections 8(b)(4)(C) and 8(b)(7)(A) thus seek to shelter an ongoing collective bargaining relationship against the pressures of recognition picketing by a minority union, subsection (B) of section 8(b)(7) goes yet further and seeks to shelter employees (and their employer) from such pressures even when they have *rejected* collective bargaining in a "valid election." Thus, that subsection bars recognition picketing by an uncertified union "where within the preceding twelve months a valid election under section 9(c) of this Act has been conducted." Since no new election can be held within that twelve-month period, pursuant to section 9(c)(3) of the Act, Congress found it appropriate to bar contemporaneously economic pressure in the form of recognition picketing. This ban applies whether the picketing union was an ousted incumbent, a rejected insurgent, or even one which was not at all on the scene at the time of the earlier election. (It should be noted, however, that the Board has held that the employer may have a duty to bargain with a union which clearly demonstrates majority support even within the election year. Conren, Inc. v. NLRB (7th Cir. 1966). Presumably, such support ought not be demonstrable by picketing in violation of section 8(b)(7).)

Just as with subsection (A), the picketing union can assert as a defense to a charge under section 8(b)(7)(B) that the election which was held within the preceding twelve months was not a "valid election" and thus collaterally attack the employer's claim to a year of "repose" against recognition picketing. If, for example, the election resulted in a victory for the employer because of the fear generated by discriminatory discharges and spurious threats of a plant shutdown, the validity of this election can be challenged not only directly, by promptly filing objections to the election, but also collaterally as a defense to a charge of illegal recognition picketing. Such defense has been sustained and no "valid election" found in cases where the appropriate bargaining unit was improperly determined, NLRB v. Teamsters Local 327 (6th Cir. 1969); where the employer instigated the filing of the decertification petition, *cf.* Lawrence Typog. Union v. McCulloch (D.C. Cir. 1965); and where an election was improperly held under the expedited-election procedures of section 8(b)(7)(C), see Local 86, Painters (1974).

The question naturally arises whether the picketing union can in the section 8(b)(7) proceeding raise defects in the election long after that election was held and its validity scrutinized on direct review. In a thorough opinion, the Court of Appeals for the Second Circuit has held that all questions relating to the validity of the election are open to review in an 8(b)(7)(B) proceeding either before the Board or the federal district court (in an action for an injunction under section 10(*l*)). NLRB v. Teamsters Local 182 (2d Cir. 1963). This rather broad permission for collateral attack is subject to at least two qualifications. The court said that the charged union fails to raise the question of the validity of the election stemming from alleged employer unfair labor practices merely by asserting (in the 8(b)(7)(B) proceeding) that it has filed charges against the employer; it must demonstrate that the alleged employer unfair labor practices in fact prevented a fair election and that any dismissal of such charges by the General Counsel was erroneous. Moreover, the Board has held that where the picketing union initially seeks direct review of the election and the Board passes upon its exceptions in the representation proceeding, that union is not entitled to have those issues relitigated in the unfair labor practice proceeding against it under section 8(b)(7)(B). United Furniture Workers (Jamestown Sterling Corp.) (1964). Of course, should the Board or court find in the section 8(b)(7)(B) case that an election within the preceding year was not "valid," that does not nullify the election but merely permits the union to continue its picketing for recognition.

§ 10.   Section 8(b)(7)(C): Purpose and Construction

The most complex subsection of section 8(b)(7), by far, is section 8(b)(7)(C). It bars recognition picketing

> where such picketing has been conducted without a petition under section 9(c) being filed within a reasonable period of time not to exceed thirty days from the commencement of such picketing: Provided, That when such a petition has been filed the Board shall forthwith, without regard to the provisions of section 9(c)(1) or the absence of a showing of a substantial interest on the part of the labor organization, direct an election in such unit as the Board finds to be appropriate and shall certify the results thereof.

A second, and even more elaborate, proviso follows; it will be considered below. Section 8(b)(7)(C) was designed to shield the employer and its employees from the adverse economic effects of protracted organizational picketing and to provide a procedure for promptly resolving the representation issue which gave rise to the picketing.

The decision which most comprehensively deals with section 8(b)(7)(C) is Hod Carriers Local 840 (Blinne Constr. Co.) (1962). The facts of *Blinne* can be simplified as follows. When confronted with a request for recognition from the union, the employer refused and intentionally transferred one of the union supporters in the belief this would destroy the union's majority. The union then picketed the employer for three announced objectives: recognition, payment of the area wage scale pursuant to the Davis-Bacon Act, and protest against the alleged unfair labor practices of discriminatory transfer and refusal to recognize. Three weeks later, the union filed charges against the employer under sections 8(a)(1), (2), (3) and (5); three weeks after that the 8(a)(2) and (5) charges were dismissed by the regional director, whereupon the union filed a petition for a representation election (all told, six weeks after the picketing began). Later, the employer entered into a settlement agreement concerning the charges under sections 8(a)(1) and (3). The Board held that the continuation of the picketing beyond thirty days in the absence of the filing of a representation petition violated section 8(b)(7)(C).

At the threshold, the Board clarified two issues raised in the prefatory passages of section 8(b)(7). First, the picketing fell within the reach of the section because "an object" was recognition, even though it also was directed at employer unfair labor practices and the refusal to meet area standards. Second, the fact that the union may have had majority support at the time of the picketing did not remove it from the reach of the section, since the union was not "currently certified" as required by the terms of that section.

The union's basic defense was that its failure to file a representation petition within thirty days of the beginning of its picketing should have been excused in view of the employer's unfair labor practices and the union's filing of charges; Congress could not have intended, asserted the union, to rush the union into a representation election the results of which would be tainted by the employer's wrongdoing. While the Board agreed that Congress would not wish to have such a tainted election held, it concluded nonetheless that the union's proper line of attack was to file the election petition promptly so as to comport with the clear mandate of subsection (C), and also to file against the employer charges which would be promptly addressed by the Board while the election was stayed. So long as a petition was filed "within a reasonable period of time not to exceed thirty days from the commencement of such picketing," the picketing would not violate the Act and could continue during the pendency of the election proceeding, even as extended by the "blocking charges" filed by the union. Once the election is held, and if it is valid, then the picketing union will either be forbidden to picket (under section 8(b)(4)(C) if another union is certified or under section 8(b)(7)(B) if no union is) or its recognition picketing will be sheltered if it is elected as the certified representative. The congressional goal of prompt filing and disposition of the union's representation claim would be thus secured. (While the Board, for technical reasons, held that the failure of the picketing union to file a representation petition *is* excused by its filing of section 8(a)(5) refusal-to-bargain charges which are thought meritorious enough to warrant the General Counsel's issuance of a complaint, it firmly stated that the filing of even meritorious charges against the employer under sections 8(a)(1), (2), (3) and/or (4) will not cleanse recognition picketing which continues beyond thirty days in the absence of a petition.) The union in *Blinne* was thus held to violate section 8(b)(7)(C): no representation petition was filed for six weeks from the beginning of the picketing; the charge against the employer under section 8(a)(5) was dismissed as nonmeritorious; and the merit of two of the other charges did not relieve the union of the thirty-day petition requirement.

It is to be noted that the ban of section 8(b)(7)(C) is imposed unless the representation petition is "filed within a reasonable period of time not to exceed thirty days" from the beginning of the picketing. The union has no guarantee that picketing on the twenty-ninth or thirtieth day is protected, for thirty days constitutes the maximum sheltered period and the union is by no means "entitled" thereto. While it is commonly held that thirty days *is* a "reasonable period," that period can be substantially reduced if the picketing is accompanied by violence, coercion and intimidation. Cuneo v. United Shoe Workers (D.N.J.1960) (picketing for ten days held unreasonable). Intermittent periods of picketing of separate durations less than thirty days have been "tacked" together and held to violate section 8(b)(7)(C) when the union picketed the employer at different jobsites, Construction Laborers Local 1207 (1963); and when two different unions were acting jointly and in concert with, and in support of, each other's demand for recognition, Kennedy v. Construction Laborers Local 383 (D.Ariz.1961).

§ 11. The Expedited-Election Proviso

In the course of its decision, the Board in *Blinne* also construed the "expedited election" proviso of section 8(b)(7)(C). In the interest not only of inducing the picketing union to file a representation petition but also of having that petition disposed of with dispatch, Congress in the proviso stated that the Board, when such a petition is filed, "shall forthwith . . . direct an election" without the full-scale hearing ordinarily held in contested election cases. Yet in *Blinne*, the Board held that since the expedited election is properly to be conducted only in the context of picketing arguably in violation of section 8(b)(7)(C), such procedure would obtain only when a charge for violation of that section is filed against the union. The Board believed that Congress would not have wanted to permit any union to circumvent the normal representation-hearing procedures merely by coordinating the filing of a petition with its picketing; nor did the Board believe that a picketing union which wants to have the benefit of the normal representation procedures was intended to lose that benefit merely because it conscientiously petitions for an election in a timely manner. Only when an employer or employee believes himself sufficiently aggrieved by the picketing to file an 8(b)(7)(C) charge will the election be expedited.

In these cases, the regional office will promptly investigate the representation petition and the regional director will (typically without any formal hearing) announce the appropriate bargaining unit and order an election therein. The major difference between the expedited and the normal election is that the expedited election procedure discards the showing-of-interest requirement, the requirement that the employer furnish the so-called *Excelsior* list of employee names and addresses, and the pre-election review by the Board of the actions of the regional director. If the election is ordered, the charge against the picketing union under section 8(b)(7)(C) will be dismissed, its primary expediting function having been served. 29 C.F. R. § 101.24(a) (1975).

§ 12. Permissible Recognition Picketing: The Informational-Picketing Proviso

In analyzing the proscriptions of section 8(b)(7)(C), one ought not lose sight of what the section *permits*. A minority union may peacefully picket to secure recognition or to secure new adherents among the employees, and in the process significantly impede the employer's business—by inducing its employees to engage in work stoppages, by inducing employees of suppliers and customers not to make deliveries or pickups, and by inducing members of the public to refrain from doing business with the employer—for as long as a month, and indeed possibly for considerably longer if there are delays in processing the election petition. This has led some critics to suggest that the statute should be read to permit the picketing to continue no longer than thirty days, even if it takes longer to process the representation petition or intervening unfair labor practice charges filed against the employer.

In any event, Congress concluded that the thirty-day shelter was in fact inadequate in the case of certain picketing appeals made by a union seeking recognition or seeking to organize—appeals which were directed not at other employees (of the picketed employer or of its suppliers or commercial customers) but at members of the public. Unions engaged in organizing activities have, since the early days of common law regulation, contended that their picketing is in large measure designed to inform the individual members of the public who would otherwise patronize the employer that a labor dispute exists there, that the employer does not recognize or bargain with the picketing union, or that the employees are not union members—and that the customer should for these reasons exercise his discretion and not patronize the employer. Indeed, for a brief period, such picketing was assimilated to freedom of speech and held constitutionally immune from state injunction. AFL v. Swing (U.S.1941). It was essentially for these reasons that in 1959 Congress—even though perhaps no longer constitutionally compelled to do so, see Teamsters Local 695 v. Vogt, Inc. (U.S.1957) (state may constitutionally bar picketing designed to force employer to pressure employees to join union) —granted immunity in the second proviso of section 8(b)(7)(C) to a class of picketing which otherwise would violate that section:

Provided further, That nothing in this subparagraph (C) shall be construed to prohibit any picketing or other publicity for the purpose of truthfully advising the public (including consumers) that an employer does not employ members of, or have a contract with, a labor organization, unless an effect of such picketing is to induce any individual employed by any other person in the course of his employment, not to pick up, deliver or transport any goods or not to perform any services.

This is the so-called "informational picketing" proviso, and its meaning and purpose have been elucidated in a number of Board and court decisions.

(1) The proviso has been held to be directed not at picketing which lacks a recognitional or organizational object but at picketing which has such an object and which thus would be proscribed under section 8(b)(7)(C) were it not for the proviso. Thus, picketing of an employer solely because it deals with Communist countries, or has discharged an employee, or pays wages less than union scale does not violate section 8(b)(7) at all, because it lacks a recognitional or organizational objective; subsection (C) and its proviso simply do not come into play. It is thus irrelevant to the legality of such picketing that it turns away employees of suppliers or of commercial customers. When, however, the union's picket signs declare to the public "that an employer does not employ members of, or have a contract with, a labor organization," the Board infers that its object is organizational or recognitional; and yet it may be sheltered by the proviso. Local Joint Exec. Bd. of Hotel Employees (Crown Cafeteria), *enf'd* (9th Cir. 1964).

(2) The union's purpose—in order to engage in "proviso picketing"—must be to communicate to individual members of the public the fact that the employer is nonunion in the hope that this will affect their decision to patronize. Its purpose must not be to "signal" to employees of the employer's suppliers or customers that a labor dispute exists and that organized and disciplined economic pressure through work stoppages should be imposed on the recalcitrant employer. As one court has noted:

> This proviso gives the union freedom to appeal to the unorganized public for spontaneous popular pressure upon the employer; it is intended, however, to exclude the invocation of pressure by organized labor groups or members of unions, as such.

> The permissible picketing is, therefore, that which through the dissemination of certain allowed representations, is designed to influence members of the unorganized public, as individuals, because the impact upon the employer by way of such individuals is weaker, more indirect and less coercive

and is thus likely to generate less pressure on the employer to coerce its employees to join the union. NLRB v. Local 3, IBEW (Picoult) (2d Cir. 1963).

(3) The distinction between "informational" and "signal" picketing in the proviso to section 8(b)(7)(C) refers to the purpose of the picketing union, rather than primarily to the effects which flow from the picketing. But the effects of the picketing—*i. e.,* whether only individual customers are turned away or whether delivery and pickup employees also refrain from working at the picketed site—are important as well. If, for example, the union pickets only at customer entrances during ordinary business hours, avoids delivery and employee entrances, and requests that delivery and pickup employees do their assigned work, and if no work stoppage results, then the evidence is persuasive that the union's purpose was to "communicate" rather than to "signal." If, however, the picketing has the effect of turning away delivery and pickup employees, then the shelter of the proviso is lost, regardless of the union's purported purpose to communicate only with individual members of the public. *Ibid.*

(4) The shelter of the proviso will not, however, be lost simply because a single deliveryman misreads the purport of what would otherwise be proviso picketing and refuses to cross the picket line to make a delivery. The Board has held, with judicial approval, that the picketing must actually disrupt, interfere with or curtail the business of the employer before it will fall outside of the proviso's protection. Barker Bros. v. NLRB (9th Cir. 1964). For example, the Board has held picketing to fall within the proviso even though (during a period when some $100,000 of merchandise was delivered to the store) a glazing contractor's employees refused to cross the picket line to install two mirrors in the store, a driver refused to deliver a shipment of electric light bulbs for use in the store, and there was a two-day delay in the repair of some floor tiles. Retail Clerks Local 1404 (1963). This construction of the Act makes good sense, even though the Congressional language—"unless an effect of such picketing is to induce any individual employed by any other person . . . not to pick up, deliver or transport any goods or not to perform any services"—is written in terms which allow little latitude in construction. Perhaps it could be argued that such occasional refusals to work are not an "effect" of the picketing but rather of a misunderstanding of the picketing. Certainly, if such an occasional refusal were to be induced by the employer, as a means of ousting the protection of the proviso, it ought not be treated as an "effect" of the picketing.

(5) With less need for ingenious construction, the proviso requires that the picketing be truthful, and that it communicate that the employer does not employ members of or have a contract with the union. If all that the union placards state is that the employer's wages and working conditions do not meet union standards, such

picketing (provided it is otherwise found to have a recognitional object) will not be sheltered by the proviso. Butchers Local 120 (1966), *enf'd per curiam* (9th Cir. 1968).

(6) The proviso applies only to subsection (C) of section 8(b)(7) and not to either subsection (A) or (B). Thus, picketing at customer entrances, announcing that the employer has no contract with the union and resulting in no work stoppages, will (since the message is presumed to evidence a recognitional object) violate section 8(b)(7) if there is a lawfully recognized incumbent union operating under a "contract bar," or if a valid election was held less than twelve months before. While this proscription might be said to raise close questions of constitutional law or at least of legislative policy akin to those under subsection (C), Congress has concluded that even an appeal to individual consumers—if the appeal is by picketing and has a recognitional object—generates undue pressure on the employer and its employees when the statutory policy is rather to ensure them a period of stability and repose.

(7) Proviso picketing, since it does not violate section 8(b)(7)(C), may continue indefinitely without the limitation of the statutory thirty-day period. Moreover, proviso picketing will not furnish a predicate for an expedited election under the first proviso to section 8(b)(7)(C), and an election thus expedited will not be treated as a "valid election" under subsection (B). Recognition picketing may continue, even immediately after the wrongly expedited election, and the charged union can by way of defense in the 8(b)(7)(B) proceeding challenge the propriety of directing an expedited election under section 8(b)(7)(C). Local 86, Painters (1974).

CHAPTER XII
SECONDARY BOYCOTTS

§ 1. Background and History

A secondary boycott may be defined as the application of economic pressure upon a person with whom the union has no dispute regarding its own terms of employment in order to induce that person to cease doing business with another employer with whom the union does have such a dispute. Thus, a union may seek to organize the employees at Company P, or may seek to extract economic concessions during a collective bargaining negotiation with Company P. An inducement of P's employees to engage in a work stoppage would be treated as "primary" concerted activity, and a request to Company S which buys the product of Company P to refrain from doing so would be a "primary" product boycott; in either situation the object is to cut off P's business and thereby to force capitulation to the union's demands. If the request to Company S, however, is unsuccessful, and the union attempts to coerce in turn that company to cease buying from (or supplying) Company P—and that coercion takes the form of appealing to S's employees to engage in a work stoppage or to S's customers to boycott S's product—the union's pressure becomes "secondary." The attempted withdrawal of services or patronage from S (generically referred to as a "boycott") pressures a person with whom the union has no underlying quarrel and whose employment relations it does not seek to alter. The object, just as in the primary boycott, is to fracture the ongoing business relationship between Company P and its suppliers or purchasers in order to make it increasingly costly for that company to resist the union's demands.

Most states at common law treated the secondary boycott as an illegal exercise of coercion against a person who was "uninvolved" in the labor dispute of another company. *E. g.,* Bricklayers' Union v. Seymour Ruff & Sons (Md.1931). Some states, however, did condone secondary activity, at least when it took the more limited form of an appeal to S's employees not to work on (and S's customers not to purchase) the goods which came from the primary employer rather than to cease working for or patronizing the secondary employer altogether. *E. g.,* Goldfinger v. Feintuch (N.Y.1937). The secondary boycott which affected the delivery or receipt of goods in interstate commerce was also consistently held to contravene the Sherman Antitrust Act and not to be saved by the labor-exempting provisions of the Clayton Act. Duplex Printing Press Co. v. Deering (U.S.1921). The United States Supreme Court, however, read the Norris-LaGuardia Act of 1932 to shelter (against antitrust injunctions and criminal proceedings) secondary boycotts effected by peaceful strikes, picketing or appeals to customers even though the employer upon whom the pressure was being immediately exerted was not the one whose labor policy the employees were trying to alter. United States v. Hutcheson (U.S.1941). Six years later, however, Congress came full circle when it declared the secondary boycott to be an unfair labor practice in violation of section 8(b)(4)(A) of the Taft-Hartley Act (since amended as 8(b)(4)(B)). The secondary boycott was condemned because it was thought unfairly to enmesh in a proliferating dispute a person who was in truth a "neutral," a "stranger" to that dispute who was "uninvolved" in the union's grievance against the primary employer.

Rather than declare illegal the "secondary boycott" in such terms, Congress in 1947 declared it an unfair labor practice for a labor organization to engage in or to induce any employees to engage in a

> strike or a concerted refusal .   .   . to use, manufacture, .   .   . handle or work on any goods .   .   . or to perform any services where an object thereof is forcing .   .   . any employer or other person to cease using, .   .   . handling, transporting, or otherwise dealing in the products of any other producer .   .   . or to cease doing business with any other person .   .   .   .

Essential to proof of the unfair labor practice is a proscribed *means*—a work stoppage (*i. e.,* among employees at Company S) or an inducement to engage in same—and a proscribed *object*—to force a person (Company S) to cease doing business with another person (Company P). Statements by the legislative draftsmen make it clear that their object was to proscribe the secondary boycott. Yet, the literal language of what is now section 8(b)(4)(B) does not fully implement the legislative purpose, for it is at once too broad and insufficiently broad in drawing a boundary between illegal secondary activity and legal primary activity. The literal text is too broad, for it would outlaw even the conventional primary strike; a strike at Company P has as its object forcing Companies P and S to cease doing business for the duration of the strike and the labor dispute. Yet the strike, and appeals by pickets at Company P that employees of Company S not cross the picket line, is lawful primary activity. NLRB v. International Rice Milling Co. (U.S.1951). And the literal text is insufficiently broad, for it would leave unforbidden picketing of the premises of Company S when the union's object is not to induce S completely to terminate business with Company P but rather to induce S in turn to induce P to re-assign work from employees represented by one union to employees represented by the picketing union. Yet such picketing at Company S has been held secondary activity in violation of section 8(b)(4)(B). NLRB v. Local 825, Operating Engineers (Burns & Roe, Inc.) (U.S.1971).

Since its adoption, then, the interpretation of section 8(b)(4)(A) as amended has been guided in only slight measure by the text and far more significantly by the legislative object of outlawing the common law secondary boycott. Thus, there is rather common agreement that a strike at one company designed to induce that company to keep certain work within the bargaining unit rather than to contract it away is primary activity. The union is seeking to preserve work for bargaining unit employees; its complaint is directly with the employees' own employer; and any potential subcontractor with which the employer refrains from doing business is an incidental victim of the work stoppage. On the other hand, there is also rather common agreement that if the union's strike has as an object the termination of business (or the refraining to do business) with another company simply because that other company will not recognize the union, the strike is secondary and unlawful. The union's complaint is not about the working conditions within the struck company but is rather that the other company operates on a nonunion basis; the strike is used to exert pressure on that other company to concede. As the Supreme Court stated in National Woodwork Mfrs. Ass'n v. NLRB (U.S.1967), a determination whether it is lawful to strike to induce a cessation of business (pursuant to a provision in a labor agreement calling for such cessation)

> cannot be made without an inquiry into whether, under all the surrounding circumstances, the Union's objective was preservation of work for [bargaining unit] . . . employees, or whether the . . . boycott [was] . . . tactically calculated to satisfy union objectives elsewhere. Were the latter the case, . . . the boycotting employer would be a neutral bystander, and the . . . boycott would, within the intent of Congress, become secondary. There need not be an actual dispute with the boycotted employer . . . for the activity to fall within this category, so long as the tactical object . . . is that employer, or benefits to other than the boycotting employees or other employees of the primary employer thus making the agreement or boycott secondary in its aim. The touchstone is whether the agreement or its maintenance is addressed to the labor relations of the contracting employer *vis-a-vis* his own employees. This will not always be a simple test to apply.

The Court's final note of caution is well taken, for there are indeed some cases in which there is serious question whether the union's object is work preservation and thus primary, or relates rather to the labor policies of some other employer. Thus, a subcontractor in the construction industry may be a party to a labor contract which bans the use of prefabricated material on the jobsite and requires instead that comparable work be done by bargaining unit employees; but the building specifications in the agreement between that subcontractor and the general contractor may require that prefabricated materials be used. Should the union induce a strike when the prefabricated materials are brought to the jobsite, there is a division of opinion as to whether the strike is primary or secondary. Most courts of appeals have held that the object of the strike is work-preservation for unit employees, that it is the labor relations of the construction subcontractor that the union seeks to influence, and that the strike is primary. Local 742, Carpenters v. NLRB (D.C.Cir. 1971). The NLRB, however, takes issue with these courts and concludes that since the subcontractor is bound by its agreement with the general contractor to use the prefabricated materials, the union's object must be to induce a change of policy on the part of the general contractor, such that the subcontractor is really a "neutral" and the strike there secondary and unlawful. Local 438, Journeymen Plumbers (Koch Sons), *enf'd* (4th Cir. 1973).

In most cases, however, it will be rather clear which is the primary employer and which is the secondary employer, and the difficult issue will be to determine whether certain inducements to a work stoppage among even secondary employees will be tolerated. In any event, it should be noted that amendments to what is now section 8(b)(4)(B) of the Labor Act since its enactment in 1947 bring within the ban of that section a secondary strike by a labor organization (that is, a union in which there is participation by "employees" within the definition of the Act) even though the "neutral" being struck is not itself an "employer" within the coverage of the Labor Act. Thus, if the Machinists' Union (which represents "employees") wishes to organize Company P and it induces a strike of workers employed by an airline company (which is covered by the Railway Labor Act and excluded from the National Labor Relations Act) which does business with Company P, the remedies given by the Labor Act against secondary boycotts may be invoked by the airline company as well as by Company P. Marriott Corp. v. NLRB (9th Cir. 1974).

§ 2.   Primary-Situs vs. Secondary-Situs Picketing

Property owned by the employer with whom the picketing employees have their dispute has traditionally been regarded as the most appropriate place for an appeal by picketers to "primary employees" to engage in a work stoppage. This kind of primary concerted activity "for the purpose of collective bargaining or other mutual aid or protection" is protected by the terms of section 7 of the Labor Act. This is true even though a necessary incident of such primary picketing is to discourage employees of other companies who are engaged in delivering goods to or picking up goods from the primary employer from crossing the picket line. NLRB v. International Rice Milling Co. (U.S.1951). The business of the secondary employer is disrupted but only to the extent to which its employees would otherwise perform services at the primary situs; this disruption would occur in any event, without picketing, if the primary strike were completely successful. If the primary employees, however, were to set up a picket patrol at the property where the secondary employer does its business, the disruption of its business would be far greater, since the inclination not to cross a picket line would be felt not only by those secondary employees who work on goods destined for or coming from the primary employer but also by other employees of the secondary employer who are doing unrelated work, as well as by suppliers and customers of the secondary employer.

Although picketing at the secondary situs is thus normally condemned, there are two major exceptions: when the secondary employer is deemed an "ally" of the primary, or when the primary employer is at work there.

§ 3.   The Ally Doctrine: Contracting Out Struck Work

If, as a means of continuing production in the face of a strike, the primary employer seeks out the services of another company to complete the work which in the absence of the strike would have been done by the primary employer, the person doing the struck work cannot assert the status of a neutral employer, one who is unconcerned with the underlying labor dispute. That company, which the primary employer is using to escape the pressure of the strike and which is deriving economic benefit from the shutdown, is treated as an "ally" rather than a neutral and is subject to all of the pressures (through inducement of its employees to strike) to which the primary employer is properly subjected, just as if its employees were replacements put to work in the primary plant.

The "ally doctrine" was announced in Douds v. Metropolitan Fed. of Architects (S.D.N.Y.1948). In that case, employees of a corporation engaged in supplying engineering services to industrial concerns went on strike in support of demands for a new labor contract. During the strike, the corporation substantially increased the amount of work which it had previously been contracting out to another company and sent its supervisory personnel to that company to oversee the subcontracted work. In a proceeding for an injunction under section 10(l) of the Labor Act to halt the picketing of the second company by the union representing the striking employees of the corporation, the court refused to issue an injunction. It held that the second company, by doing subcontracted work which but for the strike would have been done by the corporation (or primary employer), was not a "neutral" but was an "ally" of the primary employer and as such was legally subject to the same economic pressures as the primary. The court squared its conclusion with the seemingly controlling proscription in section 8(b)(4)(A) by holding that the relationship between the primary employer and the ally was not one of "doing business"; the same result might have been reached by holding that a work stoppage at the ally company forces no cessation of business with "any other person" since both companies are completely united in interest.

The ally doctrine has since been endorsed by the NLRB, Brewery Workers Union No. 8 (1964), and by the courts generally, National Woodwork Mfrs. Ass'n v. NLRB (U.S.1967). Its reach, however, is not altogether well defined. Thus, at one extreme, it will not normally be sufficient to convert a "neutral" into an "ally" that the struck primary employer simply announces to its customers that that other company is available as a substitute to satisfy their needs. United Marine Div., NMU (1961). In such a case, the Board in effect treats the neutral employer as if it were a competitor of the struck employer whose services are being sought out and paid for on the initiative of the primary employer's customers; the struck employer is not aided by the work done by the neutral but may actually be harmed, both by the loss of this particular contract and by the loss to the competitor of future contracts with the customer as well. At the other extreme, it has been held that a company doing struck work can become an "ally" even if the struck primary employer does not initiate a subcontract with it in order to tide itself through the strike; it is enough if the primary employer encourages its customers to make their own substitute arrangements and later pays the "ally" directly for the services thus rendered. NLRB v. Business Mach. Mechanics Conf. Bd. Local 459 (Royal Typewriter Co.) (2d Cir. 1955) (ally was also in a position reasonably to know that it was doing work which would have been done by the primary company in the absence of the strike).

In the intermediate case, however, the customers having a contract with the struck primary employer secure comparable services from another and unilaterally reduce their account owing to the struck employer. Such a case is Laborers Local 859 v. NLRB (Thomas S. Byrne, Inc.) (D.C.Cir. 1971). There, a building-stone supplier which ordinarily delivered stone to construction companies on its own trucks was undergoing a strike, and the construction companies made arrangements with independent truckers to make delivery and deducted the delivery cost from the contract price of the stone. Employees of the stone supplier picketed both the construction-company customers and the independent truckers. Both Board and court agreed that the customers did not, simply by securing alternative methods of having the struck work (that is, delivery of the stone) performed, become "allies" of the struck employer subject to primary picketing. But whereas the Board held that the truckers also remained "neutrals" because there was no direct contractual arrangement between them and the primary company to do the struck work, the court of appeals disagreed and held them to be allies, since they were performing struck work and the primary employer was in substance bearing the expense (by having a comparable amount deducted from the customers' contract debt). Although as a matter of economic reality, there appears to be no distinction between the three situations just discussed—all involve the satisfaction of the customer of the struck company, benefit to the "neutral" and completion of the contract at the expense of the primary employer—there will no doubt be continued disagreement in the future on the question whether an "ally" finding must rest on some financial arrangement between the primary and "secondary" companies. As likely as not, rulings on this question will turn not so much on logical analysis as on the distaste of the decisionmaker for any "unfair" extension of union pressures to locations away from the primary situs.

An "ally" finding will apparently not, however, depend on the "secondary" employer's having actual knowledge that the work it is doing is farmed-out struck work, at least when the work is done at the request of the primary employer. The Board places upon the "secondary" employer "the burden of determining whether or not he is engaged in neutral or ally type work" and thus treats it as an "ally." General Drivers Local 563 (Fox Valley Material Suppliers Ass'n) (1969), *enf'd per curiam* (7th Cir. 1971) (primary employer, in the excavating business, rented equipment and operator from another person; Board notes that the strike was widely publicized and that the lessor was advised by the union business agent that it was doing struck work). A company may also become an ally when it is given work which would otherwise be done by primary employees when those employees, although not themselves on strike, have honored at their own plant a picket line set up by a union coming from one of the primary employer's other plants. Thus, when strikers of a company's New York plant picketed at the Chicago plant, inducing Chicago employees not to load and unload trucks there, and the Chicago employer assigned the delivery work to a warehouse employer, the picketing could be extended to the warehouse which was to be treated as an ally. Madden v. Steel Fabricators Local 810 (N.D. Ill. 1963).

Of course, if the struck primary company manages to continue production and to send its goods to other employers for their usual services of re-selling or further processing, those other employers are not working on farmed-out struck goods by way of substitution for the primary employer. They are thus not deemed allies, and inducement of their employees to engage in a work stoppage is secondary and illegal (even though the inducement is limited to the "hot" goods). NLRB v. Wine Workers Local 1 (2d Cir. 1949). Nor is neutrality lost by a person who prior to the strike performed work for the primary employer pursuant to subcontract and who continues to do so during the course of the strike; that company does not secure an economic benefit by getting work which it otherwise would not have performed. Warehouse Union Local 6 (1965), *enf'd* (9th Cir. 1967) (picketing held illegal at warehouse which stocked goods of primary employer under lease agreement, when lease pre-existed the strike of the primary; warehouse held not doing struck work even though strike was triggered by primary's decision to close down own warehouse). But if the volume of work given to the subcontractor increases as a result of the strike, the subcontractor is an ally and is subject to the same labor pressures as is the primary employer. Douds v. Metropolitan Fed. of Architects (S.D.N.Y.1948).

§ 4. The Ally Doctrine: Common Ownership and Control

Section 8(b)(4)(B) requires, in order to find an illegal secondary boycott, that the union's object be to force "any person" to cease dealing or doing business with "any other person." If, for example, striking production workers at Company P induce by their picketing there a work stoppage of clerical employees of Company P, there is no "other person," no disinterested or neutral party, whose employees are being induced to engage in a work stoppage—and thus no secondary boycott. Several cases have raised the issue whether striking employees of one company who picket at another company which is owned and controlled by the same persons who own and control the struck company are engaging in illegal secondary activity, or whether the picketed company is to be treated as an "ally" such that the picketing there is lawful primary activity. There appears to be agreement that technical status as a separate business entity and a "neutral" is not lost merely because the same persons who own controlling shares of the primary employer also own controlling shares of the picketed company, or indeed merely because one company is the wholly-owned subsidiary of the other. J. G. Roy & Sons v. NLRB (1st Cir. 1958) (Board's "ally" finding reversed, although both companies were owned by five brothers, who were also the board of directors and officers); Packinghouse Employees Local 616 (Southwest Forest Indus., Inc.) (1973) (parent held not an "ally" of struck wholly-owned subsidiary). The common ownership or parent-subsidiary relationship is in itself deemed insufficient to warrant an inference of "actual" common control over the companies, as distinguished from merely "potential" control.

Beyond that, however, there is considerable disagreement within the Board, and between the Board and the courts of appeals, as to the additional relationship between the primary company and the alleged neutral which must exist before an "ally" finding is warranted. One court has stated:

> In determining whether an employer is in fact a neutral in a labor dispute, the courts have considered such factors as the extent to which a corporation is de facto under the control of another corporation, the extent of common ownership of the two employers, the integration of the business operations of the employers, and the dependence of one employer on the other employer for a substantial portion of its business.

NLRB v. Local 810, Steel Fabricators (2d Cir. 1972). The decided cases can be said to fall into something of a pattern: Two companies will be held "allied" if they are commonly owned and at least one of the following elements is present—actual common control of day-to-day business operations, actual common determination of labor relations policies, or integration of the two companies in a "straight-line" operation.

Thus, in one case, employees were on strike against a company engaged in logging and sawmill operations and picketed another company which transported the logs from the logging site to the sawmill and which was owned by substantially the same persons as the struck company and which had the same president. The integrated or straight-line operation of the companies, when added to their common ownership, was held to render the picketed company an ally of the primary employer and the picketing lawful. National Union of Marine Cooks (Irwin-Lyons Lumber Co.) (1949). One court has explained a similar result—when the struck company supplied goods for resale to a number of commonly-owned companies which were also picketed—as resting upon both common ownership and the fact that "the operation and success of each is interrelated with and heavily dependent upon the other members of the group performing their assigned tasks." NLRB v. Local 810, Steel Fabricators (2d Cir. 1972) (concurring judge requires for ally finding a combination of common ownership and "extensive economic interdependence"). It appears that the "ally" finding will be made in such cases even though the actual day-to-day operations of the two companies are controlled by different persons.

Most cases in which an ally relationship has been found between two technically distinct business enterprises reveal actual—as opposed to merely potential—common control over *either* day-to-day business decisions *or* such personnel matters as hiring and firing, determination of working conditions or collective bargaining. For example, in Milwaukee Plywood Co. v. NLRB (7th Cir. 1960), in which a strike was in progress at a parent company, the wholly-owned subsidiary was treated as an ally subject to picketing in view of the following factors: the parent company paid the salaries of the two companies' common officers and directors, advertised for and kept the corporate records of the subsidiary, hired major employees of the subsidiary and determined the commissions of the subsidiary's salesmen, and the subsidiary used the parent's property and trade-names and submitted daily business accounts to the parent. The determination whether two commonly owned companies should be treated as one because of actual common control of business operations is one which can often be made either way, as demonstrated by Sheet Metal Workers Int'l Ass'n v. Atlas Sheet Metal Co. (5th Cir. 1967), where the court of appeals sustained as reasonable a jury determination (in a section 303 action for damages) that a struck parent and a picketed subsidiary were different "persons" on the following facts: the companies had identical boards of directors and identical officers, the common president being paid only by the parent; the parent lent money and equipment to the subsidiary without security; and there was frequent consultation on business matters between the subsidiary's general manager and the common president.

In Newspaper Prod. Co. v. NLRB (5th Cir. 1974), the court and Board found an ally relationship between a newspaper production company and the company that did its engraving work—both of which were owned by the same local newspapers—in part because of the integrated business operation conducted at the same site and in part because two persons participated in collective bargaining for both companies. But before common determination of labor policy will oust a company's status as a neutral when a related company is struck, the person allegedly setting labor policy for the nonstruck company must serve in more than a merely advisory capacity and must have authority to make conclusive decisions on labor matters. Local 391, Teamsters (Vulcan Materials Co.) (1974) (parent company offered advisory labor relations services to both the struck subsidiary and a picketed subsidiary). Indeed, in an early case on this subject, a court found no ally relationship in spite of the fact that the common president of two companies negotiated for and controlled labor relations at both, since the companies produced different products with different kinds of employees, no common supervision and no employee interchange. Bachman Mach. Co. v. NLRB (8th Cir. 1959). See also J. G. Roy & Sons v. NLRB (1st Cir. 1958) (five brothers served as officers and directors of construction company and company selling lumber and building supplies; Board ally finding reversed, since there was no common supervision or interchange of employees, no interference in business or labor policy, relatively small percentage of business done mutually).

Once again, as with the "struck work" branch of the ally doctrine, there is confusion in (or absence of) rationale when one confronts a "common ownership and control" case which does not involve an alter ego pure and simple. The cases do not really explain exactly why it is that "common day-to-day control" or "common determination of labor-relations policy" should justify picketing at a nonstruck company. Relevant decisions do not support as broad an assertion as that employees striking one company should be able to picket at any other location so "controlled" by the struck company that picketing there will prevent the flow of profits into the "same pockets"; as already noted, the relationship of parent and wholly-owned subsidiary has not in itself been thought enough to warrant invoking the ally doctrine. Perhaps it is believed—beneath the level of articulation—that if the nonstruck company (presumed to have similar working conditions) can continue in business and make profits during the strike, the wages and working conditions at the struck company will be rather directly affected, and for the worse; permitting picketing of the nonstruck company would once again merely "perfect" the economic pressure upon the struck company, allowing the union fuller scope with its economic weapons in its own direct self-interest. At base, the drawing of the line in many ally cases—indeed, in secondary boycott cases generally—does involve a value judgment about the "allowable" uses of peaceful economic pressure and the striking of some balance based on a sense of "fairness." Surely the cases do not speak in these terms but it is difficult to resist the inference that such values are at work when the Board and courts draw lines in "close" cases concerning which the statute speaks only vaguely if at all.

In a rather striking development in recent years, the ally doctrine—which has been used to "fuse" the primary and technically distinct secondary employer and thus render concerted activity primary —has been read conversely, so as to split a technically single employer into distinct "persons" and thus render secondary and illegal some union pressures which would appear to be primary. The leading cases raising this issue have been in the field of mass communications, where a single enterprise can own several newspapers or radio and television stations, and can operate them either as separately incorporated businesses or as divisions which are technically a part of one company. A court applied the conventional ally doctrine, just discussed, and held that a union, striking a Miami newspaper operated as a corporate subsidiary of Knight Newspapers, engaged in a secondary boycott when it picketed an Ohio newspaper operated directly by Knight. Although the Florida newspaper was wholly owned by Knight, Knight was not to be treated as an ally, since the day-to-day operations and all labor-policy and personnel decisions were made independently by the struck Florida corporation. Miami Newspaper Pressmen's Local 46 v. NLRB (D.C.Cir. 1963).

In two other cases the complaining party was the Hearst Corporation, which operates several newspapers and radio and television stations as divisions rather than as separate corporations. In one, a strike at a Los Angeles Hearst newspaper precipitated picketing at the premises of a San Francisco Hearst newspaper. Los Angeles Newspaper Guild, Local 69 v. NLRB (9th Cir. 1971). In the other, a strike at a Hearst television station in Baltimore precipitated picketing at a Hearst newspaper in that city. AFTRA v. NLRB (D.C.Cir. 1972). The unions argued that the picketing of the newspapers was valid primary activity, since the newspaper employer in each case was the Hearst Corporation, the primary employer, and thus no "other person" was being victimized by the picketing. The Board and the two courts of appeals rejected the argument. The Hearst Corporation, while possessing potential control over the operations and policies of its divisions, did not actually exercise it. The divisions of Hearst, although technically parts of a single corporation, were held to be different "persons"; their independence of each other in day-to-day operations, in management and in the formulation and implementation of labor policy rendered each a neutral, independent and unoffending employer with regard to the others and thus within the protective policies of the secondary boycott provisions of the Labor Act. As the Board concluded, in Los Angeles Newspaper Guild, Local 69 (1970), *enf'd* (9th Cir. 1971):

> It is apparent, therefore, that if these two divisions were corporate subsidiaries instead of divisions, they would be entitled to the protection of Section 8(b)(4)(B) from each other's labor disputes. To deprive them of the protection of the statute on the technical ground that they are merely divisions of the Corporation would exalt form over substance, a result which we are convinced is not required by the statute.

Compare Local 179, Teamsters (Alexander Warehouse) (1960) (picketing of two company warehouses in support of strike at third held primary, not merely because same company but because of common supervision, integrated operation and physical proximity of three warehouses).

§ 5. Common-Situs Picketing

Even when picketing by employees engaged in a primary dispute takes place at property owned by a "neutral" company, and there is no ally relationship, the picketing may still be treated as lawful if primary employees are working at the site. The primary situs of the dispute is located wherever primary employees are found, even if that situs "roves" to the property of the secondary employer in the form of a truck or a ship owned by the primary employer and operated by its employees. In order both to allow traditional appeals to primary employees (and any incidental appeal to secondary employees with whom they work at the secondary's property) while circumscribing their impact on the business of the secondary employer, the Board in 1950 devised what has become known as the *Moore Dry Dock* standards. In Sailors' Union of the Pacific (Moore Dry Dock Co.) (1950), a ship owned by an employer engaged in a labor dispute was being serviced at a drydock (the "neutral"), and picketing was conducted at the entrance to the drydock (access having been denied to the berth for the primary's ship). The Board found the picketing there to be primary since it complied with four enunciated tests:

> (a) The picketing is strictly limited to times when the *situs* of dispute is located on the secondary employer's premises;

> (b) At the time of the picketing the primary employer is engaged in its normal business at the *situs*;

> (c) The picketing is limited to places reasonably close to the location of the *situs*; and

> (d) The picketing discloses clearly that the dispute is with the primary employer.

These rules have been applied by the courts and have been acknowledged favorably by the United States Supreme Court. Local 761, IUE v. NLRB (General Elec. Co.) (U.S.1961). Thus, if the picketing at the common situs continues when the primary employees have been removed, or if even in the presence of primary employees at the common situs the picket signs brand the secondary employer rather than the primary as "unfair," there is noncompliance with the *Moore Dry Dock* standards and the picketing will run afoul of section 8(b)(4)(B).

More accurately, compliance with these standards gives rise only to a presumption of legality and of primary activity; even when the picketing meets these tests the Board (or court in a section 303 action) will look to other factors to determine whether "an object" of the picketing was really to appeal to the secondary employer to cease doing business with the primary. Gulf Coast Bldg. & Supply Co. v. IBEW Local 480 (5th Cir. 1970). The trier of fact must make the exceedingly fine determination whether, in spite of compliance with *Moore Dry Dock,* the object of the picketing is to appeal to the employees of the primary employer and to publicize the facts of the dispute rather than in any part to "enmesh" the secondary by inducing a work stoppage of its employees. Plumbers Local 32 (A&B Plumbing, Inc.) (1968). Not only is this an elusive factual line to draw, but there is considerable question whether such a distinction comports with the decision of the Supreme Court in the so-called *General Electric* case, Local 761, IUE v. NLRB (U.S.1961), to be discussed in detail immediately below. There, the Court acknowledged that much lawful primary picketing (at least at the primary situs) is clearly designed to appeal to secondary employees to induce *them* to engage in a work stoppage, and that the central issue is not whether such an appeal is being made to secondary employees but rather the relationship between their work and the kind of work done by the primary employer. There is little wonder that the Board has been divided within itself on the legality of picketing, within the *Moore Dry Dock* standards, which is obviously addressed to secondary employees working nearby. See Teamsters Local 126 (Ready Mixed Concrete) (1972) (3 to 2 decision holding picketing illegal, with dissenters relying on the Supreme Court decision in *General Electric*).

For a period of time, the Board held that common-situs picketing ostensibly in compliance with *Moore Dry Dock* was indeed unlawfully addressed to secondary employees, by finding that the primary employer owned separate property at which an "effective" appeal to primary employees could take place. Washington Coca-Cola Bottling Works, Inc. (1953), *enf'd* (D.C.Cir. 1955). The courts rejected the Board's making this a rigid fifth requirement, and the Board itself discarded this "no separate primary situs" requirement (although treating it as a factor to be considered), in IBEW Local 861 (Plauche Elec., Inc.) (1962).

Common-situs picketing has proved to be a special problem in the construction industry, where the property on which employees are at work is generally owned by another and where many different employers (a general contractor and subcontractors) have their employees working in close proximity. The extent of allowable picketing at a construction site was determined by the Supreme Court in NLRB v. Denver Bldg. & Constr. Trades Council (U.S.1951). (Although the case was decided the year after *Moore Dry Dock,* that decision played no role in the Court's analysis.) In *Denver Building,* a general contractor awarded a subcontract for electrical work to a nonunion company; a council of unions representing construction trades posted a picket at the jobsite and informed all union members, employed by the general contractor and by other subcontractors, not to report for work until the nonunion electrical subcontractor was replaced. Because the only employees reporting to the jobsite were those of the electrical subcontractor, the general contractor to get its work done ordered the subcontractor off the job; the subcontractor filed charges against the union for violation of what was then section 8(b)(4)(A). The union argued that the "primary" employer in its dispute was the general contractor (because it used a nonunion subcontractor), and that therefore picketing of the entire jobsite was not unlawful.

The Supreme Court, however, disagreed and held that the intervention of a contract between the general contractor and the nonunion electrical subcontractor made the latter the primary employer and made the general contractor a "neutral" employer; the objective of the union was to close down the entire jobsite as a means of precipitating a termination of that subcontract. "[T]he fact that the contractor and subcontractor were engaged on the same construction project, and that the contractor had some supervision over the subcontractor's work, did not eliminate the status of each as an independent contractor or make the employees of one the employees of the other." A dissenting Justice would have permitted the picketing just as picketing would have been allowed had the general contractor performed the electrical work through nonunion employees of its own; he said that "The presence of a subcontractor does not alter one whit the realities of the situation" and that the unions have a genuine interest, not to be circumvented by "fortuitous business arrangements," in not working alongside nonunion employees on the same job.

For years, organized labor—particularly the construction unions —supported the introduction of legislation in Congress to overrule the *Denver Building* decision and thus to permit common-situs picketing by a single construction union addressed to all other crafts at the jobsite. In 1975, both Houses of Congress did indeed pass such legislation, giving reasons much like those of the dissenting Justice in *Denver Building,* most particularly the close working and economic interrelation among all unions on a construction site. The legislation became the focus of considerable public attention and criticism, in large measure because it was alleged to give undue economic power to construction unions at a time when the industry was economically depressed, and it was vetoed by President Ford.

§ 6. Primary-Situs Picketing and the Reserved Gate

Picketing which takes place at the common entrance to the primary plant has always been treated as legal, even though the picket line is respected by employees of suppliers and deliverymen, of buyers and of companies doing conventional maintenance and repair work. While such "secondary" employees are induced thereby to engage in a work stoppage or a refusal to handle, this inducement is treated as "incidental" to the primary strike or picketing and as sheltered within in a 1959 proviso to section 8(b)(4)(B): "*Provided,* That nothing contained in this clause (B) shall be construed to make unlawful, where not otherwise lawful, any primary strike or primary picketing." After the adoption of the *Moore Dry Dock* rules, however, the Board began to apply them during the 1950's to "common situs" picketing even at the primary situs. Some employers took advantage of this development and, in an effort to insulate the employees of neutral employers and independent contractors from picketing by primary employees, resorted to the cutting of separate gates onto the primary premises, with employees of other companies entering through different gates from those used by primary employees. The Board held picketing at these "secondary" gates to violate section 8(b)(4) since, there being no primary employees there, "an object" was obviously to appeal to the employees of neutrals to engage in a work stoppage.

In the *General Electric* case, Local 761, IUE v. NLRB (U.S. 1961), the Supreme Court reversed such a Board decision and held that an employer would not be permitted, by cutting separate gates, to convert into illegal secondary picketing an appeal to the kinds of employees at whom primary picketing had traditionally been "incidentally" directed—suppliers, customers and day-to-day maintenance employees whose work requires them to be at the primary situs. Legality was said by the Court to turn upon the nature of the work done by the independent contractors, and primarily upon the "relatedness" of their work to the everyday operations of the primary employer. Thus, reserved-gate picketing at the property of the primary employer would be treated as also primary and lawful unless "the work done by the men who use the gate [is] unrelated to the normal operations of the employer and the work [is] of a kind that would not, if done when the plant were engaged in its regular operations, necessitate curtailing those operations" (quoting from United Steelworkers v. NLRB (2d Cir. 1961)).

While the Court's formulation is cryptic and unexplained, it appears to be bottomed on two separate ideas in the law of secondary boycotts. If, for example, the work of the independent contractors is related to the primary employer's normal operations—such as suppliers or conventional maintenance services—then the pressure exerted on them is legal; it is comparable to that which would be exerted by a successful primary strike and a conventional picket line. Similarly, if the work of the independent contractors would necessitate shutting down the plant, such as fundamental reconstruction of the operating areas of the plant, then picketing at gates reserved for these employees is also legal; both the employer and the independent contractor are "taking advantage of the strike" to do work which could not be done while the plant was operating normally, and the "neutrality" of the contractor is a fiction—the contractor is an "ally." Reserved-gate picketing at the primary situs will be held secondary and illegal when the independent contractor is doing work which is not "related" to the everyday plant operations *and* which could be done in any event without closing down the plant. Construction work (other than in the plant itself) would be the most obvious example. To induce such construction workers to engage in a work stoppage imposes a pressure on the secondary employer far beyond that which would be felt were the primary's plant to be shut down by the strike, and the construction company cannot properly be treated as an "ally" who is taking advantage of the work stoppage in order to perform services which could not otherwise be performed.

The test of "relatedness" to everyday operations of the plant can be applied readily in many obvious cases, but the Board and the courts have provided no sure guidance in the more debatable ones. On remand in the *General Electric* case the Board treated as primary pressure picketing addressed to independent contractors engaged in such construction work as repair of roads, building of a shower room, concrete work on a warehouse building and construction of a catwalk; although these seem rather "unrelated" to and independent of the manufacture of major home appliances, the Board found them "related" since General Electric had a Central Maintenance division whose employees had previously done this kind of work or possessed the skills to do them, and thus declared the reserved-gate picketing primary. Local 761, IUE (1962). The Board has also found employees of contractors to be doing "related" work when they are engaged in repairing or improving plant machinery or physical systems, even though the repairs are major and of the "one-shot" (rather than day-to-day) variety, Chemical Workers Union (Crest, Inc.) (1969) (installation of platforms and guardrails and repair of damaged walls caused by explosion), and even though the employees of the struck employer have never performed such tasks, Oil Workers Int'l Union (Firestone Synthetic Rubber & Latex Co.) (1968) (dictum) (functioning and repair —by digging effluent ditch—of water-treatment system related to regular operations of plant).

The Supreme Court has sustained the application of the *General Electric* rules in a case in which the "reserved gate" picketing took place on property which was owned not by the struck primary employer but by a neutral railroad employer. In United Steelworkers v. NLRB (Carrier Corp.) (U.S.1964), the Court upheld as primary and legal picketing which was directed at railroad employees engaged in deliveries to the struck plant even though it took place at the entrance of a spur of track leading to the struck plant which was technically on the railroad's right-of-way. Because the railroad spur was in substance a gate to the plant and the railroad employees were making deliveries needed in the day-to-day operations of the plant, a picketing appeal directed at them was not a secondary boycott, even though no primary employees might be at the spur track and the picketing would thus not comply with the *Moore Dry Dock* rules relating to common-situs picketing.

In spite of the Court's willingness to apply the "relatedness" test to reserved-gate picketing on property other than that owned by the primary employer, the Board has limited the decision in *Carrier Corp.* to its facts and has continued, in cases in which the picketing is at the property of the secondary employer or of some third person, to apply the *Moore Dry Dock* requirements. These would make reserved-gate appeals to secondary employees unlawful, regardless of "relatedness," since by hypothesis no primary employees are moving through the gate where the picketing takes place and the picketing is clearly designed to induce secondary employees not to work. The Board so held in Building & Constr. Trades Council of New Orleans, (1965), *enf'd* (5th Cir. 1967) (Markwell & Hartz, Inc.), where a union in a dispute with a general contractor picketed the entire construction site (owned by a third person) including entrance gates reserved for subcontractors doing piledriving and electrical work. The Board's finding of illegality was affirmed by a majority of a three-judge panel of the court of appeals in a decision evoking three separate opinions. Two judges disagreed with the Board that the *General Electric* standard of "work relatedness" was inapt in the typical construction case in which the work site is owned by a third party; but one of those two judges held the work of the subcontractors "unrelated" (in the *General Electric* sense) to that of the general contractor and found the picketing illegal because not in compliance with *Moore Dry Dock,* while the other judge (in dissent) would have remanded to the Board for a determination of "relatedness." The third judge, although concluding that the piledriving and electrical employees were doing work "related" to that of the struck general contractor (which under *General Electric* would have permitted a reserved-gate appeal), held the reserved-gate picketing illegal under *Moore Dry Dock* which was thought to apply in all cases other than at a situs owned by the struck employer. Obviously, the issue of reserved-gate picketing at construction sites is not free from doubt, although the dissenting judge in *Markwell & Hartz* made the telling point that the decision of the Board and of the court majority in effect applies "more rigid standards to the construction industry than to the manufacturing industry. Any prime contractor would be able to frustrate the purposes of picketing by opening gates reserved for his subcontractors."

§ 7. Clothing Industry Proviso

The legislative history relating to the enactment of what is now section 8(b)(4)(B) shows that its draftsmen did not contemplate the outlawing of the secondary boycott as it had been employed in the clothing industry. In that industry, primary strikes and picketing could clearly be utilized to organize the jobber, who purchases and cuts the fabric, but who secures the services of a contractor to sew and press the garment, which is then returned to the jobber. The operations of the contractor were frequently under sweatshop conditions and were mobile, with sewing machines easily moved from the loft of one building to another; this, in addition to the short life of any given contract, made it difficult for unions to organize the contractor and improve the working conditions there. Unions typically achieved these objects by utilizing concerted activities against the jobber and by securing the agreement of the jobber that it would not engage nonunion contractors. Although the legislative "understanding" in 1947 was that such boycotting of the jobber in order to force it to cease doing business with the nonunion contractor was within the "ally" concept, and thus primary activity, an express exclusion of the garment industry from section 8(b)(4)(B) was written into section 8(e) in 1959. Excluded from the former section are "persons in the relation of a jobber, manufacturer, contractor, or subcontractor working on the goods or premises of the jobber or manufacturer or performing parts of an integrated process of production in the apparel and clothing industry .   .   .   ."

§ 8. "Coercion" and Consumer Picketing of Secondary Employers

Two forms of pressure on a neutral employer, to induce it to refrain from doing business with the primary employer, were not outlawed by section 8(b)(4) as written in the Taft-Hartley amendments in 1947: (1) direct coercion of the neutral by threats and other means short of an actual work stoppage of its employees, and (2) appeals to the customers of the secondary employer to cease patronizing that employer. These loopholes were meant to be plugged by Congress in 1959, when it added subsection (ii) to section 8(b)(4) declaring it illegal for a labor organization with a secondary object "to threaten, coerce, or restrain any person engaged in commerce." In two cases decided in 1964, the Supreme Court dealt with two issues involving union appeals to consumers patronizing a secondary employer in a labor dispute. In both cases, the Court read narrowly the proscriptions in the 1959 amendments, and reversed decisions by the courts of appeals against the unions.

In NLRB v. Servette, Inc. (U.S.1964), the union, engaged in a labor dispute with Servette, a distributor of food items to supermarkets, attempted to induce managers of supermarkets to refrain from stocking goods supplied by Servette and backed that inducement with threats to circulate handbills to supermarket customers making an appeal not to purchase goods distributed by Servette. The Supreme Court held such conduct lawful. Although the court of appeals had found this to be an illegal inducement under the 1947 Act of the supermarket managers not to "use" or "handle" goods supplied by the primary employer, the Supreme Court held that the statutory language was directed at a work stoppage by secondary employees and not at the exercise of their managerial discretion to stock a particular product. Further, the Court rejected the argument that the pressure on the managers violated the 1959 amendments to section 8(b)(4), holding that Congress intended to proscribe only that form of pressure directly on secondary employers which takes the form of "threat, coercion or restraint" and not simply of a request backed by a warning that the union would otherwise engage in lawful consumer handbilling.

A far more contentious issue was raised in NLRB v. Fruit & Vegetable Packers (Tree Fruits Labor Rel. Comm.) (U.S.1964), in which the union, in support of a strike against fruit packers and warehousemen, picketed the consumer entrances of supermarkets which continued to handle fruit packed by nonunion packers. The picketing was carefully circumscribed—in its text, timing and location—so as to appeal to customers not to buy Washington State apples (rather than not to patronize the supermarket at all). A divided Court sustained the legality of such consumer picketing. A substantial amount of evidence gleaned from the legislative history of the 1959 amendments supported the supermarkets' argument that Congress, in outlawing "coercion" of neutrals, intended to outlaw all consumer picketing at secondary sites—regardless of whether it takes the form of an appeal not to patronize at all or simply not to buy the "hot" product. Nonetheless, the Court refused, in light of the First Amendment to the Constitution and of section 13 of the Labor Act, to read the congressional intent that broadly. A five-man majority of the Court held consumer picketing to "coerce" the neutral employer in violation of section 8(b)(4)(ii) only if it appeals to consumers to boycott completely the distributor or user of the struck product. A consumer appeal limited to the struck product was held to be akin to a primary appeal and to have an impact on the secondary's business limited to the decline in sales of the "hot" goods.

Three other Justices read Congress to proscribe even this "product picketing," but one of those Justices concluded that the picketing could continue nonetheless since such a ban by Congress would impinge on picketing rights protected by the First Amendment. The other two Justices who construed the 1959 amendments to ban even product picketing found this constitutional and based on the sound legislative policy of sheltering the secondary employer against what would inevitably be a disruption of its business (from the picketing) in greater degree than merely the lost sales of the "hot" product. Indeed, those judges foresaw the case in which the secondary employer handled the goods of the primary employer almost exclusively, such that an appeal limited to the "hot" goods sold by the secondary employer would in fact destroy its business altogether, and thus clearly constitute unlawful "coercion."

Exactly the case envisioned did indeed arise some years later, in Local 14055, Steelworkers v. NLRB (Dow Chem. Co.) (D.C.Cir. 1975). There, the union had a dispute with the Bay Refining Division of the Dow Chemical Company, which sold Bay Gas to service stations which in turn derived between 50 and 98 percent of their business from the sale of such gasoline to their customers. The Bay strikers picketed at these service stations, appealing to customers not to buy Bay Gas or not to buy gasoline at all; there was no interruption of the services of employees or of deliveries or pickups. A divided Board found the union's product picketing at the stations to violate section 8(b)(4)(i); the majority distinguished *Tree Fruits*, where the boycotted apples constituted an insubstantial part of the business of the supermarket, since a successful consumer boycott of the Bay Gas would have the predictable effect of closing down the service stations altogether. (The Board majority also dismissed the argument that the stations were "allies" of Bay on account of their substantial economic interdependence, for the requisite common ownership or managerial control was lacking.) The court of appeals denied enforcement. While it acknowledged that several of the gas stations would be all but put out of business because they sold only Bay products, it held nonetheless that the Supreme Court's permission to picket in *Tree Fruits* was based not on the insubstantiality of the impact on the neutral supermarkets but rather upon the fact that the picketing induced a boycott which was limited to the struck product as opposed to the business of the neutral distributor. "The picketing was not a signal for conduct on the part of anyone except as an appeal to the public not to purchase Bay gas," an objective that *Tree Fruits* held not to be within the ban of section 8(b)(4)(ii). The court was also concerned that to permit product picketing when the product constitutes fifty percent of a neutral's businsss while banning it when the product constitutes some indefinably greater proportion would create hazards for unions that would pose serious constitutional questions under the First Amendment.

In spite of its willingness to permit the product picketing of the service stations, which might close them down completely, the court of appeals did give its support to a line of Board and court cases which ban consumer appeals having comparable effects on neutral companies. In those cases, goods manufactured or supplied by the primary employer become so "merged" into the goods or services of the secondary employer as to be inseparable, thus converting a boycott of the primary's goods or services in substance into a more expansive (and in some cases total) boycott of the secondary. This impact is clearest when goods or services supplied by the primary employer to the secondary employer are not passed along directly to the latter's customers. For example, in Local 254, Building Serv. Employees (1965), a union which had a dispute with a cleaning company picketed businesses whose premises were cleaned by the company, informing the public that the premises were being cleaned by nonunion workers. The Board held this picketing to violate section 8(b) (4) (ii) (B) because the secondary businesses were not "purveying to its customers—who might have been induced to respect a product boycott picket line—any goods or services furnished by the primary employer." The same analysis renders unlawful consumer picketing of an ice cream store built by a construction company with which the union has its dispute, and thus where a "product boycott would of necessity encompass the entire business of the neutral occupant's premises and, therefore, the entire business of the secondary employer." Salem Bldg. Trades Council (1967), *enf'd* (9th Cir. 1968). Even when striking bakery employees seek to induce a product boycott at secondary restaurants, picketing there will be held coercive and illegal in spite of the arguable "separability" of the struck product, since it has been held that the bread "loses its identity" and becomes an integral part of the restaurant's product and the customer, unable to choose his own brand of bread, is required either to eat his meal as served (on or with bread) or to go elsewhere. American Bread Co. v. NLRB (6th Cir. 1969).

Perhaps a more common example of illegal coercion is consumer picketing at a store which advertises itself or particular products sold by it through a newspaper or radio or television station whose employees are engaged in a strike and are picketing at the secondary site. It has been held that the advertising medium is properly treated as a producer (in part) of the products advertised and distributed by the secondary employer, since it enhances the value of such products through its infusion of capital and services. Great Western Broadcasting Corp. v. NLRB (9th Cir. 1966). Nonetheless, the "product" picketing at the secondary location is deemed coercive because it extends beyond the struck product; stores and restaurants advertise themselves as well as their products, and an appeal not to patronize the "struck goods" is in substance an appeal for a total boycott of the secondary employer. In Honolulu Typog. Union No. 37 v. NLRB (D. C.Cir. 1968), the court held:

> Here, where picketing means a total boycott, one interest must plainly yield, either the Union's desire to maximize pressure on the primary employer (the newspaper) by cutting off its markets or the neutral's desire to avoid a boycott

of his entire business. In the 1959 amendments, Congress chose protection of the neutral from this sort of disruption as the interest more deserving of protection.

It may be, however, that if the picket signs are limited to specifically named advertised products, the consumer picketing would be protected. NLRB v. San Francisco Typog. Union No. 21 (9th Cir. 1972).

§ 9.   The Publicity Proviso

When pressures on secondary employers take the form of appeals not to their employees but to their consumers, these communications typically represent not so much a "signal" to action by brethren within the labor movement as they do a source of information or publicity about the facts of a labor dispute which the consumer will presumably weigh in determining whether or not to cut off all or part of his patronage of the neutral company. Congress, concerned about the constitutional implications of outlawing consumer appeals of this kind, supplemented the "employer coercion" amendment of 1959 with the so-called publicity proviso. This proviso expressly shelters from the proscription of section 8(b)(4)

> publicity, other than picketing, for the purpose of truthfully advising the public, including consumers and members of a labor organization, that a product or products are produced by an employer with whom the labor organization has a primary dispute and are distributed by another employer

unless such publicity has the effect of inducing any secondary employee not to handle goods or perform services at the distributor's place of business. Since consumer appeals limited to the struck product were declared by the Supreme Court in *Tree Fruits* not to violate section 8(b)(4) at all because not "coercive," the proviso operates only when the appeals are coercive in nature and encourage the consumer completely to boycott the neutral employer. If such an appeal is made through picketing, it is not saved by the publicity proviso and is illegal. If, however, such coercive appeals take the form of "publicity, other than picketing"—such as, most clearly, newspapers and radio or television appeals—then the proviso will operate and any resultant deterrence of customers of the neutral will have to be tolerated because of the concern for freedom of speech. Even so, it should be noted, if these coercive non-picketing appeals result in the stoppage of deliveries or pickups at the secondary site, the proviso does not operate, and the conduct is illegal. No case appears to have considered the rather substantial constitutional issues raised by this statutory ban when the appeals are made through the media away from the secondary site.

Many coercive consumer appeals at the secondary site take the form of handbilling rather than conventional picketing (patrolling with signs), and the question has been raised whether such appeals reap the benefit of the publicity proviso. The legislative history makes it clear that handbilling was indeed to be protected and distinguished from picketing. Teamsters Local 537 (Lohman Sales Co.) (1961). In some cases, however, where the handbills are disseminated at the secondary site by groups of persons who parade back and forth at consumer entrances, the distinction between picketing and handbilling effectively vanishes and with it the protection of the publicity proviso. Service Employees Local 399 (W.J. Burns Int'l Detective Agency) (1962).

Although the proviso in its terms appears to shelter only non-picketing publicity disseminated by employees who are in a dispute with a "producer" whose "products" are distributed at the secondary site, the Supreme Court has construed that term broadly to encompass primary employers who merely distribute products rather than manufacture them. NLRB v. Servette, Inc. (U.S.1964). The Board and courts have gone yet further to cover primary employers who supply services, such as advertising or equipment maintenance, to the secondary, even though those are obviously neither "products" of the primary nor "distributed" by the secondary as those terms are commonly understood. Great Western Broadcasting Corp. v. NLRB (9th Cir. 1966) (advertising medium through its infusion of capital and services in the advertiser's product is considered a "producer" of that product).

§ 10. "Hot Cargo" Agreements: Legislative Background

Section 8(b)(4)(B) makes it an unfair labor practice for a labor organization to induce a work stoppage or to coerce a "neutral" employer where an object is to pressure, by an interruption of business, another employer with which the union has a dispute. It does not, however, outlaw a voluntary agreement between the union and the neutral employer which has that effect. Nor is it a violation of that section for a union to pressure an employer by means short of strike or "coercion" to live up to such an agreement, whether through the grievance procedure or by judicial action or by promises of a "tougher than usual" stance of the union at the next contract negotiation or grievance adjustment. Thus, a provision in a labor contract requiring the contracting employer to cease doing business with any non-union company (a "hot cargo" clause) would have been valid and enforceable under the Taft-Hartley Act of 1947; only when the union in a specific instance seeks to enforce it by inducing a work stoppage does section 8(b)(4)(B) literally apply and render such economic pressure unlawful. Carpenters Local 1976 v. NLRB (Sand Door) (U.S.1958).

In 1959, Congress moved to outlaw the "hot cargo" clause itself as well as strikes and other union coercion designed to force an employer to agree to such a clause.　It enacted section 8(e) which provides:

> It shall be an unfair labor practice for any labor organization and any employer to enter into any contract or agreement, express or implied, whereby such employer ceases or refrains . . . from handling . . . or otherwise dealing in any of the products of any other employer, or to cease doing business with any other person, and any . . . [such] agreement shall be to such extent unenforceable and void.

Section 8(b)(4)(A) was revised to outlaw work stoppages and "coercion" of employers with an object of forcing or requiring an employer "to enter into any agreement which is prohibited by section 8(e)." Thus were the Taft-Hartley "loopholes" in the secondary boycott provisions closed.　The legislative history of the 1959 Landrum-Griffin amendments demonstrates that it was the Teamsters Union which had most commonly used such "hot cargo" clauses to exert secondary pressure on trucking companies shipping goods from or to other companies with which the union was engaged in a dispute.　But the congressional ban was written so as to apply to all labor organizations and employers within the coverage of the Labor Act.　There was, however, an express exclusion from section 8(e) (and thus derivatively from 8(b)(4)(A)) for agreements concerning jobsite work in the construction industry, and a complete exemption from sections 8(e) and 8(b)(4)(B) for most employers and employees engaged in the apparel and clothing industry.

Even though section 8(e) in terms outlaws only a provision whereby the employer "ceases or refrains or agrees to cease or refrain" from handling products or doing business, the proscription has also been applied to contract clauses which take the form of employer authorization of employee decisions to refuse to handle, or of contract statements that employee refusals will not be treated as a cause for discipline or as a breach of contract.　Truck Drivers Local 413 v. NLRB (D.C.Cir. 1964).　Also within the ban of section 8(e) are provisions for premature contract termination and renegotiation in the event the signatory employer continues to deal with the boycotted primary company.　Employing Lithographers v. NLRB (5th Cir. 1962).

Section 8(e) has also been given a broad construction regarding the persons protected thereby.　In its terms, the section bans only agreements between a "labor organization" and an "employer" in which the latter agrees not to do business with any other "person." On its face, it would appear that the Act does not bar a hot cargo agreement between a union and a person excluded from the statutory definition of "employer," for example, a railroad, airline or governmental agency.　But in Marriott Corp. v. NLRB (9th Cir. 1974), the court approved the Board's invalidation under section 8(e) of an agreement between the Machinists' Union and Lufthansa Airlines in which the airline (a "person" but not an "employer") agreed to cease doing any food-concession business with Marriott, where the object was not to preserve work at Lufthansa but rather to ban Marriott as nonunion.   The Board and court read section 8(e) as intended by Congress to be coextensive with section 8(b)(4)(B) which *does* protect against a work stoppage a neutral which falls outside the statutory definition of "employer."

§ 11.   Section 8(e) and the Primary-Secondary Distinction

The text of section 8(e) and its legislative history make it clear that Congress intended to import therein the distinction between valid primary activity and illegal secondary activity which lay at the heart of section 8(b)(4)(A) as written in the Taft-Hartley Act and as construed for a decade by the Board and courts.   But the new section had the same textual deficiency as its forbear, for read literally it would proscribe even the conventional no-subcontracting provision so common in collective bargaining agreements, whereby the employer agrees to give work to bargaining-unit employees rather than to "do business" to that extent with another employer by way of subcontract. One court, in Orange Belt Dist. Council of Painters No. 48 v. NLRB (D.C.Cir. 1964), set forth the following guidelines for construing section 8(e) so as to outlaw only agreements having an unlawful secondary object:

> The test as to the "primary" nature of a subcontractor clause in an agreement with a general contractor has been phrased by scholars as whether it "will directly benefit employees covered thereby," and "seeks to protect the wages and job opportunities of the employees covered by the contract."   We have phrased the test as whether the clauses are "germane to the economic integrity of the principal work unit," and seek "to protect and preserve the work and standards [the union] has bargained for," or instead "extend beyond the [contracting] employer and are aimed really at the union's difference with another employer."   As we said in [another case], the Board may not rely on
>
> > "blanket pronouncements in respect to subcontracting clauses.   These clauses take many forms.   Some prohibit subcontracting under any circumstances; some prohibit it unless there is sufficient work in the shop to keep shop employees busy; some prohibit it except where the subcontractor maintains a wage scale and working conditions commensurate with those of the employer who is party to the collective agreement.   On the face of it, these provisions would seem to be legitimate attempts by the union to protect and preserve the work and standards it has bargained for.   In the latter supposition, for example, the union may be attempting to re-

move the economic incentive for contracting out, and thus to preserve the work for the contracting employees."

These guidelines were soon endorsed by the Supreme Court, over the lengthy dissent of four Justices, in National Woodwork Mfrs. Ass'n v. NLRB (U.S.1967). There, the Court considered a challenge under section 8(e) to a provision in a labor contract which authorized carpenters to refuse to handle doors which were pre-fitted (made ready for immediate installation) prior to shipment to the job-site; the object of this "product boycott" was to preserve the fitting work for bargaining-unit employees. The dissenters would have invalidated the clause since it was a literal agreement to refrain from handling the products of another employer and was the kind of product boycott for work-preservation purposes that Congress supposedly intended to outlaw as secondary under section 8(e). But the majority held that the union's work-preservation object rendered the provision primary and legal. The central issue for the Court was

> whether, under all the surrounding circumstances, the Union's objective was preservation of work for Frouge's [the contracting employer's] employees, or whether the agreements and boycott were tactically calculated to satisfy union objectives elsewhere. Were the latter the case, Frouge, the boycotting employer, would be a neutral bystander, and the agreement or boycott would, within the intent of Congress, become secondary. . . . The touchstone is whether the agreement or its maintenance is addressed to the labor relations of the contracting employer *vis-a-vis* his own employees [or whether it seeks to benefit "other than the boycotting employees or other employees of the primary employer"].

Since the object of the union was to preserve work for unit employees, and since it had no quarrel with the union status or other personnel relations of the door manufacturer, the contract provision was upheld.

In a companion case decided the same day, the Court pursued its logic a step further, holding that a work-preservation clause in a contract between a company and a local union could be implemented by members of a sister local working for the same company by refusing to work on "hot goods" handled by the company in violation of its contract obligation. The objective of the signatory local was clearly primary, as was the supportive work stoppage by fellow employees of the same company; the fact that the latter employees were from a different union at a different location introduced no secondary employer onto the scene. Houston Insulation Contractors Ass'n v. NLRB (U.S.1967).

As clear as it may be that an employer promise not to purchase nonunion goods is illegal, and that an employer promise not to purchase goods which unit employees have traditionally produced is legal, there are a number of intermediate contract proscriptions whose legal status is debatable. An employer promise not to work on goods which have been manufactured or shipped by another company which is presently suffering a work stoppage of its employees is an example. If the contracting employer is at the request of the struck employer working on those goods only because of the strike, and is doing work which but for the strike would be done at the other company, then the contracting employer is merely promising not to act as an "ally" of the struck employer. The union's object is thus treated as primary and the contract clause is legal—provided that it is written or clearly construed by the parties to condone only those "refusals to deal" which are countenanced by the ally doctrine. Truck Drivers Local 413 v. NLRB (D.C.Cir. 1964). If, however, the goods being shipped from the struck employer are from inventory or have been manufactured by strike replacements there, then the contracting employer is not by working on those goods reaping economic benefits which it would not have had in the absence of the strike, and the hot cargo provision is unlawful to that extent. Employing Lithographers v. NLRB (5th Cir. 1962). There is some disagreement among the courts of appeals as to whether it is proper for the Board, when a "struck work" clause is unduly broad, to "rewrite" it so as to preserve it to the extent it could be written lawfully. Compare *ibid.* (striking down the clause in its entirety) with Truck Drivers Local 413 v. NLRB (D.C.Cir. 1964).

If the contracting employer agrees not to require its employees to breach a lawful picket line at another company, this too is tantamount to a promise to cease doing business with another employer whose employees are on strike and thus on its face appears to violate section 8(e). But this circumscribed work stoppage by "secondary" employees at the site of a lawful primary strike has always been countenanced as a lawful incident of such a strike and picketing, and the contract clause will also be sustained as lawful. *Ibid.* Clearer yet is the legality of a "picket line clause" which relates only to lawful primary picket lines at other plants of the contracting employer; in such a case secondary pressures are absent. If the "picket line clause," however, is broad enough to condone employee refusal to cross through illegal secondary picket lines at the contracting employer or elsewhere, then the pressure on the contracting employer will also be regarded as secondary and the hot cargo provision held invalid. Drivers Local 695 v. NLRB (D.C.Cir. 1966).

While a contract provision barring employer dealing with a company which has not executed a labor contract (a "union signatory" clause) is secondary and illegal, the Board and the courts have come to distinguish the "union standards" clause, whereby the contracting employer agrees not to have work done by any other company which "does not observe the wages, hours and conditions of employment" which obtain within its own bargaining unit. Although this appears to be designed to exert pressure on the other company, which will because of the cessation of business by the contracting "neutral" employer be induced to better the working conditions of its own employees, it has been held that such a provision has a primary object, *i. e.,* the retention of that work and the preservation of work standards within the bargaining unit, and the removal of any inducement to subcontract that work more cheaply. Truck Drivers Local 413 v. NLRB (D.C.Cir. 1964). Of course, the more specific the "union standards" provision becomes in defining exactly what conditions of employment must obtain elsewhere, the more it may resemble an illegal "union signatory" provision. Whether the union in such cases has "an object" of using the clause for tactical purposes to pressure an employer other than the contracting company will turn upon fine factual questions. Thus, in Teamsters Local 386 (Construction Materials Trucking) (1972), the labor contract provided that in the event the employer subcontracted work covered by the contract and to be performed off the jobsite,

> he will subcontract such work only to an Employer or person who agrees that the persons performing such work will work in accordance with the schedule of hours and will receive not less than the wages and economic benefits provided in this Agreement including holidays, vacations, and pension contributions or benefits or their equivalent and any other programs or contributions required by this Agreement and who further agrees to submit any grievance or disputes concerning his performance or compliance with such undertaking to the procedures set forth in Section 15 of this Agreement.

The Board divided, three to two, on the legality of this provision under section 8(e). All appeared to agree that the union has a "legitimate interest in preventing the undermining of the work opportunities and standards of employees in a contractual bargaining unit by subcontractors who do not meet the prevailing wage scales and employee benefits covered by the contract" but that the union may not "control the employment practices of firms which seek to do business with the employer." The Board majority construed the quoted contract provision to require only that the subcontractor pay equivalent economic benefits to its employees and not that the subcontractor also accord such noneconomic benefits as union security and the hiring hall; the requirement that the subcontractor submit to grievance procedures under the labor contract was viewed as ancillary to and a mode of peacefully resolving disputes concerning the job-preservation provisions of the contract. The dissenters, pointing to the requirement that the subcontractor make available not only the stipulated economic benefits but also "any other programs" under the contract, and that it submit to the contract grievance procedure, concluded that the provision was an unlawful "union signatory" clause rather than a lawful "union standards" clause.

Similarly, a contract clause which appears on its face to be a union standards clause (or a no-subcontracting clause) may be struck down when the standards recited relate to work and skills (or to geographical jurisdiction) which are different from those which the contracting employees in fact possess. If, for example, a labor contract with painters bars the contractor from purchasing siding from any company which does not extend to its carpenters wages and other terms of employment comparable to those established by labor unions having jurisdiction over carpenters in the same geographical area, the union's object cannot be work preservation for its painters and the provision is secondary and illegal. See Teamsters Local 216 v. NLRB (Bigge Drayage Co.) (D.C.Cir. 1975) (no-subcontracting clause violated section 8(e) when it related to hauling of concrete girders, while employees under labor contract hauled only dirt, rock, debris, asphalt and other supplies).

A comparable problem has been generated by certain language employed by the Supreme Court in the *National Woodwork* case. There, the Court upheld the work-preservation clause in part because it was being used as a "shield" to retain work traditionally performed by unit employees at the jobsite rather than as a "sword" to acquire new work. A number of cases deal with the legality of a provision by which the employer agrees not to subcontract work which unit employees would perform themselves but which they have not performed before. *E. g.,* NLRB v. Local 141, Sheet Metal Workers (6th Cir. 1970) (such a clause relating to work presently performed within unit only in business emergencies, held unlawful). Where such a "work acquisition" clause would give to unit employees work which is similar to that which they already do, and which they thus have the skills to do, such work has been treated as "fairly claimable" by the union and the work acquisition clause has been held primary and not in violation of section 8(e). Sheet Metal Workers Local 223 v. NLRB (D.C.Cir. 1974) (court points out the need to determine the scope of the bargaining unit represented by the contracting union in order to determine if work sought is "fairly claimable" by unit employees). Indeed, in many such cases the "new" work sought by the union is so closely related to its "old" work that it is difficult to classify the clause as designed to preserve work or to acquire it. For example, in Canada Dry Corp. v. NLRB (6th Cir. 1970), the court upheld an agreement between a supermarket and its retail clerks which provided in substance that the shelving of certain brands of goods was henceforth to be performed by unit employees even though in the past such shelving had been done by the salesmen of those brands (who were obviously not in the bargaining unit). The court found both that the clerks in any realistic sense had the skills and experience to do this work and were thus not really seeking new job tasks, and also that the union had no secondary objective:

> There is no evidence that the union had any dispute with any of the bottlers or other suppliers; or that it was attempting to require the employees of the outside vendors to join the clerks' union; or that the union would allow the suppliers to shelve their own products provided they were represented by a union approved by the clerks. [The contract provision] . . . is no more than an attempt to preserve those work opportunities which the union had a right to protect for its members.

These cases would sustain such "work acquisition" clauses for "fairly claimable" work whether they take the form of no-subcontracting clauses or union standards clauses. While it is true that the union might be thought to be using such provisions as a "sword" rather than a "shield," it is difficult to see why that should be at all relevant in determining whether the union's object is primary or secondary; whether the union seeks to retain work already performed by unit employees, or to reach out and increase their work jurisdiction, the concern is still the protection of working conditions of unit employees and not an adjustment in the labor relations of any other employer. Indeed, a strict application of the "sword" and "shield" dichotomy would appear to render all work-jurisdiction provisions illegal—even the conventional no-subcontracting clause—when incorporated in a first collective bargaining agreement when a union and employer have undertaken a new bargaining relationship. See Sheet Metal Workers Local 223 v. NLRB (D.C.Cir. 1974) (roofers traditionally performing certain work for other employers in the area secure an initial labor contract with a union standards clause relating to that work; held lawful). Of course, if the labor agreement forbids the employer to contract out to "substandard" employers work which is far removed from that traditionally done by the unit employees and for which they cannot readily acquire the skills, it would be reasonable for the Board to assume that the union's object is not truly to acquire work but rather to pressure the signatory employer to deal only with unionized subcontractors; the provision thus is in substance a "union signatory" clause and unlawful under section 8(e). In so-called "work acquisition" cases generally, the Board appears rather inclined to find the clauses under examination illegal. See Teamsters Local 216 (Bigge Drayage Co.) (1972), *enf'd* (D.C.Cir. 1975) (3–2 Board decision that hauling of concrete girders is not "fairly claimable" by haulers of dirt, rock, asphalt and other equipment and supplies).

The same is true in cases in which the Board invokes its "right of control" doctrine. The Board has consistently held that union enforcement of what appears to be a valid work-preservation clause will be illegal, if the work sought by the union is work which the employer has agreed in a contract with a third party must be performed elsewhere, such that the signatory employer is said to have no control over the assignment of that work to unit employees. The typical case is a promise to the union by a construction subcontractor not to use prefabricated materials which the subcontractor becomes obliged to use by the terms of its bid or specifications or other stipulation in an agreement between the subcontractor and the general contractor. The Board typically assumes that a refusal to work on the prefabricated materials must, because the signatory employer cannot lawfully ignore its specifications by reassigning the work to unit employees, be directed at the general contractor in order to force that contractor to alter the specifications or otherwise sanction a reassignment. Thus, the Board presumes that such a work stoppage has a secondary object and violates section 8(b)(4)(B). Local 438, Journeymen Plumbers (Koch Sons), *enf'd* (4th Cir. 1973) (the signatory construction subcontractor is found to be the "neutral" being struck to achieve a purpose elsewhere). The Board will determine in each case not only whether the union's objective was work preservation but also whether the union's pressures were directed at their own employer or rather at another employer who has control over the assignment of work. (In such cases, what is outlawed is not the hot cargo clause itself but rather its enforcement by a work stoppage, a violation not of section 8(e) or 8(b)(4)(A) but of section 8(b)(4)(B).) Most of the courts of appeals have rejected this "right of control" doctrine and have held, taking their cue from the Supreme Court decision in *National Woodwork,* that the union will not violate section 8(b)(4)(B) if the object of the strike is work-preservation for unit employees. The fact that the signatory employer lacks the right of controlling the assignment of the work in question is acknowledged by the courts to be one factor in determining the union's object, but it is not to be treated as decisive. Local 742, Carpenters v. NLRB (D.C.Cir. 1971).

§ 12.   The Clothing and Construction Provisos to Section 8(e)

Section 8(e) excludes from its ban hot cargo clauses of two kinds: agreements by jobbers or manufacturers in the clothing industry not to subcontract work to nonunion contractors, and agreements by construction employers not to subcontract jobsite work to nonunion contractors. These two provisos in section 8(e) have somewhat different origins and reach.

In the clothing industry in the first decades of this century, manufacturers would frequently, in order to avoid unionization and higher wages, subcontract the work of cutting and sewing the fabric to "outside" contractors, whose operations were mobile, short-lived and difficult to unionize; "jobbers" also emerged, having no employees of their own but being primarily in the business of assigning work to contractors. The only practicable way for the clothing unions to improve the working conditions of the great preponderance of workers in the industry (some 80 percent worked for the contractors) was to secure agreements from the manufacturers and jobbers not to contract out work to nonunion shops. See Greenstein v. National Skirt & Sportswear Ass'n (S.D.N.Y.1959). In realization of this economic reality, and of the integrated business relationship of the subcontractor and the manufacturer or jobber, Congress authorized hot cargo clauses in the clothing industry. Indeed, it went further and in section 8(e) eliminated the clothing industry from the reach even of section 8(b)(4)(B) and thus the totality of the Act's secondary boycott prohibitions. Thus, not only is it lawful in that industry to enter into an agreement not to contract work to nonunion shops, but it is also lawful for a union to induce a work stoppage to secure such an agreement (which would, if the agreement were illegal, otherwise violate section 8(b)(4)(A)) and to induce a work stoppage the object of which is actually to force the manufacturer or jobber to cease doing business that it is presently doing with a nonunion contractor (which would, were it not for the expansive proviso, otherwise violate section 8(b)(4)(B)).

The breadth of this protective policy in the clothing industry was underlined in a recent case, in which a clothing union engaged in picketing in order to force a jobber to limit its subcontracting to unionized contractors. In Joint Bd. of Coat Workers' Unions (Hazantown, Inc.) (1974), the jobber tried to argue that the picketing—regardless of whether it was sheltered under the secondary boycott provisions of the Labor Act—had an object of securing recognition (by the contractors and, in substance, by the jobber as something of a common employer of the contractors' employees) and was thus subject to the ban of section 8(b)(7). The Board noted the broad protection given by the proviso to section 8(e) to hot cargo agreements in the clothing industry and to picketing to secure such agreements, and held that therefore section 8(b)(7) should not be read to outlaw the picketing.

Because of the frictions traditionally created by the presence in the construction industry of union and nonunion employees working side-by-side at the jobsite, section 8(e) expressly exempts from its ban hot cargo provisions "relating to the contracting or subcontracting of work to be done at the site of the construction." If, however, the construction employer agrees to refrain from accepting at the jobsite materials made elsewhere by a nonunion company, such an agreement is not sheltered by the proviso and will be held to violate section 8(e). Since a work stoppage to obtain an unlawful hot cargo agreement violates section 8(b)(4)(A), a strike to obtain a hot cargo clause relating to jobsite work is lawful, while a strike to obtain a hot cargo clause relating to work done elsewhere will violate section 8(b)(4)(A) and may be enjoined pursuant to section 10(*l*) or may be the subject of an action for damages under section 303 of the Labor Act. In contrast to the clothing industry, there is no explicit proviso in section 8(e) which removes the construction industry from the reach of section 8(b)(4) altogether. The significance is that a strike which is designed not to secure a hot cargo clause but to enforce it—and thus to sever immediately the business relationship between the employer and a nonunion contractor—will be banned by section 8(b)(4)(B). This will be true even if the nonunion employer is performing work at the jobsite; the strike to compel a cessation is unlawful, but an employer agreement is lawful, as is a lawsuit or a demand for arbitration, or any other measure short of a work stoppage or threats or coercion generated by the union. Northeastern Indiana Bldg. & Constr. Trades Council (1964), *enf't denied on other grounds* (D.C.Cir. 1965).

Since the construction industry proviso in section 8(e) shelters only hot cargo agreements dealing with the subcontracting of work at the jobsite, there is sometimes a question whether the work described in the agreement is (in the language of the Act) "work to be done at the site of the construction, alteration, painting, or repair of a building, structure, or other work." The cases appear to read this term rather narrowly, thus rendering a number of borderline hot cargo clauses subject to the ban of section 8(e). Thus, in Ohio Valley Carpenters Dist. Council (1962), the labor contract provided that prefabricated doors and windows could be used at a jobsite only if work in preparing them was performed by members of the Council at Council rates of pay; although the work referred to could have been done at the jobsite, the Board concluded that the work was essentially to be performed away from the jobsite and that the provision was therefore illegal. A more common problem arises when materials such as cement are delivered to a jobsite, then poured there by the employee who has driven the delivery truck. It has generally been held that the delivery to and pouring at the site are not to be treated as jobsite work but as simply the final acts in transportation by an off-site supplier. NLRB v. Teamsters Local 294 (2d Cir. 1965). Although unions have argued that a strict "physical test" ought to be employed in determining whether subcontracted work is jobsite work, at least one court considering such a delivery case has rejected that test by examining the policies underlying the proviso: "[T]he potential for conflict is likely to arise only when the non-union laborers are in frequent and relatively close contact with the union craftsmen." ACCO Constr. Equipment, Inc. v. NLRB (D.C.Cir. 1975).

The Supreme Court has recently imposed a limitation of significance upon the protection afforded to hot cargo agreements under the construction industry proviso to section 8(e). In Connell Constr. Co. v. Plumbers Local 100 (U.S.1975), a union seeking to organize mechanical and plumbing subcontractors in the Dallas, Texas area picketed a general contractor at one of its major construction sites, the object being to induce the general contractor to enter into an agreement to subcontract jobsite mechanical work only to companies having a labor contract with the union. The union had no intention to organize the employees of the general contractor itself. The general contractor capitulated and then promptly attacked its hot cargo agreement with the union as in violation of state and federal antitrust laws. Among its arguments that the agreement should be immune from antitrust liability, the union claimed that it was a hot cargo arrangement (admittedly secondary in nature) that was limited to jobsite work in the construction industry and that it was therefore "allowed" by Congress under the construction industry proviso. A divided Court, noting that the union was not a representative of the employees of the general contractor and that there was no conventional collective bargaining agreement between the general contractor and the union, held that these facts were fatal to the union's claim of protection by the proviso. The Court read the legislative history of the construction industry proviso to evidence a Congressional concern for the union which used the hot cargo agreement in order to eliminate the friction of having union and nonunion employees working alongside each other on a construction site. This policy was inapplicable to the union in *Connell* because that union was not seeking to protect the employees of the general contractor (whom they were not organizing) from working alongside nonunion employees, was not seeking thus to protect its own members (since the ban on subcontracting would apply even on jobsites at which these members were not yet employed, and even if they were employed the ban would not forbid the use of other nonunion subcontractors), and was not seeking to organize any particular nonunion subcontractor on the jobsite at which the picketing took place (since the objective was generally to exert pressure on mechanical subcontractors in the Dallas area). The Court doubted that Congress intended to shelter hot cargo agreements with contractors who were "strangers" to the union, thereby giving construction unions "an almost unlimited organizational weapon" in achieving "top-down" organizing against the wishes of employees. The Court concluded that the authorization given by the proviso to section 8(e) "extends only to agreements in the context of collective-bargaining relationships and . . . possibly to common-situs relationships on particular jobsites as well."

CHAPTER XIII

JURISDICTIONAL DISPUTES

§ 1. Background; Board Procedures

When two groups of employees actively assert competing claims to the same work, there exists what is known as a jurisdictional or work-assignment dispute. Riggers and machinists may each claim the right to move and assemble machinery; truckdrivers and brewery workers may each claim the right to transport beer; lathers and carpenters may each claim the right to suspend and assemble backerboard ceilings. At common law, when one or the other group engaged in a strike or picketing in support of its work-assignment claim, some states would condemn this conduct as tortious while others would refuse to interfere in light of the direct economic self-interest of the employees. *E. g.*, Pickett v. Walsh (Mass.1906) (strike by bricklayers and masons to take pointing work from pointers, held lawful competition). Apart from determining contract rights, the courts could not, of course, resolve the underlying dispute by affirmatively assigning the work to one of the embattled employee groups.

With the proliferation of jurisdictional work stoppages upon the conclusion of World War II, Congress was moved to enact as part of the 1947 Taft-Hartley amendments sections 8(b)(4)(D) and 10(k), the object of which was both to resolve the underlying inter-employee dispute and to curb attendant work stoppages. Thus, a labor organization commits an unfair labor practice when it encourages a work stoppage (and now, since the further amendment in 1959 of section 8(b)(4), when it threatens, coerces or restrains an employer directly) where an object is

> forcing or requiring any employer to assign particular work to employees in a particular labor organization or in a particular trade, craft, or class rather than to employees in another labor organization or in another trade, craft, or class, unless such employer is failing to conform to an order or certification of the Board determining the bargaining representative for employees performing such work.

Unlike the typical unfair labor practice, which culminates in a proceeding under section 10(c) and a coercive Board order, section 8(b)(4)(D) was designed to trigger a different kind of Board proceeding, one which would resolve the work-assignment dispute and thereby circumvent the need for continued economic pressure and conventional unfair labor practice remedies. Thus, under section 10(k) the Board is "empowered and directed," upon the issuance of a charge under section 8(b)(4)(D),

> to hear and determine the dispute out of which such unfair labor practice shall have arisen, unless, within ten days after

notice that such charge has been filed, the parties to such dispute submit to the Board satisfactory evidence that they have adjusted, or agreed upon methods for the voluntary adjustment of the dispute. Upon compliance by the parties to the dispute with the decision of the Board or upon such voluntary adjustment of the dispute, such charge shall be dismissed.

The filing of a charge under section 8(b)(4)(D) thus precipitates a Board hearing under section 10(k) for a determination of the claims to the disputed work. (The claims may both come from the employer's own employees, or from a subcontractor's employees demanding work also claimed by "inside" employees, or from employees of two different subcontractors.) For the first thirteen years of its administration of these provisions, the Board took a narrow view of its powers. It claimed to have no authority in a section 10(k) proceeding to overturn the employer's initial work assignment except when that assignment was contrary to a Board order or certification or to a clear and unambiguous provision of a collective bargaining agreement to which the employer was a party; the past practices of the employer and of the industry, and the skill and efficiency of the competing employees were not considered. If the work assignment comported with these rather lenient tests, the Board would declare the striking employees to be "not entitled" to strike for the disputed work; any continuing work stoppage would then be subject to the already pending 8(b)(4)(D) proceeding. The Board's position was repudiated by the Supreme Court in NLRB v. Radio & Television Broadcast Eng'rs Local 1212 (U.S.1961) (the *CBS* case). There, the Court held that Congress intended the Board to make an affirmative determination that one group of employees rather than the other was entitled to the disputed work. Even in the absence of a clear right sanctioned by a labor contract or a Board order, the Board was to make an award based upon its "experience and a knowledge of the standards generally used by arbitrators, unions, employers, joint boards and others . . . ."

The Board soon began to operate in accordance with the Supreme Court's mandate. Section 102.90 of the NLRB Rules and Regulations (29 C.F.R. § 102.90 (1975)) sets forth Board procedures in these cases. It provides that upon a finding by the regional director that a charge under section 8(b)(4)(D) has merit, he is to serve notice upon the parties of a hearing under section 10(k) to be held within ten days. He may also seek an injunction against the strike or picketing from a federal district court pursuant to section 10(*l*), which is typically done whenever the regional director reasonably believes there is a continuation or threatened resumption of conduct which violates the Act. The "10(k) hearing" is to be conducted by a hearing officer whose function it is to develop a full record which, upon the close of the hearing, is promptly transferred to the Board for resolution of the dispute.

§ 2.   Board Criteria for Work-Assignment Awards

In its first major decision on work-assignment disputes after the *CBS* case, Machinists Local 1743 (J.A. Jones Constr. Co.) (1962), the Board enumerated some of the criteria it would utilize in resolving such disputes and indicated how it conceived of the decisional process:

> At this beginning stage in making jurisdictional awards as required by the Court, the Board cannot and will not formulate general rules for making them. Each case will have to be decided on its own facts. The Board will consider all relevant factors in determining who is entitled to the work in dispute, *e. g.,* the skills and work involved, certifications by the Board, company and industry practice, agreements between unions and between employers and unions, awards of arbitrators, joint boards, and the AFL–CIO in the same or related cases, the assignment made by the employer, and the efficient operation of the employer's business. This list of factors is not meant to be exclusive, but is by way of illustration. The Board cannot at this time establish the weight to be given the various factors. Every decision will have to be an act of judgment based on common sense and experience rather than on precedent. It may be that later, with more experience in concrete cases, a measure of weight can be accorded the earlier decisions.

The Board has in a number of cases considered factors other than those enumerated in the *Jones* case, such as relative labor costs, IBEW Local 3 (1971) (Local 3 electricians' hourly rate of $16.13, compared to $5.04–$5.37 for employer's present employees); the safety record of the two groups, Operating Eng'rs Local 701 (1974); and, in cases involving the introduction of machinery, the fact that one group of employees had done that work previously and would be displaced from their job unless assigned the disputed work, *e. g.,* Typographers Local 2 (Philadelphia Inquirer) (1963).

The Board has failed, however, both to apply these criteria in a consistent manner from one case to the next and to allocate greater or lesser weight to each of the criteria. This failure has been the subject of consistent criticism in the scholarly literature and has been recently condemned by a court of appeals. NLRB v. ILWU Local 50 (Pacific Maritime Ass'n) (9th Cir. 1974) (court concedes, however, that all other courts of appeals have deferred to Board's expertise). The Board's assignments do, however, demonstrate a decided inclination to endorse that made by the employer in the first instance, even though it is arguable that giving undue weight to the employer's preference contravenes the decision of the Supreme Court in the *CBS* case and even though giving it any weight at all may be improperly to count "double" such factors as efficiency, cost-savings, skills and employer practice, all of which the employer considered when making the initial assignment. Moreover, the Board will generally make a work assignment to a group of employees whose claim rests upon a labor agreement that "clearly and unambiguously binds an employer to one (and only one) union." *Ibid*.

Conversely, the Board appears to have given unduly little weight to the decisions of private dispute-resolution agencies, such as arbitrators and, in the construction industry, the Impartial Jurisdictional Disputes Board (and, in many of the reported cases, its predecessor the National Joint Board for the Settlement of Jurisdictional Disputes), comprised of representatives from construction unions and from general and specialty contractors. When there is an arbitration award outstanding interpreting an ambiguous provision in a contract with one of the claiming unions, the NLRB frequently justifies giving little deference to such an award by noting that the other union did not appear before the arbitrator. But in the construction industry both contesting unions will commonly have submitted to the jurisdiction of the Impartial Board, which bases its decisions on prior practice, prior awards and interunion agreements. The minimal deference accorded by the NLRB to awards of the Impartial Board—both awards in earlier cases and awards in the very case before the NLRB —has unhappy implications for voluntary resort to such private agencies for dispute resolution. The Board's attitude may, however, be justified in those cases in which significant interests of the employer have not been previously considered.

§ 3. Private Resolution of the Dispute

Since Congress in section 10(k) contemplated governmental resolution of the work-assignment dispute only as a last resort in the event private resolution fails, that section provides that the hearing will not proceed at all if, within ten days of receiving notice of the filing of the section 8(b)(4)(D) charge, "the parties to such dispute submit to the Board satisfactory evidence that they have adjusted, or agreed upon methods for the voluntary adjustment of, the dispute."

In a recent case which reached the Supreme Court, two unions agreed to submit a work-assignment dispute to the Joint Board for the Settlement of Jurisdictional Disputes but the affected employer was not bound to participate and chose not to do so. The Joint Board awarded the work to members of the Plasterers' Union, who continued to picket when the employer refused to abide by the award and reverse its initial assignment to the Tile Setters. The NLRB in its Section 10(k) proceeding declined to defer to the award of the Joint Board, confirmed the employer's assignment of the work to the Tile Setters, and thereafter found the continued strike of the Plasterers to violate section 8(b)(4)(D). On review, the Plasterers argued that the NLRB was not authorized, after the decision of the Joint Board, to proceed under section 10(k) or 8(b)(4)(D) since the "parties" to the dispute, *i. e.,* the Plasterers and Tile Setters, had "agreed upon methods for the voluntary adjustment thereof." The Supreme Court rejected this argument, and held that the employer in a work-assignment dispute is also a "party" to the dispute under section 10(k), since "[a] change in work assignment may result in different terms or conditions of employment, a new union to bargain with, higher wages or costs, and lower efficiency or quality of work." NLRB v. Plasterers Local 79 (U.S.1971).

Accordingly, only when the employer and both unions voluntarily agree in advance to submit a dispute to private resolution should the Board stay its hand and suspend the section 10(k) hearing. The sequence of Board procedures is more fully set forth in section 102.93 of its Rules and Regulations. (29 C.F.R. § 102.93 (1975)). If the parties submit to the regional director satisfactory evidence that they have agreed upon methods for voluntary adjustment, he is to defer action on the charge and withdraw any notice of a pending 10(k) hearing. Should it subsequently appear to the regional director, however, that the dispute has not been adjusted in accordance with such agreed-upon methods, and that an unfair labor practice within section 8(b)(4)(D) has been or is being committed, he may issue a complaint, precipitate the hearing under section 10(k), and seek an injunction under section 10(*l*).

§ 4. Enforcement of the Work-Assignment Award

Once a section 10(k) award issues, and the charged union abides by the award and terminates its economic pressure, the section 8(b)(4)(D) charge against it will be dismissed. If that union, however, continues to induce a work stoppage or to threaten, restrain or coerce the employer in the face of the Board's award to the contrary, the 8(b)(4)(D) charge will be prosecuted and the union held to have committed an unfair labor practice. If the Board reverses the employer's initial award, and the defeated union commences to engage in conduct proscribed by section 8(b)(4)(D), a new charge may be filed against that union and its activity in the face of the Board award found illegal. Since the Board's award of work in a section 10(k) proceeding is not treated as a final "order" subject to direct appeal and judicial review, it can only be reviewed in the context of a petition to enforce or to set aside an order pursuant to section 8(b)(4)(D). *E. g.,* Bricklayers Union v. NLRB (D.C.Cir. 1973). Rather few cases have reached the courts of appeals in which the merits of a Board work-assignment award have been challenged. On review, the findings of fact made by the Board are to be sustained if supported by substantial evidence on the whole record, while its conclusions (that is, the ultimate award and the supporting reasons) are to be sustained unless "arbitrary and capricious." NLRB v. ILWU Local 50 (Pacific Maritime Ass'n) (9th Cir. 1974). The courts have, with one exception, uniformly given great deference to the Board's work assignment award. The one exception was a recent case in which the court criticized the Board for failing to "establish some rational principles governing the weight that it gives to the various factors it considers in § 10(k) hearings" and for rendering an award that was unsupported when tested against criteria the Board has found most weighty in prior cases (*i. e.*, employer preference and clear labor-contract provisions). *Ibid.* (Board's award found arbitrary and capricious).

Since the Board's work-assignment award is not an "order" to the employer, there are—somewhat strangely—no administrative sanctions which can be imposed upon an employer who refuses to reassign work in accordance with a Board award. Indeed, a literal reading of sections 8(b)(4)(D) and 10(k) would appear to require that the Board proceed against the victorious union which continues to strike or picket, since a favorable section 10(k) award is not by the terms of the statute made a defense to the unfair labor practice charge. The Board, however, under its own rules deals with the employer's resistance to the award as though it were, in the language of section 8(b)(4)(D), "failing to conform to an order or certification of the Board determining the bargaining representative for employees performing such work"; it will therefore dismiss the charge against the victorious union in spite of its continued picketing. It was the use of such economic force that Congress intended to be the sanction for employer refusal to honor the 10(k) award:

> Neither the employer nor the employees to whom he has assigned the work are legally bound to observe the § 10(k) decision, but both will lose their § 8(b)(4)(D) protection against the picketing which may . . . shut down the job. The employer will be under intense pressure, practically, to conform to the Board's decision. This is the design of the Act. Congress provided no other way to implement the Board's § 10(k) decision.

NLRB v. Plasterers Local 79 (U.S.1971). Congress presumably intended to permit such a strike or picketing as a prelude to the resolution of the work-assignment dispute though the peaceful and private processes of collective bargaining. Indeed, the Board has held that the sole recourse of a victorious union whose members had earlier been released by the employer is through continued economic pressure and not through a request for their reinstatement under section 8(a)(3) ("discrimination in regard to hire or tenure of employment . . . to encourage or discourage membership in any labor organization"). Brady-Hamilton Stevedore Co. (1972), *review denied* (9th Cir. 1974).

§ 5. Relation to Other Legislative Provisions

The jurisdictional or work-assignment dispute is closely related to other kinds of disputes under the Labor Act. It is, for example, sometimes difficult to distinguish from a representation dispute. See Carey v. Westinghouse Elec. Corp. (U.S.1964). In a representation dispute, there is no quarrel about which employees should do a certain kind of work; rather, two unions are each seeking to be the bargaining spokesman, in dealing with the employer about terms and conditions of employment, for particular employees concededly entitled to do the work they do. In a work-assignment dispute, two employee groups are quarreling about which group shall furnish the employees to do the kind of work they both seek, and the union (or nonunion) affiliation of both competing employee groups is fixed from the outset. A representation dispute will be resolved by the Board under section 9 of the Act by making a determination of the unit in which an election is to be held and by offering employees within that unit the opportunity freely to select their representative; the touchstone for grouping employees for this purpose is their community of interest, which depends in greatest measure upon their skills, training and the kind of work they do. A work-assignment dispute is handled by the Board under section 8(b)(4)(D) and section 10(k), and it need not involve a clash between two unions but between different "trades, crafts, or classes" (although a "labor organization" must be responsible for the strike or coercion in order to trigger a charge under section 8(b)(4)(D)). Of course, there may be cases in which the same set of facts gives rise to a dispute about which group of employees shall perform certain work *and* in which bargaining unit they should be included. In such cases, since employees are grouped into bargaining units depending upon the content of their jobs, a resolution of the work-assignment dispute should logically precede a resolution of the representation dispute.

Work-assignment disputes often resemble secondary-boycott disputes as well, especially when a "hot cargo" provision is involved. A union may demand that an employer terminate a subcontract and assign the work in question to unit employees. If the union strikes in support of this demand, and if the subcontractor's employees concurrently demand that they be assigned the work, there is a work-assignment dispute cognizable under the federal Labor Act; it is a "primary" strike since the striking employees seek to induce their own employer to create enhanced job opportunities for them. National Woodwork Mfrs. Ass'n v. NLRB (U.S.1967). If, however, it can be shown that the strike has as its true object an interruption of business with the subcontractor in order to pressure the subcontractor to recognize the union as spokesman for its own employees, then the strike is secondary activity illegal under section 8(b)(4)(B) and any resulting employer agreement so to pressure the subcontractor will be unenforceable and void under section 8(e). *Ibid.* The Supreme Court recently decided a case in which a construction subcontractor assigned the work of operating a welding machine to Ironworkers rather than to Operating Engineers; the Operating Engineers struck the entire construction project in support of demands to be assigned the disputed work, demands which were made both to the subcontractor in question and to the general contractor for the entire project. It was argued by the Operating Engineers that the strike could violate only section 8(b)(4)(D) and not also 8(b)(4)(B), since the union's object was to force the general contractor not to terminate the subcontract of the "primary" employer but simply to pressure it to reassign the disputed work. The Court, however, held that the object and foreseeable effect of the strike of the Operating Engineers, in the event it did not receive the disputed work, was to have the general contractor oust the primary employer from the jobsite. The Court thus enforced the Board findings of violations under both sections 8(b)(4)(B) and (D). NLRB v. Local 825, Operating Eng'rs (U.S. 1971).

Finally, there is some question as to the relationship between sections 8(b)(4)(D) and 10(k) on the one hand and section 8(a)(3) on the other in the case in which an employer, submitting to pressures of picketing or a work stoppage, ousts certain employees represented by one union from their jobs and assigns those jobs to employees represented by a second union. It is arguable that the reassignment constitutes "discrimination with regard to hire or tenure of employment . . . to encourage or discourage membership" in the two different unions, in violation of section 8(a)(3). A recent Board case put the problem in its starkest light when an employer discharged crane operators and oilers represented by the Operating Engineers in response to a refusal by Longshoremen to coordinate their work with cranes operated by members of any other union; subsequently, the ousted Operating Engineers were awarded the work in a section 10(k) proceeding. The Board, in a 3-to-2 decision, held that in a work-assignment case the section 8(a)(3) reinstatement remedy was inapt, even at the behest of the union which prevailed in the 10(k) hearing, and that the exclusive remedy of that union for the "wrongful" work assignment was utilization of economic pressure beyond the reach of section 8(b)(4)(D). The Board dissenters argued that sections 8(a)(3) and 8(b)(4)(D) should be read harmoniously and not one to the exclusion of the other, and that the Board's decision perversely relegated the victorious union to economic warfare rather than to the peaceful reinstatement remedy of section 8(a)(3). Brady-Hamilton Stevedore Co. (1972), *review denied* (9th Cir. 1974).

CHAPTER XIV

FEATHERBEDDING

§ 1. Background; Federal Criminal Legislation

"Featherbedding" is the name given to employee practices which create or spread employment by "unnecessarily" maintaining or increasing the number of employees used, or the amount of time consumed, to work on a particular job. It may take the form of minimum-crew regulations on the railroad, make-work rules such as the setting and prompt destruction of unneeded "bogus" type in the newspaper industry, stand-by pay for musicians when a radio station broadcasts music from phonograph records, or production ceilings for work on the assembly line or at the construction site. Most of these practices stem from a desire on the part of employees for job security in the face of technological improvements or, as in the case of painters going over with a dry brush pipe already painted prior to delivery to the worksite, in the face of employer subcontracting. In addition to job security, employees often justify such practices as required by minimum standards of health and safety (*e. g.*, minimum-crew and production-ceiling limitations). These practices are "enforced" against uncooperative employees by union fines or, when there is no union on the scene, by social ostracism. They are enforced against uncooperative employers by contract remedies if the practices have been incorporated in a collective bargaining agreement and also by the use of concerted activities, such as the strike, picketing and boycott.

In spite of employee assertions that these so-called featherbedding practices are directly related to job security, health and safety, most courts at common law found them to be economically wasteful and without any legitimate employee justification. *E. g.*, Austin v. Painters Dist. Council 22 (Mich.1954) (injunction granted against refusal to work with paint rollers, found not dangerous to employee health or safety); Opera on Tour, Inc. v. Weber (N.Y.1941) (injunction granted against strike induced by musicians in protest against use by traveling opera company of phonograph records rather than live orchestra). It was, indeed, not until 1942 that it was definitely held that such practices and supportive concerted activities were immune from federal antitrust proceedings under the Sherman Act; the union was held to be engaged in peaceful concerted activities in a dispute relating to conditions of employment and thus protected by the Norris-LaGuardia Act and by section 20 of the Clayton Act. United States v. American Fed'n of Musicians (N.D.Ill.1942), *aff'd per curiam* (U.S.1943).

In protest against certain particularly serious abuses committed by the musicians' union in the broadcasting industry, Congress amended the Communications Act of 1934 by the Lea Act of 1946 (or anti-Petrillo Act, named in dubious honor of the then-president of the union), 47 U.S.C.A. § 506. The Act provided for fine and imprisonment for imposing restrictions on the production of phonograph records for broadcast and, more relevantly, for inducing radio broadcasters to employ "any persons in excess of the number of employees needed . . . to perform actual services" or to pay more than once for services performed or to pay "for services . . . which are not to be performed." The Supreme Court upheld the statute against constitutional charges of vagueness (as well as against an equal-protection challenge for the allegedly irrational exclusion of employees in the broadcast industry other than musicians), United States v. Petrillo (U.S.1947); but Mr. Petrillo was nonetheless acquitted for lack of knowledge that the extra musicians for whom he sought employment were not "needed," (N.D.Ill.1948). Another federal statute makes criminal the use or attempted use of extortion of money—by "actual or threatened force, violence, or fear"—which "obstructs, delays, or affects commerce," 18 U.S.C.A. § 1951 (the Hobbs Act, an amendment to the Federal Anti-Racketeering Act of 1934). This Act has been held to outlaw threats of union force or violence designed to induce an employer to pay for unwanted services of a particular class of laborers on a construction site. United States v. Green (U.S.1956).

Both the Lea Act and the Hobbs Act have since lain dormant, unused as weapons against featherbedding, highlighting both the difficulty of drafting legislation which bars the use of all featherbedding practices thought generally to be objectionable and the unwisdom of declaring as criminal concerted activities which may be separated only slightly from peaceful pressure designed to promote the job security or safety of employees.

§ 2. Section 8(b)(6)

With at least some of these concerns in mind, Congress in 1947 enacted section 8(b)(6) of the Taft-Hartley amendments, declaring it to be an unfair labor practice for a union

> to cause or attempt to cause an employer to pay or deliver or agree to pay or deliver any money or other thing of value, in the nature of an exaction, for services which are not performed or not to be performed.

The statute renders the union subject to the usual cease-and-desist order, and to an order to repay to the employer any moneys exacted by the union in violation of the section. As with all other unfair labor practices, the Board may within its discretion seek an injunction under section 10(j) against any proscribed featherbedding, after a Board complaint has issued but pending disposition of the case by the administrative law judge and the Board. The statute does not, however, render section 8(b)(6) violations subject to the mandatory-injunction provisions of section 10(*l*) or to the tort-damages provisions of section 303 of the Taft-Hartley Act.

More significantly, section 8(b)(6) does not proscribe the causing of an employer to hire "unneeded" employees all of whom do some work. The House bill had borrowed from the Lea (anti-Petrillo) Act and would have made such conduct an unfair labor practice. But that Act had generated constitutional objections then being tested before the courts and, in any event, Senator Taft expressed the final sense of the draftsmen that the question of the number of employees "needed" to perform a job properly should be addressed on an industry-by-industry basis through collective bargaining and not by agency or court determination. Accordingly, it is not an unfair labor practice for a union to press for make-work devices or to oppose the utilization of labor-saving machinery. All that is barred is the causing of an employer to pay "for services which are not performed or not to be performed," that is, to pay for stand-by employees who will knowingly render no services whatever.

This very narrow proscription was applied in the same spirit by the United States Supreme Court in American Newspaper Pub. Ass'n v. NLRB (U.S.1953), and NLRB v. Gamble Enterprises, Inc. (U.S. 1953). In the *ANPA* case, the publishers' association challenged the longstanding practice of the typographers' union to insist upon contract provisions for the setting of "bogus" type—that is, the setting of type (including the setting of any corrections) and then the prompt destruction of the type in the melting box—for standard advertisements which were already supplied to the newspaper publishers in matrix form ready for direct use by the newspapers. In the *Gamble* case, members of "traveling bands" who were in the musicians' union refused to work for a theatre owner unless the owner also employed a local band to play overtures, during intermissions and after the performance of the traveling band. The employer resisted this attempt to impose such unwarranted services by the local bands, and filed a charge against the union under section 8(b)(6).

The Supreme Court held that although the services of the musicians and the typographers may have been unwanted and in fact unused by the employers, the unions had not violated section 8(b)(6). The unions actually sought, in good faith, to have the employees render the services in question and thus, unlike insistence upon pay for "stand-by" employees who in fact have no intention of working, did not seek pay "for services which are not performed or not to be performed." The Court noted Congress's intention to relieve the Board and courts of the task of determining whether and how many workers were "reasonably required" by the employer and held, in the *ANPA* case, that "Section 8(b)(6) leaves to collective bargaining the determination of what, if any, work, including bona fide 'made work,' shall be included as compensable services and what rate of compensation shall be paid for it."

The scope of section 8(b)(6) was further restricted in *ANPA* by the Supreme Court's unequivocal dictum that section 8(b)(6) does not outlaw union bargaining for a wide range of conventional employee benefits which might appear literally to fall within its ban, such as

> employees' wages during lunch, rest, waiting or vacation periods; payments for service on relief squads; or payments for reporting for duty to determine whether work is to be done. Such practices are recognized to be incidental to the employee's general employment and are given consideration in fixing the rate of pay for it. They are not in the nature of exactions of pay for something not performed or not to be performed.

The same exclusion would no doubt be held to apply to union demands for paid holidays, pay for time spent by union representatives in grievance adjustment and backpay for employees who are to be reinstated after discriminatory discharge. Also outside the ban of section 8(b)(6) is severance pay which, along with the reassignment or retraining of employees, is commonly utilized to cushion the blow of technological unemployment to which featherbedding has often been a response.

Section 8(b)(6) lay dormant for twenty years after the *ANPA* and *Gamble* cases, but it was recently revived by the Board in two cases in spite of the fact that the employee for whom the union demanded payment did some work at the jobsite. The Board concluded that the union's demand "falls considerably short of being a bona fide offer of the competent performance of relevant services." Local 456, Teamsters (J.R. Stevenson Corp.) (1974) (employer had no teamster work to be done, and employee's checking of truckdrivers' union card was performed as agent of the union). See Metallic Lathers Local 46 (1973) (services performed, but irrelevant to employer, by employee who was incompetent and substantially idle; pressure by union, which did not represent any company employees, was held not a good faith offer of relevant services). It is uncertain whether the Board's new emphasis upon the "relevancy" and "competency" of the services rendered will invite a substantial increase of attacks upon featherbedding practices in the future.

§ 3. Relation to Other Provisions of the Labor Act and to State Law

Other unfair labor practice provisions have been invoked in cases involving charges of featherbedding. The employer violates sections 8(a)(1) and (3), and the union violates sections 8(b)(1) and (2), when the union secures the discharge of an employee who has refused to slow down his work to a union-determined rate. Printz Leather Co. (1951). Union pressures to give to or preserve for its members work which the employer would eliminate or contract out to other parties may under some circumstances violate the good-faith bargaining requirements of section 8(b)(3), or the secondary-boycott and hot-cargo provisions of sections 8(b)(4)(A), (B), and 8(e), *e. g.,* National Woodwork Mfrs. Ass'n v. NLRB (U.S.1967), or the jurisdictional-dispute provisions of section 8(b)(4)(D). Employee slowdowns designed to change the pace of work may be unprotected activity rendering employees susceptible to discharge or other discipline not outlawed by section 8(a)(1). Elk Lumber Co. (1950).

Since peaceful union attempts to assure or to spread work are thus generally either unfair labor practices or are within the range of protected bargaining, the regulation of "featherbedding" practices has been effectively brought within the exclusive domain of the federal government. State courts are without jurisdiction to enjoin or otherwise outlaw such practices. Musicians Local 6 v. Superior Court (Cal.1968) (superior court restrained from enjoining picketing designed to induce baseball club to use live musicians at ballpark). The Supreme Court has, however, held that section 8(b)(6) does not oust the federal criminal court of jurisdiction in any case properly falling within the Hobbs Act amendment to the Anti-Racketeering Act (which requires the "wrongful use of actual or threatened force, violence, or fear"). United States v. Green (U.S.1956). Compare United States v. Enmons (U.S.1973) (Hobbs Act narrowly construed so as not to outlaw physical destruction of property designed to compel agreement to pay higher wages, since this is not a "wrongful" objective; Court rejects the Government's "semantic argument that the Hobbs Act reaches the use of violence to achieve legitimate union objectives, such as higher wages in return for genuine services which the employer seeks.").

CHAPTER XV

REMEDIES FOR UNION UNFAIR LABOR PRACTICES

§ 1. Board Remedies

The Board is empowered by section 10(c), upon the conclusion of an unfair labor practice proceeding, to

> issue and cause to be served on [the person committing the unfair labor practice] an order requiring such person to cease and desist from such unfair labor practice, and to take such affirmative action including reinstatement of employees with or without back pay, as will effectuate the policies of this Act: *Provided,* That where an order directs reinstatement of an employee, back pay may be required of the employer or labor organization, as the case may be, responsible for the discrimination suffered by him.

The typical Board order against a labor organization violating section 8(b) requires that it cease and desist from the illegal conduct and post notices which contain a recitation of that conduct and of the terms of the cease-and-desist order. Where there is evidence that the union has a "proclivity for unlawful conduct," the cease-and-desist order may bar not only continued illegal conduct directed at the employer in the case at bar, but also against any other employer in the union's jurisdiction. NLRB v. Local 138, Operating Eng'rs (2d Cir. 1967). The Board will also order such affirmative relief as to require the minority union in section 8(b)(1) cases to refund to employees dues and fees which have been unwillingly paid by employees subject to an illegal union-security agreement, Komatz Constr. Inc. v. NLRB (8th Cir. 1972); and to require the union, pursuant to the explicit proviso of section 10(c), to pay backpay to an employee whose discharge has been secured by the union in violation of section 8(b)(2). See Radio Officers' Union v. NLRB (U.S.1954) (union liability not dependent on reinstatement of employee or joinder of employer); Bricklayers Local 18 (1971) (union which enforced illegal contract provision by threat of work stoppage held liable with employer for backpay, union to bear primary liability).

Board orders are not self-executing, and assume the force of law only when formally enforced by a federal court of appeals. Such orders can, however, be enforced on a provisional basis while the court of appeals is reviewing the Board's decision under section 10(e) or (f); in such enforcement proceedings, the Act authorizes the court pending determination of the appeal "to grant such temporary relief or restraining order as it deems just and proper," relief rarely invoked by the Board, particularly in enforcement proceedings against unions. When a court enforces a Board cease-and-desist order against a union, it in effect enjoins the union, and this injunction will frequently reach union conduct (such as a peaceful secondary boycott or work-assignment strike in violation of section 8(b)(4)) which Congress took pains to shelter against injunction in the Norris-LaGuardia Act of 1932; Congress thus expressly provided in section 10(h) that the Norris-LaGuardia Act was not to limit courts in administering the National Labor Relations Act.

§ 2. Judicial Remedies: Injunction

Far more devastating to the union than the frequently protracted unfair labor practice proceeding before the Board and courts is the much more expeditiously issued preliminary injunction. In view of Congress's special objection to union unfair labor practices under sections 8(b)(4) (secondary boycotts, certain strikes and picketing for recognition, and strikes or picketing in work-assignment disputes), 8(e) (hot-cargo clauses), and 8(b)(7) (recognition picketing), Congress in 1947 (with amendments in 1959) empowered the federal district court in section 10(*l*) to enjoin unlawful conduct under those sections, under specific conditions. (1) Unlike the injunction at common law, the "10(*l*) injunction" is issued not at the request of a private party, but only on petition of the Board through a regional director; (2) a charge must have been filed under any of sections 8(b)(4)(A), (B) or (C) (and also "where such [injunctive] relief is appropriate" under section 8(b)(4)(D)), 8(e) or 8(b)(7); (3) the charge must be given priority status and investigated in the regional office; and (4) the regional office must have "reasonable cause to believe such charge is true and that a complaint should issue." If those conditions are satisfied, the regional director on behalf of the Board *must* petition the appropriate district court for injunctive relief pending the Board's issuance of an unfair labor practice complaint and disposition of that case. The Act expressly provides, however, that no such injunction shall be sought if the union is charged with a violation of section 8(b)(7) at a time when a meritorious charge has been filed against the employer under section 8(a)(2) (domination of or illegal assistance to another labor organization).

Also unlike the common law equity practice, the substantive wrong charged against the union in an injunction action under section 10(*l*) is sharply defined so as to fall within the proscription of the specifically cited sections of the Labor Act. The court, upon finding that there is reasonable cause to believe the Act has been violated and that such violations are likely to continue, "shall have jurisdiction to grant such injunctive relief or temporary restraining order as it deems just and proper, notwithstanding any other provision of law." All parties (including the person filing the charge) are to receive notice of the Board's injunction petition and may be represented by counsel; where the unavoidability of "substantial and irreparable injury" is alleged, a temporary restraining order may issue without notice, but such order expires after at most five days. In many instances, the issuance of an injunction pursuant to section 10(*l*) will effectively dispose of the controversy with the union, and the underlying unfair labor practice charges against the union will be settled and the Board proceeding mooted.

Union violations falling outside the reach of section 10(*l*) are subject to injunction—as is any unfair labor practice committed by an employer—under section 10(j). There are three features of the 10(j) injunction which distinguish it from the injunction under section 10(*l*). First, it is sought by the Board only after a formal unfair labor practice complaint has been issued, and not merely a charge. Second, the decision to seek an injunction under section 10(j) lies within the discretion of the Board (to which the regional director applies for authorization), and is not mandated by the Act. Third, although both sections provide that the court is to grant such injunctive relief "as it deems just and proper," courts are more reluctant to grant equity relief under section 10(j) than under section 10(*l*). Under the latter section, reaching most commonly the secondary boycott or illegal recognition picketing, there appears to be almost a presumption that the union's violation creates irreparable harm and should be enjoined. Schauffler v. Local 1291, Longshoremen (3d Cir. 1961). When, however, the union's (or employer's) conduct allegedly violates some other unfair labor practice provision, it is normally not considered sufficient basis for an injunction under section 10(j) that there is reasonable cause to believe the union has violated and will continue to violate the Act. (Examples of injunctions against unions under section 10(j) are for failure to comply with the notice and bargaining requirements of section 8(d), for inducement of employer discrimination against nonmembers, or for violent or mass picketing in violation of section 8(b)(1).) Some courts have suggested that it is necessary, before issuing an injunction under section 10(j), to determine whether it is dictated by the traditional balancing of equities and hardships. See Boire v. International Bhd. of Teamsters (5th Cir. 1973). There appears to be no consensus for this position, and the cases do not make it clear what conditions (other than "reasonable cause to believe") must be present for an injunction to issue. A leading case, Angle v. Sacks (10th Cir. 1967), has held that it is not necessary to demonstrate that the dispute rises to the level of a national emergency, that the industry involved is crucial to the public interest or that it encompasses a vast geographic area and many employees. That court held it sufficient to warrant an injunction under section 10(j) that delay in the issuance of an order until after the termination of unfair labor practice proceedings will frustrate the purposes of the Act, will nullify the efficacy of the Board order, or will render meaningless the administrative procedures employed by the Board—in short, that the Board's own remedies will be inadequate to restore the status quo ante.

In spite of these differences, both section 10(j) and section 10(l) are understood to require that the trial court find reasonable cause to believe that an unfair labor practice is being committed or is threatened. It is clear that the court need only find reasonable cause to believe; actually to determine whether the record facts and the applicable rules of law dictate an unfair labor practice finding would constitute a usurpation of the Board's function. As the court stated in Schauffler v. Local 1291, Longshoremen (3d Cir. 1961):

> If, in a Section 10(l) proceeding, a district court or a court of appeals undertook to finally adjudicate such questions it would not be acting consistently with the congressional policy underlying Section 10(l). That Section's usefulness as a tool with which the status quo may be preserved pending final adjudication would be diminished insofar as the Board would be required to finally litigate questions of substance at a preliminary stage. Moreover, the court would not have the benefit of the Board's opinion on questions of fact and novel questions of labor law when making its decision. Thus, the court would, to some extent, usurp the Board's function as the primary fact finder in cases arising under the Act and its function as primary interpreter of the statutory scheme.

The Board, to demonstrate reasonable cause, must present both a colorable case that the facts as alleged have taken place, Kennedy v. Teamsters Local 542 (9th Cir. 1971) (district court need only reasonably believe "that the allegations of the Regional Director's petition had been prima facie established"), and a colorable case that the applicable legal rules point toward a violation. The Board need not "conclusively show the validity of the propositions of law underlying its charge but is required to demonstrate merely that the propositions of law which it has applied to the charge are substantial and not frivolous." Schauffler v. Local 1291, Longshoremen (3d Cir. 1961). Even if the legal theories advanced by the Board are novel, and there is no clear precedent in support of those theories, the injunction should issue (if otherwise appropriate) if the Board's position on the applicable law is "not insubstantial or frivolous." Boire v. International Bhd. of Teamsters (5th Cir. 1973).

There appears to be some difference of opinion as to the scope of review by courts of appeals in cases arising under sections 10(j) and 10(l). Most courts agree that the question whether there is reasonable cause to believe that the Act has been violated is a question of fact, and therefore that a district court determination of this question is to be overturned on appeal only if clearly erroneous. Squillacote v. Graphic Arts Union Local 277 (7th Cir. 1975). At least one court of appeals has held that the "clearly erroneous" test applies only when the district court *grants* a section 10(l) injunction, but that the *deni-*

al of an injunction will be subjected to greater appellate scrutiny, given the congressional policy favoring the grant of such provisional relief when appropriate. NMU v. Commerce Tankers Corp. (2d Cir. 1972). Another and even more refined formulation of the scope of review was set forth in Boire v. International Bhd. of Teamsters (5th Cir. 1973):

> The factual findings of the District Court, *i. e.,* what happened and what will happen, are reviewable under the "clearly erroneous" standard as are all factual questions. The need for equitable relief is left to the discretion of the District Court in the first instance and is only reviewable to the extent that such discretion has been abused. The lower court's legal conclusions—here, whether the Board's legal theories are substantial and not frivolous—are subject to the same standard of review as any legal conclusion of the District Court: was it correct?

The "issue of law" before the court of appeals is thus "whether the General Counsel's theories were substantial and not whether they were correct."

§ 3. Judicial Remedies: Damages

When Congress created the National Labor Relations Board to administer the Wagner Act, it expressed a judgment that the norms of labor relations could be better developed and applied by a specialized administrative agency than by courts. The limited reintroduction of the injunction in 1947 in sections 10(j) and 10(*l*) can still be viewed as merely supportive of the Board's jurisdiction. But Congress went yet further in 1947 and enacted section 303 which as amended provides that it "shall be unlawful . . . to engage in any activity or conduct defined as an unfair labor practice in section 8(b)(4)" and that "[w]hoever shall be injured in his business or property" by reason of such unlawful conduct may sue therefor in a federal district court "without respect to the amount in controversy" or in a state court and "shall recover the damages by him sustained and the cost of the suit." In effect, Congress declared that the conduct outlawed in section 8(b)(4) shall be subject to redress not only by the Board but also as a federal tort in the federal and state courts. The dual remedial scheme was clearly designed as a deterrent to the kinds of union conduct—secondary boycott, recognition and work-assignment strikes—which Congress found most objectionable. It was hoped that the union tempted to violate section 8(b)(4) would be dissuaded for fear of suffering not merely a cease-and-desist order or possibly a preliminary injunction under section 10(*l*) but also a substantial money judgment enforceable against the union's assets (but not against those of any individual member, section 301(b)).

Given the broad language by which the statute defines the party plaintiff—"[w]hoever shall be injured in his business or property"—

it has been held that an action under section 303 in a secondary boycott situation may be brought not only by the neutral or secondary
employer, but also by the primary employer, United Brick Workers v.
Deena Artware, Inc. (6th Cir. 1952) and by employees of the primary
employer (at least when an object of the defendant union is to sever
the plaintiffs' employment), Wells v. Operating Eng'rs Local 181 (6th
Cir. 1962). It is not clear, however, how free the courts will be to
draw within the circle of allowable plaintiffs third persons (other
than the boycotted neutral) with whom the primary employer has
business dealings. Thus, the person who leased property to the primary employer was allowed to recover for physical damage to its
property as well as for business losses suffered under a percentage
lease. Gilchrist v. UMW (6th Cir. 1961). And, while business losses
suffered by a sales agent marketing the products of the primary employer were held in one case to be too remote for redress under section 303, UMW v. Osborne Mining Co. (6th Cir. 1960), a more recent
case has held to the contrary on similar facts, W.J. Milner & Co. v.
IBEW Local 349 (5th Cir. 1973). In the latter case, the court found
a cause of action to be stated by the exclusive area sales agent of the
primary employer since it was "reasonably foreseeable by the union"
that a decline in sales to the boycotted neutral contractors would be
felt by both the plaintiff and the primary employer whose "financial
fortunes . . . were closely intertwined," and since recovery of
damages by the sales agent (and others similarly situated) would not
be so oppressive to the union as to "threaten or undermine legitimate
union interests" and inhibit the exercise of the right to strike. See
also Abbott v. Local 142, United Ass'n of Journeymen (5th Cir. 1970)
(cause of action under section 303 by organizer and manager of neutral company in his individual capacity). In keeping with the general tendency of courts to apply under section 303 relevant principles of
the common law, it might well be appropriate to accord a cause of action under that section to third persons whose business relationship
with the primary or secondary employer is direct and customary in
the trade.

Assuming a proper party plaintiff, common law principles developed under the law of torts dictate liability in a section 303 action for
all injuries proximately flowing from the illegal conduct. Local 978,
Carpenters v. Markwell (8th Cir. 1962). Thus, the aggrieved party
may recover for time and money spent in attempting to have the
picketing stopped, Abbott v. Local 142 Journeymen of Pipe Fitting
Industry (5th Cir. 1970); for loss of a lease suffered because of the
illegal union activity and for loss of business profits which can be ascertained with reasonable certainty, Riverside Coal Co. v. UMW (6th
Cir. 1969), and indeed sometimes when the determination of loss of
business is necessarily rather arbitrary, Hyatt Chalet Motels, Inc. v.
Salem Bldg. & Constr. Trades Council (D.Ore.1968) (disruption of motel business, with no way to ascertain the number of possible motel

guests who refused to cross the picket line); and for such losses as the rental value of idled equipment and amounts paid as salaries of supervisory personnel for the period of the work stoppage, and daily liquidated damages under a contract with a third party to the extent that late performance resulted from the boycott, Wells v. Union of Operating Eng'rs (W.D.Ky.), *aff'd* (6th Cir. 1962). Similarly, the usual duty of the plaintiff obtains to mitigate damages. Vulcan Materials Co. v. United Steelworkers (5th Cir. 1970).

The liability of the union for the acts of its members and officials will also be governed by the usual common law principles of agency law, for section 303 incorporates section 301(e) of the Act which provides that it is not necessary to prove that "the specific acts performed were actually authorized or subsequently ratified." UMW v. Gibbs (U.S.1966) (the more onerous proof requirements of section 6 of the Norris-LaGuardia Act are inapplicable). There being no specific period of limitations set forth in the statute to govern actions under section 303, most courts have applied by "absorption" the appropriate state statute of limitations. Union of Operating Eng'rs v. Fishbach & Moore, Inc. (9th Cir. 1965).

A clear federal policy is, however, evinced by the language and legislative history of section 303 to limit the award of damages in such cases to compensation of the plaintiff; punitive damages may not be awarded for violation of that section. Teamsters Local 20 v. Morton (U.S.1964). Nor may an injunction issue, for that form of relief may be sought or issued only by the NLRB. Amalgamated Ass'n of Street Employees v. Dixie Motor Coach Corp. (8th Cir. 1948). It is possible, nonetheless, for the plaintiff to join with its federal claim a claim for certain violations of state tort law; typically, the union will be charged with strike or picketline violence, since state laws banning most forms of peaceful concerted activity are preempted by federal law. If the federal court concludes that it is proper to consider the state-law claim under its pendent jurisdiction, it does have the power to award punitive damages if such would be proper under state law. UMW v. Gibbs (U.S.1966) (district court must, however, find in ruling on the state-law claim that there is "clear proof" that the union authorized or ratified individuals' acts, as required in federal courts by section 6 of the Norris-LaGuardia Act). Indeed, even an injunction could issue against the violence, provided the court complied with the provisions of the Norris-LaGuardia Act. But neither punitive damages nor an injunction may issue against peaceful union conduct which a state declares tortious simply by virtue of its being generated by a secondary, jurisdictional or recognitional dispute. Teamsters Local 20 v. Morton (U.S.1964).

§ 4. Alternative Remedies

The option of redressing illegal union activity both before the Board under section 8(b)(4) and the courts under section 303 creates the possibility of institutional duplication and conflict. It is clear that an aggrieved party may assert a claim either by filing a charge or commencing a court action, that it is not obliged to make an election, and that it may pursue both remedies at the same time or in sequence. The Supreme Court has held, in International Longshoremen's Union v. Juneau Spruce Corp. (U.S.1952), that a court in a section 303 action need not stay its hand until the Board has first passed upon the unfair labor practice charge; although the definition of the wrong in section 303 is borrowed from section 8(b)(4), the Act specifies two different remedies before two different tribunals and each is entitled to make its own independent decision on the evidence before it. (The case for prior Board action was especially strong in *Juneau Spruce,* for the union was alleged to have engaged in picketing in a work-assignment dispute, a dispute which the Board is empowered to resolve under section 10(k) by awarding the work to a particular group of employees—which group might, indeed, be members of the defendant union in the court action. An award to its members under section 10(k) would have sheltered the union from charges under section 8(b)(4)(D) before the Board.) See also Plumbers Local 761 v. Zaich Constr. Co. (9th Cir. 1969) (*Juneau* decision not modified by 1959 amendments to Labor Act).

It is thus possible for the Board to hold that the union has not violated section 8(b)(4) at the same time as a judge and jury find the union to have violated section 303 on the same facts, and to have both decisions affirmed on appeal. This was precisely the result in NLRB v. Deena Artware, Inc. (6th Cir. 1952), in which the Board was affirmed in holding that employees who had been disciplined by the employer had not participated in an illegal secondary boycott, and United Brick Workers v. Deena Artware, Inc. (6th Cir. 1952), in which a judgment was affirmed against the union under section 303. The court of appeals noted the seeming inconsistency in affirming both decisions, but adverted to the two separate fact-finding agencies, the different witnesses in the two proceedings, the fact that cross-examination of the same witnesses had been conducted by different attorneys in the two proceedings, and the difference in the record evidence before the court in each case.

For the same reasons, it has been held that the facts found and the judgment rendered in one proceeding are not to be treated as res judicata or collateral estoppel in a subsequent proceeding in the other forum. Old Dutch Farms, Inc. v. Milk Drivers Local 584 (E.D.N.Y. 1968). Such a decision may also be supported by a belief that Congress purposely created an additional liability under section 303 in order better to deter the union by knowledge that it would always be susceptible to two proceedings regardless of a favorable outcome in the first. The more recent cases, however, clearly evidence a trend —observable in our law generally—toward a broader application of estoppel principles when the party in question has had a full and fair opportunity to present its case and when a second proceeding would in most respects be duplicative and costly to the parties and the public. This trend has been in large measure spurred by the Supreme Court decision in United States v. Utah Constr. & Mining Co. (U.S. 1966), that courts should accord res judicata effect to administrative findings fairly based. *E. g.,* Paramount Transp. Sys. v. Chauffeurs Local 150 (9th Cir. 1971) (Board finding of secondary boycott applied as res judicata in section 303 action; Supreme Court decision in *Utah Construction* is held to require collateral estoppel for "those administrative determinations that have been made in a proceeding fully complying with the standards of procedural and substantive due process that attend a valid judgment by a court" and in which the Board decision is supported by substantial evidence on the record as a whole). See Eazor Express, Inc. v. Teamsters Local 326 (D.Del. 1975) (thorough discussion of cases). While all of the reported cases appear to involve findings of union liability by the Board which are then applied against the union in the section 303 trial, a disposition before the Board which is favorable to the union after a full and fair litigation—especially when the charging employer is a party and represented by counsel—should also shelter the union in a subsequent action for damages under section 303.

THE BALANCE OF ECONOMIC WEAPONS

CHAPTER XVI

PROTECTED AND UNPROTECTED CONCERTED ACTIVITY

§ 1. Introduction

The Norris-LaGuardia Act of 1932 sheltered peaceful strikes, picketing and boycotts against injunctions issued in federal courts at the behest of the employer (or the United States attorney). It did not, however, shelter employees engaged in such concerted activities against employer self-help measures such as replacement or outright discharge. Indeed, the operative effect of the Norris-LaGuardia Act was to permit both labor and management to resort to whatever peaceful measures of economic self-help could be mustered in support of their respective claims. The Wagner Act of 1935 departed from this philosophy, announcing instead that concerted employee activities were to be affirmatively protected as a means of promoting some measure of equality of bargaining power between employee groups and management, and that employers were to be forbidden under section 8(a)(1) "to interfere with, restrain, or coerce employees in the exercise of the right" to engage in such concerted activities. The catalogue of protected activities is set forth in section 7:

> Employees shall have the right to self-organization, to form, join, or assist labor organizations, to bargain collectively through representatives of their own choosing, and to engage in other concerted activities for the purpose of collective bargaining or other mutual aid or protection . . .

to which was added in the Taft-Hartley amendments of 1947, "the right to refrain from any or all of such activities . . . ."

It is thus a violation of section 8(a)(1)—at least on the face of the statutory text—for an employer to discharge an employee solely because he has engaged in any of the activities set forth in section 7. A discharge so motivated will also (at least in cases where a union is being organized or is already on the scene) violate section 8(a)(3), which forbids an employer "by discrimination in regard to hire or tenure of employment . . . to encourage or discourage membership in any labor organization." The converse proposition is also important. An employer is free to discharge or otherwise discipline an employee, consistently with the Labor Act, for engaging in activity which is *not* protected by section 7. Whether employee activity falls within or without the shelter of section 7 is thus a definitional issue of utmost importance in the administration of the Act.

The extremely broad protective language of both section 7 and 8(a)(1) is misleading and has been narrowed over time. It has never been seriously contended that *all* concerted activity in support of collective bargaining—including industrial sabotage or destruction of property—is protected and immune from discharge as a self-help measure. Thus, a court of appeals has recently stated that concerted activity will be held protected only if it satisfies four requirements:

> (1) there must be a work-related complaint or grievance; (2) the concerted activity must further some group interest; (3) a specific remedy or result must be sought through such activity; and (4) the activity should not be unlawful or otherwise improper.

Shelly & Anderson Furniture Mfg. Co. v. NLRB (9th Cir. 1974). The last criterion had been the subject of elaboration in an earlier case, Boeing Airplane Co. v. NLRB (9th Cir. 1956), in which the court deemed unprotected concerted activity which

> falls in the classification of a slow-down, sit-down strike, wildcat strike, damage to business or to plant and equipment, trespass, violence, refusal to accept work assignment, physical sabotage, refusal to obey rules and other such activities.

The limitations upon resort to concerted activity go even further. Even if concerted activity is found to fall within the shelter of section 7, such as a peaceful strike in support of requests for a wage increase, it does not follow that the employer is barred from taking *any* measure—such as withholding wages or hiring temporary replacements—which might be said to "interfere" with that employee activity. We shall first consider the question whether certain types of concerted activity fall within or without the shelter of section 7. We shall then consider what countermeasures are available to the employer when confronted with protected concerted activity.

§ 2. "Concerted" Activity for "Mutual" Aid

Most of the reported cases involving employer discipline for exercising section 7 rights deal with employees who are engaged in union solicitation, organization or bargaining and who thus clearly fall within the statutory protection. The statutory protection obtains whether the employees are jointly seeking support for a union, or are jointly criticizing it. See Cooper Tire & Rubber Co. v. NLRB (6th Cir. 1971) (suspension of employees for drafting and circulating petition complaining of performance of union officials). When there is no union on the scene, employee conduct will be protected only if classifiable as "concerted activities for . . . mutual aid or protection." Thus, a spontaneous walkout by a group of employees who believe it is too cold to continue at work is concerted activity for "mutual aid or protection," even though there is no union which speaks for them and even though not one is a union member. NLRB v. Washington Aluminum Co. (U.S.1962). And a strike is protected, although unrelated to union organization, when its purpose is to protest the discharge of a fellow employee, even when the discharge is lawful. NLRB v. Pepsi-Cola Bottling Co. (5th Cir. 1971).

The statutory phrase has given some difficulty in instances where an employer had discharged or otherwise disciplined a single employee who was arguably acting "alone" in his own self-interest rather than in a "concerted" effort for "mutual" aid or protection. The Supreme Court has recently adopted a rather expansive definition of the latter statutory terms. In NLRB v. Weingarten, Inc. (U. S.1975), an employer insisted on interviewing an employee concerning her responsibility for missing company cash and property, in spite of the employee's repeated requests that she be accompanied by a shop steward or other union representative. The Court held that the employee's resistance to interrogation in the absence "of a union representative at an investigatory interview in which the risk of discipline reasonably inheres is within the protective ambit" of section 7, and that the employer's denial of the employee's request violates section 8(a)(1):

> This is true even though the employee alone may have an immediate stake in the outcome; he seeks "aid or protection" against a perceived threat to his employment security. The union representative whose participation he seeks is however safeguarding not only the particular employee's interest, but also the interests of the entire bargaining unit by exercising vigilance to make certain that the employer does not initiate or continue a practice of imposing punishment unjustly. The representative's presence is an assurance to other employees in the bargaining unit that they too can obtain his aid and protection if called upon to attend a like interview.

The Court analogized the case to one in which a group of employees use strike action to support the claim of only a single individual with an immediate stake in the dispute; the strikers know that they will in the future be able to rely on the support of that individual should they ever have a claim of their own. In a related case, the Court held that the discharge or other discipline of an employee for refusing to participate in such an interview without union representation (as opposed to the employer's simple insistence that the employee appear) is also a violation of section 8(a)(1). ILGWU v. Quality Mfg. Co. (U.S.1975).

The Court's analysis in *Weingarten* appears to settle as well the question whether the refusal of an individual employee to cross a picket line of another union set up at another company is to be characterized as "concerted activity for mutual aid or protection." The earlier current of decisions in the courts of appeals justified so treating the picket-line refusal, since the individual placed himself in concert with the picketers as well as with other employees who refused to cross, thus making common cause which one day would redound to his own benefit. It seems clear that the group to which he is lending his support in honoring the picket line need not be his co-employees but may simply be others within the labor movement generally. An employee may thus not be discharged for demonstrating along with employees of another company against discriminatory hiring by that other company. Washington State Serv. Employees (1971). (It should be emphasized here that this discussion relates simply to whether the conduct is "concerted activity for mutual aid or protection"; even conduct so defined may for other reasons be held unprotected, rendering the employee susceptible to discharge.)

The decisions are less clear when there is no group of employees with whom the discharged employee has made common cause. It is not at all certain why the statute protects against discharge only the employee who has engaged in "concerted" activity. The phrase is carried over from the purpose clause of the Norris-LaGuardia Act, the primary aim of which had been to overturn common law concepts of tortious and criminal conspiracy as well as federal antitrust limitations upon combinations and conspiracies in restraint of trade. There is no clear evidence that Congress, in moving to protect employees through sections 7 and 8 against not only injunctions but also employer self-help, intended to exclude from that protection employees who act alone in lodging complaints or in refusing to cross a picket line. Although such conduct was arguably thought not worthy of legislative or administrative concern because *de minimis* or merely selfish, this argument is somewhat difficult to square with the uniform willingness to treat conduct as "concerted" whenever engaged in by as few as two employees.

In any event, an individual employee may complain to the employer or to fellow employees about working conditions; the complaint may or may not relate to conditions common to other employees, and may or may not find substantiation in an existing collective bargaining agreement. The Board has in the past been protective of such individual complaints, at least if they have some potential relevance to the lot of other employees and are not the product of an idiosyncratic selfishness. Even when there is no collective bargaining agreement which furnishes the source of the asserted rights, the Board has treated the employee complaint as representing a preliminary step toward organization, calculated to induce group action to correct the grievance. See Ohio Oil Co. (1951) (protest by two employees against cutback in overtime is within section 7 both because of their number and because they reflected discontent of other employees.) More recently, however, the Board may have given evidence of a trend toward a more strict reading of the "concerted" requirement in such cases. In Maietta Trucking Co. (1971), the Board sustained a discharge of an employee for complaining about as central a working condition as wages:

> No claimed right to a particular wage under law or a collective bargaining contract is presented, nor is the situation one involving presentation of a grievance to a bargaining agent. [Since the driver] . . . was not engaged in protected concerted activities . . . his termination was not in violation of the Act, even if in retaliation for his requesting a wage increase.

The courts of appeals have tended over time also to be rigorous in applying the "concerted activity" test, NLRB v. Buddies Supermarkets, Inc. (5th Cir. 1973) (individual's complaints regarding commission payments), although there appears to be no uniformity. NLRB v. Texas Natural Gas Corp. (5th Cir. 1958) (court upholds discharge of an employee who picketed with an employee discharged the preceding day—and thus not an "employee" within the Act—to induce other employees to protest the discharge); NLRB v. Office Towel Supply Co. (2d Cir. 1953) (gripe about workload by one employee to others "too inchoate" to be protected).

A strong case for section 7 protection is made out when the individual complaint is nurtured by a provision in a collective bargaining agreement, for it is arguable that reliance upon that provision even if only by a single employee furthers the interest of the union and the collective bargaining process, and redounds to the economic benefit of other employees similarly situated. The Board tends so to hold, although there has been a mixed reception in the courts of appeals. In C & I Air Conditioning, Inc. (1971), *enf't denied* (9th Cir. 1973), an employee had complained to his employer on a number of occasions concerning safety hazards on the job, including defective truck equipment and dangerous stairway conditions. For this he was discharged. The Board held the discharge to violate section 8(a)(1), since these unsafe conditions were of concern to all employees and were the subject of provisions in the labor contract; although the employee acted alone and filed no grievance, the discharge was held to discourage collective bargaining and to demonstrate the futility of seeking to enforce the contract. The court of appeals reversed, since the employee's complaints were characterized as relating simply to his own safety. At least one court has approved the position of the Board, which has been characterized as that of "constructive concerted activity." NLRB v. Interboro Contractors (2d Cir. 1967) (complaints by single employee in reasonable belief that contract had been violated is protected, even if no other employees are interested in the issue). But other courts believe that "concerted" activity must at least require preparation for or inducement of group action or "talk looking toward group action." NLRB v. Northern Metal Co. (3d Cir.

1971). In spite of this split of opinion among the circuits, the Board reads the appellate cases strongly to support its protection for individual complaints based on labor-contract provisions. Cray-Burke Co. (1974).

There is much to be said for the *Interboro* principle of "constructive concerted activity," given the lack of any clear reason why section 7 requires "concerted" activity for mutual aid and protection, given the fact that section 7 does not require that activity in support of collective bargaining be concerted, and given the fact that the labor contract is the culmination of the collective bargaining process and is designed to be enforced through measures other than strikes and picketing. In any event, courts and the Board have found protected "concerted" activity when the individual employee asserting a contract violation is a designated union representative, Trailmobile Div., Pullman, Inc. v. NLRB (5th Cir. 1969); or is an employee who invokes the designated contract grievance procedure, NLRB v. Selwyn Shoe Mfg. Corp. (8th Cir. 1970). In a recent Supreme Court case in which several of these elements coalesced, one shop chairlady was discharged and another suspended because of their insistence on representing an employee in an interview with the employer likely to lead to discipline and, as to one of the union representatives, also because she sought to file grievances under the labor contract. The discipline was held to be for protected activity, and reinstatement and backpay sustained. ILGWU v. Quality Mfg. Co. (U.S.1975). Again, it should be noted that individual or group assertion of employee rights may be found to be concerted activity, and yet may be unprotected, for example, because it constitutes an attempt to interfere with the exclusive-representation status of the majority union. See Emporium Capwell Co. v. Western Addition Community Org'n (U.S. 1975). This issue will be discussed in greater detail below.

Even if employee conduct is found to be "concerted" there are some cases which raise the question whether it is for "mutual aid or protection." As noted above, the picket-line cases find such "mutual" aid when an individual employee from one company refuses to cross a picket line at another company. It has also been held that employees engage in protected activity when they announce support for a work stoppage at another company, NLRB v. Peter Cailler Kohler Swiss Choc. Co. (2d Cir. 1942); when they take up contributions for another company's agricultural workers, who are not even within the statutory definition of "employees," General Elec. Co. (1968); and when they (or a single employee) engage in demonstrations in protest of the discriminatory hiring policies of another employer, Washington State Serv. Employees (1971). Using a rationale difficult to reconcile with these decisions, a court of appeals has reversed a Board decision that employees are engaged in protected activity when they complain of the decisions of a credit union comprised exclusively of company employees but operated independently of the company. The court held that to be protected the protest must concern a matter having a reasonable relation to conditions of employment and on which the employees' company has some control and some power and right to ameliorate. G & W Elec. Specialty Co. v. NLRB (7th Cir. 1966). To the extent that the court may have been concerned with employee pressures directed against the employer on a matter which falls without "terms and conditions of employment," the decision might better have been explained as one in which the concerted activity was for "mutual aid" but was otherwise unprotected.

§ 3.   Concerted Activity Unprotected Because of Objective: Generally

Even though employee activities are found to be in the cause of organization or bargaining, or for other mutual aid or protection, such activities may be held unprotected, either because the employees' objective is thought to be reprehensible, typically because contrary to the terms or spirit of the Labor Act, or because the means employed for carrying out the concerted design are thought to be indefensible. Nowhere in the statute is it stated that employee activity shall be deemed unprotected for these reasons. The Board and the courts have over time developed a "common law" under section 7, much as the common law courts in injunction actions had held conduct to be tortious or not depending upon an unguided appraisal of the employees' means and objectives. Although the development of this Board-made "common law" is not altogether without statutory inspiration, there are a number of decisions—some of them of the Supreme Court—which arguably go rather far toward condemning concerted activities as unprotected simply because they are thought to be vaguely "unfair," or to impose "undue" pressures upon the employer. Exactly what makes these pressures so, and what gives the Board or the courts authority to declare them unprotected by section 7, is articulated rarely if at all. Since such decisions affect the kinds of countermeasures the employer may use in the face of such activities, they can very significantly shape the outcome of collective bargaining in particular cases. While it is arguable that it is for Congress—rather than for the Board or the courts—to draw the line between allowed and disallowed action and reaction, as it has done in writing the unfair labor practice provisions of the Act, it is too late in the day to question the authority of the Board and courts to engage in the very important "lawmaking" process of developing classes of unprotected activity.

It is, for example, well established that concerted activity loses the protection of section 7 if its objective is either to compel the employer to violate section 8(a) of the Labor Act, or is such that the union would be responsible for an unfair labor practice under section 8(b). Both of these rationales converge in a case in which employees engage in a strike designed to force the employer to discharge an employee solely because he has spoken out against the union or has neglected to attend union meetings. The object is to force the employer to violate section 8(a)(3) and the union's endorsement violates section 8(b)(2); it is thought inconsistent with the purposes of those sections of the Act to hold that employees participating in such a strike should be sheltered against discharge or other discipline.

Either of these two objectionable acts—inducing an employer unfair labor practice or participating in the commission of a union unfair labor practice—will normally suffice to render employee conduct unprotected. Thus, even before it was declared an unfair labor practice for an insurgent union to strike or picket in support of a demand for recognition when the employer was already dealing with a certified union, employees engaging in such activity were held subject to discharge. Although the activity was not prohibited by law, it was held unprotected, since the object of the union was to compel the employer to violate the Act by bargaining with a union other than the certified union thereby interfering with the rights of the majority. Thompson Prods., Inc. (1947). Similarly unprotected is a boycott designed to force the employer to recognize one of two unions presently on the ballot in a pending election. Hoover Co. v. NLRB (6th Cir. 1951) (employer recognition would violate section 8(a)(1) under the *Midwest Piping* doctrine). It has also been held that concerted activity may become unprotected when its object is to compel the employer to violate a law other than the National Labor Relations Act. Thus, in American News Co. (1944), a strike to compel the employer to grant an immediate wage increase was held unprotected because the Emergency Price Control Act of 1942 forbade wage increases prior to approval by the National War Labor Board.

§ 4.   The Union Unfair Labor Practice

Even if the employer would not violate any law by succumbing to the union's concerted pressures, employees may still lose their protection against employer self-help when their conduct would, had it been endorsed by a union, be such as to render the union liable to unfair labor practice charges. Thus, a union violates its duty to bargain in good faith when it induces a strike to force the employer to concede on a subject which is not a "term or condition of employment." See NLRB v. Wooster Div. of Borg-Warner Corp. (U.S. 1958). It has accordingly been held that employees lose the protection of section 7 when they exert pressure upon the employer concerning an item which is thought not directly to touch the employment relationship but rather to be a "management prerogative."

Frequently litigated, for example, is the employee protest against an employer decision to hire, discharge, replace or transfer a particular supervisory employee. The law in the area is not at all clear. Occasionally, there is a difficult issue of fact as to whether the employee protest was addressed to the change in supervisors or was rather in response to other objectionable working conditions more clearly within the statutory definition of jointly bargainable subjects.

So too, when the employees are unorganized and the protest spontaneous; courts sometimes find the employee protest unprotected more because of the means used (for example, an unannounced work stoppage rather than a letter or oral protest) than because of the status of the supervisor. Henning & Cheadle, Inc. v. NLRB (7th Cir. 1975). What can be said with confidence is that the Board tends to classify a protest concerning the identity of at least a low-level supervisor as protected, while the courts have tended to disagree. The position of the Board was articulated in Plastilite Corp. (1965), *mdf'd on other grounds* (8th Cir. 1967):

> We have consistently held . . . that conditions of employment are involved, and a "labor dispute" exists, if the supervisor's identity and capability have an impact on the employees' job interests . . . While we do not hold that employees may act concertedly to protest the appointment or termination of every supervisor, even a top-level management representative, it is our opinion that [invoking Dobbs Houses, Inc. (1962)] . . . "Where . . . facts establish that the identity and capability of the supervisor involved has [sic] a direct impact on the employees' own job interests and on their performance of the work they are hired to do, they are legitimately concerned with his identity. Therefore, strike or other concerted action which evidence the employees' concern is no less protected than any other strike which employees may undertake in pursuit of a mutual interest in the improvement of their conditions of employment."

The Board in *Plastilite* found a strike protected "[b]ecause of the diligent manner in which Lucore [the working supervisor] performed his duties, the willingness with which he assisted other employees, and the aid he gave the employees in helping them meet their quotas." The apparently prevailing principle in the courts of appeals is that the identity of a supervisory employee is a management prerogative, is not a bargainable issue, and any resulting protest is not for the "mutual aid or protection" of the employees. *E. g.*, American Art Clay Co. v. NLRB (7th Cir. 1964) (change in foreman linked to speed-up in production).

Even the Board is likely to find employee pressures unprotected when their object is to protest an employer decision concerning a high-level supervisor or of any supervisor who represents the employer in collective bargaining or grievance adjustment. This result is buttressed by section 8(b)(1)(B), which makes it an unfair labor practice for a union to "restrain or coerce . . . an employer in the selection of his representatives for the purposes of collective bargaining or the adjustment of grievances." See Communications Workers Local 2550 (1972) (employee walkout protesting failure to transfer supervisor violates section 8(b)(1)(B), even though part of the object was to protest working conditions; unfair labor practice decision not governed by tests for "protected" activities under section 7 and 8(a), but would be unprotected in any event, since the walkout was unreasonably disruptive particularly in light of available grievance and arbitration procedures).

Employees also forfeit the protection of section 7 when, although the employer would not violate the law by acceding to their demands, they strike with the object of altering contract terms without complying with the notice and "cooling off" provisions of section 8(d) of the Labor Act. Local 1113, United Elec. Workers v. NLRB (Marathon Elec. Mfg. Corp.) (D.C.Cir. 1955). Here, the result is much more clearly mandated by statute, for section 8(d) expressly provides: "Any employee who engages in a strike within any notice period . . . shall lose his status as an employee" and is thus subject to discharge with impunity. (This loss of protection has, however, been held not to result when the strike during the statutory sixty-day period is in protest of a significant employer unfair labor practice rather than of contract or bargaining terms. Mastro Plastics Corp. v. NLRB (U.S.1956).)

Many of the cases discussed above put what is perhaps an undue premium upon the employees' full gathering of facts and accurate assessment of what are frequently very complex legal questions. The employee becomes susceptible to discharge if, for example, he is not aware of his union's failure to give the requisite notice to federal and state mediation agencies or if he fails accurately to determine whether a discharged supervisor is sufficiently high or low level or whether a picket line he honors is primary or secondary. It is thus arguable that employees who engage in concerted activities for which the union may be held in violation of section 8(b) ought not automatically forfeit their own section 7 protection. This is especially true when the violation is a close or complex one and the employees were, without counsel, merely obedient to a union signal and acting with a good faith belief of the legality of their union's activities. There appear, however, to be no cases which adopt such a position. The Board, however, has made an effort to confine its definition of unprotected activity in these cases to conduct which squarely violates section 8(b), without condemning other related activity which is arguably protected. See Claremont Polychem. Corp. (1972) (employees unprotected when engaging in recognition picketing shortly after election in violation of section 8(b)(7)(B), but their strike for recognition is not prohibited and is indeed protected pursuant to section 13 of the Labor Act).

§ 5.   Concerted Activity Unprotected Because of Method of Protest: Violation of Federal Law

As one might imagine, the fact that industrial sabotage is carried out in the name of concerted activity for improved wages and working conditions will not render the employees immune from discharge or other discipline. The Board and the courts will find employee activity unprotected when the means utilized are characterized as illegal, reprehensible, indefensible, disloyal or inconsistent with the terms or spirit of the Labor Act.

Thus, it appears never to have been seriously questioned that, no matter how laudable the object, a secondary boycott within section 8(b)(4) is barred by the Act, and the employees so engaged are subject to discharge. The same is true when employees strike over the application or modification of the terms of a labor contract either in violation of the notice provisions of section 8(d), Mastro Plastics Corp. v. NLRB (U.S.1956), or in violation of a no-strike promise in the contract, NLRB v. Sands Mfg. Co. (U.S.1939). Cf. Local 174, Teamsters v. Lucas Flour Co. (U.S.1962) (federal law requires that a no-strike promise be implied in a labor contract in congruence with an express arbitration provision). The Supreme Court has held, however, that even the no-strike provisions of section 8(d) and of a labor contract should normally not be understood to render a strike unprotected if its purpose is to protest employer unfair labor practices rather than to extract economic concessions. Mastro Plastics Corp. v. NLRB (U.S.1956). The Board has since purported to narrow the *Mastro Plastics* exception so that even an unfair labor practice strike will be held unprotected because of section 8(d) or a contractual no-strike promise unless the employer unfair labor practice being protested is sufficiently serious and flagrant as to undermine the status of the union or the collective bargaining agreement. This limitation was announced in Arlan's Dep't Store (1961), which held a strike in violation of a no-strike agreement to be unprotected when the employer unfair labor practice, a discharge, was isolated and the product merely of a clash of personalities, and when redress for the discharge was available under the grievance and arbitration provisions of the contract. (This restriction upon the doctrine of *Mastro Plastics* has hardly ever been applied by the Board.)

In spite of this prevailing condemnation—as unprotected activity—of strikes in breach of contractual no-strike clauses, another exception is made when the walkout is in response to unsafe working conditions. This exception is rooted in section 502 of the Labor Act, enacted as part of the Taft-Hartley Act in 1947. That section provides that "the quitting of labor by an employee or employees in good faith because of abnormally dangerous conditions for work at the place of employment . . . [shall not] be deemed a strike under this Act." The Board, with court approval, has read section 502 to dictate the conclusion that such a good faith work stoppage because of "abnormally dangerous conditions for work" is also outside the ban of a contractual no-strike provision and is in spite of that ban protected activity for which the employees may not be discharged. Knight Morley Corp. (1956), enf'd (6th Cir. 1957). But even here, one may assume that the employees' fear, to render the stoppage protected, must rest not merely upon good faith but also upon "ascertainable, objective evidence." See Gateway Coal Co. v. UMW (U.S.1974) (construing section 502 in the context of an employer action to enjoin a work stoppage, assertedly because of unsafe conditions, which was in breach of an implied no-strike clause; Court holds injunction proper in spite of good-faith employee fear that supervisors assigned to coal mine would tolerate unsafe ventilation conditions).

Moreover, as is true in cases where the employees' objective contravenes federal legislation other than the Labor Act, concerted activity has been held unprotected when the means employed violate federal law even though that law is addressed to conduct rather far removed from the field of labor relations. A closely divided Supreme Court balanced the policies of section 7 and of the federal criminal code outlawing mutiny when it held, in Southern S.S. Co. v. NLRB (U.S.1942), that a strike on board ship and a refusal to follow orders were unprotected, although the ship was in port, the strike was peaceful and the strikers did not interfere with work carried on by other employees. The Court held that the NLRB in enforcing the provisions of the Labor Act should seek to effect an accommodation with other Congressional objectives. (It went on to hold that, since the strike was triggered by employer unfair labor practices, the Board had the power to reinstate the strikers as a remedy for the initial employer violations, but that such reinstatement in the circumstances of the case would not effectuate the purposes of the Labor Act.) *But see* Hamilton v. NLRB (6th Cir. 1947) (strike without notice, in violation of War Labor Disputes Act governing war production, does not oust Wagner Act protections for strikers, in light of WLDA legislative history).

§ 6. "Wildcat" and Other Minority Protests

When employees are not represented by a union, the fact that only a small group of employees in the plant engage in concerted activity does not of itself deprive that activity of section 7 protection. NLRB v. Washington Aluminum Co. (U.S.1962) (unorganized employees protest cold temperatures in plant). When, however, employees have selected an exclusive representative to bargain with their employer, concerted activity on the part of a minority of employees, not formally authorized by the union, is commonly held unprotected. (A strike in such a case is termed a "wildcat".) While such conduct falls within the literal coverage of section 7—concerted activity for mutual aid—it has been thought to be inconsistent with the philosophy of exclusive representation embodied in the Labor Act: control over bargaining, and the use of economic force as an incident thereof, should be centralized in the union, which must adjust conflicts among individuals and minority interests within the bargaining unit and speak with a single voice to the employer. In effect minority pressure to induce concessions from the employer constitutes compulsion of the employer to bargain not with the exclusive representative but directly with employees and "over the head" of the union—employer conduct which would violate section 8(a)(5) of the Act. Medo Photo Supply Corp. v. NLRB (U.S.1944). Such minority activity is also thought objectionable because it is frequently the product of intraunion dissension and is designed to protest and to induce a change in the position of the union rather than (or as well as) of the employer, and it is thought unsound thus to embroil the employer in a dispute "not its own." While this minority action is in most instances, by definition, not an unfair labor practice—since this would require attribution of wrongful conduct to a "labor organization" rather than to individual dissidents—it is unprotected and the employer may secure redress through discharge or lesser discipline.

This principle has been developed over the years in Board and appellate decisions, and has recently been endorsed by the Supreme Court in what is perhaps its most severe test: peaceful picketing and leafletting, without the authorization of the bargaining representative, by dissident employees charging the employer with racially discriminatory hiring policies.

An early and leading case which declared the wildcat strike to be unprotected activity is NLRB v. Draper Corp. (4th Cir. 1944). There, the employer discharged a minority faction of employees who had gone on strike, without the sanction of the bargaining representative, in protest of employer delays in the negotiation of a new labor contract. Sustaining the discharges, the Board noted that "Just as a minority has no right to enter into separate bargaining arrangements with the employer, so it has no right to take independent action to interfere with the course of bargaining which is being carried on by the duly authorized bargaining agent chosen by the majority." A court of appeals also found to be unprotected a work stoppage by 50 of 120 employees in the unit (the number-counting issue was, however, itself a subject of dispute), without the authorization of the certified union, just prior to a vote to be conducted among the unit employees on the acceptability of the employer's last bargaining offer. NLRB v. Sunbeam Lighting Co. (7th Cir. 1963). The prevailing rule was, however, liberalized somewhat in Western Contracting Corp. v. NLRB (10th Cir. 1963), where a spontaneous strike initiated by a minority faction concerned an issue over which the union had already protested, and the prompt ratification of the minority strike by the union and a majority of the employees converted it from its wildcat status; the walkout thus did not derogate from the position of the union as exclusive representative and was not in violation of the collective agreement. Earlier cases were distinguished and the discharges held to violate section 8(a)(3).

This decision set the stage for a wide departure from the "wildcat" principle, in NLRB v. R. C. Can Co. (5th Cir. 1964). There, a small group of employees, against the general consensus within the majority union, stopped work and picketed in order to pressure the employer to expedite ongoing negotiations with the union. The court found the activity protected and the employer's discipline (in effect, a two-week layoff) a violation of the Act. The court held the action of the minority to be in overall support for and acceptance of union policy rather than an expression of disagreement with or repudiation of the union's goals and methods in the collective bargaining process; thus, the employer was not forced to choose between conflicting demands of the union and the minority employee group. Other courts, however, held wildcat protests unprotected in spite of congruence with the union's efforts. NLRB v. Sunset Minerals, Inc. (9th Cir. 1954). While the Board has been somewhat hospitable toward the *R. C. Can* rationale for protecting minority concerted activity, the court which announced it has since narrowed the reach of that decision, in a case involving spontaneous and unauthorized minority activity in support of an apparent union objective of securing reinstatement for a discharged employee. That court stated, in NLRB v. Shop Rite Foods, Inc. (5th Cir. 1970):

> R. C. Can concerned a very narrow set of circumstances in which the minority action was directed toward a specific, previously considered and articulated union objective. If union objectives are characterized in general terms—such as wages, job security, conditions of employment and the like —one can assume that in a great majority of instances minority action will be consistent with one or more of those objectives. If R. C. Can is not applied with great care it would allow minority action in a broad range of situations and permit unrestrained undercutting of collective bargaining.

More recently, another court of appeals has rejected *R. C. Can* outright, because of the need better to accommodate the policies of section 7 with those of section 9(a), particularly as the latter section sustains the capacity of the majority union to "waive" the rights to protest which might otherwise be asserted by wildcat groups. Lee A. Consaul Co. v. NLRB (9th Cir. 1972).

The treatment of minority protests as unprotected has recently been sorely tested—and sustained—in the context of concerted activity by dissident employees directed at alleged racial discrimination by the employer. In NLRB v. Tanner Motor Livery, Ltd. (9th Cir. 1969), two employees without consulting with the union or securing its authorization engaged in picketing with the object of protesting allegedly discriminatory practices. The employees were discharged, and the Board held the employees to have been engaging in protected activity; the union was assumed to have agreed with their protest against illegal discrimination by the employer, such that the union's status as exclusive representative could not be deemed to have been "infringed, imperiled, or otherwise undermined." The court of appeals reversed, rejecting the rationale of *R. C. Can.* The court read recent Supreme Court decisions on the power of unions to fine or expel members as evidencing a concern for resolving intraunion policy disputes through internal democratic union procedures, such that the union can confront the employer at the bargaining table with a single voice and the employer can rely on allegiance of all within the union for the position espoused by that union. "The concept of orderly bargaining premised upon democratic union processes" was thought to render the unauthorized picketing unprotected.

The Supreme Court more recently reached the same conclusion, invoking a similar but somewhat more limited rationale. In Emporium Capwell Co. v. Western Addition Community Organization (U.S. 1975), the employer and union were bound by a contract which forbade racial discrimination in employment and established a grievance and arbitration procedure for the resolution of contract disputes. The union, during the contract term, levelled charges of race discrimination against the employer, held meetings with representatives of the company and of pertinent government agencies, and initiated the grievance procedure. Several employees, however, expressed their discontent with the propriety of individual grievances to remedy a pervasive employer wrong, and ultimately called a press conference and engaged in leafletting and picketing at the company premises, demanding all the while that the company president meet with them to discuss the improvement of minority employment conditions. Two of the dissidents were discharged. The Board found the discharges not to violate section 8(a)(1), but the court of appeals reversed, holding that the principle of exclusive representation could properly be subordinated to the strong national policy demanding the prompt elimination of employment discrimination. The Supreme Court reversed in turn, basing its decision on the Board's finding that the discharged employees had used concerted activity in order to compel the employer to "bargain" with them rather than with the designated bargaining representative. The Court held the Labor Act to accord exclusively to the majority union the power to "bargain" and to eliminate altogether attempts at bargaining by individuals or factions for which the union was obligated (and privileged) to speak. The Court noted that the union was already utilizing the grievance procedure available under the contract, and that attempts by groups of employees (whose claims will often be mutually antagonistic) to bypass that procedure would not only likely exacerbate racial tensions but would in any event exert undue pressure upon the employer to circumvent its obligation to bargain exclusively with the incumbent union.

The Court also rejected the argument of the court of appeals—and thereby apparently the premise of the *R. C. Can* decision as well—that the dissidents could not have been working at cross-purposes with the union which is required by law to combat racial discrimination in employment:

> This argument confuses the employees' substantive right to be free of racial discrimination with the procedures available under the NLRA for securing these rights. . . . [These rights] cannot be pursued at the expense of the orderly collective-bargaining process contemplated by the NLRA. . . . [A]n employer may have no objection to incorporating into a collective agreement the substance of his obligation not to discriminate in personnel decisions . . . . But that does not mean that he may not have strong and legitimate objections to bargaining on several fronts over the implementation of the right to be free of discrimination. . . . Similarly, while a union cannot lawfully bargain for the establishment or continuation of discriminatory practices . . . it has a legitimate interest in presenting a united front on this as on other issues and in not seeing its strength dissipated and its stature denigrated by sub-groups within the unit separately pursuing what they see as separate interests.

While the Court rested its holding of unprotected activity on the factual finding that the dissident employees sought to "bargain" with the employer, it also suggested that minority concerted activity would have been unprotected even if it was in support of a "grievance" (concerning which the Labor Act gives individual employees greater privileges than in the case of bargaining). The Court's emphasis upon the principle of exclusive representation, and upon the need to channel the views of all factions within the unit through the majority union, reinforces the prevailing view since the early 1940's that wildcat concerted activities are unprotected and render the participants susceptible to discharge.

§ 7. Methods Forbidden by State Law

It is commonly understood that employees lose the protection of section 7 when they engage in violence, assault and trespass in contravention of clearly applicable state criminal and tort law. In one of the early Supreme Court decisions under the Wagner Act, NLRB v. Fansteel Metallurgical Corp. (U.S.1939), the employees, in response to employer unfair labor practices, had physically occupied the plant by staging a sitdown strike at their work places; the trespass and violence to the employer's property continued in the face of a state-court injunction. The Court held this conduct to render the employees amenable to discharge. While today the result would be explained by the distinction between protected and unprotected activities under section 7, the Court rather relied on section 2(3) of the Wagner Act and concluded that strikers remained "employees" under that section only when the strike was legal and was not characterized by the use of illegal force. (This rationale appears no longer to be utilized in the reported cases.) The Court also held that while the discharges did not violate the Act, the Board could unless arbitrary and unreasonable require the employer to hire back the strikers as a remedy for the unfair labor practices which triggered the strike.

Although the "sitdown" strike has since *Fansteel* been branded as unprotected because illegal under state law, there will be the occasional borderline case where the issue of trespass is sufficiently close that rather than state law supplying the touchstone for determining whether concerted activity is unprotected, federal law will demand a determination that the conduct is protected and that any contrary state-law principles must be preempted. In just such a close case, a court of appeals has recently—without dealing with the issue of preemption of state law—held the principle of *Fansteel* inapplicable to a "sit-in" by ninety-seven employees who were protesting the discharge of co-workers; the employees refused to leave upon the request of the employer but did so when police were summoned, and did no violence or damage to plant equipment. The court held the sit-in not to be per se unprotected, and held the employees immune from discharge since there was no violence, no interference with nonstrikers and no "claim to hold the premises in defiance of the owner's right of possession." NLRB v. Pepsi-Cola Bottling Co. (5th Cir. 1971). Where there does exist such violence, interference and claim to possession, state law will not be preempted and the conduct will be unprotected; but short of that, it is merely question-begging to argue that state law brands concerted activity "illegal" and thus causes the forfeiture of section 7 protection.

§ 8. "Irresponsible" or "Indefensible" Methods

Closely related to the *Fansteel* principle is that which holds unprotected an employee protest which, while not trespassory, is so timed as to create a risk of injury to the employer's physical plant or equipment. For example, in NLRB v. Marshall Car Wheel Co. (5th Cir. 1955), the employees staged an unannounced walkout at a time when molten iron was being contained in a cupola and prolonged retention there would have caused costly damage to plant equipment. The court branded the conduct "irresponsible" and held it unprotected. It is interesting to note that even earlier, the Board had held that, quite apart from the protected or unprotected status of similar employee activity, the employer would not be found to violate section 8(a)(3) of the Act by "defensively" locking out its employees in anticipation of such a critically timed work stoppage; the lockout was deemed in furtherance of legitimate business ends. Duluth Bottling Ass'n (1943) (lockout to prevent sudden work stoppage resulting in spoilage of materials); Betts Cadillac Olds, Inc. (1951) (lockout to avert immobilization of automobiles brought in for repair). The

Board goes beyond these decisions when it finds these employee activities to be unprotected, for this permits the employer to discharge or otherwise discipline the employees without any business justification whatever. It is perhaps understandable that the Board should so hold in cases in which the employees create serious risks of harm or spoilage to company equipment or goods. Compare NLRB v. Leprino Cheese Co. (10th Cir. 1970) (work stoppage while converting milk to cheese, held protected; no real danger to property, though quality and value of cheese suffers).

But it has been easy to slide from the proposition that such unprotected activity is "indefensible" or "irresponsible" or "unduly offensive" in light of the union's goals, to the proposition that all activity which can be so characterized ought to be held unprotected. Thus, several cases which consider the propriety of employee protests concerning the hiring, discharge or transfer of a supervisor suggest that courts will find the protest protected if it is done by discussion or correspondence with the employer; but that it will be deemed unprotected when in the form of a work stoppage, particularly when the stoppage is unannounced and is at a peculiarly busy time of the workday. E. g., Dobbs Houses, Inc. v. NLRB (5th Cir. 1963). Apart from the threat or actuality of harm to person or property, it is not at all clear that the protection of section 7 should be ousted when employees, in pursuit of an object relating to a "term or condition of employment," engage in a protest which is unannounced, or is timed for maximum inconvenience to or impact upon the employer, or is otherwise somehow "incommensurate" to the subject matter of the protest. The Supreme Court spoke to this issue in NLRB v. Washington Aluminum Co. (U.S.1962). There, several organized employees had individually complained to the employer about the cold working conditions in the shop, and spontaneously agreed to walk off the job on a particularly cold day. The Court held:

> We cannot agree that employees necessarily lose their right to engage in concerted activities under § 7 merely because they do not present a specific demand upon their employer to remedy a condition they find objectionable. The language of § 7 is broad enough to protect concerted activities whether they take place before, after, or at the same time such a demand is made.

The Court also stated that subject to certain long-recognized restrictions—such as concerted activity which is unlawful, violent, in breach of contract, or disloyal—the issue of protection ought not turn upon an evaluation whether the decision by the employees to utilize concerted protest was or was not reasonable:

> The fact that the company was already making every effort to repair the furnace and bring heat into the shop that morning does not change the nature of the controversy that

caused the walkout. At the very most, that fact might tend to indicate that the conduct of the men in leaving was unnecessary and unwise, and it has long been settled that the reasonableness of workers' decisions to engage in concerted activity is irrelevant to the determination of whether a labor dispute exists or not.

The Board has seized upon this language to state a flat principle that, subject to the four well-recognized exceptions (noted in *Washington Aluminum*), the application of section 7 "does not depend on the *manner* in which the employees choose to press the dispute, but rather on the *matter* they are protesting." Plastilite Corp. (1965), *mdf'd on other grounds* (8th Cir. 1967). The Board there endorsed the view that ". . . we are unable to conclude that ill judgment or lack of consideration add up to illegality," and asserted that it is improper to pass upon the employees' "manner and time of making their protest." It repudiated the principle adopted by most of the courts in cases relating to protest about supervisory positions:

> [W]e must respectfully disagree with any rule which would base the determination of whether a strike is protected upon its reasonableness in relation to the subject matter of the "labor dispute."

§ 9. Insubordination and Disloyalty

Even though an employee or group of employees present or argue to the employer a cause that is normally within the scope of statutory protection, the presentation may be in a sufficiently abusive or insubordinate manner as to warrant discipline in accordance with industrial traditions. There is no clear dividing line between a "dressing down" by an employee which must be tolerated under section 7 of the Labor Act and one which crosses the line of insubordination, but it is the task of the National Labor Relations Board to draw that line, and its decision will be sustained if supported by substantial evidence on the record considered as a whole. A recent example of such a case is American Tel. & Tel. Co. v. NLRB (2d Cir. 1975), in which an employee, the union's representative in processing grievances, loudly and in the presence of other employees harangued a supervisor concerning certain data turned over by the supervisor in connection with a number of pending grievances. A disciplinary warning from the employer led to the issuance of a complaint under section 8(a)(1), which was dismissed by the administrative law judge but sustained by the Board. On review, the court of appeals acknowledged that it could readily have accepted the decision of the administrative law judge that the employee was properly disciplined for her rudeness; yet it felt constrained to enforce the Board's order to the contrary:

> A certain amount of salty language or defiance will be tolerated in bargaining sessions with respect to grievances, in

recognition of the fact that the sessions are usually held behind closed doors and "that passions run high in labor disputes and that epithets and accusations are commonplace" . . . . However, if the employee's conduct becomes so flagrant that it threatens the employer's ability to maintain order and respect in the conduct of his business, it will not be protected. . . . The responsibility for applying this balancing test, depending as it does so heavily on the facts in a particular case, rests with the Board, whose decision, if supported by substantial evidence, will not be disturbed unless it is arbitrary or illogical.

Another major category of concerted activity commonly held unprotected, for reasons much like those relating to insubordination, is conduct characterized as "disloyalty" to the employer. The basic text for the disloyalty doctrine is the Supreme Court decision in the so-called *Jefferson Standard* case, NLRB v. IBEW Local 1229 (U.S. 1953). There, employees were involved in a negotiating dispute with the Jefferson Standard Broadcasting Company concerning the renewal of an arbitration clause in the forthcoming labor contract, and the employees while still on the payroll and during their off-duty hours distributed to the public handbills which sharply criticized the quality of programming on the employer's television station. The handbills made no mention of a union, of collective bargaining, or of the disputed arbitration provision. The employer's discharge of these employees was held by the Court not to violate section 8(a)(3). The Court found that the employees' attack on the employer was "disloyal," that section 10(c) of the Labor Act bars reinstatement of one who is discharged for "cause," and that "There is no more elemental cause for discharge of an employee than disloyalty to his employer. . . . The legal principle that insubordination, disobedience or disloyalty is adequate cause for discharge is plain enough." Had the employees so acted in the absence of a labor dispute, no one would doubt that the discharge was proper, and the "fortuity of the coexistence of a labor dispute affords these technicians no substantial defense." The Court's analysis of disloyalty and cause stressed three features of the employee handbilling: (1) The handbills made no explicit reference to a labor dispute; (2) the company policies attacked in the handbill related to finance and public relations "for which management, not technicians, must be responsible"; and (3) the workers were on the company payroll and thus were obliged to protect the employer's interests.

The logic of *Jefferson Standard* is not compelling and its reach unclear. The Court borrowed the concept of "cause" from disputes arising under labor contracts, sources arguably inapt when the issue is the scope of statutory rights. As a dissenting Justice pointed out, even concededly protected activity such as refusing to work and branding the employer unfair would be "disloyal" or "cause" for discipline in the absence of a labor dispute; to label the coexisting labor dispute no more than "fortuitous" is to beg the question. But assuming the soundness of the "disloyalty" test, its reach is unclear because of the admixture of factual elements found to render the employees' conduct disloyal in *Jefferson Standard*. For example, in a subsequent case which arguably presented none of the three factual elements noted above, the Board relied on *Jefferson Standard* to hold unprotected the distribution by striking paint-company employees of circulars giving notice of the strike and warning that paint produced by temporary strike replacements might be of inferior quality. Patterson Sargent Co. (1956). The attack on the product was thought sufficiently disloyal, although the employees were on strike and not being paid, gave notice of the labor dispute, and stated that the quality of the product would return to normal once the dispute was resolved. In any event, a court has also stigmatized as indefensible, disloyal and illegal—and thus unprotected—efforts by an employee in the course of a labor dispute to serve as an employment agent to secure work for his fellow employees with competitor employers. Boeing Airplane Co. v. NLRB (9th Cir. 1956) (citing common law cases supporting employer cause of action for soliciting away employees).

Cases decided since *Jefferson Standard* may suggest that the reach of the disloyalty doctrine is becoming increasingly confined. In NLRB v. Washington Aluminum Co. (U.S.1962), involving a spontaneous walkout of employees in protest against extremely cold working conditions, the Supreme Court rejected the employer argument that an established plant rule forbidding employees to leave work without permission of the foreman rendered the walkout "cause" for discharge. Its reasoning may suggest that, while *Jefferson Standard* looks to industrial rules and traditions to determine "cause" unaffected by the "fortuity" of the coexistence of a labor dispute, the Court might now make an independent determination whether concerted activity should be protected unaffected by the coexistence of company rules and traditions which would treat that activity as "cause" for discipline. And the Board, in Edir, Inc. (1966), has reiterated the position that the fact that employees report for work and remain on the payroll is not in itself sufficient to render disloyal and thus unprotected after-hours picketing. The picketing communicates to the public information concerning the labor dispute, and protection is not lost even if the picketing impairs the image or income of the employer. The Board analogized the employee conduct to solicitation for the union on nonworking time which is, even when carried out on company property, clearly protected activity. Compare Plastilite Corp. (1965), *mdf'd on other grounds* (8th Cir. 1967) (concerted protest not rendered unprotected because means appear "unreasonable" in relation to subject matter of dispute).

Nonetheless, notions of employee disloyalty have been found relevant in determining whether or not to protect certain classes of conduct: (1) Criticism of the employer which proves to be false; (2) Unannounced and sporadic (or "quickie") work stoppages; (3) Refusals to cross picket lines at other places of business.

§ 10. False Accusations Against the Employer

An employer will on occasion discharge or discipline an employee who has, typically in the course of engaging in unionization or grievance processing or other generally protected activity, communicated to other employees information about the employer which proves to be false. Of course, if the false and defamatory statement is only a pretext for a discharge which is in truth based on other protected activity or on a desire to discourage union activity, section 8(a)(3) has been violated and the employee will be reinstated. NLRB v. Symons Mfg. Co. (7th Cir. 1964). And, even if the discharge is indeed based on the employer's belief that false and defamatory statements were made by the employee when in fact they were not, the discharge is unlawful in spite of the employer's good faith. Cusano v. NLRB (3d Cir. 1951) (protection for employee activities should not turn on employer's state of mind). Compare NLRB v. Burnup & Sims, Inc. (U. S.1964) (in spite of good faith belief that discharged employees had threatened to use dynamite to bring union into plant, which was not true, discharge violates section 8(a)(1) even if arguably not 8(a)(3)).

When, however, the discharge is for false and defamatory statements actually made by the employee in the course of unionization, collective bargaining or grievance processing, the law is not altogether clear. The Board has rather consistently held that even false statements do not lose their protection under section 7 unless they have been made maliciously or with knowledge of their falsity; but the few court decisions have not uniformly endorsed this view. See Atlantic Towing Co. (1948), *enf't denied* (5th Cir. 1950) (although Board found employee statement regarding employer preference for one of two unions to have been unintentional or negligent misstatement, court sustained discharge irrespective of employee knowledge of falsity); Bowling Green Mfg. Co. (1968), *enf't denied* (6th Cir. 1969) (although Board found employee radio statements protected because not deliberately or maliciously false, and discharge a violation of section 8(a)(1) in spite of employer belief of deliberate falsehood, court found the employee statements unprotected in large measure because untrue).

The most recent cases may indicate a growing judicial endorsement of the Board's more permissive attitude toward employee communications. Thus, in NLRB v. Cement Transp., Inc. (6th Cir. 1974), the court agreed with the Board that certain employee statements (made during organizing efforts) concerning employer bribery of union officials and employer retention of moneys earned by company drivers were not cause for discharge, even if untrue, because they were not "indefensible or reckless."

> In the context of a struggle to organize a union, "the most repulsive speech enjoys immunity provided it falls short of a deliberate or reckless untruth," so long as the allegedly offensive actions are directly related to activities protected by the Act and are not so egregious as to be considered indefensible. Linn v. United Plant Guard Workers Local 114, 383 U.S. 53, 61 (1966) . . . .

See also Owens-Corning Fibreglas Corp. v. NLRB (4th Cir. 1969) (minor misstatements are unprotected only if deliberately or maliciously false). The Board's approach has been referred to approvingly by the Supreme Court in a recent decision sheltering the use of nonmalicious epithets in union organizing campaigns. In Old Dominion Branch 496, Letter Carriers v. Austin (U.S.1974), the Court stated:

> Vigorous exercise of this right "to persuade other employees to join" must not be stifled by the threat of liability for the overenthusiastic use of rhetoric or the innocent mistake of fact. Thus, the Board his concluded that statements of fact or opinion relevant to a union organizing campaign are protected by § 7, even if they are defamatory and prove to be erroneous, unless made with knowledge of their falsity. See, e. g., Atlantic Towing Co., 75 N.L.R.B. 1169, 1171–1173 (1948) . . . .

(It may be significant that the Court failed to note that the Board's order in *Atlantic Towing* was denied enforcement by the court of appeals.)

§ 11. Intermittent Work Stoppages; Slowdowns

Employees will on occasion seek to effect a legitimate object by engaging in intermittent and unannounced work stoppages, or in "slowdowns" on the job. This device puts special pressure on the employer, which is unable to plan its production activities or to secure replacements when needed; and is particularly attractive to employees, who remain on the payroll and are not subject to the economic deprivations attendant upon an all-out strike. The Board and courts have rather consistently held such "quickie" stoppages or slowdowns to be unprotected when part of a systematic scheme by employees to extract a concession from the employer. While the cases suggest that the conduct is objectionable in part because it is unorthodox and gives the employees too much leverage, the major reason appears to be that employees who remain on the payroll are believed obligated to discharge in full the work responsibilities embodied in their contract of employment and are not entitled to pick and choose the work they wish to do. For employees to decide, contrary to the employer's instructions, to work "on their own terms" has long been thought "indefensible" and cause for discharge. See NLRB v. Montgomery Ward & Co. (8th Cir. 1946):

> It was implied in the contract of hiring that these employees would do the work assigned to them in a careful and workmanlike manner; that they would comply with all reasonable orders and conduct themselves so as not to work injury to the employer's business; that they would serve faithfully and be regardful of the interests of the employer during the term of their service, and carefully discharge their duties to the extent reasonably required. . . .
> Any employee may, of course, be lawfully discharged for disobedience of the employer's directions in breach of his contract. . . . While these employees had the undoubted right to go on a strike and quit their employment, they could not continue to work and remain at their positions, accept the wages paid to them, and at the same time select what part of their allotted tasks they cared to perform of their own volition, or refuse openly or secretly, to the employer's damage, to do other work.

Thus, since the early days of the administration of the Wagner Act, cases have condemned as unprotected a refusal by employees to work overtime, as a means of protesting excessive overtime assignments, C.G. Conn, Ltd. v. NLRB (7th Cir. 1939); a refusal by employees to work at normal capacity, as a means of protesting a change in method of wage payment, Elk Lumber Co. (1950), or as a means of avoiding an increase in the work "standard" under an incentive-pay system, General Elec. Co. (1965) (employee's urging another to limit production may not be a union unfair labor practice but is not protected either, since employer is entitled to have employees work to capacity); and a refusal to perform clerical work which would have been performed by other company employees had they not been on strike, NLRB v. Montgomery Ward & Co. (8th Cir. 1946). Indeed, it is unprotected even to threaten such repeated work stoppages. NLRB v. Kohler Co. (7th Cir. 1955).

Perhaps the two leading cases on the status of "quickie" stoppages have been decided by the Supreme Court. They represent, however, rather conflicting philosophies regarding the propriety of employees' engaging in such activities. In UAW Local 232 v. Wisconsin Employment Relations Board (Briggs-Stratton) (U.S.1949) (5–4 decision), the Court held that a state through its NLRB-like regulatory agency could forbid such "quickie" stoppages consistently with the National Labor Relations Act. There, within a five-month period, the employees had engaged in twenty-seven unannounced work stoppages, unaccompanied by reasons or demands; the employer did not discharge the employees but secured (without antiunion animus) a cease-and-desist order from the Wisconsin Employment Relations Board, as a means of keeping the plant in operation. The Supreme Court characterized the walkouts as "illegal" and found no preemption of state regulation, since section 7 was held not to protect the walkouts and section 8(b) was held not to forbid them. In sum, the conduct was held not prohibited but unprotected.

The other relevant, and more recent, decision of the Supreme Court is NLRB v. Insurance Agents' Int'l Union (U.S.1960), in which the issue was whether unannounced brief and intermittent work stoppages by insurance agents in support of bargaining positions asserted in good faith by the union at negotiations rendered the union subject to a charge of bad-faith bargaining under section 8(b)(3). Although the issue whether the stoppages were unprotected was not before the Board and Court (because the employer had not discharged or disciplined the employees), the Court stated that peaceful economic weapons having the most serious effect on an employer are nonetheless "part and parcel of the system" of free collective bargaining embodied in the federal Labor Act. The Court conceded arguendo the correctness of *Briggs-Stratton*, but went on to note that union tactics are not to be regarded as proscribed merely because they are unconventional (rather than the "traditional" total strike), or are not generally supported by public opinion, or are deserving of condemnation, or are such as to "offer maximum pressure on the employer at minimum economic cost to the union." The Court declared it improper for the Board to function "as an arbiter of the sort of economic weapons the parties can use," or to "introduce some standard of properly 'balanced' bargaining power, or some new distinction of justifiable and unjustifiable, proper and 'abusive' economic weapons into the collective bargaining duty imposed by the Act."

It is true that *Insurance Agents* addresses the issue whether the union has violated the law by inducing "quickie" stoppages, while *Briggs-Stratton* addresses the issue whether participating employees are subject to employer self-help; and that they are thus compatible in their holdings. But the more recent Supreme Court decision certainly does counsel caution in condemning as unprotected such stoppages, which are "part and parcel" of proper collective bargaining and condemnation of which, by exclusion from the shelter of section 7, may render the Board just as subject to the charge of being "arbiter of the sort of economic weapons the parties can use" as when those stoppages are included within the ban of section 8(b). As will be developed below, should "quickie" stoppages be treated as protected activity the employer is not deprived of all recourse to self-help; but the applicable law would require that the employer demonstrate some substantial business justification for its response (*e. g.*, the need to get the work done through the use of replacements), such that outright discharge might not be appropriate as is true when the employee activity is labeled "unprotected."

In any event, the Board and courts continue to characterize as unprotected a plan or program of intermittent stoppages, whether threatened or actually implemented, in support of legitimate bargaining demands.   Recent decisions reiterate that employees may not with impunity remain on the payroll while refusing overtime work but must instead, to secure the protection of the Act, assume the status of strikers, with the attendant loss of pay and risk of permanent replacement.   First Nat'l Bank of Omaha (1968), *enf'd* (8th Cir. 1969).   There have, however, been some limitations upon the condemnation of such "quickie" stoppages.   In the *Omaha Bank* case, the employer's discharge of employees for refusing to work overtime was held to violate the Act, because at the time of their refusal it was unclear whether they intended to make the walkout the first in a series of intermittent refusals to work or instead the beginning of a full-fledged continuing walkout.   The Board has also held that a single unannounced walkout will be presumed protected, and the employees will be subject to discharge "when and only when the evidence demonstrates that the stoppage is part of a plan or pattern of intermittent action which is inconsistent with a genuine strike or genuine performance by employees of the work normally expected of them by the employer."   Polytech, Inc. (1972).   This somewhat more hospitable reception to the unannounced and unanticipated stoppage will likely be of greatest use to employees who are unorganized and who are responding spontaneously and directly to particular objectionable working conditions;   this was so in the two cases last cited.   In a related development, the Board has held that three brief work stoppages, without notice or reasons given, were not planned in advance as intermittent walkouts within the reach of *Briggs-Stratton* but were rather separate and protected walkouts in response to distinct refusals by the employer to process grievances pursuant to contract;   the reviewing court disagreed, and denied enforcement of the Board's order.   Blades Mfg. Corp. (1963), *enf't denied* (8th Cir. 1965).

There also appears to be developing a more lenient attitude than in the past toward employee refusals in the course of their work to take on chores which are assigned to them because left undone by other employees currently on strike.   Contrary to an early finding that such refusals were unprotected, NLRB v. Montgomery Ward & Co. (8th Cir. 1946), a court of appeals has recently held them protected (even when engaged in by a single employee) at least when the employee stands ready to perform his normally assigned tasks, General Tire & Rubber Co. v. NLRB (1st Cir. 1971).   That such refusals to do "struck work" are protected is reinforced by the decisions under section 8(e), the so-called hot-cargo provision of the Labor Act, which hold that a term in a labor contract protecting against discipline an employee who refuses to do struck work does not violate section 8(e).   See Truck Drivers Local 413 v. NLRB (D.C.Cir. 1964) (requirement that the contract clause incorporate the "ally doctrine"). Of course, no such secondary-boycott issue exists when the striking worker and the refusing worker are employed by the same company. Nonetheless, the employee's refusal may be such as to require a readjustment by the employer of work assignments, resulting in the temporary layoff of the refusing employee; if the layoff meets the test of business justification, it will not violate section 8(a)(1) even though the employee's refusal is protected activity. General Elec. Co. (1971).

§ 12. Refusals to Cross Picket Lines

When an employee refuses to cross a legal picket line established at his own company, he is deemed—even though his decision is made without prearrangement with others—to be engaged in a legal strike in common cause with his fellow employees, whether or not represented by the same union in the same bargaining unit, and his refusal to cross is held to be protected activity. NLRB v. Union Carbide Corp. (4th Cir. 1971) (holding, however, that an employee who refrains from crossing not out of "principle," but because of fear of personal injury, is not protected). Of course, if the picket line at the employee's own plant is incident to an illegal secondary boycott, or to illegal recognition picketing, the employee's refusal is thought to implicate him in the illegal enterprise and thus to render his refusal to cross unprotected. It has already been noted that one could argue that the resulting exposure to discharge in such cases is far too harsh a sanction when the task of distinguishing between legal and illegal picketing is often a complex one and commonly forced upon the individual employee without benefit of counsel.

Any clarity in the law dissolves, however, when the employee is turned away by picketers, engaged in lawful peaceful activity, at some other company with which his employer is doing business. It has already been noted that the refusal to cross the picket line is regarded as "concerted" activity for "mutual aid or protection," even though the decision is made independently by the employee. But the question remains whether the activity is protected, or whether the employee renders himself susceptible to discharge. The Board holds that the refusal to cross a legal picket line at another company is protected activity. Some federal courts of appeals agree, while others hold the refusal unprotected.

The arguments for holding the picket-line refusal unprotected are twofold. First, it smacks of the secondary boycott; the employer of the refusing employee suffers pro tanto a work stoppage as a direct result of a labor dispute to which it is not a party and over which it has no control. Second, and perhaps the more commonly articulated reason in the cases, the refusal is assimilated to the situation just discussed concerning unannounced or intermittent refusals to work overtime or to full capacity: the employee is violating the obligation in his employment contract to work according to his employer's directions, and is without authorization choosing, while on the payroll, not to make deliveries to or pickups from the picketed employer. See NLRB v. L. G. Everist, Inc. (8th Cir. 1964).

Those who would protect the refusal to cross a picket line argue that it is perhaps the paradigmatic example of one member of the labor community making common cause with other workers and lending them the kind of support which one day he will expect them to reciprocate. Compare NLRB v. Peter Cailler Kohler Swiss Choc. Co. (2d Cir. 1942). Moreover, the Labor Act expressly excepts from the proscription of its secondary-boycott provision all primary picketing and any "refusal by any person to enter upon the premises of any employer (other than his own employer), if the employees of such employer are engaged in a strike ratified or approved by a representative of such employees whom such employer is required to recognize under this Act." (The quoted provision is from a proviso to section 8(b)(4).) Finally, the object of the refusing employee—contrary to the "quickie" stoppage—is not to exert undue economic pressure on the employer in order to extract some bargaining concession.

In what appears to have been its first encounter with the issue, the Board with passing reference to the section 8(b)(4) proviso found the refusal to cross a legal picket line to be protected activity. Cyril de Cordova & Bros. (1950). In a case which ultimately reached the Supreme Court, the Board reaffirmed this position but its order was not enforced, first by the court of appeals which held that a picket-line refusal during the working day was unprotected (without noting how unlikely it was to encounter a refusal on nonworking time) and also that the 8(b)(4) proviso did no more than render such a refusal immune from the unfair labor practice machinery of the Board; and then by the Supreme Court, but on the distinct basis that the refusal was unprotected because in breach of contract. Rockaway News Supply Co. (1951), enf't denied (2d Cir. 1952), aff'd (U.S.1953). The year of the Supreme Court decision, the Board reversed its own course and held the picket-line refusal to be unprotected, since it was tantamount to insubordination. Auto Parts Co. (1953). This change in position corresponded to a change in the composition of the Board after a national election, a coincidence which also marks the next change in Board position, in Redwing Carriers, Inc. (1962) (modifying the Board's own decision of 1961), enf'd (D.C.Cir. 1963) (not discussing this issue).

The most resounding appellate rebuff of the "protected" classification made by the "Kennedy Board" came in NLRB v. L. G. Everist, Inc. (8th Cir. 1964), where the employer had discharged several drivers who refused to make deliveries through a picket line and who were also denied reinstatement after they had made an unconditional request therefor. Although the Board found the employees' refusal protected activity and thus found the employer's decision not to reinstate a violation of section 8(a)(3), the court of appeals refused to enforce the order and held the conduct of the employees unprotected because it was sympathetic activity in support of a dispute between a company and union with which they had no relationship and because it was a violation of the "ordinary and implied obligations of employment." The Board refused to follow the *Everist* court's decision, and in Overnight Transportation Co. (1965), *enf'd in part* (D.C.Cir. 1966), it found a discharge for refusal to make a pickup at a picketed company to violate sections 8(a)(1) and (3); but on appeal the court, without making any finding on whether the refusal to cross the picket line was protected, found the discharge to violate section 8(a)(3) because the true reason for the discharge was not the refusal to pickup but rather antiunion animus. More recently, several courts of appeals have rewarded the Board for its tenacity, by holding that refusals to cross primary picket lines at other companies are indeed protected by section 7. *E. g.*, Teamsters Local 657 v. NLRB (Chemical Express, Inc.) (D.C.Cir. 1970); NLRB v. Alamo Express (5th Cir. 1970).

Thus the cases stand, rather in disarray. The characterization as either protected or unprotected is important, for the ultimate question in these cases is whether the employer, faced with a refusal to cross a picket line, may freely discharge the recalcitrant employee, or secure a permanent replacement to do the work, or in either instance refuse an unconditional request for reinstatement. If the employee conduct is unprotected, the employer may resort to any one of those measures; if the employee conduct is protected, however, the employer is limited in its response only to those measures which can be justified by its need for continuity of business operations. The matter of allowable employer responses to picket-line refusals, assuming them to be protected, is discussed in greater detail elsewhere in this work.

While there is much confusion concerning the protected status of an employee refusal to cross a lawful picket line at another company, there appears to be unanimity that a refusal is clearly unprotected if either of two conditions exist. First, if the picket line in question is an illegal one—for example, a secondary boycott in violation of section 8(b)(4) or recognition picketing in violation of section 8(b)(7)—a refusal to cross the line is tantamount to participation in such illegal activity and is deemed unprotected; this is true whether the illegal picket line is at the plant of the recalcitrant employee or at the plant of another company. Second, even if the picket line is legal, and even if it is at the plant of the recalcitrant employee, any privilege against discipline or discharge which he might otherwise have for refusing to cross the picket line may be "waived" by his union in a labor contract with the disciplining employer. If the Board or courts construe the terms of the employee's collective bargaining agreement, typically the no-strike clause, to render the picket-line refusal a breach of contract, it becomes unprotected and the employee may be discharged therefor. NLRB v. Rockaway News Supply Co. (U.S.1953). Unfortunately, the few cases interpreting such alleged "waivers" are also in considerable disarray. The Board tends—although not with unanimity—to be inhospitable toward finding such a waiver. *E. g.,* Keller-Cresent Co. (1975). The courts disagree among themselves on the degree of explicitness necessary to support such a finding of waiver. Compare Montana-Dakota Util. Co. v. NLRB (8th Cir. 1972) (typical no-strike clause should be construed broadly, in light of pro-arbitration policy of federal law, to include prohibition of picket-line refusal), with Kellogg Co. v. NLRB (6th Cir. 1972) (typical no-strike clause should be narrowly construed, in light of strike-protection policy of section 13 of Labor Act, so as not to bar picket-line refusal in absence of clear waiver by union).

Conversely, even though a court might not be prepared to hold protected a picket-line refusal at a plant of another company, it may hold that the employer's right to discipline or discharge has in certain instances been contractually relinquished. Although the so-called hot-cargo provisions of section 8(e) of the Labor Act have been construed to render void and unenforceable an employer's promise in a labor contract not to discipline any employee who refuses to cross an illegal picket line elsewhere, such a no-discipline promise is legal and enforceable when addressed to a refusal which takes place at a picket line incident to a primary peaceful labor dispute (even one which goes beyond the shelter of the section 8(b)(4) proviso because not approved or ratified by an exclusive bargaining representative). Truck Drivers Local 413 v. NLRB (D.C.Cir. 1964) (court assumed that refusal to cross a primary picket line at another company is protected activity, such that employer-union agreement not to discipline therefor would not run afoul of hot-cargo proscriptions of section 8(e)).

CHAPTER XVII

EMPLOYER COUNTERMEASURES TO CONCERTED ACTIVITY

§ 1. Employer Violence and Threats

Clearly the use of physical coercion by an employer against employees engaging in protected activity will be found to violate section 8(a)(1). Heights Thrift-Way, Inc. (1965) (president of grocery corporation beats peaceful pickets). A threat to assault pickets will also "interfere with, restrain or coerce" employees engaging in conduct protected by section 7. H.R. McBride (1959), *enf'd* (10th Cir. 1960). Of course, most employers who do effect or threaten violence do not do so personally but rather act through agents. As is discussed elsewhere, the conduct of others will be attributed to the employer under section 8(a)(1) by application of the usual principles of agency law. Thus, the employer will be charged with violence or intimidation committed by professional strikebreakers employed by the company, Remington Rand, Inc. (1937), *enf'd as mdf'd on other grounds* (2d Cir. 1938); or by nonstrikers to whom management of the plant is delegated and who threaten mass demonstrations against strikers, Sunshine Mining Co. (1938), *enf'd as mdf'd on other grounds* (9th Cir. 1940); or by a plant guard who attacks an employee picketing peacefully, Stark Ceramics, Inc. (1965), *enf'd* (6th Cir. 1967). Employer liability for the acts of others is of course most clear when the specific hostile conduct is encouraged by the employer in advance, Anchor Rome Mills, Inc. (1949) (supervisors encourage 75 to 100 nonstrikers armed with clubs, blackjacks and hatchets to assault 8 to 10 strikers). Even the conduct of local police may be attributed to the employer if it can be shown that the employer encouraged extreme action by the police which led to violence. *E. g.,* Republic Steel Corp. v. NLRB (3d Cir. 1939) (employer donated weapons to police, while foremen and nonstrikers were deputized; three strikers were killed when police stormed union hall); Oregon Worsted Co. (1937), *enf'd* (9th Cir. 1938) (employer encouraged police to club strikers). Fortunately, such blatant acts of employer violence are today extremely rare on the labor scene.

§ 2. Section 8(a)(3): Discrimination, Motive and Business Justification

The most vexing problems of statutory construction have been presented by section 8(a)(3) which, in pertinent part, declares that it shall be an unfair labor practice for an employer "by discrimination in regard to hire or tenure of employment or any term or condition of employment to encourage or discourage membership in any labor organization." The most obvious case of violation of section 8(a)(3) is the discharge of an employee whom the employer knows to be a union organizer and who is discharged specifically in order to penalize the employee, to impede the union's progress and to instill fear among other employees who would otherwise be sympathetic to the union cause. Here, there is "discrimination in regard to . . . tenure of employment," whether "discrimination" is defined so as to require antiunion motivation or, more neutrally, simply disparate treatment (regardless of motive) of one employee and all other employees with a comparable work record. Here too there is an act "to discourage membership" in a union, whether that refers to the motive for the employer's conduct or, more neutrally, simply to its effect (regardless of motive). Any employer claim of good faith is by hypothesis negated and, although the employer might argue that there is the "legitimate business justification" of freedom from the union and from the interference and wage increases which are usually attendant, the entire statutory scheme makes it clear that this is an impermissible justification. In short, a discharge motivated solely by the employee's union membership or activity is clearly *sufficient* to make out a violation of section 8(a)(3). The more difficult issue is whether such motivation is *necessary* in order to violate section 8(a)(3).

The statutory language does not speak clearly to this issue. The operative phrase, "to encourage or discourage" union membership, describes an effect of employer action and not its motive. But the section goes on to require that the discouragement (typically it will be that, rather than encouragement) be "by discrimination." "Discrimination" can have at least four meanings: (1) treating employee A different from employee B, even though the difference is warranted by business reasons, such as the skill or length of service of the two employees; (2) treating employee A different from employee B, when the difference is arbitrary and unwarranted by business reasons but is unrelated to union activity, *e. g.,* the religion or political beliefs of the two employees; (3) treating employee A different from employee B, when the difference is related to their union membership or activities; (4) treating employee A different from the way employee A would be treated were it not for his union membership or activities. Any of these forms of discrimination might discourage the union membership or activities of the discharged employee, or of his co-workers if that employee is visibly active in the union, for his removal might be perceived as an expression of antiunion animus (even if in truth it is not) and it might well remove from the scene the union's most effective spokesman. Discrimination of the third form is clearly the one Congress had most in mind when enacting section 8(a)(3) and is the form most frequently observed and articulated in the reported cases. Discrimination of the first kind—the "neutral" disparate treatment of employees based on business reasons—is obviously the kind of employer action which the statute purports to regulate the least, if at all. Such regulation would intrude most severely into the employer's business decisions, decisions made not with an eye toward ridding the employer of the union but rather bettering the efficiency, discipline or safety of the enterprise.

Nonetheless, decisions of the United States Supreme Court make it rather (although not completely) clear that—like section 8(a)(1) —the employer may be held to violate section 8(a)(3) even when the discouragement of union activities flows from conduct which is not moved by antiunion animus and which is in fact based on what the employer perceives to be sound business reasons. Both sections have been read to invite the Board to "balance" the employer's business interest and the employees' interest in free choice as to collective bargaining and concerted activities, to determine which interest is the weightier. While the differences between the two sections have largely been obliterated, the Board and the courts continue to treat certain kinds of employer action primarily or exclusively under section 8(a)(3) and purport to search for specific proof of antiunion animus to make out a violation. The Board's function is narrowed when outlawry turns upon specific proof of hostility toward employee rights, as is typically required in the conventional case of discharge or discipline; its function is broadened when it is invited to determine whether employer action taken in good faith can nonetheless be outlawed because its justification is not "substantial" when measured against the harm to protected employee rights. The major decisions of the Supreme Court do not give consistent answers to such questions as: (1) In what cases must the employer be moved by antiunion animus in order to violate the Act, and in what cases can a violation be made out even absent such animus? (2) In those cases in which employer countermeasures to union activity can be outlawed simply by striking a "balance," what are the guidelines for such balancing? (3) Is it the Board or the Supreme Court (or the Congress) which has the fundamental power and responsibility to do the balancing? Just as the Board and courts "make law" when they classify activity as "unprotected" against employer reprisal, they also "make law"— equally unguided by the terms of the Labor Act—when they determine which employer countermeasures to protected activity are allowable under sections 8(a)(1) and (3) and which are not; and like that other task, this determination can in many cases shape the outcome of collective bargaining.

An attempt will be made to trace the history of the major Supreme Court decisions on these important questions and then to set forth some governing legal principles that can be extracted from those decisions.

In NLRB v. Mackay Radio and Tel. Co. (U.S.1938), the employer continued operating during a strike by hiring replacements. When the strike ended, and six of the replacements decided to leave, the employer filled their vacancies with six of the former strikers who sought reemployment; five other strikers who had been prominent in the union were denied reinstatement. This employer discrimination —disparate treatment of more and less vigorous union supporters— was held to violate section 8(a)(3). The Court went on, however, to hold that the hiring of permanent replacements for economic strikers is not an unfair labor practice:

> [I]t does not follow that an employer, guilty of no act denounced by the statute, has lost the right to protect and continue his business by supplying places left vacant by strikers. And he is not bound to discharge those hired to fill the places of strikers, upon the election of the latter to resume their employment, in order to create places for them. The assurance by respondent to those who accepted employment during the strike that if they so desired their places might be permanent was not an unfair labor practice nor was it such to reinstate only so many of the strikers as there were vacant places to be filled.

In effect, the Court assumed that permanent replacement of economic strikers was based on legitimate business reasons and was because of that lawful—even though the employer's retention of those who refuse to strike or who abandon the strike and its replacement and termination of those who do strike is surely discrimination which discourages union activity.

The Court soon gave a more expansive reading to section 8(a)(3), in Republic Aviation Corp. v. NLRB (U.S.1945). There, an employee was discharged for passing out union application cards during lunchtime in violation of a company rule against solicitation of any kind in the plant. The Court held the no-solicitation rule to violate section 8(a)(1) to the extent it applied to nonworking time, even though the rule had been adopted before the advent of the union and had been applied nondiscriminatorily to all forms of in-plant solicitation. In spite of these latter factors, the Court went on to hold the discharge to violate section 8(a)(3): "It seems clear . . . that if a rule against solicitation is invalid as to union solicitation . . . a discharge because of violation of that rule discriminates within the meaning of § 8(3) in that it discourages membership in a labor organization." Thus, sections 8(a)(1) and (3) were viewed as congruent, the discharge was not saved because the employer believed it necessary to plant efficiency or safety, and "discouragement" alone appeared sufficient to make out a violation of section 8(a)(3) (since discrimination was thought to inhere in any such discouragement).

The Court once again gave a broad reading to section 8(a)(3) in Radio Officers' Union v. NLRB (U.S.1954). There, in three consolidated cases, the employer was found to violate that section by *encouraging* union membership. One involved a reduction in seniority and another a refusal to employ, in both cases because of failure to abide by union rules, and the third involved the employer's retroactive payment of moneys solely to union members. The Court announced that union "membership" in section 8(a)(3) should be read to embrace activities on behalf of or within the union; thus, an employer's actions might be found unlawful if, although no greater number of employees became union members, those who were members felt obliged to attend more meetings or to make monetary contributions beyond their dues. It also defined "discrimination" quite broadly: "Discrimination is not contested in these cases: involuntary reduction of seniority, refusal to hire for an available job, and disparate wage treatment are clearly discriminatory." The Court went on, however, to hold that proof of illicit purpose was essential to found a violation of section 8(a)(3). It looked to earlier Supreme Court decisions holding that "the act permits a discharge for any reason other than union activity," and to legislative history demonstrating that that section "prohibits an employer from discriminating against an employee by reason of his membership or nonmembership in a labor organization." The Court then proceeded to hold that specific proof of intent to encourage or discourage is not necessary, but that such intent may be inferred when the employer's conduct "inherently encourages or discourages union membership" or when such result is "a natural consequence of his action" and thus reasonably foreseeable. Even if the employer did not in fact intend to discourage or encourage union membership, it will in such cases be presumed that it did so intend. In the three cases before it, the Court found illicit purpose because the employer's disparate treatment was "based solely on" union membership. It held:

> The policy of the Act is to insulate employees' jobs from their organizational rights. Thus §§ 8(a)(3) and 8(b)(2) were designed to allow employees to freely exercise their right to join unions, be good, bad, or indifferent members, or abstain from joining any union without imperiling their livelihood.

(Note the similarity between this rationale and the fourth definition of discrimination set forth above.) The Court concluded by stressing the capacity and authority of the NLRB, on the basis of its experience, to infer—even in the absence of specific evidence that employees were in fact encouraged or discouraged—that such consequences were a likely product of the employer's discrimination. In short, while both the intent to discourage or encourage and that effect were necessary to establish a violation of section 8(a)(3), the Board was free to presume both simply from the conduct of the employer.

In 1961, the Court was confronted with the question whether the employer's discharge of an employee solely because he had initially not been hired by referral from the union's hiring hall—a procedure set forth in the collective bargaining agreement—was in violation of section 8(a)(3) (and the union's involvement a violation of section 8(b)(2)). Teamsters Local 357 v. NLRB (U.S.1961). The Court conceded that, although the agreement stipulated that union referral should not be based on union membership, such membership might well be encouraged by the hiring-hall arrangement. But membership is also encouraged whenever the union negotiates or processes grievances effectively, and such is not illegal. The encouragement must flow from employer discrimination, and that in turn may not be inferred unless—as in *Radio Officers*—disparate treatment of employees is *based upon* their union membership or activities. The Court upheld the nondiscriminatory hiring hall, and rejected the argument of the dissenting opinion that "discrimination" within section 8(a)(3) embraces "all differences in treatment regardless of their basis" (including the hiring of those referred by the union and the refusal to hire those who are not).

To this point, it appeared that the Court was prepared to uphold employer conduct which encouraged or discouraged union activities if reasonably related to the employer's business needs—such as working-time no-solicitation rules, permanent replacement of strikers and employment referrals through hiring halls—but not if lacking in such a business justification, such as the nonworking-time no-solicitation rule and the favored treatment of union members in such matters as seniority or wages. The Court may have spoken as though invidious purpose was essential in section 8(a)(3) cases, but it appeared that the cases might better be understood by evaluating the strength of the employer's business need for taking particular action; illicit purpose was on occasion "presumed," a sure signal that it was becoming unnecessary. The Court's developing rationale raised the question how it would rule if an employer's action was designed to advance a substantial business interest and lacked any motive of injuring or benefiting the union, but was necessarily effected by disparate treatment between union activists (*i. e.,* strikers) and non-strikers.

In NLRB v. Erie Resistor Corp. (U.S.1963), a struck company, "under intense competition and subject to insistent demands from its customers to maintain deliveries," offered permanent employment to strike replacements and, to induce them to accept, assured them that they would not be laid off at the end of the strike because of their brief tenure with the company; this was implemented by awarding strike replacements and returning strikers twenty years "superseniority" for purposes of layoff and recall. The strike ended soon after and the strikers returned to work, but a subsequent contraction in the workforce resulted in the layoff of former strikers and the retention of those who were junior in service but who had the superseniority credit. The Supreme Court affirmed the Board's finding of an 8(a)(3) violation, in the face of the trial examiner's conclusion that the superseniority had been offered as a business necessity to keep the plant in operation. The Court held that there is certain employer conduct which is so "inherently discriminatory or destructive" of employee rights that even business objectives will not save it:

> Nevertheless, his conduct *does* speak for itself—it *is* discriminatory and it *does* discourage union membership and whatever the claimed overriding justification may be, it carries with it unavoidable consequences which the employer not only foresaw but which he must have intended.

The Court made clear that parsing the motives of the employer

> is in reality the far more delicate task .   .   . of weighing the interests of employees in concerted activity against the interest of the employer in operating his business in a particular manner and of balancing in the light of the Act and its policy the intended consequences upon employee rights against the business ends to be served by the employer's conduct.

The Board had found the superseniority plan to have a far more devastating impact on the rights of employees than does permanent replacement, primarily because it added to replacement the sanction of lesser seniority for returning strikers and thus the greater fear of future layoff, a sanction which continued after the strike was settled and which would indefinitely aggravate relations within the plant with each contraction of the workforce.   The Board concluded that the employer's business purpose did not outweigh this harmful impact, and the Supreme Court held that the Board had acted within the broad range of its discretion in balancing the interests of the parties.

The Court's apparent de-emphasis of the motive requirement in section 8(a)(3) was complemented by developments under two neighboring sections of the Act.   In 1961, the Court had held in ILGWU v. NLRB (Bernhard-Altmann Texas Corp.) (U.S.1961), that an employer violates sections 8(a)(2) and (1) by recognizing and bargaining with a union as exclusive representative when that union in fact has only minority support, even though both employer and union in good faith believe it to have majority support.   In 1964, the Court decided NLRB v. Burnup & Sims, Inc. (U.S.1964) in which an employer, acting in good faith reliance upon a disclosure from an employee that two employees then engaged in soliciting for the union had threatened to dynamite the plant, promptly discharged the two suspects. In fact, the two employees had made no such threats.   The Board treated the matter, as was customary in discharge cases, under section 8(a)(3) and found that the employer violated that section by using the dynamite story as a pretext for ridding itself of the two union activists.   The Supreme Court did not deal with this issue but instead took the rare step of treating the case under section 8(a)(1) and concluded that the discharge violated that section, in spite of the employer's good faith; the employer knew the employees were engaging in organizational activities and the basis of the discharge was what proved to be nonexistent misconduct in the course of those activities. "[T]he protected activity would lose some of its immunity, since the example of employees who are discharged on false charges would or might have a deterrent effect on other employees." The Court's treatment of the case under section 8(a)(1) suggested that, whatever the purpose or motive requirement might be under section 8(a)(3), it could be avoided by framing the claim under the broader section and disposing of the case by interest balancing.

This prospect was, however, short-lived. Two years after *Erie Resistor,* the Court announced three decisions which reasserted the motive requirement in section 8(a)(3) and castigated the Board for engaging in the balancing of economic weapons in excess of its legislative authority. In Textile Workers Union v. Darlington Mfg. Co. (U.S.1965), a unanimous Court held for the first time that certain management decisions could not be subjected to the broader interest-balancing scrutiny of section 8(a)(1) and that they would violate the Act, if at all, only if specifically motivated by antiunion animus and thus a clear violation of section 8(a)(3). In that case, a union victory at the one textile mill owned by a company—which was effectively controlled, along with sixteen other textile manufacturers, by one family—precipitated the complete shutdown of that plant and the piecemeal auction sale of the plant machinery and equipment. The Board held that the owner had shut down in retaliation against the union. The Court held, nonetheless, that if the transaction was to be treated as the shutdown of an entire business, it was lawful in spite of any admitted antiunion animus. The Court first differentiated the reach of sections 8(a)(1) and (3):

> A violation of § 8(a)(1) alone . . . presupposes an act which is unlawful even absent a discriminatory motive. Whatever may be the limits of § 8(a)(1), some employer decisions are so peculiarly matters of management prerogative that they would never constitute violations of § 8(a)(1), whether or not they involved sound business judgment, unless they also violated § 8(a)(3).

Although the Court did not itemize those decisions which are "peculiarly matters of management prerogative" its opinion makes clear that at the least it was referring to the complete shutdown of a business, or to a partial shutdown, *i. e.,* the shutdown of one of a number of plants owned by the same company. Viewing the Darlington shutdown as a complete shutdown of one company, the Court found that the desire to escape the union does not render the shutdown illegal. Adverting not at all to the statement in *Radio Officers* that "The policy of the Act is to insulate employees' jobs from their organizational rights," the Court viewed the prime purpose of section 8(a)(3) as "to prohibit the discriminatory use of economic weapons in an effort to obtain future benefits" and concluded that "a complete liquidation of a business yields no such future benefit for the employer." Such benefit might, however, accrue if the one-plant shutdown were viewed as a partial shutdown within a group of plants owned by the family. The Court thus held that a partial closing violates section 8(a)(3) only "if motivated by a purpose to chill unionism in any of the remaining plants of the single employer and if the employer may reasonably have foreseen that such closing would likely have that effect." Since the findings in the record of antiunion animus and discouragement of union membership related only to employees at the plant that was shut down, the Court remanded to determine both whether that shutdown had an adverse impact upon unionization in other company plants and whether such was in fact the employer's object.

A further condonation of employer action arguably harmful to section 7 rights took place in American Ship Bldg. Co. v. NLRB (U.S.1965). There, an employer had reached an impasse in bargaining negotiations and, fearing that the union was delaying a strike until the busy season, it locked out its employees in order to induce concessions and a contract settlement. There was no evidence that the lockout was designed to evade the duty to bargain, to cripple the union as representative of the employees or to penalize the employees for unionization and collective bargaining. Overruling the Board's long-standing condemnation of the bargaining lockout as punishment for employee adherence to bargaining demands, the Supreme Court concluded that the employer had not violated either section 8(a)(1) or 8(a)(3). It held that the lockout did not interfere illegally with employee rights to bargain or to engage in concerted activities and that the Board could not avoid the need to demonstrate antiunion motive, since the lockout was not "demonstrably so destructive" of employee rights (such as would be the permanent discharge of unionized employees and their replacement with known union haters). The lockout after impasse, designed to bring about a settlement on favorable terms is not

> inherently so prejudicial to union interests and so devoid of significant economic justification that no specific evidence of intent to discourage union membership or other antiunion animus is required.

> . . . [U]se of the lockout does not carry with it any necessary implication that the employer *acted to discourage* union membership or otherwise discriminate against union members *as such*. (Emphasis added.)

In the past, the Court had deferred to the expertise of the Board when striking down the grant of superseniority as too destructive a weapon in collective bargaining and when sustaining the "defensive" lockout of employees in a multiemployer bargaining unit when one employer in the unit was the victim of a "whipsaw" strike, NLRB v. Truck Drivers Local 449 (Buffalo Linen) (U.S.1957). But in *American Ship Building*, the Court took the Board to task for construing

> its functions too expansively when it claims general authority to define national labor policy by balancing the competing interests of labor and management.
>
> . . . Sections 8(a)(1) and (3) do not give the Board a general authority to assess the relative economic power of the adversaries in the bargaining process and to deny weapons to one party or the other because of its assessment of that party's bargaining power.

The decision of the Court evoked separate opinions from certain Justices who saw it as a departure from earlier decisions which had eliminated the need for proof of animus, had endorsed the process of interest-balancing and had exalted the Board's capacity to do so.

On the same day, the Court decided NLRB v. Brown (U.S.1965). There, a strike was called against one employer in a multiemployer bargaining unit, and the other employers in the unit locked out their employees in order to dull the effectiveness of the whipsaw strike and preserve the united bargaining front of the employers. When the struck employer chose to continue operating with temporary replacements, the other employers also reopened but also by utilizing temporary replacements rather than their locked out employees. Overruling the Board's finding of illegality, the Supreme Court held that the use of temporary replacements by the non-struck employers violated neither section 8(a)(1) nor 8(a)(3). The Court appeared to hold that both sections require either proof of antiunion animus (that is, desire to evade bargaining, destroy the union or penalize the employees for bargaining) or of employer conduct which is "demonstrably so destructive of employee rights and so devoid of significant service to any legitimate business end that it cannot be tolerated consistently with the Act." Here, the impact of temporary replacement was "comparatively slight" (over and above the already lawful lockout) and it was "reasonably adapted to achieve legitimate business ends or to deal with business exigencies."

Darlington, American Ship Building and *Brown* thus appeared to destroy the independent utility of section 8(a)(1), with its interest-balancing approach, and to require proof that the employer's specific purpose was to discourage its employees' union activities. This purpose could be proved circumstantially only if the employer discriminated among employees *on the basis of* their union membership. But the Court took another twist only two years later, in NLRB v. Great Dane Trailers, Inc. (U.S.1967), and announced a formula which, while rather vague, is controlling today and has shaped the course of Board and lower court decisions since.

In *Great Dane*, after the expiration of a labor contract providing for accrual of vacation benefits, the employer took a strike and continued to operate with some remaining employees and replacements. It stated that it had no continuing liability for vacation pay under the expired contract, but announced that it would, of its own motion, grant vacation pay (according to the contract formula) to persons who had reported for work on a date some two weeks earlier during the strike. In spite of no employer proof as to its reason for thus discriminating between strikers and nonstrikers, the court of appeals reversed the Board's findings of violation of sections 8(a)(1) and (3) for lack of proof by the General Counsel of antiunion animus. The Supreme Court in turn reversed and sustained the Board's conclusions under both sections. The Court held that the payment of vacation benefits to nonstrikers and their denial to strikers is clearly "discrimination" which "no doubt" discourages union activities. It also held that section 8(a)(3) is normally read to require that the discriminatory and discouraging conduct must be motivated by antiunion purpose, and proceeded to formulate principles of proof on this issue in two different classes of cases:

> First, if it can reasonably be concluded that the employer's discriminatory conduct was "inherently destructive" of important employee rights, no proof of an antiunion motivation is needed and the Board can find an unfair labor practice even if the employer introduces evidence that the conduct was motivated by business considerations. Second, if the adverse effect of the discriminatory conduct on employee rights is "comparatively slight," an antiunion motivation must be proved to sustain the charge *if* the employer has come forward with evidence of legitimate and substantial business justifications for the conduct. Thus, in either situation, once it has been proved that the employer engaged in discriminatory conduct which could have adversely affected employee rights to *some* extent, the burden is upon the employer to establish that he was motivated by legitimate objectives since proof of motivation is most accessible to him.

Since the employer had not come forward with any business justification, both sections 8(a)(1) and (3) were held to be violated, even though no specific proof of antiunion bias was offered by the General Counsel. The Court left vague the issue whether, in the "comparatively slight" cases, the Board could find a violation even when the employer tendered a business justification should it conclude that that justification was insufficiently "legitimate and substantial"— that is, whether the Board could weigh the substantiality of the business reason against the severity (even though slight) of the impact on union activities. The Court also provided no criteria for determining whether employer conduct was "inherently destructive" or had only a "comparatively slight" impact on employee rights. (It is noteworthy that in *American Ship Building*, a majority of the Court held the bargaining lockout to have no impact whatever on protected rights, while one Justice believed it to be inherently destructive!)

Soon after, the Court decided NLRB v. Fleetwood Trailer Co. (U.S.1967), the last major statement of its position on the general criteria for decision under sections 8(a)(1) and (3). The case ironically raised issues not unlike those in the *Mackay* case, which had in 1938 upheld the legality of permanent replacements of economic strikers. In *Fleetwood Trailer*, an employer undergoing a strike drastically cut back on its production schedule, such that when the strike ended and the strikers applied for reinstatement, there were no positions available for them. Some six weeks later, when the gradual return to the pre-strike volume of business resulted in several job openings, the employer hired six new applicants rather than former strikers who had earlier applied for reinstatement. The Supreme Court disagreed with the Court of Appeals, which had held that the strikers' rights to reinstatement were to be determined as of the date of their application, and concluded that the strikers remained "employees" within the protection of the Act, and were thus entitled to an offer of reinstatement (in preference to new hires) of their former jobs so long as they did not obtain regular and substantially equivalent employment elsewhere. The employer might make an exception if it could demonstrate that a striker's job had been altogether eliminated for substantial business reasons, such as the need to adapt to changes in business conditions or to improve efficiency. Since the refusal to reinstate does discourage the exercise of section 7 rights, the burden is on the employer to justify it, and if—as in *Fleetwood*—it fails to do so, the Court held that sections 8(a)(1) and (3) are violated "without reference to intent."

It is possible to summarize the present state of the law under sections 8(a)(1) and (3) as follows:

(1) Some employer action which interferes with concerted activities may be challenged only under section 8(a)(1), either because there is no discrimination regarding working conditions (*e. g.,* employer polling of employees) or because there is no discouragement of union activities (*e. g.,* where the employee protest is spontaneous and without union support). Some employer action, "peculiarly matters of management prerogative," may be challenged exclusively or primarily only under section 8(a)(3); other than plant closings, the contours of this category are undetermined. Most employer action which interferes with concerted activities is subject to challenge under both sections.

(2) In cases tested only under section 8(a)(3), such as plant closings, the General Counsel must present specific evidence that the

employer was actually motivated by a purpose to chill unionism among its other employees and that such "chilling" was likely to occur.

(3) Although many opinions still state that proof of violation of section 8(a)(1) is easier than and different from proof of violation of section 8(a)(3)—with section 8(a)(3) requiring proof of antiunion animus and section 8(a)(1) requiring only that employer interests be outweighed by employee interests—in truth there appears to be little difference between them.

(4) If the employer action has a "devastating impact" on section 7 activities, the Board may find that action illegal, without need for proof of antiunion animus. Even if the employer was in fact motivated by a desire to preserve its business, this is not a defense. In general, conduct will be held to have a "devastating impact" if all union activists are treated in a manner inferior to all employees who are not union activists.

(5) If the employer action has only a "comparatively slight" impact on section 7 activities, then the employer must demonstrate that it had a "legitimate and substantial" business reason for taking that action. If the employer makes no such demonstration, then an unfair labor practice will be found, regardless of proof or lack of proof of antiunion bias. If the employer makes such a demonstration, then no unfair labor practice will be found unless the General Counsel proves antiunion motivation for the employer's action. In determining whether the employer's business reasons were "legitimate and substantial," the issue is not whether the employer acted in good faith and without intention to intrude on the employees' rights but whether the employer's reasons "outweigh" the harm to the employees.

(6) A determination whether employer action causes "devastating" or only "slight" harm to employee rights, and a determination whether one "outweighs" the other, falls within the area of expertise of the NLRB and is subject to only limited judicial review. (In spite of some Supreme Court statements to the contrary, these determinations give the Board considerable power—relatively unguided by the terms of the statute—to choose among the kinds of economic weapons that the parties may utilize in support of their positions in collective bargaining. This Board power thus can indirectly shape the substantive terms of the labor contract in many cases.)

(7) In any case (other than the shutdown of a business) in which the employer's action was in fact motivated by a desire to punish employees for engaging in section 7 activities, or by a desire to oust or circumvent a union as bargaining representative, the action is unlawful.

§ 3. The Distinction Between the Economic Strike and the Unfair Labor Practice Strike; the "Conversion" Doctrine

The kind of responsive action which an employer may take against its striking employees may depend on the cause of the strike. A distinction has been drawn between the unfair labor practice striker and the economic striker, and to the extent their rights differ the unfair labor practice striker is treated more favorably. Employees who engage in a work stoppage in protest against employer conduct which is found (by the NLRB) to be in violation of the Labor Act are said to be unfair labor practice strikers. Employees who engage in a work stoppage for other reasons, typically in support of bargaining demands regarding wages and working conditions or requests that the employer recognize a union, are said to be economic strikers. Determining the cause of a work stoppage is a task for the NLRB and often requires the drawing of nice factual inferences from an ambiguous record. All that can be said with confidence is that if a strike occurs shortly after the employer has committed a serious unfair labor practice, the strikers will be treated as unfair labor practice strikers, *e. g.*, NLRB v. Thayer Co. (1st Cir. 1954); but if the strike occurs many weeks later and at a point during negotiations when a strike for bargaining concessions would seem expectable, then the cause of the strike will probably be deemed economic, *e. g.*, Jordan Bus Co. (1954).

Further complications are provided by what has become known as the "conversion" doctrine: A stoppage which begins as an economic strike may be "converted" into an unfair labor practice strike by the intervening commission by the employer of an unfair labor practice which is determined (by the Board) to make the strike last longer than it otherwise would. In theory, an employee is treated as an economic striker during the period when the economic strike would have continued of its own force; he is thereafter treated as an unfair labor practice striker for the period of prolongation. Obviously, there is no litmus-paper test to determine whether a strike would have continued as long as it did even in the absence of the employer unfair labor practice or to determine exactly the date at which the conversion takes place.

Although any employer unfair labor practice can theoretically convert a strike, the Board treats certain employer conduct as more likely than others to have that effect. Thus, if the employer violates section 8(a)(2) by improperly supporting an insurgent union during an economic strike sponsored by the incumbent union, this has been held "inevitably" to convert the subsisting strike. Crosby Chems., Inc. (1949), *mdf'd on other grounds* (5th Cir. 1951). Conversion also will usually follow when the employer violates section 8(a)(5) by insisting on a nonmandatory subject of bargaining, Grand Lodge of Free & Accepted Masons (1974) (demanding that economic strikers waive their rights to reinstatement); or by unilaterally granting pay increases during negotiations, Kohler Co. (1960), *mdf'd on other grounds* (D.C.Cir. 1962); or by refusing outright to meet and discuss, Manville Jenckes Corp. (1941). These violations will commonly convert an economic strike since it can be said with some assurance that they interrupt the bargaining process and thus delay the settlement that would otherwise have been reached on economic issues. That cannot so clearly be said about employer violations of section 8(a)(3), such as discriminatory discharges because of union activities, or of section 8(a)(1), such as interrogation or surveillance of employees. Such discharges, interrogation or surveillance are of course unfair labor practices and can be remedied as such, but they do not necessarily alter the status of employees already on strike for economic reasons. The burden of proof is upon the General Counsel to demonstrate prolongation. Clinton Foods, Inc. (1955). On judicial review of the Board's determination, the court will simply decide whether the Board's conclusion is supported by substantial evidence. Rogers Mfg. Co. v. NLRB (6th Cir. 1973).

It is commonly difficult to determine not only whether there has been prolongation of the economic strike but the precise date on which the prolongation occurred. There appears to be no general rule for determining that date. In Erie Resistor Corp. (1961), *enf't denied* (3d Cir. 1962), *rev'd* (U.S.1963), the employer announced a grant of twenty-years superseniority credit to strikebreakers, and this remained a bone of contention in negotiations; two weeks after all other matters were settled, the union members voted to continue the strike to protest the superseniority program and the Board held the strike to have been converted on that date. Compare Rogers Mfg. Co. v. NLRB (6th Cir. 1973) (union unconditionally offered to return to work, employer then demanded superseniority for strikebreakers, and Board dated conversion from first union meeting thereafter). In Manville Jenckes Corp. (1941), the conversion was held to take place with the first in a long series of unfair labor practices (an outright refusal to bargain), since the employer's acts showed an uncooperative attitude toward the union that threatened the bargaining process from the outset. In Sioux Falls Stock Yards Co. (1974), conversion was set at the date the employer unilaterally offered improved benefits in violation of section 8(a)(5). This pattern appears to be quite common in cases of conversion; rather than determine the date in the future at which an economic strike would likely end, and then date the conversion from that point, the Board is generally content to conclude that conversion occurs immediately upon the commission of, for example, the employer's refusal to bargain since protest against that action is assumed to be one of the union's motives for continuing the strike thereafter. *E. g.*, Cavalier Div. of Seeburg Corp. (1971), *mdf'd on other grounds* (D.C.Cir. 1973).

In determining whether and when a strike is converted, the Board will not normally find a clear statement by the union of its reason for striking. West Coast Casket Co. (1951). Particularly in a complex bargaining situation where many issues are discussed and many compromises necessary before an economic strike will be settled, it may be difficult to ascertain whether any one issue, economic or otherwise, is preventing settlement. In such instances, the Board must turn to such evidence of union motive as union telegrams, Winter Garden Citrus Prod. Co-op. v. NLRB (5th Cir. 1956), union newspaper advertisements, Birmingham Pub. Co. (1957), statements made at union meetings, Griffin Pipe Div. of Griffin Wheel Co. (1962), and personal recollections of collective bargaining sessions.

§ 4.   Discharge and Replacement of Strikers

As an initial matter, neither the economic striker nor the unfair labor practice striker may be discharged. To do so violates sections 8(a)(1) and (3). NLRB v. International Van Lines (U.S.1972). It is difficult to discern how the severance of the employment relationship advances any legitimate business interest, while the resulting discouragement of union membership and activities is obvious. The employer may, however, seek to continue operating during the strike by hiring permanent replacements or replacements who—like supervisors, relatives or company employees outside the bargaining unit—are known to serve only temporarily pending termination of the strike. In the case of the unfair labor practice striker, the employer must, upon an unconditional request for reinstatement, reinstate the striker to his original position and oust the replacement. Mastro Plastics Corp. v. NLRB (U.S.1956). Failure to do so is itself deemed discrimination in violation of section 8(a)(3). NLRB v. Dubo Mfg. Co. (6th Cir. 1965).

The economic striker is not treated as well. In an early and major decision, NLRB v. Mackay Radio & Tel. Co. (U.S.1938), the Supreme Court held that an economic striker retains his status as an "employee" within the definition of section 2(3) of the Labor Act and thus retains the protection of the Act against intentional discrimination by the employer, such as the rehiring only of those strikers who are least active in the union. The Court went on, however, to conclude that an economic striker could be permanently replaced and was not entitled to "bump" his replacement upon the termination of the strike. The employer "has [not] lost the right to protect and continue his business by supplying places left vacant by strikers. And he is not bound to discharge those hired to fill the places of strikers, upon the election of the latter to resume their employment." In the language of the more modern Supreme Court decisions, any untoward impact of permanent replacement upon the protected right of employees to strike was deemed outweighed by the legitimate and substantial employer interest in continuing to operate its business during the work stoppage. These same principles apply when a strike has been "converted" from an economic strike to an unfair labor practice strike, and give significance to the Board's determination whether conversion occurs and the precise date on which the strike becomes prolonged by the employer unfair labor practice. The Board will not require the employer to rehire the permanently replaced striker when the replacement was effected during the period when the strike would have naturally continued had it been purely economically motivated; strikers replaced during the period of "prolongation" are, however, entitled to reinstatement. R. J. Oil & Ref. Co. (1954).

If strike replacements are hired for only a temporary period, commonly for the duration of the strike, even the economic striker is entitled to reinstatement upon making unconditional application. Pioneer Flour Mills v. NLRB (5th Cir. 1970). It violates the Act to discriminate against him by requiring him to appear for an interview, Spencer Auto Elec., Inc. (1947), or to submit an application as a new employee, Philanz Oldsmobile, Inc. (1962). The employer's characterization of the replacement as permanent rather than temporary will usually not be contradicted. Texas Co. (1951), *rev'd on other grounds* (9th Cir. 1952).

The replacement of economic and unfair labor practice strikers also has differing effects upon the eligibility of both the strikers and their replacements to vote in a collective bargaining election conducted during the strike. While both economic and unfair labor practice strikers are entitled to vote (whether or not the employer has purported to replace them), this privilege expires for the economic striker if the election is conducted beyond twelve months from the commencement of the strike as provided in section 9(c)(3) of the Labor Act. Permanent replacements for economic strikers are eligible to vote, Rudolph Wurlitzer Co. (1941), but replacements for unfair labor practice strikers are not, Tampa Sand & Material Co. (1962). These principles withdraw from the employer the power to commit an unfair labor practice and thereafter oust the union by hiring permanent replacements for the strikers. When, however, the strike is an economic strike, the hiring of permanent replacements (who may vote) may justify an employer's doubt that the union retains majority support and thus may shelter a refusal to continue recognition of the union; but in determining the extent of union support, the replaced economic strikers must be counted during the twelve-month period commencing with the strike. Pioneer Flour Mills v. NLRB (5th Cir. 1970).

The employer right permanently to replace economic strikers—although realistically dependent upon such factors as the strength of the union, the tightness of the labor market and the degree of skills required—obviously deters the exercise of the right to strike and is a severe sanction therefor. It also creates a distinction between the rights of economic and unfair labor strikers which some think unsound and indeed perverse, since the strike may be the only recourse against employer intransigence at the bargaining table while the union and employees always have available the machinery of the NLRB to redress employer unfair labor practices. The Board and the courts have since *Mackay* sharply reduced its impact—and also narrowed the distinction between economic strikers and unfair labor practice strikers—by holding that the economic striker is entitled, upon unconditional application, to preferential reinstatement status even though on the date of his application for reinstatement his position is not available due to temporary economic retrenchment resulting from the strike or to the presence of a permanent replacement.

§ 5.   Reinstatement Rights of Economic Strikers

Although the Board initially held that the employer could not deny reinstatement to a replaced economic striker whose replacement left some time after the strike, its decisions usually rested in some degree on specific evidence of antiunion discrimination in denying reinstatement. With a change in Board membership resulting from appointments made by President Eisenhower, the Board firmly ruled that the employer owes no duty (other than to accord nondiscriminatory treatment as an applicant for new employment) to an economic striker whose job, on the date of his reinstatement request, had been legitimately abolished or had been filled by a permanent replacement. Brown & Root, Inc. (1961), *enf'd as mdf'd* (8th Cir. 1963). The employer had no duty to seek out the former strikers at a later date when their job opened up again, and they were at that time entitled to no preference above a new job applicant. Another change in Board membership under President Kennedy brought a reversal of this principle, and the Supreme Court approved the change in NLRB v. Fleetwood Trailer Co. (U.S.1967).

There, an economic strike caused a sharp curtailment in production such that when the strike terminated and the strikers applied for reinstatement, their work no longer existed because of the temporary cutback. When the company's volume of business returned to normal, it hired several new applicants before reinstating the former strikers, and the Board held this to violate sections 8(a)(1) and (3). In affirming, the Supreme Court placed primary reliance upon section 2(3) of the Act, which includes within the definition of "employee" any "individual whose work has ceased as a consequence of, or in connection with, any current labor dispute   .   .   and who has not obtained any other regular and substantially equivalent employment"; and also upon the Court's earlier decision in NLRB v. Great Dane Trailers, Inc. (U.S.1967), which required the employer to demonstrate that any action which discouraged union activities was due to "legitimate and substantial business justifications." It held:

> This basic right to jobs cannot depend upon job availability
> as of the moment when the applications are filed. The right
> to reinstatement does not depend upon technicalities relating

> to application. On the contrary, the status of the striker as
> an employee continues until he has obtained "other regular
> and substantially equivalent employment." . . .
> Frequently a strike affects the level of production and the
> number of jobs. It is entirely normal for striking employees
> to apply for reinstatement immediately after the end of the
> strike and before full production is resumed. If and when a
> job for which the striker is qualified becomes available, he is
> entitled to an offer of reinstatement.

The Court cited its *Mackay* decision, permitting the hiring of permanent replacements, as an example of a "legitimate and substantial" business reason for not immediately reinstating an economic striker. It also, without deciding, adverted to the possibility that another such legitimate reason would be the elimination of the striker's job for substantial and bona fide reasons other than labor-relations considerations, such as the need to adapt to changes in business conditions or to improve efficiency.

The Court's decision in *Fleetwood* might have been read to apply only to cases of temporary retrenchment in the workforce; arguably, it was a version of the familiar case of the economic striker being only temporarily replaced (stronger yet, not replaced at all) and thus entitled to reinstatement for that reason. But the Board promptly went further, concluded that the Supreme Court meant to reject the "day of application" rule even in cases in which a permanent replacement had been hired for the economic striker, and overruled its earlier decisions to the contrary. In Laidlaw Corp. (1968), enf'd (7th Cir. 1969), the Board held that even if on the date of application for reinstatement a permanent replacement holds the striker's job, the employer must later seek out the former striker and give him priority over new applicants for any comparable job that opens by virtue of the replacement's departure. Both the Board and the court of appeals in *Laidlaw* held that the employer's attempt to terminate the "employee" status of the former striker as of the date of application, and the hiring of new applicants when reinstatement applications were still outstanding, were presumptive violations of the Act regardless of the employer's motive. The employer could defend its action only by demonstrating either that the former striker had in the meantime secured regular and equivalent employment elsewhere or that its refusal to reinstate the striker was founded on a legitimate and substantial business reason (such as a change in the employer's operations or the striker's lack of requisite skills). Even though the court conceded that the precedents applicable at the time of the employer's refusal to reinstate supported the employer—indeed, the evidence showed the employer to have acted only after securing advice of counsel—the court held that it was proper for the Board to order backpay running from that date until actual reinstatement, since the harshness of retroactivity was outweighed by the need to protect important statutory rights of employees. The Board has since made it clear that the reinstatement must be with full vested employment benefits, including seniority. Globe Molded Plastics Co. (1973) (reinstatement without former seniority lacks any business justification and is illegal without proof of antiunion animus). To reinstate to the same position at a reduced rate of pay is "inherently destructive" of protected employee rights and unlawful. Northwest Oyster Farms, Inc. (1968). It has also been clearly held that the economic striker's right of reinstatement is activated not only upon the departure of the precise individual who replaced him but whenever a job opens up for which the former striker is qualified. Little Rock Airmotive, Inc. v. NLRB (8th Cir. 1972).

The *Laidlaw* decision has been uniformly approved by the courts of appeals. See, *e. g.*, Retail Stores Union v. NLRB (Coca Cola Bottling Works, Inc.) (D.C.Cir. 1972). Several courts have also been confronted with the retroactive application of the *Laidlaw* principle to employer conduct which occurred prior to the Board decision in that case, at a time when the Board precedents were to the contrary. In spite of employer claims (as in *Laidlaw* itself) that the Board should have announced its change in rule only prospectively, and through its rulemaking procedures rather than in ad hoc adjudications, courts have nonetheless sustained such Board "retroactive" backpay orders. Compare H. & F. Binch Co. (2d Cir. 1972), and American Mach. Corp. v. NLRB (5th Cir. 1970) (both cases noting that the Supreme Court decision in *Fleetwood Trailer* had portended a change in the law), with Retail Store Union v. NLRB (Coca Cola Bottling Works, Inc. (D.C.Cir. 1972) (backpay for period prior to *Fleetwood* held improper, remand to Board to determine whether any backpay should be ordered commencing reasonable time after *Fleetwood*; on remand, the Board so ordered).

The principle announced in *Laidlaw* renders significant the question whether, at the time of a striker's request for reinstatement, a permanent replacement has already taken his position. One court has recently provided guidance:

> On the one hand, a mere offer [to a strike replacement], unaccepted when the striker seeks reinstatement, is insufficient to qualify; on the other, actual arrival on the job should not be required if an understanding has been reached that this will occur at a reasonably early date . . . .
> The standard established by the Board in earlier decisions appears to have been that a replacement has been obtained if, but only if, both the employer and the replacement understand that the latter has accepted the vacant position before the replaced striker offered to return to work. . . .
> Since such hirings are almost always oral and at will, it is not necessary that conversations should have taken a form

where the "replacement" would have a cause of action if a striker was allowed to return to work before the replacement arrived on the scene. Perhaps the Trial Examiner's phrasing, that the replacement would have reasonable "grounds for indignation" if he were subsequently denied the promised job, is about as good a formulation of the appropriate standard as can be achieved.

H. & F. Binch Co. v. NLRB (2d Cir. 1972). It will also become important in many cases to determine when, in the language of section 2(3) of the Labor Act, an economic striker has secured "regular and substantially equivalent employment" with some other employer and has thereby terminated his right to be sought out by his original employer for reinstatement upon the availability of his former position. The obvious intention of the legislation is to assure that the striker does not lose his status as "employee" of the struck employer merely because he has secured employment elsewhere as a means of "making ends meet" during the pendency of the strike. The Board has recently stated:

> The question of what constitutes "regular and substantially equivalent employment" cannot be determined by a mechanistic application of the literal language of the statute but must be determined on an *ad hoc* basis by an objective appraisal of a number of factors, both tangible and intangible, and includes the desire and intent of the employee concerned. Without attempting to set hard and fast guidelines, we simply note that such factors as fringe benefits (retirement, health, seniority for purposes of vacation, retention, and promotion), location and distance between the location of the job and an employee's home, differences in working conditions, et cetera, may prompt an employee to seek to return to his old job.

Little Rock Airmotive, Inc. (1970), *enf'd as mdf'd* (8th Cir. 1972) (trial examiner, Board, and court disagree on whether strikers had secured permanent employment elsewhere, all considering such factors as lower pay and seniority and physical incapacity at new job, and continuing notification of original employer concerning availability).

The *Laidlaw* decision also renders necessary a determination as to the duration of the striker's right to reinstatement. While it is not uncommon for collective bargaining agreements to accord to laid-off workers reinstatement rights continuing for one or two years, employers in the *Laidlaw* situation have complained of the burdens that would be imposed if the obligation to seek out former strikers for job openings were to continue indefinitely. It has nonetheless been held that the striker's status as "employee" with reinstatement privileges can extend beyond the twelve-month period from the commencement of the strike which, under section 9(c)(3), determines his eligibility to vote in a representation election. NLRB v. Hartmann Luggage (6th Cir. 1971). Nor is it relevant that at the time of the request for reinstatement, the striker's union was no longer majority representative such that its request for reinstatement on behalf of the strikers was arguably unauthorized. American Mach. Corp. v. NLRB (5th Cir. 1970). The Board has also rejected the argument that the right to reinstatement lapses one year after the termination of the strike or is congruent with a recall period for laid-off employees in the labor contract. Brooks Research & Mfg., Inc. (1973).

In that case, however, the Board did hold that reasonable recall procedures embodied in a labor contract may be utilized to limit the duration of the employer's obligation and the striker's privilege; it was sufficient that the employer give notice of recall by telephone and mail, directed to the last known address and telephone number on file, and that the employee must report to work within three working days after notification, on pain of having his name deleted from the list of applicants for reinstatement. A court has suggested that the employer might notify such applicants of a reasonable time during which their applications will be considered current, after which they must take affirmative action to maintain their status. American Mach. Corp. v. NLRB (5th Cir. 1970). (But the employer's unilateral declaration of these requirements, without bargaining with the majority union, will violate section 8(a)(5). Food Serv. Co. (1973).) The Board has also held that the employer may limit the duration of reinstatement rights as part of an agreement negotiated with the union establishing the terms on which the strike is to be concluded:

> So long, therefore, as the period fixed by agreement for the reinstatement of economic strikers is not unreasonably short, is not intended to be discriminatory, or misused by either party with the object of accomplishing a discriminatory objective, was not insisted upon by the employer in order to undermine the status of the bargaining representative, and was the result of good-faith collective bargaining, the Board ought to accept the agreement of the parties as effectuating the policies of the Act which . . . includes as a principal objective encouragement of the practice and procedure of collective bargaining as a means of settling labor disputes.

United Aircraft Corp. (1971), *enf't denied on other grounds* (2d Cir. 1975) (strike-settlement agreement, negotiated in 1960—eight years prior to the Board decision in *Laidlaw*—provided that after four and one-half months strikers would be treated as new job applicants; or appeal, court holds that waiver of right to reinstatement could no prior to *Fleetwood,* have been done knowingly).

§ 6. Remedies

The employer is not obligated for backpay to either the economic striker or the unfair labor practice striker for the period during which they voluntarily cease their work and engage in the strike. But if they wish to return to work and make an unconditional application for reinstatement, an illegal refusal to reinstate will trigger the running of backpay beginning five days after the request for reinstatement. D'Armigene, Inc. (1964), *mdf'd on other grounds* (2d Cir. 1965) (five-day period gives the employer time to communicate offer of reinstatement). Backpay will ordinarily be computed at the wage rate which obtained when the discriminatee was last on the job. Patrick F. Izzi (1966). If he would have been entitled to a raise or a bonus during the period in which he was illegally deprived of work, he is entitled in the determination of backpay to credit for that raise, Golay & Co. v. NLRB (7th Cir. 1971), or that bonus, Nabors v. NLRB (5th Cir. 1963). Entitlement to a raise or a bonus is determined by referring to the earnings of employees comparable in classification and seniority to the discriminatee.

To be entitled to backpay for a wrongful denial of reinstatement, the striker's request for reinstatement must be unconditional. It may not, for example, be conditioned upon the employer's recognizing the union as bargaining agent. Samuel Levine (1963). But the request need not come from the individual striker personally. It may be submitted on behalf of a group of employees by the union as their agent. Trinity Valley Iron & Steel Co. v. NLRB (5th Cir. 1969). The request need take no special form, such as a specific application supplied by the employer; it need only communicate to the employer the employees' desire for reinstatement. NLRB v. Fleetwood Trailer Co. (U.S.1967).

Backpay for illegal refusal to reinstate will generally cease accumulating when the employer makes an unconditional offer of reinstatement. Crossett Lumber Co., *enf'd per curiam* (8th Cir. 1938); Charley Toppino & Sons (1965), *enf'd* (5th Cir. 1966). But here too, the backpay period will not terminate when the offer to reinstate is conditioned on such acts as the employee's abandonment of a valid grievance, Thor Power Tool Co. (1964), *enf'd* (7th Cir. 1965), or is conditioned on the acceptance of employment substantially different from or inferior to that performed by the employee before, Thomas J. Aycock, Jr. (1965), *enf'd as mdf'd* (5th Cir. 1967). If no substantially equivalent work is available at the time the employee requests reinstatement (except when the application is by an unfair labor practice striker and the lack of work is because the employer has hired a replacement), the employer's liability will be tolled when it places the employee on a preferential hiring list. Ethel J. Hinz (1962). If the employer fails to offer reinstatement (or preferential hiring) to an employee entitled thereto, and that employee is reinstated pursuant to Board order, backpay liability will continue from the date of the employee's request for reinstatement until the date the employer complies by offering reinstatement. Astro Electronics, Inc. (1971), *enf'd per curiam* (9th Cir. 1972).

§ 7. The Reinstatement of Strikers Engaging in Unprotected Activity

Persons engaging in an economic strike or an unfair labor practice strike are not, by virtue of that fact, necessarily engaging in protected activity immune from discharge, for in the course of their strike they may engage in violence, or in an illegal secondary boycott, or in a breach of contract, or in some other conduct classified as "unprotected activity." (This classification is considered at length elsewhere in this work.) Engaging in unprotected activity exposes the striker to disciplinary measures, consistently with sections 8(a)(1) and (3). Thus, if an economic striker engages in violence on the picket line—for example, by assaulting a fellow employee or a supervisor—the employer is free under the Labor Act to discharge that employee for that conduct (although not for merely participating in the strike, a nice factual issue). Since the employee action is unprotected there is no violation of section 8(a)(1), which requires that the employer not coerce employees in the exercise of rights protected by section 7; a more narrowly drafted section 8(a)(3) would not be violated either, since the Board would not attribute the discharge to the employee's union membership or lawful union activities. Reinstatement cannot be secured, for the simple reason that no unfair labor practice is committed by the employer.

The situation is different when an unfair labor practice striker engages in unprotected activity and is then discharged therefor. Although the discharge is not an interference with protected activity and thus does not in itself violate the Labor Act, the employer has by hypothesis committed an unfair labor practice which precipitated or prolonged the strike, and the discharged strikers might be ordered reinstated as a remedy for the initial employer misconduct. The Court of Appeals for the First Circuit held, in NLRB v. Thayer Co. (1st Cir. 1954), that the Board erred in believing that it had no power to order the reinstatement of unfair labor practice strikers discharged for unprotected activity, and remanded the case to the Board to determine whether reinstatement of the particular dischargees given the particular conduct in which they engaged would comply with the congressional guidelines for remedies under section 10(c). That section empowers the Board to order reinstatement or other affirmative relief "as will effectuate the policies of this Act" but bars the reinstatement of any individual who "was suspended or discharged for cause." The court held that since the strike had been precipitated by employer misconduct, the issues of "effectuating the policies of the Act" and of "just cause" can be determined by the Board only by balancing the gravity of the employer unfair labor practice against the gravity of the employees' misconduct in order to determine whether reinstatement is warranted.

Although the Board was reluctant to embrace this principle, it was reasserted by another court of appeals in Local 833, UAW v. NL RB (Kohler Co.) (D.C.Cir. 1962). There, the Board found that an economic strike was prolonged by employer refusals to bargain, but refused to order reinstatement of strikers who thereafter were discharged for such conduct as "belly to back" mass picketing which barred access to the plant for six weeks, participation in large disorderly mass demonstrations at the homes of nonstrikers and obstruction of the company employment office when the company tried to hire replacements. The court remanded so that the Board could determine whether reinstatement was warranted as a remedy for the employer's refusal to bargain:

> To hold that employee "misconduct" automatically precludes compulsory reinstatement ignores two considerations which we think important. First, the employer's antecedent unfair labor practices may have been so blatant that they provoked employees to resort to unprotected action. Second, reinstatement is the only sanction which prevents an employer from benefiting from his unfair labor practices through discharges which may weaken or destroy the union.

The court noted that automatic denial of reinstatement may not be essential to protect legitimate interests of the public or of the employer, since those interests may be protected by other sanctions— criminal prosecutions, civil suits, union unfair labor practice proceedings and the anticipation that discharge might be effected and might be sustained by the Board. The court also rejected the argument that the employees' misconduct was "cause" for their discharge such that reinstatement was improper under section 10(c). It held that the Board in construing this provision of the Act must consider at least "the employer's unfair labor practices, each employee's job history, and the relationship between the acts of misconduct and fitness for continued service."

The Board, coincident with a change in its membership with new presidential appointees, reversed its former position and adopted the principle of the *Thayer* and *Kohler* cases that strikers discharged for strike misconduct, unprotected activity, may be reinstated if the strike was precipitated or prolonged by an employer unfair labor practice. Blades Mfg. Co. (1963), *enf't denied on other grounds* (8th Cir. 1965) (Board assumed arguendo that concerted activity was partial or intermittent and thus unprotected).

In spite of the generally applicable principle that employees discharged for participation in unprotected activity can secure reinstatement only if they were protesting an employer unfair labor practice, the doctrine of "condonation" has on occasion been invoked to give reinstatement rights even to economic strikers who engage in unprotected conduct. The doctrine of condonation applies in the following circumstances. Employees on strike in support of demands for a new labor contract might inflict violence on co-workers; or, in support of a grievance during the contract term, employees might strike in breach of a no-strike clause. Although this conduct in either case exposes the employees to discharge, the employer might demonstrate that it regards the infractions as minor and that it intends to invoke no sanction therefor; it could do this either prior to imposing any discipline on the strikers or by way of reconsideration after discipline has initially been imposed. The employer can evidence its willingness to "condone" the strikers' wrongdoing either by verbal statements or by permitting all or some of the perpetrators to return to work with full privileges. If, having gone this far, the employer reverses position and imposes discipline upon the strikers, adverting to their unprotected activity, such discipline may be found to violate section 8(a)(3). The rationale for the condonation doctrine is by no means evident, and the decided cases do little to articulate it. For the employees have indeed engaged in unprotected activity—in the hypotheticals, picket-line violence or breach of the contractual no-strike provision—and the employer's imposition of discipline can thus on its face not be on account of activity sheltered by sections 7, 8(a)(1) and 8(a)(3).

Two different explanations of the condonation doctrine emerge from the cases, only one of which is rather directly responsive to the text and policies of the statutory provisions normally being applied. Under that theory, when the employer—verbally or through its actions such as reinstatement—acknowledges that it forgives the violence or the breach of contract, one may infer that the employer is lacking in candor when it later discharges (or refuses to reinstate) the strikers assertedly for the "wrongdoing" that has already been condoned. In other words, the condonation warrants the inference that the asserted reason is merely a pretext for the discipline, and that the employer's true motive was rather to punish the strikers for their participation, as such, in the strike, participation which apart from the condoned wrongdoing would be protected activity. Needham Packing Co. (1970) (exhaustive treatment by trial examiner).

A second rationale for the condonation doctrine holds the employer on a theory of contract-enforcement to any implied or express promise not to discipline for the condoned activities. Holding an employer to a strike-settlement agreement by which it restores employment rights to workers engaging in unprotected activities will foster the "friendly adjustment of industrial disputes"; while permitting the employer to reneg "would contravene the basis of the strike settlement and would tend to promote another strike or other form of industrial unrest." *Ibid.* Although one may question whether the Board's unfair labor practice jurisdiction, and particularly section 8

(a) (3), is an appropriate vehicle by which to implement the statutory policy of promise-enforcement and the general promotion of industrial peace, there is judicial support for this rationale (as well as for the pretext rationale mentioned above). Jones & McKnight, Inc. v. NLRB (7th Cir. 1971) ("The primary purpose of the Act is to further industrial peace, and effectuation of this statutory policy demands that parties to a strike settlement be precluded from going behind their agreement to reopen a matter which they have waived in the interests of peace and harmony.").

In order to find that the employer has "condoned" employee wrongdoing—such that subsequent discharge or refusal to reinstate will be deemed an unfair labor practice—it is commonly held that:

> [C]ondonation may not be lightly presumed from mere silence or equivocal statements, but must clearly appear from some positive act by an employer indicating forgiveness and an intention of treating the guilty employees as if their misconduct had not occurred.

NLRB v. Marshall Car Wheel & Foundry Co. (5th Cir. 1955). The employer must agree both "to forgive the misconduct and 'wipe the slate clean'" and also "to resume the former employment relationship with the employee." NLRB v. Colonial Press, Inc. (8th Cir. 1975). The burden of clearly proving these elements is upon the General Counsel. Merck & Co. (1954). Therefore, condonation is not shown if the employer agrees to take back the strikers but only as new employees, or if the employer when discharging the strikers neglects specifically to cite the wrongdoing as a reason for the discipline. NLRB v. Marshall Car Wheel & Foundry Co. (5th Cir. 1955). An employer statement that there are "no hard feelings" unaccompanied by reinstatement will not make out condonation; nor will reinstatement alone (so a court has held) without something akin to such a statement. Retail Store Union v. NLRB (Coca Cola Bottling Works, Inc.) (D.C. Cir. 1972). Presumably, the mere willingness of the employer to resume the employment relationship, particularly in times of competitive economic pressure, will not alone warrant a finding of condonation. See NLRB v. Community Motor Bus Co. (4th Cir. 1971) (inadequate proof that employer has "wiped slate clean" when it refrains from discipline simply "to keep the peace" or when it merely tells employees that they are "needed" and wanted back). It has even been held that an offer of complete reinstatement which is spurned by the strikers does not forever waive the employer's right to refuse reinstatement. *Ibid.* (While this might make sense on a theory that no "contract" has been formed between employer and strikers, it is not clear why the "pretext" rationale would not be applicable to show that any wrongdoing committed by the strikers prior to the reinstatement offer was not the true reason for any subsequent discipline.) Court reversals of the Board in a number of cases mentioned above demonstrate that many courts are not inclined to give the Board great deference in its finding that condonation has occurred, in spite of the argument that can be made that this is a purely factual issue on which the Board's findings should be sustained if supported by "substantial evidence on the record considered as a whole."

§ 8.   Responses to Employee Refusals to Cross Picket Lines

There is a substantial amount of confusion in the cases on the question of allowable employer responses to refusals by its employees to cross picket lines encountered at other companies. Of course, if an employee is discharged or otherwise disciplined because of his lawful union activities apart from the refusal to cross, and the refusal is used only as a pretext, the employer violates section 8(a)(3); this is so even if the refusal itself is characterized as unprotected activity. See Truck Drivers Local 728 v. NLRB (Overnight Transp. Co.) (D. C.Cir. 1966). If the employer action, however, is a response solely to the refusal to cross the picket line, it will not violate the Act if the refusal is held to be unprotected activity; this is true whether the employer conduct under scrutiny is a discharge or a subsequent refusal to reinstate upon request. NLRB v. L. G. Everist, Inc. (8th Cir. 1964).

The present position of the Board, and of some appellate courts, is that the picket-line refusal is protected activity, which raises the issue of allowable employer response. Although at one time the Board adopted the anomalous position that the picket-line refusal is protected but subjects the employee to discharge, Redwing Carriers, Inc. (1962), *enf'd* (D.C.Cir. 1963), the Board has attempted to apply the philosophy of NLRB v. MacKay Radio & Tel. Co. (U.S.1938) (permanent replacement of economic strikers held lawful) so as to sustain only employer responses (such as temporary or permanent replacement) which can be justified by reference to needs of the business. Some courts have disparaged what has appeared to them to be the Board's mechanical allowance of permanent replacement but disallowance of outright discharge. NLRB v. Rockaway News Co. (U.S. 1953). The distinction is indeed somewhat awkwardly transplanted from the full-strike context of *Mackay,* particularly when the employee's refusal to pick up or deliver goods at a picketed establishment represents nonperformance of only a small part of his assigned duties. Unlike *Mackay,* it is the employer who takes the initiative in severing the work relationship by replacing the recalcitrant employee with another hire, and the employer can very frequently have the rejected work performed by making only minor adjustments in the work assignments of employees already on the payroll, without severing the employment of the recalcitrant employee altogether.

The Board thus claims to apply the discharge-replacement distinction with special attention to business realities in these cases:

> [W]e are convinced that substance, rather than form, should be controlling. That is, where it is clear from the record that the employer acted only to preserve efficient operation of his business, and terminated the services of the employees only so it could immediately or within a short period thereafter replace them with others willing to perform the scheduled work, we can see no reason for reaching different results solely on the basis of the precise words, i. e., replacement or discharge, used by the employer, or the chronological order in which the employer terminated and replaced the employees in question.

Redwing Carriers, Inc. (1962), enf'd (D.C.Cir. 1963). If an employee loses his job because of his refusal to cross a picket line elsewhere, the Board places upon the employer the burden of demonstrating that the refusal constituted a substantial interference with its business, that any such interference could not be overcome merely by assigning another employee to do the work, and that a replacement was in fact hired. Otherwise, the employer violates section 8(a)(1). This appears to be merely an application of the interest-balancing analysis endorsed by the Supreme Court in NLRB v. Great Dane Trailers, Inc. (U.S.1967), with the burden shifting to the employer upon a showing that the employee lost his job because of his refusal to cross the picket line; the absence of any independent antiunion animus will not shelter the employer against a finding of an 8(a)(1) violation, the section (rather than 8(a)(3)) under which these kinds of cases have commonly been treated. See NLRB v. Alamo Express, Inc. (5th Cir. 1970) (court looks for employee replacement as evidence of business purpose).

While in the context of a full strike, under *Mackay*, the employer is apparently conclusively presumed to have a legitimate business reason for hiring permanent replacements, the Board in the picket-line-refusal cases has required an affirmative demonstration that discharge or replacement is all but essential to avoid serious disruption of the business. In Overnite Transp. Co. (1965), the Board held that the employer must show more than that "someone else may have to do the work," a need which will always exist in the case of a refusal to go through a picket line to make pickups or deliveries; "Clearly, what is required is the balancing of two opposing rights, and it is only when the employer's business need to replace the employees is such as clearly to outweigh the employees' right to engage in protected activity that an invasion of the statutory right is justified." In *Overnight*, the Board held that the discharge of an employee for refusing to make a pickup (through a picket line) pursuant to radio-dispatched instructions violated section 8(a)(1), where the pickup was a single transaction rather than a regular and permanent assignment, the radio dispatcher was able promptly to find another truckdriver to make the disputed pickup, the recalcitrant employee was immediately given other substitute pickup assignments for a full day's work, and such adjustments in assignments within the geographic sphere of company operations appeared commonplace. The Board has also held that discharge is not justified by business needs when the lack of time and available manpower made it impossible for the employer to find a replacement for the recalcitrant employee, Swain & Morris Constr. Co. (1967), *enf'd* (9th Cir. 1970); and when conversely, a "one-shot" delivery has already been made by a supervisory employee at the time when the recalcitrant employee is informed of his discharge, Thurston Motor Lines (1967) (Board also found that one employee had already been discharged validly for refusing to make the delivery in question, and that the designation of the second employee to cross the picket line was suspect since the employer knew him to be a strong union adherent and thus a "poor replacement choice").

§ 9. The Illegal Lockout; The "Defensive" Lockout

An employer is said to "lock out" its employees when, for tactical reasons, it refuses to utilize those employees for the performance of available work. The Labor Act does not by its own terms declare the lockout lawful or unlawful. Legality depends upon the application of the general provisions of section 8(a) to the facts of any given case. Thus, if the purpose of the lockout is to punish employees for joining or designating a labor organization or otherwise to obstruct their free choice of a representative, this is clearly "discouragement of union membership" through the intentional deprivation of job opportunities and thus a violation of sections 8(a)(1) and (3). Tonkin Corp. (1966), *enf'd* (9th Cir. 1968). If the purpose of the lockout is to force a favored union on the employees, it will violate section 8(a)(2). *Ibid.* If its purpose is to evade the duty to bargain, or to force acquiescence in an illegal bargaining position, the lockout may be held to violate section 8(a)(5). See NLRB v. Wooster Div. of Borg-Warner Corp. (U.S.1958).

Other lockouts may, however, be motivated by legitimate business reasons. These have been the subject of evolving doctrine in the Board and the courts. The three most common lockouts might be labelled, somewhat conclusorily, the defensive-economic lockout, the defensive-multiemployer lockout and the offensive-bargaining lockout.

The Board has traditionally held, with judicial approval, that it is legal for an employer to lock out its employees when it is reasonably fearful of a strike which, if called at a time chosen by the union, will result in inordinate harm to the business, property, goods or goodwill of the employer. The leading Board decisions are Duluth Bottling Ass'n (1943), in which an anticipated strike would have caused spoilage of syrup to be used in the manufacture of soft drinks;

International Shoe Co. (1951), in which an entire integrated-production plant was shut down in response to intermittent "quickie" walkouts in individual departments; and Betts Cadillac Olds, Inc. (1951), in which an anticipated strike among automobile service and repair personnel would have left customers' disassembled cars stranded in the shop. The latter case held that, before the precise moment a strike occurs, the employer may take "reasonable measures, including closing down his plant, where such measures are, under the circumstances, necessary for the avoidance of economic loss or business disruption attendant upon a strike." The lockout was characterized as "defensive" and thus justified and lawful. (The employer, however, acts somewhat at its peril, since it is for the Board to determine whether the lockout was a reasonable response to a reasonably feared work stoppage. Quaker State Oil Refining Corp. v. NLRB (3d Cir. 1959).)

The defensive-economic lockout was an inherently unstable concept. It is difficult indeed to differentiate "usual" from "unusual" economic losses. Moreover, since the union will normally utilize the work stoppage to cause serious inconvenience and loss to the employer, the "defensive" lockout was used by the employer to maximize its own bargaining advantage and minimize that of the union, and to achieve thereby a more prompt settlement on more favorable terms; that is precisely the object of the offensive or bargaining lockout as well.

When several employers bargain as a group with a single union, the union will sometimes seek to maximize its bargaining leverage by striking one of the employers, which will then be induced to settle promptly and generously because of the competitive losses inflicted by the nonstruck employers. To combat this kind of "whipsaw" strike—that is, to guard against being the next victim and to "preserve the integrity" of the entire multiemployer bargaining unit—the nonstruck employers might lock out their own employees, who are members of the same union as the strikers but themselves prepared to work in order to increase the pressure on the struck company. The Board at first held this kind of lockout illegal, but reversed its position in 1954, contemporaneous with a change in its membership, and was sustained by the Supreme Court in NLRB v. Truck Drivers Local 449 (Buffalo Linen) (U.S.1957). The Court held that, like the cases of defensive lockouts to avoid unusual economic hardship, the employees' right to strike had to be balanced against a legitimate employer interest, here the interest of the nonstruck employers "in preserving multiemployer bargaining as a means of bargaining on an equal basis with a large union and avoiding the competitive disadvantages resulting from nonuniform contractual terms." The task of striking the balance was committed by Congress "primarily to the National Labor Relations Board, subject to limited judicial review," and was discharged properly by the Board in that case.

Ironically, soon after, the Court rebuked the Board for engaging in a balancing of interests within the multiemployer setting and for acting in excess of the powers given it by Congress. In NLRB v. Brown (U.S.1965), after a whipsaw strike and multiemployer lockout as in *Buffalo Linen*, the struck employer exercised its privilege to continue operating with temporary replacements; the nonstruck employers, not wanting to remain closed and yet not wanting to reinforce the pressures on the struck employer by returning their locked out employees to work, also hired replacements announced to be temporary until the strike terminated. The Court overturned the Board's finding of section 8(a)(1) and (3) violations and held the hiring of temporary replacements by the nonstruck (locking-out) employers to be justified by the preservation of the multiemployer unit and to be no more harmful to the statutory rights of the employees than was the clearly legal lockout.

Implicit in the Court's *Buffalo Linen* holding was the belief that reinforcement of the bargaining position of the locking-out employers was a legitimate business purpose. This, and the decision of the Supreme Court in NLRB v. Insurance Agents' Int'l Union (U.S.1960), that a union does not commit an unfair labor practice (by bargaining in bad faith) when it pressures the employer during negotiations by intermittent and harassing work stoppages, set the stage for sustaining the offensive or bargaining lockout.

§ 10.   The Offensive or Bargaining Lockout

For many years, the Board held illegal the lockout designed to pressure a union into a prompt and favorable settlement at the negotiating table. It rejected employer arguments that the peaceful lockout was the analogue of the peaceful bargaining strike, and held that such a lockout interfered with the employees' right to strike and punished the employees for adherence to their bargaining position, thereby violating sections 8(a)(1), (3) and usually 8(a)(5) as well. The Supreme Court dramatically reversed the Board in American Ship Bldg. Co. v. NLRB (U.S.1965), where it stated: "[W]e hold that an employer violates neither § 8(a)(1) nor § 8(a)(3) when, after a bargaining impasse has been reached, he temporarily shuts down his plant and lays off his employees for the sole purpose of bringing economic pressure to bear in support of his legitimate bargaining position." In that case, the employer, which had been the victim of strikes in previous negotiations, feared that the union would protract negotiations for a new contract until the winter, the employer's busy season, and thus immobilize customers' ships in drydock. Finding this apprehension reasonable, the trial examiner concluded that the employer's summer lockout was a defensive-economic lockout and thus lawful. The Board, however, found the employer's fear of a strike unreasonable, and concluded that the purpose of the lockout was to break the bargaining impasse and to secure more favorable contract terms, thus rendering the lockout illegal.

The Supreme Court, accepting without question the Board's reading of the employer's purpose in locking out, concluded that the bargaining lockout was not so inherently destructive of employee rights to bargain and to strike that sections 8(a)(1) and (3) could be found violated absent proof of an intention by the employer to penalize the employees for unionization, to destroy the union or to evade its duty to bargain:

> [T]he right to bargain collectively does not entail any "right" to insist on one's position free from economic disadvantage. . . .

> . . . [T]here is nothing in the statute which would imply that the right to strike "carries with it" the right exclusively to determine the timing and duration of all work stoppages. . . .

> . . . There was not the slightest evidence and there was no finding that the employer was actuated by a desire to discourage membership in the union as distinguished from a desire to affect the outcome of the particular negotiations in which it was involved.

As in NLRB v. Brown (U.S.1965), decided the same day, the Court in *American Ship Building* reprimanded the Board—which had concluded that the employer already possessed sufficient weapons in the battle of collective bargaining, such as permanent replacement, stockpiling of goods and subcontracting—for arrogating, without statutory support, "a general authority to assess the relative economic power of the adversaries in the bargaining process and to deny weapons to one party or the other because of its assessment of that party's bargaining power." Two Justices, concurring, argued against the adoption of a rule of per se legality for the post-impasse bargaining lockout and urged that the Board be empowered to weigh the conflicting interests in differing lockout situations. A third Justice, who concurred for other reasons, was apparently prepared to sustain the Board's conclusion that the bargaining lockout so interfered with protected employee rights as to be per se illegal, regardless of lack of proof of antiunion bias.

The Board promptly acknowledged that *American Ship Building* had obliterated the distinction between offensive and defensive lockouts, and concluded that neither was per se legal or per se illegal. It also concluded, in light of the intervening Supreme Court decision in NLRB v. Great Dane Trailers, Inc. (U.S.1967), that henceforth the lockout could be declared illegal only if either: (a) the employer's specific motive was to penalize employees for engaging in protected activities, or to destroy the union, or to evade the duty to bargain collectively; or (b) "the lockout in all [the] circumstances was inherently prejudicial to union interests and so devoid of significant

economic justification that no specific evidence of intent is required."
Darling & Co. (1968), *enf'd* (D.C.Cir. 1969). The Board has thus
held that absent either of these two record findings, employers who
are engaging in "joint bargaining" through a single spokesman—but
which do not technically comprise a multiemployer unit within the
shelter of *Buffalo Linen*—may lock out their employees in order to
buttress their bargaining position against a whipsaw strike, as well as
the bargaining position of other participating employers. Weyerhaeuser Co. (1967). Even when two employers were bargaining separately with the same union, with many of the same issues under
consideration in the separate negotiations, a lockout pursuant to an
agreement between the employers that one would lock out if the other were struck was held to have a "bargaining motivation" and a
"significant economic justification" and thus not to violate section
8(a)(1) or 8(a)(3). Evening News Ass'n (1967), *enf'd* (6th Cir.
1968). Indeed, the Board noted that *American Ship Building* would
have permitted a lockout in such cases even in the absence of a strike
to precipitate it. Weyerhaeuser Co. (1967).

The Board applied the same criteria in a "pure" single-employer
context, and held that a lockout even prior to an impasse in negotiations, but designed to induce a prompt settlement on favorable terms,
was legal. Darling & Co. (1968), *enf'd* (D.C.Cir. 1969). The Board
stated:

> While the finding of an impasse in negotiations may be a
> factor supporting a determination that a particular lockout
> is lawful, the absence of an impasse does not of itself make a
> lockout unlawful any more than the mere existence of an
> impasse automatically renders a lockout lawful.

The Board and the enforcing court considered the employer's good
faith bargaining before and after the lockout, the longevity of relations with and the strength of the union, the union's strike threat, a
strike some years before on a hotly contested issue which was also
disputed in the current negotiations, and the "unusual harm" that
would come from a strike timed for the employer's busy season. It
was held that proof of union animus was lacking, the lockout was not
"inherently destructive" of employee rights, it was supported by "legitimate and substantial" business reasons, and was thus not in violation of sections 8(a)(1) and (3). This case-by-case screening of the
particular circumstances showing employer justification and employee harm was viewed as consistent with the decision of the Court
in *American Ship Building* and has shaped the analysis of the Board
and the lower courts in subsequent cases.

In a recent decision expanding even further the rights of employers incidental to bargaining lockouts, the Board has held that an employer, entitled to lock out employees in support of its bargaining
position on the termination date of a contract, may lawfully lay off

employees in advance of that date if the business is such as to dictate a gradual cessation of work prior to the lockout date. Royal Packing Co. (1972) (staged layoff of slaughterers, processers and distributors of beef in order to leave storage lockers free of inventory on lockout date). The Board held that the layoffs did not themselves constitute a lockout but rather a reduction in force for lack of work, and thus did not violate the "cooling off" and notice provisions of section 8(d) of the Labor Act.

§ 11. The Lockout Plus Replacements

In NLRB v. Brown (U.S.1965), the Supreme Court held that the nonstruck employers in a multiemployer bargaining unit did not violate the Labor Act when they locked out their employees and, to compete with the struck employer which remained open with temporary replacements, hired temporary replacements of their own. The question remained whether a single employer could lock out its employees in support of its bargaining position and then proceed to operate with replacements, either temporary or permanent, either from within the plant (such as non-unit employees or supervisors) or without. On that question, the Board is sharply divided within itself, and the court decisions conflict. At first, the Board with court approval held that the use in a single-employer negotiation of temporary replacements for locked out employees was per se illegal; the deprivation of work at the same time as the employer continued to reap economic benefits would discourage the employees from collective bargaining and destroy the union's capacity for effective representation. Inland Trucking Co. (1969), enf'd (7th Cir. 1971). A change in Board membership brought a reversal of position, again with judicial approval. In Ottawa Silica Co. (1972), enf'd mem. (6th Cir. 1973), two Board members concluded that the single-employer lockout followed by temporary replacements was motivated by legitimate employer bargaining interests rather than antiunion animus and had no substantial tendency to discourage union membership; the replacements did not threaten the job security of employees upon the conclusion of the work stoppage and the lockout could be terminated whenever the employees were prepared to agree to the employer's terms. Two other Board members, relying on Inland Trucking, concluded that the employer's conduct was inherently destructive, discriminatory against unionized employees willing to work, and thus illegal without regard to motivation. The fifth Board member, refusing to find the employer's conduct either per se lawful or per se unlawful, found it lawful on the specific facts of the case by engaging in effect in a balancing process. The disparity of views persists. Inter Collegiate Press (1972), enf'd (8th Cir. 1973) (no violation of section 8(a)(1) or (3)).

The Supreme Court in American Ship Building, although it noted that the lockout was referred to in common with the strike at several places in the Taft-Hartley Act, did not hold that the employer is free to use the lockout at any time when the union would be free to use the strike. At the least it must be noted that the strike is specially protected in section 13 of the Labor Act while the lockout is not. The cases just discussed also raise doubts concerning any claim that whatever devices for self-protection the employer has when confronted with a strike are also necessarily available as a follow-up to a bargaining lockout. No case appears to raise the question whether the employer may hire temporary replacements after a defensive-economic lockout, a situation arguably not significantly different from the use of such replacements in the face of a strike. The case for temporary replacements is weaker when the employer takes the initiative with an offensive-bargaining lockout, although even here there is plausibility to the claim of business justification. When, however, the employer engages in a bargaining lockout and hires permanent replacements—a case which appears not to have arisen—such action would likely be deemed sufficient proof in itself of discriminatory motive as to be illegal per se. The discouragement of union membership and activities appears obvious, as does the capacity of the employer to oust the union by the hiring of permanent replacements. Moreover, there is not likely to be any legitimate business purpose, including bargaining leverage, which explains the use of permanent rather than temporary replacements.

§ 12. The "Partial Lockout"

An employer will typically hesitate long before implementing a lockout. Like a strike, it closes down the employer's operation, and its advantage lies only in usurping the union's control over timing. An employer might prefer to steal a march on the union by exerting lockout-like pressure on employees while at the same time keeping the plant in operation and accruing profits. This could be done, for example, by locking out only part of the workforce within the bargaining unit rather than all, or by keeping all employees at work but subject to reduced economic benefits pending settlement of negotiations. The "partial lockout" is a rather new and not frequently litigated device, and its legality is uncertain at best.

In Laclede Gas Co. (1970), it was held lawful for the employer, as the contract termination date approached, to "lock out" certain of its employees while retaining others on the payroll to do work which would ready the company for an impending work stoppage. Even though many of the locked out employees were senior in company service to many of those retained, their lockout was temporary, tactical, supported by business justification and did not discriminate on the basis of union membership or activity.

When, however, the employer's "partial" pressure takes the form of the temporary reduction of economic benefits then under negotiation, the few decisions condemn the employer action not only as bad-faith bargaining in violation of section 8(a)(5) but also as illegal discrimination in violation of sections 8(a)(1) and (3). In Local 155, Molders v. NLRB (United States Pipe & Foundry Co.) (D.C.Cir. 1971), the employer during negotiations cancelled an interim pay increase and a number of other economic benefits which had obtained under the expired contract; the employer's purpose was to bring pressure upon the union to settle, or to induce it to strike promptly rather than to continue negotiations into the summer when a stoppage would be most disruptive. Rejecting the argument that the endorsement by the Supreme Court of the lockout in *American Ship Building* necessarily included endorsement of the "lesser" pressure of reduced pay, a divided court of appeals held the employer's action, regardless of antiunion motivation, unlawfully to deprive the employees of their statutory control over the right to strike or to refrain from striking. Compare Borden, Inc. (1972) (*American Ship Building* does not protect employer's tactical cancellation of insurance benefits under section 8(a)(5), since lockout causes both employees and employer to suffer while cancellation of benefits injures only employees). Underlying such decisions may be the fear that such tactical reduction in benefits may impel employees to strike, thus rendering them subject to permanent replacement; as was suggested by one Board member in United States Pipe & Foundry Co. (1969), *enf'd* (D.C.Cir. 1971), perhaps the better solution is to permit the employer to withhold benefits, thus eliminating the severe disruption attendant upon a complete lockout, but to treat any subsequent strike as a "constructive lockout" which shelters the strikers against permanent replacement.

§ 13. Denial of Economic Benefits

If an employer refuses to pay accrued fringe benefits to employees who engage in a strike but pays those benefits to nonstrikers, there is a violation of sections 8(a)(1) and (3). There is unlawful discrimination in the clearest sense of disparate treatment of strikers and nonstrikers, and there is more than a strong likelihood that union activities will be discouraged. The employer's action will be held illegal even if there is no specific evidence that it actually was motivated by a desire to discourage the exercise of section 7 rights. In NLRB v. Great Dane Trailers, Inc. (U.S.1967) an employer announced in the midst of a bargaining strike that it would pay accrued vacation pay according to the formula in the expired contract only to persons who were at work on an earlier date during the strike; the employer introduced no reasons of business necessity for the action taken. The Supreme Court found an unfair labor practice, and set forth the rules of proof which have since governed the trial of cases under section 8(a)(3):

> First, if it can reasonably be concluded that the employer's discriminatory conduct was "inherently destructive" of important employee rights, no proof of an antiunion motiva-

tion is needed and the Board can find an unfair labor practice even if the employer introduces evidence that the conduct was motivated by business considerations. Second, if the adverse effect of the discriminatory conduct on employee rights is "comparatively slight," an antiunion motivation must be proved to sustain the charge *if* the employer has come forward with evidence of legitimate and substantial business justifications for the conduct. Thus, in either situation, once it has been proved that the employer engaged in discriminatory conduct which could have adversely affected employee rights to *some* extent, the burden is upon the employer to establish that he was motivated by legitimate objectives since proof of motivation is most accessible to him.

In *Great Dane*, the Court did not decide whether the disparate payment of accrued vacation pay had an inherently destructive or comparatively slight impact on the right to strike, since the impact that it did have was not counterbalanced by any proof at all of business justification.

Some two weeks later, the Board held that the grant of a pay increase at one store where there was no organizing activity and a denial of the increase at two other stores which were involved in an election campaign was "inherently destructive of employee interests" and thus illegal, regardless of what might have been employer good faith. Great Atl. & Pac. Tea Co. (1967). An employer was also held to have taken inherently discriminatory action when, attendant upon a shutdown of its plant for economic reasons, it paid severance pay to employees represented by two unions but denied it to employees represented by a third, one of whose members had filed a charge with the NLRB against the employer relating to an earlier lockout. To withhold severance pay pending determination of the Board proceeding on the lockout was held a violation of sections 8(a)(1), (3) and (4) ("to discharge or otherwise discriminate against an employee because he has filed charges or given testimony under this Act"). NLRB v. Darling & Co. (7th Cir. 1970). That the discrimination is unjustifiable is also clear when the employer refuses to pay a Christmas bonus to its employees pursuant to a disqualification clause in its bonus plan which provides: "In the event of a work slowdown or stoppage, any employee involved in such work slowdown or stoppage will forfeit all bonus points earned, and will be ineligible for a Christmas bonus check." Swift Serv. Stores, Inc. (1968). The Board held that to condition the bonus payment on refraining from a lawful protected strike is inherently discriminatory and illegal, even if business motivation and lack of union animus are assumed.

There are, however, cases involving denial of benefits in which the employer does not blatantly disqualify participants in protected activities, but rather effects the same result in promulgating a plan or formula which is neutral and "business-related" on its face. It is not uncommon for the employer to require that employees be at work for a stipulated number of hours or days in a stipulated period in order to qualify for vacation or holiday pay, for bonuses, for profit-sharing allotments and the like. Although such "time worked" formulas will disadvantage the striker in comparison to the nonstriker, and thus appear to be inherently discriminatory, the employer argues that there is a legitimate and substantial business reason to relate fringe benefits to time at work; there is a claimed correlation between pay and productivity, thus providing an incentive and a reward for punctuality, attendance and skills. In short, the denial of fringe benefits while arguably discriminatory is no more unlawful than the refusal to pay strikers daily wages for hours not worked during the course of the strike.

In general, the Board has not been persuaded by this argument, while the appellate courts have. (The great bulk of the cases were decided before *Great Dane*, but there is no indication that the Supreme Court formula announced there, purportedly based on earlier Court decisions, would lead to different results today.) In a typical decision, the Board endorsed the trial examiner's reliance on Board precedent in spite of appellate reversals and held that time on strike cannot be lawfully equated to an unexcused absence or "quit" leading to termination of employment or equated to an absence on a stipulated date prior to the vacation period which ousts the employees of their claim to vacation pay. Frick Co. (1966), *enf'd on this issue* (3d Cir. 1968). Absences from work because of participation in a strike were held to warrant, because of legislative policy, preferred treatment in comparison to absences from work because of illness, death in the family and the like which can precipitate a loss of benefits without violating the Labor Act.

In four appellate decisions in the early 1960's, the Board position was resoundingly—and in each instance unanimously—reversed, in cases dealing with strikes which interfered with accrual of time for probationary employees, for participation in a profit-sharing plan, for a Christmas bonus and for rehiring to seasonal jobs.

In Pittsburgh-Des Moines Steel Co. v. NLRB (9th Cir. 1960), the employer applied a five-factor formula, including group productivity within the plant, in determining its Christmas bonus and this resulted in the denial of a bonus to workers who had participated in a prolonged strike during the computation period. The Board held that the denial of the bonus was thus based upon engagement in protected activities and found it unlawful regardless of motive. The court of appeals reversed. It asserted that proof of antiunion animus could be dispensed with only when discriminatory action was "based solely upon the criterion of union membership," and that "The strike may well have caused the business condition—poor productivity—which the employer used as the criterion for its determination to withhold the bonus, but the protected union activity was not in itself the basis of the employer's discrimination." Concluding that discrimination on the basis of group productivity was not inherently illegal, and that the General Counsel failed specifically to demonstrate antiunion animus, the court set aside the Board's order.

In NLRB v. Community Shops, Inc. (7th Cir. 1962), the employer was engaged in a seasonal business and implemented a program at the beginning of the 1959 business season whereby employees who had worked during the 1958 season were to be selected for rehire in order of length of their "actual working experience" during the 1958 season. A strike during that season resulted in the loss of credit to the strikers for time lost, just as would have time lost for illness, layoff or any other cause. The employer's refusal to rehire or its delay in rehiring because of the time lost in the 1958 strike was held by the Board to be unlawful, since it foreseeably discouraged union activities. The court of appeals reversed, concluding that the "rehire formula was initiated pursuant to a legitimate business purpose" and was applied equally to both strikers and nonstrikers, and that the record offered no specific evidence that the employer was motivated by a desire to penalize the strikers or discourage union activities.

In Quality Castings Co. v. NLRB (6th Cir. 1963), the employer's profit-sharing plan disqualified any employee who had not worked fifty percent of the scheduled work time during the first nine months of the year; in the year in question, a strike resulted in the disqualification of several employees. The Board held this to violate the Act, since it foreseeably discouraged union activities and also furnished grounds for an inference of actual antiunion animus. The court of appeals reversed, finding such an inference unsupported in the record and finding also that in all other cases in which proof of motive was dispensed with, "the action complained of has been clearly discriminatory on its face; that is, it has been openly and avowedly directed solely at a group of people who have participated . . . in certain actions which are specifically protected, concerted activities . . . ." Here, the court noted that the employer treated absence because of the strike the same as absence for any other reason (even excused absences), and concluded the action was "directed at a group which is defined by other than union membership or activity criteria, and which clearly includes others who did not engage" in the strike. "[W]e think petitioner was entitled to require a minimum amount of work and consequent profit creation before it permitted an employee to participate in profit sharing."

The Board was again reversed in NLRB v. National Seal, Div. of Federal-Mogul-Bower Bearings, Inc. (9th Cir. 1964), in which several probationary employees who participated in a strike were terminated by the employer, which relied upon a collective bargaining agreement requiring sixty days of work to qualify a probationary employee for regular employment and a company practice that such probationary period had to be completed without interruption. The court, relying upon a stipulation that the employer had not been discriminatorily motivated, rejected the Board's per se rule outlawing conduct which foreseeably discouraged striking. The rule requiring a probationary period "had a reasonable and practical purpose and was reasonable in duration," had been a longstanding rule consistently applied and had been incorporated in the labor contract.

A recent decision may mark a movement by the Board toward the courts' more hospitable attitude in cases of employer denial of benefits to strikers, although the Board—as did the court in *Federal-Mogul*—placed heavy emphasis on a collective bargaining agreement provision which could be viewed as a union "waiver" of the right to full protection for strikers. In Roegelein Provision Co. (1970), the employer denied vacation benefits to all employees, including strikers, who in the preceding eligibility year had been (as provided in the labor contract) "absent from work for any reason" for two hundred hours. The trial examiner held this illegal, since it violated the Board's principle that an employer may not equate strike time with other forms of absence in the computation of benefits. The Board reversed, finding that the vacation-pay provision of the contract had been assented to by the union with knowledge of its implications for strikers, that the disqualification of the strikers resulted from good-faith collective bargaining and not union animus, and that the employer's action "could hardly be viewed as conduct discouraging union activity in any proscribed sense." Compare G. C. Murphy Co. (1973) (contract provision requiring that vacation pay take form of paid time off rather than lump-sum payment validates employer rescheduling of strikers' vacation and refusal to pay them lump-sum payments for originally scheduled vacation during strike; Labor Act does not require that strikers be given benefits beyond those given by contract to other employees).

CHAPTER XVIII

NATIONAL EMERGENCY DISPUTES

§ 1. Legislative Background

At the conclusion of the Second World War, the American economy—already disrupted by the transition from the wartime effort to production for peacetime—was disrupted even further by a rash of strikes. During the first year of peacetime, nearly 5,000 work stoppages impeded the economic conversion, affecting millions of workers and resulting in the loss of over 100 million man-days of work. The strikes hit such major industries as oil, coal and shipping. In spite of the settled history of the Wagner Act of 1935, which made the strike a protected weapon for the economic betterment of workers, President Truman and the Congress were in agreement that some legislation was necessary to limit the right to strike in major industries. The debate in Congress, which led to the enactment of the Taft-Hartley amendments of 1947, turned upon whether the limitation should extend to all major industries or only to particularly vital ones, such as transportation, communications and public utilities; and whether work stoppages should be banned only for a "cooling off" period or should be altogether replaced by a system of compulsory arbitration. Congress proclaimed, finally, that the industries affected by its anti-strike legislation should be only those which "imperil the national health or safety" (although no statutory definition of that phrase was provided), and that the strike limitation should not be permanent but should last only for a "cooling off" period of at most eighty days.

The full statutory scheme for the "national emergency" dispute is set forth in sections 206–10 of the Taft-Hartley Act, or Labor-Management Relations Act of 1947. 29 U.S.C.A. §§ 176–80. The President of the United States is authorized by the Act to appoint a board of inquiry should he believe that a threatened or actual strike or lockout, affecting an entire industry or a substantial part of an industry engaged in interstate commerce, endangers or will endanger the national health or safety. (By section 212, the industries covered by the Railway Labor Act—railroads and airlines—are exempt from these national emergency provisions.) The board of inquiry is empowered to conduct private and public hearings to gather information, and is within the time specified by the President to tender a report to him on the facts of the dispute and the parties' positions; the board is expressly forbidden to forward any recommendations. Upon receipt of the report, the President must make it public and file a copy with the Federal Mediation and Conciliation Service (an agency established by Congress also in 1947).

The President is also authorized (not required) upon receipt of the report to direct the Attorney General to petition for an injunction against the strike or lockout in any federal district court having jurisdiction over the parties, and the court is given jurisdiction to issue the injunction if it finds that the strike or lockout "affects an entire industry or a substantial part thereof" engaged in interstate commerce *and* that without an injunction the "national health or safety" will be imperiled.   (The anti-injunction provisions of the Norris-La-Guardia Act are expressly made inapplicable in such cases.)   If an injunction is issued, the parties are required by the Act to attempt to settle their dispute with the assistance of the Federal Mediation and Conciliation Service, and the President is required to reconvene the board of inquiry which at the end of sixty days (assuming there has been no settlement) reports to the President once again on the current situation, including the parties' positions and the employer's last settlement offer.   The report is once again made public, and the National Labor Relations Board (not otherwise mentioned in the national emergency provisions) is within fifteen days to conduct a secret-ballot poll of the employees involved to determine whether they approve the employer's final offer.   When the Board certifies the result of that poll within five days to the Attorney General, he is required to move the court to discharge the injunction, and the court is required to do so.   (If the parties settle at an earlier date, the Attorney General moves at that time to discharge the injunction.)

In effect, the Act empowers the President to delay a strike or lockout for no more than eighty days, with settlement in that period presumably fostered by the report of the board of inquiry, the mediation efforts of the Federal Service, the pressure of public opinion and as a last resort a vote of the employees.   If the eighty-day period passes without settlement, the Act makes no provision for a renewal of the injunction.   The strike or lockout may proceed.

In two significant decisions—not dealing directly with the application of the national emergency provisions of the Taft-Hartley Act —the Supreme Court held those provisions to circumscribe the powers of both the President and the individual states.   In Youngstown Sheet & Tube Co. v. Sawyer (U.S.1952), the Court held invalid the seizure by the President of the steel industry, an act precipitated by an impending steel strike at a time when an interruption in steel production would allegedly have crippled the military effort in Korea.   The Court relied in part on the national emergency provisions, which it held the President had no inherent power to ignore and which authorized a strike once the procedures were exhausted.   In Amalgamated Street Employees Div. 998 v. Wisconsin Employment Rel. Bd. (U.S. 1951), the Court struck down a Wisconsin anti-strike and compulsory arbitration law governing local public utilities and transit companies. It relied in part on the fact that Congress had addressed the problem of emergency disputes in 1947 and had established a procedure for resolution of such disputes which if utilized preempted state regulation and which if not utilized left the matter to the usual processes of peaceful and protected economic weapons under the federal Labor Act (once again preempting state regulation). Indeed, the reach of the national emergency provisions of Taft-Hartley is greater than that of the federal Labor Act generally, which deals with representation elections and unfair labor practices. The eighty-day strike injunction may issue against supervisors as well as rank-and-file workers, even though supervisors are not otherwise given the benefits or burdens of NLRA coverage. United States v. National Marine Eng'rs' Benef. Ass'n (2d Cir. 1961). (Nonetheless, states are free to enjoin strikes by supervisors, Hanna Mining Co. v. District 2, Marine Eng'rs Benef. Ass'n (U.S.1965); although in the event of any conflict with the federal eighty-day injunction, the latter would no doubt take precedence.)

§ 2. "Substantial Part of an Industry"

One condition for the issuance of a national emergency injunction is that the strike or lockout "affects an entire industry or a substantial part thereof" engaged in interstate commerce. A strike which would have immobilized $45\frac{1}{2}$ percent of the vessels of the United States merchant marine was held to meet the statutory "substantial part" standard. United States v. National Marine Eng'rs' Benef. Ass'n (2d Cir. 1961). The contrary result was reached in a case involving a strike which stopped foreign-bound grain shipments from Chicago, since most of the grain could be shipped from other ports and the anticipated export of $75 million worth of grain from Chicago was miniscule compared to total national annual exports of over $43 billion. United States v. ILA Local 418 (Continental Grain Co.) (N.D.Ill.1971) (treating Chicago strike as severable from strikes in other ports).

In using these quantitative tests, the courts have looked not merely to the industry that is directly affected by the work stoppage but also to other industries upon which the strike will have a derivative impact. Thus, a strike at a single plant furnishing specialized piping and heat exchange products to Atomic Energy Commission contractors to use in construction of facilities for nuclear materials was enjoined, since the court found that the atomic energy industry was affected by the strike and that the facilities being constructed were a substantial part of that industry. United States v. United Steelworkers (Locomotive Co.) (2d Cir. 1953). This "tracing" of the impact of a strike to other industries has been typically employed in cases involving defense industries, in which courts have also used the technique of declaring what would normally be considered only a sector of an industry to be a specialized industry in its own right (thus increasing the "substantiality" of the disruption). In United Steelworkers v. United States (Union Carbide) (D.C.Cir. 1966), the court of appeals upheld a district court injunction of a strike at a single Union Carbide plant which was one of two producing an alloy used in military helicopter engines, the helicopters in turn being destined for Vietnam. The court found that the relevant industry was not that of metal alloys but rather the "military aircraft engine industry" (which was then again distinguished from the civilian aircraft industry). The court found that military aircraft absorbed extensive resources in the form of capital, technical skills and manpower; and that helicopters, in light of the magnitude of the American effort in Vietnam, were a substantial part of military aircraft production.

In substance, the courts have gone beyond the use of a quantitative-percentage test in most industries to employ a "qualitative" test for determining whether a "substantial part" of the industry is affected when the industry is related to military or defense activities. In so doing, the courts may have failed adequately to distinguish the two statutory requirements under section 208 of the Taft-Hartley Act: that the strike or lockout affect a substantial part of an industry and, independently, that the national health or safety is imperiled. This failure may find its source in the brief opinion written in the only Supreme Court decision dealing directly with the national emergency strike, United Steelworkers v. United States (U.S.1959). The Court there stated that the "demonstrated unavailabiltiy of defense materials" made irrelevant the fact that only about one percent of gross steel production was needed by defense industries while over fifteen percent of steel production continued. While the Court was apparently speaking only to the question whether there was a peril to "national safety," lower courts have so construed the Act as to dictate a finding of "substantiality" in almost any case which significantly involves our defense efforts.

§ 3. "National Health or Safety"

The second requirement for a national emergency injunction is that the strike or lockout "if permitted to occur or to continue, will imperil the national health or safety." Written in the disjunctive, this provision has been read precisely to mean that the court need only find danger either to health or to safety. United Steelworkers v. United States (U.S.1959).

A threat to "national safety" has been readily found to exist when there has been an interference with production for military or defense purposes. The Supreme Court decision in the *Steelworkers* case sustained an injunction against an industrywide steel strike which was found to imperil national safety because it rendered unavailable steel products required in military and space exploration missiles, ships for the Navy, and construction such as NATO material needed for collective security. The peril to national defense need not be immediate. An injunction against a strike in the merchant marine was sustained because by law merchant marine (*i. e.*, nonmilitary) ships must be available as auxiliary to military craft in time of war and national emergency and must be prepared at all times to transport oil from foreign countries.　United States v. National Marine Eng'rs' Benef. Union (2d Cir. 1961).　Nor have the courts paused to determine whether the military could mobilize in due course even if the strike continued, or whether arrangements could be made by the parties to have the strike terminated in the future when a military challenge is confronted; it is assumed that all defense plans and schedules are required to be executed immediately.

The meaning of "national health" is not quite so clear.　In United Steelworkers v. United States (U.S.1959), where the Supreme Court found a steel strike to imperil the "national safety," it expressly declined to rule whether the "national health" refers to the physical well-being of the American people or the economic well-being of the nation.　Justice Douglas in dissent urged that Congress must have defined the phrase to mean physical well-being, since it specifically substituted it for "national welfare" in an earlier draft.　In the absence of a definitive answer by the Supreme Court, the lower courts have been inclined to read the term more broadly to mean economic well-being.　In United States v. Portland Longshoremen's Benef. Soc'y, Local 861 (D.Me.1971), the court found a dock strike to imperil both national safety and national health, with the latter finding resting largely on the impact of the strike on the national balance of payments.　In another case arising from the same nationwide disruption, a federal district court denied an injunction, finding that economic dislocation alone would not imperil the "national health" and that the effect of the strike on grain shipments was too slight to imperil physical health; but the court of appeals, while refusing to stay the district court order on appeal since the showing of economic injury was so weak, did conclude that the lower court had erred in construing "national health" to require any more than a showing that there was a national emergency by virtue of a significant adverse effect upon the "essential well-being of the economy."　United States v. Longshoremen Local 418 (7th Cir. 1971).　And a third court, issuing an injunction in the port of New York in the same dock strike, found a threat to national health and safety because the strike reduced freight shipments, endangered farm exports, resulted in lost work and wages for many, would delay defense shipments abroad, damage the balance of payments and "would affect the lives and welfare of many thousands of people in the United States, including of course the strikers themselves and many others who are dependent in some way on the continuance of our foreign trade and of our transportation system."　United States v. ILA (S.D.N.Y.1971).　Until the Supreme Court addresses the question whether "national health" means the economic as well as the physical well-being of the American people, the likely answer of the lower courts is that it does.

§ 4.　Procedures

The entire national emergency procedure is for the protection of the public generally and is invoked by public officials.　Since the board of inquiry appointed by the President is purely investigatory in nature, a party to the dispute has no right to appear before it. United States v. ILA (S.D.N.Y.1964). And, once the injunction issues, a court is without jurisdiction to cite for contempt unless that proceeding is instituted by the government; a private party lacks standing. Universal Shipping Corp. v. Local 953, Checkers (D.Md.1969). Since the contempt citation is to vindicate the public interest through the Attorney General—and not the interest of the court itself—a violation of the injunction will not furnish the basis for a contempt citation if the strike is settled before the citation issues. United States v. UMW (D.C.Cir. 1951)'.

It is also the public interest in the avoidance of national emergency disputes that dictates that once the district court finds the strike or lockout to affect a substantial part of the industry and to imperil national health or safety, it must issue the injunction, and may not require in addition that there be a further demonstration of the usual equitable prerequisites to relief. Congress made the determination in 1947, binding on the courts, that regardless of the merits of the parties' positions a national emergency strike or lockout had to be temporarily delayed in order to maximize the possibility of a peaceful settlement. United Steelworkers v. United States (U.S. 1959). That is true if the companies and unions within a given court's jurisdiction are part of a larger work stoppage in other parts of the country such that the strike as a whole meets the "substantiality" test, even if the particular defendant(s) might not. United States v. National Marine Eng'rs' Benef. Ass'n (2d Cir. 1961) (injunction "may reach all who participated . . . whether their effect was large or small"). Once the injunction is issued preserving the status quo ante, the court's role continues to be relatively mechanical for it must dissolve the injunction upon settlement of the dispute or after the expiration of eighty days upon motion of the Attorney General. See Seafarer's Union v. United States (9th Cir. 1962) (although back-to-work order would of necessity require crewmen to sign articles which might require work beyond eighty days, any contract violation after eighty days would not result in contempt citation).

The national emergency provisions have consistently been subjected to criticism, by partisans and by objective analysts alike. Some fear that they will be used too extensively, particularly as national "health" and "safety" become very loosely defined. Others believe that the injunction should not be the one required remedy, but that the President should have the discretion to seize temporarily and that the courts should have the discretion to deny the injunction in cases where the threat of a strike or lockout would more quickly terminate the dispute than would the prospect of continuity of the status quo. Some urge that an eighty-day injunction is not long enough if the dispute truly generates a national emergency; a study shows that in the period between 1947 and 1967 roughly half of the twenty-four strike injunctions ran their course without a settlement, with strikes occurring in roughly half of those. There is considerable support for authorizing the board of inquiry to make recommendations for the settlement of the dispute and for eliminating the last-offer ballot, which has been uniformly in favor of rejecting the employer's last offer and has been thought simply to induce an employer to make a low offer in the knowledge that even its best offer will be rejected.

THE DUTY TO BARGAIN IN GOOD FAITH WITH THE MAJORITY REPRESENTATIVE

CHAPTER XIX

THE PRINCIPLE OF EXCLUSIVE REPRESENTATION

§ 1. Exclusivity and Majority Rule

One of the cardinal principles of American labor law is that of exclusive representation by the majority union. Congress in 1933 enacted the National Industrial Recovery Act, which created a National Labor Board and declared that employees were to have the right to "organize and bargain collectively through representatives of their own choosing" free from employer interference, restraint or coercion. While declaring that right, the NIRA did not formally declare it illegal for an employer to interfere with it, and did not expressly set forth the principle that only one union was to be the spokesman for all employees in the bargaining unit, even for employees who were not members or who voted against it. But the predecessor to the National Labor Relations Board decided, in Houde Engineering Corp. (1934), that the employer was obligated by law to bargain in good faith with a view toward a bilateral agreement regulating working conditions for all employees in the unit, and that as a corollary the employer was not free to bargain with different unions, each for their own members, but instead had to bargain with a single union designated as bargaining representative by a majority of unit employees. The Board foresaw that any principle of plural representation—whether in the form of separate negotiations or of a single negotiation with a representative council—would be divisive within the plant and would permit the employer to bestow favors so as to foster inter-union rivalry and deprive the employees of an effective representative voice.

The philosophy of the *Houde* case was expressly written into the National Labor Relations Act in 1935, soon after the NIRA was declared unconstitutional by the Supreme Court in A.L.A. Schechter Poultry Corp. v. United States (U.S.1935). Section 8(a)(5) declares it to be an unfair labor practice for an employer "to refuse to bargain collectively with the representatives of his employees, subject to the provisions of section 9(a)," and section 9(a) provides:

> Representatives designated or selected for the purposes of collective bargaining by the majority of the employees in a unit appropriate for such purposes, shall be the exclusive representatives of all the employees in such unit for the pur-

poses of collective bargaining in respect to rates of pay, wages, hours of employment, or other conditions of employment . . . .

(Congress added a proviso in 1935, and another in 1947, that deal with the presentation and adjustment of grievances, rather than with bargaining as such, and reserve certain powers to individual employees in the resolution of grievances.) The Labor Act thus clearly adopts the principle of majoritarianism which has been a part of the American political tradition. It was, for example, early held that an employer could not lawfully insist that the majority union bargain only for its own members. Although the employer argued that it would be improper to accord exclusive recognition on behalf of all employees, since employees voting against the union in the recent election had obviously not given it any authority to bargain, it was held in effect that the statute overrode the preference of the minority within the unit, and that the employer had to accept the majority union as spokesman for all employees within the bargaining unit, regardless of their personal preferences. NLRB v. Boss Mfg. Co. (7th Cir. 1939).

Section 9(a), read in conjunction with section 8(a)(5), in substance announces both an affirmative and a negative mandate. It directs the employer affirmatively to "bargain" with the majority representative concerning all matters which can be classified as "rates of pay, wages, hours of employment, or other conditions of employment." Equally important, it directs the employer not to bargain on such matters with any person (individual or aggregate) other than the majority representative. Thus, it was early held that the employer was not entitled to recognize as their own spokesman for bargaining any and all individuals and groups within the plant. Stewart Die Casting Corp. v. NLRB (7th Cir. 1940). It was, and is, thus illegal for the employer to engage in bargaining with a minority union when there is a majority union with which it must bargain on an exclusive basis. NLRB v. National Motor Bearing Co. (9th Cir. 1939). The Supreme Court held, in Medo Photo Supply Corp. v. NLRB (U.S. 1944), that the employer could not bypass the bargaining agent and engage instead in negotiations about wages and other working conditions with individual employees in the plant, even though the employees initiated the negotiations and actually sought to deal directly rather than through the duly elected majority union. The illegality of bargaining with individuals in the unit is compounded when the union's business agent, its authorized representative for bargaining, requests to be present at the negotiations but is excluded. Adolph Coors Co. (1965). Although most of the cases banning individual bargaining arose in the early years of the Act's administration, a number of such cases continue to emerge. It has, for example, rather recently been held that the employer violates section 8(a)(5) when it discusses a wage increase with individual employees (when there is a majority representative), grants the increase and has the employees sign a separate contract, J. Zembrodt Express, Inc. (1971); or solicits a list of grievances from the employees, approves the list and has the employees sign it and grants one of the requested benefits the next day, Teledyne Dental Prods. Corp. (1974) (union had demonstrated majority by authorization cards; employer is ordered to bargain with the union).

Economic necessity or financial distress is no justification for avoiding the principle of exclusive representation by bargaining with individual employees. In Wonder State Mfg. Co. (1965), the employer sought to stave off the departure of its own employees for a competitor, and negotiated individual contracts with provisions for wages, noncompetition and nondivulging of trade secrets, and mandatory signing if the employee wished to continue employment. Even assuming the individual contracts might have been compelled by the economics of the situation, they were held to violate section 8(a)(5), since "A violation of the Act cannot be excused on the ground of private inconvenience or economic and business exigencies."

Just as the employer is forbidden, when there is a duly selected majority bargaining representative, to bargain with individual employees and minority unions concerning wages and working conditions, it is also forbidden to bargain with a constituent local union when it is the national or international union which has the statutory right to bargain, either by formal certification or employer recognition. NLRB v. General Elec. Co. (2d Cir. 1969) (it does not matter whether the employer attempts to reach a settlement with the local that is more or less generous than that offered the national union; employer may, however, keep the local informed of the course of negotiations with the national). The employer may not justify bargaining with the uncertified local union even by a good faith belief that the certified national union was refusing to bargain. Independent Stave Co. v. NLRB (8th Cir. 1965).

Perhaps the fullest explanation of the reasons behind the principle of exclusivity of representation, and the rejection of individual bargaining, is that of the Supreme Court in J. I. Case Co. v. NLRB (U.S.1944). There, the employer had not engaged in individual bargaining after a union had been certified. Instead, the union had been elected after the employer had already negotiated individual employment contracts governing wages, hours and other working conditions. When the union requested bargaining on such matters, the employer refused, claiming that the preexisting individual contracts were controlling until their expiration, and that it would negotiate presently on only those matters not addressed in the individual contracts and, on their expiration, on all other matters. The Supreme Court held this to constitute a refusal to bargain in violation of section 8(a)(5).

The Court stated that the collective bargaining agreement was not technically a contract of employment but more like "a trade agreement":

> Without pushing the analogy too far, the agreement may be likened to the tariffs established by a carrier, to standard provisions prescribed by supervising authorities for insurance policies, or to utility schedules of rates and rules for service, which do not of themselves establish any relationships but which do govern the terms of the shipper or insurer or customer relationship whenever and with whomever it may be established.

Individuals are hired, normally by the employer without restriction, and immediately become subject to the working conditions already negotiated with the union, even if these individuals would be willing to work on less favorable terms. Individual bargaining may not be utilized to forestall bargaining with the designated union or to undermine the terms of the collective agreement.

> [T]he individual contract cannot be effective as a waiver of any benefit to which the employee otherwise would be entitled under the trade agreement. The very purpose of providing by statute for the collective agreement is to supersede the terms of separate agreements of employees with terms which reflect the strength and bargaining power and serve the welfare of the group. Its benefits and advantages are open to every employee of the represented unit, whatever the type or terms of his pre-existing contract of employment.

Even some freedom of contract is to be sacrificed for the employee who could secure a better bargain for himself than did the majority union.

> The practice and philosophy of collective bargaining looks with suspicion on such individual advantages. . . . [A]dvantages to individuals may prove as disruptive of industrial peace as disadvantages. They are a fruitful way of interfering with organization and choice of representatives; increased compensation, if individually deserved, is often earned at the cost of breaking down some other standard thought to be for the welfare of the group, and always creates the suspicion of being paid at the long-range expense of the group as a whole. . . . The workman is free, if he values his own bargaining position more than that of the group, to vote against representation; but the majority rules, and if it collectivizes the employment bargain, individual advantages or favors will generally in practice go in as a contribution to the collective result.

The principle of exclusive representation in collective bargaining was recently reaffirmed by the Supreme Court in a context in which it was sorely tested—a demand for bargaining by several minority-group employees who asserted that the recognized union and the labor contract were inadequately protecting the employment rights of racial minorities. In Emporium Capwell Co. v. Western Addition Community Org'n (U.S.1975), the union charged the employer with racial discrimination, and announced its intention to process its claims through the contractual grievance procedure. Several employees, seeking a more vigorous and expeditious attack on these conditions, denounced the employer as racist, held a press conference, distributed anti-employer handbills and engaged in picketing; demands were also made that top management officials meet with the protesters to consider the problem of minority employment. When two of the protesters were discharged, a charge was filed against the employer under section 8(a)(1) for interfering with employees in the exercise of their right to engage in concerted activities protected by section 7.

The Supreme Court sustained the conclusion of the Board that the protesters were not seeking to adjust a "grievance" (which might arguably have been sheltered by the proviso to section 9(a)) but were rather demanding that the employer "bargain" with them. The Court held that concerted activity thus designed to circumvent the majority union—even on an issue as central to federal labor policy as the elimination of racial discrimination in employment—was contrary to the principles of section 9(a) and that the protesters were therefore unprotected against discharge. The Court noted that any bargaining rights accorded to the protesting employees, who were black, would also have to be extended to other groups asserting the cause of a particular race, religion or sex; the potential proliferation of conflicting demands for fair employment treatment would at worst lead to economic confrontation among these groups and the frustration of their goals, and would at least force the employer to bargain in a "field largely pre-empted by the current collective-bargaining agreement with the elected bargaining representative." Although the charging party argued that there could be no substantial conflict between the protesters and the union, since federal law directs the union to resist such discrimination, the Court responded that the substantive right to be free of discrimination "cannot be pursued at the expense of the orderly collective-bargaining process contemplated by the NLRA"; the union had already utilized that process by negotiating a contract clause barring discrimination and by invoking the contractual grievance machinery. On matters of race discrimination, as on any other matter for bargaining, the union

    has a legitimate interest in presenting a united front
    . . . and in not seeing its strength dissipated and its

stature denigrated by subgroups within the unit separately pursuing what they see as separate interests. . . .

. . . The policy of industrial self-determination as expressed in § 7 does not require fragmentation of the bargaining unit along racial or other lines in order to consist with the national labor policy against discrimination.

To sum up the reasoning in the cases which outlaw "bypassing" the majority representative and bargaining with minority unions and individual employees, the central objections are these. (1) The statute requires bargaining with the majority representative, and "bypassing" demonstrates a repudiation of the principle of collective bargaining and of the bargaining agent itself; it demonstrates as well that the employer is prepared to grant benefits even without the union and thereby undermines employee support for the elected representative. (2) Congress intended to substitute the strength of the collectivity for the weakness of the individual bargainor. Individual bargaining permits the employer to combat the progressive improvement in wages and working conditions that come more readily from an integrated group effort. (3) Bargaining on a pluralistic basis, with each individual or group speaking for itself, generates a severe risk of employer domination and interference, of divisiveness and inequality of working conditions within the plant, and of economic strife—all of which undermine the fundamental congressional objective of stabilizing industrial relations and minimizing disruptions in interstate commerce. (4) Congress gave to the majority representative the task of harmonizing and adjusting the conflicting interests of employees within the bargaining unit, no matter how diverse their skills, experience, age, race or economic level. The employer improperly usurps that function for itself—and of necessity undermines the position of the union in contract negotiation and enforcement—when it seeks to set working conditions with individuals and minority organizations within the plant.

Congress and the Board and courts have not, however, pursued the principles of majoritarianism and exclusivity without regard to the interests of the minority or of the disaffected within the unit. Accommodations of these competing interests are made at a number of points in the administration of the Labor Act, and are discussed in detail elsewhere. They may be outlined briefly here.

First, the majority union is exclusive representative, in the words of section 9(a), only for "the employees in a unit appropriate for such purposes." The Board in its unit determinations considers the "community of interest" among workers, and will exclude from the bargaining unit workers whose jobs are not linked by such a community of interest and who would otherwise have their interests submerged in the larger, and presumably unsympathetic, grouping. Employees outside the unit may speak for themselves or through their own independent representative. This is clearer yet as to persons who are not "employees" under the Labor Act at all, such as supervisors or independent contractors. For example, in Chemical Workers Local 1 v. Pittsburgh Plate Glass Co. (U.S.1971), the Supreme Court held that the employer was free to deal directly with former employees now retired, on such matters as their retirement benefits and medical insurance, without the intervention of the union representing present employees. The retirees were held to be outside the bargaining unit, and no longer "employees" within the coverage of the Labor Act. (The employer, however, runs the risk that the Board or courts will determine that the workers with whom it is dealing individually are indeed "employees" within the bargaining unit. Cooke & Jones, Inc., *enf'd* (1st Cir. 1964) (supervisors). Most obviously, the employer cannot convert unit employees into, for example, independent contractors by bargaining with them directly for this status while they are unit employees. Shamrock Dairy, Inc. (1959), *enf'd* (D.C.Cir. 1960).)

Second, the duty not to deal with individuals and minority unions applies only to "rates of pay, wages, hours of employment, or other conditions of employment." If a subject falls outside these so-called "mandatory" subjects, the employer is free to negotiate directly even with individuals within the unit, at least provided such bargaining will not directly impinge on the mandatory matters being negotiated or already dealt with in the collective bargaining agreement. Chemical Workers Local 1 v. Pittsburgh Plate Glass Co. (U.S.1971); J. I. Case Co. v. NLRB (U.S.1944).

Third, the duty not to deal with individuals applies only "for the purposes of collective bargaining." As will be developed below, if the dealings cannot be characterized as "bargaining"—but rather, for example, the presentation or adjustment of "grievances," or informal discussions or interviews—it is not improper for the employer to meet, consult and deal with individual employees (although at least as to the adjustment of grievances, the majority union must be invited and may play an active role).

Fourth, the duty to bargain with a certified or recognized union does not last indefinitely. It does last for at least one year from the date the union is certified, Brooks v. NLRB (U.S.1954); and can be extended, except in unusual circumstances, during the life of a collective bargaining agreement, NLRB v. Marcus Trucking Co. (2d Cir. 1961) (employer may not recognize outside union during contract term while contract would bar a representation election, even though a majority of the employees have repudiated the incumbent union and support recognition of the outside union). But after a period of time, not exceeding three years if there is a labor contract in effect, the employees are entitled to petition for a new representation election to test the preferences of the workers in the bargaining unit. Moreover, once a contract expires, the employer can itself decline to bargain for a new contract with a union which it believes in reasonable good faith has lost its majority status.

Fifth, the power of the majority representative to speak for all unit employees has been held to give rise to a correlative duty fairly and in good faith to represent the interests of all within the unit, whether or not they are members of or voted for that union, and whether or not they are members of some racial or ethnic minority group. The so-called "duty of fair representation" was first announced by the Supreme Court as deducible from the exclusive-representation provisions of section 9(a), Wallace Corp. v. NLRB (U.S. 1944) (dictum), and enforceable by a court action; and later by the NLRB, which declared violation of that duty to be an unfair labor practice, Miranda Fuel Co. (1962), *enf't denied* (2d Cir. 1963).

Sixth, the Landrum-Griffin Amendments of 1959 incorporate a so-called Bill of Rights for union members, which provides a number of democratic safeguards in intra-union affairs, such as the right to participate in union meetings, to vote in union elections, and to compete for union office. Through these measures, it is hoped that the voice of the minority will be heard within the union, and will help shape union policy as to the protection of the rights of all within the unit.

§ 2. Employer Communications with Employees During Bargaining

An employer will frequently wish to communicate with its employees concerning the progress of contract negotiations between it and the union. As the Board has held, in Procter & Gamble Mfg. Co. (Port Ivory) (1966):

> As a matter of settled law, Section 8(a)(5) does not, on a *per se* basis, preclude an employer from communicating, in noncoercive terms, with employees during bargaining negotiations. The fact that an employer chooses to inform employees of the status of negotiations, or of proposals previously made to the union, or of its version of a breakdown in negotiations will not alone establish a failure to bargain in good faith.

Although the employer is in such cases communicating directly with individual employees, that alone does not constitute an unlawful "bypassing" of the union in the establishment of wages, hours and working conditions. Indeed, it has been held that to outlaw noncoercive informational communications would contravene section 8(c) of the Labor Act, which provides that the expressing or dissemination of "any views, argument, or opinion" shall not constitute or be evidence of an unfair labor practice "if such expression contains no threat of reprisal or force or promise of benefit." NLRB v. Movie Star, Inc. (5th Cir. 1966).

Such communications are consistent with a good faith desire to reach a bilateral agreement with the exclusive representative, and have been sustained where there are such other indicia of good faith as sending copies of the communications to the union, refraining from setting forth offers to individual employees which exceed those offered the union and continuing to bargain with the union. Procter & Gamble Mfg. Co. (Port Ivory) (1966) (moreover, although the employer criticized the union's bargaining tactics, this was not designed to subvert the employees' choice of bargaining representative). The Board has also considered as evidence of employer good faith the fact that its communication to employees of its bargaining proposals comes at a time when employees might otherwise quit their employment for lack of normal wage increases (which had to be suspended during bargaining), NLRB v. Superior Fireproof Door & Sash Co. (2d Cir. 1961); or when employees might be attracted by higher wages offered by competing companies, NLRB v. Norfolk Shipbldg. & Drydock Corp. (4th Cir. 1952). The employer is free to appeal to its employees to vote against a strike, to work even if a strike is called, and to be aware of the likely loss of business that a strike would cause, since such an appeal in itself does not coerce employees or undermine the union. General Elec. Co., Battery Prods., Capacitor Dep't v. NLRB (5th Cir. 1968). The same tests for the legality of communications during bargaining are applied when negotiations are under way with an international or national union, certified or recognized as the bargaining representative, and the communications are directed at a constituent local union. NLRB v. General Elec. Co. (2d Cir. 1969) (communications held lawful, in spite of other bad-faith bargaining).

But direct communication with employees during bargaining will be outlawed when it is determined that, expressly or in context, it has the effect not so much of informing employees but rather of coercing them in the exercise of their right freely to select and to bargain through a representative of their choice. Wantagh Auto Sales, Inc. (1969) (employer did not appeal to employees to "abandon" their union, but simply informed them of the status of negotiations while indicating a readiness to continue bargaining with the union). Thus, direct communications with employees during bargaining will be illegal when the employer seeks to reach a separate settlement with the employees, or to enlist their support through threats of reprisal or promises of benefit, or to induce them to withdraw their support from the union. An example of unlawful direct communication to employees, objectionable on all of these grounds, is a proposal to them which exceeds the terms offered at the bargaining table to the union, or which offers terms on which there has been "no meaningful negotiation" with the union. NLRB v. J. H. Bonck Co. (5th Cir. 1970).

Another example, of considerable notoriety, is represented by the former bargaining strategy of the General Electric Company—a strategy referred to as Boulwarism—and held illegal by the Board and court in General Elec. Co. (1964), *enf'd* (2d Cir. 1969). There, the company in advance of negotiations sought to determine what economic improvements its employees desired and proceeded to work out a complex offer which it believed was "right" for the employees and which it was prepared to put before the union as a first but "firm and final" proposal. The company coordinated its "final offer" position at the bargaining table with a massive public-relations campaign, in which it used all forms of mass media in order to convince both its employees and the public generally that its proposal was the "right" one and that the company was prepared to "do right" voluntarily without the need for an exchange of artificially overstated demands and understated offers that normally characterize collective bargaining. The Board was affirmed by the court of appeals in its conclusion that the company had violated section 8(a)(5) not only by certain specific acts—such as refusing to disclose pertinent information and bargaining directly with locals rather than with the recognized international union—but also by its overall bargaining conduct, most particularly the combination of firmness at the bargaining table and the communications campaign outside.

It was held that the company had knowingly, by its well-publicized disinclination to modify its bargaining position, rendered itself incapable of engaging in genuine negotiations, which presuppose some willingness to adjust differences. The court majority was careful to note that it was not outlawing all communication with employees during negotiations, or the "best offer first" technique of bargaining; nor was it compelling "auction bargaining" or the making of concessions. The court stated its holding to be that "an employer may not so combine 'take-it-or-leave-it' bargaining methods with a widely publicized stance of unbending firmness that he is himself unable to alter a position once taken." A concurring opinion articulated more fully the evils of the company's communications campaign during negotiations, in which it was announced that "firmness" was one of the company's independent policies. First, this sealed the company into its initial bargaining position, since even if it wished to modify that position at a later date, it would be incapable of doing so while preserving its pride and reputation for truthfulness. Second, the employees were led to believe that the company was its true representative and the union superfluous. The concurring judge found this sufficient to evidence bad faith in bargaining. In the interests of preserving freedom of speech, however, he emphasized that the employer is entitled to inform the employees of its bargaining position, of the weaknesses of the union's position and of the disadvantages of a strike. Moreover:

A company, of course, can advertise its belief that its offer is fair, and that, at the particular time, it sees no reason to change its offer even to forestall a strike. This kind of statement is different from advertising that it is company policy never to change any offer in response to union pressure.

A third judge, dissenting on this issue, would have found the company's "fair, firm offer" to be sheltered by the ban in section 8(d) upon requiring concessions, and the company's communications campaign to be sheltered by the "free speech" guarantees in section 8(c).

An employer also runs a risk of violating the Act when it goes beyond merely informing employees of the progress of negotiations and actually, during negotiations, takes a formal poll of the employees in the bargaining unit concerning their preferences on certain issues under negotiation and particularly concerning their appraisal of the union's bargaining position. Here too—as with most direct communication with employees not coercive on its face—there is no clear test for determining whether such employer conduct is lawful and the Board and courts will carefully scrutinize the employer's other activities both at and away from the bargaining table. In an early case, NLRB v. Penokee Veneer Co. (7th Cir. 1948), the court of appeals, in a split decision, held that the employer could lawfully poll its employees while its plant was shut down by a strike, in order to assess their willingness to return to work under conditions which were either pre-existing or had been offered to the union at the bargaining table. The court, noting that the employer had a legitimate interest in determining whether it would be fruitful to attempt to reopen its plant, also observed that the employer had refrained from bargaining with any of the individual strikers, had exerted no compulsion on them to return to work, and had assured them that all of their rights accorded them by law would be observed. More recently, in Continental Oil Co. (1971), the employer polled its employees as to their views on the present system of distributing overtime, at a time when overtime was under negotiation with the union; the employer was careful to state that it was not intending the poll to constitute bargaining with the individual employees. The Board held the poll to be lawful. There was no evidence that any employees believed that the employer was attempting to bargain with them rather than with the union, there was no attempt to influence the employees to desert the union and there was no express or implied threat of coercion. The Board in fact concluded that the employer's desire to discover pertinent information did not undermine bargaining but rather furthered it.

However, in a case decided soon after, on facts not too different, the Board in Obie Pacific, Inc. (1972) held it a violation of section 8(a)(5) for the employer to poll its employees in a discussion with them concerning the contract requirement of using two workers for a particular job rather than one; although no union representative was present at the discussion, one was informed promptly in an atmosphere of cooperation. The Board held it improper thus to challenge a contract provision and to erode the union's position on the provision by seeking directly to determine employee sentiment rather than leave such efforts to the union.

> While under appropriate circumstances, an employer may communicate to employees the reasons for his actions and even for his bargaining objective, he may not seek to determine for himself the degree of support, or lack thereof, which exists for the stated position of the employees' bargaining agent. If we were to sanction such efforts, we would impede effective bargaining.

> Part of the task facing a negotiator for either a union or a company is effectively to coalesce an admixture of views of various segments of his constituency, and to determine, in the light of that knowledge, which issues can be compromised and to what degree. A systematic effort by the other party to interfere with this process by either surreptitious espionage or open interrogation constitutes clear undercutting of this vital and necessarily confidential function of the negotiator.

§ 3. Solicitation of Strikers

During the course of a strike, the employer may wish to communicate with individual strikers in order not merely to inform them of the course of negotiations but also to determine whether they wish to return to work, to encourage them to do so, to inform them of economic harm to the business if the strike continues, and to apprise them of the employer's intention to hire replacements to do the work of the strikers. This direct communication with strikers, commonly referred to simply as "solicitation," has often resulted in charges that the employer has engaged in an illegal bypassing of the majority representative. Just as with communications concerning developments at the bargaining table, there is no clear line that separates solicitation which is legal from that which violates section 8(a)(5) (or section 8(a)(1)). Much will depend upon the particular circumstances in which the solicitation takes place, and most particularly upon the extent to which independent employer unfair labor practices give color or of coercion to the communications with the strikers.

It has been held that, absent threats of reprisal or promises of benefit, "Communications with employees by an employer are protected under the First Amendment of the Constitution," and that the "employer is free to say to his employees that he wishes to carry on production and, that, if the employees desire so to do, they may return to work." NLRB v. Bradley Washfountain Co. (7th Cir. 1951). The court there held that the employer could inform the strikers of the working conditions he is willing to extend to them, provided it extends no greater benefits to the strikers who return than is extended generally to those who remain on strike. These noncoercive contacts with employees may be made either by general literature or by individual conversations face-to-face or by telephone. Guyan Mach. Co. (1965). The employer is also free to inform the strikers that the law gives it the right to hire permanent replacements, and to state that it will begin to exercise that right at a date certain in the future. Mc-Lean-Arkansas Lumber Co. (1954) (but employer may not state that the returning striker is no longer to consider the union its bargaining representative). But, since workers who are on strike in protest of an employer unfair labor practice (rather than an "economic striker") may not be permanently replaced, the employer violates the law by announcing its intention to replace unfair labor practice strikers. ITT Henze Valve Serv. (1967), *enf'd mem.* (5th Cir. 1971) (violation of section 8(a)(1)). And even such a warning of replacement to economic strikers will be outlawed if uttered in a threatening context of other significant coercive conduct by the employer. De Soto Hardwood Flooring Co. (1951) (section 8(a)(1)).

The Board has held, with judicial approval, that inducement of strikers to return to work becomes unlawful when it may fairly be characterized as coercive, or as an attempt at individual bargaining, or as an inducement to repudiate the majority bargaining representative. The basic principles were announced by the Board in Texas Co. (1951), *enf't denied on other grounds* (9th Cir. 1952):

> Absent a threat or promise of benefit designed to coerce the strikers into returning by the deadline date, the legality of the Respondent's individual solicitation of the strikers must be determined against the background in which [the] solicitation was done. [Apart from explicit coercion, solicitation of strikers will be illegal if] (1) The solicitation has constituted an integral part of a pattern of illegal opposition to the purposes of the Act as evidenced by the Respondent's entire course of conduct, or (2) the solicitation has been conducted under circumstances, and in a manner, reasonably calculated to undermine the strikers' collective bargaining representative and to demonstrate that the Respondent sought individual rather than collective bargaining.

Perhaps the most obvious form of an illegal inducement to return to work is the promise to grant returning strikers benefits which have not been first offered to the union, for all employees, at the bargaining table. NLRB v. J. H. Bonck Co. (5th Cir. 1970) ("no meaningful negotiation" with the union on those subjects). Even though the employer argues that such greater benefits are "necessary" in order to secure strike replacements and keep the business going, that alone will not excuse the employer from first bargaining with the union to impasse prior to instituting the increase. Glazers Wholesale Drug Co. (1974). It may therefore become important to determine whether the benefits offered directly by the employer to returning strikers are "more" than those which are presently in effect or than those which have already been offered to the union (and rejected) at the bargaining table. This issue was raised in a rather early case, Pacific Gamble Robinson Co. v. NLRB (6th Cir. 1950), in which the court of appeals, reversing the Board, held that the company did not violate the Act by paying strike replacements 98 cents an hour, at a time when the present wage for new employees was 77 cents an hour, and the employer had offered to the union an increase to 87 cents. The court observed that the 98 cents paid to replacements was a flat rate which included no such valuable features of the existing contract as seniority, paid vacation, overtime and arbitration, so that the pay increase actually implemented was within the range of the total bargaining package already offered the union. The Board has recently indicated its disinclination to follow *Pacific Gamble*, see Glazers Wholesale Drug Co. (1974), and the Supreme Court in the very significant case of NLRB v. Katz (U.S.1962), has by implication suggested that the Board may make an issue-by-issue examination in assessing whether the employer has already bargained to impasse on a proposal before implementing it.

Even when the employer has offered returning strikers no greater benefits than those already paid to its employees or already offered to the union, its solicitation of individual strikers may be held to violate section 8(a)(5) when the employer has contemporaneously evidenced its rejection of the union's representative status, as by refusing to bargain in good faith over a protracted period, American Steel Bldg. Co. (1974); or by requiring that an unconditional application for reinstatement be submitted not by the union on behalf of all of the strikers but rather by the individual strikers themselves, Chanticleer, Inc. (1966); or by requiring the returning strikers to incorporate the offered terms in individual contracts of employment, Imperial Outdoor Advertising (1971), *enf'd* (8th Cir. 1972). The Board may also find that solicitation of strikers violates section 8(a)(1) of the Act, quite apart from the duty-to-bargain requirement of section 8(a)(5), when the employer engages in such conduct as offering a wage increase if the strikers return to work and reject the union, National Furniture Mfg. Co. (1961); or threatening not to negotiate or sign any agreement with the union, Federal Dairy Co. (1961), *enf'd* (1st Cir. 1962) (employer urged that employees abandon not merely the strike but also the union).

The Board has announced that solicitation of individual strikers to return to work, even by holding out a wage increase not yet offered to the union, may be lawful when the strike is itself unlawful or otherwise unprotected. For example, in California Cotton Coop. Ass'n (1954), in which the union had induced a strike that was in violation of a no-strike clause in the collective bargaining agreement, the Board held that the duty to bargain with the union was suspended for the duration of the strike, at least on matters related to the strike; therefore, individual solicitation was held lawful. And more recently, in Publicity Engravers, Inc. (1966), in which the union had commenced a strike without notifying the state mediation agency as required by section 8(d), the Board held that an offer of higher wages to returning employees, which "might violate the Act in other circumstances," did not contravene section 8(a)(1) since it interfered only with the illegal strike and not with any protected activity. There is some question whether these precedents, or at least their reasoning, can still be regarded as authoritative. See NLRB v. Katz (U.S.1962) (Court states in dictum that the duty to bargain is not discharged during an unprotected "partial" strike).

§ 4. Presentation and Adjustment of "Grievances": Generally

The principle of exclusive representation, adopted by Congress in 1935, rests on the premise that industrial stability can be assured only when the "trade agreement" which establishes overall working conditions throughout the bargaining unit is negotiated by a single spokesman which in turn must balance and adjust the possibly divergent interests of unit employees. Instability and conflict would be the price of permitting the employer to negotiate different sets of norms—on wages, fringe benefits, seniority, promotions, grievances and the like—with different individuals, groups and representatives. No comparable dislocation was believed to follow, after the uniform rules of the contract had been set, if a single worker with a personal grievance were to present it to the employer for adjustment. Congress in 1935 therefore drew a distinction between "collective bargaining in respect to rates of pay, wages, hours of employment, or other conditions of employment," the exclusive domain of the majority representative, and the presentation of "grievances," thought to warrant a modest exception from the principle of exclusivity. To section 9(a) it added a proviso:

> Provided, That any individual employee or a group of employees shall have the right at any time to present grievances to their employer.

But while the proviso gave the right to "present" grievances, it did not in terms give the individual the right to confer and adjust the grievance. Employers thus had cause to fear that individual adjustment of grievances, without the consent or presence of the majority representative, would be just as much a violation of the Act as would individual bargaining. To address this problem, and to validate direct settlement efforts between the employer and the individual employee on grievances—regardless of the authorization of the union—Congress in 1947 augmented the scope of the proviso to section 9(a) but at the same time sought to assure the participation of the union as a guardian of the contract and of the unit as a whole:

> Provided, That any individual employee or a group of employees shall have the right at any time to present grievances to their employer and to have such grievances adjusted, without the intervention of the bargaining representative, as long as the adjustment is not inconsistent with the terms of a collective-bargaining contract or agreement then in effect: Provided further, That the bargaining representative has been given opportunity to be present at such adjustment.

Thus, the employer must give the majority union an "opportunity to be present" when a grievance is adjusted, but whether or not the union avails itself of that opportunity, the employer may adjust the grievance without being held to have "bypassed" the union by dealing with an individual employee.

Although this difference in statutory treatment between "collective bargaining" and the adjustment of "grievances" makes the definition of those terms significant, Congress has nowhere illuminated the distinction. It is arguable that every dispute, however seemingly personalized, under a collective bargaining agreement will have ramifications for other employees in the unit; this is particularly so when the grievance involves not the application of a clear contract provision to a unique set of facts but rather the interpretation of an ambiguous provision, which will then clearly govern the entire unit prospectively. The Board did indeed hold at an early date that the adjustment of grievances is very much akin—in its process and in its substantive import—to bargaining over an initial contract term. Hughes Tool Co. (1944), enf'd (5th Cir. 1945). On appeal, however, the court was more willing to endorse the more common understanding that bargaining "will fix for the future the rules of the employment for everyone in the unit," while grievances "are usually the claims of individuals or small groups that their rights under the collective bargain have not been respected." But it promptly noted that while some grievances involve "only some question of fact or conduct peculiar to the employee, not affecting the unit," others "raise a question of the meaning of the contract, or present a situation not covered by the contract," and that in the latter cases adjustment will require "bargaining." It is possible, of course, to distinguish between bargaining and grievance-processing in most cases, but in the unusual case which falls within the "penumbra" of both terms, the characterization that is given by the Board or the courts will no doubt depend upon the significance that is attached to the institutional interests of the majority union and the employer in a structured and stable relationship.

The Supreme Court has recently intimated that the distinction between bargaining and grievance processing is one of "fact" and that the Board's characterization is to be sustained if supported by substantial evidence on the record considered as a whole; the reviewing court is not to make its own appraisal de novo. In Emporium Capwell Co. v. Western Addition Community Organization (U.S. 1975), several black employees, in spite of the program of the incumbent union to challenge employment discrimination through the contract grievance machinery, insisted upon meeting with top company officials in order to eradicate perceived discrimination against racial minorities in hiring and promotion. When the employer asserted that these claims would have to be processed through the union, the employees conducted a press conference, distributed leaflets attacking the employer and picketed at company premises. Two of the protesters were discharged, and a charge was filed with the Board claiming that they were engaging in the protected activity of seeking to present and adjust a grievance within the proviso to section 9(a). The Board concluded, however, that they were engaging in the unprotected activity of using concerted effort to force the employer to bargain with them on behalf of minority employees. The Supreme Court found the Board's characterization of this activity as bargaining rather than grievance-processing to be supported by the record, given both the generality of the issue (the employer's policy toward a broad range of racial minority groups, some of which were not represented at all in its workforce), and the employees' attempt to achieve their object by picketing and by discussions with top company officials rather than by use of the contractual grievance-arbitration machinery. The Court emphasized that to permit the employer to deal with the protesters on their own terms would circumvent the authority of the majority union in adjusting conflicting interests within the unit and in combatting perceived discrimination through the negotiation of contract provisions and their enforcement in arbitration.

Once a dispute is characterized as a "grievance," section 9(a) sets forth the respective rights of the employer, the aggrieved individual and the bargaining representative. Clearly, the bargaining representative must be notified in advance of any meeting at which the employer and the individual employee will attempt to adjust the grievance, and it must be given an "opportunity to be present." As the Board has held: "Congress did not make a request by the union for an opportunity to be present a condition precedent to its right to be present at the adjustment of grievances. In other words, Congress chose not to make the union the moving party but vested in it the unqualified right" to be present. To adjust a grievance without affording this opportunity is a violation of section 8(a)(5). Valencia Baxt Express, Inc. (1963). Congress insisted on such presence, for fear that the private adjustment of grievances would too readily permit the employer to favor antiunion or nonunion employees, create rivalry, suspicion and friction among employees and induce employees to desert the collective bargaining representative. Similarly, if the union is notified of the grievance and the aggrieved worker seeks to have the assistance of union stewards in presenting and adjusting the grievance, it is an unfair labor practice for the employer to exclude them. Lee Deane Prods., Inc. (1970). The employer's duty in such a case is directly imposed by section 8(d) which includes in its definition of the duty to bargain "the negotiation of an agreement, or any question arising thereunder." It has even been held that, during contract negotiations, the employer may not lawfully insist on the incorporation of a provision which would exclude union representatives from various steps of the grievance procedure. Although the employer argued that the union can "waive" its section 9(a) right to be present at the adjustment of grievances, just as it can waive the otherwise protected right to strike during the contract term, the Board held that waiver of the union's right to be present advanced no statutory interest (in contrast to the waiver of the right to strike, which furthers the statutory interest in industrial stability and the peaceful resolution of disputes). Bethlehem Steel Co. (1950). Merely affording the union an opportunity to be present at the grievance adjustment is not sufficient to comply with the requirements of the Act; it is an unfair labor practice to adjust a grievance with an individual in a manner which conflicts with the terms of the labor contract. Hotel Corp. of Puerto Rico, Inc. (1963) (part of the grievance settlement was a withholding of exclusive recognition from the majority union).

Section 9(a) does not clearly address three issues relating to the rights of the aggrieved individual. First, does the employee have a right under the Labor Act to *require* the employer to adjust or attempt adjustment of the grievance? In other words, does the employer violate the Act if it refuses to meet with an individual to adjust his grievance? Second, does the employee have a right under the Labor Act to *require* the union to present and adjust a grievance on his behalf? Third, may the aggrieved employee present and adjust his grievance—over the objection of the bargaining representative but with the consent of the employer—through a labor organization other than the exclusive representative? With varying degrees of qualification, the basic answer to each of these three questions is negative.

§ 5. The "Right" of Individuals to Adjust Grievances

Because the first proviso to section 9(a) states that any individual employee "shall have the right at any time" to present grievances and "to have such grievances adjusted," some courts held that the Labor Act gave to the employee—whether or not the bargaining representative supported his cause—the indefeasible right to present and adjust his grievance, and imposed upon the employer the affirmative duty to confer and adjust the grievance with the individual employee. The Supreme Court has recently rejected this reading of the proviso.

In Emporium Capwell Co. v. Western Addition Community Organization (U.S.1975), a number of employees, in protest of the employer's hiring and promotion policies as these affected racial minorities, engaged in leafletting and picketing, for which they were discharged. The employer had refused to deal with the protesters directly, and had required that they pursue their claims through the incumbent union under the contract grievance machinery. The discharged employees contended that they were seeking not to bargain but to present and adjust grievances, and that the Act protected their use of leafletting and picketing to compel the employer to confer and to adjust. The Court held that this argument

> clearly misapprehends the nature of the "right" conferred by this section. The intendment of the proviso is to permit employees to present grievances and to authorize the employer to entertain them without opening itself to liability for dealing directly with employees in derogation of the duty to bargain only with the exclusive bargaining representative, a violation of § 8(a)(5) . . . . The Act nowhere protects this "right" by making it an unfair labor practice for an employer to refuse to entertain such a presentation, nor can it be read to authorize resort to economic coercion.

Thus, the proviso to section 9(a) merely gives the employer a defense to a charge of refusal to bargain with the majority union, under section 8(a)(5), when it adjusts a grievance with an individual employee or group of employees; it does not impose an affirmative duty to do so. The Court explicitly endorsed the analysis of the Court of Appeals for the Second Circuit in Black-Clawson Co. v. Machinists Lodge 355 (2d Cir. 1962), which found support in the legislative history of the proviso; in the structure of the section ("The office of a proviso is seldom to create substantive rights and obligations; it carves exceptions out of what goes before"); and in what it regarded as a sound view of industrial relations, which would find chaos in the right of all disenchanted employees to process their grievances to settlement and a preferred stability in channeling all such grievances through the union ("A union's right to screen grievances and to press only those it concludes should be pressed is a valuable right").

The Court's approach parallels that which it had earlier taken on the question whether the aggrieved employee has an indefeasible right to have the union present and adjust his grievance on his behalf through the contractual grievance and arbitration machinery. In Vaca v. Sipes (U.S.1967), the company discharged an employee, asserting that his high blood pressure rendered him physically unable to perform heavy work in the company's meatpacking plant. The union pursued a grievance through four steps of the contract grievance procedure but, after securing a new medical examination which failed to support the grievant's position, the union's executive board voted not to take the case to arbitration; it did, however, try to secure less vigorous work for the grievant and it endorsed the company's referral of the grievant to a rehabilitation center. The grievant brought an action in a state court against the union's officers, and secured a judgment for compensatory and punitive damages, on the theory that the union's decision not to process the grievance to arbitration was arbitrary and capricious. The Supreme Court reversed. It agreed that no union has the power to refuse to process a grievance if its determination is "arbitrary, discriminatory, or in bad faith," and that the so-called duty of fair representation applies to the administration of the labor contract as well as to its negotiation. (This duty is discussed in greater detail elsewhere in this work). But it also underlined the discretion of the union in good faith to decline to process grievances which it believes to lack merit.

> In providing for a grievance and arbitration procedure which gives the union discretion to supervise the grievance machinery and to invoke arbitration, the employer and the union contemplate that each will endeavor in good faith to settle grievances short of arbitration. Through this settlement process, frivolous grievances are ended prior to the most costly and time-consuming step in the grievance procedures. Moreover, both sides are assured that similar complaints will be treated consistently, and major problem areas in the interpretation of the collective bargaining contract can be isolated and perhaps resolved. And finally, the settlement process furthers the interest of the union as statutory agent and as coauthor of the bargaining agreement in representing the employees in the enforcement of that agreement.

In short, where the applicable grievance procedures empower the union, rather than the individual, to process the claim of contract breach—as is almost universally the case—the individual has no absolute right to have the union process his grievance. His only right is that the union exercise a good faith and nonarbitrary judgment as to whether to do so. The Court in *Vaca* found that regardless of whether the discharge did in fact violate the labor contract (as the state-court jury found it did after a study of the medical evidence) the union acted without hostility, made an effort to protect the aggrieved employee short of arbitration, and concluded that the claim lacked sufficient merit to proceed to arbitration. Accordingly, the union could not be held liable for breach of any statutory or contractual duty to the employee, and the employer could not be held liable for discharging the employee in violation of the contract. In a case in which the union refuses to process the individual's grievance, the proviso to section 9(a) permits the individual employee and the willing employer to adjust the grievance in spite of the union's absence. To that extent, the union's control over grievance resolution is less embracing than in matters of "bargaining."

§ 6.   The Role of Minority Unions in Grievance Adjustment

On occasion, either because the majority representative has chosen not to process a grievance or because the aggrieved employee supports a rival union, the Board and courts have had to deal with the question whether the employer is free to adjust a grievance by dealing with a minority union.   (The principle that the employer has no *duty* to adjust grievances with other than the bargaining representative has already been discussed.)   Congress in the original proviso to section 9(a), incorporated in 1935, gave the right to present and adjust grievances to "any individual employee or a group of employees," and purposefully refrained from adding the phrase "through a representative of their own choosing."   That proviso was early held to authorize the employer to adjust grievances with individuals, even with the assistance of a "more experienced friend," but not with a minority union.   Hughes Tool Co. v. NLRB (5th Cir. 1945) (unfair labor practice to adjust grievance with minority union, and also unfair labor practice to adjust grievance with an individual without notifying the bargaining representative; section 9(a) had not yet been amended expressly to incorporate the latter requirement).   After Congress in 1947 added to the section 9(a) proviso the right of the bargaining representative to be present at a grievance adjustment, and forbade adjustments inconsistent with the contract, another court of appeals concluded that this sufficiently protected the majority representative such that an employer could henceforth adjust grievances with a representative of a rival union.   The court reasoned from this that it would not be an unfair labor practice under section 8(b)(4)(C) if a minority union induced a strike in order to compel the employer to redress a contract grievance (by reinstating an employee) even though there was an incumbent majority union already certified.   Douds v. Local 1250, Retail Union (2d Cir. 1949).

Soon after, the Board declined to follow this decision.   It read the 1947 amendments to section 9(a) as merely intended to make it clear that the employee may adjust his grievance even without the majority union provided the union is given an opportunity to participate; Congress did not intend also to overrule the principle of the *Hughes Tool* case that the employer violated section 8(a)(5) by adjusting grievances with a minority union.   Federal Tel. & Radio Co. (1953).   (Although the Board at first continued to hold as well that picketing by a minority union to force the settlement of a grievance by reinstating an employee was an unfair labor practice, it later abandoned this position.   Hod Carriers Local 840 (Blinne Constr. Co.) (1962) (dictum).)   The Supreme Court, in its recent decision in Emporium Capwell Co. v. Western Addition Community Org'n (U.S.

1975), has concluded that even if a dispute can be characterized as a "grievance" rather than as "bargaining," the use of leafletting or picketing by a group of employees—and presumably also by a minority union—without the endorsement of the bargaining agent, with a purpose of compelling the employer to adjust the "grievance," is unprotected activity for which the participating employees may be discharged. The Court did not, however, consider whether an employer would violate section 8(a)(5) if it capitulated to such pressures by a minority union and adjusted a grievance with it—or did so willingly.

In sum, if the majority union acquiesces the employer if it wishes may process a grievance with a minority union. In the absence of such acquiescence, the employer—even if it wishes to—is forbidden under the Board's reading of section 8(a)(5) to adjust grievances with a minority union, although at least one court held to the contrary more than twenty-five years ago. And, if the employer resists such dealing with a minority union, that union's resort to economic pressure may not be an unfair labor practice (at least if the object is to compel immediate redress rather than ongoing discussions), but it will subject the participating employees to discharge.

§ 7. Investigatory and Disciplinary Interviews

While "collective bargaining" may be pursued with no persons other than the majority representative, and the "adjustment of grievances" may proceed only if the majority representative has been given an opportunity to be present, the law is less clear as to the role the exclusive representative is to play when the employer wishes to deal directly with its employees in other less formalized situations, such as an interview or a discussion on the plant floor. The Board has held that, just as the employer is free to discuss with individual employees their special problems under life or health insurance plans, the employer is entitled to meet with a group of employees to disseminate information regarding the profit-sharing plan negotiated with the union, and it is not unlawful to exclude the union from such a meeting. In Ingraham Indus. (1969), the General Counsel did not deny that the employer had the right to address the employees but argued that the representatives of the union were entitled to be present upon request, in order to challenge what they believed to be misleading or erroneous employer statements. The Board rejected this argument, since the employer was engaging in no negotiation and no adjustment of grievances, the employer had properly negotiated the plan originally with the union, and there was no attempt to modify or renegotiate it. See American Printing Co. (1968) (no unfair labor practice when employer meets with individual employees, without a union representative present, to tell them that their privately communicated wage requests are unreasonable and will not be granted).

The Board has announced that, among the wide range of possible contacts between an employer and its workers, certain types of employee interviews warrant the presence of the bargaining representative while others do not. The Supreme Court has given its apparent endorsement to these Board pronouncements, in NLRB v. J. Weingarten, Inc. (U.S.1975). In that case, the employer, believing that a particular employee was taking money from the company cash register, placed her under surveillance and then required her to attend an interview at which she was questioned about a particular incident by a specialist from the company's security department. Her request on several occasions for the assistance of a union steward was denied. Although the employee was ultimately exonerated, her union filed a charge with the Board alleging that the compulsion to submit without union representation to an interview which the employee reasonably fears may result in discipline constitutes a violation of section 8(a)(1). The Board agreed, and was affirmed by the Supreme Court. The Court concluded that the employee's request for representation at the interview was a "concerted activity" within the protection of section 7, since the participation of the representative would safeguard not only the single potentially aggrieved employee but also all employees in the bargaining unit; those employees would see that they too can secure union representation in a like interview and would vicariously be protected by the union representative against an employer practice of unjust punishment. To discipline an employee for insisting on union representation at such an "investigatory" interview "in which the risk of discipline reasonably inheres," or to force the employee to appear at such an interview without complying with his request for union representation, "interferes with, restrains or coerces" that employee in a protected activity and violates section 8(a)(1).

The Court on the same day also held that the employer violates sections 8(a)(1) and (3) when it discharges or otherwise disciplines a union steward for insisting on representing an individual who desires such representation at an investigatory interview. ILGWU v. Quality Mfg. Co. (U.S.1975). The employer is, however, free to take at face value the claim by an employee that he refuses to appear at an investigatory interview without union representation; the employer may choose not to conduct the investigatory interview with the employee at all, and may instead secure facts from any other sources.

While the Supreme Court has thus determined that Section 8(a)(1) will normally guarantee the presence of the union at an investigatory interview when that is requested by the interviewed employee, it has not considered whether the union is independently entitled under section 8(a)(5) to be informed of an interview and given an opportunity to appear, as is the case when a "grievance" has already come into existence. Given the reach of the decisions under section 8(a)(1) it is likely that the question under section 8(a)(5) will arise only in cases in which the interviewed employee neglects to insist on union representation, either as a matter of personal preference or simply from ignorance. In determining whether there is a duty to deal with the union, the Board has drawn a distinction between the "disciplinary" interview and the "investigatory" interview. In the "disciplinary" interview, the employee is called in order to impose discipline already decided upon, or to develop a supporting record to justify a disciplinary decision already made. Although at the time the interview commences there is as yet technically no "grievance" or alleged contract breach which entitles the union to be present pursuant to section 9(a), the purpose of the interview is to bring about a severance of employment or other modification in the employee's "conditions of employment," so that there is an obligation to confer and deal with the union (at least if the union so requests). This analysis has been rejected by at least one court of appeals, which held that, so long as the employer's purpose in conducting the interview is to elicit information, "[W]e see no reason why an employer's prior commitment to disciplinary action should necessarily transform it into a collective bargaining session requiring union representation." Texaco, Inc., Houston Prod. Div. v. NLRB (5th Cir. 1969) (reversing Board finding of section 8(a)(5) violation, also because of disagreement with Board's characterization of interview as "disciplinary").

The Board has declined to extend similar protection to the union, under section 8(a)(5), when the purpose of the interview is not to confirm or announce a disciplinary decision already made but is rather an "investigatory" interview designed to gather facts. Although the employee has reasonable cause to fear that these facts will then be used as a basis for the imposition of future discipline (and section 8(a)(1) therefore forbids employer coercion of an interview alone if the employee resists), there is no independent duty to notify and confer with the union under section 8(a)(5). Dayton Typog. Serv., Inc. (1969). Moreover, even if a union representative is present at an investigatory interview, the employer is not obligated to "confer" or "deal" with him, unlike the case of the disciplinary interview in which there is a duty to bargain; the employer may insist on conducting its investigation of the employee by hearing only his account and may limit the union to the role of assisting the employee or attempting to clarify the facts. NLRB v. J. Weingarten, Inc. (U.S. 1975) (apparently approving the Board's decisions on this issue).

These differing principles governing the investigatory and the disciplinary interview will no doubt give rise to questions of definition, and it will be necessary for the Board over time to develop clearer guidelines for distinguishing the two. See Texaco, Inc., Los Angeles Sales Terminal (1969) (decision of trial examiner).

While the rights of the employee and the union are relatively modest in the investigatory interview, not even these rights may be invoked when the employee has no reasonable fear that discipline will result from the employer's discussions. Thus, the Court in *Weingarten* quoted a passage from a Board decision regarding the right to representation:

> We would not apply the rule to such run-of-the-mill shop-floor conversations as, for example, the giving of instructions or training or needed corrections of work techniques. In such cases there cannot normally be any reasonable basis for an employee to fear that any adverse impact may result from the interview, and thus we would then see no reasonable basis for him to seek the assistance of his representative.

Here too, it will no doubt become necessary for the Board, on a case-by-case basis, to determine whether a conversation between management and an individual employee may properly be characterized as an investigatory interview, where facts are gathered which the employee reasonably believes may lead to discipline, or as less ominous discussion and questioning.

CHAPTER XX

THE DUTY TO BARGAIN IN GOOD FAITH

§ 1. Bargaining in Good Faith: General Requirements and Problems of Proof

The duty to bargain in good faith is defined in section 8(d) of the Labor Act as follows:

> For the purposes of this section, to bargain collectively is the performance of the mutual obligation of the employer and the representative of the employees to meet at reasonable times and confer in good faith with respect to wages, hours, and other terms and conditions of employment, or the negotiation of an agreement, or any question arising thereunder, and the execution of a written contract incorporating any agreement reached if requested by either party, but such obligation does not compel either party to agree to a proposal or require the making of a concession . . . .

Section 8(d) also sets forth a number of procedural requirements for notification in the event a contract is to be terminated or modified, and bars strikes and lockouts for a limited "cooling off" period during negotiations. At the heart of the section are the phrases "confer in good faith" and "wages, hours, and other terms and conditions of employment." The latter phrase outlines the so-called mandatory subjects which set the boundaries of the parties' duty to bargain; within those boundaries the duty applies, while outside them either party may decline to bargain and is free to make and implement decisions unilaterally. The scope of the mandatory subjects is discussed elsewhere in this work. This section of the work focuses on the requirement that both parties bargain, in compliance with the mandates of section 8(d).

The purpose of the Act is to bring to the bargaining table parties willing to present their proposals and articulate supporting reasons, to listen to and weigh the proposals and reasons of the other party, and to search for some common ground which can serve as the basis for a written bilateral agreement. Section 8(d) has over time been construed to ban certain rather specific conduct; examples are a refusal even to meet with the other party for purposes of collective bargaining, a refusal to execute a written contract embodying terms upon which the parties agree, a change in wages or other working conditions presently under negotiation, or a refusal to turn over information requested by the other party as an aid to intelligent bargaining. These specific acts are commonly referred to as "per se" violations of the duty to bargain. Other violations of section 8(a)(5) or 8(b)(3) may be made out only by an examination of "all of the circumstances" without particular reference to any single act of the respondent; the entire pattern of conduct, in spite of apparent compliance with the discrete physical requirements of bargaining, shows that the respondent is in truth seeking to frustrate agreement, or to disrupt negotiations, or to oust the other party of "partnership" in determining wages and working conditions.

In spite of the comfort that comes from labelling conduct unlawful per se, there is in truth no very sharp dividing line between conduct unlawful per se and conduct unlawful only upon the entire record and in all of the circumstances. Most of the duty-to-bargain cases show the respondent engaging in a "mix" of objectionable conduct, with specific wrongful conduct giving a taint to other more ambiguous activity at and away from the bargaining table. Conversely, the "circumstances" may indicate that it is proper for the Board to discount whatever excuses the respondent may put forward in an attempt to explain particular acts which on their face appear to be per se unjustifiable. But beyond the frequency with which they appear in the same record, there is no sharp analytical dividing line between the per se violation and the circumstantial violation. The per se violation is often said to be such either because the respondent's conduct warrants an automatic finding of illegality without the possibility of excuse, or because the finding is based on "objective" criteria without regard to the respondent's "subjective" state of mind, or because the finding may be made in evidentiary isolation without consideration of the record as a whole. These are all variations of the same underlying theme, a theme which is in most cases quite useful but which may not be altogether accurate. For even particular acts which are commonly treated as per se violations can, admittedly in rare circumstances, be justified by the respondent, typically by showing good faith and significant business reasons. For example, an employer's refusal to meet with the union, or its unilateral imposition of conditions upon meeting, is normally deemed a per se violation. But, as will be developed below, such conduct has not been condemned when the employer is found to have certain legitimate objections to the composition of the union's bargaining team, or when the union is currently engaging in an unlawful strike, or when the employer for good reason refuses to meet unless a stenographic transcript is made (or, in some circumstances, not made) of the proceedings. A so-called unilateral change in wages or working conditions is also usually condemned as per se illegal, although it is clear that such action is lawful when, for example, it is consistent with a "dynamic" status quo, or is authorized by a collective bargaining agreement, or within a limited range of circumstances is required by statute.

It is perhaps more accurate to say that certain conduct at (or away from) the bargaining table is in the preponderance of cases likely to disrupt or frustrate negotiations and not likely to be justified by substantial business reasons. Because of this, the Board and courts will properly presume that such conduct is unlawful, and a strong onus will fall upon the respondent to demonstrate that its conduct was in good faith and warranted in the particular circumstances of the case.   Thus, to say that conduct is illegal per se is simply to say that the General Counsel makes out a prima facie case of illegality when it shows that the respondent engaged in such conduct, that a finding of a violation of the Act may be based on that conduct alone, and that the burden of persuading the Board to the contrary rests upon the respondent.   The Supreme Court has said as much in NLRB v. Katz (U.S.1962), in branding as illegal an employer grant of pay increases and modification of sick-leave policy while those subjects were under negotiation—regardless of proof that the employer's objective was to evade its duty to bargain with the union.   The Court observed that such unilateral action

> must of necessity obstruct bargaining, contrary to the congressional policy.   It will often disclose an unwillingness to agree with the union.   It will rarely be justified by any reason of substance.   .   .   .   While we do not foreclose the possibility that there might be circumstances which the Board could or should accept as excusing or justifying unilateral action, no such case is presented here.

In other cases, where there is no such particular conduct which has been deemed grievously to disrupt or frustrate negotiations, the burden of demonstrating that the respondent has without cause otherwise brought about such disruption or frustration lies with the General Counsel, and the case is characterized as raising the question whether "in all of the circumstances" it may be inferred that the respondent was bargaining in bad faith.   This kind of case typically requires a scrutiny of the substantive positions taken by the respondent at the bargaining table.

The materials that follow will consider first (and preponderantly) the forms of conduct which have generally been treated as per se or objectively unlawful.   They will conclude with a consideration of conduct at the bargaining table which, under all of the circumstances, will be deemed to reflect subjective bad faith and an intention to frustrate negotiations.

§ 2.   Delaying or Conditioning Bargaining

The statute in unqualified terms requires the parties to "meet at reasonable times."   An employer's refusal to meet with the union at all is obviously a violation of the Act.   NLRB v. Lettie Lee, Inc. (9th Cir. 1944).   But the duty must first be triggered by a union request to meet.   American Buslines, Inc. (1967) (employer does not violate section 8(a)(5) by altering status of employees if union, after protesting the change, fails to initiate or request bargaining).   In most litigated cases, however, the employer does not refuse outright the union's demand for bargaining but rather engages in dilatory tactics which protract the intervals between meetings. In B. F. Diamond Constr. Co. (1967), *enf'd* (5th Cir. 1969), the Board indicated that delays of one month between each bargaining session were unduly long, and could not be excused merely because the company negotiator had other pressing business obligations. Six meetings of relatively short duration, roughly three hours, over a six-month period, were also held to violate the duty to meet at reasonable times. Insulating Fabricators, Inc. (1963), *enf'd* (4th Cir. 1964).

These decisions condemn the failure to meet at reasonable times as sufficient alone to violate the duty to bargain, but are careful to note that this conduct occurred in the context of other behavior which betokened bad faith, such as other unfair labor practices. Perhaps the decisions rely on "all of the circumstances" because it is otherwise difficult to determine exactly what are the "reasonable times" at which the parties must meet. This elastic concept invites the conclusion that a delay of a certain period can be "reasonable" when done in good faith but not when other indicators suggest that the purpose of the delay is to frustrate negotiations. See Radiator Specialty Co. (1963), *enf'd in part* (4th Cir. 1964) (parties met thirty-seven times in ten months, but most meetings were brief and at long intervals; court refused enforcement for lack of substantial evidence of bad faith). One court appears to have endorsed as a test "whether the Respondent would have delayed, for such a relatively long period of time, negotiations for a business contract or a bank loan it was desirous of concluding." NLRB v. Reed & Prince Mfg. Co. (1st Cir. 1953) (refusal to bargain found under all the circumstances).

A refusal to confer has also been found when the employer or union imposes unreasonable conditions upon the other as a predicate to meeting or bargaining. Thus, the employer may not insist, as a condition of submitting a contract proposal to the union, that the union agree upon accepting it on the same day, when it knows that acceptance will require that the union notify its membership and conduct a ratification vote. S & M Mfg. Co. (1967). Nor may the employer insist, as a condition of continued bargaining, that the union forgo the processing of unfair labor practice charges against the employer. Fitzgerald Mills Corp. (1961), *enf'd* (2d Cir. 1963). Indeed, the employer may not insist that bargaining be delayed until the union ceases an ongoing economic strike, since the strike is an expectable occurrence during collective bargaining and the duty to bargain to an impasse continues for the duration of the strike. As the court stated in NLRB v. J. H. Rutter-Rex Mfg. Co. (5th Cir. 1957), the calling of a strike contrary to assurances given the employer does not make the union or the members of its bargaining unit outlaws who forfeit the benefits of the Labor Act; "A strike does not in and of itself suspend the bargaining obligation." (The duty to bargain during the period of a strike is discussed in detail below.)

The Supreme Court has also clearly held that neither party is entitled to condition bargaining over mandatory subjects upon agreement to some nonmandatory term. In NLRB v. Wooster Div. of Borg-Warner Corp. (U.S.1958), the employer refused to accept the terms of a negotiated agreement unless it contained provisions for exclusive recognition of the local union (although it was the International which had been certified as bargaining representative) and for a pre-strike ballot among unit employees as to the acceptability of the employer's last offer in negotiations. The Court found both the recognition clause and the ballot clause to constitute nonmandatory terms, and held that insistence upon them was "in substance, a refusal to bargain about the subjects that are within the scope of mandatory bargaining." Although the record evidence induced the trial examiner to conclude that the company had in fact negotiated in good faith concerning all mandatory subjects, the Court announced in effect a per se principle that insistence to impasse upon nonmandatory subjects constitutes, regardless of justification, a refusal to "confer" about mandatory subjects.

A party *is* free to insist on its position on a mandatory term as a condition to reaching an agreement. But it does not follow that a party may insist on resolving certain mandatory issues before even beginning to discuss any others. It is, for example, common practice for parties to negotiate about such mandatory subjects as a recognition clause, union security clause or a grievance and arbitration clause (commonly called "non-economic" items) before negotiating about wages, vacation pay, pensions and other economic benefits. If the employer, however, refuses to discuss economic matters at all until an agreement has been reached on non-economic matters, this has been held to evidence bad faith in the context of other similar indicators. NLRB v. Patent Trader, Inc. (2d Cir. 1969), *mdf'd* (2d Cir. 1970). Indeed, the Board has recently held that such conduct by an employer is in itself a refusal to bargain in good faith. After an initial agreement to negotiate non-economic items first, and after eight months of negotiations left the parties in disagreement on management rights, union security and grievance procedures, the employer in Federal Mogul Corp. (1974), refused to abide by the union's suggestion that these issues might more readily be resolved if economic matters could be discussed contemporaneously. When the employer refused to discuss the union's wage proposal until the union agreed to the company's position on the non-economic items, the union struck. The Board held the strike to have been triggered by the employer's refusal to bargain, such that replacements for the strikers had to be discharged and the strikers reinstated. And, in Adrian Daily Telegram (1974), the employer was held to have refused to bargain when, after five months of negotiations on non-economic matters and a deadlock only on the issue of union security, the employer avoided discussing the union's economic proposals (introduced at the suggestion of a federal mediator) unless the union first agreed to an open shop.

It is also unlawful for a party to insist that negotiations cease until there is a change in the composition of the negotiating team which the other party has sent to the bargaining table. Thus, it was held in Standard Oil Co. v. NLRB (6th Cir. 1963), that the employer may not refuse to meet with the bargaining committee of the certified local union merely because that committee has among its members representatives from other locals and from the International. This issue has taken on considerable significance in recent years with the development of so-called coordinated bargaining, in which a number of unions representing different units of employees working for the same employer appoint representatives to serve in common with each union's own bargaining representatives in their separate negotiations. The avowed purpose is not to force the employer to negotiate at once with all unions for all bargaining units but simply to permit the unions to assist each other in bargaining, to enhance the flow of information among the unions having a common interest and incidentally to strengthen the bargaining position of the negotiating union. It has been held that the employer violates section 8(a)(5) when it refuses to bargain with such a coordinated bargaining team and when it conditions future bargaining with the certified union upon the expulsion of "outside" members of the bargaining team.

In General Elec. Co. v. NLRB (2d Cir. 1969), the International Union of Electrical Workers sought to bargain with the General Electric Company for its certified locals on a nationwide basis (as the International had done for many years), but it sought to have on its bargaining team representatives of seven other international unions whose locals also had agreements with the company. "The avowed purposes . . . were to coordinate bargaining in 1966 with General Electric and its chief competitor, Westinghouse Electric Corporation, to formulate national goals, and otherwise to support one another." The company asserted that this was an attempt at multi-unit companywide bargaining and, even though it was informed that the representatives of other unions were nonvoting members who were present solely to aid the IUE in negotiations and not to speak for their own union members, the company refused to meet for negotiations. This was held to violate the Labor Act. The court began by noting that the Act permits employees, in section 7, "to bargain collectively through representatives of their own choosing," and that a long line of cases had established the principle that the employer could not lawfully take exception to the union's bargaining representatives unless there was a "clear and present danger" to the bargaining process (such as specific proof of intention by the union to disrupt negotiations). The court found no such danger to exist, noting that the presence of outside negotiators could be justified by a desire to enhance bargaining expertise or to counterbalance the company's own centralized formulation of labor-relations policy so as to strengthen the bargaining position of the IUE. The court found no attempt illegally to have the bargaining expand the boundaries of the bargaining unit for which the company was obligated to negotiate and no other showing by the company that the union was structuring its bargaining team with bad faith or an ulterior motive. The court's view has been adopted in the few other decisions raising an issue under section 8(a)(5) in cases of coordinated bargaining.

As the court in the *General Electric* case noted, there have been instances in which the company has successfully justified a refusal to confer with the union because of the identity of particular members (rather than the general structure) of the union bargaining team. The Board has endorsed the principle that "employers may properly refuse to recognize or deal with *particular union representatives* whose conduct or statements reflect such underlying hostility directed against the firm as to make collective bargaining a futility." Reisman Bros. (1967), *enf'd* (2d Cir. 1968). In NLRB v. Kentucky Util. Co. (6th Cir. 1950), the union negotiator had openly expressed great personal animosity toward the employer, and in Bausch & Lomb Optical Co. (1954), the union had established a company in direct competition with the employer. Compare Adrian Daily Telegram (1974) (employer must bargain, when union-operated competing newspaper is only temporary device to keep strikers employed). The union has the same limited power to object to the company negotiator, as in NLRB v. ILGWU (Slate Belt Apparel Contractors' Ass'n) (3d Cir. 1960), in which the company, in order avowedly to "put one over on the union," added a former union official to the company bargaining team. By way of summary in General Elec. Co. v. NLRB (2d Cir. 1969), the court stated that there is a general rule favoring freedom in the designation of bargaining representatives, the limitations are narrow and infrequent, and one seeking to refuse to bargain because of an objection to the other party's bargaining spokesman "clearly undertakes a considerable burden, characterized . . . as the showing of a 'clear and present' danger to the bargaining process."

It must be noted that the *employer's* freedom to bargain through a representative of its own choosing has been memorialized in section 8(b)(1)(B) of the Labor Act, which makes it an unfair labor practice for a labor organization to "restrain or coerce . . . an employer in the selection of his representatives for the purposes of collective bargaining or the adjustment of grievances." A union violates that section by trying to force the employer out of a multiemployer bargaining association, Slate Roofers Local 36 (1968), or to force the employer to designate a multiemployer association to be its bargaining agent, Orange Belt Dist. Council of Painters No. 48 (1965). (In a case in which a section 8(b)(1)(B) complaint was dismissed, however, it was held that a union does not unlawfully compel the withdrawal of a single employer from a multiemployer unit when it seeks to bargain directly with the employer and to demand that it accept the same contract over which bargaining had stalled with the multiemployer group, provided the union continues to negotiate in good faith concurrently with that group. Cheney Calif. Lumber Co. v. NLRB (9th Cir. 1963).) And, in Los Angeles Cloak Joint Bd., ILGWU (Helen Rose Co.) (1960), a union was forbidden to picket a company to force it to dismiss an industrial relations consultant thought to be hostile to the union.

The terms of section 8(b)(1)(B) also apply when the union's coercion relates to the designation by the employer of a person who adjusts or decides grievances. In Associated Gen. Contractors of America v. NLRB (7th Cir. 1972), the union bargained to impasse and struck to compel a multiemployer association with which it was negotiating to submit jurisdictional disputes during the contract term to the National Joint Board for the Settlement of Jurisdictional Disputes, on which the employer association was not represented. The court found the Joint Board to be engaged in the adjustment of grievances, and held that the union's insistence and strike constituted coercion of the employer group in its selection of representatives for that purpose. The union also violates the Act when it attempts to compel an employer to limit its selection of foremen to persons who are members of the union. Thus, in International Typog. Union (Haverhill Gazette Co.) (1959), *enf'd* (1st Cir. 1960), *aff'd by an equally divided Court* (U.S.1961), the union demanded a contract clause requiring that the composing room foreman, who had the power to hire, fire and process grievances, be a union member. This was held to violate section 8(b)(1)(B), since the employer would be limited in the choice of its foremen and the union would be given the power to force the discharge or demotion of a foreman simply by expelling him from the union.

Several cases have raised the question whether one of the parties may condition bargaining upon the presence or absence of a person who is making an electronic or stenographic recording of the bargaining sessions. Labor relations experts have differing opinions as to the propriety of verbatim recording of bargaining sessions, with the proponents asserting that it aids in drafting the contract and in resolving subsequent disputes which turn upon the course of negotiation, and the opponents asserting that it encourages artificially "making a record" rather than candid and conciliatory give-and-take. The Board has taken note of these differing positions, and has refused to announce any unqualified or per se principle as to whether insistence on recording (or non-recording) constitutes a refusal to bargain. It holds instead that this issue, which it classifies as a "mandatory" subject for bargaining, is one on which the parties may insist provided the record demonstrates that this is done in good faith and not with a purpose of avoiding, delaying or frustrating bargaining. St. Louis Typog. Union No. 8 (1964). In that case, the Board found that in the circumstances the union did not violate section 8(b)(3) by insisting that the employer association not take a stenographic transcript of the negotiations. Two members of the Board, although concurring, urged that the issue of recording not be treated as a mandatory subject but rather as a permissive subject concerning which either party is free to adhere to its own position without discussion; they urged that insistence to impasse on one's position would frustrate negotiations on the more central mandatory issues and would necessarily inject a note of mistrust and contention into the negotiations. That concurring opinion, urging a per se rule, has not, however, prevailed, and the Board has searched the entire record in order to determine whether so conditioning negotiations is done in good faith or in bad faith. *E. g.*, Architectural Fiberglass (1967) (employer insistence on using tape recorder, over union's objection, was under the circumstances in bad faith). The few court opinions have been yet more generous to the party seeking a verbatim transcript as a condition to negotiations. One court, in NLRB v. Southern Transp., Inc. (8th Cir. 1966), catalogued the virtues of having an accurate record of negotiations and could find no meritorious objections (other than cost, which the employer there agreed to assume); it held that insistence on the presence of a court stenographer was not a per se refusal to bargain, that it could be unlawful only if demonstrably in bad faith, and that the burden of demonstrating bad faith fell upon the General Counsel.

§ 3. Reneging on Bargaining Commitments

The refusal upon request to sign a document embodying terms which have been agreed upon in collective bargaining is, without more, a refusal to bargain in violation of section 8(a)(5). Section 8(d) expressly includes within the duty to bargain "the execution of a written contract incorporating any agreement reached if requested by either party." Even before that mandate was incorporated in the Taft-Hartley Act of 1947, the Supreme Court had concluded that the bargaining duty in section 8(5) of the Wagner Act implicitly incorporated this requirement. In H. J. Heinz Co. v. NLRB (U.S.1941), the Supreme Court stated:

> A business man who entered into negotiations with another for an agreement having numerous provisions, with the reservation that he would not reduce it to writing or sign it, could hardly be thought to have bargained in good faith. This is even more so in the case of an employer who, by his refusal to honor, with his signature, the agreement which he has made with a labor organization, discredits the organization, impairs the bargaining process and tends to frustrate the aim of the statute to secure industrial peace through collective bargaining.

The Court endorsed the argument of the Board that a signed contract "serves both as recognition of the union with which the agreement is reached and as a permanent memorial of its terms," and that a refusal to sign disrupts labor relations, breeds dissatisfaction and disagreement, is tantamount to a refusal to recognize the union and deprives the employees of an authentic record of the terms agreed upon by their representative and their employer.

The Supreme Court has more recently applied what is now the express and unqualified obligation to execute an agreement, set forth in section 8(d). In NLRB v. Strong (U.S.1969), an employer, which was a member of a multiemployer association negotiating on its behalf with the roofers' union, sought to withdraw from the association after a collective bargaining agreement was reached, and refused repeated demands to sign the agreement. The Court agreed that this was a refusal to bargain in violation of section 8(a)(5), and it sustained the Board's order requiring in part that the employer sign the agreement and "pay to the appropriate source any fringe benefits provided for" therein. Although the court of appeals had refused to enforce the "payment" order, in the belief that this exceeded the Board's jurisdiction and trenched upon the authority of an arbitrator who might be appointed under the signed contract, the Supreme Court held that this was an appropriate order to remedy what the Board, clearly acting within its jurisdiction, found to be an unlawful refusal to sign and to give effect to the multiemployer agreement.

Even before all the terms of the contract are agreed upon and the employer is asked to sign, a party may be held to violate the Labor Act by reneging on commitments already made in ongoing negotiations. If, for example, a tentative agreement is reached on a number of bargaining items, a refusal to honor that agreement at a later date without good reason may be viewed as an indicator of bad faith. Thus, if the employer (or union) repudiates understandings already arrived at, abruptly changes its positions without any announced reason, or interposes new demands not raised earlier, this conduct will destroy not only amicability at the bargaining table but also the premises on which bargaining has progressed, and will protract the negotiations and delay settlement. San Antonio Mach. & Supply Corp. v. NLRB (5th Cir. 1966). Although conventional principles of contract law might authorize the withdrawal from an agreement not yet fully confirmed, such withdrawal in labor negotiations may be treated as some evidence of bad faith. Perhaps all of the cases in which such conduct has been examined by the Board and courts have involved other conduct reinforcing the inference of bad faith; it is questionable whether the withdrawal would, with nothing more, be deemed a refusal to bargain. The tactic is, however, sufficiently questionable that the burden should be placed upon the withdrawing party to assert its reasons, both to the other party during negotiations and eventually to the Board. The party in question may avoid a finding of refusal to bargain in good faith by showing that the earlier negotiations had not clearly resulted in agreement, or that an earlier understanding was intended to be conditional on the resolution of other disputed issues, or that there were good reasons to modify one's bargaining position, such as an earlier misunderstanding. Food Serv. Co. (1973).

§ 4. The Employer's Duty to Disclose Information: Generally

If the employer is in possession of information which is necessary or relevant to the union in discharging its function as bargaining representative, the employer will normally be required to turn over that information upon request of the union. Just as the employer is not free to conceal from the union its reasons for rejecting the union's bargaining demands concerning wages, hours and other working conditions, for this would without more cripple the capacity of the parties to communicate and to adjust differences, the same is true when the union is forbidden access to pertinent information. Although the Supreme Court has rejected a rule which would automatically result in a finding of bad-faith bargaining whenever the employer rejects a request for relevant information, and has endorsed a case-by-case determination, NLRB v. Truitt Mfg. Co. (U.S.1956), the Board and the courts have over time developed a number of principles which facilitate an assessment in advance of the employer's duty to disclose different kinds of information.

It is clear, for example, that the duty to disclose applies both when the union is negotiating with the employer over the terms of a new labor contract and when it is administering the terms of a labor contract already in existence. The two major cases supporting this proposition are decisions of the Supreme Court. In NLRB v. Truitt Mfg. Co., *ibid.*, the company asserted, during negotiations concerning wages under a new collective bargaining agreement, that it was financially unable to meet the union's wage demand of a ten-cent-per-hour increase and that any increase in excess of two and one-half cents would put it out of business. The union requested that the company permit it (through a certified public accountant) to examine the company's books and financial records, in order to determine its profits and its capacity to increase wages. The company's refusal was found to violate section 8(a)(5). The Court held:

> Good-faith bargaining necessarily requires that claims made by either bargainer should be honest claims. This is true about an asserted inability to pay an increase in wages. If such an argument is important enough to present in the give and take of bargaining, it is important enough to require some sort of proof of its accuracy. . . . We agree with the Board that a refusal to attempt to substantiate a claim of inability to pay increased wages may support a finding of a failure to bargain in good faith.

The Court later held that the duty to disclose "unquestionably extends beyond the period of contract negotiations and applies to labor-management relations during the term of an agreement." NLRB v. Acme Industrial Co. (U.S.1967). In the *Acme* case, the union during the term of its labor contract inferred from the employer's removal of certain machinery from the plant that the employer was committing a breach of the contract, which had provisions dealing with subcontracting and with the removal of plant equipment. The union filed grievances and requested that the company supply it with information concerning the removal of plant equipment. The company's denial was found by the Board and ultimately by the Supreme Court to violate the duty to bargain, which the Court held to continue during the process of grievance settlement under an existing labor contract. The Court also held that the union need not wait to press its claim for information in an arbitration proceeding and that the Board was properly "acting upon the probability that the desired information was relevant, and that it would be of use to the union in carrying out its statutory duties and responsibilities" of administering the collective bargaining agreement.

The range of information which the employer must disclose is broad indeed. Some cases do suggest that the information sought must be not only relevant to the union's tasks as bargaining representative but also necessary. *E. g.,* United Aircraft Corp. v. NLRB (2d Cir. 1970) (union requested names and addresses of all employees in the bargaining unit, and court considered in detail the alternative modes of communicating with unit employees that were available to union). Indeed, in *Acme Industrial,* the Supreme Court adverted to the employer's duty to disclose "information that is needed by the bargaining representative for the proper performance of its duties." But the Court in that case then proceeded to sustain the Board's "acting upon the probability that the desired information was relevant." Most of the decided cases do indeed support the proposition that the union need only demonstrate that the information sought is "relevant" to the negotiation or administration of a contract.

Moreover, widespread endorsement has been given the proposition that information concerning wages and related financial benefits are to be presumed relevant, without the need for a case-by-case assessment. One early decision, stating that "[W]e find it difficult to conceive a case in which current or immediately past wage rates would not be relevant during negotiations for a minimum wage scale or for increased wages," concluded that the union has no obligation to demonstrate the relevance of requested wage information. NLRB v. Yawman & Erbe Mfg. Co. (2d Cir. 1951). The court likened its rule to that governing discovery under modern codes of procedure, where "information must be disclosed unless it plainly appears irrelevant"; any other rule would hamper the bargaining process, with the parties constantly bickering about the collateral issue of the relevance of wage data. In another influential decision, NLRB v. Item Co. (5th Cir. 1955), the court sustained a Board finding that the employer violated the Act by refusing to furnish the union with salary and merit-pay information for each unit employee, even though a contract was in existence, there was no grievance pending, and the wage-reopener provision of the contract would not be operative for some eight months. The court held that the wage information had to be disclosed even though there was no particular existing controversy, since it appeared "reasonably necessary for 'the policing of the administration of [the] contract.'" It has been held that if the information sought is relevant to its function as bargaining representative, the union does not forfeit its right to have that information simply because it also intends to use it for some other more self-interested purpose, such as recruiting new members, Prudential Ins. Co. of America v. NLRB (2d Cir. 1969) (employer required to disclose names and addresses of employees in the unit represented by the union), or collecting dues, Utica Observer-Dispatch, Inc. v. NLRB (2d Cir. 1956) (wage information must be disclosed, since union sought it not simply to facilitate dues collection but also to bargain for new minimum wage).

The validity under the Labor Act of the presumption that a wide range of wage information is relevant and must be disclosed was sustained in Boston Herald-Traveler Corp. v. NLRB (1st Cir. 1955), which required the employer to match the names of individual employees with their ages, length of service and salaries, and which noted with approval the many cases requiring the disclosure of detailed data "with respect to individual salaries, merit increases, bonuses, dates of employment, job classifications, and the like." The employer clearly must furnish information as to wage rates and classifications, Lock Joint Pipe Co. (1963) (not sufficient for employer to furnish only minimum wage rate for each classification); merit pay increases, Otis Elevator Co. (1968); the costs of a welfare benefit plan, Sylvania Elec. Prods. v. NLRB (1st Cir. 1966) (union sought cost information not to determine whether plan could be secured more cheaply but whether employer contribution might better be paid in form of wages); and the costs and actuarial assumptions underlying the pension plan proposed by the company, Cone Mills Corp. (1968), *mdf'd on other grounds* (4th Cir. 1969). Section 8(a)(5) is violated not only by outright refusal to produce such presumptively relevant evidence but also by unreasonable delay in doing so. B. F. Diamond Constr. Co. (1967), *enf'd per curiam* (5th Cir. 1969) (company also delayed negotiations by cancelling bargaining meetings, refusing to schedule meetings and making plainly unacceptable proposals).

When the information requested by the union falls outside the area of wages and fringe benefits, it does not appear from the cases as though the presumption of relevance applies. But that simply means that the burden will fall initially upon the union to demonstrate that the information sought is pertinent to its statutory power to represent employees concerning "wages, hours and other terms or conditions of employment," the so-called mandatory subjects of bargaining. It has been held, for example, that the employer must disclose on demand information regarding overtime hours worked by unit employees, Gulf States Asphalt Co. (1969); surveys and studies resulting in changes in working conditions, Texaco, Inc. v. NLRB (7th Cir. 1969); company practices regarding probationary employees, Oliver Corp. (1967) (information sought included reasons for termination and length of employment); layoffs resulting from subcontracting, Puerto Rico Tel. Co. v. NLRB (1st Cir. 1966) (company must disclose volume of business, company earnings and wage savings, when there is grievance regarding company's right to subcontract for economic reasons); and seniority lists, NLRB v. Gulf Atl. Warehouse Co. (5th Cir. 1961). Indeed, in a number of cases in which the union was skeptical of the results of a company time study, which would determine such matters as employee workload and compensation, the Board has with court approval required the employer not simply to turn over the study to the union, J. I. Case Co. v. NLRB (7th Cir. 1958), but also, when verification of the study on its face is not possible, to permit the union to come into the plant to conduct (under reasonable rules and supervision) its own time study. Fafnir Bearing Co. v. NLRB (2d Cir. 1966) (processing of grievance); General Elec. Co. (1970) (negotiation; videotape of the company's study found not to be a valid alternative to independent union study).

It is also well settled that the information which the company must disclose need not be limited to data gathered exclusively within and about bargaining unit employees. Thus, in a dispute arising from a subcontracting provision of the labor contract, the union can secure information from the employer about its dealings with subcontractors, such as names of and correspondence with subcontractors, contract terms, and products produced. Fawcett Printing Corp. (1973). And the employer will be required to produce information about the pay and classification of employees within the company but outside the bargaining unit, when the union is asserting that the employer has improperly excluded those employees from the bargaining unit. Curtiss-Wright, Wright Aero Div. v. NLRB (3rd Cir. 1965) (employer excluded confidential and administrative employees); NLRB v. Goodyear Aerospace Corp. (6th Cir. 1968) (union claimed that employees should have been within its production unit rather than in research and development). And, if the company has an announced policy of correlating its wage structure with groups of employees outside the plant, the employer must disclose on demand the information it has about those other employees. Thus, if the employer's policy is to pay uniform wages among employees in all of its plants, the union is entitled to have data on wages paid at another company location. Hollywood Brands, Inc., *enf'd* (5th Cir. 1963). If the employer uses wage data secured from other companies upon assurance of confidentiality, even that data must be disclosed if it is used by the employer in adjusting wage rates of its own employees. General Elec. Co. (1970), *enf'd* (6th Cir. 1972) (confidentiality rejected as a defense to the disclosure of pertinent wage information). Here again, although information on matters outside the unit will not normally be presumed relevant, the union as a predicate for disclosure need only explain with some specificity why it is that this information is pertinent to its bargaining or grievance-processing activities within the unit.

The same is true for company financial data that appears not to relate directly to wages or other working conditions. Information regarding such "sensitive" matters as executive salaries, company profits, detailed breakdowns of company expenses, and even the costs to the company of employee benefit plans will normally be treated as confidential and not properly disclosable to the union on demand. As to such information, the union must show a specific need on a case-by-case basis. Thus, the Board has refused to require the employer to turn over profit data, even when the employees' Christmas bonus is calculated as a percentage of profits, when the particular bargaining-table positions of the parties have not yet made the profit figures pertinent. Until that point it would not be clear whether nondisclosure would be an obstacle to meaningful bargaining. White Furniture Co. (1966), *enf'd* (4th Cir. 1967). Similarly, the costs to the employer of company participation in a pension and insurance plan for its employees will ordinarily not have to be disclosed to the union, since the employer has no duty to bargain with the union on the question whether it is spending its money wisely. But if the union seeks this information with a view toward determining whether it would rather have this money paid in the form of direct wages, the employer may be required to disclose it. Sylvania Elec. Prods. v. NLRB (1st Cir. 1966).

Most cases requiring the disclosure of company financial data have involved employer claims at the bargaining table that it is financially unable to satisfy the union's demand for wages and fringe benefits. While this information is not presumptively relevant, it is the company's assertion of poverty that makes it relevant. For the employer to insist on its incapacity to pay but then to refuse to give the union on demand data with which the union can test the validity of the employer's claim may serve as the basis for a finding of bad-faith bargaining. As the Supreme Court stated in NLRB v. Truitt Mfg. Co. (U.S.1956):

> In their effort to reach an agreement here both the union and the company treated the company's ability to pay increased wages as highly relevant. The ability of an employ-

er to increase wages without injury to his business is a commonly considered factor in wage negotiations. . . .

> Good-faith bargaining necessarily requires that claims made by either bargainer should be honest claims. This is true about an asserted inability to pay an increase in wages. If such an argument is important enough to present in the give and take of bargaining, it is important enough to require some sort of proof of its accuracy. And it would certainly not be farfetched for a trier of fact to reach the conclusion that bargaining lacks good faith when an employer mechanically repeats a claim of inability to pay without making the slightest effort to substantiate the claim.

To make the company's financial data pertinent and disclosable, it is not necessary that the company plead that a requested wage increase will drive it out of business. It is enough that it claim, for example, that price cutting by competitors makes it imperative that labor costs be minimized in order that the company can maintain its competitive position. NLRB v. Western Wirebound Box Co. (9th Cir. 1966) (union sought figures regarding productivity, labor and material costs, and price changes).

If, however, the company states that competitors are obtaining cheaper labor and refuses because of that to grant a wage increase, it has been held that the company is merely asserting unwillingness to grant the increase and not inability. Empire Terminal Warehouse Co. (1965), *enf'd* (D.C.Cir. 1966) (throughout negotiations employer had asserted it was in strong financial condition). If the employer's alleged claim of inability to pay is not clearly such and is ambiguous, its obligation to open its books will be triggered only if the union induces the employer to dispel the ambiguity. Milbin Printing, Inc. (1975) (company negotiator said that company could not "reach" the union request for a wage increase because it needed to maintain a "proper balance," but did not assert poor financial position). In any event, data concerning production, costs and profits need not be disgorged merely because, in the absence of an employer claim making it pertinent, the union asserts that it would be "helpful" to it in bargaining. Pine Indus. Rel. Comm. (1957), *enf'd in relevant part* (D.C.Cir. 1959).

A number of cases have raised the question whether the union is entitled, either during or after negotiations, to a list of employee names and addresses. The principle appears rather well settled that the employer will normally be required to disclose such a list to the union on demand. Indeed, the court of appeals in Prudential Ins. Co. v. NLRB (2nd Cir. 1969), found such a list to be even more clearly presumptively relevant to the union's bargaining responsibilities than is wage information. The court noted that the union had a statutory obligation to represent fairly all of the employees in the bargaining unit, whether or not union members:

> This obligation, being coextensive with the sphere of activities of the exclusive bargaining representative, extends to the negotiation of new contracts and also to the administration of collective agreements already adopted. It seems manifest beyond dispute that the Union cannot discharge its obligation unless it is able to communicate with those in whose behalf it acts. Thus, a union must be able to inform the employees of its negotiations with the employer and obtain their views as to bargaining priorities in order that its position may reflect their wishes. . . . Further, in order to administer an existing agreement effectively, a union must be able to apprise the employees of the benefits to which they are entitled under the contract and of its readiness to enforce compliance with the agreement for their protection.
>
> . . . Because this information is therefore so basically related to the proper performance of the union's statutory duties, we believe any special showing of specific relevance would be superfluous.

The court treated as irrelevant the employer's contention that the union would use the names and addresses to solicit new members. It found no clear distinction between soliciting the support of nonmember employees and informing them of future or present contract benefits, and it saw no evil in membership solicitation by the union which has been designated exclusive bargaining representative of those very employees. In light of the relevance of employee names and addresses to the union's tasks as bargaining agent, it is not altogether clear why courts have tended to require that the union go further in supporting its request for this information and prove also that it is not feasible for the union to reach employees effectively through other modes of communication. Yet courts do require such a showing. United Aircraft Corp. v. NLRB (2d Cir. 1970). See also Glazers Drug Co. (1974) (names and addresses of strike replacements not presumed relevant to union during strike; lawful for employer to promise disclosure after strike ends).

§ 5. Employer Defenses to the Duty to Disclose

As already noted, the duty to disclose information to the union relates only to information which is relevant to the union's responsibilities in negotiating or administering a labor contract. If what is sought is company data on employee wages and fringe benefits, this will be presumed relevant, and the burden will fall upon the employer to demonstrate that there are other reasons why the information should not be disclosed. If what is sought is other kinds of information, the burden lies with the union to demonstrate its relevance. Should it be determined that the information sought by the union is not relevant, the employer's refusal to disclose will not be a violation of section 8(a)(5).

Even relevant information, however, need not always be disclosed. For example, if it can be shown that the reason behind the union's request for financial data is to harass or publicly to embarrass the company, this information need not be disclosed. NLRB v. Robert S. Abbott Pub. Co. (7th Cir. 1964) (inference of union's motive drawn from its false reasons for rejecting the company's offer of financial data in the only form then available to the company). And if the union's only reason for seeking presumptively relevant wage information is to facilitate dues collection, that information would not have to be disclosed. Utica Observer-Dispatch, Inc. v. NLRB (2d Cir. 1956) (dictum, since union sought the information for bargaining purposes as well). The employer may also defend against disclosure by demonstrating that there is a clear and present danger that the union will use the information to incite violence or harassment of employees. Thus, the union's demand for employee names and addresses, in the context of strike violence and of no union assurance that the list would be kept confidential, was found legitimately rejected by the employer which asserted fear of reprisals to nonstrikers. Shell Oil Co. v. NLRB (9th Cir. 1972). The employer's resistance may not, however, be based on violence that had occurred ten years earlier. United Aircraft Corp. v. NLRB (2d Cir. 1970). See also Sign & Pictorial Union v. NLRB (D.C.Cir. 1969) (no need to satisfy union's demand to examine employer payroll records which would reveal names of strikebreakers, in context of harassment, threats and assaults to strikebreakers). These cases might be characterized either as cases in which relevant information was not ordered disclosed because of fear that personal or business injury would be inflicted, or as cases in which the employer was able to rebut the presumption that the union desired this information for purposes relevant to its powers as bargaining representative.

Even clearly relevant information need not be disclosed in precisely the form requested by the union. "It is sufficient if the information is made available in a manner not so burdensome or time-consuming as to impede the bargaining process." Cincinnati Steel Castings Co. (1949) (union demanded certain information in written form; employer held to bargain in good faith by offering information orally). For example, in NLRB v. Tex-Tan, Inc. (5th Cir. 1963), it was held that the employer was not obligated to hand over to the union, in the organized fashion demanded by the union, information about the company's incentive-pay plan which would have been intricate, complex and voluminous. And in Emeryville Research Center v. NLRB (9th Cir. 1971), the court sustained the employer's refusal to disclose certain salary information which would have been very burdensome to compile and which would have disclosed the sources of salary information secured upon assurances of confidentiality from competing companies. The court noted that the employer was in all other respects bargaining in good faith, that the employer sought to determine how the union wished to use the information in order to assess whether the information could be supplied in a manner which would not be so burdensome and which would keep its sources confidential, and that the union was uncooperative and persisted merely in general avowals of the data's relevance. The court, however, emphasized that:

> Nothing in this opinion should be construed to preclude the Board from finding an unfair labor practice where a company's objection to the form in which information is requested is frivolous, or based on a belief that the law does not require its production, or made for the purpose of delay or to frustrate contemporaneous negotiations.

And any alternative mode of conveying the requested information to the union must be such as to communicate all essential information. General Elec. Co. (1970) (employer's offer of videotape of employee performing his job is inadequate to evaluate job classification; union held entitled to make in-plant evaluation). If the company does wish to assert that a request for information is too burdensome, this must be done at the time the information is requested and not for the first time during the unfair labor practice proceeding. The union must be given an opportunity at the bargaining table to discuss how the data it needs may be supplied by the company in a less burdensome form. J. I. Case Co. v. NLRB (7th Cir. 1958) (request for time-study and job-evaluation data).

As a general matter, the employer's claim that relevant information must not be disclosed to the union because of the need for confidentiality will not be sustained. This is particularly true when what is sought is wage data, and the employer asserts an employee interest in keeping that personal information secret. Curtiss-Wright, Wright Aero Div. v. NLRB (3d Cir. 1965) (confidentiality is no shield when the relevance of the information, here wages, is firmly established). But when there is a legitimate business interest in preserving confidentiality, and the union's request for information goes beyond that strictly pertinent to its task as bargaining representative, an effort will be made to strike a balance by requiring the union to narrow its request for information. Thus, in Kroger Co. v. NLRB (6th Cir. 1968), although the Board required the employer to disclose to the union information about workload and scheduling which would have also disclosed a trade secret, the court refused to enforce its order, noting that the union's request for the entire program of company information would also have exposed data on such nonrelevant matters as advertising, purchasing, pricing and capital outlay. It should be noted, however, that to warrant upholding the defense of confidentiality, the employer must demonstrate that there is a legitimate business need, that it has been bargaining in good faith and making efforts to accommodate the union's request by alternative arrangements and, apparently, that the union demand has been overbroad or its bargaining position inflexible.

On occasion, an employer will argue that although the statute does give the union the right to request pertinent information for bargaining purposes, the union has "waived" that right. This defense is rarely sustained. The Supreme Court has, for example, rejected the employer's argument that the union during the term of a labor contract may not utilize section 8(a)(5) to secure information pertinent to a grievance under consideration but must instead process its claim for information to arbitration. NLRB v. Acme Industrial Co. (U.S.1967). Although the employer argued that in effect the union's agreement to arbitrate contract disputes "waived" the statutory right to disclosure of information, the Court held that the union retains the power under the Labor Act to secure information in order to determine whether even to take the grievance to arbitration. The Supreme Court thus rejected the position taken by some courts of appeals, that construction of the labor contract is beyond the jurisdiction of the National Labor Relations Board; the Board is indeed to make a threshold determination whether the demand for information relates to a colorable grievance under the contract, but the Board is not to determine whether the claim actually has merit, which is for the arbitrator to decide. P. R. Mallory & Co. v. NLRB (7th Cir. 1969). In order that the union be deemed to waive its statutory right to information, its relinquishment of the right must be knowing, clear and unequivocal. It is not sufficient, for example, that the labor contract contain a general provision stipulating that it sets forth all of the parties' obligations for the term of the agreement, J. I. Case Co. v. NLRB (7th Cir. 1958); or that the union during contract negotiations dropped its proposal for a clause requiring disclosure of information, in the absence of clear and unmistakable language that it is forgoing this right, Timken Roller Bearing Co. v. NLRB (6th Cir. 1963) (the right to disclosure is a statutory right and is not dependent upon the contract); or even that a preceding labor contract contained a provision imposing upon the employer an affirmative duty to disclose information, and that provision was stricken by the company and union in the present labor contract, NLRB v. Perkins Mach. Co. (1st Cir. 1964).

§ 6. Compliance With Requirements of Section 8(d): Contract "Termination or Modification"

Although it is usually sufficient, in order to comply with the good-faith bargaining requirements of section 8(d), that parties negotiate on "mandatory" subjects in an earnest attempt to adjust differences and refrain from making "unilateral" changes, there are yet additional requirements when either party seeks to "terminate or modify" a collective bargaining agreement. In cases of contract termination or modification, it is necessary that notification be given to the other party and to governmental mediation agencies, and that no strike, lockout or change in contract conditions be effected within a stipulated time period. If the employer fails to comply with these notification and "cooling off" requirements, it violates section 8(a)(5). If the union fails to comply, it violates section 8(b)(3). The remedy in either case will be a cease and desist order at the least. An employer violation may also result in an order to recompense employees, for example when it has discontinued a bonus without complying with section 8(d). Perhaps the most drastic sanction for a union violation is provided explicitly in section 8(d)—employees who engage in a strike in violation of that section lose their status as employees; this subjects them to immediate discharge and jeopardizes forthwith the union's status as bargaining representative.

The requirements of section 8(d) may be summarized as follows. Where a labor contract exists, the party seeking to "terminate or modify" may not do so unless it: (1) serves notice upon the other party sixty days before the contract expiration date (or if the contract lacks such an expiration date, sixty days before the proposed termination or modification is to take effect); (2) offers to bargain with the other party; (3) within thirty days of notifying the other party, gives notice to federal and state mediation agencies in the event no agreement has yet been reached; (4) preserves the contractual status quo, without strike or lockout, for sixty days after the initial notification or until the contract expires, whichever is later. If the employer changes the status quo regarding a mandatory subject of bargaining, without notifying and bargaining with the union, that is a violation of section 8(a)(5), under the Supreme Court decision in NLRB v. Katz (U.S.1962), quite apart from any noncompliance with the procedural requirements of section 8(d). Section 8(d) does have an independent role to play, however, when the employer wishes to modify working conditions within the sixty-day period even after bargaining with the union. It also outlaws premature bargaining strikes and lockouts which would otherwise be lawful, American Ship Building Co. v. NLRB (U.S.1965) (lockout), or indeed protected (as is the peaceful strike, under section 7 of the Labor Act).

The notification and cooling-off provisions of section 8(d) apply only when a party seeks to "terminate or modify" a labor agreement. Usually, these steps are taken when a contract is about to expire and a new contract to be negotiated. But these steps must also be taken when a party seeks to "modify" the contract pursuant to an express contractual provision for a "reopener" in the middle of the contract term, as is commonly done with the subject of wages. In the case of a midterm reopener, usually at the request of the union, a union which gives timely notice to the employer of its intention to reopen (and notice to the mediation agencies) may strike sixty days thereafter, even though the contract's expiration date is many months away. Although section 8(d)(4) bars the strike "until the expiration date of such contract" if that is later than sixty days following notice, the Supreme Court in NLRB v. Lion Oil Co. (U.S.1957), held the term "expiration" to be ambiguous and construed it so as to include "the date when the contract by its own terms was subject to modification." A strike over a midterm reopener would thus not violate the Labor Act (as distinguished from the collective bargaining agreement) if the union complied with the notice requirements of section 8(d). Not to read the statute this way

> would discourage the development of long-term bargaining relationships. Unions would be wary of entering into long-term contracts with machinery for reopening them for modification from time to time, if they thought the right to strike would be denied them for the entire term of such a contract, though they imposed no such limitations on themselves.

If, however, there is no formal reopener provision in a contract for a fixed term, a strike in support of a demand for modification in midterm will violate section 8(d)—and thus section 8(b)(3)—even if the union gives notice to the employer of a desire to modify and then waits sixty days before striking. Local 3, Packinghouse Workers v. NLRB (8th Cir. 1954).

The statute does not define what the term "modification" means. Sometimes an employer may, during the contract term, take some action regarding working conditions which the union asserts "modifies" the contract. The employer argues that its action is in fact authorized by the contract and that, even if it is not so authorized, it is at worst a breach of the contract remediable by arbitration and not a "modification" remediable by the Board. Sometimes a union may strike during the contract in protest against some employer action or in support of some demand, and the employer may argue that the union is trying to "modify" the contract. Again, the union will argue that the object of the strike is not to "modify" the contract but merely to enforce it, so that it is not within the ban of section 8(d). There appears to be no very clear distinction between action which "modifies" the contract and action which merely "breaches" or "enforces" the contract.

If an employer repudiates entirely an existing contract, that would clearly be a "termination or modification" which could not be effected without notification and cooling off. But since even notification and cooling off will not cure an outright repudiation, which attacks the representative status of the union, such conduct has been held to violate section 8(a)(5) directly, without any concern for section 8(d) as such. NLRB v. Hyde (9th Cir. 1964). Most of the cases in which section 8(d) has been invoked against an employer, because of an alleged "modification," have involved midterm changes made by the employer in the general wage scale or in the manner of computing compensation. For example, in Oak Cliff-Golman Baking Co. (1974), the employer during the contract term asserted financial distress and (after notice to the union) reduced wages below those set forth in the agreement, without any claim that this change comported with the contract terms. The Board treated the employees' general wage scale as such a central element in the agreement that to alter it was a "modification" akin to outright repudiation. (The Board therefore concluded that since wages were "contained in" the agreement, even an offer to bargain would not excuse the modification, since section 8(d) also provides that modification of a "contained" term cannot be effected unless the union actually gives its consent.)

In a similar case, the employer implemented during the contract term a new wage incentive system. The Board found this to be a "modification" of the contract, subject to the unfair labor practice jurisdiction of the Board, and not merely a "breach" of the contract remediable solely through the grievance and arbitration machinery. It stated, in C & S Indus., Inc. (1966):

> Of course, the breadth of Section 8(d) is not such as to make any default in a contract obligation an unfair labor practice, for that section, to the extent relevant here, is in terms confined to the "modification" or "termination" of a contract. But there can be little doubt that where an employer unilaterally effects a change which has a continuing impact on a basic term or condition of employment, wages for example, more is involved than just a simple default in a contractual obligation. Such a change manifestly constitutes a "modification" within the meaning of Section 8(d). And if not made in compliance with the requirements of that section, it violates a statutory duty the redress of which becomes a matter of concern to the Board.

See also Kinard Trucking Co. (1965) (wage reduction is a "modification" of the contract and when effected without giving the notices required by section 8(d) it violates not only the ban in section 8(a)(5) upon unilateral action but also section 8(d) as such); California Blowpipe & Steel Co. (1975) (employer's repudiation of union-shop provision is tantamount to repudiation of union as bargaining representative, "modifies" the labor contract and "terminates" the provision).

Cases involving union-initiated "termination or modification" raise analogous problems. In one case, Communications Workers Local 1190 (Western Elec. Co.) (1973), an international union had negotiated a nationwide contract on behalf of all of its locals representing company employees, but one local protested the contract and immediately called a strike to compel renegotiation. The Board, analogizing the case to one of outright employer repudiation and finding the union's conduct to evidence a "fundamental disdain for the collective bargaining process," held the strike to constitute a demand for "modification" and within the ban of section 8(d). If the union strikes during the contract term to secure an increase in the wages set forth therein, this too constitutes a demand for a "modification" which must comply with the requirements of section 8(d). J. Zembrodt Express, Inc. (1971).

The situation is different, however, when the union's strike is in response to some action taken by the employer during the contract term. The employer may try to argue that its own action is supported by the contract, so that the union's insistence that it do otherwise is a demand for contract "modification" which requires notification and a sixty-day cooling-off period. The Board usually rejects this argument. It distinguishes between a strike to secure a modification and a strike in support of a contract grievance, and holds that the latter—even if barred by a no-strike provision in the contract or even if called without first exhausting the grievance machinery—is not governed by section 8(d). Teamsters Local 741 (Los Angeles-Seattle Motor Express) (1968). Perhaps the most detailed discussion of the distinction is that of the trial examiner (not challenged on this issue on appeal to the Board) in International Union, UMW (Boone County Coal Corp.) (1957). There, the assignment of a worker from outside the bargaining unit to a job opening precipitated a claim by the union that a unit employee should have been given the work as well as training if necessary to do it properly. A strike was called, which the employer contended was both a breach of the labor contract and a violation of section 8(b)(3), in part because the union neglected before striking to give the notification required by section 8(d). The employer claimed that the union had to comply with section 8(d) because it was seeking to "modify" the seniority and management rights provisions of the contract, but the union argued that its strike was simply over a grievance as to the meaning of the contract. The trial examiner sustained the position of the union:

> Certainly, it cannot be said in this case that the alternative demands made by the Local were so *clearly* in opposition to the contract that compliance with them could have been achieved only through contract modification. Thus, the upgrading, transfer, or training of men on the working force to fill vacant positions, although not required by the contract, was not prohibited by it either. . . . [I]t is difficult to conclude that the Local was acting in bad faith or with a deliberate purpose to alter the contract. . . .

The worst that can be said of the Local's demands is that they raised issues concerning the meaning or administration of the contract, or, if not that, at least an issue as to matters not covered by the contract. But that is different from contract modification.

The trial examiner pointed out the inconsistency between the argument that the strike violated the contract, because it involved the "meaning and application" of the contract and was thus arbitrable, and the argument that the union was seeking a contract modification. "[I]f . . . the dispute fell within the contract's framework, as a grievance matter processable under the contract machinery, then the contract already controlled the situation, and no modification within the meaning of Section 8(d) could be involved."

Thus, although the line may not always be clear, section 8(d) does not apply when the union's strike protests employer action which the union in good faith and with colorable basis asserts is in violation of the contract. In such a case, the union does not seek "termination or modification." The same is true, as the Supreme Court has held, when the union's object is to protest a serious unfair labor practice allegedly committed by the employer. In Mastro Plastics Corp. v. NLRB (U.S.1956), the incumbent union served a notice on the employer requesting modification of the contract. One month later, while negotiations were going on, the employer discharged an employee because of his support of the union and also actively and unlawfully assisted a rival union. The incumbent union called a strike within the sixty-day period and prior to the expiration of the contract, claiming that the strike was not in support of contract demands but rather in protest against the employer's unfair labor practices. The strikers were discharged, the employer relying on the provision in section 8(d) depriving workers engaged in a premature strike of their status as "employees." The Supreme Court held that the loss-of-status provision applies only to employees engaging in a strike "to terminate or modify" an existing labor contract, and does not apply when the strike is "against unfair labor practices designed to oust the employees' bargaining representative." The Court read the legislative history to demonstrate a congressional intention to bar "quickie strikes" within sixty days of notification in order to gain economic advantages and not to "relegate the employees to filing charges under a procedure too slow to be effective."

For similar reasons, a work stoppage that was undertaken by a union because of "ascertainable, objective evidence supporting its conclusion that an abnormally dangerous condition for work exists" would presumably not be deemed a strike to "terminate or modify" a contract, so that the notification and cooling-off provisions of section 8(d) would be completely inapplicable. See Gateway Coal Co. v. UMW (U.S.1974) (a work stoppage to protect employees from immediate danger will not be construed to be a violation of a contractual no-strike clause). Indeed, such a work stoppage would not even be deemed a "strike" under section 8(d), since section 502 of the Labor

Act provides: "[N]or shall the quitting of labor . . . because of abnormally dangerous conditions for work at the place of employment . . . be deemed a strike under this Act."

§ 7. The Notification and Cooling-Off Requirements of Section 8(d)

Once it is determined that the employer or the union seeks "termination or modification" of a labor contract, the notification and cooling-off provisions of section 8(d) come fully into play. Section 8(d)(1) requires the party seeking to terminate or modify the contract to give notice to the other sixty days "prior to the expiration date thereof," which refers both to the stipulated date of termination of the entire agreement and to any midterm date set by the parties as the deadline for a "reopener" (typically to permit renegotiation of wages in a longterm contract). NLRB v. Lion Oil Co. (U.S.1957). Section 8(d)(2) requires the party seeking to terminate or modify to offer "to meet and confer" with the other party. It is usually not these subsections that are the subject of litigation, since the party seeking to terminate or modify a contract will normally be moved by self-interest to give notice and to seek to bargain, even if not principally to comply with the Labor Act. What usually precipitates a charge is a unilateral change of working conditions or a lockout by the employer, or a strike by the union, and these will evoke a charge of noncompliance with section 8(d)(4) instead. Thus, a typical violation of section 8(d) is a strike by the union called within sixty days of the union's notification to the employer of its intention to terminate or modify. This violates section 8(d)(4) which prohibits a strike "for a period of sixty days after such notice [to terminate or modify] is given or until the expiration date of such contract, whichever occurs later."

The obvious purpose of this prohibition—which operates against lockouts as well—is to give the parties a period of at least sixty days within which to exert all good faith efforts to reach a settlement through peaceful negotiations and not by economic force. As the language of the Act plainly dictates, if notice is given longer than sixty days before contract expiration, no bargaining strike or lockout— even after sixty days—will be lawful if called before the contract expires. Conversely, if notice to terminate or modify is given less than sixty days before contract expiration (the parties may so provide by contract if they wish), the full sixty days must run before a bargaining strike or lockout is legal, even if the contract termination date has passed. Although it has been argued to the Board that a strike at any time after the termination date is lawful—even within sixty days of notification—because after termination the contract is not "in effect" (in the language of section 8(d)), the Board has rejected this argument and held that in order to give meaning to the sixty-day strike ban the contract is to be deemed "in effect" even after its termination date. Carpenters Dist. Council (Rocky Mountain Prestress,

Inc.) (1968). But it is sufficient that the sixty days have run since notification by either of the two parties to the contract; if one party has already given notice, it is not necessary that the other party before taking economic action serve its own notice and wait another sixty days. Royal Packing Co. (1972), *enf'd mem.* (D.C.Cir. 1974) (employer lockout more than sixty days after union's modification notice was held lawful even though the employer had not given its own notice).

The statutory objective to resolve disputes through peaceful bargaining and not by resort to economic force is reinforced further by section 8(d)(3), which requires the party seeking to terminate or modify to give notice also to the Federal Mediation and Conciliation Service and any state mediation agency within thirty days after the initial notice given to the other party. Congress determined that if no settlement is reached within thirty days after initial notification, appropriate mediation agencies should be apprised and given an opportunity to aid in a peaceful solution. For the next thirty days as well, resort to strike or lockout is barred by section 8(d)(4) as within the sixty-day cooling-off period since the initial notice. Failure to give timely notice to the mediation agencies is technically a violation of section 8(d)(3), but rarely is addressed in an unfair labor practice case in isolation. The more common question is the effect of an untimely (or nonexistent) notice to mediation agencies upon the rights of the parties to strike, lockout, or modify terms under section 8(d)(4).

If, for example, a union serves notice of intention to terminate or modify, waits more than sixty days and then strikes, without giving notice to the mediation agencies (or giving notice only after the strike begins), the strike violates section 8(d)(4) and thus also section 8(b)(3). Although the former section refers only to strikes in less than sixty days from the initial notice to the other party, it was clearly the intention of Congress to have the mediation agencies notified and given an opportunity to intervene in the bargaining prior to the use of economic weapons. Bagel Bakers Council (1969), *enf'd in relevant part* (2d Cir. 1970) (employer lockout prior to employer notice to Federal Mediation Service; no defense that Service might choose not to intervene given minimal effect of employer on interstate commerce, since this is a decision for the Service to make). Indeed, it has been held that a strike violates section 8(d)(4), even though timely notice has been given the Federal Mediation and Conciliation Service, when the union neglected to give the required notice to the state agency. Local 156, Packinghouse Workers (1957).

Since Congress obviously intended—were all notices given in a timely way—that the mediation agencies would have at least thirty days to intercede prior to a strike, it is uniformly held that a strike instituted less than thirty days from the date of (an untimely) notice to the mediation agencies will be unlawful, even though more than sixty days have passed since notification was given to the other party. Local 219, Retail Clerks v. NLRB (D.C.Cir. 1959). More divergent opinions exist on the question whether, after the union gives untimely notice to the mediation agencies, it may wait a full thirty days and then lawfully institute a strike. The strictest position is that the untimely notice not only violates section 8(d)(3) but also forever taints a later strike no matter how long delayed. Operating Eng'rs Local 181 v. Dahlem Constr. Co. (6th Cir. 1951) (section 8(d)(4) violated by strike called more than three months after untimely notice to mediation agencies). At the other extreme is the position that, even though the notice to the mediation agencies is improperly delayed, not only may the union lawfully strike after waiting thirty more days, but the thirty-day wait will also cure the violation of section 8(d)(3) stemming from the untimely notice. A third, and intermediate, position is that untimely notification to the mediation agencies will not forever taint a later strike but that in order to conduct a lawful strike thereafter, a new sixty-day notice must be served on the other party to be followed by a new and timely notification to the mediation agencies. All three of these readings of section 8(d) have been rejected by the court in Retail Clerks Local 219 v. NLRB (D.C. Cir. 1959), which found the first view unnecessarily harsh, the second unnecessarily lenient, and the third unnecessarily formalistic. That court concluded that the purpose behind sections 8(d)(3) and (4) is to apprise the mediation agencies of the bargaining deadlock and to give those agencies thirty days in which to attempt to settle the dispute prior to the calling of any work stoppage. It therefore held that the Act imposes two duties: one to give notice to the mediation agencies within thirty days of the notice of termination or modification, so that section 8(d)(3) is violated when the mediation notice is untimely; and another to wait for thirty days after the mediation notice is given before calling a strike, so that a strike thus delayed will not violate section 8(d)(4).

The question whether an untimely mediation notice necessarily taints any strike called thereafter—even beyond thirty days later—is a matter of substance, for section 8(d) goes on to provide:

> Any employee who engages in a strike within any notice period specified in this subsection . . . shall lose his status as an employee of the employer engaged in a particular labor dispute, for the purposes of sections 158 to 160 of this title . . . .

The last-mentioned sections refer to unfair labor practices and representation elections. Thus, workers engaged in a premature strike may be summarily discharged and, regardless whether they are discharged, their union may lose its status as bargaining representative of a majority of "employees" in the unit. These most serious consequences would follow were the strike after untimely notice condemned under section 8(d)(4). They do not follow if a thirty-day wait after such notice "cures" the strike (even if it fails to cure the violation of section 8(d)(3) caused by the late notice).

A question remains whether untimely notice to the mediation agencies by the party initiating negotiations will bar a strike or lock-out by the other party within thirty days, but after sixty days from the initial notification. That issue arose in NLRB v. Peoria Chapter of Painting & Decorating Contractors (7th Cir. 1974). There, the union gave notice on February 14 of its intention to renegotiate the existing contract having an expiration date of April 30; however, it delayed notifying the mediation agencies until April 10. On May 1, the employer association with which the union was negotiating gave notice of a lockout. This was after the contract expiration date and seventy-seven days after the union's initial notice, but less than thirty days from the union's untimely notice to the mediation agencies. Although a federal mediator, who had entered the negotiations, therefore had less than thirty days in which to attempt to resolve the dispute, the court upheld the right of the non-initiating party (here the employers) to resort to a lockout, since the initial sixty-day period had run. The court read all of the subsections of section 8(d) to impose limitations only upon the party initiating negotiations. It also noted that a contrary reading would permit the initiating party purposely to delay giving notice to the mediation agencies in order to bar a strike or lockout by the non-initiating party for another thirty days, a frustration of the right to time the use of the weapons which the court believed unwarranted under the Labor Act. Presumably, once the sixty-day period has run, the non-initiating party is free to resort to strike or lockout even if the notice to the mediation agencies has not been given at all.

It should be noted that liability under section 8(d) is altogether a separate matter from liability under an existing contract. For example, failure to comply with the sixty-day notice provision of section 8(d)(1) will constitute an unfair labor practice but will not in itself result in the automatic renewal or extension of the labor contract. In Crowley's Milk Co. (1948), where the contract provided for automatic renewal if notice of intention to modify were not served before thirty days of the termination date, the union—which served notice on the thirty-seventh day before termination—argued that its failure to comply with the sixty-day notice provision of section 8(d) resulted in the automatic renewal of the contract. (Its object was to establish a "contract bar" to an election petition by a rival union.) The Board rejected this argument, holding that "Section 8(d)(1) . . . and Section 8(d)(3) . . . are merely particular aspects of the definition of collective bargaining in the amended Act and do not affect the actual terms of the contract governing automatic renewal." Nor will untimely notice to the mediation agencies extend the life of a labor contract for thirty days thereafter, if the contract does not so provide; grievances arising after the stipulated contract termination date will not be arbitrable under the contract procedures, even during that thirty-day period. Proctor & Gamble Indep. Union v. Proctor & Gamble Mfg. Co. (2d Cir. 1962). The same principle applies to the cooling-off provisions of section 8(d)(4). While these may be violated by a strike within sixty days of the notice to modify (or when no notice has been given at all), such a strike will not violate the labor contract if that contract has already expired of its own terms, as will often be so when negotiations are ongoing for a new agreement. In such a case, although the strike may cause the employer economic injury, if its claim against the union rests only on a theory of unfair labor practice it may not seek injunctive or compensatory relief in the courts since their jurisdiction is preempted by that of the National Labor Relations Board. The employer is relegated either to an unfair labor practice charge (which typically leads only to a cease-and-desist order and not to damages) or to the self-help measure of discharging the strikers. Rhode Island & M Assocs. v. Local 99–99A, Operating Eng'rs (D.D.C.1974) (strike without notice to mediation agencies).

Conversely, a strike may breach an agreement but not violate the cooling-off provisions of section 8(d)(4). Thus, a union may have given timely notices to the employer and to the mediation agencies and have waited sixty days before striking, but that strike may constitute a breach of contract if the union has given enforceable assurances not to strike during negotiations. Operating Eng'rs Local 181 v. Dahlem Constr. Co. (6th Cir. 1951). The employer would have no remedy before the Board but could bring an action under section 301 of the Labor Act for violation of the union's promise and could secure judicial or arbitral relief against the strike. The same would be true if, for example, a contract containing a no-strike clause provides for automatic renewal if notice is not given ninety days before termination, and notice is given less than ninety days but more than sixty days before the contract termination date.

Since resolution of a claim of contract breach will not likely resolve the claim of violation of section 8(d), the Board has held that it will assert jurisdiction over such unfair labor practice cases and not defer action until an arbitrator has first resolved the claim of breach of contract. Communications Workers of America (Western Elec. Co.) (1973).

As already noted, section 8(d) explicitly imposes a sanction upon employees who engage in a strike "within any notice period specified in this subsection"; they are to lose their status as employees under the unfair labor practice and representation provisions of the Act (until they are reemployed). The implications of this provision are twofold. First, these employees no longer have the protection of section 7 so that they are subject to immediate discharge. This adds little to the "common law" developed by the courts and the Board that employees participating in any unfair labor practice may be discharged for such "unprotected" activity. Although it can be argued that a discharge of such strikers is nonetheless unlawful when the employer acts not in retaliation for their unprotected activity, but rather to rid itself of the union, it is likely that even antiunion animus will not make the discharge illegal, since the strikers are no longer "employees" who are at all within the shelter of the Labor Act. See Fort Smith Chair Co. (1963), *enf'd* (D.C.Cir. 1964) (only two Board members of five address this issue, and would hold that discharge is valid in spite of antiunion animus). Second, these strikers, no longer "employees," can not be counted by the union towards its majority status, so that if the strikers constitute a majority within the unit, the employer will normally be free to cease recognizing and bargaining with the union. While this loss of representative status would follow in due course if the employer were first to discharge the strikers lawfully, Electrical Workers Local 1113 v. NLRB (D.C.Cir. 1955), section 8(d) would appear to permit the employer in such a situation to withdraw recognition even without first formally discharging the employees. Graham v. Boeing Airplane Co. (W.D. Wash.1948). The strike appears automatically to sever the employment relationship, which is not restored until the strikers are permitted to return to work. UMW (McCoy Coal Co.) (1967). The burden will normally be upon the employer to demonstrate that the number of workers participating in the illegal strike constituted a majority of the bargaining unit, in order to excuse its refusal to bargain. NLRB v. Cast Optics Corp. (3d Cir. 1972).

In 1974, Congress extended the jurisdiction of the Labor Act and the NLRB to nonprofit private health care institutions; previously, the Act had applied only to such private institutions if operated for profit. In view of what Congress perceived to be a special need for resolution of bargaining disputes without interruption of services in such institutions—defined to include a hospital, clinic, nursing home "or other institution devoted to the care of sick, infirm, or aged person"—section 8(d) was amended to modify the notification and cooling-off requirements for health care institutions (whether or not operated for profit). Notification of desire to terminate or modify must be given ninety days (rather than sixty days) before the date of termination or modification, and notification to federal and state mediation agencies must be given sixty days (rather than thirty days) before. Moreover, in the case of an initial contract (where there is no "termination or modification" and which would in other industries not be subject to the notification and cooling-off requirements), the union must notify the Federal Mediation Service. Significantly, in contrast to other industries, where notification of the Federal Service imposes no obligation actually to tender or to utilize mediation, the health care amendments provide that upon receiving notice of inability to settle, the Service "shall" promptly contact the parties and use its best efforts to bring them to agreement, and the parties "shall participate fully and promptly in such meetings" undertaken by the Service.

As in section 8(d) generally, these health care notification provisions will provide notice only of intention to terminate or modify, or notice of inability to settle.   They do not in terms require notice of intention to strike.   Section 8(g) was added to the Labor Act in 1974 as well, and it does provide that any union intending to engage "in any strike, picketing, or other concerted refusal to work at any health care institution" must first give ten-days' notice to the institution and to the Federal Mediation and Conciliation Service, such notice to state the date and time such action will commence.   If a first contract is involved, this ten-day notice is to follow the thirty-day notice already given by the union to the mediation agencies, thus giving the Federal Service at least forty days within which to try to effect a settlement of the initial contract before a strike may lawfully commence.   It should be noted that section 8(g) does not require that any comparable ten-day notice be given by a health care institution should it intend to lock out its employees.   Although section 8(g) does not expressly so state, a union failure to give such a ten-day notice prior to a work stoppage will be treated as a refusal to bargain remediable under section 8(b)(3); the loss-of-status provision of section 8(d) expressly applies to persons engaging in such a work stoppage in violation of section 8(g).

Section 8(g) is ambiguous in other respects.   By requiring a ten-day notice before any strike or picketing "at any health care institution," the section leaves clouded the question whether only health care employees need give this notice.   A divided Board has read the requirement much more broadly, and has recently held that a construction union violates the Act when it fails to give notice of intention to picket a site at which its members are working on the expansion and alteration of hospital facilities.   Plumbers Local 630 (Lein-Steenberg) (1975).   Construction workers participating in such picketing have also been held to lose their status as employees under the Labor Act and have thus been declared ineligible to vote in a representation election.   Casey & Glass, Inc. (1975).   Another ambiguity stems from the applicability in section 8(g) of the strike-notice requirement to "any" work stoppage or picketing.   This broad term raises the question whether the requirement applies to concerted activity in protest of employer unfair labor practices.   Given the bargaining context of all of the notification provisions of sections 8(d) and 8(g), it may well be that the precedent of Mastro Plastics Corp. v. NLRB (U.S.1956), will be found persuasive; there, the Supreme Court held that the sixty-day notification and cooling-off requirements of section 8(d) did not apply to an unfair labor practice strike.

Section 213 of the Labor Act was also added in 1974 as part of the sections dealing with the Federal Mediation and Conciliation Service.

Its effect is to authorize the Director of the Service to go beyond mediation and to appoint an impartial board of inquiry to investigate the issues in a bargaining dispute in a health care institution. The board is also to make a written report to the parties, including recommendations for settlement, within fifteen days of its appointment. There is to be no change in the status quo—and no strike—within a fifteen-day period after the board completes its report.

§ 8.   The Use of Economic Weapons During Negotiations

While the statutory process of collective bargaining assumes that the parties must meet, state their positions, state their objections to the positions of the other party and disclose information the other party needs in order to bargain intelligently, it is clear that "[C]ollective bargaining, under a system where the Government does not attempt to control the results of negotiations, cannot be equated with an academic collective search for truth." NLRB v. Insurance Agents' Int'l Union (U.S.1960). The Supreme Court has thus confirmed that a party may engage in the most unsettling and disabling economic pressure outside of the bargaining room while in good faith and lawfully attempting to reach an agreement within. The union may engage in a work stoppage which is protected by sections 7 and 13 of the Labor Act, and it may go yet further and engage in concerted activities which are so disruptive as to be treated as "unprotected," such that the participating employees may be discharged for their participation. Yet, such conduct during bargaining does not in itself violate section 8(b)(3), and there is some doubt whether it can properly be treated as some evidence of bad faith. Conversely, a lockout of employees which is designed by the employer to force the union to an early settlement (rather than to avoid bargaining or to penalize the employees for having selected a union) does not violate section 8(a)(5). American Ship Bldg. Co. v. NLRB (U.S.1965). The Supreme Court has held that compliance with the duty to bargain is to be judged by the attitudes and conduct displayed by the parties at the bargaining table, and that it is not for the Board to outlaw specific kinds of economic pressures believed to be in themselves inconsistent with a mind open to adjustment and compromise. In the *Insurance Agents* case, the Court emphasized that:

> The presence of economic weapons in reserve, and their actual exercise on occasion by the parties, is part and parcel of the system that the Wagner and Taft-Hartley Acts have recognized. Abstract logical analysis might find inconsistency between the command of the statute to negotiate toward an agreement in good faith and the legitimacy of the use of economic weapons, frequently having the most serious effect upon individual workers and productive enterprises, to induce one party to come to the terms desired by the other. But the truth of the matter is that at the present statutory

stage of our national labor relations policy, the two factors—
necessity for good-faith bargaining between parties, and
the availability of economic pressure devices to each to
make the other party incline to agree on one's terms—exist
side by side.

In *Insurance Agents*, the union induced certain concerted on-the-
job activities at the same time as it was negotiating over a six-month
period for a new contract. The agents represented by the union
would for a time refuse to solicit new business or to comply with the
company's reporting procedures; they would report late to their offices and once there would engage in "sit-in mornings" and not perform their customary duties; they refused to appear for business
conferences, picketed and distributed leaflets, and solicited signatures
of policyholders on petitions addressed to the company. The Board
found that irrespective of any union good faith in bargaining and desire to reach an agreement, its tactics frustrated any reasoned attempts at argument, persuasion and free interchange of views. The
Supreme Court squarely rejected the Board's analysis. It held that
the purpose of sections 8(a)(5) and 8(b)(3) was primarily to assure
that the parties would, in an attempt to reach agreement, narrow the
issues and discuss them with an open mind; Congress did not intend
to have the Board intrude either upon the substantive terms of the
settlement or upon the economic weapons the parties could employ to
shape those terms. The Court viewed economic weapons as "part
and parcel" of the process of peaceful collective bargaining, and held
that the Board exceeded its powers by regulating the choice of economic weapons and equalizing disparities of bargaining power. The
Court rejected the arguments that the "partial" strike was necessarily inconsistent with good-faith bargaining merely because it might
(unlike the total strike) be unprotected activity, or because it was
not "traditional" or "normal" and placed maximum pressure on the
employer at minimum economic cost to the union. It also noted that
Congress manifested its intention to outlaw union economic weapons
by announcing its proscription specifically and narrowly; section
8(b)(3) was too broadly worded to be read as an indictment of the
partial strike. In effect, the Court held that the unfair labor practice
provisions of the Labor Act could not be utilized by the employer to
quash peaceful unprotected concerted activities in support of a union's bargaining demands. The employer could retaliate with its own
forms of self-help, most clearly discharge or other discipline since
this would not run afoul of the ban in section 8(a)(1) upon employer
interference with employee protected activity. But obviously employer self-help can be utilized only by an employer economically strong
enough to do so, and it is to be this free play of economic weapons,
shaped by the respective strength and weakness of the parties, that is
to determine the contours of the collective bargaining agreement.

Although *Insurance Agents* was a battle won by the union, an employer was successful in invoking the same arguments in American Ship Bldg. Co. v. NLRB (U.S.1965), in defense of a bargaining lockout. There, the employer began to lay off employees at its several locations after negotiations reached an impasse; although the employer argued that the shutdown was authorized by traditional Board doctrine sheltering a lockout to avoid an anticipated strike and unusual economic injury, the Court upheld the lockout even on the Board's assumption that its exclusive purpose was to pressure the union to come to terms. The primary attack on the lockout was that it violated sections 8(a)(1) and 8(a)(3) by interfering with and discriminating against employees for engaging in the protected activities of collective bargaining and of striking (potentially). The Court found no interference with any statutorily protected employee rights, and upbraided the Board—invoking the *Insurance Agents* decision—for exercising "a general authority to assess the relative economic power of the adversaries in the bargaining process and to deny weapons to one party or the other because of its assessment of that party's bargaining power." The Court found that the lockout could be outlawed only if it carried with it the "necessary implication that the employer acted to discourage union membership."

> There was no evidence and no finding that the employer was hostile to its employees' banding together for collective bargaining or that the lockout was designed to discipline them for doing so. It is therefore inaccurate to say that the employer's intention was to destroy or frustrate the process of collective bargaining. What can be said is that it intended to resist the demands made of it in the negotiations and to secure modification of these demands. We cannot see that this intention is in any way inconsistent with the employees' rights to bargain collectively.

The Court observed, in a footnote, that the Board declined to make any findings that bore directly upon an allegation in the complaint that the lockout was in violation of section 8(a)(5). It then adverted to the pertinent passages in the *Insurance Agents* decision regarding the impropriety of the Board's balancing economic weapons in collective bargaining, and held them to have "even more direct application to the § 8(a)(5) question" than they did to the question of liability under section 8(a)(3). It has since been held that a bargaining lockout even before impasse—the lockout in *American Ship* was after impasse—does not violate sections 8(a)(3) and (1) in light of circumstances of the case demonstrating the employer's good faith and lack of union animus. Lane v. NLRB (Darling & Co.) (D.C. Cir. 1969). There appears to be no doubt that the same conduct would comply with the obligation of the employer under section 8(a)(5) to bargain in good faith.

The Board and courts have, however, been unwilling to free the employer under section 8(a)(5) to use economic pressures in bargaining short of a complete lockout. For example, in Local 155, Molders v. NLRB (United States Pipe & Foundry Co.) (D.C.Cir. 1971), the employer unilaterally terminated employee benefits during negotiations in order to pressure the union to come to terms or else to precipitate a strike in the near future (rather than later during the employer's busy season). In spite of the fact that the Supreme Court in *American Ship* had sustained the seemingly "greater" employer weapon of the lockout, and had held that employees have no protected right to determine when a work stoppage is to occur, the court of appeals found the termination of benefits, motivated in part by a desire to precipitate a strike, to constitute a refusal to bargain. *American Ship* was also distinguished by the Board in Borden, Inc. (1972), where the employer during negotiations cancelled, without conferring with the union, four employee insurance plans. Although the employer argued that this was merely a temporary economic weapon to induce a favorable settlement, and was thus within the shelter of the *Insurance Agents* case, the Board instead found this to be unilateral alteration in working conditions within the proscription of NLRB v. Katz (U.S.1962). The attempt in these appellate and Board cases to distinguish away the Supreme Court decisions in *Insurance Agents* and *American Ship Building* is not wholly persuasive, and their discussion concerning the "lesser" or "greater" impact of the lockout in comparison to the denial of economic benefits invites the conclusion that the tribunal deciding the case was engaging in the kind of "picking and choosing" among allowable economic weapons for which the Board was reprimanded in those two Supreme Court decisions.

§ 9. The Duty to Bargain During a Strike

The law is clear that a strike or lockout designed to secure economic concessions does not in itself constitute a refusal to bargain. Nor does a strike or lockout excuse the other party from its duty to bargain.

It has long been held that an employer's duty to bargain with the union is not terminated when the union engages in a lawful economic strike during contract negotiations. Such a strike is an expectable and protected feature of bargaining, and is the usual method whereby the union exerts pressure to secure a favorable settlement. It would too severely disrupt the negotiation of mandatory subjects of bargaining were the employer to be excused by a strike from meeting and conferring with the union. As the court stated in NLRB v. J. H. Rutter-Rex Mfg. Co. (5th Cir. 1957):

> The strike, or threat of it, so carefully recognized as a right in the Act . . . is a means of self-help allowed to a union as pressure in the bargaining process. How or why the strike is called, or how conducted, may well have significant

effect upon the right of strikers for reinstatement or reemployment or in other respects not necessary to indicate. But the mere fact that a Union has without justification precipitated a strike does not make the union or the employees for whom it is the bargaining representative outlaws so that they forfeit all of the benefits of the Act. The calling of such a strike does not infect all that thereafter occurs with the virus of that action. A strike does not in and of itself suspend the bargaining obligation.

During a strike, therefore, the employer is not free to refuse to meet with the union or to condition further negotiations upon the cessation of the strike. General Elec. Co., Battery Prods. Dept. (1967), *enf'd in relevant part* (5th Cir. 1968). It follows, of course, that both the employer *and* the union are obligated to appear at the bargaining table for good-faith negotiations while the strike subsists.

But, in spite of the usual ban upon an employer making unilateral changes in working conditions, certain changes without consultation with the union are deemed proper as a response to the union's economic pressures. Just as it is "axiomatic" that the employer may cease paying wages to striking employees without first bargaining with the union, since they are rendering no services and the employer is said to have no duty to subsidize the strike, it has been held that the employer is free unilaterally to terminate a group insurance plan for its striking employees. Philip Carey Mfg. Co. (1963), *enf'd in part* (6th Cir. 1964). It has also been a principle of long standing that the employer has no duty to bargain with the union as to its decision permanently to replace strikers and the manner in which that replacement will be effected. Times Pub. Co. (1947). The courts have extended that principle to hold that a decision to subcontract work in order to keep business operations going during the strike is one which the employer may implement without first bargaining with the union. NLRB v. Robert S. Abbott Pub. Co. (7th Cir. 1964). Perhaps the major case on this issue is Hawaii Meat Co. v. NLRB (9th Cir. 1963), in which the court of appeals overturned the Board's holding that the employer had violated section 8(a)(5) when, without bargaining with the union, it subcontracted the work of its truckdrivers when a strike was imminent. The court stated:

> We think that when an employer is confronted with a strike, his legal position is, in some respects, different from that which exists when no strike is expected or occurs. No case holds that a struck employer may not try to keep his business operating; on the contrary, it is quite clear that he has the right to do so. He may not use the strike as an excuse for committing unfair labor practices. . . . But it does not follow that what this employer did to meet the strike was an unfair labor practice, even though it might have been one in the absence of a strike.

The court noted that the employer's capacity to meet the strike by subcontracting would be crippled were it required to make an offer to the union to bargain, for the union could accept that offer and protract the negotiations. It concluded: "An employer is under no duty to offer to bargain, after a strike starts, about a decision to hire replacements for strikers, even on a permanent basis," or about securing comparable services through subcontracting.

Since the denial of enforcement of its order in *Hawaii Meat*, the Board has narrowed the breadth of its decision in that case. It now appears to require bargaining about subcontracting during a strike only when the subcontract is intended to be permanent and thus to impair the scope of the bargaining unit and the status of the union. If, however, the subcontracting is intended as a temporary measure to aid the employer to keep its operations intact during the strike, there is no duty to bargain about the decision. Empire Terminal Warehouse Co. (1965), *enf'd* (D.C.Cir. 1966). See Southern Calif. Stationers (1967) (thorough discussion by trial examiner of pertinent cases). Indeed, the Board has made it clear that the employer does not violate the Act by unilaterally subcontracting work to tide it through a strike even if work under the subcontract continues after the termination of the strike, provided "such a contract is of reasonable duration and dictated by exigencies of the strike." Shell Oil Co. (Norco Plant) (1964). The Board has also held that section 8(a)(5) does not prevent the employer from unilaterally changing the work schedules of its employees in order to maintain production in the face of an unprotected slowdown and refusal to work overtime; the employer's conduct was characterized as a temporary response to the work stoppage and one which it would have been futile to bargain about with the union. Celotex Corp. (1964), *enf'd in part* (5th Cir. 1966) (employer may also unilaterally terminate pay for "gift time" normally given employees idled by interruption of production, when the idle time was created by union's unprotected slowdown).

The rule which requires the employer to bargain during a lawful economic strike does not apply when the strike is itself an unfair labor practice, at least when the strike constitutes a violation of the union's duty to bargain in good faith under section 8(b)(3). In the few cases raising this issue squarely, the union has initiated a strike without complying with the requirements of section 8(d) that timely notice be given to the employer and to state and federal mediation agencies; such a strike violates section 8(b)(3). District 65, Wholesale Employees (1971). An employer refusal to bargain in the face of such a strike has been justified on two theories. One theory rests on the equitable idea that the union cannot at the same time violate its own duty to bargain while insisting that the employer honor its duty under section 8(a)(5); it is the refusal to bargain which taints the union and discharges the employer's correlative duty. UEW Local 1113 v. NLRB (Marathon Elec. Mfg. Co.) (D.C.Cir. 1955) (union's strike to modify contract terms, without complying with section 8(d), entitles the employer to rescind the contract). Another theory is that, pursuant to the express terms of section 8(d), the employees who participate in such an illegal strike are themselves stripped of their statutory status as "employees"; accordingly, because they are susceptible to discharge and not properly counted toward the union's majority within the bargaining unit, the union "had lost its standing as collective-bargaining agent and the Company was at liberty to treat the employees as having severed their relations." Boeing Airplane Co. v. NLRB (D.C.Cir. 1949). It is not altogether clear whether under the second theory, the employer's duty to bargain is terminated automatically when the employees engage in such a strike without complying with section 8(d) or whether the employer must first discharge the employees, United Furniture Workers v. NLRB (Fort Smith Chair Co.) (D.C.Cir. 1964). The language of section 8(d)—"Any employee who engages in a strike within any notice period .   .   . shall lose his status as an employee . . . for the purposes of sections 8, 9, and 10 of this Act"—would appear to make formal discharge unnecessary, although presumably the disability of both the retained employee and the union will terminate when the strike does.

A number of cases have also dealt with the question whether an employer is relieved of its duty to bargain when the union engages in a strike which, while not prohibited as an unfair labor practice, is unprotected, because of violence, contract breach or other contravention of labor policy. It has been held that the employer need not continue negotiations while the union sponsors a strike characterized by violence and vandalism. Kohler Co., *enf'd in relevant part* (D.C.Cir. 1962). Most of the pertinent cases deal with strikes which contravene an express no-strike promise by the union; such a strike is not an unfair labor practice but has been characterized as not within the protection of section 7 of the Labor Act. Here too, a principle of long standing, recently reaffirmed by the Board, is that such a strike relieves the employer of its duty to bargain. The Board held rather early that the employer is free not only to refuse to discuss with the union issues relating to the strike but also unilaterally to institute wage increases. United Elastic Corp. (1949). The Board there concluded that the duty to bargain was suspended during the strike, regardless of whether the union's breach of contract (*i. e.*, the strike in violation of the no-strike clause) was held to terminate the contract in its entirety. The Board has recently held that such a strike does constitute a material breach of the labor agreement, such that the employer is not bound by its terms and may condition bargaining on the cessation of the strike. Arundel Corp. (1974).

The suspension of the employer's duty to bargain is terminated when the strike terminates. International Shoe Corp. (1965), *enf'd* (1st Cir. 1966). Of course, if the collective bargaining agreement containing the no-strike promise has terminated, and the union makes no promise to continue its pledge in effect, there is no duty not to strike and the employer cannot refuse to bargain because of a work stoppage initiated thereafter. Pepper & Tanner, Inc. (1972), *mdf'd on other grounds* (6th Cir. 1973). Similarly, the employer will be held to violate section 8(a)(5) if it repudiates a contract, and refuses to recognize the union because of a strike which is allegedly in breach of contract, should it later be determined that the no-strike clause did not in fact bar the strike in question. NLRB v. State Elec. Serv., Inc. (5th Cir. 1973).

These cases, holding that unprotected strike action by the union frees the employer of its duty to bargain, are, even though recent, of dubious vitality. First, they run counter to the policy articulated in Drake Bakeries v. Local 50, Bakery Workers (U.S.1962), which held that a strike in breach of a no-strike clause does not constitute so material a breach as to relieve the employer of its duty to arbitrate contract grievances. There appears no reason why the statutory duty to bargain (by making no unilateral departures from the agreement) is any more subject to discharge than is the contractual duty to arbitrate. NLRB v. State Elec. Serv., Inc. (5th Cir. 1973) (even if strike did breach the no-strike clause, this does not terminate the entire contract or release the employer from its duty to bargain by honoring the contract). Second, and more significantly, the Supreme Court, in NLRB v. Katz (U.S.1962), disposed by footnote of the employer's argument that its unilateral changes in working conditions during negotiations, without notice to the union, were excused by certain union-instigated slowdowns. While the Court had earlier conceded arguendo that such slowdowns were unprotected activity, it held nonetheless:

> [S]uch proof would not have justified the company's refusal to bargain. Since, as we held in Labor Board v. Insurance Agent's Union, . . . the Board may not brand partial strike activity as illegitimate and forbid its use in support of bargaining, an *employer* cannot be free to refuse to negotiate when the union resorts to such tactics. Engaging in partial strikes is not inherently inconsistent with a continued willingness to negotiate; and as long as there is such willingness and no impasse has developed, the employer's obligation continues.

It is uncertain whether the Court's analysis was intended to reach strike activity unprotected not because it is "partial" but because it is either violent or in breach of contract. But even in those latter instances, it is certainly possible for the union simultaneously to be bargaining in good faith or giving effect to the terms (or in any event most of the terms) of an existing labor contract.

§ 10. Unilateral Action

If an employer during negotiations insists that it will pay a wage increase of no more than one and one-half cents an hour, and subsequently without offering any more to the union and without consulting it announces a wage increase for all employees ranging from two cents to six cents per hour, the employer will be held to violate section 8(a)(5). The Supreme Court so held in NLRB v. Crompton-Highland Mills (U.S.1949), affirming the finding of the Board that the employer's conduct clearly manifested bad faith and disparaged the process of collective bargaining. Good faith desire to reach an agreement with the union as exclusive representative would obviously dictate that the greater benefits actually granted the employees be first offered to the union as a predicate for a wage agreement. The employer's refusal to offer the union any more than one and one-half cents an hour constitutes a repudiation of the union by demonstrating that the employees can secure greater economic benefits in direct dealings with the employer than they can in dealing through the union.

In a major decision, NLRB v. Katz (U.S.1962), the Supreme Court extended the range of illegality announced in *Crompton-Highland* by modifying its rationale. In *Katz*, the employer and the union were engaged in negotiations over such matters of employee compensation as general wages, sick-leave pay and merit pay. Without notice to the union, the employer at different times during negotiations announced a new system of automatic wage increases, a change in sick-leave policy and numerous merit increases. The Board found these unilateral grants of benefits, short of impasse and without notice to the union, to constitute of themselves a refusal to bargain, without any specific determination (as there had been in *Crompton-Highland*) that the employer was acting in bad faith. The Supreme Court enforced the Board's finding of a refusal to bargain under section 8(a)(5), which requires the parties to "meet . . . and confer in good faith" on mandatory subjects:

> Clearly, the duty thus defined may be violated without a general failure of subjective good faith; for there is no occasion to consider the issue of good faith if a party has refused even to negotiate *in fact*—"to meet . . . and confer" —about any of the mandatory subjects. A refusal to negotiate *in fact* as to any subject which is within § 8(d), and about which the union seeks to negotiate, violates § 8(a)(5) though the employer has every desire to reach agreement with the union upon an over-all collective agreement and earnestly and in all good faith bargains to that end. We hold that an employer's unilateral change in conditions of employment under negotiation is similarly a violation of §

8(a)(5), for it is a circumvention of the duty to negotiate which frustrates the objectives of § 8(a)(5) much as does a flat refusal.

The Court then showed how the employer's unilateral modification of its sick-leave plan, which might well benefit some employees in the unit and disadvantage others, would disrupt the position of the union negotiators and inhibit discussion of the issue at the bargaining table. The employer's wage increases were found to be in excess of those offered the union and thus to fall within the ban of *Crompton-Highland*; "such action is necessarily inconsistent with a sincere desire to conclude an agreement with the union." Since it was not possible to determine with certainty whether the merit-pay increases fell within the range of those customarily granted (and thus were a lawful continuation of the status quo), their grant "must be viewed as tantamount to an outright refusal to negotiate on that subject." The Court believed that the unilateral changes, without notice to the union and an opportunity to bargain about them, were so disruptive of orderly negotiations as to constitute a refusal to "confer" at all, and illegal without any inquiry into the employer's state of mind.

While it may not be literally true that the employer's unilateral grant of benefits removed those issues from the bargaining table, as would a flat refusal to bargain, one can conclude that the Court believed the employer's conduct constituted a disparagement of the collective bargaining process and of the union's statutory claim to share in the determination of wages and other conditions of employment. The Court summed up its reasoning as follows:

> [T]he Board *is* authorized to order the cessation of behavior which is in effect a refusal to negotiate, or which directly obstructs or inhibits the actual process of discussion, or which reflects a cast of mind against reaching agreement. Unilateral action by an employer without prior discussion with the union does amount to a refusal to negotiate about the affected conditions of employment under negotiation, and must of necessity obstruct bargaining, contrary to the congressional policy. It will often disclose an unwillingness to agree with the union. It will rarely be justified by any reason of substance.

Although the *Katz* case involved a unilateral change in working conditions which took the form of a grant of new benefits, the employer has also been held to violate section 8(a)(5) when during negotiations it unilaterally deprives the employees of benefits already in existence. The employer has on occasion attempted to argue that its action was designed merely as a temporary measure to exert pressure on the union and employees to reach an earlier settlement on its own terms, and not to remove the issue from the bargaining table or to disparage the status of the union or to negotiate directly with the

employees. Reliance has been placed upon the Supreme Court decisions in NLRB v. Insurance Agents' Union (U.S.1960), and American
Ship Building Co. v. NLRB (U.S.1965). In *Insurance Agents*, the
Court held that a union does not violate its duty to bargain when it
instigates partial or intermittent work stoppages as a means of inducing the employer to settle, provided it negotiates in good faith at the
bargaining table. In *American Ship*, the Court upheld the right of
the employer to lock out its employees (at least after impasse) as a
means of exerting pressure to reach an early and favorable settlement.

These employer arguments supporting "unilateral decreases"
have been rather uniformly rebuffed since *Katz*, principally in reliance on that decision. For example, in Borden, Inc. (1972), the employer during negotiations cancelled, without discussing with the union, the employees' insurance programs (relating to disability, accident, medical and life insurance). This was held to constitute an unlawful unilateral change in working conditions. It was concluded:

> There is no case which holds that an employer may in an
> American Ship Building type of situation cancel employee
> insurance plans, take away their holidays or vacations or
> sick leave, or cut their wages in order to bring economic
> pressure on them to accept the employer's offer or to aban-
> don their own demands, but, in fact, what existing law there
> is, is to the contrary.

The deprivation of the insurance benefits was believed to create more
of an atmosphere of hostility and to be a more intrusive weapon than
the lockout, since only employee benefits are withdrawn and there is
no loss of services or income to the employer. Moreover, in Local
155, Molders v. NLRB (United States Pipe & Foundry Co.) (D.C.Cir.
1971), the court found that the employer's unilateral withdrawal of
employee benefits with a view toward compelling agreement or precipitating an early strike (in order to avoid delay of a strike until the
employer's busy season) discriminatorily denied employees their protected right to control the timing of their strike and constituted a refusal to bargain in violation of section 8(a)(5).

Indeed, even before *Katz* and *American Ship*, the Board announced that the Supreme Court decision in the *Insurance Agents*
partial-strike case would not justify the employer's termination of its
payments to an employee insurance plan and the withholding of holiday pay shortly before the employees were to take a ratification vote
on the proposed contract. Crestline Co. (1961). There, it was clear
that the employer's actions were only temporary; the withholding of
holiday pay was to exert pressure in bargaining, and the employer's
refusal to continue paying premiums was "because operations without
a bargaining agreement had increased its costs and it was necessary
to effect some compensating savings." Nonetheless, the Board held

the employer's actions to disparage the union's position, to subvert its authority and its representative status, and to reject the obligation to discuss matters with the union and thus necessarily to impede the progress of negotiations. But see NLRB v. Cascade Employers Ass'n (9th Cir. 1961) (a pre-*Katz* case in which an employer member of a multiemployer association instituted a unilateral decrease in wages; the court reversed the Board's finding of a refusal to bargain for lack of proof of subjective bad faith). A unilateral decrease in benefits will be particularly objectionable when accompanied by an attempt by the employer to get the consent of individual employees to the announced changes. Tom Johnson, Inc. (1965), *enf'd* (9th Cir. 1967).

Although for obvious reasons, the charge of refusal to bargain by taking "unilateral action" on wages and working conditions is normally levelled at the employer, there are rare cases in which a union has been found to violate section 8(b)(3) by forcing a change in working conditions without bargaining with the employer. A union can secure such a change by imposing fines or other discipline upon members who refuse to follow the union's announced modification in working rules. For example, in New York Dist. Council 9, Painters v. NLRB (2d Cir. 1971), journeymen painters had been painting an average of 11.5 rooms per week; although the labor contract had no requirements as to the number of rooms to be painted, it did call for a thirty-five hour workweek. The union imposed a work quota, enforceable by fines, of ten rooms per week, causing its members to stop work for the week before having painted for thirty five hours. This was held to constitute an unlawful unilateral reduction in hours of work. See IATSE Local 702 (Deluxe General, Inc.) (1972) (union unilaterally changed seniority provisions of contract by refusing to permit certain laid-off employees to be recalled unless others were reached first). The change in working conditions which the union unilaterally secures need not necessarily relate to a practice which is expressly addressed in the formal written labor contract. For example, in NLRB v. Communications Workers Local 1170 (Rochester Tel. Co.) (2d Cir. 1972), the union—after agreeing to permit the employer to continue its past practice of making temporary assignments to supervisory positions—voted to embargo supervisory assignments and to fine members who violated the embargo. This was held to violate section 8(b)(3).

In a decision not altogether easy to reconcile with those just discussed, it was held that a union during negotiations could lawfully announce a new minimum wage scale and discipline its members who work for less. In Cutler v. NLRB (2d Cir. 1968), the court held that this action by the union was tantamount only to a demand for a change in working conditions, and not a change in itself (for that would require employer agreement to the union's demand). That the union had sufficient strength to secure the employer's acquiescence in the new wage schedule was irrelevant, since "[I]t is no violation of the Act for a labor organization to be economically powerful."

It should be noted that, in certain circumstances, a refusal by employees to perform work contractually required may be treated as "unprotected" activity, even if not as an unfair labor practice on the part of the union. Employees engaging in such activity are subject to discipline, including discharge. *E. g.*, Elk Lumber Co. (1950) (employees refused to load more than one car a day, in part to pressure employer to improve wages). This subject is discussed in greater detail elsewhere in this work.

§ 11. Employer Defenses in Cases of Unilateral Action

It should be emphasized that the duty to bargain imposed by section 8(a)(5) pertains only (in the words of section 8(d)) to "wages, hours, and other terms and conditions of employment." The parties are therefore free to make unilateral changes on matters which fall outside these "mandatory" subjects of bargaining. Thus, the Supreme Court has held that the employer may, without bargaining to impasse with the union, effect changes in the medical benefits of its already retired workers, since these workers are not "employees" under the Labor Act or within the union's bargaining unit, and the impact of such benefits on the working conditions of present employees is too remote. Allied Chem. Workers v. Pittsburgh Plate Glass Co. (U.S.1971).

At the conclusion of its opinion in NLRB v. Katz (1962), the Supreme Court, noting that unilateral action without discussion with the union will "often" disclose an unwillingness to agree and will "rarely" be justified, concluded: "[W]e do not foreclose the possibility that there might be circumstances which the Board could or should accept as excusing or justifying unilateral action." In short, the so-called per se test announced in *Katz* actually does permit of some very limited exceptions; the burden is obviously upon the employer to demonstrate that its unilateral action is justified and that it acted in good faith, without a desire to impede negotiations or to undermine the representative status of the union. The cases acknowledge some special circumstances where unilateral action on mandatory subjects will be permitted. A court might, for example, be willing to condone a unilateral change in the wages and duties of a single employee, on something akin to a de minimis principle, NLRB v. Fitzgerald Mills Corp. (2d Cir. 1963) (court suggests union may secure redress as contract violation), but the scope of that principle is surely ill-defined.

Of far more general applicability is the principle that an employer does not bargain in bad faith when, after the termination of a labor contract and during negotiations for a new one, it unilaterally terminates union-shop or agency-shop provisions which require respectively that workers within the bargaining unit become union members or pay a fee to the union for its services as bargaining representative. These provisions are made lawful under section 8(a)(3) when they are part of an "agreement," and it has therefore been held that when the contract expires the statutory underpinning for the union-security arrangement disappears, so that the employer may terminate it without bargaining to impasse. In Industrial Union of Marine Workers v. NLRB (Bethlehem Steel Co.) (3rd Cir. 1963), upon the expiration of the contract the employer unilaterally suspended the contractual grievance procedure, the provision giving preferential seniority to union officials, and the union-security and dues-checkoff clauses (authorizing the employer to deduct union dues from the employees' paychecks and pay them directly to the union). The grievance and seniority modifications were held to constitute an unlawful change of the status quo without bargaining, while the latter suspensions were authorized; the union-security provision, and the checkoff which was used as an incident thereto, were "wholly dependent upon the existence of an agreement conforming to the § 8(a)(3) proviso."

The Board has also held that when a contract expires, although the employer is normally not free unilaterally to depart from the working conditions established thereby, the employer may lawfully repudiate the grievance and arbitration procedures set forth in the expired contract without notice to the union or bargaining to impasse. Hilton-Davis Chem. Co. (1970). The Board concluded that grievance and arbitration procedures are purely a product of the voluntary and mutual agreement of the parties, and when the contract expires and the employer announces its intention no longer to process new grievances through to arbitration, the consensual underpinning for arbitration is destroyed and section 8(a)(5) is not violated. The Board emphasized that as new grievances emerge concerning working conditions, the employer is obliged to bargain with the union with a view toward their resolution; but the employer will not be obliged by section 8(a)(5) to submit them to arbitration unless it consents to do so.

Every now and again, a Board or court opinion will suggest that an employer's unilateral action, without notice to or consultation with the union, will be excused if justified by business necessity. It does not appear, however, that any such principle can be generally endorsed. Thus, although the Board sustained a "unilateral" wage increase in Exposition Cotton Mills Co. (1948), noting that other mills in the area had already implemented a comparable increase, it also emphasized that the employer had every reason to be confident that the increase, already offered to the union, would be rejected in an impending vote of the union membership upon the recommendation of the union officials. The Board placed great emphasis in sustaining the increase upon the employer's good faith, a factor which is of decidedly less importance since the Supreme Court decision in NLRB v. Katz (U.S.1962). Presumably even in situations of serious economic stress, the employer must give notice to the union of its intended change in wages and working conditions in response to the emergency, and bargain to impasse; as will be developed below, even this will not justify a change when the subject matter is already dealt with in an existing collective bargaining agreement. Compare Oak Cliff-Golman Baking Co. (1973) (section 8(d) forbids the modification of wage rates in an existing contract without union consent, regardless of employer claim of dire economic necessity). It has been held, however, that the employer is entitled—even during the term of a labor agreement—to grant wage increases to employees without notice to or consultation with the union, if that is necessary to comply with new minimum-wage provisions of the Fair Labor Standards Act. But the employer violates section 8(a)(5) when it increases the wages of employees in excess of the new minimum wage, even if only to maintain the wage differentials embodied in the existing contract. Standard Candy Co. (1964). Compare Architectural Fiberglass (1967) (wage increases for male employees held to violate section 8(a)(5), since the employer's purpose was other than its avowed desire to comply with Equal Pay Act). The cases referring to business necessity in the context of an employer's unilateral change of working conditions more uniformly stand for the principle that while such necessity may not in itself justify the unilateral change, some business justification must be present even when the change is made after an impasse has been reached; that is, the employer's grant of benefits must be motivated by business reasons and not by antiunion animus. NLRB v. Southern Coach & Body Co. (5th Cir. 1964) (promotions and wage increases, in keeping with status quo, justified by business necessity).

There are three major exceptions to the principle that the employer violates section 8(a)(5) by making "unilateral" modifications in wages, hours or other terms and conditions of employment. These are: (1) when the employer has bargained in good faith to an impasse on the issue in question; (2) when the "modifications" are actually no more than a preservation of the status quo as conceived dynamically; and (3) when the union has in effect authorized the employer to make those modifications and is thus said to have "waived" its statutory privilege to require the employer to bargain (a situation most commonly arising during the term of a collective bargaining agreement). These three situations will be discussed in turn.

§ 12. Impasse

The law is clear that an employer may, after bargaining with the union to a deadlock or impasse on an issue, make "unilateral changes that are reasonably comprehended within his pre-impasse proposals." Taft Broadcasting Co. (1967), enf'd (D.C.Cir. 1968). Another formulation is that after an impasse reached in good faith, "the employer is free to institute by unilateral action changes which are in line with or which are no more favorable than" those it offered or approved prior to impasse. Bi-Rite Foods, Inc. (1964). A detailed rationale for the post-impasse change in working conditions was set forth by the Board in Bi-Rite Foods, Inc., *ibid.*:

> This freedom of action which the employer has after, but not before, the impasse springs from the fact that having bargained in good faith to impasse, he has satisfied his statutory duty to determine working conditions, if possible, by agreement with his employees. Having fulfilled his obligation to fix working conditions by joint action, he acquires a limited right to fix them unilaterally, that is, he is limited to the confines of his preimpasse offers or proposals. Any other changes he were to institute might, if offered before or after the impasse, have led or lead to progress or success in the collective negotiations; hence unilateral action of this different scope forecloses this possibility, just as would his refusal to consider a proposal, with a violation as apparent in the one instance as in the other. In explaining this result, it is sometimes said that the employer's postimpasse action "breaks" the previous impasse, although it is perhaps more precise and less susceptible of misinterpretation to say that no impasse can be said to have been reached when the reference is to changes never introduced into the collective bargaining arena. Or, applying another familiar formulation, the employer may not be heard to say that had he offered his unilaterally-instituted changes to the employees' representative, the resulting negotiations (which could as a result have taken on new directions or scope) would nevertheless have ended in deadlock.

In effect, the employer's action is not "unilateral," since at least that much of a concession was being demanded by the union when good-faith negotiations resulted in impasse. The employer ought not be forbidden to implement such an agreed-upon concession merely because the union remains fixed in its bargaining position. The announcement implementing the change is not viewed either as an avoidance of the duty to bargain or as a disparagement of the representative status of the union. The union can take credit for the granted benefit, the employer demonstrates that it has acknowledged its duty to deal with the union and not with employees directly, and good-faith negotiations can now proceed on the residual benefits which continue to separate the parties (the "unilateral" grant being deemed to "break" the impasse). Such a grant of benefits thus differs sharply from that condemned by the Supreme Court in NLRB v. Katz (U.S.1962), where the subject matter of the benefits was still under negotiation and the union had no notice of the employer's intention to implement its grant.

Impasse is also significant for another reason. Not only is the employer free after impasse to implement changes already offered to the union, but either party is free after impasse to decline to negotiate further. Since impasse signifies that the parties have exhausted (at least temporarily) the avenues of bargaining, termination of bargaining at that point cannot be thought to demonstrate a cast of mind against reaching agreement. Cheney Calif. Lumber Co. v. NLRB (9th Cir. 1963) (union declined to bargain based on good faith and reasonable belief that impasse had been reached).

It is arguable that impasse ought not be necessary in order to allow the employer to implement an improvement in wages or working conditions which it has already offered the union but which the union has rejected. Even though the subject is still being negotiated and no deadlock has been reached, the employees can be led to understand that the union is being dealt with as bargaining representative, that it has rejected the employer's proposal as inadequate and that good-faith efforts continue to be made to reach a settlement on the issue. The Board has nonetheless required an impasse and has found the pre-impasse "unilateral" grant to be a violation of section 8(a)(5), but a court of appeals has denied enforcement of the Board's order. Bradley Washfountain (1950), *enf't denied* (7th Cir. 1951). The Board found a grant of wage and fringe benefits on three occasions, accompanied by announcements to the employees that the union had rejected these at the bargaining table, to demonstrate that the employer was "bent on undermining the Union's prestige"; the Board found, "under all the circumstances," that the grant was unnecessary and that it deprived the union of due credit and demonstrated bad faith. The court of appeals found it "well nigh impossible to see" how the employer could be said to have acted unilaterally, since it complied at least partially with the union's demands and it acted without prejudice to continued negotiations on those matters; the court found no deprivation of employee rights and no disparagement or undermining of the bargaining agent.

In NLRB v. Katz (U.S.1962), the Supreme Court, after finding illegal a pre-impasse wage increase in excess of that offered the union in negotiations, stated: "Of course, there is no resemblance between this situation and one wherein an employer, after notice and consultation, 'unilaterally' institutes a wage increase identical with one which the union has rejected as too low," citing the decision of the court of appeals in *Bradley Washfountain*. In context, the Court was speaking hypothetically of a wage increase granted after impasse, but the approving citation to *Bradley Washfountain* may be understood to countenance even a pre-impasse increase, provided it is in an amount already rejected by the union and is implemented only after notice to and consultation with the union; surely the Court's endorsement is not expressly conditioned upon the existence of an impasse. Nonetheless, the National Labor Relations Board adheres to its position that "unilateral" changes made prior to impasse, even though within the range already offered to and rejected by the union, are tantamount to a refusal to bargain. Alsey Refractories Co. (1974).

The Board's doctrine thus renders quite important the determination whether or not an impasse exists. The definition of an "impasse" is understandable enough—that point at which the parties have exhausted the prospects of concluding an agreement and further discussions would be fruitless—but its application can be difficult. Given the many factors commonly itemized by the Board and courts in impasse cases, perhaps all that can be said with confidence is that an impasse is a "state of facts in which the parties, despite the best of faith, are simply deadlocked." NLRB v. Tex-Tan, Inc. (5th Cir. 1963). The Board and courts look to such matters as the number of meetings between the company and the union, the length of those meetings and the period of time that has transpired between the start of negotiations and their breaking off. There is no magic number of meetings, hours or weeks which will reliably determine when an impasse has occurred. E. g., Tex-Tan, Inc. (1961), *mdf'd on other grounds* (5th Cir. 1963) (no impasse found after twenty-one meetings, with employer bad faith apparently a significant factor in so deciding). Also properly considered are whether the refusal to modify bargaining positions occurred only at the last meeting or has embraced several meetings before the last, whether either party has expressed a willingness to modify its position or to bargain further, and whether the parties have called in a mediator to assist negotiations (the latter is apparently generally understood to demonstrate an acknowledgment by the parties of deadlock). The Board has itself summed up the factors to be considered in determining the existence of an impasse, in Taft Broadcasting Co. (1967), *enf'd* (D.C.Cir. 1968):

> Whether a bargaining impasse exists is a matter of judgment. The bargaining history, the good faith of the parties in negotiations, the length of the negotiations, the importance of the issue or issues as to which there is disagreement, the contemporaneous understanding of the parties as to the state of negotiations, are all relevant factors to be considered in deciding whether an impasse in bargaining existed.

The fact that the parties have become deadlocked as to their negotiations on a particular issue does not necessarily mean that continued negotiation concerning other open issues would prove fruitless. Therefore bargaining on those other issues must continue. Chambers Mfg. Co. (1959), *enf'd* (5th Cir. 1960) (impasse concerning job classification, but company refused to bargain on wage rates). But sometimes a single issue will loom so large in the negotiations that a stalemate on that issue alone may legitimately be found to cripple prospects for settlement on any others. In such a situation, the Board will find an impasse, for it has noted "[A] deadlock is still a deadlock whether produced by one or a number of significant and unresolved differences in positions." Taft Broadcasting Co. (1967), *enf'd* (D.C. Cir. 1968) (parties failed, after twenty-three bargaining sessions, to reach agreement on assignment of personnel).

It is not altogether clear whether the respondent must demonstrate, as a defense to a charge of unlawful unilateral action or a refusal to continue bargaining, that an impasse existed in fact (tested against objective criteria) or merely that it had a good faith belief that an impasse existed. A court of appeals has held, in Cheney Calif. Lumber Co. v. NLRB (9th Cir. 1963), that since the Labor Act requires only bargaining in good faith, the test is "not whether, judged on a basis of hindsight, an impasse has been reached as a matter of fact." The central issue is whether the respondent "had reasonable cause to believe and did sincerely believe that an impasse had been reached." The Board appears to apply a more objective test: whether the respondent was "warranted in assuming that further bargaining would have been futile." Alsey Refractories Co. (1974).

Since it may be to the employer's advantage during bargaining to implement a "unilateral" grant of benefits, and since this can only be done after impasse, there may be a temptation on the part of the employer purposely to precipitate an impasse. It is clear, however, that the employer cannot take advantage of the impasse rule when it has contrived an impasse or when the impasse is reached because of its unfair labor practice. Industrial Union of Marine & Shipbuilding Workers v. NLRB (3d Cir. 1963) (employer insistence on a nonmandatory subject). "Generally speaking, the freedom to grant a unilateral wage increase 'is limited to cases where there has been a bona fide but unsuccessful attempt to reach an agreement with the union, or where the union bears the guilt for having broken off relations.'" Herman Sausage Co. v. NLRB (5th Cir. 1960).

An impasse is a fragile state of affairs and may be broken by a change in circumstances which suggests that attempts to adjust differences may no longer be futile. In such a case, the parties are obligated to resume negotiations and the employer is no longer free to implement changes in working conditions without bargaining. Just as there is no litmus-paper test to determine when an impasse has been created, there is none which determines when it has been broken. The Board will look to "all the circumstances." Transport Co. of Texas (1969). Most obviously, an impasse will be broken when one party announces a retreat from some of its negotiating demands. Sharon Hats, Inc. (1960), *enf'd* (5th Cir. 1961). And if, for example, a deadlock was reached concerning a union security clause because of the union's alleged lack of membership strength, or a deadlock was reached concerning wages because of the employer's financial position, a demonstrable improvement in the condition of the union or company, respectively, will be deemed to break the impasse and require renewed bargaining. Kit Mfg. Co. (1962), *enf'd* (9th Cir. 1963).

A number of cases raise the question whether a post-impasse strike will constitute a sufficient change in the bargaining equilibrium as to break the impasse. In spite of language in some early cases to the contrary, it seems rather clear that the Board does not hold per se that a strike necessarily breaks an impasse. In one case in which it announced that the determination would be made "under all the circumstances," the Board found it unlawful for the employer to refuse to resume bargaining when the union requested it to do so seven months after impasse had been reached, given the long hiatus, the collapse of an intervening strike in two days, the replacement of several of the strikers, and the grant of pay increases to a number of employees. Transport Co. of Texas (1969). The Board and courts may be inclined to find, if a strike continues for many weeks without closing down the employer's business, that this exhibition of the employer's staying power will likely soften the union's demands and thus warrant a return to the bargaining table. Jeffrey-De Witt Insulator Co. v. NLRB (4th Cir. 1937); NLRB v. United States Cold Storage Corp. (5th Cir. 1953) (three-month strike and reduction in union wage demands). The same rejection of any rule that a strike automatically breaks an impasse appears to apply whether the issue is the duty to return to the bargaining table or the duty of the employer not to grant unilateral benefits. Bi-Rite Foods, Inc. (1964) (employer may lawfully implement offer on wages and fringe benefits made to union prior to impasse, in spite of post-impasse strike).

§ 13. The Dynamic Status Quo

The Supreme Court, in NLRB v. Katz (U.S.1962), held that "an employer's unilateral change in conditions of employment" without bargaining with the union is tantamount to a refusal to bargain on that subject and violates section 8(a)(5). This rule obtains during negotiations for a new contract and during the term of an existing agreement as well. The cases make clear, however, that "conditions of employment" are to be viewed dynamically, over a period of time, and that the status quo against which the employer's "change" is considered must take account of any regular and consistent past pattern of changes in employee status. Employer modifications consistent with such a pattern are not a "change" in working conditions at all. Indeed, if the employer, without bargaining with the union, *departs* from that pattern by withholding benefits otherwise reasonably expected, this is a refusal to bargain in violation of section 8(a)(5). The employer is therefore free, without bargaining to impasse, to grant a bonus consistent with a past practice, or to award merit pay or grant other pay increases comparable to those granted consistently in the past, or to subcontract bargaining-unit work as before. Such employer action, accompanied by a willingness to bargain with the union on demand concerning the termination or modification of the past practice, does not disparage the bargaining process or "go over the head" of the bargaining representative to deal directly with the employees or reflect a state of mind resistant to adjustment and compromise.

If the employer has for many years given a bonus on a holiday or at year-end, in a consistent fixed amount or directly related to employees' earnings, this bonus becomes part of the status quo as to the employees' total wage package. It is therefore within the scope of the mandatory subjects of bargaining. An employer is not free to inaugurate a bonus plan without first bargaining with the union to impasse. Central Metallic Casket Co. (1950). But it is well established that a bonus may be "unilaterally" granted consistent with such a program of long standing. Texas Foundries, Inc. (1952), *enf't denied on other grounds* (5th Cir. 1954). A withholding of a bonus, without bargaining, will be a "change" in working conditions and unlawful, if the bonus is well established, Progress Bulletin Pub. Co. (1970), *enf'd in relevant part* (9th Cir. 1971) (Christmas bonus paid regularly for at least twenty years, unilaterally withheld by employer); but will be lawful if there is no consistent past pattern of such bonuses, NLRB v. Nello Pistoresi & Son (9th Cir. 1974).

The employer is also free to grant general wage increases if consistent with past company policy. As the court stated in NLRB v. Ralph Printing & Lithog. Co. (8th Cir. 1970):

> Where there is a well-established company policy of granting certain increases at specific times, which is a part and parcel of the existing wage structure, the company is not required to inform the union and bargain concerning these increases.

Thus, in State Farm Mut. Auto Ins. Co. (1972), the Board upheld an employer's unilateral grant during contract negotiations of cost-of-living increases, where this was pursuant to a known company policy and was tied objectively to government statistics. The same is true when the wage increase follows a pattern of automatic increases at fixed intervals. NLRB v. Southern Coach & Body Co. (5th Cir. 1964) (automatic wage increases three and six months after initial hiring). If, however, in spite of a tradition of automatic wage increases, the employer recently departed from that tradition without explaining why, and then purported to reinstate the increases during negotiations (without first bargaining on the subject with the union), the employer demonstrates that the payments are discretionary rather than automatic; they are not thus part of the status quo, and the unilateral grant constitutes an unlawful "change" in working conditions. Gray Line, Inc. (1974), *mdf'd on other grounds* (D.C.Cir. 1975).

The Supreme Court has drawn the same line between "automatic" and "discretionary" past benefits in determining whether the employer is free unilaterally to grant merit-pay increases during bargaining negotiations.   In NLRB v. Katz (U.S.1962), the employer granted merit increases to twenty of fifty unit employees, while merit pay was under discussion in the parties' contract negotiations.   The Court held that such a grant is "tantamount to an outright refusal to negotiate on that subject" unless the employer can demonstrate that it was a "mere continuation of the status quo."   No such demonstration was made, and the Court concluded:

> Whatever might be the case as to so-called "merit raises" which are in fact simply automatic increases to which the employer has already committed himself, the raises here in question were in no sense automatic, but were informed by a large measure of discretion.

The Court concluded that the large measure of discretion traditionally exercised by the employer made it impossible for the union to know "whether or not there has been a substantial departure from past practice," and the employer is therefore obligated to bargain about the "procedures and criteria for determining such increases." There is even some question whether a regular past practice will validate the unilateral grant of true "merit" payments which of necessity take into account the special competence and skills of particular employees.   The Board has apparently read *Katz* so as to require bargaining over the "amounts or timing" of such increases, even where merit increases have been consistently granted in the past.   In Oneita Knitting Mills, Inc. (1973), the Board held:

> An employer with a past history of a merit increase program neither may discontinue that program .   .   .   nor may he any longer continue to unilaterally exercise his discretion with respect to such increases, once an exclusive bargaining agent is selected. .   .   .   What is required is a maintenance of preexisting practices, *i. e.*, the general outline of the program .   .   .   [H]owever the implementation of that program (to the extent that discretion has existed in determining the amounts or timing of the increases), becomes a matter as to which the bargaining agent is entitled to be consulted.

The Board does appear willing, however, to treat a merit pay program as part of the status quo even though the company has had some discretion as to whether increases would be granted to individual employees after a merit review of their work; for it has held that an employer's termination of such a program, without bargaining, violates section 8(a)(5).   General Motors Acceptance Corp. v. NLRB (1st Cir. 1973) (court would have been reluctant to find violation had employer discontinued program in good faith effort to comply with *Katz* decision; but evidence showed motive was actually discriminatory).

The Supreme Court in Fibreboard Paper Prods. Corp. v. NLRB (U.S.1964), held that the subcontracting of maintenance work ordinarily performed within the plant by bargaining-unit employees is a mandatory subject about which the employer must bargain with the union. In a significant decision soon after, however, the Board held that *Fibreboard* did not forbid unilateral acts of subcontracting which fall within the confines of a past pattern of frequent subcontracting decisions made by the employer. In Westinghouse Elec. Corp. (Mansfield Plant) (1965), the employer had over many years entered into thousands of subcontracts for maintenance work, tool-and-die work and manufacture of components, much of which work could have been done by employees in the bargaining unit. The union had in three prior negotiations unsuccessfully sought to impose contractual restrictions on the employer's subcontracting, and all resulting contracts were silent on the issue. The union charged the company with a violation of section 8(a)(5) when it continued to enter into these subcontracts (all concededly for economic rather than antiunion reasons) without notifying or bargaining with the union. The Board dismissed the complaint. It noted that in cases like *Fibreboard* in which a violation was found, the subcontracting had significantly impaired job tenure or work opportunities and "involved a departure both conditions absent in the case before it, and cumulated the factors which pointed toward no duty to bargain:

> In sum—bearing in mind particularly that the recurrent contracting out of work here in question was motivated solely by economic considerations; that it comported with the traditional methods by which the Respondent conducted its business operations; that it did not during the period here in question vary significantly in kind or degree from what had been customary under past established practice; that it had no demonstrable adverse impact on employees in the unit; and that the Union had the opportunity to bargain about changes in existing subcontracting practices at general negotiating meetings—for all these reasons cumulatively, we conclude that Respondent did not violate its statutory bargaining obligation by failing to invite union participation in individual subcontracting decisions.

In its decisions on the duty to bargain about subcontracting, the Board has placed particularly heavy emphasis—in upholding the employer action—upon the absence of any substantial adverse impact upon the employees in the bargaining unit; but it has also given weight to the fact that the action was consistent with a company past practice. *E. g.*, Fafnir Bearing Co. (1965). This past practice may have developed pursuant to an explicit provision in a contract which authorizes the employer to engage in subcontracting, but the practice will have become part of the dynamic status quo even after that contract expires and a new contract is being negotiated. Even if during negotiations the union seeks to modify the subcontracting provisions of the prior agreement, the employer need not during the hiatus between contracts bargain with the union before implementing subcontracting decisions which do not vary materially in kind or degree from what had been customary, since that contract-authorized custom had become a "term or condition of employment." Shell Oil Co. (Norco Plant) (1964). As with union demands for a change in wages, merit pay or bonuses, the employer must bargain about "such restrictions or other changes in current subcontracting practices as the union may wish to negotiate." Westinghouse Elec. Corp. (Mansfield Plant) (1965). But such union demands do not suspend the employer's power unilaterally to subcontract as in the past, "any more than a demand by the Union to modify the existing wage structure would suspend [the company's] obligation to maintain such wage structure during negotiations." Shell Oil Co. (Norco Plant) (1964).

There may be occasions when the employer attempts to justify "unilateral" grants of pay increases or bonuses—in the absence of a past practice of such grants—on the ground that it was promised to the employees before the union was selected as bargaining representative. If the employer is able to show that such a promise has been made (for reasons other than antiunion animus), it is uniformly held that such a grant of benefits without bargaining with the later-arriving union is lawful, since "conditions of employment" are comprised not only of what the employer has granted in the past but also what it has already proposed to grant. Armstrong Cork Co. v. NLRB (5th Cir. 1954) (prior to advent of union, employer had promised wage increase conditioned only on government approval; to withdraw that promised increase during negotiations violates section 8(a)(5)). Like regularly given past benefits, these promised benefits become part of the reasonably expected conditions of work, and their grant without bargaining does not disparage negotiations or undermine the representative status of the union. Thus, a wage increase planned and announced months before the union arrived on the scene, to become effective when the company moved to a new location, may be implemented after the union is designated the bargaining representative. Briggs IGA Foodliner (1964). So too may automatic wage increases promised employees prior to their hiring, and prior to the advent of the union. Architectural Fiberglass (1967) (dictum). If, however, the employer makes such "prehire" promises, which it then refrains from granting at the time the employee expected, it in effect concedes that the payment is within its discretion, so that unilaterally granting the payment later during negotiations with the union constitutes a refusal to bargain. Gray Line, Inc. (1974).

§ 14.   The Duty to Bargain During the Contract Term

Congress originally intended that the duty to bargain was to be an incident of the duty to recognize the union. The classic case of a violation of section 8(a)(5) was a refusal by the employer to recognize and bargain with the freshly certified union, rejecting its demands to negotiate a collective bargaining agreement. The duty to bargain has, however, been extended beyond this most blatant case, and covers most typically today all negotiations for labor contracts, possibly after many years of recognizing the union and negotiating agreements. Indeed, although the anticipated end-product of the mutual duty to bargain is the bilateral agreement, that duty continues even after such an agreement is executed. It continues during the life of the contract, subject to certain modifications made necessary by the existence of a contractual framework.

Perhaps the most obvious violation of the duty to bargain during the contract term is an employer's repudiation of the union and the contract altogether. Such a wholesale attack upon the representative status of the union, and of the contract representing the "partnership" of the two parties, contravenes section 8(a)(5). NLRB v. Hyde (9th Cir. 1964). In such a case, the Board will order the employer to recognize and bargain with the union and to "honor" the collective bargaining agreement. This remedy has been sustained by the courts. *Ibid.* It is very much like the remedy enforced by the Supreme Court in NLRB v. Strong (U.S.1969), where the employer had refused to execute a labor contract negotiated by a multiemployer association on its behalf. The Court upheld an order requiring the employer not only to sign the agreement but also to pay accrued fringe benefits pursuant to the terms of that agreement. The purpose of the Board's order to "honor" the contract is merely to restore the parties to their position prior to repudiation. It does not constitute a determination of the validity of the contract provisions, and it is not tantamount to an order of specific performance, enforceable through contempt proceedings if there is an alleged breach of the contract. Any claimed breach is to be tested through the grievance and arbitration procedures set forth in the contract, for these procedures are part of the contract which the employer must honor. Crescent Bed Co., *enf'd per curiam* (D.C.Cir. 1966).

The Board has extended this doctrine concerning "outright repudiation" to cases where the employer, although not disregarding the contract in all respects, unilaterally modifies a fundamental provision without any plausible claim of contractual authority. In Oak Cliff-Golman Baking Co. (1974), the employer, during the term of the labor contract, notified the union of its intention to reduce wages and asserted that severe economic conditions made the change necessary. The union refused to acquiesce and the employer implemented the wage reductions without any claim of contract right. This was held to violate section 8(a)(5), in part because the wage system was of such pervasive significance in the contract that to disregard it was the "striking of a death blow to the contract as a whole, and is thus, in reality, a basic repudiation of the bargaining relationship." And, in California Blowpipe & Steel Co. (1975), where the employer refused to require employees to join the union and pay union dues in accordance with the contract's union-shop provision, this was held to have the effect of "terminating" that provision "in derogation of Respondent's bargaining obligation under Section 8(d) of the Act." The company's repudiation of the union-shop agreement "constitutes a death blow to the Union in its role of bargaining representative by allowing employees a 'free ride,' and, as such, comes close to repudiating the collective-bargaining relationship between Respondent and the Union."

Outright repudiation of the labor agreement during its term is, however, a rather rare occurrence. The far more common claim of employer refusal to bargain during the contract term is based upon some employer change in working conditions which the employer argues the contract authorizes it to make but which the union claims is not thus authorized but must first be negotiated to impasse. If the employer's reading of the contract and antecedent negotiations is correct, it has already discharged its duty to bargain about the matter and is not acting in violation of section 8(a)(5). If, however, the union's reading is correct, the employer cannot make the change unilaterally, but must first bargain with the union; indeed, in some instances, even bargaining will not empower the employer to make the desired change. When the duty to bargain thus turns upon a good faith dispute as to the meaning of the contract, that dispute is arguably triable either (or both) to the Board or to the arbitrator. Congress has not clearly assigned jurisdiction in such instances to one party to the exclusion of the other. All that can be said with confidence is that a breach of the labor contract does not in and of itself constitute an unfair labor practice. Congress in enacting the 1947 Taft-Hartley amendments rejected a proposal that claims of contract breach should be triable to the NLRB, and enacted instead section 301, which gives the federal courts jurisdiction to hear such claims (including claimed breaches of the promise to arbitrate), and section 203(d), which provides:

> Final adjustment by a method agreed upon by the parties is hereby declared to be the desirable method of settlement of grievance disputes arising over the application or interpretation of an existing collective-bargaining agreement.

But section 10(a) of the Labor Act also clearly states that the power to adjudicate unfair labor practice cases "shall not be affected by any other means of adjustment or prevention that has been or may be established by agreement, law, or otherwise." The Supreme

Court has indeed held that the duty to bargain does continue during the term of the contract, and that it is not always satisfied merely by relying upon some good faith assertion of contractual privilege, NLRB v. C & C Plywood Corp. (U.S.1967) (employer claimed that contract authorized change in wage rates), or upon the existence of grievance and arbitration procedures, NLRB v. Acme Industrial Co. (U.S.1967) (refusal to disclose information sought by union in processing contract grievance). The resulting institutional overlap between the Board and the parties' contract-enforcement machinery (typically an arbitrator) is discussed in detail elsewhere in this work. It suffices to say that the Board has with increasing frequency exercised its discretion to stay its hand and to defer to arbitral procedures which give promise of resolving both the contract claim and the alleged refusal to bargain.

It is section 8(d) which is most pertinent in articulating the duty to bargain during the term of a labor contract. Other than to state generally that the duty includes "the negotiation of an agreement, or any question arising thereunder," that section sets forth a number of rules:

First, during the life of the contract, neither party has a duty to discuss any proposed modification of any term "contained in" that contract, and the Board has held it a corollary that neither party may lawfully insist on such discussion. Thus, a midterm modification of any such "contained" term may be lawfully made only after the consent of the opposing party has been voluntarily given.

Second, even if not "contained in" the contract, neither party may lawfully during the contract term implement a change in wages or other working conditions unless it has first bargained with the other party, that is has given notice of the change and an opportunity to negotiate about it to impasse. (Usually, the employer will seek to make the change and the union to resist it.) In short, the duty not to make unilateral changes on mandatory bargaining subjects subsists during the contract term as well as during negotiations.

Third, if one party wishes to terminate a contract, or to "modify" it (usually this has been applied to the formal wage reopener in midterm), that party must give certain timely notices to the other party and to federal and state mediation agencies, and must maintain the status quo without striking or locking out for a stipulated period. Even bargaining to impasse will not make lawful a contract modification (or strike or lockout) undertaken without complying with the notification and "cooling off" formalities of section 8(d).

Union-Initiated Modifications During the Contract Term. Refusal-to-bargain cases which arise during the contract term will usually take one of two forms. In the first kind of case, the union seeks to raise a subject for negotiation and the employer declines to discuss it. The union asserts that the employer has an obligation to bargain while the employer asserts that by virtue of some contract provision (or other union "waiver") it is relieved of its duty to bargain on that subject on union demand during the contract term. This will be referred to as the case of union-initiated modification. In a second kind of case, much more common, the employer takes the initiative and announces its intention to make some change in working conditions. Either it offers the union an opportunity to bargain first to impasse, which the union declines; or, in the great preponderance of litigated cases, the employer simply announces the change without offering to bargain (or after refusing the union's request to do so). The union attacks the employer's implementation of the change as a failure to bargain, and once again the employer points to some contract provision or other alleged "waiver" of the union's bargaining right. This second kind of case will be referred to as the employer-initiated modification.

While the scope of the duty to bargain differs in these two kinds of cases, it should be noted at the outset that that duty applies only to the so-called mandatory subjects of bargaining, "wages, hours and other terms or conditions of employment." As to other subjects, the so-called "permissive" or "voluntary" subjects, either party is entitled adamantly to refuse to engage in bargaining. Indeed, (while there may be a claim for breach of contract) the employer is not forbidden by the Labor Act—even during the term of the contract—to modify, without negotiating with the union or securing its consent, existing terms or practices on such nonmandatory subjects. Allied Chem. Workers v. Pittsburgh Plate Glass Co. (U.S.1971) (employer does not violate section 8(a)(5) by modifying health-insurance coverage for retired workers without bargaining with union).

When a union wishes to initiate discussions concerning mandatory subjects of bargaining during the term of a labor agreement, the employer's duty to bargain depends upon whether the union's proposals relate to terms and conditions which are "contained in" the contract. If they are so contained, the employer need not bargain; if they are not so contained, the employer must bargain. This principle is founded upon Board elucidation of section 8(d), which provides in pertinent part:

> [T]he duties so imposed shall not be construed as requiring either party to discuss or agree to any modification of the terms and conditions contained in a contract for a fixed period, if such modification is to become effective before such terms and conditions can be reopened under the provisions of the contract.

This provision, giving the employer a defense against a union-initiated demand for bargaining during the contract term, was most fully explored in the decision of the Board in Jacobs Mfg. Co. (1951), enf'd (2d Cir. 1952). There, the parties in July 1948 executed a two-year labor contract which provided for a reopening in one year for discussion of "wage rates." In July 1949, the union invoked the reopener and served the company with written notice of its "wage demands," which included not only a request for a wage increase but also a request that the company assume the entire cost of an existing group insurance program (covering life and medical insurance) and a request that the company create a pension plan. The employer refused in its meetings with the union to discuss the insurance and pension demands, claiming that they fell beyond the scope of the reopener. In the 1948 negotiations leading to the execution of the current labor contract, the parties had not discussed pensions at all, but they had discussed the insurance plan (apparently including a union proposal that the employer assume all costs) and had agreed upon an increase in benefits; neither pensions nor the insurance plan were actually mentioned in the labor contract.

The Board sharply divided on the question whether the employer's refusal to bargain about the union's insurance and pension proposals in the middle of the contract term was unlawful. Two Board members would have held both issues subject to mandatory bargaining since they were not referred to expressly in the written agreement and thus were not (in the language of section 8(d)) "contained in" it. Two Board members would have held both issues outside the scope of mandatory bargaining during the contract, with one of those two members arguing that the contract closes out all issues for initial bargaining during its term regardless whether they are expressly dealt with therein. The fifth Board member concluded that the insurance demand had been bargained away by the union in the 1948 negotiations and was thus "contained in" the present contract, such that the employer had no duty to bargain about that subject during the contract term; but he held that there was a duty to bargain upon request concerning pensions, which had never been discussed before and thus were not "contained in" the contract.

The different opinions expressed sharply divergent philosophies of section 8(d). All did agree that Congress intended that section, at least in part, to overturn earlier court and Board holdings that even issues squarely covered in a written labor contract were subject to continuing renegotiation during the life of the contract. But the two members who would have found an unlawful refusal to bargain on both insurance and pensions argued that except for terms and conditions actually integrated and embodied in the writing, the earlier philosophy of continuing negotiations still obtained.

A different construction of Section 8(d) in the circumstances—one that would permit a party to a bargaining contract to avoid discussion when it was sought on subject matters not contained in the contract—would serve, at its best, only to dissipate whatever the good will that had been en-

gendered by the previous bargaining negotiations that led to
the execution of a bargaining contract; at its worst, it could
bring about the industrial strife and the production interruptions that the policy of the Act also seeks to avert.

. . . . The construction of Section 8(d)   . . .
serves also to simplify, and thus to speed, the bargaining
process. It eliminates the pressure upon the parties at the
time when a contract is being negotiated to raise those subjects that may not then be of controlling importance, but
which might in the future assume a more significant status.
It also assures to both unions and employers that, if future
conditions require some agreement as to matters about
which the parties have not sought, or have not been able to
obtain agreement, then some discussion of those matters will
be forthcoming when necessary.

Those two Board members would have placed the burden upon those
who would exclude mandatory subjects from continuing negotiation
expressly so to provide in the labor contract. (They also quoted an
example of such a "zipper" clause, in which both parties "waive" the
right to demand bargaining on any matter not dealt with in the contract, whether or not that matter was in their contemplation when
the contract was negotiated or signed.)

At the opposite pole was the view that there is no duty to bargain on any subject during the life of the contract except as its express provisions may demand. Section 8(d) was read thus to give
"stability and dignity to collective bargaining agreements."

[W]hen an employer and a labor organization have through
the processes of collective bargaining negotiated an agreement containing the terms and conditions of employment for
a definite period of time, their total rights and obligations
emanating from the employer-employee relationship should
remain fixed for that time. Stabilized therefore are the
rights and obligations of the parties with respect to all bargainable subjects whether the subjects are or are not specifically set forth in the contract. To hold otherwise and prescribe bargaining on unmentioned subjects would result in
continued alteration of the total rights and obligations under
the contract, thus rendering meaningless the concept of contract stability.

. . . . Many items are not mentioned in a collective bargaining agreement either because of concessions at
the bargaining table or because one of the parties may have
considered it propitious to forego raising one subject in the
hope of securing a more advantageous deal on another.
Subjects traded off or foregone should, under these circumstances, be as irrevocably settled as those specifically cover-

ed and settled by the agreement. To require bargaining on such subjects during midterm debases initial contract negotiations.

While the duty to bargain was conceded not to terminate altogether when a contract is executed, that duty was said to take the form simply of participating in the settlement of grievances which arise in the day-to-day administration of existing contract terms.

The "swing" member of the Board concluded that the employer was obligated to bargain about the creation of a pension plan, which was neither dealt with in the labor contract nor ever discussed in negotiations. On the proposal to have the employer pay all the costs of the insurance plan, however, that member studied the 1948 contract negotiations and discovered that the union had then made exactly that demand but withdrew it at a time when the employer agreed to an increase in insurance benefits (an agreement not reflected in the written bilateral contract). Although technically not "contained in" the contract, this understanding was certainly a "part of the contemporaneous 'bargain' " when that contract was signed.

. . . I believe that it would be an abuse of this Board's mandate to throw the weight of Government sanction behind the Union's attempt to disturb, in midterm, a bargain sealed when the original agreement was reached.

To hold otherwise would encourage a labor organization —or, in a Section 8(b)(3) case, an employer—to come back, time without number, during the term of a contract, to demand resumed discussion of issues which, although perhaps not always incorporated in the written agreement, the other party had every good reason to believe were put at rest for a definite period.

On appeal, no challenge was made to the Board's decision that the employer was free of any duty to bargain about the insurance program. But the court did enforce that part of the Board's order requiring the employer to bargain over the creation of a pension plan, since section 8(d) was not intended to relieve an employer "of the duty to bargain as to subjects which were neither discussed nor embodied in any of the terms and conditions of the contract."

There appear to be very few cases which have reached the Board and courts in which the employer has rejected a union demand for "premature" modification of contract terms, leading to a claim of violation of section 8(a)(5). In these situations, the *Jacobs* principle appears still to control. If the issue is "contained in" the contract, the employer need not bargain upon demand of the union. If the issue is not "contained in" the writing and was not discussed in negotiations, the employer must bargain upon demand. There is an exception to the duty to bargain on union demand when the union has "waived" this right, for example by a "zipper" clause in the contract.

In some cases, as in the *Jacobs* case itself, it may become both important and difficult to determine whether a term is "contained in" the contract. It is not at all clear whether the Board would today support the view of the "swing" member in *Jacobs* that an issue should be treated as "contained in" a contract whenever the union raises that issue in negotiations and then foregoes pressing it, at least when it secures some employer concession in exchange. That is tantamount to holding that the union "waives" the right to demand bargaining during the contract term about a modification on this issue when it is unsuccessful in securing a comparable term in prior negotiations. The Board's attitude on this question is in a state of flux, as is discussed below in the materials on "waiver." Surely the Board's traditional view would be that the union's failure to secure an express contract term on an issue is not tantamount to a clear intention to relinquish bargaining on that subject during the contract term. But this view may have been modified more recently, given the Board's greater willingness to defer to arbitral determinations in the context of section 8(a)(5) cases and given what may also be a greater willingness to find union waiver in its bargaining tradeoffs and in broad contract provisions (such as managements rights and so-called zipper clauses). See Radioear Corp. (1974).

It is also unclear whether the union may lawfully back its demand for a midterm modification by resorting to a strike. In many cases, the contract will itself forbid a strike during its term. But the question remains whether the Labor Act does. If the parties have expressly provided for "reopener" negotiations during the contract term on a particular issue, a strike over that issue is proper although it must of course comply with the notification and cooling-off requirements of section 8(d). NLRB v. Lion Oil Co. (U.S.1957). But if the union's demand for negotiation does not fall within a formal contract reopener provision, there is a question whether—even assuming the union notifies the employer and the appropriate mediation agencies, and waits sixty days—it may strike. Section 8(d)(4) bars a strike "for a period of sixty days after such notice is given or until the expiration date of such contract, whichever occurs later." Although a strike after sixty days but before the contract expires would appear to be illegal (technically a violation of section 8(b)(3)), the decisions give no clear answer. Compare United Packinghouse Workers (Wilson & Co.) (1950) (strike valid before contract expires provided sixty days have passed since notice to employer), with Local 3, Packinghouse Workers v. NLRB (8th Cir. 1954) (strike before contract expiration date, illegal). See also Milk Drivers Local 783 (Cream Top Creamery) (1964) (by implication, a strike which complies with notification requirements of section 8(d) is lawful, even during contract term). Since the Board has held that, to protect the union's privilege not to discuss matters "contained in" a contract, the employer violates section 8(a)(5) when it exerts economic pressure on the union to do so, C & S Indus. (1966), it might well be held that a union-induced strike during the contract term also violates the duty to bargain, at least as to matters "contained in" the contract.

Employer-Initiated Modifications During the Contract Term. The vast preponderance of cases which raise the question of the duty to bargain during the term of a labor contract deal not with union-initiated demands for bargaining but rather with employer unilateral action without first bargaining with the union. It should be noted once again that any duty not to take unilateral action during the contract term applies only to mandatory subjects, that is, "wages, hours and other terms and conditions of employment." The employer does not violate section 8(a)(5) when, during the term of a contract, it unilaterally alters or terminates altogether arrangements made with the union regarding nonmandatory subjects. The Supreme Court so held in Allied Chem. Workers v. Pittsburgh Plate Glass Co. (U.S. 1971). There, the employer and union had negotiated a health insurance plan that covered retired workers, and the employer without negotiating with the union contacted retirees individually to offer them the option to drop out of the negotiated plan and instead have the employer pay added premiums for supplemental Medicare coverage. The Court held that health insurance for workers already retired is not a subject of mandatory bargaining with the union representing workers currently employed. The Court thus concluded that the employer was free unilaterally to adjust that benefit for retirees. It also held that even if this would constitute a "modification" of the contract, there was no need for the employer to comply with the notification and cooling-off requirements of section 8(d) which the Court held applicable only to midterm modifications regarding mandatory subjects. The obligations to meet and confer under section 8(d)(2) and to notify mediation agencies under section 8(d)(3) were held to be altogether inapt to a dispute on an issue about which the employer was not obligated to bargain at all. The Court concluded that the union's remedy for a unilateral midterm modification on a permissive subject was an action for breach of the contract and not an unfair labor practice proceeding.

When the employer announces an intention to change the status quo on a mandatory subject, sections 8(a)(5) and 8(d) do play an important role. On occasion, the employer will accompany its announcement with an offer to the union to bargain; the change in working conditions is made only after the union refuses to bargain or after bargaining has reached an impasse. Whether such a post-impasse change is lawful depends once again upon whether the subject is "contained in" an existing labor agreement.

If the subject is "contained in" the agreement, it is illegal for the employer to alter working conditions in midterm—even if it has given notification to the union and to the appropriate mediation agencies and even if it has bargained to impasse. Section 8(d) clearly affords the union protection for the life of the contract against "any modification" against its will of provisions which it managed to have expressly embodied in the written agreement. To permit the employer to implement such modifications, after impasse or after a union refusal to bargain on that matter at all, would make a mockery of the directive in section 8(d) that neither party shall be required "to discuss or agree to" any proposal for midterm modification of "terms and conditions contained in a contract." C & S Indus., Inc. (1966) (unlawful to introduce incentive wage plan provisions, even assuming employer first made a sufficient offer to bargain). In short, the employer may modify a term "contained in" a labor contract only if it secures the consent of the union to do so; it is insufficient that it bargain to impasse with a union which remains intransigent and it is irrelevant that the employer asserts that the modifications are compelled by dire economic necessity. Oak Cliff-Golman Baking Co. (1974) (midterm wage reductions after notice to and discussions with union).

If, however, the employer during the contract term informs the union of its intention to change working conditions, and the conditions in question are not "contained in" the contract, the employer need not secure the union's consent to the change—but it is required to bargain with the union to impasse before it implements that change. Woodworkers Local 3–10 v. NLRB (Long Lake Lumber Co.) (D.C.Cir. 1967). This is merely the corollary of the union's power to demand bargaining upon a noncovered mandatory subject during the contract term, as sustained in the *Jacobs Mfg.* case. The few pertinent cases make it fairly clear that, if the employer's change in the status quo is deemed a "modification," it must not only notify and bargain with the union in good faith to impasse, but it must also comply with the other procedural requirements of section 8(d), at least the requirement of notice to the mediation agencies and presumably the requirement of a sixty-day waiting period from the date of notifying the union before implementing the modification. NLRB v. Huttig Sash & Door Co. (8th Cir. 1967) (midterm reduction in wage rates without bargaining and without giving section 8(d) notices; "Even if a genuine bargaining impasse had come about, this, on the facts here, does not eliminate the necessity of compliance with the notice provisions."); Kinard Trucking Co. (1965) (wage reductions implemented without notice are not only unilateral changes in violation of section 8(a)(5) but also "modifications" without complying with procedural requirements of section 8(d)). It has apparently not been held, however, that an employer's midterm modification as to matters not "contained in" the contract—after notification of the union and the mediation agencies, waiting sixty days and bargaining to impasse—will still violate section 8(a)(5) on the theory that section 8(d) requires the employer to continue in full force and effect   .   .   .   all the terms and conditions of the existing contract for a period of sixty days after such notice is given or until the expiration date of such contract, whichever occurs later.

The question whether any "modification" by the employer would be illegal prior to contract expiration, even after complying with the procedural requirements of section 8(d), was reserved by the Board in an early case. John W. Bolton & Sons (1950) (employer change from hourly pay to incentive pay, shortly after notice to union but refusal by union to bargain, violates section 8(d) because of failure to comply with section 8(d) procedures). The Board today is apparently willing to authorize such a midterm modification after negotiations, since its remedial orders in these cases merely require that the employer cease and desist from refusing to bargain about mandatory subjects.

Since an employer may implement changes after bargaining to impasse on terms not "contained in" the contract, but is forbidden to do so regarding "contained" terms, it may become important to determine whether a term or condition is "contained" in the contract. The Board has held that even though the subject of wage incentives is not expressly treated in the contract's wage provisions, "such incentives are inseparably bound up with and are thus plainly an aspect of the payment of wages, a subject expressly covered by the contract." Accordingly, the employer's implementation of a wage incentive plan was held to violate the employer's obligation under section 8(d) even on the assumption that the employer had given prior notice to the union but the union declined to bargain. C & S Indus., Inc. (1966). It has been determined, however, that a practice of long standing, such as a Monday-to-Friday workweek for a class of employees, will not be regarded as "contained in" the labor contract if not expressly reflected in its written terms; the employer is therefore not forbidden by section 8(d) to make a midterm modification in that practice provided it notifies and bargains with the union in advance. Woodworkers Local 3–10 v. NLRB (Long Lake Lumber Co.) (D.C.Cir. 1967). It is not clear whether a matter becomes "contained in" an agreement if proposals on that matter are made and then dropped (perhaps as a bargaining tradeoff) during negotiations leading to a contract.

Most of the litigated cases involving charges of refusal to bargain because of employer-initiated midterm modifications arise not in cases in which the employer first bargained with the union but in cases in which it did not. In such cases, it is unnecessary to determine whether the employer's action constitutes a "modification" of a term "contained in" a labor contract. For if it is, such a modification cannot be made even after bargaining to impasse, and the conduct is even more clearly unlawful when the employer has not bargained at all. Ibid. But even if it is not a "covered" contract term, the employer may implement a midterm change on a mandatory subject only after bargaining to impasse; to implement that change without bargaining at all is deemed a violation of the general duty under section 8(a)(5) to bargain on mandatory subjects before altering the status quo, quite apart from the notice and cooling-off requirements attendant upon a "modification" of a labor contract.

§ 15. Waiver of the Duty to Bargain

The duty to bargain is rooted in the congressional objective of requiring the employer to respect the union's status as representative of the employees in establishing wages and working conditions. Accordingly, there is little question that the union may enter into an agreement with the employer whereby, in exchange for some benefit the union desires, it relinquishes for a definite term its right to demand bargaining on all mandatory subjects. The union may "waive" the right during the contract term to raise new issues and make new demands, and may go yet further and agree not to challenge modifications made by the employer in working conditions without consulting the union. The employer does not refuse to bargain when it demands in contract negotiations that during the term of the contract the union is not to challenge employer decisions on such mandatory subjects as hiring, promotions, transfers, discharge and discipline, and work scheduling. Whether these subjects are to be handled "unilaterally" under a management rights clause, or by some method of bilateral determination, is itself a mandatory subject about which the parties must bargain in good faith and either party may insist to impasse in good faith. NLRB v. American Nat'l Ins. Co. (U.S.1952). In light of the great importance of protecting the union's representative status, however, the Board has been anxious to assure that "waiver" of the duty to bargain is done by the union consciously and clearly.

If, for example, the union agrees to an express contract clause which gives to the employer the power during the contract term, without further bargaining, to modify the amount of (or to terminate altogether) a regularly given Christmas bonus—a mandatory subject, the regularity and employee expectation making the bonus tantamount to wages—it would be unsound to permit the union to claim that a bonus modification was "unilateral" and illegal. Since the union had ceded that power to the employer, its exercise does not undermine the representative status of the union. Moreover, since the employer presumably secured the express reservation of power over the bonus only by making some concession of value to the union during the contract negotiations, the contract could not serve as a stabilizing influence if the union could during its term claim that it was entitled not only to the concession but also (through section 8(a)(5)) to claim that it was still entitled to the bonus. Thus, when the union has clearly "waived" its privilege to have the employer bargain on a particular subject during the contract term, enforcement of that waiver will further both the representational and contract-stability policies of the Labor Act.

In most litigated cases, however, the "waiver" is not made out quite so clearly, and two questions emerge: (1) Has the union indeed waived its privilege to require bargaining, either on union-initiated or employer-initiated modifications? (2) Since the question of waiver will normally turn upon an examination of the intention and understanding of the parties, and that will in turn depend upon an examination of the terms of the written contract and the history of negotiations, should the issue of waiver be determined by the National Labor Relations Board in a proceeding under section 8(a)(5) or by an arbitrator in an action for contract breach processed through the contract's grievance procedure? The law on these questions of substance and process is still in a state of evolution. Until recently, one could state with some confidence that the Board would assume for itself the task of determining whether there had been a "waiver" by the union and that it would find such a waiver only when the evidence clearly supported a finding that the union had knowingly and unequivocally relinquished to the employer its statutory privilege to demand bargaining on mandatory subjects during the contract term. More recently, however, the Board has expressed a preference to have union charges of unilateral action during the contract term processed through the grievance and arbitration provisions of the parties' contract. The Board has, in deference to a perceived national policy favoring the arbitral resolution of disputes concerning contract terms and bargaining history, deferred the exercise of its own jurisdiction under section 8(a)(5) in the expectation that submission of the dispute to arbitration will resolve—more expeditiously and through a mechanism freely designed by the parties themselves—the very dispute which lies at the heart of the unfair labor practice charge. This development, considered summarily immediately below, is treated in detail elsewhere in this work. By deferring to arbitration, where tenets of contract construction will quite commonly favor the employer more than will the "clear and unmistakable waiver" principle under the Labor Act, the Board is acquiescing in a modification of the substantive standard of "waiver" to a degree which some claim to constitute an abdication of the Board's function as a congressionally created administrative agency with a public charge.

The traditional test for union waiver of the right to bargain during the contract term is a most exacting one. In Beacon Piece Dyeing & Finishing Co. (1958), the Board stated:

[A]lthough the Board has . . . held repeatedly that statutory rights may be "waived" by collective bargaining, it has also said that such a waiver "will not readily be inferred" and that there must be "a clear and unmistakable showing" that the waiver occurred. The primary issue in this case, therefore, is whether the Union "clearly and unmistakably" waived or "bargained away" its statutory rights to bargaining on an increased workload and a general wage increase therefor.

And, in Press Co. (1958), the Board stated:

> It is well established Board precedent that, although a subject has been discussed in precontract negotiations and has not been specifically covered in the resulting contract, the employer violates Section 8(a)(5) of the Act if during the contract term he refuses to bargain, or takes unilateral action with respect to the particular subject, unless it can be said from an evaluation of the prior negotiations that the matter was "fully discussed" or "consciously explored" and the union "consciously yielded" or clearly and unmistakably waived its interest in the matter.

Although the Board during the 1950's and 1960's departed on occasion from this principle, it is fair to say that the great majority of cases dealing with the duty to bargain during the contract term reflect its application.

Since the duty to bargain is comprised of at least two obligations —the duty to negotiate on a mandatory subject when requested by the other party and the duty (most commonly that of the employer) not to institute unilateral changes in working conditions—the waiver concept may apply to both. A union might be held to waive its privilege to raise for discussion certain mandatory issues and to have the employer bargain in good faith to impasse; if so, the employer is free to disregard the union's bargaining request and to maintain the status quo. In a case of employer-initiated modification, a union waiver would authorize the employer "unilaterally" to modify working conditions without first notifying the union and bargaining to impasse. The former kind of waiver eliminates only the union's own right to precipitate an improvement in the lot of the employees beyond the status quo. The latter kind of waiver would go further and permit the employer unilaterally to withdraw employee benefits otherwise anticipated.

Given the few union-initiated modifications that have been litigated, there is sparse authority on the former kind of waiver. Presumably, it must be "clear and unequivocal," but it is possible that the Board would be more willing to find the kind of waiver that requires the union to tolerate the status quo than to find one which would authorize the employer to modify the status quo to the employees' disadvantage. This appears borne out by Jacobs Mfg. Co. (1951), enf'd (2d Cir. 1952), in which the "swing" member found a waiver of the union's privilege to demand mid-term negotiations on an employee insurance program because the union had made that same proposal during negotiations but apparently traded it off for some other employer concession; and even the two Board members most zealous of the bargaining rights of the union stated that such a waiver could have been effected by a so-called zipper or integration clause, whereby each party voluntarily and unqualifiedly waives the right, and each agrees that the other shall not be obligated, to bargain collectively regarding any matter whether or not covered in the contract.   Board decisions rendered at the same time indicate that neither a zipper clause nor foregoing a proposal during negotiations would have been held to be a waiver if the employer's violation of section 8(a)(5) was a unilateral modification of working conditions (rather than merely a refusal to discuss a union-initiated modification).

The vast preponderance of cases applying the "clear and unequivocal waiver" principle do indeed involve a charge that the employer unilaterally announced or implemented a change in the status quo without giving notice or an opportunity to bargain to the union. The Board—at least until recently—rather consistently required that a waiver be demonstrated only by proof that the union had consciously explored the issue in question during negotiations and unmistakably yielded to the employer the power to make changes on that subject unilaterally.   The employer typically asserted as a defense that the union had authorized the employer so to act, most commonly by agreeing to a management rights clause, a zipper or integration clause, a grievance and arbitration procedure (as a substitute for statutory procedures enforcing the duty to bargain), or some unwritten concession in the course of bargaining.   These alleged forms of waiver will be discussed in turn.   (Of course, the union can waive its right to complain in a yet more fundamental sense when, upon being notified of the employer's intention to take "unilateral" action, it neglects altogether to request bargaining on the matter.   NLRB v. Alva Allen Indus., Inc. (8th Cir. 1966).)

Management Rights and "Zipper" Clauses.   The clearest example of a waiver concerning an employer's "unilateral" action is an express contract clause clearly authorizing the employer to take that action.   Thus, in LeRoy Mach. Co. (1964), the Board held that the employer did not violate section 8(a)(5) when it instituted a policy, without bargaining with the union, of requiring physical examinations (by the employee's doctor at company expense) of employees with serious records of absenteeism, since the management rights clause of the contract gave to the company the specific right to determine "qualifications" for employment.   In Ador Corp. (1965), the employer without bargaining ceased manufacturing a particular line of its doors and windows and laid off the employees who had formerly done that work; no violation of the duty to bargain was found, since the management rights clause accorded the specific right to abolish or change jobs or products and to lay off employees for lack of work. And, in NLRB v. Honolulu Star-Bulletin, Inc. (9th Cir. 1967), where an explicit contract clause authorized the employer to make payments above salary, the employer was deemed authorized "unilaterally" to institute a bonus plan.

But sharp limits have been placed upon the extent to which the relinquishment of privileges to management will be treated as a waiver of the statutory right to challenge unilateral employer actions. First, the Board and courts will not conclude, from an express waiver on one subject, that the union has waived on others even though closely related. Thus, the Supreme Court has held, in NLRB v. C & C Plywood Corp. (U.S.1967), that a contract clause expressly giving the employer the power to pay at a premium rate above the contract wage rate "any particular employee for some special fitness, skill, aptitude or the like" could reasonably be found by the Board not to constitute a waiver regarding the employer's unilateral change in wage rate for an entire job classification. In Tide Water Assoc. Oil Co. (1949), although the contract had a management rights clause which gave to the company the power of decision on transferring, retiring, discharging and laying off employees, the Board found the employer to violate section 8(a)(5) by unilaterally modifying the employee retirement plan. Similarly, in Cloverleaf Div. of Adams Dairy Co. (1964), *enf't denied on other grounds* (8th Cir. 1965), where the employer had unilaterally terminated its own delivery operation and subcontracted the work to an independent contractor, the Board found this to constitute an illegal refusal to bargain, in spite of the fact that the union had earlier acquiesced in certain other changes in methods of operations, such as equalizing the volume of business on employee routes or adding a new customer to a route; the union did not by so acquiescing lose the power to challenge subcontracting or other "changes which alter the wages or other working conditions of employees in a substantial or unaccustomed way."

Second, and more commonly, the Board has refused to infer a waiver from a blanket management rights provision which fails to mention with specificity the subject on which the employer has taken unilateral action. Thus, in LeRoy Mach. Co. (1964), the contract contained the following very broad management rights provision:

> The Company retains the sole right to manage its business and direct the working force, . . . to determine whether and to what extent the work required in its business shall be performed by employees covered by this agreement . . . including the sole right . . . to hire, lay off, assign . . . employees . . . subject only to such regulations governing these rights as are expressly provided in the Agreement.
>
> The above rights of management are not all inclusive, but indicate the type of matters or rights which belong to

and are inherent to management. Any of the rights, powers, and authority the Company had prior to entering this
collective bargaining agreement are retained by the Company, except as expressly and specifically abridged, delegated,
granted, or modified by this Agreement.

Nonetheless, the Board concluded that the contract clause did not
with sufficient specificity authorize the employer to make unilateral
decisions on wage rates to be paid on newly created jobs. And, in
Proctor Mfg. Corp. (1961), where the contract said nothing about determining production quotas or piecework wage rates, and contained
a management rights clause reserving to the employer all rights not
expressly mentioned in the contract, the Board found that the union
had not waived its right to have notice of and an opportunity to bargain about the employer's newly established production quotas and
piece rates.

It is quite likely that, in a number of these cases, had the union
taken its claim of unilateral action to an arbitrator, alleging breach
of contract, the arbitrator would have read the managements rights
clause—along with a commonly endorsed theory of labor relations
that management retains all rights preexisting the contract that the
union does not expressly extract from management in a specific
clause—to permit the employer to take the action, and thus deny the
grievance. Largely for this reason—that the arbitrator's maxims of
contract construction are not necessarily responsive to the statutory
policies underlying the Board's waiver doctrine—the Board commonly accompanied its "clear and unmistakable waiver" theory with a refusal to decline its own jurisdiction in deference to the contractual
grievance procedures. (As is discussed below, this hesitancy appears
no longer to exist, at least for a majority of the Board's members.)

The same hostility toward waiver has been reflected in Board decisions in which the employer invoked a generalized "zipper" or integration clause in order to demonstrate that the union had waived its
privilege to challenge employer unilateral action during the contract
term. A zipper or integration clause purports to close out bargaining
during the contract term and to make the written contract the exclusive statement of the parties' rights and obligations. An example follows:

The parties acknowledge that during negotiations which
resulted in this Agreement, each had the unlimited right and
opportunity to make demands and proposals with respect to
any subject or matter of collective bargaining, and that the
understanding and agreements arrived at by the parties after the exercise of that right and opportunity are set forth in
this Agreement. Therefore, the Employer and the Union,
for the life of this Agreement, each voluntarily and unqualifiedly waives the right and each agree that the other shall

not be obligated to bargain collectively with respect to any subject matter not specifically referred to or covered in this Agreement, even though such subjects or matters may not have been within the knowledge or contemplation of either or both of the parties at the time they negotiated or signed this Agreement.

On occasion, the integration and waiver may be limited only to matters that were "discussed during the negotiation of this Agreement."

Such a provision may fairly be read to deprive the union of the privilege during the contract term to propose additions to the written contract and to require the employer to bargain about the union's proposals. Jacobs Mfg. Co. (1951), enf'd (2d Cir. 1952). But the clause has been held not to cede clearly and unequivocally to the employer the power to make unilateral changes in the status quo, and thus possibly to modify plant practices to the detriment of the employees, without notice to and bargaining with the union. Thus, in New York Mirror (1965), the Board held that a decision to shutdown and sell the assets of a newspaper company was a mandatory subject and that the employer had unlawfully failed to give notice to and consult with the union before announcing and implementing its decision. A contractual zipper clause was held insufficient evidence of a union waiver of the right to receive notice and to discuss the employer-initiated proposal to impasse. Nor was a zipper clause sufficient, even in the context of other possible acts of union waiver, to excuse an employer's decision without bargaining to reduce the amount of a Christmas bonus traditionally given to employees. Beacon Journal Pub. Co. (1967), enf'd in relevant part (6th Cir. 1968) (zipper clause stated generally that conditions of employment were limited to those set forth in the contract; moreover, employer assured union negotiators that zipper clause was designed to close off employee claims regarding sick pay and was not directed to the Christmas bonus).

Concessions During Negotiations. Apart from express contract provisions which arguably cede to the employer the power to make changes in working conditions without bargaining, such a waiver has also been found—although rarely—in concessions made by the union at the bargaining table. A company may, for example, have a long-standing practice of awarding a Christmas bonus to employees each year; the union may seek during negotiations to secure a provision in the contract (expressly addressed to the bonus or a more general maintenance-of-benefits clause) which would obligate the employer to pay the bonus during the contract term. If the union fails to secure such a contract provision, either because the employer simply refuses to concede or because the union trades off that demand for some other concession granted by the employer, the employer may argue that it is free thereafter "unilaterally" to discontinue the bonus since the negotiations show a union waiver of the duty to bargain. The Board has in the past generally declined to find a waiver and has instead held that the employer violates section 8(a)(5) by discontinuing the bonus without bargaining. The Board has held, in Press Co. (1958):

> It is well established Board precedent that, although a subject has been discussed in precontract negotiations and has not been specifically covered in the resulting contract, the employer violates Section 8(a)(5) of the Act if during the contract term he refuses to bargain, or takes unilateral action with respect to the particular subject, unless it can be said from an evaluation of the prior negotiations that the matter was "fully discussed" or "consciously explored" and the union "consciously yielded" or clearly and unmistakably waived its interest in the matter.

The Board gives several reasons for its conclusion that the union's failure to secure a contract limitation on a matter does not constitute an authorization to the employer to change the status quo without bargaining. First, it is sometimes held that the union has a statutory right to require the employer to bargain and to refrain from unilateral action, and that its failure to have that right written into the contract as well (as a cumulative mode of enforcement) does not oust it of the right already given by the law. Timken Roller Bearing Co. v. NLRB (6th Cir. 1963) (employer must disclose information necessary to union in processing grievances, despite union's proposal and then withdrawal of contract clause requiring disclosure of information). Second, in cases where the union's proposal is that the employer continue to grant a benefit as in the past unless the union during the contract term affirmatively consents to discontinuance, the union's foregoing of this proposal only means that it is willing to relinquish a veto power over the employer's decision; it does not also demonstrate a clear intention to relinquish the right to bargain to impasse. Cloverleaf Div. of Adams Dairy Co. (1964) (union failed to press its proposal that prior to making changes in operations affecting employees, the employer was to notify the union, discuss the proposed changes and not to make such changes until they are "mutually agreed upon"). Third, in cases where the union's proposal is that a benefit be fixed for the contract term, the employer's refusal to agree and the union's willingness to acquiesce may mean simply that the parties do not intend to have the employer contractually liable on that matter on the merits; while the employer is not bound to grant that benefit throughout the contract term, and may modify it, there is no clear relinquishment by the union of its right to have the employer first bargain to impasse before doing so. Beacon Piece Dyeing & Finishing Co. (1958). Fourth, the Board has considered the disruptive impact on negotiations that would flow from the rule suggested by the employer in these cases. In Beacon Piece Dyeing & Finishing Co., *ibid.*, the Board noted:

[I]t would encourage employers to firmly resist inclusion in contracts of as many subjects as possible, with a view to such resistance giving them a right of unilateral action thereafter on all subjects excluded from the contract, thereby impeding the collective-bargaining process and creating an atmosphere which inevitably would lead to more strikes; and . . . it would discourage unions from presenting *any* subject in negotiations, for a simple refusal by the employer to agree to the demand on the subject would leave the union in the unhappy dilemma of either giving up the demand and thereby losing its bargaining rights on the subject, or striking in support of the demand—this too would seriously impede the collective bargaining process and lead to more strikes.

The union, fearing that forgoing its position on an issue would authorize unilateral action, would be inclined to become adamant about issues which more sensibly should be left for resolution later in the parties' dealings or, conversely, to become reluctant to raise issues which it would be wise for the parties to address immediately.

For these reasons, the Board in a number of cases involving Christmas bonuses held, in the 1950's and 1960's, that the union's bargaining-table conduct did not constitute a waiver of the statutory right to demand bargaining prior to discontinuation of a traditional bonus. *E. g.*, New Orleans Bd. of Trade, Ltd. (1965). Most strikingly, the Board (with court approval) found no waiver where the employer has insisted over the years that the Christmas bonus was purely voluntary and the union never expressly disputed this claim, and where the union in the most recent negotiations had failed to secure a contract provision requiring the employer to grant the bonus and had acceded to the inclusion of a zipper clause. Beacon Journal Pub. Co. (1967), *enf'd in relevant part* (6th Cir. 1968). The Board and courts did, however, in some relatively early cases, sustain a claim of waiver in negotiations. In Speidel Corp. (1958), a bonus case with facts very much like those of *Beacon Journal, ibid.,* the Board concluded that the union had acquiesced in the employer's position that the bonus was a management prerogative which could be discontinued at any time without bargaining. And in NLRB v. Nash-Finch Co. (8th Cir. 1954), the court reversed a Board finding that the employer had unlawfully terminated insurance and bonus benefits. The Board had held that the employer's refusal in negotiations to agree to a "maintenance of benefits" provision meant only that there was no contract obligation to pay the insurance and bonus benefits but did not mean that they could be discontinued without first consulting with the union. The court, however, found that in substance the employer had bargained for complete freedom to discontinue those benefits, since the union had failed to secure an express contract limitation.

As will be noted in greater detail shortly below, the Board appears to have retreated somewhat from its traditional view that union conduct in negotiations will make out a waiver only if it has consciously explored a subject and consciously yielded unilateral control to the employer. As part of a general willingness to resolve unfair labor practice issues through the use of machinery and standards appropriate to cases of contract breach, the Board appears more willing than in the past to shift the burden somewhat to the union to preserve its statutory privilege against unilateral action by securing contract concessions from the employer. Thus, in Radioear Corp. (1974), the Board permitted the employer to terminate a holiday bonus because the union had agreed to a zipper clause in the contract while failing to secure a maintenance-of-benefits provision.

Arbitration Clauses. Since the issue of union waiver of the right to challenge alleged unilateral acts by the employer will commonly turn upon examination of contract provisions, most commonly management rights and "zipper" clauses, and upon an examination of negotiating history, the employer has commonly argued that these are matters not for the Board but rather for a privately-selected arbitrator. It is said that the parties' rights turn principally upon construction of the collective bargaining agreement and not of the Labor Act, and that during the life of the contract the duty to bargain collectively concerning working conditions is discharged when disputes are adjusted through the grievance and arbitration procedure. In effect, the employer has argued that an agreed-upon grievance procedure is equivalent to a "waiver" of the union's right to challenge unilateral action before the Board as an unfair labor practice.

Until recently, this argument was rather consistently rejected by the Board. As a threshold matter, even the employer could not argue—at least after two Supreme Court decisions of 1967—that the existence of grievance machinery and arbitration, and the pertinence of a construction of the labor agreement, actually divested the Board of jurisdiction to decide the case under section 8(a)(5). In Acme Industrial Co. (U.S.1967), the Court held that the union was entitled by section 8(a)(5) to secure information for purposes of processing a contract grievance, even though the employer argued that the issue of the right to information could itself be presented to an arbitrator under the contract's grievance procedure. The same year, in NLRB v. C & C Plywood Corp. (U.S.1967), the Court held that the Board had jurisdiction over a claim of unlawful unilateral action—a general wage increase for "glue spreaders"—even though this would require the Board to construe, as evidence of union waiver, a contract provision authorizing the employer to pay particular employees at a premium rate as a reward for special skills. Although the C & C Plywood contract had no arbitration clause, the Board's jurisdiction over section 8(a)(5) cases involving contract construction was promptly sustained even in the presence of an arbitration provision, by a court of appeals in NLRB v. Huttig Sash & Door Co. (8th Cir. 1967), and that jurisdiction has not been seriously questioned since.

The Board has not traditionally been reluctant to assert this jurisdiction to the fullest, in spite of a contractual dispute-resolution machinery said to be a substitute for, or waiver of, collective bargaining. Relatively early, in Beacon Piece Dyeing & Finishing Co. (1958), the Board strictly applied the "clear and unmistakable waiver" doctrine and held that the duty to bargain is not satisfied by the substitution of a contractual grievance procedure unless that procedure clearly and unmistakably makes mention of such an intended substitution— which, of course, few if any grievance procedures actually do. Even after the Board's receptivity to arbitration had expanded considerably, it still was prepared to conclude, in C & S Indus., Inc. (1966):

> Although it lies in the discretion of the Board to defer to arbitration, we do not regard the controversy before us as one calling for our exercise of such discretion. Here we do not have an issue which, although cast in unfair labor practice terms, is essentially one involving a contract dispute, making it reasonably probable that arbitration will put the statutory infringement finally at rest in a manner sufficient to effectuate the policies of the Act. Nor does resolution of the unfair labor practice issue here involved primarily turn on an interpretation of specific contractual provisions of ambiguous meaning, within the special competence of an arbitrator to determine. Nor has either party placed this dispute before an arbitrator or secured an award passing upon any of the issues here raised.

The Board's decision, however, attested to the significance of contract interpretation, for it held that the employer's introduction of an incentive wage plan constituted a "modification" of the contract (subject to the notification requirements of section 8(d)), wage incentives being "bound up with" the contract's express wage provisions, and that the contract also contained an express prohibition of any unilateral employer change in method of payment. See Unit Drop Forge Div., Eaton Yale & Towne, Inc. (1968), enf'd in relevant part (7th Cir. 1969) (Board decided case and found employer refusal to bargain, in face of specific clauses of contract alleged to authorize employer action, zipper clause, and arbitration provision). This disinclination to defer to arbitration was endorsed by the court of appeals in NLRB v. Huttig Sash & Door Co. (8th Cir. 1967), where the Board asserted jurisdiction to declare illegal a midterm wage reduction in the face of a contract clause concerning changed wage rates, a broad management rights clause and a grievance and arbitration procedure. The court compared the Supreme Court decisions earlier that year in Acme and C & C Plywood to the case before it, and concluded:

> The same need for avoiding inordinate delay in the recognition and implementation of a labor organization's

rights; the same recognition that there may be more than one way to settle a labor dispute; the same emphasis upon preserving rights statutorily expressed; the obvious effectiveness of the Board remedy here; the possible need to obtain it eventually anyway; Acme's emphasis . . . on the peculiar nature of the relationship between the Board and the arbitration process, and upon § 10(a) of the Act, 29 U.S.C. § 160(a); and the same desirability of not rendering unavailable the Board's expertise in its traditional area, all bear upon this aspect of the jurisdictional problem and prompt us to conclude that the presence of a contract provision for both grievance procedure and arbitration does not eliminate Board jurisdiction of an unfair labor practice charge in the present context.

Board Deference; Waiver Redefined. The Board has recently expressed a much greater willingness to give "hospitable acceptance" to arbitration awards after their rendition and even to arbitration procedures in advance of their utilization, where deference will put to rest the unfair labor practice issue as well. Contemporaneously, and for similar reasons, the Board has reassessed its substantive position on union waivers, and it is now much more willing to find a waiver on the basis of bargaining compromises by the union and general provisions in the labor contract.

The Board's jurisdictional relationship to that of the arbitrator is discussed elsewhere in this work in detail. At this point it suffices to say that in 1971, the Board decided Collyer Insulated Wire in which it was claimed that the employer had made several midterm modifications in work assignments and wage rates without bargaining with the union. The employer justified its action under a specific contract provision dealing with changes in pay rates and a management rights clause, and announced its willingness to submit the dispute to arbitration. The Board, in a split decision, maintained jurisdiction but stayed its exercise pending submission of the dispute to the arbitrator, since

> [D]isputes such as these can better be resolved by arbitrators with special skill and experience in deciding matters arising under established bargaining relationships than by the application by this Board of a particular provision of our statute.

The Board noted that the collective bargaining relationship between the company and the union had been long and productive; that the unilateral action taken was not designed to undermine the union; that the employer's action "is based on a substantial claim of contractual privilege"; that the employer has agreed to arbitrate under a provision "unquestionably broad enough to embrace this dispute"; and that "The contract and its meaning . . . lie at the center of this dispute." The Board would reassert jurisdiction only if arbitration did not proceed promptly or if, after an arbitration award was rendered, it proved to be "repugnant to the policies of the Act." In a later case, it was charged that the employer had unlawfully promulgated a rule requiring union representatives to report their movements in the plant while processing grievances. The Board extended the *Collyer* principle and deferred the case to arbitration, even though there were simultaneous charges of employer antiunion animus and even though the contract contained no provision clearly addressed to the power of the employer unilaterally to promulgate the rule in question. National Radio Co. (1972).

In Board cases arising after an arbitrator has sustained under the contract employer "unilateral" changes, the Board has deferred to the arbitral decision even though the authorization held to have been given by the union under the contract would not likely satisfy the Board's traditional criteria for a "clear and unequivocal waiver." For example, in Valley Ford Sales, Inc. (1974), over a lengthy dissent tracing the history of the "clear and unequivocal waiver" principle, the Board majority dismissed a complaint under section 8(a)(5) charging the employer with the unilateral abolition of a wage incentive plan. Without addressing on the merits the issue of waiver, the Board simply held that the arbitration proceeding was fair and the award not repugnant to the Act. The arbitrator had found that the union waived its right to object to the abolition of the plan, and he relied on the management rights provisions, the union's failure to bargain concerning the plan in a number of contract negotiations, the union's failure to challenge earlier actions by the employer modifying or discontinuing the plan, and the employer's implementation of other incentive plans without objections or negotiations. And in National Radio Co. (1973), when the Board was asked after an arbitral award to assert jurisdiction and find unlawful the employer's announcement of a rule requiring reporting by union grievance processors, the Board dismissed the complaint, even though the arbitrator had not directly addressed the issue of unilateral change but only that of antiunion discrimination. The Board held that the award effectively put to rest the unfair labor practice issue and that in any event the union had not asked the arbitrator to resolve the unilateral-change issue. In effect, the Board found a waiver when the union failed to press its refusal-to-bargain claim during a pending arbitration proceeding; it is unlikely that in earlier days this would have been treated as tantamount to a knowing concession by the union of the employer's authority to act unilaterally. Finally, in Southwestern Bell Tel. Co. (1974), the arbitrator had sustained the union's claim that the employer's unilateral changes in shifts and seniority violated the agreement, but he issued no remedy other than a declaratory judgment. The Board dismissed the complaint under section 8(a)(5). Over a dissenting opinion which argued that the unilateral act had caused harm to the union which could be remedied only by an affirmative cease and desist order, the majority found that the employer was prepared to honor the arbitrator's declaration and that the purposes of the Labor Act would be satisfied even without a Board order.

In the course of staying its hand, and requiring the parties to exhaust the contractual grievance machinery, the Board has also developed a more flexible substantive test for union waiver of the duty to bargain. In Radioear Corp. (1973), the Board stated:

> The Trial Examiner . . . [relied] on the principle that there must be a "clear and unequivocal" waiver of the right involved. We do not agree. Where the parties, as here, have engaged in the collective-bargaining process, as contemplated by the statute, and have executed a collective-bargaining agreement, setting forth the terms of their bargain, we are unwilling to ignore what has taken place at the bargaining table and decide the parties' dispute on the basis of a simplistic formula arrived at by this Board.

The Board noted that the union might fairly be held to have given up its right to complain of employer unilateral action even without a clear and unequivocal waiver:

> The answer does not, in our view, call for a rigid rule, formulated without regard for the bargaining postures, proposals, and agreements of the parties, but rather, more appropriately, should take into consideration such varied factors as (a) the precise wording of, and emphasis placed upon, any zipper clause agreed upon; (b) other proposals advanced and accepted or rejected during bargaining; (c) the completeness of the bargaining agreement as an "integration"—hence the applicability or inapplicability of the parol evidence rule; and (d) practices by the same parties, or other parties, under other collective-bargaining agreements.

The Board thus clearly appeared to make the issue of waiver congruent with the issue of the parties' mutual intentions, traditionally addressed by arbitrators but without the "overlay" of public policy embodied in section 8(a)(5) which had formerly dictated that the waiver be "clear and unequivocal."

At a later stage of the *Radioear* case (1974), the Board held that its elaborated criteria applied not only to testing an arbitral award but also to passing upon a refusal to bargain charge when confronted initially and directly by the Board itself. In *Radioear*, the employer after many years of paying $30 as "turkey money" on Thanksgiving and Christmas, refused to do so during the term of the first contract negotiated with the union. The bonus was not discussed during the negotiations and was not mentioned in the contract, which did however contain a zipper clause whereby "the Union agrees that the

Company shall not be obligated to bargain collectively with respect to any subject or matter not specifically referred to or covered in this agreement." The union had attempted during negotiations to insert a clause preserving all existing benefits, but the employer refused. The Board deferred the unilateral-change issue to the arbitrator, but when he expressly declined to deal with it the Board reasserted jurisdiction and, on these facts, found "that there was here a conscious, knowing waiver of any bargaining obligation as to nonspecified benefits such as the 'turkey money' bonus." The Board placed great weight on the zipper clause and on the union's failure to secure a maintenance-of-standards clause. It concluded:

> We do not have here evidence of unconscionable over-reaching by the Respondent in the bargaining process, nor any concealment of existing benefits which might make an application of the clause near fraudulent, or any other circumstances which persuade us that we should interfere with the integrity of what appears, in all respects, to have been an openly arrived at, fairly bargained, agreement.

It is precarious to predict the course of future Board decisions on the issue of waiver of the duty to bargain. The Board in its recent decisions has been consistently divided—both on the issue of Board deference to arbitration and on the issue of "clear and unequivocal waiver"—and not only does the Board's composition change with some frequency but also the views of the courts of appeals have not been widely articulated. What can be said is that in the late 1950's and 1960's, the Board—in the interests of protecting the union's statutory rights against inadvertent sacrifice—applied a standard for waiver which was difficult to satisfy and which rather clearly departed from the standards utilized in grievance arbitration. The Board was less willing to find a waiver in general management rights and integration clauses of the contract and in union tradeoffs in bargaining negotiations. For this reason, the Board was reluctant as well to channel the union's claim of unilateral action exclusively through the contract's arbitration machinery. So far in the 1970's, however, the Board—imbued with the spirit of recent Supreme Court decisions extolling the virtues of private arbitration—has been inclined to permit the arbitrator first to address issues which may well resolve the section 8(a)(5) case, even if there is no explicit clause on which the employer relies as a defense and even if the arbitrator's remedies are not precisely those which the Board would issue. In the process, the Board has liberalized its tests for waiver, holding in effect that if "contract construction" by an examination of the written agreement, negotiating history and past practices demonstrates that employer action is not a breach of contract, it will not likely be a violation of section 8(a)(5) either. This represents a dramatic modification of the Board's attitudes, and only time will tell whether the courts will endorse it and the Board itself will adhere to it.

§ 16. Bargaining-Table Conduct: Generally

Section 8(d) of the Labor Act includes within the duty to bargain "the performance of the mutual obligation . . . to . . . confer in good faith with respect to wages, hours, and other terms and conditions of employment." Certain "objective" conduct at or away from the bargaining table is generally condemned automatically as a refusal to bargain. Examples, discussed earlier, are a refusal to meet at all, a refusal to reduce to writing an agreement already reached and a "unilateral" alteration of working conditions without discussion with the other party. Since such actions can be justified rarely if at all and since they are so destructive of the collective bargaining relationship, they are presumed unlawful and are often referred to as per se violations of the Labor Act. But a party may just as severely repudiate the principles of collective bargaining while meeting with the other party, promising to execute any agreement reached and refraining from making unilateral changes in working conditions. Such a party may come to the bargaining table and "go through the motions" of discussing proposals and counterproposals while intending in fact to disrupt negotiations or to frustrate agreement. It is for this reason that section 8(d) requires not simply that the parties "confer" but also that they confer "in good faith." The Act requires that the parties bargain with a subjective state of mind—one receptive to the adjustment of differences and to joint responsibility for the determination of wages and other working conditions. Since parties which meet the objective standards of "conferring" but which harbor a subjective desire to frustrate negotiations and reject collective bargaining will not normally articulate that desire for others to hear, the usual mode of proving bad faith is by inference from the substantive positions of the parties at the bargaining table.

Before 1947, the Labor Act imposed no express requirement of "good faith"; it simply required the employer, in then section 8(5), to "bargain collectively" with the exclusive representative. Nonetheless, the Board early came to construe that section to require not simply the "mere meeting" with the union but also the "serious intent to adjust differences and to reach an acceptable common ground." For fear that this would require a party actually to make compromises which it in good faith believed important not to make—and which it had sufficient economic strength to resist making—Congress expressly imposed a good-faith requirement in section 8(d) in 1947 but added that "such obligation does not compel either party to agree to a proposal or require the making of a concession." Congress sought to foster free collective bargaining by parties desirous of reaching an agreement but otherwise "unrestricted by any governmental power to regulate the substantive solution of their differences." NLRB v. Insurance Agents' Int'l Union (U.S.1960).

The Board was not to sit as judge of the concessions, proposals and counterproposals either party may or may not make.

The Board's dilemma in cases demanding an investigation of subjective good faith soon became apparent. Its task was, in the words of a leading opinion, NLRB v. Reed & Prince Mfg. Co. (1st Cir. 1953) to make the determination

> whether it is to be inferred from the totality of the employer's conduct that he went through the motions of negotiation as an elaborate pretense with no sincere desire to reach an agreement if possible, or that it bargained in good faith but was unable to arrive at an acceptable agreement with the union.

But the Board's determination was to be made while complying with the congressional directive not to require the making of concessions, the resolution of differences or the making of an agreement. As the court of appeals in *Reed & Prince* decided:

> It is true . . . that the Board may not "sit in judgment upon the substantive terms of collective bargaining agreements." But at the same time it seems clear that if the Board is not to be blinded by empty talk and by the mere surface motions of collective bargaining, it must take some cognizance of the reasonableness of the positions taken by an employer in the course of bargaining negotiations.

The court was forced to conclude that some perusal of the parties' substantive bargaining positions is inevitable:

> Thus if an employer can find nothing whatever to agree to in an ordinary current-day contract submitted to him, or in some of the union's related minor requests, and if the employer makes not a single serious proposal meeting the union at least part way, then certainly the Board must be able to conclude that this is at least some evidence of bad faith, that is, of a desire not to reach an agreement with the union. In other words, while the Board cannot force an employer to make a "concession" on any specific issue or to adopt any particular position, the employer is obliged to make *some* reasonable effort in *some* direction to compose his differences with the union, if § 8(a)(5) is to be read as imposing any substantial obligation at all.

The Board and courts continue to hold that it is proper to consider whether "in all the circumstances" the parties' conduct reveals a subjective state of mind set upon disrupting negotiations or frustrating agreement, and that a bargaining position on one or more subjects may—even if not in itself sufficient evidence—in context justify an inference of bad-faith bargaining. Continental Ins. Co. v.

NLRB (2d Cir. 1974).   The context which the Board studies may be comprised of conduct, statements, bargaining history, unfair labor practices and bargaining proposals.   Architectural Fiberglass (1967). The Board has considered animosity demonstrated by the employer against the union even before it was elected the bargaining representative, "M" System, Inc. (1960); or before negotiations began, NLRB v. My Store, Inc. (7th Cir. 1965).   See NLRB v. Reed & Prince Mfg. Co. (1st Cir. 1953) (Board may take judicial notice of record in prior unfair labor practice proceedings against employer, as probative of bad faith in bargaining.)   It is improper, however, to consider isolated incidents of past misconduct which are not part of a company scheme.   Collins & Aikman Corp. v. NLRB (4th Cir. 1968) (supervisors, on their own initiative, interrogated employees and solicited withdrawal from union).   As will be discussed immediately below, the Board has placed special weight—in finding bad faith "in all the circumstances"—upon a party's unyielding insistence upon unusually harsh substantive bargaining positions.

On the whole, the Board has been sustained in its factual findings of bad faith, although there has been some inclination on the part of the courts of appeals to read the record somewhat more charitably toward the respondent.   This more charitable disposition is often accompanied by a piece-by-piece examination of the respondent's conduct, with each "piece" abstracted from its context, in contrast to the Board's prevailing practice of viewing each piece in the context of a broad range of employer conduct.   See NLRB v. General Elec. Co. (2d Cir. 1969) (".   .   .   compounded like a mosaic of many pieces, but depending not on any one alone").   Some courts have been inclined to remind the Board that "Adamant insistence on a bargaining position   .   .   .   is not in itself a refusal to bargain in good faith."   Chevron Oil Co. v. NLRB (5th Cir. 1971).   The judicial concern for free collective bargaining was eloquently put in a noted decision, NLRB v. Herman Sausage Co. (5th Cir. 1960):

> If the insistence is genuinely and sincerely held, if it is not mere window dressing, it may be maintained forever though it produce a stalemate.   Deep conviction, firmly held and from which no withdrawal will be made, may be more than the traditional opening gambit of a labor controversy.   It may be both the right of the citizen and essential to our economic legal system   .   .   .   of free collective bargaining. The Government, through the Board, may not subject the parties to direction either by compulsory arbitration or the more subtle means of determining that the position is inherently unreasonable, or unfair, or impracticable, or unsound.

As a court put it more recently, in reversing a Board finding of employer bad faith in bargaining:

> In our opinion the matter at hand resolves itself into purely a question of hard bargaining between two parties

who were possessed of disparate economic power: A relatively weak Union encountered a relatively strong Company. The Company naturally desired to use its advantage to retain as many rights as possible. We do not believe, however, that that desire is inconsistent with good faith bargaining.

Chevron Oil Co. v. NLRB (5th Cir. 1971). But even those courts which reverse Board conclusions of bad faith bargaining, as unsupported by the record considered as a whole, are quick to add, as did the court in NLRB v. Cummer-Graham Co. (5th Cir. 1960):

> We do not hold that under no possible circumstances can the mere content of various proposals and counter proposals of management and union be sufficient evidence of a want of good faith to justify a holding to that effect.

It has also been held, with judicial approval, that bad-faith bargaining may be found as to only a single issue of mandatory bargaining, and that in such a case an unfair labor practice will result in spite of good-faith bargaining on all other issues and a willingness to reach an overall agreement. United Steelworkers of America v. NLRB (Roanoke Iron & Bridge Works) (D.C.Cir. 1968) (employer refusal to grant dues checkoff, with object of ridding itself of the union).

§ 17. Adamance and Refusal to Concede

Section 8(d) provides that the duty to bargain in good faith does not "compel either party to agree to a proposal or require the making of a concession." It thus acknowledges that good faith is consistent with stubbornness and with an unwillingness to yield a position that can be backed by economic staying power in the event of strike or lockout. There can thus be little doubt that "Adamant insistence on a bargaining position . . . is not in itself a refusal to bargain in good faith." Chevron Oil Co. v. NLRB (5th Cir. 1971). But the Board is likely to find that adamance is some evidence of bad faith when it is combined with certain other bargaining-table conduct.

The Board will be skeptical, for example, of the employer's good faith if it consistently turns down every union proposal without giving any reasons, or with the mere assertion of some vague principle about which there can be no meaningful discourse. As the court noted in NLRB v. Reed & Prince Mfg. Co. (1st Cir. 1953): "[I]t may be wondered how the Company could in good faith ever expect to arrive at an agreement if the major proposals submitted by the Union are refused on principle and assent on the minor ones is withheld as a matter of bargaining technique." The Board and the courts may also find bad faith when the employer proposes and insists upon a set of proposals which are "predictably unacceptable" by any "self-respecting union," for this looks as though the proponent is not interested in furthering discussions but rather in stalling or disrupting negotiations. The Board has also stated, in Procter & Gamble Mfg. Co. (1966):

> [R]igid adherence to proposals, which are predictably unacceptable to the employee representative, may be considered in proper circumstances as evidencing a predetermination not to reach agreement, or a desire to produce a stalemate as a means of frustrating bargaining and undermining the statutory representative.

(Apparently neither Board nor court has explained why it is that a strong employer may not lawfully force a weak union to accept contract proposals which are "predictably unacceptable" to the latter. There appear to be no cases where a strong union was held to have bargained in bad faith by taking an adamant stance, backed by a strike, on proposals which were "predictably unacceptable" to the employer.) The Board has in fact found that an employer's insistence on a wage figure—when there was extrinsic evidence before the Board that the employer was indeed prepared to compromise—was in bad faith, since the employer's adamance was based not on a belief that its position was fair but rather upon a desire to convince the union that no further wage concessions were forthcoming, thus stalemating the negotiations. Cincinnati Cordage & Paper Co. (1963).

Of course, the Board will be aided in inferring bad faith from the employer's adamance in those rare instances when the employer actually verbalizes its intention to repudiate the union and frustrate the negotiations. In NLRB v. Denton (5th Cir. 1954), the Board treated as a material factor in determining bad faith the employer's making of a number of meager concessions required by law (*e. g.*, recognition, overtime pay and health and safety) and its refusal to grant any wage increase or to accede to union demands on grievance procedure, union security, dues checkoff, and paid vacations and holidays. On appeal, the court stated that such refusals to make concessions cannot in themselves be deemed to constitute bad faith, but it endorsed the Board's finding of illegality in the context of other employer hostility, including statements prior to bargaining that he "would never sign a contract with any union." In a more recent case, the employer's adamance on noneconomic issues was found illegal, in light of the employer's warning to the union that it would never agree to a contract which included such items as arbitration, checkoff, senioritybidding, safety committee and penalty clauses, and the employer's further statement that he was out to "break" the union. Wal-Lite Div. of United States Gypsum Co. (1972), *enf'd denied* (8th Cir. 1973) (court discounted the employer's statements, noting that they were isolated and made seven months before negotiations began and more than six months—the statutory limitations period—before the filing of the charge). While it might be argued that such statements evidencing pre-bargaining rigidity are not to be considered in determining an unfair labor practice, in view of section 8(c) of the Act protecting "the expressing of any views, argument, or opinion," the Board has rather consistently given them weight in order to "shed light on and explain Respondent's subsequent bargaining intransigence." *Ibid.* It is doubtful that any court would take exception to this general principle. See NLRB v. General Elec. Co. (2d Cir. 1969) (court finds employer statements concerning its intention to be firm in bargaining to fall without the shelter of section 8(c), which forbids only reliance on "irrelevant" employer statements).

Perhaps the most widely noted case on the question of adamance at the bargaining table is that growing out of a dispute in 1960 between the General Electric Company and the International Union of Electrical, Radio and Machine Workers (IUE). That year, General Electric was negotiating with the international union on behalf of all employees represented by its locals at the company's many plants. In formulating its bargaining position, the company solicited the views of its local management on the benefits desired and expected by the workforce, researched the costs and effectiveness, and attempted to arrive at a proposal which it could afford and would satisfy the employees. It then embarked upon a substantial publicity campaign, in various media, designed to convince the employees that its proposals —which it described as a "fair, firm offer"—were in the employees' best interests and would be granted without the artificial exchange of extravagant demands and feigned stinginess that characterizes conventional bargaining. The company claimed that credit for such a desirable proposal should be its own (rather than having the union claim credit for wringing it out of an unwilling employer) and that changes would not be made in the company's firm offer merely because the union disliked it but only if the union could convince the employer that its calculations had been wrong. (This strategy has been called Boulwarism, after the then vice president for personnel relations at General Electric.) In the negotiations that followed, which led to a strike, the company adhered to its "firm, fair offer" in all but the most trivial respects, and announced on a few occasions that any modification in its position would cause it to look foolish in the eyes of the employees with whom it had been communicating in its publicity campaign.

The Board, with judicial approval, found that a number of specific actions by the General Electric Company violated section 8(a)(5). These included a refusal to disclose certain information requested by the union concerning the costs of employee benefits proposed by the company, and an attempt to bargain separately and directly with local unions on matters that were properly the subject of national negotiations. The decision went further, however, and found an "overall failure to bargain in good faith" based upon a "totality of the circumstances." The central components of that "totality" were the company's "take-it-or-leave-it" position and its publicity campaign directed at the employees.   NLRB v. General Elec. Co. (2d Cir. 1969).

The case evoked three opinions from the three-judge panel of the court of appeals.   The opinion for the majority held that the company's adamance from the outset and its publicity campaign justified a finding of bad faith, since the campaign constituted both an attempt to bypass the national negotiators and to deal with the locals and the individual employees, and trapped the company into a bargaining position from which it could make no retreat "for it had by its own words and actions branded any compromise a defeat."

> A pattern of conduct by which one party makes it virtually impossible for him to respond to the other—knowing that he is doing so deliberately—should be condemned by the same rationale that prohibits "going through the motions" with a "predetermined resolve not to bulge from an initial position."

The opinion took pains to point out that it was not barring employer communications with employees during negotiations, and that it was not forbidding the "best offer first" technique of bargaining or requiring the employer to engage in "auction bargaining."

> We hold that an employer may not so combine "take-it-or-leave-it" bargaining methods with a widely publicized stance of unbending firmness that he is himself unable to alter a position once taken.

Substantially the same themes were sounded by the concurring judge, who stated: "A company may make a firm, fair offer to the union and may stand by that offer, but the company should not be permitted to advertise to its employees that it believes in the firmness of its offers for the sake of firmness."   The publicity campaign made the "company seal itself into its original position in such a way that, even if it wished to change that position at a later date, its pride and reputation for truthfulness are so at stake that it cannot do so."   It also cast the employer in the role of the employees' representative and attempted to render the union superfluous.   The judge acknowledged that such effects might flow as well from a lawful "firm, fair offer" unaccompanied by publicity, but that the combination of the two warranted an inference of bad faith.   He also acknowledged that there were "free speech benefits" in informing the employees about the weaknesses of their union's positions and the unlikelihood of a change in the employer's position in the event of a strike.   But, he continued:

> These benefits can all be reaped by a company which advertises the terms of an offer and its belief that these terms are fair, without also stating that as a matter of policy it can never be persuaded to change the advertised terms.

.   .   .   A company, of course, can advertise its belief that its offer is fair, and that, at the particular time, it sees no reason to change its offer even to forestall a strike. This kind of statement is different from advertising that it is company policy never to change any offer in response to union pressure.

The dissenting judge expressed grave concern that the decision of the Board and court seriously undermined the principles underlying sections 8(c) and 8(d). He believed that, apart from such common per se violations of the Act as an outright refusal to meet or a unilateral change in working conditions, a finding of bad faith bargaining could be made "in all the circumstances" only if the employer (or union) desired not to reach any agreement with the union or was resolved "to adhere to a position without even listening to and considering the views of the other side." He found inadequate evidence of either state of mind, concluding that the company had listened to and discussed the union's proposals and arguments but had chosen for the most part to reject them either on the merits or because of confidence in its own bargaining power. He saw no difference between the conduct of General Electric and that of any employer or union which, after negotiating a contract with another party, vows firmly to extract no less favorable an agreement from another party—conduct which, the judge believed, had never been condemned as illegal under the Labor Act. He also argued that section 8(c) forbade the condemnation of the employer's publicity campaign, which was designed to convince the employees that they should in turn pressure their bargaining representatives to accede to the employer's bargaining position. While he acknowledged that publicizing one's bargaining position could make it difficult to modify it without loss of face, and thus to some degree frustrate the making of collective agreements, "the Board has been expressly prohibited from promoting peace by restricting speech. Conformably with the dictates of the First Amendment, Congress, when it enacted § 8(c), determined the dangers that free expression might entail for successful bargaining were a lesser risk than to have the Board police employer or union speech."

No case since *General Electric* appears to have tested whether an employer (or union) is free to make a single comprehensive offer from which it in fact refuses to retreat, even after listening to proposals and arguments from the other side, when that offer may properly be characterized as "fair" or "reasonable." As will be developed immediately below, the Board has held adamance to be evidence of bad faith only when it related to proposals which the Board concluded were patently objectionable. The Board has, however, held that the announcement of a "firm" offer will not be condemned when it is made late in the negotiations, after counterproposals and concessions have been exchanged. In Philip Carey Mfg. Co. (1963), *enf'd in part*

(6th Cir. 1964), the employer announced a "final" offer at the eleventh bargaining session (at a time when it also offered a wage increase) and adhered to that position during the following seven meetings. The Board held that it was necessary to consider not only the employer's position of "finality" but also the amount of negotiation that had preceded it:

> That the Respondent regarded its offer as final is a matter of its own judgment. One need not listen to argument endlessly. There comes a point in any negotiation where the positions of the parties are set and beyond which they will not go. Where that point is obviously depends on all the facts of the case.

§ 18. Unreasonable Substantive Proposals

Although adamance at the bargaining table is generally not enough to constitute evidence of bad faith, such evidence may be found when there is adamance upon certain particular substantive proposals which the Board (or court) finds peculiarly offensive. It is at this point that the exercise of the Board's unfair labor practice jurisdiction does come dangerously close to supervising the wisdom or unwisdom of the parties' proposals, rather than leaving the substantive contours of the bargain to the negotiating skill and economic strength of the parties. For this reason, the courts have been particularly scrupulous in reviewing Board findings of bad faith when rooted in an examination of the positions espoused by the parties, even when in the context of other indicia of bad faith. Since the results in these cases turn upon an investigation of "all of the circumstances," each case is unique and generalization hazardous. It appears fair to say, however, that in those cases in which the Board has based a finding of bad faith upon the employer's substantive position at the bargaining table, the employer is insisting upon a set of terms which would place the employees and the union in a worse (or no better) economic position than had there been no contract at all—thereby demonstrating a desire to penalize the employees, or undermine the union or reject collective bargaining. Moreover, this is usually accompanied by a refusal to offer serious and specific reasons for the employer's position or by an admission (either during negotiations or before the Board) that certain requests of significance for the union could be granted at no additional cost to the employer.

The Board will sometimes find evidence of bad faith in the employer's refusal to incorporate in the contract an obligation which the employer already owes under the Labor Act or some other related statute. A notorious example is the conduct of the employer in NLRB v. Reed & Prince Mfg. Co. (1st Cir. 1953). There, the employer agreed to incorporate a recognition clause along the lines of the language in section 9(a) of the Labor Act dealing with exclusive representation, but insisted that the contract also include the language in the proviso to that section which accords to individual employees the right to present grievances without the intervention of the union; when the union agreed, but requested that the contract also incorporate that part of the proviso giving the union the right to be present at the adjustment of the grievance, the employer refused. (However, there may be good reason for the employer to resist the transmutation of a statutory duty into a contract duty, since it may fear a substantively different and more inhibiting construction from an arbitrator than from the NLRB or some other statutory agency.)

Even when the employer holds firm on a position consistent with the law, and gives its reasons, the Board will on occasion parse those reasons in order to determine their weight and validity. For example, in Alba-Waldensian, Inc. (1967), enf'd (4th Cir. 1968), the Board found unconvincing, in context, the employer's refusal to check off union dues from the wages of consenting employees when that refusal was based on the "psychological" factor of a reduced paycheck, the inconvenience and clerical burden to the company and the company's objection as a matter of policy to acting as the union's bookkeeper. The Board found that the employer's objective was in truth to avoid any appearance of aid to the union and found this in context to demonstrate a bad-faith desire to frustrate bargaining. Indeed, the Board has gone almost so far as to conclude that the employer bargains in bad faith if it declines to grant a union demand, such as a checkoff, which is essential to the continued existence of the union but is costless to the employer; the lack of a business justification is deemed to evidence an employer objective to undermine the union and to destroy negotiations as well as perhaps the union itself. H. K. Porter Co. (1965), enf'd (D.C.Cir. 1966).

A number of cases center about the employer's insistence upon a broad management rights clause and upon a promise by the union not to strike during the contract term, accompanied by a refusal to incorporate an arbitration clause or by an insistence upon a grievance or arbitration clause of extremely narrow dimension. This particular complex of positions is designed to give the employer "unilateral" control over major working conditions during the contract term while depriving the union of an effective check on employer abuses, either through arbitration or through the strike. The Supreme Court has held that the employer does not violate the Act per se by insisting upon a broad management rights provision on matters such as work schedules, promotions, hiring, discipline, merit pay and other subjects of mandatory bargaining, while seeking to limit the scope of arbitral review of such decisions. NLRB v. American Nat'l Ins. Co. (U.S. 1952). But the Board has on a number of occasions found such employer insistence to evidence bad faith when in the context of other questionable bargaining positions, or of delay in agreeing to meetings, or of refusal to turn over to the union information it needs for bargaining.

Thus, in "M" System, Inc. (1960), while the employer appeared willing to grant a provision for seniority in job preferences, it retained for itself the unreviewable power to determine whether the skill, ability and willingness to work of junior employees was sufficient to override the preference of more senior employees. The management prerogatives provision proffered by the employer would have effectively denied the union any power to process grievances, and the proposed no-strike clause would have barred a work stoppage even in cases in which the employer had violated the labor contract. It was held that the company's posture

> reflects that it approached the bargaining table with the attitude of an employer who remains unreconciled to his employees' selection of a bargaining representative, who is loathe to accept the collective-bargaining principle, who is determined not to surrender in material respects the full freedom he previously enjoyed to regulate unilaterally his labor relations, and who has no serious desire to reach agreement, except perhaps on a basis which would subvert the Union's bargaining status.
>
> .   .   .
>
> .   .   . It is no answer to say that the Respondent would have been willing to enter into a contract, if only the Union had accepted its terms. The terms the Respondent proposed were such that the Union could not accept them without violating its trust to the employees it represented.

The employer in that case was also responsible for other dubious conduct, such as delaying bargaining meetings and insisting on what was in substance individual bargaining on wage rates, and the decision of the trial examiner (adopted by the Board) made it clear that it "does not rest alone on the bargaining positions taken" by the employer.

Although one would imagine that considerable deference would be given by the courts of appeals to Board decisions concerning the employer's state of mind, made "under all of the circumstances," it is fair to say that the courts have been especially thorough in scrutinizing Board findings of bad faith and more willing than the Board to study the employer's substantive bargaining positions in isolation from context and as such to find them rather indicative of a good-faith, albeit stubborn, insistence upon continued exercise of control over the business. For example, in Chevron Oil Co. v. NLRB (5th Cir. 1971), the court reversed the Board's finding of bad faith which had been based principally on the employer's position regarding management rights as well as a no-strike no-arbitration clause. The court held that the employer, which consistently refused to adopt a number of union counterproposals on these matters, was simply utilizing its economic strength to engage in hard bargaining with a weaker union. "The Company naturally desired to use its advantage to retain as many rights as possible. We do not believe, however, that that desire is inconsistent with good faith bargaining." The court reminded the Board that it was not authorized to neutralize advantages of economic power in the name of good-faith bargaining. The *Chevron* court endorsed several earlier court decisions which had reversed Board findings of bad faith. Among these decisions was NLRB v. Cummer-Graham Co. (5th Cir. 1960), in which the employer insisted upon a no-strike clause but would not grant the union's request for an arbitration clause. There, the court conceded that in practice no-strike clauses were commonly accompanied by arbitration clauses; and that "if we were entitled to an opinion, which we are not," arbitration would be a desirable adjunct. But it concluded that a party could lawfully insist on one without the other, and that "These are matters for management and labor to resolve, if they can, at the bargaining table. If they cannot there be decided, then neither Board nor Court can compel an agreement or require a concession."

A number of other cases center about an employer refusal to grant a union's proposal to "check off" union dues by automatically deducting them from the employees' periodic pay checks and remitting them directly to the union. The checkoff is typically of importance to the union, since it saves the time and expense of collecting dues on an individual basis, and it is typically inexpensive for the employer as an accounting matter, witness the frequency of payroll deductions not only for taxes but also for insurance programs and charitable causes. The Board has therefore regarded with suspicion employer adamance in resistance to the checkoff. Sometimes, the Board has looked to such matters as the employer's history of labor relations, in order to infer that the refusal to grant the checkoff stemmed from an employer desire to see the union lose membership support and collapse altogether. United Steelworkers of America v. NLRB (Roanoke Iron & Bridge Works) (D.C.Cir. 1968). But the Board has gone further and found a refusal to grant a checkoff to constitute bad faith bargaining, even apart from any context other than the reasons proffered by the employer to the union at the bargaining table. Alba-Waldensian, Inc. (1967), *enf'd* (4th Cir. 1968) (Board discredited each of the employer's arguments for denying the checkoff). And, in H. K. Porter (1965), *enf'd* (D.C.Cir. 1966), the Board concluded that the employer's willingness to reach an agreement with the union on all other matters did not relieve it of the stigma of bad-faith bargaining on the one item of the checkoff, and also concluded that bad faith was made out by proof that the employer allowed the checkoff in its other plants, that in the plant in question it deducted other moneys from employee earnings, and that it had no legitimate business reason to resist the checkoff. (The Board's order to the employer to incorporate a checkoff provision in the contract was set aside by the Supreme Court as an improper dictation of the substantive terms of the agreement.) Indeed, on at least one occasion the Board has articulated a rationale, that of unlawful discrimination, which would appear automatically to require an employer to grant a union's request for a dues checkoff whenever it makes payroll deductions for other, nonunion, activities.   Farmers Co-op. Gin Ass'n (1966).

It is not at all clear why an employer may not—regardless of the lack of inconvenience or cost of the checkoff—resist its inclusion in the contract if it has the bargaining strength to do so or wishes to hold that concession for future bargaining.   Nor is it clear why the union is not just as responsible for the deadlock by virtue of its own insistence on a checkoff provision which it knows the employer intends not to grant.   In any event, a Board finding of bad faith because of refusal to grant a checkoff has been reversed, in a case in which the employer had met often with the union and made several counterproposals on matters other than the checkoff, and in which the union's bargaining strategy had been one of consistent bluffing and extravagant demands.   NLRB v. General Tire & Rubber Co. (5th Cir. 1964).

Another subject of bargaining upon which employer adamance has been held indicative of bad faith is the duration of the agreement. In some cases, employer insistence on a termination date very far in the future is viewed as an attempt, in bad faith, to lock the union into a humiliating agreement with no early opportunity for renegotiation.   Vanderbilt Prods., Inc., *enf'd per curiam* (2d Cir. 1961) (employer also insisted on open shop, no checkoff, no seniority and absolute right to discharge).   In other cases, the employer has been taken to task for insisting upon too short a contract term, when it is obvious that the employer seeks to have the contract terminate at the same time as the union's "certification year" has expired, so that a prompt election can be held and the union hopefully expelled.   Solo Cup Co. v. NLRB (4th Cir. 1964) (in context, bad faith to insist upon termination date within four months of contract execution, in order to coincide with anniversary of union's certification).   The issue in these cases was posed as follows, in Star Expansion Indus. Corp. (1967):

> A frequent view   .   .   . is that a demand for such simultaneous termination is evidence that an antiunion employer is anxious to test the certification at the earliest possible time.   Another view may be that a union, particularly when it is losing or has lost the support of the employees, may be deliberately uncooperative in negotiations and stall them by arbitrary demands or stand-pat positions in the hope that it will obtain a contract for at least a year following the date when agreement is reached and thus prolong its life as certified bargaining agent.

There, the employer at the twentieth bargaining meeting proposed a contract termination date less than nine months thereafter, to coincide with the end of the union's certification year; an ongoing strike had garnered the support of less than a majority of the employees in the bargaining unit. It was concluded that the employer's motive in insisting on the early termination date was not to rid itself of the union as soon as possible, and that in any event the employer did have a good faith doubt that the union any longer represented a majority of the employees.

The Board has also been confronted in a number of cases with employer adamance on contract demands other than—or in addition to—management rights, grievance and arbitration, the right to strike, dues checkoff and contract termination. For example, in Continental Ins. Co. v. NLRB (2d Cir. 1974), the employer refused to include a conventional recognition clause, and insisted on one which would force the union not to organize or represent other company employees outside the unit; it retreated from its practice of granting severance pay, first stating its flat opposition and then making a proposal "so inadequate as to be patently disingenuous"; it imposed new and stringent requirements for vacations, and took what the court characterized as the "extraordinary" position that vacations were not an earned right but were designed to enable employees to do a better job for the employer; it proposed a grievance clause which defined a grievance as limited to an alleged violation of clear and unambiguous express contract provisions, and permitted the employer to determine whether cases would go to arbitration and who the arbitrator would be; its proposals on wages would give it the right at any time to grant increases in any amounts to any employees it wished. The effect of all of these employer demands, along with a sharply restricted right to strike also proposed, would clearly have been

> to place the employees in a worse position than if they had no contract at all and to require the Union in effect to waive its right to represent employees with respect to disputes over employment conditions. The Board was fully justified in concluding that the proposal was not made in good faith.

It has also been deemed bad faith (in the context of other conduct constituting a refusal to bargain) to insist on an open shop (i. e., no requirement that employees become union members), no checkoff, no seniority, an absolute right to discharge, and a contract term of five years. Vanderbilt Prods., Inc., enf'd per curiam (2d Cir. 1961). Adamance on wages or other financial benefits figured prominently in NLRB v. Fitzgerald Mills (2d Cir. 1963), in which the employer also insisted on the retention of strike replacements in preference to strikers; and also in Wal-Lite Div. of United States Gypsum Co. (1972), enf't denied (8th Cir. 1973), which evoked a sharp disagreement between the Board and the court of appeals. In Wal-Lite, the Board found that the employer went beyond mere intransigence in proposing a slash in employee benefits (which in itself would not establish bad faith) and proposed a reduction so severe that it "could not reasonably have expected the Union to acquiesce" while neglecting to proffer any pertinent explanation for its proposal. The reviewing court, however, noted that the employer had made certain concessions at the bargaining table and concluded that it was no more adamant in refusing to forgo its bargaining position than was the union in demanding the employer's capitulation to its position.

CHAPTER XXI

THE SUBJECTS OF COLLECTIVE BARGAINING

§ 1. Background: The Distinction Between Mandatory and Permissive Subjects of Bargaining

Sections 8(a)(5) and 8(b)(3) impose upon the employer and the majority union, respectively, the duty to "bargain collectively . . . subject to the provisions of section 9(a)." Section 9(a) declares that the union selected by a majority of employees in an appropriate bargaining unit shall be the exclusive spokesman "in respect to rates of pay, wages, hours of employment, or other conditions of employment." Section 8(d) fleshes out the meaning of the duty to "bargain collectively," and like section 9(a) refers to meeting and conferring "with respect to wages, hours, and other terms and conditions of employment"; it cautions, however, that on these subjects neither party need agree to a proposal or make a concession. These are the so-called mandatory subjects, about which employer and union must bargain in good faith but about which either party may stubbornly insist on its position (if "in good faith," a concept discussed elsewhere) and back that insistence with a strike or lockout. Neither party may rely on its economic power to remove "wages, hours, and other terms and conditions of employment" from the bargaining table altogether, but once those subjects are discussed in good faith the deal that is struck is to be determined by the tradeoffs and the bargaining power of the parties. Congress left the substantive contours of these mandatory subjects to be shaped by private adjustment, at the bargaining table and when impasse is reached perhaps "on the bricks."

In NLRB v. Wooster Div. of Borg-Warner Corp. (U.S.1958), the employer refused to reach a settlement with the union unless the agreement contained two clauses: one, a "ballot clause," which required that in future negotiations the employer's last bargaining offer would be put to a vote of the employees in the unit (union and non-union) before a strike could be called; and second, a clause recognizing as bargaining agent a local of the United Automobile Workers, rather than the International which had been certified by the NLRB. After the union finally capitulated to the employer's demands, it filed a charge of violation of section 8(a)(5) which was ultimately sustained by the Supreme Court. The Court rejected the employer's claim that it was free to insist on the ballot clause and the recognition clause as a condition to an agreement, and held that such insistence was unlawful when the subject in question is not a "mandatory" subject and that the two contested clauses fell outside the range of "wages, hours and conditions of employment."

> The company's good faith has met the requirements of the statute as to the subjects of mandatory bargaining. But

that good faith does not license the employer to refuse to enter into agreements on the ground that they do not include some proposal which is not a mandatory subject of bargaining. We agree with the Board that such conduct is, in substance, a refusal to bargain about the subjects that are within the scope of mandatory bargaining. This does not mean that bargaining is to be confined to the statutory subjects. Each of the two controversial clauses is lawful in itself. Each would be enforceable if agreed to by the unions. But it does not follow that, because the company may propose these clauses, it can lawfully insist upon them as a condition to any agreement.

In substance, on other than mandatory subjects, the law forbids the "strong" party to insist on its position and to back it with the use of economic force, and permits the "weak" party to refuse to discuss the issue at all—at least in theory. Three Justices dissented on this issue and would have held that any subject that is lawful may be insisted upon to impasse; but that if the subject although lawful is not "mandatory," a party who does not *wish* to discuss it need not.

The Court held that the employer could not insist on the ballot clause because, rather than regulate the relations between the employer and the employees (which is what a "mandatory" term does), it "deals only with relations between the employees and their unions," and "relates only to the procedure to be followed by the employees among themselves before their representative may call a strike or refuse a final offer." Not only does insistence on such a term close off bargaining on mandatory subjects, but the Court appeared to find the term itself objectionable since "It substantially modifies the collective-bargaining system provided for in the statute by weakening the independence of the 'representative' chosen by the employees. It enables the employer, in effect, to deal with its employees rather than with their statutory representative." The clause recognizing the UAW local to the exclusion of the certified International was also found to circumvent the employer's statutory obligation to bargain with the certified representative. The Court thus left somewhat obscure the question whether insistence on these two clauses was objectionable because they did not fall within "wages, hours, and other terms and conditions of employment," or because they undermined a fundamental principle of the Labor Act, that of exclusive representation by the certified union.

The *Borg-Warner* decision has been criticized on several counts. It is said to intrude the law unnecessarily into the private processes of bargaining (including the peaceful use of economic force) concerning lawful contract provisions, and to inhibit the vigorous assertion of proposals which could otherwise lead to a productive settlement. When the issue under discussion is concededly permissive rather than mandatory, it makes the existence of an unfair labor practice turn upon the very nice distinction between proposing and insisting, a distinction that is foreign to the practicalities of collective bargaining. And, where there is insistence to impasse (or to strike or lockout) on a subject, its legality depends upon whether the subject is classified as mandatory or permissive, a classification which ultimately must be made by Board or court, sometimes months or years after the fact. Finally, it is doubtful that it is practicable to forbid insistence on permissive subjects, since a strong party at the bargaining table can realistically do so without much fear of legal reprisal, if only by disguising its insistence as related to a mandatory subject (and then relenting on that insistence when the other party makes a concession on the truly desired permissive subject).

In any event, *Borg-Warner* requires that bargaining proposals be divided into three categories. *Illegal* provisions may not even be voluntarily incorporated in a labor contract, and insistence upon such a provision to an impasse or as a condition of agreement constitutes a violation of the duty to bargain under section 8(a)(5) or 8(b)(3). *Mandatory* provisions lawfully regulate wages, hours and other conditions of the relationship between employer and employees (and as will be seen later between employer and union); both parties must bargain in good faith about such provisions, but either party may insist on its position to an impasse and use economic force to back its position. *Nonmandatory* or *"permissive"* provisions deal with subjects other than wages, hours and working conditions and are lawful if voluntarily incorporated in the labor contract; either party may propose such a provision, but neither party is obligated to discuss it and neither party may insist to an impasse that such a provision be incorporated in the contract.

§ 2. Mandatory Subjects: Wages

The term "wages" as used in sections 8(d) and 9(a) has been broadly construed to mean compensation for services performed or "emoluments of value" accruing from employment. As was noted shortly after the enactment of the Taft-Hartley Act (which introduced section 8(d)), in W. W. Cross & Co. v. NLRB (1st Cir. 1949):

> The word "wages," following the phrase "rates of pay" in the Act must have been intended to comprehend more than the amount of remuneration per unit of time worked or per unit of work produced. We think it must have been meant to comprehend emoluments resulting from employment in addition to or supplementary to actual "rates of pay."

A variety of items have been treated as "wages"—and thus subject to the requirement of mandatory bargaining—quite often without serious analysis. The employer may not, without consulting with the union, decrease hourly pay rates, NLRB v. Huttig Sash & Door

Co. (8th Cir. 1967), or increase them, Beacon Piece Dyeing & Finishing Co. (1958). The employer must also bargain over pay differentials for workers in different shifts. Smith Cabinet Mfg. Co. (1964) (failure to consult with union regarding pay increase for second shift), and for overtime work, NLRB v. Tom Johnson, Inc. (9th Cir. 1967). Even in certain instances where a proposal on wages appears to set the "prices" for goods or services to be charged or paid to third persons—and thus to run afoul of the antitrust laws—if in substance the union is protecting its members' pay scale, the subject is mandatory and is exempt from the regulation of the antitrust laws. American Federation of Musicians v. Carroll (U.S.1968) (union stipulation of "prices" charged by bandleaders is designed to protect wage scale of union members playing in the band, and is exempt from federal antitrust law); Local 24, Teamsters v. Oliver (U.S.1959) (provision in labor contract stipulating amount employer is to pay to independent truckers for rental of their trucks, over and above their wages, protects wage scale by preventing rentals insufficient to cover operating costs; state cannot ban under its antitrust law).

Piecework and incentive plans have been held mandatory subjects, despite employer protests that mere encouragement of productivity is a management prerogative, NLRB v. Century Cement Mfg. Co. (2d Cir. 1953) (employer instituted merit increase plan without consulting union). The Supreme Court, in NLRB v. Katz (U.S.1962), acknowledged that incentive or merit pay is a matter about which the employer must bargain, as is pay for and accumulation of sick leave. It is also well settled that regardless of whether the employer is obligated to bargain about such major decisions as going out of business, closing down one of several plants, or subcontracting work currently done by its employees, it must bargain about the effects or impact of those decisions, such as severance pay or transfer to other company jobs or locations. Severance pay is thus a mandatory subject, regardless of whether it is treated as "wages" or as a "condition of employment" (because an "effect" of job loss). Other fringe benefits in the form of cash or a cash equivalent are also mandatory subjects. These include paid holidays and vacations, Singer Mfg. Co. v. NLRB (7th Cir. 1942); group health insurance, W. W. Cross & Co. v. NLRB (1st Cir. 1949) (classified as "wages" since group insurance provides a "financial cushion" in the event of ill health at lower cost than if employees negotiated insurance contracts individually), see also Allied Chem. Workers v. Pittsburgh Plate Glass. (U.S.1971); profit-sharing plans, NLRB v. Black-Clawson Co. (6th Cir. 1954); and stock-purchase plans, Richfield Oil Corp. v. NLRB (D.C.Cir. 1956) (both a "wage" matter and a "term or condition of employment").

Somewhat more difficult to classify are Christmas or year-end bonuses which the employer may assert are not "wages" but merely "gifts" to be given within its discretion and without bargaining.

Such bonuses will be held mandatory subjects of bargaining if they appear more to be remuneration for work done. In NLRB v. Niles-Bement-Pond Co. (2d Cir. 1952), the court remarked that these alleged gifts "were so tied to the remuneration which employees received for their work that they were in fact part of it, they were in reality wages and so within the statute." More recently, another court of appeals stated that in determining whether a bonus falls within the mandatory category of "wages," it would consider the consistency and regularity with which the bonus had been paid in the past, uniformity in amount, any relationship between the bonus and the employees' usual remuneration, the taxability of the bonus as income, and the employer's financial condition and ability to pay. Radio Television Tech. School, Inc. v. NLRB (3d Cir. 1973).

Most of the bonus cases in which section 8(a)(5) violations have been found involve both regularity of payment over a substantial number of years and some relationship between the amount of the bonus and the ordinary wages of the recipients. But several cases appear to establish the principle that "regularity" alone (and not even necessarily for a very substantial period of time) will be enough to require the employer to bargain with the union in good faith before terminating or substantially modifying the bonus. In Hooker Chem. Corp. (1970), *mdf'd on other grounds* (6th Cir. 1973), the employer had paid a $25 Christmas bonus for more than twenty years; in Wittock Supply Co. (1968), *enf'd* (D.C.Cir. 1969), the employer had paid a $50 Christmas bonus for only three years; in K–D Mfg. Co. (1968), *enf'd* (5th Cir. 1969), the employer had for more than thirteen years given employees fruit, hams or turkeys; and in Wald Mfg. Co. v. NLRB (6th Cir. 1970), the court held that the employer was obligated to bargain over the discontinuance of the company's annual summer picnics and Christmas parties, given in the past for at least ten years. In none of these cases did there appear to be any direct correlation between bonus and earnings. But the bonus will be treated as a gift rather than as wages, entitling the employer to modify or dispense with it unilaterally, if it is not given on a regular basis and depends rather on the financial health of the company and if it lacks a uniform and regularized method of computation. NLRB v. Wonder State Mfg. Co. (8th Cir. 1965).

Another disputed question is whether meals or housing provided by the employer may properly be characterized as "wages" (or "working conditions") about which the employer must bargain. Although many of the cases fail to articulate a coherent rationale, it is fair to say that company-provided meals and housing (including their availability and their price) will be deemed mandatory subjects if either the cost is substantially lower than market such that the employee can be said to be receiving partial compensation *or* employee consumption of the meals or housing is effectively required, either by mandate of the employer or by the lack of practical alternatives.

NLRB v. Hart Cotton Mills (4th Cir. 1951). (In the former instance, the subject is much like "wages"; in the latter instance, the subject is in a literal sense a "condition of employment.") Thus, in Weyerhaeuser Timber Co. (1949), the employer was required to bargain about the price of meals furnished to its employees in a remote logging camp. In Westinghouse Elec. Corp. v. NLRB (4th Cir. 1967) (*en banc*), however, the court overturned the Board and held that the employer had no duty to bargain about very minor price changes in a plant cafeteria operated by a caterer; the court emphasized that the food concession was run not by the employer but by a third person, that the employees were not required to eat there, and that bargaining can be ordered only if the food prices have a "significant or material" impact on wages. See also McCall Corp. v. NLRB (4th Cir. 1970) (even though food prices are set by employer rather than third person, *Westinghouse* controls and Board finding of 8(a)(5) violation is set aside). As these cases indicate, the Board is more willing to find a duty to bargain about company food prices than are the courts, and continues to be so in the face of these appellate rebuffs. Ladish Co. (1975). See also Abingdon Nursing Center (1972) (employer ordered to reinstate hot-lunch program unilaterally terminated).

In NLRB v. Hart Cotton Mills (4th Cir. 1951), the court in dictum suggested that an employer is obligated to bargain about rent in company housing if it has been traditionally set at a figure substantially below the market price or if the employees are required, by the employer or by circumstances, to live there. The court, finding that only one-third of the employees lived in company housing and that other housing was accessible by public transportation, reversed the Board finding of a bargaining violation. In contrast, another court in American Smelting & Ref. Co. v. NLRB (9th Cir. 1969), held that the employer violated section 8(a)(5) by unilaterally increasing the rent on company housing adjacent to its mine, when all adjacent housing was owned by the company, the nearest private housing was 25 miles away (to which there was no public transportation), two-thirds of the company's employees lived in company housing and the same rents were being charged as 20 years before.

In short, company meals and lodging will not be treated as "wages" or "working conditions" as a matter of law, but their treatment will depend on the significance of and alternatives to this economic benefit. It may also be of some pertinence that the employer, in the course of its dealings with the union on wages and related matters, has pointed to such company-provided benefits as part of the overall scheme of employee compensation. NLRB v. Central Ill. Pub. Serv. Co. (7th Cir. 1963) (one-third discount to employee gas-users).

Although the content of the duty to bargain is considered at greater length elsewhere, it should be noted at this point that if a subject is classified as "mandatory" it does not follow that the employer is obliged to bargain with the union before making a decision each time that subject comes up. Stated generally, what the employer must do is to bargain about a change from the status quo concerning such subjects, and if the status quo—as defined either in the labor contract or by unwritten plant custom—demonstrates that the union has permitted the employer to make such decisions without further negotiation, then the employer is free to continue to do so without violating the Labor Act. Thus, although the grant of a bonus can often be treated as "wages," the employer may grant that bonus at the fifteenth consecutive Christmas time without first getting the union's assent; the regular grant of the bonus represents the status quo, and the employer need bargain only if it intends to change or eliminate the bonus as traditionally given. Similarly, if the labor contract itself gives the employer the power to determine merit-pay awards within a stipulated range, the union has "waived" its statutory right to force the employer to bargain with the union each time it is about to award merit pay (which is clearly "wages" and a mandatory subject) pursuant to the contract. See General Controls Co. (1950) (merit pay authorized by contract); White v. NLRB (5th Cir. 1958) (merit pay authorized by past practice). The same is true of all other mandatory subjects discussed below, which may be modified "unilaterally" by the employer if the union has explicitly or impliedly given away its right to bargain. The employer makes such changes at its peril, however, for the Board or courts may conclude that the union's conduct has not amounted to a waiver of the right to bargain, or that the employer's action does not fall within the contours of the customary practice. The employer's good faith (but erroneous) belief that its action falls within the status quo to which the union has consented is no defense to a charge of failure to bargain. NLRB v. Katz (U.S.1962) (company could not freely grant merit increases, since these were not "simply automatic" but rather "informed by a large measure of discretion").

§ 3. Mandatory Subjects: Hours

The decided cases reveal no disagreement that the period of time during which employees must work is a mandatory subject of bargaining. The Supreme Court has stated:

> [W]e think that the particular hours of the day and the particular days of the week during which employees shall be required to work are subjects well within the realm of "wages, hours and other terms and conditions of employment" about which employers and unions must bargain.

Local 189, Meat Cutters v. Jewel Tea Co. (U.S.1965). Indeed, in that case, a provision in a labor contract with a group of food stores and butcher shops which stipulated a common closing time in the evening was sustained by the Court as exempt from attack under federal antitrust law. The Court concluded that the parties' regulation of the operating hours of the store was directly related to the mandatory issues of working hours and assignment of work for union members.

§ 4.   Terms and Conditions of Employment: The Employer-Employee Relationship

More expansive than "wages and hours" is the category of mandatory bargaining denoted "other terms and conditions of employment." This category includes provisions which deal with the relationship between the employer and the employees, and has also been read to engross most aspects of the employer-union relationship.

Most work rules or plant rules the employer would promulgate unilaterally in the absence of a union must be bargained about when the employees have designated a majority union. (Again, if plant rules already exist when the union is designated, they form the status quo which the employer may implement without first bargaining with the union.) These are rules which regulate how employees are to perform their work and fall squarely within "terms and conditions of employment." A clear example is safety rules, which may not be modified by the employer without first bargaining with the union; it is not a defense that the employer is obliged by law to conform its conduct to certain minimum safety standards. NLRB v. Gulf Power Co. (5th Cir. 1967). The court of appeals there relied upon the concurring opinion of Mr. Justice Stewart in Fibreboard Paper Prods. Corp. v. NLRB (U.S.1964), which stated: "What one's hours are to be, what amount of work is expected during those hours, what periods of relief are available, what safety practices are observed, would all seem conditions of one's employment." If at the time of negotiating a new contract, the union requests that the employer bargain about the content of a manual of plant rules regulating work, discharge and safety, the employer must bargain. Miller Brewing Co. (1967), *enf'd* (9th Cir. 1969). Of course, if the employer insists upon a plant rule which is unlawful because it unduly restricts the opportunity of the employees to engage in protected activities—such as rules prescribing discipline and discharge for engaging in union solicitation on nonworking time—the insistence would be a violation of section 8(a)(5). NLRB v. Magnavox Co. (U.S.1974).

The employer must bargain over workload, Beacon Piece Dyeing & Finishing Co. (1958), and over the performance by supervisors of work which would usually be done by employees in the bargaining unit, Crown Coach Corp. (1965). Also mandatory subjects of bargaining are employee claims to time away from work, such as for holidays and vacations, NLRB v. Sharon Hats, Inc. (5th Cir. 1961); and for sick leave, NLRB v. Katz (U.S.1962). The Supreme Court in *Katz* also acknowledged, without analysis, that seniority, promotions and transfers are subjects about which both employer and union must bargain and may insist.

In accordance with the literal language of the Labor Act, the parties must bargain about the requirements or "conditions" of initial employment. The employer must thus discuss in good faith the union's demand that employees be hired through a nondiscriminatory hiring hall operated by the union. Houston Chapter, Assoc. Gen. Contractors (1963), enf'd (5th Cir. 1965). Although the employer argued that there was no obligation to bargain because the hiring hall deals with job referrals *before* the worker actually becomes an "employee," the Board held that " 'employment' connotes the initial act of employing as well as the consequent state of being employed" and that the term "employees" in section 8(d) includes prospective employees. (The Board's analysis gains strong support from the early Supreme Court decision in Phelps Dodge Corp. v. NLRB (U.S. 1941), which held that the employer may not discriminate in the hiring of job applicants on the basis of their union membership.) Presumably, then, the employer must discuss with the union the issue of racial composition of the workforce and racial adjustment in hiring practices.

Similarly, the requirements of continued employment for one already on the job are literally "conditions of employment" about which both parties must bargain. Thus, the employer may not set unilaterally—or bargain directly with individual employees about— the allowable causes of discharge and the manner in which employer decisions on discharge may be reviewed through a grievance procedure. National Licorice Co. v. NLRB (U.S.1940) (by implication). Similarly, the subject of pensions and the setting of a compulsory retirement age are mandatory subjects. In Inland Steel Co. v. NLRB (7th Cir. 1948), the employer was held to have unlawfully refused to discuss the union's grievance regarding the forced retirement, pursuant to a company modification of its retirement and pension plan, of employees reaching the age of 65. This court analogized this issue to the clearly mandatory issue of discharge for cause or for other nondiscriminatory reason:

> In either case, the employee loses his job at the command of the employer; in either case, the effect upon the "conditions" of the person's employment is that the employment is terminated, and we think in either case, the affected employee is entitled under the Act to bargain collectively through his duly selected representative concerning such termination.

The subject of layoffs—when and in what sequence—is also a "term or condition of employment." United States Gypsum Co. (1951), *mdf'd on other grounds* (5th Cir. 1953). (The employer is free, however, when confronted with a strike, to hire permanent replacements or contract out work normally performed by the strikers, as a means of keeping its business going, without first bargaining with the union.   Hawaii Meat Co. v. NLRB (9th Cir. 1963).)   The employer is not free unilaterally to require physical examinations as a condition of continued employment for workers with high absenteeism, unless the union has effectively ceded that power to the employer for the term of the labor contract.   LeRoy Mach. Co. (1964) (management prerogatives clause retained for the company the sole right to "determine the qualifications of employees").   Nor may the employer disregard union requests to bargain about the impact upon employees, or the arrangements to be made for them, in the event they are displaced by a shutdown or a subcontract—for example, their retraining, severance pay or transfer.   NLRB v. Fibreboard Paper Prods. Corp. (U.S.1964).

In a major decision rather early in the life of section 8(d), the Supreme Court considered the question whether an employer could insist that the contract include a term by which the union ceded to the employer the power during the life of the contract freely to make decisions on such mandatory matters as the selection and hiring, work scheduling, and discipline and discharge of employees.   The Court held that the employer could lawfully insist in good faith upon such a "management prerogatives" clause which gave this unilateral control to the employer without review by an arbitrator.   NLRB v. American Nat'l Ins. Co. (U.S.1952).   The Board had found—and three dissenting Justices agreed—that the employer's insistence on a management rights clause relating to mandatory subjects was in effect a refusal to bargain about those subjects, and a per se violation of section 8(a)(5) regardless of the employer's good faith in refusing to concede.   The Court, however, found the clause to be lawful in itself (even the Board had conceded this, but had held that the employer could only propose the clause and not insist on it) and found that it was "common collective bargaining practice" to give to the employer flexible control over certain working conditions during the contract term.   The effect of the Board's decision would have been to confine an employer's insistence to "provisions establishing fixed standards for work schedules or any other condition of employment" in the face of what might be a contrary practice in the industry. The Court went on to hold:

> The Board was not empowered so to disrupt collective bargaining practices.   .   .   .
>
> Congress provided expressly [in section 8(d)] that the Board should not pass upon the desirability of the substantive terms of labor agreements.   Whether a contract should contain a clause fixing standards for such matters as work scheduling or should provide for more flexible treatment of such matters is an issue for determination across the bargaining table, not by the Board.   If the latter approach is

agreed upon, the extent of union and management participation in the administration of such matters is itself a condition of employment to be settled by bargaining.

Thus, a provision which stipulates whether final authority on hiring and firing, or work scheduling and merit pay is to be exercised by the employer or by the union exclusively (provided it is to be exercised without unlawful discrimination) or by some common committee or by an arbitrator, is itself mandatory and may be insisted upon in good faith to impasse. Since in *American National Insurance*, it had been found below that the employer's insistence on the management functions clause was in good faith, the Court concluded this did not violate section 8(a)(1) or (5).

While a management prerogatives clause is itself a mandatory subject, the employer runs the risk of violating section 8(a)(5) when it insists on a management prerogatives clause that is so all-encompassing that it effectively strips the union of any voice whatever in setting working conditions. That will particularly be the case when the broad management prerogatives clause is combined with an employer demand that there be no arbitration over employer decisions during the term of the contract and that the union give up its right to strike. Although, as noted in *American National Insurance*, the Board will not ordinarily be permitted to infer bad faith from the parties' substantive proposals at the bargaining table, a violation may be found where the proposals are so obviously objectionable to the other party (and normally well out of line with the terms which are customary in the industry) that it is fair to infer that the object of the proponent was to disrupt negotiations. The Board is somewhat more likely to infer such an intention from the substantive proposals alone than are the courts. Compare Stuart Radiator Core Mfg. Co. (1968) (employer violated Act by insisting on a very broad management rights clause, a very broad clause waiving statutory bargaining rights during term of contract, and a grievance and arbitration clause confined to disputes concerning only express contract provisions), with White v. NLRB (5th Cir. 1958) (absent other unfair labor practices or other evidence of bad faith, employer may insist on contract which "could fairly be found to be one which would leave the employees in no better state than they were without it"). This issue is discussed in greater detail in the materials on good faith in bargaining.

§ 5. Terms and Conditions of Employment: The Employer-Union Relationship

Mandatory bargaining subjects include not only those that regulate the relationship between employer and employees but also those that regulate the relationship between the employer and the union. Thus, as the Supreme Court held in NLRB v. American Nat'l Ins. Co. (U.S.1952), there is a duty to bargain in good faith concerning whether the employer or the union or both will determine how working conditions are to be established during the term of the labor contract. See also Dolly Madison Indus. (1970) ("most-favored nation clause," extending to employer the benefit of any more favorable terms given by union under other contracts, is mandatory subject). Similarly, the manner in which disputes between the union and employer are to be resolved during the contract term is also a subject of mandatory bargaining. Either party may thus insist in good faith on its position concerning the grievance procedure and arbitration. NLRB v. Boss Mfg. Co. (7th Cir. 1941). The employer may also insist that the union agree to a no-strike clause. Shell Oil Co. (1948). This may be explained as a provision relating to resolution of employer-union disputes; or to the obligation of employees to report for work (and thus a regulation of the employer-employee relationship); or simply as a provision which advances the basic statutory policy of avoidance of industrial strife, Bethlehem Steel Co. (1950). The Supreme Court has held, however, that the employer is not free to insist on a clause which would forbid a strike during negotiations until the employer's last offer had been rejected in a vote of all unit employees, union and nonunion; the Court found this to regulate the relationship between the union and the employees and thus to be "permissive" only. NLRB v. Wooster Div. of Borg-Warner Corp. (U.S. 1958).

Just as arbitration procedures are mandatory subjects, so too are the procedures attending negotiations, such as the time, place and duration of meetings, and the presence or exclusion of a stenographer or other recording device. (The composition of the opponent's bargaining team is typically not, however, a mandatory subject. General Elec. Co. v. NLRB (2d Cir. 1969).) In St. Louis Typog. Union (1964), the Board noted that the presence of a stenographer has been thought to have both salutary effects, such as providing a reliable record for purposes of drafting and grievance processing, and disruptive effects, such as breeding distrust and encouraging parties to speak "for the record" rather than to speak candidly and to adjust differences. The Board concluded that it would on a case-by-case basis determine whether the insistence on the presence or exclusion of a reporter was done in good faith or for purposes of disrupting negotiations. It stated:

> It is wholly consistent with the purposes of the Act that the parties be allowed to arrive at a resolution of their differences on preliminary matters by the same methods of compromise and accommodation as are used in resolving equally difficult differences relating to substantive terms or conditions of employment. In neither case will we presume to pass upon which is the preferable position or to dictate terms of an agreement, but will, rather, concern ourselves only with whether the parties are acting in good faith.

The duration of the labor contract is also a mandatory subject. United States Pipe & Foundry Co. v. NLRB (5th Cir. 1962). So too is the right of the union during the contract term to use company bulletin boards to post notices to the employees. NLRB v. Proof Co. (7th 1957).

In spite of these rather consistent holdings that negotiation procedures and grievance-resolution procedures are subjects of mandatory bargaining, the Board has recently held that a provision for "interest arbitration"—that is, an agreement to arbitrate new contract terms in the event of a bargaining impasse—is nonmandatory. In Columbus Printing Pressmen's Union No. 252 (1975), the company and union had for some years included in their labor contract a provision that disputes over the negotiation of terms in subsequent agreements would be submitted for resolution to a neutral person. When the employer, during negotiations for a new contract, stated its intention to discard the interest-arbitration provision, the union insisted to impasse upon its inclusion, and was found to have violated section 8(b)(3). Four members of the Board, over a most thorough dissenting opinion, concluded that the interest-arbitration provision constituted an interference, contrary to federal labor policy, with collective bargaining and the unfettered availability of economic weapons, as well as with the union's status as bargaining representative for unit employees.

In addition to the generality of cases dealing with negotiation and grievance procedure, another broad range of subjects that are mandatory, and which might be said to relate to the status accorded by the employer to the union, is covered by the rubric "union security." The union will usually seek some provision which goes beyond recognizing it as bargaining agent and requires as well that all employees in the unit become union members (the union shop) or pay a fee to the union (usually equal to the initiation fee and periodic dues for members) for the service of negotiating and administering the collective bargaining agreement (the agency shop). Since the typical sanction for refusing to join the union or to pay an agency fee is discharge from employment, the rationale for treating such union-security provisions as mandatory subjects may be that they are literally a "condition of employment" which determines the relationship between employer and employee. Whatever the rationale, it has been clear for some time that the employer cannot categorically refuse to discuss the question whether the union shall be entitled to at least some form of union security. NLRB v. Andrew Jergens Co. (9th Cir. 1949) (a frequently cited case, which simply states without analysis that union security is a mandatory subject). The Supreme Court has required an employer to bargain about an agency shop proposal, since it "imposes no burden not imposed by a permissible union shop contract and compels the performance of only those duties of membership which are enforceable by discharge under a union shop arrangement." NLRB v. General Motors Corp. (U.S.1963). The parties may also bargain stubbornly on the inclusion of a "dues checkoff" provision, by which the employer agrees to deduct automatically from the paycheck of consenting employees the amount payable to the union under a union shop or agency shop clause, and to remit those moneys directly to the union. NLRB v. Reed & Prince Mfg. Co. (1st Cir. 1953). Such a provision saves the union the considerable expense of periodic individual solicitation and collection of dues. See H. K. Porter Co. v. NLRB (U.S.1970) (Court refuses to enforce Board order requiring employer to insert checkoff provision in contract, but is not asked to consider Board's finding that employer refusal to grant a checkoff was in bad faith).

A clause requiring the hiring of employees by referral on a non-discriminatory basis from the union hiring hall is also a subject of mandatory bargaining. Although the nondiscriminatory hiring hall may not technically be a form of union security, since workers are to be referred regardless of whether they are union members, it does however deal with the method of hiring and thus literally with the "conditions of employment." In NLRB v. Houston Chapter, Assoc. Gen. Contractors (5th Cir. 1965) the court found that in the construction industry, where employees move from place to place and employer to employer, the hiring hall affords a measure of job security which in other industries is afforded by seniority and that it thus regulates the relationship between employer and employee.

§ 6. The Decision to Subcontract Work or Shut Down a Plant or Business

In 1964, the Supreme Court decided Fibreboard Paper Prods. Corp. v. NLRB (U.S.1964), and it is that case which furnishes the major text for determining whether "terms and conditions of employment" can be read expansively to cover employer decisions on subcontracting, plant removal or shutdown, and sale or termination of business.

In *Fibreboard*, the union gave timely notice of its intention to negotiate a new labor contract, but four days before the expiration of the existing contract the employer informed the union that negotiations would be pointless. It stated that the maintenance work performed by the unit employees within the plant could be done at less cost through a subcontractor and that it had decided to subcontract the work and terminate the employment of the maintenance employees when the labor contract expired. When the employees were terminated and the maintenance work contracted out, the union filed charges of violation of sections 8(a)(1), (3) and (5). The trial examiner and the Board found that the decision to subcontract was economically motivated and not a product of antiunion animus; the Board thus found no violation of section 8(a)(3) and, under the law as it then was, no violation of section 8(a)(5). On rehearing, however, before a Board whose composition had changed through the appointments of a new President, the Board reversed its position and held that the employer was obligated to bargain not only about the effects of the decision to subcontract (such as severance pay or reassignment, as to which the employer had in fact bargained) but also about the decision itself, even though it was motivated by a good faith desire to effect economies. The Board ordered Fibreboard to terminate the subcontract, to reinstitute the maintenance operation with the original employees, to pay them backpay (computed from the Board's second decision) and to bargain with the union before subcontracting.

The Supreme Court enforced the Board's order, in an opinion by Chief Justice Warren. Its conclusion that the employer violated section 8(a)(5) by unilaterally deciding to subcontract the maintenance work and terminate its own maintenance employees was based on a number of different premises. First, the Court attempted to apply the statutory phrase "conditions of employment" to contracting out, and found: the phrase literally covers the assignment of work to outside employees and the termination of unit employees; requiring bargaining would advance the statutory objective of "bringing a problem of vital concern to labor and management within the framework" of peaceful private resolution; and industrial practice shows that subcontracting has been widely dealt with in collective bargaining agreements. Second, the Court held that the employer had merely replaced one group of employees with another, doing the same kind of work within the same plant. Since this "did not alter the Company's basic operation" and contemplated no capital investment, "to require the employer to bargain about the matter would not significantly abridge his freedom to manage the business." Third, the Court noted that the employer was moved to subcontract in the expectation that costs could be cut by reducing the size of the workforce, decreasing fringe benefits and eliminating overtime payments. These are clearly mandatory subjects and even if there is no guarantee that the union will be able to make concessions adequate to keep the work with the present employees, Congress has decided that the union must be given the opportunity to dissuade the employer. The Court concluded by confining the scope of its holding:

> We are thus not expanding the scope of mandatory bargaining to hold, as we do now, that the type of "contracting out" involved in this case—the replacement of employees in the existing bargaining unit with those of an independent contractor to do the same work under similar conditions of employment—is a statutory subject of collective bargaining under § 8(d). Our decision need not and does not encompass other forms of "contracting out" or "subcontracting" which arise daily in our complex economy.

Mr. Justice Stewart delivered a concurring opinion which has perhaps been more influential than the opinion of the Court. He stated that, while there was a duty to bargain about this particular form of subcontracting—the substitution of one group of workers by another, to do the same work in the same plant under the control of the same employer—the Court gave too expansive a reading to the statutory term "conditions of employment" which was in truth intended by Congress to confine the employer's duty to bargain. He argued that although "conditions of employment" might be read to include any managerial decisions harming or terminating job security, the employer should be free unilaterally to implement such decisions if they "are fundamental to the basic direction of a corporate enterprise or   .   .   .   impinge only indirectly upon employment security." Within the latter category of nonmandatory subjects are "decisions concerning the volume and kind of advertising expenditures, product design, the manner of financing, and sales"; these may have an impact on job security, but only remotely. The former category of nonmandatory subjects may indeed have a very direct impact on job security, or terminate employment entirely. The investment in labor-saving machinery or the liquidation of assets and the complete termination of business are examples given by Justice Stewart:

> Nothing the Court holds today should be understood as imposing a duty to bargain collectively regarding such managerial decisions, which lie at the core of entrepreneurial control. Decisions concerning the commitment of investment capital and the basic scope of the enterprise are not in themselves primarily about conditions of employment, though the effect of the decision may be necessarily to terminate employment.

The major issue underlying the employer's decision in *Fibreboard* was labor costs, and Justice Stewart thus believed that section 8(a)(5) was violated because the unilateral decision to subcontract frustrated bargaining on that clearly mandatory subject:

> This kind of subcontracting falls short of such larger entrepreneurial questions as what shall be produced, how capital shall be invested in fixed assets, or what the basic scope of the enterprise shall be. In my view, the Court's decision in this case has nothing to do with whether any aspects of those larger issues could under any circumstances be considered subjects of compulsory collective bargaining under the present law.

The Supreme Court decision in *Fibreboard* does not, however, mean that an employer will always violate the Labor Act by subcontracting without first bargaining with the union. As is discussed elsewhere, the union can "waive" its right to demand bargaining by clearly and unequivocally granting to the employer the power to subcontract unilaterally and at will; most clearly, a contract provision may declare that subcontracting is exclusively a function of management. Also discussed elsewhere in detail is the employer's defense that its subcontracting decision did not in fact constitute a "change in working conditions," since the employer had commonly engaged in subcontracting in the past and its present "unilateral" subcontracting decision was consistent with that past practice. While the employer is not obligated to bargain about each such decision, like in kind and degree to that which has been customary, it must bargain with the union if the union wishes to initiate changes in those subcontracting practices. The Board so held, shortly after *Fibreboard* was decided, in its significant opinion in Westinghouse Elec. Corp. (Mansfield Plant) (1965). The Board in *Westinghouse* found no duty to bargain for several reasons cumulatively, the most important of which were a long history (totalling in the thousands of employer decisions) of subcontracting maintenance and production work, and the absence of any "demonstrable adverse impact on employees in the unit."

The Board found in *Westinghouse* that the employer's most recent subcontracting decisions, challenged by the union as unlawfully unilateral, resulted in no "significant impairment of job tenure, employment security, or reasonably anticipated work opportunities for those in the bargaining unit." Thus, most clearly, if the employer subcontracts work ordinarily performed by employees outside the bargaining unit, this does not directly affect the "wages, hours, and other terms and conditions of employment" of unit employees and the employer need not bargain about the decision with their union. Fafnir Bearing Co. (1965). Similarly, even if the subcontract relates to unit work, there is no duty to bargain if no unit employee is laid off or has his working hours reduced as a result. *Ibid.* And even if there are unit employees on layoff status, a subcontract will not be held to have a significant impact on the unit if it cannot be shown that the company had the equipment, or the laid-off employees the training or capability, to perform the work that has been contracted out. Central Soya Co. (1965). Indeed, the Board has even suggested that there is an insufficient demonstration of adverse impact on the unit when all that can be shown is that the subcontracting prevents laid-off employees from being recalled and presently employed workers from being assigned overtime. Westinghouse Elec. Corp. (Bettis Atomic Power Lab.) (1965). See General Tube Co. (1965) (total loss of at most nine hours of overtime per employee in a seven-week period is not a significant enough detriment to require bargaining). In any event, the Board has held, with court approval, that so long as the subcontracting decision results in no layoffs in the bargaining unit, and unit employees are working many overtime hours, and there is in fact a number of employment openings for unit jobs, the employer need not bargain about subcontracting decisions even though the union credibly alleges that unit employees seriously fear that the subcontract will cause loss of overtime in the future and ultimately loss of jobs. The court there held, in District 50, UMW v. NLRB (Allied Chem. Corp.) (4th Cir. 1966), that the union must show an adverse impact on existing employment conditions, not merely those which might arise in the future.

The reason for the "significant adverse impact" rule appears to be that an employer decision having no such impact is, like a decision relating to employees outside the bargaining unit altogether, insufficiently related to the "terms and conditions of employment" of the employees in the bargaining unit. Compare Allied Chem. Workers v. Pittsburg Plate Glass Co. (U.S.1971). The court in Puerto Rico Tel. Co. v. NLRB (1st Cir. 1966), agreed with the Board that

> at least when the subcontracting is designed to meet some temporary or transient need rather than to alter permanently the basic structure of the enterprise, an employer is not obligated to bargain unless the subcontracting adversely affects the unit's present employees. . . . Subcontracting like many other managerial decisions, may often touch the "terms and conditions of employment" only remotely, if at all. An employer should not be required to bargain about such subcontracting any more than he is required to bargain about these other matters which have been held to be outside the scope of mandatory negotiation.

The court found that, although a number of workers were terminated during the period of the subcontracting, the total number of jobs of that description in the bargaining unit actually increased in the disputed period, and it concluded that there was no adverse impact on either the unit or any employee in it. The full reach of judicial endorsement of the Board's "adverse impact" rule is not, however, altogether clear. For example, in UAW v. NLRB (General Motors Corp.) (D.C.Cir. 1967), a subcontracting decision by General Motors (which the union conceded "achieved substantial efficiencies") resulted in the elimination of six unit jobs in a bargaining unit of more than 1,000 employees, with the displaced workers being reassigned to other positions in the plant. The Board found no significant adverse impact and thus no obligation to bargain, but the court of appeals reversed, since even though the six individuals suffered no job loss there was an adverse impact on the bargaining unit which was reduced in size by the six eliminated jobs. Apparently, the court believed that the union itself had a protectible interest as unit representative, apart from any interest of the employees in the unit, in requiring the employer to bargain.

The question remained after the Supreme Court decision in *Fibreboard* whether the NLRB and the courts would limit the holding of the Supreme Court to its facts or would expand it to cover more elaborate subcontracting arrangements, the removal of a plant to another location, the shutdown of part of a business, or the sale or liquidation of an entire business. It was also unclear whether the decisions under section 8(a)(5) would be affected by the decision of the Supreme Court in Textile Workers Union v. Darlington Mfg. Co. (U. S.1965), which held that a complete shutdown of a business even solely to escape the union would not violate section 8(a)(3), nor would a partial shutdown unless it could be demonstrated that the object and effect was to "chill" unionism among the remaining employees. The decisions in this area produce no firm or readily applicable guidelines. The Board's decisions appear inconsistent with one another, in spite of its attempt to articulate relevant distinctions. The same is true of the decisions of the courts of appeals, although the courts have been generally less willing than the Board to find these kinds of management actions "mandatory" and subject to bargaining. Any more detailed attempt at synthesis is hazardous, but perhaps some hesitant conclusions may be drawn.

(1) *Subcontracting*. If the management decision may fairly be characterized as "subcontracting," that is, the use of employees of another company (or one's own company) to perform work or services previously performed by employees in the bargaining unit, the Board will likely hold that there is a duty to bargain about the decision. The courts, however, may be reluctant to agree when the subcontracting is of work outside the plant, effectively removes the employer from supervision and is accompanied by a liquidation of company assets previously devoted to the unit work. In Kronenberger d/b/a American Needle & Novelty Co. (1973), the employer transferred the production work done in one plant to its two other plants, without bargaining with the union; the Board held this illegal, relying on *Fibreboard* and treating the case as akin to subcontracting without any significant withdrawal of capital from the business. In NLRB v. Johnson d/b/a Carmichael Floor Covering Co. (9th Cir. 1966), both the Board and the court held that the employer, in the business of selling carpets, was obligated to bargain about its decision to have installation done by an outside contractor rather than as theretofore by company employees. The Board and court pushed *Fibreboard* yet further in NLRB v. American Mfg. Co. (5th Cir. 1965), and held that the employer, a manufacturer of oilfield pumping equipment, violated the Act when it unilaterally abolished its trucking department, contracted out transportation to a carrier and sold all its trucks and related equipment. In spite of the obvious differences from *Fibreboard*, the court merely stated that the Supreme Court there required bargaining over decisions to subcontract.

In a similar case, however, another court of appeals did make the distinction and reversed the Board. In NLRB v. Adams Dairy, Inc. (8th Cir. 1965), the court concluded that the employer had no duty to bargain over the decision to terminate distribution of its dairy products by its own driver-salesmen and to sell them instead to independent contractors who distributed them in geographic areas traversed by the routes of the former driver-salesmen; the latter's trucks were sold to the independent contractors. The court of appeals quoted from the opinion of Mr. Justice Stewart in *Fibreboard*, and held:

> Contrary to the situation in Fibreboard then, there is more involved in Adams Dairy than just the substitution of one set of employees for another. In Adams Dairy there is a change in basic operating procedure in that the dairy liquidated that part of its business handling distribution of milk products. Unlike the situation in Fibreboard, there was a change in the capital structure of Adams Dairy which resulted in a partial liquidation and a recoup of capital investment. To require Adams to bargain about its decision to close out the distribution end of its business would significantly abridge its freedom to manage its own affairs.

The court also cited the recently decided *Darlington* case in the Supreme Court, and underlined the fact that the dairy's decision—which the court characterized as a "partial closing" under the *Darlington* analysis—was based solely on economics and was devoid of antiunion animus. (The court failed to explain why the employer's good faith—which was also present in *Fibreboard*—was at all relevant to the question whether a particular issue is mandatory or permissive.)

Similar questions about the duty to bargain emerge when the employer terminates bargaining unit employees not by subcontracting or by using non-unit employees of its own, but rather by replacing workers with machinery. Decided cases dealing with the duty to bargain about automation decisions have not emerged frequently. In his concurring opinion in the *Fibreboard* case, Mr. Justice Stewart, observing that "An enterprise may decide to invest in labor-saving machinery" and thus necessarily terminate employment, stated nonetheless that these were decisions "concerning the commitment of investment capital and the basic scope of the enterprise [and] are not in themselves primarily about conditions of employment . . . ." In an earlier case, however, the Board had found a violation of section 8(a)(5) when a newspaper company unilaterally decided to change its printing process from the hot-type method to the cold-type method, thereby substantially reducing costs and the need for manpower. Rochet d/b/a Renton News Record (1962) (Board ruled 3–0 that employer was obligated to bargain about the effects of the decision to automate and 2–1 that it had to bargain about the decision itself; no order issued to reinstitute the hot-type process). See also NLRB v. Columbia Tribune Pub. Co. (8th Cir. 1974) (same basic fact situation as *Renton*, with court enforcing Board order to bargain, relying on *Fibreboard* and termination of employment; ambiguous whether court analyzed issue as the impact of automation or the automation decision itself).

(2) *Relocation.* If the management decision is to relocate the plant, there will likely be an obligation to bargain about that decision when the relocation does not substantially alter the manner in which the business is conducted. In ILGWU v. NLRB (McLoughlin Mfg. Corp.) (D.C.Cir. 1972), the employer, in the ladies' garment industry, concealed from the union its decision to move its business from its antiquated plant in Indiana to new quarters in Alabama. The Board and the court found this conduct a violation of section 8(a)(5). As in *Fibreboard*, the court found the decision to relocate to be based on "long-standing dissatisfaction with its labor costs," particularly those flowing from the contract seniority provision and the 35-hour workweek; the court held "the labor relations matters involved were sufficiently important to justify an attempt at reconciliation through bargaining." Also like *Fibreboard*, the relocation did not work any significant change in the manner of operation: "the company continued to lease its premises, it manufactures the same products using the same machinery, its product is sold to the same customers, and the business is owned and managed by essentially the same persons as before." The court acknowledged (perhaps erroneously) that other courts of appeals had found an 8(a)(5) violation in similar cases only when there was also a violation of section 8(a)(3), but stated that the search in those cases for antiunion animus may have been justified by the employer having "partially liquidate[d] its investment in order to reduce its entrepreneurial risk," which was not true in the case at bar. Compare Kronenberger d/b/a American Needle & Novelty Co. (1973) (work taken from one plant and relocated in two other company plants, with no significant investment or withdrawal of capital; *Fibreboard* held controlling).

Presumably, if the relocation had brought with it the discontinuation of a product, the utilization of new production processes and the like, the court would have found this to fall within the range of "managerial prerogatives" about which there was no duty to bargain with the union. A case quite comparable to the hypothesized situation is NLRB v. Transmarine Nav. Corp. (9th Cir. 1967). There, the employer operated as a freight and steamship agent and terminal operator in Los Angeles Harbor, and certain of its employees who worked as guards in the dock warehouses were represented by a union. When a consolidation of its principal customer into a much larger company made it imperative to provide larger shipyard facilities, the employer entered into an agreement—without bargaining with the union—with two other companies to create a joint venture and to secure larger facilities further south in Long Beach. The court held that the employer had no obligation to bargain about this economically motivated decision to "discontinue its operations and relocate in a different area as a minority partner in a joint venture." The joint venture had three times the number of employees, some of whom performed work never done by the employees of the respondent; the new company had substantially greater working capital, and had far larger and more modern terminal facilities. The employer's decision wrought "fundamental changes in the direction and operation of the corporate enterprise, which greatly affected its capital, assets, and personnel" and was not, as in *Fibreboard*, merely to achieve economies by reducing the workforce and employee fringe benefits. The court did hold, however, that once the employer made its decision it was obligated to notify the union in order to afford it an opportunity to bargain about such "effects" on the displaced employees as severance pay, vacation pay, seniority and pensions.

(3) *Partial shutdown*. If the employer's decision can fairly be characterized as a "partial shutdown"—that is, the employer remains in the same business in other locations but closes out one of its plants or stores—the Board will likely require the employer to bargain about that decision. The courts may be somewhat less hospitable, however, to the union's claim. (Obviously, these cases are occasionally difficult to distinguish from the so-called subcontracting cases discussed earlier, where the employer terminates one part of its business and has it done by another company subject to varying degrees of control. Unfortunately, some cases appear to be decided merely by pinning the conclusory label of "subcontract" or "partial shutdown" or "sale" on the facts before the agency or court.)

Certainly the most thoroughly articulated decision in the area of the "partial closing" is that of the Board in Ozark Trailers, Inc. (1966). In that case the Board treated as a single integrated multi-plant enterprise three companies engaged principally in the manufacture, sale and service of refrigerated truck bodies. A decision was made by one of the companies, without notifying or bargaining with the union, to close its plant, which was consuming excessive man hours and generating defective workmanship. The Board concluded that this amounted to a "partial closing," that the *Darlington* requirement in such cases under section 8(a)(3) that the closing be motivated by antiunion animus had no relevance to the issue of the employer's duty to bargain, and that the logic of *Fibreboard* required the employer to bargain. As in *Fibreboard*, the Ozark closing terminated the work of the unit employees; it was premised on production inefficiencies which were themselves mandatory subjects of bargaining; it was a matter separating the employer and union which might peaceably be resolved through the "mediating influence of collective bargaining"; requiring bargaining would not unduly abridge the employer's freedom to manage, since the duty to bargain entails the privilege of implementing the decision once impasse is reached; and, even if some management flexibility might be lost in dealing with a special business opportunity or exigency, this would occur less frequently with shutdown decisions than with the far more common subcontracting decisions, and, in any event, Congress as to all "terms and conditions of employment" has declared that this is the necessary trade-off in order to protect the interests of employees and of the public. Perhaps most significantly, the Board in *Ozark* rejected the argument that the employer need not bargain about the partial closing because it is a "major" decision, basic to the scope of the enterprise, involving the committee of investment capital. The Board responded:

[A]n employer's decision to make a "major" change in the nature of his business, such as the termination of a portion thereof, is also of significance for those employees whose jobs will be lost by the termination. For, just as the employer has invested capital in the business, so the employee has invested years of his working life, accumulating seniority, accruing pension rights, and developing skills that may or may not be salable to another employer. And, just as the employer's interest in the protection of his capital investment is entitled to consideration in our interpretation of the Act, so too is the employee's interest in the protection of his livelihood.

The reach of the Board's rationale was so broad as arguably to encompass any major corporate decision—merger or consolidation, sale, plant removal, partial or even complete shutdown—directly causing the displacement of employees. As will be seen shortly, this did not prove to be the case.

The courts of appeals have not embraced the principle announced in *Ozark Trailers*. They have rather consistently held the "partial closing" (and management decisions resembling it) to be permissive only, and a decision which the employer may make without bargaining. In NLRB v. Royal Plating & Polishing Co. (3d Cir. 1965), the employer, faced with economic difficulties and the prospect of ouster by redevelopment authorities, closed one of its two plants, terminated the employees there and sold the plant machinery and equipment. The Board found the failure to bargain to violate section 8(a)(5), but the court of appeals reversed, reasoning that the decision was one "to recommit and reinvest funds in the business" and "involved a major change in the economic direction of the Company." (The court did hold that the employer was obligated to bargain about the effects or impact of the closing, such as severance pay, seniority and pensions.) In Morrison Cafeterias Consol., Inc. v. NLRB (8th Cir. 1970), the employer, a chain of cafeterias, closed down one of the cafeterias promptly after a union election victory there, and dealt directly with the ousted employees on questions of transfer and transportation to other cafeteria locations. The Board found the shutdown not to violate section 8(a)(3), since under the test of the Supreme Court in *Darlington* there was lacking an intention to "chill" unionism at cafeterias other than the one closed down; but found the refusal to notify and bargain with the union to violate section 8(a)(5). The court of appeals agreed that section 8(a)(3) was not violated, and concluded that *Darlington* thus also relieved the employer of the duty to bargain with the union about the closing. (Yet the court held that the employer was obligated to bargain about the effects of the closing.) The Board was also reversed in what might be considered a "partial closing" case in NLRB v. Burns Int'l Detective Agency, Inc. (8th Cir. 1965), where a private security company, with contracts in different states, decided to terminate its contract to provide guards (who were represented by a union) for Creighton University because the loss of other contracts in the Omaha area had made it unduly expensive to service the single remaining contract at the University. The court distinguished *Fibreboard* since "Burns for valid economic reasons has withdrawn completely from providing any services in the Omaha area," and was not continuing the same work in the same location through subcontractors. The court leaned on the finding that the employer had not violated section 8(a)(3) since the termination of the University contract was not for antiunion reasons, and then stated—without explanation—"the finding as to motive equally applies to the facts relevant to the § 8(a)(5) violation."

(4) *Termination or Sale of Business.* If the employer's decision can fairly be characterized as a "partial shutdown," but also takes the employer completely out of a distinct phase of its business, even the Board is likely to conclude that there is no duty to bargain about such a decision. The Board has also characterized a withdrawal from business at a particular location as a "sale" to another rather than as a shutdown, and concluded that bargaining is not required. These distinctions are quite fine, indeed one might say barely perceptible, and have created difficulties for administrative law judges trying to apply Board precedent, divisions within the Board membership itself, and uncertainty for employers.

Summit Tooling Co. (1972), involved a decision by Ace Tool Engineering Co. to close down its wholly owned subsidiary Summit Tooling; the Board treated the two companies as a single "employer" under the Labor Act, such that the demise of Summit represented a termination of the employer's only activities in the field of manufacturing tools and tooling products. The Board found the shutdown of Summit to violate section 8(a)(3) because of antiunion animus, and found several 8(a)(5) violations as well, for refusal to furnish information to the union, refusal to sign a consummated labor agreement, and refusal to bargain about the effects of the Summit closing. Nonetheless, the Board took pains to treat separately the decision itself to close Summit, and held this not to be a mandatory subject. Over a dissent which would have made *Ozark Trailers* controlling in this partial-closing case, the Board held that the "practical effect" of the decision "was to take Ace out of the business of manufacturing tool and tooling products," such that the employer (Ace) now does no business remotely resembling that previously done by the discharged employees.

A case yet more difficult to square with the Board's expansive rationale in *Ozark Trailers*—particularly because the Board majority relied exclusively on the concurring opinion of Mr. Justice Stewart in *Fibreboard* and made no mention whatever of *Ozark Trailers*, to the distress of two dissenting Board members—is General Motors Corp. (1971), *enf'd* (D.C.Cir. 1972). There, General Motors, which had been operating a truck sales and service center in Houston (as well as similar facilities elsewhere), contracted (without bargaining with the union) with Trucks of Texas to grant the latter a dealership franchise, involving the purchase by Trucks of all the personal property and its rental of the premises from General Motors. Reversing the trial examiner, who had relied on *Fibreboard*, the Board characterized the transaction as a "sale" of the business at arm's length and thus a "more elemental management decision" than subcontracting. The Board majority relied on the *Fibreboard* concurrence and rulings of the courts of appeals, holding that:

> [D]ecisions such as this, in which a significant investment or withdrawal of capital will affect the scope and ultimate direction of an enterprise, are matters essentially financial and managerial in nature. They thus lie at the very core of entrepreneurial control, and are not the types of subjects which Congress intended to encompass within "rates of pay, wages, hours of employment, or other conditions of employment." Such managerial decisions ofttimes require secrecy as well as the freedom to act quickly and decisively. They also involve subject areas as to which the determinative financial and operational considerations are likely to be unfamiliar to the employees and their representatives.

Thus did the Board appear to reject every premise of its decision in *Ozark Trailers*. It concluded: "A decision to withdraw capital from a company-operated facility and relinquish operating control to an independent dealership" is not a matter of mandatory bargaining. A divided court of appeals agreed, and while endorsing the Board's characterization of the transaction as a "sale," added that it

> . . . was in keeping with a national GM policy to switch its remaining manufacturer-owned and operated retail outlets to independent franchises or dealerships. Such a decision is "fundamental to the basic direction of a corporate enterprise." It is at the core of entrepreneurial control. There is no claim here of anti-union bias on the part of GM
>
> . . . .

Summary and Implications. Some recent attempts have been made by the Board and courts to harmonize the cases discussed above and others like them. The Board did so in Royal Typewriter Co. (1974), in which the employer, a large corporate conglomerate, shut down one of its plants without bargaining with the union, asserting doubts as to the union's majority status. The administrative law judge applied the Board's analysis in *General Motors* and held there was no duty to bargain but the Board reversed. It stated that *Ozark Trailers* had continuing validity, in spite of court decisions to the contrary, in cases involving the closing of one of several plants; that *General Motors* applied, consistently, to "an economic decision to *sell* an independent dealership"; and that *Summit Tooling* found "permissive" a decision to go out of a particular line of business. (The Board appears to have relegated to obscurity its noteworthy decision in New York Mirror (1965), to the effect that the Mirror had a duty to bargain about its decision to close down its plant, sell its assets to the New York News and go out of business completely. In spite of this "holding," however, the Board dismissed the complaint, observing that the Mirror's decision was impelled by economic hardship, that the bargaining relationship with the union had been long and effective, that the employer had bargained about the effects of the closing upon the employees, and that no party to the proceeding had sought reinstitution of the operation.)

The Court of Appeals for the District of Columbia Circuit attempted its own synthesis of the court opinions—and ignored the sometimes differing Board dispositions and perhaps overstated the harmony of the appellate decisions—in International Union, UAW v. NLRB (D.C.Cir. 1972), which enforced the decision of the Board in the *General Motors* case. Citing cases in support, the court concluded:

> If the decision appears to be primarily designed to avoid the bargaining agreement with the union or if it produces no substantial change in the operations of the employer, the courts have required bargaining. . . . If the decision resulted in the termination of a substantial portion or a distinct line of the employer's business or involved a major change in the nature of its operations, no bargaining has been required. . . . The difficult cases have been those involving a small but not insubstantial proportion of the employer's business; in these cases, the results have often hinged on hints of anti-union animus.

This synthesis is revealing in at least two respects. First, it places greatest emphasis upon the degree to which the employer's decision changes the scope or operations of the business, somewhat lesser emphasis upon the issue of antiunion animus (for no articulated reason), and no apparent emphasis upon the impact of these employer decisions on the employees (which may be equally serious in these three classes of cases). In substance, then, it adopts the rationale of the *Fibreboard* concurrence rather than of the opinion of the Court. Second, this synthesis quite usefully emphasizes the operational *results* of the different kinds of employer decisions, rather than the differing characterizations found in the opinions, such as "subcontract," "partial closing" or "sale."

It should be emphasized that a Board or court decision that subcontracting or plant shutdown is a "term or condition of employment" about which the employer must bargain does not necessarily mean that the employer's freedom of action will be substantially hampered. First, the duty to bargain does not require that the employer secure the union's agreement before it implement its decision. It must give the union notice of and an opportunity to discuss its impending decision, but it is free to implement that decision after reaching an impasse in negotiations. The Board appears willing to construe the term "impasse" with sufficient flexibility as to take account of the exigencies of the situation. And it is not uncommon to find a court reversing a Board finding of refusal to bargain, holding instead that the employer had in fact adequately met and discussed the issue with the union. *E. g.*, NLRB v. Adams Dairy, Inc. (8th Cir. 1965) (employer held to have bargained about the effects of its decision to subcontract its delivery operations).

Second, when an employer's decision to subcontract work is consistent with a past practice, it is that practice which will be treated as the status quo such that the employer's decision may continue to be made "unilaterally," with bargaining necessary only regarding a departure from that practice. In Westinghouse Elec. Corp. (Mansfield Plant) (1965), the Board noted that the violations of section 8(a)(5) found in earlier cases had involved subcontracting that was "a departure from previously established operating practices, effected a change in conditions of employment, or resulted in a significant impairment of job tenure, employment security, or reasonably anticipated work opportunities for those in the bargaining unit."

Finally, it has been held that, although the employer's duty to bargain ordinarily continues during the period of a strike in the course of negotiations, the employer is free to keep its business going during the strike by hiring permanent replacements for strikers or contracting out their work without bargaining with the union. As one court said of a decision by a newspaper company to subcontract during a strike:

> If publication may be interrupted while bargaining drags on over matters which have to do with what means the publisher may use in getting his paper on the streets and in the mail, the paper may cease to exist. It would be a startling doctrine indeed if this court were to tell companies and employers faced with extinction because of a strike, that before they can make economic business decisions to contract out work in order to continue operations, they must first consult the union that caused the threat of extinction.

NLRB v. Robert S. Abbott Pub. Co. (7th Cir. 1964). Although the Board initially held that the employer was obligated to bargain about its decision to subcontract struck work, its decision was denied enforcement, see Hawaii Meat Co. v. NLRB (9th Cir. 1963) (court, however, assuming arguendo that employer would be obliged to bargain over whether subcontracting would be continued after the strike ended). The Board appears to have retreated, and now holds that the employer, while obligated to bargain about subcontracting decisions that are likely to be permanent and to impair the bargaining unit and the union's status, need not bargain about decisions to subcontract temporarily in order to tide the company through the strike. Empire Terminal Warehouse Co. (1965). See Southern Calif. Stationers (1967) (thorough analysis by trial examiner).

§ 7. Permissive Subjects of Bargaining: Generally

Some provisions which may lawfully be incorporated in a labor contract fall nonetheless outside the area of "wages, hours and other terms and conditions of employment," and are thus not mandatory subjects of bargaining for the employer under section 8(a)(5) or the union under section 8(b)(3). Such "permissive" subjects may be proposed by either party at the bargaining table, but the proponent may not insist on its position to the point of impasse or as a condition of reaching an agreement, and the other party may decline to discuss the issue altogether without violating the law. These principles were definitively announced by the Supreme Court in NLRB v. Wooster Div. of Borg-Warner Corp. (U.S.1958), discussed in detail earlier. Unlike mandatory subjects which characteristically deal with the working relationship of the employees to the employer, permissive subjects fall for the most part into two groups: those which deal with the relationship of the employer to third persons, and are normally regarded as within the prerogative of management, and those which deal with the relationship between the union and the employees in the bargaining unit, and are normally regarded as within the internal control of the union.

The union violates section 8(b)(3) when it insists to impasse that the employer agree to contribute to an industry promotion fund; such an agreement does not touch the employer-employee relationship or regulate a "condition of employment." Detroit Resilient Floor Decorators Local 2265 (1962), *enf'd* (6th Cir. 1963). As Mr. Justice Stewart said, concurring in Fibreboard Paper Prods. Corp. v. NLRB (U.S.1964): "Decisions concerning the volume and kind of advertising expenditures, product design, the manner of financing, and sales, all may bear upon the security of the workers' jobs," but only to such a remote and speculative degree as not to warrant treatment as "conditions of employment" about which the employer must bargain. Nor may the union condition the contract on the employer's bargaining regarding a strike insurance plan involving other employers. This improperly intrudes on the employer's development of a financial base for collective bargaining negotiations, just as would employer demands regarding the union's strike funds. Operating Eng'rs Local 12 (Associated General Contractors of America, Inc.) (1970) (union proposal would have subjected any insuring employer to a strike rather than the grievance procedure in the event of a contract dispute, and required such an employer to pay "wage continuance insurance" to striking or locked out employees). On these matters, the employer may voluntarily choose to acquiesce in the union's proposal and such contract provisions would be lawful; but the union violates the law if it insists or strikes over the employer's objection.

Similarly, the employer violates the law when it insists to impasse on a provision which deals not with the employer-employee relationship but with the union-employee relationship. The Supreme Court held it unlawful for an employer to condition its agreement with the union upon a provision which would have required the union in future negotiations to submit the employer's last offer to a vote of all employees in the unit, and would have authorized a strike only in the event the employees voted down the offer. NLRB v. Wooster Div. of Borg-Warner Corp. (U.S.1958). The Court distinguished the no-strike clause, a mandatory subject, which "regulates the relations between the employer and the employees"; found the clause to deal with the union's and the employees' bargaining strategy; and also found that it "substantially modifies the collective-bargaining system provided for in the statute by weakening the independence of the 'representative' chosen by the employees. It enables the employer, in effect, to deal with its employees rather than with their statutory representative." So too, whether and how the contract negotiated by the union is to be ratified by the employees is treated as an issue for the union and its members to determine internally, and the employer violates the Act by insisting, after an agreement has been reached, that it be approved by a majority vote of the employees. Houchens Market of Elizabethtown, Inc. v. NLRB (6th Cir. 1967). And, just as the employer is free to decide unilaterally whether to participate in an industry promotion plan, the union need not discuss the employer's demand that it permit use of the union label to promote the sale of the employer's goods. As the Board held (by adopting the decision of the trial examiner) in Kit Mfg. Co. (1964):

> Whatever economic advantage the use of the union label may afford an employer, and whatever [sic] it may have upon the salability of its product, the subject can scarcely be regarded as pertaining to "rates of pay, hours of employment or other conditions of employment." . . . [T]he relationship between use of the union label and the economics of employees' wages, is too remote and speculative to hold the union label to be a mandatory subject for collective bargaining.

By treating these subjects as permissive or voluntary, the Board and courts are in effect saying that adamance or a strike or lockout over a matter that has relatively slight impact on the employees, or over a subject which "public policy" relegates to the control of one party or the other, ought not be permitted to hinder the signing of a labor contract or the single-minded discussion of subjects more central to the employer-employee relationship.

§ 8. Permissive Subjects: Representation Issues

A number of cases demonstrate a more specific public policy that issues relating principally to the representational status of the parties should be determined without disrupting negotiations—either decided voluntarily by the parties or through the machinery of the Board, but not by coercion at the hands of the stronger party. This may help to explain why the Board holds permissive certain issues bearing on the relationship between the union and the employer (which is commonly treated as a matter of mandatory bargaining).

Thus, the "ballot clause" in *Borg-Warner* could arguably have been deemed mandatory, since it determined the conditions to a work stoppage and offered a device for the peaceful resolution of labor disputes, but at the same time it threatened the representative status of the union. This was also the principal reason for holding permissive the contract provision in that case which would have extended recognition not to the International certified by the NLRB but to the uncertified local instead. The Court there concluded:

> The statute requires the company to bargain with the certified representative of its employees. It is an evasion of that duty to insist that the certified agent not be a party to the collective-bargaining contract. The Act does not prohibit the voluntary addition of a party, but that does not authorize the employee to exclude the certified representative from the contract.

The Board has long held, with judicial approval, that it is illegal to insist to impasse on a contract clause requiring the other party to post bond or afford other security against the possibility of a contract breach. This is true whether the demand is made by the employer or the union, the demanded security is in the form of a bond or cash, or the contemplated breach is of any provision in the contract or only of such clearly mandatory provisions as those dealing with wages and fringe benefits or the right to strike. NLRB v. Hod Carriers Local 1082 (E.L. Boggs Plastering Co.) (9th Cir. 1967). In part, the rationale offered is that such performance bonds or security funds do not have a discernible impact on employee-employer relations, but it is also emphasized that Congress did not require that either party—if an appropriate bargaining representative—be solvent before the other party becomes obligated to bargain about mandatory subjects.

A similar explanation is found in the several cases in which one party has demanded, as a condition of negotiating or settling, that the bargaining unit be expanded beyond that certified by the NLRB. An early and often cited case on this problem is Douds v. ILA (2d Cir. 1957), which found a violation of section 8(b)(3) when the union, certified to represent employees in the port of New York and vicinity, insisted that the contract unit be expanded to include all longshoremen working all ports from Portland, Maine to Brownsville, Texas. While the court acknowledged that the union and employer in any negotiation could by voluntary agreement expand the unit for which they bargain to some larger appropriate unit than the one certified by the Board, it held that lacking such agreement neither party had the power to disrupt negotiations on mandatory matters by demanding a change in the scope of the unit. This doctrine has been applied whether the demand is for the expansion or for the contraction of the unit. The parties' recourse on such matters when they cannot agree is to the Board by way of a petition for unit clarification.

The Board has recently applied this principle in Utility Workers Union (Ohio Power Co.) (1973), which involved, essentially, bargaining between separate companies, all subsidiaries of the same utility company, and a number of local unions which were members of a joint council. The locals were separately certified in separate-plant bargaining units, but throughout their respective bargaining negotiations insisted that the companies make identical offers for all of the units and threatened that no offer with respect to any one unit would be accepted or submitted for ratification until concurrent offers had been made for all of the plants. While acknowledging that uniformity of labor standards is a legitimate union aim, and that a union could lawfully pursue that aim by basing its demands on a contract already consummated elsewhere or by insisting within each unit on a common contract expiration date, the Board held that it was illegal for the union to insist as a condition of agreement that negotiations include other units or that the employer submit identical terms in other units. In effect, the union was refusing to bargain about mandatory subjects within its own unit and bargaining instead concerning working conditions of employees in some other unit. Indeed, the cases go beyond this rationale by forbidding insistence on working conditions outside the unit even when bargaining on "intra-unit" issues is not being forestalled. See Sperry Sys. Mgt. Div. v. NLRB (2d Cir. 1974) (union violates section 8(b)(3) by insisting that employer comply with arbitration award holding that employees in nonunion California plant must be governed by working conditions set forth in New York labor contract).

The Board has recently, with judicial approval, made an exception of uncertain breadth to what appeared to be a rather firm proscription of union insistence upon expansion of the bargaining unit.

In Newspaper Prod. Co. v. NLRB (5th Cir. 1974), a union was permitted to strike in support of a demand that a small number of production workers be added to the bargaining unit, when that union also represented those additional workers, there was no other union claiming to represent them, their inclusion would not have rendered the bargaining unit inappropriate in scope, the present unit had not been formally certified by the Board and unit size had been a subject of contract negotiations before.

A corollary of these decisions that the union may not insist on "extra-unit" demands is that the employer is not obligated to bargain over them.   Thus, in Oil Workers v. NLRB (Shell Oil Co.) (D.C.Cir. 1973), the employer refused to negotiate with the union at once for all of the nineteen units it represented within the company, in spite of the union's claim that a single unified negotiation was the only effective forum for bargaining on companywide fringe benefits.   The employer's refusal was held not to violate section 8(a)(5), since the expansion of the unit was not a mandatory subject.   This principle can work to the disadvantage of the employer on occasion, witness the situation in F. W. Woolworth Co. (1969).   There the Board held that the employer could not lawfully insist that bargaining with the union certified for culinary department employees be conditioned on the presence of the union certified to represent selling and nonselling employees, even though the employer believed joint bargaining to be dictated by common working conditions of all employees.   So too, the employer cannot normally condition its bargaining upon the *exclusion* from the union's negotiating committee of members of other unions so long as the committee seeks to bargain solely on behalf of the employees in the single unit.   General Elec. Co. v. NLRB (2d Cir. 1969). This departure from the usual principle that arrangements for negotiations are mandatory subjects is dictated by the statutory objective of assuring the parties freedom to select their own bargaining representatives.   Indeed, section 8(b)(1)(B) forbids a union "to restrain or coerce . . . any employer in the selection of his representatives for the purposes of collective bargaining or the adjustment of grievances," and a union has been held to violate that section (without any consideration of section 8(b)(3)) when it insists to impasse on a proposal to resolve a contract dispute by submission to a tribunal which the employer did not establish and on which it has no representative.   Associated Gen. Contractors v. NLRB (7th Cir. 1972). This represents a departure as well from the general principle that grievance and arbitration provisions are subjects of mandatory bargaining.

Although a union violates section 8(b)(3) when it insists that bargaining be carried out not in the unit for which it is certified but in an industrywide, companywide or other multi-unit negotiation, much the same objective can apparently be secured if two or more unions coordinate their insistence on a mandatory subject such as the duration of the collective bargaining agreement. In United States Pipe & Foundry Co. v. NLRB (5th Cir. 1962) it was held lawful for three unions representing different groups of the employer's workers in separate negotiations to demand a common contract expiration date. Although this meant that in the future the employer would be forced to bargain with the three unions simultaneously (likely about similar proposals) and would thus be exposed to a unified strike threat, the court relied on this fact not to invalidate the unions' insistence but rather to uphold it:

> Under the facts of this case viewed realistically, a common expiration date of all three contracts had a vitally important connection with the "wages, hours and other terms and conditions of employment" of the employees at each plant. Without a common expiration date, any union striking for a new contract on a different date might have to "bail with a sieve" while the employer shifted its production activities to the other plant or plants. With a common expiration date, it is obvious that each union might be able to negotiate a more advantageous new contract for the employees represented by that union.

The Board finding of a section 8(b)(3) violation was also overturned in Joint Negotiating Committee v. NLRB (Phelps Dodge) (3d Cir. 1972). There, the employer was confronted with simultaneous union demands in different negotiations for, among other things, the simultaneous settlement of all of the contracts and for a most-favored nation provision (which would require the employer to give to the signatory union the benefit of any more favorable terms extended by the employer to any of the other unions). The court concluded that the good faith insistence on the separate mandatory terms was not tantamount to a demand for uniform companywide terms and that the likelihood of an impact outside the unit was insufficient for a violation. (The union may not, however, stall negotiations over trivialities or otherwise delay submission of its contract to a ratification vote in order to have the employees vote it down because its terms are less favorable than those in a recently negotiated national agreement. Los Angeles Mailers Union No. 9 (1965).)

Finally, just as the union may not insist that the employer bargain with it for employees outside the certified unit, it may not insist on recognition as representative of persons wholly outside the coverage of the Labor Act, such as supervisors, NLRB v. Retail Clerks Int'l Ass'n (Safeway Stores) (9th Cir. 1953), or agricultural laborers, District 50, UMW (Central Soya Co.) (1963). Nor need the employer bargain with the union about the rights of former employees who are presently retired—even regarding subjects, such as health insurance, which would otherwise be mandatory. So held the Supreme Court in Allied Chem. Workers v. Pittsburgh Plate Glass (U.S.1971).

There, the employer and union had previously negotiated a health insurance plan for retirees, but when Medicare was introduced the employer wrote directly to each of the retirees informing them that it would pay the monthly premiums for supplemental Medicare coverage if the retiree would withdraw from the negotiated plan. The Board found the subject of medical insurance for retirees to be a mandatory subject concerning which the employer was not free to take such unilateral action, because retirees fell within the statutory definition of "employees" about whose wages and working conditions the employer had to bargain and also because medical benefits for retirees had a direct impact on employees presently within the bargaining unit. The Supreme Court disagreed on both counts. It concluded that the "ordinary meaning of 'employee' does not include retired workers; retired employees have ceased to work for another for hire." It also held that the employer's duty to bargain runs only to a union representing employees in an "appropriate bargaining unit," and that retirees were not included within the terms of the Board's certification (which covered only employees "working on hourly rates") and that retirees and present employees could not together form a proper unit because of their lack of community of interest in working conditions. Nor was the impact of the retirees' medical insurance on the present employees sufficiently direct to warrant mandatory bargaining with the union as representative of those employees. The Court conceded there were some exceptions to the usual principle that "matters involving individuals outside the employment relationship do not fall within [the mandatory] category," but these exceptions are based not on "whether the third-party concern is antagonistic to or compatible with the interests of bargaining-unit employees, but whether it vitally affects the 'terms and conditions' of their employment." The employer may be obligated to bargain about payments to third persons which directly threaten the wages of its own employees, or about subcontracting to third persons which directly threatens the very jobs of its own employees, but "the effect that the Board asserts bargaining in behalf of pensioners would have on the negotiation of active employees' retirement plans is too speculative a foundation on which to base an obligation to bargain."

§ 9. Illegal Subjects

For the most part, neither the National Labor Relations Act nor the NLRB dictates what shall or shall not be incorporated in a collective bargaining agreement. The normal premise of collective bargaining in American law is that the parties are free to shape their own contract in light of industrial realities and the balance of economic strength. This premise is modified somewhat by the development of the category of "permissive" proposals which may not be insisted upon as a condition of reaching an agreement; they may, however, be incorporated in an agreement if both parties wish. In rare instances, the Labor Act goes further and forbids even the inclusion in a labor contract of certain provisions which are deemed particularly contrary to the interest of the public or of the employees. To insist upon the inclusion of such a provision as a condition of agreement, or to utilize a strike or lockout in support of such a demand, is held to constitute bad-faith bargaining in violation of section 8(a)(5) or 8(b)(3). Even if many of these illegal subjects can be said to relate to wages, hours and working conditions—such that insistence would not be made illegal by virtue of the "permissive" classification of such subjects—it should surely follow that one ought not be permitted to condition discussion of mandatory subjects on the agreement of the other party to violate the law. The Board has indeed held, in NMU (Texas Co.) (1948), *enf'd* (2d Cir. 1949):

> [W]hat the Act does not permit is the insistence, as a condition precedent to entering into a collective bargaining agreement, that the other party to the negotiations agree to a provision or take some action which is unlawful or inconsistent with the basic policy of the Act. Compliance with the Act's requirement of collective bargaining cannot be made dependent upon the acceptance of provisions in the agreement which, by their terms or in their effectuation, are repugnant to the Act's specific language or basic policy.

See also NLRB v. Wooster Div. of Borg-Warner Corp. (U.S.1958) (Harlan, J., concurring: "Of course an employer or union cannot insist upon a clause which would be illegal under the Act's provisions . . . .").

The employer and the union violate the Act when they agree that only union members shall be hired. This constitutes discrimination in hiring which encourages union membership and is not protected by the union-security proviso to section 8(a)(3). A union which insists, over an employer's objection, that such a provision be included in a labor contract violates the express ban in section 8(b)(2): "It shall be an unfair labor practice for a labor organization or its agents to cause or attempt to cause an employer to discriminate against an employee in violation of subsection (a)(3) . . . ." The union has been held also to violate section 8(b)(3) by bargaining in bad faith. Amalgamated Meat Cutters Union (Great Atl. & Pac. Tea Co.) (1949). The same should be true generally of illegal union-security provisions not sheltered by the statute, including hiring hall agreements which provide that preference in job referrals shall be given to union members. The employer and the union also violate the Act when they agree to a "hot cargo" provision declared illegal by section 8(e). In substance, such a provision requires the contracting employer to refrain from doing business with some other company which the union is seeking to organize or is otherwise seeking to pressure in a labor dispute. Section 8(e) declares it an unfair labor practice for the parties to agree to such a clause, and also declares the clause itself invalid. If the union demands such a provision from a resisting employer, and backs its demands by a strike or by other forms of threat or coercion, it violates the explicit ban of section 8(b)(4)(A). Such conduct would also presumably violate the union's duty to bargain in good faith, although little of substance appears to turn on this additional explanation of illegal conduct.

Other contract provisions, although not explicitly outlawed by the Labor Act, have been deemed unlawful such that insistence on their incorporation in the labor contract will violate the duty to bargain in good faith. Thus, an employer violates section 8(a)(5) when it insists to impasse, during a strike, that "superseniority" credit be given to strikebreakers and to employees who remain at work, since such superseniority has been held by the Supreme Court to discriminate unlawfully against those engaging in union activities. Philip Carey Mfg. Co. v. NLRB (6th Cir. 1964). A union which insists on a contract clause requiring disparate job treatment of white and black employees, in violation of its duty to represent fairly all employees in the bargaining unit, has been found by the Board to violate section 8(b)(3). Hughes Tool Co. (1964). And a union which insists on a contract provision forbidding employees on their nonworking time to solicit on behalf of an opposing union will also be deemed to violate section 8(b)(3), since the Supreme Court has held that such a provision cannot be incorporated even willingly by the union and the employer in view of its interference with the communicational rights of employees. NLRB v. Magnavox Co. (U.S.1974).

In rare instances, contract clauses will be found to violate legislation other than the Labor Act, such as the federal antitrust laws. Thus, employers and unions may not agree—even freely and without coercion—to have the unions extract a wage rate from other competing employers with the object of driving those employers out of business. If over union objection, employers with this object insisted on such a wage rate, this would presumably violate not only the antitrust laws but also section 8(a)(5), even though on its face the subject in issue is within the mandatory category of "wages, hours and terms and conditions of employment." UMW v. Pennington (U.S. 1965). More clearly, union insistence on a schedule of prices to be charged by employers in the sale of their products would be unlawful, since agreement on such a term would likely violate the antitrust laws and the subject would in any event be "permissive" only (since the impact on the mandatory subject of wages would likely be considered insufficiently direct). Local 189, Meat Cutters v. Jewel Tea Co. (U.S.1965).

CHAPTER XXII

BARGAINING REMEDIES

The usual remedy issued by the Board in a case of a refusal to bargain, either by employer or union, is an order requiring that the wrongdoer cease and desist from its illegal conduct and begin instead to bargain in good faith. This is clearly authorized by section 10(c) of the Labor Act, which empowers the Board to issue any "order requiring such person to cease and desist from such unfair labor practice, and to take such affirmative action including reinstatement of employees with or without back pay as will effectuate the policies of the Act." The Board will also order the wrongdoer to post appropriate notices to employees, and in cases of particularly serious violations may order that the notice be individually mailed to all employees at their homes, and that the union be given access to company bulletin boards and to a list of employee names and addresses. IUE v. NLRB (Tiidee Prods., Inc.) (D.C.Cir. 1974). Such orders do little to deter the willful violator, since in substance they merely direct that party to begin now—after months and sometimes years have passed since the refusal to bargain—to abide by the Act's mandates in the future. The Board has thus rather recently begun to utilize additional remedies, and in fact has been called upon by certain appellate courts to be more assertive yet in fashioning remedies which will more effectively make the employees whole and in the process deprive the wrongdoer of the fruits of its illegal conduct.

To remedy the unfair labor practice of refusing to sign an already negotiated contract, the Board may order the wrongdoer to sign the contract and to make payments to employees according to its terms. Thus, in NLRB v. Strong (U.S.1969), a multiemployer association reached agreement with a union on employee compensation, but an employer member of the association attempted to withdraw and refused to sign the agreement. The Board ordered the employer to sign the agreement and to pay all fringe benefits provided for therein. Although the employer attacked this order as improperly making contract compliance an issue to be resolved by the Board rather than by an arbitrator privately selected, the Supreme Court held that it fell comfortably within the Board's power under the Labor Act to order "affirmative action . . . [to] effectuate the policies of the Act." The Board has also been held to have the power to order an employer to sign a contract when it had reached agreement on that contract but was insisting as well that the union agree to include a strike-ballot clause; since such a clause was held by the Supreme Court to be "permissive" only, such that the employer could not validly insist upon its inclusion, the Board could order the employer to abide by the negotiated contract without it. NLRB v. Central Mach. & Tool Co. (10th Cir. 1970). An order to sign may issue against a union as well as against an employer. NLRB v. Local 42, Heat & Frost Insulators (3d Cir. 1972) (union bargained with employer association and then refused to sign the agreement, making a manifestly groundless claim that association was not the proper party).

The Board may also order that the employer who has failed to bargain in good faith must pay backpay to employees whose jobs were lost as a result. Perhaps the leading case is Fibreboard Paper Prods. Corp. v. NLRB (U.S.1964). There, the employer without consulting with the union representing its maintenance employees entered into a subcontract to have the maintenance work done less expensively by an outside concern and terminated its own employees. The Supreme Court upheld the Board in finding that the employer was obligated to bargain with the union before subcontracting and sustained the Board's order requiring termination of the subcontract, reinstitution of the maintenance operation within the plant and reinstatement with backpay of the terminated employees.

The period for which backpay is computed normally begins with the date on which the employees were laid off pursuant to the employer's unilateral decision and runs until the date when the employer could have lawfully shut down if that can be determined, or until the employer "cures" its wrongdoing, by either beginning to bargain with the union or actually offering the employees reinstatement; interest will be added, and earnings elsewhere during the period deducted. Kronenberger d/b/a American Needle & Novelty Co. (1973). The passing of time between the illegal refusal to bargain and the entry of an enforceable order may make it unfair to the employees to compute backpay at the rate prevailing at the time of the refusal to bargain but unfair to the employer to compute backpay for the entire period at the rate which would have prevailed at the time of the final order. On remand, in Fibreboard Paper Prods. Corp. (1969), the Board awarded backpay over the near decade of litigation in accordance with a formula that provided an increasing amount of backpay each year. For some ten years before the subcontracting decision, the maintenance employees had been paid pursuant to the so-called Pabco Wage Formula at one dollar per day less than the "prevailing Building and Construction Crafts Scale," and the backpay order required that the pay for the illegally discharged maintenance workers keep pace during the period preceding their reinstatement—even though the final wage rate awarded by the Board was higher than that to which the union eventually assented in bargaining for the employees who actually returned to work. The Board found the Pabco formula to be the "most reasonable, acceptable, and objective approximation," drawing all inferences against the employer-respondent, whose wrongdoing had injured the employees:

> Indeed, as the Respondent contends, the Union might not
> have been able to persuade the Respondent not to contract-

out or retain the "Pabco formula." On the other hand, it is by no means clear that the parties could not have reached an agreement in 1959 which would not have eliminated the "Pabco formula." The fact that the Respondent did not give the Union an opportunity to attempt to reach such an agreement was found violative of the Act. Thus, any uncertainty with respect to what wage rates the backpay claimants would have received except for termination was created by the Respondent, which bears the risk of that uncertainty.

Compare NLRB v. Mooney Aircraft, Inc. (5th Cir. 1967) (backpay for discriminatee computed on assumption that he would have been promoted had he not been unlawfully discharged).

The Supreme Court decision in *Fibreboard* supports not only a backpay order but also an order requiring that the employer terminate its contract with a third party and reinstitute the operation that had been improperly terminated without bargaining. Presumably, the Board has the power under the Labor Act to order the reacquisition of assets and the reopening of a facility as a means of restoring the status quo, as a predicate to its order to commence bargaining in good faith or truly to make the employees whole. But just as courts have been reluctant even to find a duty to bargain when the employer has terminated an operation, the Board—even when it finds there has been a violation of the duty to bargain—will often temper its remedy, particularly when the employer's decision has been made not in order to avoid its obligation to the union but rather for genuine economic reasons. Thus, the Board has refrained from ordering a newspaper company to undo its consummated decision to switch from the hot-type composing process to cold type, when that decision had been made "to meet the demands of increased competition and expanding markets" and when an order to restore the old process would have driven the employer out of business if it did not also embrace several other employers which were not parties to the Board proceeding. Rochet d/b/a Renton News Record (1962). See New York Mirror (1965) (closing of newspaper and sale of all assets).

But in a case like *Fibreboard*, where the employer's decision—although economically motivated—does not involve the dismantling or disposition of company assets or investment in automated equipment, the Board is less reluctant to order the employer to oust the subcontractor and reinstate the dischargees. For example, in Kronenberger d/b/a American Needle & Novelty Co. (1973), in which the employer had transferred certain operations from one of its plants (which otherwise kept operating) to be absorbed in another, the Board ordered the employer to remedy its refusal to bargain by resuming its operations at the original plant and offering reinstatement to the former employees there. See also Abingdon Nursing Center (1972) (resumption of hot-lunch program). The Board has gone even further, and required an employer which had without bargaining terminated its trucking operation and sold off its trucks to repurchase the trucks and then proceed to bargain about the decision to terminate. On review, however, the court of appeals remanded, noting that although the extensive investment in reopening the transportation department would ordinarily be irrelevant to the imposition of sanctions, the record in the case failed to demonstrate that this "coerced investment" was necessary to effectuate the policies of the Act; the employer even when bargaining lawfully would have been entitled to insist on pursuing its decision to use public carriers rather than its own employees. NLRB v. American Mfg. Co. (5th Cir. 1965) (reinstatement is properly ordered only in the event the employer upon bargaining agrees to reinstitute the discontinued operation). In these cases involving "large scale" employer changes, the Board normally limits its remedy so as to include an order to bargain about reinstituting the operation, reinstating the employees in the event of reinstitution, bargaining about the effects or impact of the termination and, when the employer maintains a business elsewhere, to place the terminated employees on a preferential hiring list for comparable jobs at those other locations. When the employer has unlawfully failed to bargain about a decision to relocate its business, the Board has on occasion ordered the employer to bargain at the new location with the union that had represented the employees at the old location. In view of the possibility that this might interfere with the collective bargaining rights of the employees at the new location, some courts have been hesitant to enforce such an unconditional bargaining order. Cooper Thermometer Co. v. NLRB (2d Cir. 1967).

As broad as are the remedial powers of the Board in bargaining cases, the Supreme Court has held that those powers must be limited by other policies of the Labor Act, one of which is the impropriety of government determination of substantive contract terms. In H. K. Porter Co. v. NLRB (U.S.1970), the employer's refusal to accede to the union's demand for a contract provision for checkoff of union dues was found by the Board to be motivated not by business reasons but by a desire to frustrate negotiations and undermine the union. After a number of appeals and remands, the Board adopted the suggestion of the Court of Appeals for the District of Columbia Circuit and ordered the employer to grant to the union a contract clause providing for checkoff. The Supreme Court held that such an order, imposing a substantive contract term not actually agreed upon, exceeded the Board's powers. The Court found that the statutory policy incorporated in section 8(d) favoring private determination of contract terms and not requiring the making of concessions carried over to section 10(c) relating to the issuance of remedies:

> The Board's remedial powers under § 10 of the Act are broad, but they are limited to carrying out the policies of the Act itself. One of these fundamental policies is freedom of contract. While the parties' freedom of contract is not

absolute under the Act, allowing the Board to compel agreement when the parties themselves are unable to do so would violate the fundamental premise on which the Act is based —private bargaining under governmental supervision of the procedure alone, without any official compulsion over the actual terms of the contract.

The Board has since taken to heart the reprimand in the *Porter* case and has declined an invitation from the District of Columbia court of appeals to fashion a new and potentially most effective remedy known as the "compensatory bargaining order" or the "make-whole remedy." Such an order would require the employer which has unlawfully refused for a period of time to bargain with a majority union, and is ultimately ordered to do so, to pay an amount measured by the economic benefits which the employees would have received had the employer bargained in a lawful and timely manner. In Ex-Cell-O Corp., *enf'd* (D.C.Cir. 1970), the trial examiner had ordered such an employer to compensate each of the injured employees "the monetary value of the minimum additional benefits, if any, including wages, which it is reasonable to conclude that the Union would have been able to obtain through collective bargaining with the employer," but the Board, in a 3–2 decision, refused to adopt that part of the order. It held that such an order would be punitive, since it would amount to a penalty imposed upon an employer for utilizing the only statutory method available to challenge a Board finding in a representation case, that is, a refusal to bargain; it would also be an improperly speculative order, since the Board could not objectively determine what terms the parties would have agreed upon had the employer promptly bargained, or indeed whether any agreement would have been reached at all; and a make-whole order would exceed the Board's powers and violate the principle announced by the Supreme Court in *H. K. Porter* by determining substantive contract terms.

The same year, the Court of Appeals for the District of Columbia Circuit held that the Board was mistaken in believing it had no power to issue a make-whole order. In IUE v. NLRB (Tiidee Products) (D.C.Cir. 1970), *mdf'd* (1972), *mdf'd* (D.C.Cir. 1974), the employer had entered into an election agreement with the union in which it agreed to be bound by the results of the election and any rulings made by the regional director. The employer nonetheless repudiated the union's election victory and claimed that the regional director had acted arbitrarily and capriciously. The Board found this a refusal to bargain in good faith, and the court of appeals, finding that the employer's refusal was indeed "a clear and flagrant violation of the law" resting on "patently frivolous" objections to the election, suggested that the Board could remedy the violation by ordering make-whole relief calculated by "a determination, on the basis of all the evidence available, of what it is likely the parties would have agreed to

. . . ." The court pointed to the ineffectiveness of the prospective cease-and-desist order either to deter wrongdoing or to recompense the employees for past injury (which even the *Ex-Cell-O* Board acknowledged) and the need to discourage employers from clogging the Board and court dockets with frivolous claims. Without the make-whole order, the employer is improperly permitted to pay the employees less than it otherwise would and thus to reap the benefits of its unlawful conduct; it would also be in a position by delay to undermine employee support for the duly designated bargaining representative. The make-whole order would not violate *H. K. Porter,* concluded the court, because it would compensate only for past wrongs and not dictate contract terms for the future, and because it would be based only on a Board assessment of the terms the parties would have freely agreed upon had bargaining taken place. The court underlined the fact that the employer before it was making no good faith claim on a "debatable" issue but was flagrantly violating its duty to bargain.

This distinction between an employer refusal to bargain which is designed to test a "debatable" claim of fact or law and the flagrantly frivolous refusal has subsequently been utilized to justify the denial of make-whole relief, both in the District of Columbia, Steelworkers v. NLRB (Quality Rubber Mfg. Co.) (D.C.Cir. 1970) (court rejects Board's disinclination to draw the distinction); Joint Bd., Amal. Clothing Workers v. NLRB (Levi Strauss & Co.) (D.C.Cir. 1970) (union claim to recognition on basis of authorization cards raises factually debatable issue); and in other courts of appeals, Culinary Alliance & Bartenders Union Local 703 v. NLRB (9th Cir. 1973) (court notes that *Tiidee* holding has not been adopted elsewhere and rests denial of make-whole relief on employer's good faith); Lipman Motors v. NLRB (2d Cir. 1971) (court also reserves decision of *Tiidee* issue). Compare Amalgamated Local Union 355 v. NLRB (2d Cir. 1973) (affirmative discussion of *Tiidee* and expansion of Board remedies, in context of 8(b)(1) and (2) violations). At least one other court of appeals has in fact endorsed, in dictum, the use of the *Tiidee* remedy in the case of the flagrant violation. United Steelworkers v. NLRB (Metco, Inc.) (5th Cir. 1974) (make-whole relief necessary for Board to discharge its remedial responsibilities; not ordered here, since employer claim that union had coerced employees was fairly debatable).

Nonetheless, the Board has clung to its refusal to issue a make-whole order even in the case of a flagrant employer violation—in *Tiidee* itself, on remand. Tiidee Pros. Inc. (1972), *mdf'd* (D.C.Cir. 1974). While the Board acknowledged that the court of appeals decision was the law of the case, it concluded that it could not construct from the evidence the contract that the parties would have made but for the employer's violation of section 8(a)(5). On review once again, the court finally acquiesced in the Board's refusal to grant make-whole relief, finding that the Board's inability to devise such a remedy on the record before it was an adequate reason and also that the Board had used its expert and informed discretion to balance the difficulties of computation against the "relative ease and certainty" of calculating the award that the Board *did* grant—an order that the employer "[p]ay to the Board and the Union the costs and expenses incurred by them in the investigation, preparation and presentation of these cases before the National Labor Relations Board and the court," including "reasonable counsel fees, salaries, witness fees, transcript and record costs, printing costs, travel expenses and per diem, and other reasonable costs and expenses." (The court modified this to deny reimbursement of the Board's legal expenses and to award only those legal expenses of the union incurred prior to the Board's initial *Tiidee* decision, for after that the employer was prepared to bargain and had contested in litigation only the issue of appropriate remedies.) In addition to such litigation expenses, the Board in *Tiidee* took note of the employer's flagrant violation and required the employer to mail a copy of the Board-ordered notice to each employee, to give the union access for one year to the company's bulletin boards for the purpose of posting notices concerning union business, and to supply the union with a list of employee names and addresses kept current for a one-year period. The Board, however, refrained from granting the request of the union that it be reimbursed for dues and fees allegedly lost by reason of the employer's refusal to bargain (since this would be too much like the make-whole remedy), or for the union's expenses incurred in organizing the employees (since the union had actually been successful in the representation election).

The Supreme Court in a subsequent decision clarified the respective authority of the Board and the courts of appeals in remedying bargaining violations. In NLRB v. Food Store Employees Local 347 (Heck's, Inc.) (U.S.1974), the Board had denied an order requiring the employer to pay litigation expenses and union organizing expenses, but the court of appeals modified the order (without remanding to the Board) to include these directions; the court rested its modification on the Board's willingness in the interim in *Tiidee* to order the payment of litigation expenses and its apparent willingness expressed in that case to award organizing expenses when the record showed that the employer's unlawful conduct had added to the union's pre-election organizing expenditures. The Supreme Court reversed, holding that the court exceeded its authority by expanding the scope of the order without remanding to the Board. This was not "the exceptional situation in which crystal clear Board error renders a remand an unnecessary formality"; the Board, having primary responsibility to fashion remedies under the Act, should have been given the opportunity to exercise its discretion as to whether, for example, the taxing of litigation expenses would unduly hinder the assertion of "debatable" defenses by the employer (in *Heck's*) in contrast to the frivolous defenses asserted in *Tiidee*. The Court stated:

> Thus, when a reviewing court concludes that an agency invested with broad discretion to fashion remedies has apparently abused that discretion by omitting a remedy justified in the court's view by the factual circumstances, remand to the agency for reconsideration, and not enlargement of the agency order, is ordinarily the reviewing court's proper course. Application of that general principle in this case best respects the congressional scheme investing the Board and not the courts with the broad powers to fashion remedies that will effectuate national labor policy. It also affords the Board the opportunity, through additional evidence or findings, to reframe its order better to effectuate that policy.

On remand, the Board stated that it would award such organizing and litigation expenses only when the defenses asserted by the employer in refusing to bargain are "frivolous" but not when they are "debatable" (such as defenses which rest upon determinations of credibility of witnesses). Heck's Inc. (1974).

ENFORCEMENT OF THE COLLECTIVE BARGAINING AGREEMENT

CHAPTER XXIII

THE COLLECTIVE BARGAINING AGREEMENT AND THE DUTY TO ARBITRATE

§ 1. The Collective Bargaining Agreement

The anticipated, and usual, product of collective bargaining is a written agreement between the employer and the union. In part, this agreement sets down the relationship between those two parties, for example in provisions dealing with the recognition of the union as exclusive representative for employees in the bargaining unit or dealing with the resolution of contract disputes through a grievance procedure. In greatest measure, the labor contract sets down the relationship between the employer and its employees, and among the employees themselves. Thus, the contract will normally have provisions governing wages, hours, discipline, promotions and transfers, medical and health insurance, pensions, vacations and holidays, work assignments, seniority and the like. The labor agreement is not a contract of employment; employees are hired separately and individually, but the tenure and terms of their employment once in the unit are regulated by the provisions of the collective bargaining agreement.

The collective bargaining agreement shares with the ordinary commercial contract a number of common features of form and function. But the differences between the labor contract and the commercial contract are of far more profound significance. While the typical commercial contract is the creation of parties who have been joined in a voluntary arrangement sparked by mutual self-interest, the labor contract is the product of a bilateral relationship which is in large measure compelled by law, frequently against the wishes of one of the two parties. Most commercial contracts regulate the rights and duties of the parties for a single and transient transaction, or for a defined period of time. The labor contract, while fixed in duration, will usually govern the parties' relationship for a number of years and looks toward an indefinite period of continued dealing in the future. While the labor contract resembles the commercial contract in its form, in that it is technically an agreement between two signatory parties, it most pointedly shapes the rights and duties for a mass of third persons, the employees in the plant. Those employees spend a great part of their life doing the work which is the subject of the labor contract. By articulating or absorbing a host of rules and regulations for carrying on the day-to-day continuing activities of those employees, the labor contract functions more like a statute or a code of regulations than it does a bilateral agreement. Moreover, the union, although a legal entity with capacity to contract, does not speak for a single monolithic constituency but rather for an amalgam of workers who are skilled and unskilled, young and old, male and female, black and white, educated and uneducated, whose ambitions, needs and interests frequently come into conflict.

Because of many of these characteristics, the labor contract—burdened with the task of regulating a complex work community on a continuing basis—cannot reduce to writing each and every norm or rule that has been developed over time to govern the parties' activities. It is common to treat the collective bargaining agreement as comprised not only of the written and executed document but also of plant customs and industrial practices as well as of informal agreements and concessions made at the bargaining table but not reduced to writing. Moreover, many contract provisions contain purposeful ambiguities or silences, in the expectation that no dispute will arise over their meaning or that future disputes will be resolved in due course to the mutual satisfaction of the parties. The parties normally realize that resolution of contract disputes will require formal procedures, typically culminating in recourse to a neutral third party; by this process of grievance settlement and arbitration, the contract itself evolves and the process of collective bargaining continues. Both the labor contract and the commercial contract are negotiated subject to applicable rules of contract law and of public policy, but the labor contract is far more peculiarly enmeshed in a framework of regulatory laws—in part state law but always against the background of federal labor legislation, and in part conventional contract law but always against the background of the special history of labor-management relations in America. Because of this, there are a number of different decisionmaking agencies which are potentially implicated in the construction and application of the terms of the labor contract: state courts and federal courts, privately selected arbitrators, state administrative agencies, the National Labor Relations Board, and other federal agencies (such as the Equal Employment Opportunity Commission or the Department of Labor).

§ 2. Arbitration

Most collective bargaining agreements contain express provision for resolution of contract disputes not by a lawsuit in a civil court but rather through machinery which is internal to the plant or company. Complaints of contract breach (and frequently, any kind of complaint whether or not related to the contract) are typically brought, by the union or the individual grievant, to a low-level supervisor in the first instance, and if unresolved to higher levels of supervision. If the dispute remains unresolved at the highest level of confrontation between union officials (sometimes at the international level) and company officials (commonly at companywide levels outside the plant), it will be submitted to an arbitrator, voluntarily selected by the parties to the contract.

Most commonly, the arbitration is conducted before an individual, although occasionally it will be a three-person panel (with each party appointing one member of the panel more as an advocate than as a neutral). Typically, the arbitrator is selected on an ad hoc basis to decide only a single case. In some of the larger industrial bargaining units, however, in light of the volume of grievances, a permanent umpire or referee will be selected, to be paid an annual retainer and to handle all of the cases going to arbitration under a given contract or group of contracts. Arbitrators come most frequently from the ranks of the legal profession or the teaching profession (most commonly, professors of law or economics or industrial relations), although there will sometimes be resort to a local clergyman or other respected person in the community. There are also a relatively small number of full-time professional labor arbitrators. Government or private organizations, primarily the Federal Mediation and Conciliation Service or the American Arbitration Association, facilitate the selection of an arbitrator by supplying the parties with lists of names of qualified persons from which the parties are to choose; not surprisingly, the parties will frequently research earlier arbitration decisions rendered by the persons on the list, in an effort to determine their "leanings."

There are some important differences between the ad hoc arbitrator and the permanent umpire. The latter over the course of time develops a familiarity with the parties, with the contract, with past negotiations, with the physical set-up of the plant and with plant practices. By virtue of this familiarity, he is sometimes expected by the parties (or assumes that he is expected) to consider the long-range implications of particular decisions and the overall working relationship between the parties, rather than to render a "literal" decision within the four corners of the written document. The ad hoc arbitrator, appointed to decide a single dispute, may not have this kind of familiarity and feels constrained to take a more particularistic or legalistic attitude toward the dispute, the parties and the agreement. Whether these differing attitudes are appropriate is, however, a source of considerable disagreement within the arbitral fraternity. Some observers have pointed out another difference between the permanent and the ad hoc arbitrator, noting the greater likelihood that the ad hoc arbitrator—whose future reemployment by the parties may depend on it—will render a decision which is excessively cautious about offending one party or the other and which tends to "split the difference." Support for this claim is said to be commonly found in discharge grievances, where the arbitrator will find the discharge to have been without just cause and will order the grievant reinstated, but without imposing on the company any liability for backpay.

In any event, whether the arbitrator is designated on a permanent or an ad hoc basis, he will sometimes be required to determine whether he is properly simply a creature of the parties whose function is to determine no more than what their private-contractual intentions are, or is more like a civil judge who can (or must) consider such "external" matters as law and public policy. This issue can arise when one party relies upon an explicit provision in the agreement and the other party claims that the arbitrator must find the provision to violate the National Labor Relations Act or Title VII of the 1964 Civil Rights Act and must refuse to give it effect. Here too, the arbitration fraternity is sharply split. The matter is further complicated by the fact that, as noted above, many arbitrators are not trained in the law but are selected rather for their expertise in industrial relations or because they are a respected "lay" figure in the community. An added source of difficulty are the statements in a number of judicial opinions to the effect that an arbitrator's award will be subject to court reversal if the arbitrator strays from the agreement and bases his opinion solely upon the assumed requirements of statutory or case law.

On the whole arbitration proceedings are more informal, more expeditious and less costly than civil litigation. Frequently, the parties are not represented by lawyers (but by a full-time union representative and an industrial-relations or personnel executive for the company). Formal rules of evidence do not apply, and arbitrators tend to admit "for what it is worth" a substantial amount of evidence which would normally be objectionable as immaterial or hearsay. The presentation of written or oral evidence is commonly quite informal and unstructured. In many cases, the purpose of the proceeding is more to "ventilate" the grievance than to secure a favorable decision from the arbitrator. The arbitrator's decision, usually in writing, tends to be brief, undetailed, and untechnical; it will commonly be filed with the parties less than a month after the hearing. Written briefs are not common, and in almost all cases in which they are filed, are submitted after the hearing rather than before. Many of these informal qualities—which have always made arbitration a most attractive alternative to civil litigation—have been giving way in recent years to a greater "legalization" of the arbitration process, as lawyers have been called in to serve as arbitrators and as parties have increasingly called in legal counsel to represent them at hearings.

§ 3. Section 301 and the *Lincoln Mills* Decision

The elaborate administrative machinery created by the Wagner Act of 1935, with provisions for employee elections and for redress of employer unfair labor practices, was designed to foster collective bargaining—the bilateral regulation of conditions of employment by consensual agreement—and ultimately industrial peace. Yet Congress determined in 1947 that these goals were substantially frustrated by varying state laws of contract and procedure which made it highly impracticable if not impossible to secure judicial enforcement of promises in collective bargaining agreements. Among the major obstacles to enforcement were rules barring suit against the union as an entity and requiring instead that all members of the union be joined and served as parties defendant; common law rules barring enforcement of executory promises to arbitrate contract disputes; and statutory restrictions, like the Norris-LaGuardia Act in the federal courts and analogous laws in the states, upon the issuance of injunctions against peaceful strikes in the course of a "labor dispute," even when the union had incorporated a no-strike promise in a labor contract.

Congress, believing these obstacles to create disincentives for both employer and union to forgo the use of economic force in resolving contract disputes, enacted section 301 as part of the Taft-Hartley amendments in 1947. Section 301(a) provides:

> Suits for violation of contracts between an employer and a labor organization representing employees in an industry affecting commerce as defined in this Act, or between any such labor organizations, may be brought in any district court of the United States having jurisdiction of the parties, without respect to the amount in controversy or without regard to the citizenship of the parties.

Section 301(b) provides that "Any such labor organization may sue or be sued as an entity and in behalf of the employees whom it represents," and that any money judgment against the union "shall be enforceable only against the organization as an entity and against its assets" and not against any individual union member. Promises in labor contracts were thus made enforceable by company or union in federal courts, without regard to the usual rules governing subject matter jurisdiction. In this manner, Congress remedied the jurisdictional and procedural obstacles to the enforcement of labor contracts.

It was not, however, quite so clear that Congress had intended in section 301 to declare that the applicable rules of contract construction in these federal-court proceedings were to be independent federal substantive rules or whether conventional state contract law was to apply. Were state law indeed to apply, the least that would happen is that federal courts would be unable, for example, to order specific performance of the agreement to arbitrate grievances; the worst is that section 301 would be declared unconstitutional for giving to the federal judiciary jurisdictional power in excess of that contemplated by Article III of the Constitution. Any such doubts were dispelled by the Supreme Court decision in Textile Workers Union v. Lincoln Mills (U.S.1957), which involved an employer breach of promise to submit to arbitration (as the last step in the contract grievance procedure) certain grievances concerning employee workloads and work assignments. The Court held that section 301(a) "authorizes federal courts to fashion a body of federal law for the enforcement of these collective bargaining agreements and includes within that federal law specific performance of promises to arbitrate grievances . . . ." Only thus could the Court give effect to Congress's intention to resolve peacefully disputes during the term of the labor contract, since "plainly the agreement to arbitrate grievance disputes is the *quid pro quo* for an agreement not to strike," and a union will be encouraged to relinquish the strike only if it knows in advance that employers can be held to their promise to resolve contract disputes through arbitration. The Court continued:

> [T]he legislation does more than confer jurisdiction in the federal courts over labor organizations. It expresses a federal policy that federal courts should enforce these agreements . . . . Congress adopted a policy which placed sanctions behind agreements to arbitrate grievance disputes, by implication rejecting the common-law rule . . . . We conclude that the substantive law to apply in suits under § 301(a) is federal law, which the courts must fashion from the policy of our national labor laws. . . . Federal interpretation of the federal law will govern, not state law. . . . But state law, if compatible with the purpose of § 301, may be resorted to in order to find the rule that will best effectuate the federal policy. . . . Any state law applied, however, will be absorbed as federal law and will not be an independent source of private rights.

By applying rules of judge-made federal common law to contract actions under section 301, the federal courts would be assuming jurisdiction over cases or controversies arising within the sphere of congressional power under the Commerce Clause, free of any constitutional infirmity. Nor was the anti-injunction policy of the Norris-LaGuardia Act an impediment to specific performance of arbitration promises, since "the failure to arbitrate was not a part and parcel of the abuses against which the Act was aimed" (*i. e.,* unlike peaceful strikes or picketing, it was not explicitly sheltered by the Act against injunctive relief), and the other procedural requirements of that Act were "inapposite."

§ 4. Applicability of Section 301

In decisions subsequent to *Lincoln Mills*, the Supreme Court announced a number of significant principles concerning the impact and reach of section 301 in the enforcement of collective bargaining agreements. In Charles Dowd Box Co. v. Courtney (U.S.1962), the Court held that section 301 was not designed to oust state courts of their traditional jurisdiction to enforce labor-contract promises, and that actions under that section may be brought either in state or in federal court. Soon after, the Court held that state courts enforcing such promises must, however, refrain from applying local rules of contract law and must apply instead the principles of federal law devised under the mandate of *Lincoln Mills*. In Local 174, Teamsters v. Lucas Flour Co. (U.S.1962), a union called an eight-day strike to protest the discharge of an employee and also invoked the arbitration clause of the labor contract. In spite of the absence in the contract of any express promise by the union not to strike, the employer commenced an action against the union in the state court for damages measured by its business losses during the strike. The state court, purporting to apply local rules of contract construction, held the strike to violate the contract because it was designed to coerce the employer to relinquish its contractual power to discharge employees for unsatisfactory work. The Supreme Court affirmed, but only after concluding that the state court was obligated, in the interest of national uniformity, to apply federal rules of contract construction.

> The possibility that individual contract terms might have different meanings under state and federal law would inevitably exert a disruptive influence upon both the negotiation and administration of collective agreements. Because neither party could be certain of the rights which it had obtained or conceded, the process of negotiating an agreement would be made immeasurably more difficult by the necessity of trying to formulate contract provisions in such a way as to contain the same meaning under two or more systems of law which might some day be invoked in enforcing the contract. Once the collective bargain was made, the possibility of conflicting substantive interpretation under competing legal systems would tend to stimulate and prolong disputes as to its interpretation. Indeed, the existence of possibly conflicting legal concepts might substantially impede the parties' willingness to agree to contract terms providing for final arbitral or judicial resolution of disputes.

State law should not thus be permitted to frustrate the achievement of industrial peace through collective bargaining. The Court in *Lucas Flour* then proceeded to announce a fundamental principle of federal labor-contract law; "[A] strike to settle a dispute which a collective bargaining agreement provides shall be settled exclusively and finally by compulsory arbitration constitutes a violation of the agreement." The Court's implying a no-strike promise commensurate with the arbitration clause was thought to be required by traditional contract law as well as by "the basic policy of national labor legislation to promote the arbitral process as a substitute for economic warfare." (Presumably, the parties are free by clear and explicit language to reserve to the union the right to strike concerning grievances subject to the arbitration clause.)

The Court has also given a broad and hospitable interpretation to the terms of section 301 itself, which gives to federal courts the power to adjudicate "suits for violation of contracts between an employer and a labor organization." Although it was argued that the phrase "between an employer and a labor organization" modified the word "suits," such that an action by an individual employee for breach of the labor contract would fall without the reach of section 301, this was rejected by the Supreme Court in Smith v. Evening News Ass'n (U.S.1962). There, an employee sued his employer for violation of the provision in the labor contract barring discrimination because of union activity. The Court held, assuming that the contract gave a substantive right directly enforceable by individual employees, that such an action could be brought under section 301 and would be governed by judge-made principles of federal law. Later, in Vaca v. Sipes (U.S.1967), the Court stated that a section 301 action for breach of a contract promise by the employer may be brought directly against the employer by the aggrieved employee in the event the union wrongfully refuses to process his grievance in violation of its duty to represent the employee fairly and without arbitrary discrimination. Indeed, the Court has applied section 301 to an action to compel arbitration which was brought against not the employer which had signed the labor contract and promised to arbitrate but rather against a "successor" employer into which the predecessor company was absorbed through merger but which had never itself independently promised to arbitrate. In John Wiley & Sons v. Livingston (U.S.1964), the Court concluded that "the preference of national labor policy for arbitration as a substitute for tests of strength" must intrude somewhat on conventional contract-law policy so that the duty to arbitrate does not automatically terminate when the promisor-predecessor "disappears" by corporate acquisition.

The Supreme Court has read section 301 broadly not only with regard to the kinds of persons covered but also the kind of "contracts" covered. That term has been read, in Retail Clerks Local 128 v. Lion Dry Goods, Inc. (U.S.1962), to embrace not only conventional collective bargaining agreements but also such other labor-management agreements as a "statement of understanding" negotiated in settlement of a strike. That case also held that section 301 was not limited to suits and contracts by majority representatives but included as well actions brought by minority unions on agreements validly made with the employer.

The great majority of cases brought under section 301 are actions to enforce promises to arbitrate and actions to enforce (or set aside) arbitration awards already rendered. It has also been held that courts are given jurisdiction by section 301 over actions for a declaratory judgment brought by an employer seeking a declaration that it is not required by its contract to arbitrate; the court rejected the argument that such an action is not a "suit for violation" of a labor contract. Black-Clawson Co. v. IAM Lodge 355 (2d Cir. 1962). Moreover, section 301 and federal laws are deemed controlling even

548   ENFORCEMENT OF THE AGREEMENT   Ch. 23

when the claimed breach of the labor contract relates to some clause other than the arbitration clause. Thus, they govern actions by an employer against a union for breach of the no-strike clause, whether the relief sought is damages, Atkinson v. Sinclair Ref. Co. (U.S.1962) (employer sued union and individuals for damages, since contract gave it no power to invoke arbitration), or an injunction, Boys Markets, Inc. v. Retail Clerks Local 770 (U.S.1970) (strike injunction authorized by "accommodating" the anti-injunction provisions of the Norris-LaGuardia Act to the policies of section 301). And they govern actions against an employer for violation of a substantive contract term, such as its promise not to discriminate against employees because of their union activity. Smith v. Evening News Ass'n (U.S. 1962).

The Court in Smith v. Evening News Ass'n considerably broadened the impact of section 301 when it confirmed an important principle previously noted by the Court only cursorily—that even though the asserted contract violation in a section 301 action involves conduct which is arguably protected by section 7 or prohibited by section 8 of the Labor Act, judicial jurisdiction to enforce the contract is not preempted by the authority of the National Labor Relations Board. Thus, while principles of federal preemption ordinarily dictate that discharges for antiunion animus be tried to the NLRB and not to any other federal or state tribunal, the strong countervailing federal policy under section 301 for the private adjustment of labor-contract disputes authorizes an enforcement action if the parties have forbidden such a discharge in their contract. A court may, for example, also properly order arbitration of a claim that the employer had violated its contract by assigning work to employees represented by a different union, regardless whether such a claim could also be tested before the NLRB either through its representation (unit-clarification) procedures or its unfair labor practice procedures (governing strikes over work-assignment disputes). Carey v. Westinghouse Elec. Corp. (U.S.1964). The Court ordered arbitration even though one of the contesting unions might well not be a party before the arbitrator, since "resort to arbitration may have a pervasive, curative effect." Should the arbitrator render a decision that is consistent with the principles of the Labor Act, the Board may defer to that decision; if the Board were to disagree, its own decision would of course take precedence (and the employer freed of any liability under section 301 if its conduct is ultimately sustained by the Board). See also Arnold Co. v. Carpenters Dist. Council (U.S.1974) (state court has jurisdiction to enjoin union breach of no-strike clause, even though the breach is arguably also a violation of the work-assignment-strike provisions of section 8(b)(4)(D)).

§ 5. Federal Law Principles

The Supreme Court has announced a number of significant principles of federal contract law in actions under section 301, most finding their source in Congress's desire in enacting that section to substitute the peaceful dispute-resolution machinery of arbitration (and on occasion litigation) for that of the strike, lockout and other economic weapons. While the Court emphasizes that arbitration is a creature of the parties' voluntary agreement and is not to be imposed against their will, it also makes it clear that the collective bargaining agreement is not an ordinary contract to be governed by ordinary principles of contract law and that these principles must be adjusted in light of the imperatives of federal labor policy as principally found in the Labor Act. The first major principle of federal common law regarding labor contracts—that promises to arbitrate may be specifically enforced—was announced by the Supreme Court in Textile Workers Union v. Lincoln Mills (U.S.1957). The Court has also held that the employer's duty to arbitrate is not discharged by the union's breach of its promise not to strike about arbitrable grievances, in spite of the employer's argument that the union's breach constituted a failure of consideration or a repudiation of the grievance and arbitration provisions. Drake Bakeries, Inc. v. Local 50, American Bakery Workers (U.S.1962). The employer was held entitled to and expected to take to arbitration all claims of breach of the agreement, whether minor or as significant as a claimed breach of the no-strike clause, and the Court concluded that the employer's action for damages for breach of the no-strike clause should be tried not to the courts but to the arbitrator.

Another principle of federal judge-made law is that it is no defense to an arbitration action that the employer—a "successor" by merger to the signatory employer—had never promised the union that it would arbitrate contract disputes. In John Wiley & Sons v. Livingston (U.S.1964), a small publishing firm, under contract with the union, was absorbed by merger into a larger nonunion firm. The successor firm rebuffed the claims of the union that the employees carried over into the successor continued to have rights under the predecessor's contract and also rebuffed the union's demand to take such claims to arbitration under the predecessor's contract. The Supreme Court found that, in spite of the usual doctrine of contract law barring enforcement against nonsignatories, federal policy favoring protection of employees in times of business transfers and favoring peaceful resolution of disputes required that the union's claims be arbitrated by the successor. The Court has more recently held, however, that there may be a sufficient discontinuity between the signatory predecessor employer and the successor as to warrant freeing the successor of any alleged duty to arbitrate. Howard Johnson Co. v. Detroit Local Joint Exec. Bd. (U.S.1974). (The issue of the successor's duty to arbitrate is considered in greater detail below.)

Both contract principles and policies of federal labor law have been held by the Supreme Court to warrant implying (in the face of contractual silence) a promise by the union not to strike in protest of employer action which the contract subjects to arbitration. Local 174, Teamsters v. Lucas Flour Co. (U.S.1962). Such a promise, even if only implied, may be specifically enforced by injunction, in spite of the anti-injunction provisions of the Norris-LaGuardia Act. Gateway Coal Co. v. UMW (U.S.1974) (Court implied promise not to strike about allegedly unsafe working conditions, in light of broad arbitration clause construed to cover such disputes). And, in an action for breach of a no-strike promise, the Court has held that section 301(b) forbids suit and judgment for damages against individual officers and members of the union when the union is itself liable. Atkinson v. Sinclair Ref. Co. (U.S.1962). (This principle was subsequently extended by a court of appeals so as to bar damages even against individuals engaged in a "wildcat" strike unauthorized by the union, when the contract forbade work stoppages but the union could not be held liable. Sinclair Oil Corp. v. Oil Workers (7th Cir. 1971).)

Another important principle of federal law, relevant to actions brought by individual employees, is that the court will have no jurisdiction to try alleged employer violations of the contract before the grievance and arbitration machinery has been exhausted, unless the failure to exhaust has been precipitated by the union's failure to represent the aggrieved employee fairly and without arbitrary discrimination. Vaca v. Sipes (U.S.1967).

In spite of the willingness of the Supreme Court to announce these very significant principles as judge-made law under section 301, the Court in UAW v. Hoosier Cardinal Corp. (U.S.1966), held that it would be too "bald a form of judicial innovation" were the federal courts to develop a single uniform period of limitations for contract actions brought under section 301. Since the Court in *Lincoln Mills* had countenanced absorption of state-law principles and since disuniformity of limitations periods was thought to have little disruptive impact when contracts were being negotiated or construed, it was held that the appropriate state statute of limitations should govern, in a federal court as well as in a state court. Some confusion was introduced, however, when the Court in *Hoosier Cardinal* went on to note that a state period of limitations should not apply when it is "unreasonable or otherwise inconsistent with national labor policy"; to hold that federal principles of "characterization" would control in determining which of two possibly applicable state limitations periods (one for oral contracts and one for written contracts) was controlling; and explicitly to avoid the question whether, in the event a choice was necessary between the limitations periods of two states involved in the case, state or federal choice-of-law principles would govern. Lower federal courts have since applied general principles of common law and federal labor policy in selecting between arguably applicable state limitations periods of differing lengths. For example, in Butler v. Local 823, Teamsters (8th Cir. 1975), an action by an individual employee against an employer for breach of an employment agreement, the court applied the state's limitation period for written contracts, even though the employment contract was oral, since the outcome of the action depended upon the interpretation of the written collective bargaining agreement.

§ 6. The Courts and the Arbitrator: The Steelworkers Trilogy

Perhaps the most significant pronouncements of federal law under section 301 have dealt with the construction of the arbitration clause of the labor contract and were announced in three decisions of the Supreme Court involving the Steelworkers Union and since known as the *Steelworkers Trilogy*. In those cases, the Court exalted the role of the arbitrator as a force for industrial peace, articulated a view of the labor contract as a working arrangement between labor and management engrossing unwritten understandings and plant practices not reflected in the written terms, and announced a doctrine of judicial self-restraint in cases in which the parties have assigned the task of dispute resolution to an arbitrator privately selected.

In United Steelworkers v. American Mfg. Co. (U.S.1960), the labor contract contained a grievance procedure terminating in arbitration of all disputes "as to the meaning, interpretation and application of the provisions of this agreement" (hereinafter usually referred to as a "standard" arbitration clause). The union demanded arbitration of its claim that an employee, determined in a compensation action for a job-related injury to be permanently partially disabled, was improperly denied reinstatement to his job. The lower courts denied the union's request in a section 301 action for arbitration, the trial court on the ground that the compensation settlement constituted an estoppel against any claims for reemployment and the court of appeals on the ground that the grievance was "a frivolous, patently baseless one." The Supreme Court reversed, holding that "the agreement is to submit all grievances to arbitration, not merely those that a court may deem to be meritorious." Since the union claimed that the employer had violated a specific contract provision (dealing with seniority), this was a dispute about "the meaning, interpretation and application" of the labor contract, a dispute which the parties agreed was to be decided on the merits by an arbitrator and not by a court.

> The collective agreement calls for the submission of grievances in the categories which it describes, irrespective of whether a court may deem them to be meritorious. . . . The function of the court is very limited when the parties have agreed to submit all questions of contract interpretation to the arbitrator. It is confined to ascertaining whether the party seeking arbitration is making a claim which on its face is governed by the contract. Whether the moving party is right or wrong is a question of contract interpretation for the arbitrator.

> The courts, therefore, have no business weighing the merits of the grievance, considering whether there is equity in a particular claim, or determining whether there is particular language in the written instrument which will support the claim. The agreement is to submit all grievances to arbitration, not merely those which the court will deem meritorious. The processing of even frivolous claims may have therapeutic values of which those who are not a part of the plant environment may be quite unaware.

The Court was careful, when purporting to interpret the terms of the grievance procedure, not to usurp the function of the arbitrator to decide the merits of the grievance.

It is thus the task of the trial court to determine whether the defendant has violated not some underlying substantive provision of the labor contract—such as those dealing with wages, hours, seniority, discipline and the like—but has violated a promise to submit that substantive dispute to the jurisdiction of an arbitrator. This judicial task has been denoted that of determining "substantive arbitrability," and it requires the court to do no more than construe the arbitration clause of the collective bargaining agreement.

In United Steelworkers v. Warrior & Gulf Nav. Co. (U.S.1960), the Court, while announcing that the parties are free to draft the arbitration clause as broadly or narrowly as they wish, since arbitration is a creature not of federal law but of voluntary agreement, held that federal policy under section 301 does justify construing the arbitration clause as hospitably as possible toward sending the case to arbitration. There, the union was seeking arbitration of its claim that the company's contracting out of maintenance work violated the no-lockout clause of the labor contract, while the company resisted arbitration by pointing to a provision that "matters which are strictly a function of management shall not be subject to arbitration." The Court, fashioning new principles of contract construction, refused to apply the presumption against arbitration which obtains in commercial-contract cases and held instead that—since labor arbitration substitutes not for litigation but for "industrial strife"—the arbitration clause should be presumed to embrace the parties' underlying dispute if its language can thus be reasonably read:

> Apart from matters that the parties specifically exclude, all of the questions on which the parties disagree must . . . come within the scope of the grievance and arbitration provisions of the collective agreement . . . .
>
> . . . An order to arbitrate the particular grievance should not be denied unless it may be said with positive assurance that the arbitration clause is not susceptible of an interpretation that covers the asserted dispute. Doubts should be resolved in favor of coverage.

The Court in *Warrior & Gulf* viewed the grievance and arbitration procedure as "a part of the continuous collective bargaining process," since the contract "is an effort to erect a system of industrial self-government" which is so complex that parties must of necessity leave gaps "to be filled in by reference to the practices of the particular industry and of the various shops covered by the agreement."

> The labor arbitrator's source of law is not confined to the express provisions of the contract, as the industrial common law—the practices of the industry and the shop—is equally a part of the collective bargaining agreement although not expressed in it. The labor arbitrator is usually chosen because of the parties' confidence in his knowledge of the common law of the shop and their trust in his personal judgment to bring to bear considerations which are not expressed in the contract as criteria for judgment. The parties expect that his judgment of a particular grievance will reflect not only what the contract says but, insofar as the collective bargaining agreement permits, such factors as the effect upon productivity of a particular result, its consequence to the morale of the shop, his judgment whether tensions will be heightened or diminished. . . . The ablest judge cannot be expected to bring the same experience and competence to bear upon the determination of a grievance, because he cannot be similarly informed.

The Court concluded that the exclusion from arbitration of "matters which are strictly a function of management" did not explicitly enough exclude disputes about subcontracting from the very broad arbitration clause covering any "differences" or "any local trouble of any kind" between the company and the union. Once again, the Court cautioned against becoming "entangled in the construction of the substantive provisions of a labor agreement, even through the back door of interpreting the arbitration clause," and summarized:

> In the absence of any express provision excluding a particular grievance from arbitration, we think only the most forceful evidence of a purpose to exclude the claim from arbitration can prevail, particularly where, as here, the exclusion clause is vague and the arbitration clause quite broad.

In spite of these large principles of judicial deference and arbitral primacy announced in the *Trilogy*, one occasionally finds in the reported decisions a contrary suggestion that a court may find a claim to be so outrageous that arbitration is not to be ordered. For example, in John Wiley & Sons v. Livingston (U.S.1964), the union claimed that a successor employer (not a formal party to the labor contract with the predecessor) was bound by the predecessor's promises concerning job security and fringe benefits. The Court found these grievances substantively arbitrable under a standard arbitration clause, noting:

> It is sufficient for present purposes that the demands are not so plainly unreasonable that the subject matter of the dispute must be regarded as nonarbitrable because it can be seen in advance that no award to the Union could receive judicial sanction.

A similar suggestion for judicial screening of arbitration claims was announced in IUE v. General Elec. Co. (2d Cir. 1968), in which the court envisioned a claim by a party not merely frivolous but "so totally devoid of possible merit" or demonstrating "bad faith on its part so patent" as to warrant withholding the case from arbitration; the claim would be so unconscionable as to constitute "a perversion of the grievance procedure." These intimations are difficult to square with the holding in United Steelworkers v. American Mfg. Co. (U.S.1960), and have in fact apparently not been used as the basis for decision in any case.

The Supreme Court has announced other principles of federal law, under section 301, on the issue of arbitrability. For example, in the *Warrior & Gulf* case itself, the Court acknowledged that the parties could stipulate that the issue of substantive arbitrability—that is, the arbitrator's jurisdiction to decide a particular class of case—was to be decided not by the court but by the arbitrator himself:

> Where the assertion by the claimant is that the parties excluded from court determination not merely the decision of the merits of the grievance but also the question of its arbitrability, vesting power to make both decisions in the arbitrator, the claimant must bear the burden of a clear demonstration of that purpose.

It is in fact common industrial practice to give to the arbitrator the task of deciding his own jurisdiction, thus requiring him to construe the arbitration clause itself. The Court has also held that, contrary to the presumption that substantive arbitrability is to be decided by the trial court rather than by the arbitrator, the issue of "procedural arbitrability"—that is, whether the party demanding arbitration has complied with all of the precedent conditions set forth in the agreement—is to be resolved by the arbitrator. In John Wiley & Sons v. Livingston (U.S.1964), the defendant employer argued that the union could not properly invoke arbitration at step 3 of the grievance procedure, since it had not timely pursued the prior two steps. The Supreme Court held that, since procedural issues such as this are often bound up with the underlying merits of the contract dispute and since judicial examination of alleged procedural defaults would unduly delay settlement through arbitration, procedural arbitrability is properly to be addressed by the arbitrator. Even when delay is alleged to waive the arbitration not because the contract stipulates that it does but because of equitable policies "extrinsic" to the document, the Supreme Court has held that the arbitrator rather than the court is to pass upon the allegation. Operating Engineers Local 150 v. Flair Builders, Inc. (U.S.1972).

The third case of the *Steelworkers Trilogy* was United Steelworkers v. Enterprise Wheel & Car Corp. (U.S.1960), which considered the issue not of enforcing arbitration promises but rather enforcing arbitration awards after they have been rendered. Once again, the Court found in section 301 a policy favoring judicial deference to the contract decisions of arbitrators selected by the parties, in light of arbitral expertise and the parties' general interest in the finality of arbitral awards. In *Enterprise Wheel*, the arbitrator of a discharge grievance found that the protest staged by several employees warranted discipline but nothing as severe as discharge; he thus held that a ten-day suspension was warranted and awarded reinstatement and backpay (which extended beyond the intervening termination date of the labor contract). The Supreme Court overturned an order of the lower court which denied enforcement of that part of the arbitration award granting reinstatement and backpay beyond the contract termination date. The lower court had erred because its judgment was "not based upon any finding that the arbitrator did not premise his award on his construction of the contract. It merely disagreed with the arbitrator's construction." Courts must refuse to review the merits of arbitral awards, lest they undermine the federal policy of settling labor disputes peaceably through arbitration:

> [T]he question of interpretation of the collective bargaining agreement is a question for the arbitrator. It is the arbitrator's construction which was bargained for; and so far as the arbitrator's decision concerns construction of the contract, the courts have no business overruling him because their interpretation of the contract is different from his.

Arbitrators bring to bear, in construing the agreement and fashioning remedies, expert knowledge of plant customs and practices. Although in the case at bar the arbitrator's decision was ambiguous as to the source of its remedy—which may have been either the contract or enacted legislation—this does not warrant setting aside the award, which should be assumed to rest on the contract and thus to be within the scope of the parties' submission. The Court proceeded to accord to the courts a limited power to set aside arbitral awards:

> [A]n arbitrator is confined to interpretation and application of the collective bargaining agreement; he does not sit to dispense his own brand of industrial justice. He may of course look for guidance from many sources, yet his award

is legitimate only so long as it draws its essence from the collective bargaining agreement. When the arbitrator's words manifest an infidelity to this obligation, courts have no choice but to refuse enforcement of the award.

§ 7. Substantive Exclusions from Arbitration

Read together the Supreme Court decisions in United Steelworkers v. American Mfg. Co. (U.S.1960), and United Steelworkers v. Warrior & Gulf Nav. Co. (U.S.1960), stand for the proposition that an employer may be able to point to substantive contract provisions which make the union's grievance a frivolous one on the merits and yet the employer must combat this frivolous grievance only before an arbitrator and not by way of defense in the section 301 action to compel arbitration. The standard arbitration clause contemplates arbitral scrutiny even of employer conduct clearly authorized by the labor contract. Conversely, an explicit exclusion clause may bar from arbitration even a union claim that is clearly *supported* by the substantive provisions of the labor contract. In Communications Workers of America v. New York Telephone Co. (2d Cir. 1964), the union sued to compel arbitration of its claim that certain "temporary" promotions made by the employer violated the seniority provisions of the agreement. The contract did indeed provide that "In selecting employees for promotion . . . seniority shall govern if other necessary qualifications are substantially equal," but the court properly refrained from ordering arbitration, for the contract provision in question continued: "In no event shall any grievance or dispute arising out of this section . . . be subject to the arbitration provisions of this agreement." (When the union's claim is thus clearly excluded from arbitration, it remains to be decided—by construing the contract in some other proceeding—whether the parties contemplated enforcement of that claim by court action or no institutional enforcement at all.)

The efforts of certain parties to hedge the authority of the arbitrator have on occasion resulted in highly elaborate exclusion clauses which, as one court has said, "resemble a trust indenture." IUE v. General Elec. Co. (2d Cir. 1968). There, the parties provided for mandatory arbitration of matters involving "disciplinary action" or any "claimed violation of a specific provision" of the labor contract, but excluded from mandatory arbitration (although reserving for voluntary arbitration on mutual consent of the parties) claims relating to any "implied" obligation under the contract; the arbitration clause even went so far as to instruct any court not to apply any presumption of arbitrability in construing the arbitration and exclusion provisions. Without deciding whether private parties could thus "dilute" the *Trilogy* presumption of arbitrability, the court held that the union's grievances rested on no express provisions of the labor contract and thus were within the exclusion for "implied" employer obligations. A union will also be barred from challenging an employer's refusal to rehire former employees laid off during a negotiating strike when the contract ultimately agreed upon provided for arbitration of controversies "between the employees and the Company" and also excluded claims stemming from pre-contract disputes and claims concerning workers who had been permanently replaced prior to the contract's execution. Local 787, IUE v. Collins Radio Co. (5th Cir. 1963).

Often, the arbitration provision will not contain an explicit exclusion clause, but the court may be asked to find some exclusion from arbitration inherent in the terms of the arbitration clause itself or of some other related provision. Thus, an arbitration clause will often stipulate that "no arbitrator shall have any authority to add to, detract from, or in any way alter the provisions of this Agreement." An employer may assert as a defense in an action to compel arbitration that the union is claiming a violation of an implied employer obligation, perhaps rooted in unwritten past practice, and that such a claim ought not be submitted to arbitration since the arbitrator is being asked to "add to" or "modify" the agreement. Contracts may also provide that "no arbitrator shall have the authority to establish or modify any wage, salary or piece rate, or job classification or authority to decide the appropriate classification of any employee." An employer may assert that such a provision requires withholding from arbitration any grievances related to allegedly unauthorized pay reductions, or promotions allegedly out of seniority order, or the payment of employees at pay rates fixed for lower job classifications. The apparently prevailing view is that these limitations upon the power of the arbitrator relate only to his "authority" to issue a particular kind of award or remedy, a matter which is properly raised only after the arbitral decision has been rendered; these provisions do not deprive the arbitrator of "jurisdiction" to hear the case in the first instance. As the court stated in Carey v. General Elec. Co. (2d Cir. 1963):

> Arbitration may well contribute to industrial peace even if it results in the arbitrator's determination that he can make no valid award because of the limitations upon his authority, or that the employee has no case on the merits. . . .
> We cannot divine now, nor do we deem it proper to predict, the precise form in which the arbitrator will frame his decree. We merely hold that in each of the grievances under discussion, he has the jurisdiction to reach a decision on the merits. Should his decision or the remedy exceed the bounds of his authority as established by the collective bargaining agreement, that abuse of authority is remediable in an action to vacate the award.

It is not the province of the court to announce in advance what the precise issues are for the arbitrator and what are the allowable remedies. Retail Shoe Salesman's Union, Local 410 v. Sears, Roebuck & Co. (N.D.Cal.1960). But see Socony Vacuum Tanker Men's Ass'n v. Socony Mobil Oil Co. (2d Cir. 1966) ("As the parties have been unable to agree upon a statement of the question to be arbitrated we formulate the question as follows . . . ."). The court should thus not withhold from arbitration a grievance asserting discharge without just cause, clearly within the reach of the arbitration promise, merely because what the union is seeking is an arbitral award of reinstatement for an employee whom the employer alleges the federal government would exclude from work because of security reasons. IAM Local 2003 v. Hayes Corp. (5th Cir. 1961) (employee was engaged in maintenance and repair of military aircraft).

The respondent in the section 301 action may also try to argue that, even in the absence of a conventional exclusion provision, the affirmative directions given by the arbitration clause itself contain by negative implication a direction that all other kinds of grievances be excluded. A standard form of arbitration clause provides for arbitration of all grievances relating to the "meaning, interpretation and application of the provisions of this agreement," and on occasion a union will base its grievance on some obligation not specifically imposed in the writing but rather found either in unwritten past practice within the plant or by way of inference or implication from some written provision. Thus, a union may assert that the employer violates the agreement when it contracts out bargaining-unit work, pointing not to any explicit contract limitation on such action but rather to more general contract provisions such as the recognition, wage and seniority provisions which are asserted inferentially to protect the union and the unit employees from destruction of the unit through subcontracting. There is some authority for the proposition that the union has no right to have such a grievance arbitrated under the standard arbitration clause, since it does not rest squarely on an express contract term. In Local 483, Boilermakers v. Shell Oil Co. (7th Cir. 1966), for example, the union sought to arbitrate its claim that the employer's subcontracting had violated the seniority and hour provisions of the labor agreement, but the court read the arbitration clause covering "application or interpretation of this Agreement" not to embrace the union's claim "which 'on its face' is not governed by the agreement." (Somewhat inexplicably, and over the dissent of one judge, the court proceeded however to order arbitration of the union's claim that the subcontracting had violated a contract provision barring discrimination because of union membership.) Other courts have denied arbitration under a standard clause, for lack of any express provision upon which the union rested its rights, of claims regarding plant shutdown or severance pay, Local 30, Phila. Leather Workers v. Hyman Brodsky & Son (E.D.Pa.1964); and claims regarding the employer's discontinuance of Christmas turkeys, when the union rested these claims upon an unwritten understanding,

Boeing Co. v. UAW (E.D.Pa.1964), *aff'd mem.* (3d Cir. 1965) (court holds arbitrable only what is "part of the written labor contract").

Of course, if the arbitration provision of the contract is more narrowly drawn than the "standard" clause, there is a greater likelihood that the court will refuse to send to arbitration any claim which is rooted in an implied or otherwise unwritten obligation. Thus, in Local 210, Printing Pressmen v. Times-World Corp. (W.D.Va.1974), in which the labor contract provided for arbitration of "all disputes which may arise as to the construction to be placed on any clause herein or alleged violation thereof," the court refused to order arbitration of a union grievance regarding a pay increase given to certain foremen, since the union could point to no express contract provision allegedly violated and since the arbitration clause was "rather narrow."

It is understandable that many courts are reluctant to permit the union, by relying on unwritten understandings, to use arbitration as a means of securing contract rights which it was arguably unable to secure at the bargaining table. It is not at all clear, however, that these decisions comport with the Supreme Court's vision of the labor contract as an amalgam of written terms, unwritten understandings and past practices. A search by a trial court for explicit contract language supporting the claim of the plaintiff in a section 301 action is justified when the arbitration clause is narrowly drawn, but is questionable otherwise. In any event, the court surely errs when it reads the standard arbitration clause to exclude by implication claims which rest upon contract provisions whose meaning the court regards as beyond dispute. Although the Supreme Court clearly held in United Steelworkers v. American Mfg. Co. (U.S.1960), that even seemingly baseless interpretations of contract provisions must be submitted to arbitration under the standard arbitration clause, some courts persist in construing the substantive clause in question, finding no "dispute" about the "meaning or application of the agreement," and improperly denying arbitration. *E. g.,* Department Store Drivers Local 955 v. Bermingham-Prosser Paper Co. (W.D.Mo.1973) ("the no-strike clause is clear and unnecessary of any interpretation"); Lodge 2036, IAM v. H. D. Hudson Mfg. Co. (D.Minn.1971) (union sought arbitration of employer imposition upon employees of premiums for increased insurance benefits; court holds "the provision in the collective bargaining agreement is clear and requires the employees to bear any increase in the cost of the program. It would appear that an arbitrator would have nothing to interpret under this provision.").

Perhaps because of a desire to avoid thus passing upon the substance of the plaintiff's claim in a section 301 action, many courts have construed the standard arbitration clause to cover claims which, while perhaps not addressed explicitly in the labor contract, may be plausibly asserted by inference. In United Steelworkers v. Warrior & Gulf Nav. Co. (U.S.1960), the Supreme Court ordered arbitration of a subcontracting dispute even though no clause specifically barred sub-contracting and the union rested its claim on the "no lockout" clause of the agreement. The Court endorsed the view that:

> . . . [I]t is not unqualifiedly true that a collective-bargaining agreement is simply a document by which the union and employees have imposed upon management limit-ed, express restrictions of its otherwise absolute right to manage the enterprise, so that an employee's claim must fail unless he can point to a specific contract provision upon which the claim is founded. There are too many people, too many problems, too many unforeseeable contingencies to make the words of the contract the exclusive source of rights and duties. . . .
>
> . . . .
>
> Apart from matters that the parties specifically ex-clude, all of the questions on which the parties disagree must therefore come within the scope of the grievance and arbitration provisions of the collective agreement. The grievance procedure is, in other words, a part of the contin-uous collective bargaining process. It, rather than a strike, is the terminal point of a disagreement.

Several courts of appeals have relied on these principles and have held, for example, that a union could secure arbitration under a clause embracing "controversies . . . regarding the true intent and meaning of any provision of this Contract" of its claim that a disci-plinary suspension violated the labor contract, although the contract dealt expressly only with dismissal and not with suspension, Pacific Northwest Bell Tel. Co. v. Communications Workers of America (9th Cir. 1962) (court remanding, however, to determine whether parol evidence demonstrated an intention of the parties to keep this dispute out of arbitration); and that a union could secure arbitration under a standard clause of its "garden variety" subcontracting grievance which the union based on the general contract provisions dealing with union recognition, seniority and job descriptions, IUE v. General Elec. Co. (2d Cir. 1964) (dissenting judge challenging arbitration whenever union can merely point to some "tangential" contract pro-vision).

If the arbitration clause is written so broadly as to embrace "any disagreement arising between the company and the union under this agreement," then grievances even about past practices not written into the document will likely be sent to arbitration. Local 702, IBEW v. Central Ill. Pub. Serv. Co. (7th Cir. 1963) (unwritten past practice of furnishing gas to employees at discount).

An unusual attack against the extension of an arbitration clause was launched by the union in Gateway Coal Co. v. UMW (U.S. 1974). There, the union claimed that disputes concerning the safety of employees working in the mines were matters of such urgency and significance that they fell outside the reach of the broad arbitration clause ("any local trouble") and could be the subject of a strike. Three foremen had disregarded their responsibility for checking the air flow in the mines and made false entries in their logbooks to conceal their negligence. An investigation later revealed a perilously low airflow due to a breakdown in ventilation, and the union demanded the discharge of the foremen. When the employer insisted on keeping the foremen at work, the union induced the miners to stay out of the mine, and also refused to test the employer's action before an arbitrator. The employer brought an action under section 301 both to compel arbitration and to enjoin the strike, and the Supreme Court ordered that both requests be granted. The Court held that the broad arbitration clause embraced even safety disputes, that such disputes ought properly be resolved (if the parties have so agreed) by peaceful resolution rather than by economic force, and that arbitral expertise is just as apt in safety disputes as in all other industrial disputes. No exception was to be made to the strong presumption favoring arbitration announced in the *Steelworkers Trilogy*.

§ 8.　The Use of Bargaining History to Determine Arbitrability

Obviously, there will be cases in which the arbitration clause, or an exclusion clause, is somewhat vague, neither clearly compelling the submission of a given grievance to arbitration nor clearly excluding it. A number of courts of appeals have considered whether, in such a case, it is proper to admit evidence of bargaining history in order to dispel the ambiguity. The usual source of wisdom is United Steelworkers of America v. Warrior & Gulf Navigation Co. (U.S. 1960), in which the Supreme Court announced its support for a strong presumption of arbitrability:

> An order to arbitrate the particular grievance should not be denied unless it may be said with positive assurance that the arbitration clause is not susceptible of an interpretation that covers the asserted dispute. Doubts should be resolved in favor of coverage.
>
> .　.　.　.　.
>
> .　.　.　. In the absence of any express provision excluding a particular grievance from arbitration, we think only the most forceful evidence of a purpose to exclude the claim from arbitration can prevail, particularly where, as here, the exclusion clause is vague and the arbitration clause quite broad.

From this directive, at least one court of appeals has concluded that when the exclusion clause is vague and does not unambiguously exclude the grievance from arbitration, the proper recourse is to send the case to arbitration and not to admit parol evidence of bargaining history. A. S. Abell Co. v. Baltimore Typog. Union No. 12 (4th Cir. 1964) (holding, however, that since the parties agreed to have arbitrability determined by an arbitrator, the arbitrator was free to consider the parol evidence). A perceived virtue of this exclusionary principle is that it avoids judicial delay and limits the attention of the court to matters which can be resolved on the pleadings and on written documents, without an evidentiary hearing. Tobacco Workers Local 317 v. Lorillard Corp. (4th Cir. 1971). See also Communications Workers of America v. Southwestern Bell Tel. Co. (5th Cir. 1969) (arbitration clause should be construed without recourse to bargaining history except "where the contract claim and its relationship to the written contract is vague or unclear"). Another virtue of this judicial modesty is that it leaves matters of collective bargaining history to the arbitrator, who is generally regarded as better trained to appraise them.

Other decisions, however, have permitted the introduction of bargaining history, emphasizing the assertion by the Supreme Court in *Warrior & Gulf* that a grievance might be excluded from arbitration either by an explicit contract clause or by "other most forceful evidence." Thus, in Pacific Northwest Bell Tel. Co. v. Communications Workers of America (9th Cir. 1962), the court held that the arbitration clause did not on its face bar consideration of a grievance regarding disciplinary suspension but that, since contract terms must be understood in light of the milieu in which they are negotiated, parol evidence on the question of arbitrability should be admitted by the trial court in a section 301 action. See also Strauss v. Silvercup Bakers, Inc. (2d Cir. 1965) (intentions of parties should be determined by evidence of bargaining, where the exclusion clause reveals no clear-cut intention either to exclude or include grievance within arbitration).

If one were to attempt to elicit a "prevailing view" with which most of the more recent cases accord, it would appear to be that parol evidence of bargaining history is admissible in court where its purpose is to show the intention of the parties as to the scope and meaning of the arbitration clause; it is not admissible in court to demonstrate the intention of the parties as to the scope and meaning of the substantive contract clause which is to be construed by the arbitrator. See Associated Milk Dealers, Inc. v. Milk Drivers Local 753 (7th Cir. 1970). Thus, if the union claims that the employer must arbitrate an alleged contract breach stemming from the employer's disciplinary suspension of an employee, it is improper for the court in a section 301 action to hear parol evidence tending to show that the union acceded to all such disciplinary measures, for that goes to the merits of the parties' substantive dispute. It is, however, proper for the court to hear parol evidence tending to show that the union conceded that disciplinary suspensions were not to be reviewable by an arbitrator. Pacific Northwest Bell Tel. Co. v. Communications Workers of America (9th Cir. 1962). It has also been held improper, in determining the arbitrability of a subcontracting grievance, to consider evidence that the union failed to secure in bargaining an express limitation on the kind of work that the employer could subcontract. That may be pertinent to the arbitrator in determining whether the employer should prevail on the merits but it is not pertinent to the question whether the arbitrator has jurisdiction to adjudicate disputes about the employer's right to subcontract. IUE v. General Elec. Co. (2d Cir. 1964).

Indeed, such was the holding of the Supreme Court in the *Warrior & Gulf* case, where the Court ordered arbitration in the face of an exclusionary clause relating to matters which were a function of management and of proffered evidence that the union had failed at the bargaining table to make any explicit inroads upon the employer's subcontracting practices. The Court refused to consider the latter evidence since this would require it to address the merits of the union's subcontracting claim through the "back door" of construing the arbitration clause. At least one court of appeals, however, appears to have ignored the Court's directive and has held admissible in a section 301 action to compel arbitration of a subcontracting grievance just such evidence of union bargaining efforts relating not to the arbitration of subcontracting grievances but rather to the employer's power to subcontract. Local 483, Boilermakers v. Shell Oil Co. (7th Cir. 1966).

§ 9. Existence of a Contract

In addition to construing the arbitration and exclusion provisions to determine whether a grievance is substantively arbitrable, the courts may have to pass upon other defenses to an action under section 301 to compel arbitration. The Supreme Court held in United Steelworkers v. Warrior & Gulf Nav. Co. (U.S.1960), that "[A]rbitration is a matter of contract and a party cannot be required to submit to arbitration any dispute which he has not agreed so to submit," and courts have since held that it is a judicial function to determine whether some defect in the contract-making process invalidates the labor contract and the arbitration promise contained therein. Thus, if the defendant claims that the entire contract is unenforceable because its execution was induced by fraudulent misrepresentations, then the arbitration promise is also secured by fraud and cannot be enforced by the court. ILGWU v. Ashland Industries (5th Cir. 1974) (on review of an arbitral award).

Similarly, most courts have held that a grievance which arises after a contract terminates is not subject to the expired arbitration provisions of that contract, and that the court must thus determine whether the contract on which suit is brought has indeed expired. For example, in International Union, UAW v. International Telephone & Telegraph Corp. (8th Cir. 1975), the employer argued that its labor contract, and the included arbitration provision, terminated upon the execution of a letter agreement with the union and by the employer's move to another plant location. Although the trial court had found the letter agreement to be ambiguous on the issue of its superseding the labor contract and held this matter proper for arbitration, the court of appeals reversed, holding that it was for the trial court to determine whether the labor contract was terminated by the move—even if that meant ordering an evidentiary hearing to resolve ambiguities—for if it was then the employer could not be required to arbitrate the merits. See Oil Workers v. American Maize Prods. Co. (7th Cir. 1974) (since union had terminated contract effective July 31, employer action of August 1 could not be the subject of an arbitrable grievance).

When the grievance arises during the contract term but arbitration is not demanded until after its termination, the theory just developed might point toward denying arbitration, but the few cases on the issue hold to the contrary. General Tire & Rubber Co. v. Local 512, Rubber Workers (D.R.I.), *aff'd mem.* (1st Cir. 1961). In effect, the right of access to the grievance procedure is deemed "vested" as of the date the alleged grievance arises. In any event, it is clear that if the grievance arises and the arbitrator is designated prior to the expiration of the collective bargaining agreement, the arbitrator does not lose his authority to render an award should the contract expire before he renders his decision; the impact of contract expiration upon his authority and remedies is a matter for the arbitrator himself to decide. United Steelworkers v. Enterprise Wheel & Car Corp. (U.S.1960).

§ 10. Proper Parties

The court may also be called upon to determine whether arbitration should not proceed because the party making the demand is not the one entitled by the contract to do so, or because of the absence of some indispensable party. Many grievance and arbitration procedures are drafted on the assumption that it is the employer who makes most or all of the contract promises and that as an initial matter the employer is entitled to take disputed action which it is for the union then to challenge through the filing of a grievance. Such contracts contemplate an ultimate demand for arbitration by the union, but give no comparable power to the employer. In such a case, should the employer claim that the union has violated some contract obligation, its recourse will properly be to a court for a decision on the merits, for the union has made no promise to submit the dispute to arbitration. In Atkinson v. Sinclair Ref. Co. (U.S.1962), the employees engaged in a work stoppage to protest the employer's institution of new working rules which were allegedly in breach of the labor contract. When the employer commenced an action for damages against the union for breach of its promise not to strike, the union moved to stay that action on the theory that it was for the arbitrator to determine whether the union had violated the contract. The Supreme Court, however, held that the grievance and arbitration provisions were such as to embrace only union-initiated grievances, and that employer-initiated claims were thus beyond the jurisdiction of the arbitrator and properly to be adjudicated in a court action. See also Affiliated Food Distributors, Inc. v. Local 229, Teamsters (3d Cir. 1973) (similar fact situation to *Atkinson*). Of course, if the arbitration machinery is available at the initiation either of the employer or the union, then the employer's challenge to the union's work stoppage should be tried before the arbitrator, and its action for damages in the courts should be dismissed. Drake Bakeries, Inc. v. Local 50, American Bakery Workers (U.S.1962).

Similarly, an action for arbitration brought by an individual employee will be dismissed if the court concludes that it may properly be brought only by the union, either because the labor contract explicitly gives to the union as an institution the power to invoke the step-like procedures of the grievance and arbitration sections, Black-Clawson Co. v. IAM Lodge 355 (2d Cir. 1962); or because the court concludes that the grievance was not a "personal" grievance but rather one which, like the employer's relocation of the plant, involves a "broad policy issue" about which only the union is thought to have a direct concern, Brown v. Sterling Aluminum Prods. Corp. (8th Cir. 1966). Of course, in cases in which the parties do intend to accord arbitration rights to individual employees, an action brought by an individual for breach of the labor contract may be brought under section 301 in a state or federal court, with federal law governing. Smith v. Evening News Ass'n (U.S.1962).

Just as the absence of the proper party plaintiff may be a defense to an action to compel arbitration, so too may be the absence of additional parties whose participation in the case is necessary to a fair and expeditious arbitral disposition. This issue tends to arise when there is a work-assignment dispute between two unions, one of which has been assigned a job task and the other of which claims the work, with both resting their claims on their respective collective bargaining agreements. It has been held that the court in an action by one union to compel arbitration may properly grant the motion of the employer to join as a party the union to which the work was originally assigned. Window Glass Cutters v. American St. Gobain Corp. (3d Cir. 1970). See also Columbia Broadcasting System v. American Recording & Broadcasting Ass'n (2d Cir. 1969) (order to consolidate two arbitrations, with second union accepting the arbitrator selected by the employer and the first union). It is theoretically possible that each union will be able to rest a valid claim on its own labor contract, but presumably the courts believe that a single arbitrator will resolve the case in a manner (like interpleader) which will free the employer of inconsistent claims and dual liability. The exemplar of such a proceeding is that envisioned by the Supreme Court under the Railway Labor Act in Transportation-Communication Employees v. Union Pac. R. R. (U.S.1966), in which the Court held that the National Railway Adjustment Board lacked jurisdiction to pass upon the work-assignment claim of one union under its contract with the railroad company without also considering the claim of a second union under its own contract; here too, the object was to avoid multiple suits and conflicting awards.

§ 11.   Procedural Arbitrability

In spite of these decisions in which the courts took upon themselves the task of consolidating the claims of two unions as a condition to ordering arbitration, it might reasonably be held that such a question relates to "procedural arbitrability" which the Supreme Court has held, in John Wiley & Sons v. Livingston (U.S.1964), is to be determined by the arbitrator. In the *Wiley* case, a small unionized publishing firm (Interscience) was merged into a larger firm (Wiley), and the former Interscience union claimed that Wiley was bound to extend to former Interscience employees many of the benefits accorded by the Interscience collective bargaining agreement. The Court rejected Wiley's argument that the merger automatically terminated the successor's obligation to arbitrate under the Interscience contract as well as its argument that the substantive issues raised by the union (seniority, pensions, severance and vacation pay) fell outside the reach of the Interscience arbitration clause. It also rejected Wiley's argument that the union had failed to comply with the two grievance steps which were allegedly conditions precedent to any duty to arbitrate; the Court held that such issues of "procedural arbitrability" must be decided not by the court in a section 301 action but by the arbitrator as a predicate to deciding the merits of the dispute. The Court stated:

> Doubt whether grievance procedures or some part of them apply to a particular dispute, whether such procedures have been followed or excused, or whether the unexcused failure to follow them avoids the duty to arbitrate cannot ordinarily be answered without consideration of the merits of the dispute which is presented for arbitration.

> .   .   .   Reservation of "procedural" issues for the courts would thus not only create the difficult task of separating related issues, but would also produce frequent duplication of effort.

> In addition, the opportunities for deliberate delay and the possibility of well-intentioned but no less serious delay created by separation of the "procedural" and "substantive" elements of a dispute are clear.

Thus, even if the grievant's failure to pursue each step of the grievance procedure in a timely way is said to oust the arbitrator of jurisdiction, that issue of construction and the factual issue of compliance with the contract are to be decided by the arbitrator. Newspaper Guild of Phila., Local 10 v. Philadelphia Newspapers, Inc. (E.D. Pa.1974). Should the arbitrator find the grievance nonarbitrable because of such a procedural defect, the aggrieved party will also be denied a forum should it later seek redress for the same grievance in a court action. Chambers v. Beaunit Corp. (6th Cir. 1968).

Relying on the rule that issues of "procedural arbitrability" are for the arbitrator to decide, courts have held—unlike the joinder-of-party cases already discussed, which give this issue to the court perhaps because of the joinder rules of the Federal Rules of Civil Procedure—that it is for the arbitrator to determine whether multiple grievances are to be arbitrated before the same arbitrator (in one or several sittings) or are to be arbitrated separately. Avon Prods., Inc. v. UAW Local 710 (8th Cir. 1967). In such a case the question is not whether the grievances are arbitrable, which would be for the court to decide, but rather how the arbitration should be conducted, which is for the arbitrator to decide. American Can Co. v. United Papermakers (W.D.Pa.1973). See also Tobacco Workers Local 317 v. Lorillard Corp. (4th Cir. 1971) (arbitrator is to determine whether two grievants are entitled under the contract to file a grievance in common through one representative).

It should be noted that, contrary to part of the rationale in the *Wiley* case, issues of procedural arbitrability are commonly quite divorced from the substantive issues which the case will bring before the arbitrator. The question whether an appeal was taken within seven days rather than five, or whether the contract contemplates joint hearings of grievances—while quite often raising nice issues of construction peculiarly meet for arbitration—will often be capable of resolution without trenching upon such substantive provisions as those dealing with wages, discharge or subcontracting. Indeed, a thoughtful court of appeals decision has held that "procedural arbitrability" questions should be given to the arbitrator regardless whether they are divorced from or "intertwined" with the substantive dispute on the merits. *Ibid*.

Recently, the Supreme Court has extended the reach of its "procedural arbitrability" doctrine from disputes about compliance with specific contractual conditions precedent (as in *Wiley*) to claims by the defendant in the section 301 action that the plaintiff delayed so long in pressing its grievance that, quite apart from compliance with the terms of the labor contract, it would be inequitable to order arbitration. Although a number of courts had held that this question of laches should be resolved by the court rather than by the arbitrator, since it raised issues extrinsic to the contract and did not threaten any overlap with the decision of the underlying substantive dispute, the Court rejected this position in Operating Engineers Local 150 v. Flair Builders, Inc. (U.S.1972). There, the union and the employer had agreed in 1964 to be bound by present and future contracts between the union and a multiemployer group, and in 1966 just such a contract was negotiated, with an expansive arbitration clause; the employer was unaware of and given no notice of the terms of the multiemployer agreement. It was not until 1968 that the union appeared once more and challenged certain longstanding employer practices as in breach of the 1966 agreement. The Supreme Court rejected the employer's argument that it was for a court to deal with the defense of laches, and noted no substantial difference between this issue and the issue of failure to comply with a specific contractual precondition to arbitration. The arbitration clause of the 1966 agreement (which was found by the trial court to be binding upon the employer) provided for arbitration of "any difference" that the parties failed to settle within forty-eight hours, and the Court held that the dispute concerning the union's right to press its grievance in spite of the long delay was just such a "difference" that the parties had agreed to submit to arbitration.

It is thus not surprising that courts have come to treat as a matter of "procedural arbitrability," for the arbitrator to determine, an asserted defense that arbitration should not be ordered because the grievant has also violated the contract or has otherwise engaged in wrongful or inequitable conduct. Before its decision in *Wiley*, the Supreme Court had itself ruled upon such defense in Drake Bakeries, Inc. v. Local 50, American Bakery Workers (U.S.1962). There, the employer had brought a court action for damages against the union for breach of a no-strike clause, and countered the union's argument that such an action should lie exclusively with the arbitrator by arguing that the union's breach of the no-strike clause was so fundamental a repudiation of the contract as to discharge the employer of its duty to arbitrate. The Court took upon itself the task of determining the validity of this defense of discharge and held that the employer's obligation to arbitrate was intended, in the context of federal labor law policies, to survive asserted contract violations by the union. The question whether the strike discharged the employer's duty to arbitrate was not given to the arbitrator to decide, apparently because neither party called this matter to the Court's attention. Significantly, in a more recent case involving very much the same fact situation as in *Drake Bakeries*, a court of appeals relied on the then very recent decision of the Supreme Court in *Flair Builders*, and held that the court action for damages for breach of the no-strike clause should be dismissed with the issue of the union's repudiation and the employer's discharge from arbitration being reserved for decision by the arbitrator as a matter of procedural arbitrability. General Dynamics Corp. v. Local 5, Marine Workers (1st Cir. 1972).

§ 12. Conflict With The NLRB

A frequently litigated question is whether arbitration should not be ordered by virtue of a perceived conflict with the power of the National Labor Relations Board. In many instances, a claim of contract breach will implicate facts which raise as well unfair labor practice or representation issues which might also be triable to the Board. A discharge of an employee may allegedly be without just cause in breach of contract or for antiunion animus in violation of the Labor Act. A "unilateral" decision by the employer to subcontract work or to change wage rates may allegedly violate the contract or constitute a refusal to bargain in violation of the Labor Act. The recognition of the union and the extension of the contract (or the non-recognition and non-extension) in a new plant acquired by the employer may raise contract issues or representation issues which might plausibly be resolved either by an arbitrator or by the Board. Although there was considerable doubt for some time whether arbitration and contract enforcement would be ousted by the usual principles of Board "preemption" that apply when unfair labor practice or representation issues are raised, this doubt was resolved by the Supreme Court early in the 1960's.

The Court laid great emphasis upon Congress's desire to foster the private resolution of contract disputes through arbitration as an alternative and independent channel to Board resolution, and held that the Board's unfair labor practice jurisdiction does not preempt arbitral jurisdiction. Smith v. Evening News Ass'n (U.S.1962). The Court underlined that holding, and expanded it to representation disputes, in Carey v. Westinghouse Elec. Corp. (U.S.1964). There, a union representing production and maintenance employees filed a grievance and sought arbitration of its claim that the employer was assigning unit work to technical employees represented by a second union. The state court in which the action was brought by the union to compel arbitration dismissed the case, holding that the matter involved a definition of bargaining units and was thus within the exclusive jurisdiction of the National Labor Relations Board. The Supreme Court reversed. It held that regardless of whether the case was to be characterized as a work-assignment dispute which the Board could resolve through its unfair labor practice machinery, or a representation dispute which the Board could resolve through its election or unit-clarification machinery, arbitration of the merits should proceed. The Court noted that arbitration could result in the peaceful settlement of the inter-union dispute, even if both unions did not appear before the arbitrator, and that the Board might indeed give weight to any arbitral award in passing upon any unfair labor practice or representation case that might ultimately find its way there. The Court also noted that in the event of disagreement between the arbitrator construing the contract and the Board construing the Labor Act, "the Board's ruling would, of course, take precedence" but that "the possibility of conflict is no barrier to resort to a tribunal other than the Board." As will be developed elsewhere, it is indeed true that the Board will defer to an arbitration decision already rendered, where the procedures are fair and the award not repugnant to the Labor Act; and the Board will indeed defer to as-yet-unused arbitration machinery which is available to the parties before the Board under the terms of their labor contract when arbitration gives promise of resolving fairly substantially the same issue the Board would address.

While all courts appear to endorse this abstract proposition that possible Board jurisdiction does not preempt the jurisdiction of the arbitrator, a number of related issues are less well settled. Several courts have held that if the grievant is seeking to compel arbitration under a contract provision which the NLRB has already found to violate the Labor Act, or is seeking to have the arbitrator compel conduct which the Board has held will violate the Labor Act, the court in the section 301 action should sustain a defense to arbitration. In Oil Workers v. Cities Serv. Oil Co. (N.D.Okla.1967), the Board had ruled that the employer's newly acquired plants were not "accretions" to the existing bargaining unit represented by the union, and the union's attempt to have arbitration ordered and to have the arbitrator extend the union's contract to the newly acquired plants was rebuffed by the federal district court. (The court also noted that the union and employer had stipulated that they would abide by the Board's ruling and not assert rights arising under the contract.) Similarly, a court refused to order arbitration of a union's contract claim that it represented certain plant employees when the NLRB had already determined, in a unit-clarification proceeding, that another union was entitled to represent them. Smith Steel Workers v. A. O. Smith Corp. (7th Cir. 1969) (court also holding that union's insistence on arbitration, after contrary Board ruling, constituted bad faith bargaining in violation of section 8(b)(3)). Sometimes, however, there may be some question whether the Board has indeed addressed the same issue being presented to the arbitrator. In Buchholz v. Local 463, IUE (N.Y.1965), a divided court withheld from arbitration a claim of discharge without cause when the Board had already, in the context of a representation-election proceeding, ruled that the employee's severance did not violate the Labor Act; a dissenting opinion challenged the congruence of the statutory and contract issues.

One court has stayed arbitration pending disposition of a comparable issue by the Board, when unfair labor practice proceedings had already begun and a decision had issued from the trial examiner. Kentile, Inc. v. Local 457, Rubber Workers (E.D.N.Y.1964) (union was seeking arbitration of its demand to have the employer discharge an employee, while the trial examiner had already held that the union's demand was because of the employee's union activities and thus in violation of section 8(b)(2)). Where only a charge has been filed, however, there is likely to be greater willingness to permit the arbitration to proceed United Aircraft Corp. v. Canel Lodge No. 700, IAM (2d Cir. 1970). This seems quite sound in view of the Board's willingness to defer to arbitration machinery and awards which fairly address the same issues that would confront the Board.

The intermediate situation is where a charge has been filed and the regional director or General Counsel has made a conclusive determination that no unfair labor practice complaint should issue. In such a case, there has been a tendency to focus closely upon the difference between the Board disposition and that which an arbitrator would be asked to make. Thus it has been held that a refusal by the General Counsel to issue a complaint against a party ought not constitute a defense to a proceeding to compel arbitration of a claim that the same conduct violates the collective bargaining agreement. In Luckenbach Overseas Corp. v. Curran (2d Cir. 1968), the General Counsel refused to issue a complaint for antiunion discrimination against an employer-shipowner and the purchaser of its fleet of ships, when the crew represented by one union was completely replaced upon the change of ownership by workers represented by another union. The court nonetheless ordered arbitration of the union's claim that the displacement of its members constituted a contract violation (at least of the "no lockout" provision), since the asserted contract rights may have been quite different from those asserted under the Labor Act and since the arbitrator could conceivably render a decision which would not violate the Act. The same court, in IUE v. General Elec. Co. (2d Cir. 1968), also pointed out that not only are the legal issues different in the two proceedings but also the refusal of the General Counsel to issue a complaint is merely an administrative decision not made in an adversary or trial context. Indeed, one court has held that even if the Board finds that an employer violated its duty to bargain when it unilaterally discontinued a past practice, arbitration of that same question may proceed, since an arbitral award upholding the employer will not conflict with a Board order requiring restitution for past losses and will in fact render the discontinuation of the practice lawful *in futuro* since it would no longer be unilateral but rather the product of consensual arbitration. Local 702, IBEW v. Central Ill. Pub. Serv. Co. (7th Cir. 1963) (court affirms the decision of the NLRB and also of the district court ordering arbitration).

Whatever may be the reluctance of some courts to order arbitration in the face of an outstanding decision of the Board or of an administrative law judge, there appears to be substantial support for the proposition that, where no such decision exists, the court should not bar arbitration simply because the grievant is seeking relief which might violate the Labor Act or the clause on which the grievance is based allegedly violates the Act. For example, in Carey v. General Elec. Co. (2d Cir. 1963) the union sought to compel arbitration of its claim that the employer in making an appointment to a vacancy violated a clause in the labor contract which would strip of seniority credit employees who leave the unit to work in a nonunion plant of the employer. The trial judge refused to order arbitration, upholding the employer's argument that the clause illegally discriminated in job appointments against nonunion employees and that the relief sought by the union would require the employer to violate the Labor Act. The court of appeals reversed, and ordered arbitration, stating:

> Even if we were to assume the NLRB's position to be as clear as [the trial judge] thought, conflict with its policies is here wholly conjectural. It is by no means clear that the union's grievance will be found warranted. Further, if the arbitrator does uphold the union's construction of the seniority provision in question, he might himself decline to fashion an award based upon it for fear that he would encourage a practice banned by the labor act. We cannot construct a framework of legal principles governing arbitration on the theory that the arbitrator is ignorant or oblivious of the pronouncements of the Board and the courts. . . .
>
> Only if none of these approaches is adopted by the arbitrator would it become necessary to determine whether a court should enforce an award that clearly compels an unfair labor practice. To do so now would be to "raise an unfair labor practice question prematurely and gratuitously."

Similarly, in Federal Mogul Corp. v. UAW Local 985 (E.D.Mich. 1970), the union filed a grievance claiming that its contract with a Michigan employer required that the employer recognize the union in any newly acquired plant doing the same business, and that the employer committed a breach when it opened a plant in Ohio and refused to recognize the union there (indeed, recognized a competing union there). The employer's action seeking to enjoin arbitration was rebuffed by the court, in spite of the employer's claim that an arbitral order to recognize the union in the Ohio plant would violate section 8(a)(2) of the Labor Act. The court held that judicial review was premature, that the arbitration itself could hurt no one, that the arbitrator might well decide the case or fashion a remedy so as not to violate the Labor Act, and that the time for the employer to seek judicial protection is when the arbitrator has actually rendered a decision and award requiring the commission of an unfair labor practice. A particularly striking example of judicial deference to arbitration on questions of legality is Optical Workers Local 408 v. Sterling Optical Co. (2d Cir. 1974). There, the union claimed that the employer's subcontracting of work to a nonunion company violated a provision of the labor contract which on its face did forbid such employer action. The employer resisted arbitration, asserting that the no-subcontracting clause contravened section 8(e), the so-called hot cargo section of the Labor Act. The district court agreed and declined to grant the union's request for arbitration. The union's appeal did not frontally challenge the trial court's authority to withhold the case from arbitration, but the court of appeals—in an extended dictum resembling an advisory opinion—stated that the only issue properly before the district court was whether the union claimed a violation of a contract provision (which it had) and that the legality of the provision was in the first instance an issue not for the trial court but for the arbitrator.

These cases find support in the principles of the *Steelworkers Trilogy*: that the court should not interfere with arbitration because it believes the grievance is frivolous, that the court should not consider the merits of the grievance, and that consideration by the arbitrator of even "clear" grievances is likely to have a desirable therapeutic effect upon plant relationships.

This position is not, however, universally endorsed. In Associated Milk Dealers, Inc. v. Milk Drivers 753 (7th Cir. 1970), a union resisted arbitration under a contract provision which it claimed violated not the Labor Act but the federal antitrust laws. The court found the claim of illegality to be colorable and to warrant an evidentiary hearing in the trial court as a precondition to ordering arbitration. It held that while courts could delay intervention until the award has been rendered and a party seeks its enforcement, this delay would contravene the purposes of the Sherman Act; merely to order arbitration would make the court give "significant practical effect to the illegal clause." The court explicitly rejected the argument that arbitration should be ordered and the defense of illegality tried to the arbitrator: "Arbitrators are ill-equipped to interpret the antitrust laws and their consideration of possible violations would add little. Indeed an agreement requiring arbitration of private antitrust claims would probably be unenforceable."

In any event, should the court decide to order arbitration in the face of claims that the contract provision or the remedies sought violate the Labor Act, any arbitral decision ultimately rendered which turns out to be contradicted by a later decision of the NLRB will be superseded by the Board order, and an action to enforce the arbitrator's award will be dismissed. Local 7–210, Oil Workers v. Union Tank Car Co. (7th Cir. 1973). (The issue of judicial review of arbitration awards is discussed more fully below.)

§ 13. Interest Arbitration

The decisions of the Supreme Court in the *Lincoln Mills* case and the *Steelworkers Trilogy* all involved grievance arbitration under existing labor contracts. Both before *Lincoln Mills* and since, the question has arisen whether section 301 empowers the courts specifically to enforce agreements to arbitrate disputes regarding the fixing of new contract terms in the event bargaining negotiations reach a deadlock. Although an early and influential decision held that the enforcement of arbitration promises should be limited to grievance claims and not cover so-called interest arbitration, the clear current of the more recent opinions is to the contrary. For example, in Winston-Salem Printing Pressmen Union No. 318 v. Piedmont Pub. Co. (4th Cir. 1968), the labor contract expressly provided for arbitration in the event the parties could not successfully negotiate terms for a new agreement. The court held that the rationale of the Supreme Court decisions dictates specific performance of such a promise to submit interest disputes to arbitration, as a device selected by the parties to substitute for economic warfare. Indeed, interest arbitration has been ordered under a contract which lacked any such specific provision but contained a provision for a midterm reopener for wage negotiations, a standard arbitration clause and a clause forbidding the arbitrator to "add to" or to "change the terms of the contract." An evenly divided court of appeals sitting en banc, in Laundry Workers Local 93 v. Mahoney (8th Cir. 1974), affirmed an order compelling arbitration, with the "controlling" opinion finding no sufficiently clear exclusion of interest disputes from the standard arbitration clause governing "grievances", and a concurring judge finding that the "no change" clause limited the arbitrator's remedial authority but did not deprive him in advance of jurisdiction.

No case appears to have passed upon the question whether the new contract terms decreed by the arbitrator may be confirmed and held binding upon the parties in a section 301 action, but the implication of the above cases and the Supreme Court decisions is that the arbitrator's award must be confirmed if it finds its roots in the contract terms giving him power to act—and presumably, if the award does not compel either party to engage in illegal conduct or otherwise contain provisions which are illegal or unenforceable.

CHAPTER XXIV

ARBITRATION AND THE SUCCESSOR EMPLOYER

§ 1. The *Wiley* Decision and the Concept of Successorship

Since the 1930's, the National Labor Relations Board had been confronted with the question whether the acquisition of a business and the retention of some or all of its employees carried with it the obligation to bargain with the union representing the predecessor's employees or to remedy unfair labor practices committed by the predecessor employer. The Board—almost uniformly with judicial approval—imposed such obligations if it concluded that the new employer was either the "alter ego" of the predecessor in a sham transaction designed to evade the mandates of the Labor Act, or was the "successor" in a bona fide transaction as evidenced by continuity in the workforce, in supervision and in processes of production. Thus, the death of a partner or the transfer of controlling shares in a corporation, while they may affect technical ownership, do not justify the ouster of the bargaining representative, for in itself the change in ownership does not likely affect the attitudes of the retained employees toward unionization in general and this union in particular. (The duty of a successor employer under section 8(a)(5) to bargain with the union representing the employees of the predecessor company is discussed elsewhere in this work.)

It was against this background, and that provided by the *Steelworkers Trilogy* arbitration cases under section 301, that the Supreme Court addressed the question whether and in what circumstances an employer acquiring a business could be bound by an arbitration clause in the predecessor's labor contract. John Wiley & Sons v. Livingston (U.S.1964) involved a merger of Interscience Publishers, with 80 employees (40 represented by a union), into the nonunion 300-employee publishing firm Wiley, with the Wiley company as an enlarged entity surviving the merger. The merger was effected during the life of the Interscience labor contract, which contained a grievance and arbitration procedure but lacked any provision binding the employer's successors and assigns. When Wiley rebuffed the demands of the Interscience union to continue to extend to former Interscience employees benefits (such as seniority, vacation pay, severance pay, and pension contributions) accorded in the labor contract, the union shortly before the stipulated expiration date of the contract commenced an action under section 301 to compel Wiley to arbitrate its claims of contract breach. The Supreme Court stated that the question whether the defendant employer was contractually bound to arbitrate is an issue for the courts to decide, that the governing rules are provided by federal law, and that there was a federal interest in reducing industrial strife in the course of business acquisitions by balancing against employer rights to rearrange and transfer their businesses the interests of employees to be protected against a sudden change in the employment relationship (interests which are unrepresented when the business acquisition is negotiated). To Wiley's asserted defense that the contract did not purport to bind successors and that Wiley had neither been a party to nor assumed the contract, the Court replied that the labor contract "is not in any real sense the simple product of a consensual relationship," that merger does not automatically terminate all labor-contract obligations, and that on the facts of the case Wiley should be treated as a "successor" to Interscience's contract duty to arbitrate the union's claim that certain contract rights were "vested," surviving both the merger and the contract termination date.

What made Wiley a successor, obliged by an arbitration promise it never made, was the "substantial continuity of identity in the business enterprise before and after" the change of ownership; this in turn was evidenced by the "wholesale transfer of Interscience employees to the Wiley plant, apparently without difficulty." It was only by virtue of this "substantial continuity of identity" between Interscience and Wiley that the Court was prepared to hold that the duty to arbitrate was not being imposed from without but rather was rooted in the bargaining agreement and the acts of the parties involved. The Court noted that even when successorship is found, the union may be deemed to forfeit its right to arbitration if it fails to make its claim known promptly to the successor employer. Significantly, the Court also noted that the union was making no claim to represent the former Interscience employees in collective bargaining concerning prospective terms of employment with Wiley. While conceding that it might be disruptive to have former Interscience employees treated for any period of time better than (or merely different from) the larger group of original Wiley employees, the Court entrusted such matters to the creative processes of arbitration. (Presumably, the Court was prepared to contemplate an arbitral decision that no rights to vacations, severance pay, seniority and the like survived either the merger or the contract termination date.)

The *Wiley* decision left with only vague contours the concept of "substantial continuity of identity in the business enterprise before and after" the change of ownership. This concept has been utilized regardless of whether the employer(s) had disclaimed the carryover of contract obligations and regardless of whether the change in ownership resulted from a stock transfer, the purchase of an ongoing business, the purchase only of physical assets, a merger, a consolidation, or some amalgam of these. Over time, the courts have developed a set of important components of "continuity," which strikingly resemble those utilized by the Board in determining whether there is an obligation to bargain with the predecessor's union or to remedy the predecessor's unfair labor practices. The courts have tended to investigate the following questions: (1) Is the new employer utilizing substantially the same workforce as the old employer?   (This has been the factor most consistently emphasized.)   (2) Is there substantial temporal continuity of business operations?   (3) Is the new employer utilizing the same supervisory personnel as before?   (4) Is it continuing operations in the same plant?   (5) Is it utilizing the same machinery and equipment?   (6) Is it maintaining the same job classifications and working conditions as the former employer?   (7) Is the new employer producing the same goods or rendering the same services as the old employer?   Given somewhat less emphasis, but often mentioned, in determining successorship in arbitration cases is whether the new employer has taken on the former employer's accounts receivable, goodwill, trade name, inventory, obligations, customers, or suppliers of materials, and has completed work in progress at the time of the takeover.

Other than to reiterate the concern of the *Wiley* Court for cushioning employees against the impact of a business acquisition, the courts have really not provided a rationale which explains why these factors are important and how they should be weighted.   The common practice is to engage in an ad hoc balancing followed by a statement of conclusion; no one factor has been articulated as dispositive, and an accumulation of factors, different ones in different cases, is said to point the court in one direction or another.   Most decided cases have found successorship and have carried over the duty to arbitrate.   They emphasize the similarity, before and after the takeover, of the workforce, the supervisors, the tasks performed and the products manufactured.   Special emphasis is usually placed upon the fact that—as in *Wiley*—the bulk of the predecessor's workforce was retained by the successor, without regard to whether that group in turn represents only a small part of the successor's total workforce.

The year *Wiley* was decided, two federal appeals decisions went even further in upholding the duty of a successor to arbitrate under the predecessor's labor contract.   In Wackenhut Corp. v. International Union, United Plant Guard Workers (9th Cir. 1964), the company which was held to be a successor took no assets from the predecessor and indeed had no contractual arrangement with the predecessor. Rather, it succeeded as low bidder for a building security services contract.   Nonetheless, the court found "continuity of the business enterprise" (even if not continuity of the employer) because the successor retained the old workforce to perform the same services at the same locations for the same customers.   And in United Steelworkers v. Reliance Universal, Inc. (3d Cir. 1964), where the Federal Trade Commission ordered that a business be divested as a "going concern," the court held the purchaser bound to the seller's arbitration promise in spite of the express disclaimer in the purchase instrument of any obligations under the seller's labor contract.   The court also expressly authorized the arbitrator in light of the change of circumstances created by the transfer of ownership to depart from the express substantive terms of the predecessor's agreement if it would be inequitable to bind either of the parties thereto. See also United Steelworkers v. United States Gypsum Co. (5th Cir. 1974).

It is this same appreciation of the equities which perhaps is at the heart of a decision by another court of appeals, in Bath Iron Works Corp. v. Bath Marine Draftsmen Ass'n (1st Cir. 1968). There, the same union negotiated contracts with both a parent corporation and its subsidiary, and secured a more generous agreement from the more affluent parent. Subsequently, the subsidiary was merged into the parent, and the union—rather than demanding that the surviving parent company arbitrate under the contract of the "predecessor" subsidiary—demanded that the parent arbitrate under its own contract the issue of its obligations under that contract to the newly acquired employees. The Court held that with the demise of the poorer subsidiary, any maintenance of the disparity in the agreements between the two groups of employees would lead to industrial strife, and ordered the successor parent to arbitrate with the predecessor's union (the same as its own union) under the more generous labor contract of the parent.

§ 2. Exceptions to the Duty to Arbitrate: The Unionized Successor

The two major exceptions to the *Wiley* principle of arbitration carryover have been cases in which the successor company is itself already obligated to bargain with, and indeed has a contract with, a different union from that which represents the predecessor's employees (a situation that has confronted at least two federal appeals courts); and cases in which the successor company acquires only a small proportion of the employees who had formerly worked for the predecessor (a situation considered in a significant decision of the Supreme Court).

In McGuire v. Humble Oil & Ref. Co. (2d Cir. 1966), the Humble Oil Company, with 355 employees in its Brooklyn, New York operations, took over a division of the Weber & Quinn Company, thirteen of whose employees were integrated into the Humble labor force. Although the Humble employees were already represented (by the "Association"), the "Union" representing the former Weber employees commenced an action against Humble seeking arbitration under the Weber labor contract of certain claims under that contract. Humble then secured a unit-clarification order from the NLRB, in which the Board held that the thirteen former Weber employees constituted an accretion to the Humble unit, with the Association as their bargaining agent. The Court of Appeals for the Second Circuit refused to order Humble to arbitrate with the Union under the Weber contract, holding that—unlike in *Wiley*—the successor's employees were already represented by a labor organization, that that organization had been held by the Board to be the bargaining representative for the absorbed employees of the predecessor, that to require arbitration with the Union would expose Humble to an unfair labor practice charge of circumventing the majority union to bargain with a minority union, and that industrial strife would likely result from the Union's seeking preferential treatment for the thirteen former Weber employees.

More recently, the Court of Appeals for the Ninth Circuit, in IAM v. Howmet Corp. (9th Cir. 1972), went yet further in finding the successor's union to pose an obstacle to arbitration under the predecessor's contract. There, Menasco, already subject to labor contracts with one union, acquired two Howmet plants and expressly agreed to assume the labor contract negotiated for employees in those plants by another union. When Menasco subsequently decided to close one of the plants, it bargained with the former Howmet union about severance pay, transfer and preferential hiring at its other plants, but inability to reach an agreement led to a demand that Menasco arbitrate with the union under the Howmet contract it had assumed. In spite of the fact that at the time of the arbitration demand, the employees had not yet been dispersed among the other Menasco employees and were still validly represented by the former Howmet union, the court of appeals relied on *McGuire* and refused to order Menasco to arbitrate. The court concluded that arbitration would foster industrial strife, since any arbitral award ordering job transfers to other Menasco plants and the continuance of contract rights once there would inevitably impinge directly on Menasco's bargaining and contract duties to its own union.

While the unease of the courts in the *McGuire* and *Howmet* cases is understandable, it is not at all clear that arbitration under the predecessor's contract (especially when the contract is expressly assumed and is with a majority union in a proper unit) would constitute illegal bargaining with a minority union. The rights of the affected employees are presumably preexisting rather than being bargained afresh; they will be of short duration (until the next negotiation); as the Supreme Court noted in the *Wiley* case they may be flexibly shaped by the arbitrator so as to minimize the stresses of disparate or preferential treatment; and the successor's majority representative may be made a party to the arbitration, and will in any event be expected to protect those rights as though they were absorbed into its own contract.

There appears to be no case which directly holds that an already unionized successor may be compelled to arbitrate with the predecessor's union under the predecessor's contract, but at least two cases point in that direction. In United States Gypsum Co. v. United Steelworkers (5th Cir. 1967), a successor without its own union was ordered to arbitrate with the union representing its predecessor's employees even though after the change in ownership and during the life of the predecessor's labor contract the union was formally decertified. The court stressed that the retained employees needed a "champion" to assert their contract rights under the predecessor's agreement and noted that in a hypothetical two-union situation the "old" union might be entitled to arbitrate if the disputed claim is "wrapped up in antagonistic union policy" generated by a "new" certified union.   And, in ILWU Local 142 v. Land & Constr. Co. (9th Cir. 1974), which involved only a single employer and not a successor, the court held that an "old" union replaced by a "new" union and a new contract could still secure rights to enforce a promise to arbitrate or to enforce an arbitration award provided the court found no cause to "believe that enforcement of the arbitrator's award will foster labor unrest or create a risk to the defendant [employer] of being guilty of an unfair labor practice."   The court confirmed an award of backpay for improper layoff in an arbitration proceeding conducted by the ousted union under its old contract, concluding "that enforcement of this award will [not] jeopardize the defendant's relations with its employees or their present union."

§ 3.   Exceptions to the Duty to Arbitrate: Inadequate Workforce Carryover

The continuing signficance of *Wiley* v. *Livingston* has been called into question by the Supreme Court itself, in its recent decision in Howard Johnson Co. v. Detroit Local Joint Exec. Bd. (U.S.1974). There, the Grissom family, which had operated a motel and restaurant as franchisees of Howard Johnson, transferred the business to Howard Johnson by selling it the personal property and leasing it the real property.   Although Grissom had a labor contract covering its fifty-three employees, and that contract stipulated that it would be binding on Grissom's successors and assigns, Howard Johnson disclaimed the contract and any liabilities thereunder, and so informed the union.   The Grissom employees were told shortly before the formal transfer of the operation that they were to be terminated, and after independent and nondiscriminatory recruitment, Howard Johnson began business in exactly the same manner as before, with forty-five employees only nine of whom had worked for Grissom, and with a completely new staff of supervisors.   The union claimed that the refusal to hire the former Grissom employees was a "lockout" in violation of the Grissom contract, which the union claimed bound Howard Johnson.   While Grissom announced its willingness to arbitrate, Howard Johnson would not, and the union brought an action under section 301.

The Supreme Court refused to order arbitration.   Although the most obviously applicable precedent was *Wiley*, where the surviving company in a merger was ordered to arbitrate, the Court noted that it could not ignore its intervening decision in NLRB v. Burns Int'l Security Services (U.S.1972), a refusal-to-bargain case arising under section 8(a)(5).   In *Burns*, the Court had held that while a company which took over the operations and the employees of another company could be ordered to bargain with the predecessor's union, it could not be ordered by the NLRB to assume the obligations of the predecessor's labor agreement; such an order would run counter to the federal policy barring governmental determination of labor-contract terms and would unduly inhibit the free transfer of capital and the rejuvenation of failing businesses. The Court in *Howard Johnson* observed that these policies noted in *Burns* were as relevant in an action under section 301 to compel arbitration as it was there in an unfair labor practice proceeding before the NLRB. But the Court chose to justify its denial of arbitration in *Howard Johnson* on a distinction of *Wiley*, in the process very severely undermining the precedential strength of that decision and injecting considerable uncertainty into the law governing the successor's duty to arbitrate.

The Court emphasized two factors which distinguished *Howard Johnson*. (1) Howard Johnson acquired the business not by merger but by purchase and rental of property from a company which continues to exist after the transfer. The Court conceded that "ordinarily" the analysis of successorship problems does not turn on whether there is a merger, consolidation or purchase of assets, but—without explaining why the circumstances were out of the ordinary—then proceeded to note that the controlling state corporate law governing the Interscience-Wiley merger (which made the survivor responsible for the predecessor's obligations) made a continued duty to arbitrate "fairly within the reasonable expectations of the parties." Moreover, a merger results in the "disappearance" of the predecessor while the Grissom sale and lease left Grissom amenable to a union action for breach of its labor contract. (2) Even more important, the Court held that while "continuity of identity in the business enterprise" was demonstrated in *Wiley* by the hiring of *all* the Interscience employees, such continuity was lacking when Howard Johnson exercised its privilege (accorded by the Court in its *Burns* decision) to recruit a new workforce, without discrimination on the basis of union membership, which included only a small minority of the persons working for Grissom at the time of the transfer. The gist of the union's arbitration claim was not any vested rights of employees already hired by Howard Johnson but the right to a job by former Grissom employees *not* hired, a claim which the Court considered inconsistent with the freedom to hire elaborated in *Burns*. The Court announced an important principle:

> This continuity of identity in the business enterprise necessarily includes, we think, a substantial continuity in the identity of the work force across the change in ownership.
> . . . This view is reflected in the emphasis most of the lower courts have placed on whether the successor employer hires a majority of the predecessor's employees in determining the legal obligations of the successor in § 301 suits under *Wiley*.

Thus, the Court held that "continuity in the work force" is necessary to a finding of arbitration carryover and that central to such continuity is the hiring of at least a majority of the predecessor's employees.

The Court, in passing, announced three other principles of importance to successorship cases. First, the duty to arbitrate will, like the duty to bargain, be readily imposed when the successor takes not in a bona fide transaction at arms' length but instead as an alter ego, or "disguised continuance of the old employer," to avoid the labor contract without any substantial change in ownership or management. Second, the successor violates section 8(a)(3) when it refuses to hire the predecessor's employees because of their union membership, activity or representation. (It might follow from this that it is also illegal to avoid hiring the predecessor's employees—regardless of union proclivities—in order to avoid arbitration, but this surely would be difficult to square with the Court's desire to free business purchasers of cumbersome contracts made by the predecessor.) Third, a court errs when it decides in the abstract whether a company is a "successor" and only then decides whether it is required to arbitrate or to bargain.

> The question whether Howard Johnson is a "successor" is simply not meaningful in the abstract. Howard Johnson is of course a successor employer in the sense that it succeeded to operation of a restaurant and motor lodge formerly operated by the Grissoms. But the real question in each of these "successorship" cases is, on the particular facts, what are the legal obligations of the new employer to the employees of the former owner or their representative. The answer to this inquiry requires analysis of the interests of the new employer and the employees and of the policies of the labor laws in light of the facts of each case and the particular legal obligation which is at issue, whether it be the duty to recognize and bargain with the union, the duty to remedy unfair labor practices, the duty to arbitrate, etc. There is, and can be, no single definition of "successor" which is applicable in every legal context. A new employer, in other words, may be a successor for some purposes and not for others.

The Court is thus apparently moving toward two different successorship tests in bargaining cases under section 8(a)(5) and arbitration cases under section 301. A successor will ordinarily be required to *bargain* if a majority of *its* workforce in an appropriate unit is comprised of the predecessor's employees, while a successor will ordinarily be required to *arbitrate* under its predecessor's contract only if it has retained within its own workforce employees who had comprised a majority of the *predecessor's* workforce. In some cases, where all or most of the predecessor's employees are absorbed into a much larger successor enterprise, the duty to arbitrate will carry over but the duty to bargain will not; the *Wiley* case is an example. In other cases, however, the arbitration standard will prove to be the more stringent. When a successor hires a small proportion of the predecessor's employees but, because of a drastic contraction in the business, these constitute a majority of the successor's workforce, the successor may be required to bargain with the union but (under *Howard Johnson*) will probably not be required to arbitrate. In the latter kind of case, the Board has found the greater reluctance to order arbitration than to order bargaining to be justified, since the application of the predecessor's contract will be more confining of entrepreneurial flexibility (extolled in the *Burns* case) than will the imposition of a duty to bargain. United Maintenance & Mfg. Co. (1974).

It is clear that the Court has cut back on its broad pronouncements in *Wiley*, in the interest of unfettered transfer and development of capital and human resources in business transfers. In *Howard Johnson,* it ignored the "successors and assigns" provision in the Grissom labor contract as a possible base for arbitral relief against the successor Howard Johnson; it emphasized the technical form which the transfer of assets took; and it gave no weight to the fact that the Grissom employees retained by Howard Johnson continued to use the same skills performing the same jobs under the same working conditions as before. For all these reasons, it is unlikely that the Court in *Howard Johnson* would have ordered arbitration of the claims asserted even by the Grissom employees whom Howard Johnson retained. Arbitration of claims of both terminated and retained employees was rejected by a court of appeals, relying on the *Howard Johnson* case, in Boeing Co. v. IAM (5th Cir. 1974). The court there was not prepared to announce a firm rule that "predecessor majority" is always necessary in order to found a duty to arbitrate; but it did hold that in a case in which the successor took over through periodic competitive bidding, and thus where the only factor showing "continuity in the business enterprise" would be "continuity in the workforce," a more substantial carryover of the predecessor's employees would be necessary to justify an order to arbitrate than in the case of purchase and sale, or merger, between the two employers.

CHAPTER XXV

JUDICIAL REVIEW OF ARBITRATION AWARDS

§ 1. Background: The General Standard of Judicial Review

The Supreme Court in the *Steelworkers Trilogy* announced a very limited role for courts in actions under section 301 to enforce arbitration awards. The parties having bargained for the decision of the arbitrator on the merits, and the arbitrator having expertise concerning plant practices, courts must not set aside an arbitral award merely because it disagrees with the arbitrator on the merits. As the Court said in United Steelworkers v. Enterprise Wheel & Car Corp. (U.S.1960), "The federal policy of settling labor disputes by arbitration would be undermined if courts had the final say on the merits of the awards." But the Court also sketched out the limits of judicial deference:

> Nevertheless, an arbitrator is confined to interpretation and application of the collective bargaining agreement; he does not sit to dispense his own brand of industrial justice. He may of course look for guidance from many sources, yet his award is legitimate only so long as it draws its essence from the collective bargaining agreement. When the arbitrator's words manifest an infidelity to this obligation, courts have no choice but to refuse enforcement of the award.

The Court gave an example of the kind of arbitral award that could properly be set aside. The arbitrator had in that case ordered reinstatement and backpay for discharged employees, even though at the time he rendered his award the labor contract had expired; it was unclear from the terms of his award whether he believed the post-contract rights to have been granted by the contract itself or by federal labor law. In upholding the arbitrator's remedy, the Court stated:

> It may be read as based solely upon the arbitrator's view of the requirements of enacted legislation, which would mean that he exceeded the scope of the submission. Or it may be read as embodying a construction of the agreement itself, perhaps with the arbitrator looking to "the law" for help in determining the sense of the agreement. A mere ambiguity in the opinion accompanying an award, which permits the inference that the arbitrator may have exceeded his authority, is not a reason for refusing to enforce the award.

Although the Court held that, to be enforceable, an arbitral award must "draw its essence from the collective bargaining agreement"—as opposed, for example, to being based exclusively on legislation—it is clear that the Court's concept of the agreement is a most expansive one. In United Steelworkers v. Warrior & Gulf Nav. Co. (U.S.1960), the Court viewed the labor agreement as more than the written contract:

> The labor arbitrator's source of law is not confined to the express provisions of the contract, as the industrial common law—the practices of the industry and the shop—is equally a part of the collective bargaining agreement although not expressed in it.

Indeed, the labor agreement, thus broadly understood, may even invite the arbitrator to go beyond both the words and the unwritten plant practices to consider "such factors as the effect upon productivity of a particular result, its consequence to the morale of the shop, his judgment whether tensions will be heightened or diminished."

In short, it is the task of the court in an action to confirm or to set aside an arbitrator's award to determine whether the arbitrator has resolved the grievance by considering the proper sources—"the contract and those circumstances out of which comes the 'common law of the shop' "—but not to determine whether the arbitrator has resolved the grievance correctly. Safeway Stores v. Bakery Workers, Local 111 (5th Cir. 1968). This broad rule of deference justifies sustaining arbitration awards which at first blush may look rather unreasonable. For example, in Safeway Stores v. Bakery Workers, Local 111, *ibid,* the company departed from its practice of ending the pay week on Wednesday and issuing checks the next day, and instead ended the pay week on Friday and issued checks the following Tuesday. The first paycheck under the new system covered only Thursday and Friday, resulting in sixteen hours' pay, and the union filed a grievance charging a violation of a contract provision guaranteeing forty hours' pay each week. The arbitrator sustained the grievance and ordered the employer to pay the employees for an additional twenty-four hours of work even though no work had been performed. The court resisted "the temptation to 'reason out' a la judges the arbiter's award to see if it passes muster," and found simply that the arbitrator based his award on the terms of the contract:

> If such a result is unpalatable to an employer or his law-trained counsel who feels he had a hands-down certainty in a law court, it must be remembered that just such a likelihood is the by-product of a consensually adopted contract arrangement .   .   .   .
>
> The arbiter was chosen to be the Judge. That Judge has spoken. There it ends.

And, in IAM Dist. 145 v. Modern Air Transport, Inc. (5th Cir. 1974), the collective bargaining agreement expressly authorized subcontracting by the employer if "customarily" done before. The arbitrator held that the word "customarily" should be construed to mean "exclusively," and held that employer subcontracting of work violated the labor agreement unless that work had been done "exclusively" by subcontracting previously. The court enforced the award.

Not surprisingly, many courts have been somewhat discomfited by such a narrow standard of review and have insisted that in order to warrant judicial confirmation an award must not only be based upon the contract but must also satisfy some minimal standard of rationality. It has, for example, been stated that a court will not enforce an award which is a "capricious, unreasonable interpretation" of the agreement, Holly Sugar Corp. v. Distillery Workers Union (9th Cir. 1969); or that the award must in some "rational way be derived from the agreement, viewed in the light of its language, its context, and any other indicia of the parties' intention" and must not manifestly disregard the law, Ludwig Honold Mfg. Co. v. Fletcher (3d Cir. 1969); or that a court must determine whether "it is possible for an honest intellect to interpret the words of the contract and reach the result the arbitrator reached," Newspaper Guild v. Tribune Pub. Co. (9th Cir. 1969); or that the award must be set aside "if no judge, or group of judges, could ever conceivably have made such a ruling," Safeway Stores v. Bakery Workers, Local 111 (5th Cir. 1968). It is only the rarest case, however, in which the court will overturn the construction of a contract because it is irrational or capricious; in such cases the court will usually find that the arbitrator has committed some error other than misconstruction. Common examples, to be discussed in detail below, are absence of jurisdiction or of remedial authority, violation of law or public policy, ambiguity or incompleteness, and fraud, bias or other misconduct.

§ 2. Lack of Arbitral Jurisdiction

Since the power of the arbitrator is measured by the consent of the parties in the labor contract, a court may set aside an arbitral award which purports to resolve a dispute which the parties have not in truth empowered the arbitrator to decide. For example, an arbitrator would be held to have exceeded his jurisdiction if he were to sustain a grievance based upon a merit-pay provision of the labor contract, if the arbitration clause explicitly excludes disputes about that provision from the jurisdiction of the arbitrator. Thus, in Electrical Workers Local 278 v. Jetero Corp. (5th Cir. 1974), the arbitration clause covered disputes about the contract and all amendments thereto, and the arbitrator based his backpay order on the wage rates found in two succeeding agreements; the court of appeals, however, concluded that the second subsequent agreement was not technically an amendment and set aside as beyond the arbitrator's power the award of backpay pursuant to that second agreement.

Of course, if there is a dispute about whether a particular claim falls within the power of the arbitrator to decide, this issue of substantive arbitrability may itself be given by the parties to the arbitrator for resolution. It is not at all unusual for the parties to present both issues, of arbitral jurisdiction and of the merits, to the arbitrator to decide in sequence. In such a case, if the arbitrator's decision concerning his own jurisdiction "draws its essence" from the collective bargaining agreement (and satisfies any assumed test of "minimal rationality"), then that decision should not be set aside merely because the court would have construed the arbitration clause differently. United Steelworkers v. United States Gypsum Co. (5th Cir. 1974). The usual narrow standard of judicial review announced in United Steelworkers v. Enterprise Wheel & Car Corp. (U.S.1960) should apply whether the parties have given to the arbitrator the task of deciding jurisdiction or the task of deciding the merits. Thus, where the issue is "procedural arbitrability," and the parties try to the arbitrator the question whether untimely grievance processing by the union requires denial of arbitration, the arbitrator is free to decide that the union's delay was excused by the employer's failure to notify the union of the challenged action, and the court should defer to the arbitrator's decision. Holly Sugar Corp. v. Distillery Workers Union (9th Cir. 1969).

In some instances, the respondent in arbitration (usually the employer) will challenge the jurisdiction of the arbitrator and will, although trying the merits of the underlying contract claim, explicitly preserve its challenge to jurisdiction, to be presented to a court in the event of an adverse decision on the merits. Courts will then be inclined to determine afresh, without the usual broad rules of deference, such questions as substantive arbitrability, Bakery Workers Local 719 v. National Biscuit Co. (3d Cir. 1967) (court considers history of grievance processing to determine arbitrability, since arbitrator did, although would not have in action to compel arbitration), or indeed whether there is a binding collective bargaining agreement at all, Trudon & Platt Motor Lines, Inc. v. Local 707, Teamsters (S.D. N.Y.1969), since if the respondent is correct, it has never agreed to submit the merits to arbitral determination. Sometimes, courts go too far and re-try the issue of arbitrability which has been fairly tried before the arbitrator. E. g., District 50, UMW v. Pittston Co. (N.D.W.Va.1962) (employer raised non-arbitrability in action to enforce award, and court stated: "[W]hether defendant agreed to submit the case upon a condition that it could be heard later in court, or without such condition, the law gives the defendant the right to have the court determine if the dispute is arbitrable under the agreement .   .   .   ."). A different "jurisdictional" attack on an award was made in ILGWU v. Ashland Indus., Inc. (5th Cir. 1974), in which the arbitrator had dismissed the union's grievance, sustaining the employer's claim that the contract had been secured by fraud; in spite of the arbitral disposition of the fraud issue, the court of appeals held that the existence of a valid contract is a "legal question" to be decided by the court and not by the arbitrator and remanded to the trial court for a determination of the question of fraud.

A similar "defect of power" which is said to render an arbitral award subject to judicial reversal is the arbitrator's exceeding the "submission," or the statement of the claim, agreed upon by the parties. For example, in Electrical Workers Local 791 v. Magnavox Co. (6th Cir. 1961), the arbitrator ruled against the union on the only issue submitted to him for decison, whether the employer had unreasonably increased assembly-line quotas in violation of the labor contract. But when he then proceeded to order the parties to negotiate for engineering studies to guide future quota disputes, the court refused enforcement as beyond the scope of the grievance. See also Retail Store Employees Local 782 v. Sav-On Groceries (10th Cir. 1975) (remedy of backpay not an issue within scope of submission). Again, if the question of the scope of the submission is considered by the arbitrator and a decision is made based upon the parties' language and upon other relevant sources, the decision should be sustained on judicial review. United Steelworkers v. United States Gypsum Co. (5th Cir. 1974).

§ 3. Lack of Arbitral Authority to Decide or to Remedy

Even though an arbitrator clearly has "subject matter jurisdiction" over a particular dispute, both under the contract and the parties' submission, the contract may impose explicit limitations upon his authority to render a particular decision or fashion a particular remedy. If the arbitrator's award violates this limitation upon his authority, it may be vacated by court order under section 301. For example, in Magnavox Co. v. IUE (6th Cir. 1969), an employee, recently returned to work after extensive sick leave, refused orders to remove cabinets from an oven, asserting that his doctor had advised him not to work in extreme heat; for this refusal, he was discharged. The labor contract explicitly withheld from the arbitrator the right to

> consider, rule or enter any award with respect to disciplinary action imposed upon an employee for refusal or failure to perform assigned job tasks, except where the employee can positively establish that the performance of such task would have created a serious health hazard to him.

The arbitrator found that the work assigned to the grievant would not have seriously imperiled his health but, finding that the employee's fear was in good faith, concluded that discharge was too severe; he ordered reinstatement without backpay. The court vacated the award, concluding that once the arbitrator found a refusal to work and the absence in fact of a serious health hazard, he was powerless to mitigate the penalty. See also Truck Drivers Local 784 v. Ulry-Talbert Co. (8th Cir. 1964) (arbitrator finds discharge too severe, in spite of finding that employee had committed charged offense; court vacates, since contract forbade arbitrator to reverse a discharge unless "the Company's complaint against the employee is not supported by the facts, and   .   .   .   the management has acted arbitrarily and in bad faith or in violation of the express terms of this Agreement.").

Although the broader the limits which the parties impose on the arbitrator's authority the more assertive the court may properly be in screening the award on the merits, some courts have taken very seriously the teachings of the *Steelworkers Trilogy* and have given broad range to arbitral discretion.   Thus, in Chemical Workers Local 728 v. Imco Container Co. (S.D.Ind.1971), the contract contained not only the usual ban on the arbitrator's adding to or modifying the terms of the agreement but went on to declare: "The Arbitrator must find his decision within the terms of this Agreement rather than from any general theories of labor law, justice or wisdom which he may have."   Nonetheless, when the contract was silent as to the arbitrator's power to group dissimilar multiple grievances for hearing before a single arbitrator, the court upheld the arbitrator in his reliance on the "experience of others and his general background in labor law and arbitration."

Even in the absence of an explicit ban upon the arbitrator's construing a particular provision of the contract or issuing a particular kind of award, attempts are often made to infer such a ban from other terms of the contract.   This kind of attack upon the arbitrator's authority is most commonly made in cases in which the employer has discharged an employee for wrongdoing and the arbitrator finds that the employee did in fact commit the wrong charged against him but concludes nonetheless that discharge is too severe and that a lesser discipline (such as suspension without backpay) should be ordered.   The employer will argue that such an award exceeds the powers of the arbitrator under the labor contract and will often point to (one or) two types of contract provisions.   First is a substantive contract term explicitly giving the employer the power freely to discipline for the conceded wrongdoing.   Second is the common provision in an arbitration clause that bars the arbitrator from "adding to, subtracting from or modifying" the terms of the collective bargaining agreement.   The issue is a most difficult one.   If the employer's sole defense is a substantive contract term relating to discipline, then an arbitrator's construction of that term to mean that discharge may be too severe can normally be said—even if a dubious construction—to "draw its essence" from the contract and thus not to be subject to reversal merely because the court would construe the term differently. If, however, the contract not only purports explicitly to give the employer disciplinary powers but also forbids the arbitrator to "modify" or "subtract from" those powers, this appears to invite greater judicial scrutiny of the arbitrator's award.   Such scrutiny has sometimes been read by courts as an invitation squarely to construe the substantive discipline clause of the contract, in order to determine whether the arbitrator has "modified" it.   By reviewing the arbitrator's decision on the merits, in order to implement the rather vague restrictions of a "no addition or modification" clause, the courts would appear to be overstepping the limitations imposed upon them by the Supreme Court in United Steelworkers v. Enterprise Wheel & Car Corp. (U.S.1960).

In Textile Workers Union v. American Thread Co. (4th Cir. 1961), the employer relied on a provision in the labor contract that "Employees shall be disciplined or discharged only for just cause," and discharged an employee for careless operation of his machine. The contract also provided that "should it be determined that any employee was disciplined or discharged without just cause," the employee was to be reinstated and awarded backpay for no more than ninety days. The arbitrator concluded that the employee had indeed been careless as charged, that this was "cause" for some discipline but that discharge was too severe, and that a one-week suspension would have been just discipline. The court vacated the arbitrator's award, holding that once the arbitrator had found cause for discipline, he had no authority to consider how just was the discipline actually imposed by the employer. The court, by overruling the arbitrator in his construction of the "just cause" and remedy provisions of the labor contract, appears improperly to have ruled upon the merits of the case in the guise of hedging the authority of the arbitrator. Nonetheless, courts frequently do vacate arbitral reinstatement awards which appear flatly to contradict substantive contract provisions giving the employer the apparently unfettered power to discharge for stipulated employee wrongdoing. Thus, when a contract expressly gave the employer the power to discharge strikers and the arbitrator found the aggrieved employees to have engaged in a strike in breach of contract but nonetheless ordered reinstatement (finding that discharge was punitive and unduly severe), the court set aside the award. Amanda Bent Bolt Co. v. UAW Local 1549 (6th Cir. 1971). In a similar case, in which the arbitrator ordered reinstatement on the theory that discharge was unjust because no notice was given by the employer to the strikers, the court vacated the award; it held that the discharge provision was unambiguous and required no interpretation, and thus that the arbitrator "added to" the limits on the employer's power to discharge and exceeded his authority. UAW Local 342 v. TRW, Inc. (6th Cir. 1968). And, in Timken Co. v. Steelworkers Union (6th Cir. 1973), where the contract authorized discharge for "voluntarily quitting the service of the Company," with a voluntary quit defined as an "unauthorized absence" of seven consecutive days, the employer discharged an employee for missing one month of work when in jail on charges unrelated to his employment. The arbitrator, concluding that this kind of absence was not within the purpose of the clause allowing discharge for a voluntary quit, ordered reinstatement, but the court reversed, holding that the arbitrator had substituted his sense of justice for the terms of the contract.

Other courts, however, have in comparable cases given the arbitrator greater deference. In IAM v. Campbell Soup Co. (7th Cir. 1969), the discharged employee had committed a crime in the plant, conduct which the contract explicitly stated to be grounds for discharge. The arbitrator found some discipline to be warranted but concluded that discharge was too harsh under the circumstances. The award of reinstatement was confirmed by the court, which distinguished other decisions to the contrary (including some just discussed, *supra*) by noting that the contract in the case before it contained no explicit ban on the authority of the arbitrator to "add to" the agreement and because the arbitrator had specifically found the discharge to be without "just cause." And, in Lynchburg Foundry Co. v. Steelworkers Union (4th Cir. 1968), where the contract provided that an improper discharge was to be remedied by reinstatement with backpay, an arbitral interpretation that the contract permitted a reduction in discipline—such as reinstatement with seniority but without backpay—was sustained by the court as within the authority of the arbitrator. The court found the reinstatement clause merely to mark the outer limits of the arbitrator's remedial power, and held that broad remedial discretion should be implied in the "absence of language evidencing a clear intent to deny the arbitrator any latitude of judgment" on issues of discipline and remedy.

This theme was also sounded by a court of appeals which recently upheld an arbitrator's award of wage increases based on his projection of the wage settlement that would have resulted had the employer not violated its duty to bargain under a wage reopener provision in the contract. United Steelworkers v. United States Gypsum (5th Cir. 1974). Here, too, it was argued that such an award was forbidden by the contract, which provided that the "arbitrator shall not have jurisdiction or authority to add to, detract from, or alter in any way the provisions of this contract." But the court found no contractual bar to the arbitrator's remedy:

> The nexus between the breach of the reopener clause and the method selected to remedy that breach is sufficient to support the conclusion that the remedy "draws its essence" from the contract. Gypsum's employees were denied their right to negotiate for increased wages. Relief was given in the form of what they would have received had they negotiated. This remedy is not arbitrary, capricious nor insufficiently grounded in the contract, and it flows logically and reasonably from the breach of the reopener clause.

In United Steelworkers v. Enterprise Wheel & Car Corp. (U.S.1960), the Supreme Court underlined the need for arbitral judgment and flexibility in formulating remedies in diverse and often unforeseen contingencies. Arbitrators have been upheld in the issuance of unusual and indeed drastic remedies of the kind which the National Labor Relations Board would be loath to order in an unfair labor practice case, *e. g.,* Joint Bd., ILGWU v. Senco, Inc. (D.Mass.1968) (plant removal found to be contract breach, and employer ordered to return the business to the original location); or which would in fact be beyond the power of the Board to issue, United States Steelworkers v. United States Gypsum Co. (5th Cir. 1974) (arbitrator projects wage settlement had employer negotiated wage reopener; court confirms the award and distinguishes Supreme Court decision forbidding NLRB to issue such a remedy).

§ 4. Arbitral "Modification" of the Agreement

The very common provision barring arbitral "addition to or modification of" the agreement has also been used to strike down arbitrator's awards which are based upon sources outside the written contract, such as earlier contracts, contract negotiations and plant and industry customs and practices. Perhaps the most noteworthy example is Torrington Co. v. Metal Prods. Workers Local 1645 (2d Cir. 1966), in which the union claimed before the arbitrator that the employer had improperly terminated an unwritten practice of long standing to pay employees for one hour away from work on Election Day. The employer argued that the practice was effectively terminated when it unilaterally announced its discontinuance prior to the negotiation of a new contract, but the arbitrator concluded that the employer's liability for Election Day pay could be terminated only by securing the consent of the union and that the employer had not done so in its contract negotiations. The court reversed, holding that the arbitrator had exceeded his powers by thus finding in past practice and in negotiations an employer duty not reflected in the writing, and that the arbitrator was not free to ignore the "no additions or modifications" clause of the contract. The dissenting judge argued that the court was improperly reviewing the merits of the award, and that the parties had agreed to abide by the award of the arbitrator even if wrong, so long as his sources of decision were appropriate:

> [T]he arbitrator looked to prior practice, the conduct of the negotiation for the new contract and the agreement reached at the bargaining table to reach his conclusion that paid time off for voting was "an implied part of the contract." From all of this, I conclude that the arbitrator's award "draws its essence from the collective bargaining agreement" and his words do not "manifest an infidelity to this obligation."

In H. K. Porter Co. v. Saw Workers Union 22254 (3d Cir. 1964), the arbitrator found a single unexplained grant of a pension in the past to an employee who retired at 65 with less than 25 years of company service; in all other instances, 25 years of services was a precondition to a pension, in accordance with the contract language. In his decision, the arbitrator awarded pro rata pensions to employees who reached 65 but who had not worked for 25 years. The court vacated this part of the award, holding that it contradicted the "clear and unambiguous" terms of the writing and that the one incident was not sufficient to make out a past practice justifying modification of the "plain meaning" of the contract.

Other courts have taken the side of the dissenting judge in the *Torrington* case, *supra*. In Holly Sugar Corp. v. Distillery Workers Union (9th Cir. 1969), the court held that the arbitrator had implied authority to excuse the union's untimely processing of its grievance, even though the contract did not so provide in its terms. And, in Chemical Workers Local 728 v. Imco Container Co. (S.D.Ind.1971), the court confirmed an award grouping dissimilar multiple grievances for hearing before a single arbitrator even though the contract was silent on this matter and indeed even though it expressly provided that "The Arbitrator must find his decision within the terms of this Agreement rather than from any general theories of labor law, justice or wisdom which he may have"; the court held that the arbitrator could rely on the "experience of others and his general background in labor law and arbitration." Further support for arbitral supplementation of the written contract by past practice is found in United Steelworkers v. Warrior & Gulf Nav. Co. (U.S.1960), in which the Supreme Court stated that the collective bargaining agreement was to be found not merely in the written contract but also in the "common law of the shop," including the unwritten customs and the practices of the industry and of a particular plant. If the arbitrator in deciding the merits of the dispute has recourse only to the writing, to negotiations and to plant practices, it is doubtful that the award "adds to or modifies" the labor agreement. Any misreading of those data may constitute error but not likely an excess of arbitral authority.

§ 5. Violation of Law or Public Policy

Just as private parties cannot expect a court to enforce a contract between them to engage in conduct which is illegal or otherwise contrary to public policy, they cannot expect an intervening arbitral award approving (or ordering) that conduct to receive judicial endorsement. It is not surprising that an arbitrator will occasionally render an award which sustains an arguably illegal contract provision or which orders arguably illegal conduct. The statutory regulation of labor relations has become increasingly complex and many arbitrators are laymen, selected more for their familiarity with industrial practices or with the parties than they are for their legal acumen. Indeed, even among arbitrators with substantial legal training, there are many who believe that their sole function is to construe the agreement and determine the intentions of the parties and that the function of testing the contract for legality lies with the courts. The Supreme Court appears to have endorsed this view when it stated in United Steelworkers v. Enterprise Wheel & Car Corp. (U.S.1960), that the arbitrator who bases his decision not on the parties' agreement but on extrinsic statutory policy exceeds his powers and renders his award subject to judicial attack.

Whether or not an arbitrator believes it proper to test the contract against the requirements of law and public policy, it is commonly accepted that a court should apply those requirements in an action to vacate or enforce an arbitral award under section 301. Newspaper Guild v. Washington Post Co. (D.C.Cir.1971). In one case, in which an arbitral order to the employer was alleged to require the employer to violate state law, the court stated:

> [I]t is too plain for argument that no court will order a party to do something, if in order to comply with the court's directive, he must commit a crime. This is so despite any protestations that the party contracted to do what it is said that he should be ordered to do.

UAW Local 985 v. W. M. Chace Co. (E.D.Mich.1966). Such judicial review of arbitral awards for legality does not conflict with the Supreme Court mandate of extremely limited review announced in the *Enterprise Wheel* case. As was noted in Botany Indus., Inc. v. New York Joint Bd., Amal. Clothing Workers (S.D.N.Y.), *vacated on other grounds* (2d Cir. 1974):

> Enterprise involves only one of several grounds for vacating an arbitration award—an attack upon the arbitrator's judgment—and its pronouncements are directed to that specific ground. Thus, the Supreme Court was concerned with the review of the *merits* of an arbitrator's award; and it was concerned with the *interpretation* and *construction* of the collective bargaining agreement. . . . In the instant case, however, the nature of the attack is quite different—the award is challenged, not upon its merits, but upon the ground that the underlying agreement violates a federal law and therefore is unenforceable—and thus the nature of the court's inquiry is also quite different. This court is *not* concerned with whether the arbitrator has properly construed the collective bargaining agreement, or whether this court agrees with the arbitrator's interpretation of the agreement; but, rather, this court is concerned with whether the collective bargaining agreement and, *a fortiori*, the arbitration award is capable of being enforced. Indeed, as one court has aptly stated, the court "is concerned with the *lawfulness of its enforcing* the award and not with the *correctness of the arbitrator's* decision." (Italics in original.)

Claims of illegality of a provision in the labor contract or of an arbitration award have been made both under federal law and state law.

Federal law has been invoked most commonly by asserting that the arbitrator has ordered one of the parties to commit an unfair labor practice, but this has not been the only source of attack. In Associated Milk Dealers v. Milk Drivers Local 753 (7th Cir. 1970), the union argued that a labor-contract provision which a multiemployer association sought to enforce violated the antitrust laws. The court dealt with this argument in a proceeding to withhold the employer grievance from arbitration in the first instance, but the clear implication of the court's opinion was that an arbitral award founded on a contract provision which violated the Sherman Act would be vacated. An example of a post-arbitration attack that failed, however, is United Steelworkers v. United States Gypsum Co. (5th Cir. 1974), in which the employer argued that compliance with an arbitral order to pay to the union an amount of money equivalent to union dues— which the employer had wrongly refused to check off from employee wages—would require the employer to violate section 302 of the Labor Act, which makes it a crime for an employer to pay money to a labor organization. While the court conceded that "an adequate basis for refusing to enforce an arbitrator's award is that it would require a violation of the Act," it concluded that judicial enforcement of the award would not direct a violation of the law, since section 302(a) is designed to protect employers from extortion and to insure honest representation of employees (not to prevent dues payments from employer to union) and since, in any event, section 302(c)(2) expressly excludes from its ban payment "in satisfaction of a judgment of any court or a decision or award of an arbitrator."

A more difficult issue emerges when a court is asked to set aside an arbitral award because it will force the respondent to commit an unfair labor practice. If the court passes upon the merits of this defense, it will be construing and applying the unfair labor practice provisions of the Labor Act, a task which courts ordinarily eschew in deference to the exclusive jurisdiction of the NLRB. If, however, the court ignores this defense and orders compliance with the award, the respondent is faced with the unenviable choice of honoring the award and committing an unfair labor practice, or repudiating the award and being cited for contempt for violating the court order. Presumably because of a disinclination to place a judicial stamp of approval on an order requiring a violation of the Labor Act, the few courts that have dealt with this problem have frontally addressed the unfair labor practice issue and set aside the arbitrator's award. In Botany Indus., Inc. v. New York Joint Bd., Amal. Clothing Workers (S.D.N. Y.), *vacated on other grounds* (2d Cir. 1974), the court set aside an arbitration award which was based upon what the court found to be an illegal hot-cargo clause in violation of section 8(e) of the Labor Act and which would have required the employer to engage in an unlawful secondary boycott. The court held that it could not direct the employer to commit an illegal act and that the availability of the National Labor Relations Board to test claims of violation of section 8(e) did not preempt the jurisdiction of a court in a section 301 ac-

tion to pass upon the same issue.   (It is noteworthy that the cases relied upon by the court for its holding against preemption may be said
to stand for the principle that a court and arbitrator may construe
the labor contract even though the conduct complained of may also
independently of the contract violate the Labor Act; but the court
went beyond a reading of the contract and actually applied and construed a complex unfair labor practice provision of the Act itself.
This is normally not the task of trial judges, and would be particularly
foreign to a state court, which does have concurrent jurisdiction in
contract actions under section 301.)

The impropriety of enforcing the arbitrator's award becomes
clearer, and potential judicial interference with Board functions becomes far less significant, when at the time of the court action to set
aside the arbitral award the Board has already rendered a controlling
decision in an unfair labor practice or representation case.   The Supreme Court stated in Carey v. Westinghouse Elec. Corp. (U.S.1964)
that a later Board decision must prevail and that the respondent
in the arbitration case is not to be held liable in damages for
refusing to abide by the arbitral award.   In a state-court decision,
In re Meyers (N.Y.App.Div.1969), the court refused to enforce an
arbitration award declaring that an acquired business was an "accretion" to the union's unit covered by the labor contract and that the
employees there were to be represented by the union; for, soon after
the arbitrator rendered this award, the Board held that there was no
accretion, such that a different union could properly claim bargaining
rights.   And, in Glendale Mfg. Co. v. ILGWU Local 520 (4th Cir.
1960) the arbitrator ordered the employer to bargain with the union
pursuant to the wage-reopener provisions of the labor contract.   The
court refused to enforce this arbitral order when, shortly after the arbitrator announced his decision, the union was ousted as representative in a Board-conducted certification election.   To confirm the arbitral bargaining order would impair the section 7 rights of employees
to bargain through representatives of their own choosing.

A court will also vacate an arbitral award which requires conduct in violation of state law.   In UAW v. W. M. Chace Co. (E.D.
Mich.1966), the arbitrator properly construed the labor contract to
mandate reinstatement of a woman to a job which required the lifting
of weights in excess of those permitted by state law.   The court held it
could not compel compliance with the award if employer assignment
of those tasks would be unlawful; since the state rule (based on a
twenty-five-year-old press release) was of uncertain status, the court
set down the case for trial to determine whether that rule was indeed
binding and the arbitral award thus invalid.   But in another case, in
which the arbitrator construed the labor contract to require the assignment of overtime work to women in violation of state law, the
court upheld the award nonetheless, since the employer had agreed to
abide by it and the case presented a single private dispute without

any statewide binding effect on the state labor commissioner, who had intervened in the action. UAW v. Avco Lycoming Div. (D.Conn. 1971). The court was obviously influenced by the likely invalidity of the state law when tested against the provisions of Title VII of the 1964 Civil Rights Act barring most forms of employment discrimination on the basis of sex.

A lesser form of conflict with state or federal law may emerge when the award, although not requiring illegal conduct, is said to be inconsistent with some significant public policy. In Black v. Cutter Laboratories (Cal.1955), the arbitrator found that the aggrieved employee had been discharged from her position with a pharmaceutical firm not because she was a Communist and had falsified her employment application (which she was and which she did), as the employer claimed, but rather because of her union activity in violation of the labor contract. The arbitrator's order to reinstate was vacated by the court, which held it contrary to public policy embodied in federal and state law to compel reinstatement, in a firm producing drugs for military and civilian use, of a member of the Communist Party. This controversial decision goes beyond those cases which vacate awards said actually to compel the commission of an act which would have been unlawful even if performed voluntarily; if employer and union had voluntarily agreed that the employee should be reinstated (or initially merely suspended) such action would not have been subject to challenge as contrary to law or public policy.

This was implicitly recognized in Electrical Workers Local 453 v. Otis Elevator Co. (2d Cir. 1963), in which the employer had discharged an employee for violating a company rule against gambling in the plant, after the employee had been convicted of trafficking in policy slips on plant property. The arbitrator found the employee culpable but concluded that this was not "just cause" for as severe a discipline as discharge, considering the employee's long unblemished work record, his loss of pension rights, the impact on his family, the company's failure to discipline four other employees involved in the gambling operation and the fine imposed through the criminal justice system. The arbitral order of reinstatement was vacated by the federal trial judge who was in turn reversed, and the award confirmed, by the court of appeals. The court assumed that arbitral awards contrary to public policy are properly to be vacated by a court, but concluded that reinstatement (without seven months' backpay) would not violate public policy—the employer would not be charged with sheltering criminal activities on his property, the state's anti-gambling policy was vindicated through the criminal fine and the seven-month suspension, and reinstatement advanced the public policy of rehabilitation of criminals. The same conclusion was reached more recently in IAM v. Campbell Soup Co. (7th Cir. 1969), even though the labor contract expressly stipulated that the commission of a crime in the plant was "cause" for discipline. Courts should no doubt tread with caution when asked to set aside an award in a discipline case as contrary to public policy, since "just cause" is typically a matter for arbitral expertise, is not to be reviewed on the merits for error and could have been lawfully defined by mutual agreement of the parties so as to countenance reinstatement (or some discipline less severe than discharge) for an employee found culpable of objectionable or even illegal conduct.

§ 6. Incompleteness, Ambiguity or Inconsistency

Other substantive difficulties with an award may cause a court to balk at enforcement. An example is an award that is incomplete, ambiguous or self-contradictory. In such instances, the proper remedy is not for the court to rectify the defect in the award but rather to order the case recommitted to the arbitrator. For the court to cure the defect would intrude upon the authority of the arbitrator exclusively to determine the merits of the dispute. Hanford Atomic Metal Trades Council v. General Elec. Co. (9th Cir. 1965). Thus, the failure of the arbitrator to make a final decision on the question submitted requires the court to order a resubmission to the arbitrator. IAM v. Crown Cork & Seal Co. (3d Cir. 1962) (no arbitral disposition of the submitted question of damages). The Supreme Court endorsed such a disposition in United Steelworkers v. Enterprise Wheel & Car Corp. (U.S.1960), in which the award of backpay was held to be incomplete because of the failure to determine the amounts to be deducted (for example, for earnings elsewhere) from the award. An award does not, however, lack completeness if specific sums due can be determined by a purely mechanical arithmetic exercise. Retail Clerks Local 954 v. Lion Dry Goods, Inc. (N.D.Ohio, 1966), *aff'd* (6th Cir. 1967).

The Supreme Court in *Enterprise Wheel* also cautioned against outright judicial vacating of an arbitrator's award because of ambiguity, even in the case when the ambiguity relates not to the meaning of the award but to the sources of decision and thus ultimately to the question whether the award "draws its essence" from the labor agreement:

> A mere ambiguity in the opinion accompanying an award, which permits the inference that the arbitrator may have exceeded his authority, is not a reason for refusing to enforce the award. Arbitrators have no obligation to the court to give their reasons for an award. To require opinions free of ambiguity may lead arbitrators to play it safe by writing no supporting opinions. This would be undesirable for a well-reasoned opinion tends to engender confidence in the integrity of the process and aids in clarifying the underlying agreement.

Nonetheless, the parties do have to understand what the arbitrator's award directs them to do, in order that arbitration can effectively resolve the dispute. Thus, in Bell Aerospace Co. v. Local 516, UAW (2d Cir. 1974), the arbitrator's award in a work-assignment dispute between two unions was so worded as to describe skills of some members of each union, leaving unclear who was to perform many of the contested jobs. Although the court of appeals reversed the district court's own clarification of the award, it ordered that the award be resubmitted to an arbitrator for clarification. If, however, the award is clear at the time it is rendered, an ambiguity which arises from future application of the award to a new fact situation does not make the award unenforceable; it simply creates a new dispute which must be arbitrated.

Nor is it fatal to an award of an arbitrator that it conflicts rather squarely with an award made by another arbitrator under the same contract or a different contract in the same plant. Just as different judges or juries may each reasonably read the same facts or the same contract language different ways, so too may arbitrators, and so long as the decision of each "draws its essence" from the writing, from negotiations and from plant practices, each is within the power of the arbitrator and must be enforced. American Sterilizer Co. v. UAW Local 832 (W.D.Pa.1968) (transferred employee is to determine seniority for layoffs by time spent in unit rather than in plant, under award rendered to union in transferee unit, while in arbitration by former union, seniority held to be determined by employment in plant; in employer action for declaratory judgment, court holds both awards valid and enforceable). If the employer can foresee the likelihood of such conflicting awards in advance, it can try to induce all affected parties to participate in a single proceeding; and in some cases, it can secure a judicial order directed against two conflicting claimants to present those claims to a single arbitrator, Columbia Broadcasting System v. American Recording & Broadcasting Ass'n (2d Cir. 1969) (work-assignment dispute between two unions).

§ 7. Procedural Impropriety

To this point, attention has been given to judicial power to set aside arbitration awards which have some substantive or jurisdictional defect. Courts will also screen awards for procedural regularity and will set aside awards in which there is some procedural impropriety which denies a party fundamental fairness. Many courts have found their source of power in the United States Arbitration Act, 9 U.S.C.A. § 1 et seq., which in section 10 announces four grounds for vacating an award: corruption or fraud, evident partiality of the arbitrator, prejudicial misbehavior of the arbitrator such as refusing to hear relevant and material evidence, and the arbitrator's failure to make a final and definite award or to act within the powers given him. Before the Supreme Court held in Textile Workers Union v. Lincoln Mills (U.S.1957) that section 301 accorded to federal courts the power to fashion common law rules governing arbitration promises and awards, several courts looked to the Arbitration Act (in spite of its exemption of "contracts of employment" of workers engaged in interstate commerce) for guidelines in labor arbitration cases. *E. g.,* Signal-Stat Corp. v. UEW Local 475 (2d Cir. 1956). Since *Lincoln Mills*, courts have "absorbed" the provisions of the Arbitration Act into the corpus of federal law under section 301, and have applied them to the review of arbitration awards either specifically, Pietro Scalzitti Co. v. Operating Engineers Local 150 (7th Cir. 1965), or by analogy, Ludwig Honold Mfg. Co. v. Fletcher (3d Cir. 1969).

A clear instance in which the court will vacate an arbitral award is when the arbitrator is biased or partial. The bias may be discernible from a study of the arbitrator's actual conduct at the arbitration hearing, as reflected in the record before the court. Holodnak v. Avco Corp. (D.Conn.1974), *mdf'd on other grounds* (2d Cir. 1975) (court invokes Arbitration Act and finds "evident partiality"). The bias may be found outside the record of the hearing, when the arbitrator is clearly affiliated with or beholden to a party to the arbitration and fails to make this known to the other party. For example, in Colony Liquor Distributors, Inc. v. Teamsters Local 669 (N.Y.App. Div.1970), *aff'd* (1971), an award for the union was vacated when the arbitrator failed to inform the employer that he had served as union attorney for several years, had listed the union's address as his own only six months previously, and had one of his close relatives employed by the union. The court noted that while a prior association did not in itself disqualify an arbitrator, there existed under the circumstances a reasonable inference of bias. In Bieski v. Eastern Auto. For. Co. (3d Cir. 1968), the court set aside an award of a panel comprised of management members and union members, when the union represented both groups of conflicting employees in a seniority dispute and management clearly had an economic interest which aligned it against the aggrieved employees.

On occasion, a court will vacate an award because of unfair and prejudicial exclusion or admission of evidence. This will occur only rarely, because it is the common understanding that judicial rules of evidence do not apply in arbitration procedures; indeed, one of the great attractions of arbitration for industrial disputants is the flexible and nontechnical nature of the proceeding. It is quite common for the arbitrator to admit hearsay evidence, treating the hearsay quality as pertinent to the weight to be given to the evidence but not to its admissibility. A court will not set aside an award because the arbitrator has admitted hearsay evidence or evidence which was not presented at earlier stages of the grievance machinery. Instrument Workers Local 116 v. Minneapolis-Honeywell Regulator Co. (E.D. Pa.1963) (arbitrator more like a judge than a jury in weighing evidence of dubious credence, and court should not regulate). Similarly, arbitrators are commonly free to exclude arguably relevant evidence which they consider not to merit attention. Meat Cutters Local 540

v. Neuhoff Bros. Packers, Inc. (5th Cir. 1973) (even though contract gave employer the right to require employees to take polygraph test, arbitrator's refusal to admit the results of the test was upheld).

But if the arbitrator's exclusion of material evidence is technical, unanticipated and prejudicial, the court may set aside the award. Thus, in Harvey Aluminum v. Steelworkers Union (C.D.Cal.1967), the arbitrator refused to admit certain evidence in rebuttal, claiming that it should have been introduced if at all as part of the party's case in chief. The court found this exclusion seriously improper, since such technicalities of evidence had never been invoked in the past and since the arbitrator had not otherwise given warning of such rules; it held that, barring a restriction on admissibility in the labor contract or specific reasons for discrediting the value of evidence, the parties may assume that all relevant evidence can be presented. Section 10 of the Arbitration Act buttresses this position. Of course, the refusal to admit evidence will not warrant setting aside the arbitrator's award unless the resulting prejudice leads to an unfair hearing. Newark Stereotypers' Union No. 18 v. Newark Morning Ledger Co. (3d Cir. 1968). The same general principles apply when the claim is that the arbitrator has, conversely, relied on testimony or documents which were not formally placed into evidence. In Bell Aerospace Co. v. Local 516, UAW (2d Cir. 1974), the court upheld an arbitrator's award in spite of his reliance on an affidavit not in the record, since the document was part of the record in an NLRB case stipulated by the parties to be relevant and because the parties did not object in advance of the award when they knew the arbitrator was considering the affidavit. Compare Textile Workers Union v. American Thread Co. (4th Cir. 1961) (award vacated, in part because arbitrator relied on previous arbitral award not formally introduced but referred to during the hearing).

The arbitration award will also normally be regarded as immune from attack in spite of the introduction to the court of new evidence not introduced at the arbitration hearing which appears to show that the award was erroneous. Bridgeport Rolling Mills Co. v. Brown (2d Cir. 1963). Thus, in Newspaper Guild Local 35 v. Washington Post Co. (D.C.Cir.1971), the court refused to remand to the arbitrator when a formerly reluctant witness agreed to testify after the arbitration hearing had been closed; the court held that the arbitrator lacked power to reopen the case without the consent of the parties and, more significantly, that the utility of arbitration as a dispute-resolution mechanism would be undermined if awards could be readily opened for newly discovered evidence. One court, however, has been moved recently (and arguably erroneously) to vacate an arbitrator's award of reinstatement which was clearly bottomed on the assumption that the aggrieved employee had not been earlier suspended by the employer, when evidence presented to the court showed this crucial assumption to be contrary to fact. Electronics

Corp. of America v. IUE Local 272 (1st Cir. 1974). This decision is also difficult to square with the principle that the arbitrator is free to require in discharge cases that the employer bear the burden of proof beyond a reasonable doubt that the employee was culpable, even though the contract is silent on the issue of burden of proof and even though the court might have used a different standard had it presided at the arbitration hearing. Meat Cutters Local 540 v. Neuhoff Bros. Packers, Inc. (5th Cir. 1973).

Other serious procedural irregularities resulting in fundamental unfairness may warrant vacating an arbitral award. If, for example, the contract contemplates that the grievance will be resolved by a panel of arbitrators by majority vote, an award will be set aside if the panel fails to call meetings, review evidence and decide the issue through joint efforts. Hod Carriers Local 227 v. Sullivan (E.D.Ill. 1963) (impartial member of panel conducted all hearings and rendered award without consulting other panel members). There appears, however, to be some difference of opinion when the failure of the panel to meet and decide is caused by the noncooperation of one of the parties to the arbitration proceeding. Thus, the court in Retail Clerks Union v. Lion Dry Goods, Inc. (N.D.Ohio 1966), *aff'd* (6th Cir. 1967), affirmed an arbitral award even though one of the panel members refused to participate, the refusal being to further the strategy of one of the parties; the court observed that "we would be in a state of anarchy if the parties . . . could avoid decisions by the simple process of taking their dolls and going home." Precisely such an "anarchic" result was reached more recently in Sam Kane Packing Co. v. Meat Cutters Union (5th Cir. 1973), where each party designated a panel member but the employer's nominee refused to participate (as the contract provided) in the selection of an impartial third member. The court vacated an award rendered by the union nominee on his own, holding that such an ex parte award would generate only hostility rather than private settlement of the dispute and that the proper remedy was an action against the employer to compel compliance with the labor contract and the appointment of the impartial member.

When procedural irregularities do not undermine the validity of the arbitration process, the courts will tend to sustain the award. This sometimes occurs when the contract stipulates that the arbitrator's decision shall be filed within a certain time after the hearing, and the arbitrator fails to meet the deadline. A court is likely to sustain the award nonetheless, holding either that the deadline provision was itself subject to arbitral construction, UAW Local 971 v. Bendix-Westinghouse Auto. Air Brake Co. (N.D.Ohio 1960) (arbitrator may reasonably interpret provision requiring filing of award within thirty days of "final submission"), or that the parties waived any objection to untimeliness by not raising it prior to the filing of the award (and no actual harm resulted from the delay), Machinists Union Lodge 725

v. Mooney Aircraft Inc. (5th Cir. 1969) (award rendered 44 days after hearing rather than three days).   Similar principles were applied
to declare inapplicable a provision in a state statute establishing a
sixty-day period for the filing of an arbitration award (for failure of
which the award would be void), in a case in which the arbitrator
filed his award 108 days after the filing of the last brief.   The court
sustained the award, finding a uniform federal interest in finality of
awards which would be frustrated by the application of varying state
rules on timeliness.   In West Rock Lodge 2120, IAM v. Geometric
Tool Co. (2d Cir. 1968), the court stated:

> In adopting a uniform federal standard, we ought not to
> accept an arbitration rule which encourages post-award
> technical objections by a losing party as a means of avoiding
> an adverse arbitration decision. . . . Rather, we be-
> lieve it to be a better rule that any limitation upon the time
> in which an arbitrator can render his award be a directory
> limitation, not a mandatory one, and that it should always
> be within a court's discretion to uphold a late award if no
> objection to the delay has been made prior to the rendition
> of the award or there is no showing that actual harm to the
> losing party was caused by the delay.

CHAPTER XXVI

ENFORCEMENT OF THE NO–STRIKE CLAUSE

§ 1. Common Law and Legislative Background

At common law, the most effective weapon against concerted labor activities was the injunction. When these activities were found to violate state tort law—or federal tort law, prior to the Supreme Court's decision in Erie R.R. v. Tompkins (U.S.1938)—or federal antitrust law, an injunction could promptly put an end to the strike, picketing or boycott. Although often issued only temporarily, or pending a full hearing on the merits of the case, the injunction would usually succeed in breaking the momentum and the will of the employees and effectively terminating the activities permanently. Speed was not the only feature that made the injunction desirable, for the employer could frequently secure the injunction without notice to or hearing for the union, with proof based on dubious and stylized affidavits, with proceedings before a judge rather than a jury which might be more sympathetic to the defendant workingmen, and with broadly worded decrees which reached many persons not parties to the proceedings and many forms of employee conduct which were surely lawful (such as peaceful persuasion of customers or fellow employees). A change in social temper early in this century resulted in action by Congress and the states to limit judicial regulation of labor activities. It was thought particularly harsh that courts were banning peaceful concerted activity while furnishing no alternative means to the employees to assure fairness in the resolution of the underlying economic dispute relating to unionization or to working conditions.

Congress enacted the Clayton Act in 1914, which declared most peaceful concerted activities to be nonenjoinable by federal courts and not violations of the federal antitrust laws. Restrictive judicial reading of the Clayton Act moved Congress more clearly and comprehensively to ban injunctions against peaceful labor activities, the primary text being the Norris-LaGuardia Act of 1932. 29 U.S.C.A. §§ 101–15. The statute withdraws from federal courts all jurisdiction to issue injunctions against peacefully striking, assembling, patrolling, or publicizing facts in connection with a labor dispute (section 4); defines "labor dispute" very broadly so as to encompass disputes about organizing into unions or establishing "terms or conditions of employment" and so as to encompass all persons in the same industry or occupation or labor organization or having "a direct or indirect interest therein" (section 13); and provides that in the rare case when an injunction may issue (e. g., when the concerted activities cause or threaten to cause serious harm to person or property), the federal court must comply with stringent procedural safeguards (set forth principally in section 7), such as manner and elements of proof, duration of temporary restraining orders, posting of security by the plaintiff, narrow reach of the injunction as to persons and acts, and right to recusal of the judge and speedy jury trial in contempt proceedings. Many states followed suit and enacted what are known as "little Norris-LaGuardia Acts"; roughly half the states have such anti-injunction statutes today. The thrust of the federal anti-injunction policy was reinforced in 1935, when the Wagner Act granted to employees the right to engage in concerted activity for mutual aid and protection and shielded such activity against employer restraint and coercion.

In the years that followed, there developed a trend in the more mature bargaining relationships—facilitated by the contract-writing powers of the National War Labor Board—to incorporate in labor contracts provisions for the peaceable settlement of contract disputes, through mutually administered grievance procedures culminating in third-party arbitration, and as a correlative a promise by the union that it will not resort to the strike for the duration of the contract. Judicial enforcement of these arbitration and no-strike promises was often difficult, in view of the common law principle that arbitration promises were not specifically enforceable by injunction and the jurisdictional impediments to suit against the union as an unincorporated association. Congress moved to remedy both deficiencies when, in the Taft-Hartley amendments of 1947, it took the major step of reintroducing the judiciary to the regulation of labor disputes. In part this was done by declaring that certain labor activities—such as the secondary boycott—are unfair labor practices, remediable by NLRB cease-and-desist orders enforceable in court, by injunction proceedings precipitated by an agent of the NLRB in advance of Board adjudication and in some instances by damage actions in federal or state courts.

More pertinently, Congress in 1947 enacted section 301. Section 301(b) provides, in part: "Any . . . labor organization [representing employees in an industry affecting commerce] may sue or be sued as an entity and in behalf of the employees whom it represents in the courts of the United States." (Subsection (b) also provides that judgments against unions can be enforced only against the union and its assets and not against individual members.) Section 301(a) provides:

> Suits for violation of contracts between an employer and a labor organization representing employees in an industry affecting commerce . . . may be brought in any district court of the United States having jurisdiction of the parties, without respect to the amount in controversy or without regard to the citizenship of the parties.

The legislative history demonstrates that Congress wanted to induce both parties to the labor contract to incorporate grievance and arbitration provisions on the one hand and on the other a no-strike, no-lockout clause; this inducement came from permitting the union to sue and to be sued and to make arbitration and no-strike promises enforceable. Ten years later, in Textile Workers Union v. Lincoln Mills (U.S.1957), the Supreme Court held that an employer which had wrongfully violated its promise to submit to grievance arbitration could be ordered to do so and that such an injunction would not violate the Norris-LaGuardia Act, either section 4 (whose listed protected activities, such as assembling and patrolling, did not include the failure to arbitrate) or section 7 (whose injunction prerequisites, such as irreparable injury to property, inadequate remedy at law and inability of public officers to furnish protection, were simply declared by the Court to be "inapposite"). The *Lincoln Mills* decision is perhaps most famous for its holding that in contract-enforcement actions "the substantive law to apply in suits under § 301(a) is federal law, which the courts must fashion from the policy of our national labor laws"; the specific enforceability of arbitration promises was the first such judge-made federal substantive law fashioned by the Court.

Not long after, the Court—in the three cases known as the *Steelworkers Trilogy*, United Steelworkers v. American Mfg. Co. (U.S. 1960), United Steelworkers v. Warrior & Gulf Nav. Co. (U.S.1960), United Steelworkers v. Enterprise Wheel & Car Corp. (U.S.1960)— announced its second major principle of substantive contract law, that promises to arbitrate contract grievances should (contrary to the common law construction) be broadly construed so as to engross all disputes concerning the terms of the labor contract, unless the parties clearly negate such construction. The Court's exuberance for arbitration was based on the assumed expertness of the arbitrator, the fact that labor arbitration (unlike commercial arbitration) is a substitute not for litigation but for the use of disruptive economic weapons, and the fact that the quid pro quo for the arbitration promise of the employer is the union's unqualified promise not to strike about contract grievances of all kinds.

§ 2. Remedies Available for Breach of the No-Strike Clause: Arbitration, Damages, Injunction

In three cases decided on the same day in 1962, the Supreme Court addressed the question of the different remedies available to the employer for the union's breach of a no-strike provision in a contract which also provides for arbitration of claimed contract violations. In Drake Bakeries v. Local 50, American Bakery Workers (U.S.1962), the union induced a refusal to work on days rescheduled by the employer at Christmas and New Year's time. The employer's action for damages for breach of a no-strike clause was held premature. The Court read the arbitration procedure to cover asserted breaches of the no-strike clause and to be invokable by the employer; arbitration rather than damages was the proper remedy for the union's alleged breach.   In Atkinson v. Sinclair Ref. Co. (U.S.1962), the Court distinguished *Drake Bakeries* and held that an action for damages under section 301 would lie for an alleged breach of the union's no-strike promise; here, the arbitration procedure could be invoked only by the union for employee grievances, and the employer's only means of enforcing the union's promise not to strike concerning a dispute which the union could take to arbitration was by a direct action in the courts.   The Court also held that section 301(b) of the Labor Act has made it clear that no cause of action for damages can be stated against union officials or members personally for participating in an unlawful strike authorized by the union.   A court of appeals has more recently held that section 301(b), embodying Congress's strong distaste for money judgments enforceable directly against individual laborers, should also bar an action against employees who engage in a work stoppage in violation of a no-strike clause when that stoppage is a wildcat strike unauthorized by and against the orders of the majority union.   Sinclair Oil Corp. v. Oil Workers (7th Cir. 1971).   In such cases, the primary sanction against the wildcat stoppage is discharge or other discipline by the employer (since the walkout in breach of contract is unprotected activity) or a fine by the union.

In Sinclair Ref. Co. v. Atkinson (U.S.1962), decided by the Supreme Court on the same day as the *Drake Bakeries* and *Atkinson* cases, the employer, claiming a union violation of its no-strike promise, sought not damages but an injunction against the strike.   The Court was thus presented with the question whether the policies of section 301, favoring peaceful resolution of contract disputes through arbitration and the enforcement of no-strike promises, could be accommodated with the Norris-LaGuardia ban upon injunctions of peaceful strikes, when the union had promised not to strike in protest against employer action which could be challenged in arbitration. The Court held that the anti-injunction provisions of section 4 of the Norris-LaGuardia Act directly applied to peaceful work stoppages, that Congress (in contrast to other provisions of the Taft-Hartley Act) had not expressly repealed the Norris-LaGuardia Act when it enacted section 301, that indeed the legislative history shows the deletion of a measure which would have expressly repealed the Norris-LaGuardia Act in section 301 cases, and that any exceptions to the strong labor-protective provisions of the Norris-LaGuardia Act must be made not by the judiciary but by the Congress.

A dissenting opinion for three Justices made a number of points which subsequently proved convincing to a majority of the Court when it was asked to reconsider the *Sinclair* holding soon after.   The dissenters urged that an effort be made to "accommodate" the seemingly conflicting mandates of section 301 of the Labor Act and section 4 of the Norris-LaGuardia Act.   They stated that the primary mischief to which the latter Act was addressed was the injunction which "strips labor of its primary weapon without substituting any reasonable alternative," and noted that this mischief is not present when the union voluntarily makes an express contractual commitment not to strike and has secured in exchange for that commitment the "reasonable alternative" of the employer's specifically enforceable obligation to arbitrate. The dissenters noted the irony that the quest for uniformity in labor-contract cases (mandated by section 301) would, as a result of the Court's denial of injunctive power in the federal courts, be frustrated since employers would henceforth seek strike injunctions in state courts; the state courts would apply varied local laws and would become the "preferred instruments to protect the integrity of the arbitration process," the "kingpin of federal labor policy." They also predicted that employers would now be more reluctant to agree to arbitration provisions, since the injunction was not available in federal courts to enforce the employer's quid pro quo, the no-strike clause. Consistent with its own rationale, the dissenting opinion would have made an injunction available only when the strike in breach of contract was in protest against employer action which the union could challenge in arbitration.

Other Supreme Court decisions rendered at or soon after the time of *Sinclair* ultimately induced the Court to reconsider and reverse the holding in that case. Dowd Box Co. v. Courtney (U.S. 1962), held that jurisdiction of section 301 suits to enforce labor contracts was not exclusive in the federal courts and that state courts had concurrent jurisdiction; Congress was held not to intend disturbing the pre-existing jurisdiction of state courts over such contract actions. In such cases arising under section 301, the state courts would have to apply federal principles of labor law, in the interest of uniformity and certainty in labor-contract negotiation and enforcement. Teamsters Local 174 v. Lucas Flour Co. (U.S.1962). However, in Avco Corp. v. Lodge 735, IAM (U.S.1968), the Court held that a union sued in a state court for violation of a no-strike clause (and subject to an injunction under state law) could remove the case to a federal court (since that court would have had initial jurisdiction over that action under section 301) which would not have the power to enjoin the strike because of the Norris-LaGuardia Act and the *Sinclair* decision.

Dowd Box and *Avco* in combination set the stage for Boys Markets, Inc. v. Retail Clerks Local 770 (U.S.1970), which overruled *Sinclair*. The contract in *Boys Markets* provided for arbitration of disputes concerning the interpretation or application of contract terms, and barred work stoppages, lockouts, picketing and boycotts. The employer's resistance to a union claim that bargaining-unit work had been improperly done by supervisors precipitated a strike and picketing. When the employer brought an action in the state court and secured a temporary restraining order, the union removed the case to a federal court which, in spite of *Sinclair*, ordered the parties to arbitrate the underlying dispute and enjoined the continuation of the strike and picketing. The Supreme Court sustained the injunction. It reiterated the views of the *Sinclair* dissenters, and went on to note that the "practical effect of *Avco* and *Sinclair* taken together is nothing less than to oust state courts of jurisdiction in § 301(a) suits where injunctive relief is sought for breach of a no-strike clause," an ouster which "is wholly inconsistent with our conclusion in *Dowd Box* that the congressional purpose embodied in § 301(a) was to *supplement*, and not to encroach upon, the pre-existing jurisdiction of the state courts." The Court also noted that to the extent that state courts would retain jurisdiction in injunction actions, widely disparate remedies would be available in state and federal courts, such that forum-shopping would become rampant and the federal policy of a uniform labor law would be frustrated. The Court conceded that the exodus from the state courts and the disparity of remedies could be cured not by overruling *Sinclair* (which would then make injunctions available in both forums) but rather by applying the principles of the Norris-LaGuardia Act and *Sinclair* to the state courts. It concluded, however, that neither Norris-LaGuardia nor section 301 was intended to deprive state courts of pre-existing injunctive powers and that the denial altogether of injunctive relief for breach of no-strike clauses would destroy the employer's incentive to arbitrate and would aggravate industrial strife. The Court also noted that it was not by its decision usurping congressional prerogatives but merely accommodating the unchanged Norris-LaGuardia Act, originally enacted to promote nascent unionization, with the more modern federal legislation encouraging collective bargaining to peacefully resolve industrial disputes. The Court made clear, however, that it had not abandoned the Norris-LaGuardia Act and that its holding was a narrow one. It held that an injunction may issue only when the labor contract "contains a mandatory grievance adjustment or arbitration procedure" and not as a matter of course but only when injunctive relief would be appropriate apart from the Norris-LaGuardia Act:

> When a strike is sought to be enjoined because it is over a grievance which both parties are contractually bound to arbitrate, the District Court may issue no injunctive order until it first holds that the contract *does* have that effect; and the employer should be ordered to arbitrate, as a condition of his obtaining an injunction against the strike. Beyond this, the District Court must, of course, consider whether issuance of an injunction would be warranted under ordinary principles of equity—whether breaches are occurring and will continue, or have been threatened and will be committed; whether they have caused or will cause irreparable injury to the employer; and whether the employer will suffer more from the denial of an injunction than will the union from its issuance.

§ 3. The Boys Markets Injunction: Prerequisites to Relief

The history of the no-strike injunction since the 1970 decision in *Boys Markets* has essentially been that of elucidation of the injunction requirements set forth in that case.

(1) There must be a collective bargaining agreement in effect between the parties. It has been held by some courts that if, at the time of the injunction action, the labor contract has expired, such that there is no present duty to refrain from striking or to arbitrate, an injunction cannot issue; indeed, if there is doubt about whether the contract has expired, that issue is to be determined by the court and not by the arbitrator. Pullman, Inc. v. Brotherhood of Boilermakers (E.D.Pa.1972). Where, however, the post-expiration strike concerns a grievance which arose during the contract term—and thus is subject to arbitration even after the termination date—the strike has been held to be "over a grievance which both parties are contractually bound to arbitrate" and thus subject to a *Boys Markets* injunction. Kauai Elec. Co. v. IBEW Local 1260 (D.Haw.1971).

(2) The contract must contain a mandatory arbitration procedure. Since *Boys Markets* required, as a condition to an injunction, that the strike be "over a grievance which both parties are contractually bound to arbitrate," it was later argued that a strike injunction could not issue if the labor contract provided only that the union could initiate arbitration (while giving no such right to the employer); it was urged that the arbitration clause was thus for the benefit of the union only, and that an employer should not be able to force the union to arbitration by using the leverage of an injunction against the strike. This argument has been rejected by the courts of appeals for the Third Circuit, in Avco Corp. v. Local 787, UAW (1972), and for the Fourth Circuit in Monongahela Power Co. v. Local 2332, IBEW (1973). *Boys Markets* requires not that the employer be able to initiate arbitration but only that it be bound to arbitrate; and just as the employer is bound by its promise to arbitrate, the union is bound by its promise not to strike which was given in exchange. Moreover, the court's injunction in such cases does not require the union to arbitrate but only that it refrain from striking, and also requires that the employer arbitrate only if and when the union chooses to pursue that remedy. The same analysis obtains even when there is no express no-strike promise by the union, but one is implied coincident with the union's right to demand arbitration. George A. Hormel & Co. v. Local No. P–31 (N.D.Iowa 1972). Of course, if the contract expressly reserves the right to the union to strike, or reserves to it the option either to arbitrate or to exert "economic pressure," then the *Boys Markets* requirement is not satisfied and no injunction may issue. Associated Gen. Contractors v. Illinois Conf. of Teamsters (7th Cir. 1972). Where, however, there is no reservation of the right to strike and the contract provides that either party "may" submit disputes to arbitration, this will be read to mean that

the parties have simply reserved discretion as to how far to press a grievance and that there is a duty to go to arbitration when invoked by the other party, thus justifying the issuance of a strike injunction. Amstar Corp. v. Amalgamated Meat Cutters (E.D.La.), *rev'd on other grounds* (5th Cir. 1972).

No court appears to have considered the availability of a strike injunction under a contract which has a grievance procedure which does not end in binding arbitration. Even if the union expressly reserves the right to strike, it is arguable that *Boys Markets* would permit the injunction of any strike which takes place prior to the exhaustion of the grievance procedure to finality. *Boys Markets* dealt, in the Court's words, "with the situation in which a collective bargaining contract contains a mandatory grievance adjustment *or* arbitration procedure," (emphasis added) so it is arguable that the union impliedly agreed not to strike at least while the quid pro quo relinquished by the employer (*i. e.,* the grievance procedure) can be invoked by the union.

(3) The dispute which is the subject of the strike or concerted activity must be one which is included within the mandatory arbitration provision. Since the union is deemed, under *Boys Markets,* susceptible to injunction only for a strike concerning a subject which it could take to arbitration, it becomes necessary for the federal trial court to determine what the underlying dispute is and whether the parties have brought that kind of dispute within the arbitration procedure. This problem of "substantive arbitrability" was addressed by the Supreme Court in the Steelworkers Trilogy cases involving not no-strike clauses and injunctions but simply actions to compel an employer to submit an underlying contract dispute to arbitration. In those cases, the Court concluded that, under the standard arbitration clause requiring arbitration of all disputes concerning the interpretation or application of the provisions of the agreement, all alleged contract breaches must be sent by the court to arbitration, unless the arbitration clause clearly and unambiguously excludes the dispute. Although it was held by at least one court of appeals that the Trilogy's strong presumption of arbitrability should not be imported in strike-injunction cases, this view has been effectively repudiated by the Supreme Court. In Gateway Coal Co. v. UMW (U.S.1974), the Mine Workers Union had called a work stoppage among the workers in the Gateway mine, alleging that hazardous working conditions were created by the presence of two foremen, responsible for keeping records on the air flow within the mine, who had recently been convicted of falsely preparing records so as to indicate no inadequacy of air flow. The labor contract contained a provision for arbitration of "any local trouble of any kind aris[ing] at the mine," which the Court held to give rise to an implied duty not to strike on any arbitrable matter. In determining that the presence of the two foremen was indeed an arbitrable matter, the Court relied both on the very broad language

of the contractual arbitration clause and on the "now well-known pre-sumption of arbitrability" enunciated in the Steelworkers Trilogy and the reasons underlying that presumption. The Court rejected the conclusion of the court of appeals that the presumption of arbitrability did not apply to disputes about employee safety, holding that arbitrators appreciate—or can be selected with a view toward their appreciation of—problems of safety and that such problems are not better resolved by resort to economic weapons (which would make "the safety of the workshop . . . depend on the relative economic strength of the parties rather than on an informed and impartial assessment of the facts"). The Court thus sustained the trial court's injunction against the strike, along with its suspension of the two foremen pending a final arbitral decision.

An issue that has arisen in a number of decisions is whether a court may enjoin a strike which is not in protest of a company decision which can be challenged through arbitration but is rather itself the alleged breach of contract which the employer seeks to challenge under the arbitration procedures of the collective agreement. Thus, the agreement may have both a no-strike and an arbitration clause, and the covered employees may refuse to cross a picket line which has been set up by some other union, either at the same company or at a different company. The employer may claim that the refusal to cross violates the union's no-strike pledge and may seek an injunction pending arbitration of the claim of breach. There is a sharp division of opinion among the courts on the question whether such an injunction should issue. It appears that most courts of appeals hold (usually with accompanying dissenting opinions) that *Boys Markets* contemplates that an injunction is to issue against the refusal to cross the picket line. *E.g.,* NAPA Pittsburgh, Inc. v. Chauffeurs Local 926 (3d Cir. 1974) (*en banc*); Monongahela Power Co. v. Local 2332, IBEW (4th Cir. 1973). These courts reason that the refusal to cross is itself arguably a breach of the contractual no-strike clause and is thus a matter which the parties intended to be resolved peaceably through arbitration. Since arbitration is available, the work stoppage should be enjoined. This result has been reached even when the contract is completely silent on the union's right to strike or to honor the picket line. Island Creek Coal Co. v. UMW (3d Cir. 1975).

Other courts, however, have read *Boys Markets* to authorize a strike injunction only when there is some underlying dispute between the union and the employer other than the strike itself, and when the union is thus using the strike to induce the employer to concede on the underlying dispute rather than to have that dispute resolved through arbitration. When the union's "strike" is not generated or prolonged by some other arbitrable issue, the *Boys Markets* policy of fostering arbitration is not undermined if the union is permitted by the court to continue honoring the picket line; the union's conduct is itself the arbitrable issue which can be resolved by a neutral third party even while it continues. As the court noted in Buffalo Forge Co. v. United Steelworkers (2d Cir. 1975):

> A strike not seeking to pressure the employer to yield on a disputed issue is not an attempt to circumvent arbitration machinery established by the collective bargaining agreement. Accordingly, it does no violence to the federal pro-arbitration policy to require federal courts to refrain from enjoining such strikes.

See also Amstar Corp. v. Amalgamated Meat Cutters (5th Cir. 1972). The effect of an injunction in the setting of the *Boys Markets* case is to preserve the status quo while the merits of the underlying dispute are being tried before the arbitrator, while an injunction in the picket-line cases effectively resolves the only disputed substantive issue, that is, the propriety of the work stoppage. This view appears to be the sounder one. In any event, it is rather certain that the sharp division within the courts of appeals will invite resolution of the matter by the Supreme Court.*

(4) The agreement must give rise to an obligation on the part of the union to refrain from a strike or other concerted activity. Obviously, *Boys Markets* contemplates the issuance of an injunction only when the union has actually agreed to substitute the grievance and arbitration procedures for the strike as a means of resolving a contract dispute. Usually, the substitution is made explicit, with the union both giving up the strike and agreeing to take disputes to arbitration. On occasion, however, the contract will contain an arbitration clause but will not explicitly proscribe the strike. In Local 174, Teamsters v. Lucas Flour Co. (U.S.1962), an action initiated in a state court for damages for a strike, the contract contained an arbitration clause but no no-strike clause. The Supreme Court held that the presence of the arbitration provision gave rise to an implied obligation on the part of the union not to strike over any dispute which was subject to arbitration; if the union wished to retain the right to strike about an arbitrable grievance, it would have to do so by explicit reservation.

Any uncertainty whether an implied no-strike clause would be read into the contract as a basis for an injunction (rather than damages as in *Lucas Flour*) was resolved by the Supreme Court in Gateway Coal Co. v. UMW (U.S.1974). There, the union induced a work stoppage among miners, asserting that it was hazardous for them to work in the mine while it was tended by two foremen who had recently been convicted of falsifying their records to show a normal airflow in the mines (when in truth the airflow had been dangerously low). Although the contract provided for the arbitration of "any local trouble of any kind aris[ing] at the mine," it contained no explicit promise not to strike. The Court, after holding that the work-safe-

* The *Buffalo Forge* decision was affirmed by the Supreme Court in July 1976.

ty dispute was subject to arbitration, concluded that it was proper as in *Lucas Flour* to imply such a promise; the policy reasons favoring injunctive enforcement of the implied no-strike promise were found as compelling as the reasons in actions for damages:

> It would be unusual, but certainly permissible, for the parties to agree to a broad mandatory arbitration provision yet expressly negate any implied no-strike obligation. Such a contract would reinstate the situation commonly existing before our decision in *Boys Market*. Absent an explicit expression of such an intention, however, the agreement to arbitrate and the duty not to strike should be construed as having coterminous application.

Although the union urged that certain provisions in the contract should be read so as to negate any implied no-strike obligation, the Court disagreed.

The Court noted however, that certain provisions of the law might shelter against injunction a work stoppage which on its face appeared to violate an express or implied no-strike clause. Such a provision is section 502 of the Labor Act which provides in part: "[N]or shall the quitting of labor by an employee or employees in good faith because of abnormally dangerous conditions for work at the place of employment of such employee or employees be deemed a strike under this chapter." But to invoke that provision, and thus avoid a strike injunction, the union would have had to demonstrate more than a "generalized doubt in the competence and integrity of company supervisors." The "union seeking to justify a contractually prohibited work stoppage under § 502 must present 'ascertainable, objective evidence supporting its conclusion that an abnormally dangerous condition for work exists.'"

(5) The employer seeking a strike injunction must submit to the arbitration procedure established in the collective agreement. Such an employer will normally be prepared to go to arbitration, and courts will often incorporate in the injunctive decree a condition that the plaintiff (or both parties) submit the underlying dispute to arbitration. Such a conditional order is contemplated in the *Boys Markets* decision itself (quoting from the *Sinclair* dissent, ". . . the employer should be ordered to arbitrate, as a condition of his obtaining an injunction against the strike"), and is within the spirit of section 8 of the Norris-LaGuardia Act ("No restraining order or injunctive relief shall be granted to any complainant who has failed to . . . make every reasonable effort to settle such dispute either by negotiation . . . or voluntary arbitration"). Some courts have read this requirement perhaps too strictly, and have denied injunctive relief to employers because they did not adequately trigger the union's duty to arbitrate by making a formal demand, prior to commencing the injunction action. Elevator Mfr's Ass'n v. Elevator Constructors Local 1 (S.D.N.Y.1971).

(6) An injunction must be tested under ordinary principles of equity: threat of continuing breach, irreparable injury to the plaintiff, the employer will suffer more from denial of the injunction than the union will from its issuance. In order that the court issue an injunction there must of course be a substantive contract violation by the defendants. There will be no cause of action at all against the union if, for example, the employees engaged in the strike or picketing are not subject to the no-strike clause of the agreement, Mac-Fadden-Bartell Corp. v. Local 1034, Teamsters (S.D.N.Y.1972) (no injunction against picketing by former employees on layoff, since not covered by the agreement), or the defendant union did not encourage, sanction or authorize the work stoppage, Ourisman Chevrolet Co. v. Automotive Lodge No. 1486 (D.D.C.1971) (employees' refusal to cross another union's picket line found to be a decision of individual conscience by particular employees). But it is not necessary that there already be a consummated work stoppage. An injunction may thus issue against the future implementation of a union resolution that its members not do overtime work, Avco Corp. v. Local 787, UAW (3d Cir. 1972), or against a stoppage which is yet hours away, Amstar Corp. v. Sugar Workers Local 9 (E.D.N.Y.1972). There need simply be a showing that the union's conduct is in breach of the no-strike promise and will cause the employer irreparable harm; the latter may follow almost immediately upon showing of a breach, since the usual standard of irreparable harm is inadequacy of damages to redress the wrong, and the Supreme Court has stated in *Boys Markets* that "an award of damages after a dispute has been settled is no substitute for an immediate halt to an illegal strike." The balancing of harms to the employer from denial of the injunction and to the union from its grant also appears rather automatic, for by hypothesis the union is culpable of a breach of the agreement and any "harm" that may flow to it from the issuance of the injunction ought not be legally cognizable.

§ 4. Procedures in Strike-Injunction Cases

There is some question concerning the applicable procedures when the federal court considers a request for a strike injunction under *Boys Markets*. Rule 65 of the Federal Rules of Civil Procedure normally regulates injunction procedures, but Rule 65(e) provides that "these rules do not modify any statute of the United States relating to temporary restraining orders and preliminary injunctions in actions affecting employer and employee .   .   .   ." It would appear, then, that although section 4 of the Norris-LaGuardia Act, barring altogether injunctions of peaceful strikes, has been "accommodated" away by the conflicting mandate of section 301 of the Labor Act, the other sections of the Norris-LaGuardia Act remain in full force. These sections deal with such matters as the duration of the temporary restraining order, the procedures by which it shall be issued, the bond to be posted, the requirements of proof and the scope of the injunction; these requirements are in several respects more stringent and more protective of the defendant than under Federal Rule 65. Nonetheless, several courts have issued ex parte temporary restraining orders against strikes in breach of contract without adverting to the procedural and duration requirements of section 7 of the Norris-LaGuardia Act. United States Steel Corp., Am. Bridge Div. v. Operating Eng'rs Local 18 (S.D.Ohio 1972) (express application of Rule 65). Other courts, specifically adverting to the question of the applicability of the Norris-LaGuardia Act in *Boys Markets* cases, have expressed doubt as to whether that statute governs or Rule 65 governs in actions brought against unions under section 301. Associated Gen. Contractors v. Illinois Conf. of Teamsters (7th Cir. 1973). Since, however, the *Boys Markets* decision—which the Court itself characterized as a "narrow" departure from Norris-LaGuardia —addresses only the question of the power of the federal court to enjoin, it should not be read to imply that the historically developed procedural safeguards of the other sections of that Act are to be discarded in bulk.

This view was adopted in United States Steel Corp. v. UMW (3d Cir. 1972), in which defendant labor unions moved, after all parties had stipulated to the indefinite continuance of the injunction action, that it should be awarded all reasonable costs of litigation including attorneys' fees. The federal district court had required the posting of bond in the amount of $4,000, while stipulated fees and expenses proved to be in excess of $11,000. The court of appeals found the bond inadequate and held the defendants entitled to the full amount of their expenses, including attorneys' fees, resting on section 7 of the Norris-LaGuardia Act which (unlike Rule 65) expressly requires that the plaintiff file a bond in an amount adequate to cover such expenses. The court rejected the argument that all provisions of the Norris-LaGuardia Act—and not merely section 4—are irrelevant in a section 301 action to enforce a no-strike promise, and held instead that all Norris-LaGuardia procedural safeguards are to apply in such actions except those which are obviously inappropriate (giving as an example the need for proof that the police cannot furnish adequate protection) or are in conflict with the Taft-Hartley Act. The notice, hearing and bonding requirements of section 7 were thus held applicable in a *Boys Markets* proceeding. In several cases, the Court of Appeals for the Second Circuit has held that the Norris-LaGuardia Act sets forth the controlling procedures in section 301 injunction actions on such matters as the requisite proof for and the duration of a temporary restraining order, Emery Air Freight Corp. v. Local 295, Teamsters (2d Cir. 1971) (order should have been limited to five days and issued upon testimony under oath rather than affidavits, and bond of $1,000 was clearly inadequate under Norris-LaGuardia standards); the breadth and generality of the injunction, New York Tel. Co. v. Communications Workers (2d Cir. 1971) (injunction too broad under section 9 of Norris-LaGuardia, which requires prohibition only of specific acts complained of and found by court to have been wrongfully committed); and the requirement of a hearing and specific findings of fact, Hoh v. Pepsico, Inc. (2d Cir. 1974) (injunction action against employer to prevent plant shutdown).

§ 5.   State-Court Injunction Proceedings

There appears to be no case since *Boys Markets* was decided which directly passes upon the question whether state courts in strike-injunction proceedings are obligated to mirror the result which would obtain in the federal courts. The issue can arise in at least two distinct (and converse) forms. In one, the state has some version of the Norris-LaGuardia Act, or some other legislative or judge-made ban upon labor injunctions, which bars a state-court injunction in a case where a federal court would issue an injunction under section 301 and in the face of the federal Norris-LaGuardia Act. In another, the state court would issue an injunction which is far more intrusive on the conduct of the defendant union than would be an injunction issuing from a federal court, perhaps because it enjoins a more general range of conduct or is a temporary order issued without a hearing and to last more than five days. The latter issue—state law contemplating more judicial regulation than federal law—was addressed in different guise before *Boys Markets*, at a time when the Norris-LaGuardia Act was held to bar an injunction while many states permitted its issuance. It was rather uniformly held that the *Sinclair* no-injunction principle was based solely on the Norris-LaGuardia Act and was thus applicable only in the federal courts and not in the state courts; section 301 was understood to supplement rather than displace traditional contract-enforcement remedies in the states. Shaw Elec. Co. v. IBEW Local 98 (Pa.1965); McCarroll v. Los Angeles County Dist. Council of Carpenters (Cal.1957).

But the *Boys Markets* injunction finds its rationale in section 301 which does generate a body of federal law binding on the states, Charles Dowd Box Co. v. Courtney (U.S.1962), and which because of the great importance of the availability of the injunction (and not merely damages) to enforce no-strike promises may thus require that states make available strike injunctions where the conditions of *Boys Markets* are satisfied—and in no other cases. Under this theory, the state courts would strive to mirror the federal courts in strike-injunction cases, just as they do under section 301 in actions for orders compelling arbitration. The Supreme Court recently brushed against this issue, but did not have to decide it, in a case in which a state court issued a temporary restraining order and the action was removed to a federal court, with the issue being whether the duration of the order in the removed case was to be determined by state law or federal law. In Granny Goose Foods, Inc. v. Teamsters Local 70 (U.S.1974), the Supreme Court held that the order could remain in force no longer than it would under state law but in no event longer than the time limitations of Federal Rule 65(b) measured from the date of removal; under either body of law, the order would have lapsed. It remains speculative whether, had the case not been removed, the duration of the temporary restraining order would have been circumscribed by state law or instead by section 7 of the Norris-LaGuardia Act (no more than five days). Since the Supreme Court has also clearly held that state courts can issue strike injunctions, even when the union's activity is not only a contract breach but also an unfair labor practice, William E. Arnold Co. v. Carpenters Dist. Council (U.S.1974), the issue will likely arise whether the *Boys Markets* criteria and procedures (whatever they may be) which obtain in federal courts will also bind the states; the availability to the union of removal to the federal courts may, however, eliminate many such problems.

§ 6. The Strike Which is an Unfair Labor Practice or Protests an Unfair Labor Practice

It has been undisputed for some time that the jurisdiction of courts to enforce contract promises under section 301—whether in state court or federal court—is not preempted merely because the alleged contract breach is actually or arguably also an unfair labor practice. Smith v. Evening News Ass'n (U.S.1962) ("The authority of the Board to deal with an unfair labor practice which also violates a collective bargaining contract is not displaced by Section 301, but it is not exclusive and does not destroy the jurisdiction of courts in suits under Section 301."). This principle was definitively applied by the Supreme Court to the strike-injunction action in William E. Arnold Co. v. Carpenters Dist. Council (U.S.1974). There, a union-induced strike in support of a work-assignment claim was arguably a violation of section 8(b)(4)(D), yet the Supreme Court held that the state court erred in finding its jurisdiction preempted by that of the NLRB; it held that preemption was inappropriate in contract actions under section 301, regardless of whether the requested relief was an injunction or damages.

The converse situation would be one in which the union defends against an injunction on the ground that the employer was both violating the agreement and committing an unfair labor practice, and that the union's strike was an "unfair labor practice strike" which should not be understood to be within the ban of the contractual no-strike clause. In a related context, in Mastro Plastics Corp. v. NLRB (U.S.1956), the employer discharged employees who engaged in an unfair labor practice strike during the term of a contract containing a no-strike clause. The Court held the discharges illegal, concluding that the contract clause (which would have rendered the strike unprotected and the strikers subject to discharge) was not intended in the absence of clear language to the contrary to bar strikes in protest against serious unfair labor practices. The Board in Arlan's Dept. Store (1961), held that the no-strike clause should, however, be read to embrace strikes against minor employer unfair labor practices which can also be redressed as contract breaches through the grievance and arbitration procedures. These decisions suggest that a court in a proceeding for a strike injunction may conclude that a no-strike promise was not violated by a strike in protest against particular employer unfair labor practices, and therefore that the strike is not enjoinable or indeed even compensable in damages.

This argument has, however, been rejected in Southwestern Bell Tel. Co. v. Communications Workers Local 6222 (S.D.Tex.1972). There, a strike during the contract term was in protest against allegedly illegal unilateral action by the employer in staffing a new facility with part-time employees on a separate seniority schedule. The court held—in spite of an existing decision by a trial examiner that the employer's unilateral action constituted an unlawful refusal to bargain—that the challenged employer action could have been tested by the union through the contractual arbitration procedures, and that the strong federal policy favoring arbitration and the recently announced willingness of the NLRB to defer to pertinent arbitration decisions dictate that the union invoke those arbitration procedures rather than strike. (Interestingly, the court also granted the counterclaim of the union for an injunction against the employer's implementation of its new staffing plan, pending arbitral determination of its propriety under the labor contract.) Perhaps a more grievous employer unfair labor practice, for example a repudiation of the union, the contract and the grievance procedure will induce the courts to conclude that a responsive strike is not barred by the contract and is thus not enjoinable. The same result could be reached under section 8 of the Norris-LaGuardia Act which requires that the party seeking an injunction have recourse to negotiation and arbitration as a precondition to its issuance.

§ 7. Court Enforcement of an Arbitral Cease and Desist Order

An employer may succeed in securing from an arbitrator a decision that the union has engaged in a work stoppage in violation of a no-strike clause in the labor contract, and an order that the union end the stoppage. If the union refuses, the employer may seek in a section 301 action to have the arbitrator's award confirmed and thus made the basis for a contempt citation should the union continue the strike. In the regime of Sinclair Ref. Co. v. Atkinson (U.S.1962), when the Norris-LaGuardia Act was thought to prevent a federal court from issuing a no-strike injunction, it was questionable whether the court could enforce an arbitral award having precisely that effect. The few cases addressing the issue held that a court could confirm the arbitrator's order against the union, whether in state court, Ruppert v. Egelhofer (N.Y.1958) (state version of the Norris-LaGuardia

Act), or in federal court, New Orleans S.S. Ass'n v. Longshore Workers Local 1418 (5th Cir. 1968). The court's order was held, rather conclusorily, to be something other than an injunction. Since *Boys Markets* it is clearer yet that there is no obstacle to such judicial enforcement of an arbitral cease-and-desist award. Pacific Maritime Ass'n v. International Longshoremen's Ass'n (9th Cir. 1971).

CHAPTER XXVII

LABOR AND THE ANTITRUST LAWS

§ 1. Common Law and Statutory Regulation: Before the Norris-LaGuardia Act

At common law, throughout the nineteenth century, most courts regarded labor unions as unlawful conspiracies in restraint of trade, and punishable criminally or liable civilly. Unions, and the collective activities mustered in their behalf—strikes, picketing and boycotts—were viewed as unnaturally elevating either the price of labor (*i. e.,* wages), Philadelphia Cordwainers (Commonwealth v. Pullis) (Philadelphia Mayor's Court 1806), or the price of the commodity which they were employed to manufacture, People v. Fisher (N.Y.1835). Even after the influential opinion of Chief Justice Shaw in Commonwealth v. Hunt (Mass.1842) had held that criminal liability could not be imposed on unions without specific consideration of the legality of the union's objectives and means, civil liability and injunctive relief were commonly sustained in the last quarter of the century by state courts holding that a work stoppage which was legal for one person became illegal when carried out by a combination of workers, *e. g.,* Vegelahn v. Guntner (Mass.1896).

In 1890, Congress passed the Sherman Act, section 1 of which declared illegal "[e]very contract, combination . . . or conspiracy in restraint of trade"; such arrangements were declared to be federal crimes, to be enjoinable by district attorneys of the United States, and to be subject to actions for treble damages at the behest of injured private parties. A provision which would have excluded labor unions from the Act was eliminated in the course of a major streamlining of the bill in committee, but the legislative history is not at all clear as to whether it was proper to infer that the Sherman Act was indeed designed to cover unions or was intended to leave the possibility of exclusion to be determined by the courts. The courts in fact proceeded to hold unions liable for antitrust violations in more instances than manufacturers or distributors, which were the obvious objects of concern in the Sherman Act. The Supreme Court sustained the applicability of the Act to unions and union activities in Loewe v. Lawlor (U.S.1908), the famous *Danbury Hatters* case. There, the United Hatters of North America, seeking to organize a Connecticut hat manufacturer, struck the factory and urged the public to boycott both the hats and the other persons who sold the hats. The Court found this secondary boycott to fall within the Act's ban on (in the Court's words) "any combination whatever to secure action which essentially obstructs the free flow of commerce between the states, or restricts, in that regard, the liberty of a trader to engage in business."

The award of treble damages was entered not against the union but its individual members.

In part because of the resentment generated by the *Danbury Hatters* case, substantial pressure was exerted on Congress for a labor exemption to the Sherman Act, and in 1914 the Clayton Act was passed. It added to the remedies for federal antitrust violations a private action for an injunction by an injured person. But it also contained two sections which appeared to place unions and concerted activities outside the reach of the antitrust laws. Section 6 of the Clayton Act declared:

> That the labor of a human being is not a commodity or article of commerce. Nothing contained in the antitrust laws shall be construed to forbid the existence and operation of labor . . . organizations, instituted for the purposes of mutual help . . . or to forbid or restrain individual members of such organizations from lawfully carrying out the legitimate objects thereof; nor shall such organizations, or the members thereof, be held or construed to be illegal combinations or conspiracies in restraint of trade, under the antitrust laws.

Section 20 forbade a federal court, in any dispute between employers and employees concerning "terms or conditions of employment," to grant any injunction against the following frequently employed concerted activities:

> [T]erminating any relation of employment, . . . ceasing to perform any work or labor, . . . recommending, advising, or persuading others by peaceful means so to do; . . . attending at any place . . . for the purpose of peacefully obtaining or communicating information, . . . peacefully persuading any person to work or to abstain from working; . . . ceasing to patronize . . . any party to such dispute, or . . . recommending, advising, or persuading others by peaceful and lawful means so to do . . . .

That section concluded by declaring that all such nonenjoinable conduct should also not be held to be substantive violations of any federal law. In short, the Clayton Act appeared to declare exempt from the antitrust laws all unions, all collective bargaining, and all peaceful concerted activities.

This appearance was dispelled in Duplex Printing Press Co. v. Deering (U.S.1921), involving a secondary boycott by machinists working for newspaper publishers in New York in support of an attempt by machinists in Michigan to unionize a printing-press manufacturer there, the only one of four major national printing-press manufacturers remaining unorganized. A private injunction action was held available to the Michigan manufacturer against the New York machinists because the boycott constituted an illegal restraint of interstate trade, under Loewe v. Lawlor, and because it was not sheltered by the labor exemption of the Clayton Act; sections 6 and 20 were read to do no more than incorporate the common law protections for "legitimate" union activities (which the secondary boycott was not) and to be not applicable at all to disputes between an employer and persons not in a direct employment relationship (which the secondary boycott was). An influential dissenting opinion by Mr. Justice Brandeis reproached the Court for having overridden the intention of Congress to remove the federal courts from the adjudication of antitrust claims arising from peaceful labor activities. Relying on *Duplex,* however, the Court subsequently held in violation of the antitrust laws secondary boycotts taking the form of refusals by union members to work on materials furnished by another employer which the union was seeking to organize. United States v. Brims (U.S.1926) (unionized manufacturers of millwork and construction contractors secure labor-contract provision barring union handling of nonunion millwork); Bedford Cut Stone Co. v. Stone Cutters' Ass'n, (U.S.1927) (union rule forbids members to work on nonunion stone supplied to construction sites). It was no defense that the union's object was not to interfere with the flow of products in the market but was rather to exert pressure on nonunion companies to recognize the union, improve the lot of its employees and protect gains secured among unionized companies.

In another line of antitrust cases against unions, not involving secondary boycotts, the courts dealt with primary strikes and picketing designed directly to organize an employer. The Supreme Court acknowledged that any strike might have the effect of stopping the flow of goods in interstate commerce, but that this effect was not sufficient to invoke the ban of the antitrust laws; the Court's notion of "interstate commerce" at this time was such as to render the interruption of production a "local" rather than interstate restraint upon commerce. But even the local strike might be banned if it could be specifically demonstrated that it was the union's actual intention to restrain the interstate flow of goods. The Court announced these principles in two phases of a single lawsuit involving a violent strike designed to organize a nonunion coal mine in Arkansas. The coal company, formerly unionized, had altered its corporate identity, hired nonunion workers, paid them less than union scale and thus transported into commerce lower-priced coal than that supplied by unionized mines in neighboring states. At first, the Court suggested that the strike was merely "local," since it appeared that the union's object was simply to return the ousted union to the now nonunion mine. Coronado Coal Co. v. UMW (Coronado I) (U.S.1922). On remand, however, facts were introduced to demonstrate that the union's specific objective was to stop the entry of Coronado coal into the interstate market in competition with the more expensive coal produced by unionized companies. The Court, in Coronado Coal Co. v. UMW (U. S.1925), held this evidence sufficient to show an antitrust violation, since "the purpose of the destruction of the mines was to stop the production of non-union coal and prevent its shipment to markets of other States   .   .   . where it would by competition tend to reduce the price of the commodity and affect injuriously the maintenance of wages for union labor in competing mines."

The *Coronado* decisions left with courts and juries the power to determine whether the union's motive was the "local" one of improving working conditions in the struck company or the unlawful one of buttressing against competition union gains secured elsewhere. In fact, these motives commonly coexisted and were inseparable. For that reason, the antitrust laws were most effective weapons against organizational strikes or picketing precipitated by a minority union. See Alco-Zander Co. v. Amalgamated Clothing Workers (E.D.Pa. 1929) (injunction issued against members of New York union picketing for organizational purposes at nonunion Philadelphia clothing manufacturers competing with higher priced union-made goods from New York).

§ 2.   The Norris-LaGuardia Act and the "Labor Exemption"

To make clearer what had appeared to be its intention in sections 6 and 20 of the Clayton Act of 1914, Congress in 1932 enacted the Norris-LaGuardia Act. Addressed on its face only to the injunctive jurisdiction of the federal courts, it forbade the issuance of injunctions, in cases involving labor disputes, against

> ceasing or refusing to perform any work   .   .   .; giving publicity to the existence of, or the facts involved in, any labor dispute, whether by advertising, speaking, patrolling, or by any other method not involving fraud or violence;   .   .   . assembling peaceably to act or to organize to act in promotion of their interests in a labor dispute   .   .   .   .

When injunctions could issue, for example against picket-line violence or destruction of property, the Norris-LaGuardia Act required that the court abide by very strict procedural requirements of notice, fair hearing and proof. It also made express that a "labor dispute" could exist even in the absence of a direct employment relationship between the complaining company and the defendant workers: "labor dispute" was defined to include "any controversy concerning terms or conditions of employment, or concerning the association or representation of persons in negotiating   .   .   . terms or conditions of employment, regardless of whether or not the disputants stand in the proximate relation of employer and employee," and the Act was stated to extend not only to employees complaining of their own working conditions but also to "persons who are engaged in the same industry, trade, craft, or occupation; or have direct or indirect interests therein; or who are employees of the same employer; or who are members of the same or an affiliated organization of employers or employees . . . ."

Since the Norris-LaGuardia Act spoke only of protection of unions against injunctions in federal courts, it did not initially stem the tide of private treble damages actions under the antitrust laws. But in the 1940 decision in Apex Hosiery Co. v. Leader (U.S.1940), the Supreme Court construed the Sherman Act—and "reinterpreted" Court precedents under that Act—so as to accord to unions a wide range of immunity from antitrust liability. In that case, a hosiery workers union sought a closed-shop agreement from a large Philadelphia manufacturer, although it represented only eight company employees; the company's resistance precipitated the forcible seizure of the plant by other Philadelphia union members, a sitdown strike, the stoppage of $800,000 worth of finished hosiery ready for shipment, and extensive damage to plant and equipment. A jury verdict against the union and its leaders for treble damages was overturned by the Supreme Court. The Court first stated that the violent possession of the plant and of the finished hosiery, although obviously interfering with the flow of goods in interstate commerce, was not in itself sufficient to violate the antitrust laws, any more than would a conspiracy to derail and rob a train carrying goods across state lines.

The Court, examining the purpose of Congress in enacting the Sherman Act, concluded that it was directed against any "restraint upon commercial competition in the marketing of goods or services . . . ," and against contracts

> for the restriction or suppression of competition in the market, agreements to fix prices, divide marketing territories, apportion customers, restrict production and the like practices, which tend to raise prices or otherwise take from buyers or consumers the advantages which accrue to them from free competition in the market.

The Court noted that labor unions inevitably restrained competition among employees regarding the price (or wage) at which they sold their services, but held that this was not the kind of market restraint at which the Sherman Act was aimed. It also noted that unions, by standardizing wages and working conditions among many employers in the same industry, might operate to reduce or eliminate competition even in the product market to the extent that the price of products is determined by the cost to employers of the labor utilized in production. But even this was held by the Court to fall outside the ban of the Sherman Act. "[A]n elimination of price competition based on differences in labor standards is the objective of any national labor organization. But this effect on competition has not been considered to be the kind of curtailment of price competition prohibited by the Sherman Act." The Court buttressed its conclusion by pointing to the Norris-LaGuardia Act of 1932, the Railway Labor Act of 1934, and the National Labor Relations Act of 1935, all of which were designed to foster unionization and collective bargaining in order to permit laborers to establish industrywide standards for the elimination of labor conditions thought oppressive. The authority of the older Court cases outlawing the organizing strike to suppress competition and the secondary boycott was left in an uncertain status. Although the Court admitted that these were indeed instances, respectively, of intended restraint and actual interference in interstate commerce, it suggested that the "rule of reason" in general antitrust law might shelter such union activity in view of the union's purpose to strengthen its bargaining position rather than to eliminate business competition. Since the Philadelphia sitdown strike was simply "local," and was not intended specifically to (nor did it in fact) restrain interstate commerce in any substantial way, it was not an antitrust violation; the attendant violence did not make it so, and was to be remedied by appropriate state police authority.

While *Apex* addressed the question whether union activity imposed the kinds of restraints on commerce outlawed in the Sherman Act, the Supreme Court the following year afforded labor a different sort of immunity from antitrust liability by invoking the so-called "labor exemption" embodied in the Clayton and Norris-LaGuardia Acts. In United States v. Hutcheson (U.S.1941), the Court was confronted with a criminal prosecution against officials of the carpenters' union who, in support of work-assignment demands conflicting with those of machinists working for the Anheuser-Busch brewery in St. Louis, precipitated picketing of Anheuser-Busch and of another company renting Anheuser-Busch property, a strike of carpenters doing construction work for other companies on both properties, and a boycott of Anheuser-Busch beer. Rather than use the *Apex* decision to determine whether the strike and boycott were illegal restraints upon the product market, a majority of the Court instead looked directly to the asserted exemption of the labor union for peaceful concerted activities under section 20 of the Clayton Act and section 4 of the Norris-LaGuardia Act. The Court held the concerted activities to be among those listed in the Clayton Act, which both sheltered them against injunctions and—a crucial factor in this criminal proceeding—against any charge of federal illegality, including criminal liability. It noted, however, that since the defendant union officials were not employees of Anheuser-Busch, it could be argued they could not take advantage of the Clayton Act. Nonetheless, the Court proceeded to hold that they were within the class of defendants sheltered by the more encompassing definitions of the Norris-LaGuardia Act, that the 1932 Act was intended by Congress to override the narrow judicial reading of the Clayton Act, and that thus the anti-injunction provisions of the later Act should be read in context to shelter the defendants against criminal prosecution as well.

> The Norris-LaGuardia Act reasserted the original purpose of the Clayton Act by infusing into it the immunized trade union activities as redefined by the later Act. In this light § 20 removes all such allowable conduct from the taint of being a "violation of any law of the United States," including the Sherman Law.

Only thus could the Court give effect to the congressional intention to divest the federal courts of the long-abused power to identify, weigh and evaluate the objectives of a union which underlay its use of peaceful economic weapons. In an often-quoted passage, the Court declared:

> So long as a union acts in its self-interest and does not combine with non-labor groups, the licit and the illicit under § 20 are not to be distinguished by any judgment regarding the wisdom or unwisdom, the rightness or wrongness, the selfishness or unselfishness of the end of which the particular union activities are the means.

Since the Supreme Court announced this broad exemption for labor-union activities and sharpened the requirement of product-market restraint necessary to make out a substantive antitrust violation, the Sherman Act has played a rather limited role in the regulation of unions. But the extent of the role, while elaborated by the Court in several subsequent cases, remains unclear.

§ 3. The Union-Abetted Employer Conspiracy: The Allen Bradley and Pennington Cases

One rather clear case for a union violation is that which was envisioned by the decisions in both *Apex* and *Hutcheson*, and which actually came before the Court soon after—that is, a case in which manufacturers or distributors enter into an agreement to fix price, or to bar the entry of competing firms, or to allocate customers, and the union knowingly becomes a party to the agreement and actually utilizes economic weapons for the purpose of carrying out its terms. In Allen Bradley Co. v. Local 3, IBEW (U.S.1945), an agreement was reached between New York City manufacturers of electrical equipment, New York City electrical contractors who purchased electrical equipment for installation on construction sites, and Local 3 of the Electrical Workers, which represented the employees of both the manufacturers and contractors and had jurisdiction only in the New York City metropolitan area. The contractors agreed to purchase equipment only from the New York City manufacturers recognizing Local 3, and the manufacturers agreed to confine their sales in New York to contractors recognizing Local 3. The effect was to bar the sale to contractors in New York City of electrical equipment produced outside, thus leading to an extraordinary increase in the business of the New York manufacturers (who were not subject to out-of-city competition), a dramatic increase in the price of their electrical equipment (and a disparity between their prices in and out of New York City), increased profits for both the manufacturers and the contractors (who also engaged in bid-rigging) and an increase in wages for electricians in New York City. The union both joined in the agreement and perfected its own control over the supply of electricians by striking for closed shops among all manufacturers and contractors.

The Court had no difficulty holding that the combination of manufacturers and contractors, viewed in isolation, was in violation of the Sherman Act, since it restrained trade in and controlled the price of electrical equipment and allocated customers. The Court proceeded to hold that antitrust policy would be too severely undermined were the employers to be relieved of liability merely because a union was party to their agreement, and that the labor union also violates the Sherman Act when—even though its purpose is to increase members' wages—it "aids and abets" businessmen in doing prohibited acts such as creating business monopolies or controlling the marketing of goods and services. In dictum, the Court still managed to give broad-ranging powers to a union acting within the reach of the Norris-LaGuardia Act. It stated that the facts of the case showed a "labor dispute" to exist, and thus that a peaceful strike in support of a union-initiated boycott would not have been illegal or enjoinable by a federal court, since this was conduct clearly specified in the Clayton and Norris-LaGuardia Acts; it followed that the employer's acquiescence, in a collective bargaining agreement provision, in the form of a refusal to buy nonunion materials might also be assumed legal under the antitrust laws, if standing alone:

> But it did not stand alone. It was but one element in a far larger program in which contractors and manufacturers united with one another to monopolize all the business in New York City, to bar all other business men from that area, and to charge the public prices above a competitive level. It is true that victory of the union in its disputes, even had the union acted alone, might have added to the cost of goods, or might have resulted in individual refusals of all of their employers to buy electrical equipment not made by Local No. 3. So far as the union might have achieved this result acting alone, it would have been the natural consequence of labor union activities exempted by the Clayton Act from the coverage of the Sherman Act. . . . But when the unions participated with a combination of business men who had complete power to eliminate all competition among themselves and to prevent all compe-

tition from others, a situation was created not included within the exemptions of the Clayton and Norris-LaGuardia Acts.

.   .   .   .

Our holding means that the same labor union activities may or may not be in violation of the Sherman Act, dependent upon whether the union acts alone or in combination with business groups.

The Court thus sustained the issuance of an injunction against the union, but only as related to its conduct in concert with nonlabor groups.

As of 1945, then, one could read *Hutcheson* and *Allen Bradley* together to stand for the proposition that a union's activity or a collective bargaining provision is exempt from antitrust attack if related to the union's "self interest" and if not a knowing part of a larger combination of businessmen designed to increase price or regulate supply in the product market. Three more recent Supreme Court decisions have, however, seriously fragmented the Court and have cast doubt upon the validity of such an unqualified proposition. Two of those cases, decided in 1965, split the Justices into three different groups writing separate opinions. UMW v. Pennington (U.S.1965) raised once again the question of union-abetted employer conspiracies to drive competitors from the market. Local 189, Meat Cutters v. Jewel Tea Co. (U.S.1965) raised the question of a "union initiated" agreement limiting the marketing hours of supermarkets (a limit that arguably did not relate sufficiently to the union's "self interest"). The third Supreme Court decision, Connell Constr. Co. v. Plumbers Local 100 (U.S.1975), involved an agreement (secured by picketing) with a single employer barring the subcontracting of work to companies which did not recognize that union as bargaining representative; the Court's conclusion that antitrust immunity was not available to the union for this "union initiated" and "self interested" agreement raises new and difficult questions about the application of the antitrust laws to union activity.

In UMW v. Pennington (U.S.1965), a small coal company alleged that the United Mine Workers had, since a major wage agreement in 1950, agreed with the large mine operators to move toward mechanization of the coal mines, with a concomitant reduction in the mine labor force and an increase in their wages (to match increased productivity through mechanization). It was further alleged that the UMW agreed to impose the increased wage scale on small companies, outside the bargaining unit, even though they lacked financial resources and would be driven out of business. A jury trial against the union resulted in a treble damages award for violation of the antitrust laws. The Supreme Court remanded the case on unrelated issues, but sustained the conclusion that on the alleged and proven facts, the agreement between the Mine Workers Union and the large operators was not within the labor exemption to the antitrust laws. The Court divided into three camps, each with three Justices.

The opinion designated as that of the Court was penned by Mr. Justice White. It assumed that an agreement even between a single union and single employer setting the price at which the employer was to sell its goods would constitute a direct restraint on the product market and would violate the antitrust laws. An agreement on wages is, however, within the union's central concerns and will ordinarily fall within the labor exemption; this is true even if the union on its own initiative makes uniform wage demands on different employers knowing that some of them cannot afford to pay and will likely be driven out of business. What ousts the exemption in the case of the UMW, however, is that it bound itself in an agreement with the large operators to make certain wage demands upon employers in a different bargaining unit. Thus to confine one's bargaining flexibility is contrary to the policies of both the labor law and the antitrust law. While he concluded that the UMW wage agreement was nonexempt, it was not clear whether Justice White intended to require, for a substantive antitrust violation, that the union and the large employers also have been motivated by a "predatory intent" actually to drive the small operators out of business.

Three other Justices, speaking through Justice Douglas, did indeed understand the Court to require, for an antitrust violation, a joint purpose of union and large owners to destroy certain of their competitors; an industrywide agreement with a wage scale exceeding the ability of some operators to pay would be prima facie evidence of such illegal intention. Justice Goldberg, speaking for three Justices, would have held the agreement exempt, since it clearly represented a reasonable union attitude toward wages and mechanization, squarely within the "terms and conditions of employment" about which unions and employers must bargain, and since the condemnation of union-employer understandings concerning the extra-unit implications of their contract and court scrutiny of union wage demands and bargaining purposes are unrealistic and improper intrusions by judges (and juries) in the machinery of collective bargaining. Justice Goldberg did, however, concede that the congressional concern for unfettered negotiation concerning "mandatory" subjects, such as wages and hours, "is clearly lacking where the subject of the agreement is price-fixing and market allocation. Moreover, such [latter] activities are at the core of the type of anticompetitive commercial restraint at which the antitrust laws are directed."

On remand, the Supreme Court decision in *Pennington* was read to require proof of "a conspiracy between employers and labor formed with the intention of driving competitors out of business," and not to make it a per se violation of the Sherman Act for a union and employers merely to agree "to impose a particular wage scale on other employers" without such "predatory intent." Lewis v. Pennington (6th Cir. 1968). (Similarly, it has been held that a so-called most-favored-nation clause in a collective bargaining agreement—which permits the signatory employer automatically to adopt the terms of any contract between the union and any other employer when such terms are more advantageous to the other employer—does not per se violate the antitrust laws; it can be held to do so only if there is proof of a predatory purpose on the part of the signatory union and employer to force some other employer out of business. Associated Milk Dealers, Inc. v. Milk Drivers Local 753 (7th Cir. 1970).)

The reach of the *Pennington* decision has recently been extended by a court of appeals in Embry-Riddle Aeronautical Univ. v. Ross Aviation, Inc. (5th Cir. 1974). There, Ross Aviation, rendering flight training services for the Army, recognized and contracted with a union shortly after it had been announced that Ross would be replaced by another company, Embry, which had submitted the low bid for the successor contract with the Army. The evidence demonstrated that Ross had previously resisted unionization, but that it seized upon the opportunity—knowing that Embry would retain the Ross employees when it took over the Army contract—to negotiate a wage agreement that Embry would not be able to afford, in order to force Embry to relinquish the Army contract; there was also evidence that the union knowingly acceded to this scheme. The court of appeals sustained a judgment against both Ross and the union for violation of the antitrust laws, relying on the "predatory intent" rationale of the *Pennington* decision. It rejected the arguments of the union that its contract was only with Ross, a single employer, and thus not part of a multiemployer conspiracy as in *Pennington*; and that the labor contract was not designed to have "extra-unit" effects but was simply to be extended to Embry, a successor employer in the same bargaining unit.

§ 4. "Union-Instigated" Agreements on Mandatory Subjects and Unionization: The Jewel Tea and Connell Cases

In Local 189, Meat Cutters v. Jewel Tea Co. (U.S.1965), a union representing butchers and meat cutters negotiated an agreement with independent meat-market owners and with owners of supermarkets operating self-service meat counters. One provision in the labor contract forbade the owners to operate their stores after 6 p. m.; this was part of a longstanding union campaign against night work for its members. Jewel Tea Co., one of the supermarkets, sought to remain open on Friday nights, but when confronted with a strike vote on the issue signed a contract with the union containing the marketing-hours provision. It then brought an action against the union, some of its officers and an employer trade association which had signed a similar contract, seeking to have the marketing-hours provisions invalidated under the Sherman Act. The Supreme Court—relying on the findings of the lower court after trial that supermarket self-service meat operations after 6 p. m. would require that butchers working there either do more work during the day or work at night, or lose work at night to members of other unions—concluded that the marketing-hours provision and a strike threat to secure it fell within the labor exemption.

Justice White's opinion for the Court noted that the case did not involve a union-employer conspiracy against Jewel; the union effort to bar Jewel from operating after 6 p. m. (thus removing convenience of shopping hours as a source of competition among the companies) was not the "result of a bargain between the unions and some employers directed against other employers, but pursuant to what the unions deemed to be in their own labor union interests." Although liability could thus not be made out on a *Pennington*-type theory, however, the Court observed that even a contract between a single union and a single employer (unencumbered by a conspiracy between either and other employers) could fall outside the labor exemption if it dealt with a subject such as the price to be charged for the employer's product. It held that, in view of the interest of supermarket meat cutters in not having the self-service counters operate after 6 p. m., the marketing-hours restriction was not like the fixing of product prices but was rather "intimately related to wages, hours and working conditions"; this "immediate and direct" concern of union members outweighed whatever effect the marketing-hours restriction may have had upon competition in the product market. Mr. Justice White stated in dictum that had there been no relationship between the contract restriction and the workload of the butchers, the contract would then fall without the labor exemption and would be subjected to the usual scrutiny (including the "rule of reason") to determine whether it constituted a substantive antitrust violation.

Justice Goldberg, concurring for three Justices, again urged that an agreement on mandatory-bargaining subjects should be exempt from antitrust regulation, and that the opinion of the Court too narrowly construed the union's legitimate economic interests and too broadly asserted the power of the Court to scrutinize union bargaining objectives. Justice Douglas, dissenting for three Justices, argued that the marketing-hours provision in the multiemployer agreement should be treated as evidence of an illegal conspiracy between union and storeowners to prevent Jewel Tea from using late-shopping convenience as a form of product or service competition, and should thus be deemed illegal under *Allen Bradley*.

Treating the *Pennington* and *Jewel Tea* cases together, one could with considerable hesitation attempt to extract some general principles concerning the use of antitrust law to regulate labor union activities. If a group of employers agree to fix price, allocate customers or exclude entry into the product market, and use a collective bargaining agreement to pursue such goals, *Allen Bradley* rather clearly dictates that the employers violate the antitrust laws, the union does so also, the tainted clauses will be unenforceable and illegal and—somewhat in the face of the Norris-LaGuardia Act—union concerted activity to implement the clauses will be unlawful and enjoinable. *Pennington* makes rather clear that the legal posture of such an agreement or such concerted activities will not be altered even when the sought-after anticompetitive effects in the product market are secured by dealing on subjects of mandatory bargaining, such as wages. All nine Justices would appear to agree that there is no labor exemption, and there is an illegal restraint of trade, when a union—even one acting on its own initiative and pursuing its own bargaining policy with different employers, one at a time—seeks or secures a provision in a labor contract which deals not with mandatory subjects but directly with prices, allocation of customers, and the like; for the impact on the product market is substantial and the benefits to the union thought to be remote.

But there will often be instances, particularly in multiemployer bargaining units, where there is no specific conspiracy to tinker with competition in the product market, but where one can foresee that an anticompetitive effect will flow from an agreement on matters which touch upon legitimate subjects of union concern (*i. e.,* upon mandatory subjects of bargaining). Apex Hosiery Co. v. Leader (U.S.1940) would still appear to control in such a case, and to warrant the invocation of the labor exemption, since any reduction in product competition would flow from lawful union attempts to eliminate competition between employers concerning wages, hours and other labor standards. Thus, in a case (decided prior to the 1965 Supreme Court cases) in which a dairy sought to compete with other large dairies making house-to-house deliveries by making bulk deliveries to supermarkets, the union representing the dairy employees negotiated a wage provision which so sharply increased the earnings of the employees making supermarket deliveries (avowedly as a health and work-spreading measure) as likely to discourage or encumber that form of competition. The federal court of appeals, finding no conspiracy by the union with the employers, concluded that "the union acted alone in seeking legitimate labor objectives," and sustained the agreement against antitrust attack by the affected dairy. Adams Dairy Co. v. St. Louis Dairy Co. (8th Cir. 1958).

Whatever the confusion in understanding that reigned after the Supreme Court decisions in *Pennington* and *Jewel Tea,* further complexity was introduced by the Court's five-to-four decision in Connell Constr. Co. v. Plumbers Local 100 (U.S.1975), ten years later. That case raised perplexing questions concerning the reach of the antitrust exemption for labor unions and even about the reach of the *Apex Hosiery* decision. In *Connell,* a construction union representing mechanical and plumbing employees in the Dallas, Texas area, sought to expand its membership by securing agreements from general contractors to refrain from subcontracting mechanical and plumbing work at the construction site to persons not recognizing the union as bargaining representative. Such an agreement is known as a hot cargo agreement and is ordinarily a violation of section 8(e) of the Labor Act; an exception is made in the Act, however, for such an agreement in the construction industry relating to jobsite work. When Connell, a general contractor, refused to enter into such an agreement—which was aimed at organizing not Connell's own employees but only employees of Connell's subcontractors—the union picketed one of Connell's major construction sites and ultimately secured the company's agreement. Connell promptly sought an injunction against both the picketing and the enforcement of the hot cargo agreement, asserting a violation of the state and federal antitrust laws. Although the Court held (unanimously) that state antitrust laws were preempted by the provisions of the National Labor Relations Act dealing with union organizing and unfair labor practices, the Court majority held that federal antitrust regulation was not ousted and that the remedies under the Labor Act for unfair labor practices (NLRB orders and Board-initiated injunction proceedings, along with compensatory damages in some cases) did not supplant antitrust remedies. (In the instant case, this was held to authorize the issuance of an injunction at the behest of a private party; presumably in appropriate cases, treble damages could also be secured.)

The Court majority concluded that under the circumstances of the case the hot cargo agreement, although apparently designed merely to extend the organizational power of the union, was not within the labor exemption to the federal antitrust laws. The Court remanded for a determination whether the agreement actually constituted a restraint upon trade within the ban of the Sherman Act. The Court stated that the Norris-LaGuardia Act provided an explicit exemption from the antitrust laws for certain union concerted activities and that the policies of the Labor Act warranted an extension in the form of a "nonstatutory" exemption for certain union-employer agreements, but only those which had an anticompetitive impact on the product market traceable to the elimination of competition in wages and working conditions. The hot cargo agreement executed by Connell "indiscriminately excluded nonunion subcontractors from a portion of the market, even if their competitive advantages were not derived from substandard wages and working conditions but rather from more efficient operating methods." The union could also attempt to use the hot cargo agreement, and its control over the extent of its own organizing, to exclude certain targeted subcontractors from the market for reasons wholly extrinsic to their wages and working conditions. Although the record was devoid of any evidence of such union intention or of such "spillover" anticompetitive effects, and although the Court conceded that the "record contains no evidence that the union's goal was anything other than organizing as many subcontractors as possible," it concluded that a developed record might show such an intention or effect and that a nonstatutory immunity was thereafter unwarranted and remand compelled. (Because the union's picketing had stopped, and there was no indication that it would resume, the Court expressly reserved the question whether picketing to secure such a hot cargo agreement would fall within the statutory exemption of the Norris-LaGuardia Act.) In an important aside, the Court emphasized that the hot cargo agreement was not part of an overall labor contract between Connell and the union as a representative of Connell's own employees, and avoided the question whether such an overall agreement would bring the hot cargo clause within the shelter of the "federal policy favoring collective bargaining." Although the union asserted that the hot cargo agreement fell within the construction-industry proviso to section 8(e) of the Labor Act and was therefore "allowed," the Court held to the contrary, again for the reason that Connell was a "stranger" to the union.

How far the *Connell* analysis will extend beyond the reach of the facts of that case is uncertain. Its implications are quite broad, in a number of respects. It intimates that even union picketing or other concerted activity might fall outside the shelter of the labor exemption in the Norris-LaGuardia Act; it holds that, even though the goal of the union—extending its membership and organizing the employees of subcontractors within its trade—is lawful, the union is not necessarily entitled to achieve that goal through collective bargaining; it holds that there need be no evidence whatever of employer "complicity" to divest the union of its antitrust exemption. Perhaps most fundamentally, the *Connell* decision—in a number of somewhat opaque sentences—raises new uncertainty as to the protection given in the *Apex Hosiery* case for union attempts to organize and to eliminate disparities in wages and working conditions among competing employers. Finally, the Court has clearly rejected the claim—on which the dissenting Justices placed so much weight—that the remedies available under the Labor Act for a conceded unfair labor practice by the union are not meant to preclude the far more intrusive remedies available to the injured party under the federal antitrust laws.

It remains to be seen whether *Connell* betokens a rebirth of antitrust regulation of labor unions. Given the complexity of the issues, the divisions within the Court and the arguably narrow grounds for the Court's decision, it is likely that the antitrust laws will continue to play a fairly modest role as a component of federal labor law.

§ 5. Quantum of Proof

Two other significant issues in the field of antitrust have been addressed by the Supreme Court in recent years. The first is the quantum of proof necessary to make out a case that a union has committed a substantive antitrust violation. Ramsey v. UMW (U.S.

1971), was a case much like *Pennington*. Evidence was introduced at trial to support the claim of the plaintiffs, small coalmine operators, that the union had conspired with the larger companies, in their 1958 wage agreement, to drive the smaller companies out of business. The trial court held that the contract and its negotiation did not give "clear proof" of the illegal conspiracy; "clear proof" was a more taxing standard of proof than the usual "preponderance of evidence" in a civil case, and was thought required by section 6 of the Norris-La-Guardia Act, which provides in pertinent part that no labor organization "shall be held responsible or liable in any court of the United States for the unlawful acts" of its agents "except upon clear proof of actual . . . authorization of, such acts, or of ratification of such acts after actual knowledge thereof." Over the claim of four dissenting Justices that Norris-LaGuardia requires clear proof not only of union authorization or ratification but also of "the unlawful acts," the Court held that the language and legislative history of section 6 show that it was intended specifically to curb the inclination of the federal courts to impose vicarious liability on unions for any wrongful conduct committed during labor disputes, even conduct which was not specifically authorized or ratified. It is not to be construed as requiring clear proof of elements of the antitrust cause of action other than those of "agency."

> The section neither expressly nor by implication requires satisfaction of the clear proof standard in deciding factual issues concerning the commission *vel non* of acts by union officers or by members alleged to constitute a conspiracy, or the inferences to be drawn from such acts, or concerning overt acts in furtherance of the conspiracy, the impact on the relevant market or the injury to plaintiffs' businesses.

On such factual issues other than authorization or ratification, the Court held that the standard of proof was the lesser—and usual—one of "preponderance of evidence."

§ 6. "Unions" Regulating "Employers"

Another major issue addressed in the antitrust decisions of the Supreme Court is that of the extent to which persons who are "really" employers can organize as a "union" and thereby restrict competition among each other and from outsiders on matters which look like wages, working hours and the like but which are really restraints upon the product market by businessmen on matters of price, supply and customer allocation.

The Supreme Court had little difficulty in sustaining an injunction against a group of fishermen on the Pacific Coast, independent businessmen, who organized a "union" which bargained collectively with fish processors and canners concerning the sale of fish. The union demanded that the processors and canners agree in their contract of purchase from the fishermen not to buy fish from nonmembers of the union. The Court held that the contract dispute was one among businessmen regarding the sale of commodities and did not relate to the working conditions of the fishermen or to the relationship between employer and employee. Accordingly, there was no "labor dispute" within the Norris-LaGuardia Act, and an injunction could issue barring the fishermen's attempted monopolization of the northwest fish industry in violation of the Sherman Act. Columbia River Packers Ass'n v. Hinton (U.S.1942).

In Los Angeles Meat Drivers Union v. United States (U.S.1962), "grease peddlers" who purchased grease from restaurants and other sources of supply and sold them to grease processors became organized in a union along with drivers employed by the grease processors themselves, who both purchased from the peddlers and also used their own drivers to make pick-ups directly from sources of supply. The union fixed the prices at which the peddlers were to buy from sources and were to sell to the processors; it also allocated accounts and territories, circulated among the processors blacklists of nonunion peddlers, and used strikes and boycotts to enforce its program. The union conceded that these practices violated the Sherman Act and were enjoinable, but challenged the order of the trial court terminating their membership in the union. The Supreme Court held the order proper, in view of the fact that the processors had never replaced or threatened to replace their drivers with the peddlers and there was thus no "wage or job competition, or .   .   . any other economic interrelationship between the grease peddlers and the other members of the union" which would otherwise justify the unionization of peddlers along with drivers.

A different result was reached in American Fed'n. of Musicians v. Carroll (U.S.1968). There, the union promulgated bylaws and regulations which, among other things, prescribed prices which members serving as bandleaders on one-time engagements (such as weddings or commencements) could charge the purchaser of the musical entertainment; the price was to be the total of the union wage scale for each of the instrumentalists or "sidemen" plus scale for the leader (usually twice that of the sidemen) plus eight percent to cover insurance and other expenses. Although members would typically act on different days in the capacity sometime of leader and sometime of sideman, the four complainants against the union usually acted as leaders and had employed office personnel to advertise and solicit for engagements. They asserted that the union regulations constituted price fixing in violation of the Sherman Act. The Supreme Court rejected the argument, holding that the "price" regulations fell within the labor exemption since they were in substance designed to preserve the wage scale of persons employed as leaders or as sidemen for their services as musicians and thus to eliminate price competition through the allowable means of avoiding competition in the labor market. "The price of the product—here the price for an orchestra for a club-date—represents almost entirely the scale wages of the sidemen and the leader. Unlike most industries, except for the 8% charge, there are no other costs contributing to the price. Therefore, if leaders cut prices, inevitably wages must be cut." There was evidence to support the conclusion that if the leader did not charge the amount stipulated by the union, including a charge for his out-of-pocket expenses and the wages of all instrumentalists (and himself), "he will, in fact, not pay the sidemen the prescribed scale." In short, the seeming price regulation was really an exempt attempt to shield sidemen from the leaders' cutting of their wages below union scale, and could not be the subject of an order for an injunction or treble damages.

The Court found the case indistinguishable from Teamsters Local 24 v. Oliver (U.S.1959), in which it had held that a state could not forbid under its antitrust laws a labor-contract provision setting the prices which an employer would pay to independent-contractor truckdrivers for the rental of their trucks; this was found necessary to preserve the wage scale of the employer's own truckdrivers against competition by the independent contractors who could, by charging a rent which did not cover their operating and maintenance (i. e., nonwage) expenses, effectively receive less than union scale for their driving services. This contract clause was held to deal squarely with employee wages, to fall within the "mandatory" subjects of bargaining contemplated by the Labor Act, and thus to fall outside the allowable area of state proscription.

A similar result was reached in Scott Paper Co. v. Gulf Coast Pulpwood Ass'n (S.D.Ala.1973), aff'd (5th Cir. 1974), in which members of certain associations of pulpwood producers engaged in a work stoppage and picketing directed at pulpwood dealers, for whom the producers cut, hauled and loaded the wood; the dealers supplied the wood in turn to paper companies. Certain paper companies brought an action to enjoin the activities of the pulpwood producers, alleging that the producers were independent contractors and not employees of the dealers, and that their activities violated the Sherman Act. The court, after examining the economic relationship of the producers and dealers, concluded that the former were employees, that there thus existed a "labor dispute" within the Norris-LaGuardia Act and that therefore no injunction could issue against the strike and picketing. The court distinguished the Columbia River and Los Angeles Meat Drivers cases as involving "unions" of persons who were in truth independent entrepreneurs rather than employees.

THE UNION AND THE INDIVIDUAL EMPLOYEE

CHAPTER XXVIII

UNION SECURITY AGREEMENTS

§ 1. Background: Varieties of Union Security Agreements

Many of a union's objectives can be secured if it counts among its members a bare majority of employees in a plant or company, for this gives it the right under the federal Labor Act to serve as the exclusive bargaining representative for those employees and all other employees (even nonmembers) included in the bargaining unit. This bargaining authority may be used to improve the lot of the workers in the unit, and also to shore up union gains in other plants or companies which would otherwise be threatened by competition from a nonunion unit. But the union would like to assure that all employees in the unit, and not just the majority, become union members. If all employees were required to join the union, this would protect the union against employer attempts to woo employees away and against "raiding" by other unions; would assure a reliable source of funds for union activities, including collective bargaining and grievance processing, which inure to the benefit of all employees in the unit; would strengthen the union in bargaining (since even reluctant workers might more readily support a strike call because of peer pressure and formal discipline within the union); and would tend to promote stability in the relationship between employer and union, which sometimes brings more responsible union leadership to the fore but sometimes also entrenches irresponsible leadership. These often diverging interests of the unions, the employees and the public make "union security" a volatile issue, the treatment of which under the law has followed a complex and evolving path.

At common law, when courts typically enjoined strikes and picketing directed at objects believed by the judges to be antisocial, injunctions frequently issued against concerted activities designed to coerce all employees to join the union or to coerce the employer to coerce in turn its employees to join the union. The closed-shop agreement was widely regarded as a proscribed object. *E. g.*, Plant v. Woods (Mass.1900). In 1934, Congress, considering amendments to the Railway Labor Act, enacted a provision strongly supporting employee freedom of union affiliation; just as no employer could contractually bind an employee *not* to join a union (the so-called yellow dog contract), no employer could contractually require that an employee join. At that time, the attitude of railway unions concerning union security was rather ambivalent, since some employers were using union shop agreements to compel membership in inside or company unions and thus to oust the independent unions. The following year, in the Wagner Act of 1935, Congress expressed greater concern for union stability in the face of employer coercion and declared that, in spite of the ban in section 8(3) upon an employer's discrimination in hire or tenure of employment to encourage or discourage union membership, an employer could lawfully agree to hire and retain only union members (provided the union was selected by a majority of employees in the bargaining unit and was not employer dominated or assisted). Thus was the closed-shop agreement legalized.

By 1947, union membership had greatly increased, as had disruptive union activity. Congress also became aware of the use of the closed shop by union leadership arbitrarily to oust dissenters from their jobs merely by severing their union membership. The closed shop agreement, which requires that persons be union members before they are even hired, also was thought to give the union (rather than the employer) effective control over hiring as well as "monopoly control" over the total composition of the workforce in an entire craft which could be manipulated by union membership requirements (such as initiation fees). This explains both the enactment in twelve states between 1944 and 1947 of so-called right-to-work laws (forbidding the conditioning of employment on union membership) and the enactment by Congress in the Taft-Hartley amendments of 1947 of new provisos to what is now section 8(a)(3) of the Labor Act, which bars discrimination in hire or tenure of employment to encourage or discourage union membership:

> *Provided,* That nothing in this Act, or in any other statute of the United States, shall preclude an employer from making an agreement with a labor organization . . . to require as a condition of employment membership therein on or after the thirtieth day following the beginning of such employment or the effective date of such agreement, whichever is the later, . . . ; *Provided further,* That no employer shall justify any discrimination against an employee for nonmembership in a labor organization (A) if he has reasonable grounds for believing that such membership was not available to the employee on the same terms and conditions generally applicable to other members, or (B) if he has reasonable grounds for believing that membership was denied or terminated for reasons other than the failure of the employee to tender the periodic dues and the initiation fees uniformly required as a condition of acquiring or retaining membership . . . .

(In 1951, the Railway Labor Act, now governing employees in both the railroad and airline industries, was amended so as to discard the right-to-work orientation of the 1934 law and to permit instead the execution of union shop agreements like those permitted under Taft-Hartley, with the principal exception being that there is a required waiting period of sixty rather than thirty days. The history of union security under the Railway Labor Act is recounted in considerable detail in IAM v. Street (U.S.1961).)

The Taft-Hartley provisions of 1947 effectively limited union security in two ways: (1) the employer could hire persons other than union members (although they could be required to join the union within thirty days) and thus deprive the union of control over the referral of job applicants; and (2) once hired, an employee need not, in order to retain his job, attend union meetings, refrain from criticizing union leadership and otherwise maintain good standing in the union, but need merely "tender the periodic dues and the initiation fees uniformly required" of union members. Two other significant limitations were placed upon union security provisions. As written in 1947, the Act required the bargaining representative, as a condition to concluding a union security agreement, to secure employee authorization; a majority of unit employees eligible to vote (not merely a majority of those actually voting) had to so authorize the union. Early experience with the authorization ballot showed that the Board was flooded with such elections and the union prevailed in the overwhelming preponderance of cases. In 1951, Congress reversed the procedure. A union security agreement within the section 8(a)(3) proviso is automatically lawful, but it may be terminated by a vote of the unit employees under section 9(e) to "deauthorize" the union. A more important limitation on union security is found in section 14(b), enacted in 1947:

> Nothing in this Act shall be construed as authorizing the execution or application of agreements requiring membership in a labor organization as a condition of employment in any State or Territory in which such execution or application is prohibited by State or Territorial law.

The effect of this section is to retreat from the all-embracing federal principles which characterize the Labor Act and to permit the twenty states which have enacted right-to-work laws to invalidate union security provisions which are otherwise legal under the section 8(a)(3) provisos.

The term "union security" embraces a number of different kinds of arrangements designed to bolster the membership and finances of a union:

The *closed shop*—which might provide, "The employer hereby agrees to employ only members in good standing of the Union"—gives greatest power to the union, because it permits the union to determine the eligibility of job applicants (as well as retention of a job already held) by controlling admission to union membership and by expelling from membership persons who fail to comply with internal

rules and regulations.   The closed shop is illegal, since it discriminates in hire or tenure of employment so as to encourage union membership but is not sheltered by the proviso to section 8(a)(3).

The *union shop* does not condition initial employment on union
membership but requires that employees join the union after a grace
period on the job and remain union members during the term of the
agreement.   The proviso to section 8(a)(3) forbids a grace period
shorter than 30 days.   A union shop clause might provide:

> Each employee covered by this agreement shall, as a condi-
> tion of continued employment, become and remain a member
> of the Union on and after the thirtieth day following the be-
> ginning of his employment or following the effective date of
> this agreement, whichever is the later.

The *agency shop* requires that an employee, rather than assuming "full" union membership in good standing after thirty days, simply pay the union for services rendered by the union to employees
within the bargaining unit as the employees' "agent" in negotiating
and administering the labor contract.   The Labor Act permits—and
most agency shop agreements provide for—the exaction of a service
fee which is equivalent in amount to the initiation fees and periodic
dues which are paid by full union members.   The rationale is that
even nonmembers reap the benefit of union representation and should
not be permitted a "free ride."

The *maintenance of membership* clause, a yet more tepid form of
union security, imposes no obligation to join a union but merely an
obligation to remain a member once having voluntarily become one.
Such a clause might provide:

> All employees who are members of the Union in good stand-
> ing, and those employees who may hereafter become mem-
> bers, shall, as a condition of employment, remain members
> of the Union in good standing during the term of the agree-
> ment.

A *dues checkoff* provision in itself requires no one to join a union or retain membership in a union, but simply provides that the
employer shall deduct from the earnings of union members (just as it
would for taxes, insurance premiums or charitable contributions) the
periodic membership dues and shall pay that amount directly to the
union.   The checkoff is commonly utilized in conjunction with some
more effective union security provision.   It relieves the union of the
burden in time and expense of collecting membership dues.   Such a
clause might provide:

> Upon receipt, by the Company, of a signed authoriza-
> tion, the Company will deduct the Union initiation or rein-
> statement fees and monthly dues from the pay of each of its

employees who have authorized or who may hereafter authorize such deductions. The sum so deducted shall be paid monthly to the appropriate financial officer of the Union, together with an itemized statement showing the source of each deduction.

The *hiring hall* is utilized in certain industries—most commonly, maritime, longshore and construction—where jobs tend to be unpredictable, of short duration, and not with any single employer. It amounts to a device for job security in industries in which seniority with any single employer cannot realistically determine job rights, and serves as a union-operated clearinghouse which matches employers seeking a transitory workforce and employees seeking work. The union and employer may agree that the union hall is to be the exclusive mode for job referrals or that the employer is free to hire through other sources. A typical hiring hall agreement might provide:

> The Union shall establish and maintain open and non-discriminatory employment lists for employment of workmen covered by this agreement. The Employer shall notify the Union of all vacancies and shall call the Union for employees. The Union agrees to the best of its ability to supply to the Employers competent help at all times.

> Applicants for employment shall be referred by the Union to the Employer on a non-discriminatory basis and such referrals shall not be based on, or in any way affected by, Union membership or lack of such membership or by Union By-Laws, rules, regulations, constitutional provisions, or any other aspect or obligations of Union membership, policies or requirements. It is understood and agreed that the Employer prefers experienced employees and therefore preference on referral shall be given to persons who have had at least 2000 hours of experience in the industry in the area covered by this agreement within the five-year period preceding the date of this agreement.

> The Employer shall be the sole judge of the qualifications of all applicants and retains the right to reject any applicant for employment referred by the Union.

> In the event the Unions are unable to supply competent employees that are satisfactory to the Employer, the Employer shall then have the right to employ help from any source at the regular wage rates herein specified.

The law regulates the extent to which the union may use its authority as a referral agency to favor union members in good standing and thus to encourage membership unlawfully.

These various union security devices, and their regulation by law, are the subject of the following discussion.

§ 2.   Union Shop, Agency Shop and Maintenance of Membership: A Comparison

The union shop, the agency shop and the maintenance of membership clause have very much in common. While the union shop clause purports to require membership in the union as a condition of employment, it in substance can exact no greater fealty to the union than does the agency shop provision, which requires the payment of union dues and initiation fees but not full membership. And, while joining the union or paying dues is not required under a maintenance of membership provision standing by itself, such a provision often accompanies a union shop clause, and it in any event does become its equivalent for employees who do choose to join the union of their own volition during the term of the labor agreement.

In a case that reached the Supreme Court, the employer argued that the proviso to section 8(a)(3) permitted only union security agreements requiring "membership" in a labor organization, and that while a union shop or maintenance of membership clause was thus lawful under the Act, that was not true of the agency shop, which required not membership but merely payment of dues. In spite of the anomalous conclusion that the more onerous exaction of full membership as a condition of employment was lawful, while the more tepid agency shop clause was not, the employer so argued in order to defend its refusal to bargain with the union concerning the agency shop. (The union had proposed an agency shop clause because this had been held valid under the Indiana right-to-work law, while the union shop had not.) The National Labor Relations Board had held the agency shop to be within the priviso and lawful, in American Seating Co. (1952). The Supreme Court announced its agreement some eleven years later, in NLRB v. General Motors Corp. (U.S.1963). The Court held that the provisos to section 8(a)(3) had two objectives: first, to eliminate the closed shop, and second, to permit an employer and union to agree to eliminate the "free rider" by exacting payment for the union's services as exclusive bargaining agent for all within the unit. Federal law thus validated, as a stabilizing force in collective bargaining, the exaction of an agency fee from all unit employees. The "membership" which Congress authorized the parties to demand of all employees is, in the words of the Court, "whittled down to its financial core." (A corollary of the Court's holding that the agency shop does indeed require "membership" as Congress understood that term is that states may enact or construe their right-to-work laws to bar the agency shop as well as the union shop. The Court held that section 14(b) of the Taft-Hartley Act gave the states this authority to override the federally protected contract provision, in Retail Clerks, Local 1625 v. Schermerhorn (U.S.1963), decided the same day as *General Motors*.)

The Court's analysis of the *agency* shop complements the statutory language in the second proviso to section 8(a)(3), which bars the enforcement of a *union* shop provision if the employer has reason to believe that "membership was denied or terminated for reasons other than the failure of the employee to tender the periodic dues and the initiation fees uniformly required as a condition of acquiring or retaining membership." This means that the parties are forbidden by law to require under a union shop clause, as a condition of employment, that the employee do any more than he would be required to do under an agency shop clause—that is, to pay dues. (The "reason to believe" requirement is designed to afford a defense to the employer who is told contrary to fact that denial of or ouster from membership is based on the failure to pay dues and reasonably believes this. In such a case, the employee will have no reinstatement or backpay remedy against the employer but may secure backpay from the union for violation of section 8(b)(2).) In effect, if the employee is denied membership because of his color or because he is disliked by the union leadership, or is ousted from membership because he fails to attend union meetings regularly (or at all), regardless whether the union considers him a member in good standing he may not lawfully be discharged pursuant to a contractual union shop provision. As the Supreme Court stated in NLRB v. General Motors Corp. (U.S.1963):

> It is permissible to condition employment upon membership, but membership, insofar as it has significance to employment rights, may in turn be conditioned only upon payment of fees and dues. "Membership" as a condition of employment is whittled down to its financial core.

Since the employer and union are thus permitted to exact, as a condition of employment, only the payment of dues but not full membership (which brings with it susceptibility to union discipline for violation of union rules), it may fairly be said that the strongest union security provision that can be enforced by job-related sanctions is the agency shop. Loss (or denial) of "membership in good standing" for reasons other than delinquent dues may, under the National Labor Relations Act, lawfully result in the union's denying access to meetings, denying the right to vote or to run for office in union elections, or denying the right to vote on the ratification of union agreements; but it cannot lawfully result in discharge. This is true whether it is the union which refuses to admit a willing employee, Local 1104, Communications Workers v. NLRB (N.Y.Tel.Co.) (2d Cir. 1975) (union denied membership to nonstrikers, who then refused to tender dues), or it is the employee who tenders an amount equivalent to dues and fees but refuses to comply with any other obligations of union membership in good standing, NLRB v. Hershey Foods Corp. (9th Cir. 1975). It follows that, even under a maintenance of membership clause, an employee who joins the union during the contract term is free to withdraw his name from the union rolls without fear of discharge, provided he satisfies his "membership" obligation there-after by tendering the requisite dues and fees. Marlin Rockwell Corp. (1955).

Whatever the form of union security upon which the parties have agreed—union shop, agency shop, or maintenance of member-ship—there are problems of statutory construction which are present-ed by the provisos to section 8(a)(3). Some relate to pertinent time periods—when an employee is to take on the obligations of "member-ship" and when thereafter he may become susceptible to discharge. Others relate to the nature of the payments which may be exacted.

§ 3.   The Statutory "Grace Period"

The first proviso to section 8(a)(3) authorizes the parties to make an agreement requiring as a condition of employment that all employees secure membership in the union "on or after the thirtieth day following the beginning of such employment or the effective date of such agreement, whichever is the later . . . ." This lan-guage clearly forbids the parties to condition employment on one's having been a union member prior to the effective date of the con-tract. In an early case which tested under the proviso the validity of a maintenance of membership clause, it was held that any attempt to give the clause "retroactive effect" would "substantially impair free-dom of choice at a time when the statute requires such freedom." Colonie Fibre Co. v. NLRB (2d Cir. 1947). Nor does the require-ment of union membership, which is lawful under the 8(a)(3) provi-so only when part of an agreement by the parties, continue in exist-ence when the contract is terminated. Teamsters, Local 70 (Sea-Land of Cal., Inc.) (1972), enf'd (3d Cir. 1973) (insufficient proof that parties had impliedly continued all contract terms beyond ex-press termination date). Nor can the duty to remain a "member" under a maintenance of membership agreement be extended beyond the date when one's employment is terminated. Thus, in Carpenters Local 2498 (Weyerhauser Timber Co.) (1953), it was held that a worker's duty under such a provision to remain a member necessarily rests upon his status as an employee, and it is not renewed when the former employee is later re-employed during the term of the agree-ment.

In a number of cases, the Board has given a rather strict reading to the thirty-day grace period in the proviso. Thus, requiring em-ployees immediately upon commencement of their employment simply to apply for membership, even if actual membership is not required for thirty days, is illegal. NLRB v. Hribar Trucking, Inc. (7th Cir. 1964). Similarly, the thirty-day period has been held to begin to run only with the actual effective date of the contract, and not an earlier retroactive date. Teamsters Local 70 (Sea-Land of Cal., Inc.) (1972), enf'd (3d Cir. 1973).

In other instances, the Board has applied the statutory grace period more leniently. A contract requiring membership "within 30 days" has been held to be equivalent to the statutory language ("on or after the thirtieth day"). NLRB v. Television & Radio Broadcasting Studio Employees Local 804 (3d Cir. 1963). The Board has also looked to the unwritten practices of the parties in order to save a union shop provision whose terms arguably failed to comport with the 8(a)(3) proviso. Thus, where a contract failed expressly to provide the thirty-day grace period, but the parties stipulated in the contract that rights under the Labor Act were not intended to be abridged and had also made no attempt to implement a grace period shorter than thirty days, the Board upheld the contract provision. American Seating Co. (1952). The Board has also held that employees who are union members when the contract becomes effective need not be given a thirty-day grace period within which to withdraw from the union (prior to rejoining); the concern reflected in the proviso to ban the closed shop is inapt when the employee is already a union member, and the congressional willingness to have the parties eliminate "free riders" is apt during the month in question. Krausse Milling Co. (1951) (overruling a Board decision to the contrary made the year before). Of course, the parties are free to agree to a grace period longer than thirty days; if so, this will supplant the statutory period and a discharge of the employee for noncompliance will be lawful only if it complies with the procedures and time limit stipulated in the contract. Local 776, IATSE (Film Editors) (1959), *enf'd as mdf'd* (9th Cir. 1962).

In one industry—building and construction—the statute takes account of special circumstances and reduces the grace period for acquiring union "membership" under a union shop provision or for beginning to pay union dues under an agency shop provision. In the building and construction industry, a given employer works on different jobs in different localities, performs work of brief duration and hires a transient workforce (often through a union-controlled hiring hall) typically highly organized along craft lines. A construction employer also must be in a position to know what wage rates to anticipate in different places in order that it may intelligently compute its contract bids. These factors render unsuitable the full-dressed representation election conducted by the NLRB and the usual month-long statutory grace period for union security provisions, and invite dealing with a particular union even before the employee complement has been hired. Congress therefore, in the Landrum-Griffin amendments of 1959, enacted section 8(f) of the Labor Act in order to broaden the powers of construction employers and unions to make union security agreements (like all others, subject to outlawry by state right-to-work laws) in two pertinent respects. The agreement will be lawful even if:

(1) the majority status of such labor organization has not been established under the provisions of section 9 of this Act

prior to the making of such agreement, or (2) such agreement requires as a condition of employment, membership in such labor organization after the seventh day following the beginning of such employment or the effective date of the agreement, whichever is later .   .   .   .

Since these union shop arrangements may be negotiated before the union demonstrates majority support within the employer bargaining unit, and indeed before employees are hired at all, they are known as "pre-hire agreements."

There is an understandable hesitancy to accord such contracts all of the sanctity normally attaching to collective bargaining agreements negotiated after a majority representative has been freely chosen.   Thus, section 8(f) itself expressly provides that a pre-hire contract shall not be a bar to a representation election under section 9(c) during the life of the contract or to a deauthorization election under section 9(e).   The Board has gone yet further.   Although an employer normally violates the Act when it repudiates the union and its contract in the midst of the contract term, a construction employer is free to do just that in the case of a pre-hire agreement negotiated with a minority union.   The ordinary presumption that a contracting union continues to have majority support during the life of the contract is held by the Board not to apply in such a case, so that the employer is free to test the union's status not only by petitioning for an election (as expressly authorized in section 8(f)) but also by repudiating the agreement, making unilateral changes in working conditions and even bargaining with another union.   These decisions have, however, been overturned by the courts of appeals, which have held that Congress intended to authorize an employer challenge to the section 8(f) pre-hire agreement only through an election petition when after a reasonable time it believes that the union still represents only a minority of employees in the unit.   One court found that the employer could not abrogate a pre-hire contract which contained a union shop provision which had apparently induced the unit employees to join the once-minority union.   NLRB v. Irvin (3d Cir. 1973).   Another court held that the employer must honor the pre-hire contract, even absent a union security provision, until the union is ousted in a Board election.   Operating Eng'rs Local 150 v. NLRB (R. J. Smith Constr. Co.) (D.C.Cir.1973).   In any event, the Board and the courts agree that section 8(f) empowers a construction employer to make a contract with a minority union and to abide by that contract if it chooses—and also to require union membership within seven days of employment rather than the usual thirty.

Even if the labor agreement affords the employee the proper statutory grace period (whether thirty or seven days) for beginning to assume the obligations of union membership, there may be a question whether the employee at some point during the life of the agreement has in fact timely paid the dues required of him. In several cases, a union has requested that the employer discharge an employee for delinquency in the payment of dues, but the employee then tenders the delinquent amount prior to the employer taking formal disciplinary action. The Board initially held that a discharge after such a belated tender was unlawful, reasoning that "a full and unqualified tender made anytime prior to actual discharge, and without regard as to when the request for discharge may have been made, is a proper tender . . . ." Aluminum Workers Local 135 (1955). This principle was not endorsed in the courts of appeals, which concluded that it would be too great a source of instability in the enforcement of valid union security clauses to have the employer's delay in acting convert a lawful union request for discharge into an unlawful discharge. IAM v. NLRB (New Britain Machine Co.) (2d Cir. 1957). The Board has since acquiesced in the position of the courts, expressly overruled *Aluminum Workers,* and concluded that if the union's reason for demanding discharge is indeed dues delinquency, a discharge even after a belated tender of dues by the employee is lawful. General Motors Corp. (1961). The Board concluded that the union's reason was at the time legitimate, that the employer had no cause to believe that the union's motives were unlawful and discriminatory, and that the belated tender does not in itself justify an inference that the parties had acted with illicit motive in violation of sections 8(a)(3) and 8(b)(2).

Of course, when there is in such cases other record evidence—such as the disparate treatment of delinquent dues-payers—that supports the contention that the discharge was for reasons other than the failure timely to tender dues and fees, then the discharge may be held to violate the Act (since it would fall outside the shelter of the proviso to section 8(a)(3)). NLRB v. Woodworkers of America (9th Cir. 1959) (the union accepted two late applications for membership, but insisted on discharge of third late applicant). And, if the union actually accepts the belated tender—or if union regulations permit a delayed tender—the union will be deemed to have "waived" any claim it might have under the labor contract for the employee's discharge. *Ibid.* The Board has also protected the delinquent member who tenders his late dues *before* the union *makes* a demand that the employer discharge him. Machinists Lodge 558 (Lockheed Missiles & Space Co.) (1971) (orderly administration of the union security arrangement is not undermined to the degree it would be if belated tender had to be accepted *after* the union's demand).

Before an employee is discharged for failure to tender the required dues and fees, he must be given reasonable notice that his delinquency renders him liable to discipline. The union seeking to enforce the union security clause owes the employee a fiduciary duty to deal with him fairly. NLRB v. Local 182, Teamsters (2d Cir. 1968). The problem of notice is most pressing when the agreement of which the union security provision is a part is oral. In such cases the Board has placed a heavy burden on the employer and union:

> Parties, who would defend action taken on the basis of such oral agreements, must therefore satisfy a stringent burden of proof in establishing the existence and precise terms and conditions of the agreement and in further establishing that affected employees have been fully and unmistakably notified thereof.

Pacific Iron & Metal Co. (1969).

§ 4. Periodic Dues and Initiation Fees; the Significance of Section 8(b)(5)

It has already been noted that the "membership" obligation which may be required of an employee under a union security agreement as a condition of employment is limited to a financial obligation only, and that this is true under a union shop, an agency shop, or a maintenance of membership clause. It thus becomes critical to determine what are, in the words of the second proviso to section 8(a)(3), "the periodic dues and the initiation fees uniformly required" of union members, failure to tender which may subject an employee to discharge. Employees may be required to pay—in addition to regular dues—an amount representing a percentage of earnings, thus taxing the higher-paid employees to a greater degree than others. These are treated as "periodic dues," since they meet the Board's criteria that the financial obligation be periodic, regular, uniform and general. Local 409, IATSE (RCA Service Co.) (1963). But periodic dues include only those accruing to the union subsequent to the making of the collective bargaining agreement containing the union shop provision; they do not include overdue payments owing by the employee when the contract is signed and they do not include fines imposed by the union. NLRB v. Eclipse Lumber Co. (9th Cir. 1952). Nor do they include assessments by the union for such funds as strike benefits for members. NLRB v. Die & Tool Makers (7th Cir. 1956). (Section 2, Eleventh of the Railway Labor Act does permit union security provisions which require the payment not only of initiation fees and dues but also of "assessments (not including fines and penalties)" uniformly required of members.) If the payments which the employee fails to tender, such as initiation fees, are not uniformly required, he may not lawfully be discharged; the notion of "uniformity" provides leeway for Board interpretation. NLRB v. Kaiser Steel Corp. (9th Cir. 1974) (initiation fees payable upon transfer from one job to another within a multi-union unit are not uniformly required, since employees who do not transfer need pay only a single initiation fee).

A particularly controversial issue concerning the interpretation of "periodic dues" is whether the union may exact the same monthly dues from all persons within the unit, members and nonmembers, and then refund a certain amount from those dues to members who attend union meetings.   Such a refund invites the charge that employment is being conditioned on the payment of a fine (measured by the amount of the refund) for nonattendance at union meetings, and that dues are not being "uniformly" exacted.   In Leece-Neville Co. (1963), *enf'd* (6th Cir. 1964), the Board invoked earlier decisions and held that the union had illegally "created a dues structure based upon attendance or nonattendance at Union meetings" and that, while distinctions in the calculation of dues could be made if reasonably based, "[a] classification of employees based upon attendance or nonattendance at Union meetings [is] not a reasonable classification."   Four years later, this decision was overruled by the Board, in a case in which an employee was threatened with discharge for failure to pay $6.00 monthly dues to the union, which regularly refunded $2.00 if the member attended the union meeting.   The $2.00 refund was held not to be tantamount to a fine for nonattendance but rather analogous to the door prizes, refreshments and entertainment which have traditionally been supported by unions from their own funds as a means of promoting attendance at union business meetings.   Relying on the fact that "the public's interest is served best when the memberships of labor organizations that are the exclusive statutory representatives of employees take an active and responsible role in governing their unions and formulating union policy," the Board held the refund "a legitimate device, aimed at achieving a salutary objective," and stated that to hold otherwise would constitute "an unwarranted intrusion into Respondent Union's internal affairs   .   .   .   ."   Local 171, Ass'n of Western Pulp Workers (Boise Cascade Corp.) (1967).   As yet, no court appears to have given its approval to the *Boise Cascade* holding, and the *Leece-Neville* court would no doubt reject it.

When an employer operating under a union shop provision is not certain whether the money requested by the union is actually for periodic dues and fees or rather for fines or other assessments, it may be faced with the alternative of discharging the employee and risking an unfair labor practice violation, on the one hand, and on the other of refusing to discharge the employee and hazarding a strike or some other form of union reprisal (at the least the filing of a grievance). The Labor Act does not, however, require that the employer engage in an extensive investigation to determine whether or not the employee is actually delinquent in the payment of dues.   NLRB v. Leece-Neville Co. (6th Cir. 1964).   Section 8(a)(3) is violated only if the employer has "reasonable grounds for believing" that the union is using the union shop provision to exact obligations beyond the payment of periodic dues.   The employer will normally be sustained if it acts reasonably in resolving a question of credibility.   Ferro Stamping & Mfg. Co. (1951).

Since sections 8(a)(3) and 8(b)(2) authorize the employer and union to condition employment upon the payment of "the periodic dues and the initiation fees uniformly required" of members, a union might still be in a position—by the manipulation of its initiation fee —so drastically to curtail admission to membership as to control access to employment as well and in substance to create a closed shop. In order to address this problem, Congress in the 1947 Taft-Hartley amendments enacted section 8(b)(5), which makes it an unfair labor practice for a labor organization which is a party to a lawful union security agreement to require

> the payment, as a condition precedent to becoming a member of such organization, of a fee in an amount which the Board finds excessive or discriminatory under all the circumstances. In making such a finding, the Board shall consider, among other relevant factors, the practices and customs of labor organizations in the particular industry, and the wages currently paid to the employees affected . . . .

If the initiation fee unreasonably discriminates against particular applicants or classes of applicants for union membership, their union-induced discharge for nonpayment would violate the Labor Act, even if the fee charged cannot be condemned as "excessive" in itself. The discharge would violate not only section 8(b)(5) but also sections 8(b)(2) and 8(a)(3) since, in the words of those latter sections, the discriminatory initiation fee is not "uniformly required." But a union is not altogether forbidden to require different initiation fees from different classes of members, provided the classifications are reasonable. Thus, a union violates section 8(b)(5) when its initiation fees for persons employed after the effective contract date are lower than those charged persons who were already employed on that date but had not yet become union members. Such discrimination is tantamount to a reprisal for the exercise by the latter employees of their right under section 7 to refrain from joining a union prior to the thirty-day grace period of section 8(a)(3). Ferro Stamping & Mfg. Co. (1951). The union may, however, give more generous treatment in setting initiation fees to veterans of the armed forces, and may give more (or less) generous treatment to former members of that union than to new members (although the Board's distinction of such a case from its holding in *Ferro* may not be altogether persuasive). Food Mach. & Chem. Corp. (1952) (longstanding practice of charging greater initiation fee or reinstatement charge to former members of other locals of the union).

Section 8(b)(5) has not been held to forbid the practice of waiving initiation fees as an inducement to join the union promptly. But if the union grants a waiver only to employees who join before an impending representation election, while promising to exact the full fee from those joining after, this has been held by the Supreme Court to be a misleading inducement which justifies overturning a union election victory. NLRB v. Savair Mfg. Co. (U.S.1973) (union could otherwise buy endorsements and "paint a false portrait of employee support" during the campaign). The Board has, however, held that the union does have sufficient interest, in overcoming employee reluctance to pay out money before receiving any union benefits, to warrant upholding an initiation-fee waiver which is available to unit employees who join after the election as well as to those who join before. B. F. Goodrich Tire Co. (1974) (union told employees that they could join after the election on paying a fee of $10 rather than the standard fee of $50).

Section 8(b)(5) bars not only fees which are discriminatory but also fees which are "excessive." A union which as a technical matter opens membership to all interested employees may as a practical matter exclude newcomers by imposing an extremely onerous initiation fee. Should an employee subject to a valid union shop provision be unable to afford payment of that fee, he may seek to have the fee overturned in an unfair labor practice proceeding. This has occurred in such industries as longshoring, where automation induced the union to try to limit the number of casual workers on the docks, Longshore Workers Local 1419 (New Orleans S.S. Ass'n) (1970); and broadcasting, where the union tried to limit the number of part-time nonunion employees, NLRB v. Television Broadcasting Studio Employees Local 804 (3d Cir. 1963). If the union's motive for a dramatic fee increase is thus to block access to membership and ultimately to jobs, the Board will find this to be discriminatory as between present members and prospective members, thus subjecting both employer and union to unfair labor practice charges for conditioning employment on the payment of fees not "uniformly required." Ferro Stamping & Mfg. Co. (1951). The Board will also find such fees to be "excessive" in violation of section 8(b)(5). Longshore Workers Local 1419 (New Orleans S.S. Ass'n) (1970) (since fee is excessive in violation of section 8(b)(5), it also violates sections 8(b)(1)(A) and 8(b)(2)). Section 8(b)(5) states that the Board is to consider the fees paid to comparable labor organizations, as well as the employees' earnings; it has been held that an initiation fee in an amount equal to the pay earned in a month or a month and a half by a starting worker is suspect on its face. *Ibid.* The union may, however, demonstrate that seemingly excessive fees result not from a desire to promote a closed union, but rather from financial necessity or the cost of providing increased membership benefits. Motion Picture Screen Cartoonists Local 839 (1958).

§ 5. Union Security and Board Elections: The Contract Bar and Deauthorization Elections

Under the Board's rules governing the conduct of representation elections, discussed elsewhere, an existing collective bargaining agreement will bar the holding of such an election for a period as long as three years. The "contract bar" will, however, fall and an election petition will be deemed timely if the labor contract contains an invalid union security provision. While the Board does not treat every illegal contract provision as reason to overlook the normal principles of contract bar, the illegal union security clause is thought particularly objectionable since it coerces employees in their choice of bargaining representative and is thus thought to give no promise of representational stability.

Over time, the Board has vacillated on the question whether an arguably illegal union security agreement should be treated as a contract bar or should be presumed illegal and the bar dropped. At first, the Board held that a contract containing a clause not explicitly complying with the provisos to section 8(a)(3) should nonetheless bar an election petition if the clause could be construed so as not to violate the Act and had been lawfully implemented in practice. American Seating Co. (1952). The Board changed its position in Keystone Coat, Apron & Towel Supply Co. (1958), and held that the union security provision had to conform on its face to the requirements of section 8(a)(3); it in fact proceeded to set forth the text of a clause which it was prepared to tolerate as the maximum form of union security. The Board believed this would short-circuit lengthy unfair labor practice proceedings, for the legality of the clause could be tested in an election proceeding and would be determined without resort to extrinsic evidence. It was not long, however, before the Board repudiated the *Keystone* doctrine, holding that it unjustifiably created a presumption of illegality for any union security provision not expressly reflecting the precise language of the statute. In Paragon Prods. Corp. (1961), the Board announced the rule which obtains today, that "only those contracts containing a union-security provision unlawful on its face, or which has been found to be unlawful in an unfair labor practice proceeding, may not bar a representation petition." This taint extends only to provisions whose terms unequivocally go beyond the limited form of union security permitted by section 8(a)(3) and are incapable of lawful interpretation. No extrinsic evidence as to practice under the disputed provision is relevant to this determination.

Even if a union security clause is legal, the labor contract will not bar the special kind of NLRB election known as a deauthorization election. From 1947 to 1951, a union security agreement complying with the provisos to section 8(a)(3) could not be executed unless a majority of employees in the unit specifically so authorized in an election. The fact that the overwhelming proportion of employees voted in the affirmative convinced Congress to lighten the Board's burden by reversing the election sequence, that is, by permitting the parties to make a lawful union security agreement subject to a later Board election taking away that authority. Section 9(e)(1), amended in 1951, now reads:

> Upon the filing with the Board, by 30 percentum or more of the employees in a bargaining unit covered by an agreement between their employer and a labor organization made pursuant to section 8(a)(3), of a petition alleging their desire that such authority be rescinded, the Board shall take a secret ballot of the employees in such unit and certify the results thereof to such labor organization and to the employer.

Early in the life of this provision, unions argued that the contract bar should apply to deauthorization as well as to representation elections, and that, even if not, an election supporting deauthorization should not abrogate the existing union security provision but merely bar the union from negotiating such a provision in future contracts. The Board rejected both these arguments in Great Atl. & Pac. Tea Co. (1952). The Board understood Congress to permit immediate rescission of the unwanted union security clause. The only bar to such a deauthorization election is that set forth in section 9(e)(2): "No election shall be conducted pursuant to this subsection in any bargaining unit or any subdivision within which, in the preceding twelve-month period, a valid election shall have been held." The Board has held that a representation election does not bar a deauthorization election within a year; only another deauthorization election does. Monsanto Chem. Co. (1964). A deauthorization election is appropriate even if the union security clause is illegal, Andor Co. (1957) (illegal clauses ought not be treated more leniently than legal clauses, and the more protracted unfair labor practice proceeding would subject employees to the illegal clause longer than under an election); and applies to agency shop provisions as well as union shop provisions, Monsanto Chem. Co. (1964).

§ 6. Compulsory Political Contributions

Compulsory membership in a union or compulsory financial contributions to a union have consistently been challenged by union dissidents as interfering with their freedom of thought, conscience and association protected by the Bill of Rights to the Federal Constitution. (While the first and fifth amendments bar only action of the federal government, it is argued that such action is sufficiently implicated in the proviso to section 8(a)(3) which empowers employers and unions to agree to require union membership as a condition of employment.) Such a challenge first reached the Supreme Court in Railway Employes' Dept. v. Hanson (U.S.1956). The labor contract there contained a union shop provision, authorized by Section 2, Eleventh of the Railway Labor Act in language substantially identical to that of the federal Labor Act (except that the grace period for securing membership is sixty days, and that employees may be required to pay not only periodic dues and initiation fees but also "assessments (not including fines and penalties)"). The Court first rejected the argument that the contract provision was invalid under the Nebraska right-to-work law. The Railway Labor Act authorizes such union security agreements, explicitly notwithstanding the laws of any state, and the constitutional supremacy clause warranted the subordination of state law to a valid enactment of Congress under its commerce power designed to assure stability in the railroad industry. (The Railway Labor Act has no analogue to section 14(b) of the Taft-Hartley Act permitting states to outlaw union shop agreements.) The Court also rejected the claim that the union shop unconstitutionally interfered with the freedom of thought and association of dissidents coerced into membership. The Court held that Section 2, Eleventh on its face, did no more than permit the employer and union to require financial support for all persons benefitted by the union's services as bargaining representative. Such limited compulsory "membership" does not on its face impair freedom of expression, although some specific record in some other case might more directly raise the issue of dues exactions "used as a cover for forcing ideological conformity."

Precisely that issue arose five years later, in IAM v. Street (U. S.1961), another case arising under the Railway Labor Act. There, certain employees subject to a multi-carrier, multi-union labor contract resisted the payment of dues, fees and assessments to their union, "alleging that the money each was thus compelled to pay to hold his job was in substantial part used to finance the campaigns of candidates for federal and state offices whom he opposed, and to promote the propagation of political and economic doctrines, concepts and ideologies with which he disagreed." The issue posed was no longer the "facial" invalidity of Section 2, Eleventh but rather the federally authorized exaction of moneys to be used not directly in collective bargaining and grievance administration but for political causes opposed by dissident union members. A fragmented Court managed to cluster a majority about the holding that, since constitutional issues should be avoided by means of a reasonable construction of legislation, the Railway Labor Act should be construed in light of its object of eliminating "free riders" so as "to deny unions, over an employee's objection, the power to use his exacted funds to support political causes which he opposes."

> Its use to support candidates for public office, and advance political programs, is not a use which helps defray the expenses of the negotiation or administration of collective agreements, or the expenses entailed in the adjustment of grievances and disputes. In other words, it is a use which falls clearly outside the reasons advanced by the unions and accepted by Congress why authority to make union-shop agreements was justified.

Four Justices acknowledged that unions do commonly spend membership moneys to support political causes and candidates and that it would be a distortion of the statute to "construe" it as though such expenses could not come from the contributions of objecting members; yet two of those Justices held the statute properly construed to be unconstitutional while two others held it constitutional (and indeed not even government action sufficient to trigger the restrictions of the Bill of Rights).

The Court's construction of the Act thus required that a distinction be made between "the negotiation or administration of collective agreements, or the expenses entailed in the adjustment of grievance and disputes," the costs of which may be taxed against even objecting members of the bargaining unit, and the support of "political causes," which may not. While the state court had altogether enjoined the enforcement of the union shop provision, the Supreme Court overturned this remedy as far too broad, since the gist of the employees' claim lay not in the collection of moneys but in their expenditure, and since state-court injunction of the collection of union dues would interfere with the unions' "performance of those functions and duties which the Railway Labor Act places upon them to attain its goal of stability in the industry." Even an injunction against all union expenditures on political causes would sweep too broadly, and might offend the constitutional ban on state interference with political expression by the union majority. The Court suggested two possible remedies:

> One remedy would be an injunction against expenditure for political causes opposed by each complaining employee of a sum, from those moneys to be spent by the union for political purposes, which is so much of the moneys exacted from him as is the proportion of the union's total expenditures made for such political activities to the union's total budget. . . . A second remedy would be restitution to each individual employee of that portion of his money which the union expended, despite his notification, for the political causes to which he had advised the union he was opposed.

Two years after its decision in the *Street* case, the Supreme Court clarified its position on the appropriate remedies, in Brotherhood of Ry. Clerks v. Allen (U.S.1963). The Court held that while no claim is made out against the union unless the employee makes known to the union his objection to the expenditure of his dues money for political causes, "It would be impracticable to require a dissenting employee to allege and prove each distinct union political expenditure to which he objects; it is enough that he manifests his opposition to *any* political expenditures by the union." To implement the Court's earlier suggested remedies, a determination must be made of what expenditures in the record are political expenditures and the proportion which such expenditures bear to total union expenditures; "basic considerations of fairness" compel the union, with access to the pertinent facts and records, to prove the ratio of political to total expenditures, and not the individual employees. A comparable amount of the individual's total dues and fees could be ordered refunded if already paid; and future exactions could be reduced accordingly. The Court invited the defendant unions to consider the adoption of some internal union plan providing for the designation of political expenditures, the manifestation of objections by members unwilling to contribute to such expenditures and an appropriate reduction in the moneys exacted from such objecting members. A small number of unions have in fact adopted such plans, thereby providing an internal remedy for members (or nonmembers subject to valid agency shop agreements) to challenge the use of their dues money for political causes they oppose.

One such plan was recently sustained against employee attack in Reid v. UAW Dist. Lodge 1093 (10th Cir. 1973). There, plaintiff employees argued that the union had violated its duty of fair representation to unit employees by misappropriating agency fees for objectionable political expenditures. The court rejected this charge, relying on the recent amendment to the UAW constitution which accorded both members and payers of agency fees an intra-union procedure for objecting to the use of their dues for such purposes. The union constitution provided:

> Any member shall have the right to object to the expenditure of a portion of his dues money for activities or causes primarily political in nature. The approximate proportion of dues spent for such political purposes shall be determined by a committee of the International Executive Board, which shall be appointed by the President, subject to the approval of said Board. The member may perfect his objection by individually notifying the International Secretary-Treasurer of his objection by registered or certified mail; provided, however, that such objection shall be timely only during the first fourteen (14) days of Union membership and during the fourteen (14) days following each anniversary of Union membership. An objection may be continued from year-to-year by individual notifications given during each annual fourteen (14) day period.

> If an objecting member is dissatisfied with the approximate proportional allocation made by the committee of the International Executive Board, or the disposition of his objection by the International Secretary-Treasurer, he may appeal directly to the full International Executive Board and the decision of the International Executive Board shall be appealable to the Public Review Board or the Convention Appeals Committee at the option of said member.

A more recent case sustained a similar intra-union procedure (of the International Association of Machinists) against an employee fair-representation charge, rejecting the argument that the union was unfairly acting as both "judge and jury" of the claim of the protesting employee. Seay v. McDonnell Douglas Corp. (C.D.Cal.1973). The court held, "As long as the union is not administering the　.　.　. procedure in a manner that is 'arbitrary, discriminatory, or in bad faith,' it is not in breach of the duty of fair representation."

The *Seay* court also made an attempt, in extended dictum, to deal with the elusive problem left unresolved by the Supreme Court of defining the kinds of "political" expenses which cannot lawfully be taxed against an unconsenting employee. The court stated:

> Dissenting employees in an agency fee situation should not be required to support financially union expenditures as follows:
>
> One, for payments to or on behalf of any candidate for public office in connection with his campaign for election to such public office, or
>
> Two, for payments to or on behalf of any political party or organization, or
>
> Three, for the holding of any meeting or the printing or distribution of any literature or documents in support of any such candidate or political party or organization.
>
> [E]xpenditures for other purposes　.　.　. are sufficiently germane to collective bargaining to require dissenting employees who are subject to union shop or agency fee agreements to bear their share of that burden.

§ 7.　Other Constitutional Challenges: Freedom of Speech and Religion

Other constitutional attacks on the compulsory payment of union dues and fees have been levelled by two groups committed to full freedom of individual thought: radio and television commentators and Seventh Day Adventists. In Buckley v. AFTRA (2d Cir. 1974), a noted television commentator (and sometime political candidate) argued that the requirement that he pay union dues and fees before being allowed to broadcast is a denial of free speech. The court avoided the question whether there is governmental action at all when Congress in the federal Labor Act permits private parties to implement union security agreements, and held instead that such agreements could reasonably be deemed by Congress to achieve the legitimate legislative goals of minimizing industrial strife and fostering the union's ability to perform its bargaining function and eliminating the "free rider."

The courts have also sustained the union security sections of both the NLRA and the Railway Labor Act against attack on constitutional grounds by Seventh Day Adventists, who assert that their religious tenets—principally the belief that social wrongs must be cured by the conscience of the individual and not by organized group action—prevent them from financially supporting a union against their will. While acknowledging that employees have an interest in the free exercise of their religion, the courts have sustained discharge from employment for nonpayment, deeming the employees' interest to be outweighed by the governmental interest in maintaining industrial peace. Further, the union shop assessment is treated merely as a "tax" in support of the collective bargaining services of the exclusive employee representative, which does not force an employee to subscribe to any religious or political tenet or doctrine. Linscott v. Millers Falls Co. (1st Cir. 1971) (court holds that NLRA authorization of private union shop agreements constitutes governmental action; employee is not entitled to satisfy dues-paying requirement by offering to pay an equivalent amount to charity); Gray v. Gulf, M. & O.R.R. (5th Cir. 1970) (Railway Labor Act case; sets forth full statement of creed of Seventh Day Adventists).

Congress has not been unmindful of these religious claims, however, and has taken the most unusual step of sustaining them in only a single industry subject to the National Labor Relations Act. After almost forty years of exclusion from the coverage of the Labor Act, nonprofit private health care institutions were brought within the Act and the jurisdiction of the NLRB in 1974. As part of its legislative action, Congress also (in a new section 19) decreed an exception to the Act's union security provisions:

> Any employee of a health care institution who is a member of and adheres to established and traditional tenets or teachings of a bona fide religion, body, or sect which has historically held conscientious objections to joining or financially supporting labor organizations shall not be required to join or financially support any labor organization as a condition of employment; except that such employee may be required, in lieu of periodic dues and initiation fees, to pay sums equal to such dues and fees to a nonreligious charitable fund . . . .

The only apparently pertinent explanation in the legislative history of this conscientious-objector section is that it would be unduly disruptive or unfair to require the dismissal of many Seventh Day Adventists already employed in an industry which has for many years operated on the assumption of the inapplicability of the union security authorization in the proviso to section 8(a)(3) of the Labor Act. The charitable-contribution alternative appears to represent an uneasy compromise of the policies of religious freedom and abolition of the "free rider." It is, however, a compromise which arguably commends itself as much to businesses other than hospitals and nursing homes, and there is good reason to expect that employees in other industries will challenge Congress's limitation of the conscientious-objector exception to health care institutions as an unconstitutional denial of equal protection of the laws.

§ 8. State Right-To-Work Laws

Between 1944 and 1947—when the proviso to section 8(3) of the Wagner Act sheltered union security agreements as potent as the closed shop—twelve states enacted so-called right-to-work laws (either by statute or by constitutional amendment) which provided in substance that employees were not to be required to join a union as a condition of receiving or retaining a job. Today, such laws obtain in nineteen states, most of them in the more agricultural areas of the south and midwest. (These states are Alabama, Arizona, Arkansas, Florida, Georgia, Iowa, Kansas, Mississippi, Nebraska, Nevada, North Carolina, North Dakota, South Carolina, South Dakota, Tennessee, Texas, Utah, Virginia, and Wyoming; Louisiana's law applies only to agricultural workers, who fall outside the reach of the federal Labor Act.) The wording of these state provisions varies a good deal, with some states generally barring discrimination in employment so as to encourage union membership, others more vaguely barring an employment "monopoly" by a labor union, but most expressly barring the requirement of union membership (or paying dues to a union) as a condition of employment. The purpose of these laws appears in part to be the protection of employee freedom and in part to be the attraction of new business to a union-free and thus presumably lower-wage environment. The question whether these state laws could flourish under a federal law that authorized the union shop as a force for industrial stability was definitively addressed by Congress in the Taft-Hartley amendments of 1947. In spite of the strong preemptive implications of the Wagner Act (not articulated to any substantial degree by the Supreme Court until the mid-1950's), Congress established a preserve for state right-to-work laws by enacting section 14(b) of the Labor Act:

> Nothing in this Act shall be construed as authorizing the execution or application of agreements requiring membership in a labor organization as a condition of employment in any State or Territory in which such execution or application is prohibited by State or Territorial law.

Shortly after the Taft-Hartley Act, a union's constitutional attack on a state right-to-work law was rebuffed by the Supreme Court in Lincoln Fed. Union 19129 v. Northwestern Iron & Metal Co. (U.S. 1949). Just as, some years before, the Court had endorsed the union argument that a state constitutionally could, in the reasonable pursuit of industrial peace, outlaw contracts which *forbade* joining a union (the so-called yellow dog contract), the Court now marshalled the same considerations to reject the union argument that states could not constitutionally outlaw contracts which *compelled* the joining of a union. It only remained to determine how these state laws were to be interwoven with the federal statutory fabric, and on this issue the Supreme Court was to speak in two 1963 decisions, once again giving rather broad scope to the right-to-work laws.

In Retail Clerks Local 1625 v. Schermerhorn (U.S.1963), the state court had interpreted its right-to-work law to outlaw not only the union shop (requiring employees to become members) but also the agency shop (requiring employees to give the union only financial support). The union argued that section 14(b) did not cede to the states the power to invalidate the agency shop since this was not an agreement "requiring membership in a labor organization." The Court quickly rejected this argument, holding that the only kind of "membership" which may lawfully be demanded of an employee is his payment of a service fee to the union measured by periodic dues and initiation fees, and that thus the agency shop is the "practical equivalent" of an agreement requiring "membership," both under the proviso to section 8(a)(3), NLRB v. General Motors (U.S.1963), which made the agency shop lawful under federal law, and under section 14(b), which authorized states to prohibit it. The Court proceeded to address the union's second argument which was that, even if its agency shop provision was invalid—because banned by the state right-to-work law—its execution and enforcement would violate sections 8(a)(3) and 8(b)(2) and could thus be attacked only before the National Labor Relations Board. By 1963, the law of federal preemption had become sufficiently developed and rather clearly compelled the ouster of state-court jurisdiction over conduct which arguably or actually was a federal unfair labor practice. San Diego Bldg. Trades Council v. Garmon (U.S.1959). On this issue, the Court sought the benefit of reargument and the views of the NLRB.

After reargument, the Court, in Retail Clerks Local 1625 v. Schermerhorn (U.S.1963), concluded that the state-court injunction against the enforcement of the agency shop agreement was a valid remedy. Congress, by acknowledging that states could prohibit union security agreements which the federal law would protect, "chose to abandon any search for uniformity in dealing with the problems of state laws barring the execution and application of agreements authorized by Section 14(b) and decided to suffer a medley of attitudes and philosophies on the subject." Congress gave the states such overriding power that it would be anomalous to conclude that only the NLRB had the power to implement state policy. But the Court was cautious to note that the state-court injunction may run only against the "execution or application" (in the words of section 14(b)) of a union security agreement; the state is not free to enjoin a strike or picketing the object of which is to *secure* a union shop or agency shop agreement. While it may seem strange to direct the states to permit concerted activity for a contract clause while authorizing the states to enjoin the enforcement of the clause after the concerted activity has been successful, the Court took no note of an anomaly and merely reiterated that state power "begins *only with actual negotiation and execution of the type of agreement described by Section 14(b)*. Absent such an agreement, conduct arguably an unfair labor practice would be a matter for the National Labor Relations Board under *Garmon*." Perhaps the Court was concerned that certain concerted activity which Congress clearly sought to protect —such as peaceful picketing designed to induce employees to become members, at least when not outlawed by section 8(b)(7), and peaceful informational picketing designed to communicate to the public that a company is nonunion—would be too readily outlawed by state courts, particularly when a number of state right-to-work laws are extremely broadly drawn and provide in some instances for severe sanctions (including criminal penalties).

In summary, state right-to-work laws in nineteen states prohibit the *union* shop. Where such laws are vague on the question whether the *agency* shop is prohibited, state courts are free thus to construe them, and courts in the states with right-to-work laws now on the books have indeed uniformly held them to ban the agency shop. Ficek v. Boilermakers Local 647 (N.D.1974). Whether states may lawfully prohibit the *maintenance of membership* agreement has apparently not been judicially determined. In a case which arose prior to the enactment of section 14(b) (but reached the Supreme Court afterward) the Court intimated that that section would legitimate state regulation of such an agreement. Algoma Plywood Co. v. Wisconsin Bd. (U.S.1949). The union might argue that the maintenance of membership agreement does not fall within state power since, with employees free to decide whether or not to join the union, it is not an agreement "requiring membership"; the contrary argument is perhaps more compelling since, although employees are not required to join in the first instance, they are forbidden for the duration of the contract to resign membership once it is secured. There also appears to be no definitive answer to the question whether a state may prohibit a union security agreement which in substance requires only that employees pay to the union a pro rata share of the union's expenses specifically allocable to negotiating and administering the collective bargaining agreement; this would be less than membership dues and fees which also pay for social and educational programs and benefit plans which are available only to union members. It does, however, seem fairly clear that state law may not prohibit a *hiring-hall* agreement which, because the union in making referrals of employees does not discriminate on the basis of union membership, is valid under federal law. Such an agreement would not be one "requiring membership in a labor organization as a condition of employment." NLRB v. Houston Chapter, Assoc. Gen. Contractors (5th Cir.

1965). When a state may and does prohibit a union security agreement, it may remedy the violation by an injunction against its enforcement, by an order of reinstatement and backpay for the benefit of the discharged employee (or rejected applicant), or by criminal proceedings.

§ 9.   The Union Hiring Hall: Generally

In certain industries—most notably, maritime, longshoring and construction—unions provide what is in effect a job-referral service and act as a clearinghouse between employees seeking work and employers seeking workers. These industries are characterized by irregular and short-lived employment opportunities. For example, an electrical subcontractor in the construction business may have no regular employee force but rather seek qualified electricians to go to the jobsite on one date to install wires across the studded substructure of the house and will later send electricians (not always the same ones) back after the walls have been completed in order to install switchplates and fixtures. A shipowner may seek to employ a crew for a transoceanic run and return, or for a shorter run to some port along the same coast; after a long time at sea, the crewmen may not wish to ship out again but may rather prefer some days on shore to be spent with family or friends. It would be time-consuming and uneconomical for the many employers in these industries to hire on their own and for the many employees individually to search for employment.

The solution that has been worked out over time is the union-operated hiring hall, which receives from the employers requests for workers and provides workers who are qualified and available. The service can be rendered at no cost to the employer, and the union recoups its cost from membership dues and from hiring-hall fees of nonmembers. The union and employer may agree that the hiring hall is "nonexclusive," that is, that the employer is free to reject persons referred by the union and may hire from other sources; or may agree to make the hiring hall the exclusive method of recruitment. The union is expected to distribute work opportunities in accordance with some equitable principle; work on board ship will commonly be assigned in accordance with the seniority of the workers in their service within the hall's jurisdiction, and work on shore in loading and unloading ships will commonly be on a rotational basis, with work assigned to the employees who earliest completed their last preceding job and are thus at the top of a first-come first-served list. In industries where seniority with a given employer cannot be utilized to achieve job security, the union hiring hall can afford comparable benefits.

Union control over the referral process has occasionally, however, tempted union officials to engage in invidious discrimination—to give preference in referrals to union members rather than to nonmembers, or to give preference to those union members who are most zealous in their attendance at meetings or in their support of the incumbent officials, or simply to friends, relatives or persons of the same color. The union-operated hiring hall thus frequently went hand-in-hand with the closed shop, where union membership in good standing was a condition of referral and thus of employment; the union could control the volume and qualifications of the workforce at the source. To the extent that the parties make union membership a condition of referral and employment, such an agreement would clearly constitute a violation by the employer of section 8(a)(3)— since it would lack the thirty-day grace period for joining the union, which makes the union shop lawful under the proviso to that section —and a violation of section 8(b)(2) by the union. But exclusive referral or preference of union members is not a necessary adjunct of the union-operated hiring hall, and it has been the task of the Board and the courts to test the hiring hall against the directive in those two sections barring "discrimination." Section 8(a)(3) forbids the employer "by discrimination in regard to hire or tenure of employment . . . to encourage or discourage membership in any labor organization"; and section 8(b)(2) forbids the union "to cause or attempt to cause an employer to discriminate against an employee in violation of subsection (a)(3) or to discriminate against an employee with respect to whom membership in such organization has been denied or terminated on some ground other than his failure to tender" dues and initiation fees. The key issue is thus whether the hiring hall arrangement, as written or as implemented in practice, works a union-induced discrimination which encourages union membership.

In 1959, the Board—in the face of several appellate decisions— held that the exclusive hiring hall did indeed violate sections 8(a)(3) and 8(b)(2). In Mountain Pac. Chap. of Assoc. Gen. Contractors, Inc. (1957), *enf't denied* (9th Cir. 1959), a group of construction companies contracted with a local of the Hodcarriers' Union and provided that "The recruitment of employees shall be the responsibility of the Union . . . . The Employers will call upon the Local Union in whose territory the work is to be accomplished to furnish qualified workmen in the classifications herein contained." The employers reserved the right to look elsewhere for workmen if the union could not refer anyone within forty-eight hours. The Board found the agreement to be illegal on its face, without regard to extrinsic evidence of actual union favoritism for union members, since the employer had completely relinquished the hiring function to the union. Such an arrangement enhances union power and creates an inescapable inference of encouragement of union membership, for "it is reasonable to infer that the Union will be guided in its concession by an eye towards winning compliance with a membership obligation or union fealty in some other respect" and that employees will feel constrained to offer such fealty. The Board was prepared to uphold some hiring hall agreements, but only if on their face they negated the inference of encouragement of union membership by explicitly providing that: (1) selection of applicants for referral to jobs shall be on a non-discriminatory basis without regard to union membership; (2) the employer is free to reject any applicant referred by the union; and (3) the parties are to post notices informing all employees and job applicants of these safeguards and the functioning of the hiring hall.

The Supreme Court soon had the opportunity to consider the Board's ruling that, absent these three explicit safeguards, the exclusive hiring hall is illegal per se. The Court ruled otherwise, in Local 357, Teamsters v. NLRB (U.S.1961). There, an agreement between the union and a group of motor truck operators required that hiring of casual employees be done through the union's dispatching service, with workers being referred on a seniority basis "irrespective of whether such employee is or is not a member of the Union." An employee who secured casual employment without being dispatched by the union was subsequently discharged on union request, and the Board found the parties to have violated sections 8(a)(3) and 8(b)(2) for failure of the agreement on its face to comply with the *Mountain Pacific* requirements. The Supreme Court denied enforcement, pointing out that the agreement specifically provided for referrals on a nondiscriminatory basis, that the discharged worker was in fact a union member, that Congress understood the hiring hall to serve a useful economic purpose, that while operation of the hiring hall might encourage membership, the Labor Act bars only such encouragement as is brought about by "discrimination," and that there was no record support for the Board's inference that the dispatching service was used invidiously to discriminate contrary to its express terms. "[T]he Board is confined to determining whether discrimination has in fact been practiced. If hiring halls are to be subjected to regulation that is less selective and more pervasive, Congress not the Board is the agency to do it."

§ 10. Criteria for Hiring-Hall Referral

The *Local 357* case holds, in effect, that unless a hiring-hall agreement is on its face discriminatory, the Board may hold it unlawful only if there is specific evidence from which likely discrimination and encouragement of union membership may be inferred. As the Board recently stated in Local 99, IBEW (Crawford Elec. Constr. Co.) (1974), union favoritism for its own members in hiring-hall referrals

> is no less unlawful when accomplished by discriminatory administration of benign contract provisions or by fashioning seemingly objective criteria for referral priority which in fact only union members can meet.

It is, for example, clear that the union violates the Labor Act when it induces (or attempts to induce) the employer to depart from the "benign" and nondiscriminatory terms of the labor contract in order to afford preferential hiring treatment to union members. Local 1332, Longshoremen (1965). On the other hand, it is not unlawful for the parties to provide, whether in writing or by custom, that referrals shall depend upon a period of work experience or residence within the particular geographical area. Such referral criteria lack sufficient relationship to union membership or activities to warrant any inference of discrimination encouraging such membership or activities.

There are, however, a number of cases in which the contract terms and practices are neither so clearly discriminatory nor so clearly lawful, and the Board must scrutinize referral criteria with care in order to assure that seemingly impartial criteria are not being employed to give union members a preference in referral or hiring. Thus, in one case, a union gave preference in referrals from an exclusive hiring hall to persons presently unemployed because their bargaining representative had called a strike or because some other employees' strike had resulted in their loss of work, and assigned so-called "casual" workers to a lower referral category. In Pacific Maritime Ass'n (1968), this arrangement was upheld by the Board, which overturned the findings of the trial examiner that the employer had violated sections 8(a)(1) and (3) and that the union had violated sections 8(b)(1) and (2). The Board found no evidence that the preferred category consisted principally of union members, the preference in referral did not depend on the applicant's actual participation in a strike, and the record showed that the preferred workers were more dependable, more capable and safer workers than the "casuals."

Similarly, a hiring-hall provision which requires as a condition of referral that the worker have passed a union-administered skills test will not be unlawful, provided the test is open to all workers regardless of union membership and is administered fairly. Local 42, Heat Insulators (Catalytic Constr. Co.) (1967). Of course, if the union will not administer the test unless the worker has applied for union membership, that is unlawful. Local 99, IBEW (Crawford Elec. Constr. Co.) (1974). And if the test is available only to those who satisfy certain work-experience requirements, and those requirements in turn can be satisfied only by union members (by virtue of an earlier illegal union security agreement), then the testing criterion, neutral on its face, will be held discriminatory. Local 269, IBEW (Arthur J. Hazeltine) (1964), enf'd (3d Cir. 1966) (union discriminated in violation of section 8(b)(2), and employer is charged with knowledge thereof and violates section 8(a)(3)). Similarly, while it is lawful for the employer and the union to agree that priority in referral shall be given to employees who have previously worked for the signatory employer (or more typically for one or more members of an employer association), J–M Co. (1969), it is discriminatory and unlawful to place an applicant in a lower referral category or to refuse to refer him altogether because he has not previously worked in a bargaining unit covered by a labor contract to which the signatory union was a party, Photographers Local 659 (MPO–TV) (1972), *enf'd per curiam* (D.C.Cir. 1973). In short, it is lawful to favor those who have previously worked for the employer but not to favor those who have previously been members of the union.

In the construction industry, where the hiring hall is a pervasive institution, the principles just set forth have been endorsed by Congress which in 1959 enacted section 8(f):

> It shall not be an unfair labor practice . . . for an employer engaged primarily in the building and construction industry to make an agreement covering employees engaged (or who, upon their employment, will be engaged) in the building and construction industry with a labor organization of which building and construction employees are members . . . because . . . such agreement specifies minimum training or experience qualifications for employment or provides for priority in opportunities for employment based upon length of service with such employer, in the industry or in the particular geographical area . . . .

Just as the union may not use its referral power under a hiring hall arrangement to induce nonmembers to join, it may not use that power to induce union members to become diligent union members. It is unlawful, for example, for the union to deny referral to a union member because of his failure to pay a fine which is due the union. On its face, this rule "encourages union membership" under section 8(b)(2), which contemplates a broad reading of "membership" to include union activities and obligations; to immunize any such "facially" discriminatory practice, the union bears the burden of demonstrating that its refusal to refer is "necessary to its effective function in representing employees." Carpenters Local 1437 (1974). As already noted, even the union shop agreement—the strongest lawful union security arrangement—may not lawfully be used to extract payment of fines as a condition of employment.

The union is, however, entitled to exact certain obligations from the employee that are directly related to the service of the hiring hall, as a condition of referral or of continued employment. Thus, if the hiring hall is exclusive, an employer's hiring or retention of an employee who has not been referred through the hiring hall is a contract violation, which the union may challenge by requiring that the employee be discharged; this will not violate section 8(b)(2). Operating Eng'rs Local 542 (Ralph A. Marino) (1965) (employer had brought current employee from different geographic area into area covered by labor contract). The union may also lawfully exact from the job applicant a reasonable fee for the use of the services of the hiring hall. The union and employer may therefore agree that no person shall be eligible for referral to a job if he has been late eight or more times in paying his pro rata share of the hiring hall operating expenses. Pacific Maritime Ass'n (1965). Indeed, there is no illegal discrimination when a hiring hall fee is charged, as is the custom, only to nonmembers of the union; union members support the hiring hall through their initiation fees and periodic dues. Local 825, Operating Eng'rs (H. John Homan Co.) (1962) (members paid, in addition to initiation fees and assessments, monthly dues of $10, with $1.10 remitted to the international; while hiring hall service fee charged to nonmembers was $9.00).

It remains somewhat unclear, however, what the union may fairly charge nonmembers as a fee for the use of the hiring hall. The Board initially was willing to permit the union to charge as a condition of referral a monthly fee equivalent to the monthly dues paid by union members. The Board suggested that the union was according to the nonmember the benefits not only of referral from the hiring hall but also economic benefits negotiated for the entire bargaining unit which were available to the worker during and after his employment. *Ibid.* Soon after, however, in a case in which the union's only justification for the amount of its fee to nonmembers was its intention to exact an amount equivalent to monthly union dues, the Board was reversed by the court of appeals, which held that the hiring hall fee could not lawfully exceed the worker's pro rata share of the union's direct expenses of operating the hall as well as some amount of the union's general expenses reasonably chargeable thereto. Local 138, Operating Eng'rs v. NLRB (2d Cir. 1963). On remand, the Board ordered that the union reimburse the employee to the extent that the monthly service fee ($10.00) exceeded this pro rata share; effectively, the employee's reimbursement of $3.50 per month represented his share of the union's "institutional" expenses, such as the per capita taxes paid to the international, litigation expenses, advertisements, conventions, entertainment, members' death benefits and union pins. J. J. Hagerty, Inc. (1965), *enf'd* (2d Cir. 1967). The Board rather clearly permitted the union to tax the nonmember for its expenses in policing the existing labor contract, but the court of appeals (although enforcing the Board's reimbursement order) appeared just as clearly to suggest that this was excessive; it stated the union had committed an unfair labor practice "to the extent it charged the permit men a fee not reasonably related to the cost of providing the job referral service."

Of course, most of these difficulties may be avoided—at least after the applicant is hired—if the union is in a position to secure from the employer a union shop or agency shop agreement as well as a hiring hall agreement, for then all employees will be required to pay the union an amount equivalent to dues and initiation fees uniformly paid by union members. (As noted above, section 8(f) permits construction unions and employers to shorten the pre-membership grace period to seven days.)   While the union normally enforces these union security arrangements after the employee has been at work, by demanding his discharge for nonpayment after the grace period, a hiring hall agreement in certain circumstances may permit their enforcement "at the hiring hall level," that is by a refusal to refer for work in the first instance.   Thus, where a union represented employees in a multiemployer unit, and an employee working for one employer had been delinquent in paying his initiation fee under a lawful union shop agreement, the union lawfully refused to refer him when he sought to transfer to another employer within the unit; it would have been unnecessarily cumbersome to require that the union first refer the employee and then promptly demand his discharge, as it could lawfully do for his fee delinquency.   Mayfair Coat & Suit Co. (1963).

§ 11.   Dues Checkoff

The collection of membership dues can be a most time-consuming and costly enterprise for a union.   The administrative expense can be drastically reduced if the employer agrees to deduct from the earnings of union members—as it would deduct amounts for taxes, insurance and charitable contributions—an amount equal to union dues and to pay that amount for all members directly to the union.   Such an agreement, which most commonly accompanies a union shop, agency shop or maintenance of membership provision, is known as a dues checkoff.   Like union security provisions generally, the checkoff is a subject about which the employer must bargain in good faith if the union wishes to discuss it at the negotiating table.   United States Gypsum Co. (1951), *enf'd as mdf'd on other grounds* (5th Cir. 1953). But the checkoff is a relatively mild form of union security, for it does not require that an employee join or remain a member of a union, or pay union dues; it simply prescribes the manner in which dues shall be paid, by deductions from earnings rather than by a monthly check directly from the employee to the union.   Because of this difference, the checkoff is not an agreement that is sheltered by the proviso to section 8(a)(3), and if the employer and union agree that an employee, without his authorization freely given, must pay dues through checkoff on pain of job-related discipline, this constitutes discrimination to encourage union membership (broadly understood) and is a violation of section 8(a)(3) by the employer and of section 8(b)(2) by the union.   NLRB v. Brotherhood of Ry. Clerks (Yellow Cab Co.)   (5th Cir. 1974).   The illegality is aggravated when the involuntary checkoff benefits a minority union, for then the employer is extending improper assistance in violation of section 8(a)(2), Hampton Merchants Ass'n (1965), particularly when a question of representation has been generated by the demands of a second union, Guy's Food, Inc. (1966), *enf'd* (D.C.Cir. 1967).

In short, a dues checkoff is lawful only if it is voluntarily authorized by the particular employee. Whether there is voluntary authorization is often a difficult question. The Board has held that the union is not free to induce employees to authorize the checkoff by limiting the employees' alternative to the cumbersome personal delivery of dues to the out-of-state offices of the international union. American Screw Co. (1958). Nor will a checkoff authorization—unless in explicit terms—be interpreted to authorize the employer to deduct assessments, beyond periodic dues, collected by the union to support strikers at other locals. NLRB v. Food Fair Stores (3d Cir. 1962). The allowable duration of the checkoff also depends upon the authorization given by the employee. Thus, if his employment is terminated, so too is the authority to checkoff, and it is not automatically revived if the employee is subsequently rehired. NLRB v. Brotherhood of Ry. Clerks (Yellow Cab Co.) (5th Cir. 1974) (if employee quits, subjective reasons or intention to return are not relevant). Where, however, there has been an interruption in service, it may be a factual question whether the employment relationship has actually been severed; if it has not, the earlier authorization remains effective. NLRB v. Industrial Towel & Uniform Serv. (6th Cir. 1973) (authorization not terminated when employee left work because of illness and returned at pay rate higher than normal for new employees and without union charge of customary initiation fee).

Even in the midst of the period for which the employee has authorized checkoff, the authorization may be revoked if the union has lost a deauthorization election under section 9(e), a majority of unit employees having voted to rescind the union's authority to make a union shop or agency shop agreement. The Board has noted that the checkoff authorization was at its inception premised on the employee's obligation under the labor contract to join the union or to pay union dues, and once this obligation is terminated by the deauthorization election, the employee should be free immediately to terminate the payment of dues by checkoff. Penn Cork & Closures, Inc. (1965). If, however, the union is voted out in a representation election held during the term of its contract, that alone does not destroy the contract or any union shop or checkoff provision contained therein, and the employer is obliged to continue the checkoff pursuant to employee authorization, at least until a new contract is executed by the new representative. Fender Musical Instruments (1969) (the timing of a representation election during a contract term is designed to foster contract stability, while the deauthorization election is designed to permit employees to veto the union security provision).

As a practical matter, the duration of an employee's checkoff authorization will be limited to one year or, if sooner, the termination date of the contract. That is because direct payment of dues by employer to union beyond that anniversary date is unlawful and exposes both parties to criminal liability. Such is the mandate of section 302 of the Labor Act, enacted as part of the Taft-Hartley amendments of 1947, a provision designed to counter employer bribery of union officials and union extortion directed against employers. Section 302(a) declares that "It shall be unlawful for any employer . . . to pay, lend, or deliver, or agree to pay, lend, or deliver, any money or other thing of value . . . to any representative of any of his employees who are employed in an industry affecting commerce"; and section 302(b) declares it unlawful for a union representative (indeed, for "any person") to "request, demand, receive, or accept, or agree to receive or accept, any payment, loan, or delivery of any money or other thing of value prohibited by subsection (a)." Section 302(d) declares a willful violation of these sections to be a misdemeanor punishable by a fine of not more than $10,000 or imprisonment for not more than one year, or both. In order to shelter employer payments to a union under a checkoff authorization, section 302(c)(4) provides:

> The provisions of this section shall not be applicable . . . with respect to money deducted from the wages of employees in payment of membership dues in a labor organization: Provided, That the employer has received from each employee, on whose account such deductions are made, a written assignment which shall not be irrevocable for a period of more than one year, or beyond the termination date of the applicable collective agreement, whichever occurs sooner . . . .

These provisions are enforceable by the Department of Justice rather than the NLRB.

In keeping with the usual maxim of stricter construction of criminal statutes than civil statutes, and in view of the different purposes of sections 8(a)(3) and 302(c)(4), the term "membership dues" in the latter section has been interpreted to permit the employer lawfully to deduct (and pay to the union) fines and assessments as well as periodic dues and initiation fees; payment of fines and assessments may not, however, be treated as "membership" obligations upon which an employee's job may depend under the proviso to section 8(a)(3). Mine Workers Local 515 v. American Zinc, Lead & Smelting Co. (9th Cir. 1963). Indeed, the principle has been firmly established that the question of legality of a checkoff arrangement under section 302 is completely independent of its implications under section 8 (unfair labor practices) or section 9 (representation elections) of the NLRA. Crown Prods. Co. (1952) (labor contract bars election, in spite of checkoff provision illegal under section 302). As the Board said in Salant & Salant, Inc. (1950):

> [T]he Act itself and its legislative history compel the conclusion that Congress did not intend the newly created limitations on checkoff in Section 302 to have any impact on the

unfair labor practice jurisdiction of this Board under Section 8, so as either to create or not create a *per se* violation of Section 8 solely on the basis of a violation of those limitations. In our opinion, the intent of Congress was rather to leave undisturbed the application by the Board to checkoff, as well as other conduct not specifically proscribed by amendments to Section 8, its preexisting criteria for determining whether such conduct as is engaged in constitutes a violation of the broad proscriptions of Section 8. The intent was neither to supplement, nor to detract from, such proscription of checkoff as Section 8 imposes completely apart from, and independently of, the restrictions on checkoff in Section 302.

It is not necessary, in order to avoid criminal liability under section 302, that the checkoff authorization terminate automatically after one year. So long as the employee is given at the end of the year some reasonable period in which to exercise his statutory power to revoke, the union and employer may provide that the authorization will be automatically renewed after each anniversary date if the employee is silent. Monroe Lodge 770, IAM v. Litton Bus. Systems (W. D.Va.1971), *remanded on other grounds* (4th Cir. 1972).

Unlike a union shop or an agency shop, the checkoff does not in itself "require membership" in the union, so that while the former two kinds of union security may pursuant to section 14(b) of the Labor Act be outlawed or regulated by state right-to-work laws, the states are not permitted to modify the rules of federal law that apply to the checkoff. Thus, a labor contract provision for checkoff of dues under voluntary authorizations irrevocable for a year is valid under federal law and may not be struck down under a state statute barring any period of irrevocability. Sea Pak v. Industrial Employees (S.D. Ga.1969), *opinion adopted and aff'd per curiam* (5th Cir. 1970). But certain important relationships between the checkoff and the union shop or agency shop should be noted. As stated above, when the checkoff accompanies the union or agency shop in a labor contract, the employee is free to revoke the checkoff authorization (even in mid-term) whenever the union security agreement is dissolved by a deauthorization election under section 9(e). Moreover, if the labor contract does contain both a union security and a checkoff provision, the authorization of checkoff is equivalent to the tender of dues to the union; a union request for discharge of that employee will violate section 8(b)(2) and the employer will not be able to assert as a defense to a section 8(a)(3) charge that it was unaware that the union's request for discharge was for reasons other than failure to tender dues. Electric Auto-Lite Co. (1950).

§ 12.   Procedure: Parties, Remedies, Period of Limitations

In most instances in which it is held that a union security agreement unlawfully encourages union membership, liability will rest with both the employer under section 8(a)(3) (and often section 8(a)(2) for illegal assistance to the union) and the union under section 8(b)(2).   Either may be the party charged before the NLRB, whether individually or jointly.   On occasion, the employer will claim that any participation on its part in an illicit union security arrangement was unknowing and without discriminatory intent.   Thus, the employer may seek to impose exclusive liability for an illegal hiring hall agreement upon the union, asserting that it was the union which discriminated in its referrals from the hall and that the company merely accepted the union referrals in good faith.   This will normally not be a defense to the employer.   As the court held in Lummus Co. v. NLRB (D.C.Cir. 1964):

> [W]here an employer who is a party to an exclusive hiring hall agreement either has actual notice, or may reasonably be charged with notice, that an applicant has been unlawfully denied referral by the union, the employer's refusal to hire, if based upon the applicant's failure to obtain referral, is a violation of § 8(a)(3) and (1).   And, where the agreement itself, either on its face or by reference to another agreement or to union rules, requires discrimination, or where the discriminatory acts were widespread or repeated or notorious, the employer might reasonably be charged with notice of those acts.

The remedy for illegal discharge requires that the company or union or both are to cease and desist, to post notices, and "jointly and severally" to pay backpay.   Pinkerton's Nat'l Detective Agency, Inc. (1950), enf'd (9th Cir. 1953).   If the employer is a party before the Board, reinstatement may of course be ordered; if only the union is a party, it may be ordered to notify the employee and the company that it has no objection to reinstatement.   Pen & Pencil Workers Local 19593 (1950).   If the union is sole respondent, it may also be required to bear full liability for backpay.   Radio Officers' Union v. NLRB (U.S.1954).   It is also proper, given the comparative degree of culpability, to impose primary liability for backpay on one party and only secondary (or surety) liability on the other.   NLRB v. Local 138, Operating Eng'rs (2d Cir. 1961) (union primarily liable).

The one rather controversial remedy is the so-called Brown-Olds remedy, requiring the reimbursement of all dues and fees collected pursuant to an illegal union security agreement.   The Board imposed this remedy upon the union in Plumbing & Pipefitters Local 231 (Brown-Olds Plumbing & Heating Corp.) (1956), regardless whether the employees paying the dues had done so willingly (indeed had been union members prior to the execution of the agreement) or had been coerced into doing so. Forcing the union to disgorge all initiation fees and dues for all of its members, often covering a very substantial period of time, was commonly conceded to be a drastic remedy, sometimes costing the union tens of thousands of dollars, and clearly designed to discourage illegal union security agreements. The Supreme Court soon found this to be punitive to the extent the record failed to demonstrate that the employees had been coerced by the agreement into becoming or remaining members. Carpenters Local 60 v. NLRB (U.S.1961). Without such record evidence, " 'reimbursing a lot of old-time union men' by refunding their dues is not a remedial measure in the competence of the Board to impose." The Board has the discretion—with a view toward the particular party or parties before it as respondent—to impose an order of reimbursement of dues and fees either upon the employer, the union, both jointly and severally, or both pursuant to some method of apportionment depending upon culpability. Komatz Constr., Inc. v. NLRB (8th Cir. 1972). Thus, in Burgreen Contracting Co. (1972), the order of reimbursement was directed exclusively against the union which used economic coercion to force an unwilling employer to enter into an unlawful agreement.

The Board has been imaginative in issuing remedies for a union's discriminatory operation of a hiring hall. In J. J. Hagerty, Inc. (1962), *enf'd as mdf'd* (2d Cir. 1963), the Board ordered the union to set up a nondiscriminatory hiring and referral system in consultation with the Board's regional director, to keep permanent records of its hiring and referral operation and to make those records available to the regional director for a one-year period, to submit quarterly reports about the employment of named discriminatees (indicating when and how often they applied for referral and were in fact referred by the union, and the duration of each employment), and to permit the regional director to make spot checks of the union's hiring and referral system. On appeal, the court deleted only the first of the Board's listed remedies, concluding that the Board could not require a union to set up a hiring hall.

Several cases raise a question as to the timeliness of an attack upon a union security agreement when tested by the six-month limitations period of section 10(b) of the Labor Act. In Local Lodge 1424, IAM v. NLRB (Bryan Mfg. Co.) (U.S.1960), the union and employer had executed a union security agreement at a time when the union lacked majority status. The employees filed an unfair labor practice charge some ten months later, claiming that the violation was a continuing wrong extending into the six-month limitations period. The Supreme Court disagreed, and announced a significant distinction between two kinds of unfair labor practices:

> The first is one where occurrences within the six-month limitations period in and of themselves may constitute, as a substantive matter, unfair labor practices. There, earlier

events may be utilized to shed light on the true character of matters occurring within the limitations period; and for that purpose Section 10(b) ordinarily does not bar such evidentiary use of anterior events. The second situation is that where conduct occurring within the limitations period can be charged to be an unfair labor practice only through reliance on an earlier unfair labor practice. There the use of the earlier unfair labor practice is not merely "evidentiary," since it does not simply lay bare a putative current unfair labor practice. Rather, it serves to cloak with illegality that which was otherwise lawful.

The Court found the alleged wrongdoing in the case before it to be entirely dependent upon the union's lack of majority status when the agreement was signed ten months before. Accordingly, the charge was untimely and the case dismissed.

CHAPTER XXIX

UNION DISCIPLINE OF MEMBERS

§ 1. Background: Supreme Court Decisions Under Section 8(b) (1)(A)

Section 8(b)(1)(A) of the Labor Act declares that it shall be an unfair labor practice for a union "to restrain or coerce employees in the exercise of their rights guaranteed in section 7." Section 7 accords employees the right to form, join or assist unions and the right to engage in concerted activities, and also "the right to refrain from any or all of such activities." Congress's central intention was to forbid the use by unions against nonmembers of the kinds of intrusive economic and physical threats sometimes used by employers against union supporters and barred by section 8(a)(1). Congress also forbade union attempts at disciplining nonmembers or recalcitrant members which took the form of inducing the employer to revoke job benefits (or indeed to terminate the job itself). Congress addressed this problem in section 8(b)(2), which declares it unlawful for a union "to cause or attempt to cause an employer to discriminate against an employee in violation of" section 8(a)(3). Historically, however, the major form of union discipline has been neither threats of physical reprisal nor inducement of discharge from employment but rather internal union sanctions, such as expulsion, suspension of fine. Union constitutions and bylaws commonly itemize membership wrongs against the union, stipulate the possible sanctions and provide for procedures within the union for charges, trial and penalties. Congress in 1947 declared an apparent intention not to interfere with these "internal" union measures by enacting as a part of section 8(b)(1)(A) a proviso: "Provided, That this paragraph shall not impair the right of a labor organization to prescribe its own rules with respect to the acquisition or retention of membership therein."

In a number of cases initiated before the National Labor Relations Board, complaints have been brought against unions for using expulsion, fines and court proceedings against members who have engaged in conduct arguably protected by section 7. These cases present a conflict between the congressional desire not to intrude upon internal union policing of its membership and of their obligations to the collectivity, on the one hand, and on the other the congressional desire to shelter employees who choose to assert their independence of the union by filing unfair labor practice charges against it, by petitioning for its decertification, by crossing its picket line, or by flouting its rules relating to productivity on the job. In an effort to accommodate these policies, the Board and courts have dramatically departed from the literal text of section 8(b)(1)(A) and have created what might be called a "common law" of union discipline.   (In addition, section 101(a) of the Landrum-Griffin Act of 1959 gives union members court-enforceable immunities from discipline for stipulated improper reasons, such as for freely expressing controversial views at union meetings, and court-enforceable rights to fair procedures in disciplinary trials within the union.   29 U.S.C.A. § 411(a).)

The first major decision in the development of that common law was that of the Supreme Court in NLRB v. Allis-Chalmers Mfg. Co. (U.S.1967).   There, members of two locals of the United Automobile Workers crossed the union's picket lines to work during a strike, and were fined (in accordance with due union procedures) in amounts ranging from $20 to $100 for violation of the UAW constitution and bylaws by "conduct unbecoming a Union member."   Some of the members refused to pay and one of the locals secured a judgment in a state court against one of its members in the amount of the fine.   Although the Board, in dismissing the complaint against the union under section 8(b)(1)(A), relied upon the proviso, the Supreme Court held instead that the underlying ban on union restraint and coercion was altogether irrelevant to union fines for strikebreaking.   The Court emphasized that membership support of a union strike effort is central to the union's success in collective bargaining and that Congress had no intention to interfere with union measures designed to implement internal discipline.   While expulsion from membership for strikebreaking was clearly a lawful sanction, given the proviso, the fine—which was court-enforceable as part of a "contract" between union and members—should also be deemed proper, since for the strong union it is a less harsh sanction than is expulsion and for the weak union it may be the only effective means for maintaining discipline.   The majority opinion emphasized that Congress's object has been to outlaw only two forms of union discipline: coercive threats of reprisal (commonly directed against nonmembers) and attempts to affect the relationship between the employee and his employer through job discipline.   A fine against a member, backed by a threat or actuality of litigation, is neither.   A dissenting opinion for four Justices concluded that court-enforceable fines for refusing to join the strike were "restraint or coercion" against employees who would wish to "refrain from" engaging in concerted activities, and that such fines were not sheltered by the proviso, which excused only expulsion from membership.

Remarkably, the Court in its next major decision in this area held that the union could violate section 8(b)(1)(A) by expulsion from membership.   In NLRB v. Industrial Union of Marine Workers (U.S.1968), a union member seeking to challenge the conduct of his local president failed to exhaust the internal union remedy afforded by the union constitution and proceeded instead to file an unfair labor practice charge against the union, for which the union expelled him from membership. The expulsion in turn produced a charge of violation of section 8(b)(1)(A), which was upheld by the NLRB and ultimately by the Supreme Court. The Court held that while section 8(b)(1) does not interfere with union self-regulation "where its legitimate internal affairs are concerned," there are "considerations of public policy" that come into play when a union rule penalizes a member for filing an unfair labor practice charge. The six-month statute of limitations upon the filing of charges and the incapacity of the Board to institute its own proceedings highlight the need for unobstructed recourse of private individuals to the Board. "Any coercion used to discourage, retard, or defeat that access is beyond the legitimate interests of a labor organization." The decision represented an evolution beyond *Allis-Chalmers*. First, the Court acknowledged that certain methods of discipline wholly "internal" to the union in their operation could be "coercion," even when it is expulsion from membership which is so clearly addressed by the proviso to section 8(b)(1)(A). Second, quite apart from the method of discipline, the Court announced that the object of the discipline could be policed for consistency with undefined "considerations of public policy."

The next year, the Court formulated a more comprehensive statement of principle in Scofield v. NLRB (U.S.1969). There, members of the UAW who worked for the Wisconsin Motor Corporation on a piecework basis were subject to a union rule which had since 1938 imposed a ceiling on the wages that members could earn each day in excess of the negotiated machine rate; if daily piecework earnings exceeded that ceiling, a member could not collect them immediately but had to have the employer "bank" them for a future day when earnings fell below the ceiling. When several union members demanded and received immediate payment for work above the ceiling rate, the union fined them between $50 and $100, suspended them from membership and, when several refused to pay the fines, commenced an action for their collection in state court. Their claim that the union's conduct violated section 8(b)(1)(A) was rejected by the Board and ultimately by the Supreme Court. The Court announced a principle which has since been relied upon by Board and courts:

> . . . § 8(b)(1) leaves a union free to enforce a properly adopted rule which reflects a legitimate union interest, impairs no policy Congress has imbedded in the labor laws, and is reasonably enforced against union members who are free to leave the union and escape the rule.

The Court found the union rule, designed to limit productivity under a piecework system, to reflect a "legitimate union interest" in deterring employer speedups, fostering health and safety and promoting collective bargaining strength. Nor did the rule and the fine contravene any public policy, a standard which the Court articulated with greater specificity than in *Marine Workers:*

> The union rule here left the collective bargaining process unimpaired, breached no collective contract, required no pay for unperformed service, induced no discrimination by the employer against any class of employees and presents no dereliction by the union of its duty of fair representation. In light of this, and the acceptable manner in which the rule was enforced, vindicating a legitimate union interest, it is impossible to say that it contravened any policy of the act.

§ 2. Limitations Upon Union Power to Discipline

On the basis of *Allis-Chalmers, Marine Workers* and *Scofield,* and with a glance at the Board and court decisions that have followed, one may draw the following conclusions about the power of a union to promulgate and enforce a rule disciplining members whose conduct appears to be protected by section 7.

The union may not enforce otherwise legitimate internal rules, for example forbidding members to engage in strikebreaking, by threatening or effecting job-related sanctions, such as demotion or transfer to a less desirable position, discharge, or blacklisting with future employers. Teamsters Local 1040 (Dr. Pepper Bottling Co.) (1969) (threat to blacklist). Nor may the union threaten to enforce an otherwise legitimate rule by threats of physical violence. National Cash Register Co. v. NLRB (6th Cir. 1972). Nor may a union that has lawful grounds for imposing a fine use those grounds as a defense when in truth the fine was imposed for impermissible reasons. Carpenters Local 22 (Graziano Constr. Co.) (1972) (union rules used as pretext to fine member impermissibly for opposing union candidate).

To be valid, a union rule must further a "legitimate union interest." Presumably, it will be necessary that the rule further, or prevent hindrance of, the union's fulfilling its duty as exclusive bargaining agent. Examples are a rule banning the crossing of the union's picket line, since solidarity in a strike is essential to the union's use of economic power in support of bargaining demands, as the Supreme Court observed in *Allis-Chalmers;* or a rule banning the crossing of a lawful picket line erected by a sister union, since this will induce reciprocal support by the sister union for one's own picket line, see American Newspaper Guild Local 35 (Washington Post Co.) (1970); or a rule, such as the productivity ceiling in *Scofield,* which bars a worsening of working conditions by speedups or unsafe procedures. It has also been held that the union may permissibly punish members who work with nonunion employees, Glasser v. NLRB (2d Cir. 1968) (members of musicians' union fined for playing alongside nonmembers); or who disrupt the operation of the union's hiring hall, Carpenters Local 1913 (Fixtures Unlimited) (1971), *enf'd mem.* (9th

Cir. 1972) (loud and abusive criticism of hiring hall officials, in presence of other members); or (although as will be noted shortly below, this may be a dubious precedent) who fail to attend union meetings, Minneapolis Star & Tribune Co. (1954).

The bulk of the case law dealing with union discipline develops a number of restrictions upon the kind of member conduct for which the union may fine or expel, and these restrictions are explained either by finding that the union's interest is not a "legitimate" one or, what amounts to the same thing, that the discipline contravenes the policies of the Labor Act.

(1) *Union rules restricting a member's access to the NLRB.* The Supreme Court in NLRB v. Industrial Union of Marine Workers (U.S.1968) held that a union may not by threat of expulsion from membership block or even require a temporary delay in the filing of unfair labor practice charges against the union; this, in spite of the proviso to section 8(b)(1)(A) which purports to shelter union rules regarding acquisition or retention of employment. The Board has also held that it is an unfair labor practice for the union to impose a fine upon a member for filing charges. Local 138, Operating Eng'rs (Skura) (1964) (union required exhaustion of internal appeals). The Board reasoned that no private group is free to exclude access to the NLRB to redress a violation of the Act, and the union fine coerces just as much as does an employer reprisal for filing a charge, which constitutes a violation of section 8(a)(4). Relief against the union may also be sought directly by the aggrieved member in a federal court action for violation of section 101(a)(4) of the Labor Management Reporting and Disclosure Act of 1959 (the Landrum-Griffin Act), which provides that "No labor organization shall limit the right of any member thereof to institute an action in any court, or in a proceeding before any administrative agency, irrespective of whether or not the labor organization or its officers are named as defendants or respondents in such action or proceeding . . . ." (29 U.S.C.A. § 411(a)(4).) The Board and courts have extended the protection of section 8(b)(1) to the member who merely encourages another to file a charge. Philadelphia Moving Pictures Mach. Operators Local 307 (1966), *enf'd* (3d Cir. 1967).

Somewhat curiously, the Board and courts have been more tolerant of union discipline of members who attack the union's status before the NLRB not in unfair labor practice proceedings but instead by petitioning to decertify the union as bargaining representative. The reason given is that the union has a more legitimate interest when "union members have resorted to the Board for the purpose of attacking the very existence of their union rather than as an effort to compel it to abide by the act." Tawas Tube Prods., Inc. (1965). (The distinction is not altogether convincing, since there seems to be little difference, from the point of view of furthering the policies of the Labor Act, between challenging the majority status of the union through representation proceedings or through the filing of a charge under section 8(b)(1) for union coercion or 8(a)(2) for employer assistance to a minority union.) With greater refinement yet, a distinction has been drawn between suspension or expulsion, which is allowable in such decertification cases, Price v. NLRB (9th Cir. 1967), and a fine, which is unlawful, International Molders Local 125 (Blackhawk Tanning Co.) (1969), enf'd (7th Cir. 1971). Similarly, a member who solicits authorization cards in support of a rival union may be expelled from membership but not fined. Tri-Rivers Marine Eng'rs Union (1971). See Independent Shoe Workers (United States Shoe Corp.) (1974) (fine is illegal even when the member's signing and soliciting authorization cards for a rival union were arguably "premature" since decertification petition could not lawfully be filed for another year).

The distinction between expulsion and fine for seeking to oust the union is deemed justified by the fact that the fine will be a greater deterrent to the member than will expulsion from a union which he would prefer to see replaced as his bargaining representative; and, perhaps more important, by the fact that the exclusive function of a fine must be merely to punish or make an example of the member whereas expulsion serves the legitimate "defensive" union function of excluding the member from meetings at which the union will plan its strategy against the decertification effort. For similar reasons, it is regarded as legitimate defensive action for the union, if the member attacking it is a union officer, to remove that person from office. United Lodge 66, IAM (Smith-Lee Co.) (1970). The same principles apply when the member or officer seeks not to have the union decertified altogether but rather, in a "deauthorization" election, to have it stripped of its power while bargaining representative to enter into a union security agreement with the employer requiring all unit members to join or pay dues to the union. Tool & Die Makers Lodge 113 (Mid-West Am. Dental Div.) (1973).

A union member will also be protected against discipline if rather than file an unfair labor practice charge or election petition, he merely testifies at proceedings before the NLRB. Automotive Salesmen's Ass'n (Spitler-Demmer, Inc.) (1970) (fine imposed for testimony at unfair labor practice hearing). And, in light of the "importance of preserving the integrity of arbitration," fines may not lawfully be levied against a member who testifies before an arbitrator in the trial of a contract grievance. Teamsters Local 788 (San Juan Islands Cannery) (1971).

(2) *Union rules encouraging violation of the Labor Act or of a collective bargaining agreement.* In Scofield v. NLRB (U.S.1969), the Supreme Court held it would sustain union discipline which "left the collective bargaining process unimpaired, breached no collective contract, required no pay for unperformed service, induced no discrimination by the employer against any class of employees and repre-

sents no dereliction by the union of its duty of fair representation." The Board has subsequently struck down union rules which require members to violate the Labor Act or a labor contract; often the discipline violates not only section 8(b)(1)(A) but some other section of the Act as well.

Thus, a union fine of members to induce them to engage in a secondary boycott is a direct violation of section 8(b)(4)(B), which the Board may remedy by ordering the union to reimburse the unlawfully exacted fines (in addition to the usual cease-and-desist order). Bricklayers Local 2 (Weidman) (1967). The Board has also held a union to violate section 8(b)(1)(A) for disciplining members who cross and work behind a picket line in support of an unlawful secondary boycott, on the theory that it would be inconsistent with the policies of the Labor Act to permit a union thus to punish members for refusing to engage in illegal concerted activity. On appeal, however, the Board was reversed and the union sustained in imposing a fine backed by expulsion; the court supported its holding by noting that the proviso to section 8(b)(1)(A) explicitly shelters expulsion as a union sanction and that the secondary boycott could be reached directly by an action for an injunction under section 10(l) of the Labor Act or for damages under section 303. NLRB v. Local 10, Operating Eng'rs (B. D. Morgan & Co.) (6th Cir. 1974). The court's holding thus confronts the union member with the very vexing dilemma of either crossing the secondary picket line and provoking a fine or expulsion, or refusing to cross and provoking discharge (for engaging in unprotected secondary activity). In any event, the Board appears prepared to adhere to its position, and different courts of appeals have given it strong support. Thus, subsequent to the decision in the secondary boycott case, the Board was upheld in its finding that a union, which had called a strike without giving the notices required by section 8(d), violated section 8(b)(1)(A) by denying admission to membership to employees who had refused to participate in the strike. (Some who crossed the picket lines had never been members while others had previously resigned their membership.) Although the union argued that the proviso to section 8(b)(1)(A) entitled it to deny membership to the strikebreakers, the Board and court—noting that the strike was itself an unfair labor practice—held that the proviso ought not be used by a union "to maintain loyalty in its ranks to exclude those who could have demonstrated their allegiance only by participating in unlawful activity"; such union rules would frustrate national labor policy. Local 1104, Communications Workers (N.Y. Tel. Co.) (2d Cir. 1975) (court also holds that if employees who are denied membership refuse to pay union dues, as otherwise required by a union security provision in the labor contract, they may not lawfully be discharged therefor). See also NLRB v. Retail Clerks Local 1179 (Alpha Beta Markets) (9th Cir. 1975) (illegal to fine retail clerks for crossing of picket line established by Teamsters Union in violation of section 8(b)(7)).

On an occasion when the union member is also acting temporarily in the capacity of an employer with the power to hire, the union may not fine him in the event he abides by the law's mandate to hire without discrimination and in the process violates a union rule requiring the hiring of only other union members. Glasser v. NLRB (2d Cir. 1968) (dictum, regarding member of musicians' union serving as bandleader when union rules forbid playing alongside nonmembers). Such discipline would clearly violate section 8(b)(2) as well, since it would be an attempt to induce an employer to discriminate in hiring. And the union directly violates section 8(b)(1)(B) when it disciplines a supervisory worker (who retains his membership) for his actions as management's representative in collective bargaining or grievance adjustment. Florida Power & Light Co. v. IBEW (U.S. 1974). A union rule, backed by discipline, unilaterally declaring (without bargaining with the employer) a low production ceiling when none has existed before would be a direct violation of the union's duty under section 8(b)(3) to bargain in good faith about working conditions. Painters Dist. Council 9 v. NLRB (2d Cir. 1971). The discipline itself would presumably violate section 8(b)(1)(A). Scofield v. NLRB (U.S.1969) (dictum).

The Supreme Court in *Scofield* also suggested that had the union-imposed productivity ceiling and "banking" rule violated a collective bargaining agreement, discipline of members for disobedience would have violated section 8(b)(1)(A). The Board has also held that union members who, consistent with the no-strike provision in their labor contract, cross a picket line to perform their assigned work, may not be disciplined—whether the picket line is the union's own, Glaziers Local 1162 (Tusco Glass, Inc.) (1969) (fines), or that of a sister union, Local 12419, UMW (National Grinding Wheel Co.) (1969) (contract construed to bar a work stoppage in the form of honoring the picket line of another union).

(3) *Union rules restricting participation in internal union affairs.* The Landrum-Griffin Act, or the Labor-Management Reporting and Disclosure Act of 1959, declares that all union members are to have the right to vote and be eligible for office in union elections, to meet and freely express views with other members and to speak out on issues before the union at formal meetings. (29 U.S.C.A. §§ 411, 412, 481.) It is unlawful under these sections for a union to discipline a member for speaking against union policies, Cole v. Hall (2d Cir. 1972), *aff'd on other issues* (U.S.1973), or against particular candidates for union office, Retail Clerks Local 648 v. Retail Clerks Int'l Ass'n (D.D.C.1969). Although these Landrum-Griffin policies are not directly enforceable by the National Labor Relations Board, the Board has recently held that it would take them into account and strike down as in violation of section 8(b)(1)(A) a fine which was

imposed on a member who sought to compete against an incumbent union official in running for the position of delegate to the international convention.   In Carpenters Local 22 (Graziano Constr. Co.) (1972), the Board stated:

> [T]he Board is charged with considering the full panoply of congressional labor policies in determining the legality of a union fine.   Here the Union, in the guise of enforcing internal discipline, has sought to deprive its members of the right, as guaranteed by the Labor-Management Reporting and Disclosure Act, to participate fully and freely in the internal affairs of his own union.   A fine for that purpose not only in our opinion fails to reflect a legitimate union interest but rather in fact impairs a policy that Congress has imbedded in the labor laws.

The Board held that in spite of the differentiation between its own jurisdiction and the powers of the Labor Department to enforce the LMRDA union-election provisions, it was obligated, in determining legitimacy of union interests, to look not just to the NLRA but to "take into account *all* Federal policies."

§ 3.   Susceptibility to Union Discipline: "Membership" and Resignation

Even if a union rule serves a legitimate union interest and contravenes no public policy, it may only be applied to persons who are members of the union.   The union's power to discipline is rooted in the contractual relationship that arises when one becomes a member; as to persons outside the union, "the union has no more control . . . than it has over the man in the street."   NLRB v. Granite State Joint Bd., Textile Workers Local 1029 (U.S.1972).   In NLRB v. Allis-Chalmers Mfg. Co. (U.S.1967), where the Court upheld the union's imposition of a court-enforceable fine for strikebreaking, the members had executed the pledge of allegiance to the UAW constitution and had taken the oath of full membership; some had participated in meetings where strike votes were taken; none had purported to resign his membership at the time he breached the picket lines. The Court thus concluded that they were "full members" when they violated the union rules.

It explicitly left undecided the question whether an unfair labor practice would have been committed "if the locals had imposed fines on members whose membership was in fact limited to the obligation of paying monthly dues," that is, persons subject to the equivalent of an "agency shop" agreement.   Such agreements are expressly permitted by the proviso to section 8(a)(3) in order that the union may eliminate the "free riders" in the bargaining unit who secure the benefits of contract negotiation and grievance processing by the union but who would choose not to pay the union a reasonable fee for those services.   (Such agency shop agreements may, however, be outlawed by particular states, under section 14(b) of the Labor Act.)   It is likely that such compulsory "membership" will be understood to subject the "member" only to the payment of a service fee equivalent to union dues and initiation fees and not also to other union rules which are sanctioned by court-enforceable fines.   This would seem most compatible with decisions of the Board and the Supreme Court empowering the member to resign from "full" membership in the union, in order to avoid subjection to union discipline, while fulfilling his obligation to pay a service fee equivalent to union dues in order to avoid discharge from employment.   NLRB v. Hershey Foods Corp. (9th Cir. 1975).   To make amenability to union discipline turn upon whether the employee has "full" membership status or "dues only" status may, however, prove rather artificial, since many employees subject to a union security provision in a labor agreement may believe that they are obliged to assume full membership and may be unaware that by doing so they are exposed to a significant range of union disciplinary penalties.

More clearly settled is the principle that, at least in the absence of union constitutional or bylaw provisions expressly to the contrary, a union member may resign from "full" membership and automatically escape the power of the union to impose court-enforceable fines for post-resignation conduct.   In NLRB v. Granite State Joint Bd., Textile Workers Union, Local 1029 (U.S.1973), union members who participated in a strike vote decided—some, six weeks after the strike began and others six months later and beyond—to return to work, and did so after sending letters of resignation from the union.   After notice and trial within the union, the former members were fined an amount equivalent to a day's wages for each day worked during the strike, and lawsuits were filed to collect the fines.   The Court found the imposition of court-enforceable fines for post-resignation strike-breaking to violate section 8(b)(1)(A).   The Court found no constitution or bylaw provisions limiting the right to resign and held that the amenability to union discipline was to be determined by basic principles of freedom of association (and resignation):

> Where a member lawfully resigns from a union and thereafter engages in conduct which the union rule proscribes, the union commits an unfair labor practice when it seeks enforcement of fines for that conduct.   That is to say, when there is a lawful dissolution of a union-member relation, the union has no more control over the former member than it has over the man in the street.

The Court concluded that post-resignation freedom to cross the picket line was not relinquished when the members participated in the vote to strike, since the economic hardship and likelihood of permanent replacement in an unforeseeably lengthy strike might properly cause a member to reconsider his decision. The same year, in Booster Lodge 405, IAM v. NLRB (U.S.1973), the Court held that fines for post-resignation strikebreaking could not be justified by a union constitutional provision that expressly prohibited strikebreaking by members, since this provision did not explicitly enough purport to limit the conduct of members after they resign. In both *Granite State* and *Booster Lodge,* the Court expressly refrained from confronting the question whether the union *could* curtail the freedom of a member to resign.

In most cases, unions respond to infraction of their rules not by court action but by expulsion directly or by a fine the nonpayment of which will result in expulsion. Thus, if a member resigns and then violates a union rule, for example against strikebreaking, the union may declare its condemnation by expulsion or suspension, either alone or in combination with a fine. Obviously such a sanction holds far less dread for the former member than does a court-enforceable fine, for he has already decided that his union membership means little and he has resigned; he will presumably bear suspension or expulsion with equanimity, and will not bother to pay the fine (which is by hypothesis not court-enforceable). Although in truth there may be a modicum of "coercion" for having breached the picket line, since the former member might wish readmission to the union sooner than the expulsion or suspension would permit, the Board and courts have held that it is lawful for a union to impose a fine for post-resignation strikebreaking and to condition readmission to membership upon its payment. Local 1255, IAM v. NLRB (5th Cir. 1972). It is also lawful for a union to punish post-resignation strikebreaking by a "suspension" from union membership and union activities for a five-year period, NLRB v. District Lodge 99, IAM (1st Cir. 1974) (reversing a Board finding that while expulsion is permitted, suspension is illegal because it creates the impression that the resigning member is still subject to union control), or by expulsion, Pattern Makers' Ass'n (Lietzau Pattern Co.) (1972). These decisions rest on the proviso to section 8(b)(1)(A), according the union the privilege to make rules with respect to the acquisition or retention of membership. Just as the union would be free to deny membership in the first instance to the "man in the street" who has made a habit of strikebreaking elsewhere, the union should be free to deny readmission to former members for strikebreaking after resignation. To that extent, the Supreme Court appears to have spoken too broadly in *Granite State* when it stated that "when a member lawfully resigns from the union, its power over him ends."

Since a member's amenability to discipline may depend upon whether he effectively resigned prior to engaging in the challenged conduct, several cases have had to deal with the question whether an alleged resignation was effective. The Board has held that when a union's constitution is silent on the issue "a member is free to resign at will by clearly conveying to the union his unequivocal intent to resign." District Lodge 99, IAM (General Elec. Co.) (1972), *mdf'd on other grounds* (1st Cir. 1974). No specific steps are required; one need simply let the union clearly know. An effective resignation has been found where the member, in a discussion with the union president, crumbled up and discarded his union card and said "I quit," Mechanical Workers Local 444 (Pneumatic Scale Corp.) (1968), *enf'd* (1st Cir. 1970); and where the member returned his membership card to the union and revoked his dues checkoff authorization, Communications Workers Local 6135 (Southwestern Bell Tel. Co.) (1971). But cancelling a dues checkoff authorization—which merely means that the employee chooses not to have his dues deducted by the employer from his paycheck—is consistent with paying one's dues personally and together with the member's statements to a union official that he is merely thinking of resigning is not a sufficiently unequivocal manifestation of intention to resign. District Lodge 99, IAM (General Elec. Co.) (1972), *mdf'd on other grounds* (1st Cir. 1974). A member's resignation will be deemed effective at the time when it is received by the union. Thus, the Board has held that the union may validly fine a member for crossing a picket line on the same day that the union received word of his resignation, since the evidence did not show whether the resignation or the strikebreaking occurred first. United Constr. Workers Local 10 (Erhardt Constr. Co.) (1971).

In NLRB v. Granite State Joint Bd., Textile Workers Local 1029 (U.S.1972), the Supreme Court raised but did not decide the question whether a union might validly restrict a member's right to resign, in order that it could retain the power to discipline—particularly at the time of strikes, when the union's need for solidarity and a member's temptation to violate union rules are the greatest. Although the Court had said in Scofield v. NLRB (U.S.1969), that section 8(b)(1) "leaves a union free to enforce a properly adopted rule which reflects a legitimate union interest, impairs no policy Congress has imbedded in the labor laws, and is reasonably enforced against union members who are free to leave the union and escape the rule," the implicit suggestion that members must be free at all times to resign and thereby avoid discipline was dictum and must be regarded as questionable authority. Compare NLRB v. Boeing Co. (U.S.1973) (NLRB has no power to determine whether union disciplinary fines are unreasonable in amount; "we recede from the implications of the dicta" in *Scofield* that section 8(b)(1) authorizes only reasonable fines). It is likely, however, that the Board and courts will restrict in some manner the freedom of unions to dictate in their constitutions unreasonable limitations upon the right of members to resign. Indeed, the Board has recently, relying on *Scofield,* held unreasonable a constitutional provision of the United Auto Workers which permitted resignations only within the ten-day period before the end of the union's January 1 fiscal year (with resignations becoming effective 60 days thereafter). This would have precluded resignations at the time of a strike coincident with termination of the contract in June and could not be asserted by the union to justify its discipline of attempted resignees. UAW Local 647 (General Elec. Co.) (1972).

It is not likely, however, that all restrictions on resignation will be struck down as unreasonable, for they do promote legitimate union interests in unified support for economic pressure and in financial stability; and, subject to notions of unconscionability and lack of notice, they are consistent with the Supreme Court's analysis of the union-member relationship as one rooted in contract. Perhaps these union and contract interests will eventually be balanced against those of the individual member (witness the concern of the Court in *Granite State* for the member and his family when confronted with the hardships of an unexpectedly long strike), and some principle developed whereby the union will be permitted to bar resignation (or instead to bar stipulated post-resignation conduct) for a period shortly before and shortly after the commencement of a strike.

§ 4. The Reasonableness of Disciplinary Fines

In NLRB v. Boeing Co. (U.S.1973), the Supreme Court held that since a disciplinary fine for strikebreaking advances a legitimate union interest, violates no federal labor policy and does not impair the employer-employee relationship, such a fine does not violate section 8(b)(1)(A), regardless of its amount. The reasonableness of the fine is to be determined not by the Board but rather by the state courts applying state law, in an action by the union to collect the fine or by the employee to avoid it, "upon the basis of the law of contracts, voluntary associations, or such other principles of law as may be applied in a forum competent to adjudicate the issue." The Court held that state courts would be more expert than the Board in such matters, and that since state courts would pass on reasonableness in any event in the context of actions between the union and its member, Board power to pass on reasonableness would not create uniformity but rather generate further conflict (should both forums be called upon to review the same fine in different proceedings). The Court majority did not address two other issues raised by three Justices in dissent: that many union members will be unable to bear the financial burden of a state-court lawsuit on the question of reasonableness (while he bears no expense in an NLRB proceeding); and that union fines can be so excessive as to wipe out the member's earnings during the strike and thus be equivalent to the clearly unlawful job-related penalty of withholding of wages.

§ 5. Union Discipline of Supervisors

In certain industries, notably construction and printing, supervisors are members of the union that represents the rank-and-file workers. In part, particularly in the construction industry, this is because jobs are mobile and short-lived and a person working one day as a supervisor may work the next in a nonsupervisory position; in part, membership is retained because it carries with it economic benefits in the form of old-age or retirement pay or life insurance and death benefits which have been accruing while working in the rank and file. On occasion, one's membership in the union—with the attendant amenability to union rules and discipline—may create a conflict with the loyalty normally due an employer by one serving as a supervisor. The union may, for example, consider it a breach of the duties of membership for a supervisor to make a job assignment or apply a provision in a labor contract in a manner that is injurious to fellow members in the bargaining unit or, yet more dramatically, for a supervisor to cross a union picket line in time of a strike in order to function as a supervisor or indeed as a strikebreaker by doing rank-and-file struck work. Section 8(b)(1)(A) will in most instances not be a plausible bar to such union rules—or to the supporting sanctions of fine, suspension or expulsion from membership—since it forbids a union "to restrain or coerce employees" in the exercise of their section 7 rights, and "supervisors" are excluded from the definition of "employee" in section 2(3) of the Labor Act and also necessarily from the protections of section 7.

The more relevant provision is section 8(b)(1)(B), declaring it to be an unfair labor practice for a labor organization "to restrain or coerce an employer in the selection of his representatives for the purposes of collective bargaining or the adjustment of grievances." The primary purpose of the provision was explained in the accompanying Senate Report in the course of formulation of the Taft-Hartley amendments:

> [A] union or its responsible agents could not, without violating the law, coerce an employer into joining or resigning from an employer association which negotiates labor contracts on behalf of its members; also, this subsection would not permit a union to dictate who shall represent an employer in the settlement of employee grievances, or to compel the removal of a personnel director or supervisor who has been delegated the function of settling grievances.

The union most clearly violates section 8(b)(1)(B) when it seeks to coerce the employer directly, rather than the supervisory employee; when the object is to affect the choice or identity of the supervisor or employer representative; and when a central part of that representative's function is collective bargaining or grievance processing, rather than merely the day-to-day direction and appraisal of the work of rank-and-file unit employees. Thus, unions have been found to violate the Act when they compel an employer to join or resign from a multiemployer bargaining association, Slate Workers Local 36

(1968); or to dismiss an industrial relations consultant believed to be hostile to the union, Los Angeles Cloak Joint Bd. ILGWU (1960); or to confine its selection of foremen, with the power to process grievances, to union members only, International Typog. Union (Haverhill Gazette Co.) (1959), *enf'd on this issue* (1st Cir. 1960), *aff'd on this issue by an equally divided Court* (U.S.1961); or even to agree to a contract which establishes the supervisors' working conditions, International Longshoremen's Ass'n (Westchester Marine Shipping Co.) (1975) (such picketing interferes with selection and loyalty of deck officers).

In a major decision in 1968, the Board read section 8(b)(1)(B) to proscribe a far wider range of union action than that outlined in the Senate Report, and went on (with the approval of the courts of appeals) to render a number of expansive opinions the soundness of which has recently been questioned by the Supreme Court. In San Francisco-Oakland Mailers' Union No. 18 (1968), the union had cited and fined certain members who, as foremen, had allegedly assigned bargaining-unit work in breach of the labor contract to supervisors or to others outside the unit. The Board conceded that the union's coercion was not directly on the employer but indirectly by fining the supervisors, and that the object was to force a change not of the supervisors but merely in their application of the collective bargaining agreement; yet the Board found a violation of section 8(b)(1)(B):

> That Respondent may have sought the substitution of attitudes rather than persons, and may have exerted its pressure upon the Charging Party [the employer] by indirect rather than direct means, cannot alter the ultimate fact that pressure was exerted here for the purpose of interfering with the Charging Party's control over its representatives. Realistically, the Employer would have to replace its foremen or face de facto nonrepresentation by them.

The Board also noted that the union's object was "to compel the Employer's foremen to take pro-union positions in interpreting the collective-bargaining agreement" and thus fell within the ban of the Act.

In several decisions that followed, the Board and courts found union discipline of supervisors to constitute coercion of the employer "in the selection of his representatives for the purposes of collective bargaining or the adjustment of grievances" when the supervisors' conduct related only remotely to their status as administrators of the labor contract. *E. g.*, Houston Typog. Union 87 (1970) (union fined supervisor for selecting nonunion employee as night foreman, claiming the process of selection violated the labor contract); NLRB v. Lithographers Local 15-P (6th Cir. 1971) (union fined supervisor for reporting for work during strike, claiming the work exceeded the maximum allowed by the labor contract). The usual mode of analysis was that, since the union was disciplining the supervisor for his interpretation of the labor contract, this would foreseeably pressure the supervisor always to adopt the position espoused by the union in future contract disputes, such that the employer would be losing a loyal advocate in grievance processing and contract administration. The Board and courts also found it objectionable that the purpose of the union discipline was not to affect the relationship between the member and the union (a so-called "internal" effect, as with rules against strikebreaking) but rather to affect the relationship between the union and the employer (a so-called "external" effect of the discipline) embodied in the labor contract. NLRB v. Safeway Stores, Inc. (D.C.Cir. 1972) (supervisor followed employer's instructions regarding new method of meat procurement and implemented resulting layoff of unit employees).

The net effect of these decisions was to bar union discipline of supervisors for any actions performed by them within the general scope of their supervisory or managerial responsibilities or in the course of representing the interests of their employer—even though contract negotiation or grievance processing was not realistically implicated. The Board pushed its rationale further yet when it held that a union violated section 8(b)(1)(B) by fining a supervisor for crossing a union picket line in order to perform the struck work of rank-and-file unit employees. The supervisor was performing work in the employer's interest and the fine threatened the supervisor's loyalty to which his employer was entitled (this entitlement being found in section 8(b)(1)(B)), particularly at a time when a new labor contract was being shaped by economic combat. The Supreme Court, in a 5–4 decision, refused to find an unfair labor practice and declined to enforce the Board's order. Florida Power & Light Co. v. IBEW Local 641 (U.S.1974). The Court read the legislative history to demonstrate that "Congress was exclusively concerned with union attempts to dictate to employers who would represent them in collective bargaining and grievance adjustment."

> Nowhere in the legislative history is there to be found any implication that Congress sought to extend protection to the employer from union restraint or coercion when engaged in any activity other than the *selection* of its representatives for the purposes of collective bargaining and grievance adjustment. The conclusion is thus inescapable that a union's discipline of one of its members who is a supervisory employee can constitute a violation of § 8(b)(1)(B) only when that discipline may adversely affect the supervisor's conduct in performing the duties of, and acting in his capacity as, grievance adjuster or collective bargainer on behalf of the employer.

> We may assume without deciding that the Board's *Oakland Mailers'* decision fell within the outer limits of this test,

but its decisions in the present cases clearly do not. For it is certain that these supervisors were not engaged in collective bargaining or grievance adjustment, or in any activities related thereto, when they crossed union picket lines during an economic strike to engage in rank and file struck work.

As to the likelihood that the fining of supervisors for performing struck rank-and-file work will deprive the employer of the full loyalty of its supervisors, quite apart from any direct impact on their functions as negotiators or grievance adjusters, the Court held that Congress gave the employer appropriate safeguards in other sections of the Labor Act. Congress excluded the supervisor from the definition of "employees" who are protected by the Act, and the employer is free to refrain from hiring union members as supervisors, to discharge supervisors for union activity and to refuse to bargain collectively with them. If, however, the employer chooses to hire union members as supervisors, and to bargain with a union on their behalf, section 8(b)(1)(B) cannot be used as a general protection, beyond its terms and purpose, against the union using its disciplinary power to command the loyalty of its supervisor-members.

The Board has given *Florida Power & Light* a rather narrow reading. Although there are sharp divisions within the Board on the issue, the present position of the Board majority is that a union may discipline a member supervisor for working during a strike only if the supervisor performs a substantial amount of rank-and-file work *and* the amount of that rank-and-file work done by the supervisor increases as a result of the strike. Newspaper Guild, Local 187 (Times Pub. Co.) (1976). A union may not lawfully fine the supervisor for performing rank-and-file work when he has done only a "minimal" amount of such work and spends substantially all of his time during the strike on his normal supervisory activities, Chicago Typog. Union No. 16 (Hammond Publishers, Inc.) (1975); and the fine will be held illegal by the Board even when the supervisor performs a rather substantial amount of rank-and-file work during the strike when he had performed that kind of work prior to the strike and it did not increase as a result of the strike, Wisconsin River Valley Dist. Council, Carpenters (Skippy Enterprises, Inc.) (1975) (union illegally fined supervisor who, both before and during the union's strike call, spent thirty percent of his time at rank-and-file work). The Board holds that discipline in these latter cases is reasonably likely to carry over and affect the supervisor in his performance of duties as a contract negotiator or grievance adjuster. It remains to be seen whether the courts of appeals will read this narrowly the permission given by the Supreme Court in *Florida Power* for the discipline of supervisors.

In any event, at least one court of appeals has since *Florida Power* read that case to require that, in order to make out a violation of section 8(b)(1)(B), there must be specific proof that the disciplined supervisor was actually empowered to negotiate a contract or process grievances on behalf of the employer. It was not deemed sufficient that that individual was "likely" to be chosen to bargain or to adjust grievances "at some later date."   NLRB v. Rochester Musicians Ass'n Local 66 (2d Cir. 1975) (union suspended and fined orchestra conductor for recommending the discharge of orchestra members he deemed musically incompetent: discipline did not violate section 8(b)(1)(B)).

CHAPTER XXX

THE UNION'S DUTY OF FAIR REPRESENTATION

§ 1. Origin and Statutory Basis

The Supreme Court first announced the principle that a bargaining representative must represent fairly all employees within the bargaining unit—regardless of race and regardless of membership in the union—in Steele v. Louisville & N.R.R. (U.S.1944), a case arising under the Railway Labor Act. There, a railroad company and the union representing its firemen negotiated several contract provisions which set a ceiling upon the number of black employees to be assigned to work within the bargaining unit and restricted altogether the access of black workers to certain positions. A substantial minority of unit employees were black, and were because of their color barred from membership in the union which was their bargaining representative under the Act. An action was brought against both the railroad and the union on behalf of a number of black firemen who had been ousted from their jobs because of the defendants' racially discriminatory agreement. The state courts ruled that the authority of the statutory bargaining representative to negotiate and modify the job rights of employees within the unit was plenary, and dismissed the complaint as stating no cause of action. The Supreme Court reversed.

The Court observed that the union was given the power by the Railway Labor Act to bargain for all firemen employed by the railroad, including the black plaintiffs, and that the statute forbade the workers within the unit to bargain individually or to select a minority union to represent them. Since Congress could not have intended the minority within the unit to be stripped of all means of protecting their own interests:

> The fair interpretation of the statutory language is that the organization chosen to represent a craft is to represent all its members, the majority as well as the minority, and it is to act for and not against those whom it represents. It is a principle of general application that the exercise of a granted power to act in behalf of others involves the assumption toward them of a duty to exercise the power in their interest and behalf, and that such a grant of power will not be deemed to dispense with all duty toward those for whom it is exercised unless so expressed.

The Court found implied in the Railway Labor Act a duty to refrain from "hostile discrimination" against any minority group within the bargaining unit, and concluded that "discriminations based on race alone are obviously irrelevant and invidious" and therefore in violation of the Act. The Court acknowledged that the union had the right to determine eligibility for its own membership, but that it was nonetheless obligated in collective bargaining "to represent non-union or minority union members of the craft without hostile discrimination, fairly, impartially, and in good faith." There being no statutory agency created by the Railway Labor Act to enforce this kind of claim against the union, the Court concluded that it was to be enforced in the courts, by damages as well as appropriate injunctive relief, and that relief could be secured not only against the union but against any employer implicated in the union's wrongful activities.

The Court in *Steele* did note, however, that the bargaining representative was not necessarily forbidden to make contracts which might have an unfavorable effect upon some of the employees in the bargaining unit:

> Variations in the terms of the contract based on differences relevant to the authorized purposes of the contract in conditions to which they are applied, such as differences in seniority, the type of work performed, the competence and skill with which it is performed, are within the scope of the bargaining representation of a craft, all of whose members are not identical in their interest or merit.

This power of the union to exercise its discretion in contract negotiations to draw reasonable distinctions among groups of employees was emphasized and expanded in Ford Motor Co. v. Huffman (U.S.1953). There, the company and the United Automobile Workers agreed after World War II to give seniority credit for military service to employees who had not worked for Ford before the war; this went beyond the requirement of a federal statute that seniority continue to accrue for persons whose service for Ford was interrupted by military duty. This preemployment seniority credit was challenged by several employees who were disadvantaged thereby, and who claimed that the union had violated its duty of fair representation by discriminating on the basis of a factor not ordinarily considered directly relevant to wages and working conditions. The Supreme Court stressed the discretion of the union to make reasonable distinctions among employees and held that the seniority credit was "within reasonable bounds of relevancy." The Court observed:

> Inevitably differences arise in the manner and degree to which the terms of any negotiated agreement affect individual employees and classes of employees. The mere existence of such differences does not make them invalid. The complete satisfaction of all who are represented is hardly to be expected. A wide range of reasonableness must be allowed a statutory bargaining representative in serving the unit it represents, subject always to complete good faith and honesty of purpose in the exercise of its discretion.

. . . . Seniority rules governing promotions, transfers, layoffs and similar matters may, in the first instance, revolve around length of competent service. Variations acceptable in the discretion of bargaining representatives, however, may well include differences based upon such matters as the unit within which seniority is to be computed, the privileges to which it shall relate, the nature of the work, the time at which it is done, the fitness, ability or age of the employees, their family responsibilities, injuries received in course of service, and time or labor devoted to related public service, whether civil or military, voluntary or involuntary.

Implicit in the decision of the Supreme Court in the *Huffman* case was the extension of the duty of fair representation to unions functioning as bargaining agents under the National Labor Relations Act, rather than the Railway Labor Act. The Court first actually held that a union violated a duty of fair representation imposed by the National Labor Relations Act in a per curiam opinion in Syres v. Oil Workers Local 23 (U.S.1955). There, the Court did no more than cite several cases decided under the Railway Labor Act, and reversed the ruling below that a federal court had no jurisdiction (in the absence of diversity of citizenship) over a claim of discrimination in seniority as between white and black employees.

The Court has also extended the union's duty beyond the negotiation of a new agreement to its administration of and processing grievances under an existing agreement. Thus, a union representing two groups of employees in different locations was held to have a duty to act in good faith in adjusting the rights of these groups in the event of a merger. Humphrey v. Moore (U.S.1964) (cause of action stated by claim of deceit by union in agreeing to "dovetail" both groups of employees on basis of individual seniority). And, although a collective bargaining agreement was lawful on its face as to the rights of all employees regardless of race, the duty of fair representation was held to outlaw a refusal by the union (pursuant to a plan with the employer) to process grievances asserted by black workers discharged by the employer, allegedly because of their race. Conley v. Gibson (U.S.1957). Most recently, the Supreme Court has acknowledged that the duty of fair representation is not satisfied merely by taking an employee's grievance to arbitration; the union must continue to act in good faith and without arbitrariness in the preparation and trial of the case before the arbitrator. Obvious examples of wrongful union conduct in arbitration are the manufacturing of evidence or the corruption of the arbitrator, to the detriment of the disfavored employee. Hines v. Anchor Motor Freight, Inc. (U.S. 1976).

Indeed, although most of the decided cases appear to treat the union's duty of fair representation as comparable when it negotiates and when it administers a collective bargaining agreement, there are suggestions both in decided cases and in the scholarly literature that the extent of the union's duty—*i. e.,* the limitation of its discretion in adjusting employee interests—is greater in administering an existing contract than in negotiating a new one. *E. g.,* Price v. Teamsters (3d Cir. 1972) (joint employer-union committee agreed to dovetail seniority after a plant shutdown, thus reducing the job status of the plaintiffs; court found this a rational solution, noting that the union must not "ignore provisions embodied in the agreement: the basic contract rights must be enforced"). This distinction will be explored below.

In any event, the Supreme Court could say in its leading decision in Vaca v. Sipes (U.S.1967), that it was "well established" that a bargaining representative under the National Labor Relations Act has a duty, both in its collective bargaining and in its enforcement of the resulting labor contract, "to serve the interests of all members without hostility or discrimination toward any, to exercise its discretion with complete good faith and honesty, and to avoid arbitrary conduct." The Court reiterated the position it took in the *Steele* case that the Labor Act should be thus construed in order to avoid the constitutional problems that would arise if the Act were read to destroy the rights of the individual to bargain while permitting the union (designated under the statute) to use its power in the cause of discrimination or hostility against minorities or individuals within the bargaining unit.

§ 2. Jurisdiction: The National Labor Relations Board

Breach of the duty of fair representation was initially held to give rise to an action in the federal or state courts. The Supreme Court so held in 1944 under the Railway Labor Act in Steele v. Louisville & N.R.R. (U.S.1944), and eleven years later under the National Labor Relations Act in Syres v. Oil Workers Local 23 (U.S. 1955). It was not until 1962 that the National Labor Relations Board held that the union's duty, rooted by the Supreme Court in the exclusive-representation provisions of section 9(a) of the Labor Act, could be enforced by the Board through the unfair labor practice provisions of the NLRA. This principle was announced in Miranda Fuel Co. (1962), *enf't denied* (2d Cir. 1963). There, an employee left for a six-month leave of absence three days early, which provoked certain fellow union members to pressure the union's officials in turn to pressure the company to drop that employee to the bottom of the company's seniority list. The company complied with the union's request, even though the contract had no provision for loss of seniority in such instances, and demoted the employee, who filed a charge with the NLRB. The Board found the employee to have been a victim of arbitrary and unfair discrimination by the union, in which the employer participated, and held the conduct of both the union and the employer to be an unfair labor practice.

The Board in *Miranda* first considered the right given to employees by section 7 of the Labor Act "to bargain collectively through representatives of their own choosing," and reasoned from section 9(a) that such a right would necessarily embrace freedom from unfair, irrelevant or invidious treatment at the hands of the statutory bargaining representative in matters affecting the employment relationship. Sections 8(a)(1) and 8(b)(1)(A) prohibit interference by the employer and union with the exercise of this section 7 right. Accordingly, if the union treats any workers it represents in an unfair manner, it unlawfully restrains employees in the exercise of their rights; if the employer participates in such unfair action, it also commits an unfair labor practice. Moreover, section 8(a)(3) bars employer discrimination to encourage union activity and section 8(b)(2) bars union inducement of such employer action. Since unjustified or arbitrary reduction in seniority, at the union's insistence, will foreseeably encourage membership in or loyalty to the union, those two sections were also held violated under the facts of the *Miranda* case. In so holding, the case marked a step beyond the many cases which outlaw union inducement of and employer imposition of job-related discipline because of an employee's activities in (or against) the union; in *Miranda*, it was held sufficient that the respondent union had taken "hostile action, for irrelevant, unfair or invidious reasons" regardless of whether those reasons were union-related.

The Court of Appeals for the Second Circuit refused to enforce the Board's order in *Miranda,* in a two-to-one decision. Only two of the judges directly considered the question whether the union commits an unfair labor practice by inducing employer reprisals against a worker for reasons other than that worker's union membership or activities, and on that question they disagreed, leaving the question still open in that Circuit. One judge (who helped form a majority for reversing the Board) concluded that sections 8(a)(1) and (3) and sections 8(b)(1) and (2) are not violated by action in violation of the duty of fair representation which is "unrelated to 'union membership, loyalty . . . or the performance of union obligations'." He argued that the Board and its unfair labor practice remedies "are not suited to the task of deciding general questions of private wrongs, unrelated to union activities, suffered by employees as a result of tortious conduct by either employers or labor unions." The dissenting judge did not consider whether the right to be treated fairly was within section 7 or whether the union automatically violated section 8(b)(1) by taking hostile action unrelated to union membership, but he did conclude that the record showed a violation of sections 8(a)(3) and 8(b)(2). He would have held that "discrimination" in section 8(a)(3) should be read broadly to embrace any distinction made without sufficient reasons—thus including any differential treatment based on invidious or arbitrary considerations—and that the union's demonstration of power would "encourage" nonmembers to join the union and existing members to become good members rather than bad or indifferent ones.

In spite of the setback in *Miranda,* the Board continues to treat a union's violation of the duty of fair representation as an unfair labor practice. Indeed, in Independent Metal Workers Local 1 (Hughes Tool Co.) (1964), a case involving a union's refusal to process the grievance of a black employee for reasons of race, the Board expanded its arsenal and held that such union conduct violated not only sections 8(b)(1) and (2), but also section 8(b)(3) as a refusal to bargain in good faith; it concluded that the duty to bargain was owed not only to the employer but to the employees in the bargaining unit as well.

The Board's assertion of jurisdiction over violations of the duty of fair representation has been sustained by at least three circuit courts of appeals, although the courts do not in every case embrace the precise rationale set forth by the Board. Thus, in Local 12, Rubber Workers v. NLRB (5th Cir. 1966), the Board held that the union violated sections 8(b)(1)(A), (2) and (3) by refusing to process the grievances of several black employees concerning separate seniority lists for blacks, white and females and separate sanitary facilities in the plant for black and white workers. The Board ordered the union to process the grievances and to propose to the employer, and bargain for, contract provisions which would eliminate such racially discriminatory conduct by the employer. The court enforced the Board's order, holding that the union's conduct violated section 8(b)(1)(A) and that it was therefore unnecessary to consider the issues under sections 8(b)(2) and 8(b)(3). In Truck Drivers Local 568 v. NLRB (D.C.Cir. 1967) (Red Ball Motor Freight, Inc.), two companies were in the process of merging, and the union representing the larger group of employees promised them that if it (the union) were selected the bargaining representative of the combined unit, it would oppose the "dovetailing" of the absorbed employees and would instead insist that they be "endtailed" at the bottom of the combined seniority list. The court found that the union's actual bargaining to "endtail" would be premised exclusively on the political strength of the favored group, rather than upon any reasoned basis, and would thus violate the duty to represent all unit employees fairly. But it rested its specific holding on the union's advance threat to endtail, while it was campaigning, which could only coerce the employees in the favored group to support it and coerce the employees in the absorbed group to oppose it, in each instance possibly contrary to the actual preferences of the employees. The court held this threat to violate section 8(b)(1)(A).

Most recently, a court of appeals has sustained a Board finding of a section 8(b)(1)(A) violation, stemming from the union's maintenance of two separate locals to represent employees in the bargaining unit—one local for men and one for women. Even though bargaining was done by a committee comprised of representatives from both locals, and the resulting labor contract was not discriminatory in any way, the union was held to violate the Act by the mere fact that its locals were segregated and by the refusal of each local to process the grievances of employees who were members of the other. NLRB v. Local 106, Glass Bottle Blowers (6th Cir. 1975) (Board may order the union to merge the two locals, in spite of the proviso to section 8(b)(1)(A) permitting unions to prescribe their own membership qualifications; Board found no violation of section 8(b)(2) since the union had not induced the employer to discriminate in any respect).

The Board's *Miranda* holding—that breach of the duty of fair representation is an unfair labor practice—was bolstered somewhat when the Supreme Court, for purposes of a lengthy analysis of preemption of court jurisdiction, assumed arguendo in Vaca v. Sipes (U.S.1967), that the Board did indeed have jurisdiction over such cases.

The number of fair-representation cases initiated before the Board is far fewer than those initiated in the courts, in spite of the fact that a charging party before the Board need not bear the expense of preparing and litigating the case, a task that falls to the General Counsel. This may be attributable to a number of factors: the six-month statute of limitations for unfair labor practices, the discretion of the General Counsel whether to issue a complaint, the apparent hesitation of the Board to press the fair-representation theory with vigor in several instances, the uncertainty (within the Board and among the courts of appeals) regarding the need to find that the union's and employer's discrimination is related to the union activities of the charging party, and perhaps some belief that the Board's remedial authority is more limited than that of courts. In any event, it should be noted that many cases which are at base fair-representation cases are quite commonly brought before the Board but are not so denominated; these are cases in which the union's hostile or invidious action is based on the employee's union membership or activities (or lack thereof). This is clearly a violation of section 8(b)(1)(A) and (2) and has been traditionally treated as such. Other than such "conventional" Board cases, most of its fair-representation cases deal with discrimination on the basis of race (and more recently, on the basis of sex), and rather few can be said to rest simply on claims of "pure" personal animosity or political preference.

§ 3. Jurisdiction: The Courts

As already noted, jurisdiction to enforce the duty of fair representation was first held to rest with the courts. In Steele v. Louisville & N.R.R. (U.S.1944), the Supreme Court held that a union violated an implied duty under the Railway Labor Act when it negotiated a contract which discriminated against black workers in hiring and seniority, and that the Act provided no effective administrative relief—that Act made no provision for a proceeding by an employee against his union before the Railway Adjustment Board, that Board had consistently declined to process claims brought by an individual against a railroad employer when that employee was represented by a union, and regional adjustment boards staffed by representatives of railroad employers and unions could not be expected fairly to consider claims of unfair discrimination levelled against them. To vindicate the employee's right, the Court held that judicial relief would have to be made available, and its remand to the courts of the State of Alabama made it clear that there would be concurrent jurisdiction over such federal claims in state and federal courts (in the latter instance, regardless of diversity of citizenship). In spite of the fact that Congress did create an administrative agency under the NLRA, and did give it jurisdiction in 1947 to consider union unfair labor practices, the Supreme Court tersely held not long after that a judicial remedy was appropriate even under the exclusive-representation provisions of the NLRA. Syres v. Oil Workers Local 23 (U.S.1955) (per curiam). The Court there reversed the decision of a federal appeals court that discriminatory seniority lists could be challenged only in a contract action, over which federal courts had no jurisdiction absent diversity of citizenship.

The Supreme Court has held that when an employee brings an action against his union for improperly agreeing to "dovetail" the seniority of other employees brought into the company by merger, and this is alleged to violate a provision of the labor contract to which the union is a party, this states a claim under section 301 of the Labor Act ("suits for violation of contracts between an employer and a labor organization"). Humphrey v. Moore (U.S.1964). Such actions may be brought by an individual in a federal court regardless of diversity of citizenship, and are to be governed by federal principles of substantive law. Smith v. Evening News Ass'n (U.S.1962).

Most courts agree, however, that the proper jurisdictional basis for court actions to enforce the duty of fair representation lies under 28 U.S.C.A. § 1337 (actions "arising under any Act of Congress regulating commerce"), although little of substance appears to turn upon the jurisdictional foundation. Thus, one court has held that if the claim against the union is not that it actually violated the labor contract in representing unfairly, but that it improperly enforced or administered the contract as written, there is no claim under section 301 and jurisdiction must rest on 28 U.S.C.A. § 1337. Mumford v. Glover (5th Cir. 1974). That same court has in fact pointed out that the duty of fair representation does not rest at all upon a labor contract, since it is derived directly from the National Labor Relations Act and applies even before any contract exists. Smith v. Local 25, Sheet Metal Workers (5th Cir. 1974). That view certainly appears to be sound, and does not in any way undermine the principle that would obtain in a section 301 action that the substantive rules for determining the duty of fair representation are rules of federal law. In any event, at least one plaintiff (a supervisor) has made creative use of section 301 by bringing an action under that section against his union, which represented only supervisory employees, for delay in processing his discharge grievance; since the union was not bargaining for "employees" within the Labor Act, it had no duty derivable from section 9(a) of the Labor Act which could be enforced under 28 U.S.C.A. § 1337, but the court held the labor contract to be within the reach of section 301. Dente v. Masters, Mates & Pilots Local 90 (9th Cir. 1973).

The Board's declaration in 1962 in Miranda Fuel Co., *enf't denied* (2d Cir. 1963), that it would assume unfair labor practice jurisdiction over fair-representation charges generated the question whether the courts would thereafter be preempted from hearing such cases. The Supreme Court only a few years before had declared, in San Diego Bldg. Trades Council v. Garmon (U.S.1959), that neither state nor federal courts have jurisdiction over suits directly involving activity which is arguably protected by section 7 of the Labor Act or arguably prohibited by section 8 of the Act. With hostile or arbitrary discrimination by unions now treated as violations of section 8(b) (1), (2) and (3), some courts concluded that the institutional conflict which the *Garmon* rule sought to avoid required courts to close their door to fair-representation claims and plaintiffs to file charges with the Board instead. The Supreme Court held to the contrary, and sustained the traditional jurisdiction of the courts in fair-representation cases, in Vaca v. Sipes (U.S.1967). There, an employee with a poor medical history was discharged from a job requiring heavy work. Although the union took a grievance on his behalf through three steps of the contract grievance procedure, a new medical examination convinced the union's executive board not to process the case to arbitration but instead to encourage the grievant to accept the company's offer of referral to a rehabilitation center. When the grievant insisted that the union take the case to arbitration, the union refused and the grievant brought an action against union officers in a state court, where he secured a substantial jury verdict. Among other issues before the Supreme Court, the defendants challenged the jurisdiction of the state court on the ground that the union's alleged conduct was arguably an unfair labor practice and thus within the exclusive jurisdiction of the NLRB.

The Court rejected this jurisdictional attack, giving a number of reasons. First, it noted that fair-representation lawsuits would not undermine a primary justification for the preemption doctrine—"the need to avoid conflicting rules of substantive law in the labor relations area and the desirability of leaving the development of such rules to the administrative agency created by Congress for that purpose." The doctrine of fair representation was initially developed by the courts, and the Board has since merely adopted and applied the doctrine as developed by those courts. Moreover, the Board does not ordinarily review the kinds of issues raised in a fair-representation case—"the substantive positions taken and policies pursued by a union in its negotiation of a collective bargaining agreement and in its handling of the grievance machinery"—so that the Board has no special competence not possessed by the courts. Second, the Court noted the need for a forum for the aggrieved individual whose charge was not pursued by the Board's General Counsel or who otherwise found the Board unwilling or unable to remedy the union's breach of duty. Third, the Court observed that the question of fair representation would frequently arise (as in the instant case) in the context of a claim by an individual against his employer for breach of the labor contract, for example, for wrongful discharge; in such an action under section 301, the employer commonly argues that the employee has failed to pursue his contractual remedies through the union, and the employee will commonly attempt to excuse this failure by proving that the union's refusal to process the grievance stemmed from hostility or bad faith toward the employee. The Court had earlier held that judicial jurisdiction of an action against the employer for contract breach was not preempted by the possibility that the employer's conduct was also an unfair labor practice, and it similarly concluded in *Vaca* that jurisdiction over such contract actions against the employer was proper even though it was the union that had committed an unfair labor practice. (The Court assumed arguendo that the violation of the duty of fair representation was indeed an unfair labor practice, as the Board had earlier held in *Miranda*.) The Court concluded its line of argument by holding that jurisdiction in the courts should thus be sustained even when the employee joins the union as a party to his action against the employer, and when—as in the case before the Court—the employee chooses to sue the union separately, for breach of its duty of fair representation.

The Court's final justification for rejecting the preemption argument—that a claim regarding the union's duty of fair representation was often incident to a contract claim against the employer—led some courts to conclude that their jurisdiction would indeed be preempted when the claim against the union was unrelated to an employer breach of contract, for example, was a claim for bad-faith negotiation of contract terms initially. This would have led to an anomalous division of responsibility between the Board and the courts, and would have disregarded the other reasons given by the Court in *Vaca* for finding the preemption doctrine inapt. The Supreme Court has in fact in dictum read *Vaca* quite broadly to hold

> that an action seeking damages for injury inflicted by a
> breach of a union's duty of fair representation was judicially
> cognizable .   .   .   even if the conduct complained of was

arguably protected or prohibited by the National Labor Relations Act and whether or not the lawsuit was bottomed on a collective agreement.

Amalgamated Ass'n of Street Employees v. Lockridge (U.S.1971). It would appear to follow that fair-representation suits may be brought in state or federal courts, regardless of concurrent NLRB jurisdiction, whether the claim relates to the union's conduct in negotiating or administering the contract, and whether the union's unfairness relates to race discrimination, personal hostility or even to discrimination based upon union membership or activities (a classic violation of the unfair labor practice provisions traditionally administered by the NLRB).

§ 4. The Nature of the Duty: Range of Application

The duty of the majority bargaining representative to represent fairly all employees within the bargaining unit was initially formulated in a case involving the negotiation of the terms of a comprehensive labor contract. In Steele v. Louisville & N.R.R. (U.S.1944), the union representing locomotive firemen negotiated contract provisions which were designed to give priority in hiring and promotions to white employees over black employees (who were excluded from membership in that union). The duty does not, however, end when the contract has been executed. As the Supreme Court stated in Conley v. Gibson (U.S.1957):

> Collective bargaining is a continuing process. Among other things, it involves day-to-day adjustments in the contract and other working rules, resolution of new problems not covered by existing agreements, and the protection of employee rights already secured by contract. The bargaining representative can no more unfairly discriminate in carrying out these functions than it can in negotiating a collective agreement.

The duty of fair representation thus exists whether the union is negotiating a new agreement, formally amending or modifying an existing agreement, or processing grievances initiated by itself or by members of the bargaining unit.

The duty may be violated as much by the union's failure to act as by its acts of commission. Thus, a union's refusal altogether to process a grievance may violate the duty of fair representation when the refusal is because of the grievant's race, Local 12, Rubber Workers v. NLRB (5th Cir. 1966); this is true even if the union's conduct purports to be sanctioned by the labor contract itself. The union also has been held to have an affirmative obligation to facilitate the understanding of the contract and grievance procedure on the part of employees whose national origin and native tongue are such as to frustrate such an understanding. Retana v. Apartment & Elevator Operators Local 14 (9th Cir. 1972) (Spanish-speaking employees; the court also stated in dictum that a union which arbitrarily declined to advise employees of their right to file a grievance, or failed to compel an employer to make payments to a health and welfare fund, might also be deemed to violate the duty of fair representation). Most of the cases involving the duty of fair representation find the courts or the Board screening the union's substantive position in negotiation or grievance settlement, but others demonstrate that even a union position reasonable on its face may be subject to attack when the processes of the union in formulating that position fail to satisfy the requisite statutory standard. For example, it has been held that a union's decision to secure the "endtailing" (rather than "dovetailing") of seniority of a group of employees absorbed in a business acquisition may violate the Labor Act if it was a product simply of the play of political forces within the union. Truck Drivers Local 568 v. NLRB (Red Ball Motor Freight, Inc.) (D.C.Cir. 1967).

While the duty of fair representation is thus quite comprehensive, there are certain limits to the union's accountability. Most clearly, since the duty is derived from the union's power as exclusive representative in bargaining and grievance-processing, it is only in those activities that the duty of fair representation applies. It is not, therefore, a violation of that duty simply to exclude certain bargaining-unit employees from membership in the union, if that exclusion is not reflected in the employee's wages, hours or working conditions; there must be an "injury to the employment relationship or to rights granted by the National Labor Relations Act." Smith v. Local 25, Sheet Metal Workers (5th Cir. 1974). But in a case of potentially great significance, the Board recently held—with judicial approval—that a union violated section 8(b)(1)(A) by maintaining two separate locals in the bargaining unit, one limited to men and the other limited to women, even though it was found that the labor contract with the employer did not discriminate against women and that the grievances of women employees were fully processed (albeit only by a committee within the all-female local). NLRB v. Local 106, Glass Bottle Blowers (Owens-Illinois, Inc.) (6th Cir. 1975). The separate locals, as reinforced by the separate grievance processing, were deemed inherently to generate an adverse impact on the employees' working conditions. Much the same point was made in Retana v. Apartment & Elevator Operators Local 14 (9th Cir. 1972), in which the court found a cause of action to be stated by a complaint alleging, among other things, that the union failed to provide Spanish-speaking liaison between the union and its members, failed to provide a copy of the labor contract in Spanish, and failed to explain to union members the rights and responsibilities of membership. While the union argued that these claims bore only upon the union's "internal" policies and practices, the court responded:

> As a practical matter, intra-union conduct could not be wholly excluded from the duty of fair representation, for . . . internal union policies and practices may have a substantial impact upon the external relationships of members of the unit to their employer.

Not only must the union's conduct relate in some manner to the employees' working conditions, either through bargaining or grievance processing, but the duty under section 9(a) of the Labor Act is applicable only when the union is being dealt with as majority representative for the determination of such working conditions. Thus, if the employer's dealings with the union are limited to the voluntary use of that union as a referral agency, but there is no labor contract or bargaining relationship between the parties, it has been held that the union has no obligation under the Labor Act to abstain from unfair discrimination in its referral rules. Gonzalez v. Longshoremen Local 1581 (5th Cir. 1974) (union preference given to members of particular department; employer, the Port of Houston, was forbidden by state law to negotiate a labor contract with the union). But the Supreme Court has held, in what may well be a rule limited to its unique factual situation, that once there is such a collective bargaining relationship, the duty of fair representation can extend to protect employees who are altogether outside the bargaining unit. In Brotherhood of R.R. Trainmen v. Howard (U.S.1952), a white union representing railroad brakemen negotiated an agreement to discharge black employees who were designated "train porters" but who were in fact doing the work of brakemen. Although the union argued that the aggrieved black employees were not members of the craft which the union was empowered to represent under the Railway Labor Act, the Court held nonetheless that a union given the statutory power to bargain was duty-bound not to "destroy colored workers' jobs in order to bestow them on white workers"; such unions "must execute their trust without lawless invasions of the rights of other workers." See Jones v. Trans World Airlines, Inc. (2d Cir. 1974) (union and employer executed an agreement which discriminated against formerly nonunion passenger-relations agents who were absorbed into the bargaining unit).

§ 5. Discrimination for Race, Sex, Union Membership, or Personal Hostility

The clearest cases of breach of the duty of fair representation are those in which the union, in negotiating a contract or processing grievances, has been moved by considerations of the race or sex of members of the bargaining unit or of their union membership or activities. Such union action is variously characterized as unfair, invidious, discriminatory, hostile or in bad faith.

A union acts unlawfully when it implements a policy of race discrimination when negotiating a new agreement for unit members, Steele v. Louisville & N.R.R. (U.S.1944) (lawsuit in state court for violation of implied duty in Railway Labor Act); or when processing or refusing to process grievances, Local 12, Rubber Workers v. NLRB (5th Cir. 1966) (Board finding of violations under NLRA); or even when taking work away from employees outside the bargaining unit in order to preserve it for unit members, Brotherhood of Railroad Trainmen v. Howard (U.S.1952) (all-white union representing brakemen secured the discharge of black train porters doing brakemen's work). Although most of the law on fair representation has come from cases of race discrimination, several more recent cases have involved discrimination in job rights on the basis of sex. Thus, the Board has held that a union which operates a hiring hall jointly with the employer, and which refuses to refer women applicants for jobs as casual dockworkers, violates sections 8(b)(1)(A) and 8(b)(2) of the Labor Act. Pacific Maritime Ass'n (1974) (employer violates sections 8(a)(1) and (3)). And when the union agrees with the employer that certain positions in the plant are to be assigned only to male employees, women employees have a cause of action against the union when upon layoff they are denied the right to "bump" into such a position then occupied by a less senior male worker. Petersen v. Rath Packing Co. (8th Cir. 1972). Indeed, even in a situation in which women were hired along with men and were given all of the rights given by the labor contract to male employees it has been held that the bargaining representative violates its duty of fair representation when it maintains segregated locals for male and female workers and when female workers are permitted to process their grievances only through officers of the female local (with male employees subject to a comparable limitation); even in the absence of specific proof of inferior working conditions for women, the court was prepared to sustain the Board's inference that the separate membership eligibility and grievance processing along sex lines would inevitably result in disparate working conditions. NLRB v. Local 106, Glass Bottle Blowers (Owens-Illinois, Inc.) (6th Cir. 1975).

Some rather early decisions evinced a willingness to tolerate union-negotiated distinctions along the lines of sex (but not, apparently, along racial lines) because of a colorably plausible justification in more neutral terms. Thus, in Hartley v. Brotherhood of Railway Clerks (Mich.1938) (cited approvingly by the Supreme Court in Ford Motor Co. v. Huffman (U.S.1953)), the court upheld a union decision, in time of economic recession and resulting layoffs, to renegotiate a contract in order to void the seniority rights of married women, on the theory that the male spouse would already be providing a source of income. Although the female plaintiff was harmed by the decision, the union was held to have the power to meet economic exigencies so as to satisfy the general interest of its members. Compare

Nedd v. UMW (3d Cir. 1968) (dictum regarding legality of favoring active employees over retirees). Given our changing social and legal attitudes toward equality in employment for women, it is doubtful that the same decision would be rendered today. Indeed, in NLRB v. Longshoremen Local 1581 (Manchester Terminal Corp.) (5th Cir. 1974), the union was held to have engaged in unlawful invidious discrimination by downgrading an employee simply because he was a Mexican national whose family was still living in Mexico; the reason offered by the union, that upgrading of American citizens and downgrading of foreign citizens whose families lived outside the United States would maximize the employees' benefits under the company's family health-insurance plan, was deemed improper (even assuming that it, rather than simple ethnic prejudice, was the true reason).

Another example of invidious and irrelevant discrimination by a union in bargaining or grievance processing is favoritism for union members rather than nonmembers, or for active and cooperative members rather than indifferent or obstreperous members. Although the Supreme Court, on the same day it decided the *Steele* case, noted that a union had a duty under the National Labor Relations Act to represent the interest of all employees in the unit and not merely its own members, Wallace Corp. v. NLRB (U.S.1944), some courts remained uncertain whether the duty of fair representation was to apply in cases other than those involving race discrimination. It is now clear that a union is forbidden to induce discrimination in working conditions on the basis of union membership or activities, regardless of the race of the aggrieved employees. As the court held in Thompson v. Brotherhood of Sleeping Car Porters (4th Cir. 1963):

> A union has no more justification to discriminate injuriously in its representation on the ground of non-membership, or instability of membership, or even because of persistent and vocal complaints or other obnoxious behavior, than it has to discriminate on account of skin pigmentation. None of these circumstances is relevant to the fair and proper discharge of a union's duty to those it is empowered to represent and whose employment is governed by its binding agreements.

Fair representation for nonmembers is, however, different from fair representation for racial or ethnic minorities, in a significant respect. While union inducement of employer discrimination on account of race, sex or national origin is not explicitly forbidden by the National Labor Relations Act, such inducement on account of union membership is explicitly forbidden—by section 8(b)(2). If an employer and union agree to accord preference in hiring or seniority to union members (or to particularly "loyal" members), the employer violates section 8(a)(3) and the union violates section 8(b)(2). Radio Officers' Union v. NLRB (U.S.1954). Therefore, the need to rely upon a theory of fair representation for the nonmember is not as great, and indeed most such cases are brought through the conventional channel of filing an unfair labor practice charge under section 8(b)(2) with the NLRB.

There remain, however, some situations in which the nonmember-discriminatee may choose to formulate a claim of breach of the duty of fair representation. First, it may be thought desirable to secure a judicial forum for one's claim, rather than the NLRB; although a case before the Board is tried by the General Counsel and need cost the aggrieved employee nothing, it is possible that the General Counsel will refuse to issue a complaint and, in any event, the statute of limitations before the NLRB is six months while that in a court action may run for as long as one to six years. Second, the nonmember or the dissident member may choose to frame his case as one of unfair representation—either before the Board or the court—when it is not completely clear that the "arbitrary" criterion invoked by the union is the employee's union status or is rather some other personal activity or attribute. Thus, even if a person retains his membership, he may still show a violation of the duty of fair representation if the union has sought his discharge in actuality as a reprisal for his complaints within the union concerning the union's failure effectively to protect his seniority, Cunningham v. Erie R.R. (2d Cir. 1959), or for his vocal criticism at union meetings of the position of the union's business manager concerning the company's overtime policy, NLRB v. Local 485, IUE (Automotive Plating Corp.) (2d Cir. 1972) (union in effect "swapped" away the employee's grievance protesting wrongful discharge). Since such criticisms of union policies are within the protection of section 7, such cases if involving employers under the NLRA may be tried as conventional violations of sections 8(b)(1)(A) or 8(b)(2). *Ibid.* That the union's action is in reprisal for the exercise of section 7 rights is, however, less clear when, for example, the union induces a loss in seniority for employees absorbed from some other bargaining unit (which coincidentally was represented by a different union), Jones v. Trans World Airlines, Inc. (2d Cir. 1974) (Railway Labor Act); or gives priority in referrals to persons sponsored by a "fully registered" longshoreman (who is invariably a union member), Longshore Workers Local 13 (1970). In the latter case, although the Board noted that the applicant would have to be acquainted with and sponsored by a union member—and might have inferred that this would have unlawfully encouraged union membership on the part of the applicant—it chose instead to base its finding of a violation of sections 8(b)(1) and (2) on the fact that the applicant's meeting or knowing such a person was a patently arbitrary qualification for a job referral.

Aside from discrimination on account of race, sex, national origin or union membership or activities, the bargaining representative may violate the Labor Act if it bargains for adverse working conditions, or refuses to process a grievance, solely because of personal animosity toward the aggrieved employee. It is rare that such a case arises, apart from the more invidious forms of discrimination just listed. Perhaps the most well-known example is Miranda Fuel Co. (1962), *enf't denied* (2d Cir. 1963), the case in which the NLRB first declared that a violation of the union's duty of fair representation was an unfair labor practice within the jurisdiction of the Board. There, one Lopuch secured the employer's consent to leave for vacation three days before the labor contract arguably permitted, and because of illness returned from vacation some three weeks later than originally anticipated (also with the employer's consent). For obscure reasons, several union members induced the officers of the union to demand that Lopuch be dropped to the bottom of the company's seniority list (in spite of his eight or nine years of service with the company); at first, the union relied on his late return from vacation, but when that proved attributable to an excused illness, the union relied instead upon his early departure. Lopuch was a union member, and had apparently taken no action disloyal to the union or in violation of its rules; nor apparently was he a troublemaker. The Board therefore held that the union's demand for his loss of seniority—in which the employer finally acquiesced—was due to "whim or caprice," was "hostile" and was for "irrelevant, unfair or invidious reasons." The Board concluded that the union's action deprived Lopuch of his right under section 7 to be free of invidious and hostile union discrimination (a right derivable from the exclusive-representation provisions of section 9(a) of the Labor Act), and was therefore a violation of section 8(b)(1)(A). It also found that the employer's acquiescence was "discrimination" (because wholly arbitrary) and that submission to the union's demands could only encourage union membership and union loyalty; accordingly, the employer's action violated sections 8(a)(1) and (3) and the union's inducement violated section 8(b)(2). The court of appeals reversed in a split decision, although only one judge specifically rejected the Board's conclusion that union and employer discrimination for reasons other than Lopuch's union activities —even though unexplained or indeed capricious and invidious—could constitute an unfair labor practice. While the Board (which remains split within its own membership on this issue) continues to adhere to the principles of its *Miranda* decision, it appears that no case since, either before the Board or the courts, has raised the question of "pure" personal animosity on the part of the union as a violation of the duty of fair representation.

The issue of bad faith or invidious discrimination has surfaced in a number of cases in which an employee's grievance has been "swapped" by the union in exchange for some concession by the employer on some other grievance or some matter under negotiation. The union will prevail if the "swapped" grievance was honestly appraised by it and found to lack merit, but will be held liable if the employee was sacrificed because of his activities within or against the union or because of personal animosity. In Local 13, Longshoremen v. Pacific Maritime Ass'n (9th Cir. 1971), the complaint asserted that the union had improperly participated in an arbitration proceeding which resulted in the "deregistration" of the grievant, thus depriving him of all longshore work on the Pacific Coast, while it had on the same day secured (in a "swap") a favorable arbitration award concerning the packing of heavy sacks; it was alleged that the union was motivated by the fact that the individual grievant was disliked by union officals, who presumably regarded him as a troublemaker. The court held that summary judgment for the defendant was improper, since the facts proffered could demonstrate either that the union acted from personal hostility or that its conduct on the deregistration grievance stemmed from a "good-faith choice between interpretations" of the provisions of the contract. The court held that it would be unlawful for the union deliberately to sacrifice a particular individual's meritorious grievance, and that while it would ordinarily refrain from second-guessing the union on the merit of the grievance, it might be prepared to find unfair representation were the union to agree "to an interpretation patently lacking in merit." It summed up its position as follows: A union may decline to initiate a grievance or may settle it short of arbitration

> if its decision is made in good faith, based upon an evaluation of the merits of the employee's claim and of the most advantageous expenditure of the union's energies and resources. .   .   .   What we hold is that a union may not agree with an employer, either expressly or tacitly, to exchange a meritorious grievance of an individual employee for some other supposed benefit.

See Simberland v. Long Island R.R. (2d Cir. 1970) (complaint under the Railway Labor Act properly dismissed after trial, when evidence showed that union, which had withdrawn grievances in exchange for a wage increase for all within the unit, had acted without personal animosity and had determined that grievances lacked merit).

There is even some question whether a union violates its duty of fair representation when it "swaps" away a grievance which most would regard as meritorious, provided its decision is made openly, honestly and in an effort to gain a benefit of significance for the generality of workers in the bargaining unit. Such appears to be the message of Union News Co. v. Hildreth (6th Cir. 1961), in which the employer, concerned about shortages in cash receipts, proposed to discharge all of its employees to rid itself of the elusive culprit; the union, after exploring a number of alternatives, prevailed upon the company to attempt to preserve the jobs of half of the unit employees by laying off the other half, the layoff to become permanent if the cash shortages were ended. The employer agreed, the shortages ended, the layoffs were made final, and the union refused to process the grievances of several of the discharged employees. Although it is likely that the employer would have failed to convince an arbitrator of "just cause" for the discharge of any one of the employees, and that each grievance could thus be fairly deemed meritorious, the court held that an employee's court action against the employer lacked merit and that the union's conduct was not unlawful. Although the trial evidence showed no dishonesty or malfeasance on the part of the plaintiff grievant, neither did it show "fraud, bad faith or collusion" by the union in agreeing to terminate the plaintiff's employment. The court observed: "Unless such bilateral decisions, made in good faith, and after unhurried consideration, between a Union and an employer, be sustained in court, the bargaining process is a mirage . . . ." The court concluded that the union had acted honestly to benefit as many employees in the unit as it believed feasible. As will be developed immediately below, the courts have become more willing to scrutinize such union decisions and to test them against a more exacting standard than that of "fraud, bad faith or collusion," and it is not at all clear how far the decision and rationale of the *Hildreth* case can be extended. A similar rationale has, however, been applied by a federal district court which recently permitted a union to cease processing an apparently meritorious case short of arbitration—without even "swapping" it for another grievance— when the union honestly decided that in spite of the merit of the grievance, arbitration would be unduly costly when measured against the union's precarious financial condition. Curth v. Faraday, Inc. (E.D.Mich.1975).

§ 6. Arbitrary or Perfunctory Union Action

The Supreme Court has made it clear that—even though a union has not singled out an individual or group within the bargaining unit for invidious or hostile treatment—that alone will not shelter the union against charges of violating its duty to represent all within the unit "fairly." In Vaca v. Sipes (U.S.1967), the Court rejected the argument that the union's obligation in determining whether to process or settle a grievance is merely "to refrain from patently wrongful conduct such as racial discrimination or personal hostility." Instead, the Court stated that even "arbitrary" decisions by the union could found a cause of action, and that in the context of grievance processing "a union may not arbitrarily ignore a meritorious grievance or process it in perfunctory fashion." Both the Board and the courts of appeals have viewed the Supreme Court's formulation as an intentional expansion of the union's duty of fair representation in order to offer minimal representation to all employees it serves, even when there is no evidence of deliberate wrongdoing. Beriault v. Local 40, Super Cargoes & Checkers (9th Cir. 1974).

The requirement goes beyond a negative mandate to refrain from acting invidiously, and imposes an affirmative obligation to give some reason for the union's actions. The court of appeals in Griffin v. UAW (4th Cir. 1972), although conceding that "negligence in handling grievances has not been identified as breaching the union's duty of fair representation," went on to impose upon the union an obligation to make reasoned decisions:

> Without any hostile motive of discrimination and in complete good faith, a union may nevertheless pursue a course of action or inaction that is so unreasonable and arbitrary as to constitute a violation of the duty of fair representation. A union may refuse to process a grievance or handle the grievance in a particular manner for a multitude of reasons, but it may not do so without reason, merely at the whim of someone exercising union authority. A union must especially avoid capricious and arbitrary behavior in the handling of a grievance based on a discharge—the industrial equivalent of capital punishment.

That court concluded that the union violated its duty of fair representation in processing a discharge grievance arising from a fight between the grievant and a supervisor, when the union had an option to file the grievance with a different supervisor but chose instead to file it with the grievant's victim; it held that the union's action "cannot be justified," that it showed a "stubborn refusal to recognize the inequity of placing the matter in the hands of a hostile person," and that although the union may have acted in good faith the jury could properly find the union to have arbitrarily ignored or perfunctorily handled the grievance.

The National Labor Relations Board endorsed the position of the court in *Griffin*, which it finds comparable to its own requirement in Miranda Fuel Co. (1962), *enf't denied* (2d Cir. 1963), that the union refrain from arbitrary action (however well motivated) and accord "fair and impartial treatment" to unit employees. As the Board recently held, in Truck Drivers Local 315 (Rhodes & Jamieson, Ltd.) (1975):

> The prohibition of decisionmaking supported by no reason, as well as decisionmaking for impermissible reasons, is a modest enough beginning for us. Although an employer may discharge an employee for no reason at all without violating the Act, we held in *Miranda Fuel* that unions have obligations to employees they represent that employers do not. And if a duty to avoid arbitrary conduct, as part of an affirmative, fiduciary responsibility, means anything, it must mean at least that there be a reason for action taken. Sometimes the reason will be apparent, sometimes not. When it is not the circumstances may be such that we will

have no choice but to deem the conduct arbitrary if the union does not tell us what it is.

The Board there stated that this requirement "that there be a reason
for action taken" applies when the contract is negotiated, when grievances are processed and when contract rights are adjusted or modified outside the grievance process. It went on to hold that a union
which declined to enforce contractually provided "bumping" rights
after an employee's job was eliminated violated section 8(b)(1)(A),
since the union's decisionmaking process—submitting the issue to a
vote of other unit employees who might be "bumped" from their jobs
by persons comparable to the grievant—"could express, not fairness,
but only the conflict of interest of each member of the electorate."

A similar attack has been launched—with some success—upon
union decisions regarding the adjustment of seniority rights in cases
of merger or consolidation or other acquisition of a business. Usually, some agreement will be reached between the union and the surviving company that provides for some form of "dovetailing" of seniority in order to mesh the two seniority groups. On occasion, the union
may seek the placement of the absorbed workers at the bottom of the
joint seniority list, simply because that group is outnumbered in the
union by employees who would be advantaged by such "endtailing."
A leading case on this question is Truck Drivers Local 568 v. NLRB
(D.C.Cir. 1967). There, the employer, whose workers were represented by the United Transportation Employees (UTE), acquired a
smaller facility represented by the Teamsters, and merged the two
groups. The employer and both unions agreed to an election to determine which union would bargain for the combined unit. The UTE
promptly gave assurances that if elected it would never permit the seniority of the former Teamster employees to be "dovetailed" in
amongst the original workforce and that it would bargain for their
placement at the bottom of the seniority list. These assurances were
found to violate section 8(b)(1)(A), since they coerced employees,
regardless of their true union sympathies, to vote for the UTE or the
Teamsters exclusively on the basis of their fears concerning seniority
placement. The court also held that the endtailing in itself would be
illegal, as a violation of the duty of fair representation, as "union action taken solely for considerations of political expediency, and unsupported by any rational argument whatsoever"; it condemned the
UTE for making no "good faith effort" to reconcile the interests of
the minority faction, for raising no questions as to the merits of dovetailing, and for coming forward with no reason for favoring endtailing "other than the purely political motive of winning an election."
See Ferro v. Railway Express Agency, Inc. (2d Cir. 1961) (international union bargained for job transfers for members of stronger local
but not for weaker local; held, not proper to draw distinctions between employees "based upon their political power within the union").

These decisions demonstrate that even the use of democratic processes within the union will not shelter it against a finding of violation of the duty of fair representation. Indeed, the democratic process within the union has induced these courts to accord special scrutiny to decisions which worsen the job status of workers whose only common characteristic—while not as invidious as their color, sex or national origin—is their minority status within the union. This is especially true when the decision within the union is made at such a time that one's vote for or against endtailing will be based not on the merits of the issue in the abstract but rather upon the preordained dictates of self interest after a consolidation has already occurred. The fact that the political status of a group within the union determines what seniority positions it will occupy may appear sufficiently "arbitrary" and sufficiently related to "union discrimination" as to tip the scales in favor of court or Board supervision. Of course, if the union agrees to endtail workers, or refuses to process their colorable grievance concerning endtailing, specifically because they are not members of the union, it violates the Labor Act. NLRB v. Local 396, Teamsters (United Parcel Serv.) (9th Cir. 1975) (violation of section 8(b)(1) to refuse to process endtailing grievance because worker is not a union member and filed an unfair labor practice charge against the union; union ordered to take the grievance to arbitration and also to pay the employee's fees for separate counsel).

Since favoring either group of employees in such merger or consolidation cases might be thought to place the union in an unavoidable conflict of interest, a union might decide to take no position at all on the question of dovetailing; such neutrality would presumably not be deemed a violation of the duty of fair representation. Bieski v. Eastern Auto. Forwarding Co. (3d Cir. 1968). But such neutral inaction is surely not required by the Labor Act. Dovetailing is a commonly accepted practice in cases of business acquisitions and would no doubt be presumed reasonable. Humphrey v. Moore (U.S.1964). The union would even more clearly be sustained when, before approving dovetailing, the officers give the opponents "an opportunity to make their case and then decide the question honestly and impartially" upon "full and protracted consideration to the arguments of both sides." Price v. International Bhd. of Teamsters (3d Cir. 1972). Even endtailing was sustained as having "some reason," in an early case in which an AFL union represented both groups of employees when one company of 1,000 employees acquired another company of 100 employees; when the union advocated dovetailing, the larger group simply shifted affiliation to a CIO union, which thereupon bargained for endtailing. In Britt v. Trailmobile Co. (6th Cir. 1950), the court upheld the union's action, simply by noting that it was the product of bargaining and had "some basis." It is likely that today, even if such a decision would not be rejected outright, the burden would be upon the union to demonstrate that some effort was made to consider on the merits and to accommodate the interests of the minority group of employees.

Even when the union has not been motivated by the political balance of power within its membership and has acted in apparent good faith in protecting employee interests through grievance processing or litigation, it has been found to violate its duty of fair representation by "arbitrary" or "perfunctory" conduct. For example, in Holodnak v. Avco-Lycoming Div., Avco Corp. (D.Conn.1974), *mdf'd on other grounds* (2d Cir. 1975) (court of appeals adopting by implication the "perfunctory" standard), an employee who had published a letter in a local newspaper of a political group was discharged for violating a company rule barring false or malicious statements concerning the company; the letter had attacked, among others, the company, the union, judges and arbitrators. The union provided an attorney for the grievant and took the case to arbitration, but the arbitrator sustained the discharge. The court concluded that the union had not accorded the grievant fair representation, entered a judgment against the union and the company, and set aside the arbitrator's award. It characterized the conduct of the union's attorney as "arbitrary," "sadly lacking" and "passive." The court pointed out that the attorney too willingly conceded the validity of the company's rule, failed to insist upon a very narrow construction, and failed to object when the arbitrator questioned the grievant in a manner which the court regarded as offensive and inquisitorial.

In Figueroa de Arroyo v. Sindicato de Trabajadores Packinghouse (1st Cir. 1970), the union neglected to process through the grievance procedure claims of senior employees displaced by automation; the union believed that the rights of these employees could be protected through a pending proceeding against the employer before the NLRB regarding layoffs resulting from company subcontracting. The court held that a cause of action was stated against the union: there was no evidence that it had "ever investigated or made any judgment concerning the merits" of the grievances; even though the grievants had not clearly outlined their seniority claims to the union these would have been obvious had the union "given anything but the most perfunctory attention to these grievances"; and the union's belief that these layoffs from automation would be redressed in the NLRB proceeding regarding layoffs from subcontracting was "inexplicable." (The court ruled out bad faith, hostility, discrimination or dishonesty, and noted the reputation of the union official involved as a "dedicated" union leader.) See Thompson v. Machinists Lodge 1049 (E.D.Va.1966) (international union represented grievant in unsuccessful arbitration; court holds that although "taken singly the union's omissions might not constitute lack of fair representation," its failure to give the employee notice of the arbitration hearing, when he was the only witness in support of his case, coupled with its inadequate preparation and presentation, did subject the union to liability).

As these cases demonstrate, the courts appear willing—in policing union conduct that is "arbitrary and perfunctory"—to look beyond the question whether the union in fact pursues an employee's grievance (contractual or statutory) and to determine whether the union has made a full investigation, has given the grievant notice and an opportunity to participate, has mustered colorable arguments and has refuted insubstantial arguments by the employer. Indeed, although the Board and the courts generally utilize the same formula or definition of fair representation regardless of whether the union's conduct is in the negotiation or the administration of the collective bargaining agreement, there have been occasional suggestions in the decided cases that the union owes its constituents a more exacting duty when it is enforcing an existing contract than when it is negotiating a contract in the first instance. Negotiation embraces the power to formulate general contract principles of future applicability, while grievances raise questions of arguably vested rights under the specific terms of an existing agreement. Elgin, J. & E. Ry. v. Burley (U.S.1945) (Railway Labor Act provides for intervention of National Mediation Board in "major" disputes regarding contract negotiation, while Railway Adjustment Board determines "minor" disputes regarding contract grievances; union has no statutory authority to compromise a grievance without the participation and consent of the individual). The Supreme Court has suggested, in a decision of uncertain reach, that—at least when the union and employer purport to resolve a grievance pursuant to a particular contract provision, rather than by formal amendment—a court may screen the union's construction of the contract for reasonableness. Humphrey v. Moore (U.S.1964) (union held reasonable in adjusting seniority rights by "dovetailing" in a business merger; a thorough concurring opinion of Justice Goldberg, taking issue with the Court, would assimilate the adjustment of grievances to the process of contract amendment or negotiation, with union powers the same). In another case, Price v. International Bhd. of Teamsters (3d Cir. 1972), also involving the dovetailing of seniority lists, the court read the terms of the labor contract to impose sharp limitations upon the union's discretion in the processing of grievances. It held:

> A court will defer to arbitrators or committees when they are exercising their delegated power to decide unforeseen or unresolved problems arising out of gaps or [sic] content in the contract. However, it will not allow them to ignore provisions embodied in the agreement: the basic contract rights must be enforced.

While the reasons for this attitude are not commonly articulated in the reported cases, they may rest on some of these factors: in contract administration and grievance adjustment, the aggrieved employees usually have a more particularized expectation of arguably "vested" contract rights; many grievances involve such matters as discharge and discipline, or seniority in relation to such matters as promotion, layoff and recall, all of which are of essential importance to the individual employee; often, the employee's claims can be adjusted without creating a harmful precedent of any kind and without compromising the interests of other employees in the bargaining unit; administration and grievance adjustment are performed by the union at a much lower "level of visibility" and generality than contract negotiation, and are thus more readily subject to "manipulation" by a willful union and more readily garbed with appearances of good faith or mere carelessness; section 9(a) of the Labor Act itself evinces a greater congressional concern for the rights of the individual in grievance adjustment than in contract negotiation, witness the grant to the individual employee of the right to present and adjust grievances directly with the employer.

It is rare that the reported decisions actually articulate a more exacting duty of the union in cases of grievance processing than in cases of negotiation. Nonetheless, cases charging failure to represent fairly in the processing of grievances are increasing in volume, and it is in these cases that the courts have—while using the same verbal formula—slowly expanded the duty to avoid action which is arbitrary or perfunctory or, in substance, careless. The law has not yet reached the point, however, at which the union is obligated to process all apparently meritorious grievances through the entire grievance procedure to arbitration, for it has been held that a union may weigh the merit of a grievance against the cost of arbitration and is entitled honestly to conclude that it is financially unable to bear that cost; in a recent case, such union action was held not to be arbitrary or perfunctory. Curth v. Faraday, Inc. (E.D.Mich.1975) (union may give weight to "high cost of arbitration and the financial difficulties of the local").

§ 7. Union Negligence?

A number of cases have stated that negligent conduct by the union does not breach its duty of fair representation. Several courts of appeals have so held. Dente v. Masters, Mates & Pilots Local 90 (9th Cir. 1973) (union's delay in processing grievance was at worst negligent; held, no liability); Bazarte v. United Transp. Union (3d Cir. 1970) ("proof that the union may have acted negligently or exercised poor judgment is not enough to support a claim of unfair representation"). The Board has agreed, witness its decision in Local 18, Operating Eng'rs (Ohio Pipe Line Constr. Co.) (1963). There, a union agent assured an employee that his name had been registered with the union-operated hiring hall, when in fact this was not so; by relying on the union's representation, the employee was overlooked for a number of job referrals. The Board dismissed an unfair labor practice complaint against the union, stating that "Mere forgetfulness or inadvertent error is not the type of conduct that the principles of *Miranda* were intended to reach." More recently, the Board affirmed this doctrine by dismissing an unfair labor practice complaint against a union for failure to process a grievance when only negligence was alleged. Teamsters Local 692 (1974).

In substance, however, a number of courts have found the union liable for failing to process, or for improperly processing, a grievance when the union's action can fairly be described as no worse than negligent; indeed, the reference in the Supreme Court decision in Vaca v. Sipes (U.S.1967), to "perfunctory" processing of grievances invites the finding of a violation when injury is caused by union carelessness without more. As already described, in Holodnak v. Avco-Lycoming Div., Avco Corp. (D.Conn.1974), *mdf'd on other grounds* (2d Cir. 1975), the court found that the union's attorney representing the grievant in arbitration had overlooked obvious legal arguments and had not been sufficiently aggressive in protecting the grievant against questioning by the arbitrator (a not indelicate task). In Figueroa de Arroyo v. Sindicato de Trabajadores Packinghouse (1st Cir. 1970), the court found that the union had overlooked the legal theory underlying the grievants' complaints and had unwisely relied upon NLRB procedures to vindicate the grievants' unrelated contract rights; in Thompson v. Machinists Lodge 1049 (E.D.Va.1966), the court took the union to task for poor preparation, poor responses to the arguments of the employer and inadequate attempts to safeguard the procedural rights of the grievant.

For all practical purposes, the distinction between "arbitrary" union action, clearly outlawed under the duty of fair representation, and "negligent" action was broken down in Ruzicka v. General Motors Corp. (6th Cir. 1975), where a union agent processing a discharge case neglected to file with the company a "notice of unadjusted grievance," thus permitting the company to refuse pursuant to the labor contract to submit to arbitration. The court held "such negligent handling of the grievance, unrelated as it was to the merits of [the employee's] case," to violate the duty of fair representation. It continued: "[W]hen a union makes no decision as to the merit of an individual's grievance but merely allows it to expire by negligently failing to take a basic and required step towards resolving it, the union has acted arbitrarily and is liable   .   .   .   ." The concurring judge more clearly asserted that the union's conduct was not arbitrary or perfunctory but should be deemed in any event to violate the duty of fair representation; he did not invite the court to screen all union actions for their wisdom, but argued that a total failure to act except for a proper reason was sufficiently egregious as to warrant union liability.

It remains to be seen whether, just as over the years there has been a gradual liberalizing from a requirement of hostility or invidious discrimination to one of arbitrary or perfunctory conduct, courts will more openly acknowledge that a union—at least in the processing of grievances as opposed to the negotiation of a new contract—owes the employees it represents a duty of due care in the protection of their interests.

§ 8. Remedies: In the Courts

In Steele v. Louisville & N.R.R. (U.S.1944), the Supreme Court held that the union violated the duty of fair representation by negotiating for the elimination of the jobs of black workers. It also held that this duty was enforceable by a judicial action for injunction and damages, there being no appropriate administrative agency under the Railway Labor Act to vindicate the rights of the employees, and that the Norris-LaGuardia Act was not a bar to any such injunction against the enforcement of the discriminatory agreement. Injunctive relief may be mandatory as well as negative. Thus, in Central of Ga. Ry. v. Jones (5th Cir. 1956), not only did the court enjoin the union and company from enforcing the contract and operating practices which denied blacks the right to compete and train for certain railroad jobs, but it also affirmatively required them to grant to black workers the same seniority rights, training privileges, assignments and opportunities for those jobs as white persons of similar continuous service would enjoy. And, when the union's breach of duty occurs not in negotiation but in the administration of an existing contract, an injunction may issue against the union requiring it to process the grievance through the contract procedure, including arbitration. Vaca v. Sipes (U.S.1967) ("an order compelling arbitration should be viewed as one of the available remedies when a breach of the union's duty is proved"). Indeed, a union has been ordered not to process grievances of other employees when those grievances would strip contract rights from an employee whom the union had unfairly represented. Butler v. Local 823, Teamsters (8th Cir. 1975) (no violation found of the rights of the other, absent, employees since union had in effect vigorously represented their interests throughout the grievance procedure and the instant litigation).

Even when the employer is not in common cause with the union in the union's failure to represent fairly (which the employer was in the *Steele* case, for example), an injunction may issue against the employer alone when there is proof of some independent employer wrong arising from the same transaction. Perhaps the clearest example is a wrongful discharge in breach of the employer's duty under the labor contract, combined with a union failure to process the employee's grievance in a manner consistent with its duty of fair representation. Even though the employer does not participate directly in the union's breach, the employee is entitled to sue the employer on the contract for wrongful discharge, because the employee's failure to satisfy the requirement which normally obtains to press his claim through the grievance procedure to arbitration is excused by the union's wrongful action. Vaca v. Sipes (U.S.1967). In the action against the employer, which is a contract-enforcement action within the jurisdiction of the federal courts under section 301 of the Labor Act, the court may order the employer to reinstate the employee. Such injunctive relief in a federal court is not banned by section 4(a) of the Norris-LaGuardia Act, which directs the court not to issue an injunction prohibiting persons from "ceasing or refusing . . . to remain in any relation of employment." Figueroa de Arroyo v. Sindicato de Trabajadores Packinghouse (1st Cir. 1970) (statutory language was designed to bar injunctions against striking employees, forcing them to remain in an employment relationship; "the reemployment of improperly discharged employees can hardly be said to be one of the abuses sought to be eliminated by the Norris-LaGuardia Act").

Compensatory damages may also be awarded against the union for breach of its duty of fair representation. Such damages may recompense not only for past economic injury resulting from the union's breach; in the event that preferred injunctive relief (such as reinstatement) is not available to rectify the wrong prospectively, the union may be required to pay for future damages, such as loss of future earnings, as well. *Ibid.* (six-year delay since discharge may make reinstatement impractical). But the court must distinguish, typically in the case of a union failure to challenge an alleged employer breach of contract, the injury to the grievant caused by the union's breach of duty of fair representation from the injury caused by the employer's underlying violation of the labor contract. The leading case on this issue is Vaca v. Sipes (U.S.1967), in which an employee was discharged because of poor health, and the union after processing the case through several steps of the grievance procedure chose not to seek arbitration, believing the grievance to lack merit. The Court stated that if the union's failure to process the grievance had been wrongful, the employee could sue the union for that wrong and could also sue the employer (in the same or a separate proceeding) for breach of the labor contract stemming from the wrongful discharge. While the Court conceded that a trial judge could properly order the union to arbitrate, it also found that such a remedy might not make the employee whole, particularly if much of his injury was attributable to the union's conduct—conduct which would not normally be remediable before an arbitrator. In such cases, the court may take jurisdiction and award damages against the union, but not for harm attributable solely to the employer's breach of contract:

> Though the union has violated a statutory duty in failing to press the grievance, it is the employer's unrelated breach of

contract which triggered the controversy and which caused this portion of the employee's damages. The employee should have no difficulty recovering these damages from the employer . . . . It could be a real hardship on the union to pay these damages, even if the union were given a right of indemnification against the employer. With the employee assured of direct recovery from the employer, we see no merit in requiring the union to pay the employer's share of the damages.

. . . [D]amages attributable solely to the employer's breach of contract should not be charged to the union, but increases if any in those damages caused by the union's refusal to process the grievance should not be charged to the employer.

In *Vaca*, the Court concluded that the union was not a participant in the employer's allegedly wrongful discharge and that the employer was not a participant in the union's alleged wrongful refusal to process the grievance; thus, joint liability for either wrong would have been unwarranted.

It appears that in most grievance cases, the bulk of the damages will be assessed against the employer rather than the union, since the major harm to the employee is his severance from work (or his improper transfer, demotion, or suspension). When, however, the union's delay in processing his grievance, or its refusal altogether, increases or contributes to the damages flowing from the discharge— for example, by prolonging the loss of earnings or by effectively preventing reinstatement altogether—the union may be taxed accordingly. Figueroa de Arroyo v. Sindicato de Trabajadores Packinghouse (1st Cir. 1970.)

In appropriate cases, which are likely to be rare, damages for mental distress might also be recovered by the grievant. *Ibid.* (court states in dictum that federal law would permit such a recovery against either the employer or the union in a case of its "extreme conduct"). Punitive damages might also be awarded, either against the employer for its contract breach or against the union for breach of its duty of fair representation. Such damages will likely be awarded but rarely, especially in an action against the employer which sounds in contract, where punitive damages are awarded only if there is a "willful abuse of a duty imposed as a result of the defendant's position of authority or trust, as well as a breach of contract," Holodnak v. Avco-Lycoming Div., Avco Corp. (2d Cir. 1975), but even in an action against the union which sounds more in tort. Thus, in Butler v. Local 823, Teamsters (8th Cir. 1975), the court rejected the grievant's claim for punitive damages against his union, which had declined to process a grievance stemming from his loss of seniority after his company was merged into another. The court assumed that punitive damages could be awarded in a contract action under section 301 or in an action for breach of the duty of fair representation, but held:

> The local's conduct was not the type of outrageous or extraordinary conduct for which extraordinary remedies are needed; rather, it amounted to the commonly encountered policy of favoring one group of members over another, which lies in the mainstream of unfair representation litigation. Butler was not subjected to threats of violence, harassment, physical abuse, or the scorn and ridicule of his coworkers, and there was no showing that the Local acted with any malice directed specifically at him. . . . The federal courts should fashion remedies under the labor statutes which are necessary to achieving the goal of industrial peace. . . . The plaintiff did not establish that punitive damages were needed to deter future misconduct or to prevent industrial strife.

Since the union's wrongful failure to process a grievance may force the employee to litigate, it has been held that the employee may recover reasonable counsel fees, to be allocated as appropriate between employer and union defendants. The court will consider the significance of the vindicated employee rights for other employees in the bargaining unit, the need to attract competent counsel and the importance of making the employee whole. Holodnak v. Avco-Lycoming Div., Avco Corp. (D.Conn.1974), *mdf'd on other grounds* (2d Cir. 1975) (counsel fees and expenses taxed two-thirds to the company and one-third to the union). It would appear that such an award of counsel fees will continue to be proper, in the absence of express statutory authorization therefor, even after the decision of the Supreme Court in the *Alaska Pipeline* case, Alyeska Pipeline Serv. Co. v. Wilderness Soc'y (U.S.1975). There, although the Court limited the power to award counsel fees when the plaintiff was serving as a "private attorney general," it endorsed such other and distinct justifications for counsel fees as redressing or deterring bad faith by the losing party (which forced the prevailing party to litigate) or as taxing a common fund (*i. e.*, the union treasury) for the plaintiff's rendering of a common benefit to other persons who have contributed to that fund. Most successful unfair-representation actions will fall within either (or both) of these justifications for the award of counsel fees.

There is considerable disagreement among the courts of appeals concerning the appropriate statute of limitations to be applied in an action against a union for violation of its duty of fair representation. What is clear is that there is no single federal limitations period in such actions; the Labor Act specifies no directly pertinent period (not surprisingly, since this kind of action is itself not set forth in the Act), and the six-month limitations period for unfair labor practices has been considered inapt. Vaca v. Sipes (U.S.1967). Instead, the courts have taken their cue from UAW v. Hoosier Cardinal Corp. (U.S.1966), which held that in actions brought under section 301 of the Labor Act, the court is to apply the applicable state statute of limitations. Even in those courts which do not characterize fair representation actions as jurisdictionally rooted in section 301, it has been held appropriate to incorporate state limitations law. Figueroa de Arroyo v. Trabajadores Packinghouse (1st Cir. 1970). The confusion arises in determining (even assuming the transaction is limited to one state) which of several possible limitations periods should be adopted; *Hoosier Cardinal* concludes that this "characterization" is itself a matter of federal law.

Some courts characterize the action against the union as a tort action, and apply what is generally a shorter statute of limitations than that which obtains in any employee action against the employer for breach of contract. These decisions note the seeming incongruity of permitting a suit against the employer at a time when a suit against the union would be barred, particularly when the union's violation of the duty of fair representation will be an element in the suit against the employer. But they hold nonetheless that the union's duty is akin to, although less rigorous than, the duty of due care normally associated with tort actions; that there is a federal policy favoring prompt litigation when no manifest injustice will result; and that plaintiff employees should not be able to prolong the life of their claim against the union by bringing an "incidental" claim in contract against the employer. *Ibid.* Other courts have employed a contracts characterization, at least when the employer and union are joined as defendants, noting that the same facts relating to the union's conduct must be proved even in the action against the employer (so that the "stale evidence" objection supporting the shorter limitations period is not really applicable), and that fair remedies can be applied against the union and the employer only if both defendants are subject to an equal period of vulnerability to suit. Butler v. Local 823, Teamsters (8th Cir. 1975) (holding that the proper contracts limitations period is the one for written contracts rather than oral contracts, relying more on the written labor agreement than on the oral contract of individual employment). Under a third theory, the court is to turn to the state period of limitations governing suits to enforce a liability "created by statute." Gray v. Heat & Frost Insulators Local 51 (6th Cir. 1969).

§ 9. Remedies: Before the NLRB

If the Board finds a union to have committed an unfair labor practice by violating its duty of fair representation, it may of course issue a conventional cease and desist order. Local 1367, Longshoremen (1964), *enf'd per curiam* (5th Cir. 1966). If the employer has, in complicity with the union, violated section 8(a)(3) by discriminating in retention of employees so as to encourage union membership, it may be ordered to reinstate the aggrieved employee with full back-pay and seniority; the union may be held jointly liable for such back-pay. Miranda Fuel Co. (1962), *enf't denied* (2d Cir. 1963). And, where the union violated its duty of fair representation by agreeing with the employer to accord inferior seniority and separate physical facilities to black employees, the Board has ordered the union actually to proffer and to bargain for specific proposals designed to eliminate such race discrimination within the plant; the union's refusal to press individual employee grievances against such conditions was remedied by ordering the union to press for such desegregation through the contractual grievance procedure, including arbitration. Local 12, Rubber Workers v. NLRB (5th Cir. 1966). (The Board, rather than decide the merits of the contract claim directly, will be inclined to require the union to process the grievance.) Indeed, because of a natural skepticism that the union which has been held responsible for wrongful conduct will in fact vigorously represent the interests of the aggrieved employee (especially when the union in the past acted instead as spokesman for others in the unit who continue to have an adverse interest), the Board has gone beyond ordering the union to take the case to arbitration and has ordered as well that it pay the expenses of the aggrieved employee in securing his own independent representation. NLRB v. Local 396, Teamsters (United Parcel Serv.) (9th Cir. 1975) (section 8(b)(1)(A) violation; on subsequent remand, Board concluded that although union would ordinarily use a full-time paraprofessional union employee to represent the grievant, comparable expertise outside the union could be provided only by a practicing attorney, and award of fees should be determined accordingly).

In an extraordinary case, in which the Board found that the union had committed an unfair labor practice by maintaining separate locals for men and women and processing their grievances separately (although the labor contract was not facially discriminatory), the Board ordered the union to merge the two locals. The court of appeals sustained this order as within the Board's broad remedial powers, in spite of the proviso to section 8(b)(1)(A) preserving to the union the right "to prescribe its own rules with respect to the acquisition or retention of membership therein." NLRB v. Local 106, Glass Bottle Blowers (Owens-Illinois, Inc.) (6th Cir. 1975).

The Board has also taken steps to redress violations of the duty of fair representation in election proceedings as well as in unfair labor practice proceedings. Thus, although an executed collective bargaining agreement will normally bar the holding of a representation election during its term (up to three years), the Board will dispense with this contract-bar rule when the labor contract contains provisions which are racially discriminatory on their face. Pioneer Bus

Co. (1962) (separate contracts for black and white employees). This will facilitate the possible ouster of a union which has violated the duty of fair representation in contract negotiations. Such a sanction will, however, not seriously injure the union which has sufficient power within the bargaining unit to win another election. The Board has therefore taken further steps to undermine the representational status of the majority union which unlawfully discriminates. The Board will revoke the certification of a union which is shown to discriminate on the basis of race in contract negotiation or grievance processing or, indeed, to discriminate on the basis of race in its qualifications for membership (which does not automatically violate the duty of fair representation). Metal Workers Local 1 (Hughes Tool Co.) (1964) (union discrimination in negotiating and grievance processing is an unfair labor practice; such discrimination and, independently, the exclusion, classification or segregation in membership on racial grounds, warrant loss of certification).

A splintered Board has held that certain forms of union discrimination may be attacked by the employer even prior to certification. In Bekins Moving & Storage Co. (1974), although all members of the Board agreed that no such attack should be permitted prior to the holding of an election (in view of the desire for a speedy tally and the possible mootness of the attack were the union to lose the election), two members of the Board concluded that the union would be disqualified from certification if the employer could demonstrate, promptly after the union's election victory, that it discriminated *in membership* along lines of race, sex or national origin; one member would permit such pre-certification disqualification only for discrimination in membership along lines of race or national origin, but not sex (since certification in only the former two instances was believed to raise problems of unconstitutionality); but two members would limit all such attacks to post-certification proceedings to revoke the union's certification in the event the union violates its duty of fair representation. The two principal issues dividing the members of the Board were whether the Board could, consistent with the limitations in the federal Constitution upon invidious discrimination by government, certify and thus legitimize a union so discriminating in membership; and whether as a matter of policy it was wiser to deny certification at the outset when the union's discrimination in membership made it probable that it would later proceed to violate its duty of fair representation, or was wiser to certify the union and thus impose the burden and afford the opportunity to represent all employees in the unit regardless of race, national origin or sex. See Bell & Howell Co. (1974) (no pre-certification hearing concerning charges of sex discrimination).

Even in cases in which the Board does hear evidence that the winning union ought not be certified because of discrimination in membership (or when bargaining for employees in other units), the

Board has made it clear that the employer will fail if it proves only that there is a wide statistical disparity between employable individuals of that race or nationality and union members or officers of that race or nationality. The fact that the union has no members or officers of that race or nationality may simply suggest that there are few such individuals working for that employer or in that industry, and may show only that the employer or industry—but not the union —has discriminated invidiously. The Board has suggested, however, that statistical evidence (rather common in actions under Title VII of the 1964 Civil Rights Act) might be probative of union discrimination if it could be shown that the union effectively controls access to employment or that it deliberately discriminates in membership. Grants Furniture Plaza, Inc. (1974) (employer attack on underrepresentation of Spanish-speaking workers in union membership).

Even denial or revocation of certification is not altogether an effective sanction against union discrimination—either in membership or in bargaining and grievance processing—since the employer is generally obligated to bargain with a union which is conceded to have majority support, regardless of certification. The United States Court of Appeals for the Eighth Circuit has recently held, however, that an employer may assert as a defense to a refusal to bargain (even with a majority union) the union's discrimination in membership on the basis of race. NLRB v. Mansion House Center Mgt. Corp. (8th Cir. 1973). The court held that the Constitution forbade the Board to issue a bargaining order at the behest of a union which so discriminated, since such an order would reinforce the union's discrimination with the imprimatur of a federal governmental agency. It appears that no other court of appeals has actually held the principle of *Mansion House* to apply within its circuit, and that the Board has thus far avoided applying *Mansion House* directly in any other case. See Hawkins Constr. Co. (1974) (no need to determine applicability of *Mansion House*, since evidence fails to show union discrimination).

REGULATORY CONFLICT AND ACCOMMODATION

CHAPTER XXXI

THE ARBITRATOR AND THE NATIONAL LABOR RELATIONS BOARD

§ 1. Dual Jurisdiction

A single transaction involving an employer, its employees and their union, may give rise to two kinds of claims: one for breach of contract under the parties' collective bargaining agreement, and the other for application of the provisions of the National Labor Relations Act. A change in wages or working conditions announced by the employer may breach a contract provision and may also violate the duty to bargain under section 8(a)(5). The discharge or other discipline of an employee may violate the contract's "just cause" provision and section 8(a)(3) of the Labor Act barring discrimination for antiunion reasons. An employer refusal to recognize a union as spokesman for its employees at a newly acquired plant may generate a claim of breach of contract or may be processed before the NLRB either through its unfair labor practice machinery or its procedures for representation elections. (Indeed, there may be yet other agencies, such as the Equal Employment Opportunity Commission, before which certain employer or union action may be challenged, in addition to the arbitrator and the NLRB.) The availability of both contractual and statutory machinery for the resolution of disputes creates the possibility of at least duplicative procedures and at worst of conflicting results, and has given rise in the past to the belief that either the Board or the arbitrator ought to be "preempted" from exercising its jurisdiction in these areas of institutional overlap.

The argument against preemption, however, is that each of the two institutions for dispute-resolution has special characteristics which justify maintaining an independent jurisdiction. The Board is a public agency charged with administering a statutory mandate; its task is not so much to implement the private trades struck at the bargaining table but to protect the rights of employees in the public interest (which on occasion may be undermined by the private contract). The Board will thus be sensitive to the policies and values imbedded in our labor law to which the arbitrator may be indifferent. Board proceedings are conducted by a public official, through the Office of the General Counsel, and are therefore perhaps the only effective machinery for individual employees who may lack the financial resources to institute arbitral or judicial proceedings. On the other hand, our society ordinarily places a premium on the resolution of disputes through private machinery freely created by the parties rather than by the intervention of government. Arbitration, an extension of the collective bargaining process, is more attuned to the private interests of the parties and more commonly achieves an accommodation of those interests so as to secure a healthy bargaining relationship for the future. The arbitrator is normally better acquainted with the parties, their contract, their pattern of negotiations and their plant practices. Arbitration is also, in comparison to Board proceedings, normally more informal and expeditious.

Congress has taken no steps to compel preemption of either the Board or the arbitrator in these cases of jurisdictional overlap. Indeed, Congress has underlined the responsibility of each agency in its own sphere. Section 10(a), after reiterating the Board's authority to adjudicate unfair labor practice cases, provides: "This power shall not be affected by any other means of adjustment or prevention that has been or may be established by agreement, law, or otherwise." And section 203(d) of the Act provides: "Final adjustment by a method agreed upon by the parties is hereby declared to be the desirable method for settlement of grievance disputes arising over the application or interpretation of an existing collective-bargaining agreement." Accordingly, it has been the task of the courts to determine whether the Board is to be stripped of jurisdiction whenever a case before it requires the construction of a labor contract or could be effectively resolved by arbitration as a breach-of-contract claim, and to determine whether the arbitrator is to be stripped of jurisdiction whenever a contract case grows from a transaction which raises problems of application of the Labor Act. The Supreme Court has clearly determined that neither agency has exclusive jurisdiction in these matters. It has, however, acknowledged that the Board has discretion to "defer" to the arbitrator when this would foster the expeditious resolution of disputes consistent with the Labor Act, and has also stated that in the event of a conflict between the decision of an arbitrator under the contract and the decision of the Board under the Labor Act, the Board's decision must prevail.

The Court rejected the claim that conduct violating the Labor Act could be prosecuted only before the NLRB and not also as a contract breach, in Smith v. Evening News Ass'n (U.S.1962). There the employer during a strike by one union refused to permit members of another union to report to work but did permit nonunion employees to report to work and paid them (even though no work was available). It was argued that this was in breach of a contract clause providing: "[T]here shall be no discrimination against any employee because of membership or activity" in the signatory union. Without any elaborate reasoning, the Court simply stated that while the Board retains authority to deal with this employer discrimination, which was conceded to be an unfair labor practice, that authority is not exclusive and does not displace claims of contract breach under section 301. (In the *Smith* case, there was no arbitration procedure which had to be exhausted before a lawsuit could be brought, and the Court remanded for a judicial determination of the contract claim on the merits).

The question whether the arbitrator was to be preempted was more thoroughly considered by the Court in Carey v. Westinghouse Elec. Corp. (U.S.1964). There, an electrical union representing production and maintenance employees sought to compel arbitration of its claim that the employer was assigning unit work to "salaried, technical" employees in another unit represented by a different union. The employer refused to arbitrate, claiming that the dispute was a representational one within the exclusive jurisdiction of the NLRB. The highest court of the state of New York agreed, but it was reversed by the Supreme Court. The Court acknowledged that the dispute could be characterized either as a representation dispute, with the question being which union was to bargain for the particular employees doing the jobs in question, or as a jurisdictional or work-assignment dispute, with the question being whether those employees should be ousted from the job and the work assigned instead to other employees already represented by the electrical union. The Board resolves the former kind of dispute by a unit determination in the context of a representation proceeding; in certain circumstances it can resolve the latter kind of dispute through unfair labor practice proceedings and a work-assignment hearing. But, continued the Court, however the dispute is to be characterized, it may also properly be adjudicated by an arbitrator under the contract covering the production and maintenance unit, which provided for the exclusive recognition of the electrical union. The Court held that arbitration—even when the only parties are the employer and the electrical union, but not the union representing the salaried employees—"may as a practical matter end the controversy or put into movement forces that will resolve it." The Court emphasized that arbitration, like collective bargaining generally, advances the statutory objective of promoting industrial peace and stability. It also noted that arbitration would help to avoid fragmentation of the dispute, since "the Board shows deference to the arbitral award, provided the procedure was a fair one and the results were not repugnant to the Act." The Court also addressed the problem of conflicting decisions should the Board choose to exercise its undoubted jurisdiction in an unfair labor practice or representation case:

> Should the Board disagree with the arbiter, by ruling, for example, that the employees involved in the controversy are members of one bargaining unit or another, the Board's ruling would, of course, take precedence; and if the employer's action had been in accord with that ruling, it would not be liable for damages under § 301.

Soon after the *Carey* case established that arbitration ought not be precluded because the conduct in question also falls within the jurisdiction of the NLRB, the Court decided that the Board was not ousted of its jurisdiction to hear a case merely because it would require the Board to construe the provisions of a collective bargaining agreement or because the dispute could also be resolved by arbitration. In NLRB v. Acme Industrial Co. (U.S.1967), the union demanded that the employer furnish it with information concerning the movement of equipment out of the plant, in order to assist it in formulating and processing a grievance concerning the rights of employees who would be demoted or laid off because of the relocation of equipment. The employer refused to disclose the information, and the Board's finding of an unfair labor practice was reversed by the court of appeals, which held that the Board was foreclosed from acting because it was for the arbitrator to determine whether the information was pertinent to a meritorious grievance. The Supreme Court reversed, approving the Board's assertion of jurisdiction and its conclusion that the employer had a duty to disclose the information. The Court held (relying on section 10(a) of the Labor Act) that the availability of arbitration did not affect the Board's power to adjudicate unfair labor practice charges, that in any event the Board in ordering production of the information did not make "a binding construction of the labor contract" but acted only on the probability that it would be relevant to the grievance, and that rather than intrude upon the domain of the arbitrator the Board assisted the arbitral process by permitting the union in advance to "sift out unmeritorious claims" after studying the pertinent information in the hands of the employer.

When the Board was indeed called upon to construe a labor contract, in NLRB v. C & C Plywood Corp. (U.S.1967), the Court nonetheless sustained the Board's jurisdiction in a case of "unilateral action" by the employer in violation of section 8(a)(5). There, the employer instituted without bargaining a premium pay plan for certain employees during the contract term, and relied on a contract provision which reserved to the employer the right to pay a premium rate "to reward any particular employee for some special fitness, skill, aptitude or the like." The court of appeals held that the employer's defense that the union thus authorized its action would require a construction of the contract, and that this was beyond the Board's jurisdiction. The Supreme Court acknowledged that Congress had purposely chosen not to make all contract breaches remediable before the Board as unfair labor practices, but rather to leave contract actions to the usual machinery, courts and arbitration; the object was to avoid governmental regulation of contract terms. But the Board in this case was not construing the labor agreement to determine the extent of contract rights and was not imposing its view of the contract terms upon the parties. The Board merely examined the contract to determine whether the union had given up its statutory right to establish new wage rates through collective bargaining. The Court buttressed its conclusion by noting that the contract failed to provide for arbitration of claimed breaches, so that the union's recourse against the employer's action was either a strike or an extended court action, neither of which was as desirable as prompt Board resolution. The Court also held, on the merits, that the Board did not err in finding that the contract provision in question did not authorize the employer to institute a generalized program of premium pay.

Although the Court in both *Acme* and *C & C Plywood* preserved the Board's jurisdiction while at the same time avoiding any direct clash with the jurisdiction of an arbitrator, it should have been clear from the Court's decisions that the Board would not be ousted from construing a contract clause even when an arbitrator was available to do precisely the same thing. A court of appeals in fact so held, the same year, in NLRB v. Huttig Sash & Door Co. (8th Cir. 1967), and the principle has not been seriously questioned since. In *Huttig*, the employer reduced the wages of certain employees, claiming that such action was permitted by the transfer and management-rights provisions of the labor contract. The court, however, upheld the Board's finding that the employer violated section 8(a)(5), and also held that the Board's jurisdiction was not preempted merely because the unfair labor practice issue turned upon a construction of the terms of the contract. The court read the *Acme* and *C & C Plywood* decisions to hold, in effect, that "of itself, neither the presence of a problem of contract interpretation nor the presence of an arbitration provision in the contract deprives the Board of jurisdiction." The court also found in those two Supreme Court decisions an acceptance of multiple channels for settling labor disputes, a desire for expeditious settlement, a respect for the Board's expertise, and an emphasis upon protection of statutory rights (even though there are aspects of contract interpretation which are secondary or incidental).

Once it is determined that both the Board and the arbitrator have jurisdiction or power to announce rights and obligations emerging from the same transaction, it becomes necessary to consider how that dual power is to be accommodated. Principles of priority and of deference have been developed. As the Supreme Court stated in Carey v. Westinghouse Elec. Corp. (U.S.1964), in the event of a conflict between an arbitral interpretation of a contract and a Board interpretation of the Labor Act (even when that involves contract construction), the Board as guarantor of the public interest must prevail. Such conflict has been rare, however, because arbitrators and the Board have worked out means of accommodation and deference. The impact of Board action upon the decisions of the arbitrator is discussed elsewhere in this work. Perhaps the more significant development has been the willingness of the Board to defer to decisions already rendered by an arbitrator and, more recently, its willingness to delay exercising its undoubted jurisdiction when the parties can have recourse to contractual grievance and arbitration machinery, as yet unused. That development, which has been encouraged by the Supreme Court, is the subject of the materials immediately following.

§ 2. Board Deference to Arbitration Awards: Generally

Although the National Labor Relations Board is not stripped of its jurisdiction to decide unfair labor practice or representation cases merely because a contract issue may be implicated, the Board has exercised its discretion to "defer" to arbitration awards already rendered when those awards effectively dispose of the unfair labor practice or representation issue. The Board's criteria for thus deferring to an existing award were set forth in Spielberg Mfg. Co. (1955), which has given its name to the so-called *Spielberg* doctrine. In that case, the company and union submitted to arbitration the company's refusal to reinstate four strikers accused of misconduct, and the arbitration board sustained the company. Charges filed thereafter against the employer for violation of sections 8(a)(1) and (3) were dismissed by the Board, which deferred to the arbitral finding that the refusals to reinstate were legitimately motivated:

> [T]he proceedings appear to have been fair and regular, all parties had agreed to be bound, and the decision of the arbitration panel is not clearly repugnant to the purposes and policies of the Act. In these circumstances we believe that the desirable objective of encouraging the voluntary settlement of labor disputes will be best served by our recognition of the arbitrators' award.

The *Spielberg* doctrine was elaborated further in International Harvester Co. (1962), *enf'd* (7th Cir. 1964). There, the union filed a grievance claiming that the employer had violated the labor agreement by not discharging an employee, one Ramsey, who was allegedly two months in default in his dues payments. When the arbitrator concluded that Ramsey should have been discharged pursuant to the contract, and sustained the grievance to that extent, Ramsey filed charges against the employer under section 8(a)(3) and the union under section 8(b)(2). Although the trial examiner sustained the charges, the Board reversed, and held that the award should have been respected and the complaint dismissed. The Board noted that while the arbitration award did not deprive it of its unfair labor practice jurisdiction, it was prepared to stay its hand if that would "serve the fundamental aims of the Act." One of the aims of the Act was deemed to be the elimination of economic strife and the promotion of industrial stability through the arbitral enforcement of labor contracts:

> If complete effectuation of the Federal policy is to be achieved, we firmly believe that the Board, which is entrust-

ed with the administration of one of the many facets of national labor policy, should give hospitable acceptance to the arbitral process as "part and parcel of the collective bargaining process itself," and voluntarily withhold its undoubted authority to adjudicate alleged unfair labor practice charges involving the same subject matter, unless it clearly appears that the arbitration proceedings were tainted by fraud, collusion, unfairness, or serious procedural irregularities or that the award was clearly repugnant to the purposes and policies of the Act.

Although it was contended that a fair proceeding was lacking, since Ramsey was not given notice of and did not participate in the arbitration hearing, the Board disagreed and found that "his interests were vigorously defended there by the Company" which had at all times resisted the claims of the union that Ramsey had to maintain his union membership or be discharged.

The following year, the Board applied the doctrine of deferral to arbitration in a representation case. In Raley's Inc. (1963), the Board dismissed as untimely an election petition filed by a union seeking an election among a group of employees who had earlier been found by an arbitrator to be included within a contract between the company and a different union. In spite of the fact that the contract had no express provision covering the disputed workers, that the "absorption" of those workers into the contract unit effectively deprived them of a choice of bargaining representative, and that the petitioning union was not a party to the arbitration proceeding, the Board found the proceeding fair and the award not repugnant to the Act. Applying the *Spielberg* tests, the Board concluded that the position of the petitioning union (that is, for non-inclusion of the employees under the contract) was "vigorously defended" by the employer at the arbitration hearing, and that the award was like many Board "accretion" decisions in other similar representation cases. With the employees included under the contract, there was thus a "contract bar" which rendered the other union's election petition untimely.

The Supreme Court has acknowledged with approval the Board's policy of deferring to arbitration, both concerning unfair labor practice issues, NLRB v. C & C Plywood Corp. (U.S.1967), and representation issues, Carey v. Westinghouse Elec. Corp. (U.S.1964). The policy has also been explicitly upheld by the courts of appeals. Associated Press v. NLRB (D.C.Cir. 1974).

If the decision of the arbitrator meets the *Spielberg* standards, the Board will defer even though the respondent before the Board has refused to abide by the decision of the arbitrator. The Board has held, with judicial approval, that the proper recourse of the prevailing party in arbitration is not to relitigate the issues before the Board but rather to secure judicial enforcement of the award under section 301 of the Labor Act. As the court stated in Local 715, IBEW v. NLRB (Malrite of Wisconsin, Inc.) (D.C.Cir. 1974):

> The policy established by *Spielberg* is to withhold Board processes where private methods of settlement are adequate. In this case, the arbitration process has foundered, but it has not proven inadequate. The union may yet obtain compliance with the award by means of a suit for its enforcement. As long as the remedy of judicial enforcement is available, the force of the *Spielberg* doctrine is not diminished by one party's disregard for the arbitral award.

§ 3. The Board's Prerequisites for Deference

Consonance With the Labor Act. The Board will refuse to defer to an arbitral award which it finds repugnant to the policies of the Labor Act. Perhaps the clearest example is Virginia-Carolina Freight Lines, Inc. (1965), in which a charge was filed alleging that an employee had been discharged because of his stated intention to resort to the NLRB in a contract dispute with the employer. An arbitrator had earlier passed upon the discharge and had sustained it, concluding that the employee had violated the duties of employment by enlisting a federal agency in his dispute with the company. The Board summarily noted that the employee was given precisely this privilege by section 8(a)(4), and that the arbitral award was clearly repugnant to the Act; the Board found an unfair labor practice and ordered the employee's reinstatement. The Board also declined to defer, because of repugnancy to the Act, in NLRB v. Hribar Trucking, Inc. (7th Cir. 1969), where an arbitrator ordered reinstatement of a truckdriver but imposed the condition that the driver promptly obtain his own insurance. The Board found that the employer had initially imposed the insurance requirement on the employee as a form of discrimination for his union activities, and that to honor that requirement in the arbitration would thus be repugnant to the Act.

Somewhat in contrast, the Board has recently deferred to an arbitration award which found that the employee had indeed been discharged for union activity but which ordered reinstatement only, without backpay, since the employee had been shown to have falsified his employment application by not setting forth his criminal record. The Board held, in spite of the usual award of reinstatement and full backpay for a violation of section 8(a)(3), that it would defer to the award omitting backpay, because such an award would not be repugnant to the Act in light of the employee's falsification. Ohio Ferro-Alloys Corp. (1974). See also Howard Elec. Co. (1967) (Board dismisses section 8(a)(3) complaint in deference to arbitral award ordering backpay but, because of employer's contract power over hiring, not reinstatement). The Board has also deferred to an arbitration award which held the employer responsible for conduct (a proposed unilateral change in shift assignments) which would violate the

Labor Act even though the arbitrator imposed no remedies on the employer. Southwestern Bell Tel. Co. (1974) (employer withdrew proposed action, and thus no need for a cease-and-desist order).

In another case involving a unilateral change of working conditions, the Board did find the arbitral award to be repugnant to the Labor Act. In Radio Television Tech. School, Inc. v. NLRB (3d Cir. 1973), the employer without bargaining discontinued the practice of giving its employees a Christmas bonus. In spite of a number of Board and court precedents treating such longstanding bonuses as "mandatory" subjects about which the employer was not free to act unilaterally, the arbitrator ruled that the bonus was merely a gift which the employer could withdraw at any time. The Board, with court approval, treated the award as repugnant to well-established precedent under the Act, refused to defer, and found a violation of section 8(a)(5).

The Board has also found "repugnancy" quite frequently in representation cases. In a case hardly distinguishable from Raley's Inc. (1963), the Board refused to defer to an arbitral award requiring the employer to recognize one union when that award was rendered after another union had petitioned for an election among the same employees. Hotel Employers' Ass'n (1966). The arbitrator was held not to have considered the fact that the petition filed with the Board by the opposing union raised a substantial question of representation, and the Board concluded that it was in a better position to deal with the more statutorily oriented issues of unit determination and competing majority claims. Indeed, the Board has been rather insistent in representation cases that an arbitral award, in order to warrant deference, "must clearly reflect the use of and be consonant with Board standards" on such matters as the appropriate bargaining unit. Westinghouse Elec. Corp. (1967).

Fair Procedures. More frequently, non-deferral is justified not by repugnancy to the Act but by the irregularity or unfairness of the procedures utilized in the arbitration. An example of such unfairness —although it is stated in the *Spielberg* case as an independent criterion ("all parties had agreed to be bound")—is the absence from the arbitration proceeding of one of the parties to the Board proceeding, and the absence as well of some other party who would "vigorously defend" the same substantive position. In International Harvester Co. (1962), *enf'd* (7th Cir. 1964), where the union was the object of a charge under section 8(b)(2), and the union's position before the arbitrator had been opposed to that of the employee, the Board held that the employee's lack of notice of the arbitration was not fatal to deference, because the employer had "vigorously defended" the employee's interest. But if one of the interested parties before the Board is not thus "represented" before the arbitrator, the Board is unlikely to defer to the arbitration award. This will most commonly occur when the issue before the Board relates to a representational or work-assignment conflict between two unions, only one of which was a party to the arbitration, or relates to the claim of a discharged employee that both the employer and the union are allied in interest against him.

The Board decided, in Raley's Inc. (1963), that an arbitration award "absorbing" a group of employees under a union's contract would be honored by the Board, in spite of the absence of the union which was now before the Board petitioning for an election, since the employer had vigorously argued before the arbitrator for non-inclusion. But when a similar situation reached the Board several years later, in Horn & Hardart Co. (1968), the Board noted that it was unclear exactly how vigorously the employer argued before the arbitrator for non-inclusion of a group of cashier employees; the Board noted that certain important facts supporting exclusion of the cashiers, such as their duties within the store and the lack of success on the part of the arbitrating union in organizing the cashiers independently, were not presented to the arbitrator. Because of the absence of the petitioning union from the arbitration, and the lack of certainty that its interests were effectively presented there, the Board refused to defer. It found, contrary to the arbitrator, that the cashiers were not an "accretion" to the contractual bargaining unit. Both the Board's refusal to defer and its unit determination were subsequently sustained on appeal in an unfair labor practice case. NLRB v. Horn & Hardart Co. (2d Cir. 1971). And, in Waterfront Guard Ass'n, Local 1852 (Amstar Corp.) (1974), the arbitrator had found that the employees of a security-guard company were an accretion to the unit in the plant where they worked, although the security-guard company was not a party to the arbitration. The Board refused to defer to what was in effect an arbitral determination that the guard company was a joint employer and its employees an accretion, both because that company was not represented in the arbitration and the Board's accretion precedents were to the contrary.

A number of discrimination cases before the Board have found either the company or the union or both, as charged parties, relying on an arbitration proceeding sustaining the employee's discharge but at which the employee's position was not represented, either personally or by one of the parties. In such cases, the Board will uniformly decline to defer, and will make an independent factual determination as to the cause of the discharge. For example, in Roadway Express, Inc. (1963), the discharged employee had been active in attacking both the union and the employer and in organizing a rival labor organization; the award sustaining his discharge was rendered by a bipartite committee comprised only of union and employer representatives, without any third-party neutral. The Board refused to defer, holding that while the absence of a neutral third party was not fatal to the fairness and regularity of the arbitration proceeding, the alliance in interest of both employer and union was. It stated:

> Where contract grievance procedures simply provide for the submission of a dispute to a bipartite committee, composed of representatives of the contracting parties, the absence of a public, or impartial, member will not necessarily foreclose the exercise of our discretion to give binding effect to decisions to the committee; for each representative is customarily prepared to argue for or against the merits of the employee's grievance. However, where in addition to the absence of an impartial or public member it appears from the evidence that all members of the bipartite panel may be arrayed in common interest against the individual grievant, strong doubt exists as to whether the procedures comport with the standards of impartiality that we expect to find in arbitration.

In light of the grievant's opposition to both the union and the employer, the Board found that the "arbitration tribunal was constituted with members whose common interests were adverse" to the grievant and therefore sustained the trial examiner's decision to proceed to the merits of the case (which were in any event resolved against the discharged employee). See also T.I.M.E.—DC, Inc. v. NLRB (5th Cir. 1974) (no deference to award of bipartite committee denying grievance of employee reduced in seniority when transferring to different company job; Board found both employer and union biased against employee, and proceeded to find violations of sections 8(a)(3) and 8(b)(2)).

In such cases of union hostility to the employee on whose behalf it processed the grievance, deference to an award sustaining the discharge will be yet more unlikely when the employee affirmatively refuses to participate in the arbitration hearing. NLRB v. Auburn Rubber Co. (10th Cir. 1967) (Board upheld in not deferring in section 8(a)(3) discharge case, but court finds abuse of Board discretion in not deferring in section 8(a)(1) case regarding employer interrogation when union had earlier joined employer in stipulating to judicial confirmation of arbitration award). There is, however, some likelihood that the Board, in a discrimination case against the employer and the union, will defer to an arbitration award adverse to the employee grievant—even though the union and the employee were obviously at odds in the arbitration—if the employee is represented before the arbitrator by his own counsel. Operating Engineers Local 18 (Frazier-Davis Constr. Co.) (1964).

The Board has on occasion found other procedural defects in the arbitration proceeding sufficiently serious as to warrant no deference and to require complete relitigation. For example, in Gateway Transp. Co. (1962), the Board refused to defer to an arbitration award sustaining the discharge of an employee, when two days after the discharge the employee was notified of a union-initiated appeal to be tried two days later, the union counsel announced at the arbitration hearing that he would not represent the grievant, and the employee lodged a futile protest concerning his incapacity to prepare his case and contact witnesses. And, in Illinois Ruan Transp. Corp. (1967), *enf't denied on other grounds* (8th Cir. 1968), the Board refused, in a case under section 8(a)(1), to defer to a decision of a bipartite tribunal which merely set forth the conclusion that the discharge was sustained but gave no supporting reasons.

Congruent Issues. Not long after the *Spielberg* case was decided, the Board announced a requirement for deference in addition to procedural fairness and "non-repugnance" to the Labor Act; the Board held that the arbitrator must in addition have considered the very issue that would be before the Board for decision. In Monsanto Chem. Co. (1961), the arbitrator in an earlier discharge grievance had found the discharge to comport with the requirements of the contract but had explicitly stated that he did not pass upon the issue of the employer's antiunion animus as would the Board in an unfair labor practice case. The Board therefore declined to defer to the arbitral award, since it was clear that it did not address the pretext issue —that is, whether the avowed reason for the discharge, sustained by the arbitrator, was in truth merely a "cover" for illegal discrimination. The Board has very frequently refused to defer to arbitral awards in section 8(a)(3) cases—even in the absence of an explicit arbitral disclaimer—because of the failure of the evidence introduced before the arbitrator, or the opinion of the arbitrator, to raise the issue of pretext. *E. g.,* Star Expansion Indus. Corp. (1967), *enf'd* (D. C.Cir. 1969) (arbitrator held only that the employer had not violated the contract, had not caused injury to the union; he failed to give consideration to the question of pretext and to the interest of the aggrieved employee or of the public). The Board's refusal to defer in such cases was upheld by the courts of appeals as within its discretion. John Klann Moving & Trucking Co. v. NLRB (6th Cir. 1969).

Whether pretext was actually before the arbitrator was often difficult to tell, given the rarity of hearing transcripts and the frequent terseness of arbitral opinions. The Board in fact has encouraged arbitrators to state clearly the issues they decide and those they do not; otherwise, "we will look to the evidence and contentions which have been presented to him together with the language of his award in an effort to determine whether he has in fact disposed of the unfair labor practice issue." Gulf States Asphalt Co. (1972). For a while, the Board vacillated, articulating a rule which would put upon the party urging deference the burden of demonstrating that the unfair labor practice issue was actually considered by the arbitrator, Yourga Trucking, Inc. (1972) (that party has the strongest interest in establishing the prior litigation of the issue, and also the more ready access to proof through documents or witnesses); but in practice, scanning the arbitration award in the search for an affirmative indication that the arbitrator had *not* considered that issue, Gulf States Asphalt Co. (1972) (much evidence as to motive had been introduced before the arbitrator).

In 1974, the Board concluded that it was being insufficiently deferential to arbitral awards; but in the same year, the Court of Appeals for the District of Columbia Circuit rebuked the Board for being too deferential. In Electronic Reprod. Serv. Corp. (1974), the Board deferred to an arbitral award sustaining a discharge although it appeared that the union knowingly refrained from introducing proof before the arbitrator on the issue of antiunion animus and that the arbitrator did not consider that issue in his opinion and award. The Board acknowledged that its earlier decisions had required, as conditions for deference, that the arbitrator have considered the issue of pretext or motive and that this be demonstrated by the party urging the Board to stay its hand. It overruled those decisions, noting that they frustrated the expeditious resolution of disputes by inducing the parties to separate artificially the "just cause" issue, which would be tried to the arbitrator, and the discrimination issue, which would be tried in a substantially duplicative proceeding before the Board. The Board found this practice to be "detrimental both to the arbitration process and to our own processes and to be a means of furthering the very multiple litigation which Spielberg . . . [was] designed to discourage." The Board held that parties would ordinarily be expected, in discharge arbitrations, to introduce all evidence regarding any possible claim of antiunion discrimination, and concluded:

> [W]e should give full effect to arbitration awards dealing with discipline or discharge cases, under Spielberg, except when unusual circumstances are shown which demonstrate that there were bona fide reasons, other than a mere desire on the part of one party to try the same set of facts before two forums, which caused the failure to introduce such evidence at the arbitration proceeding.

In effect, the Board majority—over the strong dissent of two members—adopted a principle akin to collateral estoppel in unfair labor practice proceedings on questions of employer motive which could have been tried to the arbitrator, regardless of whether they in fact were. See also National Radio Co. (1973) (Board deferred to arbitrator and dismissed complaint under section 8(a)(5) for unilateral employer action in promulgating rule, although arbitrator did not address this issue directly; his award on related issues resolved the parties' dispute and was not repugnant to the Act, and the union did not place the issue clearly before the arbitrator). The Board did acknowledge that its rule requiring deference to arbitration proceedings as to untried issues of antiunion discrimination was subject to exception in "unusual circumstances," and it suggested what these might be: the arbitrator specifically declines to pass on issues which he regards as statutory; both parties agree to exclude statutory issues from the arbitration proceeding; the facts giving rise to the alleged discrimination did not occur, or were not discovered, until after the time of arbitration. See Local 715, IBEW v. NLRB (Malrite of Wisconsin, Inc.) (D.C.Cir. 1974) (bargaining with individuals after arbitration hearing; Board deferral held improper).

While the Board was, in *Electronic Reproduction,* moving away from its earlier requirement that the arbitrator decide the same issue presented to the Board, the Court of Appeals for the District of Columbia Circuit was embracing that requirement with vigor. In Banyard v. NLRB (D.C.Cir. 1974), the court held that it was not sufficient to justify Board deferral that the arbitrator's award be merely procedurally fair and not repugnant to the statute. In addition, the arbitrator must have addressed the very same issue that would be before the Board in the unfair labor practice proceeding, and the arbitrator's construction of the contract must not depart from the construction which the Board would give the Labor Act. (The court also stated that the arbitrator had to be "competent" to pass upon the issue, but it is not altogether clear what the court had in mind. Presumably, a determination whether a contract clause on its face violated the Labor Act would not be one within arbitral competence to which the Board ought defer.) The court concluded that deference is warranted only when the decision of the arbitrator resolves both the contract issue and the statutory issue; if his award addresses only the former, then Board "deferral   .   .   .   approaches abdication."

Given the change in Board membership since these decisions, and the multiplicity of appellate court panels, it is not at all clear whether and when the requirements for post-arbitral deference will be firmly established. The Board's collateral estoppel position can surely be attacked as sacrificing statutory rights upon the altar of litigative efficiency and creating severe risks that the interests of the individual and the public will be too readily jeopardized by carelessness in the preparation and presentation of cases before the arbitrator. On the other hand, the directive of the Court of Appeals for the District of Columbia that deference is an abuse of discretion unless the arbitrator's decision is congruent to the Board's, both as to issues and disposition, will effectively destroy the use of arbitral resources to resolve overlapping questions of contractual and statutory breach; the temptation will be very great indeed for the party losing before the arbitrator to try the case again before the Board. Perhaps the soundest approach rests somewhere between these two positions, as was the situation prior to 1974: the Board sought some evidence that the arbitrator in fact passed upon an issue that was controlling in the Board proceeding, and would be more inclined to defer when contract construction was at the heart of the case (as in unilateral changes in working conditions under section 8(a)(5)) but markedly less so when the central issues had a purely statutory foundation (as in representation cases involving unit determinations). In any event, it is ironic that both the *Electronic Reproduction* holding and the *Banyard* holding will have the likely effect of furthering the "legalization" of arbitration proceedings so as to have the issues there approximate those which would be placed before the Board and as to have the arbitrator analyze the case both in terms of the contract and of the Labor Act.

§ 4.   Deference to Discrimination and Bargaining Decisions

Perhaps the most frequent reliance on the *Spielberg* doctrine is found in cases arising under section 8(a)(3) charging antiunion discrimination by the employer. The Board will dismiss a complaint under that section—or under section 8(b)(2), charging union inducement of employer discrimination so as to encourage union support—if an arbitrator has already considered the issue of discrimination in a discharge or discipline case. Of course, the proceedings before the arbitrator must have been fair, with the position of the discriminatee having been asserted personally or through one of the parties to the contract, and the award must not be repugnant to the policies of the Labor Act. For example, in Operating Engineers Local 18 (Frazier-Davis Constr. Co.) (1964), where the issue before the arbitrator was whether the grievant had been barred from registering under a hiring hall agreement because of his opposition to the union or because of his failure to inform the union within twenty-four hours of being hired (a rule contained within the agreement), the arbitrator held that it was for the latter reason and denied the grievance. In a proceeding under section 8(b)(2), the Board, noting that the employee had appeared through counsel at the arbitration proceeding, deferred to the arbitration award and dismissed the complaint. The Board will defer to awards against the grievant even when the arbitration panel is comprised exclusively of representatives of employers and unions in the industry (as is common in the trucking industry) without any "neutral" member; the grievant need not be present at the hearing, provided his position is vigorously presented by one of the parties. Eazor Express, Inc. (1968) (section 8(a)(3) case, with union having presented employee's position in the grievance hearing; arbitration panel dismissed grievance without explanation or rationale).

Although the arbitration awards considered by the Board are generally adverse to the grievant and charging party, the Board will also defer when the arbitration award sustains the grievance, even if the Board would normally issue an order against the employer that is more severe than that ordered by the arbitrator. Howard Elec. Co. (1967) (arbitrator had ordered backpay but no reinstatement; Board dismissed complaint under section 8(a)(3)); Ohio Ferro-Alloys Corp.

(1974) (arbitrator found discharge for union activities, and awarded reinstatement without backpay because of employee's false statements on job application; Board found this not repugnant to the Labor Act and dismissed section 8(a)(3) complaint).

The Board has, however, refused to defer to arbitration decisions in a substantial proportion of cases charging discrimination to discourage or encourage union membership. The most common reasons are that the arbitral award was repugnant to the Labor Act, or that the interest of the discriminatee was not effectively represented at the arbitration proceeding, or that the arbitrator did not consider the question whether the true motivation for discipline was the grievant's union (or antiunion) activities. Examples of repugnance to the Labor Act are arbitral decisions holding that an employer has cause to discharge an employee who resorts to the National Labor Relations Board in a dispute with the employer, Virginia-Carolina Freight Lines, Inc. (1965) (Board finds violation of section 8(a)(4)); or that the employee in order to preserve his job must insure his own truck, even though the insurance requirement had originally been imposed by the employer for antiunion reasons, NLRB v. Hribar Trucking, Inc. (7th Cir. 1969). An example of procedures unfair to the discriminatee is Jacobs Transfer, Inc. (1973), in which an employee, a candidate for president of a "reform" group within the union, was discharged for "disloyalty" for distributing a pamphlet critical of management. A bipartite arbitration panel, with no third-party neutral, heard a grievance filed by the union over the protest of the employee (who announced his refusal to be bound by the result) and sustained the discharge for disloyalty. The Board found that both union and employer representatives were arrayed in interest against the grievant, and found the discharge in fact to have been for protected employee activities in violation of section 8(a)(3). See NLRB v. Auburn Rubber Co. (10th Cir. 1967) (discriminatees and their union chose not to appear in arbitration case prosecuted by Teamsters, and Board need not defer concerning charges of employer discrimination; but since Teamsters stipulated to court confirmation of arbitral award concerning interrogation, Board should have deferred on that issue).

Until recently, the Board had also refused to defer to an arbitration award in a discrimination case unless the respondent could affirmatively demonstrate that the arbitrator had actually considered the question whether antiunion (or prounion) animus had motivated the discipline, rather than some supposed business reason asserted merely as a pretext. Yourga Trucking, Inc. (1972). The Board has since departed from this principle and has announced that even if the issue of discrimination is not presented to and considered by the arbitrator, it will nonetheless dismiss in deference to the decision of an arbitrator in a discipline case that is not otherwise repugnant to the Labor Act or unfair in its procedures. Electronic Reprod. Serv.

Corp. (1974). In that case, the Board did allow of certain exceptions to its rule that the pretext issue must be presented to the arbitrator or be sacrificed before the Board: if the discrimination does not occur until after the arbitration proceeding, or if the arbitrator expressly declines to pass on the pretext issue, or if the parties mutually agree to exclude the issue from arbitration, or if the discrimination issue turns upon evidence newly discovered or unavailable at the time of the arbitration. The courts, however, have consistently endorsed the Board's earlier refusal to defer when the arbitrator has failed to address the issue of discrimination and pretext. *E. g.*, John Klann Moving & Trucking Co. v. NLRB (6th Cir. 1969). And the Court of Appeals for the District of Columbia Circuit recently emphasized the indispensability of such arbitral consideration and refused to enforce a Board dismissal, since it was unclear whether the arbitration committee had considered a contract issue that was "congruent" to the statutory issue in the section 8(a)(3) case. The court, in Banyard v. NLRB (D.C.Cir. 1974), required as a condition of deference that the arbitrator "clearly decided" the discrimination issue that would be before the Board and also, apparently, that the arbitrator utilize the same criteria for analysis that the Board would.

The issue of Board deferral to arbitration awards has been raised somewhat less frequently in cases charging unilateral employer actions in violation of the duty to bargain under section 8(a)(5). The Board has traditionally been reluctant to cede to arbitrators the question whether the union during the contract term "waived" its statutory right to have the employer bargain before changing working conditions, even though the question of waiver turned upon an analysis of contract provisions and bargaining history. *E. g.*, Cloverleaf Div. of Adams Dairy (1964) (arbitration not yet invoked). Since it announced a policy of pre-arbitral deferral in Collyer Insulated Wire (1972), however, the Board has been more hospitable to arbitration decisions already rendered in which the arbitrator has held that the employer's change in working conditions was authorized under the contract and that the union thus waived its right to demand that the employer bargain to impasse before making the change. For example, in Valley Ford Sales (1974), the employer was charged with a violation of section 8(a)(5) for "unilaterally" rescinding a wage incentive plan during the contract term. Such action would traditionally be deemed illegal in the absence of bargaining to impasse—and indeed arguably illegal even after bargaining if the union refused to give its consent. Yet the arbitrator dismissed the union's grievance, concluding that the employer's action was authorized by a contractual management rights clause, the past practice of the parties and the history of their contract negotiations. The Board dismissed the complaint under section 8(a)(5), concluding that the arbitrator's decision had satisfied the *Spielberg* standards and had utilized the standards the Board would in determining a waiver of the duty to bargain. A dissenting opinion by two Board members recounted at length the history of the Board's traditional doctrine of "clear and unequivocal waiver," which the dissenters argued was being overturned by the majority's deference to the decision of the arbitrator.

As in cases under section 8(a)(3), the Board has refused in section 8(a)(5) cases to defer to arbitration awards which it deems repugnant to the policies of the Labor Act. For example, in Radio Television Tech. School v. NLRB (3d Cir. 1973), the employer had discontinued a bonus of long standing without bargaining with the union, and the arbitrator found this to be within the employer's power because as a bonus it was merely discretionary. The Board declined to defer to this award, since it ignored a consistent line of Board and court precedents declaring that bonuses given regularly and in proportion to earnings are "mandatory" subjects about which the employer must bargain prior to termination. Accordingly, the award was held repugnant to the Act and after considering the case on the merits, the Board found a violation of section 8(a)(5). Moreover, although the Board has said that it will defer to an arbitral award which considers contract terms, prior practices and negotiating history to determine if the union has waived its right to complain of unilateral action—that is, although the Board apparently now treats the statutory and contract issues as "congruent" in unilateral-action cases—it will clearly not defer when the arbitrator explicitly refrains from addressing the statutory question of duty to bargain. Radioear Corp. (1974).

§ 5. Nondeference to Representation and Work-Assignment Decisions

The Board has been least inclined to defer to arbitration awards when the case represents a clash between two unions. In one kind of case, two unions are competing to be the bargaining representative for the workers presently holding particular jobs; this is known as a representation dispute and is resolved by the Board through bargaining-unit determinations and elections. In another kind of case, two unions are claiming that their members are entitled to perform certain kinds of work, and typically one union is claiming that the disputed work should be taken away from those to whom the employer has already assigned it. This is known as a jurisdictional or work-assignment dispute and is resolved by the Board in special hearings in which it sits very much as does an arbitrator, although its criteria for assigning the work go beyond those found in collective bargaining negotiations and agreements. The Board is reluctant to defer to prior arbitration decisions in both the representation and work-assignment areas, in part because the arbitrator's criteria for decision are usually not those employed by the Board and in part because the arbitrator will usually not have before him all of the competing parties.

The representation issue on which the Board has most frequently been asked to defer to an arbitration award is that of the appropriate bargaining unit, in particular the "accretion" issue. A collective bargaining agreement between the employer and Union A may provide that the union is to be recognized as bargaining representative for all of the company's employees, including those employed in new plants to be acquired in the future no matter where they are located geographically. A new plant opens, and a second union (Union B) seeks to represent the employees there and petitions the Board to conduct a representation election. Union A intervenes in the election proceeding and claims that the Board should dismiss the petition of Union B, since an arbitrator has already held that the original contract between the company and Union A entitles that union to recognition at the new plant. If the employees at the new plant are indeed to be treated as an "accretion" to the company bargaining unit, then the contract will bar a fresh election there.

In the Board's first application of the *Spielberg* doctrine to a representation case of this kind, Raley's Inc. (1963), it deferred to the arbitrator's finding that certain disputed janitors were to be absorbed under a contract which did not expressly provide for their inclusion in the unit; the Board therefore dismissed the election petition under the contract-bar rule. It noted that the arbitral award was not repugnant to the Labor Act, since the Board had found an "accretion" in similar cases in the past, and also noted that the position of the petitioning or insurgent union had in effect been "vigorously defended" by the employer, although that union was not a party to the arbitration. The Board the same year even deferred to an arbitral finding of "contract absorption" although the employer had refused to participate in the arbitration hearing, so that the substantive position of the insurgent union was wholly unrepresented. Insulation & Specialties, Inc. (1963) (Board refuses to permit arbitration to be frustrated by the nonappearance of a party; employer had in any event sent exhibits from the pending Board case to the arbitrator after the arbitration hearing).

Very soon after, however, the Board moved away from its policy of deference in accretion cases. In Hotel Employers' Ass'n (1966), the arbitrator included a group of employees under the contract of Union A at the very time that an election petition filed by Union B was pending before the Board. The Board refused to defer, noting that while the arbitrator concluded that the employer and Union A intended the contract to engross the disputed employees, it was the Board which was better equipped to deal with the pertinent statutory issues of appropriate bargaining unit and the conflicting majority claims of the two unions. And in Westinghouse Elec. Corp. (1967), the Board refused to defer to an arbitral decision which had resolved the competing representation claims of two unions by dividing the disputed group of employees between the two unions on the basis of the skills needed to perform their work. The Board concluded:

> [T]he ultimate issue of representation could not be decided by the Arbitrator on the basis of his interpreting the contract under which he was authorized to act, but could only be resolved by utilization of Board criteria for making unit determinations. In such cases the arbitrator's award must clearly reflect the use of and be consonant with Board standards.

The Board found the arbitrator's award deficient in its failure to go beyond an examination of the employees' skills to consider as well other criteria relevant to the issue of unit determination: bargaining history, integration of operations, lines of promotion within the group, and the possible adverse effects (upon both employer and employees) of splitting the group. On the merits, the Board included the employee group as an entity in the bargaining unit represented by the union which had not been a party to the earlier arbitration proceeding.

The Board has since consistently held that while it is the task of the arbitrator to determine whether the employer and the incumbent union intended to absorb the disputed employees, this is not controlling upon the Board in making an accretion determination. The Board is concerned about the freedom of the employees to select their bargaining representative, while the contract may have the effect of frustrating that freedom. Indeed in one case in which the arbitrator purported to go beyond the terms of the labor contract and to apply the Board's statutory accretion criteria, the Board refused to defer, since the arbitrator's interpretation was "not clearly consonant with Board precedent." Combustion Engineering, Inc. (1972) ("His award relied on factors to which the Board gives little or no weight and makes no reference to factors ordinarily deemed controlling, such as lack of employee interchange, functional autonomy, dissimilarities in wages and fringe benefits, and the difference between the products of both."). In short, the Board's test for non-repugnance in unit-determination cases is very strict indeed, and no deference will be given the arbitrator unless the Board determines that his decision was a correct one. Unlike cases arising under section 8(a)(5), which turn upon construction of contract provisions and prior negotiations, and cases arising under section 8(a)(3), which turn upon factual issues such as cause for discharge, the arbitrator has no special competence or expertise to determine representation issues. It is the Board which has the special competence, and therefore deference is regarded as improper, regardless of the fairness and regularity of the arbitral proceeding.

On occasion, however, where the arbitrator has decided (or is about to decide) an issue which is incidental to a Board representation proceeding, and which rests more squarely on contract rather than statutory interpretation, the Board will defer. For example, in Pacific Tile & Porcelain Co. (1962), the Board postponed ruling on the voting eligibility of certain strikers in order that an arbitrator could first determine the validity of their discharges.

The Board has sometimes justified its refusal to defer by questioning how vigorously the employer argued the position of the union not represented before the arbitrator, and thus the fullness of the record before the arbitrator. Horn & Hardart Co. (1968) (facts were omitted before the arbitrator regarding the duties of the disputed employees and the unsuccessful attempts of the incumbent union, appearing at the arbitration, to organize them). See NLRB v. Horn & Hardart Co. (2d Cir. 1971). In two recent accretion cases, where the arbitrator absorbed disputed workers technically employed by a distinct business entity, the Board declined to defer, in one case partly because the other entity, an alleged joint employer, was not a party to the arbitration, Waterfront Guard Ass'n Local 1852 (Amstar Corp.) (1974); and in the other case, Pix Mfg. Co. (1970), even though it was a party. In the latter case, a division of a company relocated its plant, and was represented at the arbitration hearing between the company and its union, at which the arbitrator held that the relocation brought it within the company's labor agreement. In spite of the representation at the arbitration of all concerned parties, the Board refused to defer, since its traditional "accretion" criteria were improperly applied.

The Board is also reluctant to defer to arbitration awards in cases of work-assignment disputes between unions, unless all three parties—the two unions and the employer—have agreed to be bound by the arbitration. Unlike other unfair labor practice and representation issues, as to which the statute is silent on matters of Board deference, the Labor Act, in section 10(k), explicitly directs the Board to dismiss any charge filed under section 8(b)(4)(D) if "the parties to such dispute submit to the Board satisfactory evidence that they have adjusted, or agreed upon methods for the voluntary adjustment of, the dispute." Congress in 1947 empowered the Board not merely to issue cease and desist orders against strikes and picketing in a work-assignment dispute, but actually to pass upon the merits of that dispute, as would an arbitrator, in a Board hearing under section 10(k). But if an arbitrator has already been given authority to resolve the case by "the parties to such dispute," the congressional purpose in seeing the dispute resolved peaceably would be achieved and Board action rendered unnecessary.

The Supreme Court has held that the employer is a "party to such dispute," such that the Board is required to defer to an arbitrator's award of the disputed work only if the employer was represented before the arbitrator; if the unions' competing claims persist, the Board is not to stay its hand in conducting a hearing under section

10(k) if the unions were party to the arbitration proceeding but the employer was not. NLRB v. Plasterers Local 79 (U.S.1971). The strong endorsement recently given by the Court to arbitration agreements was held to be premised on their voluntary nature, as a product of free collective bargaining. The Court found in the 1947 legislative history a congressional purpose to have the Board decide work-assignment disputes rather than to require "compelled arbitration" by some private agency against the will of an interested party. Since the employer in the *Plasterers* case did not voluntarily participate in the arbitration between the two unions, the Court bowed to the congressional preference for Board resolution and ordered the Board to determine the dispute, with the employer afforded a chance to participate:

> [I]f union agreements to arbitrate are sufficient to terminate § 10(k) proceedings, there is no assurance that these private procedures will always be open to employer participation, that an employer will be afforded a meaningful chance to participate, or that all relevant factors will be properly considered.

The Court also noted that the arbitral board utilized by unions in the construction industry to resolve jurisdictional disputes has traditionally placed greatest emphasis upon agreements between unions at the international level as well as established industrial practices and, more recently, upon costs and efficiency; but the Board goes well beyond these criteria to consider such factors as the skills and work involved, NLRB certifications, agreements between the employer and the unions, arbitration awards in the same and similar cases, and the assignment made by the employer.

In sum, if the two competing unions and the employer have submitted the dispute to arbitration (or have agreed to do so in the future), the Board will quash the notice of hearing under section 10(k). Local 1, IBEW (Sundermeyer Painting Co.) (1965). If there is no such tripartite agreement, the Board will reach the merits in the hearing, and will give weight to any existing arbitration award between two of the parties. IAM Lodge 1743 (J. A. Jones Constr. Co.) (1962). "An award by a joint board of standing and experience, following procedures of fairness and impartiality, cannot fail to be helpful to the Board in making a jurisdictional determination if it is ultimately required to do so." Millwrights Local 1102 (Don Cartage Co.) (1965). But such a two-party arbitral award will not be given conclusive weight, in part because the award will commonly neglect to consider the same range of criteria utilized by the Board in resolving work-assignment disputes, and in part because the interests of the absent party may well not be vigorously brought to the attention of the arbitration tribunal. NLRB v. Teamsters Local 631 (Reynolds Elec. & Eng. Co.) (9th Cir. 1968). Indeed, it may well be that the absent union in an arbitration is asserting rights against the employer under its own contract, such that it is possible to have two conflicting arbitration awards based on plausible readings of different labor contracts. In any event, if an arbitrator awards the work to one of the unions, and the Board decides in a section 10(k) proceeding that the work should be awarded to the other union, the Board's award will take precedence. New Orleans Typog. Union No. 17 v. NLRB (5th Cir. 1966) (consolidated appeal from arbitration award and from Board order in section 8(b)(4)(D) case).

§ 6.   Board Deferral to Arbitration Machinery: Generally

In Spielberg Mfg. Co. (1955), the Board announced its policy of dismissing an unfair labor practice complaint in deference to an arbitration award already rendered, provided the arbitral procedures were fair and the award was not repugnant to the policies of the Labor Act. In Raley's Inc. (1963), the Board extended the *Spielberg* principle to representation cases, and dismissed a union's election petition when an arbitrator had already ruled that the employees in question were subsumed under a contract between the employer and another union. The principle of deference to arbitration awards already rendered was extended to pending arbitration proceedings in Dubo Mfg. Corp. (1963), in which the Board deferred action on charges against an employer for discriminatory discharge and refusal to reinstate, when a federal district court had already ordered the employer to arbitrate similar allegations under the parties' labor contract. In these cases, the Board emphasized the statutory policy favoring the utilization of contractual grievance machinery, particularly arbitration, in resolving disputes falling within the reach of both the contract and the Labor Act. The Supreme Court in several cases cited the Board's deferral policy with approval, noting that the Board has discretion to respect an arbitration award and that arbitration of disputes contributes to industrial peace and stability. *E. g.*, Carey v. Westinghouse Elec. Corp. (U.S.1964).

The Board's policy concerning arbitration machinery not yet invoked was not quite so hospitable. The Board did, on several occasions beginning as early as 1943, decline to assert its jurisdiction in cases in which the parties could have treated the matter as a contract breach to be processed through their grievance machinery; the Board's declination of authority was designed to foster collective bargaining and private machinery for dispute resolution. Consolidated Aircraft Corp. (1943), *enf'd* (9th Cir. 1944). For the most part, however, the Board was prepared to assert jurisdiction even though the respondent claimed that its conduct was consistent with its labor contract (or affirmatively authorized by it) and that arbitration machinery was available to test that claim. *E. g.,* Cloverleaf Div. of Adams Dairy (1964).

The Board dramatically reversed course in 1971 with its divided decision in Collyer Insulated Wire (1971). The employer in that case was charged under section 8(a)(5) with unilaterally changing certain working conditions during the contract term: increasing the wage rate for certain skilled maintenance employees, directing that the removal and cleaning of a certain gear be performed by a single maintenance machinist rather than by two as in the past, and changing wage rates for extruder operators. Before the trial examiner, the employer argued that these changes were authorized by the contract (particularly certain wage-adjustment provisions) and by the parties' practices under the contract. Although the trial examiner reached the merits, the Board on review held this to be error, since the dispute was essentially "over the terms and meaning of the contract" and should have been resolved pursuant to the contractual grievance and arbitration machinery. Even though arbitration had not yet been invoked, the Board found the circumstances to warrant a dismissal of the complaint; it retained jurisdiction, however, in order to assure that the dispute was either settled or was promptly submitted to arbitration and that any arbitration procedure would be fair and its result not repugnant to the Labor Act.

The Board in *Collyer* set forth its reasons for deferring further action until arbitration was attempted: (1) The parties had a "long and productive collective-bargaining relationship" and "for 35 years, mutually and voluntarily resolved the conflicts which inhere in collective bargaining." (2) There was no claim of enmity by the company to the employees' protected rights, no unlawful conduct or aggravated circumstances of any kind, no employer design to undermine the union. (3) The employer "credibly asserted its willingness to resort to arbitration" and urged the union to do so. (4) The contract obligates each party to submit contract disputes to arbitration and makes the results binding, and the arbitration provisions are "unquestionably broad enough to embrace this dispute." (5) "The contract and its meaning . . . lie at the center of this dispute," which involves "substantive contract interpretation almost classical in its form." Each party asserted a reasonable claim under the contract in good faith, and the employer's position "is not patently erroneous but rather is based on a substantial claim of contractual privilege." (6) The arbitrator can construe the agreement so as to resolve both the contract dispute and the unfair labor practice dispute; the Labor Act comes into play only if the employer's conduct is held not to be sanctioned by the labor agreement.

Two Board members dissented, as they continued to do in every subsequent case in which the Board invoked or expanded upon the *Collyer* principle of deferral to unused arbitral procedures. They asserted that the parties to the contract did not intend, by providing for arbitration of their contract disputes, to sacrifice their public forum of the NLRB under the Labor Act; that the Board was more qualified than the arbitrator to pass upon the disputed issues, and that arbitration proceedings were becoming increasingly expensive and time-consuming; that Board deferral was tantamount to a form of "compulsory arbitration" (most obviously in cases where, as in *Collyer*, the time limit for invoking arbitration had passed); and that consistent Board precedent required that the union not be held to have "waived" its statutory rights simply by incorporating an arbitration clause in its contract.

Collyer was a most natural case for deferral to future arbitration, since the employer's defense under section 8(a)(5) was that the union by specific contract provisions and past practices had authorized its action. A Board decision would have required an analysis of contract terms, bargaining history and plant practices—precisely the task normally given to arbitrators, for which the Supreme Court has consistently held them specially qualified. Put simply, contract interpretation was a condition to any unfair labor practice determination. Subsequent to *Collyer*, however, the Board significantly expanded the scope of its doctrine of pre-arbitral deferral.

First, in unilateral-action cases under section 8(a)(5), the Board has deferred even though the rights of the parties do not turn upon the construction of a specific contract provision. Thus, if the union has unsuccessfully negotiated for an explicit limitation on employer action, and management relies in the section 8(a)(5) case upon the union's agreement to a management prerogatives clause, or a "zipper" or integration clause, the Board will have the case submitted to arbitration first. Radioear Corp. (1972) (unilateral termination of holiday bonus).

Second, the Board has even deferred in unilateral-action cases in which the employer cannot point to any contract term which allegedly gives it a privilege to change working conditions. For example, in Great Coastal Express (1972), the employer unilaterally revoked the privilege of employees to park in the company lot; the contract made no mention of parking privileges but did require the employer to maintain all existing working conditions in effect during the contract term. Although no reasonable construction of the contract would sanction the company's conduct, the Board deferred since the arbitrator might construe the "maintenance of benefits" provision so as to resolve the issue. Presumably the Board believes that if there is no contract provision on which the respondent can rely, the arbitrator will render a decision which in substance sustains the unfair labor practice charge and thus renders further Board action unnecessary. See also Bethlehem Steel Corp. (1972) (Board defers on employer's unilateral subcontracting, although contract is silent on right to subcontract; employer relied on historical practice and business necessity).

Third, and perhaps most significantly, the Board will defer in a case arising under section 8(a)(3) charging employer discrimination

—or section 8(b)(2) charging union inducement of discrimination—even though the unfair labor practice issue is not dependent upon any construction of the contract but requires an application simply of the mandates of the Labor Act. The case announcing this principle is National Radio Co. (1972), in which it was alleged that the employer had enforced a rule regulating grievance processing within the plant when that rule had been promulgated for reasons of antiunion animus. It was clear that the issue before the Board would turn not upon contract construction but rather upon findings of fact concerning the promulgation of the rule and the employer's motive, and the application of the statutory standard in section 8(a)(3) of "discrimination . . . to discourage union membership." The Board acknowledged that deferral on the issue of discriminatory discharge would not "rest on any presumed primacy of an arbitrator to interpret an ambiguous or contested contract provision." Nonetheless, the Board concluded that an arbitrator could test the discharge for violation of the company's rule against the "just cause" requirement of the contract, and that this could resolve the dispute in a manner not "repugnant to purposes and policies of the Act." In effect, the Board reformulated its basic conditions for a pre-arbitral deferral as follows: (1) the "asserted wrong is remediable in both a statutory and a contractual forum" and (2) it must be reasonable to assume that "the arbitration procedure will resolve [the] dispute in a manner consistent with the standards of *Spielberg*." See also Eastman Broadcasting Co. (1972).

In sum, the Board appears willing to apply the pre-arbitral deferral policy of the *Collyer* case to disputes which are susceptible of resolution by grievance arbitration in a manner which conforms to the Labor Act, regardless of whether questions of interpretation of ambiguous contract provisions are at the heart of the dispute. Indeed, although the Board's position on the matter is not wholly clear, it has even deferred to arbitration machinery where the central issue is one of pure statutory analysis, such as whether dues checkoff authorizations relied upon by the union conform to section 302 of the Labor Act, Norfolk, Portsmouth Wholesale Beer Distributors Ass'n (1972); and whether participation in an unprotected work stoppage was "condoned" by the employer, Tyee Constr. Co. (1973).

Its nuances to one side, the Board's general policy of pre-arbitral deferral has been endorsed (although not by way of strict holding) by the Supreme Court in William E. Arnold Co. v. Carpenters Dist. Council (U.S.1974), in which the Court held that a state court had jurisdiction to enjoin a strike in breach of contract even though the strike might also constitute an unfair labor practice which the Board could remedy. The Court approvingly quoted from the *Collyer* decision those passages in which the Board emphasized the propriety of withholding its jurisdiction in cases in which a dispute could also be resolved through voluntary contractual settlement procedures. Moreover, the appellate courts which have considered the issue—a majority of all of the federal courts of appeals—have uniformly sustained the discretion of the Board to defer to unused arbitral machinery. *E. g.*, Local 2188, IBEW v. NLRB (Western Elec. Co.) (D.C.Cir. 1974). The Court of Appeals for the District of Columbia Circuit has, however, stated that deferral would be improper if arbitration "would impose an undue financial burden upon one of the parties," so that a remedy is effectively denied, or if the possibility of a number of differing results in successive arbitrations would prevent "an orderly exposition of the law." That court was also concerned that Board abstention might constitute "not deference, but abdication" in cases in which there was no "congruence" between the contractual dispute and the issue before the Board. *Ibid.*

§ 7.   Criteria for Pre-Arbitral Deferral

As is demonstrated by the cases just discussed, the Board will normally decline to exercise its power to rule on unfair labor practice cases when the parties may invoke an arbitration procedure which is also likely to resolve the dispute. Although this deferral policy was first announced in an unfair labor practice case which turned directly upon the construction of a specific contract provision, it has also been applied when the respondent relies upon a vague contract provision (such as a "zipper" clause) or upon an unwritten past practice, and has indeed been applied when the issue before the Board is rooted completely in construction of the Labor Act and not of the contract (for example, whether an employee has been discharged for antiunion reasons). The Board has spelled out a number of conditions upon its willingness to defer.

Availability of Arbitration. To warrant Board deferral to contractual arbitration machinery, there must of course be a collective bargaining agreement in existence which on its face gives some protection to the interests of the aggrieved party before the NLRB (referred to hereafter as the "charging party," even though technically the charge may be filed by a person other than the one directly aggrieved by the action of the respondent employer or union). Thus, where the employer and union both agree that the contract does not extend to the employees at the jobsite at which the unfair labor practice issue arose, the Board will not defer. Pauley Paving Co. (1972), *enf'd mem.* (4th Cir. 1974). Assuming the charging party to be covered by the contract, there must exist in that contract an arbitration clause which can be invoked by the charging party or by another with a common interest. District 10, IAM (Ladish Co.) (1972) (one of the contending unions in a work-assignment dispute is not a party to the contract, which had no provision for arbitration). Thus, the Board will not likely defer, in a refusal-to-bargain case brought against a union, when the labor contract does not clearly permit the employer (the charging party) to file grievances and demand arbitration. Communications Workers of America (Western Elec. Co.) (1973). Nor will it defer if arbitral review of management action is left by the contract to the ad hoc agreement of the parties, Tulsa-Whisenhunt Funeral Homes, Inc. (1972); presumably the Board will also not defer if the results of the arbitration are advisory only rather than binding.

To justify deferral, the Board need not be convinced that the dispute is clearly encompassed by the arbitration procedure; it is sufficient that it be "arguably" encompassed, since the question of arbitrability should itself be determined by the arbitrator. Urban N. Patman, Inc. (1972), enf'd (9th Cir. 1974). The Board appears willing to give considerable breadth to the standard arbitration clause which covers disputes concerning the "interpretation or application" of the provisions of the contract, and to construe narrowly contract restrictions on the power of the arbitrator. E. g., Western Elec., Inc. (1972), enf'd (D.C.Cir. 1974). The Board will leave the case to the arbitrator even when there appears to be no contract provision on which the respondent relies as a defense, or when the respondent's interpretation of the contract is patently erroneous; so long as the claim of the charging party rests upon a construction of the contract, including negotiating history or past practices, deferral will be appropriate. Wrought Washer Mfg. Co. (1972).

Since the *Collyer* policy of deferral assumes the availability of an arbitration procedure, the Board will not defer if the respondent refuses to express its willingness to arbitrate the dispute or if both parties mutually agree not to seek arbitration. A classic example of such a case is one in which the union has failed to invoke the grievance or arbitration procedure in a timely manner, and the respondent employer refuses to waive the arbitration defense of untimely filing. Detroit Edison Co. (1973) (union failed to demand arbitration of vacation-pay grievance). But the Board will defer if the respondent indicates that it will waive the defense of untimeliness and proceed to arbitration forthwith. Columbus & S. Ohio Elec. Co. (1973). Indeed, even though the respondent has engaged in "foot dragging" in the processing of grievances against it, the Board will defer if the union has already obtained a court order requiring the employer to submit such grievances to arbitration. Medical Manors, Inc. (1972).

Award Will be Honored. Not only must there be an applicable arbitration procedure before the Board will defer the exercise of its jurisdiction, but it must be likely that the respondent will respect the award and the collective bargaining relationship generally. In the Board's leading decision in Collyer Insulated Wire (1971), it noted that the charging union had made no claim of employer enmity to the employees' exercise of protected rights, that the situation was "wholly devoid of unlawful conduct or aggravated circumstances of any kind" and that the employer's action was not "designed to undermine the union." The Board will thus look to the relationship between the company and the union—both in the past and in the situation under litigation—in order to determine whether it has been characterized by disputatiousness, instability or illegality, or has instead been characterized by overall stability and mutual respect. The record of harmonious dealings need not be lengthy in order to convince the Board that deferral is justified. E. g., Coppus Engineering Corp. (1972) (union certified in March 1969, negotiations begin in August, contract executed in December, and union filing of section 8(a)(5) charge in May 1970). The Board will consider such factors as prior unfair labor practice violations and settlements, lawsuits to enforce contract provisions, strikes and lockouts, and experience with arbitration (particularly compliance with awards). If, for example, in spite of some history of litigiousness, there is evidence through arbitral settlement of similar cases in the recent past that the collective bargaining relationship has matured, the Board will be willing to defer the case pending arbitration; "the parties' agreed-upon grievance and arbitration machinery can reasonably be relied on to function properly and to resolve the current disputes fairly," and will not be "unpromising or futile." United Aircraft Corp. (Pratt & Whitney Div.) (1973), enf'd (2d Cir. 1975).

If, however, there is a "rocky" history of bargaining in the recent past—characterized by strikes, distrust, bickering, and a proliferation of unresolved grievances—the Board may conclude that arbitration will not likely provide stability, and will proceed to determine the merits itself. Columbus Coated Fabrics (1973). The most obvious instances in which the Board will decline to defer to arbitration because of the parties' record of bargaining are those in which the respondent has repudiated the contract outright and thus demonstrated pervasive hostility to the collective bargaining process. While this is obviously more likely to occur when the respondent is an employer, e. g., Mountain State Constr. Co. (1973) (employer allegedly terminated contract with incumbent union and executed a "sweetheart" agreement with favored union, in violation of sections 8(a)(1), (2), (3), and (5)), the Board has acted similarly when the repudiation was by the incumbent union, Communications Workers of America (Western Elec. Co.) (1973) (binding contract negotiated by international union was immediately rejected by local, which urged its members to strike to modify the agreement, thus showing "a fundamental disdain for the collective-bargaining process"). See Jos. T. Ryerson & Sons (1972) (Board refuses to defer case arising under section 8(a)(1) for threatening union official because of his processing of grievances, since employer's alleged conduct "strikes at the foundation" of the grievance and arbitration mechanism).

To warrant deferral, there must also be a prospect that the arbitration will be before a panel sufficiently neutral that its decision would be given deference under the requirements of Spielberg Mfg. Co. (1955). Thus, the Board has refused to defer a charge that an

association of football clubs (the National Football League) violated
section 8(a)(5) by unilaterally promulgating fines for on-the-field
fights, when the arbitrator under the league's labor agreement was
the Commissioner of Football, who had himself suggested the rule
and was responsible for its enforcement.   National Football League
Mgt. Council (1973), *remanded on other grounds* (8th Cir. 1974).
But it is not necessary that the arbitration panel have a third-party
neutral apart from representatives of both labor and management;   a
bipartite panel composed of equal numbers of representatives will be
a sufficient guarantor of procedural regularity to warrant deference
in advance.   Teamsters Local 70 (National Biscuit Co.) (1972), *enf'd*
(2d Cir. 1973) (alleged union violation of section 8(b)(3) by unilaterally setting working conditions).

   Even when the arbitrator is a neutral, however, the Board will
not defer in advance if both the employer and the union are allied in
interest against the charging party.   This will occur most frequently
when the charge before the Board is in the nature of a section
8(a)(3) violation by the employer and a section 8(b)(2) violation by
the union, and both are alleged to have discriminated against the
charging party.   Where, for example, a discharge was precipitated by
the employee's outspoken opposition to both the union and the company, the Board will not defer to arbitration between those two parties.   Kansas Meat Packers (1972).   Indeed, the Board has extended
this principle by looking behind what might appear to be divergent
interests of the union and the company to determine whether there
will be in truth an adversary presentation before the arbitrator.   In
NLRB v. Railway Clerks (Yellow Cab Co.) (5th Cir. 1974) (charges
under sections 8(b)(1)(A) and 8(b)(2)), for example, in which the
union had demanded that the charging parties be held to the dues
checkoff authorization they had executed prior to leaving and then
rejoining the company, the Board refused to defer to arbitration,
since the interests of the employees and their union were in direct
conflict and it was unlikely that the employer would vigorously assert
in arbitration the interest of the employees.   Nor will the Board defer to unused arbitration machinery in work-assignment disputes between two unions, since no single arbitration clause will bring all parties before a single tribunal.   Inter-union arbitration will not bind the
employer (although presumably its interest will be asserted with vig-
or by one of the competing unions), and arbitration pursuant to a
contract between the employer and one of the unions will not likely
address in full the interests of the nonrepresented union, which may
rest its own claim to the work on a completely separate labor contract with the employer.   Steelworkers Local 4454 (Continental Can
Co.) (1973).

   Deferral has, however, been held proper when the interests of
the charging party—even though he may not be a party in the arbitration proceeding—are in substantial harmony with the interests of

one of the parties to the labor contract, and that party is willing and able to invoke arbitration and assert the position of the charging party before the arbitrator. (Presumably, applying the *Spielberg* tests, even then deferral will be improper if the charging party announces in advance that it objects to or refuses to be bound by the arbitration proceeding.) Thus, in a case arising under section 8(a)(3) for discharge of a union steward for processing grievances in the plant, the Board noted that "the interests of the employee and his representative are in substantial harmony," that the union in protecting the steward protects itself, and that therefore "we see no ground to assume that [his] interests will be inadequately represented under the contractual procedures." National Radio Co. (1972). A court of appeals has also held that the Board may properly defer—even in a section 8(b)(2) case involving the validity of a contractual union-security provision—when it is clear that the employer will assert in arbitration a position similar to that of the aggrieved employees. Enterprise Pub. Co. v. NLRB (1st Cir. 1974).

Congruence of Issues. The Board has also invoked—although neither with clarity nor consistency—another significant criterion before deferring to arbitration machinery: there must be a "sufficient identity" between the contract issue that would be placed before the arbitrator and the statutory issue placed before the Board. There need not be an exact identity, for the Board has held that it will defer a discharge case arising under section 8(a)(3) even though the contract provision to be construed by the arbitrator is a broad "just cause" provision and not one which more specifically tracks the statutory language, "discrimination to discourage union membership." As the Board said in such a case, deferral was appropriate since it was reasonable to assume "that the arbitration procedure will resolve this dispute in a manner consistent with the standards of *Spielberg*." National Radio Co. (1972). See also Houston Mailers Union No. 36 (1972) (Board defers case under section 8(b)(1)(B), involving union fine of foreman, where the contract forbade union discipline of any foreman "for carrying out the instructions" of the employer). But when construction of the contract would in substance leave unresolved the central issue which confronts the Board, the Board will not defer but will promptly decide the case on the merits. A clear example is the case in which the employer and union have agreed to sweep within the bargaining unit all after-acquired plants of the employer, and the issue before the Board is whether—regardless of the parties' attempt to deprive new employees of a free choice of representative—a new plant constitutes a distinct and appropriate bargaining unit. Germantown Dev. Co. (1973) (signatory employer acquired control of another company through purchase of stock).

The Board explained in some detail its reluctance to defer in Communications Workers of America (Western Elec. Co.) (1973). There a binding contract, with a no-strike clause, was negotiated by an international union on behalf of a local, which promptly rejected the contract and struck for improved benefits. The Board, in a case brought against the local for bad-faith bargaining, refused to defer to arbitration under the no-strike clause. It noted that there was no "sufficient identity" or "parallelism" between the unfair labor practice issue and the contract issue, since regardless of any breach of the no-strike clause the strike would be unlawful if its object was to modify the contract and it was called without compliance with the notification and cooling-off requirements of section 8(d); these latter issues would not at all determine, or be determined by, any decision under the contract. The Board thus proceeded to decide the merits, since the "necessary parallelism of the arbitrable issue and the statutory issue does not exist in this case." This rationale helps to explain the Board's refusal to defer when the issue in a section 8(a)(1) case was whether an employer had unlawfully threatened a union official for processing grievances, and it was unlikely that the contract forbade any employer action short of formal discipline of the employee, Jos. T. Ryerson & Sons (1972); when the issue in a section 8(a)(1) case was the reinstatement rights of strikers, and the parties appeared to concede that the only plausibly relevant contract provision governing recall after layoff was in fact inapplicable, Bio-Science Laboratories (1974) (issue is a matter of law for the Board to decide); when the issue in a section 8(a)(5) case was the employer's duty to disclose information to assist the union in processing grievances, and the duty was based exclusively on the Labor Act while the contract was silent on the matter of disclosure, American Standard, Inc. (1973); and when the issue in a section 8(b)(1)(B) case was whether the union had unlawfully incited a strike to force the employer to improve the benefits of a "supervisor," and the contract made no mention of the separate statutory status of supervisors and included them in the bargaining unit, Sheet Metal Workers Local 17 (Geo. Koch Sons) (1972), enf'd mem., (1st Cir. 1973) (the arbitrator would not be "considering the issue which we are called on to decide," i. e., the worker's "status as an 'employee' or 'supervisor' as defined in the Act which we administer").

It is not at all clear what the Board means by "parallelism" or "congruence" between the contractual and statutory issues, or when it is that the Board will invoke that requirement. For example, in Communications Workers of America (Western Elec. Co.) (1973), discussed just above, the employer's challenge to the union's strike could have been promptly tested before an arbitrator as a breach of contract, and an arbitral award in favor of the employer would presumably have put to rest the refusal-to-bargain issue as well; after the rendition of such an award, a charge against the union under section 8(b)(3) would surely have been dismissed under the Spielberg principle, in spite of the lack of congruence between the contract issue and the statutory issue. Indeed, the Board has even deferred to an arbitration decision already rendered when the central issue had apparently never been raised before or adjudicated by the arbitrator. Electronic Reprod. Serv. Corp. (1974). Given the uncertainty currently surrounding the significance of the "same issue" requirement in post-arbitration Board cases, it is likely that there will be comparable uncertainty under *Collyer* in the pre-arbitration stage. At least one court of appeals has emphasized the need for "congruence between the contractual dispute and the overlying unfair labor practice charge," lest Board abstention constitute "not deference, but abdication." Local 2188, IBEW v. NLRB (Western Elec. Co.) (D.C.Cir. 1974).

In any event, there is little doubt that the Board will refuse to defer cases in which the charge is that a contract provision is itself clearly unlawful under the Labor Act. The Board will likely assume that the arbitrator will feel obliged to construe the provision as written, such that deferral will not relieve the Board from the ultimate task of determining whether the provision is repugnant to the Act, a matter on which the Board is presumably far more qualified than is the arbitrator. The Board has in fact held, in a case against a union for entering into an allegedly unlawful "hot cargo" agreement requiring a secondary boycott, that it would not defer to an arbitrator. The Board stated, in Operating Engineers Local 701 (Oregon-Columbia Chap., Assoc. Gen. Contractors) (1975):

> Deferral is not appropriate in a dispute where the contract provisions governing the dispute are as here unlawful on their face or by their express terms call for a result inconsistent with Board policy under the Act.

It remains to be seen whether the Board will defer when the claim is that a contract term is illegal as construed or applied rather than on its face. The Board may be willing to defer such a case to arbitration, on the assumption that the arbitrator may—indeed ought to—interpret the provision in a manner not repugnant to the Act, thus perhaps eliminating altogether the need for a Board proceeding.

§ 8. Subject Matter of Deferred Cases

The Board has deferred to arbitration machinery in cases which have arisen under many different sections of the Labor Act, against unions as well as against employers. It has, for example, deferred in a case arising under section 8(a)(1), where the charge was that the employer had unlawfully reprimanded a union official for handling grievances on company time, a problem explicitly considered in the collective bargaining agreement. Jos. T. Ryerson & Sons (1972). The Board also has stayed its hand in cases arising under section 8(a)(2) when, for example, at issue is the propriety of the employer's continuing to check off union dues from employee wages after a contract has expired and before a new one is negotiated. Associated Press (1972), *enf'd* (D.C.Cir. 1974). Similar charges may be brought in such cases against the union under section 8(b)(2) for inducing the employer to discharge employees who refuse to pay dues during the hiatus between contracts; here too, Board deferral to arbitration has secured judicial approval, particularly if it is probable that the employer will vigorously assert the interests of the employees in the arbitration proceeding. Enterprise Pub. Co. v. NLRB (1st Cir. 1974). If a contract contains a provision barring discharge without "just cause" or for union activities, the Board will defer charges arising under section 8(a)(3), as in National Radio Co. (1972), in which the Board first extended the *Collyer* doctrine to a case of discharge because of grievance-processing activities on behalf of the union.

Of course, the initial use of the doctrine of deferral to arbitration machinery was in a case arising under section 8(a)(5), in which the employer was charged with having unilaterally altered working conditions during the contract term without bargaining with the union, and the employer claimed that the union had expressly authorized the employer in the contract to make such changes "unilaterally." Collyer Insulated Wire (1971). Indeed, the Board has deferred in unilateral-action cases under section 8(a)(5) even though the employer relies not on express contract provisions but simply on unwritten past practice and bargaining history, and even though the Board is willing to concede that such reliance is unfounded. Peerless Pressed Metal Corp. (1972).

The Board has also deferred to arbitration in the rather rare case of a refusal-to-bargain charge brought against a union for setting working conditions unilaterally. In Nabisco, Inc. v. NLRB (2d Cir. 1973), the union directed its members to cease making cash collections upon delivery of goods to the company's customers, in light of the increase of robberies from and assaults upon company deliverymen. The employer claimed that the union's action was a modification of the contract's provisions dealing with the receipt of money and with the continuation of past practices, in violation of section 8(b)(3), and that the union's threats to fine uncooperative members violated section 8(b)(1)(A). In spite of the reversal of the usual roles—with the union relying on the arbitration machinery as a defense to refusal-to-bargain and coercion charges—the Board found the case to be fully controlled by *Collyer*, and deferred the exercise of its jurisdiction on both charges, with judicial approval. The Board will also defer when the fine is imposed on a supervisor, thus raising an issue under section 8(b)(1)(B)—which bars union coercion of an employer in the selection of its representatives for bargaining or grievance-processing—when the contract as well bars union discipline of supervisors for carrying out the instructions of the employer. Houston Mailers Union No. 36 (1972) (union, claiming violation of bylaws, fined foreman for making a work assignment sought by more senior employees).

In spite of this broad range of cases in which the Board has deferred, there has also developed a pattern of cases under particular sections of the Labor Act as to which it will not defer to available arbitration machinery but will proceed forthwith to adjudicate the merits. In discrimination cases, for example, the Board will not defer to arbitration between the employer and the union when both those parties are aligned in interest against the discriminatee employee, Kansas Meat Packers (1972), or when the employee and his union representative are mutually antagonistic and the employer is not likely to assert the interest of the employee vigorously in arbitration, NLRB v. Railway Clerks (Yellow Cab Co.) (5th Cir. 1974) (union charged with violating sections 8(b)(1)(A) and 8(b)(2) for demanding that employee who left the unit be automatically subject to the contract's checkoff requirement upon his return). Nor will the Board defer when the employer is charged with discrimination against an employee specifically for his recourse to the Board itself to redress a statutory violation by the employer, McKinley Transp. Ltd. (1975) (Board finds violation of section 8(a)(4)), or for his use of the grievance and arbitration provisions of the contract. In Jos. T. Ryerson & Sons (1972), the employer threatened a union officer with reprisal for handling a grievance that the employer believed to be unmeritorious. The Board noted that the contract appeared to give the arbitrator no power to review employer interference with the grievance procedure other than in cases of discharge, and it gave as another reason for refusing deferral that the charged violation "strikes at the foundation of that grievance and arbitration mechanism upon which we have relied in the formulation of our *Collyer* doctrine"; the Board held deferral to be proper only when arbitral procedures promised to be "fair and regular" and "open, in fact, for use by the disputants," without access being inhibited or precluded by the respondent.

Although the Board will usually defer in refusal-to-bargain cases charging unilateral modifications in working conditions—either by the employer or the union—it has tended not to defer in several other kinds of bargaining cases. It will not defer when the statutory violation is an outright repudiation of the collective bargaining relationship and the labor contract. In Mountain State Constr. Co. (1973), the Board held deferral to arbitration unwarranted when the employer attempted to withdraw from an employer association which had already negotiated a labor contract, and then declared it was no longer bound by the contract and purported to contract with a different union. The Board concluded that this was a complete rejection of the principles of collective bargaining and of the self-organizational rights of employees, and that deferral to the arbitration machinery of the repudiated contract would be improper. The Board reached the same conclusion when a union was the respondent in a case arising under section 8(b)(3). In Communications Workers of America (Western Elec. Co.) (1973), the Board found the strike call of a local union which sought to modify an agreement ratified that day (after binding negotiation by the international union) to show a "fundamental disdain for the collective-bargaining process" and not to warrant deferral to arbitration:

> Such a wholesale repudiation amounts to a renunciation of the most basic of collective-bargaining principles. We are not inclined to defer when a party's actions indicate an unwillingness to accept in any measure a bargain once reached.

The Board will also be disinclined to defer to arbitration when the employer is charged with refusing to disclose to the union information which is relevant to the union's tasks of evaluating and processing grievances. The Board in such cases asserts that the union's request for information rests not upon the contract but rather upon the Labor Act, and that the Board's decision to require disclosure will not trench upon the jurisdiction of the arbitrator to construe the contract but will rather facilitate the processing and settlement of grievances. United-Carr Tenn. (1973). (The Board may defer, however, when there is an explicit provision of the labor contract which deals with the disclosure of information. United Aircraft Corp. (Pratt & Whitney Div.) (1973).) See Columbus Printing Pressmen's Union No. 252 (1975) (Board refuses to defer to arbitration machinery the question whether the union's insistence to impasse upon an interest-arbitration provision in a new contract constitutes a refusal to bargain; the issue in the section 8(a)(5) case turns upon whether the provision is a mandatory subject of bargaining, and does not involve a construction of the agreement).

Finally, just as the Board tends to make its own assessment of the merits in cases of representation or work-assignment disputes, even after arbitral decisions have already been rendered, it will also not defer to unused arbitration machinery in such cases. For example, in a work-assignment dispute in which each of two unions is claiming that its own members should be given certain jobs—with each union perhaps resting its claim on its own separate collective bargaining agreement—the Board will not withhold the exercise of its own jurisdiction (unless all parties agree to some settlement procedure) because no single arbitration under either union's contract will likely resolve the dispute or bind all parties. United Steelworkers (Continental Can Co.) (1973). And the Board has consistently declined to leave to an arbitrator the responsibility to determine whether employees at a newly acquired plant are to be swept in (as an "accretion") to an existing bargaining unit already governed by a collective bargaining agreement. The Board believes that the employer and the union cannot at will deprive newly acquired employees of their rights to self-organization and that the task of making unit determinations lies within the expertise of the Board and not of the arbitrator. For these reasons, the Board has refused to defer action on representation and unit-clarification petitions even when relevant issues of contract construction are already before an arbitrator in a pending proceeding (but no decision has yet been issued). Germantown Dev. Co. (1973) (union bargaining with a multiemployer association sought to include employees of a wholly owned subsidiary of one of the employer members of the association).

CHAPTER XXXII

PREEMPTION OF STATE REGULATION

§ 1. Overview

The most common form of governmental regulation of labor-management disputes until 1935 was state-court relief by injunction or damages against concerted activities, typically through application of general principles of tort, property and contract law. When the Supreme Court held in Thornhill v. Alabama (U.S.1940), that peaceful picketing was essentially akin to "free speech" protectible against governmental intrusion by the United States Constitution, it appeared as though state regulation of peaceful concerted activities was largely to become constitutionally preempted. Although the Court was soon to limit sharply this class of constitutionally protected labor activity, there simultaneously emerged the doctrine that the federal Labor Act (by virtue of the Supremacy Clause of the Constitution) worked an even more pervasive preemption of potentially conflicting state regulation. Congress, in enacting the Wagner Act in 1935, had expressed a belief that the economic disruptions worked by labor-management disputes have an untoward impact on interstate commerce and that the varied (and commonly anti-collective bargaining) policies embodied in state law were properly to be replaced by a single uniform scheme of regulation the object of which was the fostering of collective bargaining. Congress did not, however, address the full preemptive implications of its labor legislation and has for the most part continued to this day to leave to the courts the task of accommodating the imperatives of the federal scheme with the diverse and particular local needs of the states. The Supreme Court has considered this issue in no fewer than thirty cases since 1945, and its decisions have been somewhat unclear if not inconsistent.

The Supreme Court has recently reaffirmed the position taken in San Diego Bldg. Trades Council v. Garmon (U.S.1959), which held that a state could neither enjoin nor award damages against minority-union picketing designed to induce an employer to enter into a union-shop agreement against the wishes of its employees. The Court (under the then existing law) concluded that the concerted activity was arguably protected against employer reprisals under section 7 and also arguably prohibited as a union unfair labor practice under section 8, with redress in either case properly limited to the National Labor Relations Board:

> When it is clear or may fairly be assumed that the activities which a State purports to regulate are protected by § 7 of the National Labor Relations Act, or constitute an unfair labor practice under § 8, due regard for the federal en-

actment requires that state jurisdiction must yield. To leave the States free to regulate conduct so plainly within the central aim of federal regulation involves too great a danger of conflict between power asserted by Congress and requirements imposed by state law. . . . At times it has not been clear whether the particular activity regulated by the States was governed by § 7 or § 8 or was, perhaps, outside both these sections. But courts are not primary tribunals to adjudicate such issues. It is essential to the administration of the Act that these determinations be left in the first instance to the National Labor Relations Board. . . . [T]he failure of the Board to define the legal significance under the Act of a particular activity does not give the States the power to act. In the absence of the Board's clear determination that an activity is neither protected nor prohibited or of compelling precedent applied to essentially undisputed facts, it is not for this Court to decide whether such activities are subject to state jurisdiction.

The Court has rested its holdings for preemption of state regulation of labor activities on two grounds. First, there is a potential conflict between the substantive provisions of federal law and those of state law. A state might outlaw concerted activity which the federal government seeks to protect and will thus frustrate the federal policy favoring employee organization or free collective bargaining. Second, and avowedly the more dominant note in the Supreme Court decisions, is the potential conflict between state enforcement bodies (courts or agencies) and the specialized enforcement agency established to administer the Labor Act—even though there might appear to be no conflict whatever in the substantive rules sought to be enforced. As the Supreme Court stated in Amalgamated Ass'n of Street Employees v. Lockridge (U.S.1971):

[I]n matters of dispute concerning labor relations a simple recitation of the formally prescribed rights and duties of the parties constitutes an inadequate description of the actual process for settlement Congress has provided. The technique of administration and the range and nature of those remedies that are and are not available is a fundamental part and parcel of the operative legal system established by the National Labor Relations Act. . . .

The rationale for preemption, then, rests in large measure upon our determination that when it set down a federal labor policy Congress plainly meant to do more than simply to alter the then-prevailing substantive law. It sought as well to restructure fundamentally the processes for effectuating that policy, deliberately placing the responsibility for applying and developing this comprehensive legal system in the hands of an expert administrative body rather than the federalized judicial system.

Congress prescribed for the Board "a particular procedure for investigation, complaint and notice, and hearing and decision, including judicial relief pending a final administrative order," thereby seeking "to obtain uniform application of its substantive rules and to avoid these diversities and conflicts likely to result from a variety of local procedures and attitudes toward labor controversies." Garner v. Teamsters Local 776 (U.S.1953).

Over the years, there has been a strong strain in Supreme Court opinions, almost uniformly in concurring or dissenting opinions, which argues for the more limited form of preemption that only bars states from inhibiting conduct which the federal Act actually protects. This view would therefore tolerate state remedies which are cumulative to federal remedies for conduct which the federal Act declares to be an unfair labor practice. The preemption theory which presently is endorsed by a majority of the Court is more all-embracing, since as just outlined it would bar even cumulative state remedies against concerted activities concededly in violation of federal law. The existence of a federal administrative agency fashioning rather limited remedies is itself thought to preempt other state (or even federal) judicial or administrative regulation. It is predictable that the "narrow" preemption view, more hospitable to relief through agencies other than the NLRB, will continue to have supporters on the Court. It is less predictable whether it will ultimately prevail over the now dominant "broad" preemption theory.

In any event, whatever the rationale for preemption—whether "substantive" or "administrative"—there are a host of exceptions to the doctrine. Many of the exceptions are based on the Court's inability to discern a congressional intention to oust the states of the power to regulate matters of deep local concern or matters with which the federal Act is concerned only peripherally. In such cases, state regulation is sustained, the Court according "due regard for the presuppositions of our embracing federal system, including the principle of diffusion of power not as a matter of doctrinaire localism but as a promoter of democracy . . . ." San Diego Bldg. Trades Council v. Garmon (U.S.1959). All agree that the regulation of criminal or tortious violence is within that exception, but the outer limits of the exception remain undefined. Another class of case in which preemption doctrine is overcome is that in which there is some strong federal policy which is to be implemented by state or federal courts regardless of whether the NLRB might regulate the conduct as well. Examples are lawsuits to enforce promises in collective bargaining agreements, to redress union violations of the duty of fair representation to employees in the bargaining unit, and to remedy race or sex discrimination in employment.

Of course, the concerns that underlie the doctrine of preemption are normally called into play only with regard to activities of persons who are within the coverage of the federal Labor Act and the jurisdiction of the NLRB. State law will thus generally operate freely when regulating governmental employees or agricultural workers, who are excluded from the Act by sections 2(2) and 2(3) respectively. The Supreme Court has dealt on several occasions with the question whether concerted activities aimed at foreign shipowners and their foreign crews fall without the jurisdiction of the NLRB and whether state courts are free to enjoin or otherwise regulate such activities. The Court has found that certain action directed at such shipowners does not "affect commerce" and that Congress did not intend to authorize the Board to regulate such matters, which touch upon our international relations. Curiously, the Court has inferred from this denial of Board jurisdiction that the diverse laws of the states can be applied instead. The Court first held that picketing by American unions in support of the wage demands of foreign crewmen against a foreign shipowner was not regulable by the NLRB, and that an action for damages by the shipowner (in a federal court because of diversity of citizenship) would lie. Benz v. Compania Naviera Hidalgo (U.S.1957). The Court also held to be beyond the jurisdiction of the Board the conduct of a representation election among foreign crews of foreign flagships, McCulloch v. Sociedad Nacional (U.S. 1963), and picketing of a foreign ship in an effort to organize the foreign crew, Incres S. S. Co. v. International Maritime Workers (U.S. 1963) (state court finding of preemption reversed). The same is true of dockside picketing by American unions publicizing and protesting the payment of wages to foreign crewmen which are inferior to those of American crewmen on other ships; since the object of the picketing is to affect the wages paid by foreign shipowners to the foreign crew, the dispute is not "in commerce," the Board is without jurisdiction, and state courts may enjoin. There is state-court jurisdiction whether the action is brought by the foreign shipowner, Windward Shipping (London) Ltd. v. American Radio Ass'n (U.S.1974), or by American stevedoring companies whose attempts to service the ship are frustrated by the picketing, American Radio Ass'n v. Mobile S. S. Ass'n (U.S.1974) (5–4 decision, with dissenters arguing that involvement of American plaintiff as object of arguable secondary boycott in violation of section 8(b)(4) preempts state-court jurisdiction). Where, however, the picketing protests wages paid by a foreign shipowner to American employees, such as nonunion American longshoremen, the dispute can be resolved by a wage decision by the shipowner which affects only wages paid to American workers, is therefore "in commerce" and within the jurisdiction of the NLRB, and is beyond the power of the states to regulate. Longshoremen's Local 1416 v. Ariadne Shipping Co. (U.S.1970).

The operation of preemption doctrine will be separately considered in the context of activities which are affirmatively protected under section 7 of the national Labor Act, or are prohibited under the section 8 unfair labor practice provisions of the Act, or are without both sections 7 and 8 of the Act (so-called unprotected activities).

§ 2. Protected Activity: The Reach of Preemption

Employee rights defined by section 7 are protected against employer reprisal by section 8(a)(1), but the Labor Act in its terms does not address the question of the power of states to regulate, by civil, criminal or administrative remedies, such "protected" activities. When Florida enacted legislation requiring the qualification and licensing of union business agents, and the state attorney general secured a state-court injunction against a union and business agent acting as such for failure to secure a state license, the Supreme Court reversed and held that the Florida law and injunction interfered with the freedom of employees to select a bargaining representative of their own choice. Hill v. Florida (U.S.1945). In effect, section 7 rights were held "protected" against state as well as employer sanction. A state is also barred from enacting "strike vote" legislation which prohibits the calling of a strike until a specific statutory procedure has been exhausted. UAW v. O'Brien (U.S.1950) (state-court refusal to enjoin criminal prosecution; statute required filing of notice within stipulated time periods before strike or lockout, with majority vote in support of strike a prerequisite to strike).

The Court has also held invalid state legislation declaring it a misdemeanor for utility employees to engage in a strike causing an interruption of an essential service; when the employer is within the coverage of the federal Act, such a strike is a protected activity and cannot consistently with the Labor Act and the Supremacy Clause be barred by state law. Street Employees Div. 998 v. Wisconsin Employment Rel. Bd. (U.S.1951). Nor can a state by the application of its antitrust laws declare invalid a provision in a labor contract which regulates the rental price which the trucking employer is to pay to independent owners of trucks, when the purpose of the contract provision was in truth to protect the negotiated union wage scale against possible undermining by subcontracting and was thus a subject about which the parties were required to bargain by federal labor law. Local 24, Teamsters v. Oliver (U.S.1959).

In these cases, state jurisdiction was preempted upon a finding that the conduct sought to be regulated was *actually* protected by the federal Labor Act. The Supreme Court decisions, however, go further and purport to oust state regulation of conduct which is only "arguably protected" under section 7 (or "arguably prohibited" under section 8). This has been held to follow from the Court's emphasis upon the "primary jurisdiction" of the Board to determine whether such conduct is not merely arguably protected but is actually protected. The alternative to preemption for arguably protected activities would be to give the state court the task of determining whether the activities are in fact protected (as a predicate to the grant or denial of relief), and this is apparently believed to be an inadequate means for protecting federal rights (particularly when Supreme Court review would be necessarily exercised but sparingly). The result of this broad preemption theory is effectively to shelter against state regulation conduct which is not in fact actually protected under section 7, for a Board decision on the issue of actual protection cannot always be readily obtained. The Board does not decide whether conduct is actually protected except in the context of an unfair labor practice proceeding in which an employer has been charged with coercing its employees in the exercise of their "protected" rights; thus, the only way in which an employer can secure from the Board a conclusive determination that employee activity is not protected, and is thus possibly subject to state regulation, is by discharging the employees. Indeed, if the concerted activities, such as "stranger picketing" for organizational purposes, are carried on by others than the employer's own employees, a determination that they are "protected" may well be impossible to secure from the Board. It is essentially for these reasons that certain members of the Court have urged that state restriction of concerted activities be barred only when those activities are specifically determined to be actually protected rather than merely arguably protected. See the concurring opinion of Mr. Justice White in Longshoremen's Local 1416 v. Ariadne Shipping Co. (U.S.1970) (Court reversed state injunction of peaceful primary picketing, since arguably protected). In any event, the Court's current preemption doctrine bars the state court and the federal court in diversity cases from determining whether the defendants' claim of federal protection under section 7 is meritorious; it is sufficient that the conduct be arguably protected. Amalgamated Ass'n of Street Employees v. Lockridge (U.S.1971).

§ 3.   Method of Challenging State Jurisdiction

That concerted activities are protected by the Labor Act and are thus sheltered against state prohibition is a defense which is most commonly raised by the employees or union in the state-court proceeding. In addition, there are instances in which the state-court proceeding has been attacked collaterally, not by the employees but by the National Labor Relations Board. The Supreme Court has held that the NLRB may secure an injunction in a federal court against the enforcement by an employer of an order issued by a state court enjoining employee conduct which is in part protected and in part an unfair labor practice. The federal-court order was held proper under 28 U.S.C.A. § 2283, which provides, "A court of the United States may not grant an injunction to stay proceedings in a State court except . . . where necessary in aid of its jurisdiction," since the federal court itself had been asked by the Board to enjoin the union under the preliminary-injunction provisions of section 10(*l*) of the Labor Act. Capital Serv., Inc. v. NLRB (U.S.1954). The Court subsequently went far beyond this holding, to sustain a federal court injunction issued at the behest of the Board when the activity enjoined by the state court had not been the subject of unfair labor practice charges filed by the employer or of a preliminary injunction under section 10 of the federal Labor Act. In NLRB v. Nash-Finch Co. (U.S.1971), the federal injunction against the state-court proceeding was held proper (even though not "in aid of the jurisdiction" of the federal court) simply on general grounds of statutory preemption, in order "to prevent frustration of the policies of the Act." The Court's conclusion that the Board could secure the injunction of state action "where its federal power pre-empts the field" obviously applies to state-court injunctions against arguably protected concerted activities as much as against arguably prohibited concerted activities. Such an injunction is not, however, available upon petition of the union. Amalgamated Clothing Workers v. Richman Bros. (U.S.1955).

The Supreme Court has also held that a person enjoined by a state court from engaging in protected activity may not be held in contempt of court for violating that order, at least if there is no opportunity afforded for that person to argue to the state court that the injunction was preempted by federal law. In re Green (U.S.1962) (lawyer advised union client to disregard state-court injunction issued without hearing against strike which although arguably in violation of contract no-strike clause was arguably protected as a protest against alleged employer refusal to bargain; Court broadly holds: "[A] state court is without power to hold one in contempt for violating an injunction that the state court had no power to enter by reason of federal pre-emption").

§ 4. Protected Activity: Allowable State Regulation?

In spite of these strong Supreme Court precedents for preemption of state jurisdiction, the Court appears to recognize that certain local regulatory policies within the states may warrant some incursion upon the exercise of even "protected" activities. In Local 24, Teamsters v. Oliver (U.S.1959), in which state antitrust law was preempted to the extent it curtailed bargaining on such mandatory subjects as wages and hours, the Supreme Court noted that "We have not here a case of a collective bargaining agreement in conflict with a local health or safety regulation; the conflict here is between the federally sanctioned agreement and state policy which seeks specifically to adjust relationships in the world of commerce." While the distinction is elusive, the Court is apparently prepared to sustain the application of state laws concerning, for example, industrial safety practices and perhaps even wage and hour legislation which inhibits the bargaining freedom of parties covered by the national Act. It is not sufficient to sustain state regulation that it is based on some general societal policy having nothing to do specifically with labor relations. Weber v. Anheuser-Busch, Inc. (U.S.1955) (injunction of arguably protected activity barred, although state law deals generally with restraint of trade).

It may well be that the "health and safety" rationale will shelter the payment to strikers of state welfare benefits or unemployment compensation. It has been argued that such payments constitute state assistance to persons engaged in protected activities (unlike the cases already discussed of state prohibition of such activities) so as to frustrate the intention underlying the federal Labor Act of leaving the parties to their own economic resources in resolving bargaining disputes. The Court of Appeals for the First Circuit has been presented with two such cases, and has considered them to raise first the question whether the payment of welfare or unemployment benefits reflects a deeply rooted state interest and then the question whether, assuming such a state interest, there is too great a frustration of a federal purpose found in the national Labor Act. The court found the record evidence inadequate to decide these issues, and in one case affirmed the denial of an injunction against welfare payments, ITT Lamp Div. v. Minter (1st Cir. 1970); and in the other case held it error to dismiss an action for an injunction against payment of unemployment compensation to strikers, Grinnell Corp. v. Hackett (1st Cir. 1973) (six-week waiting period before strikers received such compensation).

The converse concern, for the economic wellbeing of the employer, has been held to justify the avoidance by a trustee in bankruptcy of a duly negotiated collective bargaining agreement, in the face of claims that such avoidance would frustrate the statutory rights of employees by giving the employer the power to violate the National Labor Relations Act (by refusing to execute an agreement already reached or by repudiating outright an executed agreement). Shopmen's Local 455, Bridge Workers v. Kevin Steel Prods., Inc. (2d Cir. 1975). But even in that case, where the power of avoidance was given by the federal Bankruptcy Act—such that subordination to the NLRA was not mandated by the Supremacy Clause of the Constitution—the court concluded that the policies of the Labor Act were such as to justify extreme caution by the bankruptcy court in permitting the trustee to avoid the labor contract:

> The decision to allow rejection should not be based solely on whether it will improve the financial status of the debtor. Such a narrow approach totally ignores the policies of the Labor Act and makes no attempt to accommodate to them. .   .   . [A] bankruptcy court should permit rejection of a collective bargaining agreement "only after thorough scrutiny, and a careful balancing of the equities on both sides, for,

in relieving a debtor from its obligations under a collective bargaining agreement, it may be depriving the employees affected of their seniority, welfare and pension rights, as well as other valuable benefits which are incapable of forming the basis of a provable claim for money damages."

Of course, unlike the federal Bankruptcy Act, state laws designed to relieve debt-ridden companies would have to be tested under the Supremacy Clause when arguably in conflict with the federal Labor Act.

In any event, whatever may be the reach of the "health and safety" rationale as an incursion upon the jurisdiction and policies of the National Labor Relations Board, it is doubtful that it would be carried so far as to require a reconsideration of the Court's early holding that states may not bar the strike in private industries providing an essential public service. Street Employees Div. 1287 v. Missouri (U.S.1963) (Court sets aside injunction of strike among employees of transit system initially privately owned but temporarily taken over by state which declared public emergency).

Somewhat less clear is the applicability of state trespass laws to bar peaceful concerted activity on company property. It has long been held that federal law in certain circumstances requires an employer to open its property even to nonemployees if such is necessary to bring to employees information about unionization. NLRB v. Babcock & Wilcox Co. (U.S.1956). Presumably, in such cases, the employer could not rely upon state trespass laws to eject these non-employee organizers whose access to its property is sheltered by sections 7 and 8(a)(1). The Supreme Court has not, however, clearly determined whether employees and nonemployees may come onto the company's private property in order to engage in other normally protected activities, such as picketing, free from the restraints of state trespass laws. In Taggart v. Weinacker's, Inc. (U.S.1970), where the Court dismissed the writ of certiorari as improvidently granted, one Justice asserted that the fundamental state interest in its trespass law could not be preempted for organizational picketing on company property, while two other Justices asserted that the *Garmon* decision clearly requires preemption of the trespass claim.

More recently, however, the Court rendered a decision pertinent to this question in Hudgens v. NLRB (U.S.1975). There, employees striking at the warehouse of a shoe company engaged in picketing at one of the company's retail shoe stores which was operated pursuant to a lease in an enclosed shopping mall. Although the Court held that the shopping center property had not sufficiently taken on the attributes of public property, and thus that the strikers had no constitutional right to picket there, it remanded so that the Board could address the question whether the right to picket on the privately owned mall property was statutorily protected by section 7.

If such picketing is indeed protected, so that the employer would be barred under section 8(a)(1) from resorting to self-help to discipline the employees, presumably a state-court injunction resting on the state's trespass law would be barred as well. If, however, the picketing need not take place on private property in order to foster the objectives of the Labor Act, it will—even though peaceful—presumably be subject to injunction under state law. In view of the fact that the legal standards are very unclear as to whether picketing on private property is or is not protected activity, a strong case can be made that such picketing falls within the *Garmon* principle, and that preemption should operate.

§ 5.   Prohibited Activity: The Reach of Preemption

Unlike the case of protected activity, it is not quite so obvious that conduct prohibited by the federal Act—*i. e.*, union unfair labor practices—should also be free from state regulation. Yet the Supreme Court has held that even though the substantive goals of state and federal law may be alike, there is a potential conflict with the federal scheme merely by virtue of two different law-enforcing authorities implementing differing remedial schemes. In Garner v. Teamsters Local 776 (U.S.1953), the Court affirmed the overturning of a state-court injunction against organizational picketing which effectively cut off all the business of a trucking concern. It concluded that this picketing, designed to coerce the company into compelling its employees to join the union, fell within the unfair labor practice jurisdiction of the Board and thus beyond the jurisdiction of state courts:

> Congress evidently considered that centralized administration of specially designed procedures were [sic] necessary to obtain uniform application of its substantive rules and to avoid these diversities and conflicts likely to result from a variety of local procedures and attitudes toward labor controversies. . . . A multiplicity of tribunals and a diversity of procedures are quite as apt to produce incompatible or conflicting adjudications as are different rules of substantive law.

The Court was thus concerned that different states would remedy federal unfair labor practices with differing degrees of severity, contrary to the congressional design. The Court in *Garner* also set forth a second rationale for preemption: the challenged union conduct might *not* in truth be an unfair labor practice (which is a matter for the NLRB to decide) and might for that reason be intended by Congress to be unimpeded by state restrictions:

> The detailed prescription of a procedure for restraint of specified types of picketing would seem to imply that other picketing is to be free of other methods and sources of re-

straint. For the policy of the national Labor Management Relations Act is not to condemn all picketing but only that ascertained by its prescribed processes to fall within its prohibitions. Otherwise, it is implicit in the Act that the public interest is served by freedom of labor to use the weapon of picketing. For a state to impinge on the area of labor combat designed to be free is quite as much an obstruction of federal policy as if the state were to declare picketing free for purposes or by methods which the federal Act prohibits.

Some years later, in San Diego Bldg. Trades Council v. Garmon (U.S.1959), again involving minority-union recognition picketing, the Court attempted to formulate a systematic approach to preemption of conduct arguably protected or arguably prohibited by the national Labor Act. The Court's formulation rested on the first rationale of *Garner, i. e.*, that the NLRB must determine whether conduct is prohibited by section 8 of the Labor Act and that

> Congress has entrusted administration of the labor policy for the Nation to a centralized administrative agency, armed with its own procedures, and equipped with its specialized knowledge and cumulative experience.   .   .

> Administration is more than a means of regulation: administration is regulation. We have been concerned with conflict in its broadest sense; conflict with a complex and interrelated federal scheme of law, remedy, and administration.

It followed that the state could not regulate the minority picketing (which the state courts assumed was an unfair labor practice) either by injunction—akin to the prospective remedy normally granted by the NLRB—or by an award of damages. Although the employer argued that damages should not be ousted, since they address past economic harm to the employer with which the Board is typically unconcerned, the Court responded: "In fact, since remedies form an ingredient of any integrated scheme of regulation, to allow the State to grant a remedy here which has been withheld from the National Labor Relations Board only accentuates the danger of conflict [with federal policy]."

The policy of preemption applies to state regulation of prohibited activities even though the state announces its rule by some manner other than conventional tort law or an independent body of labor relations law. For example, in Connell Constr. Co. v. Plumbers Local 100 (U.S.1975), a plumbers union picketed a general contractor in the construction industry until it secured an agreement that the contractor would not utilize nonunion subcontractors to do mechanical work at its jobsites. The employer sought an injunction against enforcement of the contract, claiming a violation of the federal and state antitrust laws. The Court, which ultimately concluded that the union's activities were secondary and illegal, held nonetheless that they could be subjected to the federal antitrust laws, which Congress had carefully tailored in order to accommodate to its labor policies regarding union organizing. State antitrust laws, however, could not be assumed to accord with those federal labor policies, and were therefore to be preempted as to union contracts and concerted activities in aid of organizing.

> State antitrust laws generally have not been subjected to this process of accommodation. If they take account of labor goals at all they may represent a totally different balance between labor and antitrust policies. Permitting state antitrust law to operate in this field could frustrate the basic federal policies favoring employee organization and allowing elimination of competition among wage earners, and interfere with the detailed system Congress has created for regulating organizational techniques.

The Court appears concerned, in cases involving conduct even concededly prohibited as an unfair labor practice, that independent state remedies will prove to be far more harsh than is contemplated by the federal scheme. For example, the fact that Board remedies— at least in cases of coercive organizational picketing—are normally prospective only (without compensation to the injured employer) may evince a substantive policy of limited financial liability and the tolerance of "one free bite" by the respondent. There may also be a concern that too great a dependence on more attractive state remedies may encourage the employer too readily to ignore the preferred federal remedial processes.

Since the *Garmon* holding relegates to the "primary jurisdiction" of the Board both the remedy for unfair labor practices and, obviously, the determination whether the conduct of the employees is prohibited at all (as a predicate to applying the remedies), the Court has ousted the states of jurisdiction to regulate conduct not only *actually* prohibited by section 8 but also conduct which is *arguably* prohibited. Unlike the case of arguably *protected* activities, the employer can fairly readily seek a Board determination whether the employee conduct is actually prohibited merely by filing unfair labor practice charges; if determined by the Board not to be prohibited, the conduct may well then be subject to state regulation as beyond the concern of the NLRB. Even here, however, the implications of primary jurisdiction are not wholly happy, since the employer's self-interest (*e. g.*, the prospect of a substantial damage award in a state court) may be such as to dictate an affirmative hope that the charged union will succeed before the Board (albeit not succeed to the point of convincing the Board that the conduct is protected); and since the Board's determination may be long in coming and may in any event prove to be completely inconclusive on the question of federal prohibition (*e. g.*, an unexplained refusal by the General Counsel to issue a complaint). Perhaps a sounder rationale for barring state regulation of conduct arguably prohibited may be found in the second rationale of the *Garner* case: that such conduct is also arguably *not* prohibited and thus is intended by Congress to be free from governmental regulation altogether, either because it is in truth "protected" under section 7 or "permitted" as a legitimate economic weapon in organizing or bargaining subject only to corresponding self-help measures by the employer (but not by direct judicial or administrative measures). See Weber v. Anheuser-Busch, Inc. (U.S.1955) (arguable secondary activity is possibly protected and thus not enjoinable). It is this rationale which has been invoked by the Court under the Railway Labor Act—which has no formal unfair labor practice provisions and no agency which can assert "primary jurisdiction" on such matters—to bar a state-court injunction of union activity which might be characterized as a secondary boycott but which might also be characterized as economic force "permitted" by Congress after the exhaustion of stipulated bargaining procedures. Brotherhood of R. R. Trainmen v. Jacksonville Terminal Co. (U.S.1969) (with the Railway Labor Act affording no standards for distinguishing primary from secondary activity, an injunction might mistakenly bar conduct which Congress intended to protect).

In any event, the law is rather clear that state remedies may not issue against concerted activities which are actually or arguably forbidden by the unfair labor practice provisions of the national Act. In most cases involving claims of "arguably" prohibited activities, there is no dispute that the parties are within the jurisdiction of the NLRB and what is arguable is the substantive legality of the defendants' conduct. But it is also possible to find that conduct is "arguably" prohibited when there is a dispute on the question whether the persons engaging in that conduct are within the coverage of the national Labor Act. Thus, in Marine Eng'rs Benef. Ass'n v. Interlake S.S Co. (U.S.1962), the Court overturned a state injunction against conduct which was arguably an illegal secondary boycott under the Labor Act in spite of the employer's claim that the boycotting marine engineers were all supervisors whose union would not be an "employee organization" capable of violating section 8(b)(4). The Court found the marine engineers were arguably "employees," and held that state courts must "concede that a union is an 'employee organization' for section 8(b) purposes whenever a reasonably arguable case is made to that effect." As in the case of protected activities, the issue of arguable or actual prohibition may be asserted by the defendants in the state court proceeding or by the National Labor Relations Board in seeking an injunction from a federal court against the implementation of any state-court injunction against the concerted activity. NLRB v. Nash-Finch Co. (U.S.1971).

§ 6. Prohibited Activity: Allowable State Regulation

In spite of the general rule of preemption of state regulation of conduct actually or arguably prohibited as an unfair labor practice, the Supreme Court has allowed two notable exceptions: "[W]here the activity regulated was a merely peripheral concern of the Labor Management Relations Act . . . [o]r where the regulated conduct touched interests so deeply rooted in local feeling and responsibility that, in the absence of compelling congressional direction, we could not infer that Congress had deprived the States of the power to act." San Diego Bldg. Trades Council v. Garmon (U.S.1959). The clearest examples of the latter involve acts of physical violence or concerted conduct imminently threatening violence. While picket-line violence which intimidates employees may violate section 8(b)(1), the states through the exercise of traditional police powers may quell such violence by injunction, Youngdahl v. Rainfair, Inc. (U.S.1957) (injunction limited to physical obstruction and threats of violence as distinguished from picketing generally), or by holding the union liable for compensatory damages (limited to harm caused by the violence as distinguished merely from the work stoppage) and punitive damages, UAW v. Russell (U.S.1958) (action by employee), United Constr. Workers v. Laburnum Constr. Corp. (U.S.1954) (action by employer). Although the Court in the latter two cases sustained the state remedies because they were unlike, and not likely to conflict in purpose with, those available from the NLRB, and because the state law reflected a general societal policy rather than one specifically addressed to labor relations, the *Garmon* decision more narrowly reformulated the rationale as that of "deeply rooted local feeling."

Arguably prohibited conduct which has been held to be a "peripheral concern" of the federal Labor Act and thus subject to state substantive law is that of a union which expels a member in violation of the "contract" between the union and the member as embodied in the union constitution and bylaws. The law is rather nebulous in this area, for an expulsion from membership may not only constitute a contract breach but may also have implications for the employee's job security and may thus fall within the reach of section 8(a)(3) which bars employer discrimination in hire and tenure encouraging union membership and of section 8(b)(2) which bars union inducement of such employer discrimination. The Supreme Court has drawn a most elusive line between employee claims against the union the gist of which is wrongful expulsion and the prime requested relief is reinstatement to membership, and claims against the union the gist of which is wrongful inducement of employer discrimination as to job security and the prime requested relief is reimbursement from the union for the loss of job rights. In the former class of case, state relief is held not to be preempted, since contract-based disputes relating to union membership are deemed of "peripheral concern" to the NLRB; in the latter class of case, NLRB jurisdiction under sections

8(a)(3) and 8(b)(2) is deemed preemptive. Compare IAM v. Gonzales (U.S.1958) (potential conflict with NLRB too contingent when state court awards reinstatement of union membership, damages for mental and physical suffering resulting from expulsion—which NLRB could not do—and damages for loss of wages resulting from expulsion), with Local 100, Plumbers v. Borden (U.S.1963), and Iron Workers Local 207 v. Perko (U.S.1963) (in both cases, gist of action was interference with existing or prospective employment relations rather than internal union matters, and there was absent a specific claim for restoration of membership to which an award of damages for loss of earnings could be subordinated).

The significance of the *Gonzales* holding was sharply curtailed by the Supreme Court in its synthesis of the earlier pertinent cases in Amalgamated Ass'n of Street Employees v. Lockridge (U.S.1971), which requires a court to characterize the "crux" of the case as relating either to internal union matters or to job discrimination. While this appears to put a premium on artful pleading, the tone of the *Lockridge* opinion is such that it will likely be understood effectively to bar state court actions against unions for wrongful expulsion when the expulsion has brought with it some significant impairment of employment status, or when the rights of the employee-member turn not exclusively upon the union's constitution or bylaws but also upon the terms of the collective bargaining agreement. Further complications lie in the fact that expulsion from membership for certain reasons believed grossly in contravention of statutory values can constitute a violation by the union of section 8(b)(1), thus reinforcing the *Lockridge* thrust toward preemption; and many of these cases will also involve claims against the employer of breach of the labor contract and against the union of breach of its duty of fair representation, both of which claims have been unqualifiedly held by the Court *not* to be preempted by actual or potential NLRB jurisdiction, as will be noted further below.

The Supreme Court has invoked both the "deep local feeling" and "peripheral concern" justifications in sustaining the power of states to hold defamatory and subject to damages the making of certain statements by or about employees, unions or employers in the context of a labor-election campaign. In Linn v. Plant Guard Workers Local 114 (U.S.1966), a company official brought a libel action against an employee, his union and two union officials to recover damages for statements made in a leaflet concerning illegal and otherwise improper conduct by the plaintiff and other supervisors. The Court conceded that certain defamatory statements have been held by the NLRB to be protected, even though erroneous; the use of epithets such as "scab," "unfair" or "liar" is commonplace in labor organizing campaigns and cannot properly provoke discharge or discipline. The Court also conceded that certain defamatory statements might violate section 8(b) or might justify the Board's setting aside of an election if sufficiently coercive, misleading or inflammatory. Nonetheless, in spite of the Board's capacity to deal with such defamatory statements, the Court held that there was a deeply rooted state interest in outlawing defamatory statements made knowingly or recklessly and that such regulation was only a peripheral concern of the NLRB which, in remedying coercive, misleading or inflammatory statements, accords no redress for the injury to the reputation of the defamation victim.

In order, however, to avoid "unwarranted intrusion upon free discussion in election campaigns," the Court in *Linn* announced two essential elements of proof for recovery under state law: (1) the defamatory statements must have been published with "malice," defined as knowledge of their falsity or reckless disregard of their truth or falsity, and (2) the plaintiff must introduce specific evidence of injury, "which may include general injury to reputation, consequent mental suffering, alienation of associates, specific items of pecuniary loss, or whatever form of harm would be recognized by state tort law." The Court has since made clear that it is error to define "malice" for the jury as simply personal spite or ill will; that the protection of the *Linn* doctrine extends to union statements designed to pressure unit employees to join, even though there may be no "labor dispute" between union and employer and even though the statements are made after the union has been designated bargaining representative rather than before; and that the union's use of the term "scab" to describe nonmembers "was protected under federal law and cannot be the basis of a state libel judgment." Old Dominion Branch 496, Letter Carriers v. Austin (U.S.1974) (defamation action by nonmembers, labelled "scabs" and "traitors" in union newsletter; although governed by federal executive order, employees and union were held entitled to protections comparable to national Labor Act).

The *Linn* case, in substance, demonstrates that federal concerns in labor-management relations may be effectuated not merely by barring state jurisdiction altogether but rather by shaping an independent federal rule of substantive law which either state or federal courts may be empowered to apply. Just as the Court in *Linn* created what was in essence a federal defamation standard (requiring malice and specific injury), it is likely—although no case appears directly to have raised this issue—that in a state-court action to enjoin or to award damages for picket-line violence, the question whether "violence" occurred or was threatened such that the state could properly regulate it would be determined by federal law. An isolated shove, or the use of abusive epithets, on the picket line might be regarded as so commonplace in labor disputes that they ought to be treated as protected, not only against employer discharge but also against state judicial or administrative remedies. The states should not be heard to assert a "deeply felt local interest" in enjoining picket-line conduct of which the Board or Supreme Court might be more solicitous. Compare NLRB v. Pepsi-Cola Bottling Co. (5th Cir. 1971) (sit-in protest by employees, involving no violence or interference with nonstrikers or claim of possession of employer premises, does not per se subject employee protesters to discharge).

Indeed, many of the exceptions to the doctrine of NLRB preemption involve the application, by state or federal courts, of federal substantive law in the face of claims that the challenged conduct is also an unfair labor practice. Actions for enforcement of promises in collective bargaining agreements, under section 301 of the federal Act, are governed by federal law and are not preempted merely because the same conduct which allegedly violates the contract is also prohibited by section 8 as an unfair labor practice. Smith v. Evening News Ass'n (U.S.1962). The same is true of employee actions against the union for breach of the duty of fair representation in negotiating labor contracts, Steele v. Louisville & N. R. R. (U.S. 1944), and in enforcing them, Vaca v. Sipes (U.S.1967). Section 303 of the federal Act expressly declares the violation of section 8(b)(4) to be "unlawful" and remediable by the injured party (held to include either the primary or the secondary employer) in a federal or state court action for compensatory damages. The contours of this federally created "tort" are set by the text of section 8(b)(4), and this text is to be interpreted and applied by judges and juries regardless of whether the Board has already passed on the case and, indeed, even in the face of a Board ruling squarely opposite to that made by the court. United Brick & Clay Workers v. Deena Artware, Inc. (6th Cir. 1952); Longshoremen v. Juneau Spruce Corp. (U.S.1952). But state law may not go further in actions covered by section 303 and award punitive damages. Local 20, Teamsters v. Morton (U.S.1964).

§ 7. Unprotected Activity

Certain employee activities—such as sit-down strikes, "quickie" and unscheduled work stoppages, strikes in breach of contract, and disloyalty—have been classified as conduct which is neither protected by section 7 nor prohibited by section 8. As such, the participating employees are not sheltered by section 8(a)(1) from employer reprisals and this conduct has been denoted "unprotected" activity. In one of its earliest decisions raising the question of preemption of state remedies, the Supreme Court held that unscheduled and sporadic "quickie" strikes were neither protected under section 7 nor remediable by the NLRB under section 8, and thus inferred that:

> Policing of such conduct is left wholly to the states. . . . There is no existing or possible conflict or overlapping between the authority of the Federal and State Boards, because the Federal Board has no authority either to investigate, approve or forbid the union conduct in question. This conduct is governable by the State or it is entirely ungoverned.

The order of the State Board requiring that the union cease and desist from the quickie stoppages was approved, since Congress had not "clearly manifested" an intention to oust states from the exercise of their police powers. UAW Local 232 v. Wisconsin Employment Rel. Bd. (Briggs & Stratton) (U.S.1949).

Subsequently, the Court retreated, and moved more directly in a preemptionist direction in this area of "unprotected" activities. First, it repudiated the *Briggs & Stratton* case to the extent that the Court there determined for itself whether the defendants' conduct was unprotected activity: "In the absence of the Board's clear determination that an activity is neither protected nor prohibited or of compelling precedent applied to essentially undisputed facts, it is not for this Court to decide whether such activities are subject to state jurisdiction." San Diego Bldg. Trades Council v. Garmon (U.S.1959). Second, even when there is such an available definitive Board ruling that the conduct is neither protected nor prohibited, it does not automatically follow that the states are free to regulate; Congress' declaration in the Labor Act that the activities should be free from federal regulation may in some cases evince an intention to free such activities from all other governmental regulation as well.

This theme was firmly sounded in Garner v. Teamsters Local 776 (U.S.1953), involving minority-union organizational picketing designed to compel the employer to induce employees to join the union. The highest state court, concluding that the picketing was within the ban of the Labor Act, dissolved a lower court injunction, and the Supreme Court affirmed. It suggested that, if indeed the picketing was not actually forbidden by federal law, it ought also be sheltered from state restraints:

> The detailed prescription of a procedure for restraint of specified types of picketing would seem to imply that other picketing is to be free of other methods and sources of restraint. For the policy of the national Labor Management Relations Act is not to condemn all picketing but only that ascertained to fall within its prohibitions. Otherwise, it is implicit in the Act that the public interest is served by freedom of labor to use the weapon of picketing. For a state to impinge on the area of labor combat designed to be free is quite as much an obstruction of federal policy as if the state were to declare picketing free for purposes or by methods which the federal Act prohibits.

It is thus necessary, when conduct of employees is found to be "unprotected" against employer self-help, to determine whether Congress intended the employee conduct to fall within "the area of labor combat designed to be free" from direct judicial or administrative restrictions.

The Court made this determination in Local 20, Teamsters v. Morton (U.S.1964), an action in a federal court under section 303 of the federal Act for certain secondary boycott activities, including inducement of a work stoppage among the employees of a customer of the primary employer and direct persuasion (without threat or coercion) of the customer to refrain from doing business with the primary employer. The Supreme Court affirmed the award of compensatory damages for inducing the work stoppage, but it reversed the award of damages under state tort law (adjudicated as pendent to the section 303 claim) for the peaceful inducement of the customer. It concluded that this inducement was not prohibited under section 8 of the Labor Act, but assumed arguendo that it was not protected either; it referred to such direct persuasion of the secondary employer as therefore "permitted by federal law," as a "part of the balance struck by Congress between the conflicting interests of the union, the employees, the employer and the community." Relying on the *Garner* decision, the Court held:

> If the Ohio law of secondary boycott can be applied to proscribe the same type of conduct which Congress focused upon but did not proscribe when it enacted § 303, the inevitable result would be to frustrate the congressional determination to leave this weapon of self-help available, and to upset the balance of power between labor and management expressed in our national labor policy.

This analysis in the *Morton* case, along with an important Supreme Court decision on the function of the National Labor Relations Board in the area of "unprotected" activities, make it highly doubtful that the Court would today endorse its decision in the *Briggs & Stratton* case that the states are free to enjoin unprotected work stoppages. In NLRB v. Insurance Agents' Int'l Union (U.S.1960), the Court reversed a determination of the NLRB that intermittent and unannounced work stoppages during contract negotiations constituted bargaining in bad faith by the union. It held that, while such stoppages are not protected by section 7 against employer self-help measures, they are "part and parcel" of the federal scheme of collective bargaining, and also that the Board exceeds its powers when it deprives employees of this weapon in an effort to "equalize" the economic weapons of the parties. The logic of the *Insurance Agents* decision would seem to dictate that state courts should also be barred from intruding upon this concerted activity, since such intrusion would (in the words of the *Morton* case) "frustrate the congressional determination to leave this weapon of self-help available, and . . . upset the balance of power between labor and management expressed in our national labor policy." This analysis has, however, been recently rejected by the Wisconsin Supreme Court in upholding the jurisdiction of the state Employment Relations Commission to enjoin a union-induced refusal by employees to work overtime. The union argued that such activity was "permitted" by the relevant Supreme Court cases. The state court, however, read the *Insurance Agents* case to have "left regulation of strike tactics to the states" and concluded that although Congress may have "permitted" concerted activity upon which it "focused" and did not outlaw, the Labor Act nowhere "focuses upon" the matter of strike tactics. Lodge 76, IAM v. Wisconsin Employment Rel. Comm. (Wis.1975).*

In any event, the Supreme Court has utilized a theory of congressionally intended laissez faire between labor and management in a recent case involving an action for damages by several supervisors against an employer which had discharged them for joining a union. Beasley v. Food Fair, Inc. (U.S.1974). The state trial court relied on the state right-to-work law in holding the employer liable for the supervisors' discharge, but the Supreme Court held that the text and legislative history of the Labor Act demonstrate an affirmative congressional intention to free the employer of the obligation to bargain with unionized supervisors and to permit the employer freely to rid itself of supervisors with divided loyalties. (The Court placed heavy emphasis upon section 14(a) of the Labor Act which provides, in part, that "no employer subject to this Act shall be compelled to deem individuals defined herein as supervisors as employees for the purpose of any law, either national or local, relating to collective bargaining.") Thus, for a state to impede—by an award of damages—an employer's discharge of unionized supervisors would frustrate the congressional intention to leave this weapon of self-help available to the employer.

A Supreme Court decision in the converse situation shows that the Court is willing to find that certain unprotected activity *can* be regulated by the states, consistent with the congressional design. Thus, in Hanna Mining Co. v. Marine Engineers Dist. 2 (U.S.1965), the Court held that state courts had the power to enjoin, at the behest of the employer, concerted organizing activity by persons working for it but held by the NLRB to be "supervisors" (such that their conduct was neither arguably protected nor prohibited "employee" activity under the federal Act). Once again, the Court stated that the "propelling intention" behind Congress's exclusion of supervisory employees from the reach of the Labor Act "was to relieve employers from any compulsion under the Act and under state law to countenance or bargain with any union of supervisory employees," and relied on that intention not to bar state remedies (as in *Beasley*) but rather to countenance them when used by the employer against the supervisors. Similarly, the fact that malicious libel in the course of an election campaign is neither protected nor prohibited does not

* This decision was reversed by the United States Supreme Court in June 1976.

evince a Congressional intention to foster (or even tolerate) such conduct, and state law to that extent will not be preempted. Linn v. Plant Guard Workers Local 114 (U.S.1966).

§ 8. Summary and Prospectus

The preemption formula presently endorsed by the Supreme Court is broad. No state may use judicial or administrative remedies to inhibit or bar conduct which is, under the national Labor Act, actually or arguably protected by section 7 or actually or arguably prohibited by section 8. Indeed, it is likely that the preemption obtains when the conduct is unprotected, at least if it appears that Congress intended to leave the parties to their respective self-help measures in economic combat. These principles are, however, riddled with exceptions. States may regulate when there is a deeply-rooted state interest (violence) or when the matter is one of peripheral concern to the NLRB (intra-union disputes). Moreover, claims based on federal substantive law will frequently overcome the normal preemptive thrust of sections 7 and 8; examples are contract actions under section 301, tort actions for damages under section 303 for violations of section 8(b)(4), actions for breach of the duty of fair representation, actions for malicious defamation, some actions under the federal antitrust laws, and proceedings in bankruptcy to avoid an existing collective bargaining agreement. Further confusion is added by the fact that over time the rationale underlying preemption has shifted, although it today appears to rest fairly firmly on the motion of uniform administration of the Labor Act through the exclusive jurisdiction of the NLRB. Nonetheless, even this rationale has been subjected to increasing attack in the separate opinions of different Justices, who appear to be more tolerant of state regulation of labor activities. Some Justices would oust state regulation only when the conduct in question is actually protected by section 7, with the latter determination made by the state court itself; others would subordinate even clearly protected concerted activity to local trespass laws governing the property of the employer or to local safety and health regulations. All that can be said with confidence is that the contours of the preemption doctrine have not been firmly settled and are likely to change in the future, if only with the changing composition of the Supreme Court.

APPENDIX A

SHERMAN ANTITRUST ACT

26 Stat. 209 (1890), as amended, 15 U.S.C. §§ 1–7 (1970).

Sec. 1. Every contract, combination in the form of trust or otherwise, or conspiracy, in restraint of trade or commerce among the several States, or with foreign nations, is hereby declared to be illegal * * *. Every person who shall make any contract or engage in any combination or conspiracy hereby declared to be illegal shall be deemed guilty of a misdemeanor, and, on conviction thereof, shall be punished by fine not exceeding fifty thousand dollars, or by imprisonment not exceeding one year, or by both said punishments, in the discretion of the court.

Sec. 2. Every person who shall monopolize, or attempt to monopolize, or combine or conspire with any other person or persons, to monopolize any part of the trade or commerce among the several States, or with foreign nations, shall be deemed guilty of a misdemeanor, and, on conviction thereof, shall be punished by fine not exceeding fifty thousand dollars, or by imprisonment not exceeding one year, or by both said punishments, in the discretion of the court.

Sec. 4. The several district courts of the United States are invested with jurisdiction to prevent and restrain violations of this act; and it shall be the duty of the several United States attorneys, in their respective districts, under the direction of the Attorney General, to institute proceedings in equity to prevent and restrain such violations. Such proceedings may be by way of petition setting forth the case and praying that such violation shall be enjoined or otherwise prohibited. When the parties complained of shall have been duly notified of such petition the court shall proceed, as soon as may be, to the hearing and determination of the case; and pending such petition and before final decree, the court may at any time make such temporary restraining order or prohibition as shall be deemed just in the premises.

Sec. 7. Any person who shall be injured in his business or property by any other person or corporation by reason of anything forbidden or declared to be unlawful by this act, may sue therefor in any circuit court of the United States in the district in which the defendant resides or is found, without respect to the amount in controversy, and shall recover threefold the damage by him sustained, and the costs of suit, including a reasonable attorney's fee.*

Sec. 8. The word "person," or "persons," wherever used in this act shall be deemed to include corporations and associations existing under or authorized by the laws of either the United States, the laws of any of the Territories, the laws of any State, or the laws of any foreign country.

CLAYTON ANTITRUST ACT

38 Stat. 730 (1914), as amended, 15 U.S.C. §§ 15, 17, 26 (1970),
29 U.S.C. § 52 (1970).

Be it enacted by the Senate and House of Representatives of the United States of America in Congress Assembled, That "antitrust laws," as used herein, includes the Act entitled "An Act to protect trade and commerce against unlawful restraints and monopolies," approved July second, eighteen hundred and ninety [Sherman Act] * * *.

Sec. 4. That any person who shall be injured in his business or property by reason of anything forbidden in the antitrust laws may sue therefor in any district court of the United States in the district in which the defendant resides or is found or has an agent, without respect to the amount in controversy, and shall recover threefold the damages by him sustained, and the cost of suit, including a reasonable attorney's fee.

Sec. 6. That the labor of a human being is not a commodity or article of commerce. Nothing contained in the antitrust laws shall be construed to forbid the existence and operation of labor, agricultural, or horticultural organizations, instituted for the purposes of mutual help, and not having capital stock or conducted for profit, or to forbid or restrain individual members of such organizations from lawfully carrying out the legitimate objects thereof; nor shall such organizations, or the members thereof, be held or construed to be illegal combinations or conspiracies in restraint of trade, under the antitrust laws.

Sec. 16. That any person, firm, corporation, or association shall be entitled to sue for and have injunctive relief, in any court of the United States having jurisdiction over the parties, against threatened loss or damage by a violation of the antitrust laws, including sections 2, 3, 7, and 8 of this Act, when and under the same conditions and prin-

---

* Section 7 was repealed by 69 Stat. 283 (1955), without, however, adversely affecting the remedies available for antitrust violations since Section 4 of the Clayton Antitrust Act of 1914, infra, independently authorizes suits for treble damages.

ciples as injunctive relief against threatened conduct that will cause loss or damage is granted by courts of equity, under the rules governing such proceedings, and upon the execution of proper bond against damages for an injunction improvidently granted and a showing that the danger of irreparable loss or damage is immediate, a preliminary injunction may issue: *Provided*, That nothing herein contained shall be construed to entitle any person, firm, corporation, or association, except the United States, to bring suit in equity for injunctive relief against any common carrier subject to the provisions of the Act to regulate commerce, approved February fourth, eighteen hundred and eighty-seven, in respect of any matter subject to the regulation, supervision, or other jurisdiction of the Interstate Commerce Commission.

Sec. 20. That no restraining order or injunction shall be granted by any court of the United States, or a judge or the judges thereof, in any case between an employer and employees, or between employers and employees, or between employees, or between persons employed and persons seeking employment, involving, or growing out of, a dispute concerning terms or conditions of employment, unless necessary to prevent irreparable injury to property, or to a property right, of the party making the application, for which injury there is no adequate remedy at law, and such property or property right must be described with particularity in the application, which must be in writing and sworn to by the applicant or by his agent or attorney.

And no such restraining order or injunction shall prohibit any person or persons, whether singly or in concert, from terminating any relation of employment, or from ceasing to perform any work or labor, or from recommending, advising, or persuading others by peaceful means so to do; or from attending at any place where any such person or persons may lawfully be, for the purpose of peacefully obtaining or communicating information, or from peacefully persuading any person to work or to abstain from working; or from ceasing to patronize or to employ any party to such dispute, or from recommending, advising, or persuading others by peaceful and lawful means so to do; or from paying or giving to, or withholding from, any person engaged in such dispute, any strike benefits or other moneys or things of value; or from peaceably assembling in a lawful manner, and for lawful purposes; or from doing any act or thing which might lawfully be done in the absence of such dispute by any party thereto; nor shall any of the acts specified in this paragraph be considered or held to be violations of any law of the United States.

NORRIS–LAGUARDIA ACT

47 Stat. 70 (1932), 29 U.S.C. §§ 101–15 (1970).

AN ACT

To amend the Judicial Code and to define and limit the jurisdiction of courts sitting in equity, and for other purposes.

Sec. 1. Issuance of restraining orders and injunctions; limitation; public policy.

No court of the United States, as herein defined, shall have jurisdiction to issue any restraining order or temporary or permanent injunction in a case involving or growing out of a labor dispute, except in a strict conformity with the provisions of this Act; nor shall any such restraining order or temporary or permanent injunction be issued contrary to the public policy declared in this Act.

Sec. 2. Public policy in labor matters declared.

In the interpretation of this Act and in determining the jurisdiction and authority of the courts of the United States, as such jurisdiction and authority are herein defined and limited, the public policy of the United States is hereby declared as follows:

Whereas under prevailing economic conditions, developed with the aid of governmental authority for owners of property to organize in the corporate and other forms of ownership association, the individual unorganized worker is commonly helpless to exercise actual liberty of contract and to protect his freedom of labor, and thereby to obtain acceptable terms and conditions of employment, wherefore, though he should be free to decline to associate with his fellows, it is necessary that he have full freedom of association, self-organization, and designation of representatives of his own choosing, to negotiate the terms and conditions of his employment, and that he shall be free from the interference, restraint, or coercion of employers of labor, or their agents, in the designation of such representatives or in self-organization or in other concerted activities for the purpose of collective bargaining or other mutual aid or protection; therefore, the following definitions of and limitations upon the jurisdiction and authority of the courts of the United States are enacted.

Sec. 3. Nonenforceability of undertakings in conflict with public policy; "yellow dog" contracts.

Any undertaking or promise, such as is described in this section, or any other undertaking or promise in conflict with the public policy declared in section 2 of this Act is hereby declared to be contrary to the public policy of the United States, shall not be enforceable in any court of the United States and shall not afford any basis for the granting of legal or equitable relief by any such court, including specifically the following:

Every undertaking or promise hereafter made, whether written or oral, express or implied, constituting or contained in any contract or agreement of hiring or employment between any individual, firm, company, association, or corporation, and any employee or prospective employee of the same, whereby

(a) Either party to such contract or agreement undertakes or promises not to join, become, or remain a member of any labor organization or of any employer organization; or

(b) Either party to such contract or agreement undertakes or promises that he will withdraw from an employment relation in the event that he joins, becomes, or remains a member of any labor organization or of any employer organization.

Sec. 4. Enumeration of specific acts not subject to restraining orders or injunctions.

No court of the United States shall have jurisdiction to issue any restraining order or temporary or permanent injunction in any case involving or growing out of any labor dispute to prohibit any person or persons participating or interested in such dispute (as these terms are herein defined) from doing, whether singly or in concert, any of the following acts:

(a) Ceasing or refusing to perform any work or to remain in any relation of employment;

(b) Becoming or remaining a member of any labor organization or of any employer organization, regardless of any such undertaking or promise as is described in section 3 of this Act;

(c) Paying or giving to, or withholding from, any person participating or interested in such labor dispute, any strike or unemployment benefits or insurance, or other moneys or things of value;

(d) By all lawful means aiding any person participating or interested in any labor dispute who is being proceeded against in, or is prosecuting, any action or suit in any court of the United States or of any State;

(e) Giving publicity to the existence of, or the facts involved in, any labor dispute, whether by advertising, speaking, patrolling, or by any other method not involving fraud or violence;

(f) Assembling peaceably to act or to organize to act in promotion of their interests in a labor dispute;

(g) Advising or notifying any person of an intention to do any of the acts heretofore specified;

(h) Agreeing with other persons to do or not to do any of the acts heretofore specified; and

(i) Advising, urging, or otherwise causing or inducing without fraud or violence the acts heretofore specified, regardless of any such undertaking or promise as is described in section 3 of this Act.

Sec. 5. Doing in concert of certain acts as constituting unlawful combination or conspiracy subjecting person to injunctive remedies.

No court of the United States shall have jurisdiction to issue a restraining order or temporary or permanent injunction upon the ground that any of the persons participating or interested in a labor dispute constitute or are engaged in an unlawful combination or conspiracy because of the doing in concert of the acts enumerated in section 4 of this Act.

Sec. 6. Responsibility of officers and members of associations or their organizations for unlawful acts of individual officers, members, and agents.

No officer or member of any association or organization, and no association or organization participating or interested in a labor dispute, shall be held responsible or liable in any court of the United States for the unlawful acts of individual officers, members, or agents, except upon clear proof of actual participation in, or actual authorization of, such acts, or of ratification of such acts after actual knowledge thereof.

Sec. 7. Issuance of injunctions in labor disputes; hearings; findings of court; notice to affected persons; temporary restraining order; undertakings.

No court of the United States shall have jurisdiction to issue a temporary or permanent injunction in any case involving or growing out of a labor dispute, as herein defined, except after hearing the testimony of witnesses in open court (with opportunity for cross-examination) in support of the allegations of a complaint made under oath, and testimony in opposition thereto, if offered, and except after findings of fact by the court, to the effect—

(a) That unlawful acts have been threatened and will be committed unless restrained or have been committed and will be continued unless restrained, but no injunction or temporary restraining order shall be issued on account of any threat or unlawful act excepting against the person or persons, association, or organization making the threat or committing the unlawful act or actually authorizing or ratifying the same after actual knowledge thereof;

(b) That substantial and irreparable injury to complainant's property will follow;

(c) That as to each item of relief granted greater injury will be inflicted upon complainant by the denial of relief than will be inflicted upon defendants by the granting of relief;

(d) That complainant has no adequate remedy at law; and

(e) That the public officers charged with the duty to protect complainant's property are unable or unwilling to furnish adequate protection.

Such hearing shall be held after due and personal notice thereof has been given, in such manner as the court shall direct, to all known persons against whom relief is sought, and also to the chief of those public officials of the county and city within which the unlawful acts have been threatened or committed charged with the duty to protect complainant's property: *Provided, however,* That if a complainant shall also allege that, unless a temporary restraining order shall be issued without notice, a substantial and irreparable injury to complainant's property will be unavoidable, such a temporary restraining order may be issued upon testimony under oath, sufficient, if sustained, to justify the court in issuing a temporary injunction upon a hearing after notice. Such a temporary restraining order shall be effective for no longer than five days and shall become void at the expiration of said five days. No temporary restraining order or temporary injunction shall be issued except on condition that complainant shall first file an undertaking with adequate security in an amount to be fixed by the court sufficient to recompense those enjoined for any loss, expense, or damage caused by the improvident or erroneous issuance of such order or injunction, including all reasonable costs (together with a reasonable attorney's fee) and expense of defense against the order or against the granting of any injunctive relief sought in the same proceeding and subsequently denied by the court.

The undertaking herein mentioned shall be understood to signify an agreement entered into by the complainant and the surety upon which a decree may be rendered in the same suit or proceeding against said complainant and surety, upon a hearing to assess damages of which hearing complainant and surety shall have reasonable notice, the said complainant and surety submitting themselves to the jurisdiction of the court for that purpose. But nothing herein contained shall deprive any party having a claim or cause of action under or upon such undertaking from electing to pursue his ordinary remedy by suit at law or in equity.

Sec. 8. Noncompliance with obligations involved in labor disputes or failure to settle by negotiation or arbitration as preventing injunctive relief.

No restraining order or injunctive relief shall be granted to any complainant who has failed to comply with any obligation imposed by law which is involved in the labor dispute in question, or who has failed to make every reasonable effort to settle such dispute either by negotiation or with the aid of any available governmental machinery of mediation or voluntary arbitration.

Sec. 9. Granting of restraining order or injunction as dependent on previous findings of fact; limitation on prohibitions included in restraining orders and injunctions.

No restraining order or temporary or permanent injunction shall be granted in a case involving or growing out of a labor dispute, except on the basis of findings of fact made and filed by the court in the record of the case prior to the issuance of such restraining order or injunction; and every restraining order or injunction granted in a case involving or growing out of a labor dispute shall include only a prohibition of such specific act or acts as may be expressly complained of in the bill of complaint or petition filed in such case and as shall be expressly included in said findings of fact made and filed by the court as provided herein.

Sec. 10. Review by Court of Appeals of issuance or denial of temporary injunctions; record; precedence.

Whenever any court of the United States shall issue or deny any temporary injunction in a case involving or growing out of a labor dispute, the court shall, upon the request of any party to the proceedings and on his filing the usual bond for costs, forthwith certify as in ordinary cases the record of the case to the court of appeals for its review. Upon the filing of such record in the court of appeals, the appeal shall be heard and the temporary injunctive order affirmed, modified, or set aside with the greatest possible expedition, giving the proceedings precedence over all other matters except older matters of the same character.

Sec. 11. Contempts; speedy and public trial; jury.

In all cases arising under this Act in which a person shall be charged with contempt in a court of the United States (as herein defined), the accused shall enjoy the right to a speedy and public trial by an impartial jury of the State and district wherein the contempt shall have been committed: *Provided,* That this right shall not apply to contempts committed in the presence of the court or so near thereto as to interfere directly with the administration of justice or to apply to the misbehavior, misconduct, or disobedience of any officer of the court in respect to the writs, orders, or process of the court.*

Sec. 12.* Contempts; demand for retirement of judge sitting in proceeding.

The defendant in any proceeding for contempt of court may file with the court a demand for the retirement of the judge sitting in the

---

* Sections 11 and 12 were repealed by Act of June 25, 1948 (62 Stat. 862), a codification of the provisions of Title 18 of the United States Code. The substance of Section 11 was reenacted in the same Act (62 Stat. 844, 18 U.S.C. § 3692 (1970)); the substance of Section 12 is now found in Rules 42(a) and (b) of the Federal Rules of Criminal Procedure.

proceeding, if the contempt arises from an attack upon the character or conduct of such judge and if the attack occurred elsewhere than in the presence of the court or so near thereto as to interfere directly with the administration of justice. Upon the filing of any such demand the judge shall thereupon proceed no further, but another judge shall be designated in the same manner as is provided by law. The demand shall be filed prior to the hearing in the contempt proceeding.

Sec. 13. Definitions of terms and words used in chapter.

When used in this Act, and for the purposes of this Act—

(a) A case shall be held to involve or to grow out of a labor dispute when the case involves persons who are engaged in the same industry, trade, craft, or occupation; or have direct or indirect interests therein; or who are employees of the same employer; or who are members of the same or an affiliated organization of employers or employees; whether such dispute is (1) between one or more employers or associations of employers and one or more employees or associations of employees; (2) between one or more employers or associations of employers and one or more employers or associations of employers; or (3) between one or more employees or associations of employees and one or more employees or associations of employees; or when the case involves any conflicting or competing interests in a "labor dispute" (as hereinafter defined) of "persons participating or interested" therein (as hereinafter defined).

(b) A person or association shall be held to be a person participating or interested in a labor dispute if relief is sought against him or it, and if he or it is engaged in the same industry, trade, craft, or occupation in which such dispute occurs, or has a direct or indirect interest therein, or is a member, officer, or agent of any association composed in whole or in part of employers or employees engaged in such industry, trade, craft, or occupation.

(c) The term "labor dispute" includes any controversy concerning terms or conditions of employment, or concerning the association or representation of persons in negotiating, fixing, maintaining, changing, or seeking to arrange terms or conditions of employment, regardless of whether or not the disputants stand in the proximate relation of employer and employee.

(d) The term "court of the United States" means any court of the United States whose jurisdiction has been or may be conferred or defined or limited by Act of Congress, including the courts of the District of Columbia.

Sec. 14.   Separability of provisions.

If any provision of this Act or the application thereof to any person or circumstance is held unconstitutional or otherwise invalid, the remaining provisions of this Act and the application of such provisions to other persons or circumstances shall not be affected thereby.

Sec. 15.   Repeal of conflicting acts.

All acts and parts of acts in conflict with the provisions of this Act are repealed.

NATIONAL LABOR RELATIONS ACT

49 Stat. 449 (1935), as amended by 61 Stat. 136 (1947), 65 Stat. 601 (1951), 72 Stat. 945 (1958), 73 Stat. 541 (1959), 88 Stat. 395 (1974) ; 29 U.S.C. §§ 151–69.

FINDINGS AND POLICIES

Sec. 1.   The denial by some employers of the right of employees to organize and the refusal by some employers to accept the procedure of collective bargaining lead to strikes and other forms of industrial strife or unrest, which have the intent or the necessary effect of burdening or obstructing commerce by (a) impairing the efficiency, safety, or operation of the instrumentalities of commerce; (b) occurring in the current of commerce; (c) materially affecting, restraining, or controlling the flow of raw materials or manufactured or processed goods from or into the channels of commerce, or the prices of such materials or goods in commerce; or (d) causing diminution of employment and wages in such volume as substantially to impair or disrupt the market for goods flowing from or into the channels of commerce.

The inequality of bargaining power between employees who do not possess full freedom of association or actual liberty of contract, and employers who are organized in the corporate or other forms of ownership association substantially burdens and affects the flow of commerce, and tends to aggravate recurrent business depressions, by depressing wage rates and the purchasing power of wage earners in industry and by preventing the stabilization of competitive wage rates and working conditions within and between industries.

Experience has proved that protection by law of the right of employees to organize and bargain collectively safeguards commerce from injury, impairment, or interruption, and promotes the flow of commerce by removing certain recognized sources of industrial strife and unrest, by encouraging practices fundamental to the friendly adjustment of industrial disputes arising out of differences as to wages, hours, or other working conditions, and by restoring equality of bargaining power between employers and employees.

Experience has further demonstrated that certain practices by some labor organizations, their officers, and members have the intent or the necessary effect of burdening or obstructing commerce by preventing the free flow of goods in such commerce through strikes and other forms of industrial unrest or through concerted activities which impair the interest of the public in the free flow of such commerce. The elimination of such practices is a necessary condition to the assurance of the rights herein guaranteed.

It is hereby declared to be the policy of the United States to eliminate the causes of certain substantial obstructions to the free flow of commerce and to mitigate and eliminate these obstructions when they have occurred by encouraging the practice and procedure of collective bargaining and by protecting the exercise by workers of full freedom of association, self-organization, and designation of representatives of their own choosing, for the purpose of negotiating the terms and conditions of their employment or other mutual aid or protection.

DEFINITIONS

Sec. 2. When used in this Act—

(1) The term "person" includes one or more individuals, labor organizations, partnerships, associations, corporations, legal representatives, trustees, trustees in bankruptcy, or receivers.

(2) The term "employer" includes any person acting as an agent of an employer, directly or indirectly, but shall not include the United States or any wholly owned Government corporation, or any Federal Reserve Bank, or any State or political subdivision thereof, or any person subject to the Railway Labor Act, as amended from time to time, or any labor organization (other than when acting as an employer), or anyone acting in the capacity of officer or agent of such labor organization.

(3) The term "employee" shall include any employee, and shall not be limited to the employees of a particular employer, unless the Act explicitly states otherwise, and shall include any individual whose work has ceased as a consequence of, or in connection with, any current labor dispute or because of any unfair labor practice, and who has not obtained any other regular and substantially equivalent employment, but shall not include any individual employed as an agricultural laborer, or in the domestic service of any family or person at his home, or any individual employed by his parent or spouse, or any individual having the status of an independent contractor, or any individual employed as a supervisor, or any individual employed by an employer subject to the Railway Labor Act, as amended from time to time, or by any other person who is not an employer as herein defined.

(4) The term "representatives" includes any individual or labor organization.

(5) The term "labor organization" means any organization of any kind, or any agency or employee representation committee or plan, in which employees participate and which exists for the purpose, in

whole or in part, of dealing with employers concerning grievances, labor disputes, wages, rates of pay, hours of employment, or conditions of work.

(6) The term "commerce" means trade, traffic, commerce, transportation, or communication among the several States, or between the District of Columbia or any Territory of the United States and any State or other Territory, or between any foreign country and any State, Territory, or the District of Columbia, or within the District of Columbia or any Territory, or between points in the same State but through any other State or any Territory or the District of Columbia or any foreign country.

(7) The term "affecting commerce" means in commerce, or burdening or obstructing commerce or the free flow of commerce, or having led or tending to lead to a labor dispute burdening or obstructing commerce or the free flow of commerce.

(8) The term "unfair labor practice" means any unfair labor practice listed in section 8.

(9) The term "labor dispute" includes any controversy concerning terms, tenure or conditions of employment, or concerning the association or representation of persons in negotiating, fixing, maintaining, changing, or seeking to arrange terms or conditions of employment, regardless of whether the disputants stand in the proximate relation of employer and employee.

(10) The term "National Labor Relations Board" means the National Labor Relations Board provided for in section 3 of this Act.

(11) The term "supervisor" means any individual having authority, in the interest of the employer, to hire, transfer, suspend, lay off, recall, promote, discharge, assign, reward, or discipline other employees, or responsibly to direct them, or to adjust their grievances, or effectively to recommend such action, if in connection with the foregoing the exercise of such authority is not of a merely routine or clerical nature, but requires the use of independent judgment.

(12) The term "professional employee" means—

(a) any employee engaged in work (i) predominantly intellectual and varied in character as opposed to routine mental, manual, mechanical, or physical work; (ii) involving the consistent exercise of discretion and judgment in its performance; (iii) of such a character that the output produced or the result accomplished cannot be standardized in relation to a given period of time; (iv) requiring knowledge of an advanced type in a field of science or learning customarily acquired by a prolonged course of specialized intellectual instruction and study in an institution of higher learning or a hospital, as distinguished from a general academic education or from an apprenticeship or from training in the performance of routine mental, manual, or physical processes; or

(b) any employee, who (i) has completed the courses of specialized intellectual instruction and study described in clause (iv) of paragraph (a), and (ii) is performing related work under the supervision of a professional person to qualify himself to become a professional employee as defined in paragraph (a).

(13) In determining whether any person is acting as an "agent" of another person so as to make such other person responsible for his acts, the question of whether the specific acts performed were actually authorized or subsequently ratified shall not be controlling.

(14) The term "health care institution" shall include any hospital, convalescent hospital, health maintenance organization, health clinic, nursing home, extended care facility, or other institution devoted to the care of sick, infirm, or aged person.

NATIONAL LABOR RELATIONS BOARD

Sec. 3. (a) The National Labor Relations Board (hereinafter called the "Board") created by this Act prior to its amendment by the Labor Management Relations Act 1947 is hereby continued as an agency of the United States, except that the Board shall consist of five instead of three members, appointed by the President by and with the advice and consent of the Senate. Of the two additional members so provided for, one shall be appointed for a term of five years and the other for a term of two years. Their successors, and the successors of the other members, shall be appointed for terms of five years each, excepting that any individual chosen to fill a vacancy shall be appointed only for the unexpired term of the member whom he shall succeed. The President shall designate one member to serve as Chairman of the Board. Any member of the Board may be removed by the President, upon notice and hearing, for neglect of duty or malfeasance in office, but for no other cause.

(b) The Board is authorized to delegate to any group of three or more members any or all of the powers which it may itself exercise. The Board is also authorized to delegate to its regional directors its powers under section 9 to determine the unit appropriate for the purpose of collective bargaining, to investigate and provide for hearings, and determine whether a question of representation exists, and to direct an election or take a secret ballot under subsection (c) or (e) of section 9 and certify the results thereof, except that upon the filing of a request therefor with the Board by any interested person, the Board may review any action of a regional director delegated to him under this paragraph, but such a review shall not, unless specifically ordered by the Board, operate as a stay of any action taken by the regional director. A vacancy in the Board shall not impair the right of the remaining members to exercise all of the powers of the Board, and three members of the Board shall, at all times, constitute a quorum of the Board, except that two members shall constitute a quorum of any group designated pursuant to the first sentence hereof. The Board shall have an official seal which shall be judicially noticed.

(c) The Board shall at the close of each fiscal year make a report in writing to Congress and to the President stating in detail the cases it has heard, the decisions it has rendered, the names, salaries, and duties of all employees and officers in the employ or under the supervision of the Board, and an account of all moneys it has disbursed.

(d) There shall be a General Counsel of the Board who shall be appointed by the President, by and with the advice and consent of the Senate, for a term of four years. The General Counsel of the Board shall exercise general supervision over all attorneys employed by the Board (other than trial examiners and legal assistants to Board members) and over the officers and employees in the regional offices. He shall have final authority, on behalf of the Board, in respect of the investigation of charges and issuance of complaints under section 10, and in respect of the prosecution of such complaints before the Board, and shall have such other duties as the Board may prescribe or as may be provided by law. In case of a vacancy in the office of the General Counsel the President is authorized to designate the officer or employee who shall act as General Counsel during such vacancy, but no person or persons so designated shall so act (1) for more than forty days when the Congress is in session unless a nomination to fill such vacancy shall have been submitted to the Senate, or (2) after the adjournment *sine die* of the session of the Senate in which such nomination was submitted.

Sec. 4. (a) Each member of the Board and the General Counsel of the Board shall receive a salary of $12,000 * a year, shall be eligible for reappointment, and shall not engage in any other business, vocation, or employment. The Board shall appoint an executive secretary, and such attorneys, examiners, and regional directors, and such other employees as it may from time to time find necessary for the proper performance of its duties. The Board may not employ any attorneys for the purpose of reviewing transcripts of hearings or preparing drafts of opinions except that any attorney employed for assignment as a legal assistant to any Board member may for such Board member review such transcripts and prepare such drafts. No trial examiner's report shall be reviewed, either before or after its publication, by any person other than a member of the Board or his legal assistant, and no trial examiner shall advise or consult with the Board with respect to exceptions taken to his findings, rulings, or recommendations. The

* Pursuant to Public Law 90–206, 90th Cong., 81 Stat. 644, approved Dec. 16, 1967, and in accordance with Sec. 225 (f)(ii) thereof, effective in 1969, the salary of the Chairman of the Board shall be $40,000 per year and the salaries of the General Counsel and each Board member shall be $38,000 per year.

Board may establish or utilize such regional, local, or other agencies, and utilize such voluntary and uncompensated services, as may from time to time be needed. Attorneys appointed under this section may, at the direction of the Board, appear for and represent the Board in any case in court. Nothing in this Act shall be construed to authorize the Board to appoint individuals for the purpose of conciliation or mediation, or for economic analysis.

(b) All of the expenses of the Board, including all necessary traveling and subsistence expenses outside the District of Columbia incurred by the members or employees of the Board under its orders, shall be allowed and paid on the presentation of itemized vouchers therefor approved by the Board or by any individual it designates for that purpose.

Sec. 5. The principal office of the Board shall be in the District of Columbia, but it may meet and exercise any or all of its powers at any other place. The Board may, by one or more of its members or by such agents or agencies as it may designate, prosecute any inquiry necessary to its functions in any part of the United States. A member who participates in such an inquiry shall not be disqualified from subsequently participating in a decision of the Board in the same case.

Sec. 6. The Board shall have authority from time to time to make, amend, and rescind, in the manner prescribed by the Administrative Procedure Act, such rules and regulations as may be necessary to carry out the provisions of this Act.

RIGHTS OF EMPLOYEES

Sec. 7. Employees shall have the right to self-organization, to form, join, or assist labor organizations, to bargain collectively through representatives of their own choosing, and to engage in other concerted activities for the purpose of collective bargaining or other mutual aid or protection, and shall also have the right to refrain from any or all of such activities except to the extent that such right may be affected by an agreement requiring membership in a labor organization as a condition of employment as authorized in section 8(a)(3).

UNFAIR LABOR PRACTICES

Sec. 8. (a) It shall be an unfair labor practice for an employer—

(1) to interfere with, restrain, or coerce employees in the exercise of the rights guaranteed in section 7;

(2) to dominate or interfere with the formation or administration of any labor organization or contribute financial or other support to it: *Provided,* That subject to rules and regulations made and published by the Board pursuant to section 6, an employer shall not be

prohibited from permitting employees to confer with him during working hours without loss of time or pay;

(3) by discrimination in regard to hire or tenure of employment or any term or condition of employment to encourage or discourage membership in any labor organization: *Provided,* That nothing in this Act, or in any other statute of the United States, shall preclude an employer from making an agreement with a labor organization (not established, maintained, or assisted by any action defined in section 8(a) of this Act as an unfair labor practice) to require as a condition of employment membership therein on or after the thirtieth day following the beginning of such employment or the effective date of such agreement, whichever is the later, (i) if such labor organization is the representative of the employees as provided in section 9(a), in the appropriate collective-bargaining unit covered by such agreement when made, and (ii) unless following an election held as provided in section 9(e) within one year preceding the effective date of such agreement, the Board shall have certified that at least a majority of the employees eligible to vote in such election have voted to rescind the authority of such labor organization to make such an agreement: *Provided further,* That no employer shall justify any discrimination against an employee for nonmembership in a labor organization (A) if he has reasonable grounds for believing that such membership was not available to the employee on the same terms and conditions generally applicable to other members, or (B) if he has reasonable grounds for believing that membership was denied or terminated for reasons other than the failure of the employee to tender the periodic dues and the initiation fees uniformly required as a condition of acquiring or retaining membership;

(4) to discharge or otherwise discriminate against an employee because he has filed charges or given testimony under this Act;

(5) to refuse to bargain collectively with the representatives of his employees, subject to the provisions of section 9(a).

(b) It shall be an unfair labor practice for a labor organization or its agents—

(1) to restrain or coerce (A) employees in the exercise of the rights guaranteed in section 7: *Provided,* That this paragraph shall not impair the right of a labor organization to prescribe its own rules with respect to the acquisition or retention of membership therein; or (B) an employer in the selection of his representatives for the purposes of collective bargaining or the adjustment of grievances;

(2) to cause or attempt to cause an employer to discriminate against an employee in violation of subsection (a)(3) or to discriminate against an employee with respect to whom membership in such organization has been denied or terminated on some ground other than his failure to tender the periodic dues and the initiation fees uniformly required as a condition of acquiring or retaining membership;

(3) to refuse to bargain collectively with an employer, provided it is the representative of his employees subject to the provisions of section 9(a);

(4) (i) to engage in, or to induce or encourage any individual employed by any person engaged in commerce or in an industry affecting commerce to engage in, a strike or a refusal in the course of his employment to use, manufacture, process, transport, or otherwise handle or work on any goods, articles, materials, or commodities or to perform any services; or (ii) to threaten, coerce, or restrain any person engaged in commerce or in an industry affecting commerce, where in either case an object thereof is:

(A) forcing or requiring any employer or self-employed person to join any labor or employer organization or to enter into any agreement which is prohibited by section 8(e);

(B) forcing or requiring any person to cease using, selling, handling, transporting, or otherwise dealing in the products of any other producer, processor, or manufacturer, or to cease doing business with any other person, or forcing or requiring any other employer to recognize or bargain with a labor organization as the representative of his employees unless such labor organization has been certified as the representative of such employees under the provisions of section 9: *Provided*, That nothing contained in this clause (B) shall be construed to make unlawful, where not otherwise unlawful, any primary strike or primary picketing;

(C) forcing or requiring any employer to recognize or bargain with a particular labor organization as the representative of his employees if another labor organization has been certified as the representative of such employees under the provisions of section 9;

(D) forcing or requiring any employer to assign particular work to employees in a particular labor organization or in a particular trade, craft, or class rather than to employees in another labor organization or in another trade, craft, or class, unless such employer is failing to conform to an order or certification of the Board determining the bargaining representative for employees performing such work:

Provided, That nothing contained in this subsection (b) shall be construed to make unlawful a refusal by any person to enter upon the premises of any employer (other than his own employer), if the employees of such employer are engaged in a strike ratified or approved by a representative of such employees whom such employer is required to recognize under this Act: *Provided further,* That for the purposes of this paragraph (4) only, nothing contained in such paragraph shall be construed to prohibit publicity, other than picketing, for the purpose of truthfully advising the public, including consumers and members of a labor organization, that a product or products are produced by an employer with whom the labor organization has a primary dispute and are distributed by another employer, as long as such publicity does not have an effect of inducing any individual employed by any person other than the primary employer in the course of his employment to refuse to pick up, deliver, or transport any goods, or not to perform any services, at the establishment of the employer engaged in such distribution;

(5) to require of employees covered by an agreement authorized under subsection (a) (3) the payment, as a condition precedent to becoming a member of such organization, of a fee in an amount which the Board finds excessive or discriminatory under all the circumstances. In making such a finding, the Board shall consider, among other relevant factors, the practices and customs of labor organizations in the particular industry, and the wages currently paid to the employees affected;

(6) to cause or attempt to cause an employer to pay or deliver or agree to pay or deliver any money or other thing of value, in the nature of an exaction, for services which are not performed or not to be performed; and

(7) to picket or cause to be picketed, or threaten to picket or cause to be picketed, any employer where an object thereof is forcing or requiring an employer to recognize or bargain with a labor organization as the representative of his employees, or forcing or requiring the employees of an employer to accept or select such labor organization as their collective bargaining representative, unless such labor organization is currently certified as the representative of such employees:

(A) where the employer has lawfully recognized in accordance with this Act any other labor organization and a question concerning representation may not appropriately be raised under section 9(c) of this Act,

(B) where within the preceding twelve months a valid election under section 9(c) of this Act has been conducted, or

(C) where such picketing has been conducted without a petition under section 9(c) being filed within a reasonable period of time not to exceed thirty days from the commencement of such picketing: *Provided,* That when such a petition has been filed the Board shall forthwith, without regard to the provisions of section 9(c)(1) or the absence of a showing of a substantial interest on the part of the labor organization, direct an election in such unit as the Board finds to be appropriate and shall certify the results thereof: *Provided further,* That nothing in this subparagraph (C) shall be construed to prohibit any picketing or other publicity for the purpose of truthfully advising the public (including consumers) that an employer does not employ members of, or have a contract with, a labor organization, unless an effect of such picketing is to induce any individual employed by any other person in the course of his employment, not to pick up, deliver or transport any goods or not to perform any services.

Nothing in this paragraph (7) shall be construed to permit any act which would otherwise be an unfair labor practice under this section 8(b).

(c) The expressing of any views, argument, or opinion, or the dissemination thereof, whether in written, printed, graphic, or visual form, shall not constitute or be evidence of an unfair labor practice under any of the provisions of this Act, if such expression contains no threat of reprisal or force or promise of benefit.

(d) For the purposes of this section, to bargain collectively is the performance of the mutual obligation of the employer and the representative of the employees to meet at reasonable times and confer in good faith with respect to wages, hours, and other terms and conditions of employment, or the negotiation of an agreement, or any question arising thereunder, and the execution of a written contract incorporating any agreement reached if requested by either party, but such obligation does not compel either party to agree to a proposal or require the making of a concession: *Provided,* That where there is in effect a collective-bargaining contract covering employees in an industry affecting commerce, the duty to bargain collectively shall also mean that no party to such contract shall terminate or modify such contract, unless the party desiring such termination or modification—

(1) serves a written notice upon the other party to the contract of the proposed termination or modification sixty days prior to the expiration date thereof, or in the event such contract contains no expiration date, sixty days prior to the time it is proposed to make such termination or modification;

(2) offers to meet and confer with the other party for the purpose of negotiating a new contract or a contract containing the proposed modifications;

(3) notifies the Federal Mediation and Conciliation Service within thirty days after such notice of the existence of a dispute, and simultaneously therewith notifies any State or Territorial agency established to mediate and conciliate disputes within the State or Territory where the dispute occurred, provided no agreement has been reached by that time; and

(4) continues in full force and effect, without resorting to strike or lockout, all the terms and conditions of the existing contract for a period of sixty days after such notice is given or until the expiration date of such contract, whichever occurs later:

The duties imposed upon employers, employees, and labor organizations by paragraphs (2), (3), and (4) shall become inapplicable upon an intervening certification of the Board, under which the labor organization or individual, which is a party to the contract, has been superseded as or ceased to be the representative of the employees subject to the provisions of section 9(a), and the duties so imposed shall not be construed as requiring either party to discuss or agree to any modification of the terms and conditions contained in a contract for a fixed period, if such modification is to become effective before such terms and conditions can be reopened under the provisions of the contract. Any employee who engages in a strike within any notice period specified in this subsection, or who engages in any strike within the appropriate period specified in subsection (g) of this section shall lose his status as an employee of the employer engaged in the particular labor dispute, for the purposes of sections 8, 9, and 10 of this Act, as amended, but such loss of status for such employee shall terminate if and when he is reemployed by such employer. Whenever the collective bargaining involves employees of a health care institution, the provisions of this section 8(d) shall be modified as follows:

(A) The notice of section 8(d)(1) shall be ninety days; the notice of section 8(d)(3) shall be sixty days; and the contract period of section 8(d)(4) shall be ninety days;

(B) Where the bargaining is for an initial agreement following certification or recognition, at least thirty days' notice of the existence of a dispute shall be given by the labor organization to the agencies set forth in section 8(d)(3).

(C) After notice is given to the Federal Mediation and Conciliation Service under either clause (A) or (B) of this sentence, the Service shall promptly communicate with the parties and use its best efforts, by mediation and conciliation, to bring them to agreement. The parties shall participate fully and promptly in such meetings as may be undertaken by the Service for the purpose of aiding in a settlement of the dispute.

(e) It shall be an unfair labor practice for any labor organization and any employer to enter into any contract or agreement, express or implied, whereby such employer ceases or refrains or agrees to cease or refrain from handling, using, selling, transporting or otherwise dealing in any of the products of any other employer, or to cease doing business with any other person, and any contract or agreement entered into heretofore or hereafter containing such an agreement shall be to such extent unenforceable and void: *Provided,* That nothing in this subsection (e) shall apply to an agreement between a labor organization and an employer in the construction industry relating to the contracting or subcontracting of work to be done at the site of the construction, alteration, painting, or repair of a building, structure, or other work: *Provided further,* That for the purposes of this subsection (e) and section 8(b)(4)(B) the terms "any employer", "any person engaged in commerce or in industry affecting commerce", and "any person" when used in relation to the terms "any other producer, processor, or manufacturer", "any other employer", or "any other person" shall not include persons in the relation of a jobber, manufacturer, contractor, or subcontractor working on the goods or premises of the jobber or manufacturer or performing parts of an integrated process of production in the apparel and clothing industry: *Provided further,* That nothing in this Act shall prohibit the enforcement of any agreement which is within the foregoing exception.

(f) It shall not be an unfair labor practice under subsections (a) and (b) of this section for an employer engaged primarily in the building and construction industry to make an agreement covering employees engaged (or who, upon their employment, will be engaged) in the building and construction industry with a labor organization of which building and construction employees are members (not established, maintained, or assisted by any action defined in section 8(a) of this Act as an unfair labor practice) because (1) the majority status of such labor organization has not been established under the provisions of section 9 of this Act prior to the making of such agreement, or (2) such agreement requires as a condition of employment, membership in such labor organization after the seventh day following the beginning of such employment or the effective date of the agreement, whichever is later, or (3) such agreement requires the employer to notify such labor organization of opportunities for employment with such employer, or gives such labor organization an opportunity to refer qualified applicants for such employment, or (4) such agreement specifies minimum training or experience qualifications for employment or provides for priority in opportunities for employment based upon length of service with such employer, in the industry or in the particular geographical area: *Provided,* That nothing in this subsection shall set aside the final proviso to section 8(a)(3) of this Act: *Provided further,* That any agreement which would be invalid, but for clause (1) of this subsection, shall not be a bar to a petition filed pursuant to section 9(c) or 9(e).*

(g) A labor organization before engaging in any strike, picketing, or other concerted refusal to work at any health care institution shall, not less than ten days prior to such action, notify the institution in writing and the Federal Mediation and Conciliation Service of that intention, except that in the case of bargaining for an initial agreement following certification or recognition the notice required by this subsection shall not be given until the expiration of the period specified in clause (B) of the last sentence of section 8(d) of this Act. The notice shall state the date and time that such action will commence.

---

* Sec. 8(f) was inserted in the Act by subsec. (a) of Sec. 705 of Public Law 86–257. Sec. 705(b) provides:

Nothing contained in the amendment made by subsection (a) shall be construed as authorizing the execution or application of agreements requiring membership in a labor organization as a condition of employment in any State or Territory in which such execution or application is prohibited by State or Territorial law.

The notice, once given, may be extended by the written agreement of both parties.

REPRESENTATIVES AND ELECTIONS

Sec. 9. (a) Representatives designated or selected for the purposes of collective bargaining by the majority of the employees in a unit appropriate for such purposes, shall be the exclusive representatives of all the employees in such unit for the purposes of collective bargaining in respect to rates of pay, wages, hours of employment, or other conditions of employment: *Provided,* That any individual employee or a group of employees shall have the right at any time to present grievances to their employer and to have such grievances adjusted, without the intervention of the bargaining representative, as long as the adjustment is not inconsistent with the terms of a collective-bargaining contract or agreement then in effect: *Provided further,* That the bargaining representative has been given opportunity to be present at such adjustment.

(b) The Board shall decide in each case whether, in order to assure to employees the fullest freedom in exercising the rights guaranteed by this Act, the unit appropriate for the purposes of collective bargaining shall be the employer unit, craft unit, plant unit, or subdivision thereof: *Provided,* That the Board shall not (1) decide that any unit is appropriate for such purposes if such unit includes both professional employees and employees who are not professional employees unless a majority of such professional employees vote for inclusion in such unit; or (2) decide that any craft unit is inappropriate for such purposes on the ground that a different unit has been established by a prior Board determination, unless a majority of the employees in the proposed craft unit vote against separate representation or (3) decide that any unit is appropriate for such purposes if it includes, together with other employees, any individual employed as a guard to enforce against employees and other persons rules to protect property of the employer or to protect the safety of persons on the employer's premises; but no labor organization shall be certified as the representative of employees in a bargaining unit of guards if such organization admits to membership, or is affiliated directly or indirectly with an organization which admits to membership, employees other than guards.

(c) (1) Wherever a petition shall have been filed, in accordance with such regulations as may be prescribed by the Board—

(A) by an employee or group of employees or any individual or labor organization acting in their behalf alleging that a substantial number of employees (i) wish to be represented for collective bargaining and that their employer declines to recognize their representative as the representative defined in section 9(a), or (ii) assert that the individual or labor organization, which has been certified or is being currently recognized by their employer as the bargaining representative, is no longer a representative as defined in section 9(a); or

(B) by an employer, alleging that one or more individuals or labor organizations have presented to him a claim to be recognized as the representative defined in section 9(a);

the Board shall investigate such petition and if it has reasonable cause to believe that a question of representation affecting commerce exists shall provide for an appropriate hearing upon due notice. Such hearing may be conducted by an officer or employee of the regional office, who shall not make any recommendations with respect thereto. If the Board finds upon the record of such hearing that such a question of representation exists, it shall direct an election by secret ballot and shall certify the results thereof.

(2) In determining whether or not a question of representation affecting commerce exists, the same regulations and rules of decision shall apply irrespective of the identity of the persons filing the petition or the kind of relief sought and in no case shall the Board deny a labor organization a place on the ballot by reason of an order with respect to such labor organization or its predecessor not issued in conformity with section 10(c).

(3) No election shall be directed in any bargaining unit or any subdivision within which, in the preceding twelve-month period, a valid election shall have been held. Employees engaged in an economic strike who are not entitled to reinstatement shall be eligible to vote under such regulations as the Board shall find are consistent with the purposes and provisions of this Act in any election conducted within twelve months after the commencement of the strike. In any election where none of the choices on the ballot receives a majority, a run-off shall be conducted, the ballot providing for a selection between the two choices receiving the largest and second largest number of valid votes cast in the election.

(4) Nothing in this section shall be construed to prohibit the waiving of hearings by stipulation for the purpose of a consent election in conformity with regulations and rules of decision of the Board.

(5) In determining whether a unit is appropriate for the purposes specified in subsection (b) the extent to which the employees have organized shall not be controlling.

(d) Whenever an order of the Board made pursuant to section 10(c) is based in whole or in part upon facts certified following an investigation pursuant to subsection (c) of this section and there is a petition for the enforcement or review of such order, such certification and the record of such investigation shall be included in the transcript of the entire record required to be filed under section 10(e) or 10(f), and thereupon the decree of the court enforcing, modifying, or setting aside in whole or in part the order of the Board shall be made and entered upon the pleadings, testimony, and proceedings set forth in such transcript.

(e) (1) Upon the filing with the Board, by 30 per centum or more of the employees in a bargaining unit covered by an agreement between their employer and a labor organization made pursuant to section 8(a)(3), of a petition alleging they desire that such authority be rescinded, the Board shall take a secret ballot of the employees in such unit and certify the results thereof to such labor organization and to the employer.

(2) No election shall be conducted pursuant to this subsection in any bargaining unit or any subdivision within which, in the preceding twelve-month period, a valid election shall have been held.

PREVENTION OF UNFAIR LABOR PRACTICES

Sec. 10. (a) The Board is empowered, as hereinafter provided, to prevent any person from engaging in any unfair labor practice (listed in section 8) affecting commerce. This power shall not be affected by any other means of adjustment or prevention that has been or may be established by agreement, law, or otherwise: *Provided,* That the Board is empowered by agreement with any agency of any State or Territory to cede to such agency jurisdiction over any cases in any industry (other than mining, manufacturing, communications, and transportation except where predominantly local in character) even though such cases may involve labor disputes affecting commerce, unless the provision of the State or Territorial statute applicable to the determination of such cases by such agency is inconsistent with the corresponding provision of this Act or has received a construction inconsistent therewith.

(b) Whenever it is charged that any person has engaged in or is engaging in any such unfair labor practice, the Board, or any agent or agency designated by the Board for such purposes, shall have power to issue and cause to be served upon such person a complaint stating the charges in that respect, and containing a notice of hearing before the Board or a member thereof, or before a designated agent or agency, at a place therein fixed, not less than five days after the serving of said complaint: *Provided,* That no complaint shall issue based upon any unfair labor practice occurring more than six months prior to the filing of the charge with the Board and the service of a copy thereof upon the person against whom such charge is made, unless the person aggrieved thereby was prevented from filing such charge by reason of service in the armed forces, in which event the six-month period shall be computed from the day of his discharge. Any such complaint may be amended by the member, agent, or agency conducting the hearing or the Board in its discretion at any time prior to the issuance of an order based thereon. The person so complained of shall have the right to file an answer to the original or amended complaint and to appear in person or otherwise and give testimony at the place and time fixed in the complaint. In the discretion of the member, agent, or agency conducting the hearing or the Board, any other person may be allowed to intervene in the said proceeding and to present testimony. Any such proceeding shall, so far as practicable, be conducted in accordance with the rules of evidence applicable in the district courts of the United States under the rules of civil procedure for the district courts of the United States, adopted by the Supreme Court of the United States pursuant to the Act of June 19, 1934 (U.S.C., title 28, secs. 723–B, 723–C).

(c) The testimony taken by such member, agent, or agency or the Board shall be reduced to writing and filed with the Board. Thereafter, in its discretion, the Board upon notice may take further testimony or hear argument. If upon the preponderance of the testimony taken the Board shall be of the opinion that any person named in the complaint has engaged in or is engaging in any such unfair labor practice, then the Board shall state its findings of fact and shall issue and cause to be served on such person an order requiring such person to cease and desist from such unfair labor practice, and to take such affirmative action including reinstatement of employees with or without back pay, as will effectuate the policies of this Act: *Provided,* That where an order directs reinstatement of an employee, back pay may be required of the employer or labor organization, as the case may be, responsible for the discrimination suffered by him: *And provided further,* That in determining whether a complaint shall issue alleging a violation of section 8(a)(1) or section 8(a)(2), and in deciding such cases, the same regulations and rules of decision shall apply irrespective of whether or not the labor organization affected is affiliated with a labor organization national or international in scope. Such order may further require such person to make reports from time to time showing the extent to which it has complied with the order. If upon the preponderance of the testimony taken the Board shall not be of the opinion that the person named in the complaint has engaged in or is engaging in any such unfair labor practice, then the Board shall state its findings of fact and shall issue an order dismissing the said complaint. No order of the Board shall require the reinstatement of any individual as an employee who has been suspended or discharged, or the payment to him of any back pay, if such individual was suspended or discharged for cause. In case the evidence is presented before a member of the Board, or before an examiner or examiners thereof, such member, or such examiner or examiners, as the case may be, shall issue and cause to be served on the parties to the proceeding a proposed report, together with a recommended order, which shall be filed with the Board, and if no exceptions are filed within twenty days after service thereof upon such parties, or within such further period as the Board may authorize, such recommended order shall become the order of the Board and become effective as therein prescribed.

(d) Until the record in a case shall have been filed in a court, as hereinafter provided, the Board may at any time, upon reasonable notice and in such manner as it shall deem proper, modify or set aside, in whole or in part, any finding or order made or issued by it.

(e) The Board shall have power to petition any court of appeals of the United States, or if all the courts of appeals to which application may be made are in vacation, any district court of the United States, within any circuit or district, respectively, wherein the unfair labor practice in question occurred or wherein such person resides or transacts business, for the enforcement of such order and for appropriate temporary relief or restraining order, and shall file in the court the record in the proceedings, as provided in section 2112 of title 28, United States Code. Upon the filing of such petition, the court shall cause notice thereof to be served upon such person, and thereupon shall have jurisdiction of the proceeding and of the question determined therein, and shall have power to grant such temporary relief or restraining order as it deems just and proper, and to make and enter a decree enforcing, modifying, and enforcing as so modified, or setting aside in whole or in part the order of the Board. No objection that has not been urged before the Board, its member, agent, or agency, shall be considered by the court, unless the failure or neglect to urge such objection shall be excused because of extraordinary circumstances. The findings of the Board with respect to questions of fact if supported by substantial evidence on the record considered as a whole shall be conclusive. If either party shall apply to the court for leave to adduce additional evidence and shall show to the satisfaction of the court that such additional evidence is material and that there were reasonable grounds for the failure to adduce such evidence in the hearing before the Board, its member, agent, or agency, the court may order such additional evidence to be taken before the Board, its member, agent, or agency, and to be made a part of the record. The Board may modify its findings as to the facts, or make new findings, by reason of additional evidence so taken and filed, and it shall file such modified or new findings, which findings with respect to questions of fact if supported by substantial evidence on the record considered as a whole shall be conclusive, and shall file its recommendations, if any, for the modification or setting aside of its original order. Upon the filing of the record with it the jurisdiction of the court shall be exclusive and its judgment and decree shall be final, except that the same shall be subject to review by the appropriate United States court of appeals if application was made to the district court as hereinabove provided, and by the Supreme Court of the United States upon writ of certiorari or certification as provided in section 1254 of title 28.

(f) Any person aggrieved by a final order of the Board granting or denying in whole or in part the relief sought may obtain a review of such order in any circuit court of appeals of the United States in the circuit wherein the unfair labor practice in question was alleged to have been engaged in or wherein such person resides or transacts business, or in the United States Court of Appeals for the District of Columbia, by filing in such court a written petition praying that the order of the Board be modified or set aside. A copy of such petition shall be forthwith transmitted by the clerk of the court to the Board, and thereupon the aggrieved party shall file in the court the record in the proceeding, certified by the Board, as provided in section 2112 of title 28, United States Code. Upon the filing of such petition, the court shall proceed in the same manner as in the case of an application by the Board under subsection (e) of this section, and shall have the same jurisdiction to grant to the Board such temporary relief or restraining order as it deems just and proper, and in like manner to make and enter a decree enforcing, modifying, and enforcing as so modified, or setting aside in whole or in part the order of the Board; the findings of the Board with respect to questions of fact if supported by substantial evidence on the record considered as a whole shall in like manner be conclusive.

(g) The commencement of proceedings under subsection (e) or (f) of this section shall not, unless specifically ordered by the court, operate as a stay of the Board's order.

(h) When granting appropriate temporary relief or a restraining order, or making and entering a decree enforcing, modifying, and enforcing as so modified, or setting aside in whole or in part an order of the Board, as provided in this section, the jurisdiction of courts sitting in equity shall not be limited by the Act entitled "An Act to amend the Judicial Code and to define and limit the jurisdiction of courts sitting in equity, and for other purposes," approved March 23, 1932 (U.S.C., Supp. VII, title 29, secs. 101–115).

(i) Petitions filed under this Act shall be heard expeditiously, and if possible within ten days after they have been docketed.

(j) The Board shall have power, upon issuance of a complaint as provided in subsection (b) charging that any person has engaged in or is engaging in an unfair labor practice, to petition any district court of the United States (including the District Court of the United States for the District of Columbia), within any district wherein the unfair labor practice in question is alleged to have occurred or wherein such person resides or transacts business, for appropriate temporary relief or restraining order. Upon the filing of any such petition the court shall cause notice thereof to be served upon such person, and thereupon shall have jurisdiction to grant to the Board such temporary relief or restraining order as it deems just and proper.

(k) Whenever it is charged that any person has engaged in an unfair labor practice within the meaning of paragraph (4)(D) of section 8(b), the Board is empowered and directed to hear and determine the dispute out of which such unfair labor practice shall have arisen, unless, within ten days after notice that such charge has been filed, the parties to such dispute submit to the Board satisfactory evidence that they have adjusted, or agreed upon methods for the voluntary adjustment of, the dispute. Upon compliance by the parties to the dispute with the decision of the Board or upon such voluntary adjustment of the dispute, such charge shall be dismissed.

(*l*) Whenever it is charged that any person has engaged in an unfair labor practice within the meaning of paragraph (4)(A), (B), or (C) of section 8(b), or section 8(e) or section 8(b)(7), the preliminary investigation of such charge shall be made forthwith and given priority over all other cases except cases of like character in the office where it is filed or to which it is referred. If, after such investigation, the officer or regional attorney to whom the matter may be referred has reasonable cause to believe such charge is true and that a complaint should issue, he shall, on behalf of the Board, petition any district court of the United States (including the District Court of the United States for the District of Columbia) within any district where the unfair labor practice in question has occurred, is alleged to have occurred, or wherein such person resides or transacts business, for appropriate injunctive relief pending the final adjudication of the Board with respect to such matter. Upon the filing of any such petition the district court shall have jurisdiction to grant such injunctive relief or temporary restraining order as it deems just and proper, notwithstanding any other provision of law: *Provided further,* That no temporary restraining order shall be issued without notice unless a petition alleges that substantial and irreparable injury to the charging party will be unavoidable and such temporary restraining order shall be effective for no longer than five days and will become void at the expiration of such period: *Provided further,* That such officer or regional attorney shall not apply for any restraining order under section 8(b)(7) if a charge against the employer under section 8(a)(2) has been filed and after the preliminary investigation, he has reasonable cause to believe that such charge is true and that a complaint should issue. Upon filing of any such petition the courts shall cause notice thereof to be served upon any person involved in the charge and such person, including the charging party, shall be given an opportunity to appear by counsel and present any relevant testimony: *Provided further,* That for the purposes of this subsection district courts shall be deemed to have jurisdiction of a labor organization (1) in the district in which such organization maintains its principal office, or (2) in any district in which its duly authorized officers or agents are engaged in promoting or protecting the interests of employee members. The service of legal process upon such officer or agent shall constitute service upon the labor organization and make such organizations a party to the suit. In situations where such relief is appropriate the procedure specified herein shall apply to charges with respect to section 8(b)(4)(D).

(m) Whenever it is charged that any person has engaged in an unfair labor practice within the meaning of subsection (a)(3) or (b)(2) of section 8, such charge shall be given priority over all other cases except cases of like character in the office where it is filed or to which it is referred and cases given priority under subsection (*l*).

INVESTIGATORY POWERS

Sec. 11. For the purpose of all hearings and investigations, which, in the opinion of the Board, are necessary and proper for the exercise of the powers vested in it by section 9 and section 10—

(1) The Board, or its duly authorized agents or agencies, shall at all reasonable times have access to, for the purpose of examination, and the right to copy any evidence of any person being investigated or proceeded against that relates to any matter under investigation or in question. The Board, or any member thereof, shall upon application of any party to such proceedings, forthwith issue to such party subpenas requiring the attendance and testimony of witnesses or the production of any evidence in such proceeding or investigation requested in such application. Within five days after the service of a subpena on any person requiring the production of any evidence in his possession or under his control, such person may petition the Board to revoke, and the Board shall revoke, such subpena if in its opinion the evidence whose production is required does not relate to any matter under investigation, or any matter in question in such proceedings, or if in its opinion such subpena does not describe with sufficient particularity the evidence whose production is required. Any member of the Board, or any agent or agency designated by the Board for such purposes, may administer oaths and affirmations, examine witnesses, and receive evidence. Such attendance of witnesses and the production of such evidence may be required from any place in the United States or any Territory or possession thereof, at any designated place of hearing.

(2) In case of contumacy or refusal to obey a subpena issued to any person, any district court of the United States or the United States courts of any Territory or possession, or the District Court of the United States for the District of Columbia, within the jurisdiction of which the inquiry is carried on or within the jurisdiction of which said person guilty of contumacy or refusal to obey is found or resides or transacts business, upon application by the Board shall have jurisdiction to issue to such person an order requiring such person to appear before the Board, its member, agent, or agency, there to produce evidence if so ordered, or there to give testimony touching the matter under investigation or in question; and any failure to obey such order of the court may be punished by said court as a contempt thereof.

(3)*

(4) Complaints, orders, and other process and papers of the Board, its member, agent, or agency, may be served either personally or by registered mail or by telegraph or by leaving a copy thereof at the principal office or place of business of the person required to be served. The verified return by the individual so serving the same setting forth the manner of such service shall be proof of the same, and the return post office receipt or telegraph receipt therefor when registered and mailed or telegraphed as aforesaid shall be proof of service of the same. Witnesses summoned before the Board, its member, agent, or agency, shall be paid the same fees and mileage that are paid witnesses in the courts of the United States, and witnesses whose depositions are taken and the persons taking the same shall severally be entitled to the same fees as are paid for like services in the courts of the United States.

(5) All process of any court to which application may be made under this Act may be served in the judicial district wherein the defendant or other person required to be served resides or may be found.

(6) The several departments and agencies of the Government, when directed by the President, shall furnish the Board, upon its request, all records, papers, and information in their possession relating to any matter before the Board.

Sec. 12. Any person who shall willfully resist, prevent, impede, or interfere with any member of the Board or any of its agents or agencies in the performance of duties pursuant to this Act shall be punished by a fine of not more than $5,000 or by imprisonment for not more than one year, or both.

LIMITATIONS

Sec. 13. Nothing in this Act, except as specifically provided for herein, shall be construed so as either to interfere with or impede or diminish in any way the right to strike, or to affect the limitations or qualifications on that right.

Sec. 14. (a) Nothing herein shall prohibit any individual employed as a supervisor from becoming or remaining a member of a labor organization, but no employer subject to this Act shall be compelled to deem individuals defined herein as supervisors as employees for the purpose of any law, either national or local, relating to collective bargaining.

(b) Nothing in this Act shall be construed as authorizing the execution or application of agreements requiring membership in a labor organization as a condition of employment in any State or Territory in which such execution or application is prohibited by State or Territorial law.

---

* Sec. 11(3) was repealed by Sec. 234, Public Law 91–452, 91st Cong., S. 30, 84 Stat. 926, Oct. 15, 1970. See Title 18, U.S.C. Sec. 6001, *et seq.*

(c) (1) The Board, in its discretion, may, by rule of decision or by published rules adopted pursuant to the Administrative Procedure Act, decline to assert jurisdiction over any labor dispute involving any class or category of employers, where, in the opinion of the Board, the effect of such labor dispute on commerce is not sufficiently substantial to warrant the exercise of its jurisdiction: *Provided,* That the Board shall not decline to assert jurisdiction over any labor dispute over which it would assert jurisdiction under the standards prevailing upon August 1, 1959.

(2) Nothing in this Act shall be deemed to prevent or bar any agency or the courts of any State or Territory (including the Commonwealth of Puerto Rico, Guam, and the Virgin Islands), from assuming and asserting jurisdiction over labor disputes over which the Board declines, pursuant to paragraph (1) of this subsection, to assert jurisdiction.

Sec. 15. Wherever the application of the provisions of section 272 of chapter 10 of the Act entitled "An Act to establish a uniform system of bankruptcy throughout the United States," approved July 1, 1898, and Acts amendatory thereof and supplementary thereto (U.S.C., title 11, sec. 672), conflicts with the application of the provisions of this Act, this Act shall prevail: *Provided,* That in any situation where the provisions of this Act cannot be validly enforced, the provisions of such other Acts shall remain in full force and effect.

Sec. 16. If any provision of this Act, or the application of such provision to any person or circumstances, shall be held invalid, the remainder of this Act, or the application of such provision to persons or circumstances other than those as to which it is held invalid, shall not be affected thereby.

Sec. 17. This Act may be cited as the "National Labor Relations Act."

Sec. 18. No petition entertained, no investigation made, no election held, and no certification issued by the National Labor Relations Board, under any of the provisions of section 9 of the National Labor Relations Act, as amended, shall be invalid by reason of the failure of the Congress of Industrial Organizations to have complied with the requirements of section 9(f), (g), or (h) of the aforesaid Act prior to December 22, 1949, or by reason of the failure of the American Federation of Labor to have complied with the provisions of section 9(f), (g), or (h) of the aforesaid Act prior to November 7, 1947: *Provided,* That no liability shall be imposed under any provision of this Act upon any person for failure to honor any election or certificate referred to above, prior to the effective date of this amendment: *Provided, however,* That this proviso shall not have the effect of setting aside or in any way affecting judgments or decrees heretofore entered under section 10(e) or (f) and which have become final.

INDIVIDUALS WITH RELIGIOUS CONVICTIONS

Sec. 19.   Any employee of a health care institution who is a member of and adheres to established and traditional tenets or teachings of a bona fide religion, body, or sect which has historically held conscientious objections to joining or financially supporting labor organizations shall not be required to join or financially support any labor organization as a condition of employment; except that such employee may be required, in lieu of periodic dues and initiation fees, to pay sums equal to such dues and initiation fees to a nonreligious charitable fund exempt from taxation under section 501(c)(3) of the Internal Revenue Code, chosen by such employee from a list of at least three such funds, designated in a contract between such institution and a labor organization, or if the contract fails to designate such funds, then to any such fund chosen by the employee.

LABOR MANAGEMENT RELATIONS ACT

61 Stat. 136 (1947), as amended by 73 Stat. 519 (1959), 83 Stat. 133 (1969),
87 Stat. 314 (1973), 88 Stat. 396 (1974) ; 29 U.S.C. §§ 141–97 (1970).

AN ACT

To amend the National Labor Relations Act, to provide additional facilities for the mediation of labor disputes affecting commerce, to equalize legal responsibilities of labor organizations and employers, and for other purposes.

Be it enacted by the Senate and House of Representatives of the United States of America in Congress assembled,

SHORT TITLE AND DECLARATION OF POLICY

Sec. 1.   (a) This Act may be cited as the "Labor Management Relations Act, 1947."

(b) Industrial strife which interferes with the normal flow of commerce and with the full production of articles and commodities for commerce, can be avoided or substantially minimized if employers, employees, and labor organizations each recognize under law one another's legitimate rights in their relations with each other, and above all recognize under law that neither party has any right in its relations with any other to engage in acts or practices which jeopardize the public health, safety, or interest.

It is the purpose and policy of this Act, in order to promote the full flow of commerce, to prescribe the legitimate rights of both employees and employers in their relations affecting commerce, to provide orderly and peaceful procedures for preventing the interference by either with the legitimate rights of the other, to protect the rights of individual employees in their relations with labor organizations whose activities affect commerce, to define and proscribe practices on the part of labor and management which affect commerce and are inimical to the general welfare, and to protect the rights of the public in connection with labor disputes affecting commerce.

TITLE I

AMENDMENT OF NATIONAL LABOR RELATIONS ACT

Sec. 101. The National Labor Relations Act is hereby amended to read as follows: [The text of the National Labor Relations Act as amended is set forth supra.]

TITLE II

CONCILIATION OF LABOR DISPUTES IN INDUSTRIES AFFECTING COMMERCE; NATIONAL EMERGENCIES

Sec. 201. That it is the policy of the United States that—

(a) sound and stable industrial peace and the advancement of the general welfare, health, and safety of the Nation and of the best interests of employers and employees can most satisfactorily be secured by the settlement of issues between employers and employees through the processes of conference and collective bargaining between employers and the representatives of their employees;

(b) the settlement of issues between employers and employees through collective bargaining may be advanced by making available full and adequate governmental facilities for conciliation, mediation, and voluntary arbitration to aid and encourage employers and the representatives of their employees to reach and maintain agreements concerning rates of pay, hours, and working conditions, and to make all reasonable efforts to settle their differences by mutual agreement reached through conferences and collective bargaining or by such methods as may be provided for in any applicable agreement for the settlement of disputes; and

(c) certain controversies which arise between parties to collective-bargaining agreements may be avoided or minimized by making available full and adequate governmental facilities for furnishing assistance to employers and the representatives of their employees in formulating for inclusion within such agreements provision for adequate notice of any proposed changes in the terms of such agreements, for the final adjustment of grievances or questions regarding the application or interpretation of such agreements, and other provisions designed to prevent the subsequent arising of such controversies.

Sec. 202. (a) There is hereby created an independent agency to be known as the Federal Mediation and Conciliation Service (herein referred to as the "Service," except that for sixty days after the date of the enactment of this Act such term shall refer to the Conciliation Service of the Department of Labor). The Service shall be under the direction of a Federal Mediation and Conciliation Director (hereinafter referred to as the "Director"), who shall be appointed by the President by and with the advice and consent of the Senate. The Director shall receive compensation at the rate of $12,000 * per annum. The Director shall not engage in any other business, vocation, or employment.

(b) The Director is authorized, subject to the civil-service laws, to appoint such clerical and other personnel as may be necessary for the execution of the functions of the Service, and shall fix their compensation in accordance with chapter 51 and subchapter III of chapter 53 of title 5, and may, without regard to the provisions of the civil-service laws, appoint such conciliators and mediators as may be necessary to carry out the functions of the Service. The Director is authorized to make such expenditures for supplies, facilities, and services as he deems necessary. Such expenditures shall be allowed and paid upon presentation of itemized vouchers therefor approved by the Director or by any employee designated by him for that purpose.

(c) The principal office of the Service shall be in the District of Columbia, but the Director may establish regional offices convenient to localities in which labor controversies are likely to arise. The Director may by order, subject to revocation at any time, delegate any authority and discretion conferred upon him by this Act to any regional director, or other officer or employee of the Service. The Director may establish suitable procedures for cooperation with State and local mediation agencies. The Director shall make an annual report in writing to Congress at the end of the fiscal year.

(d) All mediation and conciliation functions of the Secretary of Labor or the United States Conciliation Service under section 8 of the Act entitled "An Act to create a Department of Labor," approved March 4, 1913 (U.S.C., title 29, sec. 51), and all functions of the United States Conciliation Service under any other law are hereby transferred to the Federal Mediation and Conciliation Service, together with the personnel and records of the United States Conciliation Service. Such transfer shall take effect upon the sixtieth day after the date of enactment of this Act. Such transfer shall not affect any proceedings pending before the United States Conciliation Service or any certification, order, rule, or regulation theretofore made by it or by the Secretary of Labor. The Director and the Service shall not be subject in any way to the jurisdiction or authority of the Secretary of Labor or any official or division of the Department of Labor.

---

* As of February 14, 1969, the salary of the Director became $40,000. See 5 U.S.C. § 5315 (and note following) (1970).

FUNCTIONS OF THE SERVICE

Sec. 203. (a) It shall be the duty of the Service, in order to prevent or minimize interruptions of the free flow of commerce growing out of labor disputes, to assist parties to labor disputes in industries affecting commerce to settle such disputes through conciliation and mediation.

(b) The Service may proffer its services in any labor dispute in any industry affecting commerce, either upon its own motion or upon the request of one or more of the parties to the dispute, whenever in its judgment such dispute threatens to cause a substantial interruption of commerce. The Director and the Service are directed to avoid attempting to mediate disputes which would have only a minor effect on interstate commerce if State or other conciliation services are available to the parties. Whenever the Service does proffer its services in any dispute, it shall be the duty of the Service promptly to put itself in communication with the parties and to use its best efforts, by mediation and conciliation, to bring them to agreement.

(c) If the Director is not able to bring the parties to agreement by conciliation within a reasonable time, he shall seek to induce the parties voluntarily to seek other means of settling the dispute without resort to strike, lock-out, or other coercion, including submission to the employees in the bargaining unit of the employer's last offer of settlement for approval or rejection in a secret ballot. The failure or refusal of either party to agree to any procedure suggested by the Director shall not be deemed a violation of any duty or obligation imposed by this Act.

(d) Final adjustment by a method agreed upon by the parties is hereby declared to be the desirable method for settlement of grievance disputes arising over the application or interpretation of an existing collective-bargaining agreement. The Service is directed to make its conciliation and mediation services available in the settlement of such grievance disputes only as a last resort and in exceptional cases.

Sec. 204. (a) In order to prevent or minimize interruptions of the free flow of commerce growing out of labor disputes, employers and employees and their representatives, in any industry affecting commerce, shall—

(1) exert every reasonable effort to make and maintain agreements concerning rates of pay, hours, and working conditions, including provision for adequate notice of any proposed change in the terms of such agreements;

(2) whenever a dispute arises over the terms or application of a collective-bargaining agreement and a conference is re-

quested by a party or prospective party thereto, arrange promptly for such a conference to be held and endeavor in such conference to settle such dispute expeditiously; and

(3) in case such dispute is not settled by conference, participate fully and promptly in such meetings as may be undertaken by the Service under this Act for the purpose of aiding in a settlement of the dispute.

Sec. 205. (a) There is hereby created a National Labor-Management Panel which shall be composed of twelve members appointed by the President, six of whom shall be selected from among persons outstanding in the field of management and six of whom shall be selected from among persons outstanding in the field of labor. Each member shall hold office for a term of three years, except that any member appointed to fill a vacancy occurring prior to the expiration of the term for which his predecessor was appointed shall be appointed for the remainder of such term, and the terms of office of the members first taking office shall expire, as designated by the President at the time of appointment, four at the end of the first year, four at the end of the second year, and four at the end of the third year after the date of appointment. Members of the panel, when serving on business of the panel, shall be paid compensation at the rate of $25 per day, and shall also be entitled to receive an allowance for actual and necessary travel and subsistence expenses while so serving away from their places of residence.

(b) It shall be the duty of the panel, at the request of the Director, to advise in the avoidance of industrial controversies and the manner in which mediation and voluntary adjustment shall be administered, particularly with reference to controversies affecting the general welfare of the country.

NATIONAL EMERGENCIES

Sec. 206. Whenever in the opinion of the President of the United States, a threatened or actual strike or lock-out affecting an entire industry or a substantial part thereof engaged in trade, commerce, transportation, transmission, or communication among the several States or with foreign nations, or engaged in the production of goods for commerce, will, if permitted to occur or to continue, imperil the national health or safety, he may appoint a board of inquiry to inquire into the issues involved in the dispute and to make a written report to him within such time as he shall prescribe. Such report shall include a statement of the facts with respect to the dispute, including each party's statement of its position but shall not contain any recommendations. The President shall file a copy of such report with the Service and shall make its contents available to the public.

Sec. 207. (a) A board of inquiry shall be composed of a chairman and such other members as the President shall determine, and shall have power to sit and act in any place within the United States and to conduct such hearings either in public or in private, as it may deem necessary or proper, to ascertain the facts with respect to the causes and circumstances of the dispute.

(b) Members of a board of inquiry shall receive compensation at the rate of $50 for each day actually spent by them in the work of the board, together with necessary travel and subsistence expenses.

(c) For the purpose of any hearing or inquiry conducted by any board appointed under this title, the provisions of sections 9 and 10 (relating to the attendance of witnesses and the production of books, papers, and documents) of the Federal Trade Commission Act of September 16, 1914, as amended (U.S.C. 19, title 15, secs. 49 and 50, as amended), are hereby made applicable to the powers and duties of such board.

Sec. 208. (a) Upon receiving a report from a board of inquiry the President may direct the Attorney General to petition any district court of the United States having jurisdiction of the parties to enjoin such strike or lock-out or the continuing thereof, and if the court finds that such threatened or actual strike or lock-out—

(i) affects an entire industry or a substantial part thereof engaged in trade, commerce, transportation, transmission, or communication among the several States or with foreign nations, or engaged in the production of goods for commerce; and

(ii) if permitted to occur or to continue, will imperil the national health or safety, it shall have jurisdiction to enjoin any such strike or lock-out, or the continuing thereof, and to make such other orders as may be appropriate.

(b) In any case, the provisions of the Act of March 23, 1932, entitled "An Act to amend the Judicial Code and to define and limit the jurisdiction of courts sitting in equity, and for other purposes," shall not be applicable.

(c) The order or orders of the court shall be subject to review by the appropriate United States court of appeals and by the Supreme Court upon writ of certiorari or certification as provided in sections 239 and 240 of the Judicial Code, as amended (U.S.C., title 29, secs. 346 and 347).

Sec. 209. (a) Whenever a district court has issued an order under section 208 enjoining acts or practices which imperil or threaten to imperil the national health or safety, it shall be the duty of the parties to the labor dispute giving rise to such order to make every effort to adjust and settle their differences, with the assistance of the Service created by this Act. Neither party shall be under any duty to accept, in whole or in part, any proposal of settlement made by the Service.

(b) Upon the issuance of such order, the President shall reconvene the board of inquiry which has previously reported with respect to the dispute. At the end of a sixty-day period (unless the dispute has been settled by that time), the board of inquiry shall report to the President the current position of the parties and the efforts which have been made for settlement, and shall include a statement by each party of its position and a statement of the employer's last offer of settlement. The President shall make such report available to the public. The National Labor Relations Board, within the succeeding fifteen days, shall take a secret ballot of the employees of each employer involved in the dispute on the question of whether they wish to accept the final offer of settlement made by their employer as stated by him and shall certify the results thereof to the Attorney General within five days thereafter.

Sec. 210. Upon the certification of the results of such ballot or upon a settlement being reached, whichever happens sooner, the Attorney General shall move the court to discharge the injunction, which motion shall then be granted and the injunction discharged. When such motion is granted, the President shall submit to the Congress a full and comprehensive report of the proceedings, including the findings of the board of inquiry and the ballot taken by the National Labor Relations Board, together with such recommendations as he may see fit to make for consideration and appropriate action.

COMPILATION OF COLLECTIVE BARGAINING AGREEMENTS, ETC.

Sec. 211. (a) For the guidance and information of interested representatives of employers, employees, and the general public, the Bureau of Labor Statistics of the Department of Labor shall maintain a file of copies of all available collective-bargaining agreements and other available agreements and actions thereunder settling or adjusting labor disputes. Such file shall be open to inspection under appropriate conditions prescribed by the Secretary of Labor, except that no specific information submitted in confidence shall be disclosed.

(b) The Bureau of Labor Statistics in the Department of Labor is authorized to furnish upon request of the Service, or employers, employees, or their representatives, all available data and factual information which may aid in the settlement of any labor dispute, except that no specific information submitted in confidence shall be disclosed.

EXEMPTION OF RAILWAY LABOR ACT

Sec. 212. The provisions of this title shall not be applicable with respect to any matter which is subject to the provisions of the Railway Labor Act, as amended from time to time.

CONCILIATION OF LABOR DISPUTES IN THE HEALTH CARE INDUSTRY

Sec. 213. (a) If, in the opinion of the Director of the Federal Mediation and Conciliation Service a threatened or actual strike or lockout affecting a health care institution will, if permitted to occur or to continue, substantially interrupt the delivery of health care in the locality concerned, the Director may further assist in the resolution of the impasse by establishing within 30 days after the notice to the Federal Mediation and Conciliation Service under clause (A) of the last sentence of section 8(d) (which is required by clause (3) of such section 8(d)), or within 10 days after the notice under clause (B), an impartial Board of Inquiry to investigate the issues involved in the dispute and to make a written report thereon to the parties within fifteen (15) days after the establishment of such a Board. The written report shall contain the findings of fact together with the Board's recommendations for settling the dispute, with the objective of achieving a prompt, peaceful and just settlement of the dispute. Each such Board shall be composed of such number of individuals as the Director may deem desirable. No member appointed under this section shall have any interest or involvement in the health care institutions or the employee organizations involved in the dispute.

(b)(1) Members of any board established under this section who are otherwise employed by the Federal Government shall serve without compensation but shall be reimbursed for travel, subsistence, and other necessary expenses incurred by them in carrying out its duties under this section.

(2) Members of any board established under this section who are not subject to paragraph (1) shall receive compensation at a rate prescribed by the Director but not to exceed the daily rate prescribed for GS–18 of the General Schedule under section 5332 of title 5, United States Code, including travel for each day they are engaged in the performance of their duties under this section and shall be entitled to reimbursement for travel, subsistence, and other necessary expenses incurred by them in carrying out their duties under this section.

(c) After the establishment of a board under subsection (a) of this section and for 15 days after any such board has issued its report, no change in the status quo in effect prior to the expiration of the contract in the case of negotiations for a contract renewal, or in effect prior to the time of the impasse in the case of an initial bargaining negotiation, except by agreement, shall be made by the parties to the controversy.

(d) There are authorized to be appropriated such sums as may be necessary to carry out the provisions of this section.

TITLE III

SUITS BY AND AGAINST LABOR ORGANIZATIONS

Sec. 301. (a) Suits for violation of contracts between an employer and a labor organization representing employees in an industry affecting commerce as defined in this Act, or between any such labor organizations, may be brought in any district court of the United States having jurisdiction of the parties, without respect to the amount in controversy or without regard to the citizenship of the parties.

(b) Any labor organization which represents employees in an industry affecting commerce as defined in this Act and any employer whose activities affect commerce as defined in this Act shall be bound by the acts of its agents. Any such labor organization may sue or be sued as an entity and in behalf of the employees whom it represents in the courts of the United States. Any money judgment against a labor organization in a district court of the United States shall be enforceable only against the organization as an entity and against its assets, and shall not be enforceable against any individual member or his assets.

(c) For the purposes of actions and proceedings by or against labor organizations in the district courts of the United States, district courts shall be deemed to have jurisdiction of a labor organization (1) in the district in which such organization maintains its principal office, or (2) in any district in which its duly authorized officers or agents are engaged in representing or acting for employee members.

(d) The service of summons, subpena, or other legal process of any court of the United States upon an officer or agent of a labor organization, in his capacity as such, shall constitute service upon the labor organization.

(e) For the purposes of this section, in determining whether any person is acting as an "agent" of another person so as to make such other person responsible for his acts, the question of whether the specific acts performed were actually authorized or subsequently ratified shall not be controlling.

RESTRICTIONS ON PAYMENTS TO EMPLOYEE REPRESENTATIVES

Sec. 302. (a) It shall be unlawful for any employer or association of employers or any person who acts as a labor relations expert, adviser, or consultant to an employer or who acts in the interest of an employer to pay, lend, or deliver, or agree to pay, lend, or deliver, any money or other thing of value—

(1) to any representative of any of his employees who are employed in an industry affecting commerce; or

(2) to any labor organization, or any officer or employee thereof, which represents, seeks to represent, or would admit to membership, any of the employees of such employer who are employed in an industry affecting commerce; or

(3) to any employee or group or committee of employees of such employer employed in an industry affecting commerce in excess of their normal compensation for the purpose of causing such employee or group or committee directly or indirectly to influence any other employees in the exercise of the right to organize and bargain collectively through representatives of their own choosing; or

(4) to any officer or employee of a labor organization engaged in an industry affecting commerce with intent to influence him in respect to any of his actions, decisions, or duties as a representative of employees or as such officer or employee of such labor organization.

(b) (1) It shall be unlawful for any person to request, demand, receive, or accept, or agree to receive or accept, any payment, loan, or delivery of any money or other thing of value prohibited by subsection (a).

(2) It shall be unlawful for any labor organization, or for any person acting as an officer, agent, representative, or employee of such labor organization, to demand or accept from the operator of any motor vehicle (as defined in part II of the Interstate Commerce Act) employed in the transportation of property in commerce, or the employer of any such operator, any money or other thing of value payable to such organization or to an officer, agent, representative or employee thereof as a fee or charge for the unloading, or in connection with the unloading, of the cargo of such vehicle: *Provided,* That nothing in this paragraph shall be construed to make unlawful any payment by an employer to any of his employees as compensation for their services as employees.

(c) The provisions of this section shall not be applicable (1) in respect to any money or other thing of value payable by an employer to any of his employees whose established duties include acting openly for such employer in matters of labor relations or personnel administration or to any representative of his employees, or to any officer or employee of a labor organization, who is also an employee or former employee of such employer, as compensation for, or by reason of, his service as an employee of such employer; (2) with respect to the payment or delivery of any money or other thing of value in satisfaction of a judgment of any court or a decision or award of an arbitrator or impartial chairman or in compromise, adjustment, settlement, or release of any claim, complaint, grievance, or dispute in the absence of fraud or duress; (3) with respect to the sale or purchase of an article or commodity at the prevailing market price in the regular course of business; (4) with respect to money deducted from the wages of employees in payment of membership dues in a labor organization: *Provided*, That the employer has received from each employee, on whose account such deductions are made, a written assignment which shall not be irrevocable for a period of more than one year, or beyond the termination date of the applicable collective agreement, whichever occurs sooner; (5) with respect to money or other thing of value paid to a trust fund established by such representative, for the sole and exclusive benefit of the employees of such employer, and their families and dependents (or of such employees, families, and dependents jointly with the employees of other employers making similar payments, and their families and dependents): *Provided*, That (A) such payments are held in trust for the purpose of paying, either from principal or income or both, for the benefit of employees, their families and dependents, for medical or hospital care, pensions on retirement or death of employees, compensation for injuries or illness resulting from occupational activity or insurance to provide any of the foregoing, or unemployment benefits or life insurance, disability and sickness insurance, or accident insurance; (B) the detailed basis on which such payments are to be made is specified in a written agreement with the employer, and employees and employers are equally represented in the administration of such fund, together with such neutral persons as the representatives of the employers and the representatives of employees may agree upon and in the event the employer and employee groups deadlock on the administration of such fund and there are no neutral persons empowered to break such deadlock, such agreement provides that the two groups shall agree on an impartial umpire to decide such dispute, or in event of their failure to agree within a reasonable length of time, an impartial umpire to decide such dispute shall, on petition of either group, be appointed by the district court of the United States for the district where the trust fund has its principal office, and shall also contain provisions for an annual audit of the trust fund, a statement of the results of which shall be available for inspection by interested persons at the principal office of the trust fund and at such other places as may be designated in such written agreement; and (C) such payments as are intended to be used for the purpose of providing pensions or annuities for employees are made to a separate trust which provides that the funds held therein cannot be used for any purpose other than paying such pensions or annuities; (6) with respect to money or other thing of value paid by any employer to a trust fund established by such representative for the purpose of pooled vacation, holiday, severance or similar benefits, or defraying costs of apprenticeship or other training programs: *Provided,* That the requirements of clause (B) of the proviso to clause (5) of this subsection, shall apply to such trust funds; or (7) with respect to money or other thing of value paid by any employer to a pooled or individual trust fund established by such representative for the purpose of (A) scholarships for the benefit of employees, their families, and dependents for study at educational institutions, or (B) child care centers for pre-school and school age dependents of employees: *Provided,* That no labor organization or employer shall be required to bargain on the establishment of any such trust fund, and refusal to do so shall not constitute an unfair labor practice: *Provided further,* That the requirements of clause (B) of the proviso to clause (5) of this subsection shall apply to such trust funds, or (8) with respect to money or any other thing of value paid by any employer to a trust fund established by such representative for the purpose of defraying the costs of legal services for employees, their families, and dependents for counsel or plan of their choice: *Provided,* That the requirements of clause (B) of the proviso to clause (5) of this subsection shall apply to such trust funds: *Provided further,* That no such legal services shall be furnished: (A) to initiate any proceeding directed (i) against any such employer or its officers or agents except in workman's compensation cases, or (ii) against such labor organization, or its parent or subordinate bodies, or their officers or agents, or (iii) against any other employer or labor organization, or their officers or agents, in any matter arising under the National Labor Relations Act, as amended, or this Act; and (B) in any proceeding where a labor organization would be prohibited from defraying the costs of legal services by the provisions of the Labor-Management Reporting and Disclosure Act of 1959.

(d) Any person who willfully violates any of the provisions of this section shall, upon conviction thereof, be guilty of a misdemeanor and be subject to a fine of not more than $10,000 or to imprisonment for not more than one year, or both.

(e) The district courts of the United States and the United States courts of the Territories and possessions shall have jurisdiction, for cause shown, and subject to the provisions of section 17 (relating to notice to opposite party) of the Act entitled "An Act to supplement existing laws against unlawful restraints and monopolies, and for other purposes," approved October 15, 1914, as amended (U.S.C., title 28, section 381), to restrain violations of this section, without regard to the provisions of sections 6 and 20 of such Act of October 15, 1914, as amended (U.S.C., title 15, section 17, and title 29, section 52), and the provisions of the Act entitled "An Act to amend the Judicial Code and to define and limit the jurisdiction of courts sitting in equity, and for other purposes," approved March 23, 1932 (U.S.C., title 29, sections 101–115).

(f) This section shall not apply to any contract in force on the date of enactment of this Act, until the expiration of such contract, or until July 1, 1948, whichever first occurs.

(g) Compliance with the restrictions contained in subsection (c) (5) (B) upon contributions to trust funds, otherwise lawful, shall not be applicable to contributions to such trust funds established by collective agreement prior to January 1, 1946, nor shall subsection (c) (5) (A) be construed as prohibiting contributions to such trust funds if prior to January 1, 1947, such funds contained provisions for pooled vacation benefits.

BOYCOTTS AND OTHER UNLAWFUL COMBINATIONS

Sec. 303. (a) It shall be unlawful, for the purpose of this section only, in an industry or activity affecting commerce, for any labor organization to engage in any activity or conduct defined as an unfair labor practice in section 8(b) (4) of the National Labor Relations Act, as amended.

(b) Whoever shall be injured in his business or property by reason of any violation of subsection (a) may sue therefor in any district court of the United States subject to the limitations and provisions of section 301 hereof without respect to the amount in controversy, or in any other court having jurisdiction of the parties, and shall recover the damages by him sustained and the cost of the suit.

RESTRICTION ON POLITICAL CONTRIBUTIONS

Sec. 304. Section 313 of the Federal Corrupt Practices Act, 1925 (U.S.C., 1940 edition, title 2, sec. 251; Supp. V, title 50, App., sec. 1509), as amended, is amended to read as follows:

Sec. 313. It is unlawful for any national bank, or any corporation organized by authority of any law of Congress, to make a contribution or expenditure in connection with any election to any political office, or in connection with any primary election or political convention or caucus held to select candidates for any political office, or for any corporation whatever, or any labor organization to make a contribution or expenditure in connection with any election at which Presidential and Vice Presidential electors or a Senator or Representative in, or a Delegate or Resident Commissioner to Congress are to be voted for, or in connection with any primary election or political convention or caucus held to select candidates for any of the foregoing offices, or for any candidate, political committee, or other person to accept or receive any contribution prohibited by this section. Every corporation or labor organization which makes any contribution or expenditure in violation of this section shall be fined not more than $5,000; and every officer or director of any corporation, or officer of any labor organization, who consents to any contribution or expenditure by the corporation or labor organization, as the case may be, *and any person who accepts or receives any contribution,* in violation of this section shall be fined not more than $1,000 or imprisoned for not more than one year, or both; *and if the violation was willful, shall be fined not more than $10,000 or imprisoned not more than two years, or both.* For the purposes of this section "labor organization" means any organization of any kind, or any agency or employee representation committee or plan, in which employees participate and which exist for the purpose, in whole or in part, of dealing with employers concerning grievances, labor disputes, wages, rates of pay, hours of employment, or conditions of work.

TITLE IV

CREATION OF JOINT COMMITTEE TO STUDY AND REPORT ON BASIC PROBLEMS AFFECTING FRIENDLY LABOR RELATIONS AND PRODUCTIVITY

* * *

TITLE V

DEFINITIONS

Sec. 501. When used in this Act—

(1) The term "industry affecting commerce" means any industry or activity in commerce or in which a labor dispute would burden or obstruct commerce or tend to burden or obstruct commerce or the free flow of commerce.

(2) The term "strike" includes any strike or other concerted stoppage of work by employees (including a stoppage by reason of the expiration of a collective-bargaining agreement) and any concerted slow-down or other concerted interruption of operations by employees.

(3) The terms "commerce", "labor disputes", "employer", "employee", "labor organization", "representative", "person", and "supervisor" shall have the same meaning as when used in the National Labor Relations Act as amended by this Act.

SAVING PROVISION

Sec. 502. Nothing in this Act shall be construed to require an individual employee to render labor or service without his consent, nor shall anything in this Act be construed to make the quitting of his labor by an individual employee an illegal act; nor shall any court issue any process to compel the performance by an individual employee of such labor or service, without his consent; nor shall the quitting of labor by an employee or employees in good faith because

of abnormally dangerous conditions for work at the place of employment of such employee or employees be deemed a strike under this
Act.

SEPARABILITY

Sec. 503. If any provision of this Act, or the application of such
provision to any person or circumstance, shall be held invalid, the
remainder of this Act, or the application of such provision to persons
or circumstances other than those as to which it is held invalid, shall
not be affected thereby.

APPENDIX B

Official National Labor Relations Board Forms

(1) Petition for Election.
(2) Unfair Labor Practice Charge Against Employer.
(3) Unfair Labor Practice Charge Against Union.

Form NLRB-502
(11-64)

UNITED STATES OF AMERICA
NATIONAL LABOR RELATIONS BOARD

PETITION

Form Approved.
Budget Bureau No. 64-R002.14

DO NOT WRITE IN THIS SPACE
CASE NO.
DATE FILED

INSTRUCTIONS.—Submit an original and four (4) copies of this Petition to the NLRB Regional Office in the Region in which the employer concerned is located.
If more space is required for any one item, attach additional sheets, numbering item accordingly.

The Petitioner alleges that the following circumstances exist and requests that the National Labor Relations Board proceed under its proper authority pursuant to Section 9 of the National Labor Relations Act.

1. Purpose of this Petition (If box RC, RM, or RD is checked and a charge under Section 8(b)(7) of the Act has been filed involving the Employer named herein, the statement following the description of the type of petition shall not be deemed made.)

(Check one)

☐ RC-CERTIFICATION OF REPRESENTATIVE —A substantial number of employees wish to be represented for purposes of collective bargaining by Petitioner and Petitioner desires to be certified as representative of the employees.

☐ RM-REPRESENTATION (EMPLOYER PETITION)—One or more individuals or labor organizations have presented a claim to Petitioner to be recognized as the representative of employees of Petitioner.

☐ RD-DECERTIFICATION — A substantial number of employees assert that the certified or currently recognized bargaining representative is no longer their representative.

☐ UD-WITHDRAWAL OF UNION SHOP AUTHORITY—Thirty percent (30%) or more of employees in a bargaining unit covered by an agreement between their employer and a labor organization desire that such authority be rescinded.

☐ UC-UNIT CLARIFICATION—A labor organization is currently recognized by employer, but petitioner seeks clarification of placement of certain employees. (Check one) ☐ In unit not previously certified
☐ In unit previously certified in Case No. _____

☐ AC-AMENDMENT OF CERTIFICATION—Petitioner seeks amendment of certification issued in Case No. _____

Attach statement describing the specific amendment sought.

2. NAME OF EMPLOYER	EMPLOYER REPRESENTATIVE TO CONTACT	PHONE NO.

3. ADDRESS(ES) OF ESTABLISHMENT(S) INVOLVED (Street and number, city, State, and ZIP Code)

4a. TYPE OF ESTABLISHMENT (Factory, mine, wholesaler, etc.)	4b. IDENTIFY PRINCIPAL PRODUCT OR SERVICE

5. Unit Involved (In UC petition, describe PRESENT bargaining unit and attach description of proposed clarification.)

Included

Excluded

6a. NUMBER OF EMPLOYEES IN UNIT

PRESENT _____

PROPOSED (BY UC/AC) _____

6b. IS THIS PETITION SUPPORTED BY 30% OR MORE OF THE EMPLOYEES IN THE UNIT?
☐ YES ☐ NO
*Not applicable in RM, UC, and AC

(If you have checked box RC in 1 above, check and complete EITHER item 7a or 7b, whichever is applicable)

7a. ☐ Request for recognition as Bargaining Representative was made on .... (Month, day, year) .... and Employer
declined recognition on or about .... (If no reply received, so state)
(Month, day, year)

7b. ☐ Petitioner is currently recognized as Bargaining Representative and desires certification under the act.

8. Recognized or Certified Bargaining Agent (If there is none, so state)

NAME	AFFILIATION
ADDRESS	DATE OF RECOGNITION OR CERTIFICATION

9. DATE OF EXPIRATION OF CURRENT CONTRACT, IF ANY (Show month, day, and year)	10. IF YOU HAVE CHECKED BOX UD IN 1 ABOVE, SHOW HERE THE DATE OF EXECUTION OF AGREEMENT GRANTING UNION SHOP (Month, day, and year)

11a. IS THERE NOW A STRIKE OR PICKETING AT THE EMPLOYER'S ESTABLISHMENT(S) INVOLVED? YES ...... NO	11b. IF SO, APPROXIMATELY HOW MANY EMPLOYEES ARE PARTICIPATING?

11c. THE EMPLOYER HAS BEEN PICKETED BY OR ON BEHALF OF .... A LABOR
(Insert name)

ORGANIZATION, OF .... SINCE ....
(Insert address)   (Month, day, year)

833

12. ORGANIZATIONS OR INDIVIDUALS OTHER THAN PETITIONER (AND OTHER THAN THOSE NAMED IN ITEMS 8 AND 11c), WHICH HAVE CLAIMED RECOGNITION AS REPRESENTATIVES AND OTHER ORGANIZATIONS AND INDIVIDUALS KNOWN TO HAVE A REPRESENTATIVE INTEREST IN ANY EMPLOYEES IN THE UNIT DESCRIBED IN ITEM 5 ABOVE (IF NONE, SO STATE)

NAME	AFFILIATION	ADDRESS	DATE OF CLAIM (Required only if Petition is filed by Employer)

I declare that I have read the above petition and that the statements therein are true to the best of my knowledge and belief.

....
(Petitioner and affiliation, if any)

By..   ....
     (Signature of representative or person filing petition)   *(Title, if any)*

Address ....
      (Street and number, city, State, and ZIP Code)   *(Telephone number)*

WILLFULLY FALSE STATEMENT ON THIS PETITION CAN BE PUNISHED BY FINE AND IMPRISONMENT (U.S. CODE, TITLE 18, SECTION 1001)   [B3400]

FORM NLRB-508
(12-65)

UNITED STATES OF AMERICA
NATIONAL LABOR RELATIONS BOARD

CHARGE AGAINST LABOR ORGANIZATION OR ITS AGENTS

Form Approved
Budget Bureau No. 64-R003.12

INSTRUCTIONS: File an original and 3 copies of this charge and an additional copy for each organization, each local and each individual named in item 1 with the NLRB regional director for the region in which the alleged unfair labor practice occurred or is occurring.

DO NOT WRITE IN THIS SPACE
Case No.
Date Filed

1. LABOR ORGANIZATION OR ITS AGENTS AGAINST WHICH CHARGE IS BROUGHT

a. Name	b. Union Representative to Contact	c. Phone No.

d. Address (Street, city, State and ZIP code)

e. The above-named organization(s) or its agents has (have) engaged in and is (are) engaging in unfair labor practices within the meaning of section 8 (b), subsection(s) ———— (List Subsections) ———— of the National Labor Relations Act, and these unfair labor practices are unfair labor practices affecting commerce within the meaning of the Act.

2. Basis of the Charge (Be specific as to facts, names, addresses, plants involved, dates, places, etc.)

3. Name of Employer

4. Location of Plant Involved (Street, city, State and ZIP code)

5. Type of Establishment (Factory, mine, wholesaler, etc.)	6. Identify Principal Product or Service	7. No. of Workers Employed

8. Full Name of Party Filing Charge

9. Address of Party Filing Charge (Street, city, State and ZIP code)	10. Telephone No.

11. DECLARATION

I declare that I have read the above charge and that the statements therein are true to the best of my knowledge and belief.

By _____   _____
(Signature of representative or person making charge)   (Title or office, if any)

Address _____   _____
(Telephone number)   (Date)

WILLFULLY FALSE STATEMENTS ON THIS CHARGE CAN BE PUNISHED BY FINE AND IMPRISONMENT (U.S. CODE, TITLE 18, SECTION 1001)

[B32011]

FORM NLRB-501
(2-67)

Form Approved
Budget Bureau No. 64-R001.12

UNITED STATES OF AMERICA
NATIONAL LABOR RELATIONS BOARD

CHARGE AGAINST EMPLOYER

INSTRUCTIONS: File an original and 4 copies of this charge with NLRB regional director for the region in which the alleged unfair labor practice occurred or is occurring.	DO NOT WRITE IN THIS SPACE
	Case No.
	Date Filed

1. EMPLOYER AGAINST WHOM CHARGE IS BROUGHT

a. Name of Employer	b. Number of Workers Employed

c. Address of Establishment (Street and number, city, State, and ZIP code)	d. Employer Representative to Contact	e. Phone No.

f. Type of Establishment (Factory, mine, wholesaler, etc.)	g. Identify Principal Product or Service

h. The above-named employer has engaged in and is engaging in unfair labor practices within the meaning of section 8(a), subsections (1) and _____ of the National Labor Relations Act,
(List subsections)
and these unfair labor practices are unfair labor practices affecting commerce within the meaning of the Act.

2. Basis of the Charge (Be specific as to facts, names, addresses, plants involved, dates, places, etc.)

By the above and other acts, the above-named employer has interfered with, restrained, and coerced employees in the exercise of the rights guaranteed in Section 7 of the Act.

3. Full Name of Party Filing Charge (If labor organization, give full name, including local name and number)

4a. Address (Street and number, city, State, and ZIP code)	4b. Telephone No.

5. Full Name of National or International Labor Organization of Which It Is an Affiliate or Constituent Unit (To be filled in when charge is filed by a labor organization)

6. DECLARATION

I declare that I have read the above charge and that the statements therein are true to the best of my knowledge and belief.

By _____ _____
(Signature of representative or person filing charge)   (Title, if any)

Address _____ _____ _____
(Telephone number)   (Date)

WILLFULLY FALSE STATEMENTS ON THIS CHARGE CAN BE PUNISHED BY FINE AND IMPRISONMENT (U.S. CODE, TITLE 18, SECTION 1001)

[B3202]

APPENDIX C

CHAPTER I

A. Blum, A History of the American Labor Movement (1972).

D. Bok and J. Dunlop, Labor and the American Community (1970).

A. Cox, Law and the National Labor Policy (1960).

C. Gregory, Labor and the Law (2d Ed. 1958, with 1961 supplement).

H. Millis & E. Brown, From the Wagner Act to Taft-Hartley (1950).

H. Millis and R. Montgomery, Organized Labor (1945).

H. Wellington, Labor and the Legal Process (1968).

CHAPTER II

Bernstein, "The NLRB's Adjudication-Rule Making Dilemma Under the Administrative Procedure Act," 79 Yale L.J. 571 (1970).

F. McCulloch and T. Bornstein, The National Labor Relations Board (1974).

K. McGuiness, How To Take a Case Before the National Labor Relations Board (4th Ed. 1975).

Murphy, "The National Labor Relations Board—An Appraisal," 52 Minn. L.Rev. 819 (1968).

Peck, "The Atrophied Rule-Making Powers of the National Labor Relations Board," 70 Yale L.J. 729 (1961).

Shapiro, "The Choice of Rulemaking or Adjudication in the Development of Administrative Policy," 78 Harv.L.Rev. 921 (1965).

CHAPTER III

H. Millis and E. Brown, From the Wagner Act to Taft-Hartley (1950).

Rosenthal, "Exclusions of Employees Under the Taft-Hartley Act," 4 Ind. & Lab.Rel.Rev. 556 (1951).

CHAPTER IV

Cushman, The Duration of Certifications by the National Labor Relations Board and the Doctrine of Administrative Stability, 45 Mich.L.Rev. 1 (1946).

Freidin, "The Board, the 'Bar' and the Bargain," 59 Colum.L.Rev. 61 (1959).

Goldberg, "District Court Review of NLRB Representation Proceedings," 42 Ind.L.J. 455 (1967).

CHAPTER V

J. Abodeely, The NLRB and the Appropriate Bargaining Unit (1971).

Note, "Craft Severance: NLRB's New Approach," 42 Ind.L.J. 554 (1967).

Note, "The Board and Section 9(c)(5): Multilocation and Single-Location Bargaining Units in the Insurance and Retail Industries," 79 Harv.L. Rev. 811 (1966).

C. Rehmus, Multiemployer Bargaining (1965).

Sharp, "Craft Certification: New Expansion of an Old Concept," 33 Ohio St.L.J. 102 (1972).

A. Weber, The Structure of Collective Bargaining (1961).

CHAPTER VI

Affeldt, "Bargaining Orders without an Election: The National Labor Relations Board's 'Final Solution,'" 57 Ky.L.J. 151 (1969).

Christensen and Christensen, *"Gissel Packing* and 'Good Faith Doubt': The Gestalt of Required Recognition of Unions Under the NLRA," 37 U.Chi.L.Rev. 411 (1970).

Goldberg, "The Labor Law Obligations of a Successor Employer," 63 Nw. U.L.Rev. 735 (1969).

Note, *"NLRB v. Gissel Packing Co.*: Bargaining Orders and Employee Free Choice," 45 N.Y.U.L.Rev. 318 (1970).

Pogrebin, "NLRB Bargaining Orders since Gissel: Wandering from a Landmark," 46 St. John's L.Rev. 193 (1971).

Slicker, "A Reconsideration of the Doctrine of Employer Successorship— A Step Toward a Rational Approach," 57 Minn.L.Rev. 1051 (1973).

CHAPTER VII

Aaron, "Employer Free Speech: The Search for a Policy," in Public Policy and Collective Bargaining 28 (Shister, Aaron & Summers, eds. 1962).

Bok, "The Regulation of Campaign Tactics in Representation Elections Under the National Labor Relations Act," 78 Harv.L.Rev. 38 (1964).

Christensen, "Free Speech, Propaganda and the National Labor Relations Act," 38 N.Y.U.L.Rev. 243 (1963).

Getman, "Section 8(a)(3) of the NLRA and the Effort to Insulate Free Employee Choice," 32 U.Chi.L.Rev. 735 (1965).

Getman & Goldberg, "The Behavioral Assumptions Underlying NLRB Regulation of Campaign Misrepresentations: An Empirical Evaluation," 28 Stan.L.Rev. 263 (1976).

Getman, Goldberg & Herman, "NLRB Regulation of Campaign Tactics: The Behavioral Assumptions on Which the Board Regulates," 27 Stan. L.Rev. 1465 (1975).

Helm, "Union Waiver of Initiation Fees During the Organizational Campaign," 63 Ky.L.J. 841 (1975).

Pollitt, "The National Labor Relations Board and Race Hate Propaganda in Union Organization Drives," 17 Stan.L.Rev. 373 (1965).

R. Williams, P. Janus, & K. Huhn, NLRB Regulation of Election Conduct (1974).

CHAPTER VIII

Daykin, "Employees' Right to Organize on Company Time and Company Property," 42 Ill.L.Rev. 301 (1947).

Gould, "The Question of Union Activity on Company Property," 18 Vand. L.Rev. 73 (1964).

Note, "Collectively Bargained Waiver of Plant-Site Solicitation and Distribution," 56 Iowa L.Rev. 152 (1970).

Vanderheyden, "Employee Solicitation and Distribution—A Second Look," 14 Lab.L.J. 781 (1963).

CHAPTER IX

Getman, "The *Midwest Piping* Doctrine," 31 U.Chi.L.Rev. 292 (1964).

Note, "New Standards for Domination and Support Under Section 8(a) (2)," 82 Yale L.J. 510 (1973).

Note, "Section 8(a)(2): Employer Assistance to Plant Unions and Committees," 9 Stan.L.Rev. 351 (1957).

CHAPTER X

Cox, "Strikes, Picketing and the Constitution," 4 Vand.L.Rev. 574 (1951).

Cox, "The Influence of Mr. Justice Murphy on Labor Law," 48 Mich.L.Rev. 767 (1950).

Dodd, "Picketing and Free Speech: A Dissent," 56 Harv.L.Rev. 513 (1943).

Gregory, "Constitutional Limitations on the Regulation of Union and Employer Conduct," 49 Mich.L.Rev. 191 (1950).

Jones, "Free Speech: Pickets on the Grass, Alas! Amidst Confusion, a Consistent Principle," 29 S.Cal.L.Rev. 137 (1956).

Samoff, "Picketing and the First Amendment: 'Full Circle' and 'Formal Surrender,'" 9 Lab.L.J. 889 (1958).

CHAPTER XI

Comment, "Picketing for Area Standards: An Exception to Section 8(b) (7)," Duke L.J. 767 (1968).

Dunau, "Some Aspects of the Current Interpretation of Section 8(b)(7)," 52 Geo.L.J. 220 (1964).

Meltzer, "Organizational Picketing and the NLRB: Five on a Seesaw," 30 U.Chi.L.Rev. 78 (1962).

Rosen, "Area Standards Picketing," 23 Lab.L.J. 67 (1972).

Shawe, "Federal Regulation of Recognition Picketing," 52 Geo.L.J. 248 (1964).

CHAPTER XII

Asher, "Secondary Boycott—Allied, Neutral and Single Employers," 52 Geo.L.J. 406 (1964).

Comment, "Hot Cargo Clauses: The Scope of Section 8(e)," 71 Yale L.J. 158 (1961).

Comment, "Subcontracting Clauses and Section 8(e) of the National Labor Relations Act," 62 Mich.L.Rev. 1176 (1964).

Engel, "Secondary Consumer Picketing—Following the Struck Product," 52 Va.L.Rev. 189 (1966).

Feldacker, "Subcontracting Restrictions and the Scope of Sections 8(b) (4)(A) and (B) and of 8(e) of the National Labor Relations Act," 17 Lab.L.J. 170 (1966).

Goetz, "Secondary Boycotts and the LMRA: A Path Through the Swamp," 19 U.Kan.L.Rev. 651 (1971).

Hickey, "Subcontracting Clauses Under Section 8(e) of the NLRA," 40 Notre Dame Lawyer 377 (1965).

Lesnick, "Job Security and Secondary Boycotts: The Reach of NLRA §§ 8(b)(4) and 8(e)," 113 U.Pa.L.Rev. 1000 (1965).

Lesnick, "The Gravamen of the Secondary Boycott," 62 Colum.L.Rev. 1363 (1962).

Levin, " 'Wholly Unconcerned': The Scope and Meaning of the Ally Doctrine under Section 8(b)(4) of the NLRA," 119 U.Pa.L.Rev. 283 (1970).

Lewis, "Consumer Picketing and the Court—The Questionable Yield of *Tree Fruits*," 49 Minn.L.Rev. 479 (1965).

Note, "Picketing and Publicity Under Section 8(b)(4) of the LMRA," 73 Yale L.J. 1265 (1964).

Note, "A Rational Approach to Secondary Boycotts and Work Preservation," 57 Va.L.Rev. 1280 (1971).

Ross, "An Assessment of the Landrum-Griffin Act's Secondary Boycott Amendments to the Taft-Hartley Act, 22 Lab.L.J. 675 (1971).

St. Antoine, "Secondary Boycotts and Hot Cargo: A Study in Balance of Power," 40 U.Det.L.J. 189 (1962).

St. Antoine, "What Makes Secondary Boycotts Secondary?", Southwestern Legal Foundation, 11th Annual Institute on Labor Law 5 (1965).

Shalov, "The Landrum-Griffin Amendments: Labor's Use of the Secondary Boycott," 45 Cornell L.Q. 724 (1960).

Zimmerman, "Secondary Picketing and the Reserved Gate: The *General Electric* Doctrine," 47 Va.L.Rev. 1164 (1961).

CHAPTER XIII

Atleson, "The NLRB and Jurisdictional Disputes: The Aftermath of CBS," 53 Geo.L.J. 93 (1964).

Cohen, "The NLRB and Section 10(k): A Study of the Reluctant Dragon," 14 Lab.L.J. 905 (1963).

Farmer & Powers, "The Role of the National Labor Relations Board in Resolving Jurisdictional Disputes," 46 Va.L.Rev. 660 (1960).

Leslie, "The Role of the NLRB and the Courts in Resolving Union Jurisdictional Disputes," 75 Colum.L.Rev. 1470 (1975).

O'Donoghue, "Jurisdictional Disputes in the Construction Industry Since *CBS*," 52 Geo.L.J. 314 (1964).

Player, "Work Assignment Disputes Under Section 10(k): Putting the Substantive Cart Before the Procedural Horse," 52 Texas L.Rev. 417 (1974).

Sussman, "Section 10(k): Mandate for Change?", 47 B.U.L.Rev. 201 (1967).

CHAPTER XIV

Aaron, "Governmental Restraints on Featherbedding," 5 Stan.L.Rev. 680 (1953).

Note, "Drafting Problems and the Regulation of Featherbedding—an Imagined Dilemma," 73 Yale L.J. 812 (1964).

CHAPTER XV

K. Huhn & D. McDowell, NLRB Remedies for Unfair Labor Practices (1976).

Note, "Sections 8(b)(4) and 303: Independent Remedies Against Union Practices Under the Taft-Hartley Act," 61 Yale L.J. 745 (1952).

CHAPTER XVI

Cantor, "Dissident Worker Action, After *The Emporium*," 29 Rutgers L. Rev. 35 (1975).

Cox, "The Right to Engage in Concerted Activities," 26 Ind.L.J. 319 (1951).

Getman, "The Protection of Economic Pressure by Section 7 of the National Labor Relations Act," 115 U.Pa.L.Rev. 1195 (1967).

Gould, "The Status of Unauthorized and 'Wildcat' Strikes Under the National Labor Relations Act," 52 Cornell L.Q. 672 (1967).

Schatzki, "Some Observations and Suggestions Concerning a Misnomer— 'Protected' Concerted Activities," 47 Texas L.Rev. 378 (1969).

CHAPTER XVII

Baird, "Lockout Law: The Supreme Court and the NLRB," 38 Geo.Wash. L.Rev. 396 (1970).

Bernhardt, "Lockouts: An Analysis of Board and Court Decisions Since Brown and American Ship," 57 Cornell L.Rev. 211 (1972).

Christensen & Svanoe, "Motive and Intent in the Commission of Unfair Labor Practices: The Supreme Court and the Fictive Formality," 77 Yale L.J. 1269 (1968).

Feldesman & Koretz, "Lockouts," 46 B.U.L.Rev. 329 (1966).

Getman, "Section 8(a)(3) of the NLRA and the Effort to Insulate Free Employee Choice," 32 U.Chi.L.Rev. 735 (1965).

Janofsky, "New Concepts in Interference and Discrimination Under the NLRA—The Legacy of *American Ship Building & Great Dane Trailers*," 70 Colum.L.Rev. 81 (1970).

Martin, "The Rights of Economic Strikers to Reinstatement: A Search for Certainty," 1970 Wis.L.Rev. 1062.

Meltzer, "Lockouts Under the LMRA: New Shadows on an Old Terrain," 28 U.Chi.L.Rev. 614 (1961).

Note, "Intent, Effect, Purpose, and Motive as Applicable Elements to § 8(a) (1) and § 8(a)(3) Violations of the National Labor Relations Act," 7 Wake Forest L.Rev. 616 (1971).

Note, "the Unfair Labor Practice Strike: A Critique and a Proposal for Change," 46 N.Y.U.L.Rev. 988 (1971).

Oberer, "Lockouts and the Law: The Impact of American Shipbuilding and Brown Food," 51 Cornell L.Q. 193 (1966).

Oberer, "The Scienter Factor in Sections 8(a)(1) and (3) of the Labor Act: of Balancing, Hostile Motive, Dogs and Tails," 52 Cornell L.Q. 491 (1967).

CHAPTER XVIII

Cox, "Seizures in Emergency Disputes," in Emergency Disputes and National Policy 224 (Bernstein et al., eds., 1955).

Jones, "Toward a Definition of 'National Emergency Dispute,'" 1971 Wis. L.Rev. 700 (1971).

Kleiler, "Presidential Seizures in Labor Disputes," 6 Ind. & Lab.Rel.Rev. 547 (1953).

Rehmus, "The Operation of the National Emergency Provisions of the Labor Management Relations Act of 1947," 62 Yale L.J. 1047 (1953).

CHAPTER XIX

Comment, "Union Presence in Disciplinary Meetings," 41 U.Chi.L.Rev. 329 (1974).

Schatzki, "Majority Rule, Exclusive Representation, and the Interests of Individual Workers: Should Exclusivity be Abolished?", 123 U.Pa.L. Rev. 897 (1975).

Weyand, Majority Rule in Collective Bargaining, 45 Colum.L.Rev. 556 (1945).

CHAPTER XX

Anker, "Pattern Bargaining, Antitrust Laws and the National Labor Relations Act," N.Y.U. 19th Annual Conf. on Labor 81 (1967).

Benetar, "Coalition Bargaining Under the NLRA," and Abramson, "Coordinated Bargaining by Unions," N.Y.U. 20th Annual Conf. on Labor 219, 231 (1968).

Comment, "Impasse in Collective Bargaining," 44 Texas L.Rev. 769 (1966).

Cooper, "Boulwarism and the Duty to Bargain in Good Faith," 20 Rutgers L.Rev. 653 (1966).

Cox, "The Duty to Bargain in Good Faith," 71 Harv.L.Rev. 1401 (1958).

Cox & Dunlop, "Regulation of Collective Bargaining by the National Labor Relations Board," 63 Harv.L.Rev. 389 (1950).

Cox & Dunlop, "The Duty to Bargain Collectively During the Term of an Existing Agreement," 63 Harv.L.Rev. 1097 (1950).

Duvin, "The Duty to Bargain: Law in Search of Policy," 64 Colum.L.Rev. 248 (1964).

Fleming, "The Obligation to Bargain in Good Faith," 47 Va.L.Rev. 988 (1961).

Goldberg, "Coordinated Bargaining Tactics of Unions," 54 Cornell L.Rev. 897 (1969).

Gross, Cullen & Hanslowe, "Good Faith in Labor Negotiations: Tests and Remedies," 53 Cornell L.Rev. 1009 (1968).

Huston, "Furnishing Information as an Element of Employer's Good Faith Bargaining," 35 U.Det.L.J. 471 (1958).

Miller, "Employer's Duty to Furnish Economic Data to Unions—Revisited," 17 Lab.L.J. 272 (1966).

H. Northrup, Boulwarism (1964).

Note, "Boulwareism: Legality and Effect," 76 Harv.L.Rev. 807 (1963).

Schatzki, "NLRB Resolution of Contract Disputes Under Section 8(a) (5)," 50 Texas L.Rev. 225 (1972).

Schatzki, "The Employer's Unilateral Act—A Per Se Violation—Sometimes," 44 Texas L.Rev. 470 (1966).

Wollett, "The Duty to Bargain Over the 'Unwritten' Terms and Conditions of Employment," 36 Texas L.Rev. 863 (1958).

CHAPTER XXI

Christensen, "New Subjects and New Concepts in Collective Bargaining," ABA Section of Labor Relations Law Proceedings 245 (1970).

Cox and Dunlop, "Regulation of Collective Bargaining by the National Labor Relations Board," 63 Harv.L.Rev. 389 (1950).

Goetz, "Current Problems in Application of Federal Labor Law to Welfare and Pension Plans," Southwestern Legal Foundation, 16th Annual Inst. on Labor Law 107 (1970).

Note, "Proper Subjects for Collective Bargaining: Ad Hoc v. Predictive Definition," 58 Yale L.J. 803 (1949).

Oldham, "Organized Labor, the Environment and the Taft-Hartley Act," 71 Mich.L.Rev. 936 (1973).

Platt, "The Duty to Bargain as Applied to Management Decisions," 19 Lab.L.J. 143 (1968).

Rabin, "Fibreboard and the Termination of Bargaining Unit Work: The Search for Standards in Defining the Scope of Duty to Bargain," 71 Colum.L.Rev. 803 (1971).

Rabin, "The Decline and Fall of Fibreboard," N.Y.U. 24th Annual Conf. on Labor 237 (1972).

Schwarz, "Plant Relocation or Partial Termination—The Duty to Decision-Bargain," 39 Fordham L.Rev. 81 (1970).

CHAPTER XXII

Gross, Cullen & Hanslowe, "Good Faith in Labor Negotiations: Tests and Remedies," 53 Cornell L.Rev. 1009 (1968).

McCulloch, "Past, Present and Future Remedies Under Section 8(a)(5) of the NLRA," 19 Lab.L.J. 131 (1968).

St. Antoine, "A Touchstone for Labor Board Remedies," 14 Wayne L.Rev. 1039 (1968).

CHAPTER XXIII

Cox, "Reflections Upon Labor Arbitration," 72 Harv.L.Rev. 1482 (1959).

Cox, "Rights Under a Labor Agreement," 69 Harv.L.Rev. 601 (1956).

Cox, "The Legal Nature of Collective Bargaining Agreements," 57 Mich. L.Rev. 1 (1958).

Edwards, "Due Process Considerations in Labor Arbitration," 25 Arb.J. 141 (1970).

F. Elkouri & E. Elkouri, How Arbitration Works (3d ed. 1973).

O. Fairweather, Practice & Procedure in Labor Arbitration (1973).

Feller, "A General Theory of the Collective Bargaining Agreement," 61 Calif.L.Rev. 663 (1973).

R. Fleming, The Labor Arbitration Process (1965).

P. Hays, Labor Arbitration: A Dissenting View (1966).

Lesnick, "Arbitration as a Limit on the Discretion of Management, Union, and NLRB: The Year's Major Developments," N.Y.U. 18th Ann. Conf. on Labor 7 (1966).

Shulman, "Reason, Contract, and Law in Labor Relations," 68 Harv.L.Rev. 999 (1955).

Smith & Jones, "The Impact of the Emerging Federal Law of Grievance Arbitration on Judges, Arbitrators, and Parties," 52 Va.L.Rev. 831 (1966).

Smith & Jones, "The Supreme Court and Labor Dispute Arbitration: The Emerging Federal Law," 63 Mich.L.Rev. 751 (1965).

Summers, "Collective Agreements and the Law of Contracts," 78 Yale L.J. 525 (1969).

C. Updegraff, Arbitration and Labor Relations (3d ed. 1970).

CHAPTER XXIV

Goldberg, "The Labor Law Obligations of a Successor Employer," 63 Nw. L.Rev. 735 (1969).

Morris & Gaus, "Successorship and the Collective Bargaining Agreement: Accommodating *Wiley* and *Burns*," 59 Va.L.Rev. 1359 (1973).

Note, "Contract Rights and the Successor Employer: The Impact of *Burns Security*," 71 Mich.L.Rev. 571 (1973).

Note, "Contractual Successorship: The Impact of *Burns*," 40 U.Chi.L.Rev. 617 (1973).

Platt, "The NLRB and the Arbitrator in Sale and Merger Situations," N.Y.U. 19th Annual Conf. on Labor 375 (1967).

Slicker, "A Reconsideration of the Doctrine of Employer Successorship—A Step Toward a Rational Approach," 57 Minn.L.Rev. 1051 (1973).

CHAPTER XXV

Aaron, "Judicial Intervention in Labor Arbitration," 20 Stan.L.Rev. 41 (1967).

Dunau, "Three Problems in Labor Arbitration," 55 Va.L.Rev. 427 (1969).

Jones, "The Name of the Game is Decision—Some Reflections on 'Arbitrability' and 'Authority' in Labor Arbitration," 46 Texas L.Rev. 865 (1968).

Meltzer, "Ruminations About Ideology, Law, and Labor Arbitration," 34 U.Chi.L.Rev. 545 (1967).

CHAPTER XXVI

Axelrod, "The Application of the *Boys Markets* Decision in the Federal Courts," 16 B.C.Ind. & Com.L.Rev. 893 (1975).

Fairweather, "Employer Actions and Options in Response to Strikes in Breach of Contract," N.Y.U. 18th Annual Conf. on Labor 129 (1966).

Gould, "On Labor Injunctions, Unions, and the Judges: the Boys Market Case," 1970 Sup.Ct.Rev. 215.

Vladeck, *"Boys Markets* and National Labor Policy," 24 Vand.L.Rev. 93 (1970).

CHAPTER XXVII

Cox, "Labor and the Antitrust Laws—A Preliminary Analysis," 104 U.Pa.L. Rev. 252 (1955).

Cox, "Labor and the Antitrust Laws: Pennington and Jewel Tea," 46 B.U.L.Rev. 317 (1966).

Meltzer, "Labor Unions, Collective Bargaining, and the Antitrust Laws," 32 U.Chi.L.Rev. 659 (1965).

St. Antoine, "Collective Bargaining and the Antitrust Laws," Industrial Relations Research Ass'n, 19th Annual Winter Meeting Proceedings 66 (1966).

St. Antoine, *"Connell*: Antitrust Law at the Expense of Labor Law," 62 Va.L.Rev. 603 (1976).

Sovern, "Some Ruminations on Labor, the Antitrust Laws and *Allen Bradley*," 13 Lab.L.J. 957 (1962).

Winter, "Collective Bargaining and Competition: The Application of Antitrust Standards to Union Activities," 73 Yale L.J. 14 (1963).

CHAPTER XXVIII

Fenton, "Union Hiring Halls Under the Taft-Hartley Act," 9 Lab.L.J. 505 (1958).

Grodin & Beeson, "State Right-to-Work Laws and Federal Labor Policy," 52 Calif.L.Rev. 95 (1964).

Henderson, "The Confrontation of Federal Preemption and State Right to Work Laws," 1967 Duke L.J. 1079.

Hopfl, "The Agency Shop Question," 49 Cornell L.Q. 478 (1964).

Kuhn, "Right-to-Work Laws—Symbols or Substance?", 14 Ind. & Lab.Rel. Rev. 587 (1961).

Mayer, "Union Security and the Taft-Hartley Act," 1961 Duke L.J. 505.

F. Meyers, Right to Work in Practice (1959).

Rains, "Construction Trades Hiring Halls," 10 Lab.L.J. 363 (1959).

Rosenthal, "The National Labor Relations Act and Compulsory Unionism," 1954 Wis.L.Rev. 53.

P. Sultan, Right-to-Work Laws (1958).

CHAPTER XXIX

Archer, "Allis-Chalmers Recycled: A Current View of a Union's Right to Fine Employees for Crossing a Picket Line," 7 Indiana L.Rev. 498 (1974).

Atleson, "Union Fines and Picket Lines: The NLRA and Union Disciplinary Power," 17 U.C.L.A.L.Rev. 681 (1970).

Craver, "The *Boeing* Decision: A Blow to Federalism, Individual Rights and Stare Decisis," 122 U.Pa.L.Rev. 556 (1974).

Gould, "Some Limitations Upon Union Discipline Under the National Labor Relations Act: The Radiations of *Allis-Chalmers*," 1970 Duke L.J. 1067.

Note, "Union Power to Discipline Members Who Resign," 86 Harv.L.Rev. 1536 (1973).

Silard, "Labor Board Regulation of Union Discipline After Allis-Chalmers, Marine Workers, and Scofield," 38 Geo.Wash.L.Rev. 187 (1969).

CHAPTER XXX

Blumrosen, "Legal Protection for Critical Job Interests: Union-Management Authority Versus Employee Autonomy," 13 Rutgers L.Rev. 631 (1959).

Blumrosen, "The Worker and Three Phases of Unionism: Administrative and Judicial Control of the Worker-Union Relationship," 61 Mich.L.Rev. 1435 (1963).

Clark, "The Duty of Fair Representation: A Theoretical Structure," 51 Texas L.Rev. 1119 (1973).

Cox, "Rights Under a Labor Agreement," 69 Harv.L.Rev. 601 (1956).

Cox, "The Duty of Fair Representation," 2 Vill.L.Rev. 151 (1957).

Dunau, "Employee Participation in the Grievance Aspects of Collective Bargaining," 50 Colum.L.Rev. 731 (1950).

Hanslowe, "The Collective Agreement and the Duty of Fair Representation," 14 Lab.L.J. 1052 (1963).

Leiken, "The Current and Potential Equal Employment Role of the NLRB," 1971 Duke L.J. 833.

Lewis, "Fair Representation in Grievance Administration: Vaca v. Sipes," 1967 Sup.Ct.Rev. 81.

Murphy, "The Duty of Fair Representation Under Taft-Hartley," 30 Mo.L. Rev. 373 (1965).

Sherman, "Union's Duty of Fair Representation and the Civil Rights Act of 1964," 49 Minn.L.Rev. 771 (1965).

Sovern, "The National Labor Relations Act and Racial Discrimination," 62 Colum.L.Rev. 563 (1962).

Summers, "Individual Rights in Collective Agreements and Arbitration," 37 N.Y.U.L.Rev. 362 (1962).

Wellington, "Union Democracy and Fair Representation: Federal Responsibility in a Federal System," 67 Yale L.J. 1327 (1958).

CHAPTER XXXI

Atleson, "Disciplinary Discharges, Arbitration and NLRB Deference," 20 Buffalo L.Rev. 355 (1971).

Getman, "Collyer Insulated Wire: A Case of Misplaced Modesty," 49 Ind. L.J. 57 (1973).

Isaacson and Zifchak, "Agency Deferral to Private Arbitration of Employment Disputes," 73 Colum.L.Rev. 1383 (1973).

Nash, Wilder & Banov, "The Development of the *Collyer* Deferral Doctrine," 27 Vand.L.Rev. 23 (1974).

Schatzki, "NLRB Resolution of Contract Disputes Under Section 8(a)(5)," 50 Texas L.Rev. 225 (1972).

Sovern, "Section 301 and the Primary Jurisdiction of the NLRB," 76 Harv. L.Rev. 529 (1963).

Wollett, "The Agreement and the National Labor Relations Act: Courts, Arbitrators and the NLRB—Who Decides What?", 14 Lab.L.J. 1041 (1963).

Zimmer, "Wired for Collyer: Rationalizing NLRB and Arbitration Jurisdiction," 48 Ind.L.J. 141 (1973).

CHAPTER XXXII

Bryson, "A Matter of Wooden Logic: Labor Law Preemption and Individual Rights," 51 Texas L.Rev. 1037 (1973).

Cohen, "Congress Clears the Labor No Man's Land," 56 Nw.U.L.Rev. 333 (1961).

Come, "Federal Preemption of Labor-Management Relations: Current Problems in the Application of *Garmon*," 56 Va.L.Rev. 1435 (1970).

Cox, "Federalism in the Law of Labor Relations," 67 Harv.L.Rev. 1297 (1954).

Cox, "Labor Law Preemption Revisited," 85 Harv.L.Rev. 1337 (1972).

Lesnick, "Preemption Reconsidered: The Apparent Reaffirmation of *Garmon*," 72 Colum.L.Rev. 469 (1972).

McCoid, "Notes on a 'G-String': A Study of the 'No Man's Land' of Labor Law," 44 Minn.L.Rev. 205 (1959).

Meltzer, "The Supreme Court, Congress and State Jurisdiction Over Labor Relations," 59 Colum.L.Rev. 6, 269 (1959).

Michelman, "State Power to Govern Concerted Employee Activities," 74 Harv.L.Rev. 641 (1961).

*

TABLE OF CASES

References are to Pages

Court cases in which the National Labor Relations Board is a party are listed under the name of the company or union which is the adversary party. Cases in which the United States is a party are listed under "United States." Companies bearing the name of a person are listed by the first name or initials (e. g., "L. B. Foster Co."). Union names are listed by the first word indicating a craft or industry (e. g., "Teamsters" or "Oil Workers"); within that entry, cases in which the international union is a party are listed first, followed by references to union locals in numerical sequence.

American Steel Foundries v. Tri-City
Council, 257 U.S. 184 (1921), 221

American Sterilizer Co. v. UAW Local
832, 278 F.Supp. 637 (W.D.Pa.1968),
590

American Tel. & Tel. Co. v. NLRB, 521
F.2d 1159 (2d Cir. 1975), 314

American Thread Co., NLRB v., 204 F.
2d 169 (5th Cir. 1953), 135

American Thread Co., Textile Workers
Union v., 291 F.2d 894 (4th Cir.
1961), 590, 601

American Tube Bending Co., NLRB v.,
134 F.2d 993 (2d Cir.), cert. denied,
320 U.S. 768 (1943), 151

American Zinc, Lead & Smelting Co..
Mine Workers Local 515 v., 311 F.2d
565 (9th Cir. 1963), 672

Amstar Corp. v. Amalgamated Meat Cutters, 337 F.Supp. 810 (E.D.La.),
rev'd, 468 F.2d 1372 (5th Cir. 1972),
611, 613

Amstar Corp. v. Sugar Workers Local 9,
345 F.Supp. 331 (E.D.N.Y.1972), 615

Anchor Motor Freight, Inc., Hines v.,
96 S.Ct. 1048 (1976), 697

Anchor Rome Mills, Inc., 86 N.L.R.B.
1120 (1949), 326

Andor Co., 119 N.L.R.B. 925 (1957), 655

Andrew Jergens Co., NLRB v., 175 F.2d
130 (9th Cir.), cert. denied, 338 U.S.
827 (1949), 508

Angle v. Sacks, 382 F.2d 655 (10th Cir.
1967), 289

Anheuser-Busch, Inc., Weber v., 348 U.
S. 468 (1955), 773, 778

A. O. Smith Corp., Smith Steel Workers
v., 420 F.2d 1 (7th Cir. 1969), 570

A. Paladini, Inc., 168 N.L.R.B. 952 (1967),
30

Apartment & Elevator Operators Local
14, Retana v., 453 F.2d 1018 (9th Cir.
1972), 706

Apex Hosiery Co. v. Leader, 310 U.S. 469
(1940), 4, 625, 633

Appalachian Shale Prods. Co., 121 N.L.
R.B. 1160 (1958), 55

Arbie Mineral Feed Co. v. NLRB, 438
F.2d 940 (8th Cir. 1971), 102

Architectural Fiberglass, 165 N.L.R.B.
238 (1967), 407, 445, 454, 483

Ariadne Shipping Co., Longshoremen's
Local 1416 v., 397 U.S. 195 (1970),
769, 771

Arlan's Dept. Store, 133 N.L.R.B. 802
(1961), 306, 619

Armstrong Cork Co. v. NLRB, 211 F.2d
843 (5th Cir. 1954), 454

Arnold Co. v. Carpenters Dist. Council,
417 U.S. 12 (1974), 548

Arundel Corp., 210 N.L.R.B. 525 (1974),
437

A. S. Abell Co. v. Baltimore Typog. Union
No. 12, 338 F.2d 190 (4th Cir. 1964),
562.

Ashland Industries, Inc., ILGWU v., 488
F.2d 641 (5th Cir.), cert. denied, 419
U.S. 840 (1974), 563, 587

Asociacion de Trabajadores Agricolas v.
Green Giant Co., 518 F.2d 130 (3d
Cir. 1975), 189

Associated Gen. Contractors of America
v. NLRB, 465 F.2d 327 (7th Cir.
1972), cert. denied, 409 U.S. 1108
(1973), 406, 527

Assoc. Gen. Contractors of America,
Houston Chapter, 143 N.L.R.B. 409
(1963), enf'd, 349 F.2d 449 (5th Cir.
1965), cert. denied, 382 U.S. 1026
(1966), 504, 509, 663

Associated Gen. Contractors of Illinois
v. Illinois Conf. of Teamsters, 454
F.2d 1324 (7th Cir. 1972), on remand
345 F.Supp. 1296, affirmed 486 F.2d
972 (1973), 610, 616

Associated Press, 199 N.L.R.B. 1110
(1972), enf'd, 492 F.2d 662 (D.C.Cir.
1974), 761

Associated Press v. NLRB, 492 F.2d
662 (D.C.Cir. 1974), 735

Astro Electronics, Inc., 188 N.L.R.B. 572
(1971), enf'd per curiam, 463 F.2d
176 (9th Cir. 1972), 349

Athbro Precision Eng'r Corp., NLRB v.,
423 F.2d 573 (1st Cir. 1970), 63

Atkinson, Sinclair Ref. Co. v., 370 U.S.
195 (1962), 607, 619

Atkinson v. Sinclair Ref. Co., 370 U.S.
238 (1962), 548, 550, 564, 607

Atlantic Towing Co., 75 N.L.R.B. 1169
(1948), enforcement denied 179 F.2d
497 (5th Cir. 1950), 317, 318

Atlas Sheet Metal Co., Sheet Metal Workers Int'l Ass'n v., 384 F.2d 101 (5th
Cir. 1967), 248

Auburn Rubber Co., NLRB v., 384 F.2d
1 (10th Cir. 1967), 739, 744

Austin, Old Dominion Branch 496, Letter
Carriers v., 418 U.S. 264 (1974), 318,
781

*

INDEX

References are to Pages